Business Studies 1
Volume 2

PEARSON CUSTOM PUBLISHING

Business Studies 1
Volume 2

Compiled from:

Corporate Financial Management
Fifth Edition
by Glen Arnold

Employment Relations
Third Edition
by Ed Rose

Management & Organisational Behaviour
Ninth Edition
by Laurie J. Mullins
with Gill Christy

PEARSON

Harlow, England • London • New York • Boston • San Francisco • Toronto • Sydney • Auckland • Singapore • Hong Kong
Tokyo • Seoul • Taipei • New Delhi • Cape Town • Sao Paulo • Mexico City • Madrid • Amsterdam • Munich • Paris • Milan

Pearson Education Limited
Edinburgh Gate
Harlow
Essex CM20 2JE

And associated companies throughout the world

Visit us on the World Wide Web at:
www.pearsoned.co.uk

This Custom Book Edition © Pearson Education Limited 2014

Compiled from:

Corporate Financial Management, Fifth Edition
by Glen Arnold
ISBN 978 0 273 75883 9
© Financial Times Professional Limited 1998
© Pearson Education Limited 2002, 2005, 2008, 2013

Employment Relations, Third Edition
by Ed Rose
ISBN 978 0 273 71008 0
© Pearson Education Limited 2001, 2008

Management & Organisational Behaviour, Ninth Edition
by Laurie J. Mullins with Gill Christy
ISBN 978 0 273 72408 7
Laurie J. Mullins 1985, 1989, 1993, 1996, 1999, 2002, 2005, 2007, 2010
Chapters 4, 6 © Linda Carter and Laurie J. Mullins 1993, 1996, 1999, 2002, 2005, 2007
Chapter 5 © Linda Carter 1993, 1996, 1999, 2002, 2005, 2007
Chapter 16 © Peter Scott 2010
Chapter 17 © David Preece 1999, 2002, 2005, 2007

ISBN 978 1 78376 451 8

Printed and bound in Great Britain by Clays Ltd, Bungay, Suffolk.

Contents

Section 3: Organisational Behaviour 559

Section 1:

Corporate Finance

The financial world

LEARNING OUTCOMES

At the end of this chapter the reader will have a balanced perspective on the purpose and value of the finance function, at both the corporate and the national level. More specifically, the reader should be able to:

■ describe alternative views on the purpose of the business and show the importance to any organisation of clarity on this point;

■ describe the impact of the divorce of corporate ownership from day-to-day managerial control;

■ explain the role of the financial manager;

■ detail the value of financial intermediaries;

■ show an appreciation of the function of the major financial institutions and markets.

MyFinanceLab *Complete your diagnostic test for Chapter 1 now to create your personal study plan.*

Introduction

Before getting carried away with specific financial issues and technical detail, it is important to gain a broad perspective by looking at the fundamental questions and the place of finance in the overall scheme of things. The finance function is a vital one, both within an individual organisation and for society as a whole. In the UK, for example, the financial services industry accounts for a larger proportion of national output than the whole of manufacturing industry. There are now over 6 million UK employees in banking, finance, insurance and other finance-related businesses. By contrast there are only 3 million in manufacturing. As recently as 1993 both sectors employed 4.4 million, so you can see that there has been an enormous shift in demand and resources in recent times. To some this is a cause of great alarm and regret but, given that this trend has occurred at a time when free choice in the marketplace largely dictates what is produced, presumably there must be something useful that financial firms are providing. We will examine the key role played by financial intermediaries and markets in a modern economy, and how an efficient and innovative financial sector contributes greatly to the ability of other sectors to produce efficiently. One of the vital roles of the financial sector is to encourage the mobilisation of savings to put them to productive use through investment. Without a vibrant and adaptable financial sector all parts of the economy would be starved of investment and society would be poorer.

This chapter also considers the most fundamental question facing anyone trying to make decisions within an organisation: what is the objective of the business? Without clarity on this point it is very difficult to run a business in a purposeful and effective manner. The resolution of this question is somewhat clouded in the large, modern corporation by the tendency for the owners to be distant from the running of the enterprise. Professional managers are usually left in control and they have objectives which may or may not match those of the owners.

Finally, to help the reader become orientated, a brief rundown is given of the roles, size and activities of the major types of financial institutions and markets. A little bit of jargon busting early on will no doubt be welcomed.

The objective of the firm

Xstrata, widely regarded as one of the best-managed companies in the world, has a clear statement of its objective ('aim') in its 2010 Annual Report – *see* **Case study 1.1**.

Case study 1.1 **Xstrata plc**

'We will grow and manage a diversified portfolio of metals and mining businesses with the single aim of delivering industry-leading returns for our shareholders.

We can achieve this only through genuine partnerships with employees, customers, shareholders, local communities and other stakeholders, which are based on integrity, cooperation, transparency and mutual value creation.

Our businesses maintain a meaningful position in seven major international commodity markets: copper, coking coal, thermal coal, ferrochrome, nickel, vanadium and zinc . . . The Group also comprises a growing platinum group metals business, iron ore projects, recycling facilities and a suite of global technology products, many of which are industry leaders.

We believe that operating to leading standards of health, safety and environmental management, contributing to the development of sustainable communities and engaging with our stakeholders in two-way dialogue, regardless of our location, enhances our corporate reputation and is a source of competitive advantage. We balance social, environmental, ethical and economic considerations in how we manage our businesses.'

Source: Xstrata plc Annual Report 2010.

Notice that there is not a confusion of objectives (as there is in many companies) with no one knowing which of a long list of desirable outcomes is the dominant purpose of the firm. Xstrata does not confuse the objective with the strategy to be employed to achieve the objective. Many managerial teams believe that it is their objective to operate within a particular market or take particular actions. They seem unable to distinguish market positions or actions from the ultimate purpose for the existence of the organisation. This will not only lead to poor strategic decisions but frequently makes intelligent financial decisions impossible.

This book is all about practical decision making in the real world. When people have to make choices in the harsh environment in which modern businesses have to operate, it is necessary to be clear about the purpose of the organisation; to be clear about what objective is set for management to achieve. A multitude of small decisions is made every day; more importantly, every now and then major strategic commitments of resources are made. It is imperative that the management teams are aware of, respect and contribute to the fundamental objective of the firm in all these large and small decisions. Imagine the chaos and confusion that could result from the opposite situation where there is no clear, accepted objective. The outcome of each decision, and the direction of the firm, will become random and rudderless. One manager on one occasion will decide to grant long holidays and a shorter working week, believing that the purpose of the institution's existence is to benefit employees; while on another occasion a different manager sacks 'surplus' staff and imposes lower wages, seeing the need to look after the owner's interests as a first priority. So, before we can make decisions in the field of finance we need to establish what it is we are trying to achieve.

You have probably encountered elsewhere the question, 'In whose interests is the firm run?' This is a political and philosophical as well as an economic question and many books have been written on the subject. Here we will provide a brief overview of the debate because of its central importance to making choices in finance. The list of interested parties in Exhibit 1.1 could be extended, but no doubt you can accept the point from this shortened version that there are a number of claimants on a firm.

Sound financial management is necessary for the survival of the firm and for its growth. Therefore all of these stakeholders, to some extent, have an interest in seeing sensible financial decisions being taken. Many business decisions do not involve a conflict between the objectives of each of the stakeholders. However, there are occasions when someone has to decide which claimants are to have their **objectives maximised**, and which are merely to be **satisficed** – that is, given just enough of a return to make their contributions.

There are some strong views held on this subject. The pro-capitalist economists, such as Friedrich Hayek and Milton Friedman, believe that making shareholders' interests the paramount objective will benefit both the firm and society at large. This approach is not quite as extreme as it sounds because these thinkers generally accept that unbridled pursuit of shareholder returns, to the point of widespread pollution, murder and extortion, will not be in society's best interest and so add the proviso that maximising shareholder wealth is the desired objective provided that firms

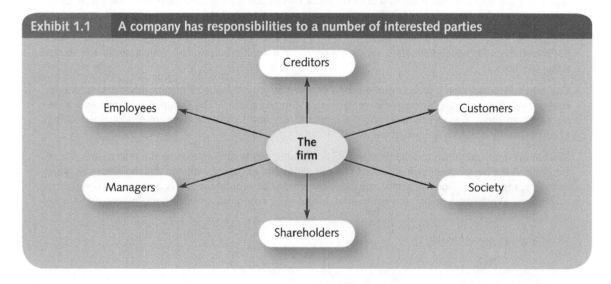

Exhibit 1.1 A company has responsibilities to a number of interested parties

remain within 'the rules of the game'. This includes obeying the laws and conventions of society, and behaving ethically and honestly.

At the opposite end of the political or philosophical spectrum are the left-wing advocates of the primacy of workers' rights and rewards. The belief here is that labour should have its rewards maximised. The employees should have all that is left over, after the other parties have been satisfied. Shareholders are given just enough of a return to provide capital, suppliers are given just enough to supply raw materials and so on.

Standing somewhere in the middle are those keen on a balanced stakeholder approach. Here the (often conflicting) interests of each of the claimants are somehow maximised but within the constraints set by the necessity to compromise in order to provide a fair return to the other stakeholders.

Some possible objectives

A firm can choose from an infinitely long list of possible objectives. Some of these will appear noble and easily justified, others remain hidden, implicit, embarrassing, even subconscious. The following represent some of the most frequently encountered.

- *Achieving a target market share* In some industrial sectors to achieve a high share of the market gives high rewards. These may be in the form of improved profitability, survival chances or status. Quite often the winning of a particular market share is set as an objective because it acts as a proxy for other, more profound objectives, such as generating the maximum returns to shareholders. On other occasions matters can get out of hand and there is an obsessive pursuit of market share with only a thin veneer of shareholder wealth espousement. The founder of easyJet thinks that the current directors are expanding excessively – *see* Exhibit 1.2.

- *Keeping employee agitation to a minimum* Here, return to the organisation's owners is kept to a minimum necessary level. All surplus resources are directed to mollifying employees. Managers would be very reluctant to admit publicly that they place a high priority on reducing workplace tension, encouraging peace by appeasement and thereby, it is hoped, reducing their own stress levels, but actions tend to speak louder than words.

 Some companies have tried to reduce workplace tension by giving workers a large proportion of the shares, i.e. making them part-owners. But, as the example of *Le Monde* shows, allowing workers to organise the firm in their own interests *can* result in financial disaster – *see* Exhibit 1.3.

- *Survival* There are circumstances where the overriding objective becomes the survival of the firm. Severe economic or market shock may force managers to focus purely on short-term

Exhibit 1.2

EasyJet reacts to Stelios onslaught

Carolyn McCall must be wondering what she has let herself in for. When easyJet's new chief executive arrives on 1 July, she will wade into a bitter battle over corporate strategy that has moved out of the boardroom and into the public domain.

To the City's bewilderment, founder Sir Stelios Haji-Ioannou last week announced his decision to resign as non-executive director 'in order to lead shareholder activism'. He believes that in the face of rising oil prices, easyJet's aggressive capacity expansion plans are no longer appropriate. Instead,

he thinks the airline's primary focus should be on improving profit margins and returning cash to him and other investors. His forcefully worded statement accuses management of 'squandering shareholders' funds on more expensive aircraft that will probably destroy shareholder value'.

European airlines still desperately need to cut capacity. We agree with Sir Stelios that a more mature airline industry being run for profits and dividends would be welcome.

Exhibit 1.3

Cap in hand

France's most respected newspaper teeters on the edge of bankruptcy

Ever since Charles de Gaulle called for the launch of *Le Monde*, first published in 1944, to replace *Le Temps*, a once prestigious daily tainted by collaboration with German invaders, the paper has prided itself on its independence.

Uniquely among leading newspapers, its journalists control it, and have the right to veto the choice not only of editor but also of the company's chief executive. But the lossmaking firm has just a few months to avert bankruptcy by finding fresh capital – and the price may be the abolition of the writers' powers.

. . . potential bidders may be having second thoughts after looking at the accounts, according to people close to the firm. It has nearly €100m ($120m) of debt, €25m of which comes due in 2011. Management says that €60m–70m is required to reduce this burden and put the firm on a footing for growth. But others, pointing to ongoing losses, including more than €10m in 2009, reckon the firm needs as much as €100m–150m.

Blame for *Le Monde's* situation rests chiefly with its journalists, business-people argue. The firm racked up debts in the late 1990s and early 2000s

with a series of acquisitions designed to create a broader media group around the flagship paper. But it was not profitable enough to sustain the expansion, mainly because the editorial staff resisted moves to improve efficiency. 'Unlike the *New York Times* or the *Wall Street Journal*', says Philippe Micouleau, the ex-boss of *La Tribune*, a business daily, 'neither the current nor the former management of Le Monde SA have been able to implement radical restructuring plans because of strong internal resistance.'

Raising €60m or more of new capital will mean that the internal shareholders which control Le Monde SA – notably the journalists' association – will have their control diluted. It is still just possible, some people reckon, that the journalists will refuse to cede power, forcing the group to seek bankruptcy protection. Otherwise they will try to hang on to some trappings of independence, such as their veto over the editor.

If other bidders pull out by June 14th, however, the rescuer will have more power to dictate terms. A new backer would certainly insist on full commercial freedom to break with the lossmaking past.

The Economist, 12 June 2010.

issues to ensure the continuance of the business. In firefighting they end up paying little attention to long-term growth and return to owners. However, this focus is clearly inadequate in the long run – there must be other goals. If survival were the only objective then putting all the firm's cash reserves into a bank savings account might be the best option. When managers say that their objective is survival, what they generally mean is the avoidance of large risks which endanger the firm's future. This may lead to a greater aversion to risk, and a rejection of activities that shareholders might wish the firm to undertake. Shareholders are in a position to diversify their investments: if one firm goes bankrupt they may be disappointed but they have other companies' shares to fall back on. However, the managers of that one firm may have the majority of their income, prestige and security linked to the continuing existence of that firm. These managers may deliberately avoid high-risk/high-return investments and therefore deprive the owners of the possibility of large gains.

- *Creating an ever-expanding empire* This is an objective which is rarely discussed openly, but it seems reasonable to propose that some managers drive a firm forward, via organic growth or mergers, because of a desire to run an ever-larger enterprise. Often these motives become clearer with hindsight; when, for instance, a firm meets a calamitous end the post-mortem often reveals that profit and efficiency were given second place to growth. The volume of sales, number of employees or overall stock market value of the firm have a much closer correlation

with senior executive salaries, perks and status than do returns to shareholder funds. This may motivate some individuals to promote growth.

- *Maximisation of profit* This is a much more acceptable objective, although not everyone would agree that maximisation of profit should be the firm's purpose.

- *Maximisation of long-term shareholder wealth* While many commentators concentrate on profit maximisation, finance experts are aware of a number of drawbacks of profit. The maximisation of the returns to shareholders in the long term is considered to be a superior goal. We look at the differences between profit maximisation and wealth maximisation later.

This list of possible objectives can easily be extended but it is not possible within the scope of this book to examine each of them. Suffice it to say, there can be an enormous variety of objectives and significant potential for conflict and confusion. We have to introduce some sort of order.

The assumed objective for finance

The company should make investment and financing decisions with the aim of maximising long-term shareholder wealth. Throughout the remainder of this book we will assume that the firm gives primacy of purpose to the wealth of shareholders. This assumption is made mainly on practical grounds, but there are respectable theoretical justifications too.

The practical reason

If one may assume that the decision-making agents of the firm (managers) are acting in the best interests of shareholders then decisions on such matters as which investment projects to undertake, or which method of financing to use, can be made much more simply. If the firm has a multiplicity of objectives, imagine the difficulty in deciding whether to introduce a new, more efficient machine to produce the firm's widgets, where the new machine will both be more labour efficient (thereby creating redundancies) and eliminate the need to buy from one half of the firm's suppliers. If one focuses solely on the benefits to shareholders, a clear decision can be made. This entire book is about decision-making tools to aid those choices. These range from whether to produce a component in-house, to whether to buy another company. If for each decision scenario we have to contemplate a number of different objectives or some vague balance of stakeholder interests, the task is going to be much more complex. Once the basic decision-making frameworks are understood within the tight confines of shareholder wealth maximisation, we can allow for complications caused by the modification of this assumption. For instance, shareholder wealth maximisation is clearly not the only consideration motivating actions of organisations such as the Co-operative Bank, with publicly stated ethical principles and a goal of benefiting its members. The John Lewis Partnership has been a very successful employee-owned company, but recognises the need for a rational financial decision-making framework – *see* Exhibit 1.4.

Exhibit 1.4

Partners hold key to John Lewis success

By Andrea Felsted, Senior Retail Correspondent

For Gill Armstrong, manager of a Waitrose supermarket in the Oxfordshire town of Witney, having a share in the ownership of the upmarket grocery chain makes a big difference to the way that she runs the store, and oversees another in nearby Wantage.

'When you are thinking about the decisions you make, you are thinking, "this is my business, this is my shop, what should I be doing?",' says Ms Armstrong who has been with the John Lewis Partnership, the employee-owned organisation that includes Waitrose and the John Lewis department stores, for 31 years.

When it came to whether to open until 10pm over the Christmas period, Ms Armstrong says: 'Most people would think 'no way, I want to get my bus home at 5pm'. Partners think about it differently.

▶

Exhibit 1.4 (continued)

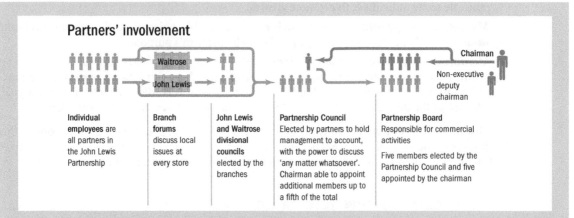

Partners' involvement

Individual employees are all partners in the John Lewis Partnership

Branch forums discuss local issues at every store

John Lewis and Waitrose divisional councils elected by the branches

Partnership Council Elected by partners to hold management to account, with the power to discuss 'any matter whatsoever'. Chairman able to appoint additional members up to a fifth of the total

Partnership Board Responsible for commercial activities

Five members elected by the Partnership Council and five appointed by the chairman

Given that this is my shop, do I want to close my doors and turn customers away, or do I want to kick them open and welcome them in?'

Such an attitude has helped John Lewis and Waitrose trounce the competition in the crucial Christmas and new year trading period.

The John Lewis Partnership is even helping the government on how its model could be applied to the public sector.

According to Charlie Mayfield, chairman, the unusual structure that sees the 75,000 partners, as they are known, own the business, is key to this success.

'Unlike other companies who have shareholders who are outside the business, and only own [the shares] for a short time, our shareholders work in the business. They spend, in some cases, their whole careers with us. They care deeply about it. Their livelihoods and happiness are all tied up within it,' he says.

The group's senior managers say this structure – put in place by founder John Spedan Lewis in 1929 – fosters better customer service, lower staff turnover and trust among customers.

'We don't tell people to do things, we ask them to do things, because they are owners of the business,' says Mark Price, managing director of Waitrose.

Ownership also means that once a year, partners receive a bonus, paid as a percentage of salary.

This is decided by the board, based on the surplus after investment is subtracted from the final profit for the year. Last year, the bonus was 15 per cent of salary...

'It reinforces that sense of common purpose. Everyone is in this together,' says Mr Mayfield.

But according to one seasoned retail analyst, the John Lewis Partnership has injected a 'pragmatism' into its business.

He says the 'triumvirate' of Mr Mayfield, Andy Street running John Lewis, and Mr Price, are 'as true to the founders' principles as commercial realities will allow'.

The new dynamism includes investing in online for the past 10 years – a move now paying off with more than £500m of sales for the first time in the year from February 1 2010.

On Friday, John Lewis said it would open beauty spas in stores.

But it also includes initiatives that the analyst says would have been considered 'taboo' in the past, such as John Lewis stores cutting jobs and outsourcing parts of after sales service.

'Cutting costs and cutting staff is alien to the John Lewis culture,' says Neil Saunders, consulting director of Verdict.

Mr Mayfield argues that both paternalism and commercialism are inherent in the model. 'We are not a charity. We were not created just as a nice place. The belief that sits behind it is a very commercial one. That is a point that is often overlooked,' he says.

'The partnership model was founded expressly because it was a better way to run a business. It was intended as a competitive idea, one that would beat the competition, not just be nice.'

But could this pragmatism go too far?

'A business can't be set in aspic,' says Mr Street, managing director of John Lewis. 'If we take the right business decisions [partners] will all share in that process.'

He adds that some 90 per cent of people affected by job cuts are redeployed elsewhere in the business.

The theoretical reasons

The 'contractual theory' views the firm as a network of contracts, actual and implicit, which specifies the roles to be played by various participants in the organisation. For instance, the workers make both an explicit (employment contract) and an implicit (show initiative, reliability, etc.) deal with the firm to provide their services in return for salary and other benefits, and suppliers deliver necessary inputs in return for a known payment. Each party has well-defined rights and pay-offs. Most of the participants bargain for a limited risk and a fixed pay-off. Banks, for example, when they lend to a firm, often strenuously try to reduce risk by making sure that the firm is generating sufficient cash flow to repay, that there are assets that can be seized if the loan is not repaid and so on. The bankers' bargain, like that of many of the parties, is a low-risk one and so, the argument goes, they should be rewarded with just the bare minimum for them to provide their service to the firm. Shareholders, on the other hand, are asked to put money into the business at high risk. The deal here is, 'You give us your £10,000 nest egg that you need for your retirement and we, the directors of the firm, do not promise that you will receive a dividend or even see your capital again. We will try our hardest to produce a return on your money but we cannot give any guarantees. Sorry.' Thus the firm's owners are exposed to the possibilities that the firm may go bankrupt and all will be lost. Because of this unfair balance of risk between the different potential claimants on a firm's resources it seems reasonable that the owners should be entitled to any surplus returns which result after all the other parties have been satisfied.

Another theoretical reason hinges on the practicalities of operating in a free market system. In such a capitalist system, it is argued, if a firm chooses to reduce returns to shareholders because, say, it wishes to direct more of the firm's surplus to the workers, then this firm will find it difficult to survive. Some shareholders will sell their shares and invest in other firms more orientated towards their benefit. In the long run those individuals who do retain their shares may be amenable to a takeover bid from a firm which does concentrate on shareholder wealth creation. The acquirer will anticipate being able to cut costs, not least by lowering the returns to labour. In the absence of a takeover the company would be unable to raise more finance from shareholders and this might result in slow growth and liquidity problems and possibly corporate death, throwing all employees out of work.

For over 200 years it has been argued that society is best served by businesses focusing on returns to the owner. Adam Smith (1776) expressed the argument very effectively:

> The businessman by directing . . . industry in such a manner as its produce may be of the greatest value, intends only his own gain, and he is in this, as in many other cases, led by an invisible hand to promote an end which was no part of his intention. Nor is it always the worse for society that it was no part of it. By pursuing his own interest he frequently promotes that of the society more effectually than when he really intends to promote it. I have never known much good done by those who affected to trade for the public good. It is an affectation, indeed, not very common among merchants.
>
> *Source:* Adam Smith, *The Wealth of Nations*, 1776, p. 400.

Adam Smith's objection to businessmen affecting to trade for the public good is echoed in Michael Jensen's writings in which he attacks the stakeholder approach (and its derivative, the Balanced Scorecard of Kaplan and Norton (1996)). His main worry is the confusion that results from having a multiplicity of targets to aim for, but he also takes a sideswipe at managers who are able to use the smokescreen of the stakeholder approach to cloak their actions in pursuit of benefits for themselves, or their pet 'socially beneficial' goals:

> Stakeholder theory effectively leaves managers and directors unaccountable for their stewardship of the firm's resources . . . [it] plays into the hands of managers by allowing them to pursue their own interests at the expense of the firm's financial claimants and society at large. It allows managers and directors to devote the firm's resources to their own favorite causes – the environment, arts, cities, medical research – without being held accountable . . . it is not surprising that stakeholder theory receives substantial support from them.
>
> (*Source:* Jensen, 2001)

However, Jensen goes on to say that companies cannot create shareholder value if they ignore important constituencies. They must have good relationships with customers, employees, suppliers, government and so on. This is a form of corporate social responsibility (CSR), within an overall framework of shareholder wealth maximisation. (Some of the CSR officers, consultants and departments take this a stage further to a belief that the firm must balance all the stakeholder interests

to fulfil its social role – something Jensen disagrees with.) **Exhibit 1.5** illustrates one of the outcomes of the pressure applied by shareholders, who, despite being keenly interested in the returns generated from the shares they hold, nevertheless want companies to act responsibly with regard to climate change, obesity, access by African AIDS patients to medicines, etc. They are acutely aware of reputational risk, the potential backlash against 'heartless capitalists', and litigation (take BP following the Gulf oil spill in 2010), but there are more positive reasons for the shift: people working within organisations are more committed if they feel the firm is 'a force for good in the world'. This is a way to attract and retain good staff, leading to improved business performance. A similar positive opinion about the firm can be generated in the minds of customers, encouraging sales.

Also, simply to tell people to maximise shareholder value may not be enough to motivate them to deliver value. They must be turned on by a vision or a strategy, e.g. to put a PC on every desk, to produce a drug to cure AIDs or to build a state-of-the-art aeroplane. Shareholder value can measure how successful you are, but it does not create superior vision or strategy – you need additional (but subsidiary) goals and measures, which may be identified and supported through a Balanced Scorecard approach, because it allows a greater understanding of what creates value.

Exhibit 1.5

European drugs groups do most for poor

By Andrew Jack in London

Europe-based pharmaceuticals groups led by GlaxoSmithKline are outperforming US and Japanese rivals in efforts to ensure medicines reach the poor, according to an independent evaluation to be published on Monday.

UK-based GSK retained its prime position in the second Access to Medicines Index, while Merck of the US, known for its efforts on HIV and donations to treat river blindness, came next, ahead of Novartis, Gilead and Sanofi-Aventis . . .

The assessment – which analyses research on treatments for diseases of the poor, marketing, pricing and drug donations – reflects a desire by

drug groups to improve their image after suing the South African government to retain their control of HIV drugs a decade ago.

It comes at a time of interest by investors in the potential of emerging markets and strategies to boost volumes by cutting prices and extending sales to those on lower incomes . . .

Andrew Witty, GSK chief executive, said: 'Long-term value creation will come from keeping in step with society. I don't want to look back . . . and say I was in a pretty unusual position to improve healthcare around the world and didn't take advantage of it.'

 Financial Times, 21 June 2010.

John Kay also points out that firms going directly for 'shareholder value' may actually do less well for shareholders than those that focus on vision and excellence first and find themselves shareholder wealth maximisers in an **oblique way**. He argues that Boeing, in the 1990s, sacrificed its vision of being a company always on the cutting edge of commercial plane design, breaking through technological and marketplace barriers. This reduced the vibrancy of the pioneering spirit of the organisation, as it refocused on short-term financial performance measures – *see* **Exhibit 1.6**. However, it is possible to argue that Boeing's managers in the 1990s were not, in fact, shareholder wealth maximisers because they forgot the crucial 'long-term' focus. Being daring and at the cutting edge may be risky, but it often leads to the highest long-term shareholder wealth. Concentrating on short-term financial goals and presenting these as shareholder wealth-maximising actions can lead to slow pace and market irrelevance. So, being too fastidious in requiring immediately visible and quantifiable returns in an uncertain world can result in the rejection of extremely valuable projects that require a leap into the unknown by a team of enthusiasts. Where would Google be today if, when it was starting out, it had required a positive

Exhibit 1.6

Forget how the crow flies

If you want to go in one direction, the best route may involve
going in the other. Paradoxical as it sounds, goals are more likely
to be achieved when pursued indirectly. So the most profitable
companies are not the most profit-oriented, and the happiest
people are not those who make happiness their main aim. The
name of this idea? Obliquity

By John Kay

. . . I once said that Boeing's grip on the world civil aviation market made it the most powerful market leader in world business. Bill Allen was chief executive from 1945 to 1968, as the company created its dominant position. He said that his spirit and that of his colleagues was to eat, breathe, and sleep the world of aeronautics. 'The greatest pleasure life has to offer is the satisfaction that flows from participating in a difficult and constructive undertaking', he explained . . .

The company's largest and riskiest project was the development of the 747 jumbo jet. When a non-executive director asked about the expected return on investment, he was brushed off: there had been some studies, he was told, but the manager concerned couldn't remember the results.

It took only 10 years for Boeing to prove me wrong in asserting that its market position in civil aviation was impregnable. The decisive shift in corporate culture followed the acquisition of its principal US rival, McDonnell Douglas, in 1997. The transformation was exemplified by the CEO, Phil Condit. The company's previous preoccupation with meeting 'technological challenges of supreme magnitude' would, he told Business Week, now have to change. 'We are going into a value-based environment where unit cost, return on investment and shareholder return are the measures by which you'll be judged. That's a big shift.'

The company's senior executives agreed to move from Seattle, where the main production facilities were located, to Chicago. More importantly, the more focused business reviewed risky investments in new civil projects with much greater scepticism. The strategic decision was to redirect resources towards projects for the US military that involved low financial risk. Chicago had the advantage of being nearer to Washington, where government funds were dispensed.

So Boeing's civil orderbook today lags behind that of Airbus, the European consortium whose aims were not initially commercial but which has, almost by chance, become a profitable business. . . . And what was the market's verdict on the company's performance in terms of unit cost, return on investment and shareholder return? Boeing stock, $48 when Condit took over, rose to $70 as he affirmed the commitment to shareholder value; by the time of his enforced resignation in December 2003 it had fallen to $38 . . .

At Boeing, the attempt to focus on simple, well defined objectives proved less successful than management with a broader, more comprehensive conception of objectives . . .

Obliquity gives rise to the profit-seeking paradox: the most profitable companies are not the most profit-oriented. Boeing illustrates how a greater focus on shareholder returns was self-defeating in its own narrow terms . . .

Collins and Porras compared the philosophy of George Merck ('We try never to forget that medicine is for the people. It is not for the profits. The profits follow, and if we have remembered that, they have never failed to appear. The better we have remembered it, the larger they have been') with that of John McKeen of Pfizer ('So far as humanly possible, we aim to get profit out of everything we do').

The individuals who are most successful at making money are not those who are most interested in making money. This is not surprising. The principal route to great wealth is the creation of a successful business, and building a successful business demands exceptional talents and hard work. There is no reason to think these characteristics are associated with greed and materialism: rather the opposite. People who are

▶

Exhibit 1.6 *(continued)*

obsessively interested in money are drawn to get-rich-quick schemes rather than to business opportunities, and when these schemes come off, as occasionally they do, they retire to their villas in the sun . . .

Although we crave time for passive leisure, people engaged in watching television reported low levels of contentment. Csikszentmihalyi's systematic finding is that the activities that yield the highest for satisfaction with life require the successful performance of challenging tasks.

FT John Kay, *Financial Times Magazine*, 17 January 2004, pp. 17–21. Reproduced with kind permission of the Financial Times. (Also see Kay, J. (2010) *Obliquity*, Profile Books.)

number popping out of a rigorous financial analysis of the prospects for its search engine when the internet was relatively primitive? Paul Polman, chief executive of Unilever, is an obliquity man – *see* Exhibit 1.7.

In an interview in 2003 Milton Friedman focused on the main benefit of encouraging businesses to pursue high returns for owners. He said that this results in the best allocation of investment capital among competing industries and product lines. This is good for society because consumers end up with more of what they want because scarce investment money is directed to the best uses, producing the optimum mix of goods and services. 'The self-interest of employees in retaining their jobs will often conflict with this overriding objective.' He went on:

> the best system of corporate governance is one that provides the best incentives to use capital efficiently. . . . You want control . . . in the hands of those who are residual recipients [i.e. shareholders bear the residual risk when a company fails] because they are the ones with the direct interest in using the capital of the firm efficiently.
>
> *Source*: Simon London, *Financial Times Magazine*, 7 June 2003, p. 13.

One final and powerful reason for advancing shareholders' interests above all others (subject to the rules of the game) is very simple: they own the firm and therefore deserve any surplus it produces. The Companies Act 2006 reinforces this by stating that directors' primary duty is to promote the success of the company for the benefit of its members, that is, the shareholders. Yet in the fulfilment of that duty directors should have regard to the interests of employees, suppliers, customers, the environment and corporate reputation. Thus in closing a factory, say, the interests of shareholders trump those of employees, but the latter concerns should not be completely ignored. *The Economist* presents a series of arguments in favour of shareholder supremacy in Exhibit 1.8.

Exhibit 1.7

The outsider in a hurry to shake up his company

By Stefan Stern

. . . Mr Polman makes it clear that shareholders are not exactly the first thing on his mind. 'I do not work for the shareholder, to be honest; I work for the consumer, the customer,' he says. 'I discovered a long time ago that if I focus on doing the right thing for the long term to improve the lives of consumers and customers all over the world,

the business results will come. . . . I'm not driven and I don't drive this business model by driving shareholder value. I drive this business model by focusing on the consumer and customer in a responsible way, and I know that shareholder value can come.'

FT *Financial Times*, 5 April 2010.

Exhibit 1.8

The good company

Companies today are exhorted to be 'socially responsible'. What, exactly, does this mean?

It will no longer do for a company to go quietly about its business, telling no lies and breaking no laws, selling things that people want, and making money. That is so passé. Today, all companies, but especially big ones, are enjoined from every side to worry less about profits and be socially responsible instead. Surprisingly, perhaps, these demands have elicited a willing, not to say avid, response in enlightened boardrooms everywhere. Companies at every opportunity now pay elaborate obeisance to the principles of corporate social responsibility. They have CSR officers, CSR consultants, CSR departments, and CSR initiatives coming out of their ears. A good thing, too, you might think. About time. What kind of idiot or curmudgeon would challenge the case for businesses to behave more responsibly? Thank you for asking.

Cynics and believers

The practices that caring, progressive CEOs mention when speaking at conferences on CSR come in all shapes and sizes. Treat your employees well; encourage loyalty among your customers and suppliers; avoid investing in 'unethical' industries, or in countries where workers are paid low wages or denied decent benefits; take care to save energy and recycle used envelopes; and so on. The range of such policies makes it hazardous to generalise. Some of them advance the interests of shareholders and of the wider world as well; others make everyone, except the office bureaucrats paid to dream them up, worse off. Motives vary too. Some CSR advocates are cynics: they pay lip service to the idea but are chuckling quietly. Others are true believers, born-again champions of a kinder, gentler capitalism.

The one thing that all the nostrums of CSR have in common is that they are based on a faulty – and dangerously faulty – analysis of the capitalist system they are intended to redeem. Admittedly, CSR is now so well entrenched and amply funded that to complain about it may be pointless. We are concerned that it may even be a socially irresponsible use of scarce newsprint. Nonetheless, if businessmen had a clearer understanding of the CSR mindset and its defects, they would be better at their jobs and everybody else would be more prosperous.

Simply put, advocates of CSR work from the premise that unadorned capitalism fails to serve the public interest. The search for profit, they argue, may be a regrettable necessity in the modern world, a sad fact of life if there is to be any private enterprise. But the problem is that the profits of private enterprise go exclusively to shareholders. What about the public good? Only if corporations recognise their obligations to society – to 'stakeholders' other than the owners of the business – will that broader social interest be advanced. Often, governments can force such obligations on companies, through taxes and regulation. But that does not fully discharge the enlightened company's debt to society. For that, one requires CSR.

This is wrong. The goal of a well-run company may be to make profits for its shareholders, but merely in doing that – provided it faces competition in its markets, behaves honestly and obeys the law – the company, without even trying, is doing good works. Its employees willingly work for the company in exchange for wages; the transaction makes them better off. Its customers willingly pay for the company's products; the transaction makes them better off also. All the while, for strictly selfish reasons, well-run companies will strive for friendly long-term relations with employees, suppliers and customers. There is no need for selfless sacrifice when it comes to stakeholders. It goes with the territory.

Thus, the selfish pursuit of profit serves a social purpose. And this is putting it mildly. The standard of living people in the West enjoy today is due to little else but the selfish pursuit of profit. It is a point that Adam Smith emphasised in 'The Wealth of Nations': 'It is not from the benevolence of the butcher, the brewer, or the baker, that we expect our dinner, but from their regard to their own interest.' This is not the fatal defect of capitalism, as CSR-advocates appear to believe; it is the very reason capitalism works.

Maybe so, those advocates might reply, but perhaps the system would work even better if there were a bit more benevolence in the boardroom and a bit less self-interest. In some cases, that might be so, but in general (as Smith also noted) one should be wary of businessmen proclaiming their

▶

Exhibit 1.8 (*continued*)

benevolence. A question to ask of all outbreaks of corporate goodness is, who is paying? Following the Indian Ocean tsunami, many companies made generous donations to charities helping the victims. There could be no worthier cause – but keep in mind that, in the case of public companies, the managers authorising those donations were giving other people's money, not their own. Philanthropy at others' expense, even in a cause as good as that one, is not quite the real thing.

All things considered, there is much to be said for leaving social and economic policy to governments. They, at least, are accountable to voters. Managers lack the time for such endeavours, or should do. Lately they have found it a struggle even to discharge their obligations to shareholders, the people who are paying their wages. If they want to make the world a better place – a commendable aim, to be sure – let them concentrate for the time being on that.

The Economist, 22 January 2005.

This is not the place to advocate one philosophical approach or another which is applicable to all organisations at all times. Many organisations are clearly not shareholder wealth maximisers and are quite comfortable with that. Charities, government departments and other non-profit organisations are fully justified in emphasising a different set of values to those espoused by the commercial firm. The reader is asked to be prepared for two levels of thought when using this book. While it focuses on corporate shareholder wealth decision making, it may be necessary to make small or large modifications to be able to apply the same frameworks and theories to organisations with different goals.

However, beware of organisations that try to balance a number of objectives. Take, for example, football clubs that have floated on the stock market. They have at least two parties to satisfy: (i) shareholders looking for good return on their savings: (ii) fans looking for more spending on players and lower ticket prices. It is very difficult to satisfy both – hence the dramatic tensions and suspicions at so many clubs.

What is shareholder wealth?

Maximising wealth can be defined as maximising purchasing power. The way in which an enterprise enables its owners to indulge in the pleasures of purchasing and consumption is by paying them dividends. The promise of a flow of cash in the form of dividends is what prompts investors to sacrifice immediate consumption and hand over their savings to a management team through the purchase of shares. Shareholders are interested in a flow of dividends over a long time horizon and not necessarily in a quick payback. Take the electronics giant Philips: it could raise vast sums for short-term dividend payouts by ceasing all research and development (R&D) and selling off surplus sites. But this would not maximise shareholder wealth because, by retaining funds within the business, it is believed that new products and ideas, springing from the R&D programme, will produce much higher dividends in the future. Maximising shareholder wealth means maximising the flow of dividends to shareholders *through time* – there is a long-term perspective.

Profit maximisation is not the same as shareholder wealth maximisation

Profit is a concept developed by accountants to aid decision making, one decision being to judge the quality of stewardship shown over the owner's funds. The accountant has to take what is a continuous process, a business activity stretching over many years, and split this into accounting periods of, say, a year, or six months. To some extent this exercise is bound to be artificial and fraught with problems. There are many reasons why accounting profit may not be a good proxy for shareholder wealth. Here are five of them:

● *Prospects* Imagine that there are two firms that have reported identical profits but one firm is more highly valued by its shareholders than the other. One possible reason for this is that recent profit figures fail to reflect the relative potential of the two firms. The stock market

will give a higher share value to the company which shows the greater future growth outlook. Perhaps one set of managers has chosen a short-term approach and raised profits in the near term but have sacrificed long-term prospects. One way of achieving this is to raise prices and slash marketing spend – over the subsequent year profits might be boosted as customers are unable to switch suppliers immediately. Over the long term, however, competitors will respond and profits will fall.

● *Risk* Again two firms could report identical historic profit figures and have future prospects which indicate that they will produce the same average annual returns. However, one firm's returns are subject to much greater variability and so there will be years of losses and, in a particularly bad year, the possibility of bankruptcy. **Exhibit 1.9** shows two firms which have identical average profit but Volatile Joe's profit is subject to much greater risk than that of Steady Eddie. Shareholders are likely to value the firm with stable income flows more highly than one with high risk.

● *Accounting problems* Drawing up a set of accounts is not as scientific and objective as some people try to make out. There is plenty of scope for judgement, guesswork or even cynical manipulation. Imagine the difficulty facing the company accountant and auditors of a clothes retailer when trying to value a dress which has been on sale for six months. Let us suppose the dress cost the firm £50. Perhaps this should go into the balance sheet and then the profit and loss account will not be affected. But what if the store manager says that he can sell that dress only if it is reduced to £30, and contradicting him the managing director says that if a little more effort was made £40 could be achieved? Which figure is the person who drafts the financial accounts going to take? Profits can vary significantly depending on a multitude of small judgements like this.

● *Communication* Investors realise and accept that buying a share is risky. However, they like to reduce their uncertainty and nervousness by finding out as much as they can about the firm. If the firm is reluctant to tell shareholders about such matters as the origin of reported profits, then investors generally will tend to avoid those shares. Fears are likely to arise in the minds of poorly informed investors: did the profits come from the most risky activities and might they therefore disappear next year? Is the company being used to run guns to unsavoury regimes abroad? The senior executives of large quoted firms spend a great deal of time explaining their strategies, sources of income and future investment plans to the large institutional shareholders to make sure that these investors are aware of the quality of the firm and its prospects. Firms that ignore the importance of communication and image in the investment community may be doing their shareholders a disservice as the share price might fall.

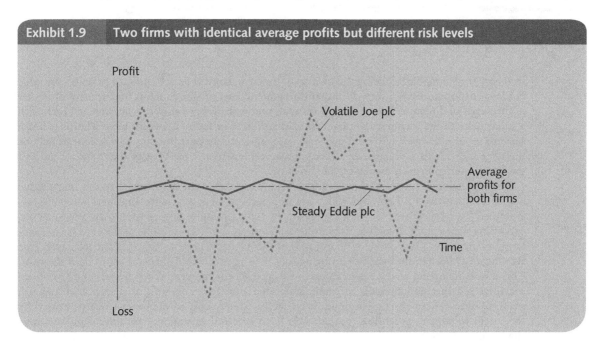

Exhibit 1.9 Two firms with identical average profits but different risk levels

- **Additional capital** Profits can be increased simply by making use of more shareholders' money. If shareholders inject more money into the company or the firm merely retains profits (which belong to shareholders) their future profits can rise, but the *return* on shareholders' money may fall to less than what is available elsewhere for the same level of risk. This is shareholder wealth destructive. For more on this see Chapter 14.

Exhibit 1.10 shows what some leading European companies say about their objectives.

Exhibit 1.10

What companies state as their objective

'Our mission is to make a meaningful difference to patient health through great medicines. We are committed to acting responsibly and to the sustainable development of our business. Our mission requires us to do things in the right way – to behave in accordance with our values and to act with integrity. We believe that our approach delivers lasting value for patients, society and our shareholders.'

AstraZeneca Annual Report 2010

Chief executive's review: 'Our objective remains to build a platform on which we can deliver steady and sustainable long-term growth and value for shareholders. We remain on track to deliver on this objective.'

Tate and Lyle Annual Report 2011

'We aim to constantly increase the value of our company by profitable growth and to remain the number one in chemistry. With innovation and new technologies, we open up new market opportunities. We combine economic success with environmental protection and social responsibility. To realize our goals everyday and across the company, the BASF team aligns its activities with four guidelines: 1. We earn a premium on our cost of capital. 2. We help our customers to be even more successful. 3. We form the best team in the industry. 4. We ensure sustainable development.'

BASF – The Chemical Company, corporate website

'Our strategy seeks to reinforce our position as a leader in the oil and gas industry in order to provide a competitive shareholder return while helping to meet global energy demand in a responsible way.'

Royal Dutch Shell Annual Report 2010

Author's note: This section took longer to complete than expected because most annual reports examined failed to state any objective for the organisation so the search for something to quote was extended. Perhaps this is the most telling fact to emerge!

Corporate governance

In theory the shareholders, being the owners of the firm, control its activities. In practice, the large modern corporation has a very diffuse and fragmented set of shareholders and control often lies in the hands of directors. It is extremely difficult to marshall thousands of shareholders, each with a small stake in the business, to push for change. Thus in many firms we have what is called a separation, or a divorce, of ownership and control. In times past the directors would usually be the same individuals as the owners. Today, however, less than 1 per cent of the shares of most of the largest quoted firms is owned by the directors.

The separation of ownership and control raises worries that the management team may pursue objectives attractive to them, but which are not necessarily beneficial to the shareholders – this is termed 'managerialism' or 'managementism' – for example, raising their own pay or perks, expanding their empire, avoiding risky projects, boosting short-term results at the expense of long-term performance. This conflict is an example of the principal–agent problem. The principals (the shareholders) have to find ways of ensuring that their agents (the managers) act in their interests. This means incurring costs, 'agency costs', to (a) monitor managers' behaviour, and (b) create incentive schemes and controls for managers to encourage the pursuit of shareholders' wealth maximisation. These costs arise in addition to the agency cost of the loss of wealth caused by the extent to which prevention measures do not work and managers continue to pursue non-shareholder wealth goals.

Corporate governance means the system by which companies are managed and controlled. Its main focus is on the responsibilities and obligations placed on the executive directors and the non-executive directors, and on the relationships between the firm's owners, the board of directors and the top tier of managers. The interaction between these groups leads to the defining of the corporate objective, the placing of constraints on managerial behaviour and the setting of targets and incentive payments based on achievement.

The board of directors has the responsibility of overseeing the company, acting as a check on managerialism, so that shareholders' best interests are appropriately prioritised. The board sets company-wide policy and strategic direction, leaving the executive directors to manage day-to-day activities. It also decides who will be an executive director (subject to shareholder vote) and sets their pay. In addition the board oversees the reporting of accounting results to shareholders. The board should also take a keen interest in the ethical behaviour of senior managers.

Annual general meeting

The board is expected to organise an annual general meeting (AGM) at which shareholders are encouraged by the directors to engage in dialogue with the directors, and can vote to change the board of directors if they are dissatisfied. Proxy votes may be assigned if a shareholder cannot attend, i.e. they ask someone else, usually the chairman of the company, to vote in a particular way on their behalf. In theory the shareholders can strongly influence the strategic and operational decisions. However, this power is usually weakened:

- The cost of attending a meeting (or even sending in a proxy form) outweighs the benefit for many shareholders, leading to many (most) votes being unused.

- Many fund managers do not take their 'ownership' of stakes in a corporation seriously, and given that most shares quoted on public stock markets are now owned by institutional investors (e.g. pension funds, insurance funds), when faced with the issue of what to do with a poor board of directors and senior management, rather than acting to remove them, most fund managers find it easier simply to sell the shares and move on.

Corporate governance regulations

There is a considerable range of legislation and other regulatory pressures designed to encourage directors to act in shareholders' interests. In the UK the Companies Act 2006 requires certain minimum standards of behaviour, as does the London Stock Exchange (LSE). For example, directors are forbidden to use their position to profit at the expense of shareholders, e.g. they cannot buy shares in their own company just before announcing unexpectedly high profits. There is the back-up of the financial industry regulator, the Financial Services Authority (FSA) (to be the Financial Conduct Authority (FCA), in 2013) and the Financial Reporting Council (FRC), an accounting body.

Following a number of financial scandals, guidelines of best practice in corporate governance were issued. These are now consolidated in the UK Corporate Governance Code, which is backed by the FSA, the LSE and the FRC.

Under the code, directors of companies listed[1] on the Main Market of the LSE are required to state in the annual report how the principles of the code have been applied. If the principles have not been followed they have to state why – the 'comply or explain' approach. The principles include:

- The board should include a balance of executive and non-executive directors (and in particular independent[2] non-executive directors) such that no individual or small group of individuals can dominate the board's decision taking. For large companies (the largest 350 on the LSE) at least half the board, excluding the chairman, should comprise non-executive

1 Overseas companies listed on the Main Market are required to disclose the significant ways in which their corporate governance practices differ from those set out in the Code.
2 The board should determine whether the director is independent in character and judgement and whether there are relationships or circumstances which are likely to affect, or could appear to affect, the director's judgement. To be independent the non-executive directors generally should not, for example, be a customer, ex-employee, supplier, or a friend of the founding family or the chief executive.

directors determined by the board to be independent. The independent non-executive directors can act as a powerful counterweight to the executive directors. These directors are not full-time and not concerned with day-to-day management. They may be able to take a broader view than executive directors, who may become excessively focused on detail. The experienced individuals who become non-executive directors are not expected to be dependent on the director's fee for income and can therefore afford to be independently minded. They are expected to 'constructively challenge and help develop proposals on strategy . . . scrutinize the performance of management in meeting agreed goals and objectives and monitor the reporting of performance' (The UK Code at www.frc.org.uk, p. 11).

- No one individual on the board should be able to dominate and impose their will. The running of the board of directors (by a chairman) should be a separate responsibility conducted by a person who is not also responsible for running the business, i.e. the chief executive officer (CEO) or managing director (MD). (This is frequently ignored in practice, which is permitted, if a written justification is presented to shareholders.)

- There should be transparency on directors' remuneration, requiring a remuneration committee consisting exclusively of non-executive directors, independent of management. No director should be involved in deciding his or her remuneration. A significant proportion of remuneration should be linked to corporate and individual performance.

- The procedure for the appointment of board directors should be formal (nomination committee), rigorous, objective (based on merit) and transparent (information on the terms and conditions made available). Directors are to retire by rotation every year – they may be re-elected.

- The audit committee (responsible for validating financial figures, e.g. by appointing effective external auditors, and for the system of corporate reporting, risk management and internal control principles) should consist exclusively of independent non-executive directors, otherwise the committee would not be able to act as a check and balance to the executive directors.

- Directors are required to communicate with shareholders, e.g. meetings arranged between major shareholders and directors or using the annual general meeting to explain the company's performance and encourage discussion.

The 'comply or explain' approach is in contrast to many other systems of regulation of corporate governance around the world – these are often strict rule-based systems with lawyers to the fore (e.g. Sarbanes–Oxley regulations in the US, which have frightened companies away from listing on a US stock market). The code specifically allows companies to deviate from the guideline, so long as this can be justified with reference to shareholder well-being: 'It is recognised that an alternative to following a provision [of the code] may be justified in particular circumstances if good governance can be achieved by other means. A condition of doing so is that the reasons for it should be explained clearly and carefully to shareholders, who may wish to discuss the position with the company and whose voting intentions may be influenced as a result' (The UK Code at www.frc.org.uk, p. 4). Furthermore, some of the provisions do not apply to companies smaller than the largest 350 listed on the LSE. However, failure to comply or explain properly will result in suspension from the stock exchange.

www.ecgi.org displays corporate governance codes in a range of countries.

There are various other (complementary) methods used to try to align the actions of senior management with the interests of shareholders, that is, to achieve 'goal congruence'.

- ***Linking rewards to shareholder wealth improvements*** A technique widely employed in industry is to grant directors and other senior managers share options. These permit managers to purchase shares at some date in the future at a price which is fixed now. If the share price rises significantly between the date when the option was granted and the date when the shares can be bought, the manager can make a fortune by buying at the pre-arranged price and then selling in the marketplace. For example, in 2013 managers might be granted the right to buy shares in 2019 at a price of £1.50. If the market price moves to, say, £2.30 in 2019, the managers can buy and then sell the shares, making a gain of 80p. The managers under such a scheme have a clear interest in achieving a rise in share price and thus congruence comes about to

some extent. An alternative method is to allot shares to managers if they achieve certain performance targets, for example growth in earnings per share or return on assets. Many companies have **long-term incentive plans (LTIPs)** for senior executives which at the end of three years or more pay bonuses if certain targets are surpassed, e.g. share price rise or high profit achieved. **Exhibit 1.11** discusses share option schemes and other ways of encouraging managers to promote the interests of shareholders.

Exhibit 1.11

How to encourage managers to act more like owners

By Stefan Stern

What would your customers say if they could see your expenses claim? The abstemious can rest easy. But extravagant restaurant receipts, first-class travel and accommodation, huge taxi fares – such things might not endear you to the people you are supposed to be serving. You should expect a tough conversation about the prices you charge if customers get the impression you are enjoying the high life with their money.

That is why smart business leaders advise their colleagues to imagine they are spending their own money when they are out on company business. Act like an owner, the adage goes. Be responsible. Think before you splash the company's cash about.

This is a micro-level example of what has been called the 'principal-agent problem'. Even the most senior managers are not, usually, the owners of the business they are working for. It may not be easy for them to think and act like an owner. At the same time, can owners be confident that managers are working in the company's best interests and not simply pursuing their own selfish agenda?

This question was explored by two academics, Michael Jensen and William Meckling, in a famous 1976 paper ('Theory of the firm: managerial behaviour, agency costs and ownership structure'), which popularised so-called agency theory. Their answer to the problem? Among other things, try to align the interests of managers and shareholders. Use share options to give managers 'skin in the game', a personal interest in the success – or failure – of the company. Incentives work: they should be deployed to get people working towards the same end.

There have been, to put it at its gentlest, regrettable unintended consequences to the spread of this theory. It turns out that the simple solution of share options does not solve the complicated problem of how to encourage and reward effective, responsible management.

For one thing, senior managers may not have the same time horizons as owners. A chief executive might reasonably calculate that he or she will be given no more than three or four years to run the business before their time is up. You would understand it if that CEO worked pretty hard to get the share price up fast in order to make those share options more valuable. And the longer-term consequences for the business in engineering such a rapid share price rise? Not necessarily the CEO's problem.

The shareholder base will, in any case, reflect a wide range of characters with varying priorities. There will be long-term institutional investors and hedge funds working in their own unique way. You can't easily be aligned with all of these people at the same time.

Prof Jensen conceded in 2002, in the wake of the dotcom crash, that the incentives he regarded as crucial could do terrible harm. 'In the bubble, the carrots (options) became managerial heroin, encouraging a focus on short-term prices with destructive long-term consequences,' he said. 'It also encouraged behaviour that actually reduced the value of some firms to their shareholders.'

Stewardship – steady, long-term leadership that may not be reflected in rapid rises in the share price – is harder to reward with remuneration schemes based on stock markets.

In an important critique published in 2004 ('Bad management theories are destroying good management practices'), Sumantra Ghoshal condemned agency theory as an example of all that was wrong with modern management. Amoral theories taught in business schools, he said, had 'actively freed their students from any sense of moral responsibility'. Agency theory served to convert 'collective pessimism about managers into realised pathologies in management behaviours'.

▶

Exhibit 1.11 *(continued)*

According to this critique, the theory seems to launch a cycle of distrust. Managers are knaves, out for themselves, who have to be tied in with share options. But managers who feel regarded in this way can become unmotivated and in the end untrustworthy. Why has executive pay exploded over the past 20 years? Partly, Prof Ghoshal suggested, because managers have sunk to reach the low expectations people have for them.

So is the idea of managers acting like owners a futile dream? Not necessarily. Drawing on pointers given to him by a former boss, Phil Gerbyshak, a management blogger, has posted some apparently humdrum but, in fact, sensible thoughts on how managers could live up to that goal (my paraphrasing):

- Always act professionally. You never know who is going to hear what you're saying or see what you're doing.
- Treat everyone you talk to with respect, regardless of their position. Nothing and nobody is beneath you.
- A little overtime won't hurt. Work until the job is done.
- If you're the last one in the room, turn out the light.
- Be on time for meetings. Time is money. Why would you waste time?

Less exciting, perhaps, than holding plenty of in-the-money options. But more likely to do long-term good to a business.

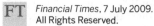

- *Sackings* The threat of being sacked with the accompanying humiliation and financial loss may encourage managers not to diverge too far from the shareholders' wealth path. However, this method is employed in extreme circumstances only. It is sometimes difficult to implement because of the difficulties of making a coordinated shareholder effort. It is made easier if the majority of directors are independent of the executives.

- *Selling shares and the takeover threat* Over 70 per cent of the shares of the typical company quoted on the London stock market are owned by financial institutions such as pension and insurance funds. These organisations generally are not prepared to put large resources into monitoring and controlling all the hundreds of firms of which they own a part. Quite often their first response, if they observe that management is not acting in what they regard as their best interest, is to sell the share rather than intervene. This will result in a lower share price, making the raising of funds more difficult. It may also lower rewards to managers whose remuneration partly depends on the share price level. If this process continues the firm may become vulnerable to a merger bid by another group of managers, resulting in a loss of top management posts. Fear of being taken over can establish some sort of backstop position to prevent shareholder wealth considerations being totally ignored.

- *Information flow* The accounting profession, the stock exchange and the investing institutions have conducted a continuous battle to encourage or force firms to release more accurate, timely and detailed information concerning their operations. The quality of corporate accounts and annual reports has generally improved, as has the availability of other forms of information flowing to investors and analysts, such as company briefings and company announcements (which are available from financial websites, e.g. www.uk.advfn.com). All this helps to monitor firms, and identify early any wealth-destroying actions by wayward managers, but as a number of recent scandals have shown, matters are still far from perfect.

In some countries the interests of shareholders are often placed far below those of powerful people – *see* Exhibit 1.12.

Exhibit 1.12

Satyam sums up Asian governance failings

By Kevin Brown in Singapore

In January last year, India's corporate establishment was rocked by one of the biggest scandals yet to emerge in Asia – the admission by B. Ramalinga Raju, chairman of Satyam, that he had invented $1bn of cash on the company's books, not to mention 13,000 employees.

Mr Raju is now on trial. But the scandal at Satyam, once one of India's top five IT companies, is still unfolding. The company, later acquired by the Mahindra group, disclosed a few days ago that the total financial irregularities involved amount to $1.7bn.

It also faces a $68m shareholders' lawsuit in New York, and a possible civil suit from the US Securities and Exchange Commission.

The Satyam case is extraordinary in its scale and its direct effect on the company's workforce, now halved from a peak of 50,000. But in the contempt it displays for the rights of minority shareholders and other stakeholders it reflects the dire state of corporate governance in much of Asia.

Sometimes this contempt is political. In China, a group of top executives at China Eastern Airlines, Air China and China Southern Airlines, suddenly swapped jobs in late 2008 without warning nor explanation, on orders from the Communist party. It made no difference that the three airlines are listed in Hong Kong. Sometimes it is nationalistic. Lee Kun-hee, convicted on corruption charges two years ago, was reinstated as chairman of Samsung in March after being granted a pardon by President Lee Myung-bak. The aggressively pro-big business president said Mr Lee was needed to help win the 2018 Winter Olympic Games for Pyeongchang.

Sometimes it is crudely financial. Hong Kong regulatory proposals that would have prevented directors benefiting from inside knowledge when trading their own companies' shares were scrapped when the territory's powerful tycoons revolted against an extension of the existing short closed period for such trades.

In much of the region, corporate governance is a low priority for both companies and governments, largely because both have bought the argument that the people most likely to run a company well over the long term are its majority owners, especially when they rely on dividends for income.

The result, in many countries, is weak legislation, underpowered regulators and, often, poor access to the courts for minorities seeking redress. Truly independent directors are a rarity, related party transactions are common, and regulators often have few sanctions.

There are bright spots. Two years ago, Hong Kong became the first and only Asian jurisdiction to introduce mandatory voting by poll for all resolutions at all shareholder meetings. In Thailand, most votes at general meetings are now by poll.

Hong Kong's Securities and Futures Commission is taking an increasingly tough line against insider trading, with several successful prosecutions. For the first time, it has won a court order disqualifying directors for non-disclosure of material information.

In Singapore, the central bank last month won its first civil suit judgment against a fund manager for manipulating the share price of a listed company to raise its own net asset value.

Elsewhere, Japan has toughened up disclosure rules and introduced a requirement for at least one independent director to sit on boards of listed companies. On the other hand, audit committees remain almost unknown and most shareholder votes include only proxies, mainly representing institutions.

Corporate governance matters because it protects small investors from big ones, restricts opportunities for criminal or questionable behaviour and attracts capital by reassuring investors they will not lose their holding because the finance director has decamped with the treasury.

But there is also evidence that it improves share performance. CLSA, a Hong Kong brokerage, said in a report published last month that a survey of 875 companies over six years from 2004 showed a clear correlation between good governance standards and stock market performance, after isolating other factors.

Nevertheless, Asia is failing to catch up with global standards. Jamie Allen, secretary-general of the Asia Corporate Governance Association, an institutional lobbying and research group, says that even the leading jurisdictions – Singapore, Hong Kong and Tokyo – remain well behind London and New York.

▶

Exhibit 1.12 *(continued)*

That needs to change. Governments must set clear standards, and companies need to grasp that good governance is in their own interests, in the long term if not the short. But ticking the right boxes is not enough. For all its faults, Satyam had an independent audit committee. It just was not looking in the right places.

Kevin Brown is the FT's Asia Regional Correspondent.

Primitive and modern economies

A simple economy

Before we proceed to discuss the role of the financial manager and the part played by various financial institutions it is useful to gain an overview of the economy and the place of the financial system within society. To see the role of the financial sector in perspective it is, perhaps, of value to try to imagine a society without any financial services. Imagine how people would go about their daily business in the absence of either money or financial institutions. This sort of economy is represented in Exhibit 1.13. Here there are only two sectors in society. The business sector produces goods and services, making use of the resources of labour, land and commodities which are owned by the household sector. The household sector is paid with the goods and services produced by the business sector.

Exhibit 1.13 Flows within a simple economy – production level

Resources: land, labour, commodities

Household sector

Business sector

Output of goods and services

In this economy there is no money and therefore there are two choices open to the household sector upon receipt of the goods and services:

1 *Consumption* Commodities can be consumed now either by taking those specific items provided from the place of work and enjoying their consumption directly, or, under a barter system, by exchanging them with other households to widen the variety of consumption.

2 *Investment* Some immediate consumption could be forgone so that resources can be put into building assets which will produce a higher level of consumption in the future. For instance, a worker takes payment in the form of a plough so that in future years when he enters the productive (business) sector he can produce more food per acre.

The introduction of money

Under a barter system much time and effort is expended in searching out other households interested in trade. It quickly becomes apparent that a tool is needed to help make transactions more

efficient. People will need something into which all goods and services received can be converted. That something would have to be small and portable, it would have to hold its value over a long period of time and have general acceptability. This will enable people to take the commodities given in exchange for, say, labour and then avoid the necessity of, say, carrying the bushels of wheat to market to exchange them for bricks. Instead **money** could be paid in exchange for labour, and money taken to the market to buy bricks. Various things have been used as a means of exchange ranging from cowry shells to cigarettes (in prisons particularly) but the most popular used to be a metal, usually gold or silver. (Now it is less tangible such as credit and debit card transactions.) The introduction of money into the system creates monetary as well as real flows of goods and services – *see* Exhibit 1.14.

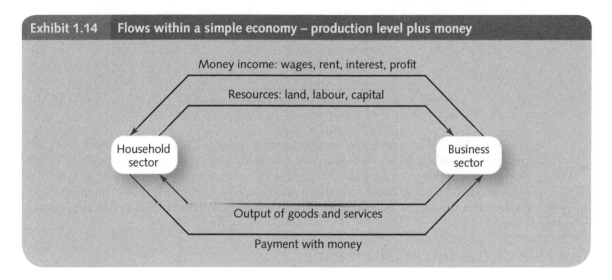

Exhibit 1.14 Flows within a simple economy – production level plus money

Money income: wages, rent, interest, profit

Resources: land, labour, capital

Household sector

Business sector

Output of goods and services

Payment with money

Investment in a money economy

Investment involves resources being laid aside now to produce a return in the future, for instance, today's consumption is reduced in order to put resources into building a factory and the creation of machine tools to produce goods in later years. Most investment is made in the business sector but it is not the business sector consumption which is reduced if investment is to take place, as all resources are ultimately owned by households. Society needs individuals who are prepared to sacrifice consumption now and to wait for investments to come to fruition. These capitalists are willing to defer consumption and put their funds at risk within the business sector but only if they anticipate a suitable return. In a modern, sophisticated economy there are large-scale flows of investment resources from the ultimate owners (individuals who make up households) to the business sector. Even the profits of previous years' endeavours retained within the business belong to households – they have merely permitted firms to hold on to those resources for further investments on their behalf.

Investment in the twenty-first century is on a grand scale and the time gap between sacrifice and return has in many cases grown very large. This has increased the risks to any one individual investor and so investments tend to be made via pooled funds drawing on the savings of many thousands of households. A capital market has developed to assist the flow of funds between the business and household sectors. Among their other functions the financial markets reduce risk through their regulatory regimes and insistence on a high level of disclosure of information. In these more advanced financial structures businesses issue securities which give the holder the right to receive income in specified circumstances. Those that hold debt securities have a relatively high certainty of receiving a flow of interest (except those holding Greek debt!). Those that buy a security called a share have less certainty about what they will receive but, because the return is based on a share of profit, they expect to gain a higher return than if they had merely lent money to the firm.

In Exhibit 1.15 we can see household savings going into business investment. In exchange for this investment the business sector issues securities which show the claims that households have

Exhibit 1.15 Flows within a modern economy

Securities are issued and a return received, e.g. shares, bonds

Money income: wages, rent, interest, profit

Resources: land, labour, capital

Household sector

Business sector

Output of goods and services

Payment with money

Savings of households going into productive investment

over firms. This exhibit shows three interconnected systems. The first is the flow of real goods and services. The second is a flow of money. The third is the investment system which enables production and consumption to be increased in the future. It is mainly in facilitating the flow of investment finance that the financial sector has a role in our society. The financial system increases the efficiency of the real economy by encouraging the flow of funds to productive uses.

The role of the financial manager

To be able to carry on a business a company needs **real assets**. These real assets may be tangible, such as buildings, plant, machinery, vehicles and so on. Alternatively a firm may invest in intangible real assets, for example patents, expertise, licensing rights, etc. To obtain these real assets corporations sell financial claims to raise money; to lenders a bundle of rights are sold within a loan contract, to shareholders rights over the ownership of a company are sold as well as the right to receive a proportion of profits produced. The financial manager has the task of both raising finance by selling financial claims and advising on the use of those funds within the business. This is illustrated in Exhibit 1.16.

The financial manager plays a pivotal role in the following.

Interaction with the financial markets

In order to raise finance, knowledge is needed of the financial markets and the way in which they operate. To raise share (equity) capital, awareness of the rigours and processes involved in 'taking a new company to market' might be useful. For instance, what is the role of an issuing house? What services do brokers, accountants, solicitors, etc. provide to a company wishing to float? Once a company is quoted on a stock market it is going to be useful to know about ways of raising additional equity capital – what about rights issues and open offers? Knowledge of exchanges such as the Alternative Investment Market (AIM) (UK) or the European market Euronext might be valuable. If the firm does not wish to have its shares quoted on an exchange perhaps an investigation needs to be made into the possibility of raising money through the private equity industry.

Understanding how shares are priced and what it is that shareholders are looking for when sacrificing present consumption to make an investment could help the firm to tailor its strategy, operations and financing decisions to suit its owners. These, and dozens of other equity finance questions, are part of the remit of the finance expert within the firm. All other managers need a working knowledge of these issues too.

Another major source of finance comes from banks. Understanding the operation of banks and what concerns them when lending to a firm may enable you to present your case better, to negoti-

Exhibit 1.16 The flow of cash between capital markets and the firm's operations

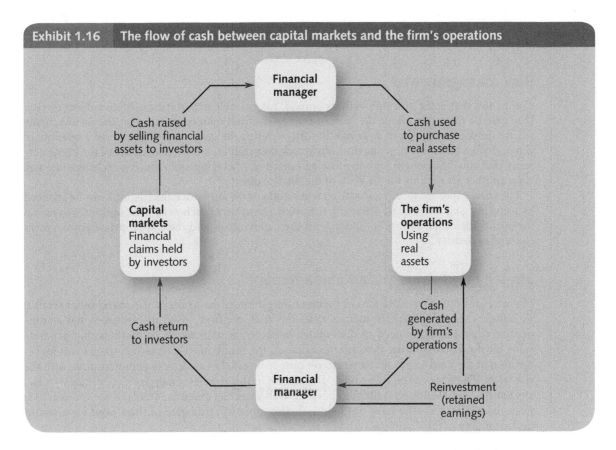

ate improved terms and obtain finance which fits the cash-flow patterns of the firm. Then there are ways of borrowing which by-pass banks. Bonds could be issued either domestically or internationally. Medium-term notes, commercial paper, leasing, hire purchase and factoring are other possibilities (all described in Chapters 11 and 12).

Once a knowledge has been gained of each of these alternative financial instruments and of the operation of their respective financial markets, then the financial manager has to consider the issue of the correct balance between the different types. What proportion of debt to equity? What proportion of short-term finance to long-term finance and so on?

Perhaps you can already appreciate that the finance function is far from a boring 'bean-counting' role. It is a dynamic function with a constant need for up-to-date and relevant knowledge. The success or failure of the entire business may rest on the quality of the interaction between the firm and the financial markets. The financial manager stands at the interface between the two.

Investment

Decisions have to be made concerning how much to invest in real assets and which specific projects to undertake (**capital budgeting decisions** or **capital expenditure (capex)**). Managers need knowledge of both analytical techniques to aid these sorts of decisions and to be aware of a wide variety of factors which might have some influence on the wisdom of proceeding with a particular investment. These range from corporate strategy and budgeting restrictions to culture and the commitment of individuals likely to be called upon to support an activity.

There is also the opposite of investment – **divestment** or **disinvestment**. Assets, such as a factory or subsidiary, that are no longer contributing to shareholder wealth need to be disposed of to release capital.

Treasury management

The management of cash may fall under the aegis of the financial manager. Many firms have large sums of cash which need to be managed properly to obtain a high return for shareholders. Other

areas of responsibility might include inventory control, creditor and debtor management, and issues of solvency and liquidity.

Risk management

Companies that enter into transactions abroad, for example exporters, are often subject to risk: they may be uncertain about the sum of money (in their own currency) that they will actually receive on the deal. Three or four months after sending the goods they may receive a quantity of yen or dollars but at the time the deal was struck they did not know the quantity of the home currency that could be bought with the foreign currency. Managing and reducing exchange rate risk is yet another area calling on the skills of the finance director.

Likewise, exposure to interest rate changes and commodity price fluctuations can be reduced by using hedging techniques. These often employ instruments such as futures, options, swaps and forward agreements. Failure to understand these derivatives and their appropriate employment can lead to disaster.

Strategy and value-based management

Managers need to formulate and implement long-term plans to maximise shareholder wealth. This means selecting markets and activities in which the firm, given its resources, has a competitive edge. Managers need to distinguish between those products or markets that generate value for the firm and those that destroy value. At the centre of **value-based management** is recognition of the need to produce a return on money invested in an activity commensurate with the risk taken. The financial manager has a pivotal role in this strategic analysis.

Financial knowledge is essential to perform well as a chief executive (CEO) – see **Exhibit 1.17**. Even those directors who have not held a finance post will be aware of their need for a sound understanding of the discipline.

Exhibit 1.17

Finance directors step on to centre stage

By Alison Smith and Gill Plimmer

It has been a season to put a spring in the step of finance directors. Within a couple of months earlier this year, no fewer than five became chief executives at FTSE 250 companies.

David Sleath, who took the helm at office and warehouse developer Segro at the annual meeting in late April, is the most recent in a clutch of chief financial officer promotions that began with John Hunter becoming chief executive at software group SDL in February.

The fashion for finance officers is not confined to movement within a company. Ian Dyson was finance director at Marks and Spencer before becoming chief executive of Punch Taverns, while Colin Day left household goods group Reckitt Benckiser and then became chief executive of cigarette filter maker Filtrona.

They are in good company. Analysis by headhunters Spencer Stuart shows that about one-third of FTSE 100 chief executives have a financial background, 15

of them being former chief financial officers. They include Peter Voser at Royal Dutch Shell, Jeremy Darroch at BSkyB, and Tidjane Thiam at Prudential.

Tim Burrage, a consultant at Spencer Stuart, says that the proportion of CFOs who go on to become chief executive is pretty consistent over time, though their routes to the top jobs have changed.

'It is much rarer for someone to have come up through a 25-year career at a single organisation,' he says, 'and more common for someone to have had a career across three, four or five companies taking in at least one big general management role along the way.'

Other headhunters see a different pattern. Mark Freebairn, partner and head of the CFO recruitment practice at Odgers Berndtson, says the promotion of CFOs varies according to economic conditions. 'Typically they are appointed when the market is slowing because shareholders want to see the business led by someone who can manage

Exhibit 1.17 *(continued)*

the cost base. But when the market starts to grow, businesses worry that the CFO is too dull and grey. Then they appoint a sales director or marketing manager because they are the creative visionaries who are much more exciting.'

Headhunters cite two main factors pushing finance directors to the fore when it comes to recent chief executive appointments.

The first is a rise of a generation of finance directors who have made a point of managing their careers so they gain wider skills on their way to the C-suite. 'Many have acquired experience leading significant operational change to complement their technical and corporate finance expertise,' says Aidan Bell of Spencer Stuart.

'A lot of CFOs will have had at least one non-executive position,' says Peter Waine, partner at Hanson Green.

Second is the change in the finance function itself, which has become both broader and more prominent during the past decade. 'Finance directors have got much more involved in strategic operations,' Mr Freebairn says. 'They have got

heavily involved in pricing, product development and margin management.'

'A CFO is now much more like a partner with the CEO than at a lower place in the hierarchy,' says Marie Hollein, president and chief executive of Financial Executives International, a professional association for senior financial officers.

Perhaps in keeping with the image of CFOs becoming cautious CEOs, they rarely seem to feature as high-profile corporate hero or villain.

However, headhunters are conscious that while the route for a CFO becoming a CEO may be becoming clearer, stories do not always have a happy ending.

Mr Burrage is clear that some CFOs should recognise their talents may not lie in taking centre stage.

'There are examples of outstanding financial executives who have sought out commercial opportunities and have CEO capability in their DNA,' he says. 'But finance directors who don't have those instincts should not try and reinvent themselves as chief executives when they would do better to stay as world-class financial officers.'

 Financial Times, 15 May 2011.

The flow of funds and financial intermediation

Exhibit 1.16 looked at the simple relationship between a firm and investors. Unfortunately the real world is somewhat more complicated and the flow of funds within the financial system involves a number of other institutions and agencies. Exhibit 1.18 is a more realistic representation of the financial interactions between different groups in society.

Households generally place the largest proportion of their savings with **financial institutions**. These organisations then put that money to work. Some of it is lent back to members of the household sector in the form of, say, a mortgage to purchase a house, or as a personal loan. Some of the money is used to buy securities issued by the business sector. The institutions will expect a return on these loans and shares, which flows back in the form of interest and dividends. However, they are often prepared for businesses to retain profit within the firm for further investment in the hope of greater returns in the future. The government sector enters into the financial system in a number of ways, two of which are shown in Exhibit 1.18. Taxes are taken from businesses and this adds a further dimension to financial decisions – for example, taking taxation into account when selecting sources of finance and when analysing investment proposals. Second, governments usually fail to match their revenues with their expenditure and therefore borrow significant sums from the financial institutions. The diagram in Exhibit 1.18 remains a gross simplification – it has not allowed for overseas financial transactions, for example – but it does demonstrate a crucial role for financial institutions in an advanced market economy.

Primary investors

Typically the household sector is in financial surplus. This sector contains the savers of society. It is these individuals who become the main providers of funds used for investment in the business

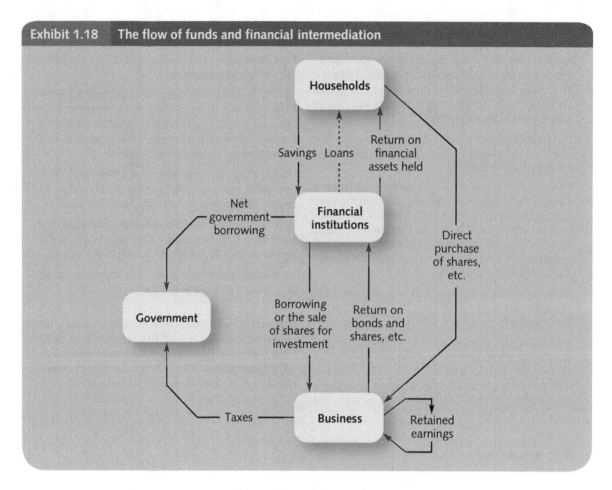

Exhibit 1.18 The flow of funds and financial intermediation

sector. **Primary investors** tend to prefer to exchange their cash for financial assets which (a) allow them to get their money back quickly should they need to (with low transaction cost of doing so) and (b) have a high degree of certainty over the amount they will receive back. That is, primary investors like high **liquidity** and low risk. Lending directly to a firm with a project proposal to build a North Sea oil platform which will not be sold until five years have passed is not a high-liquidity and low-risk investment. However, putting money into a sock under the bed is (if we exclude the possibility of the risk of sock theft).

Ultimate borrowers

In our simplified model the **ultimate borrowers** are in the business sector. These firms are trying to maximise the wealth generated by their activities. To do this companies need to invest in real plant, equipment and other assets, often for long periods of time. The firms, in order to serve their social function, need to attract funds for use over many years. Also these funds are to be put at risk, sometimes very high risk. (Here we are using the term 'borrower' broadly to include all forms of finance, even 'borrowing' by selling shares.)

Conflict of preferences

We have a **conflict of preference** between the primary investors wanting low-cost liquidity and certainty, and the ultimate borrowers wanting long-term risk-bearing capital. A further complicating factor is that savers usually save on a small scale, £100 here or £200 there, whereas businesses are likely to need large sums of money. Imagine some of the problems that would occur in a society which did not have any financial intermediaries. Here lending and share buying will occur only as a result of direct contact and negotiation between two parties. If there were no

organised market where financial securities could be sold on to other investors the fund provider, once committed, would be trapped in an illiquid investment. Also the costs that the two parties might incur in searching to find each other in the first place might be considerable. Following contact a thorough agreement would need to be drawn up to safeguard the investor, and additional expense would be incurred obtaining information to monitor the firm and its progress. In sum, the obstacles to putting saved funds to productive use would lead many to give up and to retain their cash. Those that do persevere will demand exceptionally high rates of return from the borrowers to compensate them for poor liquidity, risk, search costs, agreement costs and monitoring costs. This will mean that few firms will be able to justify investments because they cannot obtain those high levels of return when the funds are invested in real assets. As a result few investments take place and the wealth of society fails to grow. Exhibit 1.19 shows (by the top arrow) little money flowing from saving into investment.

The introduction of financial intermediaries

The problem of under-investment can be alleviated greatly by the introduction of financial institutions (e.g. banks) and financial markets (e.g. a stock exchange). Their role is to facilitate the flow of funds from primary investors to ultimate borrowers at a low cost. They do this by solving the conflict of preferences. There are two types of financial intermediation: the first is an agency or brokerage type operation which brings together lenders and firms, the second is an asset-transforming type of intermediation, in which the conflict is resolved by creating intermediate securities which have the risk, liquidity and volume characteristics which the investors prefer. The financial institution raises money by offering these securities, and then uses the acquired funds to purchase primary securities issued by firms.

Brokers

At its simplest an intermediary is a 'go-between', someone who matches up a provider of finance with a user of funds. This type of intermediary is particularly useful for reducing the search costs for both parties. Stockbrokers, for example, make it easy for investors wanting to buy shares in a newly floated company. Brokers may also have some skill at collecting information on a firm and monitoring its activities, saving the investor time. They also act as middlemen when an investor wishes to sell to another, thus enhancing the liquidity of the fund providers. Another example is the Post Office, which enables individuals to lend to the UK government in a convenient and cheap manner by buying National Savings Income Bonds or Premium Bonds.

Asset transformers

Intermediaries, by creating a completely new security, the intermediate security, increase the opportunities available to savers, encouraging them to invest and thus reducing the cost of finance for the productive sector. The transformation function can act in a number of different ways.

Risk transformation

For example, instead of an individual lending directly to a business with a great idea, such as installing wind turbines in the English Channel, a bank creates a deposit or current account with relatively low risk for the investor's savings. Lending directly to the firm the saver would demand compensation for the probability of default on the loan and therefore the business would have to pay a very high rate of interest which would inhibit investment. The bank, acting as an intermediary, creates a special kind of security called a bank account agreement. The intermediary then uses the funds attracted by the new financial asset to buy a security issued by the wind farm owner (the primary security) when it obtains long-term debt capital. Because of the extra security that a lender has by holding a bank account as a financial asset rather than by making a loan direct to a firm, the lender is prepared to accept a lower rate of interest and the ultimate borrower obtains funds at a relatively low cost. The bank is able to reduce its risk exposure to any one project by diversifying its loan portfolio among a number of firms. It can also reduce risk by building up

Exhibit 1.19 Savings into investment in an economy without financial intermediaries

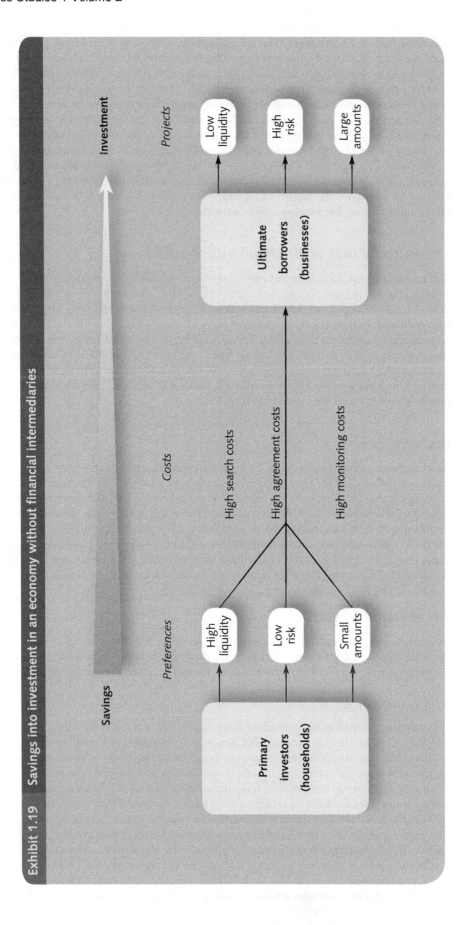

expertise in assessing and monitoring firms and their associated risk. Another example of **risk transformation** is when unit or investment companies (*see* later in this chapter) take savers' funds and spread these over a wide range of company shares.

Maturity (liquidity) transformation

The fact that a bank lends long term for a risky venture does not mean that the primary lender is subjected to illiquidity. Liquidity is not a problem because banks maintain sufficient liquid funds to meet their liabilities when they arise. You can walk into a bank and take the money from your account at short notice because the bank, given its size, exploits economies of scale and anticipates that only a small fraction of its customers will withdraw their money on any one day. Banks and building societies play an important role in borrowing 'short' and lending 'long'.

Volume transformation

Many institutions gather small amounts of money from numerous savers and re-package these sums into larger bundles for investment in the business sector. Apart from the banks and building societies, unit trusts are important here. It is uneconomic for an investor with, say, £50 per month, who wants to invest in shares, to buy small quantities periodically. Unit trusts gather together hundreds of individuals' monthly savings and invest them in a broad range of shares, thereby exploiting economies in transaction costs.

Intermediaries' economies of scale

An intermediary, such as a bank, is able to accept lending to (and investing in shares of) companies at a relatively low rate of return because of the economies of scale enjoyed compared with the primary investor. These **economies of scale** include:

(a) *Efficiencies in gathering information* on the riskiness of lending to a particular firm. Individuals do not have access to the same data sources or expert analysis.

(b) *Risk spreading* Intermediaries are able to spread funds across a large number of borrowers and thereby reduce overall risk. Individual investors may be unable to do this.

(c) *Transaction costs* They are able to reduce the search, agreement and monitoring costs that would be incurred by savers and borrowers in a direct transaction. Banks, for example, are convenient, safe locations with standardised types of securities. Savers do not have to spend time examining the contract they are entering upon when, say, they open a bank account. How many of us read the small print when we opened a bank account?

The reduced **information costs**, convenience and passed-on benefits from the economies of operating on a large scale mean that primary investors are motivated to place their savings with intermediaries.

Apart from linking savers with ultimate borrowers there are financial services within the household sector and within the business sector. For example, transferring money between bank accounts or providing financial advice.

Financial markets

A financial market, such as a stock exchange, has two aspects: there is the **primary market** where funds are raised from investors by the firm, and there is the **secondary market** in which investors buy and sell securities, such as shares and bonds, between each other. The securities sold into the primary market are generally done so on the understanding that repayment will not be made for many years, if ever, and so it is beneficial for the original buyer to be able to sell on to other investors in the secondary market. In this way the firm achieves its objective of raising finance that will stay in the firm for a lengthy period and the investor has retained the ability to liquidate (turn into cash) a holding by selling to another investor. In addition a well-regulated exchange encourages investment by reducing search, agreement and monitoring costs – *see* **Exhibit 1.20**.

Exhibit 1.20 Savings into investment in an economy with financial intermediaries and financial markets

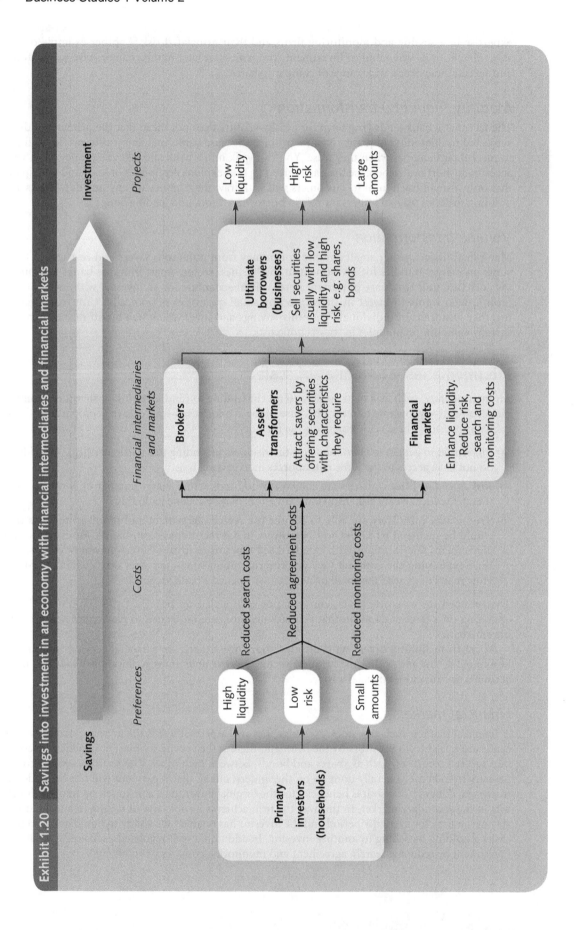

Growth in the financial services sector

The financial services sector has grown rapidly in the post-war period. It now represents a significant proportion of total economic activity, not just in the UK, but across the world. We define the core of the financial sector as banking (including building societies), insurance and various investment services. There are one or two other activities, such as accounting, which may or may not be included depending on your perspective. Firms operating in the financial services sector have, arguably, been the most dynamic, innovative and adaptable companies in the world over the past 40 years.

Some reasons for the growth of financial services in the UK

There are a number of reasons for the growth of the financial services sector. These include:

1 *High income elasticity.* This means that as consumers have become increasingly wealthy the demand for financial services has grown by a disproportionate amount. Thus a larger share of national income is devoted to paying this sector fees etc. to provide services because people desire the benefits offered. Firms have also bought an ever-widening range of financial services from the institutions which have been able to respond quickly to the needs of corporations.

2 *International comparative advantage.* London is the world's leading financial centre in a number of markets, for instance cross-border lending and international bond dealing. It is the place where the most currency transactions take place – about £1,000bn per day. It is also a major player in the fund management, insurance and derivatives markets. It is certainly Europe's leading financial centre. One of the reasons for London maintaining this dominance is that it possesses a comparative advantage in providing global financial services. This advantage stems, not least, from the critical mass of collective expertise which it is difficult for rivals to emulate – *see* Exhibit 1.21.

Exhibit 1.21

London tops financial services league

By Brooke Masters, Chief Regulation Correspondent

London, New York and Hong Kong have solidified their positions as the world's top three cities for banking and other financial services, with London retaining its slight lead over the other two cities, according to the latest Global Financial Centres Index.

The twice-yearly ranking of 75 world cities by Z/Yen group, the think-tank, is based on surveys of industry professionals and objective factors such as office rental rates, airport satisfaction and transport.

Sponsored by the Qatar Financial Centre Authority, the GFCI is a closely watched barometer within the financial services sector.

London has led every survey, but New York and more recently Hong Kong have slowly closed the gap. In the ninth report, due to be released today, London has 775 points to New York's 769 and Hong Kong's 759.

However, Singapore, which had been closing the gap in previous surveys, dropped six points to 722.
. . .

London's cheerleaders greeted the rankings with relief, saying they reflected a growing sense that the capital is emerging from the financial crisis with its global reputation intact, despite tougher regulation, new taxes on banks and higher earners and a spate of 'banker-bashing' by top politicians.

'It all got a bit shaky about nine months ago but it's settled down. It is politically convenient to kick the banking industry but there is more recognition that this is an important industry,' said Stuart Fraser, chairman of the policy committee for the City of London.

'We're getting a lot of interest in City property and all the tall buildings that were put on ice are back on again,' he added.

Exhibit 1.21 *(continued)*

Overall, the survey reflected the growing interest in Asia – Seoul leapt 25 points and eight places to enter the top 20 for the first time, and there are now eight Asian cities in the top 20, up from three four years ago. Paris, meanwhile, lost eight points and fell to 20th place, and offshore centres such as Jersey and the Cayman Islands continued their slide.

Mark Yeandle, the Z/Yen associate director who runs the survey, said he believed that London and Hong Kong would hold on to their primacy.

'What distinguishes the top centres is their ability to attract the dealmakers and people who add value. The other centres are rising because of the Chinese economy. It's going to be a real struggle to attract the really high fliers,' he said.

This edition of the GFCI was the first to look at how the various cities are perceived by different-sized businesses. While New York did best among people at companies with 2,000 or more employees, London was top among smaller enterprises with fewer than 500 employees, such as boutique advisory and professional services firms and hedge fund managers.

In the ranking for particular sectors, London led for asset management, wealth management, government and regulatory and professional services. New York was preferred for banking and Hong Kong was the leading city for insurance.

Dynamism, innovation and adaptation – four decades of change

Since the 1970s there has been a remarkably proactive response by the financial sector to changes in the market environment. New financial instruments, techniques of intermediation and markets have been developed with impressive speed. Instruments which even in the 1990s did not exist have sprung to prominence to create multi-billion-pound markets, with thousands of employees serving that market. *See* Exhibit 1.22.

There has been a general trend towards deregulation and liberalisation for institutions, while recognising that individual investors need protection.

Until the mid-1970s there were clearly delineated roles for different types of financial institutions. Banks did banking, insurance firms provided insurance, building societies granted mortgages and so on. There was little competition between the different sectors, and cartel-like arrangements meant that there was only limited competition within each sector. Some effort was made in the 1970s to increase the competitive pressures, particularly for banks. The arrival of large numbers of foreign banks in London helped the process of reform in the UK but the system remained firmly bound by restrictions, particularly in defining the activities firms could undertake.

Exhibit 1.22	Main features of change in financial services
1970s	• Roles strictly demarcated
1980s	• Deregulation • Competitive invasions of market segments • Globalisation
1990s and 2000s	• Continuation of boundary blurring • Increasing internationalisation • Disintermediation • New products (e.g. ever more exotic derivatives) • Internet services and trading • Growth of hedge e-funds and private equity funds

The real breakthrough came in the 1980s. The guiding philosophy of achieving efficiency through competition led to large-scale deregulation of activities and pricing. There was widespread competitive invasion of market segments. Banks became much more active in the mortgage market and set up insurance operations, stockbroking arms, unit trusts and many other services. Building societies, meanwhile, started to invade the territory of the banks and offered personal loans, credit cards, cheque accounts. They even went into estate agency, stockbroking and insurance underwriting. The Stock Exchange was deregulated in 1986 (in what is known as the 'Big Bang') and this move enabled it to compete more effectively on a global scale and reduce the costs of dealing in shares, particularly for the large institutional investors.

The 1970s and early 1980s were periods of volatile interest rates and exchange rates. This resulted in greater uncertainty for businesses. New financial instruments were developed to help manage risk. The volume of trading in LIFFE (the London International Financial Futures and Options Exchange) has rocketed since it was opened in 1982 – it now handles around £2,000bn worth of business every day. (Euronext bought LIFFE in 2002 and it is now called 'NYSE Liffe' following the merger of the New York Stock Exchange with Euronext.) Likewise the volume of swaps, options, futures, etc. traded in the informal 'over-the-counter' market (i.e. not on a regulated exchange) has grown exponentially.

Through the 1980s the trend towards globalisation in financial product trading and services continued apace. Increasingly a worldwide market was established. It became unexceptional for a company to have its shares quoted in New York, London, Frankfurt and Tokyo as well as its home exchange in Africa. Bond selling and trading became global and currencies were traded 24 hours a day. International banking took on an increasingly high profile, not least because the multinational corporations demanded that their banks provide multifaceted services ranging from borrowing in a foreign currency to helping manage cash.

Vast investments have been made in computing and telecommunications systems to cut costs and provide improved services. Automated teller machines (ATMs), banking by telephone and Internet, and payment by EFTPOS (electronic funds transfer at point of sale) are now commonplace. A more advanced use of technological innovation is in the global trading of the ever-expanding range of financial instruments. It became possible to sit on a beach in the Caribbean and trade pork belly futures in Chicago, interest rate options in London and shares in Singapore. In the 1990s there was a continuation of the blurring of the boundaries between different types of financial institutions to the point where organisations such as JPMorgan Chase and Barclays are referred to as 'financial supermarkets' (or '**universal banks**' or '**financial services companies**') offering a wide range of services. The irony is that just as this title was being bandied about, the food supermarket giants such as Sainsbury's and Tesco set up comprehensive banking services, following a path trodden by a number of other non-banking corporations. Marks and Spencer provides credit cards, personal loans and even pensions. The Internet has provided a new means of supplying financial services and lowered the barrier to entry into the industry. New banking, stockbroking and insurance services have sprung up. The Internet allows people to trade millions of shares at the touch of a button from the comfort of their home, to transfer the proceeds between bank accounts and to search websites for data, company reports, newspaper reports, insurance quotations and so on – all much more cheaply than ever before.

The globalisation of business and investment decisions has continued, making national economies increasingly interdependent. Borrowers use the international financial markets to seek the cheapest funds, and investors look in all parts of the globe for the highest returns. Some idea of the extent of global financial flows can be gained by contrasting the *daily* turnover of foreign exchange (approximately £2,500bn)[3] with the *annual* output of all the goods and services produced by the people in the UK of less than this. Another effect of technological change is the increased mobility of activities within firms. For example, banks have transferred a high proportion of their operations to India, as have insurance companies and other financial firms.

Another feature of recent years has been the development of **disintermediation** – in other words, cutting out the middleman. This means borrowing firms bypassing the banks and obtaining debt finance by selling debt securities, such as bonds, in the market. The purchasers can be individuals but are more usually the large savings institutions such as pension funds, insurance

3 Bank for International Settlement: www.BIS.org

funds and hedge funds. Banks, having lost some interest income from lending to these large firms, have concentrated instead on fee income gained by arranging the sale and distribution of these securities as well as underwriting their issue (guaranteeing to buy if no one else will). Hedge funds, for example, (free from most regulatory control) now account for a high proportion of financial market trading whereas they were barely heard of 20 years ago. Private equity funds, which invest in shares and other securities of companies outside a stock exchange, have grown tremendously over the last 20 years, owning stakes in companies which employ millions of workers.

The financial system

To assist with orientating the reader within the financial system and to carry out more jargon busting, a brief outline of the main financial services sectors and markets is given here.

The institutions

The banking sector

Retail banks

Put at its simplest, the retail banks take (small) deposits from the public which are re-packaged and lent to businesses and households. This is generally high-volume and low-value business which contrasts with wholesale (investment) banking which is low volume but each transaction is for high value. The distinction between retail and investment banks has become blurred over recent years as the large institutions have diversified their operations. The retail banks operate nationwide branch networks and a subset of banks provides a cheque-clearance system (transferring money from one account to another) – these are the clearing banks. The five largest UK clearing banks are Barclays, Lloyds, Royal Bank of Scotland (including NatWest), HSBC and Santander. Loans, overdrafts and mortgages are the main forms of retail bank lending. The trend up until 2009 was for retail banks to reduce their reliance on retail deposits and raise more wholesale funds from the financial markets. But this has partially been reversed as banks found wholesale funding less reliable than obtaining funds to lend from deposits in bank accounts. They get together with other banks if a large loan is required by a borrower (say £150m) rather than provide the full amount themselves as this would create an excessive exposure to one customer – this is called syndicate lending, discussed in Chapter 11.

Investment banks[4]

The terms wholesale bank, merchant bank and investment bank are often used interchangeably. There are subtle differences but for most practical purposes they can be regarded as the same. These institutions tend to deal in large sums of money – at least £250,000 – although some have set up retail arms. They concentrate on dealing with other large organisations, corporations, institutional investors and governments. While they undertake some lending their main focus is on generating commission or trading income by providing advice and facilitating deals. There are five main areas of activity:

- **Raising external finance for companies** These banks provide advice and arrange finance for corporate clients. Sometimes they provide loans themselves, but often they assist the setting up of a bank syndicate or make arrangements with other institutions. They will advise and assist a firm issuing a bond, they have expertise in helping firms float on a stock exchange and make rights issues. They may 'underwrite' a bond or share issue. This assures the corporation that it will receive the funds it needs for its investment programme.

- **Broking and dealing** They act as agents for the buying and selling of securities on the financial markets, including shares and bonds. Some also have market-making arms which quote prices

4 There is much more on investment banks as well as many other financial organisations in Arnold (2012).

they are willing to buy or sell from or to, say, a shareholder or a bond holder, thus assisting the operation of secondary markets (*see* Chapter 9). They also trade in the markets on their own account and assist companies with export finance.

- *Fund management (asset management)* The investment banks offer services to rich individuals who lack the time or expertise to deal with their own investment strategies. They also manage unit and investment trusts as well as the portfolios of some pension funds and insurance companies. In addition corporations often have short-term cash flows which need managing efficiently (treasury management).

- *Assistance in corporate restructuring* Investment banks earn large fees from advising acquirers on mergers and assisting with the merger process. They also gain by helping target firms avoid being taken over too cheaply. Corporate disposal programmes, such as selling off a division, may also need the services of an investment bank.

- *Assisting risk management using derivatives* Risk can be reduced through hedging strategies using futures, options, swaps and the like. However, this is a complex area with large room for error and terrible penalties if a mistake is made (*see* Chapters 21 and 22). The banks may have specialist knowledge to offer in this area.

International banks

There are two main types of international banking in the UK:

- Foreign banking transactions (lending/borrowing, etc.) in the host country currency with overseas residents and companies, e.g. transactions in sterling with non-UK residents by UK banks.

- Eurocurrency banking for transactions in a currency outside the jurisdiction of the country of that currency, e.g. yen transactions in Canada (Chapter 11 considers this further).

The major part of international banking these days is borrowing and lending in foreign currencies. There are about 250 non-UK banks operating in London, the most prominent of which are American, German, Swiss and Japanese. Their initial function was mainly to provide services for their own nationals, for example for export and import transactions, but nowadays their main emphasis is in the Eurocurrency market and international securities (shares, bonds, etc.) trading. Often funds are held in the UK for the purpose of trading and speculation on the foreign exchange market.

Building societies

Building societies collect funds from millions of savers by enticing them to put their money in interest-bearing accounts. The vast majority of that deposited money is then lent to people wishing to buy a home – in the form of a mortgage. Thus, they take in short-term deposits (although they also borrow on the wholesale financial markets) and they lend money for long periods, usually for 25 years. More recently building societies have diversified their sources of finance (e.g. using the wholesale financial markets) and increased the range of services they offer.

Finance houses[5]

Finance houses are responsible for the financing of hire purchase agreements and other instalment credit, for example leasing. If you buy a large durable good such as a car or a washing machine you often find that the sales assistant also tries to get you interested in taking the item on credit, so you pay for it over a period of, say, three years. It is usually not the retailer that provides the finance for the credit. The retailer usually works with a finance house which pays the retailer the full purchase price of the good and therefore becomes the owner. You, the customer, get to

5 The term 'finance house' is also used for broadly based financial service companies carrying out a wide variety of financial activities from share brokerage to corporate lending. However, we will confine the term to instalment credit and related services.

use the good, but in return you have to make regular payments to the finance house, including interest. Under a **hire purchase** agreement, when you have made enough payments you will become the owner. Under **leasing** the finance house retains ownership (for more detail *see* Chapter 12). Finance houses also provide **factoring** services – providing cash to firms in return for receiving income from the firms' debtors when they pay up. Most of the large finance houses are subsidiaries of the major conglomerate banks.

Long-term savings institutions

Pension funds

Pension funds are set up to provide pensions for members. For example, the University Superannuation Scheme (USS), to which university lecturers belong, takes 7.5 per cent of working members' salaries each month and puts it into the fund. In addition the employing organisation pays money into the scheme. When a member retires the USS will pay a pension. Between the time of making a contribution and payment in retirement, which may be decades, the pension trustees oversee the management of the fund. They may place some or all of the fund with specialist investment managers. This is a particularly attractive form of saving because of the generous tax relief provided. The long time horizon of the pension business means that large sums are built up and available for investment – currently around £1,100bn in the UK funds. A typical allocation of a fund is:

- 30–35 per cent in UK shares;
- 20–30 per cent lending to the UK government by buying bonds and bills and by lending via corporate bonds issued by UK firms;
- 20–30 per cent overseas company shares;
- 3–6 per cent in bonds issued by foreign organisations;
- 5–15 per cent other (e.g. property, cash and overseas bonds).

Insurance funds

Insurance companies engage in two types of activities:

- *General insurance* This is insurance against specific contingencies such as fire, theft, accident, generally for a one-year period. The money collected in premiums is mostly held in financial assets which are relatively short term and liquid so that short-term commitments can be met (totalling around £100bn in the UK).
- *Life assurance* With **term assurance**, your life is assured for a specified period. If you die your beneficiaries get a payout. If you live you get nothing at the end of the period. With **whole-of-life policies**, the insurance company pays a capital sum upon death whenever this occurs. **Endowment policies** are more interesting from a financial systems perspective because they act as a savings vehicle as well as cover against death. The premium will be larger but after a number of years have passed the insurance company pays a substantial sum of money even if you are still alive. The life company has to take the premiums paid over, say, 10 or 25 years, and invest them wisely to satisfy its commitment to the policy holder. Millions of UK house buyers purchase with an endowment mortgage. They simply pay interest to the lender (e.g. a building society) while also placing premiums into an endowment fund. The hope is that after 25 years or so the value of the accumulated fund will equal or be greater than the capital value of the loan.

Life assurance companies also provide **annuities**. Here a policy holder pays an initial lump sum and in return receives regular payments in subsequent years. They have also moved into pensions. Indeed, the majority of their business is now pension related.

UK life assurance companies have over £1,500bn under management. A typical fund allocation is:

- 30–50 per cent UK shares;
- 10–15 per cent lending to the UK government;

- 5–10 per cent property;
- 15–25 per cent overseas securities;
- 5–10 per cent other.

The risk spreaders

These institutions allow small savers a stake in a large diversified portfolio.

Unit trusts

Unit trusts are 'open-ended' funds, so the size of the fund and the number of units depend on the amount of money investors wish to put into the fund. If a fund of one million units suddenly doubled in size because of an inflow of investor funds it would become a fund of two million units through the creation and selling of more units. The buying and selling prices of the units are determined by the value of the fund. So if a two-million unit fund is invested in £2m worth of shares in the UK stock market, the value of each unit will be £1. If over a period the value of the shares rises to £3m, the units will be worth £1.50 each. Unit holders sell units back to the managers of the unit trust if they want to liquidate their holding. The manager will then either sell the units to another investor or sell some of the underlying investments to raise cash to pay the unit holder. The units are usually quoted at two prices depending on whether you are buying (higher) or selling. There is also an ongoing management charge for running the fund. Trustees supervise the funds to safeguard the interests of unit holders but employ managers to make the investment decisions.

There is a wide choice of unit trusts specialising in different types of investments ranging from Japanese equities to privatised European companies. Of the £500bn or so invested in unit trusts and their cousins, OEICs, 50–60 per cent is devoted to shares (one-half of which are non UK) with 20 per cent devoted to bonds. Instruments similar to unit trusts are called mutual funds in other countries.

Investment trusts

Investment trusts differ from unit trusts because they are companies able to issue shares and other securities. Investors can purchase these securities when the investment company is launched or purchase shares in the secondary market from other investors. These are known as closed-end funds because the company itself is closed to new investors – if you wished to invest your money you would go to an existing investor (via a broker) and not buy from the company. Investment trusts usually spread the investors' funds across a range of other companies' shares. They are also more inclined to invest in a broader range of assets than unit trusts – even property and shares not listed on a stock market. Approximately one-half of the money devoted to the 400 or so UK investment companies (£80bn) is put into UK securities, with the remainder placed in overseas securities. The managers of these funds are able to borrow in order to invest. This has the effect of increasing returns to shareholders when things go well. Correspondingly, if the value of the underlying investments falls, the return to shareholders falls even more, because of the obligation to meet interest charges.

Open-ended investment companies (OEICs)

Open-ended investment companies are hybrid risk-spreading instruments which allow an investment in an open-ended fund. Designed to be more flexible and transparent than either investment companies or unit trusts, OEICs have just one price. However, as with unit trusts, OEICs can issue more shares, in line with demand from investors, and they can borrow.[6]

Exchange-traded funds (ETFs)

ETFs are set up as companies issuing shares, and the money raised is used to buy a range of securities such as a collection of shares in a particular stock market index or sector, say the FTSE 100 or pharmaceutical shares. Thus if BP comprises 8 per cent of the total value of the FTSE 100 and the ETF has £100m to invest, it will buy £8m of BP shares; if Whitbread is 0.15 per cent of the FTSE, the ETF buys £150,000 of Whitbread shares. (Alternatively, many ETFs do not buy the actual shares

6 There is much more on unit trusts, investment trusts, OEICs and ETFs in Arnold (2010).

but gain exposure to the share returns through the purchase of derivatives of the shares.) They are open-ended funds – the ETF shares are created and cancelled as demand rises or falls. However, they differ from unit trusts and OEICs in that the pricing of ETF shares is left up to the market-place. ETFs are quoted companies and you can buy and sell their shares at prices subject to change throughout the day (unlike unit trusts and OEICs, where prices are set by a formula once a day). Globally, there are more than 2,000 different ETFs listed on over 40 exchanges with a total value over $1,000bn. In the US alone more than 800 ETFs are traded on the stock markets. They have become so significant there that around 30 per cent of New York Stock Exchange trading is in ETFs.

The risk takers

Private equity funds

These are funds that invest in companies that do not have a stock market trading quote for their shares. The firms are often young and on a rapid growth trajectory, but private equity companies also supply finance to well-established companies. The funds usually buy shares in these companies and occasionally supply debt finance. Frequently the private equity funds are themselves funded by other financial institutions, such as a group of pension funds. Private equity has grown tremendously over the last 20 years to the point where now over one-fifth of non-government UK workers are employed by a firm financed by private equity. Private equity is discussed in Chapter 10.

Hedge funds

Hedge funds gather together investors' money and invest it in a wide variety of financial strategies largely outside of the control of the regulators, being created either outside the major financial centres or as private investment partnerships. The investors include wealthy individuals as well as institutions, such as pension funds, insurance funds and banks. By being outside normal regulatory control hedge funds are not confined to investing in particular types of security, or to using particular investment methods. For example, they have far more freedom than unit trusts in 'going short', i.e. selling a security first and then buying it later, hopefully at a lower price. They can also borrow many times the size of the fund to punt on a small movement of currency rates, or share movements, orange juice futures, or whatever they judge will go up (or go down). If the punt goes well (or rather, a series of punts over the year) the fund managers earn million-pound bonuses (often on the basis of 2 per cent of funds under management fee plus 20 per cent of the profit made for client investors).

Originally, the term 'hedge' made some sense when applied to these funds. They would, through a combination of investments, including derivatives, try to hedge (lower or eliminate) risk while seeking a high absolute return (rather than a return relative to an index). Today the word 'hedge' is misapplied to most of these funds because they generally take aggressive bets on the movements of currencies, equities, interest rates, bonds, etc. around the world. For example, one fund, Amaranth, bet on the movement of the price of natural gas, and lost US$6bn in a matter of days in 2006. Their activities would not be a concern if they had remained a relatively small part of the investment scene. However, today they command enormous power and billions more are being placed in these funds every week. Already over £1,300bn is invested in these funds. Add to that the borrowed money – sometimes ten times the fund's base capital – and you can see why they are to be taken very seriously. Up to 50 per cent of the share trades on a typical day in London is said to be due to hedge funds, for example.

The markets

The money markets

The money markets are wholesale markets (usually involving transactions of £500,000 or more) which enable borrowing on a short-term basis (less than one year). The banks are particularly active in this market – both as lenders and as borrowers. Large corporations, local government bodies and non-banking financial institutions also lend when they have surplus cash and borrow when short of money.

The bond markets

While the money markets are concerned with short-term lending the capital markets deal with longer-term (> 1 year) debt (e.g. bond) and equity instruments. A **bond** is merely a document which sets out the borrower's promise to pay sums of money in the future – usually regular interest plus a capital amount upon the maturity of the bond. These are securities issued by a variety of organisations including governments and corporations. The UK bond markets are over three centuries old and during that time they have developed very large and sophisticated primary and secondary sub-markets encompassing gilts (UK government bonds), corporate bonds, local authority bonds and international bonds, among others. Bonds as a source of finance for firms will be examined in Chapter 11.

The foreign exchange markets (forex or FX)

The **foreign exchange markets** are the markets in which one currency is exchanged for another. They include the *spot* **market** where currencies are bought and sold for 'immediate' delivery (in reality, one or two days later) and the *forward* **markets**, where the deal is agreed now to exchange currencies at some fixed point in the future. Also currency *futures* and *options* and other forex derivatives are employed to hedge risk and to speculate. The forex markets are dominated by the major banks, with dealing taking place 24 hours a day around the globe. Chapter 22 looks at how a company could use the forex market to facilitate international trade and reduce the risk attached to business transactions abroad.

The share markets

All major economies now have share markets. The London Stock Exchange is an important potential source of long-term equity (ownership) capital for UK companies and for hundreds of overseas companies. Chapters 9 and 10 examine stock markets and the raising of equity capital.

The derivative markets

A **derivative** is a financial instrument the value of which is derived from other financial securities or some other underlying asset. For example, a **future** is the right to buy something (e.g. currency, shares, bonds) at some date in the future at an agreed price. This *right* becomes a saleable derived financial instrument. The performance of the derivative depends on the behaviour of the underlying asset. Companies can use these markets for the management and transfer of risk. They can be used to reduce risk (hedging) or to **speculate**. **NYSE Liffe** trades options and futures in shares, bonds and interest rates. This used to be the only one of the markets listed here to have a trading floor where face-to-face dealing took place on an **open outcry system** (traders shouting and signalling to each other, face to face in a trading pit, the price at which they are willing to buy and sell). Now all the financial markets (money, bond, forex, derivatives and share markets) are conducted using computers (and telephones) from isolated trading rooms located in the major financial institutions. In the derivative markets a high proportion of trade takes place on what is called the **over-the-counter (OTC)** market rather than on a regulated exchange. The OTC market flexibility allows the creation of tailor-made derivatives to suit a client's risk situation. The practical use of derivatives is examined in Chapters 21 and 22.

Concluding comments

We now have a clear guiding principle set as our objective for the myriad financial decisions discussed later in this book: maximise shareholder wealth. Whether we are considering a major investment programme, or trying to decide on the best kind of finance to use, the criterion of creating value for shareholders over the long run will be paramount. A single objective is set primarily for practical reasons to aid exposition in this text; however, many of the techniques described in later chapters will be applicable to organisations with other purposes as they stand; others will need slight modification.

There is an old joke about financial service firms: they just shovel money from one place to another, making sure that some of it sticks to the shovel. The implication is that they contribute little to the well-being of society. Extremists even go so far as to regard these firms as parasites on the 'really productive' parts of the economies. And yet very few people avoid extensive use of financial services. Most have bank and building society accounts, pay insurance premiums and contribute to pension schemes. People do not put their money into a bank account unless they get something in return. Likewise building societies, insurance companies, pension funds, unit trusts, investment banks and so on can survive only if they offer a service people find beneficial and are willing to pay for. Describing the mobilisation and employment of money in the service of productive investment as pointless or merely 'shovelling it around the system' is as logical as saying that the transport firms which bring goods to the high street do not provide a valuable service because of the absence of a tangible 'thing' created by their activities.

Key points and concepts

- Firms should clearly define the **objective** of the enterprise to provide a focus for decision making.

- **Sound financial management** is necessary for the achievement of all **stakeholder** goals.

- Some stakeholders will have their returns **satisficed** – given just enough to make their contribution. One (or more) group(s) will have their returns **maximised** – given any surplus after all others have been satisfied.

- The assumed objective of the firm for finance is to **maximise shareholder wealth**. Reasons:

 - **practical**, a single objective leads to clearer decisions;
 - the **contractual theory**;
 - **survival** in a competitive world;
 - it is better for **society**;
 - counters the tendency of managers to pursue goals for their own benefit;
 - they **own** the firm.

- **Maximising shareholder wealth** is **maximising purchasing power** or **maximising the flow of discounted cash flow** to shareholders over a long time horizon.

- **Profit maximisation** is not the same as shareholder wealth maximisation. Some factors a profit comparison does not allow for:

 - future prospects;
 - risk;
 - accounting problems;
 - communication;
 - additional capital.

- **Corporate governance**. Large corporations usually have a **separation of ownership and control**. This may lead to **managerialism** where the agent (the managers) takes decisions primarily with their interests in mind rather than those of the principals (the shareholders). This is a **principal–agent problem**. Some solutions:

 - corporate governance regulation;
 - link managerial rewards to shareholder wealth improvement;
 - sackings;
 - selling shares and the takeover threat;
 - improve information flow.

- **Financial institutions and markets** encourage growth and progress by **mobilising savings** and encouraging investment.

- Financial managers contribute to firms' success primarily through **investment and finance decisions**. Their knowledge of financial markets, investment appraisal methods, treasury, risk management and value analysis techniques is vital for company growth and stability.

- Financial institutions encourage the flow of saving into investment by acting as **brokers** and **asset transformers**, thus alleviating the **conflict of preferences** between the **primary investors** (households) and the **ultimate borrowers** (firms).

- **Asset transformation** is the creation of an intermediate security with characteristics appealing to the primary investor to attract funds, which are then made available to the ultimate borrower in a form appropriate to them. Types of asset transformation:

 - risk transformation;
 - maturity transformation;
 - volume transformation.

- Intermediaries are able to transform assets and encourage the flow of funds because of their **economies of scale** *vis-à-vis* the individual investor:
 - efficiencies in gathering information;
 - risk spreading;
 - transaction costs.

- The **secondary markets** in financial securities encourage investment by enabling investor liquidity (being able to sell quickly and cheaply to another investor) while providing the firm with long-term funds.

- The **financial services sector** has grown to be of great economic significance in the UK. Reasons:
 - high income elasticity;
 - international comparative advantage.

- The financial sector has shown remarkable **dynamism**, **innovation** and **adaptability** over the last three decades. Deregulation, new technology, globalisation and the rapid development of new financial products have characterised this sector.

- **Banking sector:**
 - **Retail banks** – high-volume and low-value business.
 - **Wholesale investment banks** – low-volume and high-value business. Mostly fee based.
 - **International banks** – mostly Eurocurrency transactions.
 - **Building societies** – still primarily small deposits aggregated for mortgage lending.
 - **Finance houses** – hire purchase, leasing, factoring.

- **Long-term savings institutions:**
 - **Pension funds** – major investors in financial assets.

 - **Insurance funds** – life assurance and endowment policies provide large investment funds.

- **The risk spreaders:**
 - **Unit trusts** – genuine trusts which are open-ended investment vehicles.
 - **Investment trusts** – companies which invest in other companies' financial securities, particularly shares.
 - **Open-ended investment companies** (OEICs) – a hybrid between unit and investment trusts.
 - **Exchange traded funds (ETFs)** – set up as companies to invest in a range of securities.

- **The risk takers:**
 - **Private equity funds** – invest in companies not quoted on a stock exchange.
 - **Hedge funds** – wide variety of investment or speculative strategies outside regulators' control.

- **The markets:**
 - **The money markets** are short-term wholesale lending and/or borrowing markets.
 - **The bond markets** deal in long-term bond debt issued by corporations, governments, local authorities and so on, and usually have a secondary market.
 - **The foreign exchange market** – one currency is exchanged for another.
 - **The share market** – primary and secondary trading in companies' shares takes place.
 - **The derivatives market** – NYSE Liffe dominates the 'exchange-traded' derivatives market in options and futures in the UK. However, there is a flourishing over-the-counter (OTC) market.

References and further reading

Students of finance, or any managerial discipline, should get into the habit of reading the *Financial Times* and *The Economist* to (a) reinforce knowledge gained from a course, and (b) appreciate the wider business environment.

Aggarwal, R., Erel, I., Stulz, R. and Williamson, R. (2010) 'Differences in governance practices between U.S. and foreign firms: measurement, causes, and consequences', *Review of Financial Studies*, Vol. 23, No. 3, pp. 3131–69.
　The higher the level of protection afforded to shareholders with only a small percentage of a company (minority shareholders) the greater the firm value

Ang, J., Cole, R. and Lin, J. (2000) 'Agency costs and ownership structure', *Journal of Finance*, Vol. 55, No. 1, pp. 81–106.
　Examines 1,708 companies and finds higher agency costs when an outsider (low shareholding by managers) rather than an insider manages the firm.

Anthony, R.N. (1960) 'The trouble with profit maximisation', *Harvard Business Review*, Nov.–Dec., pp. 126–34.
　Challenges the conventional economic view of profit maximisation on grounds of realism and morality.

Arnold, G. (2000) 'Tracing the development of value-based management'. In Glen Arnold and Matt Davies (eds), *Value-based Management: Context and Application*. London: Wiley.
A more detailed discussion of the objective of the firm is presented.

Arnold, G. (2010) *The Financial Times Guide to Investing*. 2nd edn. Harlow: FT Prentice Hall.
This provides much more on the financial system and instruments.

Arnold, G. (2012) *Modern Financial Markets and Institutions*. Harlow: FT Prentice Hall.
A textbook describing financial instruments, markets and institutions.

Atanassov, J. and Kim, E.H. (2009) 'Labor and corporate governance: international evidence from restructuring decisions', *Journal of Finance*, Vol. 64, No. 1, pp. 341–74.
The effect of strong union laws on corporate governance with greater benefits to the workforce and managers. Easy to follow.

Bebchuk, L., Cohen, A. and Ferrell, A. (2009) 'What matters in corporate governance?' *Review of Financial Studies*, Vol. 22, No. 2, pp. 783–827.
Six governance factors seem to have a great impact on firm valuation.

Becht, M., Mayer , C. and Rossi, S. (2010) 'Returns to shareholder activism: evidence from a clinical study of the Hermes UK Focus Fund', *Review of Financial Studies*, Vol. 23, Issue 3, pp. 3093–129.
Describes the extent of intervention by a fund in its investee companies. It outperforms, and the authors attribute this to the high level of engagement with management in companies.

Berle, A.A. and Means, G.C. (1932) *The Modern Corporation and Private Property*. New York: Macmillan.
An early discussion of the principal–agent problem and corporate governance.

Doidge, C, Andrew Karolyi, G. and Stulz, R. (2007) 'Why do countries matter so much for corporate governance?' *Journal of Financial Economics*, Vol. 86, No. 1, pp. 1–39.
Tests a model of how protections for minority shareholders at the national legal level influence firms' costs and benefits in implementing corporate governance improvements.

Donaldson, G. (1963) 'Financial goals: management vs. stockholders', *Harvard Business Review*, May–June, pp. 116–29.
Clear and concise discussion of the conflict of interest between managers and shareholders.

Donghui L., Moshirian, F., Pham, P. and Zein, J. (2006) 'When financial institutions are large shareholders: the role of macro corporate governance environments', *Journal of Finance*, Vol. 61, No. 6, pp. 2975–3007.
In countries with strong shareholder rights, effective legal enforcement and extensive financial disclosure there are larger percentage holdings of shares in companies.

Dyck, A. and Zingales, L. (2004) 'Private benefits of control: an international comparison', *Journal of Finance*, Vol. 59, No. 2, pp. 537–600.
Someone who controls a company (without owning all the shares) can appropriate value for him/herself.

Fama, E.F. (1980) 'Agency problems and the theory of the firm', *Journal of Political Economy*, Spring, pp. 288–307.
Explains how the separation of ownership and control can lead to an efficient form of economic organisation.

Friedman, M. (1970) 'The social responsibility of business is to increase its profits', *New York Times Magazine*, 30 Sept.
A viewpoint on the objective of the firm.

Galbraith, J. (1967) 'The goals of an industrial system' (excerpt from *The New Industrial State*). Reproduced in H.I. Ansoff, *Business Strategy*. London: Penguin, 1969.
Survival, sales and expansion of the 'technostructure' are emphasised as the goals in real-world corporations.

Ghoshal, S. (2005) 'Bad management theories are destroying good management practices', *Academy of Management's Learning and Education*, Vol. 4, No. 1, pp. 75–91.
Argues that the encouragement of shareholder wealth maximisation is wrong.

Global Financial Centres Index (every six months), Z/Yen Group, available at www.zyen.com.
Provides a summary of professional opinion of leading financial centres.

Fich, E.M. and Shivdasani, A. (2006) 'Are busy boards effective monitors?' *Journal of Finance*, Vol. LXI, No. 2, April.
Evidence that if non-executive directors hold three or more directorships then weaker governance occurs.

Hart, O.D. (1995a) *Firms, Contracts and Financial Structure*. Oxford: Clarendon Press.
A clear articulation of the principal–agent problem.

Hart, O.D. (1995b) 'Corporate governance: some theory and implications'. *Economic Journal*, 105, pp. 678–9.
Principal–agent problem discussed.

Hayek, F.A. (1969) 'The corporation in a democratic society: in whose interests ought it and will it be run?' Reprinted in H.I. Ansoff, *Business Strategy*. London: Penguin, 1969.
Objective should be long-run return on owners' capital subject to restraint by general legal and moral rules.

Jensen, M.C. (1986) 'Agency costs of free cash flow, corporate finance and takeovers', *American Economic Review*, Vol. 76, pp. 323–9.
Agency cost theory applied to the issue of the use to which managers put business cash inflows.

Jensen, M.C. (2001) 'Value maximisation, stakeholder theory, and the corporate objective function', *Journal of Applied Corporate Finance*, Vol. 14, No. 3, Fall.
Cogently argues against simple stakeholder balancing or a Balance Scorecard approach to directing a company

because of the violation of the proposition that a single-valued objective is a prerequisite for purposeful or rational behaviour by any organisation, thus politicising the corporation and leaving managers empowered to exercise their own preferences.

Jensen, M.C. and Meckling, W.H. (1976) 'Theory of the firm: managerial behavior, agency costs and ownership structure', *Journal of Financial Economics*, Oct., Vol. 3, pp. 305–60.
 Seminal work on agency theory.

John, K., Litov, L. and Yeung, B., (2008) 'Corporate governance and risk-taking', *Journal of Finance*, Vol. 63, No. 4, pp. 1679–1728.
 Some evidence that better investor protection mitigates against managers' natural tendency to reduce firm risk and slow down its growth.

Kaplan, R. and Norton, D.P. (1996) *The Balanced Scorecard*. Boston, MA: Harvard Business School Press.
 The managerial equivalent of stakeholder theory in which multiple measures are used to evaluate performance.

Kay, J. (2004) 'Forget how the crow flies', *Financial Times Magazine*, 17–18 January, pp. 17–21.
 An imporant argument on obliquity is presented.

Kay, J. (2010) *Obliquity: Why our goals are best achieved indirectly*. London: Profile Books.
 An excellent set of ideas on obliquity with frequent reference to companies and other aspects of our lives where obliquity can be applied. Very easy to read.

Kim, K., Kitsabunnarat-Chatjuthamard, P. and Nofsinger, J. (2007) 'Large shareholders, board independence, and minority shareholder rights: evidence from Europe', *Journal of Corporate Finance*, Vol. 13, No. 5, pp. 859–80.
 Countries with stronger shareholder protection rights have firms with more independent directors. Also ownership concentration and board independence are negatively related.

Klein, A. and Zur, E. (2009) 'Entrepreneurial shareholder activism: hedge funds and other private investors', *Journal of Finance*, Vol. LXIV, No. 1, pp. 187–229.
 If the funds are pushing for change they lift the target share price and often gain seats on the board.

La Porta, R., Lopez-de-Silanes, F., Shleifer, A. and Vishny, R. (2000) 'Investor protection and corporate governance', *Journal of Financial Economics*, Vol. 58, No. 1/2, pp. 3–27.
 Describes the differences in laws and their effectiveness across countries.

Leuz, C., Lins, K. and Warnock, F. (2009) 'Do foreigners invest less in poorly governed firms?' *Review of Financial Studies*, Vol. 22, No. 8, pp. 3245–85.
 The answer is 'Yes'.

London, S. (2003) 'The long view: lunch with the FT, Milton Friedman', *Financial Times Magazine*, 7–8 June, pp. 12–13.

Masulis, R., Wang, C. and Xie, F. (2009) 'Agency problems at dual-class companies', *Journal of Finance*, Vol. 64, No. 4, pp. 1697–1727.
 Managers with more control over the cash of the firm are more prone to pursue their own benefits at shareholders' expense – higher pay, etc., and empire-building.

Maury, B. (2006) 'Family ownership and firm performance: empirical evidence from Western European corporations', *Journal of Corporate Finance*. Vol. 12, Issue 2, pp. 321–41.
 Active family control is associated with higher profitability.

McKinsey and Company: Koller, T., Goedhart, M. and Wessels, D. (2010) *Valuation*. 5th edn. New York: John Wiley & Sons Ltd.
 Contends that shareholder wealth should be the focus of managerial actions.

Simon, H.A. (1959) 'Theories of decision making in economics and behavioural science', *American Economic Review*, June.
 Traditional economic theories are challenged, drawing on psychology. Discusses the goals of the firm: satisficing vs. maximising.

Simon, H.A. (1964) 'On the concept of organisational goals', *Administrative Science Quarterly*, 9(1), June, pp. 1–22.
 Discusses the complexity of goal setting.

Smith, A. (1776) *The Wealth of Nations*. Reproduced in 1910 in two volumes by J.M. Dent, London.
 An early viewpoint on the objective of the firm.

The Economist (2005) 'A survey of corporate social responsibility', 22 January.
 A forcefully argued piece on the dangers of advocating corporate social responsibility if that means less attention to shareholder wealth.

Tirole, J. (2005) *The Theory of Corporate Finance*. Princeton: Princeton University Press.
 Provides a thorough overview of the principal–agent problem and corporate governance.

UK Corporate Governance Code (2010) Available at the Financial Reporting Council website (www.frc.org.uk).
 A clearly and concisely written set of principles, updated regularly.

Wen, S. and Zhao, J. (2011) 'Exploring the rationale of enlightened shareholder value in the realm of UK company law – the path dependence perspective', *International Trade and Business Law Review*, Vol. XIV, pp. 153–73.
 A discussion of the impact of the Companies Act 2006 on the primacy of shareholder interests in the British company.

Williamson, O. (1963) 'Managerial discretion and business behaviour', *American Economic Review*, 53, pp. 1033–57.
 Managerial security, power, prestige, etc. are powerful motivating forces. These goals may lead to less than profit-maximising behaviour.

Case study recommendations

See www.pearsoned.co.uk/arnold for case study synopses. Also see Harvard University: http://hbsp.harvard.edu/product/cases

- Goldman Sachs: A Bank for All Seasons (A) (2010) Authors: Lena Genello Goldberg and Tiffany Obenchain. Harvard Business School.

- Financial Networks and Informal Banking in China: From Pawnshops to Private Equity (2009) Author: Elizabeth Köll. Harvard Business School.

- Rural Credit Cooperatives in India (2007) Authors: Bidhan Parmar and Wei Li Darden, University of Virginia. Available from Harvard Business School website.

- The Japanese Financial System: From Postwar to the New Millennium (2001) Author: Ulrike Schaede. Harvard Business School.

- YES BANK: Mainstreaming Development into Indian Banking (2010) Authors: Michael Chu and Namrata Arora. Harvard Business School.

- China's Financial Markets: 2007 (2009) Authors: Li Jin and Bingxing Huo. Harvard Business School.

Websites

Alternative Investment Management Association (Hedge funds) www.aima.org
Association of British Insurers www.abi.org.uk
Association of Investment Companies www.theaic.co.uk or www.aitc.co.uk
Bank for International Settlement www.bis.org
Bank of England www.bankofengland.co.uk
British Bankers Association www.bba.org.uk
British Venture Capital Association www.bvca.co.uk
Building Societies Association www.bsa.org.uk
City of London financial and business information www.cityoflondon.gov.uk
Companies House www.companieshouse.gov.uk
European Corporate Governance Institute www.ecgi.org

Finance and Leasing Association www.fla.org.uk
Financial Times www.FT.com
Financial Reporting Council www.frc.org
Institute of Financial Services www.ifslearning.org
Investment Management Association www.investment-funds.org.uk
National Association of Pension Funds www.napf.co.uk
NYSE Liffe www.euronext.com
London Stock Exchange www.londonstockexchange.com
Securities Industry and Financial Markets Association www.sifma.org
The Banker www.thebanker.com
The City UK www.thecityuk.com
UK Corporate Governance Code www.frc.org.uk

Self-review questions

1 Why is it important to specify a goal for the corporation?

2 How can 'goal congruence' for managers and shareholders be achieved?

3 How does money assist the well-being of society?

4 What are the economies of scale of intermediaries?

5 Distinguish between a primary market and a secondary market. How does the secondary market aid the effectiveness of the primary market?

6 Illustrate the flow of funds between primary investors and ultimate borrowers in a modern economy. Give examples of intermediary activity.

7 List as many financial intermediaries as you can. Describe the nature of their intermediation and explain the intermediate securities they create.

8 What is the principal–agent problem?

9 What is the 'contractual theory'? Do you regard it as a strong argument?

10 What difficulties might arise in state-owned industries in making financial decisions?

11 Briefly describe the following types of decisions (give examples):
a Financing
b Investment
c Treasury

d Risk management
e Strategic.

c The foreign exchange markets
d The share markets
e The derivatives markets.

12 Briefly explain the role of the following:
a The money markets
b The bond markets

Questions and problems

MyFinanceLab *Questions with an icon are also available for practice in MyFinanceLab with additional supporting resources.*

Answers to most questions can be found at www.pearsoned.co.uk/Arnold.

1 Explain the rationale for selecting shareholder wealth maximisation as the objective of the firm. Include a consideration of profit maximisation as an alternative goal.

2 What benefits are derived from the financial services sector which have led to its growth over recent years in terms of employment and share of gross domestic produce (GDP)?

3 What is managerialism and how might it be incompatible with shareholder interests?

4 Why has an increasing share of household savings been channelled through financial intermediaries?

5 Discuss the relationship between economic growth and the development of a financial services sector.

6 Firm A has a stock market value of £20m (number of shares in issue × share price), while firm B is valued at £15m. The firms have similar profit histories:
Provide some potential reasons why, despite the same total profit over the last five years, shareholders regard firm A as being worth £5m more (extend your thoughts beyond the numbers in the table).

	Firm A £m	Firm B £m
2004	1.5	1.8
2005	1.6	1.0
2006	1.7	2.3
2007	1.8	1.5
2008	2.0	2.0

7 The chief executive of Geight plc receives a salary of £80,000 plus 4 per cent of sales. Will this encourage the adoption of decisions which are shareholder wealth enhancing? How might you change matters to persuade the chief executive to focus on shareholder wealth in all decision making?

MyFinanceLab *Now retake your diagnostic test for Chapter 1 to check your progress and update your study plan.*

Assignments

1 Consider the organisations where you have worked in the past and the people you have come into contact with. List as many objectives as you can, explicit or implicit, that have been revealed to, or suspected by, you. To what extent was goal congruence between different stakeholders achieved? How might the efforts of all individuals be channelled more effectively?

2 Review all the financial services you or your firm purchase. Try to establish a rough estimate of the cost of using each financial intermediary and write a balanced report considering whether you or your firm should continue to pay for that service.

Visit www.pearsoned.co.uk/arnold to get access to Gradetracker diagnostic tests, podcasts, Excel spreadsheet solutions, *FT* articles, a flashcard revision tool, web links, a searchable glossary and more.

Project appraisal:
net present value and internal rate of return

LEARNING OUTCOMES

By the end of the chapter the reader should be able to demonstrate an understanding of the fundamental theoretical justifications for using discounted cash flow techniques in analysing major investment decisions, based on the concepts of the time value of money and the opportunity cost of capital. More specifically the reader should be able to:

■ calculate net present value and internal rate of return;

■ show an appreciation of the relationship between net present value and internal rate of return;

■ describe and explain at least three potential problems that can arise with internal rate of return in specific circumstances;

■ demonstrate awareness of the propensity for management to favour a percentage measure of investment performance and be able to use the modified internal rate of return.

MyFinanceLab *Complete your diagnostic test for Chapter 2 now to create your personal study plan*

Introduction

Shareholders supply funds to a firm for a reason. That reason, generally, is to receive a return on their precious resources. The return is generated by management using the finance provided to invest in real assets. It is vital for the health of the firm and the economic welfare of the finance providers that management employ the best techniques available when analysing which of all the possible investment opportunities will give the best return.

Someone (or a group) within the organisation may have to take the bold decision on whether it is better to build a new factory or extend the old; whether it is wiser to use an empty piece of land for a multi-storey car park or to invest a larger sum and build a shopping centre; whether shareholders would be better off if the firm returned their money in the form of dividends because shareholders can obtain a better return elsewhere, or whether the firm should pursue its expansion plan and invest in that new chain of hotels, or that large car showroom, or the new football stand.

These sorts of decisions require not only brave people, but informed people; individuals of the required calibre need to be informed about a range of issues: for example, the market environment and level of demand for the proposed activity, the internal environment, culture and capabilities of the firm, the types and levels of cost elements in the proposed area of activity, and, of course, an understanding of the risk appertaining to the project.

BMW and Nissan presumably considered all these factors before making their massive investments in factories to produce cars in the UK – *see* Exhibit 2.1.

Exhibit 2.1

Mini investment drives revival in carmaking

By John Reed, Motor Industry Correspondent

BMW has said the UK will remain the 'heart' of its burgeoning Mini luxury small-car brand in a morale boosting decision for the government as it seeks ways to drive manufacturing growth.

The industry's largest premium carmaker said on Thursday that it would invest another £500m in its UK operation over the next three years, mostly to build the next generation of Mini cars at its plant in Oxford.

The decision will bring BMW's investment in the UK, its biggest production centre in Europe after Germany, to £1.5bn. The Munich-based producer said the move would safeguard more than 5,000 jobs in Oxford and at its pressings plant in Swindon and engine plant at Hams Hall in Warwickshire.

The announcement came a day after Nissan said it would invest £192m to build the next version of its Qashqai vehicle in Sunderland.

 Financial Times, 10 June 2011, p. 3.
All Rights Reserved.

Bravery, information, knowledge and a sense of proportion are all essential ingredients when undertaking the onerous task of investing other people's money, but there is another element which is also of crucial importance, that is, the employment of an investment appraisal technique which leads to the 'correct' decision; a technique which takes into account the fundamental considerations.

This chapter examines two approaches to evaluating investments within the firm.[1] Both emphasise the central importance of the concept of the time value of money and are thus described as discounted cash flow (DCF) techniques. Net present value (NPV) and internal rate of return (IRR) are in common usage in most large commercial organisations and are regarded as more complete than

1 The selection of investment projects is called capital expenditure – 'capex' – or capital budgeting.

the traditional techniques of payback and accounting rate of return (e.g. return on capital employed – ROCE). The relative merits and demerits of these alternative methods are discussed in Chapter 4 alongside a consideration of some of the practical issues of project implementation. In this chapter we concentrate on gaining an understanding of how net present value and internal rate of return are calculated, as well as their theoretical underpinnings.

Value creation and corporate investment

If we accept that the objective of investment within the firm is to create value for its owners then the purpose of allocating money to a particular division or project is to generate cash inflows in the future, significantly greater than the amount invested. Thus, put most simply, the project appraisal decision is one involving the comparison of the amount of cash put into an investment with the amount of cash returned. The key phrase and the tricky issue is 'significantly greater than'. For instance, would you, as part-owner of a firm, be content if that firm asked you to swap £10,000 of your hard-earned money for some new shares so that the management team could invest it in order to hand back to you, in five years, the £10,000 plus £1,000? Is this a significant return? Would you feel that your wealth had been enhanced if you were aware that by investing the £10,000 yourself, by, for instance, lending to the government, you could have received a 5 per cent return per year? Or that you could obtain a return of 10 per cent per annum by investing in other shares on the stock market? Naturally, you would feel let down by a management team that offered a return of less than 2 per cent per year when you had alternative courses of action which would have produced much more.

This line of thought is leading us to a central concept in finance and, indeed, in business generally – the **time value of money**. Investors have alternative uses for their funds and they therefore have an opportunity cost if money is invested in a corporate project. The *investor's* **opportunity cost** is the sacrifice of the return available on the best forgone alternative.

Investments must generate at least enough cash for all investors to obtain their required returns. If they produce less than the investor's opportunity cost then the wealth of shareholders will decline.

Exhibit 2.2 summarises the process of good investment appraisal. The achievement of value or wealth creation is determined not only by the future cash flows to be derived from a project but also by the timing of those cash flows and by making an allowance for the fact that time has value.

Exhibit 2.2 Investment appraisal: objective, inputs and process

The time value of money

When people undertake to set aside money for investment something has to be given up now. For instance, if someone buys shares in a firm or lends to a business there is a sacrifice of consumption. One of the incentives to save is the possibility of gaining a higher level of future consumption by sacrificing some present consumption. Therefore, it is apparent that compensation is required to induce people to make a consumption sacrifice. Compensation will be required for at least three things:

- *Impatience to consume* That is, individuals generally prefer to have £1.00 today than £1.00 in five years' time. To put this formally: the utility of £1.00 now is greater than £1.00 received five years hence. Individuals are predisposed towards impatience to consume, thus they need an appropriate reward to begin the saving process. The rate of exchange between certain future consumption and certain current consumption is the pure rate of interest – this occurs even in a world of no inflation and no risk. If you lived in such a world you might be willing to sacrifice £100 of consumption now if you were compensated with £102 to be received in one year. This would mean that your pure rate of interest is 2 per cent.

- *Inflation* The price of time (or the interest rate needed to compensate for impatience to consume) exists even when there is no inflation, simply because people generally prefer consumption now to consumption later. If there is inflation then the providers of finance will have to be compensated for that loss in purchasing power as well as for time.

- *Risk* The promise of the receipt of a sum of money some years hence generally carries with it an element of risk; the payout may not take place or the amount may be less than expected. Risk simply means that the future return has a variety of possible values. Thus, the issuer of a security, whether it be a share, a bond or a bank account, must be prepared to compensate the investor for impatience to consume, inflation and risk involved, otherwise no one will be willing to buy the security.[2]

Take the case of Mrs Ann Investor who is considering a £1,000 one-year investment and requires compensation for three elements of time value. First, a return of 2 per cent is required for the pure time value of money. Second, inflation is anticipated to be 3 per cent over the year. At time zero (t_0) £1,000 buys one basket of goods and services. To buy the same basket of goods and services at time t_1 (one year later) £1,030 is needed. To compensate the investor for impatience to consume and inflation the investment needs to generate a return of 5.06 per cent, that is:

$$(1 + 0.02)(1 + 0.03) - 1 = 0.0506$$

The figure of 5.06 per cent may be regarded here as the risk-free return (RFR), the interest rate which is sufficient to induce investment assuming no uncertainty about cash flows.

Investors tend to view lending to reputable governments through the purchase of bonds or bills as the nearest they are going to get to risk-free investing, because these institutions have an almost unlimited ability to raise income from taxes or to create money. The RFR forms the bedrock for time value of money calculations as the pure time value and the expected inflation rate affect all investments equally. Whether the investment is in property, bonds, shares or a factory, if expected inflation rises from 3 per cent to 5 per cent then the investor's required return on all investments will increase by 2 per cent.

2 A further factor (which to some extent could be seen as a form of risk) is that once the lender has committed the funds to a borrower for a set period of time they have to face the risk that at some point they may need the funds. With some investments there are ways of releasing the money – converting the instrument to cash – quickly, at low transaction cost and with certainty over the amount that would be released. This can be achieved by insisting that the borrower repays or from selling the right to receive interest, etc. to another investor in a market. That is, there is high liquidity and therefore low liquidity risk. If lenders/ investors do not have access to the possibility of quick, low-cost conversion to cash – high liquidity risk – then they are likely to demand an additional return in compensation.

However, different investment categories carry different degrees of uncertainty about the outcome of the investment. For instance, an investment on the Russian stock market, with its high volatility, may be regarded as more risky than the purchase of a share in Tesco with its steady growth prospects. Investors require different **risk premiums** on top of the RFR to reflect the perceived level of extra risk. Thus:

Required return = **RFR + Risk premium**
(Time value of money)

In the case of Mrs Ann Investor, the risk premium pushes up the total return required to, say, 10 per cent, thus giving full compensation for all three elements of the time value of money.

Discounted cash flow

The net present value and internal rate of return techniques, both being **discounted cash flow** methods, take into account the time value of money. **Exhibit 2.3**, which presents Project Alpha, suggests that on a straightforward analysis, Project Alpha generates more cash inflows than outflows. An outlay of £2,000 produces £2,400.

Exhibit 2.3	Project Alpha, simple cash flow	
	Points in time (yearly intervals)	**Cash flows (£)**
	0 Now	–2,000
	1 (1 year from now)	+600
	2	+600
	3	+600
	4	+600

However, we may be foolish to accept Project Alpha on the basis of this crude methodology. The £600 cash flows occur at different times and are therefore worth different amounts to a person standing at time zero. Quite naturally, such an individual would value the £600 received in one year more highly than the £600 received after four years. In other words, the present value of the pounds (at time zero) depends on when they are received.

It would be useful to convert all these different 'qualities' of pounds to a common currency, to some sort of common denominator. The conversion process is achieved by **discounting** all future cash flows by the time value of money, thereby expressing them as an equivalent amount received at time zero. The process of discounting relies on a variant of the **compounding** formula:

$$F = P(1 + i)^n$$

where
- F = future value
- P = present value
- i = interest rate
- n = number of years over which compounding takes place

Note It will be most important for many readers to turn to Appendix 2.1 at the end of this chapter at this point to get to grips with the key mathematical tools which will be used in this chapter and throughout the rest of the book. Readers are also strongly advised to attempt the Appendix 2.1 exercises (answers for which are provided in Appendix VI at the end of the book).

If a saver deposited £100 in a bank account paying interest at 8 per cent per annum, after three years the account will contain £125.97:

$$F = 100(1 + 0.08)^3 = £125.97$$

This formula can be changed so that we can answer the following question: 'How much must I deposit in the bank now to receive £125.97 in three years?' We need to rearrange the formula so that we are calculating for present value, P.

$$P = \frac{F}{(1 + i)^n} \text{ or } F \times \frac{1}{(1 + i)^n}$$

$$P = \frac{125.97}{(1 + 0.08)^3} = 100$$

In this second case we have discounted the £125.97 back to a present value of £100. If this technique is now applied to Project Alpha to convert all the money cash flows of future years into their present value equivalents the result is as follows (assuming that the time value of money is 10 per cent) – *see* Exhibit 2.4.

Exhibit 2.4	Project Alpha, discounted cash flow	
Points in time (yearly intervals)	**Cash flows (£)**	**Discounted cash flows (£)**
0	−2,000	−2,000.00
1	+600	$\frac{600}{1 + 0.10}$ = +545.45
2	+600	$\frac{600}{(1 + 0.10)^2}$ = +495.87
3	+600	$\frac{600}{(1 + 0.10)^3}$ = +450.79
4	+600	$\frac{600}{(1 + 0.10)^4}$ = +409.81

We can see that, when these future pounds are converted to a common denominator, this investment involves a larger outflow (£2,000) than inflow (£1,901.92). In other words the return on the £2,000 is less than 10 per cent.

Technical aside

If your calculator has a 'powers' function (usually represented by x^y or y^x) then compounding and discounting can be accomplished relatively quickly. Alternatively, you may obtain discount factors from the table in Appendix II at the end of the book. If we take the discounting of the fourth year's cash flow for Alpha as an illustration:

$$\frac{1}{(1 + 0.10)^4} \times 600$$

Calculator: Input 1.10
Press y^x (or x^y)
Input 4
Press =
Display 1.4641
Press $1/_x$
Display 0.6830
Multiply by 600
Answer 409.81

Using Appendix II, look down the column 10% and along the row 4 years to find discount factor of 0.683:

$0.683 \times £600 = £409.81$

(This approach works on some calculators but not others – check the instructions.)

Net present value and internal rate of return

Net present value: examples and definitions

The conceptual justification for, and the mathematics of, the net present value and internal rate of return methods of project appraisal will be illustrated through an imaginary but realistic decision-making process at the firm of Hard Decisions plc. This example, in addition to describing techniques, demonstrates the centrality of some key concepts such as opportunity cost and time value of money and shows the wealth-destroying effect of ignoring these issues.

Imagine you are the finance director of a large publicly quoted company called Hard Decisions plc. The board of directors have agreed that the objective of the firm should be shareholder wealth maximisation. Recently, the board appointed a new director, Mr Brightspark, as an 'ideas' man. He has a reputation as someone who can see opportunities where others see only problems. He has been hired especially to seek out new avenues for expansion and make better use of existing assets. In the past few weeks Mr Brightspark has been looking at some land that the company owns near the centre of Birmingham. This is a ten-acre site on which the flagship factory of the firm once stood; but that was 30 years ago and the site is now derelict. Mr Brightspark announces to a board meeting that he has three alternative proposals concerning the ten-acre site.

Mr Brightspark stands up to speak: Proposal 1 is to spend £5m clearing the site, cleaning it up, and decontaminating it. [The factory that stood on the site was used for chemical production.] It would then be possible to sell the ten acres to property developers for a sum of £12m in one year's time. Thus, we will make a profit of £7m over a one-year period.

Proposal 1: Clean up and sell – Mr Brightspark's figures

Clearing the site plus decontamination, payable t_0	−£5m
Sell the site in one year, t_1	£12m
Profit	£7m

The chairman of the board stops Mr Brightspark at that point and turns to you, in your capacity as the financial expert on the board, to ask what you think of the first proposal. Because you have studied assiduously on your financial management course you are able to make the following observations:

Point 1 This company is valued by the stock market at £100m because our investors are content that the rate of return they receive from us is consistent with the going rate for our risk class of shares; that is, 15 per cent per annum. In other words, the opportunity cost for our shareholders of buying shares in this firm is 15 per cent. (Hard Decisions is an all-equity firm, no debt capital has been raised and this is the best capital structure.) The alternative to investing their money with us is to invest it in another firm with similar risk characteristics yielding 15 per cent per annum. Thus, we may take this **opportunity cost of capital** as our minimum required return from any project we undertake. This idea of opportunity cost can perhaps be better explained by the use of a diagram (*see* **Exhibit 2.5**).

If we give a return of less than 15 per cent then shareholders will lose out because they can obtain 15 per cent elsewhere and will, thus, suffer an opportunity cost.

We, as managers of shareholders' money, need to use a discount rate of 15 per cent for any project of the same risk class that we analyse. The discount rate is the opportunity cost of investing in the project rather than the capital markets, for example, buying shares in other firms giving a 15 per cent return. Instead of accepting this project the firm can always give the cash to the shareholders and let them invest it in financial assets.

Point 2 I believe I am right in saying that we have received numerous offers for the ten-acre site over the past year. A reasonable estimate of its immediate sale value would be £6m. That is, I could call up one of the firms keen to get its hands on the site and squeeze out a price of about £6m.

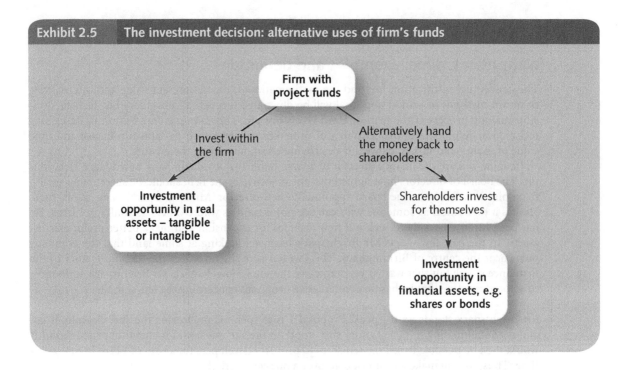

Exhibit 2.5 The investment decision: alternative uses of firm's funds

This £6m is an opportunity cost of the project, in that it is the value of the best alternative course of action. Thus, we should add to Mr Brightspark's £5m of clean-up costs the £6m of opportunity cost because we are truly sacrificing £11m to put this proposal into operation. If we did not go ahead with Mr Brightspark's proposal, but sold the site as it is, we could raise our bank balance by £6m, plus the £5m saved by not paying clean-up costs.

Proposal 1: Clean up and sell – Year t_0 cash flows

Immediate sale value (opportunity cost)	£6m
Clean-up, etc.	£5m
Total sacrifice at t_0	£11m

Point 3 I can accept Mr Brightspark's final sale price of £12m as being valid in the sense that he has, I know, employed some high-quality experts to derive the figure, but I do have a problem with comparing the initial outlay *directly* with the final cash flow on a simple *nominal* sum basis. The £12m is to be received in one year's time, whereas the £5m is to be handed over to the clean-up firm immediately, and the £6m opportunity cost sacrifice, by not selling the site, is being made immediately.

 If we were to take the £11m initial cost of the project and invest it in financial assets of the same risk class as this firm, giving a return of 15 per cent, then the value of that investment at the end of one year would be £12.65m. The calculation for this:

$$F = P(1 + k)$$

where k = the opportunity cost of capital:

$$11(1 + 0.15) = £12.65m$$

This is more than the return promised by Mr Brightspark.

Another way of looking at this problem is to calculate the **net present value** of the project. We start with the classic formula for net present value:

$$NPV = CF_0 + \frac{CF_1}{(1 + k)^n}$$

where CF_0 = cash flow at time zero (t_0), and
CF_1 = cash flow at time one (t_1), one year after time zero:

$$NPV = -11 + \frac{12}{1 + 0.15} = -11 + 10.435 = -£0.565m$$

All cash flows are expressed in the common currency of pounds at time zero. Thus, everything is in present value terms. When the positives and negatives are netted out we have the *net present value*. The decision rules for net present value are:

NPV \geq 0 Accept
NPV $<$ 0 Reject

Project proposal 1's negative NPV indicates that a return of less than 15 per cent per annum will be achieved.

An investment proposal's net present value is derived by discounting the future net cash receipts at a rate which reflects the value of the alternative use of the funds, summing them over the life of the proposal and deducting the initial outlay.

In conclusion, Ladies and Gentlemen, given the choice between:

(a) selling the site immediately raising £6m and saving £5m of expenditure – a total of £11m, or

(b) developing the site along the lines of Mr Brightspark's proposal,

I would choose to sell it immediately because £11m would get a better return elsewhere.
The chairman thanks you and asks Mr Brightspark to explain Project proposal 2.

Proposal 2: Office complex – Mr Brightspark's figures

Mr Brightspark: Proposal 2 consists of paying £5m immediately for a clean-up. Then, over the next two years, spending another £14m building an office complex. Tenants would not be found immediately on completion of the building. The office units would be let gradually over the following three years. Finally, when the office complex is fully let, in six years' time, it would be sold to an institution, such as a pension fund, for the sum of £40m (*see* Exhibit 2.6).

Mr Brightspark claims an almost doubling of the money invested (£25m invested over the first two years leads to an inflow of £47m).
The chairman turns to you and asks: Is this project really so beneficial to our shareholders?
You reply: The message rammed home to me by my finance textbook was that the best method of assessing whether a project is shareholder wealth enhancing is to discount all its cash flows at the opportunity cost of capital. This will enable a calculation of the net present value of those cash flows.

$$NPV = CF_0 + \frac{CF_1}{1 + k} + \frac{CF_2}{(1 + k)^2} + \frac{CF_3}{(1 + k)^3} \dots + \frac{CF_n}{(1 + k)^n}$$

So, given that Mr Brightspark's figures are true cash flows, I can calculate the NPV of Proposal 2 – *see* Exhibit 2.7. Note that we again use a 15 per cent discount rate, which implies that this

Exhibit 2.6	Project 2: Mr Brightspark's figures	

Points in time (yearly intervals)	Cash flows (£m)	Event
0 (now)	−5	Clean-up costs
0 (now)	−6	Opportunity cost
1	−4	Building cost
2	−10	Building cost
3	+1	Net rental income $\frac{1}{4}$ of offices let
4	+2	Net rental income $\frac{1}{2}$ of offices let
5	+4	Net rental income All offices let
6	+40	Office complex sold
Total	+22	Inflow £47m Outflow £25m
Profit	£22m	

Note: Mr Brightspark has accepted the validity of your argument about the opportunity cost of the alternative 'project' of selling the land immediately and has quickly added this −£6m to the figures

Exhibit 2.7	Proposal 2: Net present value	

Points in time (yearly intervals)	Cash flows (£m)		Discounted cash flows (£m)
0	−5		−5
0	−6		−6
1	−4	$\dfrac{-4}{(1 + 0.15)}$	−3.48
2	−10	$\dfrac{-10}{(1 + 0.15)^2}$	−7.56
3	1	$\dfrac{1}{(1 + 0.15)^3}$	0.66
4	2	$\dfrac{2}{(1 + 0.15)^4}$	1.14
5	4	$\dfrac{4}{(1 + 0.15)^5}$	1.99
6	40	$\dfrac{40}{(1 + 0.15)^6}$	17.29
Net present value			−0.96

(An Excel spreadsheet version of this calculation is shown at www.pearsoned.co.uk/arnold)

project is at the same level of risk as project 1 and the same as the average of the existing set of risk projects carried out by the firm. If it is subject to higher risk an increased rate of return would be demanded (the calculation of the required rate of return is discussed in Chapter 16).

Proposal 2:　Net present value

Because the NPV is less than 0, we would serve our shareholders better by selling the site and saving the money spent on clearing and building and putting that money into financial assets yielding 15 per cent per annum. Shareholders would end up with more in Year 6.

The chairman thanks you and asks Mr Brightspark for his third proposal.

Proposal 3:　Worldbeater manufacturing plant

Mr Brightspark: Proposal 3 involves the use of the site for a factory to manufacture the product 'Worldbeater'. We have been producing 'Worldbeater' from our Liverpool factory for the past ten years. Despite its name, we have confined the selling of it to the UK market. I propose the setting up of a second 'Worldbeater' factory which will serve the European market. The figures are as follows (*see* Exhibit 2.8).

Exhibit 2.8	Proposal 3: Mr Brightspark's figures	
Points in time (yearly intervals)	Cash flows (£m)	Event
0	–5	Clean-up
0	–6	Opportunity cost
1	–10	Factory building
2	0	
3 to infinity	+5	Net income from additional sales of 'Worldbeater'

Note: Revenue is gained in Year 2 from sales but this is exactly offset by the cash flows created by the costs of production and distribution. The figures for Year 3 and all subsequent years are net cash flows, that is, cash outflows are subtracted from cash inflows generated by sales.

The chairman turns to you and asks your advice.

You reply: Worldbeater is a well-established product and has been very successful. I am happy to take the cash flow figures given by Mr Brightspark as the basis for my calculations, which are set out in Exhibit 2.9.

This project gives an NPV that is positive, and therefore is shareholder wealth enhancing. The third project gives a rate of return which is greater than 15 per cent per annum. It provides a return of 15 per cent plus a present value of £5.5m. Based on these figures I would recommend that the board looks into Proposal 3 in more detail.

The chairman thanks you and suggests that this proposal be put to the vote.

Mr Brightspark (interrupts): Just a minute, are we not taking a lot on trust here? Our finance expert has stated that the way to evaluate these proposals is by using the NPV method, but in the firms where I have worked in the past, the internal rate of return (IRR) method of investment appraisal was used. I would like to see how these three proposals shape up when the IRR calculations are done.

The chairman turns to you and asks you to explain the IRR method, and to apply it to the figures provided by Mr Brightspark.

Exhibit 2.9 **Proposal 3: Net present value**

Points in time (yearly intervals)	Cash flows (£m)		Discounted cash flows (£m)
0	−11		−11
1	−10	$\dfrac{-10}{(1 + 0.15)}$	−8.7
2	0		
3 to infinity	5	Value of perpetuity at time t_2: $P = \dfrac{F}{k} = \dfrac{5}{0.15} = 33.33.$ This has to be discounted back two years: $\dfrac{33.33}{(1 + 0.15)^2}$	= 25.20
Net present value			+5.5

(An Excel spreadsheet version of this calculation is shown at www.pearsoned.co.uk/arnold)
Note: If these calculations are confusing you are advised to read the mathematical Appendix 2.1 at the end of this chapter.

Note

The perpetuity formula $\left(\dfrac{F}{k}\right)$ can be used on the assumption that the first payment arises one year from the time at which we are valuing. So, if the first inflow arises at time 3 we are valuing the perpetuity as though we are standing at time 2. The objective of this exercise is not to convert all cash flows to time 2 values, but rather to time 0 value. Therefore, it is necessary to discount the perpetuity value by two years.

Before continuing this boardroom drama it might be useful at this point to broaden the understanding of NPV by considering two worked examples.

Worked example 2.1 Camrat plc

Camrat plc requires a return on investment of at least 10 per cent per annum over the life of any proposed project with the same risk as its existing projects in order to meet the opportunity cost of its shareholders (Camrat is financed entirely by equity and this is the optimal capital structure). The dynamic and thrusting strategic development team have been examining the possibility of entering the new market area of mosaic floor tiles. This will require an immediate outlay of £1m for factory purchase and tooling-up, which will be followed by *net* (i.e. after all cash outflows, e.g. wages, variable costs, etc.) cash inflows of £0.2m in one year, and £0.3m in two years' time. Thereafter, annual net cash inflows will be £180,000.

Required

Given these cash flows, will this investment provide a 10 per cent return (per annum) over the life of the project? Assume for simplicity that all cash flows arise on anniversary dates and the project has the same risk level as the existing set of projects.

Answer

First, lay out the cash flows with precise timing. (Note: the assumption that all cash flows arise on anniversary dates allows us to do this very simply.)

Points in time (yearly intervals)	0	1	2	3 to infinity
Cash flows (£)	−1m	0.2m	0.3m	0.18m

▶

Second, discount these cash flows to their present value equivalents.

Points in time	0	1	2	3 to infinity
	CF_0	$\dfrac{CF_1}{1+k}$	$\dfrac{CF_2}{(1+k)^2}$	$\dfrac{CF_3}{k} \times \dfrac{1}{(1+k)^2}$
	$-1m$	$\dfrac{0.2}{1+0.1}$	$\dfrac{0.3}{(1+0.1)^2}$	$\dfrac{0.18}{0.1}$

This discounts back two years:

$$\dfrac{0.18/0.1}{(1+0.1)^2}$$

	$-1m$	0.1818	0.2479	$\dfrac{1.8}{(1.1)^2} = 1.4876$

Third, net out the discounted cash flows to give the net present value.

$$
\begin{array}{r}
-1.0000 \\
+0.1818 \\
+0.2479 \\
+1.4876 \\
\hline
\end{array}
$$

Net present value $\qquad +0.9173$

Conclusion

The positive NPV result demonstrates that this project gives not only a return of 10 per cent per annum but a large surplus above and beyond a 10 per cent per annum return. This is an extremely attractive project: on a £1m investment the surplus generated beyond the opportunity cost of the shareholders (their time value of money) is £917,300; thus, by accepting this project, we would increase shareholder wealth by this amount.

(An Excel spreadsheet version of this calculation is shown at www.pearsoned.co.uk/arnold)

Worked example 2.2	Actarm plc

Actarm plc is examining two projects, A and B. The cash flows are as follows:

	A £	B £
Initial outflow, t_0	240,000	240,000
Cash inflows:		
Time 1 (one year after t_0)	200,000	20,000
Time 2	100,000	120,000
Time 3	20,000	220,000

Using discount rates of 8 per cent and then 16 per cent, calculate the NPVs and state which project is superior. Why do you get a different preference depending on the discount rate used?

Answer

Using 8 per cent as the discount rate

$$NPV = CF_0 + \frac{CF_1}{1+k} + \frac{CF_2}{(1+k)^2} + \frac{CF_3}{(1+k)^3}$$

Project A

$$-240,000 + \frac{200,000}{1+0.08} + \frac{100,000}{(1+0.08)^2} + \frac{20,000}{(1+0.08)^3}$$

$$-240,000 + 185,185 + 85,734 + 15,877 = +£46,796$$

Project B

$$-240{,}000 + \frac{20{,}000}{1 + 0.08} + \frac{120{,}000}{(1 + 0.08)^2} + \frac{220{,}000}{(1 + 0.08)^3}$$

$$-240{,}000 + 18{,}519 \; + \; 102{,}881 \; + \; 174{,}643 \quad = +\pounds56{,}043$$

Using an 8 per cent discount rate both projects produce positive NPVs and therefore would enhance shareholder wealth. However, Project B is superior because it creates more value than Project A. Thus, if the accepting of one project excludes the possibility of accepting the other then B is preferred.

Using 16 per cent as the discount rate

Project A

$$-240{,}000 + \frac{200{,}000}{1.16} + \frac{100{,}000}{(1.16)^2} + \frac{20{,}000}{(1.16)^3}$$

$$-240{,}000 + 172{,}414 + 74{,}316 \; + 12{,}813 = +\pounds19{,}543$$

Project B

$$-240{,}000 + \frac{20{,}000}{1.16} + \frac{120{,}000}{(1.16)^2} + \frac{220{,}000}{(1.16)^3}$$

$$-240{,}000 + 17{,}241 + 89{,}180 \; + 140{,}945 = +\pounds7{,}366$$

With a 16 per cent discount rate Project A generates more shareholder value and so would be preferred to Project B. This is despite the fact that Project B, in pure undiscounted cash flow terms, produces an additional £40,000.

The different ranking (order of superiority) occurs because Project B has the bulk of its cash flows occurring towards the end of the project's life. These large distant cash flows, when discounted at a high discount rate, become relatively small compared with those of Project A, which has its high cash flows discounted by only one year.

(An Excel spreadsheet showing these calculations is available at www.pearsoned.co.uk/arnold)

NPV is used by many people besides corporate finance teams. For example, as **Exhibit 2.10** shows, stockbrokers sometimes calculate NPV to help estimate share values.

Exhibit 2.10

Churchill Mining in focus

By Neil Hume and Bryce Elder

Churchill Mining was in focus on Monday. Its shares rose 5.9 per cent to 111¾p on the back of reports that claimed the mining company was talking to several Indian power companies with a view to selling its East Kutai thermal coal project in Indonesia.

Northland Capital Partners said the news was significant and a sale would put a higher price on East Kutai than currently implied by Churchill's share price.

'Whilst not conclusive at this stage, this is potentially significant positive newsflow,' the broker said.

'The current market valuation accords less than 10 per cent of the $1.8bn net present value [of the project] suggested by the feasibility study, suggesting significant scope for upside.'

Internal rate of return

We now return to Hard Decisions plc. The chairman has asked you to explain internal rate of return (IRR).

You respond: The **internal rate of return** is a very popular method of project appraisal and it has much to commend it. In particular it takes into account the time value of money. I am not surprised to find that Mr Brightspark has encountered this appraisal technique in his previous employment. Basically, what the IRR tells you is the rate of return you will receive by putting your money into a project. It describes by how much the cash inflows exceed the cash outflows on an annualised percentage basis, taking account of the timing of those cash flows.

The internal rate of return is the rate of return which equates the present value of future cash flows with the outlay (or, for some projects, it equates discounted future cash outflows with initial inflow):

Outlay = Future cash flows discounted at rate r

Thus:

$$CF_0 = \frac{CF_1}{1 + r} + \frac{CF_2}{(1 + r)^2} + \frac{CF_3}{(1 + r)^3} \cdots \frac{CF_n}{(1 + r)^n}$$

IRR is also referred to as the 'yield' of a project.

Alternatively, the internal rate of return, r, can be viewed as the discount rate at which the net present value is zero. It is the value for r which makes the following equation hold:

$$CF_0 + \frac{CF_1}{1 + r} + \frac{CF_2}{(1 + r)^2} + \frac{CF_3}{(1 + r)^3} \cdots \frac{CF_n}{(1 + r)^n} = 0$$

(*Note*: in the first formula CF_0 is expressed as a positive number, whereas in the second it is usually a negative.)

These two equations amount to the same thing. They both require knowledge of the cash flows and their precise timing. The element which is unknown is the rate of return which will make the time-adjusted outflows and inflows equal to each other.

I apologise, Ladies and Gentlemen, if this all sounds like too much jargon. Perhaps it would be helpful if you could see the IRR calculation in action. Let's apply the formula to Mr Brightspark's Proposal 1.

Proposal 1: Internal rate of return

Using the second version of the formula, our objective is to find an r which makes the discounted inflow at time 1 of £12m plus the initial £11m outflow equal to zero:

$$CF_0 + \frac{CF_1}{1 + r} = 0$$

$$-11 + \frac{12}{1 + r} = 0$$

The method I would recommend for establishing r is trial and error (assuming we do not have the relevant computer program available). So, to start with, simply pick a discount rate and plug it into the formula. (You can pick any (reasonable) discount rate to begin with in the trial and error approach.)

Let us try 5 per cent:

$$-11 + \frac{12}{1 + 0.05} = £0.42857\text{m or }£428,571$$

A 5 per cent rate is not correct because the discounted cash flows do not total to zero. The surplus of approximately £0.43m suggests that a higher interest rate will be more suitable. This will reduce the present value of the future cash inflow.

Try 10 per cent:

$$-11 + \frac{12}{1 + 0.1} = -0.0909 \text{ or } -£90,909$$

Again, we have not hit on the correct discount rate.

Try 9 per cent:

$$-11 + \frac{12}{1 + 0.09} = +0.009174 \text{ or } +£9,174$$

The last two calculations tell us that the discount rate which causes the discounted future cash flow to equal the initial outflow lies somewhere between 9 per cent and 10 per cent. The precise rate can be found through interpolation.

Interpolation for Proposal 1

First, display all the facts so far established (*see* **Exhibit 2.11**).

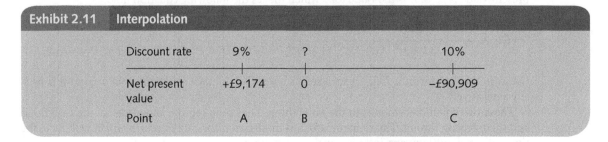

Exhibit 2.11	Interpolation			
Discount rate	9%	?		10%
Net present value	+£9,174	0		−£90,909
Point	A	B		C

Exhibit 2.11 illustrates that there is a yield rate (r) which lies between 9 per cent and 10 per cent which will produce an NPV of zero. The way to find that discount rate is to first find the distance between points A and B as a proportion of the entire distance between points A and C.

$$\frac{A \to B}{A \to C} = \frac{9,174 - 0}{9,174 + 90,909} = 0.0917$$

Thus the ? lies at a distance of 0.0917 away from the 9 per cent point.

Thus, IRR:

$$= 9 + \left(\frac{9,174}{100,083}\right) \times (10 - 9) = 9.0917 \text{ per cent}$$

To double-check our result:

$$-11 + \frac{12}{1 + 0.090917}$$

$$-11 + 11 = 0$$

Internal rate of return decision rules

The rule for internal rate of return decisions is:

If $k > r$ reject

If the opportunity cost of capital (k) is greater than the internal rate of return (r) on a project then the investor is better served by not going ahead with the project and applying the money to the best alternative use.

If $k \leq r$ accept

Here, the project under consideration produces the same or a higher yield than investment elsewhere for a similar risk level.

The IRR of Proposal 1 is 9.091 per cent, which is below the 15 per cent opportunity cost of capital used by Hard Decisions plc for projects of this risk class. Therefore, using the IRR method as well as the NPV method, this project should be rejected.

It might be enlightening to consider the relationship between NPV and IRR. **Exhibits 2.12** and **2.13** show what happens to NPV as the discount rate is varied between zero and 10 per cent for Proposal 1. At a zero discount rate the £12m received in one year is not discounted at all, so the NPV of £1m is simply the difference between the two cash flows. When the discount rate is raised to 10 per cent the present value of the year 1 cash flow becomes less than the current outlay. Where the line crosses the x axis, i.e. when NPV is zero, we can read off the internal rate of return.

It should be noted that in the case of Project proposal 1 the NPV/discount rate relationship is nearly a straight line. This is an unusual case. When cash flows occur over a number of years the line is likely to be more curved and concave to the origin.

Exhibit 2.12	The relationship between NPV and the discount rate (using Proposal 1's figures)

Discount rate (%)	NPV
10	−90,909
9.0917	0
9	9,174
8	111,111
7	214,953
6	320,755
5	428,571
4	538,462
3	650,485
2	764,706
1	881,188
0	1,000,000

Exhibit 2.13	The relationship between NPV and the discount rate for Project proposal 1

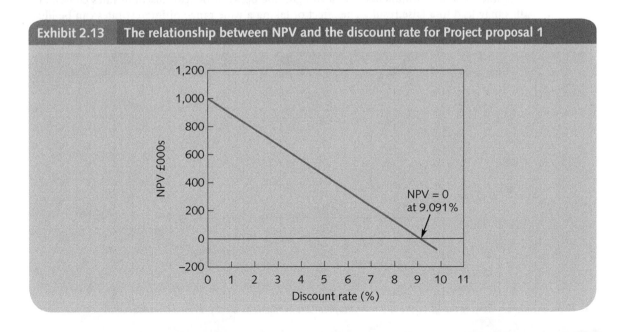

If the board will bear with me I can quickly run through the IRR calculations for Project proposals 2 and 3.

Proposal 2: IRR

To calculate the IRR for Proposal 2 we first lay out the cash flows in the discount formula:

$$-11 + \frac{-4}{(1+r)} + \frac{-10}{(1+r)^2} + \frac{1}{(1+r)^3} + \frac{2}{(1+r)^4} + \frac{4}{(1+r)^5} + \frac{40}{(1+r)^6} = 0$$

Then we try alternative discount rates to find a rate, r, that gives a zero NPV:

Try 14 per cent:

NPV (approx.) = –£0.043 or –£43,000

At 13 per cent:

NPV = £932,000

Interpolation is required to find an internal rate of return accurate to at least one decimal place (*see* **Exhibit 2.14**).

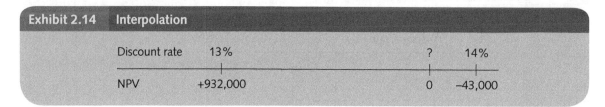

Exhibit 2.14	**Interpolation**		
Discount rate	13%	?	14%
NPV	+932,000	0	–43,000

$$13 + \frac{932,000}{975,000} \times (14 - 13) = 13.96\%$$

From **Exhibit 2.15**, we see that this project produces an IRR less than the opportunity cost of shareholders' funds (15 per cent); therefore it should be rejected under the IRR method. The curvature of the line is exaggerated to demonstrate the absence of linearity and emphasise the importance of having a fairly small gap in trial and error interest rates prior to interpolation. The interpolation formula assumes a straight line between the two discount rates chosen and this may lead to a false result. The effect of taking a wide range of interest rates can be illustrated if we calculate on the basis of 5 per cent and 30 per cent – *see* **Exhibit 2.16**.

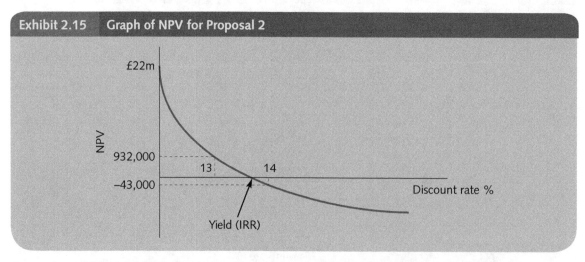

Exhibit 2.15 Graph of NPV for Proposal 2

(*An Excel spreadsheet showing the IRR calculation for Proposal 2 is available at www.pearsoned.co.uk/arnold*)

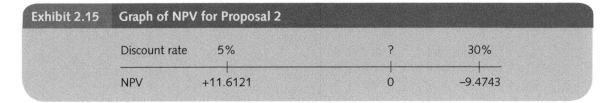

| Exhibit 2.15 | Graph of NPV for Proposal 2 |

Discount rate	5%	?	30%
NPV	+11.6121	0	−9.4743

At 5 per cent, NPV of Project 2 = £11.6121m.
At 30 per cent, NPV of Project 2 = −£9.4743m.

$$5 + \left(\frac{11.6121}{11.6121 + 9.4743} \right)(30 - 5) = 18.77\%$$

From Exhibit 2.17 we see that the non-linearity of the relationship between NPV and the discount rate has created an IRR almost 5 per cent removed from the true IRR. This could lead to an erroneous acceptance of this project given the company's hurdle rate of 15 per cent. In reality this project yields less than the company could earn by placing its money elsewhere for the same risk level.

| Exhibit 2.17 | The accuracy of the IRR calculated may depend on the size of the gap between the discount rates used in the interpolation calculation |

Proposal 3: IRR

$$CF_0 + \frac{CF_1}{1 + r} + \frac{CF_3/r}{(1 + r)^2} = 0$$

Try 19 per cent:

$$-11 + \frac{-10}{1 + 0.19} + \frac{5/0.19}{(1 + 0.19)^2} = -£0.82m$$

Try 18 per cent:

$$-11 + \frac{-10}{1 + 0.18} + \frac{5/0.18}{(1 + 0.18)^2} = £0.475m$$

Project 3 produces an internal rate of return of 18.37 per cent which is higher than the opportunity cost of capital and therefore is to be commended.

We can lay out the facts that we have discovered – *see* Exhibit 2.18.

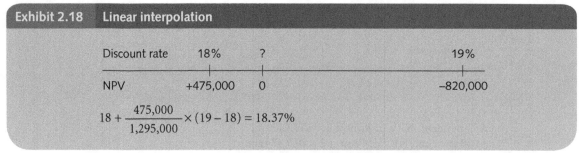

Exhibit 2.18	Linear interpolation

Discount rate 18% ? 19%

NPV +475,000 0 −820,000

$$18 + \frac{475,000}{1,295,000} \times (19 - 18) = 18.37\%$$

(An Excel spreadsheet showing the IRR calculation for proposed project 3 is available at www.pearsoned.co.uk/arnold)

IRR is a commonly used metric in business. Gerald Ronson, one of the richest people in the property business, uses it to make decisions – *see* **Exhibit 2.19**.

Exhibit 2.19

Bullish Ronson defies slump to carry on building apace

By Daniel Thomas

Gerald Ronson strolls out of his Mercedes – the 'workhorse' he uses to cover 40,000 miles a year visiting his various projects in the UK – in front of his office building in Marylebone looking every inch the fighter that his reputation makes out.

He's in characteristically bullish mood. Heron, the property company he started with his father in 1965, is in robust health considering the extent of the property slump, which has wiped out the value of some properties by half over the past two years.

Heron, partly because it sold its UK investments and partly because European markets have performed relatively well, has held its net asset value almost static, and is looking for opportunities.

Mr Ronson says that most deals cross his large mahogany desk early on, but so far there have been few of interest. He has almost £140m to spend when the time is right.

'There will be interesting opportunities over the next 18–24 months but I have yet to see a deal that I consider we want to do. This is not the time to overpay, and you need to see a respectable return. We [want] to see a return over 20 per cent on an IRR basis with low gearing,' he adds.

We temporarily leave the saga of Mr Brightspark and his proposals to reinforce understanding of NPV and IRR through the worked example of Martac plc.

Problems with internal rate of return

We now return to Hard Decisions plc.

Mr Brightspark: I have noticed your tendency to prefer NPV to any other method. Yet, in the three projects we have been discussing, NPV and IRR give the same decision recommendation. That is, reject Projects 1 and 2 and accept Project 3. So, why not use IRR more often?

You reply: It is true that the NPV and IRR methods of capital investment appraisal are closely related. Both are **'time-adjusted' measures of profitability**. The NPV and IRR methods gave the same result in the cases we have considered today because the problems associated with the IRR method are not present in the figures we have been working with. In the appraisal of other projects we may encounter the severe limitations of the IRR method and therefore I prefer to stick to the theoretically superior NPV technique.

Worked example 2.3	Martac plc

Martac plc is a manufacturer of *Martac-aphro*. Two new automated process machines used in the production of *Martac-aphro* have been introduced to the market, the CAM and the ATR. Both will give cost savings over existing processes:

£000s	CAM	ATR
Initial cost (machine purchase and installation, etc.)	120	250
Cash flow savings: At Time 1 (one year after the initial cash outflow)	48	90
At Time 2	48	90
At Time 3	48	90
At Time 4	48	90

All other factors remain constant and the firm has access to large amounts of capital. The required return on projects is 8 per cent. Production ceases after four years and the machines will then have a zero scrap value.

Required

(a) Calculate the IRR for CAM.
(b) Calculate the IRR for ATR.
(c) Based on IRR, which machine would you purchase?
(d) Calculate the NPV for each machine.
(e) Based on NPV, which machine would you buy?
(f) Is IRR or NPV the better decision tool?

Answers

In this problem the total cash flows associated with the alternative projects are not given. Instead the incremental cash flows are provided, for example, the additional savings available over the existing costs of production. This, however, is sufficient for a decision to be made about which machine to purchase.

(a) IRR for CAM

$$CF_0 + \frac{CF_1}{1+r} + \frac{CF_2}{(1+r)^2} + \frac{CF_3}{(1+r)^3} + \frac{CF_4}{(1+r)^4} = 0$$

Try 22 per cent:

$$-120{,}000 + 48{,}000 \times \text{annuity factor (af) for 4 years @ 22\%}$$

(*See* Appendix 2.1 to this chapter for annuity calculations and Appendix III at the end of the book for an annuity table.)

The annuity factor tells us the present value of four lots of £1 received at four annual intervals. This is 2.4936, meaning that the £4 in present value terms is worth just over £2.49.

$$-120{,}000 + 48{,}000 \times 2.4936 = -£307.20$$

Try 21 per cent:

$$-120{,}000 + 48{,}000 \times \text{annuity factor (af) for 4 years @ 21\%}$$

$$-120{,}000 + 48{,}000 \times 2.5404 = +£1{,}939.20$$

See Exhibit 2.20.

Exhibit 2.20	Interpolation				
Discount rate		21%		?	22%
NPV		1,939.2		0	−307

$$21 + \left(\frac{1939.2}{1939.2 + 307}\right) \times (22 - 21) = 21.86\%$$

(b) IRR for ATR

Try 16 per cent:

$$-250{,}000 + 90{,}000 \times 2.7982 = +£1{,}838$$

Try 17 per cent:

$$-250{,}000 + 90{,}000 \times 2.7432 = -£3{,}112$$

See Exhibit 2.21.

Exhibit 2.21	Interpolation			
Discount rate		16%	?	17%
NPV		+1,838	0	−3,112

$$16 + \left(\frac{1{,}838}{1{,}838 + 3{,}112}\right) \times (17 - 16) = 16.37\%$$

(c) Choice of machine on basis of IRR

If IRR is the only decision tool available then as long as the IRRs exceed the discount rate (or cost of capital) the project with the higher IRR might appear to be the preferred choice. In this case CAM ranks higher than ATR.

(d) NPV for machines: CAM

$$-120{,}000 + 48{,}000 \times 3.3121 = +£38{,}981$$

NPV for ATR

$$-250{,}000 + 90{,}000 \times 3.3121 = +£48{,}089$$

(e) Choice of machine on basis of NPV

ATR generates a return which has a present value of £48,089 in addition to the minimum return on capital required. This is larger than for CAM and therefore ATR ranks higher than CAM if NPV is used as the decision tool.

(f) Choice of decision tool

This problem has produced conflicting decision outcomes, which depend on the project appraisal method employed. NPV is the better decision-making technique because it measures in absolute amounts of money. That is, it gives the increase in shareholder wealth available by accepting a project. In contrast IRR expresses its return as a percentage which may result in an inferior low-scale project being preferred to a higher-scale project. So, if you cannot undertake both projects, the one that returns most to shareholders is the one with the highest NPV rather than the highest IRR.

(An Excel spreadsheet showing this calculation is shown at www.pearsoned.co.uk/arnold)

I will illustrate three of the most important problems, **multiple solutions**, **ranking** and confusion between **investing-type decisions** and **financing-type decisions**.

Multiple solutions

There may be a number of possible IRRs. This can be explained by examining the problems Mr Flummoxed is having (*see* Worked example 2.4).

Worked example 2.4	Mr Flummoxed

Mr Flummoxed of Deadhead plc has always used the IRR method of project appraisal. He has started to have doubts about its usefulness after examining the proposal, 'Project Oscillation'.

Project Oscillation

Points in time (yearly intervals)	0	1	2
Cash flow	−3,000	+15,000	−13,000

Internal rates of return are found at 11.56 per cent *and* 288.4 per cent.

Given that Deadhead plc has a required rate of return of 20 per cent, it is impossible to decide whether to implement Project Oscillation using an unadjusted IRR methodology. If there are a number of possible IRRs this means they are all meaningless.

The cause of multiple solutions is **unconventional cash flows**. Conventional cash flows occur when an outflow is followed by a series of inflows or a cash inflow is followed by a series of cash outflows. Unconventional cash flows are a series of cash flows with more than one change in sign. In the case of Project Oscillation the sign changes from negative to positive once, and from positive to negative once. Multiple yields can be adjusted for whilst still using the IRR method, but the simplest approach is to use the NPV method.

Ranking

The IRR decision rule does not always rank projects in the same way as the NPV method. Sometimes it is important to find out, not only which project gives a positive return, but which

Exhibit 2.22	Illustration of the IRR ranking problem

Project	Cash flows £m		IRR%	NPV (at 15%)
	Time 0	One year later		£
A	−20	+40	100%	+14.78m
B	−40	+70	75%	+20.87m

NPV at different discount rates

Discount rate (%)	Project A	Project B
0	20	30
20	13.33	18.33
50	6.67	6.67
75	2.86	0
100	0	−5
125	−2.22	−8.89

one gives the greater positive return. For instance, projects may be mutually exclusive, that is, only one may be undertaken and a choice has to be made. The use of IRR alone sometimes leads to a poor choice (*see* Exhibit 2.22).

From **Exhibit 2.23**, it is clear that the ranking of the projects by their IRRs is constant at 75 per cent and 100 per cent, regardless of the opportunity cost of capital (discount rate). Project A is always better. On the other hand, ranking the projects by the NPV method is not fixed. The NPV ranking depends on the discount rate assumed. Thus, if the discount rate used in the NPV calculation is higher than 50 per cent, the ranking under both IRR and NPV would be the same, i.e. Project A is superior. If the discount rate falls below 50 per cent, Project B is the better choice. One of the major elements

Exhibit 2.23 NPV at different discount rates

leading to the theoretical dominance of NPV is that it takes into account the scale of investment; thus the shareholders are made better off by undertaking Project B by £20.87m because the initial size of the project was larger. NPVs are measured in absolute amounts.

John Kay discusses the ranking problem of IRR in a FT article – *see* **Exhibit 2.24**.

Exhibit 2.24

How not to measure a business

By John Kay

Would you rather have a 20 per cent return on £1,000 or a 25 per cent return on £500? Ideally, you would like to find a company that would offer a 25 per cent yield on any capital you invested in it, but such opportunities do not exist. If you could not do that, you would like to have both the 20 per cent and the 25 per cent projects, but you will often have to choose between alternative routes to the same objective, or different financial models for the same business. So should you always choose the higher return on equity? The answer is not obvious. If you can expect to earn at least a 15 per cent return on your other investments, then you will be better off taking the 25 per cent proposition. If you cannot – and you probably cannot – then the lower, but still exhilarating, 20 per cent return on the larger amount is a better choice.

All good introductory finance texts explain that ranking projects by their rate of return is not an appropriate means of choosing between them. Most suggest an alternative way of approaching the problem. Measure the opportunity cost of funds, based on the risk adjusted returns available elsewhere. In a world in which even long-term borrowing by the US Treasury costs less than 4 per cent, that figure is unlikely to be very high – let's put it at 7 per cent. Then investing £1,000 at 20 per cent yields £200 a year, and investing £500 at 25 per cent and £500 at 7 per cent only £160. And £200 is always better than £160. Money, not percentages (or relative performance), pays the grocer and the yacht chandler.

But that simple message has not got through. Large companies think their investment appraisal techniques are sophisticated if they compute internal rates of return. It is more and more common for them to highlight the rate of return on their equity in their annual reports.

Confusion over investing-type decisions versus financing-type decisions

Hard Decisions plc's Proposal 1 required a cash outflow of £11m at time zero followed by a cash inflow of £12m one year later. This resulted in an IRR of 9.0917 per cent and negative NPV of −£0.565m, thus the project is rejected under both methods given the required rate of return of 15 per cent. This is an investing-type decision, because the initial cash flow is an outflow. Now consider a project that resulted in £11m being *received* at time zero and £12m *flowing out* at time 1 (one year later). Here we have a financing-type decision. You need to be careful in interpreting the results of a financing-type decision IRR. The IRR is again 9.0917 and given the opportunity cost of capital there is a danger of automatically rejecting the project if you have it stuck in your mind that the IRR must exceed 15 per cent for the project to be accepted. This would be wrong because you are being offered the chance to receive £11m, which can then be invested at 15 per cent per year at that risk level. This will outweigh the outflow that occurs at time one of £12m. In other words, this project gives a positive NPV and should be accepted.

$$NPV = £11m − £12m/(1.15) = +£0.565m$$

This leads us to reverse the IRR rules for a financing-type situation. To avoid confusion use NPV.

Exhibit 2.25 Characteristics of NPV and IRR

NPV	IRR
● It recognises that £1 today is worth more than £1 tomorrow.	● Also takes into account the time value of money.
● In conditions where all worthwhile projects can be accepted (i.e. no mutual exclusivity) it maximises shareholder utility. Projects with a positive NPV should be accepted since they increase shareholder wealth, while those with negative NPVs decrease shareholder wealth.	● In situations of non-mutual exclusivity, shareholder wealth is maximised if all projects with a yield higher than the opportunity cost of capital are accepted, while those with a return less than the time value of money are rejected.
● It takes into account investment size – absolute amounts of wealth change.	● Fails to measure in terms of absolute amounts of wealth changes. It measures percentage returns and this may cause ranking problems in conditions of mutual exclusivity, i.e. the wrong project may be rejected.
● It is not as intuitively understandable as a percentage measure.	● It is easier to communicate a percentage return than NPV to other managers and employees, who may not be familiar with the details of project appraisal techniques. The appeal of quick recognition and conveyance of understanding should not be belittled or underestimated.
● It can handle non-conventional cash flows.	● Non-conventional cash flows cause problems, e.g. multiple solutions.
● Additivity is possible: because present values are all measured in today's £s they can be added together. Thus the returns (NPVs) of a group of projects can be calculated.	● Additivity is not possible. ● Financing-type decisions may result in misinterpretation of IRR results.
● It assumes that cash inflows arising during the life of a project are reinvested at the opportunity cost of capital – a reasonable assumption.	● IRR implicitly assumes that cash flows received, say halfway through a project, can be invested elsewhere at a rate equal to the IRR until the end of the project's life – see next section for more detail on this problem.

The board of directors of Hard Decisions are now ready for a coffee break and time to digest these concepts and techniques. The chairman thanks you for your clarity and rigorous analysis. He also thanks Mr Brightspark for originating three imaginative and thought-provoking proposals to take the business forward towards its goal of shareholder wealth enhancement.

Modified internal rate of return

The fourth characteristic listed for IRR in Exhibit 2.25 is a powerful force driving its adoption in the practical world of business where few individuals have exposed themselves to the rigours of financial decision-making models, and therefore may not comprehend NPV. These issues are examined in more detail in Chapter 4, but it is perhaps worth explaining now the consequences of sticking rigidly to IRR.

One problem centres on the reinvestment assumption. With NPV it is assumed that cash inflows arising during the life of the project are reinvested at the opportunity cost of capital. In contrast the IRR implicitly assumes that the cash inflows that are received, say, half-way through a project can be reinvested elsewhere at a rate equal to the IRR until the end of the project's life. This is intuitively unacceptable. In the real world, if a firm invested in a very high-yielding project and some cash was returned after a short period, this firm would be unlikely to be able to deposit this cash elsewhere until the end of the project and reach the same extraordinary high yield, and yet this is what the IRR implicitly assumes. The more likely eventuality is that the intra-project cash inflows will be invested at the 'going rate' or the opportunity cost of capital. In other words, the firm's normal discount rate is the better estimate of the reinvestment rate. The effect of this erroneous reinvestment assumption is to inflate the IRR of the project under examination.

For example, Project K below has a very high IRR, at 61.8 per cent; thus the £1,000 received after one year is assumed to be taken back into the firm and then placed in another investment, again yielding 61.8 per cent until time 2. This is obviously absurd: if such an investment existed, why has the firm not already invested in it – given its cost of capital of only 15 per cent?

Project K (required rate of return 15 per cent)

Points in time (yearly intervals)	0	1	2
Cash flows (£)	–1,000	+1,000	+1,000

IRR

Try 60 per cent: NPV = 15.63.
Try 62 per cent: NPV = –1.68.

Interpolation

Exhibit 2.26	Project K

Discount rate	60%			?	62%
NPV	15.63			0	–1.68

$$60 + \left(\frac{15.63}{15.63 + 1.68} \right) \times (62 - 60) = 61.8\%$$

The reinvestment assumption of 61.8 per cent, for the £1,000 receivable at time 1, is clearly unrealistic, especially in the light of the fact that most investors can obtain a return of only 15 per cent for taking this level of risk.

The IRR of Project K assumes the following:

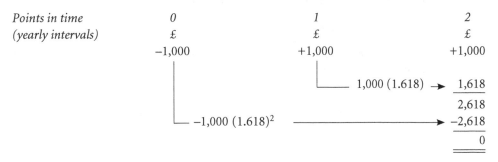

The £2,618 compounded cash flows at the terminal date of the project are equivalent to taking the original investment of £1,000 and compounding it for two years at 61.8 per cent. However, an NPV calculation assumes that the intra-project cash inflow is invested at 15 per cent:

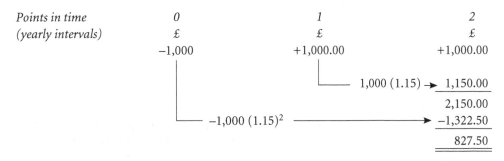

Discounting £827.50 back two years gives the NPV of £625.71.

If, for reasons of pragmatism or communication within the firm, it is necessary to describe a project appraisal in terms of a percentage, then it is recommended that the **modified internal rate of return (MIRR)** is used. This takes as its starting point the notion that, for the sake of consistency with NPV, any cash inflows arising during the project are reinvested at the opportunity cost of funds. That is, at the rate of return available on the next best alternative use of the funds in either financial or real assets. The MIRR is the rate of return, m, which, if used to compound the initial investment amount (the original cash outlay), produces the same terminal value as the project's cash inflows. The value of the project's cash inflows at the end of the project's life after they have been expressed in the terminal date's £s is achieved through compounding at the opportunity cost of funds. In other words, the common currency this time is not time 0 £s but time 4, or time 6, or time 'n' £s.

What we are attempting to do is find that rate of compounding which will equate the terminal value of the intra-project cash flows with the terminal value of the initial investment.

Modified internal rate of return for Project K

First, calculate the terminal value of the cash flows excluding the t_0 investment using the opportunity cost of capital.

		Terminal value (£)
t_1 1,000 (1.15)		1,150.00
t_2 1,000	already expressed as a terminal value because it occurs on the date of termination	1,000.00
	Total terminal value	2,150.00

The modified internal rate of return is the rate of compounding applied to the original investment necessary to produce a future (terminal) value of £2,150.00 two years later.

$$1,000 \, (1 + m)^2 = 2,150$$

Solve for m. (The mathematical tools – *see* Appendix 2.1 – may be useful here.) Divide both sides of the equation by 1,000:

$$(1 + m)^2 = \frac{2,150}{1,000}$$

Then, take roots to the power of 2 of both sides of the equation:

$$\sqrt[2]{(1 + m)^2} = \sqrt[2]{\frac{2,150}{1,000}}$$

$$m = \sqrt[2]{\frac{2,150}{1,000}} - 1 = 0.466 \text{ or } 46.6\%$$

or more generally:

$$m = \sqrt[n]{\frac{F}{P}} - 1$$

Thus, the MIRR is 46.6 per cent compared with the IRR of 61.8 per cent. In the case of Project K this reduced rate is still very high and the project is accepted under either rule. However, in a number of situations, the calculation of the MIRR may alter the decision given under the IRR method. This is true in the worked example of Switcharound plc for projects Tic and Cit, which are mutually exclusive projects and thus ranking is important.

Worked example 2.5 Switcharound plc

The business development team of Switcharound plc has been working to find uses for a vacated factory. The two projects it has selected for further consideration by senior management both have a life of only three years, because the site will be flattened in three years when a new motorway is constructed. On the basis of IRR the business development team is leaning towards acceptance of Cit but it knows that the key senior manager is aware of MIRR and therefore feels it is necessary to present the data calculated through both techniques. The opportunity cost of capital is 10 per cent.

Cash flows

Points in time (yearly intervals)	0	1	2	3	IRR
Tic (£m)	−1	0.5	0.5	0.5	23.4%
Cit (£m)	−1	1.1	0.1	0.16	27.7%

However, on the basis of MIRR, a different preference emerges.

Tic: MIRR

		Terminal value £m
t_1	$0.5 \times (1.1)^2$	0.605
t_2	0.5×1.1	0.550
t_3	0.5	0.500
Total terminal value		1.655

$$1,000,000 \, (1 + m)^3 = 1,655,000$$

$$m = \sqrt[n]{\frac{F}{P}} - 1$$

$$m = \sqrt[3]{\frac{1,655,000}{1,000,000}} - 1 = 0.183 \text{ or } 18.3\%$$

Cit: MIRR

		Terminal value £m
t_1	$1.1 \times (1.1)^2$	1.331
t_2	0.1×1.1	0.110
t_3	0.16	0.16
Total terminal value		1.601

$$1{,}000{,}000 \ (1 + m)^3 = 1{,}601{,}000$$

$$m = \sqrt[n]{\frac{F}{P}} - 1$$

$$m = \sqrt[3]{\frac{1{,}601{,}000}{1{,}000{,}000}} - 1 = 0.17 \text{ or } 17\%$$

Of course, a more satisfactory answer can be obtained by calculating NPVs, but the result may not be persuasive if the senior management team do not understand NPVs.

NPVs for Tic and Cit

Tic $-1 + 0.5 \times$ annuity factor, 3 years @ 10%
$-1 + 0.5 \times 2.4869 = 0.24345$ or £243,450

Cit $-1 + \dfrac{1.1}{1 + 0.1} + \dfrac{0.1}{(1 + 0.1)^2} + \dfrac{0.16}{(1 + 0.1)^3} = 0.202855$ or £202,855

Therefore, Tic contributes more towards shareholder wealth.

Summary table

Ranking

	NPV	IRR	MIRR
Tic	£243,450 (1)	23.4% (2)	18.3% (1)
Cit	£202,855 (2)	27.7% (1)	17.0% (2)

Concluding comments

This chapter has provided insight into the key factors for consideration when an organisation is contemplating using financial (or other) resources for investment. The analysis has been based on the assumption that the objective of any such investment is to maximise economic benefits to the owners of the enterprise. To achieve such an objective requires allowance for the opportunity cost of capital or time value of money as well as robust analysis of relevant cash flows. Given that time has a value, the precise timing of cash flows is important for project analysis. The net present value (NPV) and internal rate of return (IRR) methods of project appraisal are both discounted cash flow techniques and therefore allow for the time value of money. However, the IRR method does present problems in a few special circumstances and so the theoretically preferred method is NPV. On the other hand, NPV requires diligent studying and thought in order to be fully understood, and therefore it is not surprising to find in the workplace a bias in favour of communicating a project's viability in terms of percentages. Most large organisations, in fact, use three or four methods of project appraisal, rather than rely on only one for both rigorous analysis and communication – *see* Chapter 4 for more detail. If a percentage approach is regarded as essential in a particular organisational setting then the MIRR is to be preferred to the IRR. Not only does the MIRR rank projects more appropriately and so is useful in mutual exclusivity situations, it also avoids biasing upward expectations of returns from an investment. The fundamental conclusion of this chapter is that the best method for maximising shareholder wealth in assessing investment projects is net present value.

- **Time value of money** has three component parts each requiring compensation for a delay in the receipt of cash:
 - the pure time value, or impatience to consume,
 - inflation,
 - risk.

- **Opportunity cost of capital** is the yield forgone on the best available investment alternative – the risk level of the alternative being the same as for the project under consideration.

- Taking account of the time value of money and opportunity cost of capital in project appraisal leads to **discounted cash flow analysis** (DCF).

- **Net present value** (NPV) is the present value of the future cash flows after netting out the initial cash flow. Present values are achieved by discounting at the opportunity cost of capital.

$$NPV = CF_0 + \frac{CF_1}{1+k} + \frac{CF_2}{(1+k)^2} + \dots \frac{CF_n}{(1+k)^n}$$

- **The net present value decision rules** are:

 $NPV \geq 0$ accept
 $NPV < 0$ reject

- **Internal rate of return** (IRR) is the discount rate which, when applied to the cash flows of a project, results in a zero net present value. It is an 'r' which results in the following formula being true:

$$CF_0 + \frac{CF_1}{1+r} + \frac{CF_2}{(1+r)^2} + \dots \frac{CF_n}{(1+r)^n} = 0$$

- **The internal rate of return decision rule** is:

 IRR \geq opportunity cost of capital – accept
 IRR $<$ opportunity cost of capital – reject

- IRR is poor at handling situations of unconventional cash flows. **Multiple solutions** can be the result.

- There are circumstances when IRR ranks one project higher than another, whereas NPV ranks the projects in the opposite order. This **ranking problem** becomes an important issue in situations of mutual exclusivity.

- The IRR decision rule is reversed for financing-type decisions.

- NPV measures in **absolute amounts of money**. IRR is a percentage measure.

- IRR assumes that intra-project cash flows can be invested at a rate of return equal to the IRR. This biases the IRR calculation.

- If a percentage measure is required, perhaps for communication within an organisation, then the **modified internal rate of return** (MIRR) is to be preferred to the IRR.

Appendix 2.1 Mathematical tools for finance

The purpose of this appendix is to explain essential mathematical skills that will be needed for this book. The author has no love of mathematics for its own sake and so only those techniques of direct relevance to the subject matter of this textbook will be covered in this section.

Simple and compound interest

When there are time delays between receipts and payments of financial sums we need to make use of the concepts of simple and compound interest.

Simple interest

Interest is paid only on the original principal. No interest is paid on the accumulated interest payments.

Example 1

Suppose that a sum of £10 is deposited in a bank account that pays 12 per cent per annum. At the end of year 1 the investor has £11.20 in the account. That is:

$$F = P(1 + i)$$
$$11.20 = 10(1 + 0.12)$$

where F = Future value, P = Present value, i = Interest rate.

The initial sum, called the principal, is multiplied by the interest rate to give the annual return. At the end of five years:

$$F = P(1 + in)$$

where n = number of years. Thus,

$$16 = 10(1 + 0.12 \times 5)$$

Note from the example that the 12 per cent return is a constant amount each year. Interest is not earned on the interest already accumulated from previous years.

Compound interest

The more usual situation in the real world is for interest to be paid on the sum which accumulates – whether or not that sum comes from the principal or from the interest received in previous periods.

Example 2

An investment of £10 is made at an interest rate of 12 per cent with the interest being compounded. In one year the capital will grow by 12 per cent to £11.20. In the second year the capital will grow by 12 per cent, but this time the growth will be on the accumulated value of £11.20 and thus will amount to an extra £1.34. At the end of two years:

$$F = P(1 + i) (1 + i)$$
$$F = 11.20(1 + i)$$
$$F = 12.54$$

Alternatively,

$$F = P(1 + i)^2$$

Exhibit 2.27 displays the future value of £1 invested at a number of different interest rates and for alternative numbers of years. This is extracted from Appendix I at the end of the book.

From the second row of the table in Exhibit 2.27 we can read that £1 invested for two years at 12 per cent amounts to £1.2544. Thus, the investment of £10 provides a future capital sum 1.2544 times the original amount:

$$£10 \times 1.2544 = £12.544$$

Exhibit 2.27	The future value of £1				
		Interest rate (per cent per annum)			
Year	1	2	5	12	15
1	1.0100	1.0200	1.0500	1.1200	1.1500
2	1.0201	1.0404	1.1025	1.2544	1.3225
3	1.0303	1.0612	1.1576	1.4049	1.5209
4	1.0406	1.0824	1.2155	1.5735	1.7490
5	1.0510	1.1041	1.2763	1.7623	2.0114

Over five years the result is:

$$F = P(1 + i)^n$$
$$17.62 = 10(1 + 0.12)^5$$

The interest on the accumulated interest is therefore the difference between the total arising from simple interest and that from compound interest:

$$£17.62 - £16.00 = £1.62$$

Almost all investments pay compound interest and so we will be using compounding throughout the book.

Present values

There are many occasions in financial management when you are given the future sums and need to find out what those future sums are worth in present-value terms today. For example, you wish to know how much you would have to put aside today which will accumulate, with compounded interest, to a defined sum in the future; or you are given the choice between receiving £200 in five years or £100 now and wish to know which is the better option, given anticipated interest rates; or a project gives a return of £1m in three years for an outlay of £800,000 now and you need to establish if this is the best use of the £800,000. By the process of discounting, a sum of money to be received in the future is given a monetary value today.

Example 3

If we anticipate the receipt of £17.62 in five years' time we can determine its present value. Rearrangement of the compound formula, and assuming a discount rate of 12 per cent, gives:

$$P = \frac{F}{(1 + i)^n} \text{ or } P = F \times \frac{1}{(1 + i)^n}$$

$$10 = \frac{17.62}{(1 + 0.12)^5}$$

Alternatively, discount factors may be used, as shown in **Exhibit 2.28** (this is an extract from Appendix II at the end of the book). The factor needed to discount £1 receivable in five years when the discount rate is 12 per cent is 0.5674.

Therefore the present value of £17.62 is:

$$0.5674 \times £17.62 = £10$$

Exhibit 2.28 The present value of £1

| Year | Interest rate (per cent per annum) | | | | | |
	1	5	10	12	15	17
1	0.9901	0.9524	0.9091	0.8929	0.8696	0.8547
2	0.9803	0.9070	0.8264	0.7972	0.7561	0.7305
3	0.9706	0.8638	0.7513	0.7118	0.6575	0.6244
4	0.9610	0.8227	0.6830	0.6355	0.5718	0.5337
5	0.9515	0.7835	0.6209	0.5674	0.4972	0.4561
20	0.8195	0.3769	0.1486	0.1037	0.0611	0.0433

Examining the present value table in Exhibit 2.28 you can see that as the discount rate increases, the present value goes down. Also the further into the future the money is to be received, the less valuable it is in today's terms. Distant cash flows discounted at a high rate have a small present value; for instance, £1,000 receivable in 20 years when the discount rate is 17 per cent has a present value of £43.30. Viewed from another angle, if you invested £43.30 for 20 years it would accumulate to £1,000 if interest compounds at 17 per cent.

Determining the rate of interest

Sometimes you wish to calculate the rate of return that a project is earning. For instance, a savings company may offer to pay you £10,000 in five years if you deposit £8,000 now, when interest rates on accounts elsewhere are offering 6 per cent per annum. In order to make a comparison you need to know the annual rate being offered by the savings company. Thus, we need to find i in the discounting equation.

To be able to calculate i it is necessary to rearrange the compounding formula. Since:

$$F = P(1 + i)^n$$

first, divide both sides by P:

$$F/P = (1 + i)^n$$

(The Ps on the right side cancel out.)

Second, take the root to the power n of both sides and subtract 1 from each side:

$$i = \sqrt[n]{[F/P]} - 1 \text{ or } i = [F/P]^{1/n} - 1$$

$$i = \sqrt[5]{£10,000/£8,000} - 1 = 0.046 \text{ or } 4.6\%$$

Not a good deal compared with accounts offering 6 per cent.

Example 4

In the case of a five-year investment requiring an outlay of £10 and having a future value of £17.62 the rate of return is:

$$i = \sqrt[5]{\frac{17.62}{10}} - 1 \quad i = 12\%$$

$$i = [17.62/10]^{1/5} - 1 \quad i = 12\%$$

Technical aside

You can use the $\sqrt[x]{y}$, the $\sqrt[y]{x}$ button or a combination of the y^x and $\frac{1}{x}$ buttons depending on the calculator.

Alternatively, use the future value table, an extract of which is shown in Exhibit 2.27. In our example, the return on £1 worth of investment over five years is:

$$\frac{17.62}{10} = 1.762$$

In the body of the future value table look at the year 5 row for a future value of 1.762. Read off the interest rate of 12 per cent.

An interesting application of this technique outside finance is to use it to put into perspective the pronouncements of politicians. For example, in 1994 John Major made a speech to the Conservative Party conference promising to double national income (the total quantity of goods and services produced) within 25 years. This sounds impressive, but let us see how ambitious this is in terms of an annual percentage increase.

$$i = \sqrt[25]{\frac{F}{P}} - 1$$

F, future income, is double P, the present income.

$$i = \sqrt[25]{\frac{2}{1}} - 1 = 0.0281 \text{ or } 2.81\%$$

The result is not too bad compared with the previous 20 years. However, performance in the 1950s and 1960s was better and countries in the Far East have annual rates of growth of between 5 per cent and 10 per cent.

The investment period

Rearranging the standard equation so that we can find n (the number of years of the investment), we create the following equation:

$$F = P(1 + i)^n$$
$$F/P = (1 + i)^n$$
$$\log(F/P) = \log(1 + i)n$$

$$n = \frac{\log(F/P)}{\log(1 + i)}$$

Example 5

How many years does it take for £10 to grow to £17.62 when the interest rate is 12 per cent?

$$n = \frac{\log(17.62/10)}{\log(1 + 0.12)} \text{ Therefore } n = 5 \text{ years}$$

An application outside finance How many years will it take for China to double its real national income if growth rates continue at 10 per cent per annum?
Answer:

$$n = \frac{\log(2/1)}{\log(1 + 0.1)} = 7.3 \text{ years}$$ (quadrupling in less than 15 years. At this rate it won't be long before China overtakes the USA as the world's biggest economy)

Annuities

Quite often there is not just one payment at the end of a certain number of years. There can be a series of identical payments made over a period of years. For instance:

- bonds usually pay a regular rate of interest;
- individuals can buy, from saving plan companies, the right to receive a number of identical payments over a number of years;
- a business might invest in a project which, it is estimated, will give regular cash inflows over a period of years;
- a typical house mortgage is an annuity.

An annuity is a series of payments or receipts of equal amounts. We are able to calculate the present value of this set of payments.

Example 6

For a regular payment of £10 per year for five years, when the interest rate is 12 per cent, we can calculate the present value of the annuity by three methods.

Method 1

$$P_{an} = \frac{A}{(1+i)} + \frac{A}{(1+i)^2} + \frac{A}{(1+i)^3} + \frac{A}{(1+i)^4} + \frac{A}{(1+i)^5}$$

where A = the periodic receipt.

$$P_{10,5} = \frac{10}{(1.12)} + \frac{10}{(1.12)^2} + \frac{10}{(1.12)^3} + \frac{10}{(1.12)^4} + \frac{10}{(1.12)^5} = £36.05$$

Method 2

Using the derived formula:

$$P_{an} = \frac{1 - 1/(1+i)^n}{i} \times A$$

$$P_{10,5} = \frac{1 - 1/(1 + 0.12)^5}{0.12} \times 10 = £36.05$$

Method 3

Use the 'present value of an annuity' table. (*See* Exhibit 2.29, an extract from the more complete annuity table at the end of the book in Appendix III.) Here we simply look along the year 5 row and 12 per cent column to find the figure of 3.605 (strictly 3.6048). This refers to the present value of five annual receipts of £1, which comes to £3.605. Therefore we multiply by £10:

$$3.605 \times £10 = £36.05$$

Exhibit 2.29	The present value of an annuity of £1 per annum				
	Interest rate (per cent per annum)				
Year	**1**	**5**	**10**	**12**	**15**
1	0.9901	0.9524	0.9091	0.8929	0.8696
2	1.9704	1.8594	1.7355	1.6901	1.6257
3	2.9410	2.7232	2.4869	2.4018	2.2832
4	3.9020	3.5460	3.1699	3.0373	2.8550
5	4.8534	4.3295	3.7908	3.6048	3.3522

The student is strongly advised against using Method 1. This was presented for conceptual understanding only. For any but the simplest cases, this method can be very time consuming.

Perpetuities

Some contracts run indefinitely and there is no end to a series of identical payments. Perpetuities are rare in the private sector, but certain government securities do not have an end date; that is, the amount paid when the bond was purchased by the lender will never be repaid, only interest payments are made. For example, the UK government has issued Consolidated Stocks or War

Loans which will never be redeemed. Also, in a number of project appraisals or share valuations it is useful to assume that regular annual payments go on for ever. Perpetuities are annuities which continue indefinitely. The value of a perpetuity is simply the annual amount received divided by the interest rate when the latter is expressed as a decimal.

$$P = \frac{A}{i}$$

If £10 is to be received as an indefinite annual payment then the present value, at a discount rate of 12 per cent, is:

$$P = \frac{10}{0.12} = £83.33$$

It is very important to note that in order to use this formula we are assuming that the first payment arises 365 days after the time at which we are standing (the present time or time zero).

Discounting semi-annually, monthly and daily

Sometimes financial transactions take place on the basis that interest will be calculated more frequently than once a year. For instance, if a bank account paid 12 per cent nominal return per year, but credited 6 per cent after half a year, in the second half of the year interest could be earned on the interest credited after the first six months. This will mean that the true annual rate of interest will be greater than 12 per cent.

The greater the frequency with which interest is earned, the higher the future value of the deposit.

Example 7

If you put £10 in a bank account earning 12 per cent per annum then your return after one year is:

$$10(1 + 0.12) = £11.20$$

If the interest is compounded semi-annually (at a nominal annual rate of 12 per cent):

$$10(1 + [0.12/2])(1 + [0.12/2]) = 10(1 + [0.12/2])^2 = £11.236$$

In Example 7 the difference between annual compounding and semi-annual compounding is an extra 3.6p. After six months the bank credits the account with 60p in interest so that in the following six months the investor earns 6 per cent on the £10.60.

If the interest is compounded quarterly:

$$10(1 + [0.12/4])^4 = £11.255$$

Daily compounding:

$$10(1 + [0.12/365])^{365} = £11.2747$$

Example 8

If £10 is deposited in a bank account that compounds interest quarterly and the nominal return per year is 12 per cent, how much will be in the account after eight years?

$$10(1 + [0.12/4])^{4 \times 8} = £25.75$$

Continuous compounding

If the compounding frequency is taken to the limit we say that there is continuous compounding. When the number of compounding periods approaches infinity the future value is found by

$F = Pe^{in}$ where e is the value of the exponential function. This is set as 2.71828 (to five decimal places, as shown on a scientific calculator).

So, the future value of £10 deposited in a bank paying 12 per cent nominal compounded continuously after eight years is:

$$10 \times 2.71828^{0.12 \times 8} = £26.12$$

Converting monthly and daily rates to annual rates

Sometimes you are presented with a monthly or daily rate of interest and wish to know what that is equivalent to in terms of annual percentage rate (APR) (or effective annual rate (EAR)).

If m is the monthly interest or discount rate, then over 12 months:

$$(1 + m)^{12} = 1 + i$$

where i is the annual compound rate.

$$i = (1 + m)^{12} - 1$$

Thus, if a credit card company charges 1.5 per cent per month, the APR is:

$$i = (1 + 0.015)^{12} - 1 = 19.56\%$$

If you want to find the monthly rate when you are given the APR:

$$m = (1 + i)^{1/12} - 1 \text{ or } m = \sqrt[12]{(1 + i)} - 1$$
$$m = (1 + 0.1956)^{1/12} - 1 = 0.015 = 1.5\%$$

Daily rate:

$$(1 + d)^{365} = 1 + i$$

where d is the daily discount rate.

The following exercises will consolidate the knowledge gained by reading through this appendix (answers are provided at the end of the book in Appendix VI).

Exercise **Mathematical tools exercises**

1 What will a £100 investment be worth in three years' time if the rate of interest is 8 per cent, using: (a) simple interest? (b) annual compound interest? **?**

2 You plan to invest £10,000 in the shares of a company.

 a If the value of the shares increases by 5 per cent a year, what will be the value of the shares in 20 years?

 b If the value of the shares increases by 15 per cent a year, what will be the value of the shares in 20 years? **?**

3 How long will it take you to double your money if you invest it at: (a) 5 per cent? (b) 15 per cent? **?**

4 As a winner of a lottery you can choose one of the following prizes:

 a £1,000,000 now.

 b £1,700,000 at the end of five years.

 c £135,000 a year for ever, starting in one year.

 d £200,000 for each of the next 10 years, starting in one year.

 If the time value of money is 9 per cent, which is the most valuable prize?

5 A bank lends a customer £5,000. At the end of 10 years he repays this amount plus interest. The amount he repays is £8,950. What is the rate of interest charged by the bank? **?**

6 The Morbid Memorial Garden company will maintain a garden plot around your grave for a payment of £50 now, followed by annual payments, in perpetuity, of £50. How much would you have to put into an account which was to make these payments if the account guaranteed an interest rate of 8 per cent? **?**

7 If the flat (nominal annual) rate of interest is 14 per cent and compounding takes place monthly, what is the effective annual rate of interest (the annual percentage rate)? **?**

8 What is the present value of £100 to be received in 10 years' time when the interest rate (nominal annual) is 12 per cent and (a) annual discounting is used? (b) semi-annual discounting is used? **?**

9 What sum must be invested now to provide an amount of £18,000 at the end of 15 years if interest is to accumulate at 8 per cent for the first 10 years and 12 per cent thereafter? **?**

10 How much must be invested now to provide an amount of £10,000 in six years' time assuming interest is compounded quarterly at a nominal annual rate of 8 per cent? What is the effective annual rate? **?**

11 Supersalesman offers you an annuity of £800 per annum for 10 years. The price he asks is £4,800. Assuming you could earn 11 per cent on alternative investments, would you buy the annuity? **?**

12 Punter buys a car on hire purchase paying five annual instalments of £1,500, the first being an immediate cash deposit. Assuming an interest rate of 8 per cent is being charged by the hire purchase company, how much is the current cash price of the car? **?**

References and further reading

Bierman, H. and Smidt, S. (2006) *The Capital Budgeting Decision*, 9th edn. London: Routledge.
 A clear introductory exposition of the concepts discussed in this chapter.

Bierman, H. and Smidt, S. (2006) *Advanced Capital Budgeting*. London: Routledge.
 A book for those interested in pursuing the technical issue in depth.

Dean, J. (1951) *Capital Budgeting*. New York: Columbia University Press.
 Dean introduced an analytical framework for a systemised approach to investment within the firm based on discounted cash flow. Easy to read.

Fama, E.F. and Miller, M.H. (1972) *The Theory of Finance*. New York: Holt, Rinehart & Winston.
 A more detailed consideration of IRR and NPV.

Fisher, I. (1930) *The Theory of Interest*. Reprinted in 1977 by Porcupine Press.
 Originator of the present value rule.

Hirshleifer, J. (1958) 'On the theory of optimal investment decision', *Journal of Political Economy*, 66 (August), pp. 329–52.
 Early theory.

Hirshleifer, J. (1961) 'Risk, the discount rate and investment decisions', *American Economic Review*, May, pp. 112–20.
 Theoretical justification for the use of net present value.

McDaniel, W.R., McCarty, D.E. and Jessell, K.A. (1988) 'Discounted cash flow with explicit reinvestment rates: Tutorial and extension', *The Financial Review*, August.
 Modified internal rate of return discussed in more detail as well as other theoretical developments.

Solomon, E. (1963) *The Theory of Financial Management*. New York: Columbia University Press.
 An early advocate of net present value.

Wilkes, F.M. (1980) 'On multiple rates of return', *Journal of Business Finance and Accounting*, 7(4).
 Theoretical treatment of a specific issue.

Case study recommendations

Please see www.pearsoned.co.uk/arnold for case study synopses.

- Ginny's Restaurant: An introduction to capital investment valuation. Author: Mark Mitchell (2001) Harvard Business School.

- Tree Values. Authors: R.S. Ruback and K.S. Luchs (2000) Harvard Business School.

Websites

Investopedia www. investopedia.com
As well as tutorials on finance this website has quick definitions and quick calculators, e.g. for NPV.

Self-review questions

1 What are the theoretical justifications for the NPV decision rules?

2 Explain what is meant by conventional and unconventional cash flows and what problems they might cause in investment appraisal.

3 Define the time value of money.

4 What is the reinvestment assumption for project cash flows under IRR? Why is this problematical? How can it be corrected?

5 Rearrange the compounding equation to solve for: (a) the annual interest rate, and (b) the number of years over which compounding takes place.

6 What is the 'yield' of a project?

7 Explain why it is possible to obtain an inaccurate result using the trial and error method of IRR when a wide difference of two discount rates is used for interpolation.

Questions and problems

MyFinanceLab	*Questions with an icon are also available for practice in MyFinanceLab with additional supporting resources.*

Answers to most questions can be found at www.pearsoned.co.uk/Arnold.
Answers to questions marked with an asterisk are to be found only in the Lecturer's Guide.

1 Proast plc is considering two investment projects whose cash flows are:

Points in time (yearly intervals)	Project A	Project B
0	−120,000	−120,000
1	60,000	15,000
2	45,000	45,000
3	42,000	55,000
4	18,000	60,000

The company's required rate of return is 15 per cent.

a Advise the company whether to undertake the two projects.

b Indicate the maximum outlay at time 0 for each project before it ceases to be viable.

(An Excel spreadsheet solution to the question is at www.pearsoned.co.uk/arnold)

2 Highflyer plc has two possible projects to consider. It cannot do both – they are mutually exclusive. The cash flows are:

Points in time (yearly intervals)	Project A	Project B
0	−420,000	−100,000
1	150,000	75,000
2	150,000	75,000
3	150,000	0
4	150,000	0

Highflyer's cost of capital is 12 per cent. Assume unlimited funds. These are the only cash flows associated with the projects.

a Calculate the internal rate of return (IRR) for each project.

b Calculate the net present value (NPV) for each project.

c Compare and explain the results in (a) and (b) and indicate which project the company should undertake and why.

(An Excel spreadsheet solution to the question is at www.pearsoned.co.uk/arnold)

3* Mr Baffled, the managing director of Confused plc, has heard that the internal rate of return (IRR) method of investment appraisal is the best modern approach. He is trying to apply the IRR method to two new projects.

	Cash flows		
Year	0	1	2
Project C	−3,000	+14,950	−12,990
Project D	−3,000	+7,500	−5,000

a Calculate the IRRs of the two projects.

b Explain why Mr Baffled is having difficulties with the IRR method.

c Advise Confused whether to accept either or both projects. (Assume a discount rate of 25 per cent.)

4 Using a 13 per cent discount rate, find the NPV of a project with the following cash flows:

Points in time (yearly intervals)	t_0	t_1	t_2	t_3
Cash flow (£)	−300	+260	−200	+600

Explain the difficulties you might have analysing this project using the IRR method.

5 a Find the total terminal value of the following cash flows when compounded at 15 per cent. Cash flows occur at annual intervals and the fourth year's cash flow is the last.

Points in time (yearly intervals)	t_1	t_2	t_3	t_4
Cash flow (£)	+200	+300	+250	+400

b If £900 is the initial cash outflow at time 0, calculate the compounding rate that will equate the initial cash out-
flow with the terminal value as calculated in (a) above.

c You have calculated the modified internal rate of return (MIRR), now calculate the IRR for comparison.

6 a If the cost of capital is 14 per cent, find the modified internal rate of return for the following investment and state
if you would implement it.

Points in time (yearly intervals)	t_0	t_1	t_2	t_3	t_4
Cash flow	−9,300	5,400	3,100	2,800	600

b Is this project to be accepted under the internal rate of return method?.

7* Seddet International is considering four major projects which have either two- or three-year lives. The firm has raised all
of its capital in the form of equity and has never borrowed money. This is partly due to the success of the business in gen-
erating income and partly due to an insistence by the dominant managing director that borrowing is to be avoided if at
all possible. Shareholders in Seddet International regard the firm as relatively risky, given its existing portfolio of projects.
Other firms' shares in this risk class have generally given a return of 16 per cent per annum and this is taken as the oppor-
tunity cost of capital for the investment projects. The risk level for the proposed projects is the same as that of the existing
range of activities.

Project				
		Net cash flows		
Points in time (yearly intervals)	t_0	t_1	t_2	t_3
A	−5,266	2,500	2,500	2,500
B	−8,000	0	0	10,000
C	−2,100	200	2,900	0
D	−1,975	1,600	800	0

Ignore taxation and inflation.

a The managing director has been on a one-day intensive course to learn about project appraisal techniques.
Unfortunately, during the one slot given over to NPV he had to leave the room to deal with a business crisis, and
therefore does not understand it. He vaguely understands IRR and insists that you use this to calculate which of
the four projects should be proceeded with, if there are no limitations on the number which can be undertaken.

b State which is the best project if they are mutually exclusive (i.e. accepting one excludes the possibility of accept-
ing another), using IRR.

c Use the NPV decision rule to rank the projects and explain why, under conditions of mutual exclusivity, the
selected project differs from that under (b).

d Write a report for the managing director, detailing the value of the net present value method for shareholder
wealth enhancement and explaining why it may be considered of greater use than IRR

MyFinanceLab *Now retake your diagnostic test for Chapter 2 to check your progress and
update your study plan.*

Assignments

1 Try to discover the extent to which NPV, IRR and MIRR are used in your organisation. Also try to gauge the degree of appreciation of the problems of using IRR.

2 If possible, obtain data on a real project, historical or proposed, and analyse it using the techniques learned in this chapter.

Visit www.pearsoned.co.uk/arnold to get access to Gradetracker diagnostic tests, podcasts, Excel spreadsheet solutions, *FT* articles, a flashcard revision tool, web links, a searchable glossary and more.

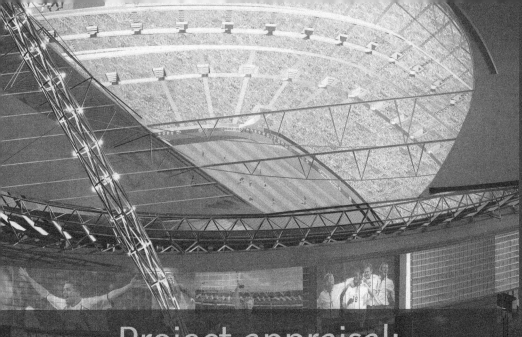

Project appraisal:
Cash flow and applications

LEARNING OUTCOMES

By the end of this chapter the reader will be able to identify and apply relevant and incremental cash flows in net present value calculations. The reader will also be able to recognise and deal with sunk costs, incidental costs and allocated overheads and be able to employ this knowledge to the following:

- the replacement decision/the replacement cycle;
- the calculation of annual equivalent annuities;
- the make or buy decision;
- optimal timing of investment;
- fluctuating output situations.

MyFinanceLab *Complete your diagnostic test for Chapter 3 now to create your personal study plan*

Introduction

The last chapter outlined the process of project evaluation. This required consideration of the fundamental elements; first, recognition of the fact that time has a value and that money received in the future has to be discounted at the opportunity cost of capital; second, the identification of relevant cash flows that are to be subject to the discounting procedure. It is to this second issue that we now turn.

This chapter examines the estimation of the cash flows appropriate for good decision making. The relevant cash flows are not always obvious and easy to obtain and therefore diligent data collection and rigorous analysis are required. Defining and measuring future receipts and outlays accurately is central to successful project appraisal.

In **Case study 3.1** Airbus would have had to consider carefully which projected cash flows are, and are not, relevant to the decision whether to go ahead with producing an aircraft capable of carrying 555 passengers.

Case study 3.1 **Will it fly?**

Airbus's superjumbo

(This case study describes the difficult decision to go ahead and produce the A380. Chapter 6 describes what happened afterwards – it was not all plain sailing!)

Surely one of the biggest investment appraisal decisions ever made was when Airbus decided to go ahead and produce the A380 superjumbo. This is one of those 'bet the company' type investments. A massive £6,500 million was needed to create this monster aircraft.

It was touch and go all through 2000 as to whether Airbus would dare to invest so much money. Before they said 'yes let's do it' they had to have firm orders for at least 50 aircraft. Finally, just before Christmas the sixth major buyer signed up, to take the order book to 50 'definites' and 42 on option (the airlines have the right to buy, but not the obligation).

The A380 is significantly larger than Boeing's highly successful 747. It carries 555 passengers (compared with 416). It also cuts direct operating costs for the airlines by 15–20 per cent compared with Boeing's B747–400 and is able to fly 10 per cent further (8,150 nautical miles).

So, where is all the money on development and build going? This is a project at the cutting edge of technology. The remarkable innovations cost a tremendous amount in terms of up-front cost but the benefit will be spread out over many decades.

Some of the innovations include improved aerodynamics and weight-saving materials such as carbon-fibre, aluminium and glass-fibre.

Having completed the essential groundwork the chapter moves on to demonstrate the practical application of the net present value (NPV) method. This deals with important business decisions, such as whether to replace a machine with a new more efficient (but expensive) version or whether it is better to persevere with the old machine for a few more years despite its rising maintenance costs and higher raw material inputs. Another area examined is replacement cycles, that is, if you have machinery which costs more to run as it gets older and you know that you will continue to need this type of machine and therefore have to replace it at some stage, should you regularly replace after one year or two, three or four years? An example is a car hire company that replaces its fleet of cars on a regular cycle. Other topics include the make or buy decision and optimal timing for the implementation of a project.

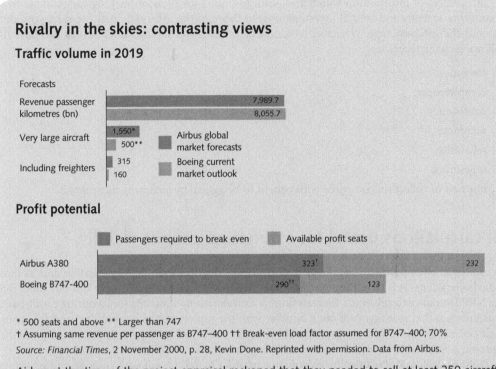

Rivalry in the skies: contrasting views

Traffic volume in 2019

Forecasts

Revenue passenger kilometres (bn): 7,989.7 / 8,055.7

Very large aircraft: 1,550* / 500**
Including freighters: 315 / 160

- Airbus global market forecasts
- Boeing current market outlook

Profit potential

- Passengers required to break even
- Available profit seats

	Passengers required to break even	Available profit seats
Airbus A380	323[†]	232
Boeing B747-400	290[††]	123

* 500 seats and above ** Larger than 747
† Assuming same revenue per passenger as B747–400 †† Break-even load factor assumed for B747–400; 70%

Source: Financial Times, 2 November 2000, p. 28, Kevin Done. Reprinted with permission. Data from Airbus.

Airbus at the time of the project appraisal reckoned that they needed to sell at least 250 aircraft to break even in cash-flow terms (presumably meaning that nominal cumulative cash inflows equal nominal cumulative cash outflows). To achieve a positive net present value would require the sale of hundreds more aircraft. Each aircraft has a list price of around $216m–$230m – but don't pay too much attention to that, as airlines receive substantial discounts. At full capacity something like 96,000 people are needed to work on this aircraft.

And yet it could so easily have been abandoned. Boeing had decided not to develop a superjumbo because it estimated the maximum market at 500 aircraft – they believe that airlines are generally content to continue using the 747. Airbus estimated the market for jumbos and superjumbos at 1,550. It expects to take two-thirds of that business, worth $400bn in today's prices.

This is a high-impact project appraisal if ever there was one. Many of the techniques you have learned in Chapter 2 and will learn in this chapter will have been employed by the management of Airbus to help them decide whether or not to press the button to 'go' or the button to 'stop'.

Quality of information

Good decisions are born of good information. This principle applies to all types of business decisions but is especially appropriate in the case of capital investment decisions in which a substantial proportion of the firm's assets can be put at risk. Obtaining relevant and high-quality information reduces the extent of the risk for the enterprise. Information varies greatly in its reliability, which often depends upon its source. The financial manager or analyst is often dependent on the knowledge and experience of other specialists within the organisation to supply data. For example, the marketing team may be able to provide an estimate of likely demand while the production team could help establish the costs per unit. Allowance will have to be made for any bias that may creep into the information passed on; for instance, a manager who is particularly keen on encouraging the firm to expand in a particular geographical area might tend to be over-optimistic concerning market demand. For some elements of a project there might be high-quality information, whereas other aspects have a lower quality. Take the case of the investment in a new lorry for a courier firm; the cost of purchase can be estimated with high precision, whereas the reaction of competitor firms is subject to much more uncertainty.

The sources of information which are useful as inputs for decision making vary widely; from accounting systems and special investigations, to those of the informal, 'just-between-you-and-me-and-the-gatepost' type. Whatever its source all information should, as far as possible, have the following characteristics:

- relevance;
- completeness;
- consistency;
- accuracy;
- reliability;
- timeliness;
- low cost of collection compared with benefit to be gained by gathering more detail.

Are profit calculations useful for estimating project viability?

Accountants often produce a wealth of numerical information about an organisation and its individual operations. It is tempting to simply take the profit figures for a project and put these into the NPV formula as a substitute for cash flow. A further reason advanced for favouring profit-based evaluations is that managers are often familiar with the notion of 'the bottom line' and frequently their performance is judged using profit. However, as was noted in Chapter 1, determining whether a project is 'profitable' is not the same as achieving shareholder wealth maximisation.

Profit is a concept developed by accountants in order to assist them with auditing and reporting. Profit figures are derived by taking what is a continuous process, a change in a company's worth over time, and allocating these changes to discrete periods of time, say a year (*see* Exhibit 3.1). This is a difficult task. It is a complex task with rules, principles and conventions in abundance.

Profit uses two carefully defined concepts: income and expenses. Income is not cash inflow, it is the amount earned from business activity whether or not the cash has actually been handed over. So, if a £1,000 sofa has been sold on two years' credit the accountant's income arises in the year of sale despite the fact that cash actually flows in two years later. Expense relates the use of an asset to a particular time period whether or not any cash outflow relating to that item occurs in that period. If a firm pays immediately for a machine which will have a ten-year useful life it does not write off the full cost of the machine against the first year's profit, but allocates a proportion of the cost to each of the ten years. The cash outflow occurs in the first year but the expense (use) of the asset occurs over ten years.

Shareholders make current consumption sacrifices, or they give up the return available elsewhere when they choose to invest their money in a firm. They do this in anticipation of receiving more £s in the future than they laid out. Hence what is of interest to them are the future cash flows and the precise timing of these cash flows. The accountant does a difficult and important job but the profit figures produced are not suitable for project appraisal. Profit is a poor approach for two main reasons, first, depreciation and second, working capital.

Exhibit 3.1	Business activity is a continuous process; this is difficult to capture in periodic accounts

Business activity

A continuous process of change in a company's wealth . . .

Year 1	Year 2	Year 3	Year 4	Year 5 . . .

Depreciation

Accounting profit is calculated after deducting depreciation, whereas what we are interested in is net cash inflows for a year. Depreciation should not be deducted to calculate net cash inflows. For example, if a firm buys a machine for £20,000 which is expected to be productive for four years and have a zero scrap value, the firm's accountant may allocate the depreciation on the machine over the four years to give the profit figures of, say, a stable £7,000 per year (*see* Exhibit 3.2). The reason for doing this may be so that the full impact of the £20,000 payout in the first year is not allocated solely to that year's profit and loss account, but is spread over the economic life of the asset. This makes good sense for calculating accounting profit. However, this is not appropriate for project appraisal based on NPV because these figures are not true cash flows. We need to focus on the cash flows at the precise time they occur and should not discount back to time zero the figure of £7,000, but cash flows at the time they occur.

Exhibit 3.2	ABC plc: An example of adjustment to a profit and loss projection

Machine cost £20,000, at time 0. Productive life of four years.

Accountant's figures				
Year	1	2	3	4
	£	£	£	£
Profit before depreciation	12,000	12,000	12,000	12,000
Depreciation	5,000	5,000	5,000	5,000
Profit after depreciation	7,000	7,000	7,000	7,000

Cash flow					
Point in time (yearly intervals)	0	1	2	3	4
	£	£	£	£	£
Cash outflow	−20,000				
Cash inflow		12,000	12,000	12,000	12,000

Working capital

When a project is accepted and implemented the firm may have to invest in more than the large and obvious depreciable assets such as machines, buildings, vehicles and so forth. Investment in a new project often requires an additional investment in working capital, that is, the difference between short-term assets and liabilities. The main short-term assets are cash, stock (inventories) and debtors (receivables). The principal short-term liabilities are creditors (trade payables).

So, a firm might take on a project which involves an increase in the requirements for one of these types of working capital. Each of these will be taken in turn.

Cash floats

It may be that the proposed project requires the firm to have a much higher amount of cash float. For instance, a firm setting up a betting shop may have to consider not only the cash outflow for building or refurbishment, but also the amount of extra cash float needed to meet minute-by-minute betting payouts. Thus, we have to take into account this additional aspect of cash inputs when evaluating the size of the initial investment. This is despite the fact that the cash float will be recoverable at some date in the future (for instance, when the shop is closed in, e.g., three years' time). The fact that this cash is being used to lubricate day-to-day business and is therefore not

available to shareholders means that a sacrifice has been made at a particular point. The owners of that money rightfully expect to receive a suitable return while that money is tied up and unavailable for them to use as they wish.

Stock (inventories)

Examples of stock are raw materials and finished goods. If a project is undertaken which raises the level of inventories then this additional cash outflow has to be allowed for. So, for a retail business opening a number of new shops the additional expenditure on stock is a form of investment. This extra cash being tied up will not be recognised by the profit and loss accounts because all that has happened is that one asset, cash, has been swapped for another, inventory. However, the cash use has to be recognised in any NPV calculation. With some projects there may be a reduction in inventory levels. This may happen in the case of the replacement of an inefficient machine with a new piece of equipment. In this case the stock reduction releases cash and so results in a positive cash flow.

Debtors (receivables)

Accounting convention dictates that if a sale is made during a year it is brought into the profit and loss account for that year. But in many cases a sale might be made on credit and all the firm has is a promise that cash will be paid in the future; the cash inflow has not materialised in the year the sale was recorded. Also, at the start of the financial year this firm may have had some outstanding debtors, that is, other firms or individuals owing this firm money, and in the early months of the year cash inflow is boosted by those other firms paying off their debt.

If we want to calculate the cash flow for the year then the annual profit figure has to be adjusted to exclude the closing balance of debtors (cash owed by customers at the end of the year but not yet paid over), and include the opening balance of debtors (cash owed by the customers at the beginning of the year which is actually received in this year for sales that took place the previous year).

Creditors (trade payable)

Whether suppliers send input goods and services to this firm for payment on 'cash on delivery terms' or 'credit terms' the accountant, rightly, records the value of these as an expense (if they are used up this year), and deducts this from the profit and loss account, in the year of delivery. The cash flow analyst needs to make an adjustment here because the full amount of the expense may not yet have flowed out in cash. So, if creditor balances increase we need to recognise that the profit and loss account has overstated the outflow of cash. We need then to add back the extent to which the creditor amount outstanding has increased from the beginning of the year to the end to arrive at the cash flow figure.

Thus we may have four working capital adjustments to make to the profit and loss account figures to arrive at cash flow figures. The value of the firm's investment in net working capital, associated with a project, is found by the:

increase in cash floats

increase in stocks

increase in debtors

less the increase in creditors

Net operating cash flow

The **net operating cash flow** associated with a new investment is equal to the profit, with depreciation[1] added back plus or minus any change in working capital. If the project results in an increase in working capital then:

Net operating cash flow	=	Profit before depreciation	−	Periodic investment in net working capital

An example of the differences between profit and cash flow

We now turn to an example of the firm, ABC plc, carrying out a project appraisal. The finance manager has been provided with forecast profit and loss accounts and has to adjust these figures to arrive at cash flow (*see* **Exhibit 3.3**). This project will require investment in machinery of £20,000 at the outset. The machinery will have a useful life of four years and a zero scrap value when production ceases at the end of the fourth year.

ABC's business involves dealing with numerous customers and the cash flows within any particular week are unpredictable. It therefore needs to maintain a cash float of £5,000 to be able to pay for day-to-day expenses. (Note: this cash float is not used up, and cannot therefore be regarded as a cost – in some weeks cash outflows are simply greater than cash inflows and to provide adequate liquidity £5,000 is needed for the firm to operate efficiently. The £5,000 will not be needed when output ceases.)

To produce the product it will be necessary to have a stock of raw materials close to hand. The investment in this form of inventory together with the cash committed to work in progress and finished goods amounts to £2,000 at the beginning of production. However, more cash (an extra £1,000) is expected to be required for this purpose at the end of the second year. When the new business is begun a large proportion of raw materials will come from suppliers who will grant additional credit. Therefore the level of creditors will rise by £1,000 over the period of the project.

To illustrate some of the differences between profit and cash flow there follows a conversion from projected accounting figures to cash flow. First it is necessary to add back the depreciation and instead account for the cost of the machine at time 0, the start date for the project when the cash actually left the firm. To capture the cash flow effect of the investment in inventories (stock) we need to see if any additional cash has been required between the beginning of the year and its end. If cash has been invested in inventory then the net stock adjustment to the cash flow calculation is negative. If cash has been released by the running down of inventory the cash flow effect is positive.

Now we turn to creditors. The accounting profit is derived after subtracting the expense of all inputs in a period, whether or not the payment for those inputs has been made in that period. If at the start ABC's suppliers provide goods and services to the value of £1,000 without requiring immediate payment then £1,000 needs to be added to the accountant's figures for true cash flow at that point. If the creditor's adjustment is not made then we are denying that of the £2,000 of stock delivered on the first day of trading half is bought on credit. It is not necessary for ABC to pay £2,000 at the start to suppliers; they pay only £1,000 and thus the creditor adjustment shows a positive cash flow at time 0, offsetting the outflow on stock. (In other examples, later in the book, it may be assumed that all stock is bought on trade credit and therefore there would not be a cash outflow for stock payments at time 0. In these examples all creditor and debtor adjustments are made at the year ends and not at time 0.) In subsequent years the prior year's creditor debts actually paid match the amount outstanding at the year end, thus no net cash flow effect adjustment is necessary.

In this simplified example it is assumed that after exactly four years all production ceases and outstanding creditors and debtors are settled on the last day of the fourth year. Also on the last day of the fourth year the money tied up in cash float and stock is released. Furthermore, the net cash

1 Other non-cash deductions such as for amortisation of intangible assets may also be added back.

Exhibit 3.3	ABC plc: an example of profit to cash flow conversion

- Machinery cost £20,000 at time 0, life of four years, zero scrap value.
- Extra cash floats required: £5,000, at time 0.
- Additional stock: £2,000 at time 0, £3,000 at time 2.
- Increase in creditors: £1,000.

ABC plc		Accounting year			
Point in time (yearly intervals)	0	1	2	3	4
	£	£	£	£	£
Accounting profit		7,000	7,000	7,000	7,000
Add back depreciation		5,000	5,000	5,000	5,000
		12,000	12,000	12,000	12,000
Initial machine cost	−20,000				
Cash float	−5,000				5,000
Stock					
Closing stock	2,000	2,000	3,000	3,000	0
Opening stock		2,000	2,000	3,000	3,000
Net stock adjustment (Outflow −tive, Inflow +tive)	−2,000	0	−1,000	0	+3,000
Creditors					
End of year	1,000	1,000	1,000	1,000	0
Start of year		1,000	1,000	1,000	−1,000
Cash flow effect of creditors (Outflow −tive, Inflow +tive)	+1,000	0	0	0	−1,000
Net operating cash flow	−26,000	12,000	11,000	12,000	19,000
Point in time (yearly intervals)	0	1	2	3	4
Cash flow	−26,000	12,000	11,000	12,000	19,000

Cost of capital 12%

$$NPV = -26,000 + \frac{12,000}{(1 + 0.12)} + \frac{11,000}{(1 + 0.12)^2} + \frac{12,000}{(1 + 0.12)^3}$$

$$+ \frac{19,000}{(1 + 0.12)^4} = +£14,099$$

This project produces a positive NPV, i.e. it generates a return which is more than the required rate of 12%, and therefore should be accepted.
(An Excel spreadsheet version of this calculation is available at www.pearsoned.co.uk/arnold)

flows from each year's trading all arrive on the last day of the respective year. These assumptions are obviously slightly unrealistic, but to make the example more realistic would add unneccessarily to its complexity.

Strictly speaking we should allow for the fact that a business generally receives and pays cash flows fairly evenly through the year rather than assume that all cash flows occur at the end of the year. So, in theory, we should discount cash flows weekly or even daily (365 discount calculations per year!).

The practice of simplifying to one net cash flow per year, followed by most managers, is justified on the grounds of practical necessity to avoiding over-complicated calculations. Furthermore, by assuming cash comes in at the end of the year, and not any earlier, managers are, if anything, under-estimating NPV. This more conservative estimate of project viability encourages greater confidence in the likelihood of project acceptance boosting shareholder wealth. An alternative is to assume cash inflows half-way through the year, in which case the discount factor becomes $\frac{1}{(1+r)^{0.5}}$, $\frac{1}{(1+r)^{1.5}}$, etc.

Incremental cash flows

A fundamental principle in project appraisal is to include only **incremental cash flows**. These are defined as the cash flows dependent on the project's implementation. Only those cash flows that are induced by the investment at time 0 and in subsequent years are regarded as incremental. Some of these cash flows are easy to establish but others are much more difficult to pin down.

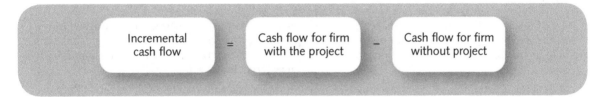

Here are some guideposts for finding relevant/incremental cash flows.

Include all opportunity costs

The direct inputs into a project are generally easy to understand and measure. However, quite often a project uses resources which already exist within the firm but which are in short supply and which cannot be replaced in the immediate future. That is, the project under consideration may be taking resources away from other projects. The loss of net cash flows from these other projects is termed an opportunity cost. For example, a firm may be considering a project that makes use of a factory which at present is empty. Because it is empty we should not automatically assume that the opportunity cost is zero. Perhaps the firm could engage in the alternative project of renting out the factory to another firm. The forgone rental income is a cost of the project under consideration.

Likewise if a project uses the services of specialist personnel this may be regarded as having an opportunity cost. The loss of these people to other parts of the organisation may reduce cash flows on other projects. If they cannot be replaced with equally able individuals then the opportunity cost will be the lost net cash flows. If equally able hired replacements are found then the extra cost imposed, by the additional salaries, etc., on other projects should be regarded as an opportunity cost of the new project under consideration.

For a third example of opportunity cost, imagine your firm bought, when the price was low, a stock of platinum to use as a raw material. The total cost was £1m. It would be illogical to sell the final manufactured product at a price based on the old platinum value if the same quantity would now cost £3m. An alternative course of action would be to sell the platinum in its existing state, rather than to produce the manufactured product. The current market value of the raw platinum (£3m) then is the opportunity cost.

Include all incidental effects

It is possible for a new project to either increase or reduce sales of other products of the company. Take the case of an airline company trying to decide whether to go ahead with a project to fly between the USA and Japan. The direct cash flows of selling tickets, etc. on these flights may not give a positive NPV. However, it could be that the new service generates additional net revenue not only for USA–Japan flights but also on existing routes as customers switch to this airline because it now offers a more complete worldwide service. If this additional net cash flow is included the project may be viable.

On the other hand if a clothes retailer opens a second or a third outlet in the same town, it is likely to find custom is reduced at the original store. This loss elsewhere in the organisation becomes a relevant cash flow in the appraisal of the *new* project, that is, the new shop.

In the soft drink business the introduction of a new brand can reduce the sales of the older brands. This is not to say that a company should never risk any cannibalisation, only that if a new product is to be launched it should not be viewed in isolation. All incidental effects have to be allowed for, including those effects not directly associated with the new product or service.

In the article in Exhibit 3.4 Sir David Rowlands makes a plea for attention to be paid to incidental effects of a new high-speed rail route in the UK.

Exhibit 3.4

New lines needed to justify second high-speed rail route

By Robert Wright

A new, high-speed rail line in the UK 'may struggle' to justify itself under traditional measures, the man in charge of investigating options for a route admits.

Sir David Rowlands nevertheless looks poised to recommend building a high-speed route from London to Manchester via Birmingham, based on more sophisticated assessment techniques.

Sir David, formerly permanent secretary at the Department for Transport, was put in charge of High Speed 2 – the company set up to investigate options for a new, north-south high-speed line – in January.

His comments in an interview underline the challenge facing backers of a second dedicated high-speed line in the UK following the completion in 2007 of High Speed 1 from the Channel Tunnel to London St Pancras. As the country's largest population centres are relatively near each other and rapid, frequent trains already have substantial market shares on many routes, traditional economic models produce too few benefits to justify the economic and social costs of construction.

On the prospect of supplementing the southern part of the London-to-Glasgow west coast main line with a dedicated high-speed route, Sir David says: 'Building a business case on a very traditional basis in terms of how transport projects are appraised, it may struggle.'

However, he adds, London Underground's Jubilee Line Extension also failed to justify itself in cost-benefit terms until civil servants started using novel analysis techniques. These measured 'agglomeration benefits' – the improved efficiency and competitiveness gained by connecting people better to each other. That project is now widely recognised as a success.

The case for a high-speed line is likely to be based on factors similar to those for the Jubilee Line, Sir David says, including a new route's ability to free up the existing west coast main line for more freight and commuter traffic.

'For HS2, you need to explore how sensibly you can go beyond existing appraisal techniques,' Sir David says. 'It's something to do with capturing the benefits of reliable train services; it's something to do with the benefits to the existing west coast; and it's something to do with the connectivity benefits that we may generate by drawing Scotland, Yorkshire, the north-west, Midlands and London closer together.'

 Financial Times, 15 June 2009, p. 2.
All Rights Reserved.

Ignore sunk costs

Do not include sunk costs. For example, the project to build Concorde involved an enormous expenditure in design and manufacture. At the point where it had to be decided whether to put the aeroplane into service, the costs of development became irrelevant to the decision. Only incremental costs and inflows should be considered. The development costs are in the past and are bygones; they should be ignored. The money spent on development is irrecoverable, whatever the decision on whether to fly the plane. Similarly with Eurotunnel, the fact that the overspend runs into billions of pounds and the tunnel service is unlikely to make a profit does not mean that the incremental cost of using some electricity to power the trains and the cost of employing some train

drivers should not be incurred. The £9bn+ already spent is irrelevant to the decision on whether to transport passengers and freight between France and the UK. So long as incremental costs are less than incremental benefits (cash flows when discounted) then the service should operate.

A common mistake in this area is to regard pre-project survey work already carried out or committed to (market demand screening, scientific study, geological survey, etc.) as a relevant cost. After all, the cost would not have been incurred but for the *possibility* of going ahead with the project. However, at the point of decision on whether to proceed, the survey cost is sunk – it will be incurred whether or not implementation takes place, and it therefore is not incremental. Sunk costs can be either costs for intangibles (such as research and development expenses), or costs for tangibles that may not be used for other purposes (such as the cost of the Eurotunnel). When dealing with sunk costs it is sometimes necessary to be resolute in the face of comments such as 'good money is being thrown after bad' but always remember the 'bad' money outflow happened in the past and is no longer an input factor into a rigorous decision-making process.

Be careful with overheads

Overheads consist of such items as managerial salaries, rent, light, heat, etc. These are costs that are not directly associated with any one part of the firm or one item produced. An accountant often allocates these overhead costs amongst the various projects a firm is involved in. When trying to assess the viability of a project we should only include the incremental or extra expenses that would be incurred by going ahead with a project. Many of the general overhead expenses may be incurred regardless of whether the project takes place.

There are two types of overhead. The first type is truly incremental costs resulting from a project. For example, extra electricity, rental and administrative staff costs may be incurred by going ahead rather than abstaining. The second type of overhead consists of such items as head office managerial salaries, legal expertise, public relations, research and development and even the corporate jet. These costs are not directly associated with any one part of the firm or one project and will be incurred regardless of whether the project under consideration is embarked upon. The accountant generally charges a proportion of this overhead to particular divisions and projects. When trying to assess the viability of a project only the incremental costs incurred by going ahead are relevant. Those costs which are unaffected are irrelevant.

Dealing with interest

Interest on funds borrowed to invest does represent a cash outflow. However, it is wrong to include this element in the cash flow calculations. **To repeat, interest should not be deducted from the net cash flows.** This is because if it were subtracted this would amount to double counting because the opportunity cost of capital used to discount the cash flows already incorporates a cost of these funds. The net cash flows are reduced to a present value by allowing for the weighted average cost of finance to give a return to shareholders and lenders. If the undiscounted cash flows also had interest deducted there would be a serious understatement of NPV. For more details see Chapter 16 on the calculation of the firm's discount rate (cost of capital).

Worked example 3.1	Tamcar plc

The accountants at Tamcar plc, manufacturers of hairpieces, are trying to analyse the viability of a proposed new division, 'Baldies heaven'. They estimate that this project will have a life of four years before the market is blown away by the lifting of the present EU import ban on hairpieces. The estimated sales, made on three months' credit, are as follows:

Year	Sales (£)	
20X1	1.5m	There are no bad debts.
20X2	2.0m	
20X3	2.5m	Costs of production can be assumed to be paid
20X4	3.0m	for on the last day of the year. There are no creditors.

Year	Cost of production (£)
20X1	0.75m
20X2	1.00m
20X3	1.25m
20X4	1.50m

At the start of the project an investment of £1m will be required in buildings, plant and machinery. These items will have a net worth of zero at the end of this project. The accountants depreciate the buildings and machinery at 25 per cent per annum on a straight line basis.

A cash float of £0.5m will be required at the start. Also stocks will increase by £0.3m. These are both recoverable at the end of the project's life.

A £1m invoice for last year's scientific study of 'Baldies heaven' hairpiece technology (e.g. wind resistance and combability) has yet to be paid.

The head office always allocates a proportion of central expenses to all divisions and projects. The share to be borne by 'Baldies heaven' is £500,000 per annum. The head office costs are unaffected by the new project.

The accountants have produced the following projected profit and loss accounts:

Year	20X1 £m	20X2 £m	20X3 £m	20X4 £m
Sales	1.50	2.00	2.50	3.00
Costs of production	0.75	1.00	1.25	1.50
Depreciation	0.25	0.25	0.25	0.25
Scientific survey	0.25	0.25	0.25	0.25
Head office	0.50	0.50	0.50	0.50
Profit/loss	−0.25	0	0.25	0.50

Accountants' summary

Investment: £2m Return: £0.5m over 4 years

$$\text{Average Return on Investment (ROI)} = \frac{\text{Average profit}}{\text{Investment}} = \frac{0.5 \div 4}{2} = 0.0625 \text{ or } 6.25\%$$

Recommendation: do not proceed with this project as 6.25% is a poor return.

Required

Calculate the Net Present Value and recommend whether to accept this project or invest elsewhere.

Assume

- No tax.
- The return required on projects of this risk class is 11%.
- Start date of the project is 1.1.20X1.

Answer

- Depreciation is not a cash flow and should be excluded.
- The scientific survey is a sunk cost. This will not alter whether Tamcar chooses to go ahead or refuses to invest – it is irrelevant to the NPV calculation.
- Head office costs will be constant regardless of the decision to accept or reject the project, they are not incremental.

The sales figures shown in the first line of the table below are not the true cash receipts for each of those years because three months' credit is granted. Thus, in year 1 only three-quarters of £1.5m is actually received. An adjustment for debtors shows that one-quarter of the first year's sales are deducted. Thus £375,000 is received in the second year and therefore this is added to time 2's cash flow. However, one-quarter of the £2m of time 2's sales is subtracted because this is not received until the following year.

An assumption has been made concerning the receipt of debtor payments after production and distribution has ceased. In 20X4 sales are on the last day and given the three months' credit, cash is received after three months at time 4.25.

Time (annual intervals)	Tamcar cash flows					
	0 start 20X1	1 end 20X1	2 end 20X2	3 end 20X3	4 end 20X4	4.25
Year						20X5
Sales		+1.5	+2.0	+2.5	+3.0	
Buildings, plant, machinery	−1.0					
Cash float	−0.5				+0.5	
Stocks	−0.3				+0.3	
Costs of production		−0.75	−1.0	−1.25	−1.50	
Adjustment for debtors:						
Opening debtors	*0*	*0*	*0.375*	*0.500*	*0.625*	*0.75*
Closing debtors	*0*	*0.375*	*0.500*	*0.625*	*0.750*	*0*
Cash flow adjustment for debtors		−0.375	−0.125	−0.125	−0.125	+0.75
Cash flow	−1.8	+0.375	+0.875	+1.125	+2.175	+0.75

$$\text{Net present value} \quad -1.8 + \frac{0.375}{(1.11)} + \frac{0.875}{(1.11)^2} + \frac{1.125}{(1.11)^3} + \frac{2.175}{(1.11)^4} + \frac{0.75}{(1.11)^{4.25}}$$

	−1.8	+0.338	+0.710	+0.823	+1.433	+0.481

NPV = + £1.985m

This is a project that adds significantly to shareholder wealth, producing £1.985m more than the minimum rate of return of 11 per cent required by the firm's finance providers.

(An Excel spreadsheet version of the calculation is available at www.pearsoned.co.uk/arnold)

Worked example 3.2 The International Seed Company (TISC)

As the newly appointed financial manager of TISC you are about to analyse a proposal for the marketing and distribution of a range of genetically engineered vegetable seeds which have been developed by a bio-technology firm. This firm will supply the seeds and permit TISC to market and distribute them under a licence.

Market research, costing £100,000, has already been carried out to establish the likely demand. After three years TISC will withdraw from the market because it anticipates that these products will be superseded by further bio-technological developments.

The annual payment to the bio-technology firm will be £1m for the licence; this will be payable at the end of each accounting year.

Also £500,000 will be needed initially to buy a fleet of vehicles for distribution. These vehicles will be sold at the end of the third year for £200,000.

There will be a need for a packaging and administrative facility. TISC is large and has a suitable factory with offices, which at present are empty. Head office has stated that they will let this space to your project at a reduced rent of £200,000 per annum payable at the end of the accounting year (the open market rental value is £1m p.a.).

The project would start on 1.1.20X1 and would not be subject to any taxation because of its special status as a growth industry. A relatively junior and inexperienced accountant has prepared forecast profit and loss accounts for the project as shown in the following table.

Year	20X1	20X2	20X3
	£m	£m	£m
Sales	5	6	6
Costs			
Market research	0.1		
Raw material (seeds)	2.0	2.4	2.4
Licence	1.0	1.0	1.0
Vehicle fleet depreciation	0.1	0.1	0.1
Direct wages	0.5	0.5	0.5
Rent	0.2	0.2	0.2
Overhead	0.5	0.5	0.5
Variable transport costs	0.5	0.5	0.5
Profit	0.1	0.8	0.8

By expanding its product range with these new seeds the firm expects to attract a great deal of publicity which will improve the market position, and thus the profitability, of its other products. The benefit is estimated at £100,000 for each of the three years.

Head office normally allocates a proportion of its costs to any new project as part of its budgeting/costing process. This will be £100,000 for this project and has been included in the figures calculated for overhead by the accountant. The remainder of the overhead is directly related to the project.

The direct wages, seed purchases, overhead and variable transport costs can be assumed to be paid at the end of each year. Most of the sales revenue may be assumed to be received at the end of each year. However, the firm will grant two months' credit to its customers which means that for some of the sales recorded by the accountant for a year the actual cash is received in the following year. An initial cash float of £1m will be needed. This will be returned at the end of the third year.

Assume no inflation. An appropriate discount rate is 15 per cent.

Required

Assess the viability of the proposed project using the discounted cash flow technique you feel to be most appropriate.

Suggestion

Try to answer this question before reading the model answer.

Answer

Notes

- Market research cost is non-incremental.
- Opportunity cost of factory is £1m per annum.
- Vehicle depreciation does not belong in a cash flow calculation.
- The effect on TISC's other products is an incidental benefit.
- Head office cost apportionment should be excluded.

Hynix, Samsung and Toshiba had to pay a great deal of attention to the estimated relevant cash flows associated when building and operating massive factories for the production of chips. It remains to be seen if they have overestimated demand (*see* **Exhibit 3.5**).

£m	20X1 start	20X1 end	20X2 end	20X3 end	20X3 end	20X4 2 months
Cash flows						
Inflows						
Sales		5.0	6.0	6.0		
Benefit to divisions		0.1	0.1	0.1		
Cash at end					1.0	
Vehicles					0.2	
Total inflows	0	5.1	6.1	6.1	1.2	0
Outflows						
Licence		1.0	1.0	1.0		
Vehicles	0.5					
Property rent (opportunity cost)		1.0	1.0	1.0		
Raw materials		2.0	2.4	2.4		
Direct wages		0.5	0.5	0.5		
Overheads		0.4	0.4	0.4		
Variable transport		0.5	0.5	0.5		
Initial cash	1.0					
Cash flows after outflows	−1.5	−0.3	0.3	0.3	1.2	0
Adjustment for debtors						
Debtor: start		0	0.833	1.00		1.0
end		0.833	1.000	1.00		0
Cash flow effect of debtors		−0.833	−0.167	0	0	+1.0
Cash flows	**−1.5**	**−1.133**	**+0.133**	**+0.3**	**+1.2**	**+1.0**
Net present value						

$$NPV = -1.5 + \frac{-1.133}{(1.15)} + \frac{0.133}{(1.15)^2} + \frac{0.3}{(1.15)^3}$$

$$+ \frac{1.2}{(1.15)^3} + \frac{1.00}{(1.15)^{3.167}}$$

$$NPV = -1.5 - 0.985 + 0.101 + 0.197 + 0.789 + 0.642 = -£0.756$$

Conclusion

Do not proceed with the project as it returns less than 15 per cent.

(An Excel spreadsheet version of the calculation is available at www.pearsoned.co.uk/arnold)

Exhibit 3.5

Hynix set for capital spending spree

By Song Jung-a in Seoul

Hynix Semiconductor, the world's second-largest memory chipmaker, yesterday said it would raise its capital expenditure by a third to Won3,050bn ($2.5bn) this year to take advantage of a strong recovery in the global technology sector.

Global chipmakers are rushing to expand production facilities on the back of robust sales of new mobile gadgets such as smartphones and tablet personal computers.

▶

Exhibit 3.5 *(continued)*

The move by Hynix to increase spending this year comes two weeks after industry leader Samsung Electronics doubled its investment for semiconductors to Won11,000bn in an effort to cement its technology lead over rivals.

This month, Japan's Toshiba said it would boost capital spending, mainly in its chip and infrastructure business.

Hynix had previously earmarked an initial budget of Won2,300bn for this year. Its capital spending amounted to Won1,000bn last year.

The South Korean group said the move was needed to accelerate technology migration and focus on developing next-generation products.

Hynix plans to increase the portion of more advanced 40-nano chips from 15 per cent of its output to 50 per cent by the end of this year to improve productivity and cost competitiveness.

The aggressive investments by chipmakers underline the industry's confidence in future demand. However, there are fears it could lead to oversupply, as happened a few years ago. The memory chip industry suffered net losses due to a glut of chips for more than two years before returning to profits last year.

Financial Times, 1 June 2010, p. 21.
All Rights Reserved.

The replacement decision

In the dynamic and competitive world of business it is important to review operations continually to ensure efficient production. Technological change brings with it the danger that a competitor has reduced costs and has leaped ahead. Thus, it is often wise to examine, say, the machinery used in the production process to see if it should be replaced with a new improved version. This is a continual process in many industries, and the frustrating aspect is that the existing machine may have years of useful life left in it. Despite this the right decision is sometimes to dispose of the old and bring in the new. If your firm does not produce at lowest cost, another one will.

In making a **replacement decision** the increased costs associated with the purchase and installation of the new machine have to be weighed against the savings from switching to the new method of production. In other words the incremental cash flows are the focus of attention. The worked example of Amtarc plc demonstrates the incremental approach.

Replacement cycles

Many business assets, machinery and vehicles especially, become increasingly expensive to operate and maintain as they become older. This rising cost burden prompts the thought that there must be a point when it is better to buy a replacement than to face rising repair bills. Assets such as vehicles are often replaced on a regular cycle, say every two or three years, depending on the comparison between the benefit to be derived by delaying the replacement decision (that is, the postponed cash outflow associated with the purchase of new assets) and the cost in terms of higher maintenance costs (and lower secondhand value achieved with the sale of the used asset).

Consider the case of a car rental firm which is considering a switch to a new type of car. The cars cost £10,000 and a choice has to be made between four alternative (mutually exclusive) projects (four alternative regular replacement cycles). Project 1 is to sell the cars on the second-hand market after one year for £7,000. Project 2 is to sell after two years for £5,000. Projects 3 and 4 are three-year and four-year cycles and will produce £3,000 and £1,000 respectively on the secondhand market. The cost of maintenance rises from £500 in the first year to £900 in the second, £1,200 in the third and £2,500 in the fourth. The cars are not worth keeping for more than four years because of the bad publicity associated with breakdowns. The revenue streams and other costs are unaffected by which cycle is selected. We will focus on achieving the lowest present value of the costs.

| Worked example 3.3 | Amtarc plc |

Amtarc plc produces Tarcs with a machine which is now four years old. The management team estimates that this machine has a useful life of four more years before it will be sold for scrap, raising £10,000.

Q-leap, a manufacturer of machines suitable for Tarc production, has offered its new computer-controlled Q-2000 to Amtarc for a cost of £800,000 payable immediately.

If Amtarc sold its existing machine now, on the secondhand market, it would receive £70,000. (Its book (accounting) value, after depreciation, is £150,000.) The Q-2000 will have a life of four years before being sold for scrap for £20,000.

The attractive features of the Q-2000 are its lower raw material wastage and its reduced labour requirements. Selling price and variable overhead will be the same as for the old machine.

The accountants have prepared the figures shown below on the assumption that output will remain constant at last year's level of 100,000 Tarcs per annum.

| | Profit per unit of Tarc | |
| | Old machine | Q-2000 |
	£	£
Sale price	45	45
Costs		
Labour	10	9
Materials	15	14
Variable overhead	7	7
Fixed overhead		
Factory admin., etc.	5	5
Depreciation	0.35	1.95
Profit per Tarc	7.65	8.05

The depreciation per unit has been calculated as follows:

$$\frac{\text{Total depreciation for a year}}{\text{Output for a year}}$$

Old machine: $\dfrac{(150,000 - 10,000)/4}{100,000} = £0.35$

Q-2000: $\dfrac{(800,000 - 20,000)/4}{100,000} = £1.95$

An additional benefit of the Q-2000 will be the reduction in required raw material buffer stocks – releasing £120,000 at the outset. However, because of the lower labour needs, redundancy payments of £50,000 will be necessary after one year.

Assume

- No inflation or tax.
- The required rate of return is 10 per cent.
- To simplify the analysis sales, labour costs, raw material costs and variable overhead costs all occur on the last day of each year.

Required

Using the NPV method decide whether to continue using the old machine or to purchase the Q-2000.

Hints

Remember to undertake incremental analysis. That is, analyse only the difference in cash flow which will result from the decision to go ahead with the purchase. Remember to include the £10,000 opportunity cost of scrapping the old machine in four years if the Q-2000 is purchased.

Answers

Stage 1

Note the irrelevant information:

1 Depreciation is not a cash flow and should not be included.
2 The book value of the machine is merely an accounting entry and has little relationship with the market value. Theoretically book value has no influence on the decision. (In practice, however, senior management may be reluctant to write off the surplus book value through the profit and loss account as this may prejudice an observer's view of their performance – despite there being no change in the underlying economic position.)

Stage 2

Work out the annual incremental cost savings.

	Savings per Tarc		
	Old machine £	Q-2000 £	Saving £
Labour	10	9	1
Materials	15	14	1
Total saving			2

Total annual saving £2 × 100,000 = £200,000.

Stage 3 Incremental cash flow table

Time £000s	0	1	2	3	4
Purchase of Q-2000	−800				
Scrap of old machine	+70				
Raw material stocks	+120				
Opportunity cost (old machine)					−10
Redundancy payments		−50			
Sale of Q-2000					+20
Annual cost savings		+200	+200	+200	+200
	−610	+150	+200	+200	+210

Stage 4 Calculate NPV

$$\text{Discounted cash flows} \quad -610 + \frac{150}{1.1} + \frac{200}{(1.1)^2} + \frac{200}{(1.1)^3} + \frac{210}{(1.1)^4}$$

NPV = −£14,660.

The negative NPV indicates that shareholder wealth will be higher if the existing machine is retained.

If we make the simplifying assumption that all the cash flows occur at annual intervals then the relevant cash flows are as set out in Exhibit 3.6.

Exhibit 3.6	Relevant cash flows					
	Point in time (yearly intervals)	0	1	2	3	4
Project 1		£	£	£	£	£
Replace after	Purchase cost	−10,000				
one year	Maintenance		−500			
	Sale proceeds		+7,000			
	Net cash flow	−10,000	+6,500			
Project 2						
Replace after	Purchase cost	−10,000				
two years	Maintenance		−500	−900		
	Sale proceeds			+5,000		
	Net cash flow	−10,000	−500	+4,100		
Project 3						
Replace after	Purchase cost	−10,000				
three years	Maintenance		−500	−900	−1,200	
	Sale proceeds				+3,000	
	Net cash flow	−10,000	−500	−900	+1,800	
Project 4						
Replace after	Purchase cost	−10,000				
four years	Maintenance		−500	−900	−1,200	−2,500
	Sale proceeds					+1,000
	Net cash flow	−10,000	−500	−900	−1,200	−1,500

Assuming a discount rate of 10 per cent the Present Values (PVs) of costs of one cycle of the projects are:

$$PV_1 \quad -10,000 \quad + \quad \frac{6,500}{1.1} \qquad\qquad = -4,090.90$$

$$PV_2 \quad -10,000 \quad - \quad \frac{500}{1.1} \quad + \quad \frac{4,100}{(1.1)^2} \qquad = -7,066.12$$

$$PV_3 \quad -10,000 \quad - \quad \frac{500}{1.1} \quad - \quad \frac{900}{(1.1)^2} \quad + \quad \frac{1,800}{(1.1)^3} \qquad = -9,845.98$$

$$PV_4 \quad -10,000 \quad - \quad \frac{500}{1.1} \quad - \quad \frac{900}{(1.1)^2} \quad - \quad \frac{1,200}{(1.1)^3} \quad - \quad \frac{1,500}{(1.1)^4} = -13,124.44$$

At first sight the figures in Exhibit 3.6 might suggest that the first project is the best. Such a conclusion would be based on the normal rule with mutually exclusive projects of selecting the one with the lowest present value of costs. However, this is not a standard situation because purchases and sales of vehicles have to be allowed for far beyond the first round in the replacement cycle. If we can make the assumption that there are no increases in costs and the cars can be replaced with identical models on regular cycles in the future[2] then the pattern of cash flows for the third project, for example, are as shown in Exhibit 3.7.

2 This is a bold assumption. More realistic assumptions could be made, e.g. allowing for inflation, but the complexity that this produces is beyond the scope of this book.

Exhibit 3.7	Cash flows for Project 3							
Time (years)	**0**	**1**	**2**	**3**	**4**	**5**	**6**	**7 ...**
Cash flows (£)								
1st generation	−10,000	−500	−900	+1,800				
2nd generation				−10,000	−500	−900	+1,800	
3rd generation							−10,000	−500 ...

One way of dealing with a long-lived project of this kind is to calculate the present values of numerous cycles stretching into the future. This can then be compared with other projects' present values calculated in a similarly time-consuming fashion. Fortunately there is a much quicker technique available called the annual equivalent annuity method (AEA). This third project involves three cash outflows followed by a cash inflow within one cycle as shown in Exhibit 3.8.

Exhibit 3.8	Cash outflows and cash inflow in one cycle			
Time (years)	**0**	**1**	**2**	**3**
Cash flows (£)	−10,000	−500	−900	+1,800

This produces a one-cycle present value of −£9,845.98. The **annual equivalent annuity (AEA)**[3] method finds the amount that would be paid in each of the next three years if each annual payment were identical and the three payments gave the same (equivalent) present value of −£9,845.98, that is, the constant amount which would replace the ? in Exhibit 3.9.

Exhibit 3.9	Using the AEA				
Time (years)	**0**	**1**	**2**	**3**	**Present value**
Actual cash flows (£)	−10,000	−500	−900	+1,800	−9,845.98
Annual equivalent annuity (£)		?	?	?	−9,845.98

(Recall that the first cash flow under an 'immediate' annuity arises after one year.)

To find the AEA we need to employ the annuity table in Appendix III. This table gives the value of a series of £1 cash flows occurring at annual intervals in terms of present money. Normally these 'annuity factors' (af) are multiplied by the amount of the cash flow that is received regularly, the annuity (A), to obtain the present value, PV. In this case we already know the PV and we can obtain the af by looking at the three-year row and the 10 per cent column. The missing element is the annual annuity.

$$PV = A \times af$$

$$or\ A = \frac{PV}{af}$$

In the case of the three-year replacement:

$$A = \frac{-£9,845.98}{2.4869} = -£3,959.14$$

3 Also called equivalent annual annuity and equivalent annual cash flow.

Thus, two alternative sets of cash flows give the same present value (*see* Exhibit 3.10).

Exhibit 3.10	Cash flow 1 and Cash flow 2			
Time (years)	**0** **£**	**1** **£**	**2** **£**	**3** **£**
Cash flow 1	–10,000	–500	–900	+1,800
Cash flow 2		–3,959.14	–3,959.14	–3,959.14

The second generation of cars bought at the end of the third year will have a cost of –£9,845.98 when discounted to the end of the third year (assuming both zero inflation and that the discount rate remains at 10 per cent). The present value of the costs of this second generation of vehicle is equivalent to the present value of an annuity of –£3,959.14. Thus replacing the car every three years is equivalent to a cash flow of –£3,959.14 every year to infinity (*see* Exhibit 3.11).

Exhibit 3.11	Replacing the car every three years							
Time (years)	**0**	**1**	**2**	**3**	**4**	**5**	**6**	**7 ...**
Cash flows (£)								
First generation	10,000	–500	–900	+1,800				
Second generation				–10,000	–500	–900	+1,800	
Third generation							–10,000	–500 ...
Annual equivalent annuity	0	–3,959.14	–3,959.14	–3,959.14	–3,959.14	–3,959.14	–3,959.14	–3,959.14

If all the other projects are converted to their annual equivalent annuities a comparison can be made (*see* Exhibit 3.12).

Exhibit 3.12	Using AEAs for all projects		
Cycle	**Present value of one cycle (PV)**	**Annuity factor (af)**	**Annual equivalent annuity (PV/af)**
1 year	–4,090.90	0.9091	–4,498.96
2 years	–7,066.12	1.7355	–4,071.52
3 years	–9,845.98	2.4869	–3,959.14
4 years	–13,124.44	3.1699	–4,140.33

Thus Project 3 requires the lowest equivalent annual cash flow and is the optimal replacement cycle. This is over £540 per year cheaper than replacing the car every year.

A valid alternative to the annual equivalent annuity is the **lowest common multiple (LCM) method**. Here the alternatives are compared using the present value of the costs over a timespan equal to the lowest common multiple of the cycle lengths. So the cash flow for 12 cycles of Project 1 would be discounted and compared with six cycles of Project 2, four cycles of Project 3 and three cycles of Project 4. The AEA method is the simplest and quickest method in cases where the lowest common multiple is high. For instance the LCM of five-, six- and seven-year cycles is 210 years, and involves a great many calculations.

Worked example 3.4 Brrum plc

Suppose the firm Brrum has to decide between two machines, A and B, to replace an old worn-out one. Whichever new machine is chosen it will be replaced on a regular cycle. Both machines produce the same level of output. Because they produce exactly the same output we do not need to examine the cash inflows at all to choose between the machines; we can concentrate solely on establishing the lower-cost machine.

Brrum plc
- Machine A costs £30m, lasts three years and costs £8m a year to run.
- Machine B costs £20m, lasts two years and costs £12m a year to run.

Cash flows

Point in time (yearly intervals)	0	1	2	3	PV (6%)
Machine A (£m)	−30	−8	−8	−8	−51.38
Machine B (£m)	−20	−12	−12	−	−42.00

Because Machine B has a lower PV of cost, should we jump to the conclusion that this is the better option? Well, Machine B will have to be replaced one year before Machine A and, therefore, there are further cash flows to consider and discount.

If we were to assume a constant discount rate of 6 per cent and no change in costs over a number of future years, then we can make a comparison between the two machines. To do this we need to convert the total PV of the costs to a cost per year. We convert the PV of the costs associated with each machine to the equivalent annuity.

Machine A
Machine A has a PV of −£51.38m. We need to find an annuity with a PV of −£51.38m which has regular equal costs occurring at years 1, 2 and 3.

Look in the annuity table along the row of 3 years and down the column of 6% to get the three-year annuity factor.

PV = Annual annuity payment (A) × 3-year annuity factor (af)

$$-51.38 = A \times 2.673$$
$$A = -51.38/2.673 = -£19.22\text{m per year}$$

Point in time (yearly intervals)	0	1	2	3	PV (6%)
Cash flows (£m)	−30	−8	−8	−8	−51.38
Equivalent 3-year annuity (£m)		−19.22	−19.22	−19.22	−51.38

When Machine A needs to be replaced at the end of the third year, if we can assume it is replaced by a machine of equal cost we again have a PV of costs for the end of year 3 of £51.38m. This too has an equivalent annuity of −£19.22m. Thus, the −£19.22m annual costs is an annual cost for many years beyond year 3.

Machine B
$$PV = A \times af$$
$$-42 = A \times 1.8334$$
$$A = -42/1.8334 = -£22.908\text{m}$$

Point in time (yearly intervals)	0	1	2	PV (6%)
Cash flows (£m)	−20	−12	−12	−42
Equivalent 2-year annuity (£m)		−22.91	−22.91	−42

Again, if we assume that at the end of two years the machine is replaced with an identical one, with identical costs, then the annuity of −£22.91m can be assumed to be continuing into the future.

▶

Comparing the annual annuities
 Machine A: −£19.22m.
 Machine B: −£22.91m.

When we compare the annual annuities we see that Machine A, in fact, has the lower annual cost and is therefore the better buy.

When to introduce a new machine

Businesses, when switching from one kind of a machine to another, have to decide on the timing of that switch. The best option may not be to dispose of the old machine immediately. It may be better to wait for a year or two because the costs of running the old machine may amount to less than the equivalent annual cost of starting a regular cycle with replacements. However, eventually the old machine is going to become more costly due to its lower efficiency, increased repair bills or declining secondhand value. Let us return to the case of the car rental firm. It has been established that when a replacement cycle is begun for the new type of car, it should be a three-year cycle. The existing type of car used by the firm has a potential further life of two years. The firm is considering three alternative courses of action. The first is to sell the old vehicles immediately, raising £7,000 per car, and then begin a three-year replacement cycle with the new type of car. The second possibility is to spend £500 now to service the vehicles ready for another year's use. At the end of the year the cars could be sold for £5,200 each. The third option is to pay £500 for servicing now, followed by a further £2,000 in one year to maintain the vehicles on the road for a second year, after which they would be sold for £1,800. The easiest approach for dealing with a problem of this nature is to calculate NPVs for all the possible alternatives. We will assume that the revenue aspect of this car rental business can be ignored as this will not change regardless of which option is selected. The relevant cash flows are shown in Exhibit 3.13. Note that the annual equivalent annuity cash flow, rather than the actual cash flows for the three-year cycle of new cars, is incorporated and is assumed to continue to infinity. It is therefore a perpetuity.

(Note that the sums of £3,959.14 are perpetuities starting at times 1, 2 and 3, and so are valued at times 0, 1 and 2. The latter two therefore have to be discounted back one and two years respectively.) The net present value calculations are as set out in Exhibit 3.14. The switch to the new cars

Exhibit 3.13	Cash flow per car (excluding operating revenues, etc.)				
Point in time (yearly intervals)		0 £	1 £	2 £	3 → ∞ £
Option 1 – sell old car at time 0	Secondhand value	+7,000			
	New car		−3,959.14	−3,959.14	−3,959.14
	Net cash flow	+7,000	−3,959.14	−3,959.14	−3,959.14
Option 2 – sell old car after one year	Secondhand value		+5,200		
	Maintenance	−500			
	New car			−3,959.14	−3,959.14
	Net cash flow	−500	+5,200	−3,959.14	−3,959.14
Option 3 – sell old car after two years	Secondhand value			+1,800	
	Maintenance	−500	−2,000		
	New car				−3,959.14
	Net cash flow	−500	−2,000	+1,800	−3,959.14

Exhibit 3.14	Present value calculations

Option 1 $+ \quad 7{,}000 \quad - \quad \dfrac{3{,}959.14}{0.1} \quad = -£32{,}591.4$

Option 2 $-500 \quad + \quad \dfrac{5{,}200}{1.1} \quad - \quad \dfrac{3{,}959.14}{0.1} \times \dfrac{1}{1.1} \quad = -£31{,}764.91$

Option 3 $-500 \quad - \quad \dfrac{2{,}000}{1.1} \quad + \quad \dfrac{1{,}800}{(1.1)^2} \quad - \quad \dfrac{3{,}959.14}{0.1} \times \dfrac{1}{(1.1)^2} \quad = -£33{,}550.74$

should take place after one year. Thereafter the new cars should be replaced every three years. This policy is over £800 cheaper than selling off the old cars immediately.

Drawbacks of the annual equivalent annuity method

It is important to note that annual equivalent annuity analysis relies on there being a high degree of predictability of cash flows stretching into the future. While the technique can be modified reasonably satisfactorily for the problems caused by inflation we may encounter severe problems if the assets in question are susceptible to a high degree of technical change and associated cash flows. An example here would be computer hardware where simultaneously over short time periods both technical capability increases and cost of purchase decreases. The absence of predictability means that the AEA approach is not suitable in a number of situations. The requirement that identical replacement takes place can be a severe limitation but the AEA approach can be used for approximate analysis, which is sufficient for practical decisions in many situations – provided the analyst does not become too preoccupied with mathematical preciseness and remembers that good judgement is also required.

Timing of projects

In some industries the mutually exclusive projects facing the firm may simply be whether to take a particular course of action now or to make shareholders better off by considering another possibility, for instance, to implement the action in a future year. It may be that taking action now would produce a positive NPV and is therefore attractive. However, by delaying action an even higher NPV can be obtained. Take the case of Lochglen distillery. Ten years ago it laid down a number of vats of whisky. These have a higher market value the older the whisky becomes. The issue facing the management team is to decide in which of the next seven years to bottle and sell it. The table in **Exhibit 3.15** gives the net cash flows available for each of the seven alternative projects.

Exhibit 3.15	Lochglen distillery's choices

		Year of bottling					
Point in time (yearly intervals)	0	1	2	3	4	5	6
Net cash flow £000s per vat	60	75	90	103	116	129	139
Percentage change on previous year		25%	20%	14.4%	12.6%	11.2%	7.8%

The longer the firm refrains from harvesting, the greater the size of the money inflow. However, this does not necessarily imply that shareholders will be best served by delaying as long as possible. They have an opportunity cost for their funds and therefore the firm must produce

an adequate return over a period of time. In the case of Lochglen the assumption is that the firm requires a 9 per cent return on projects. The calculation of the NPVs for each project is easy (*see* Exhibit 3.16).

Exhibit 3.16	NPVs for Lochglen distillery's choices						
		Year of bottling					
Point in time (yearly intervals)	**0**	**1**	**2**	**3**	**4**	**5**	**6**
£000s per vat		$\dfrac{75}{1.09}$	$\dfrac{90}{(1.09)^2}$	$\dfrac{103}{(1.09)^3}$	$\dfrac{116}{(1.09)^4}$	$\dfrac{129}{(1.09)^5}$	$\dfrac{139}{(1.09)^6}$
Net present value	60	68.8	75.8	79.5	82.2	83.8	82.9

As shown in Exhibit 3.16, the optimal point is at Year 5 when the whisky has reached the ripe old age of 15. Note also that prior to the fifth year the value increased at an annual rate greater than 9 per cent. After Year 5 (or 15 years old) the rate of increase is less than the cost of capital. Another way of viewing this is to say that if the whisky was sold when at 15 years old, the cash received could be invested elsewhere (for the same level of risk) and receive a return of 9 per cent, which is more than the 7.8 per cent available by holding the whisky one more year.

The make or buy decision

A perennial issue that many organisations need to address is whether it is better to buy a particular item, such as a component, from a supplier or to produce the item in-house. If the firm produces for itself it will incur the costs of set-up as well as the ongoing annual costs. These costs can be avoided by buying in but this has the potential drawback that the firm may be forced to pay a high market price. This is essentially an incremented cash flow problem. We need to establish the difference between the costs of set-up and production in-house and the costs of purchase. Take the case of Davis and Davies plc who manufacture fishing rods. At the moment they buy in the 'eyes' for the rods from I'spies plc at £1 per set. They expect to make use of 100,000 sets per annum for the next few years. If Davis and Davies were to produce their own 'eyes' they would have to spend £40,000 immediately on machinery, setting up and training. The machinery will have a life of four years and the annual cost of production of 100,000 sets will be £80,000, £85,000, £92,000 and £100,000 respectively. The cost of bought-in components is not expected to remain at £1 per set. The more realistic estimates are £105,000 for year 1, followed by £120,000, £128,000 and £132,000 for years 2 to 4 respectively, for 100,000 sets per year. The new machinery will be installed in an empty factory the open market rental value of which is £20,000 per annum and the firm's cost of capital is 11 per cent. The extra cash flows associated with in-house production compared with buying in are as set out in Exhibit 3.17.

Exhibit 3.17	Cash flows for producing 'eyes' in-house				
Points in time (yearly intervals) **£000s**	**0**	**1**	**2**	**3**	**4**
1 Cash flows of self-production	40	80	85	92	100
2 Plus opportunity costs		20	20	20	20
3 Relevant cash flows of making	40	100	105	112	120
4 Costs of purchasing component		105	120	128	132
Incremented cash flow due to making (line 4 – line 3)	–40	5	15	16	12

▶

Net present value of incremental cash flows

$$-40 \; + \; \frac{5}{1.11} \; + \; \frac{15}{(1.11)^2} \; + \; \frac{16}{(1.11)^3} \; + \; \frac{12}{(1.11)^4}$$

NPV = −£3,717

As the incremental NPV is negative Davis and Davies should continue to purchase 'eyes'. The present values of the future annual savings are worth less than the initial investment for self-production. An example of this sort of buy-in or build decision is shown for JCB in Exhibit 3.18.

Exhibit 3.18

JCB to buck trend and build engines

By Dan Roberts, Industrial Editor

JCB is due to buck the trend in British engineering decline by launching one of the first new engines designed and built entirely in the UK for over a decade.

The Staffordshire manufacturer of construction equipment says signs of recovery in several of its main export markets have encouraged it to commit £50m to replace existing diesel engines bought from foreign-owned suppliers.

Although the capital expenditure is small by global standards, it reflects growing confidence in one of the UK's biggest privately-owned companies and contradicts warnings that the specialist expertise required has been lost . . .

'Until recently we have never had the volume of sales to support the development of a new engine but we have been developing the project in secret for the last four years', said Mr Patterson . . .

JCB says annual vehicle sales are more than 30,000, up from 11,000 in 1993 . . .

 Financial Times, 29 August 2003, p. 4.
All Rights Reserved.

Fluctuating output

Many businesses and individual machines operate at less than full capacity for long periods of time. Sometimes this is due to the nature of the firm's business. For instance, electricity demand fluctuates through the day and over the year. Fluctuating output can produce some interesting problems for project appraisal analysis. Take the case of the Potato Sorting Company, which grades and bags potatoes in terms of size and quality. During the summer and autumn its two machines work at full capacity, which is the equivalent of 20,000 bags per machine per year. However, in the six months of the winter and spring the machines work at half capacity because fewer home grown potatoes need to be sorted. The operating cost of the machine per bag is 20 pence. The machines were installed over 50 years ago and can be regarded as still having a very long productive life. Despite this they have no secondhand value because modern machines called Fastsort now dominate the market. Fastsort has an identical capacity to the old machine but its running cost is only 10 pence per bag. These machines are also expected to be productive indefinitely, but they cost £12,000 each to purchase and install. The new production manager is keen on getting rid of the two old machines and replacing them with two Fastsort machines. She has presented the figures given in Exhibit 3.19 to a board meeting on the assumption of a cost of capital of 10 per cent.

Exhibit 3.19 Comparison of old machines with Fastsort

Cost of two old machines

Output per machine = per year	rate of 20,000 p.a. for six months 20,000 × 0.5	=	10,000
+	rate of 10,000 p.a. for six months 10,000 × 0.5	=	$\dfrac{5,000}{15,000}$

15,000 bags @ 20p × 2 = £6,000.

Present value of a perpetuity of £6,000: $\dfrac{6,000}{0.1}$ = £60,000

Cost of the Fastsorts
Annual output – same as under old machines, 30,000 bags p.a.

Annual operating cost 30,000 × 10p = £3,000

Present value of operating costs $\dfrac{3,000}{0.1}$ = £30,000

Plus initial investment	£24,000
Overall cost in present value terms	£54,000

The production manager has identified a way to save the firm £6,000 and is duly proud of her presentation. The newly appointed finance director thanks her for bringing this issue to the attention of the board but thinks that they should consider a third possibility. This is to replace only one of the machines. The virtue of this approach is that during the slack six months only the Fastsort will be used and can be supplemented with the old machine during the busy period, thus avoiding £12,000 of initial investment. The figures work out as set out in Exhibit 3.20.

The board decides to replace only one of the machines as this saves £8,000 compared with £6,000 under the production manager's proposal.

Exhibit 3.20 Replacing only one old machine

	Fastsort		Old machine	
Output	20,000 bags		10,000 bags	
Initial investment	£12,000			
Operating costs	10p × 20,000	= £2,000	20p × 10,000	= £2,000
Present value of operating costs	$\dfrac{2,000}{0.1}$	= £20,000	$\dfrac{2,000}{0.1}$	= £20,000
Total present value of costs	£12,000	+ £20,000	+ £20,000	= £52,000

Concluding comments

Finding appropriate cash flows to include in a project appraisal often involves some difficulty in data collection and requires some thoughtfulness in applying the concepts of incremental cash flow. The reader who has diligently worked through this chapter and has overcome the barriers to understanding may be more than a little annoyed at being told that the understanding of these issues is merely one of the stages leading to successful application of net present value to practical business problems. The logical, mathematical and conceptual knowledge presented above has to be married to an appreciation of real-world limitations imposed by the awkward fact that it is people who have to be persuaded to act to implement a plan. This is an issue examined in the next chapter. Further real-world complications such as the existence of risk, of inflation and taxation and of limits placed on availability of capital are covered in subsequent chapters.

Key points and concepts

- **Raw data** have to be checked for accuracy, reliability, timeliness, expense of collection, etc.

- **Depreciation** is not a cash flow and should be excluded.

- **Profit** is a poor substitute for cash flow. For example, working capital adjustments may be needed to modify the profit figures for NPV analysis.

- Analyse on the basis of **incremental cash flows**. That is the difference between the cash flows arising if the project is implemented and the cash flows if the project is not implemented:

 - **opportunity costs** associated with, say, using an asset which has an alternative employment are relevant;
 - **incidental effects**, that is, cash flow effects throughout the organisation, should be considered along with the obvious direct effects;
 - **sunk costs** – costs which will not change regardless of the decision to proceed are clearly irrelevant;

 - **allocated overhead** is a non-incremental cost and is irrelevant;
 - **interest** should not be double counted by both including interest as a cash flow and including it as an element in the discount rate.

- **The replacement decision** is an example of the application of incremental cash flow analysis.

- **Annual equivalent annuities (AEA)** can be employed to estimate the **optimal replacement cycle** for an asset under certain restrictive assumptions. The **lowest common multiple (LCM)** method is sometimes employed for short-lived assets.

- Whether to repair the old machine or sell it and buy a new machine is a very common business dilemma. Incremental cash flow analysis helps us to solve these types of problems. Other applications include **the timing of projects**, the issue of **fluctuating output** and the **make** or **buy decision**.

References and further reading

Bierman, H. and Smidt, S. (2006) *The Capital Budgeting Decision*, 9th edn. London: Routledge.
 Contains some good chapters for the beginner.

Bierman, H. and Smidt, S. (2006) *Advanced Capital Budgeting*. London: Routledge.
 Good for those wanting to pursue these topics in more depth.

Carsberg, B.V. (1975) *Economics of Business Decisions*. Harmondsworth: Penguin.
 An economist's perspective on relevant cash flows.

Coulthurst, N.J. (1986) 'The application of the incremental principle in capital investment project evaluation', *Accounting and Business Research*, Autumn.
 A discussion of the theoretical and practical application of the incremental cash flow principle.

Gordon, L.A. and Stark, A.W. (1989) 'Accounting and economic rates of return: a note on depreciation and other accruals', *Journal of Business Finance and Accounting*, 16(3), pp. 425–32.
 Considers the problem of depreciation – an algebraic approach.

Pohlman, R.A., Santiago, E.S. and Markel, F.L. (1988) 'Cash flow estimation practices of larger firms', *Financial Management*, Summer.
> Evidence on large US corporation cash flow estimation practices.

Reinhardt, U.E. (1973) 'Break-even analysis for Lockheed's Tristar: an application of financial theory', *Journal of Finance*, 28, pp. 821–38, September.
> An interesting application of the principle of the opportunity cost of funds.

Case study recommendations

Please see www.pearsoned.co.uk/arnold for case study synopses.

- Tottenham Hotspur. Authors: L. Cohen, J. Coval and C. Malloy (2009) Harvard Business School.

- Vereinigung Hamburger Schiffsmakler und Schiffsagenten e.V. (VHSS): Valuing Ships. Authors: B.C. Esty and A. Sheen (2011) Harvard Business School.

- USEC Inc. Authors: K. Eades, L. Doe and B. Mackovjak (2008) Darden School of Business. Available from Harvard Case Study website.

- Hansson Private Label, Inc.: Evaluating an investment in expansion. Authors: E. Stafford, J.L. Heilprin and J. DeVolder (2010) Harvard Business School.

- Replacement Decision: Getting It Right. Author: H.E. Kierulff (2007) Business Horizons. Available from Harvard Case Study website.

- TechnoServe and the Tanzanian Specialty Coffee Industry. Authors: P.A. Hecht and S. Haji (2004) Harvard Business School.

- Wabash Music, Inc. Author: T. Luehrman (2005) Harvard Business School.

Self-review questions

1 Imagine the Ministry of Defence have spent £50m researching and developing a new guided weapon system. Explain why this fact may be irrelevant to the decision on whether to go ahead with production.

2 'Those business school graduates don't know what they are talking about. We have to allocate overheads to every department and activity. If we simply excluded this cost there would be a big lump of costs not written off. All projects must bear some central overhead.' Discuss this statement.

3 What is an annual equivalent annuity?

4 What are the two main techniques available for evaluating mutually exclusive repeated projects with different lengths of life? Why is it not valid simply to use NPVs?

5 Arcmat plc owns a factory which at present is empty. Mrs Hambicious, a business strategist, has been working on a proposal for using the factory for doll manufacture. This will require complete modernisation. Mrs Hambicious is a little confused about project appraisal and has asked your advice about which of the following are relevant and incremental cash flows.

 a The future cost of modernising the factory.
 b The £100,000 spent two months ago on a market survey investigating the demand for these plastic dolls.
 c Machines to produce the dolls – cost £10m payable on delivery.
 d Depreciation on the machines.

 e Arcmat's other product lines are expected to be more popular due to the complementary nature of the new doll range with these existing products – the net cash flow effect is anticipated at £1m.
 f Three senior managers will be drafted in from other divisions for a period of a year.
 g A proportion of the US head office costs.
 h The tax saving due to the plant investment being offset against taxable income.
 i The £1m of additional raw material stock required at the start of production.
 j The interest that will be charged on the £20m bank loan needed to initiate this project.
 k The cost of the utility services installed last year.

6 In a 'make or buy' type of decision should we also consider factors not easily quantified such as security of supply, convenience and the morale of the workforce? (This question is meant to start you thinking about the issues discussed in Chapter 4. You are not expected to give a detailed answer yet.)

7 'Depreciation is a cost recognised by tax authorities so why don't you use it in project appraisal?' Help the person who asked this question.

8 A firm is considering the implementation of a new project to produce slippers. The already owned equipment to be used has sufficient spare capacity to allow this new production without affecting existing product ranges. The production manager suggests that because the equipment has been paid for it is a sunk cost and should not be included in the project appraisal calculations. Do you accept his argument?

Questions and problems

Answers to most questions can be found at www.pearsoned.co.uk/Arnold.
Answers to questions marked with an asterisk are to be found only in the Lecturer's Guide.

1 The Tenby-Saundersfoot Dock company is considering the reopening of one of its mothballed loading docks. Repairs and new equipment will cost £250,000 payable immediately. To operate the new dock will require additional dock-side employees costing £70,000 per year. There will also be a need for additional administrative staff and other overheads such as extra stationery, insurance and telephone costs amounting to £85,000 per year. Electricity and other energy used on the dock is anticipated to cost £40,000 per year. The London head office will allocate £50,000 of its (unchanged) costs to this project. Other docks will experience a reduction in receipts of about £20,000 per year due to some degree of cannibalisation. Annual fees expected from the new dock are £255,000 per year.

Assume

– all cash flows arise at the year ends except the initial repair and equipment costs which are incurred at the outset;
– no tax or inflation;
– no sales are made on credit.

a Lay out the net annual cash flow calculations. Explain your reasoning.
b Assume an infinite life for the project and a cost of capital of 17 per cent. What is the net present value?

2 A senior management team at Railcam, a supplier to the railway industry, is trying to prepare a cash flow forecast for the years 20X2–20X4. The estimated sales are:
These sales will be made on three months' credit and there will be no bad debts.

Year	20X1	20X2	20X3	20X4	20X5
Sales (£)	20m	22m	24m	21m	25m

There are only three cost elements. First, wages amounting to £6m per year. Second, raw materials costing one-half of sales for the year. Raw material suppliers grant three months of credit. Third, direct overhead (only incurred if the project is undertaken) at £5m per year. Start date: 1.1.20X1.
Calculate the net operating cash flow for the years 20X2–20X4. **?**

3 (*Examination level*) Pine Ltd have spent £20,000 researching the prospects for a new range of products. If it were decided that production is to go ahead an investment of £240,000 in capital equipment on 1 January 20X1 would be required.
 The accounts department has produced budgeted profit and loss statements for each of the next five years for the project. At the end of the fifth year the capital equipment will be sold and production will cease.
 The capital equipment is expected to be sold for scrap on 31.12.20X5 for £40,000.

	Year end 31.12.20X1	Year end 31.12.20X2	Year end 31.12.20X3	Year end 31.12.20X4	Year end 31.12.20X5
Sales	400	400	400	320	200
Materials	240	240	240	192	120
Other variable costs	40	40	40	32	20
Overheads	20	20	24	24	24
Depreciation	40	40	40	40	40
Net profit/(loss)	60	60	56	32	(4)

(All figures in £000s)

When production is started it will be necessary to raise material stock levels by £30,000 and other working capital by £20,000.

Both the additional stock and other working capital increases will be released at the end of the project.

Customers receive one year's credit from the firm.

The overhead figures in the budgeted accounts have two elements – 60 per cent is due to a reallocation of existing overheads, 40 per cent is directly incurred because of the take-up of the project.

For the purposes of this appraisal you may regard all receipts and payments as occurring at the year end to which they relate, unless otherwise stated. The company's cost of capital is 12 per cent.

Assume no inflation or tax.

Required

a Use the net present value method of project appraisal to advise the company on whether to go ahead with the proposed project.

b Explain to a management team unfamiliar with discounted cash flow appraisal techniques the significance and value of the NPV method.

(In addition to the standard solution given at www.pearsoned.co.uk/Arnold there is an Excel spreadsheet solution available at www.pearsoned.co.uk/arnold) **?**

4* (*Examination level*) Mercia plc owns two acres of derelict land near to the centre of a major UK city. The firm has received an invoice for £50,000 from consultants who were given the task of analysis, investigation and design of some project proposals for using the land. The consultants outline the two best proposals to a meeting of the board of Mercia.

Proposal 1 is to spend £150,000 levelling the site and then constructing a six-level car park at an additional cost of £1,600,000. The earthmoving firm will be paid £150,000 on the start date and the construction firm will be paid £1.4m on the start date, with the balance payable 24 months later.

It is expected that the car park will be fully operational as from the completion date (365 days after the earth-movers first begin).

The annual income from ticket sales will be £600,000 to an infinite horizon. Operational costs (attendants, security, power, etc.) will be £100,000 per annum. The consultants have also apportioned £60,000 of Mercia's central overhead costs (created by the London-based head office and the executive jet) to this project.

The consultants present their analysis in terms of a commonly used measure of project viability, that of payback.

This investment idea is not original; Mercia investigated a similar project two years ago and discovered that there are some costs which have been ignored by the consultants. First, the local council will require a payment of £100,000 one year after the completion of the construction for its inspection services and a trading and environmental impact licence. Second, senior management will have to leave aside work on other projects, resulting in delays and reduced income from these projects amounting to £50,000 per year once the car park is operational. Also, the proposal is subject to depreciation of one-fiftieth (1/50) of the earthmoving and construction costs each year.

Proposal 2 is for a health club. An experienced company will, for a total cost of £9m payable at the start of the project, design and construct the buildings and supply all the equipment. It will be ready for Mercia's use one year after construction begins. Revenue from customers will be £5m per annum and operating costs will be £4m per annum. The consultants allocate £70,000 of central general head office overhead costs for each year from the start. After two years of operating the health club Mercia will sell it for a total of £11m.

Information not considered by the consultants for Proposal 2

The £9m investment includes £5m in buildings not subject to depreciation. It also includes £4m in equipment, 10 per cent of which has to be replaced each year. This has not been included in the operating costs.

A new executive will be needed to oversee the project from the start of the project – costing £100,000 per annum.

The consultants recommend that the board of Mercia accept the second proposal and reject the first.

Assume

– If the site was sold with no further work carried out it would fetch £100,000.

– No inflation or tax.

– The cost of capital for Mercia is 10 per cent (this is the relevant rate for this project).

– It can be assumed, for simplicity of analysis, that all cash flows occur at year ends except those occurring at the start of the project.

Required

a Calculate the net present value of each proposal.
 State whether you would recommend Proposal 1 or 2.
b Calculate the internal rate of return for each proposed project.

(In addition to the solution given in the Lecturer's Guide there is an Excel spreadsheet solution available at www.pearsoned.co.uk/arnold (Lecturer's Guide)) **?**

5* (*Examination level*) Mines International plc
The Albanian government is auctioning the rights to mine copper in the east of the country. Mines International plc (MI) is considering the amount they would be prepared to pay as a lump sum for the five-year licence. The auction is to take place very soon and the cash will have to be paid immediately following the auction.
 In addition to the lump sum the Albanian government will expect annual payments of £500,000 to cover 'administration'. If MI wins the licence, production would not start until one year later because it will take a year to prepare the site and buy in equipment. To begin production MI would have to commission the manufacture of specialist engineering equipment costing £9.5m, half of which is payable immediately, with the remainder due in one year.
 MI has already conducted a survey of the site which showed a potential productive life of four years with its new machine. The survey cost £300,000 and is payable immediately.
 The accounts department have produced the following projected profit and loss accounts.

	Year				
Projected profit and loss (£m)	1	2	3	4	5
Sales	0	8	9	9	7
Less expenses					
Materials and consumables	0.6	0.4	0.5	0.5	0.4
Wages	0.3	0.7	0.7	0.7	0.7
Overheads	0.4	0.5	0.6	0.6	0.5
Depreciation of equipment	0	2.0	2.0	2.0	2.0
Albanian govt. payments	0.5	0.5	0.5	0.5	0.5
Survey costs written off	0.3				
Profit (loss) excluding licence fee	(2.1)	3.9	4.7	4.7	2.9

The following additional information is available:
a Payments and receipts arise at the year ends unless otherwise stated.
b The initial lump sum payment has been excluded from the projected accounts as this is unknown at the outset.
c The customers of MI demand and receive a credit period of three months.
d The suppliers of materials and consumables grant a credit period of three months.
e The overheads contain an annual charge of £200,000 which represents an apportionment of head office costs. This is an expense which would be incurred whether or not the project proceeds. The remainder of the overheads relate directly to the project.
f The new equipment will have a resale value at the end of the fifth year of £1.5m.
g During the whole of Year 3 a specialised item of machinery will be needed, which is currently being used by another division of MI. This division will therefore incur hire costs of £100,000 for the period the machinery is on loan.
h The project will require additional cash reserves of £1m to be held in Albania throughout the project for operational purposes. These are recoverable at the end of the project.
i The Albanian government will make a one-off refund of 'administration' charges one and a half months after the end of the fifth year of £200,000.

The company's cost of capital is 12 per cent.
Ignore taxation, inflation and exchange rate movements and controls.

Required

a Calculate the maximum amount MI should bid in the auction.
b What would be the Internal Rate of Return on the project if MI did not have to pay for the licence?

c The board of directors have never been on a finance course and do not understand any of the finance jargon. However, they have asked you to persuade them that the appraisal method you have used in (a) above can be relied on. Prepare a presentation for the board of directors explaining the reasoning and justification for using your chosen project appraisal technique and your treatment of specific items in the accounts. You will need to explain concepts such as the time value of money, opportunity cost and sunk cost in plain English. **?**

6 Find the annual equivalent annuity at 13 per cent for the following cash flow:

Point in time (yearly intervals)	0	1	2	3
Cash flow (£)	−5,000	+2,000	+2,200	+3,500

?

7* (*Examination question if combined with Question 8*) Reds plc is attempting to decide a replacement cycle for new machinery. This machinery costs £10,000 to purchase. Operating and maintenance costs for the future years are:

Point in time (yearly intervals)	0	1	2	3
Operating and maintenance costs (£)	0	12,000	13,000	14,000

The values available from the sale of the machinery on the secondhand market are:

Point in time (yearly intervals)	0	1	2	3
Secondhand value (£)	0	8,000	6,500	3,500

Assume

– replacement by an identical machine to an infinite horizon;
– no inflation, tax or risk;
– the cost of capital is 11 per cent.

Should Reds replace this new machine on a one-, two- or three-year cycle? **?**

8* The firm Reds plc in Question 7 has not yet purchased the new machinery and is considering postponing such a cash outflow for a year or two. If it were to replace the existing machine now it could be sold immediately for £4,000. If the firm persevered with the old machine for a further year then £2,000 would have to be spent immediately to recondition it. The machine could then be sold for £3,000 in 12 months' time. The third possibility is to spend £2,000 now, on reconditioning, and £1,000 on maintenance in one year, and finally sell the machine for £1,500, 24 months from now. Assuming all other factors remain constant regardless of which option is chosen, which date would you recommend for the commencement of the replacement cycle? **?**

9 Quite plc has an ageing piece of equipment which is less efficient than more modern equivalents. This equipment will continue to operate for another 15 years but operating and maintenance costs will be £3,500 per year. Alternatively it could be sold, raising £2,000 now, and replaced with its modern equivalent which costs £7,000 but has reduced operating and maintenance costs at £3,000 per year. This machine could be sold at the end of its 15-year life for scrap for £500. The third possibility is to spend £2,500 for an immediate overhaul of the old machine which will improve its efficiency for the rest of its life, so that operating and maintenance costs become £3,200 per annum. The old machine will have a zero scrap value in 15 years, whether or not it is overhauled. Quite plc requires a return of 9 per cent on projects in this risk class. Select the best course of action. (Assume that cash flows arise at the year ends.) **?**

10* The managing director of Curt plc is irritated that the supplier for the component widgets has recently increased prices by another 10 per cent following similar rises for each of the last five years. Based on the assumption that this pattern will continue, the cost of these widgets will be:

Points in time (yearly intervals)	1	2	3	4	5
Payments for widgets (£)	100,000	110,000	121,000	133,100	146,410

The managing director is convinced that the expertise for the manufacture of widgets exists within Curt. He therefore proposes the purchase of the necessary machine tools and other items of equipment to produce widgets in-house, at a cost of £70,000. The net cash outflows associated with this course of action are:

Points in time (yearly intervals)	0	1	2	3	4	5
Cash outflows	70,000	80,000	82,000	84,000	86,000	88,000

Note: The figures include the £70,000 for equipment and operating costs, etc.

The machinery has a life of five years and can be sold for scrap at the end of its life for £10,000. This is not included in the £88,000 for year 5. The installation of the new machine will require the attention of the technical services manager during the first year. She will have to abandon other projects as a result, causing a loss of net income of £48,000 from those projects. This cost has not been included in the above figures.

The relevant discount rate is 16 per cent, and all cash flows occur at year ends except the initial investment.

Help Curt plc to decide whether to produce widgets for itself. What other factors might influence this decision?

11 The Borough Company is to replace its existing machinery. It has a choice between two new types of machine having different lives. The machines have the following costs:

Points in time (yearly intervals)		Machine X	Machine Y
0	Initial investment	£20,000	£25,000
1	Operating costs	£5,000	£4,000
2	Operating costs	£5,000	£4,000
3	Operating costs	£5,000	£4,000
4	Operating costs		£4,000

Machine X ceases to operate and is worth nothing after three years. Machine Y ceases to operate and is worth nothing after four years.

Each machine will be replaced at the end of its life by identical machines with identical costs. This cycle will continue indefinitely. The cost of capital is 13 per cent.

Which machine should Borough buy? **?**

12* Netq plc manufactures Qtrans, for which demand fluctuates seasonally. Netq has two machines, each with a productive capacity of 1,000 Qtrans per year. For four months of the year each machine operates at full capacity. For a further four months the machines operate at three-quarters of their full capacity and for the remaining months they produce at half capacity. The operating cost of producing a Qtran is £4 and the machines are expected to be productive to an indefinite horizon. Netq is considering scrapping the old machines (for which the firm will receive nothing) and replacing them with new improved versions. These machines are also expected to last forever if properly maintained but they cost £7,000 each. Each has an annual capacity of 1,000 Qtrans. Operating costs (including maintenance) will, however, fall to £1.80 per Qtran. The appropriate cost of capital is 13 per cent. Should Netq replace both of its machines, one of them, or neither? Assume output is the same under each option and that the new machines have the same productive capacity as the old. **?**

13 Clipper owns 100 acres of mature woodland and is trying to decide when to harvest the trees. If it harvests immediately the net cash flow, after paying the professional loggers, will be £10,000. If it waits a year the trees will grow, so that the net cash flow will be £12,000. In two years, £14,000 can be obtained. After three years have elapsed, the cash flow will be £15,500, and thereafter will increase in value by £1,000 per annum.

Calculate the best time to cut the trees given a cost of capital of 10 per cent. **?**

14* (*Examination level*) Opti plc operates a single machine to produce its output. The senior management are trying to choose between four possibilities. First, sell the machine on the secondhand market and buy a new one at the end of one year. Second, sell in the secondhand market and replace at the end of two years. The third is to replace after three years. Finally, the machine could be scrapped at the end of its useful life after four years. These replacement cycles are expected to continue indefinitely. The management team believe that all such replacements will be for financially identical equipment, i.e. the cash inflows produced by the new and old equipment are the same. However, the cost of maintenance and operations increases with the age of the machine. These costs are shown in the table, along with the secondhand and scrap values.

Points in time (yearly intervals)	0	1	2	3	4
Initial outlay (£)	20,000				
Operating and maintenance costs (£)		6,000	8,000	10,000	12,000
Secondhand/scrap value (£)		12,000	9,000	6,000	2,000

Assume

– The cost of capital is 10 per cent.
– No inflation.
– No technological advances.
– No tax.
– All cash flows occur on anniversary dates.

Required

Choose the length of the replacement cycle which minimises the present values of the costs of an infinite number of cycles. **?**

15 (*Examination level*) Hazel plc produces one of the components used in the manufacture of car bumpers. The production manager is keen on obtaining modern equipment and he has come to you, the finance director, with details concerning two alternative machines, A and B.

The cash flows and other assumptions are as follows.

Points in time (yearly intervals)	0	£000s 1	£000s 2	£000s 3
Machine A	−200	+220	+242	0
Machine B	−240	+220	+242	+266

Machine A would have to be replaced by an identical machine on a two-year cycle.
Machine B would be replaced by an identical machine every three years.
It is considered reasonable to assume that the cash flows for the future replacements of A and B are the same as in the above table.
The opportunity cost of capital for Hazel is 15 per cent.
Ignore taxation.
The acceptance of either project would leave the company's risk unchanged.
The cash flows occur on anniversary dates.

Required

a Calculate the net present value of Machine A for its two-year life.
b Calculate the net present value of Machine B for its three-year life.
c Calculate the annual equivalent annuities for Machines A and B and recommend which machine should be selected.
d You are aware that the production manager gets very enthusiastic about new machinery and this may cloud his judgement. You suggest the third possibility, which is to continue production with Machine C which was purchased five years ago for £400,000. This is expected to produce +£160,000 per year. It has a scrap value now of £87,000 and is expected to last another five years. At the end of its useful life it will have a scrap value of £20,000. Should C be kept for another five years?
e The production manager asks why you are discounting the cash flows. Briefly explain the time value of money and its components. **?**

MyFinanceLab

Now retake your diagnostic test for Chapter 3 to check your progress and update your study plan.

Assignments

1 Try to obtain budgeted profit and loss accounts for a proposed project and by combining these with other data produce cash flow estimates for the project. Calculate the NPV and contrast your conclusions on the viability of the project with that suggested by the profit and loss projections.

2 Examine some items of machinery (e.g. shopfloor machine tools, vehicles, computers). Consider whether to replace these items with the modern equivalent, taking into account increased maintenance costs, loss or gain of customer sales, secondhand values, higher productivity, etc.

3 Apply the technique of annual equivalent annuities to an asset which is replaced on a regular cycle. Consider alternative cycle lengths.

Visit www.pearsoned.co.uk/arnold to get access to Gradetracker diagnostic tests, podcasts, Excel spreadsheet solutions, *FT* articles, a flashcard revision tool, web links, a searchable glossary and more.

The decision-making process for investment appraisal

LEARNING OUTCOMES

The main outcome expected from this chapter is that the reader is aware of both traditional and discounted cash flow investment appraisal techniques and the extent of their use. The reader should also be aware that these techniques are a small part of the overall capital-allocation planning process. The student is expected to gain knowledge of:

■ the empirical evidence on techniques used;

■ the calculation of payback, discounted payback and accounting rate of return (ARR);

■ the drawbacks and attractions of payback and ARR;

■ the balance to be struck between mathematical precision and imprecise reality;

■ the capital-allocation planning process.

MyFinanceLab *Complete your diagnostic test for Chapter 4 now to create your personal study plan*

Introduction

An organisation may be viewed simply as a collection of projects, some of which were started a long time ago, some only recently begun, many being major 'strategic' projects and others minor operating-unit-level schemes. It is in the nature of business for change to occur, and through change old activities, profit centres and methods die, to be replaced by the new. Without a continuous process of regeneration firms will cease to progress and be unable to compete in a dynamic environment. It is vital that the processes and systems that lead to the development of new production methods, new markets and products, and so on are efficient. That is, both the project appraisal techniques and the entire process of proposal creation and selection lead to the achievement of the objective of the organisation. Poor appraisal technique, set within the framework of an investment process that does not ask the right questions and which provides erroneous conclusions, will destroy the wealth of shareholders.

The payback and accounting rate of return (ARR) methods of evaluating capital investment proposals have historically been, and continue to be, very popular approaches. This is despite the best efforts of a number of writers to denigrate them. It is important to understand the disadvantages of these methods, but it is also useful to be aware of why practical business people still see a great deal of merit in observing the outcome of these calculations.

The employment of project appraisal techniques must be seen as merely one of the stages in the process of the allocation of resources within a firm. The appraisal stage can be reached only after ideas for the use of capital resources have been generated and those ideas have been filtered through a consideration of the strategic, budgetary and business resource capabilities of the firm. Following the appraisal stage are the approval, implementation and post-completion auditing stages.

Any capital allocation system has to be viewed in the light of the complexity of organisational life. This aspect has been ignored in Chapters 2 and 3, where mechanical analysis is applied. The balance is corrected in this chapter. Investment, as in the case of Petrobras's oil business (*see* Exhibit 4.1), needs to be thoroughly evaluated. This chapter considers the process of project development, appraisal and post-investment monitoring.

Exhibit 4.1

Oil: Dominance of Petrobras may slow development

By Jonathan Wheatley

When Petrobras, Brazil's national oil company, raised $70bn in equity in September, it was not only the biggest share issue ever undertaken. It was also an affirmation of the enormous investor interest in Brazil and of its huge potential as an oil producing nation.

The industry is undergoing transformational change. Petrobras has overseen the development of the national oil and gas sector for more than half a century, enjoying a monopoly on production and exploration until private sector competition was permitted in the late 1990s.

Petrobras continues to dominate the industry, partly through its privileged position and partly because of world-class expertise in deepwater exploration, acquired as the company pushed further away from the coast into more challenging environments.

It is setting out to test that expertise in the 'pre-salt' fields, discovered in 2007 and so called because they are under several kilometres of seawater, rock and a hard-to-penetrate layer of salt.

At the same time it has embarked on an ambitious $224bn investment programme for 2010 to 2014. As well as exploration and production in and outside

▶

Exhibit 4.1 *(continued)*

the pre-salt region, this includes refining, energy generation, biofuels and other activities.

Many analysts think Petrobras will be overstretched, especially because regulations currently before Brazil's congress would make it the sole lead operator in all future consortia working in the pre-salt fields.

Petrobras says it has all the expertise needed to develop the pre-salt fields alone – and that other companies only want to take part in order to gain access to its proprietary technology.

It also says it is preparing to train 250,000 workers, even giving them basic schooling if necessary.

Petrobras will also be obliged to take a minimum 30 per cent stake in any consortia operating in the pre-salt fields and may have to fund up to 100 per cent at the government's discretion.

Some analysts believe Petrobras will quickly run out of funds and be forced to return to capital markets for more equity within two or three years.

The share issue itself raised other questions. As part of the process, the government sold Petrobras the rights to 5bn barrels of pre-salt oil, for which the government received $42.5bn worth of new shares in the company.

Since the government controls Petrobras – it has a majority of voting stock but a minority of total capital – many investors were concerned about what they said was a conflict of interest, as the government was the biggest party on both sides of the transaction.

Investors also complained about a lack of transparency in the way the price Petrobras paid for the 5bn barrels was arrived at and that the price itself, of $8.51 per barrel, was too high, as it would result in a rate of return similar to Petrobras's cost of funding.

'The net present value of the investment is zero,' says one fund manager.

Financial Times, 14 November 2010.
All Rights Reserved.

Evidence on the employment of appraisal techniques

A number of surveys enquiring into the appraisal methods used in practice have been conducted. The results from surveys conducted by Pike, by the author jointly with Panos Hatzopoulos and by Alkaraan and Northcott are displayed in Exhibit 4.2. Some striking features emerge from these and other studies. Payback remains in wide use, despite the increasing application of discounted cash flow techniques. Internal rate of return is popular, but net present value is the preferred method in large companies. Accounting rate of return continues to be the laggard, but is still used in over 50 per cent of large firms. One observation that is emphasised in many studies is the tendency for decision makers to use more than one method. In the Arnold and Hatzopoulos study 67 per cent of firms use three or four of these techniques. These methods are regarded as being complementary rather than competitors.

There is an indication in the literature that while some methods have superior theoretical justification, other, simpler methods are used for purposes such as communicating project viability and gaining commitment throughout an organisation. It is also suggested that those who sponsor and advance projects within organisations like to have the option of presenting their case in an alternative form which shows the proposal in the best light.

Another clear observation from the literature is that small and medium-sized firms use the sophisticated formal procedures less than their larger brethren.

Payback

The **payback** period for a capital investment is the length of time before the cumulated stream of forecasted cash flows equals the initial investment.

The decision rule is that if a project's payback period is less than or equal to a predetermined threshold figure it is acceptable.

Exhibit 4.2	Appraisal techniques used

Proportion of companies using technique

	Pike surveys[a]				Arnold and Hatzopoulos survey[b]				Alkaraan & Northcott[c]
	1975 %	1980 %	1986 %	1992 %			**1997**		**2002**
					Small %	Medium %	Large %	Total %	Large %
Payback	73	81	92	94	71	75	66	70	96
Accounting rate of return	51	49	56	50	62	50	55	56	60
Internal rate of return	44	57	75	81	76	83	84	81	89
Net present value	32	39	68	74	62	79	97	80	99

Capital budget (per year) for companies in Arnold and Hatzopoulos study approx. Small: £1–50m. Medium: £51–100m. Large: £100m+.

Notes

(a) Pike's studies focus on 100 large UK firms.

(b) In the Arnold and Hatzopoulos study (2000), 300 finance directors of UK companies taken from The Times 1000 (London: Times Books), ranked according to capital employed (excluding investment trusts), were asked dozens of questions about project appraisal techniques, sources of finance and performance measurement. The first 100 (Large size) of the sample are the top 100; another 100 are in the rankings at 250–400 (Medium size); the final 100 are ranked 820–1,000 (Small size). The capital employed ranges between £1.3bn and £24bn for the large firms, £207m and £400m for the medium-sized firms, and £40m and £60m for the small companies. Ninety-six usable replies were received: 38 large, 24 medium and 34 small.

(c) Alkaraan and Northcott focus on UK manufacturing companies each with at least a turnover of £100m, 1,000 employees and assets of £50m. 83 companies returned questionaires.

Sources: Pike (1988 and 1996), Arnold and Hatzopoulos (2000) and Alkaraan and Northcott (2006)

Consider the case of Tradfirm's three mutually exclusive proposed investments (*see* Exhibit 4.3).

Exhibit 4.3	Tradfirm

Cash flows (£m)

Points in time (yearly intervals)	0	1	2	3	4	5	6
Project A	−10	6	2	1	1	2	2
Project B	−10	1	1	2	6	2	2
Project C	−10	3	2	2	2	15	10

Note: Production ceases after six years, and all cash flows occur on anniversary dates.

There is a boardroom battle in Tradfirm, with older members preferring the payback rule. They set four years as the decision benchmark. For both A and B the £10m initial outflow is recouped after four years. In the case of C it takes five years for the cash inflows to cumulate to £10m. Thus payback for the three projects is as follows:

Project A: 4 years
Project B: 4 years
Project C: 5 years

If the payback rule is rigidly applied, the older members of the board will reject the third project, and they are left with a degree of indecisiveness over whether to accept A or B. The younger members prefer the NPV rule and are thus able to offer a clear decision.

As **Exhibit 4.4** shows, Project A has a positive NPV and is therefore shareholder wealth enhancing. Project B has a negative NPV; the firm would be better served by investing the £10m in the alternative that offers a 10 per cent return. Project C has the largest positive NPV and is therefore the one that creates most shareholder wealth.

Exhibit 4.4	Tradfirm: Net Present Values (£m)

Project A $\quad -10 + \dfrac{6}{1.1} + \dfrac{2}{(1.1)^2} + \dfrac{1}{(1.1)^3} + \dfrac{1}{(1.1)^4} + \dfrac{2}{(1.1)^5} + \dfrac{2}{(1.1)^6} = £0.913m$

Project B $\quad -10 + \dfrac{1}{1.1} + \dfrac{1}{(1.1)^2} + \dfrac{2}{(1.1)^3} + \dfrac{6}{(1.1)^4} + \dfrac{2}{(1.1)^5} + \dfrac{2}{(1.1)^6} = -£0.293m$

Project C $\quad -10 + \dfrac{3}{1.1} + \dfrac{2}{(1.1)^2} + \dfrac{2}{(1.1)^3} + \dfrac{2}{(1.1)^4} + \dfrac{15}{(1.1)^5} + \dfrac{10}{(1.1)^6} = £12.208m$

Note: The discount rate is 10 per cent.

Drawbacks of payback

The first drawback of payback is that it makes no allowance for the time value of money. It ignores the need to compare future cash flows with the initial investment after they have been discounted to their present values. The second drawback is that receipts beyond the payback period are ignored. This problem is particularly obvious in the case of Project C. A third disadvantage is the arbitrary selection of the cut-off point. There is no theoretical basis for setting the appropriate time period and so guesswork, whim and manipulation take over.

Discounted payback

With **discounted payback** the future cash flows are discounted prior to calculating the payback period. This is an improvement on the simple payback method in that it takes into account the time value of money. In **Exhibit 4.5** the *discounted* cash inflows are added together to calculate payback. In the case of Project B the discounted cash inflows never reach the level of the cash outflow.

This modification tackles the first drawback of the simple payback method but it is still necessary to make an arbitrary decision about the cut-off date and it ignores cash flows beyond that date.

Exhibit 4.5	Discounted payback: Tradfirm plc (£m)							
Points in time (yearly intervals)	0	1	2	3	4	5	6	Discounted payback
Project A								
Undiscounted cash flow	−10	6	2	1	1	2	2	
Discounted cash flow	−10	5.45	1.65	0.75	0.68	1.24	1.13	Year 6
Project B								
Undiscounted cash flow	−10	1	1	2	6	2	2	Outflow −10m
Discounted cash flow	−10	0.909	0.826	1.5	4.1	1.24	1.13	Inflow +£9.7m
Project C								
Undiscounted cash flow	−10	3	2	2	2	15	10	
Discounted cash flow	−10	2.73	1.65	1.5	1.37	9.3	5.64	Year 5

Note: The discount rate is 10 per cent.

Reasons for the continuing popularity of payback

Payback remains a widely used project appraisal method despite its drawbacks. This requires some explanation. The first fact to note is that payback is rarely used as the primary investment technique, but rather as a secondary method which supplements the more sophisticated methods. Although it appears irrational to employ payback when the issue is examined in isolation, we may begin to see the logic behind its use if we take into account the organisational context and the complementary nature of alternative techniques. For example, payback may be used at an early stage to filter out projects which have clearly unacceptable risk and return characteristics. Identifying those projects at a preliminary stage avoids the need for more detailed evaluation through a discounted cash flow method, thus increasing the efficiency of the appraisal process. This early sifting has to be carefully implemented so as to avoid premature rejection.

Payback also has one extraordinarily endearing quality to busy managers and hard-pressed students alike – it is simple and easy to use. Executives often admit that the payback rule, used indiscriminately, does not always give the best decisions, but it is the simplest way to communicate an idea of project profitability. NPV is difficult to understand and so it is useful to have an alternative measure which all managers can follow. In the workplace a project's success often relies on the gaining of widespread employee commitment. Discussion, negotiation and communication of ideas often need to be carried out in a simple form so that non-quantitative managers can make their contribution and, eventually, their commitment. Communication in terms of the sophisticated models may lead to alienation and exclusion and, ultimately, project failure.

Another argument advanced by practitioners is that projects which return their outlay quickly reduce the exposure of the firm to risk. In the world beyond the simplifications needed in academic exercises, as described in Chapters 2 and 3, there is a great deal of uncertainty about future cash flows. Managers often distrust forecasts for more distant years. Payback has an implicit assumption that the risk of cash flows is directly related to the time distance from project implementation date. By focusing on near-term returns this approach uses only those data in which management have greatest faith. Take the case of the web-based music download industry. Here, competitive forces and technology are changing so rapidly that it is difficult to forecast for eight months ahead, let alone for eight years. Thus, managers may choose to ignore cash flow projections beyond a certain number of years. They accept only those projects immune to the risk of total market collapse a few years down the line or the risk of company failure due to an inability to meet debts as they become due. Those who advocate NPV counter this approach by saying that risk is accounted for in a better way in the NPV model than is done by simply excluding data – it certainly does not completely ignore cash flows beyond the payback period. Risk analysis applied to NPV is examined in Chapter 6.

There is some evidence that payback is more popular in companies which measure and reward executive performance through accounting profit numbers. Payback tends to be high when there are high near-term cash flows/profits.

A further advantage of payback, as perceived by many managers, is its use in situations of capital shortage. If funds are limited, there is an advantage in receiving a return on projects earlier rather than later, as this permits investment in other profitable opportunities. Theoretically this factor can be allowed for in a more satisfactory way with the NPV method; capital rationing is discussed in Chapter 5.

This section is not meant to promote the use of payback. It remains a theoretically inferior method to the discounted cash flow approaches. Payback has a number of valuable attributes, but the primary method of project appraisal in most organisations should take into account all of the relevant cash flows and then discount them.

Accounting rate of return

The **accounting rate of return (ARR)** method may be known to readers by other names such as the **return on capital employed (ROCE)** or **return on investment (ROI)**. The ARR is a ratio of the accounting profit to the investment in the project, expressed as a percentage.

The *decision rule* is that if the ARR is greater than, or equal to, a hurdle rate then accept the project.

This ratio can be calculated in a number of ways but the most popular approach is to take profit after the deduction of depreciation. For the investment figure we regard any increases in working capital as adding to the investment required. Three alternative versions of ARR are calculated for Timewarp plc which give markedly different results (*see* Worked example 4.1). Note: these are just three of all the possible ways of calculating ARR – there are many more.

Worked example 4.1 Timewarp plc

Timewarp is to invest £30,000 in machinery for a project which has a life of three years. The machinery will have a zero scrap value and will be depreciated on a straight-line basis.

Accounting rate of return, version 1 (annual basis)

$$\text{ARR} = \frac{\text{Profit for the year}}{\text{Asset book value at start of year}} \times 100$$

Time (year)	1 £	2 £	3 £
Profit before depreciation	15,000	15,000	15,000
Less depreciation	10,000	10,000	10,000
Profit after depreciation	5,000	5,000	5,000
Value of asset (book value)			
Start of year	30,000	20,000	10,000
End of year	20,000	10,000	0

Accounting rate of return	$\frac{5,000}{30,000} = 16.67\%$	$\frac{5,000}{20,000} = 25\%$	$\frac{5,000}{10,000} = 50\%$

On average the ARR is: $1/3 \times (16.67 + 25 + 50)\% = 30.55\%$.
Note the illusion of an annual rise in profitability despite profits remaining constant year on year.

Accounting rate of return, version 2 (total investment basis)

$$\text{ARR} = \frac{\text{Average annual profit}}{\text{Initial capital invested}} \times 100$$

$$\text{ARR} = \frac{(5,000 + 5,000 + 5,000)/3}{30,000} \times 100 = 16.67\%$$

Accounting rate of return, version 3 (average investment basis)

$$\text{ARR} = \frac{\text{Average annual profit}}{\text{Average capital invested}} \times 100$$

$$\text{Average capital invested:} \frac{30,000}{2} = 15,000$$

(At time 0 the machinery has a value of £30,000, three years later it has a value of zero. If we assume constant devaluation then the average value of the machinery is £15,000.)

$$\text{ARR} = \frac{(5,000 + 5,000 + 5,000)/3}{15,000} \times 100 = 33.33\%$$

If we now make the example slightly more sophisticated by assuming that the machinery has a scrap value of £8,000 at the end of year 3, then the average capital invested figure becomes:

0.5 (initial outlay + scrap value)
0.5 (30,000 + 8,000) = 19,000

The profit figures also change.

	Year 1 £	Year 2 £	Year 3 £
Profit before depreciation	15,000	15,000	15,000
Depreciation	7,333	7,333	7,333
Profit after depreciation	7,667	7,667	7,667

The ARR (version 3) is: $\dfrac{7,667}{19,000} \times 100 = 40.35\%$

Drawbacks of accounting rate of return

The number of alternative ARR calculations can be continued beyond the three possibilities described in Worked example 4.1. Each alternative would be a legitimate variant and would find favour with some managers and accountants. The almost wide-open field for selecting profit and asset definitions is a major weakness of ARR. This flexibility may tempt decision makers to abuse the technique to suit their purposes. Secondly, as explained in Chapter 3, the inflow and outflow of cash should be the focus of investment analysis appraisals. Profit figures are very poor substitutes for cash flow. The most important criticism of accounting rate of return is that it fails to take account of the time value of money. There is no allowance for the fact that cash received in year 1 is more valuable than an identical sum received in year 3. Also there is a high degree of arbitrariness in defining the cut-off or hurdle rate. There is no reason for selecting 10, 15 or 20 per cent as an acceptable ARR. This arbitrariness contrasts with NPV, which has a sound theoretical base to its decision rule: accept if the project's cash flows deliver more than the finance provider's opportunity cost of capital.

Accounting rate of return can lead to some perverse decisions. For example, suppose that Timewarp use the second version, the total investment ARR, with a hurdle rate of 15 per cent, and the appraisal team discover that the machinery will in fact generate an additional profit of £1,000 in a fourth year. Common sense suggests that if all other factors remain constant this new situation is better than the old one, and yet the ARR declines to below the threshold level (15 per cent) because the profits are averaged over four years rather than three and the project is therefore rejected.

The original situation is:

$$\text{ARR} = \frac{(5,000 + 5,000 + 5,000)/3}{30,000} = 16.67\%. \text{ Accepted}$$

The new situation is:

$$\text{ARR} = \frac{(5,000 + 5,000 + 5,000 + 1,000)/4}{30,000} = 13.33\%. \text{ Rejected}$$

An alternative way of viewing this problem is to think of two projects that are identical except that one offers the additional £1,000. If only one project can be accepted, which will the managers go for? If they are motivated by ARR (e.g. by bonuses related to ARR achieved) they may be inclined to accept the project that offers the higher ARR even if this means sacrificing £1,000 of shareholders' money.

Reasons for the continued use of accounting rate of returns

Exhibit 4.2 showed that over one-half of large firms calculate ARR when appraising projects and so the conclusion must be that, in the practical world of business, some merit is seen in this technique. One possible explanation is that managers are familiar with this ancient and extensively used profitability measure. The financial press regularly report accounting rates of return. Divisional performance is often judged on a profit-to-assets-employed ratio. Indeed, the entire firm is often analysed and management evaluated on this ratio. Because performance is measured in this way, managers have a natural bias towards using it in appraising future projects. Conflicting signals are sometimes sent to managers controlling a division. They are expected to use a discounted cash flow approach for investment decisions, but find that their performance is being monitored on a profit-to-investment ratio basis. This dichotomy may produce a resistance to proposed projects which produce low returns in the early years and thus report a low ARR to head office. This may result in excellent long-term opportunities being missed. (Some additional reasons for the continued use of ARR and payback are given in the Arnold and Hatzopoulos (2000) paper.)

Exhibit 4.6 illustrates what can happen if too much emphasis is placed on accounting numbers.

Exhibit 4.6

More EU lunacy

By John Plender

Mrs Loyola de Palacio, the European Union's transport commissioner, complains bitterly that the International Accounting Standards Board and the European Financial Reporting Advisory Group pose a threat to the development of Europe's infrastructure. They are, she believes, too academic in dealing with the time gap between the vast negative cash flow incurred during construction and the subsequent revenue build-up.

The fear is that enormous accounting losses will have to be recognised in the early years of projects,

while in the later years 'exaggerated' profits will appear.

The laughable assumption underlying this latest attempt by the European Commission to subvert standard setting in accountancy is that entrepreneurs and financial institutions are incapable of doing **net present value** calculations. So to recognise what she calls the reality of 'the construction sector' Mrs de Palacio wants the accountants to distort economic reality and cook the books.

 Financial Times, 8 November 2004, p. 22.

Internal rate of return: reasons for continued popularity

Exhibit 4.2 showed that firms use IRR as much as the theoretically superior NPV. Given the problems associated with IRR described in Chapter 2, this may seem strange. It is all the more perplexing if one considers that IRR is often more difficult to calculate manually than NPV (although, with modern computer programs, the computational difficulties virtually disappear). Some possible explanations follow.

- *Psychological* Managers are familiar with expressing financial data in the form of a percentage. It is intuitively easier to grasp what is meant by an IRR of 15 per cent than, say, an NPV of £2,000.

- *IRR can be calculated without knowledge of the required rate of return* Making a decision using the IRR involves two separate stages. Stage 1 involves gathering data and then computing the IRR. Stage 2 requires comparing this with the cut-off rate. By contrast, it is not possible to calculate NPV without knowing the required rate of return. The proposal has to be analysed in one stage only. In a large company it is possible for senior managers to request that profit centres and

divisions appraise projects on the basis of their IRRs, while refusing to communicate in advance the rate of return required. This has at least two potential advantages. First, the required rate may change over time and it becomes a simple matter of changing the cut-off comparison rate at head office once the IRR computations are received from lower down the organisation. With NPV, each project's cash flows would need to be calculated again at the new discount rate. Secondly, managers are only human and there is a tendency to bias information passed upwards so as to achieve their personal goals. For instance, it has been known for ambitious managers to be excessively optimistic concerning the prospects for projects that would lead to an expansion of their domain. If they are provided with a cut-off rate prior to evaluating projects you can be sure that all projects they sponsor will have cash flows 'forecasted' to produce a return greater than the target. If the head office team choose not to communicate a cut-off rate, this leaves them free to adjust the required return to allow for factors such as over-optimism. They may also adjust the minimum rate of return for perceived risk associated with particular projects or divisions.

- *Ranking* Some managers are not familiar with the drawbacks of IRR and believe that ranking projects to select between them is most accurately and most easily carried out using the percentage-based IRR method. This was, in Chapter 2, shown not to be the case.

The managerial 'art' of investment appraisal

This book places strong emphasis on the formal methods of project appraisal, so a word of warning is necessary at this point. Mathematical technique is merely one element needed for successful project appraisal. The quantitative analysis is only the starting point for decision making. In most real-world situations there are many qualitative factors which need to be taken into account. The techniques described in Chapters 2 and 3 cannot be used in a mechanical fashion. Management is largely an art form with a few useful quantitative techniques to improve the quality of the art. For instance, in generating and evaluating major investments the firm has to take into account:

- *Strategy* The relationship between the proposed project and the strategic direction of the firm is very important. A business-unit investment isolated from the main thrust of the firm may be a distraction in terms of managerial attention and financial resources. A project that looks good at divisional level may not be appropriate when examined from the whole-firm perspective. It may even be contradictory to the firm's goals. For example, luxury goods companies are sometimes enticed to produce lower-priced items for the mass market or to stretch the brand into unrelated areas. The project, when judged on its own, appears to have a very high NPV. But there is the danger of losing the premium brand (expensive and exclusive) strategic position in the existing product ranges by association with something that does not quite fit the image the firm has nurtured.

- *Social context* The effect on individuals is a crucial consideration. Projects require people to implement them. Their enthusiasm and commitment will be of central importance. Neglecting this factor may lead to resentment and even sabotage. Discussion and consensus on major project proposals may matter more than selecting the mathematically correct option. In many cases, quantitative techniques are avoided because they are precise. It is safer to sponsor a project in a non-quantified or judgemental way at an early stage in its development. If, as a result of discussion with colleagues and superiors, the idea becomes more generally accepted and it fits into the pervading view on the firm's policy and strategy, the figures are presented in a report. Note here the order of actions. First, general acceptance. Second, quantification. A proposal is usually discussed at progressively higher levels of management before it is 'firmed up' into a project report. One reason for this is that continuing commitment and support from many people will be needed if the project is to succeed. In order to engender support and to improve the final report it is necessary to start the process in a rather vague way, making room for modifications in the light of suggestions. Some of these suggestions will be motivated by shareholder wealth considerations, others will be motivated by goals closer to the hearts of key individuals. Allowing adaptability in project development also means that if circumstances change, say, in the competitive environment, the final formal appraisal takes account of this. The sponsor or promoter of a capital investment has to be aware of, and to adjust for, social sub-systems within the organisation (see Ekanem (2005) for eight case studies showing the importance of social context).

- *Expense* Sophisticated project evaluation can cost a considerable amount of money. The financial experts' input is costly enough, but the firm also has to consider the time and trouble managers throughout the organisation might have to devote to provide good-quality data and make their contribution to the debate. In a firm of limited resources it may be more efficient to search for projects at an informal or judgement level, thus generating a multitude of alternative avenues for growth, rather than to analyse a few in greater quantitative depth.

- *Stifling the entrepreneurial spirit* Excessive emphasis on formal evaluatory systems may be demotivating to individuals who thrive on free thinking, fast decision making and action. The relative weights given to formal approaches and entrepreneurialism will depend on the context, such as the pace of change in the marketplace.

 A leading businessman describes the problems arising from overemphasis on accounting [or should that be finance?] numbers – *see* Exhibit 4.7.

Exhibit 4.7

Entrepreneur fires broad attack

By Peter Marsh

British manufacturers have failed to invest enough in marketing and given too much management control to accountants, according to Edward Atkin, one of the country's most successful engineering entrepreneurs of the past decade.

Until recently Mr Atkin was the managing director and majority owner of Avent, one of the world's biggest makers of babies' bottles.

He sold Avent to a venture capital company for £300m, of which £225m (minus advisers' fees) came to Mr Atkin and his family. The entrepreneur is now weighing up several ideas about ways in which to invest some of the cash in innovative businesses.

In a speech to the Institution of Electrical Engineers Mr Atkin will say that most successful manufacturers require a stable investment climate and an interest in making world beating products.

These factors are more likely to be in place if the businesses are owned privately, and also have people with an interest in engineering at the helm, rather than accountants.

'As soon as financial criteria become the main method used for evaluating investment opportunities, the company is almost certainly doomed,' Mr Atkin will say.

'It is impossible to forecast variables like volumes, competitive pricing, raw material costs, interest rates or currencies three or five years out,' Mr Atkin will say. 'What is very easy, however, is to appreciate that speeding up a process, reducing waste, eliminating direct labour and improving tolerances and reliability will enhance both the products and their manufacturer, as well as the experience of the end-user. These benefits will be long-term and valid, irrespective of the output, exchange rate, raw material costs and all the other variables.'

Successful manufacturers such as US semiconductor maker Intel, and BMW and Toyota, two of the world's biggest car producers, have made as a centre of their businesses 'an unbroken trend of consistent [product] development, decade after decade.'

This is a culture, Mr Atkin will say, that makes it relatively easy to build up strong teams of engineering and marketing experts within the company that will stay for long periods. It also makes it easier to establish long-term brand loyalty.

- *Intangible benefits* Frequently, many of the most important benefits that flow from an investment are difficult to measure in money terms. Improving customer satisfaction through better service, quality or image may lead to enhanced revenues, but it is often difficult to state precisely the quantity of the increased revenue flow. For example, new technology often provides a number of intangible benefits, such as reduced time needed to switch machine tools to the production of other products, thereby reducing risk in fluctuating markets, or a quicker response to customer choice. These non-quantifiable benefits can amount to a higher value than the more obvious tangible benefits (see Alkaraan and Northcott (2006) for a survey of just how important

these factors are for UK firms). An example of how intangible benefits could be allowed for in project appraisal is shown through the example of Crowther Precision plc.

Worked example 4.2 Crowther Precision plc

Crowther Precision plc produces metal parts for the car industry, with machinery that is now more than 20 years old. With appropriate maintenance these machines could continue producing indefinitely. However, developments in the machine tool industry have led to the creation of computer-controlled multi-use machines. Crowther is considering the purchase of the Z200 which would provide both quantifiable and non-quantifiable benefits over the old machine. The Z200 costs £1.2m but would be expected to last indefinitely if maintenance expenditure were increased by £20,000 every year forever.

The quantifiable benefits are:

(a) reduced raw material requirements, due to lower wastage, amounting to £35,000 in each future year;
(b) labour cost savings of £80,000 in each future year.

These quantifiable benefits are analysed using the NPV method (*see* Exhibit 4.8).

Exhibit 4.8 Incremental net present value analysis of Z200

		Present value £
Purchase of machine		−1,200,000
Present value of raw material saving	$\dfrac{35,000}{0.1}$	+350,000
Present value of labour saving	$\dfrac{80,000}{0.1}$	+800,000
Less present value of increased maintenance costs	$\dfrac{20,000}{0.1}$	−200,000
Net present value		−250,000

Note: Assume discount rate of 10 per cent, all cash flows arise at the year ends, zero scrap value of old machine.

Examining the quantifiable elements in isolation will lead to a rejection of the project to buy the Z200. However, the non-quantifiable benefits are:

● reduced time required to switch the machine from producing one version of the car component to one of the other three versions Crowther presently produces;
● the ability to switch the machine over to completely new products in response to changed industry demands, or to take up, as yet unseen, market opportunities in the future;
● improved quality of output leading to greater customer satisfaction.

It is true that the discounted cash flow analysis has failed to take into account all the relevant factors, but this should not lead to its complete rejection. In cases where non-quantifiable elements are present, the problem needs to be separated into two stages.

1 Analyse those elements that are quantifiable using NPV.
2 If the NPV from Stage 1 is negative, then managerial judgement will be needed to subjectively assess the non-quantifiable benefits. If these are judged to be greater than the 'loss' signalled in Stage 1 then the project is viable. For Crowther, if the management team consider that the intangible benefits are worth more than £250,000 they should proceed with the purchase of the Z200.

This line of thought is continued in Chapter 6 (pp. 203–12), where operational and strategic decisions with options (real options) are considered. As the article in Exhibit 4.9 shows, the decision to commit to an investment means the loss of options. While reading it you might like to relate the ideas presented to Airbus's commitment to the A380 (case study 3.1 on page 93). It is committed, while Boeing has greater freedom to act.

Exhibit 4.9

Tyranny of time

By their very nature capital investment decisions threaten to place a straitjacket on companies. There is no easy way out.

By Peter Martin

When you make a capital investment decision, you freeze time. In fast-moving industries, this may be the most important aspect of the decision – more important than its actual content. But it is rarely assessed in this light.

There is any amount of theory about how to take capital investment decisions.

All such approaches assume that there are financial and easily quantifiable costs of taking the decision; and less measurable benefits to set against it. The techniques all revolve around ways of making imponderable future benefits more tangible. There is a reason for this: managers usually want to take investment decisions while their superiors usually do not. So the techniques are ever more elaborate ways of capturing the discounted value of blue sky.

But there are also intangible costs of taking the decision, and they are not given the attention they deserve. The cost of freezing time is one of the most important.

Here is how it works. When you make a big capital investment decision, it will usually take between 18 months and five years to bring the plant fully into operation. The cost of tying up capital for that time is reflected in the investment appraisal. But the broader implications of tying up the company are not.

When you have committed yourself to a big new plant, you have not just signed a cheque for the money. You have also sold your soul to this technology, on this scale, in this site. That is what freezing time means. Until the plant is complete, and it is clear whether it works and whether there is a market for its products, time stands still. For you, but not for your rivals.

They are free to react, to adjust technology, to play around with the pricing and volume. You are not. Unless you have built an implausibly flexible new plant, you are on a convergence course with a straitjacket.

Once your new plant is up and running, you can start to adjust the pattern of its output, and strive to reduce its costs. But until then, your options are more limited: press on, or give up.

The semiconductor industry illustrates this dilemma in a big way. In the mid-1990s, the UK looked like a good home for a bunch of new chip plants. Siemens, LG Group and Hyundai all targeted the British regions for big state-of-the-art factories. One of them – Siemens' factory on Tyneside – opened and promptly shut down again. The other two have never made it into production, and look more questionable by the moment: the Asian crisis undermined their parents and their markets simultaneously.

The decisions all three companies had to make were unenviable, because they were all or nothing. Technology had moved on while the plants were being prepared. Once the Siemens plant came into production, it was clear that it was the wrong plant, making the wrong sort of chip, in the wrong place.

So the company shut it down, at vast cost – only to invest another huge sum in a different plant to make different chips in France. For LG and Hyundai the moment of decision comes even before they have had the satisfaction of seeing their plants up and running.

The problem is not so much the risk that a plant's technology may prove inappropriate, or that its markets may not meet expectations: these are the

Exhibit 4.9 *(continued)*

normal risks of doing business in a capital intensive industry. It is more that the process of building the factory shuts out other alternatives, freezing the company's options and its internal clock.

What can companies do to avoid this risk? First, look for investment decisions that can be made piece by piece, and implemented quickly, minimising the freezing effect. Engineers usually hate this approach, because it means they are never designing plants at the cutting edge of the technology, or at maximum efficient scale. That's tough.

Second, once an investment has been approved, managers must resist the temptation to make the decision sacrosanct. It needs revisiting, in the light of changing technology and markets, just as much as plants that are already operating. This is a difficult balance to strike, because every big investment decision usually had to be made in the teeth of the

opposition of a faction that wanted something bigger, smaller, older, newer, or somewhere else. This group of dissidents will never be happy with the decision, and they may even be right.

Third, keep a close eye on the relationship between the product cycle time in your industry and the time it takes to get a new plant commissioned.

If the former is shrinking while the latter is lengthening – a common feature of any high-technology industry that has to cater to retail consumers – there will come a point at which the price of freezing time will outstrip the benefits of new plant.

If you cannot keep going by patching the old factory, it is time to think of some revolutionary new process that will replace one big capital investment decision with a lot of small ones. Or give up.

The investment process

There is a great deal more to a successful investment programme than simply project appraisal. As Exhibit 4.10 demonstrates, project appraisal is one of a number of stages in the investment process. The emphasis in the academic world on ever more sophistication in appraisal could be seriously misplaced. Attention paid to the evolution of investment ideas, their development and sifting may produce more practical returns. Marrying the evaluation of projects once screened with strategic, resource and human considerations may lead to avoidance of damaging decisions. Following through the implementation with a review of what went right, what went wrong, and why, may enable better decision making in the future.

Investment by a firm is a process often involving large numbers of individuals up and down an organisational hierarchy. It is a complex and infinitely adaptable process which is likely to differ from one organisation to another. However, we can identify some common threads.

Generation of ideas

A firm is more likely to founder because of a shortage of good investment ideas than because of poor methods of appraisal. A good investment planning process requires a continuous flow of ideas to regenerate the organisation through the exploitation of new opportunities. Thought needs to be given to the development of a system for the encouragement of idea generation and subsequent communication through the firm. Indeed, one of the central tasks of senior management is to nurture a culture of search for and sponsorship of ideas. In the absence of a well-functioning system, the danger remains that investment proposals only arise in a reactive manner. For example, a firm examines new product possibilities only when it is realised that the old product is becoming, or has become, obsolete. Or else the latest technology is installed in reaction to its adoption by a competitor. A system and culture is needed to help the firm 'get ahead of the game' and be proactive rather than reactive.

One of the main inputs into a more systematic search for ideas is likely to be an environment-scanning process. It is also helpful if all potential idea-generators are made aware of the general strategic direction of the firm and the constraints under which it operates. Idea-generators often become sponsors of their proposals within the organisation. These individuals, in a poorly operating system, can see themselves taking a high risk for very little reward. Their reputation and career

Exhibit 4.10 The investment process

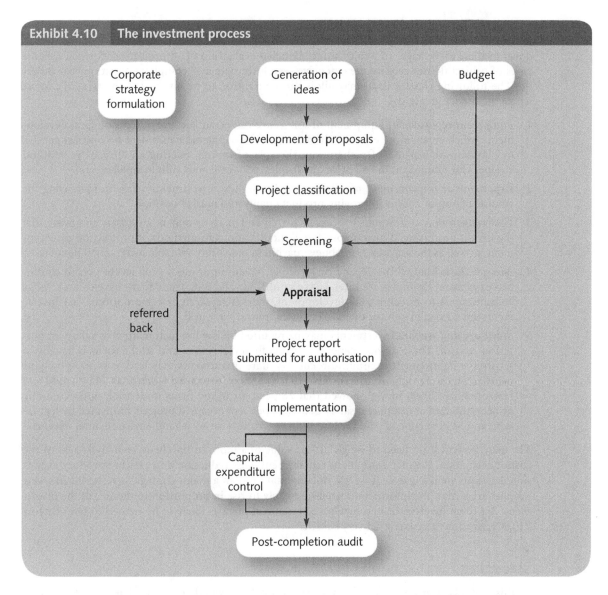

prospects can be intimately associated with a project. If it goes badly then they may find themselves blamed for that failure. In a system with such poor incentives the natural response of most people would be to hold back from suggesting ideas and pushing them through, and concentrate on day-to-day management. This defensive attitude could be bad for the organisation and it is therefore incumbent on senior management to develop reward systems that do not penalise project idea-generators and sponsors.

Development and classification

As the sponsor or the division-level team gather more data and refine estimates, some degree of early filtering takes place. Ideas that may have looked good in theory do not necessarily look so good when examined more closely. In a well-functioning system, idea generation should be propagated in an unstructured, almost random manner, but the development phase starts to impose some degree of order. Many firms like to have a bottom-up approach, with ideas coming from plant level and being reviewed by divisional management before being presented to senior management. At the development stage the sponsor elaborates and hones ideas in consultation with colleagues. The divisional managers may add ideas, ask for information and suggest alternative scenarios. There may also be division-level projects which need further consideration. As the discussions and data gathering progress the proposal generally starts to gain commitment from a number of people who become drawn in and involved.

The classification stage involves matching projects to identified needs. Initially, there may be a long list of imaginative project ideas or solutions to a specific problem, but this may be narrowed down in these early stages to two or three. Detailed evaluation of all projects is expensive. Some types of project do not require the extensive search for data and complex evaluation that others do. The following classification may allow more attention to be directed at the type of project where the need is greatest:

1 *Equipment replacement* Equipment obsolescence can occur because of technological developments which create more efficient alternatives, because the old equipment becomes expensive to maintain or because of a change in the cost of inputs, making an alternative method cheaper (for example, if the oil price quadruples, taxi firms may shift to smaller cars).

2 *Expansion or improvement of existing products* These investments relate to increasing the volume of output and/or improving product quality and market position.

3 *Cost reduction* A continuous process of search and analysis may be necessary to ensure that the firm is producing at lowest cost. Small modifications to methods of production or equipment, as well as the introduction of new machines, may bring valuable incremental benefits.

4 *New products* Many firms depend on a regular flow of innovatory products to permit continued expansion. Examples are Intel, GlaxoSmithKline and 3M. These firms have to make huge commitments to research and development, market research and promotion. Vast investments are needed in new production facilities around the world.

5 *Statutory and welfare* Investments may be required by law for such matters as safety, or pollution control. These do not, generally, give a financial return and so the focus is usually to satisfy the requirement at minimum cost. Welfare investments may lead to some intangible benefits which are difficult to quantify, such as a more contented workforce. The Arnold and Hatzopoulos (2000) survey showed that 78 per cent of the firms undertook non-economic projects directed at health and safety issues; 74 per cent accepted projects motivated by legislation; and 54 per cent had paid for uneconomic projects for social and environmental reasons.

The management team need to weigh up the value of a more comprehensive analysis against the cost of evaluation. Regular equipment replacement, cost reduction and existing product expansion decisions are likely to require less documentation than a major strategic investment in a new product area. Also, the information needs are likely to rise in proportion to the size of the investment. A £100m investment in a new pharmaceutical plant is likely to be treated differently to a £10,000 investment in a new delivery vehicle.

Screening

At this stage, each proposal will be assessed to establish whether it is sufficiently attractive to receive further attention through the application of sophisticated analysis. Screening decisions should be made with an awareness of the strategic direction of the firm and the limitations imposed by the financial, human and other resources available. There should also be a check on the technical feasibility of the proposal and some preliminary assessment of risk.

Strategy

Capital allocation is a pivotal part of the overall strategic process. A good investment appraisal system must mesh with the firm's long-term plan. The managers at plant or division level may not be able to see opportunities at a strategic level, such as the benefits of combining two divisions, or the necessity for business-unit divestment. Thus, the bottom-up flow of ideas for investment at plant level should complement the top-down strategic planning from the centre. Each vantage point has a valuable contribution to make.

Budget

Most large firms prepare capital budgets stretching over many years. Often a detailed budget for capital expenditure in the forthcoming year is set within the framework of an outline plan for the next

five years. Individual projects are required to conform to the corporate budget. However, the budget itself, at least in the long run, is heavily influenced by the availability of project proposals. The Arnold and Hatzopoulos (2000) survey shows the use of budgets by UK firms (*see* Exhibit 4.11).

Exhibit 4.11	Capital expenditure budgets for UK firms		
	Small firms %	Medium-sized firms %	Large firms %
Outline capital expenditure budgets are prepared for:			
1 year ahead	18	8	–
2 years ahead	18	25	13
3 years ahead	35	50	18
4 years ahead	9	–	5
More than 4 years ahead	21	13	61
Blank	–	4	3
Detailed capital expenditure budgets are prepared for:			
1 year ahead	70	79	55
2 years ahead	21	13	21
3 years ahead	9	4	8
4 years ahead	–	–	5
More than 4 years ahead		4	11

Note: 96 firms completed the survey questionnaire.

Source: Arnold and Hatzopoulos (2000).

Appraisal

It is at the appraisal stage that detailed cash flow forecasts are required as inputs to the more sophisticated evaluation methods, such as net present value. Manuals provide detailed checklists which help the project sponsor to ensure that all relevant costs and other factors have been considered. These manuals may explain how to calculate NPV and IRR and may also supply the firm's opportunity cost of capital. (If risk adjustment is made through the discount rate there may be more than one cost of capital and the sponsor then has to classify the project into, say, high-, medium- or low-risk categories – *see* Chapter 6.) The project promoter may seek the aid of specialists, such as engineers, accountants and economists, in the preparation of the formal analysis.

Report and authorisation

Many firms require that project proposals are presented in a specific manner through the use of **capital appropriation request forms**. Such forms will detail the nature of the project and the amount of finance needed, together with the forecasted cash inflows and the NPV, IRR, ARR and/ or payback. Some analysis of risk and a consideration of alternatives to the proposed course of action may also be required.

Expenditure below a threshold, say £100,000, will gain authorisation at division level, while that above the threshold will need approval at corporate level. At head office a committee consisting of the most senior officers (chairman, chief executive, finance director, etc.) will meet on a regular basis to consider major capital projects. Very few investment proposals are turned down by this committee, mainly because these project ideas will have already been through a number of stages of review and informal discussion up and down the organisation, and the obviously non-viable will have been eliminated. Also, even marginally profitable projects may get approval to give a vote of confidence to the sponsoring management team. The alternative of refusal may damage motivation and may cause loss of commitment to developing other projects. If the senior management had

had doubts about a proposal they would have influenced the sponsoring division(s) long before the proposal reached the final report stage. In most cases there is a long period of consultation between head office and division managers, and informal pressures to modify or drop proposals can be both more efficient and politically astute ways of proceeding than refusal at the last hurdle.

Implementation

Capital expenditure controls

Firms must keep track of investment projects so as to be quickly aware of delays and cost differences compared with the plan. When a project is authorised there is usually a specified schedule of expenditure, and the accountants and senior management will keep a watchful eye on cash outflows. During the installation, purchasing and construction phases, comparisons with original estimates will be made on a periodic basis. Divisions may be permitted to overspend by, say, 10 per cent before a formal request for more funds is required. A careful watch is also kept on any changes to the projected start and completion dates. Deviations from projected cash flows are often caused by the following two factors:

a inaccuracy in the original estimate, that is, the proposal report did not reflect reality perfectly;

b poor control of costs.

It is often difficult to isolate each of these elements. However, deviations need to be identified and explained as the project progresses. This may permit corrective action to be taken to avoid further overspending and may, in extreme circumstances, lead to the cancellation of the project.

Post-completion audit

Post-completion auditing is the monitoring and evaluation of the progress of a capital investment project through a comparison of the actual cash flows and other costs and benefits with those forecasted at the time of authorisation. Companies need a follow-up procedure which examines the performance of projects over a long timespan, stretching over many years. It is necessary to isolate and explain deviations from estimated values.

Exhibit 4.12 shows the extent of the use of post-competition audits by UK companies.

Exhibit 4.12	Replies to the question: 'Does your company conduct post-audits of major capital expenditure?'			
	Small %	Medium-sized %	Large %	Composite %
Always	41	17	24	28
Sometimes/on major projects	41	67	71	59
Rarely	12	17	5	10
Never	6	–	–	2

Note: 96 companies responded to the survey.

Source: Arnold and Hatzopoulos (2000).

There are three main reasons for carrying out a post-completion audit:

1 *Financial control mechanism* This monitoring process helps to identify problems and errors evident in a particular project. A comparison with the original projections establishes whether the benefits claimed prior to approval actually materialise. If a problem is encountered then modifications or abandonment may be possible before it is too late.

2 *Insight gained may be useful for future capital investment decisions* One benefit of auditing existing projects is that it might lead to the identification of failings in the capital investment process generally. It may be discovered that data collection systems are inadequate or that appraisal methods are poor. Regular post-completion auditing helps to develop better decision making. For instance, past appraisals may have paid scant regard to likely competitor reaction; once recognised this omission will be corrected for in all future evaluations.

3 *The psychological effect* If potential project sponsors are aware that implemented proposals are monitored and reviewed they may be encouraged to increase their forecasting accuracy. They may also be dissuaded from playing 'numbers games' with their project submission, designed to draw more resources to their divisions or pet schemes unjustifiably. In addition, they may take a keener interest in the implementation phase.

Senior managers must conduct a careful balancing act because the post-completion audit may encourage another sort of non-optimal behaviour. For instance, if middle managers are judged on the extent to which project outcomes exceed original estimates, there will be a tendency to deliberately understate the forecast. Also, if the audit is too inquisitorial, or if it too forcefully apportions blame for results which are only partially under the control of managers, then they may be inclined to suggest only relatively safe projects with predictable outcomes. This may result in a loss of opportunities. Ideally, regular post-completion reviews are needed, but many firms settle for an audit one year after the asset has been put in place. This may be inadequate for projects producing returns over many years. Some firms do manage an annual review of progress, and some even go as far as monthly monitoring during the first year followed by annual reviews thereafter. On the other hand, many projects involve only minor commitment of resources and are routine in nature. The need for post-completion auditing is not as pressing for these as it would be for strategic projects requiring major organisational resource commitment. Given the costs involved in the auditing process, many firms feel justified in being highly selective and auditing only a small proportion. Another reason for not carrying out a post-completion audit in all cases is the difficulty of disentangling the costs and benefits of a specific project in a context of widespread interaction and interdependence.

Exhibit 4.13 describes the attitude taken by the CEO of Roche to encouraging risk-taking and post-event judgement of the decision-takers.

Exhibit 4.13

A healthy attitude to risk-taking

By Andrew Jack and Haig Simonian

Since becoming chief executive of Roche in April, the 40-year-old Austrian Severin Schwan has been on a whirlwind tour to gauge for himself what is widely viewed as the world's most successful big pharmaceuticals company.

His career began in finance and continued through administration, including stints at foreign subsidiaries.

Mr Schwan stresses his suspicion of metrics and the importance of teamwork – both to define his management style and what Roche requires.

Collaboration is paramount for Roche. The group has a decentralised structure and a hands-off relationship with subsidiaries that analysts say has been a major contribution to its success. The federated structure has fostered focused research,

with each company concentrating on specific areas, but has also been supple enough for collaboration on marketing.

Development of Avastin, for example, the breakthrough cancer treatment discovered by Genentech, was accelerated by a division of labour between it and Roche, with each concentrating on different types of the disease.

Mr Schwan says such teamwork is essential in a knowledge-based business such as pharmaceuticals, where scientists need the freedom to think. 'When I toured our labs, I grasped the potential and the enthusiasm of our people. We have to capitalise on that. If you tell your people all the time what to do, don't be surprised if they don't come up with new ideas. Innovative people need air to breathe.'

Exhibit 4.7 *(continued)*

He accepts there has to be broad guidance too and makes clear that teamwork also requires results. 'Our culture of working together at Roche is based on mutual trust and teamwork. An informal, friendly manner supports this: at the same time, this must not lead to negligence or shoddy compromises – goals must be achieved and, at times, tough decisions have to be implemented.'

His strategic priority now as chief executive is to reinforce the co-operation between Roche's scientists involved in discovering new drugs and their counterparts in diagnostics.

He tried to encourage teamwork when still rising up the ladder in diagnostics. 'But such efforts were largely on a one-off project basis. After taking over diagnostics in 2006, I tried to do things more systematically. And, as chief executive of the group, I now want to do that more than ever.'

'This also has to do with encouraging people to take risks: innovation needs courage. And if something goes wrong, let's put the issue on the table, learn from it and resolve it together. In our sort of business, it's extremely important to be willing to celebrate failure.'

Celebrating failure may sound extraordinary coming from the chief executive of a company with SFr46.1bn (£22bn) in sales and SFr11.4bn in net profits. But Mr Schwan uses a recent example to illustrate his point. For much of last year, Roche was locked in a bitter legal dispute with its US rival Amgen over the intellectual property rights to their two competing drugs for anaemia associated with chronic kidney disease.

Roche's lawyers were convinced of the merits of their case and pushed the legal battle to the limits. In the end, a US court sided with Amgen, barring Roche's Mircera drug from the all important US market.

Mr Schwan did not admonish the lawyers for poor judgment: just the opposite. He cracked open the champagne, congratulating them for pursuing what they believed was the correct outcome. 'No one in group legal has been punished or censured,' he says.

'Risk aversion is typical of the culture of a big company. People believe they'll never advance by sticking their necks out. We want to develop a culture of encouraging risks to distinguish ourselves. We want quality, not quantity.'

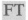 *Financial Times*, 4 August 2008, p. 14.

Concluding comments

The typical student of finance will spend a great deal of time trying to cope with problems presented in a mathematical form. This is necessary because these are often the most difficult aspects of the subject to absorb. However, readers should not be misled into thinking that complex computations are at the centre of project investment in the practical world of business. Managers are often either ignorant of the principles behind discounted cash flow techniques or choose to stress more traditional rule-of-thumb techniques, such as payback and accounting rate of return, because of their communicatory or other perceived advantages. These managers recognise that good investment decision making and implementation require attention to be paid to the social and psychological factors at work within an organisation. They also know that formal technical appraisal takes place only after a long process of idea creation and development in a suitably nurturing environment. There is also a long period of discussion and commitment forming, and continuous re-examination and refinement. The real art of management is in the process of project creation and selection and not in the technical appraisal stage.

Key points and concepts

- **Payback and ARR** are widely used methods of project appraisal, but discounted cash flow methods are the most popular.

- Most large firms use **more than one appraisal method**.

- **Payback** is the length of time for cumulated future cash inflows to equal an initial outflow. Projects are accepted if this time is below an agreed cut-off point.

▶

- **Payback has a few drawbacks:**
 - no allowance for the time value of money;
 - cash flows after the cut-off are ignored;
 - arbitrary selection of cut-off date.

- **Discounted payback** takes account of the time value of money.

- **Payback's attractions:**
 - it complements more sophisticated methods;
 - simple, and easy to use;
 - good for communication with non-specialists;
 - makes allowance for increased risk of more distant cash flows;
 - projects returning cash sooner are ranked higher. Thought to be useful when capital is in short supply.

- **Accounting rate of return** is the ratio of accounting profit to investment, expressed as a percentage.

- **Accounting rate of return has a few drawbacks:**
 - it can be calculated in a wide variety of ways;
 - profit is a poor substitute for cash flow;
 - no allowance for the time value of money;
 - arbitrary cut-off rate;
 - some perverse decisions can be made.

- **Accounting rate of return attractions:**
 - familiarity, ease of understanding and communication;
 - managers' performances are often judged using ARR and therefore they wish to select projects on the same basis.

- **Internal rate of return** is used more than NPV:
 - psychological preference for a percentage;
 - can be calculated without cost of capital;
 - thought (wrongly) to give a better ranking.

- **Mathematical technique is only one element** needed for successful project appraisal. Other factors to be taken into account are:
 - strategy;
 - social context;
 - expense;
 - entrepreneurial spirit;
 - intangible benefits.

- **The investment process** is more than appraisal. **It has many stages:**
 - generation of ideas;
 - development and classification;
 - screening;
 - appraisal;
 - report and authorisation;
 - implementation;
 - post-completion auditing.

References and further reading

Alkaraan, F. and Northcott, D. (2006) 'Strategic capital investment decision-making: a role for emergent analysis tools? A study of practice in large UK manufacturing companies', *British Accounting Review*, 38, pp. 149–73.
 As well as providing survey evidence on appraisal techniques used this paper considers the issue of using alternative techniques for strategies investments.

Arnold, G.C. and Hatzopoulos, P.D. (2000) 'The theory–practice gap in capital budgeting: evidence from the United Kingdom', *Journal of Business Finance and Accounting*, 27(5) and (6), June/July, pp. 603–26.
 Evidence of techniques used by UK firms, discussion of reasons for continued use of rule-of-thumb methods.

Arya, A., Fellingham, J.C. and Glover, J.C. (1998) 'Capital budgeting: some exceptions to the net present value rule', *Issues in Accounting Education*, 13(3), August, pp. 499–508.
 Discussion on the use of NPV.

Bierman, H. and Smidt, S. (2006) *The Capital Budgeting Decision*, 9th edn. London: Routledge.
Beginner's guide.

Bierman, H. and Smidt, S. (2006) *Advanced Capital Budgeting*. London: Routledge.
 For those who need more depth.

Boardman, C.M., Reinhard, W.J. and Celec, S.G. (1982) 'The role of the payback period in the theory and application of duration to capital budgeting', *Journal of Business Finance and Accounting*, 9(4), Winter, pp. 511–22.
 Payback critically assessed.

Bromwich, M. and Bhimani, A. (1991) 'Strategic investment appraisal', *Management Accounting*, March.
 Short article describing appraisal of non-quantifiable benefits of a project.

Brounen, D., de Jong, A. and Koedijk, K. (2004) 'Corporate finance in Europe: confronting theory with practice', *Financial Management*, Winter, pp. 71–101.
 A pan-European survey of the use of appraisal techniques – payback is still popular (unfortunately < 5 per cent surveyed replied).

Dixit, A.K. and Pindyck, R.S. (1994) *Investment Under Uncertainty*. Princeton, NJ: Princeton University Press.
 Higher-level discussion.

Ekanem, I. (2005) '"Bootstrapping": the investment decision-making process in small firms', *British Accounting Review*, 37, pp. 299–318.
 Describes how investment decisions are made in eight small firms – somewhat differently to textbook theory.

Emmanuel, C., Otley, D. and Merchant, K. (1990) *Accounting for Management Control*, 2nd edn. London: Chapman and Hall.
 An advanced accounting text that deals with investment appraisal.

Finnie, J. (1988) 'The role of financial appraisal in decisions to acquire advanced manufacturing technology', *Accounting and Business Research*, 18(70), pp. 133–9.
 Argues that better management of the appraisal process is required for projects using advanced manufacturing technology.

Fisher, F.M. and McGowan, J.I. (1983) 'On the misuse of accounting rates of return to infer monopoly profits', *American Economic Review*, 73, March, pp. 82–97.
 Highlights a number of problems with ARR.

Gadella, J.W. (1992), 'Post-project appraisal', *Management Accounting*. March, pp. 52 and 58.
 Post-completion auditing discussion.

Gordon, L.A. and Myers, M.D. (1991) 'Postauditing capital projects', *Management Accounting* (US), January, pp. 39–42.

Graham, J.R. and Harvey, C.R. (2001) 'The theory and practice of corporate finance: evidence from the field', *Journal of Financial Economics*, 60(2–3), May, pp. 187–243.
 Provides evidence of US corporate use of project appraisal techniques together with an easy-to-follow discussion.

Hajdasinski, M.M. (1993) 'The payback period as a measure of profitability and liquidity', *Engineering Economist*, 38(3), Spring, pp. 177–91.
 Payback's usefulness.

Hansen, H., Huhn, W., Legrand, O., Steiners, D. and Vahlenkamp, T. (2009) *Capex Excellence: Optimising fixed asset investing*. Chichester: John Wiley and Sons.
 McKinsey consultants' perspective on capital expenditure decisions. Easy to read with some food for thought, but I find the emphasis on return on invested capital rather than the DCF disturbing, as is their 'strategic analysis'.

Ho, S.M. and Pike, R.H. (1991) 'Risk analysis techniques in capital budgeting contexts', *Accounting and Business Research*, 21(83).
 Survey of 146 UK firms' project risk analysis practices.

Kaplan, R.S. (1986) 'Must CIM be justified by faith alone?', *Harvard Business Review*, March/April, pp. 87–95.
 DCF analysis applied to computer-integrated manufacturing projects – interesting application of principles.

Kaplan, R.S. and Atkinson, A.A. (1998) *Advanced Management Accounting*, International Edition. Englewood Cliffs, NJ: Prentice-Hall.
 Theory–practice gap explored.

Kay, J.A. (1976) 'Accountants, too, could be happy in a golden age: the accountant's rate of profit and the internal rate of return', *Oxford Economic Papers*, 28, pp. 447–60.
 A technical/mathematical consideration of the link between ARR and IRR.

Kee, R. and Bublitz, B. (1988) 'The role of payback in the investment process', *Accounting and Business Research*, 18(70), pp. 149–55.
 Value of payback discussed.

Kennedy, A. and Mills, R. (1990) *Post Completion Audit of Capital Expenditure Projects*. London: CIMA. Management Accounting Guide 9.
 Post-completion auditing evidence.

Kennedy, A. and Mills, R. (1992) 'Post completion auditing: a source of strategic direction?', *Management Accounting* (UK), May, pp. 26–8.
 Post-completion auditing evidence.

Kennedy, A. and Mills, R. (1993a) 'Post completion auditing in practice', *Management Accounting*, October, pp. 22–5.
 Post-completion auditing evidence.

Kennedy, A. and Mills, R. (1993b) 'Experiences in operating a post-audit system', *Management Accounting*, November.
 Post-completion auditing evidence.

Lawrence, A.G. and Myers, M.D. (1991) 'Post-auditing capital projects', *Management Accounting*, January, pp. 39–42.
 Survey of 282 large US firms' post-auditing objectives, method and thoroughness.

Lefley, F. (1997) 'The sometimes overlooked discounted payback method', *Management Accounting* (UK), November, p. 36.
 Payback's virtues.

Longmore, D.R. (1989) 'The persistence of the payback method: a time-adjusted decision rule perspective', *Engineering Economist*, 43(3), Spring, pp. 185–94.
 Payback's use.

Lowenstein, L. (1991) *Sense and Nonsense in Corporate Finance*. Reading, MA: Addison Wesley.
 Criticism of over-preciseness in project appraisal and the underplaying of unquantifiable elements.

Lumijärvi, O.P. (1991) 'Selling of capital investments to top management', *Management Accounting Research*, 2, pp. 171–88.
 Describes a real-world case of a lower-level manager influencing superiors so that desired investment funds are received.

McIntyre, A.D. and Coulthurst, N.J. (1986) *Capital Budgeting Practices in Medium-Sized Businesses – A Survey*. London: Institute of Cost and Management Accountants.
 Interesting survey of investment appraisal practices in UK medium-sized firms. More detailed than the later (1987) article.

McIntyre, A.D. and Coulthurst, N.J. (1987) 'Planning and control of capital investment in medium-sized UK companies', *Management Accounting*, March, pp. 39–40.
Interesting summary of empirical work explaining the capital budgeting processes in 141 medium-sized firms with turnovers in the range £1.4m–£5.75m.

Mills, R.W. and Herbert, P.J.A. (1987) 'Corporate and divisional influence in capital budgeting', Chartered Institute of Management Accountants, Occasional Paper Series.
Internal issues associated with capital budgeting.

Neale, B. and Holmes, D. (1988) 'Post-completion audits: the costs and benefits', *Management Accounting*, March, pp. 27–30.
Post-completion audits discussion.

Neale, C.W. and Holmes, D.E.A. (1988) 'Post-completion audits: the costs and benefits', *Management Accounting*, 66(3).
Benefits of post-completion auditing. Evidence from a survey of 384 UK and USA large firms.

Pike, R.H. (1982) *Capital Budgeting in the 1980s*. London: Chartered Institute of Management Accountants.
Clearly describes evidence on the capital investment practices of major British companies.

Pike, R.H. (1983) 'A review of recent trends in formal capital budgeting processes', *Accounting and Business Research*, Summer, pp. 201–8.
More evidence.

Pike, R.H. (1985) 'Owner–manager conflict and the role of payback', *Accounting and Business Research*, Winter, pp. 47–51.
Comparison of methods.

Pike, R.H. (1988) 'An empirical study of the adoption of sophisticated capital budgeting practices and decision-making effectiveness', *Accounting and Business Research*, 18(72), Autumn, pp. 341–51.
Observes the trend within 100 large UK firms over 11 years towards sophisticated methods – NPV, post-completion audits, probability analysis.

Pike, R.H. (1996) 'A longitudinal survey of capital budgeting practices', *Journal of Business Finance and Accounting*, 23(1), January.

Excellent, short and clear article surveying appraisal methods in UK large firms.

Pike, R.H. and Wolfe, M. (1988) *Capital Budgeting in the 1990s*. London: Chartered Institute of Management Accountants.
Some interesting evidence on appraisal methods used in practice. Clearly expressed.

Ross, S.A. (1995) 'Uses, abuses, and alternatives to the net-present-value rule', *Financial Management*, 24(3), Autumn, pp. 96–102.
Discussion of the value of NPV.

Sangster, A. (1993) 'Capital investment appraisal techniques: a survey of current usage', *Journal of Business Finance and Accounting*, 20(3), April, pp. 307–33.
Evidence of use.

Scapens, R.W., Sale, J.T. and Tikkas, P.A. (1982) *Financial Control of Divisional Capital Investment*. London: Institute of Cost and Management Accountants, Occasional Papers Series.
Good insight into the capital investment process in large UK and US companies.

Statman, M. and Sepe, J.F. (1984) 'Managerial incentive plans and the use of the payback method', *Journal of Business Finance and Accounting*, 11(1), Spring, pp. 61–5.
Payback's usefulness.

Steele, R. and Albright, C. (2004) 'Games managers play at budget time', *MIT Sloan Management Review*, Spring, pp. 81–4.
Executive game-play tactics revealed.

Tyrrall, D.E. (1998) 'Discounted cash flow: rational calculation or psychological crutch?', *Management Accounting* (UK), February, pp 46–8.
Discussion of theory–practice relationship.

Wooley, S. (2009) *Sources of Value: A practical guide to the art and science of valuation*. Cambridge University Press.
An easy to read introduction to traditional DCF, followed by distinct ideas on practical implementation.

Zimmerman, J.L. (2010) *Accounting for Decision Making and Control*, 7th edn. Boston: Irwin/McGraw-Hill.
Contains a useful discussion on discounted cash flow methods.

Case study recommendations

Please see www.pearsoned.co.uk/arnold for case study synopses.

- Twilight Acre Farms Limited. Authors: Mary Heisz and Stephen Rene Frey (2009). Richard Ivey School of Business Foundation. Available on Harvard Business School website.

- Target Corporation. Authors: Kenneth Eades, David Ding and Saul Yeaton (2008). Darden School of Business. Available on Harvard Business School website.

- Innocent Drinks. Authors: W.A. Sahlman and D. Heath, (November 2004) Harvard Business School.

- Super Project. Author: H.E. Wyman (May 2004) Harvard Business School.

Self-review questions

1 Payback is dismissed as unsound. Discuss.

2 Define accounting rate of return and compare it with net present value.

3 Describe discounted payback.

4 Do you believe the arguments for using IRR are strong enough to justify relying on this technique alone?

5 Why is investment project generation, selection and implementation closer to an art form than a science?

6 How would you appraise a project with a high proportion of non-quantifiable benefits?

7 If you were chief executive of a large corporation, how would you encourage project idea generation, communication and sponsorship?

8 Why is project screening necessary?

9 Invent five projects, each of which falls into a different project category.

10 Why are few projects rejected at the report stage?

11 When do capital expenditure controls and post-completion audits become an excessive burden, and when are they very important?

12 Comment on the following statement:

'The firm should choose the investment with a short payback rather than one with a larger net present value.'

Questions and problems

MyFinanceLab *Questions with an icon are also available for practice in MyFinanceLab with additional supporting resources.*

Answers to most questions can be found at www.pearsoned.co.uk/Arnold.
Answers to questions marked with an asterisk are to be found only in the Lecturer's Guide.

1 For the following projects, calculate the payback and the discounted payback.

Point in time (yearly intervals)	0 £	1 £	2 £	3 £	4 £	5 £	6 £	7 £
A	−3,000	500	500	500	500	500	500	500
B	−10,000	2,000	5,000	3,000	2,000	–	–	–
C	−15,000	5,000	4,000	4,000	5,000	10,000	–	–
D	−4,000	1,000	1,000	1,000	1,000	7,000	7,000	7,000
E	−8,000	500	500	500	2,000	5,000	10,000	–

The cost of capital is 12 per cent.

2 A project has a £10,000 initial investment and cash inflows of £3,334 per year over six years. What is the payback period? What will be the payback period if the receipts of £3,334 per year occur for only three years? Explain the significance of your answer.

3* (*Examination level*) Oakland plc is considering a major investment project. The initial outlay of £900,000 will, in subsequent years, be followed by positive cash flows, as shown below. (These occur on the anniversary dates.)

Year	1	2	3	4	5
Cash flow (£)	+50,000	+120,000	+350,000	+80,000	+800,000

After the end of the fifth year this business activity will cease and no more cash flows will be produced.

The initial £900,000 investment in plant and machinery is to be depreciated over the five-year life of the project using the straight-line method. These assets will have no value after Year 5.

The management judge that the cash inflows shown above are also an accurate estimation of the profit before depreciation for each of the years. They also believe that the appropriate discount rate to use for the firm's projects is 10 per cent per annum.

The board of directors are used to evaluating project proposals on the basis of a payback rule which requires that all investments achieve payback in four years.

As the newly appointed executive responsible for project appraisal you have been asked to assess this project using a number of different methods and to advise the board on the advantages and disadvantages of each. Do this in the following sequence.

(i) a Calculate the payback period.
 b Calculate the discounted payback period.
 c Calculate an accounting rate of return.
 d Calculate the internal rate of return.
 e Calculate the net present value.

(ii) Compare the relative theoretical and practical merits and demerits of each of the methods used.

 Assume: No tax or inflation.

4 A firm is considering investing in a project with the following cash flows:

Year	1	2	3	4	5	6	7	8
Net cash flow (£)	1,000	1,500	2,000	1,750	1,500	1,000	500	500

The initial investment is £6,250. The firm has a required rate of return of 10 per cent. Calculate:

a the payback period;
b the discounted payback;
c the net present value.

What are the main objections to the use of payback? Why does it remain a very popular method?

5 Maple plc is considering which of two mutually exclusive projects to accept, each with a five-year life. Project A requires an initial expenditure of £2,300,000 and is forecast to generate annual cash flows before depreciation of £800,000. The equipment purchased at time zero has an estimated residual value after five years of £300,000. Project B costs £660,000 for equipment at the start. This has a residual value of £60,000 after five years. Cash inflows before depreciation of £250,000 per annum are anticipated. The company has a straight-line depreciation policy and a cost of capital of 15 per cent (relevant for projects of this risk class). You can assume that the cash flows are also equal to the profits before depreciation. Calculate:

a an accounting rate of return;
b the net present value.

What are the disadvantages of using ARR?

6 Explain why empirical studies show that, in practice, firms often prefer to evaluate projects using traditional methods.

7 Camelia plc has been run in an autocratic style by the chief executive and main shareholder, Mr Linedraw, during its 40-year history. The company is now too large for Mr Linedraw to continue being involved in all decisions. As part of its reforms the firm intends to set up a structured programme of capital investment. You have been asked to compile a report which will guide management. This will detail the investment process and will not be confined to appraisal techniques.

8 'The making of good investment decisions is as much about understanding human psychology as it is about mathematics.' Explain this statement.

9 Explain how each of the following can lead to a sub-optimal investment process:

a relying on top-down idea generation;
b managers being judged solely on accounting rate of return;
c a requirement that projects have a quick payback;
d post-auditing once only, one year after completion;
e post-auditing conducted by managers from 'rival' divisions;
f over-optimism of project sponsors.

MyFinanceLab *Now retake your diagnostic test for Chapter 4 to check your progress and update your study plan.*

Assignment

Investigate the capital investment process in a firm you know well. Relate the stages and methods used to the process outlined in this chapter. Consider areas for improvement.

Visit www.pearsoned.co.uk/arnold to get access to Gradetracker diagnostic tests, podcasts, Excel spreadsheet solutions, *FT* articles, a flashcard revision tool, web links, a searchable glossary and more.

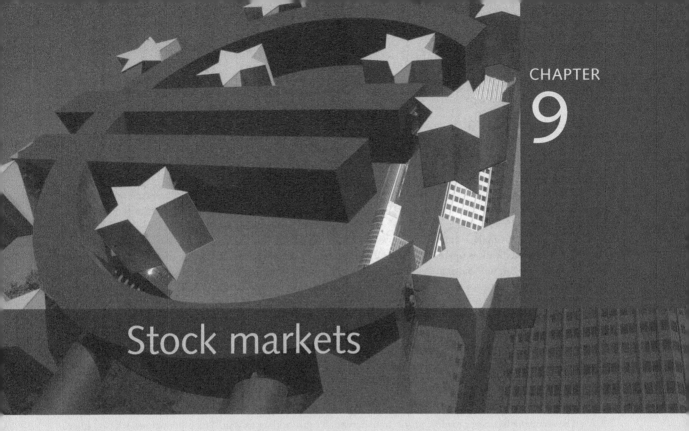

Stock markets

LEARNING OUTCOMES

An appreciation of the rationale and importance of a well-organised stock market in a sophisticated financial system is a necessary precursor to understanding what is going on in the world around us. To this end the reader, having read this chapter, will be able to:

■ describe the scale of stock market activity around the world and explain the reasons for the widespread adoption of stock exchanges as one of the foci for a market-based economy;

■ explain the functions of stock exchanges and the importance of an efficiently operated stock exchange;

■ give an account of the stock markets available to UK firms and describe alternative share trading systems;

■ demonstrate a grasp of the regulatory framework for the UK financial system;

■ be able to understand many of the financial terms expressed in the broadsheet newspapers (particularly the *Financial Times*);

■ outline the UK corporate taxation system.

MyFinanceLab *Complete your diagnostic test for Chapter 9 now to create your personal study plan*

Case study 9.1 Using the stock market both to create wealth and to treat disease

Oxford BioMedica

Alan and Sue Kingsman started an Oxford University-backed company called Oxford BioMedica in 1995. This company develops technologies to treat diseases including cancer, wet age-related muscular degeneration and Parkinson's disease. The aim is to replace faulty genes and target cancer cells.

Alan and Sue are biochemistry academics who lacked the finance needed for future research and development. They raised seed finance in June 1996 (small amounts of start-up money) and then raised £5.1bn by floating on the Alternative Investment Market (AIM) in December 1996. Later AIM shareholders bought another £23.6m of shares from the company which was then able to ramp up research.

Oxford BioMedica was upgraded to the Official List of the London Stock Exchange in April 2001 following a successful £35.5m fund-raising. In 2003 a further £20.4 million was raised through a rights issue (selling more shares to existing shareholders) followed by £30.1m in 2005. The company has a number of products in trial. TroVax® is an anti-cancer vaccine. It also has gene therapy approaches to Parkinson's disease (ProSavin®) and loss of eyesight (RetinoStat®). It is even testing a way of treating Motor Neurone Disease.

Oxford BioMedica's proprietary gene delivery system, called the LentiVector® platform technology, was invented initially through pioneering work at Oxford University and then through in-house development. Lentiviruses can deliver a significant amount of genetic information into cells very efficiently. Oxford BioMedica also works on the 5T4 tumour antigen, which is a unique protein found on most common types of solid cancer. The company raised £20m via a share placing and open offer in January 2011, bringing the total raised from outside investors to £137.3m.

The company has never made a profit, but shareholders are willing to wait. The potential rewards are huge, running into billions of pounds if successful treatments are created. The rewards to patients could be beyond price.

Sources: Based on various articles in the *Financial Times* and *Investors Chronicle*, and Oxford BioMedica's website.

Introduction

This chapter is concerned with the role and value of stock markets in the modern economy. It also looks more specifically at the workings of the London Stock Exchange. Imagine the difficulties Sue and Alan Kingsman would have getting their venture off the ground in a world without some form of market where long-term risk capital can be raised from investors, and where those investors are able to sell on their holdings to other risk takers whenever they wish. There would certainly be a much smaller pool of money made available to firms with brilliant ideas and society would be poorer.

Stock exchanges around the world

Stock exchanges are markets where government and industry can raise long-term capital and investors can buy and sell securities. Stock exchanges[1] grew in response to the demand for funds to finance investment and (especially in the early days) ventures in overseas trade. The risky sea-voyage trading businesses of the sixteenth, seventeenth and eighteenth centuries often required the raising of capital from large numbers of investors. Until the Napoleonic Wars the Dutch capital markets were pre-eminent, raising funds for investment abroad and loans for governments and businesses, and developing a thriving secondary market in which investors could sell their financial securities to other investors. This transferability of ownership of financial assets was an important breakthrough for the development of sophisticated financial systems. It offered the investor liquidity, which encouraged the flow of funds to firms, while leaving the capital in the business venture untouched.

1 Stock exchange and stock market will be used interchangeably. Bourse is an alternative word used particularly in Continental Europe.

The Napoleonic Wars led to a rapid rise in the volume of British government debt sold to the public. Trading in this debt tended to take place in coffee houses in London and other cities. Much of the early industrialisation was financed by individuals or partnerships, but as the capital requirements became larger it was clear that joint-stock enterprises were needed, in which the money of numerous investors was brought together to give joint ownership with the promise of a share of profits. Canal corporations, docks companies, manufacturing enterprises, railways and insurance companies were added to the list of firms with shares and bonds traded on the stock exchanges of Europe, America and a few places in Asia in the nineteenth century.

The second major breakthrough was the introduction of limited liability for shareholders in 1855.[2] This meant that the owners of shares were not responsible for the debts of the firm – once they had handed over the money to purchase the shares they could not be called on to contribute any further, regardless of the demands of creditors to a failed firm. This encouraged an even greater flow of funds into equity (ownership) capital and aided the spectacular rise of Victorian Britain as an economic powerhouse. Similar measures were taken in other European and North American countries to boost the flow of funds for investment. Outside the Western economies the value of limited liability and a stock exchange was quickly recognised – for example, Bombay and Johannesburg opened stock markets while still part of the British Empire.

Growth of stock markets

Stock markets have prospered and expanded globally. New markets have appeared in developing countries to join and rival the traditional stock markets. Exhibit 9.1 details the relative size of stock markets around the world according to the total market capitalisation (number of shares multiplied by share price) of the companies traded on them.

The world has changed dramatically in the last 30 years. Liberalisation towards greater free market capitalism and the accelerating wave of privatisation pushed stock markets to the forefront of developing countries' tools of economic progress. The strong ideological opposition to

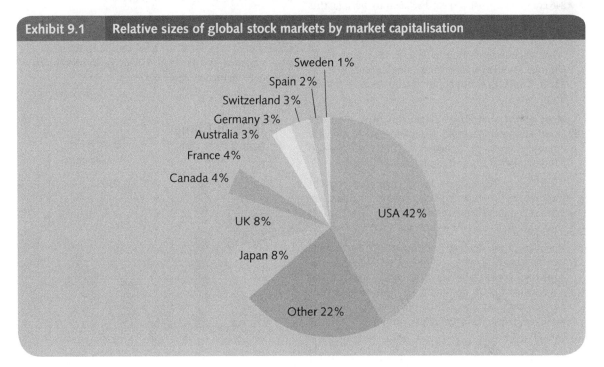

Exhibit 9.1 Relative sizes of global stock markets by market capitalisation

Source: from *Global Investment Returns Yearbook 2011*, Credit Suisse Research Institute (Dimson, E., Marsh, P. and Staunton, M. 2011) © Elroy Dimson, Paul Marsh and Mike Staunton.

2 The first limited liability law was introduced in the USA in 1811.

capitalism has been replaced with stock markets in Moscow, Warsaw and Sofia. Even countries which still espouse communism, such as China and Vietnam, now have thriving and increasingly influential stock exchanges designed to facilitate the mobilisation of capital and its employment in productive endeavour, with – 'horror of horrors' to some hard-line communists – a return going to the capital providers. Laos and Cambodia also joined the club of ex-communist countries with stock markets in 2011.

China has two thriving stock exchanges, in Shanghai and Shenzhen, with over 2000 companies listed. There are now tens of millions of Chinese investors who can only be properly described as 'capitalists' given that they put at risk their savings on the expectations of a reward on their capital. **Exhibit 9.2** describes the rivalry between China's two main markets. (Initial public offerings are when shares are sold for the first time on the market.)

Exhibit 9.2

Shenzhen takes over as China's listing hub

By Robert Cookson in Hong Kong

For years, Shanghai has been the undisputed king of China's equity markets, vitalised by a steady stream of initial public offerings from the country's biggest and best state-owned enterprises.

But this year Shanghai has been outgunned by Shenzhen, its less glamorous rival in the south of China, because of an extraordinary boom there in IPOs by The Shenzhen Stock Exchange has seen 246 companies raise a record $33.6bn by listings this year, triple last year's total and much more than the $24.1bn raised in Shanghai.

'This tells us something of epic proportions about China,' says Peter Fuhrman, chairman of China First Capital, a boutique investment bank in Shenzhen.

Most of the companies listing in Shenzhen are small and medium-sized groups owned by private entrepreneurs, as opposed to the state-owned behemoths that typically gravitate to Shanghai.

'Chinese policymakers have seen the central importance to the country's future of allowing private companies greater access to private flows of equity capital,' says Mr Fuhrman.

The China Securities Regulatory Commission, which controls stock market listings in the country, appears to have sharply accelerated approvals of IPOs in Shenzhen this year. Market participants say the CSRC has also become less involved in decisions about size, timing and pricing of share sales.

Shenzhen's IPO boom represents a substantial fresh source of capital for smaller private companies, which have typically been starved of

funds by a state-owned banking system that has preferred to lend to other organs of the government.

The bourse is also an increasingly attractive place for private equity groups to make lucrative exits from their investments in China.

Goldman Sachs made a near 200-fold profit on its original $5m investment in Hepalink, when the drugmaker listed in Shenzhen in April.

Shenzhen is still a relatively small part of China's financial system – the Rmb220bn ($33bn) raised by IPOs there this year is dwarfed by the Rmb6,000bn-plus in new loans that Chinese banks have extended during the same period.

IPOs in China
Amount raised ($bn)

Shanghai
Shenzhen

Year to date

Source: Dealogic

Importance of stock exchanges

Today the important contribution of stock exchanges to economic well-being is recognised from Uzbekistan to Uruguay. There are now over 140 countries with exchanges and many of these countries have more than one exchange. Many exchanges have been amalgamated with larger ones – the London Stock Exchange (LSE) merged with the Borsa Italiana in 2007; the NYSE merged in 2006 with the Euronext group, itself a merger of the Paris, Amsterdam, Brussels and Lisbon exchanges and in 2008 with the American Stock Exchange; the US market NASDAQ merged in 2007 with OMX, the Scandanavian and Baltic group of exchanges (Stockholm, Helsinki, Copenhagen and Iceland, and Estonia, Latvia, Lithuania and Armenia) and also with the Boston and Philadelphia exchanges, with the result that NASDAQ OMX is the largest US electronic exchange, listing over 2,700 companies in the US and another 778 in Europe. In addition to actual mergers, many stock exchanges have holdings in other exchanges or have mutual trading agreements. For instance, the Tokyo Stock Exchange has a 4.9 per cent shareholding in the Singapore exchange.

More mergers and alliances between exchanges are bound to follow, not least because the major financial institutions that operate across the globe desire a seamless, less costly way of trading shares over borders.

Exhibit 9.3 focuses on the share trading aspect of 20 of these markets, but most markets usually also trade bonds and other securities. Note the size and importance now of markets outside Europe and North America.

A comparison of the major markets

Until quite recently the LSE was the leading stock exchange in the world for trading shares in overseas companies and one of the biggest for the trading of domestic company shares. However, the electronic revolution and mergers have dramatically increased the market in foreign equity trading in the US, and NYSE Euronext and NASDAQ OMX now head the field in both foreign and domestic trading – see Exhibits 9.4 and 9.5. Looking only at domestic (home-grown companies') equity, China's domestic trading has shown a huge increase as it opens itself to capitalism.

Clearly, stock markets are regarded as an important element in the intricate lattice work of a modern and sophisticated society. Not only are they a vital meeting place for investors and a source of investment capital for businesses, they permit a more appropriate allocation of resources within society – that is, an optimum mix of goods and services produced to satisfy people.

Multilateral trading facilities (MTFs)

Traditional stock exchanges had virtual monopoly positions for the trading of shares and other securities in their home countries. They had little incentive to cut fees or to improve their trading technology. This resulted in the main users, institutional investment funds, banks, brokers and hedge funds, becoming frustrated with the raw deal they were getting.

Starting in the US in the early 2000s they determined that the national stock exchanges could do with some competition, so they got together, chipped in a few million for start-up costs and created new trading platforms. These were equipped with nimbler technology and required far fewer staff than the traditional exchanges. They had narrower differences between the price to buy (bid) and the price to sell (offer) a share, lower execution (transaction) costs, and the time between sending an order and the order being complete was much faster than the traditional exchanges. Not only did the institutions now have a cheaper way of trading shares but they could also use the presence of the new trading platforms to force the old exchanges to change their ways.

The Americans called these platforms **electronic communications networks (ECNs)**. They are also known as **multilateral trading facilities** (MTFs, a term more favoured in Europe) and they have certainly had an effect. As recently as 2003 about 80 per cent of the trading volume in the shares listed on the NYSE was handled by the NYSE itself. Today less than one-quarter of the trades go through the NYSE; the rest are traded through new trading systems, mostly MTFs including BATS, Direct Edge and ArcaEx. NYSE is not alone; NASDAQ has lost a lot of trade to the new venues as well.

| Exhibit 9.3 | The world's twenty largest stock exchanges at the end of 2010, ranked according to domestic market capitalisation of equities | | | | |

End of 2010	Domestic equities market capitalisation[1]	Total share trading in year	Number of listed companies		
	$ million	$ million	Total	Domestic	Foreign
NYSE Euronext (US element only)	13,394,082	17,795,600	2,317	1,799	518
NASDAQ OMX (US element only)	3,889,370	12,659,198	2,778	2,480	298
Tokyo SE Group	3,827,774	3,787,952	2,293	2,281	12
London SE Group	3,613,064	2,741,325	2,966	2,362	604
NYSE Euronext (Europe)	2,930,072	2,018,077	1,135	983	152
Shanghai SE	2,716,470	4,496,194	894	894	NA
Hong Kong Exchanges	2,711,316	1,496,433	1,413	1,396	17
TSX (TMX) Group (Canada)	2,170,433	1,368,954	3,741	3,654	87
Bombay SE	1,631,830	258,696	5,034	5,034	NA
National Stock Exchange India	1,596,625	801,017	1,552	1,551	1
BM&FBOVESPA (Brazil)	1,545,566	868,813	381	373	8
Australian SE	1,454,491	1,062,650	1,999	1,913	86
Deutsche Börse	1,429,719	1,628,496	765	690	75
Shenzhen SE	1,311,370	3,572,529	1,169	1,169	0
SIX Swiss Exchange	1,229,357	788,361	296	246	50
BME Spanish Exchanges	1,171,625	1,360,910	3,345	3,310	35
Korea Exchange	1,091,911	1,607,247	1,798	1,781	17
NASDAQ OMX Nordic Exchange (European element)	1,042,154	750,279	778	752	26
MICEX (Russia)	949,149	408,078	250	249	1
Johannesburg SE	925,007	340,025	397	352	45

[1] The total value, at market prices, of all issued shares of companies quoted on the stock market.

Sources: World Federation of Exchanges: www.worldexchanges.org.

| Exhibit 9.4 | Value of equity trading in foreign companies on stock exchanges in year |

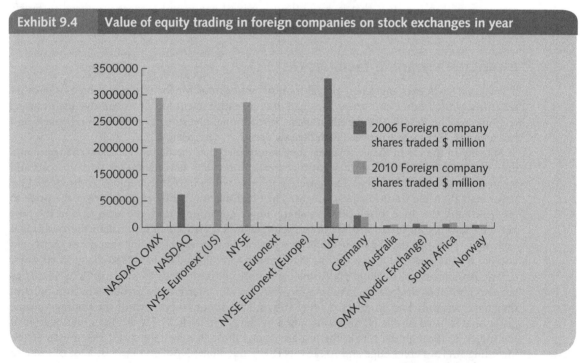

Source: World Federation of Exchanges.

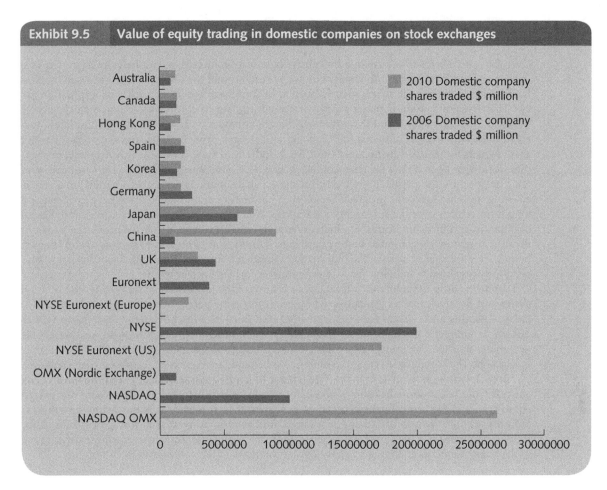

Exhibit 9.5 Value of equity trading in domestic companies on stock exchanges

Source: World Federation of Exchanges.

A major breakthrough in Europe occurred in November 2007, with the introduction of the EU's **Markets in Financial Instruments Directive (Mifid)**, which has the aim of providing a 'harmonised regulatory regime for investment services across the 30 member states of the European Economic Area.' The main objectives of the Directive are 'to increase competition and consumer protection in investment services'. Following this Directive, brokers acting on behalf of share (and other security) buyers and sellers must now demonstrate that they are achieving the keenest price and using the most efficient, cost-effective trading venues.[3] This encouraged the establishment of cheaper and faster electronic trading platforms to challenge the old ones. And, of course, European institutional investors were just as keen as their US counterparts to have alternatives to the national exchanges.

Traditional stock markets have lost a lot of trade to the new generation of European MTFs (such as BATS Europe, Chi-X and Turquoise). These trade the shares from companies quoted on a variety of national exchanges across Europe, and they are far less strictly regulated than stock markets. As recently as 2007 shares in the FTSE100 index were traded largely through the LSE. Today MTFs have taken around one-third share of continental European share trading and about half of trading in large UK companies' shares, causing a drop in volume of trading at the LSE and other traditional stock exchanges.

The proliferation of trading venues means that prices are increasingly being set for shares in a number of different places. In 2007, Rolls-Royce's shares were publicly traded in one place; now they are bought and sold on 14 platforms.[4]

3 'Best execution', a requirement of Mifid, of a trade means demonstrating that the broker obtained the best price, low cost of execution, speed and the likelihood of settlement of the trade going well.

4 For more on the consequences of the shift towards MTFs consult Arnold (2012a) Chapter 8.

Globalisation of financial flows

Over the last 20 years of the twentieth century there was an increasing emphasis on share (equity) finance and stock exchanges. An 'equity culture' spread around the world. Given that stock markets have been around for centuries, what happened in those years to spark such a widespread interest? The first explanation is that a greatly increased number of companies sought a stock market quotation for their shares and there were deliberate attempts by governments to stimulate interest in share ownership. Following the Thatcher and Reagan privatisations, and the push for wider share ownership in 1980s Britain and the USA, hundreds of state-owned or privately held companies worldwide floated their shares on stock exchanges. Governments the world over, regardless of their position on the political spectrum, promoted share markets and other financial markets as enabling tools for economic progress. Secondly, it became apparent that equities had provided good long-term returns over the first eighty years of the twentieth century – returns significantly ahead of inflation and those on bonds. So, increasingly, those with responsibility for providing pensions decades from now concentrated on buying shares. Thirdly, the 1980s and 1990s was one of the best periods ever for share returns. The bull market stimulated interest from millions of investors who previously preferred to hold less risky, lower-return securities, such as bonds.

Despite the drop-off in interest after the poor returns of the first decade of the twenty-first century, shares and the stock market remain very important for many people across the globe. In the USA, Japan, Australia and Canada for instance, about one-third of households now own shares (either directly or indirectly through mutual funds and pension funds). One-eighth of British households own shares directly. The equity culture has grown so strongly in Germany that over 12 million people hold shares. The Scandinavian countries and the Netherlands are even more 'equitised' than Germany.

Financial globalisation means the integration of capital markets throughout the world. The extent of the internationalisation of the equity markets is illustrated by the volume of foreign equity trades in the major financial centres (*see* Exhibit 9.4). It is evident in the fact that a substantial proportion of pension fund and insurance fund money is invested in foreign equities. Also, today a corporation is not limited to raising funds in a capital market where it is domiciled. Three of the major elements encouraging cross-border financial activity are shown in Exhibit 9.6.

Deregulation

The 1980s and 1990s was a period when government deregulation of financial markets was seen as a way of enabling financial and corporate entities to compete in the global marketplace and benefit consumers. The limits placed on the purchase and sale of foreign currency (**foreign exchange controls**) have been eliminated or lowered in most advanced economies. This has encouraged the flow of investment capital. Cartel-like arrangements for fixing the minimum commissions paid by investors for buying and selling shares have been eroded, as have the restrictions on ownership of

Exhibit 9.6 Globalisation of financial flows

Deregulation

Technology

Globalisation of financial flows

Institutionalisation

financial firms and brokers by foreigners. Now, more than ever, domestic securities can be purchased by individuals and institutional funds from another country. Commercial banks have found the barriers preventing participation in particular markets being demolished. Tax laws have been modified so as not to discourage the flow of funds across borders for investment, and the previously statutorily enforced 'single-activity' financial institutions (in which, for example, banks did banking, building societies did mortgage lending) have ventured into each others' markets, increasing competition and providing a better deal for the consumer.

Technology

The rapid transmission of vast quantities of financial information around the globe has transformed the efficiency of financial markets. Securities can be monitored, analysed and dealt in on hundreds of share, bond, commodity and derivative exchanges at the touch of a button from almost anywhere in the world. The combination of powerful computers and extensive telecommunication networks allows accelerated integration, bringing with it complex trading strategies and enormous daily capital flows.

Institutionalisation

Forty years ago most shares were owned by individuals. Today, the markets are dominated by financial institutions (pension funds, insurance companies, hedge funds, the 'mutual funds' such as unit and investment trusts and private equity funds (*see* Chapter 10)). Whereas the individual, as a shareholder, tended to be more parochial and to concentrate on national company shares, the institutions have sufficient knowledge and strength to seek out the rewards from overseas investments. They also appreciate the diversification benefits which accrue due to the low level of correlation of returns between some financial markets (*see* Chapter 7).

Why do companies list their shares on more than one exchange?

There are hundreds of companies which pay for the privilege of having their shares listed for trading on stock exchanges in other countries instead of, or as well as, on their local exchange. Exhibit 9.3 shows that the most popular secondary listings locations are the USA and the UK. There are also substantial numbers of foreign shares listed on most of the northern European exchanges, as well as on those of Canada, Australia, Japan, Mexico, Switzerland and Singapore. This dual or triple listing can be a costly business and the regulatory environment can be stringent so there must be some powerful motivating factors driving managers to globalise their investor base. Here are some reasons for listing abroad:

- ***To broaden the shareholder base*** By inviting a larger number of investors to subscribe for shares it may be possible to sell those shares for a higher price and thus raise capital more cheaply (that is, a lower return will be required per £ invested). *See* the case of Prudential (*see* Exhibit 9.7).

Exhibit 9.7

Pru accelerates its Hong Kong listing ahead of $20bn rights issue

By Paul J Davies, Insurance Correspondent

Prudential plans to list in Hong Kong ahead of its $20bn (£13.3bn) rights issue, in a surprise move that could encourage local investors to buy the life assurer's shares in support of its $35.5bn agreed deal to acquire AIA, AIG's Asian business.

Plenty of Asian investors, many of whom were being lined up for the initial public offering of AIA, are keen to invest in the combined group, said people familiar with the deal.

Exhibit 9.7 *(continued)*

A Hong Kong listing would make it easier for Asian investors to buy into the Pru ahead of its rights issue. The company is hoping that the listing will support its share price, which fell almost 14 per cent last week after news of the deal.

'While [the dual listing] does not offer instant additional liquidity, it does mean that any selling of the shares in London could be more easily taken up by finding new investors in Hong Kong,' said Marcus Barnard, analyst at Oriel Securities.

Asia has been the fastest-growing part of the Pru's business for several years and the AIA deal would see the region become the biggest contributor to the group's new business profits.

Additional reporting by Philip Stafford in London and Robert Cookson in Hong Kong

- *The domestic stock exchange is too small or the firm's growth is otherwise constrained* Some companies are so large relative to their domestic stock markets that they have no choice but to obtain equity finance from abroad. When Ashanti Goldfields, the Ghanaian gold-mining company, was privatised it was valued at about $1.7bn, which was more than ten times the capitalisation of the Accra stock market. A listing in London was a great success and the company expanded its activities in other African countries; it also listed in New York, Toronto, Zimbabwe, Ghana and London. Prada chose to list on the Hong Kong market where more money for growth was available (*see* Exhibit 9.8).

- *To reward employees* Many employees of foreign-owned firms are rewarded with shares in the parent company. If these shares are locally listed the share-ownership plans can be better managed and are more appealing to employees.

- *Investors in that particular market may understand the firm better* This point is illustrated with the case of Caparo (Exhibit 9.9). AIM is one of the markets organised by the London Stock Exchange.

- *To raise awareness of the company* For example, Standard Chartered listed on the Bombay Stock Exchange as well as London and Hong Kong to strengthen its brand (*see* Exhibit 9.10).

Exhibit 9.8

Prada draws up plans for Hong Kong IPO

By Rachel Sanderson in Milan

Prada, the Italian fashion group, is set to list on the Hong Kong stock exchange as early as May as it seeks to tap voracious Asian demand for luxury goods.

The decision by the group, which is majority owned by designer Miuccia Prada, her family and her chief executive husband Patrizio Bertelli, is a first for the European luxury goods and fashion industry.

It underlines Hong Kong's rising status as a destination for international listings. Analysts say that in a buoyant Hong Kong market, the whole group could be worth as much as €5bn–€6bn ($6.8bn-$8.2bn), whereas a listing in Milan, among the worst-performing markets in the past year, would have less chance of achieving that.

In a move that was closely watched by European luxury goods groups, L'Occitane, a French cosmetics and perfumery company, listed in Hong Kong last May as part of an Asian expansion strategy.

The company raised $704m in an offer that attracted strong demand from institutional investors. Its shares have since surged in value. Bernstein Research expects demand from Asia, outside of Japan, for bags, shoes and watches to drive luxury goods consumption until at least 2015. Prada has abandoned several attempted listings in Milan in the past decade, citing unfavourable market conditions and gaining a reputation in the process for volatility.

Exhibit 9.9

Indian business opts for Aim

By David Blackwell

Aim is enjoying an Indian summer as companies from the sub-continent opt to join the junior market.

On Tuesday, Caparo Energy will become the third Indian company in a month to float on Aim.

Caparo, which has raised about £50m ($80m), is planning to develop a portfolio of wind farms. Investors include Blackrock and Henderson.

Ravi Kailas, chief executive, said the company had looked at raising the money from private equity groups, but London's institutional investors were aware of the Indian energy sector on Aim and a flotation on the junior market would leave other options open.

 Financial Times, 11 October 2010.

Exhibit 9.10

StanChart eyes 'small' listings in China and India

By Sharlene Goff, Retail Banking Correspondent

Standard Chartered, the Asia-focused bank, is targeting stock market listings in Mumbai and Shanghai as it seeks to strengthen its brand in key local markets.

Peter Sands, chief executive, said a listing in India could be launched in the first half of next year, while plans for a listing in China were less advanced.

Speaking to the Financial Times following the bank's trading update, Mr Sands said: 'These two markets are incredibly important to us. We are actively pursuing a listing in India and how we could make it work effectively. Plans for China are at an earlier stage.'

He said the additional listings would be 'relatively small' and were 'not driven by the quantum of capital but what they would do to reinforce the profile and positioning of the bank'.

Mr Sands said he had no plans to relocate from London.

This differs to the strategy of HSBC, which is also primarily focused on Asia and recently decided to move its chief executive to Hong Kong.

Standard Chartered, which derives more than 90 per cent of earnings from Asia, Africa and the Middle East, is on track for record profits this year.

 Financial Times, 30 October 2009.

- *Discipline* Not only have Chinese companies seen the benefit of tapping capitalistic share capital, they have also been made aware of the managerial rigour demanded by stock markets and their investors. Many Russian companies have also listed in London to gain respectability through the enforcement by Western investors of good corporate governance and transparency of information (they have also listed in London to gain some protection against arbitrary actions by the Russian government).

- *To understand better the economic, social and industrial changes occurring in major product markets.* This is illustrated by the Toyota article (*see* Exhibit 9.11).

Exhibit 9.11

Toyota to list in New York and London

Toyota, Japan's third-largest company by market capitalisation, plans to list its shares in New York and London this month.

The issue is aimed at attracting international investors, meeting the needs of the increasingly global industry and boosting Toyota's image, said Yuji Araki, senior managing director.

The move is the latest in a series of global offers by Japanese companies, which are aimed at increasing the international element of their shareholder base . . .

Mr Araki said the company decided to list in New York and London not only to increase its investor base but also to be able to judge whether Toyota's performance met western standards.

'If they don't, we will have to change ourselves', he said.

Listing in the two cities would also help Toyota sense the changes in foreign stock markets more quickly and from those changes, the economic, social and industrial changes occurring in those markets, Mr Araki said.

Foreigners own a relatively low proportion of Toyota – just 8.8 per cent. But Mr Araki emphasised that the company had no fixed target for foreign shareholders . . .

In addition to New York, Toyota decided to list in London because 'in order to attract international investors it is essential to list in London', he added . . .

However, over the next two to three years, changes would be introduced in Japanese reporting requirements, which would bring them much closer to SEC standards, Mr Araki said.

FT Michiyo Nakamoto and Paul Abrahams, *Financial Times*, 8 September 1999, p. 26.

The importance of a well-run stock exchange

A well-run stock exchange has a number of characteristics. It is one where a 'fair game' takes place; that is, where it is not possible for some investors and fund raisers to benefit at the expense of other participants – all players are on 'a level playing field'. It is a market which is well regulated to avoid abuses, negligence and fraud in order to reassure investors who put their savings at risk. It is also one on which it is reasonably cheap to carry out transactions. In addition, a large number of buyers and sellers are likely to be needed for the efficient price setting of shares and to provide sufficient liquidity, allowing the investor to sell at any time without altering the market price. There are six main benefits of a well-run stock exchange.

1 Firms can find funds and grow

Because investors in financial securities with a stock market quotation are assured that they are, generally, able to sell their shares quickly, cheaply and with a reasonable degree of certainty about the price, they are willing to supply funds to firms at a lower cost than they would if selling was slow, or expensive, or the sale price was subject to much uncertainty. Thus stock markets encourage investment by mobilising savings. As well as stimulating the investment of domestic savings, stock markets can be useful for attracting foreign savings and for aiding the privatisation process.

2 Allocation of capital

One of the key economic problems for a nation is finding a mechanism for deciding what mixture of goods and services to produce. An extreme solution has been tried and shown to be lacking in sophistication – that of a **totalitarian directed economy** where bureaucratic diktat determines the exact quantity of each line of commodity produced. The alternative method favoured in most nations (for the majority of goods and services) is to let the market decide what will be produced and which firms will produce it.

An efficiently functioning stock market is able to assist this process through the flow of investment capital. If the stock market was poorly regulated and operated then the mis-pricing of shares and other financial securities could lead to society's scarce capital resources being put into sectors which are inappropriate given the objective of maximising economic well-being. If, for instance, the market priced the shares of a badly managed company in a declining industrial sector at a high level then that firm would find it relatively easy to sell shares and raise funds for further investment in its business or to take over other firms. This would deprive companies with better prospects and with a greater potential contribution to make to society of essential finance.

To take an extreme example: imagine the year is 1910 and on the stock market are some firms which manufacture horse-drawn carriages. There are also one or two young companies which have taken up the risky challenge of producing motor cars. Analysts will examine the prospects of the two types of enterprise before deciding which firms will get a warm reception when they ask for more capital in, say, a rights issue. The unfavoured firms will find their share prices falling as investors sell their shares, and will be unable to attract more savers' money. One way for the older firm to stay in business would be to shift resources within the firm to the production of those commodities for which consumer demand is on a rising trend.

More recently there has been a dramatic shift in finance resources as markets supplied hundreds of billions to high-technology industries, such as mobile phone chip technology, e.g. the Cambridge-based company, ARM plc, that designs and licenses 95 per cent of the world's chips for mobiles, or Skype in Internet telephony.

3 For shareholders

Shareholders benefit from the availability of a speedy, cheap secondary market if they want to sell. Not only do shareholders like to know that they can sell shares when they want to, they may simply want to know the value of their holdings even if they have no intention of selling at present. By contrast, an unquoted firm's shareholders often find it very difficult to assess the value of their holding.

Founders of firms may be particularly keen to obtain a quotation for their firms. This will enable them to diversify their assets by selling a proportion of their holdings. Also, venture capital firms which fund unquoted firms during their rapid growth phase often press the management to aim for a quotation to permit the venture capitalist to have the option of realising the gains made on the original investment, or simply to boost the value of their holding by making it more liquid.

4 Status and publicity

The public profile of a firm can be enhanced by being quoted on an exchange. Banks and other financial institutions generally have more confidence in a quoted firm and therefore are more likely to provide funds at a lower cost. Their confidence is raised because the company's activities are now subject to detailed scrutiny. The publicity surrounding the process of gaining a quotation may have a positive impact on the image of the firm in the eyes of customers, suppliers and employees and so may lead to a beneficial effect on their day-to-day business.

5 Mergers

Mergers can be facilitated better by a quotation. This is especially true if the payments offered to the target firm's shareholders for their holdings are shares in the acquiring firm. A quoted share has a value defined by the market, whereas shares in unquoted firms are difficult to assess.

The stock exchange also assists what is called 'the **market in managerial control**'. This is a mechanism in which teams of managers are seen as competing for control of corporate assets. Or, to put it more simply, mergers through the stock market permit the displacement of inefficient management with a more successful team. Thus, according to this line of reasoning, assets will be used more productively and society will be better off. This 'market in managerial control' is not as effective as is sometimes claimed (it tends to be over-emphasised by acquiring managers) (*see* Chapter 20 for further discussion).

6 Improves corporate behaviour

If a firm's shares are traded on an exchange, the directors may be encouraged to behave in a manner conducive to shareholders' interests. This is achieved through a number of pressure points. For example, to obtain a quotation on a reputable exchange, companies are required to disclose a far greater range and depth of information than is required by accounting standards or the Companies Acts. This information is then disseminated widely and can become the focus of much public and press comment. In addition, investment analysts ask for regular briefings from senior managers and continuously monitor the performance of firms. Before a company is admitted to the Stock Exchange the authorities insist on being assured that the management team are sufficiently competent and, if necessary, additional directors are appointed to supplement the board's range of knowledge and skills. Directors are required to consult shareholders on important decisions, such as mergers, when the firm is quoted. They also have to be very careful to release price-sensitive information in a timely and orderly fashion and they are strictly forbidden to use inside information to make a profit by buying or selling the firm's shares.

The London Stock Exchange

The London Stock Exchange (LSE) started in the coffee houses of eighteenth-century London where the buying and selling of shares in joint stock companies took place. In 1773 the volume of trade was sufficiently great for the brokers to open a subscription room in Threadneedle Street. They called the building the Stock Exchange.[5] During the nineteenth century, over twenty other stock exchanges were formed in the rapidly expanding industrial towns of Britain. They amalgamated in 1973 to become a unified Stock Exchange. All of the old trading floors of the regional exchanges and in London, where market members would meet face to face to exchange shares, are now obsolete. Today, there is no physical marketplace. The dealing rooms of the various finance houses are linked via telephone and computer, and trading takes place without physical contact. Having abandoned **floor trading** in 1986 the LSE found itself with an overly large building. In 2004 it finally moved within the City's square mile to Paternoster Square next to St Paul's Cathedral.

Securities traded

The volume of trade has expanded enormously in recent years. **Exhibit 9.12** indicates the types of securities sold on the Exchange. There are five types of *fixed-interest securities* traded in London: gilts, local authority bonds, foreign government bonds, sterling corporate bonds and Eurobonds. The government bond or 'gilts' market (lending to the UK government) is big, with a weekly turnover of over £90bn in 2011. In that year the UK government raised over £130bn through selling gilt-edged securities. Sterling bonds issued by companies (corporate bonds) comprise a relatively small market – just a few billion. Specialist securities, such as warrants and covered warrants, are normally bought and traded by a few investors who are particularly knowledgeable in investment matters. (Warrants are discussed in Chapter 10.) During 2011, 2317 new Eurobonds were listed in London by UK companies, raising a total of £196bn.

The Specialist Fund Market was launched in 2007. It creates a market in single strategy hedge funds, certain emerging market funds, specialist property and private equity funds for institutional investors (not for individuals, who may be less aware of the risks of investing in these funds).

There has been the rapid development of the **depositary receipt** market over the last ten years. These are certificates which can be bought and sold, which represent evidence of ownership of a company's shares held by a depositary. Thus, an Indian company's shares could be packaged in, say, groups of five by a depositary (usually a bank) which then sells a certificate representing the bundle of shares. The depositary receipt can be denominated in a currency other than the corporation's domestic currency and dividends can be received in the currency of the depositary receipt (say, pounds) rather than the currency of the original shares. These are attractive securities for histicated international investors because they may be more liquid and more easily traded than

5 It moved in 1801 to Capel Court and in 1972 to Throgmorton Street.

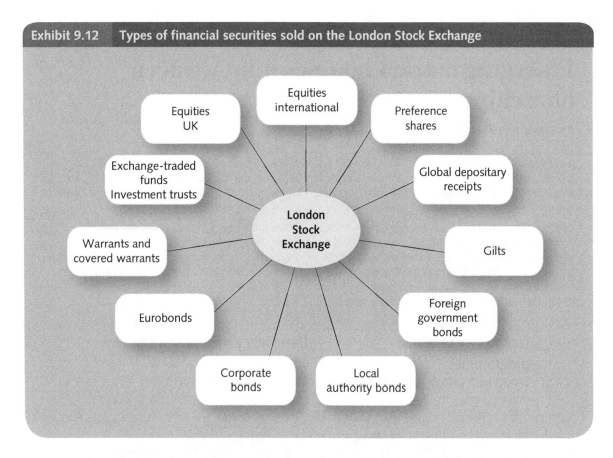

Exhibit 9.12 Types of financial securities sold on the London Stock Exchange

the underlying shares. They may also be used to avoid settlement (*see* later) or foreign exchange and foreign ownership difficulties (government restrictions on investment by foreigners) which may exist in the company's home market. From the company's point of view depositary receipts are attractive because they allow a market in the company's shares (even though they are wrapped up in a depositary receipt) permitting fund raising and the other benefits of a quotation on a regulated global capital market without the company needing to jump the regulatory hurdles necessary to join the Main Market (Official List) in London. DRs have been very useful as a means for companies in emerging countries (such as Kazakhstan, Brazil or India) to raise capital from the developed world's exchanges. However, emerging nations have developed to such an extent that they now have wealthy investors looking to invest in the developed world – *see* Exhibit 9.13.

Our main concern in this chapter is with the market in ordinary shares and it is to this we now turn. The London Stock Exchange is both a primary market and a secondary market. The primary market is where firms can raise new finance by selling shares to investors. The secondary market is where existing securities are sold by one investor to another.[6]

The primary market (equities)

Large sums of money flow from the savers in society via the Stock Exchange to firms wanting to invest and grow. In 2011 there were over 1,000 UK companies on the Main Market and over 80 UK companies on the techMARK (also run by the London Stock Exchange). There were also over 1,100 companies on the Exchange's market for smaller and younger companies, the Alternative Investment Market (AIM). In addition, there were over 300 foreign companies. During 2011, UK-listed firms raised new capital amounting to over £200bn by selling equity and fixed interest securities on the LSE. Included in this figure was £9bn raised by companies coming to the Stock

6 Confusion can arise here with the terms 'primary listing' (when a company's shares are traded on more than one market its primary listing is on its main market and it is subject to stringent regulations there) and 'secondary listing' where the shares are traded outside its main market.

Exhibit 9.13

Emerging market bourses hunt western blue chips

By Steve Johnson

A swathe of emerging market stock exchanges are lining up to launch depositary receipt programmes, allowing local investors to access foreign companies without leaving their home market.

The move would also ease the way for western companies to raise capital from increasingly wealthy emerging market investors, mirroring a trend that has seen emerging market companies raise almost $200bn (£125bn, €151bn) by launching American and (European-listed) global depositary receipts since 2005.

In May, Standard Chartered, the UK-headquartered but emerging market-focused bank, blazed a trail by listing the first Indian depositary receipt – raising $500m in the process.

Telefónica, the Spanish telecoms company, and Dufry Group, a Swiss retailer, have listed Brazilian depositary receipts, while a number of Indian companies have launched DRs in Singapore.

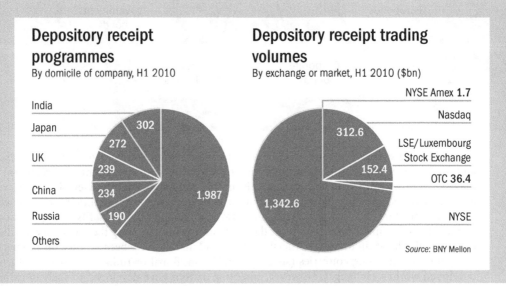

Depository receipt programmes
By domicile of company, H1 2010

India — 302
Japan — 272
UK — 239
China — 234
Russia — 190
Others — 1,987

Depository receipt trading volumes
By exchange or market, H1 2010 ($bn)

NYSE Amex **1.7**
Nasdaq — 312.6
LSE/Luxembourg Stock Exchange — 152.4
OTC **36.4**
NYSE — 1,342.6

Source: BNY Mellon

Exchange for the first time by selling shares. Companies already quoted on the Main Market (Official List of the LSE) sold a further £2.5bn of shares through events such as rights issues and other securities such as bonds. AIM companies sold £3.66bn of shares. UK companies also raised money by selling convertible bonds, debentures, loans and preference shares (*see* Chapters 10 and 11 for discussion on these securities and Exhibit 9.14 for a summary of the money raised by UK companies).

Each year there is great interest and excitement inside dozens of companies as they prepare for flotation. The year 2011 was a watershed year for 21 UK companies which joined the Main Market and 90 which joined AIM. The requirements for joining the Main Market are stringent. The listing particulars should give a complete picture of the company; its trading history, financial record, management and business prospects. It should (normally) have at least a three-year trading history and has to make at least 25 per cent of its ordinary shares publicly available (*see* Chapter 10 for more detail). Given the costs associated with gaining a listing, it may be surprising to find that the total value of the ordinary shares of the majority of quoted companies is less than £100m (*see* Exhibit 9.15).

Exhibit 9.14	Money raised by UK companies, 1999–2011							
	New companies issuing shares		Other issues of shares and other securities		Eurobonds		AIM	
	No. of Co.'s	Money raised (£m)	No. of issues	Money raised (£m)	No. of issues	Money raised (£m)	No. of new companies joining AIM	Money raised* (£m)
1999	106	5,353	893	9,917	1,022	85,515	102	934
2000	172	11,399	895	13,979	1,012	100,556	277	3,092
2001	113	6,922	866	14,824	935	83,342	177	1,128
2002	59	5,082	763	11,696	815	86,657	160	976
2003	32	2,445	618	4,920	1,096	118,755	162	2,095
2004	58	3,610	690	8,621	1,170	127,508	355	4,656
2005	86	6,078	772	8,099	1,099	148,309	519	8,942
2006	82	9,088	665	14,445	1,500	216,495	462	15,678
2007	73	7,613	477	8,995	2,025	165,924	284	16,184
2008	53	3,110	402	51,666	2,101	432,445	114	4,332
2009	17	458	378	73,907	1,858	254,571	36	5,602
2010	57	6,998	380	12,360	2096	184,465	102	6,958
2011	21	9,240	580	2,462	2,312	196,442	90	4,269

* Includes non-UK companies

Source: London Stock Exchange, www.londonstockexchange.com. Reproduced courtesy of London Stock Exchange plc.

Exhibit 9.15	Distribution of UK companies by equity market value at August 2011 for Main Market and TechMARK. The AIM numbers include non-UK companies

Source: www.londonstockexchange.com, statistics section. Reproduced courtesy of London Stock Exchange plc.

The LSE is clearly an important source of new finance for UK corporations and for companies around the world. However, it is not the most significant source. The most important source of funds is generally from within the firm itself (**internal finance**). This is the accumulated profits retained within the firm and not distributed as dividends. In an average year retained profits account for about one-half of the new funds for UK firms.

These retained earnings are also equity capital because this is money that belongs to shareholders – they have merely allowed companies to use it within the business rather than paying it out to

the owners. Thus the amount of equity capital devoted to a firm can grow to be worth millions of pounds largely through the retention of profits, despite the fact that it might have raised only a few thousands by selling shares to investors at its start. The sale of ordinary shares rarely accounts for a significant proportion of capital raised (it is usually less than 15 per cent of funds raised). Following retained earnings, bank loans are often very important for companies, but this does vary significantly. The sale of bonds and preference shares combined generally accounts for less than 5 per cent of new capital put into UK companies.

The secondary market in equities

The LSE operates and regulates a secondary market for the buying and selling of UK shares between investors in which an average of about 600,000 bargains, worth over £25bn, are completed in a typical day. In addition to these domestic equities a similar value of foreign shares were traded on a typical day. The secondary market turnover far exceeds the primary market sales. This high level of activity ensures a liquid market enabling shares to change ownership speedily, at low cost and without large movements in price – one of the main objectives of a well-run exchange.

The UK equity markets available to companies

The Main Market (Official List)

Companies wishing to be listed have to sign a **Listing Agreement** which commits directors to certain high standards of behaviour and levels of reporting to shareholders. This is a market for medium and large established firms with a reasonably long trading history. The costs of launching even a modest new issue runs into hundreds of thousands of pounds and therefore small companies are unable to justify a full main market listing. The regulations and the process of floating on the Main Market are discussed in Chapter 10.

The Alternative Investment Market (AIM)

There is a long-recognised need for equity capital by small, young companies which are unable to afford the costs of full Official listing. Many stock exchanges have **alternative equity markets** that set less stringent rules and regulations for joining or remaining quoted (often called '**second-tier markets**').

Lightly regulated or unregulated markets have a continuing dilemma. If the regulation is too lax scandals of fraud or incompetence will arise, damaging the image and credibility of the market, and thus reducing the flow of investor funds to companies. (This happened to the German market for small companies, **Neuer Markt**, which had to close in 2002 because of the loss in investor confidence.) On the other hand, if the market is too tightly regulated, with more company investigations, more information disclosure and a requirement for longer trading track records prior to flotation, the associated costs and inconvenience will deter many companies from seeking a quotation.

The driving philosophy behind **AIM** is to offer young and developing companies access to new sources of finance, while providing investors with the opportunity to buy and sell shares in a trading environment run, regulated and marketed by the LSE. Efforts are made to keep the costs down and make the rules as simple as possible. In contrast to the Main Market there is no requirement for AIM companies to be a minimum size, to have traded for a minimum period of three years or for a set proportion of their shares to be in public hands – if they wish to sell a mere 1 per cent or 5 per cent of the shares to outsiders then that is acceptable. They do not have to ensure that 25 per cent of the shares are in public hands (that is, not in the hands of dominant shareholders or connected persons). However, investors have some degree of reassurance about the quality of companies coming to the market. These firms have to appoint, and retain at all times, a nominated adviser and nominated broker. The **nominated adviser** ('**nomad**') is selected by the corporation from a Stock Exchange approved register. These advisers have demonstrated to the Exchange that they have sufficient experience and qualifications to act as a 'quality controller',

confirming to the LSE that the company has complied with the rules. Unlike with Official List companies there is no pre-vetting of admission documents by the UK Listing Authority (or the Exchange) as a lot of weight is placed on the nominated advisers' investigations and informed opinion about the company.

Nominated brokers have an important role to play in bringing buyers and sellers of shares together. Investors in the company are reassured that at least one broker is ready to trade or do its best to match up buyers and sellers. They also represent the firm to the Market (public relations). The adviser and broker are to be retained throughout the company's life on AIM. They have high reputations and it is regarded as a very bad sign if either of them abruptly refuses further association with a firm. AIM companies are also expected to comply with strict rules regarding the publication of price-sensitive information and the quality of annual and interim reports. Upon flotation an '**AIM admission document**' is required; this is similar to a prospectus required for companies floating on the Main Market, but less detailed (see Chapter 10). The admission documentation even goes so far as to state the directors' unspent convictions and all bankruptcies of companies where they were directors. The LSE charges companies an annual fee to maintain a quotation on AIM. If to this is added the cost of financial advisers, brokers and of management time spent communicating with institutions and investors the annual cost of being quoted on AIM runs into tens of thousands of pounds. This can be a deterrent for some companies.

However, there are cost savings compared with the Main Market. The flotation prospectus is less detailed and therefore cheaper. The annual expense of managing a quotation is less. For example AIM companies do not have to disclose as much information as companies on the Main Market. Price-sensitive information will have to be published but normally this will require only an electronic message from the adviser to the Exchange rather than a circular to shareholders. AIM companies are not bound by the Listing Rules administered by the UKLA but instead are subject to the AIM rules, written and administered by the LSE.

Note also that there are tax advantages for shareholders investing in AIM companies via venture capital trusts and the Enterprise Investment Scheme (*see* Chapter 10) or through the reduction in inheritance tax for some investors.

Offsetting the cost advantages AIM has over the Official List is the fact that the higher level of regulation and related enhanced image, prestige and security of Official List companies means that equity capital can usually be raised at a lower required rate of return (the shares can be sold for more per unit of projected profit).

AIM is not just a stepping-stone for companies planning to graduate to the Official List. It has many attractive features in its own right. Indeed, many Official List companies have moved to AIM in recent years.

techMARK

At the end of 1999, at the height of high technology fever, the London Stock Exchange launched a 'market-within-a-market' called **techMARK**. This is part of LSE's Main Market and is therefore technically not a separate market. It is a grouping of technology companies on the LSE. One of the reasons for its creation was that many companies lacking the minimum three-year account history required to join the Main Market had relatively high market values and desired the advantages of being on a prestigious market. The LSE relaxed its rule and permitted a listing if only one year of accounts is available for techMARK companies. This allowed investors to invest through a well-regulated exchange in companies at an early stage of development, such as Freeserve and lastminute.com. The LSE does insist that all companies joining techMARK have at least 25 per cent of their shares in a **free float** (in public hands).

PLUS–quoted shares

PLUS is a stock exchange based in London, and is used by companies that do not want to pay the costs of a flotation on one of the markets run by the LSE. Companies quoted on PLUS provide a service to their shareholders, allowing them to buy and sell shares at reasonable cost. It also allows the company to gain access to capital, for example by selling more shares in a rights issue, without

submitting to the rigour and expense of a quotation on the LSE. The downside is that trading in PLUS-quoted shares can be illiquid (not many buyers or sellers), with high dealing costs (bid/offer spreads – *see* later – are frequently 30–50 per cent).

PLUS (originally called Ofex) was set up by the broker J.P. Jenkins in 1995 and is owned by PLUS-Markets group (www.plusmarketsgroup.com). Joining fees range from a minimum of £15,000 to £100,000 for the largest companies, and annual fees are between £5,665 and £51,500. In addition there are Corporate Adviser's fees of around £20,000, plus an annual retainer. If new money is to be raised there will be additional advisory and other costs. PLUS companies are generally small and often brand new, but there are also some long-established and well-known firms, such as Thwaites and Adnams.

Many companies gain a quotation on PLUS without raising fresh capital simply to allow a market price to be set and current shareholders to trade. If no money is raised, no formal admission document or prospectus is required, but the Corporate Adviser (to be retained by the company at all times) will insist that good accounting systems are in place, with annual audited accounts and semi-annual accounts. The Corporate Adviser will also ensure that the company has at least one non-executive director and adequate working capital. There are about 150 companies with a combined market capitalisation of around £2bn quoted on the PLUS exchange.

In addition to the 150 or so shares that are listed on the PLUS-quoted system, PLUS Market provides a trading platform for all UK-listed shares, plus some European shares and some unlisted shares.

PLUS is often seen as a nursery market for companies that eventually grow big enough for AIM or Main Market. Despite this many companies are happy to remain on PLUS for many years and have no desire to increase their costs by moving up to the LSE markets. Indeed, some companies have come off AIM and joined PLUS.

Tasks for stock exchanges

Traditionally, exchanges perform the following tasks in order to play their valuable role in a modern society:

- Supervision of trading to ensure fairness and efficiency.
- The authorisation of market participants such as brokers and market makers.
- Creation of an environment in which prices are formed efficiently and without distortion (**price discovery** or **price formation**). This requires not only regulation of a high order and low transaction cost but also a liquid market in which there are many buyers and sellers, permitting investors to enter or exit quickly without moving the price.
- Organisation of the clearing and **settlement** of transactions (after the deal has been struck the buyer must pay for the shares and the shares must be transferred to the new owners).
- The regulation of the admission of companies to the exchange and the regulation of companies on the exchange.
- The dissemination of information, e.g. trading data, prices and company announcements. Investors are more willing to trade if prompt and complete information about trades, companies and prices is available.

In recent years there has been a questioning of the need for stock exchanges to carry out all these activities. In the case of the LSE the settlement of transactions was long ago handed over to CREST (discussed later in this chapter). Also the responsibility for authorising the listing of companies was transferred to the UK Listing Authority arm of the Financial Services Authority (the principal UK regulator). The LSE's Regulatory News Service (which distributes important company announcements and other price-sensitive news) now has to compete with other distribution platforms outside the LSE's control as listed companies are now able to choose between competing providers of news dissemination platforms. Despite all this upheaval the LSE still retains an important role in the distribution of trading and pricing information.

How stock exchanges work

Types of trading

Traditionally shares were traded between two traders, face to face. A few stock exchanges around the world still have a place where buyers and sellers (or at least their representatives) meet to trade. For example, the NYSE continues to make some use of a large trading floor, with thousands of face-to-face deals taking place every working day (**open outcry trading**). This is the traditional image of a stock market, and if television reporters have a story about what is going on in the world's security markets, they often show an image of traders rushing around, talking quickly amid a flurry of small slips of paper on the NYSE trading floor. Most trading now, however, is conducted silently in front of banks of computers, with deals being completed in nano-seconds. The stress levels for those dealing remain as high, if not higher, than ever, as now a slight mistake with a finger on a keyboard can cause mayhem.

Quote-driven trading is how most stock exchanges were operated. With this type of approach, **market makers** give a price at which they will buy (lower price) or sell (higher price), and they make their profits on the margins between buying and selling. Traditionally they operated in 'trading pits' and used an open outcry system of trading, i.e. shouting and using hand signals to make trades, much like you might see bookmakers at a small horse race meeting. They were able to adjust their prices according to what other traders were doing. Although this type of trading does still take place, it has been superseded by electronic trading. Market makers input their prices ('bid' is the price at which they are willing to buy and 'offer' or 'ask' is the price at which they are willing to sell) to a computer system and dealing takes place electronically.

Market makers, also known as **dealers**, fulfil a crucial role in the markets: in those securities in which market makers agree to make a market there will always be (in trading hours) someone available who will quote a price at which they will buy or sell – as a purchaser or seller you may not like the price but at least someone is making a trade possible. To take share trading as an example, imagine if you wanted to invest in a small company's shares and there were no market makers, then you might hesitate because the shares would fail to have the important quality of liquidity. Investors in companies lacking an active secondary market will demand higher rates of return (lower share prices) to compensate for the inability to quickly find a counterparty willing to trade.

The idea is that in a market with competing market makers, if the gap between the bid and offer prices gets too wide then clients will be lured away by better prices being offered by other market makers in that security.[7] The difference between the prices is known as the **trader's spread** or **bid–offer spread**. Many of these prices are displayed on electronic systems so that clients can see them displayed on their computer screens throughout the day. Other security bid–offer prices are given to you only if you telephone the market maker and ask for a quote.

Market makers take a considerable risk: they have to hold inventories of shares and other securities to supply those who want to buy. Tying up a lot of money in inventories of shares, bonds, etc. can be very expensive, and there is always the possibility of downward movement in price while they hold millions of pounds or euros in inventory. The degree of risk varies from one security to another and this helps explain the differences in the size of the bid–offer spread. For some securities it is significantly less than 1 per cent of the value, in others it can be 20 per cent or more. The other major factor influencing the spread is the volume of trade that takes place relative to the amount that has to be held in inventory – high volume gives access to a liquid market for the market maker. Thus Marks & Spencer has millions of shares traded every day and so the market maker is not likely to have M&S shares on its hands for long because they are going out of the door as fast as they are coming in – spreads here can be around one-tenth of 1 per cent. Shares of a small engineering company, meanwhile, might trade in lots of only a few hundred at two- or three-day intervals. Thus the market maker has money tied up for days before selling and is fearful of a price fall between trading days.

7 Unfortunately, in many cases there is only one market maker willing to make a market in a security.

We can see how the quote-driven system works through **Exhibit 9.16**. This could apply to markets in a wide variety of securities and instruments, from bonds to commodities, but we will assume that it is company shares. The demand curve shows that as the price declines, the amount demanded to buy from the market maker rises. The supply curve shows rising volume offered by investors with higher prices. The **clearing price** is 199p – this is where the demand from clients wanting to buy and supply of the securities from those wanting to sell are evenly matched. Naturally, the market makers in this security will be taking a spread around this clearing price, so the true price to the buying client might be 199.5p, whereas the price that a seller to the market makers can obtain is only 198.5p.

| Exhibit 9.16 | Supply and demand in a quote-driven market |

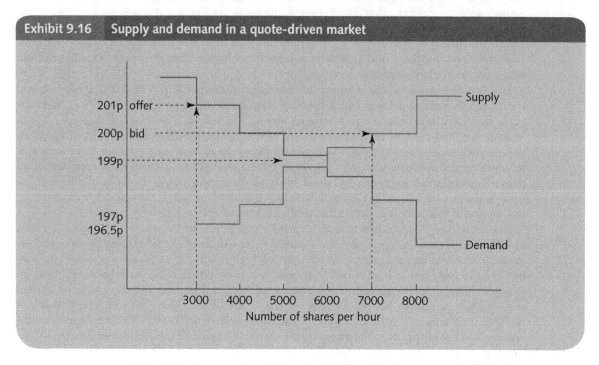

If one of the market makers is currently quoting prices of 200p–201p (offering to buy at 200p and sell at 201p) then he will experience a flood of orders from sellers because investors are willing to sell 7,000 shares per hour if offered 200p. On the other hand, demand at 201p is a mere 3,000 shares. The market maker will thus end up buying a net 4,000 shares per hour if he takes all the trade. In fact, it is even worse than this for our market maker because the potential buyers can pick up their shares for only 199.5p from other market makers and so he ends up buying 7,000 per hour and not selling any.

Even if our market maker is exceptionally optimistic about the market equilibrium price rising significantly above 201p in the next few hours he is not doing himself any favours by quoting such high prices because he could buy a large number of the shares he wants at a price a lot less than this – there are 5,000 per hour going through other market makers at 199.5p, for example. Thus there is a strong incentive for our market maker to move his prices down towards the intersection of the supply and demand curves.

Now consider a market maker who quotes 197p–196.5p. She will experience a flood of buy orders from clients given the prices offered by other market makers in this competitive market. Under the rules governing market makers she is obliged to deal at the prices quoted up to a maximum number of shares (decided by the exchange that controls this particular market). Perhaps this obligation to sell 8,000 shares per hour to clients when she is attracting few (no) clients to sell to her may lead to problems in satisfying demand. She will thus be tempted (unless she has a lot of shares to shift) to move her bid and offer prices to around the market equilibrium price.

A market maker who tries to maintain a large bid–offer spread will fail when there are many market makers for a security. For example, consider the five market makers offering the following prices:

Market maker	Bid price	Offer price
1	198.5p	199.5p
2	197.3p	199.5p
3	197.0p	200.0p
4	198.5p	199.7p
5	198.3p	202.0p

Any potential seller (or broker for the seller) would look at the various market makers' prices and conclude that they would like to trade with either market maker 1 or 4 at 198.5p. Any buyer of shares would want to trade with 1 or 2. Market maker 4 may be temporarily under-stocked with these shares and is content to see inventory build up – he is not going to get many to buy from him at 199.7p when buyers can get away with paying only 199.5p. Market maker 2, mean-while, will see more sales than purchases – perhaps she has excessive inventory and wishes to allow an outflow for a while.

Of course, for most securities the intersection of the supply and demand 'curves' moves over time. Perhaps the company announces at 2pm that it has won a large export order. Immediately the investors see this news on their computer screen and the demand curve shifts upwards while the supply curve shifts downwards. Market makers also read the news and anticipate the shifts and quickly move their price quotes to where they think they can trade with a reasonable balance between bid deals and offer deals, aiming for a large number of each making a profit on the spread.

Criticism of trading systems based on market makers quoting bid and offer prices focused on the size of the middleman's (the market maker's) margin led to the development of **order-driven trading**, where buyers trade with sellers at a single price so that there is no bid–offer spread. Most stock exchanges in the world now operate this type of system. These markets allow buy and sell orders to be entered on a central computer, and investors are automatically matched (they are sometimes called **matched-bargain systems** or **order book trading**). In 1997, the LSE introduced an order-driven service known as **SETS (Stock Exchange Electronic Trading System)** and I will use this as an example to explain how order-driven trading works.

SETS

SETS electronic order book uses powerful computer systems to execute millions of trades a day in milliseconds. Traders (via brokers) enter the prices at which they are willing to buy or sell as well as the quantity of shares they want to trade. They can then wait for the market to move to the price they set as their limit. Alternatively they can instruct brokers to transact immediately at the best price currently available on the order book system. Trades are then executed by the system if there is a match between a buy order price and a sell order price. These prices are displayed anonymously to the entire market. An example of prices and quantities is shown in the lower half of **Exhibit 9.17** – a reproduction of a SETS screen as seen by brokers.

The buy orders are shown on the left and the sell orders on the right. So, we can observe for Lloyds Bank someone (or more than one person) has entered that they are willing to buy 100,000 shares at a maximum price of 69.92p (bottom line on screen). Someone else has entered that they would like to sell 6,930 shares at a minimum price of 70.53p. Clearly the computer cannot match these two orders and neither of these two investors will be able to trade. They will either have to adjust their limit prices or wait until the market moves in their favour.

As we travel up the screen we observe a closing of the gap between the prices buyers are will-ing to pay and the offering price of sellers. On the eighth line from the bottom we see that buyers want 36,060 shares at 70.17p whereas sellers are prepared to accept 70.20p for 87,116 shares. Now we are getting much closer to a match. Indeed, if we look above the **yellow strip** we can see the price where buyers and sellers were last matched – the 'last traded price' is 70.18p. These screens are available to market participants at all times and so they are able to judge where to pitch their price limits. For example, if I was a buyer of 5,000 shares entering the market I would not be inclined to offer more than 70.2p given the current state of supply and demand. However, if I was a seller of 5,000 shares I would recognise that the price offered would not have to fall

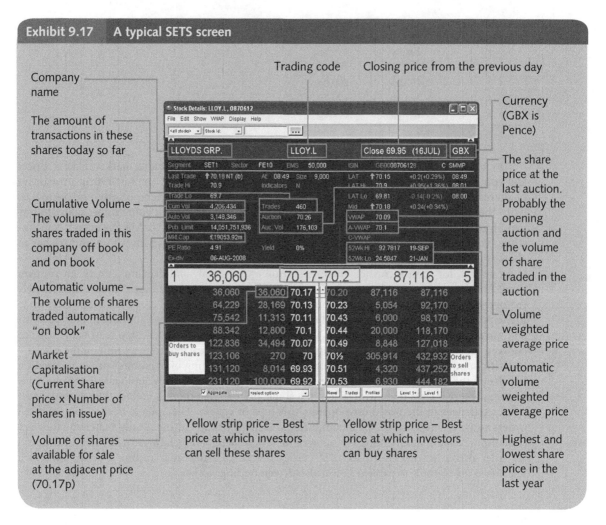

Exhibit 9.17 A typical SETS screen

Source: London Stock Exchange.

below 70.17p to attract buyers. If I was a buyer of 110,000 shares rather than just 5,000 I have two options: I could set a maximum price of 70.2p, in which case I would transact for 87,116 immediately but would leave the other 22,884 unfilled order in the market hoping for a general market price decline; alternatively, I could set my limit at 70.44p, in which case I could transact with those investors prepared to sell at 70.2p, 70.23p, 70.43p and 70.44p. The unfilled orders of the sellers at 70.44p (118,170–110,000) are carried forward on SETS.

Supporters of the older quote-driven system say that a major problem with the order-driven system is that there may be few or no shares offered at prices close to a market clearing rate and so little trade can take place. In other words, the market can be very illiquid. There may indeed be times when no sellers are posting sensible prices and other times when buyers are scarce. This is when the quote-driven system may be more liquid because market makers who make a book in a company's shares must continuously offer prices and are obliged to trade at the price shown (up to a certain quantity of shares). By way of counter-criticism, it is alleged there have been times when it has been difficult to contact market makers to trade at their displayed prices, even though in theory they are obliged to make themselves available to quote and trade at bid and offer prices throughout the trading day. To improve trading liquidity on SETS, in 2007 the system was modified so that market makers can now post prices on it. Thus it offers a continuous order book with automatic execution (via computer rather than market maker systems), but also has market makers providing continuous bid and offer prices for many shares (but these trades are executed through the automatic system). It is thought that by having the two systems combined there will be tighter bid–offer spreads, greater transparency of trades and improved liquidity.

Clearing and settlement

When a trade has been completed and reported to the exchange it is necessary to clear the trade. That is, the exchange ensures that all reports of the trade are reconciled to make sure all parties are in agreement as to the number and the price of shares traded. The exchange also checks that the buyer and seller have the cash and securities to do the deal. Also the company registrar is notified of the change in ownership. Later the transfer of ownership from seller to buyer has to take place; this is called settlement. These days clearing frequently does not just mean checking that a buyer and a seller agree on the deal; the clearing house also acts as a 'central counterparty' which acts as a buyer to every seller and as a seller to every buyer. This eliminates the risk of failure to complete a deal by guaranteeing that shares will be delivered against payment and vice versa. Clearing houses and central counterparties (CCPs in Europe, central counterparty clearing (CCCs) in the USA) provide an invaluable service – they execute and guarantee every aspect of the transaction. Instead of having to wait for cheque clearance, or for documents to be signed and arrive by post, traders set up accounts with clearing houses and CCPs, so that transactions can be carried out immediately, with the CCP absorbing any loss should either default. With a CCP, investors can also 'net' their trades, so that if one part of the investing institution has bought 1m shares while another has sold 1.5m, the trades are paired so that settlement is for only 500,000 shares.

For the LSE, as in most of Europe, share settlement is T+3, which means that shares are transferred to new owners three days after the trade takes place, but there is pressure to move to T+2 – *see* Exhibit 9.18.

To facilitate settlement a company called Euroclear UK & Ireland uses the CREST system and acts as a central securities depository (CSD) for the UK and Ireland. CREST enables dematerialisation by keeping an electronic register of the shares and a record of shares traded on stock markets, and providing an electronic means of settlement and registration. This system is cheaper and quicker than the old one which used paper – ownership is now transferred with a few strokes on a keyboard. The volume of this trading is huge, around 1.3m transactions daily in over 16,000 securities, with a value in excess of £1.4tn. Under the CREST system shares are usually held in

Exhibit 9.18

Brussels eyes faster times for settlement

By Jeremy Grant in London and Nikki Tait in Brussels

European regulators are considering ways to cut the time it takes for securities to be processed after trades are done in a bid to reduce risks to the system in the event of defaults and other large financial failures.

Reducing the so-called 'settlement cycle' would be one of the biggest moves taken by regulators in the wake of the 2008 financial crisis since proposed reforms of the over-the-counter derivatives markets, recently finalised by the European Commission.

Settlement is the post-trade process that ensures securities are exchanged for cash, completing a transaction such as the trading of stocks and shares.

Currently settlement in most of Europe takes place three days after the trade is made, in a system known as 'T+3'. Germany uses T+2.

Reducing the cycle by a day would cut by a third the time it takes for a deal to be finalised – and thus reduce the scope for failures such as defaults while transactions work their way through settlement and custody processes. It would also make it easier for the region to handle corporate actions such as rights issues and takeover bids.

The idea of reducing the settlement cycle was identified before the financial crisis as a way of harmonising pan-European post-trade structures to make the region's capital markets more efficient.

But the issue has received fresh impetus since the collapse of Lehman Brothers, whose default raised alarm over counterparty risk.

the name of a nominee company rather than in the name of the actual purchaser. Brokers and investment managers run these nominee accounts. Thus, when an investor trades, their broker holds their shares electronically in their (the broker's) nominee account and arranges settlement through their membership of the CREST system. This increases the speed of transactions enormously. There might be dozens of investors with shares held by a particular nominee company. The nominee company appears as the registered owner of the shares as far as the company (say, Sainsbury or BT) is concerned. Despite this, the beneficial owners receive all dividends and any sale proceeds. Some investors oppose the CREST system because under such a system they do not automatically receive annual reports and other documentation, such as an invitation to the annual general meeting. They also potentially lose the right to vote (after all, the company does not know who the beneficial owners are). Those investors who take seriously their ownership of a part of a company can insist on remaining outside of CREST. In this way they receive share certificates and are treated as the real owners of the business. This is more expensive when share dealing, but that is not a great concern for investors who trade infrequently.

There is a compromise position: personal membership of CREST. The investor is then both the legal owner and the beneficial owner of the shares, and also benefits from rapid (and cheap) electronic share settlement. The owner will be sent all company communications and retain voting rights. However, this is more expensive than the normal CREST accounts.

SETSqx

Trading on SETS is for companies whose trading is liquid, i.e. large companies with a high proportion of the shares held by a wide range of investors (a large free float), so there are plenty of shares traded each day.[8] There are other means of trading for less frequently traded shares. SETSqx (Stock Exchange Electronic Trading Service – quotes and crosses) trades in Main Market (and a few AIM) shares which are less liquid and not traded on SETS. SETSqx combines order book technology (similar to the SETS method of trading) with the best of the LSE's existing quote-driven trading. On SETSqx a single market maker's quote can be displayed if a market maker is interested in quoting a price. (Ideally, the exchange would like many market makers quoting prices so that competition encourages keener prices for share owners.)

An investor wanting to trade with a market maker can do so in the normal way, but also can connect, usually via brokers, to the electronic system and put onto the system's screen display an order for shares stating a price at which they would like to trade, either to sell or to buy – particularly useful if there are no market makers in that share. If someone else on the system likes the displayed price, they can phone the originator and a deal is done.

This may still leave some orders for trades unexecuted (i.e. no one phones up and trades at the advertised price). To cope with this, or to trade shares anonymously, there are four auctions per day (at 08.00, 11.00, 15.00 and 16.35) in which investors make bids and the system matches up buyers and sellers. Now all Main Market shares trade on either SETS or SETSqx.

Quote-driven trading

The LSE's Stock Exchange Automated Quotation (SEAQ) system deals mainly in smaller, less liquid companies not on its Main Market. It is the LSE's quote-driven service that allows market makers to quote prices in AIM securities (those AIM securities not traded on SETS or SETSqx) as well as a number of fixed-interest securities. It lists hundreds of companies on its electronic notice board where market makers display prices at which they are willing to buy or sell.

The SEAQ computer gathers together the bid–offer quotes from all the market makers that make a market in that particular share. These competing quotations are then available to brokers and other financial institutions linked up to the SEAQ system.

Exhibit 9.19 goes through the stages in buying or selling on the LSE's SEAQ system. What happens when you, as an investor, telephone your broker to buy shares is this: when you mentioned

8 It trades FTSE 100, FTSE 250 and FTSE Small Cap constituents (see later) plus ETFs (*see* Chapter 1).

Exhibit 9.19 The SEAQ quote-driven system

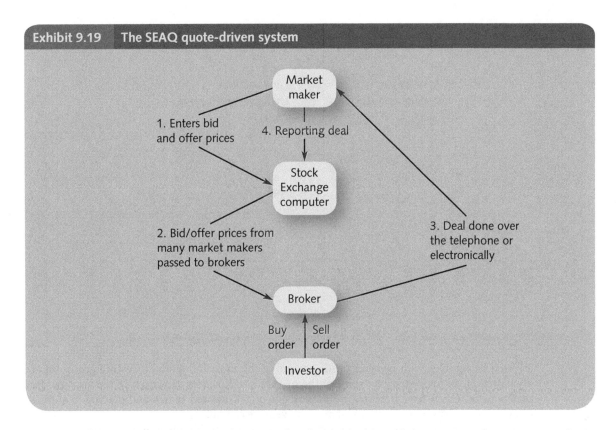

the company name the broker immediately punched into their computer the company code. So within a second of your mentioning your interest in the company the broker has on their screen all the prices that different market makers are willing to pay as well as all the prices at which they are willing to sell the shares. It can be confusing and time consuming for the broker to look at all the prices to find the best current rates. Fortunately they do not have to do this as the screen displays a 'yellow strip' above the market makers' prices, which provides the identity of the market makers offering the best bid and offer prices (these are called **touch prices**). It is the price in the yellow strip that the broker will immediately report to you over the telephone. So, you might be told 105–109. If you were happy with 109p you would then instruct your broker to buy, say, 1,000 shares.

The market makers are obliged to deal (up to a certain number of shares) at the price quoted, but they have the freedom to adjust prices after deals are completed. Transactions may be completed by the broker speaking to the market maker on the telephone, but an increasing number of trades are completed electronically. All trades are reported to the exchanges's central electronic computer and are disseminated to market participants (usually within three minutes) so that they are aware of the price at which recent trades were completed.

The underlying logic of the quote-driven system is that through the competitive actions of numerous market makers, investors are able to buy or sell at any time at the best price. A problem arises for some very small or infrequently traded firms. Market makers are reluctant to commit capital to holding shares in such firms, and so for some there may be only one market maker's quote, while for others there may be none. These shares have a better trading environment on SETSqx.

The ownership of UK shares

The latest figures from the Office for National Statistics (ONS) give the ownership of UK shares from 1963 to 2010, and some dramatic changes can be seen – *see* **Exhibit 9.20**.

The tax-favoured status of pension funds made them a very attractive vehicle for savings, resulting in billions of pounds being put into them each year. Most of this money used to be

Exhibit 9.20 Percentage ownership of UK shares 1963–2010

Source: from Office for National Statistics, Source: Office for National Statistics licensed under the Open Government Licence v.1.0.

invested in equities, with pension funds becoming the most influential investing group on the stock market, taking nearly one-third of the market in UK shares. However, in the last two decades pension funds have been taking money out of UK quoted shares and placing it in other investments such as bonds, overseas shares and venture capital.

Insurance companies similarly rose in significance, increasing their share of quoted equities from 10 per cent to about one-quarter by the 1990s, after which they, too, moved their investments to bonds and overseas equities.

Small personal investors used to dominate the market, with 54 per cent of quoted shares in 1963. This sector has shown a continuous gradual decline, falling to 11.5 per cent, but the reason for the decline is not that individual investors have become disinterested in the stock market but that they have shown a tendency to switch from direct investment to collective investment vehicles, so probably the same number of people (if not more) are investing, but in a different way. They gain benefits of diversification and skilled management by putting their savings into unit and investment trusts or into endowment and other savings schemes offered by the insurance companies. Although the mode of investment has changed from direct to indirect, Britain remains a society with a deep interest in the stock market. Very few people are immune from the performance of the LSE. The vast majority of the UK population have a pension plan or endowment savings scheme, or a unit trust investment.

The most remarkable trend has been the increasing share of equities held by overseas investors: only 7 per cent in 1963, but over 41 per cent in 2010. This increase partly reflects international mergers where the new company is listed in the UK, and foreign companies sometimes floating their UK subsidiaries but holding on to a large shareholding. It also reflects an increasing tendency among investors to buy shares in overseas markets. In addition, large sovereign wealth funds are investing, say oil money, in shares around the world. The rising internationalisation of share ownership is not just manifest in the UK – for each of the following countries more than 30 per cent of the domestic company shares are owned by overseas organisations: the Netherlands, Switzerland, Greece, Portugal, Poland, France, Norway, Sweden, Spain, Austria and Denmark.

Also note the rise in the 'other' category in Exhibit 9.20 over the last decade. This is largely due to the growing importance of hedge funds and venture capital companies.

Regulation

Financial markets need high-quality regulation in order to induce investors to place their trust in them. There must be safeguards against unscrupulous and incompetent operators. There must be an orderly operation of the markets, fair dealing and integrity. However, the regulations must not be so restrictive as to stifle innovation and prevent the markets from being competitive internationally.

London's financial markets have a unique blend of law, self-regulation and custom to regulate and supervise their members' activities. Interestingly, the UK regulatory system is going through something of an upheaval at the time of writing. For over a decade the Financial Services Authority (FSA) has dominated the scene. It is a 'super-regulator' with oversight of an amazing range of financial sectors. In 2013 the FSA will split in two. The main body, the Financial Conduct Authority (FCA), will still be a super-regulator covering a very wide range of financial services – *see* Exhibit 9.21. One important function, that of the individual regulation of the 2,200 biggest banks, insurers and brokers on the issue of safety and soundness (micro-prudential supervision), will be transferred to the new Prudential Regulatory Authority (PRA), a subsidiary of the Bank of England. It will be responsible for granting permission for their activities and approving their senior management. It will have the powers to impose additional capital requirements (plenty of assets relative to liabilities) and, limit leverage (e.g. not too much borrowing).

The Bank of England previously had the responsibility, together with the FSA and the Treasury, of ensuring the systemic safety of the banking system; that is, setting rules on capital and liquidity reserves (plenty of cash and near cash to cope with sudden outflows) for banks across the sector as a whole and imposing other rules to reduce the risk that the failure of one bank leads on to the failure of many. Following the 2008 financial crisis it was thought wise to concentrate this macro-prudential regulation in the hands of one regulator together with the micro-prudential regulation of individual banks (and other finance businesses) rather than have the 'tripartite' approach where people in the Bank of England, the Treasury and the FSA are not quite clear which of them should be taking charge when a systemic threat arises – as was the case up to 2008. The additional consideration is that these systemically important institutions might need access to central bank funding in an emergency and so it is best if they are regulated by the Bank of England.

The FCA retains responsibility for protecting consumers and preserving market integrity, covering:

- investor protection, including that for bank customers;
- market supervision and regulation;
- business conduct of banks and financial services, including approval of consumer-related managers and the supervision of investment managers and other firms whose failure would be non-systemic (they would not cause a contagious collapse of a number of firms);
- civil and criminal enforcement of market abuse rules;
- UK Listing Authority – supervision of initial public offerings and subsequent monitoring of listed companies (*see* Chapter 10).

The Bank of England also has the Monetary Policy Committee to set interest rates and adjust the money supply.

The FSA/FCA can be described as semi-detached from government: it is financed by the industries it regulates, but its powers come from legislation; it often consults the financial services companies before deciding on principles, rules and codes of conduct, but it has basic principles approved by the government and it is answerable to the Treasury, which appoints its board, and through them to Parliament.[9]

With regard to the stock markets: the FSA/FCA supervises exchanges, clearing houses and settlement houses. It also conducts market surveillance and monitors transactions on seven Recognised Investment Exchanges (RIEs). The recognised exchanges work with the FSA/FCA to protect investors and maintain the integrity of markets. Much of the monitoring and enforcement is delegated to the RIEs. The London Stock Exchange, LSE, for example, vets new stockbrokers and tries to ensure

9 For more on financial regulation consult Arnold (2012a).

Exhibit 9.21 UK financial service industry regulation

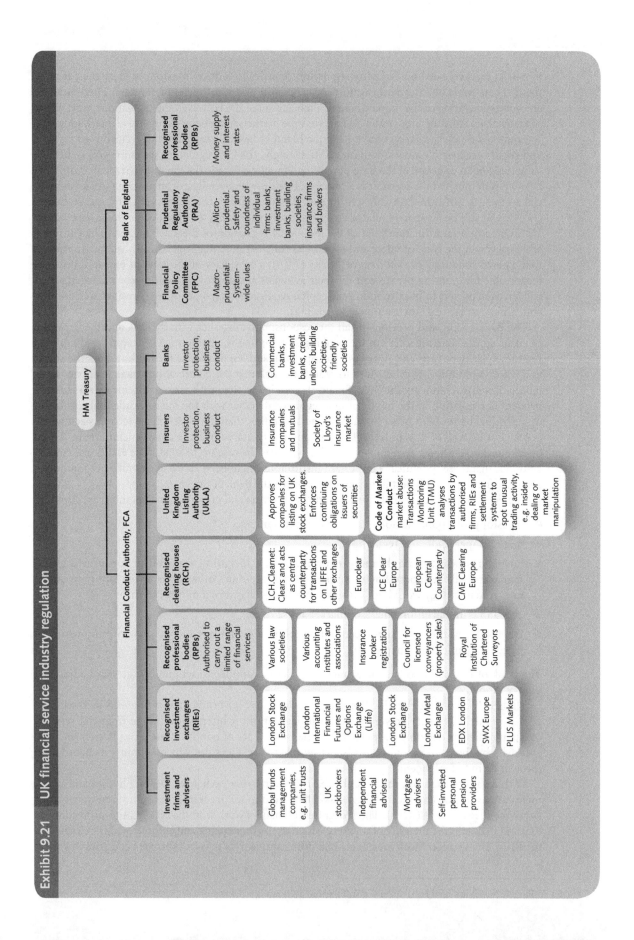

compliance with LSE rules, aimed at making sure members (e.g. market makers and brokers) act with the highest standards of integrity, fairness, transparency and efficiency. It monitors market makers' quotations and the price of actual trades to ensure compliance with its dealing rules. It is constantly on the lookout for patterns of trading that deviate from the norm with the aim of catching those misusing information (e.g. insider dealing), creating a false or misleading impression to the disadvantage of other investors or some other market-distorting action. The LSE in partnership with the FSA/FCA also requires companies to disseminate all information that could significantly affect their share prices.

Outside the FSA/FCA structure there are numerous ways in which the conduct of firms and financial institutions is put under scrutiny and constraint. The media keep a watchful stance – always looking to reveal stories of fraud, greed and incompetence. There is legislation prohibiting insider dealing, fraud and negligence. Companies Acts regulate the formation and conduct of companies and there are special Acts for building societies, insurance companies and unit trusts. The **Competition Commission (CC)** and the **Office of Fair Trading (OFT)** attempt to prevent abuse of market power. The **Panel on Takeovers and Mergers** determines the manner in which acquisitions are conducted for public companies (*see* Chapter 20). In addition European Union regulations are an increasing feature of corporate life. Accountants also function, to some extent, as regulators helping to ensure companies do not misrepresent their financial position. In addition any member of the public may access the accounts of any company easily and cheaply at **Companies House** (or via Companies House's website or the postal system). **The Serious Fraud Office (SFO)** investigates cases of serious or complex fraud.

Understanding the figures in the financial pages

Financial managers and investors need to be aware of what is happening on the financial markets, how their shares are affected and which measures are used as key yardsticks in evaluating a company. The financial pages of the broadsheet newspapers, particularly the *Financial Times*, provide some important statistics on company share price performance and valuation ratios. These enable comparisons to be made between companies within the same sector and across sectors. **Exhibit 9.22** shows extracts from two issues of the *Financial Times*. The information provided in the Monday edition is different from that provided on the other days of the week.

Indices

Information on individual companies in isolation is less useful than information set in the context of the firm's peer group, or in comparison with quoted companies generally. For example, if Tesco's shares fall by 1 per cent on a particular day, an investor might be keen to learn whether the market as a whole rose or fell on that day, and by how much. The *Financial Times* (FT) joined forces with the Stock Exchange (SE) to create **FTSE International** in November 1995, which has taken over the calculation (in conjunction with the Faculty and Institute of Actuaries) of a number of **equity indices**. These indicate the state of the market as a whole or selected sectors of the market and consist of 'baskets' of shares so that the value of that basket can be compared at different times. Senior managers are often highly sensitive to the relative performance of their company's share price. One reason for this is that their compensation package may be linked to the share price and in extreme circumstances managers are dismissed if they do not generate sufficiently high relative returns.

To calculate the indices shown in **Exhibit 9.23** each component share contributes to the index level. However, the shares do not have an equal weight in calculating the average. Rather, the average is derived by weighting each share by the size of the company; by its market capitalisation. Thus a 2 per cent movement in the share price of a large company has a greater effect on an index than a 2 per cent change in a small company's share price.[10] The characteristics of some of these indices are as follows.

10 The weighting for some shares is reduced if a high proportion of the shares are held not in a free float but in the hands of people closely connected with the business, e.g. directors, major shareholders.

Exhibit 9.22 London Share Service extracts: Aerospace and Defence

WEDNESDAY OCTOBER 5 2011

Notes	Price	Chng	52 Week High	52 Week Low	Yld	P/E	Vol '000s
Aerospace & Defence							
AvonRub..†	259	-17.75	340	156	1	13	51
BAE Sys....	254	-6	372.90	241	7.1	7.4	19,439
Chemring.†	519	-9.50	740	470.30	2.4	10.8	557
Cobham...†	168.50	-4.50	247.40	167	3.7	12.4	3,109
Hampson...	9.43	+0.03	41	9.22	-	1.1	1,374
Meggitt...†	322.30	-8.10	400.90	124	3	13.4	16,880
RollsRyc.✠	571	-27	666.61	314.06	2.6	6.3	10,410
Senior.....†	137	-5.60	193.60	128.60	2.4	10.3	3,114
UltraElc...†	£15.32	+0.11	£19.03	£12.65	2.3	14.4	159
UMECO.....	310.75xd	-6.25	512.50	305.71	5.9	22.4	7

MONDAY OCTOBER 3 2011

Notes	Price	Wks% Chng	Div	Div Cov	Mcap £m	Last xd
Aerospace & Defence						
AvonRub..†	258	-2.0	2.50	8.0	87.6	10.8
BAE Sys....	267.30	-2.4	18	1.9	8,889.2	20.4
Chemring.†	528.50	+1.0	12.40-	3.9	1,025.5	13.7
Cobham...†	174.80	-2.6	6.17	2.2	1,912.9	4.5
Hampson...	9.50	-13.6	-	-	26.5	9.10
Meggitt...†	334.90	+5.7	9.55	2.5	2,603.0	10.8
RollsRyc.✠	595	-0.2	14.85	6.2	11,139.7	27.10
Senior.....†	144.50	+6.6	3.27	4.1	581.2	4.5
UltraElc...†	£15.05	+0.9	35.70	3.0	1,035.6	17.8
UMECO.....	319.25xd	+0.7	18.25	0.8	153.8	7.9

Price/earnings ratio (PER) – share price divided by the company's earnings (profits after tax) per share in the latest twelve-month period. A much examined and talked about measure

$$PER = \frac{share\ price}{earnings\ per\ share}$$

Market price – this is the mid-price (midway between the best buying and selling prices) quoted at 4.30 pm on the previous day

Change in closing price on day before (Tuesday) compared with previous trading day

The highest and lowest prices during the previous 52 weeks

Dividend yield – the dividend divided by the current share price expressed as a percentage

$$\frac{dividend\ per\ share}{current\ share\ price} \times 100$$

Volume of trade in those shares on the day

Share price change over the previous week

The dividend paid in the company's last full year – it is the cash payment in pence per share (after deduction of 10% tax for UK firms)

Dividend cover – profit after tax divided by the dividend payment, or earnings per share divided by dividend per share

$$Dividend\ cover = \frac{earnings\ per\ share}{dividend\ per\ share}$$

Market capitalisation is calculated by multiplying the number of shares by their market price

Ex-dividend date is the last date on which the share went ex-dividend (new buyers of the shares will not receive the recently announced dividend after this date) 17th August in this case

FT *Financial Times*, 3 October and 5 October 2011
All Rights Reserved.

Exhibit 9.23 FTSE Actuaries Shares Indices

FTSE Actuaries Share Indices

UK series

Produced in conjunction with the Institute and Faculty of Actuaries

www.ft.com/equities

	£ Stlg Oct 4	Day's chge%	Euro Index	£ Stlg Oct 3	£ Stlg Sept 30	Year ago	Div yield%	Cover	P/E ratio	Xd. adj	Total Return
FISE 100 (100)	4944.44	−2.58	4473.25	5075.50	5128.48	5635.76	3.92	3.24	7.87	163.89	3322.88
FTSE 250 (250)	9425.93	−3.33	8527.67	9750.56	9819.38	10681.96	3.15	2.29	13.83	255.25	5852.95
FTSE 250 ex Inv Co (204)	9837.54	−3.43	8900.05	10186.65	10257.46	11215.24	3.38	2.39	12.38	284.62	6215.85
FTSE 350 (350)	2612.83	−2.68	2363.84	2684.80	2711.63	2976.05	3.82	3.14	8.34	84.56	3560.06
FTSE 350 ex Inv Co (304)	2599.61	−2.68	2351.87	2671.13	2697.96	2963.14	3.86	3.16	8.21	84.98	1822.01
FTSE 350 Higher Yield (112)	2772.19	−2.01	2508.01	2829.00	2844.16	2959.22	4.91	2.70	7.53	113.72	3683.68
FTSE 350 Lower Yield (238)	2193.04	−3.58	1984.05	2274.50	2311.34	2709.49	2.32	4.40	9.78	49.88	2118.11
FTSE SmallCap (268)	2709.70	−2.89	2451.47	2790.36	2805.30	3029.01	2.92	2.00	17.16	61.78	3325.53
FTSE SmallCap ex Inv Co (156)	2174.87	−3.24	1967.61	2247.58	2263.05	2482.05	3.46	2.42	11.92	58.45	2793.19
FTSE All-Share (618)	2557.82	−2.69	2314.07	2628.41	2654.38	2912.18	3.79	3.12	8.45	82.19	3529.05
FTSE All-Share ex Inv Co (460)	2537.27	−2.69	2295.48	2607.28	2633.36	2892.17	3.85	3.15	8.24	82.72	1808.72
FTSE All-Share ex Multinatl (548)	736.09	−2.75	551.94	756.91	761.45	857.59	3.82	2.18	11.99	22.31	1097.61
FTSE Fledgling (141)	4183.63	−1.58	3784.95	4250.74	4302.30	4267.59	3.88	0.45	57.87	93.29	6776.36
FTSE Fledgling ex Inv Co (88)	4888.02	−1.98	4422.21	4986.65	5041.28	4966.76	5.09	0.32	62.04	131.11	7760.42
FTSE All Small (409)	1873.87	−2.79	1695.29	1927.56	1938.93	2076.95	3.00	1.83	18.20	42.60	2953.50
FTSE All-Small ex Inv Co (244)	1616.16	−3.14	1462.14	1668.61	1680.59	1824.74	3.58	2.20	12.68	43.33	2632.18
FTSE AIM All-Share (818)	657.79	−4.16	595.10	686.35	700.34	790.18	0.81	1.66	74.61	4.73	677.98
FTSE Sector Indices											
Oil & Gas (28)	**7516.51**	**−3.36**	**6800.21**	**7777.91**	**7876.85**	**8050.92**	**3.48**	**5.70**	**5.04**	**220.77**	**5278.66**
Of & Gas Producers (19)	7136.40	−3.26	6456.33	7376.66	7465.17	7606.19	3.54	5.75	4.92	211.11	5172.07
Oil Equipment & Servicestion (7)	17824.16	−6.24	16125.57	19010.77	19628.18	21740.21	1.97	3.49	14.53	409.94	11560.78
Basic Materials (36)	**5301.96**	**−3.56**	**4796.70**	**5497.53**	**5589.46**	**7127.09**	**2.51**	**8.55**	**4.65**	**137.30**	**4529.37**
Chemicals (7)	6178.25	−4.67	5589.48	6481.08	6498.58	6705.05	2.78	2.49	14.49	147.70	4841.03
Forestry & Paper (1)	5290.26	−4.80	4786.12	5557.07	5567.65	6264.63	4.82	3.11	6.66	257.86	4869.54
Industrial Metals & Mining (3)	4428.91	−7.43	4006.85	4784.47	4775.83	7664.37	0.76	18.80	6.97	33.93	3594.85
Mining (25)	16500.42	−3.46	14927.98	17091.77	17395.06	22393.40	2.49	8.99	4.47	426.77	7328.78
Industrials (113)	**2591.61**	**−3.30**	**2344.64**	**2679.95**	**2719.31**	**2872.49**	**3.19**	**2.66**	**11.76**	**60.69**	**2307.00**

- *FTSE 100* The 'Footsie™' index is based on the 100 largest companies (generally over £2bn market capitalisation). Large and relatively safe companies are referred to as 'blue chips'. This index has risen five-fold since it was introduced at the beginning of 1984 at a value of 1,000. This is the measure most watched by investors. It is calculated in real time (every 15 seconds) and so changes can be observed throughout the day. The other international benchmarks are: for the USA, the Dow Jones Industrial average (DJIA) (30 share) index, the Standard & Poor's 500 index and the NASDAQ Comp; for the Japanese market the Nikkei 225 index; for France the CAC-40; for Hong Kong the Hang Seng index; and for Germany the Xetra Dax index. For Europe as a whole there is FTSEurofirst 300 and Euro Stoxx 50 and for the world FTSE All World.

- *FTSE All-Share* This index is the most representative in that it reflects the average movements of over 600 shares representing 98 per cent of the value of the London market. This index is broken down into a number of industrial and commercial sectors, so that investors and companies can use sector-specific yardsticks, such as those for mining or chemicals. Companies in the FTSE All-Share index have market capitalisations (roughly) above £40m. It is an aggregation of the FTSE 100, FTSE 250 and the FTSE SmallCap.

- *FTSE 250* This index is based on 250 firms which are in the next size range after the top 100. Capitalisations are generally between £250m and £2bn. (It is also calculated with investment trusts excluded.)

- *FTSE 350* This index is based on the largest 350 quoted companies. It combines the FTSE 100 and the FTSE 250. This cohort of shares is also split into two to give high and low dividend yield groups. A second 350 index excludes investment trusts.

- *FTSE SmallCap* This index covers companies (268 of them in October 2011) included in the FTSE All-Share but excluded from the FTSE 350, with a market capitalisation of about £40m to £250m.
- *FTSE Fledgling* This includes companies listed on the Main Market but too small to be in the FTSE All-Share Index.
- *FTSE AIM All-Share* Index of all AIM companies (except those with a low free float and low liquidity).
- *FTSE All-small* Combines companies in FTSE SmallCap with those in the FTSE Fledgling (409 companies in October 2011).

The indices in the first column in Exhibit 9.23 are price indices only (share price movements only are reflected in the indices). The final column, 'Total return', shows the overall performance with both share price rises and dividends reinvested in the portfolio.

Taxation and corporate finance

Taxation impacts on financial decisions in at least three ways.

1 *Capital allowances* At one time it was possible for a firm to reduce its taxable profit by up to 100 per cent of the amount invested in certain fixed assets. So if a firm made a profit of £10m, and in the same year bought £10m worth of approved plant and equipment, HM Revenue and Customs would not charge any tax because the capital allowance of £10m could be subtracted from the profit to calculate taxable profit. The idea behind this generosity was to encourage investment and thus stimulate economic growth. Today, the type of expenditure subject to 100 per cent capital allowances is very restricted and the capital allowance is generally 18 per cent of the value of the investment in the first year and 18 per cent on a declining balance for subsequent years.

 Capital allowances in project appraisal were discussed in Chapter 5.

2 *Selecting type of finance* The interest paid on borrowed capital can be used to reduce the taxable profit and thus lower the tax bill. On the other hand, payments to shareholders, such as dividends, cannot be used to reduce taxable profit. This bias against share capital may have some impact on the capital structure decision – *see* Chapter 18.

3 *Distribution of profit UK* Companies pay corporation tax on profits nine months after the end of the accounting period (except very large companies which pay quarterly instalments earlier than that). The profits are calculated after all costs have been deducted, including interest but excluding dividends. The proportion of taxable profit paid to the tax authorities is 24 per cent if taxable profit exceeds £1,500,000, and 20 per cent where it is less than £300,000 (a sliding scale applies between £300,000 and £1.5m).

 Standard-rate taxpayers (those with a marginal tax rate of 20 per cent on normal income) are liable to pay 10 per cent income tax on dividends. The rate of income tax on dividends for higher rate taxpayers is 32.5 per cent. The 10 per cent rate is deemed to be paid by the company when it pays corporation tax. Therefore, standard-rate taxpayers do not have to pay tax on dividends received. The higher-rate taxpayer can offset the 10 per cent tax paid against the total tax they are due to pay on dividends.

Concluding comments

Stock markets are major contributors to the well-being of a modern financially sophisticated society. They have great value to a wide variety of individuals and institutions. For savers they provide an environment in which savings can be invested in real productive assets to yield a return both to the saver and to society at large. The powerful pension and insurance funds rely on a well-regulated and broadly based stock exchange to enable the generation of income for their members. The mobilisation of savings for investment is a key benefit of a well-run exchange; so too is the improved allocation of scarce resources in society, and this results in a more satisfying mixture of goods and services being produced. The stock market has a part to play in directing investment to

those parts of the economy which will generate the greatest level of utility for consumers. If people want cars rather than horse-drawn transport then savings will be directed to permit investment in factories and production lines for cars. If they demand tablets rather than notebooks then the computer firm supplying tablets will find it easier to raise fresh finance than will the notebook firm.

Companies value stock markets for their capacity to absorb new issues of financial securities permitting firms to expand, innovate and produce wealth. Entrepreneurs can reap the rewards of their efforts by having access to a flourishing secondary share market and employees can be rewarded with shares which become more appealing because they can be quickly priced by looking at reports in the financial press. Managers often acknowledge the disciplinary benefits of a stock market which insists on high levels of information disclosure, integrity, competence and the upholding of shareholder interests. Governments are aware of the range of social benefits listed above and so should value an exchange on these grounds alone. However, they also see more direct advantages in a fit and proper market. For example, they are able to raise finance to cover the difference between taxes and expenditure, and they are able to tap the market in privatisations and thereby not only fill government coffers but encourage wider share ownership and allow the market to pressurise managers to run previously state-owned businesses in a more efficient manner.

Having gained some background knowledge of the workings of the London Stock Exchange, we now need to turn to the question of how equity funds are actually raised on the Main Market of the LSE and on AIM. The next chapter will examine this. It will also describe sources of equity finance available to firms which are not quoted.

Key points and concepts

- **Stock exchanges** are markets where government and industry can raise long-term capital and investors can buy and sell securities.

- **Two breakthroughs in the rise of capitalism**:
 - thriving secondary markets for securities;
 - limited liability.

- **Over 140 countries now have stock markets**. They have grown in significance due to:
 - disillusionment with planned economies
 - recognition of the key role of stock markets in a liberal pro-market economic system in mobilising saving and allocating resources.

- The **largest** domestic stock markets are in the USA, Japan and the UK.

- Electronic communication networks (ECNs) or multilateral trading facilities (MTFs) are alternative trading venues for shares quoted on the major national stock exchanges of the USA and Europe.

- The **globalisation** of equity markets has been driven by:
 - deregulation;
 - technology;
 - institutionalisation.

- Companies **list on more than one exchange** for the following reasons:
 - to broaden the shareholder base and lower the cost of equity capital;
 - the domestic market is too small or the firm's growth is otherwise constrained;
 - to reward employees;

 - investors in particular markets may understand the firm better;
 - to raise awareness of the company;
 - to discipline the firm and learn to improve performance;
 - to understand better the economic, social and industrial changes occurring in major product markets.

- **A well-run stock exchange**:
 - allows a 'fair game' to take place;
 - is regulated to avoid negligence, fraud and other abuses;
 - allows transactions to take place cheaply;
 - has enough participants for efficient price setting and liquidity.

- **Benefits** of a well-run stock exchange:
 - firms can find funds and grow;
 - society can allocate capital better;
 - shareholders can sell speedily and cheaply. They can value their financial assets and diversify;
 - increase in status and publicity for firms;
 - mergers can be facilitated by having a quotation. The market in managerial control is assisted;
 - corporate behaviour can be improved.

- The **London Stock Exchange** regulates the trading of **equities** (domestic and international) and **debt instruments** (e.g. gilts, corporate bonds and Eurobonds, etc.) and **other financial instruments** (e.g. warrants, depositary receipts and preference shares).

- The **primary market** is where firms can raise finance by selling shares (or other securities) to investors.

- The **secondary market** is where existing securities are sold by one investor to another.

- **Internal funds** are generally the most important source of long-term capital for firms. **Bank borrowing** varies greatly and **new share or bond issues** account for a minority of the funds needed for corporate growth.

- LSE's **Main Market** is the most heavily regulated UK exchange.

- The **Alternative Investment Market (AIM)** is the lightly regulated exchange designed for small, young companies.

- **techMARK** is the sector of the Official List focused on technology-led companies. The rules for listing are different for techMARK companies than for other OL companies.

- **PLUS** provides a share trading facility for companies, less costly than the LSE.

- Stock exchanges undertake most or all of the following **tasks** to play their role in a modern society:
 - supervise trading;
 - authorise market participants (e.g. brokers, market makers);
 - assist price formation;
 - clear and settle transactions;
 - regulate the admission of companies to and companies on the exchange;
 - disseminate information.

- A **quote-driven** share trading system is one in which **market makers** quote a bid and an offer price for shares. An **order-driven** system is one in which investors' buy and sell orders are matched without the intermediation of market makers.

- The **ownership of quoted shares** has shifted from dominance by individual shareholders in the 1960s to dominance by institutions, many of which are from overseas.

- **High-quality regulation** generates confidence in the financial markets and encourages the flow of savings into investment.

- The **Financial Services (Conduct) Authority** is at the centre of UK financial regulation.

- **Dividend yield:**

$$\frac{\text{Dividend per share}}{\text{Share price}} \times 100$$

- **Price-earnings ratio (PER):**

$$\frac{\text{Share price}}{\text{Earnings per share}}$$

- **Dividend cover:**

$$\frac{\text{Earnings per share}}{\text{Dividend per share}}$$

- **Taxation** impacts on financial decisions in at least three ways:
 - capital allowances;
 - selecting type of finance;
 - corporation tax.

References and further reading

Arnold, G. (2010) *The Financial Times Guide to Investing.* 2nd edn. Harlow: FT Prentice Hall.
 Contains more information on the financial markets.

Arnold, G. (2012a) *Modern Financial Markets and Institutions.* Harlow: FT Prentice Hall.
 Contains more on equity and other markets.

Arnold, G. (2012b) *The Financial Times Guide to Financial Markets.* Harlow: FT Prentice Hall.
 More on equity and other markets.

Credit Suisse Global Investment Returns Yearbook.
 An annual publication discussing returns on shares and other financial assets for leading exchanges over 110 years. Downloadable for free. www.credit-suisse.com/uk

Grout, P.A., Megginson, W.L. and Zalewska, A. (2009) *One Half-Billion Shareholders and Counting – Determinants of individual share ownership around the world.* Available at www.ssrn.com
 An extensive survey of the proportions of country populations owning shares.

London Stock Exchange Website.
 An excellent overview of the role and activities of the LSE. Great graphics and illustrations.

Office for National Statistics (2012) Ownership of UK quoted shares 2010. www.ons.gov.uk.
 The ONS is a great source of statistics – free on the internet.

Vaitilingam, R. (2010) *The Financial Times Guide to Using the Financial Pages.* 6th edn. London: FT Prentice Hall.
 Excellent introduction to the mysteries of the financial pages.

Case study recommendations

See www.pearsoned.co.uk/arnold for case study synopses. Also see Harvard University: http://hbsp.harvard.edu/product/cases

- CalPERS' Emerging Equity in the Markets Principles. Authors: Robert G. Eccles and Aldo Sesia (2009). Harvard Business School.

- Microstrategy, Incorporated: PIPE. Authors: Richard Crawford and Susan Chaplinsky (2003). Darden, University of Pennsylvania. Available at Harvard website.

- Freeport-McMoRan: Financing an acquisition. Authors: David P. Stowell and Peter Rossman (2009). Kellogg School of Management. Available at Harvard website.

- Note on Depositary Receipts. Author: Walter Kuemmerle (2004). Harvard Business School.

- Cross-Border Listings and Depositary Receipts. Authors: Mithir Desai, Kathleen Luchs, Mark F. Veblen, Ami Dave and Maria Raga-Frances (2004). Harvard Business School.

Websites

ADVFN www.advfn.com
Companies House www.companieshouse.gov.uk
CREST ww.euroclear.com
Financial Services Authority www.fsa.gov.uk
Financial Times www.ft.com
FTSE Group www.ftse.com
Hemmington Scott www.hemscott.com
Investors Chronicle www.investorschronicle.co.uk
London Clearing House, LCH.Clearnet www.lchclearnet.com

London Stock Exchange www.londonstockexchange.com
Morgan Stanley Capital www.msci.com
NASDAQ www.nasdaq.com
NYSE Euronext www.euronext.com or www.nyse.com
Office of National Statistics www.ons.gov.uk
PLUS Markets Group www.plusmarketsgroup.com
Proshare Investment clubs www.proshareclubs.co.uk
World Federation of Exchanges www.world-exchanges.org

Video presentations

Chief executives and finance directors describe their current policy on raising funds on Cantos.com (www.cantos.com) – this is free to view.

Self-review questions

1 Name the largest (by volume of share turnover on the secondary market) share exchanges in the USA, Europe and Asia.

2 What is a depositary receipt and why are they created?

3 Explain why finance has been 'globalised' over the past 30 years.

4 What are the characteristics of, and who benefits from, a well-run exchange?

5 What securities, other than shares, are traded on the London Stock Exchange?

6 Why is a healthy secondary market good for the primary share market?

7 Explain the acronyms AIM, NASDAQ, SETS, RIE and FCA.

8 What is the most important source of long-term finance for companies generally?

9 Why has it been necessary to have more share exchanges than simply the Main Market of the London Stock Exchange in the UK?

10 Why is a nominated adviser appointed to a firm wishing to join AIM?

11 Why might you be more cautious about investing in a company listed on PLUS, than a company on the Main Market of the London Stock Exchange?

12 What is CREST?

13 What have been the main trends in UK share ownership over the past 30 years?

14 Explain the following: FTSE 100, FT All-Share, FTSE Fledgling.

Questions and problems

> **MyFinanceLab** *Questions with an icon are also available for practice in MyFinanceLab with additional supporting resources.*

1 'Stock markets are capitalist exploitative devices giving no benefit to ordinary people.' Write an essay countering this argument.

2 Describe what a badly run stock exchange would be like and explain how society would be poorer as a result.

3 Many countries, for example Peru and Germany, are encouraging small investors to buy quoted shares. Why are they doing this?

4 Explain why firms obtain a share listing in countries other than their own.

5 Describe the trading systems of the London Stock Exchange and outline the advantages and disadvantages of the alternative methods of trading shares.

6 In the USA some firms have bypassed the formal stock exchanges and have sold their shares directly to investors over the internet (e.g. Spring Street Brewing). What advantages are there to this method of raising funds compared with a regulated exchange? What are the disadvantages, for firms and shareholders?

7 Discuss some of the consequences you believe might follow from the shift in UK share ownership over the past 30 years.

8 Describe the network of controls and restraints on the UK financial system to prevent fraud, abuse, negligence, etc.

9 Frame-up plc is considering a flotation on the Official List of the London Stock Exchange. The managing director has asked you to produce a 1,000-word report explaining the advantages of such a move.

10 Collasus plc is quoted on the London Stock Exchange. It is a large conglomerate with factories and sales operations in every continent. Why might Collasus wish to consider obtaining additional quotations in other countries?

11 'The City is still far too clubby and gentlemanly. They are not rigorous enough in rooting out wrongdoing. What we need is an American type of system where the government takes a lead in setting all the detailed rules of behaviour.' Consider the advantages and disadvantages of a self-regulatory system so decried by this speaker.

> **MyFinanceLab** *Now retake your diagnostic test for Chapter 9 to check your progress and update your study plan.*

Assignments

1 Carry out a comparative study in your firm (or any quoted firm) using information provided by the *Financial Times*. Compare PERs, dividend yields, dividend cover and other key factors, with a peer group of firms and the stock market as a whole. Try to explain the differences.

2 If your firm has made use of the stock market for any reason, put together a report to explain the benefits gained and some estimate of the costs of membership.

> Visit www.pearsoned.co.uk/arnold to get access to Gradetracker diagnostic tests, podcasts, Excel spreadsheet solutions, *FT* articles, a flashcard revision tool, web links, a searchable glossary and more.

Long-term debt finance

LEARNING OUTCOMES

An understanding of the key characteristics of the main categories of debt finance is essential to anyone considering the financing decisions of the firm. At the end of this chapter the reader will be able to:

■ explain the nature and the main types of bonds, their pricing and their valuation;

■ describe the main considerations for a firm when borrowing from banks;

■ give a considered view of the role of mezzanine and high-yield bond financing as well as convertible bonds, sale and leaseback, securitisation and project finance;

■ demonstrate an understanding of the value of the international debt markets;

■ explain the term structure of interest rates and the reasons for its existence.

MyFinanceLab *Complete your diagnostic test for Chapter 11 now to create your personal study plan*

Introduction

The concept of borrowing money to invest in real assets within a business is a straightforward one, yet in the sophisticated capital markets of today with their wide variety of financial instruments and forms of debt, the borrowing decision can be bewildering. Should the firm tap the domestic bond market or the Eurobond market? Would bank borrowing be best? If so, on what terms, fixed or floating rate interest, a term loan or a mortgage? And what about syndicated lending, mezzanine finance and high-yield bonds? The variety of methods of borrowing long-term finance is infinite. This chapter will outline the major categories and illustrate some of the fundamental issues a firm may consider when selecting its finance mix. As you can see from the extract from the annual accounts of GlaxoSmithKline (Exhibit 11.1) a firm may need knowledge and understanding of a great many different debt instruments. The terms floating rate note, medium-term notes, and commercial paper mentioned in the extract are explained in this chapter. Lease finance and overdrafts are examined in Chapter 12.

Exhibit 11.1 Loans and other borrowings for GlaxoSmithKline plc, 2009 and 2010

Net debt	Listing exchange	2010 £m	2009 £m
Short-term borrowings:			
US$ Floating Rate Note 2010	New York Stock Exchange	–	(621)
Commercial paper		–	(621)
Bank loans and overdrafts		(259)	(182)
Loan stock		–	(7)
Obligations under finance leases		(32)	(40)
		(291)	(1,471)
Long-term borrowings:			
3.00% € European Medium Term Note 2012	London Stock Exchange	(640)	(662)
5.125% € European Medium Term Note 2012	London Stock Exchange	(1,919)	(1,985)
4.85% US$ US Medium Term Note 2013	New York Stock Exchange	(1,599)	(1,548)
4.375% US$ US Medium Term Note 2014	London Stock Exchange	(1,049)	(990)
3.875% € European Medium Term Note 2015	London Stock Exchange	(1,358)	(1,404)
5.625% € European Medium Term Note 2017	London Stock Exchange	(1,062)	(1,100)
5.65% US$ US Medium Term Note 2018	New York Stock Exchange	(1,756)	(1,701)
4.00% € European Medium Term Note 2025	London Stock Exchange	(632)	(653)
5.25% £ European Medium Term Note 2033	London Stock Exchange	(981)	(979)
5.375% US$ US Medium Term Note 2034	London Stock Exchange	(318)	(308)
6.375% US$ US Medium Term Note 2038	New York Stock Exchange	(1,744)	(1,689)
6.375% £ European Medium Term Note 2039	London Stock Exchange	(694)	(693)
5.25% £ European Medium Term Note 2042	London Stock Exchange	(985)	(984)
Bank loans		(1)	–
Obligations under finance leases		(71)	(90)
		(14,809)	(14,786)
Net debt		(8,859)	(9,444)

Source: GlaxoSmithKilne Annual Report 2010.

Some fundamental features of debt finance

Put at its simplest, **debt** is something that has to be repaid. Corporate debt repayments have taken the form of interest and capital payments as well as more exotic compensations such as commodities and shares. The usual method is a combination of a regular interest, with capital (principal) repayments either spread over a period or given as a lump sum at the end of the borrowing. Debt finance is less expensive than equity finance, due to the lower rate of return required by finance providers, lower transaction costs of raising the funds (for example, arrangement fees with a bank or the issue costs of a bond) and the tax deductibility of interest. The lower required returns arise because investors recognise that investing in a firm via debt finance is less risky than investing via shares. It is less risky because interest is paid out before dividends are paid so there is greater certainty of receiving a return than there would be for equity holders. Also, if the firm goes into liquidation, the holders of a debt type of financial security are paid back before shareholders receive anything.

Offsetting these plus-points for debt are the facts that lenders do not, generally, share in the value created by an extraordinarily successful business and there is an absence of voting power – although debt holders are able to protect their position to some extent through rigorous lending agreements.

There are dangers associated with raising funds through debt instruments. Creditors are often able to claim some or all of the assets of the firm in the event of non-compliance with the terms of the loan. This may result in liquidation. Institutions which provide debt finance often try to minimise the risk of not receiving interest and their original capital. They do this by first of all looking to the earning ability of the firm, that is, the pre-interest profits and cash flows in the years over the period of the loan. As a back-up they often require that the loan be secured against assets owned by the business, so that if the firm is unable to pay interest and capital from profits the lender can force the sale of the assets to receive their legal entitlement. The matter of security has to be thought about carefully before a firm borrows capital. It could be very inconvenient for the firm to grant a bank a **fixed charge** on a specific asset – say a particular building – because the firm is then limiting its future flexibility to use its assets as it wishes. For instance, it will not be able to sell that building, or even rent it without the consent of the bank or the bondholders.

Bonds

A **bond** is a long-term contract in which the bondholders lend money to a company. In return the company (usually) promises to pay the bond owners predetermined payments (usually a series of **coupons**) until the bond matures. At **maturity** the bondholder receives a specified principal sum called the **par** (**face** or **nominal**) value of the bond. This is usually £100 in the UK and $1,000 in the USA. The time to maturity is generally between seven and 30 years although a number of firms, for example Disney, IBM and Reliance of India, have issued 100-year bonds.

Bonds may be regarded as merely IOUs (I owe you) with pages of legal clauses expressing the promises made. Most corporate bonds are sufficiently **liquid** (many transactions, so able to sell/buy at low cost without moving the price) to be *listed* on the London Stock Exchange and other exchanges in Europe, Asia and the Americas but the majority of *trading* occurs in the over-the-counter (OTC) market directly between an investor and a bond dealer. Access to a secondary market means that the investor who originally provided the firm with money does not have to hold on to the bond until the maturity date (the **redemption date**). However, because so many investors buy and then hold to maturity rather than trade in and out bonds generally have very thin secondary markets compared with shares. The amount the investor receives in the secondary market might be more or less than what he/she paid. For instance, imagine an investor paid £99.80 for a bond which promised to pay a coupon of 9 per cent per year on a par value of £100 and to pay the par value in seven years. If one year after issue interest rates on similar bonds are 20 per cent per annum no one will pay £99.80 for a bond agreement offering £9 per year for a further six years plus £100 on the redemption date. We will look at a method for calculating exactly how much they might be willing to pay later in the chapter.

These **negotiable** (that is tradable in a secondary market) instruments come in a variety of forms. The most common is the type described above with regular (usually semi-annual or annual) fixed coupons and a specified redemption date. These are known as **straight**, **plain vanilla** or **bullet bonds**. Other bonds are a variation on this. Some pay coupons every three months, some pay no coupons at all (called **zero coupon bonds** – these are sold at a large discount to the par value and the investor makes a capital gain by holding the bond), some bonds do not pay a fixed coupon but one which varies depending on the level of short-term interest rates (**floating-rate** or **variable-rate bonds**), some have interest rates linked to the rate of inflation. In fact, the potential for variety and innovation is almost infinite. Bonds issued in the last few years have linked the interest rates paid or the principal payments to a wide variety of economic events, such as the price of silver, exchange-rate movements, stock market indices, the price of oil, gold, copper – even to the occurrence of an earthquake. These bonds were generally designed to let companies adjust their interest payments to manageable levels in the event of the firm being adversely affected by some economic variable changing. For example, a copper miner pays lower interest on its finance if the copper price falls. Sampdoria, the Italian football club, issued a €3.5m bond that paid a higher rate of return if the club won promotion to the 'Serie A' division (2.5 per cent if it stayed in Serie B, 7 per cent if it moved to Serie A). If the club rose to the top four in Serie A the coupon would rise to 14 per cent. The John Lewis bond described in Exhibit 11.2 provides shopping vouchers in addition to coupon payments.

Exhibit 11.2

Companies sweeten offerings to investors

By Mark Wembridge

Dividends, capital gains and the chance to partake in tea and biscuits at the annual meeting are not the only perks offered to shareholders of publicly listed companies.

Many UK companies offer little-publicised sweeteners to encourage retail investors to buy their shares, including discount cards and vouchers.

On Monday John Lewis, the employee-owned department store group, launched its own investor perk by offering discount vouchers to buyers of a £50m ($80.4m) retail bond issue.

The retailer is offering a 6.5 per cent return to investors in the five-year bond, with a 4.5 per cent annual interest rate and a further 2 per cent to be paid in vouchers that can be spent at Waitrose, the upmarket grocer it owns.

John Lewis staff and customers will be able to invest lump sums of between £1,000 and £10,000, and investors will receive £32 in cash and £20 in vouchers every year for each £1,000 invested.

Retailers are not the only companies to offer incentives to investors.

Investors who hold 1,000 shares in housebuilder Persimmon for at least a year can claim a 2 per cent discount on the purchase of a new home, capped at £4,000.

Mulberry, the Somerset-based luxury handbag retailer, gives holders of 500 or more ordinary shares a 20 per cent discount card every year.

Holders of more than 200 shares in British Airways, now part of International Consolidated Airlines Group, are eligible for a 10 per cent discount on some flights booked online.

Debentures and loan stocks

The most secured type of bond is called a **debenture**. They are usually secured by either a fixed or a floating charge against the firm's assets. A fixed charge means that specific assets are used as security which, in the event of default, can be sold at the insistence of the debenture bond-holder and the proceeds used to repay them. Debentures secured on property may be referred to as **mortgage debentures**. A **floating charge** means that the loan is secured by a general charge on

all the assets of the corporation (or a class of the firm's assets such as inventory or debtors). In this case the company has a high degree of freedom to use its assets as it wishes, such as sell them or rent them out, until it commits a default which 'crystallises' the floating charge. If this happens a **receiver** will be appointed with powers to dispose of assets and to distribute the proceeds to the creditors. Even though floating-charge debenture holders can force a **liquidation**, fixed-charge debenture holders rank above floating-charge debenture holders in the payout after insolvency.

The terms bond, debenture and **loan stock** are often used interchangeably and the dividing line between debentures and loan stock is a fuzzy one. As a general rule debentures are secured (have the backing of collateral) and loan stock is unsecured but there are examples which do not fit this classification. If liquidation occurs the unsecured loan stockholders rank beneath the debenture holders and some other categories of creditors such as the tax authorities. In the USA, Canada and some other countries the definitions are somewhat different and this can be confusing. There a debenture is an unsecured bond and so the holders become general creditors who can only claim assets not otherwise pledged. In the USA the secured form of bond is referred to as the mortgage bond and unsecured shorter-dated issues (less than 10 years) are called **notes**.

Bonds are often referred to collectively as **fixed-interest securities**. While this is an accurate description for many bonds, others do not offer *regular* interest payments that are *fixed* amounts. Nevertheless, they are all lumped together as fixed interest to contrast these types of loan instrument with equities that do not carry a promise of a return (Warren Buffett, the financialist, uses the term 'fixed maturity securities').

Trust deeds and covenants

Bond investors are willing to lower the interest they demand if they can be reassured that their money will not be exposed to a high risk. This reassurance is conveyed by placing risk-reducing restrictions on the firm. A **trust deed** (or bond indenture) sets out the terms of the contract between bondholders and the company. The **trustee** (if one is appointed) ensures compliance with the contract throughout the life of the bond and has the power to appoint a receiver (to liquidate the firm's assets). If a trustee is not appointed the usual practice is to give each holder an independently exercisable right to take legal action against a delinquent borrower. The loan agreement will contain a number of **affirmative covenants**. These usually include the requirements to supply regular financial statements, interest and principal payments. The deed may also state the fees due to the lenders and details of what procedures are to be followed in the event of a technical **default**, for example non-payment of interest.

In addition to these basic covenants are the **negative (restrictive) covenants**. These restrict the actions and the rights of the borrower until the debt has been repaid in full. Some examples are:

- *Limits on further debt issuance* If lenders provide finance to a firm they do so on certain assumptions concerning the riskiness of the capital structure. They will want to ensure that the loan does not become more risky due to the firm taking on a much greater debt burden relative to its equity base, so they limit the amount and type of further debt issues – particularly debt which is higher ('**senior debt**') ranking for interest payments and for a liquidation payment. **Subordinated debt** – with low ranking on liquidation – is more likely to be acceptable.

- *Dividend level* Lenders are opposed to money being taken into the firm by borrowing at one end, while being taken away by shareholders at the other. An excessive withdrawal of shareholder funds may unbalance the financial structure and weaken future cash flows.

- *Limits on the disposal of assets* The retention of certain assets, for example property and land, may be essential to reduce the lenders' risk.

- *Financial ratios* A typical covenant here concerns the **interest cover**, for example: 'The annual pre-interest pre-tax profit will remain four times as great as the overall annual interest charge'. Other restrictions might be placed on working capital ratio levels, and the debt to net assets ratio.

While negative covenants cannot provide completely risk-free lending they can influence the behaviour of the management team so as to reduce the risk of default. The lenders' risk can be further reduced by obtaining guarantees from third parties (for example, **guaranteed loan stock**). The guarantor is typically the parent company of the issuer.

Repayments

The principal on many bonds is paid entirely at maturity. However, there are bonds which can be repaid before the final redemption date. One way of paying for redemption is to set up a **sinking fund** that receives regular sums from the firm which will be sufficient, with added interest, to redeem the bonds. A common approach is for the company to issue bonds where it has a range of dates for redemption; so a bond dated 2020–2024 would allow a company the flexibility to repay the principal in cash over four years. Another way of redeeming bonds is for the issuing firm to buy the outstanding bonds by offering the holder a sum higher than or equal to the amount originally paid. A firm is also able to purchase bonds on the open market.

Some bonds are described as 'irredeemable' as they have no fixed redemption date. From the investor's viewpoint they may be irredeemable but the firm has the option of repurchase and can effectively redeem the bonds.

Bond variations

Bonds which are sold at well below the par value are called **deep discounted bonds**, the most extreme form of which is the zero coupon bond. It is easy to calculate the rate of return offered to an investor on this type of bond. For example, if a company issues a bond at a price of £60 which is redeemable at £100 in eight years the annualised rate of return (r) is:

$$60(1 + r)^8 = 100$$

$$r = \sqrt[8]{\frac{100}{60}} - 1 = 0.066 \text{ or } 6.6\%$$

(Mathematical tools of this kind are explained in Appendix 2.1 to Chapter 2).

These bonds are particularly useful for firms with low cash flows in the near term, for example firms engaged in a major property development which will not mature for many years.

A major market has developed over the past two decades called the floating-rate note (FRN) market (also called the variable-rate note market). Two factors have led to the rapid growth in FRN usage. First, the oscillating and unpredictable inflation of the 1970s and early 1980s caused many investors to make large real-term losses on fixed-rate bonds as the interest rate fell below the inflation rate. As a result many lenders became reluctant to lend at fixed rates on a long-term basis. This reluctance led to floaters being cheaper for the issuer because it does not need to offer an interest premium to compensate the investor for being locked into a fixed rate. Secondly, a number of corporations, especially financial institutions, hold assets which give a return that varies with the short-term interest rate level (for example, bank loans and overdrafts) and so prefer to have a similar floating-rate liability. These instruments pay an interest that is linked to a benchmark rate – such as the **LIBOR (London Inter-Bank Offered Rate** – the rate that banks charge each other for borrowed funds). The issuer will pay, say, 70 basis points (0.7 of a percentage point) over six-month LIBOR. The coupon is set for (say) the first six months at the time of issue, after which it is adjusted every six months; so if LIBOR was 5 per cent, the FRN would pay 5.7 per cent for that particular six months. (There are LIBOR rates for various lengths of time, for example, lending/borrowing between high reputation banks for a few hours (overnight LIBOR), or three months.)

There are many other variations on the basic vanilla bond, two of which will be examined later – high-yield bonds and convertible bonds. We now turn to another major source of long-term debt capital – bank borrowing.

Bank borrowing

An alternative to going to the capital markets to raise money via a public bond issue or a private bond placement is to borrow directly from a bank. In this case a tradable security is not issued. The bank makes the loan from its own resources and over time the borrowing company repays the bank with interest. Borrowing from banks is attractive to companies for the following reasons.

- *Administrative and legal costs are low* Because the loan arises from direct negotiation between borrower and lender there is an avoidance of the marketing, arrangement, regulatory and underwriting expenses involved in a bond issue.

- *Quick* The key provisions of a bank loan can be worked out speedily and the funding facility can be in place within a matter of hours.

- *Flexibility* If the economic circumstances facing the firm should change during the life of the loan banks are generally better equipped – and are more willing – to alter the terms of the lending agreement than bondholders. Negotiating with a single lender in a crisis has distinct advantages. Bank loans are also more flexible in the sense that if the firm does better than originally expected a bank loan can often be repaid without penalty. Contrast this with many bonds with fixed redemption dates, or hire purchase/leasing arrangements with fixed terms.

- *Available to small firms* Bank loans are available to firms of almost any size whereas the bond market is for the big players only.

Factors for a firm to consider

There are a number of issues a firm needs to address when considering bank borrowing.

Costs

The borrower may be required to pay an **arrangement fee**, say 1 per cent of the loan, at the time of the initial lending, but this is subject to negotiation and may be bargained down.[1] The interest rate can be either fixed or floating. If it is floating then the rate will generally be a certain percentage above the banks' **base rate** or LIBOR. Because the borrowing corporation is not as safe as a high quality bank taking out the borrowing in the interbank market a corporation will pay say 1 per cent (or 100 basis points) more than LIBOR if it is in a good bargaining position. In the case of base-rate-related lending the interest payable changes immediately the bank announces a change in its base rate. This moves irregularly in response to financial market conditions, which are heavily influenced by the **Bank of England** in its attempt to control the economy. For customers in a poorer bargaining position offering a higher-risk proposal the rate could be 5 per cent or more over the base rate or LIBOR. The interest rate will be determined not only by the riskiness of the undertaking and the bargaining strength of the customer but also by the degree of security for the loan and the size of loan – economies of scale in lending mean that large borrowers pay a lower interest rate. A generation ago it would have been more normal to negotiate fixed-rate loans but most loans today are 'variable rate'.

Floating-rate borrowings have advantages for the firm over fixed-rate borrowings:

- If interest rates fall the cost of the loan falls.

- At the time of arrangement fixed rates are usually above floating rates (to allow for lenders' risk of misforecasting future interest rates).

- Returns on the firm's assets may go up at times of higher interest rates and fall at times of lower interest rates, therefore the risk of higher rates is offset. For example, a bailiff firm may prosper in a high interest rate environment.

However, floating rates have some disadvantages:

- The firm may be caught out by a rise in interest rates if, as with most businesses, its profits do not rise when interest rates rise. Many have failed because of a rise in interest rates at an inopportune time.

- There will be uncertainty about the precise cash outflow impact of the interest. Firms need to plan ahead; in particular, they need to estimate amounts of cash coming in and flowing out, not least so that they can pay bills on time. Fixed rates contribute to greater certainty on cash flows.

1 And indeed the firm should always try, where possible, to negotiate terms each year, or as and when the financial position of the company improves.

Security

When banks are considering the provision of debt finance for a firm they will be concerned about the borrower's competence and honesty. They need to evaluate the proposed project and assess the degree of managerial commitment to its success. The firm will have to explain why the funds are needed and provide detailed cash forecasts covering the period of the loan. Between the bank and the firm stands the classic gulf called 'asymmetric information' in which one party in the negotiation is ignorant of, or cannot observe, some of the information which is essential to the contracting and decision-making process. The bank is unable to assess accurately the ability and determination of the managerial team and will not have a complete understanding of the market environment in which they propose to operate. Companies may overcome bank uncertainty to some degree by providing as much information as possible at the outset and keeping the bank informed of the firm's position as the project progresses.

The finance director and managing director need to consider both the quantity and quality of information flows to the bank. An improved flow of information can lead to a better and more supportive relationship. Firms with significant bank financing requirements to fund growth will be well advised to cultivate and strengthen understanding and rapport with their bank(s). The time to lay the foundations for subsequent borrowing is when the business does not need the money, so that when loans are required there is a reasonable chance of being able to borrow the amount needed on acceptable terms.

Another way for a bank to reduce its risk is to ensure that the firm offers sufficient collateral for the loan. Collateral provides a means of recovering all or the majority of the bank's investment should the firm fail. If the firm is unable to meet its loan obligations then holders of fixed-charge collateral can seize the specific asset used to back the loan. Also, on liquidation, the proceeds of selling assets will go first to the secured loan holders, including floating-charge bank lenders. Collateral can include stocks, debtors and equipment as well as land, buildings and marketable investments such as shares in other companies. In theory banks often have this strong right to seize assets or begin proceedings to liquidate. In practice they are reluctant to use these powers because the realisation of full value from an asset used as security is sometimes difficult and such draconian action can bring adverse publicity. Banks are careful to create a margin for error in the assignment of sufficient collateral to cover the loan because, in the event of default, assigned assets usually command a much lower price than their value to the company as a going concern. A quick sale at auction produces bargains for the buyers of liquidated assets and usually little for the creditors.

Another safety feature applied by banks is the requirement that the firm abide by a number of loan covenants which place restrictions on managerial action in a similar fashion to bond covenants (*see* section on bonds earlier in this chapter). Exhibit 11.3 discusses National Express' net-debt-to-profits ratio covenant.

Exhibit 11.3

National Express in debt talks

By Gill Plimmer

National Express is in talks with bankers to renegotiate terms on part of its £1.2bn debt amid fears that the bus and rail operator will breach loan conditions in December.

The group is expected to pass a key test of whether it is meeting the terms of its debt at the end of this month. But it is still seeking greater flexibility as it struggles with a slowdown in passenger revenues on its East Coast train franchise and rising payments to the Department for Transport to run the services.

The company hopes to have announced an agreement by the time it issues a trading update on July 1 over an easing of a debt condition, or covenant, requiring that net debt cannot be more than 3½ times underlying earnings.

Jez Maiden, finance director, has said recently he was confident that a programme of 'self-help' aimed at improving cash flows by £100m this year will bolster the group's finances.

The company has slashed its dividend and cut costs, shedding jobs and selling its £33m London bus business to raise cash last month.

But speculation that it will be forced to launch a £400m rights issue continues to rise.

Exhibit 11.3 *(continued)*

The company is struggling under the weight of the most expensive rail franchise in the industry.

Under the terms of a contract negotiated in 2007 at the height of the economic boom, National Express is contracted to pay the government £1.4bn to run train services between London and Edinburgh until 2015, with the amount rising steeply from £85m in 2008 to £395m this year.

Financial Times, 17 June 2009.

Finally, lenders can turn to the directors of the firm to provide additional security. They might be asked to sign **personal guarantees** that the firm will not default. Personal assets (such as homes) may be used as collateral. This erodes the principle of limited liability status and is likely to inhibit risk-taking productive activity. However, for many smaller firms it is the only way of securing a loan and at least it demonstrates the commitment of the director to the success of the enterprise.[2]

Repayment

A firm must carefully consider the period of the loan and the repayment schedules in the light of its future cash flows. It could be disastrous, for instance, for a firm engaging in a capital project which involved large outlays for the next five years followed by cash inflows thereafter to have a bank loan which required significant interest and principal payments in the near term. For situations like these **repayment holidays** or **grace periods** may be granted, with the majority of the repayment being made once cash flows are sufficiently positive.

It may be possible for a company to arrange a **mortgage-style repayment schedule** in which monthly payments from the borrower to the lender are constant throughout the term.

A **term loan** is a business loan with an original maturity of more than one year and a specified schedule of principal and interest payments. It may or may not be secured and has the advantage over the overdraft of not being repayable at the demand of the bank at short notice (*see* Chapter 12). The terms of the loan are usually tailored to the specific needs of the individual borrower and these are capable of wide variation. A proportion of the interest and the principal can be repaid monthly or annually and can be varied to correspond with the borrower's cash flows. It is rare for there to be no repayment of the principal during the life of the loan but it is possible to request that the bulk of the principal is paid in the later years. Banks generally prefer **self-amortising term loans** with a high proportion of the principal paid off each year. This has the advantage of reducing risk by imposing a programme of debt reduction on the borrowing firm.

The repayment schedule agreed between bank and borrower is capable of infinite variety – four possibilities are shown in **Exhibit 11.4**.

The retail and investment banks are not the only sources of long-term loans. Insurance companies and other specialist institutions such as private equity funds (*see* Chapter 10) will also provide long-term debt finance.

Syndicated loans

For large loans a single bank may not be able or willing to lend the whole amount. To do so would be to expose the bank to an unacceptable risk of failure on the part of one of its borrowers. Bankers like to spread their lending to gain the risk-reducing benefits of diversification. They prefer to participate in a number of syndicated loans in which a few banks each contribute a portion of the overall loan. So, for a large multinational company loan of, say, £500m, a single bank may provide £30m, with perhaps 100 other banks contributing the remainder. The bank originating the loan will usually manage the syndicate and is called the **lead manager** (there might be one or more lead

2 Indeed, when the author recently contacted a number of banks to negotiate a loan for a company he controls, the corporate loan officers were all amazed at his cheek in not accepting a personal guarantee clause – 'but we normally get a personal guarantee, it is just standard practice', they declared. Don't accept this line if you have a strong business plan and strong financial structure.

Exhibit 11.4	Examples of loan repayment arrangements

In all four schemes £10,000 is borrowed, repayable over four years with interest at 10% p.a. (assuming annual payments, not monthly)

(a) Time period (years)	1	2	3	4
Payment (£)	3,155	3,155	3,155	3,155

(b) Time period (years)	1	2	3	4
Payment (£)	1,000	1,000	1,000	11,000

(c) Time period (years)	1	2	3	4
Payment (£)	0	0	0	14,641

(d) Time period (years)	1	2	3	4
Payment (£)	0	1,000	6,000	6,831

banks). This bank (or these banks) may invite a handful of other banks to co-manage the loan who then persuade other banks to supply much of the funding. That is, they help the process of forming the syndicate group of banks in the general syndication. The managing bank also underwrites much of the loan while inviting other banks to underwrite the rest – that is, guaranteeing to provide the funds if other banks do not step forward.[3] Syndicated loans are available at short notice and can be provided discreetly (helpful if the money is to finance a merger bid, for example). Syndicated loans generally offer lower returns than bonds, but as they rank above most bonds on liquidation payouts there is less risk. The loans carry covenants similar to those on bond agreements. The volume of new international syndicated loans now runs into hundreds of billions of pounds per year.

Credit rating

Firms often pay to have their bonds and other loans rated by specialist **credit-rating** organisations. The debt rating depends on the likelihood of payments of interest and/or capital not being paid (that is, default) and, in some cases, on the extent to which the lender is protected in the event of a default (an estimate is made of the likelihood of recouping a proportion of money in the event of insolvency or bankruptcy, the recoverability of the debt). Government bonds from the reputable leading countries have an insignificant risk of default whereas unsecured subordinated corporate loan stock has a much higher risk. We would expect that firms in stable industries and with conservative accounting and financing policies and a risk-averse business strategy would have a low risk of default and therefore a high credit rating. Companies with a high total debt burden, a poor cash flow position, in a worsening market environment causing lower and more volatile earnings, will have a high default risk and a low credit rating. The leading organisations providing credit ratings are Moody's, Standard & Poor's (S&P) and Fitch. The highest rating is AAA or Aaa (triple-A rated). Such a rating indicates very high quality. The capacity to repay interest and principal is extremely strong. Single A indicates a strong capacity to pay interest and capital but there is some degree of susceptibility to impairment as economic events unfold. BBB indicates adequate debt service capacity but vulnerability to adverse economic conditions or changing circumstances. B and C rated debt has predominantly speculative characteristics. The lowest is D which indicates the firm is in default. Ratings of BBB- (or Baa3 for Moody's) or above are regarded as '**investment grade**' – this is important because many institutional investors are permitted to invest in investment grade bonds only (*see* **Exhibit 11.5**). Bonds rated below this are

3 The term 'mandated lead arranger' or MLA is often used for the managing bank(s). Also 'book runner' or 'bookrunner group' indicates those who solicit interest in the loan from lenders and gather offers of support. They gradually 'build a book' – a list of confirmed buyers. They do the syndication.

Standard & Poor's	Moody's	Fitch's	Grades	
AAA	Aaa	AAA	Prime, maximum safety	
AA+	Aa1	AA+	High grade, high quality	
AA	Aa2	AA		
AA–	Aa3	AA–		
A+	A1	A+	Upper medium	Investment grade bonds
A	A2	A		
A–	A3	A–		
BBB+	Baa1	BBB+	Lower medium	
BBB	Baa2	BBB		
BBB–	Baa3	BBB–		
BB+	Ba1	BB+	Speculative	
BB	Ba2	BB		
BB–	Ba3	BB–		
B+	B1	B+	Highly speculative	
B	B2	B		
B–	B3	B–		Non-investment grade, high-yield or 'junk' bonds
CCC+	Caa1	CCC+	Substantial risk	
CCC	Caa2	CCC	In poor standing	
CCC–	Caa3	CCC–		
CC	Ca	CC	Extremely speculative	
C	C	C	May be in default	
D		D	Default	

Exhibit 11.5 A comparison of Moody's, Standard & Poor's and Fitch's rating scales

called **high-yield** (or **junk**) **bonds**. Generally, the specific loan is rated rather than the borrower. If the loan does not have a rating it could be that the borrower has not paid for one, rather than implying anything sinister.

The rating and re-rating of bonds is followed with great interest by borrowers and lenders and can give rise to some heated argument. Credit ratings are of great concern to the borrowing corporation or government because bonds with lower ratings tend to have higher costs Exhibit 11.6 describes the grave situation for Portugal and Greece in 2011 and emphasises the power of the credit rating agencies. (Deficit refers to the shortfall in taxes to cover government spending.)

Exhibit 11.6

Downgrade blow knocks wind out of Portugal

By Peter Wise in Lisbon, Peter Spiegel in Brussels and Ben Hall in London

In an unguarded moment caught on camera on Wednesday, Pedro Passos Coelho, Portugal's prime minister, described Moody's downgrade of the country's sovereign debt to junk status as 'a punch in the stomach'.

The blow has knocked the wind out of his new centre-right coalition less than a week after it presented a government programme aimed at demarcating Portugal's economic woes from the deep crisis that has engulfed Greece.

Vítor Gaspar, finance minister, criticised the US rating agency for failing to take into account austerity measures and a 'broad political consensus' in support of the country's €78bn bail-out deal with the European Union and International Monetary Fund.

Despite these protestations, Portugal was forced to follow Greece and Ireland in seeking a bail-out as its credit ratings were cut and its bond yields soared to unsustainable levels. By suggesting that

Exhibit 11.6 (continued)

Portugal is likely to follow Greece in seeking a second bail-out deal and failing to meet its deficit-reduction commitments, Moody's has stung the Portuguese into an angry response.

Moody's four-notch downgrade was 'immoral and insulting', said Fernando Faria de Oliveira, chief executive of state-owned Caixa Geral de Depósitos, Portugal's largest bank by deposits.

Moody's said moves to involve private investors in a new rescue plan for Greece made it likely that the EU would require the same preconditions for Portugal. This would discourage new private sector lending, decreasing the likelihood that Portugal could resume financing its debt in international markets in two years, as envisaged in the bail-out deal, the agency said.

Moody's also cited 'heightened concerns' that Portugal would not be able to meet the deficit-reduction targets it has agreed to in the rescue package. This was because of the 'formidable challenges' facing the new centre-right coalition government to cut spending, increase tax revenue, lift growth and support the banking system.

 Financial Times, 7 July 2011, p. 6.

Bond default rates

Exhibit 11.7 shows the proportion of bonds that have defaulted one, two, three, four, five and ten years after issue over the period 1990–2010. Notice the large differences in default rates between the ratings. After five years only 0.17 per cent of AA bonds defaulted, whereas 11.68 per cent of B bonds defaulted. When examining data on default rates it is important to appreciate that default is a wide-ranging term and could refer to any number of events, from a missed payment to bankruptcy. For some of these events all is lost from the investor's perspective; for other events a very high percentage, if not all, of the interest and principal is recovered. Hickman (1958) observed that defaulted publicly held and traded bonds tended to sell for 40 cents on the dollar. This average recovery rate rule of thumb seems to have held over time – in approximate terms – with senior secured bank loans returning more than 60 per cent and subordinated bonds less than 30 per cent.

Mezzanine finance and high-yield (junk) bonds

Mezzanine debt is a loan offering a high return with a high risk. It may be either unsecured or secured but ranks behind senior loans for payment of interest and capital. This type of debt generally offers interest rates two to nine percentage points more than that on senior debt and frequently gives the lenders some right to a share in equity values should the firm perform well. It is a kind of **hybrid finance** ranking for payment below straight debt but above equity – it is thus described alternatively as *subordinated*, *intermediate* or *low grade*. One of the major attractions of this form of finance for the investor is that it often comes with equity warrants (*see* Chapter 10) or share options (see Chapter 4) attached which can be used to obtain shares in the firm – this is known as an '**equity kicker**'. These may be triggered by an event such as the firm joining the stock market.

Exhibit 11.7	Fitch Global Corporate Finance average cumulative default rates 1990–2010					
Rating	1 year	2 years	3 years	4 years	5 years	10 years
	%	%	%	%	%	%
'AAA'	0	0	0	0	0	0
'AA'	0	0	0	0.08	0.17	0.32
'A'	0.04	0.17	0.37	0.54	0.81	2.12
'BBB'	0.26	0.83	1.48	2.10	2.78	5.13
'BB'	1.12	2.74	4.15	5.23	6.04	12.33
'B'	3.10	7.72	9.93	10.55	11.68	15.21
'CCC to 'C	30.98	41.26	43.22	44.70	45.36	57.89
Investment grade	0.14	0.47	0.84	1.20	1.60	2.95
High yield	3.69	6.91	8.55	9.53	10.43	14.98
All Industrials	1.11	2.18	2.83	3.27	3.71	5.37

Source: Fitch Ratings Global Corporate Finance 2010 Transition and Default Study www.fitchratings.com/creditdesk/reports/report_frame.cfm?rpt_id=606665

Mezzanine finance tends to be used when bank borrowing limits are reached and the firm cannot or will not issue more equity. It is more expensive than bank borrowing, but is cheaper (in terms of required return) than would be available on the equity market; and it allows the owners of a business to raise large sums of money without sacrificing control. It is a form of finance which permits the firm to move beyond what is normally considered acceptable debt:equity ratios (gearing or leverage levels).

Crucially, unlike most bank loans, which usually involve annual repayments, mezzanine is often like an interest-only mortgage with no capital repayments until the end of the loan. Also mezzanine lenders, which are often specialist funds rather than banks, are usually prepared to lend against the company's prospects in terms of expected cash flows, rather than insisting on security (collateral), as banks tend toward. Mezzanine funds were hit hard by the recession following the 2008 financial crisis – *see* Exhibit 11.8.

Exhibit 11.8

Hunger for funds spurs mezzanine debt revival

By Daniel Schäfer and Robin Wigglesworth in London

Mezzanine funds are preparing themselves for a revival of their market after the collapse of high-yield financings prompts private equity groups to tap alternative sources of deal funding.

Banks financing the recent buy-out of Swedish alarm group Securitas Direct raised €393.5m in mezzanine funding this week, in the biggest such deal this year.

This mezzanine investment looks set to be the first in a string of such funding deals, say bankers, as it provides a way for banks to relieve some of the pain from highly leveraged buy-out loans that are stuck on their balance sheets.

Mezzanine investments rank between senior bank debt and equity in terms of risk profile for the lender and in terms of costs for the borrower.

Recent market turbulence has dented investor appetite for European high-yield bonds, leaving banks potentially unable to refinance large bridge loans they handed out to buyers of companies such

Exhibit 11.8 *(continued)*

as Securitas Direct, Polkomtel and Coditel in the run-up to the summer.

'We will see more deals like Securitas getting done where one or a club of mezzanine investors will provide capital,' says Fred Goltz, head of mezzanine investment at Kohlberg Kravis Roberts & Co, the alternative asset manager.

'This is better for banks and private equity groups than having to deal with a hung bridge loan.'

It comes as mezzanine investors are raising vast amounts of fresh money this year in anticipation of a revival of their long dormant market. About 65 mezzanine funds globally are currently targeting to collect $27.1bn in fresh capital from investors,

according to data by Preqin, a private equity research group.

This includes Blackstone Group's GSO Capital, London-listed Intermediate Capital Group and KKR, which is currently vying to raise a $1bn fund according to Preqin.

The asset class has been a mere shadow of its high times in 2006 and 2007, when record amounts of more than $35bn had been deployed annually in deals such as the vast $20.6bn mezzanine loan financing the takeover of Hilton Hotels by buy-out group Blackstone.

Last year, only $2.67bn was invested in mezzanine deals globally, according to data from Dealogic, excluding the recent Securitas Direct deal. In the first half of this year, hardly any new deals got done as mezzanine money had been very expensive compared with buoyant high-yield markets.

But with demand for risky assets in the high-yield markets quickly evaporating in the past few months, mezzanine has regained its long-gone appeal to buy-out chiefs. 'The high-yield market is choppy in Europe, but there are alternatives. Mezzanine investors remain hungry for deals,' says Peter Bacon, head of European capital markets at Morgan Stanley, which had arranged the Securitas mezzanine financing.

With typical coupons of between 12 and 14 per cent, bankers say that mezzanine suddenly looks almost cheap. It also gives buy-out managers more flexibility in terms of refinancing at a later stage and paying the interest rates at the end of the maturity.

Mezzanine loans have yet to recover post crisis

Total global mezzanine loans

Bonds with high-risk and high-return characteristics are called high-yield (junk) bonds (they are rated below investment grade by rating agencies with ratings of Bs and Cs). These may be bonds which started as apparently safe investments but have now become riskier ('**fallen angels**') or they may be bonds issued specifically to provide higher-risk finance instruments for investors. This latter type began its rise to prominence in the USA in the 1980s and is now a market with over $100bn issued per year. The rise of the US junk bond market meant that no business was safe from the threat of takeover, however large – *see* **Case study 11.1** on Michael Milken.

The high-yield bond is much more popular in the USA than in Europe because of the aversion (constrained by legislation) to such instruments in the major financial institutions. The European high-yield bond market is in its infancy. The first high-yield bonds denominated in European currencies were issued as recently as 1997 when Geberit, a Swiss/UK manufacturer, raised DM 157.5m by selling 10-year bonds offering an interest rate which was 423 basis points (4.23 per cent) higher than the interest rate on a 10-year German government bond (bund). Since then there have been hundreds of issues. However, the European high-yield market remains about one-quarter the size of the US one but it is growing rapidly.

While studying at Wharton Business School in the 1970s Michael Milken came to the belief that the gap in interest rates between safe bonds and high-yield bonds was excessive, given the relative risks. This created an opportunity for financial institutions to make an acceptable return from junk bonds, given their risk level. At the investment banking firm Drexel Burnham Lambert, Milken was able to persuade a large body of institutional investors to supply finance to the junk bond market as well as provide a service to corporations wishing to grow through the use of junk bonds. Small firms were able to raise billions of dollars to take over large US corporations. Many of these issuers of junk bonds had debt ratios of 90 per cent and above – for every $1 of share capital $9 was borrowed. These gearing levels concerned many in the financial markets. It was thought that companies were pushing their luck too far and indeed many did collapse under the weight of their debt. The market was dealt a particularly severe blow when Michael Milken was convicted, sent to jail and ordered to pay $600m in fines. Drexel was also convicted, paid $650m in fines and filed for bankruptcy in 1990. The junk bond market was in a sorry state in the early 1990s, with high levels of default and few new issues. However, it did not take long for the market to recover.

Mezzanine finance is usually a private form of debt (e.g. loan), rather than a publicly traded bond form of debt. However, mezzanine notes are sometimes issued which are tradable in a secondary market. Mezzanine finance (and **second lien** loans – whose owners, by definition, would be in line behind senior secured creditors in a liquidation) has proved to be particularly useful to managers involved in a management buy-out (MBO) which by necessity requires high levels of debt, that is, **leveraged buy-outs (LBOs)**. A typical LBO would have a financial structure as follows:

- 50–60 per cent from senior bank or other debt providers;
- 25–30 per cent from subordinated debt – for example, mezzanine finance, unsecured low-ranking bonds and/or preference shares;
- 10–25 per cent equity.

Fast-growing companies also make use of mezzanine finance and junk bonds. They have been particularly attractive sources for cable television companies, telecommunications and some media businesses which require large investments in the near term but also offer a relatively stable profits flow in the long term. Mezzanine loans have the advantage over bonds in flexibility on exit. That is, high yield bonds typically have a life of five to seven years, making it expensive to repay early. Mezzanine does not carry large penalties for early repayment.

Mezzanine financing and high-yield bonds have been employed by firms 'gearing themselves up' to finance merger activity, and also for **leveraged recapitalisations**. For instance, a firm might have run into trouble, defaulted and its assets are now under the control of a group of creditors, including bankers and bondholders. One way to allow the business to continue would be to persuade the creditors to accept alternative financial securities in place of their debt securities to bring the leverage (financial gearing) to a reasonable level. They might be prepared to accept a mixture of shares and mezzanine finance. The mezzanine instruments permit the holders to receive high interest rates in recognition of the riskiness of the firm, and they open up the possibility of an exceptionally high return from warrants or share options should the firm get back to a growth path. The alternative for the lenders may be a return of only a few pence in the pound from the immediate liquidation of the firm's assets.

Mezzanine finance/junk bond borrowing usually leads to high debt levels resulting in a high fixed cost imposition on the firm. This can be a dangerous way of financing expansion and therefore the use of these types of finance has been criticised. On the other hand, some commentators have praised the way in which high gearing and large annual interest payments have focused the minds of managers and engendered extraordinary performance (*see* Chapter 18). Also, without this finance, many takeovers, buyouts and financial restructurings would not take place. As **Exhibit 11.9** makes clear, high yield bond finance has grown significantly in recent years.

Exhibit 11.9

Resurgence of UK corporate bond issues

By Robin Wigglesworth and Richard Milne

A flurry of UK corporate bond issuance is providing a healthy respite for bankers in London after a lacklustre 18 months.

Last week was the busiest for investment-grade sterling bonds since July last year, according to Barclays Capital, with cinema chain Odeon & UCI and carmaker Jaguar Land Rover and airports operator BAA selling debt.

'I can't remember the last time the sterling market has been this busy,' says Marco Baldini, head of European corporate syndicate at Barclays Capital. 'It's all pointing to a very robust year.'

Bond issuance has been far more muted in the UK and continental Europe compared with the US as companies have been reluctant to borrow money they did not necessarily need. Bankers say that US businesses by contrast have been more keen to lock in the record low interest rates on offer.

'We think that [European] corporates filled their boots coming out of the credit crunch. There hasn't been a wholesale ringing of the bell where [chief executives] are out there being aggressive,' says Denis Coleman, head of European credit finance at Goldman Sachs.

Places for People, the social housing association, on Monday became the latest group to issue in sterling, increasing the size of its 20-year bond from £150m to £175m due to strong demand.

Mr Baldini says one reason is that the UK represents something of a haven as opposed to the crisis-wracked continent. 'UK investors are a bit more removed from the European situation. The tone of the market is more positive, while Europe is still being affected by Greece.'

Nick Gartside, international chief investment officer for fixed income at JPMorgan Asset Management, points to the difference in returns between low-yielding cash and government debt on the one hand and corporate debt on the other: 'I believe assets compete against each other. My biggest competitor is cash.'

The rebound in activity among investment-grade companies is also reflected in issuance by high-yield companies, those with lower credit ratings. As banks have largely shunned lending to the riskier companies, bond markets have filled the gap in the UK and continental Europe.

The volumes may lag behind those in the US but bankers are excited by signs that the long-awaited move away from bank finance in Europe could be slowly happening.

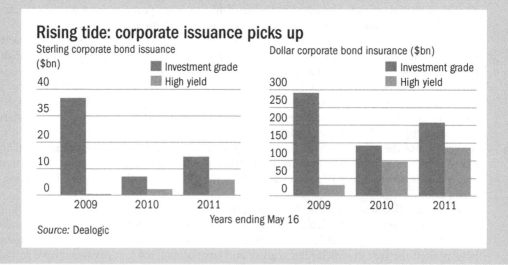

Rising tide: corporate issuance picks up

Sterling corporate bond issuance ($bn) — Investment grade / High yield
40, 35, 20, 10, 0 — 2009, 2010, 2011

Dollar corporate bond insurance ($bn) — Investment grade / High yield
300, 250, 200, 150, 100, 50, 0 — 2009, 2010, 2011

Years ending May 16

Source: Dealogic

Financing a leveraged buy-out

If the anticipated cash flows are reasonably stable then a highly leveraged buy-out may give an exceptional return to the shareholders. Take the case of Sparrow, a subsidiary of Hawk plc (*see* Exhibit 11.10). The managers have agreed a buy-out price of £10m, equal to Sparrow's assets. They are able to raise £1m from their own resources to put into equity capital and have borrowed £9m. The debt pays an interest rate of 14 per cent and the corporate tax rate is 25 per cent (payable one year after year-end). Profits before interest and tax in the first year after the buy-out are expected to be £1.5m and will grow at 25 per cent per annum thereafter. All earnings will be retained within the business to pay off debt.

Exhibit 11.10 Sparrow – Profit and Loss Account and Balance Sheet (£000s)

	Years					
	1	2	3	4	5	6
Profit before interest and taxes (after depreciation)	1,500	1,875	2,344	2,930	3,662	4,578
Less interest	1,260	1,226	1,144	999	770	433
	240	649	1,200	1,931	2,892	4,145
Tax	0	60	162	300	483	723
Profits available to pay off debt	240	589	1,038	1,631	2,409	3,422

Balance Sheet		Year					
	Opening	1	2	3	4	5	6
Equity	1,000	1,240	1,829	2,867	4,498	6,907	10,329
Debt	9,000	8,760	8,171	7,133	5,502	3,093	0
Assets	10,000	10,000	10,000	10,000	10,000	10,000	10,329

Notes: Past tax liabilities have been accepted by Hawk. Money set aside for depreciation is used to replace assets to maintain £10m of assets throughout. Also depreciation equals capital allowances used for tax purposes.

In the first few years the debt burden absorbs a large proportion of the rapidly increasing profits. However, it only takes six years for the entire debt to be retired. The shareholders then own a business with assets of over £10m, an increase of over tenfold on their original investment. The business is also producing a large annual profit which could make a stock market flotation attractive, in which case the value of the shares held by the management will probably be worth much more than £10m.[4]

Convertible bonds

Convertible bonds (or convertible loan stocks) carry a rate of interest in the same way as vanilla bonds, but they also give the holder the right to exchange the bonds at some stage in the future

4 This example is designed to show the effect of leverage. It does lack realism in a number of respects; for example, it is unlikely that profits will continue to rise at 25 per cent per annum without further investment. This can be adjusted for – the time taken to pay off the debt lengthens but the principles behind the example do not alter.

into ordinary shares according to some prearranged formula.[5] The owner of these bonds is not obliged to exercise this right of conversion and so the bonds may continue until redemption as interest-bearing instruments. Usually the conversion price is 10–30 per cent greater than the existing share price. So if a £100 bond offered the right to convert to 40 ordinary shares the conversion price would be £2.50 (that is, £100/40) which, given the current market price of the shares of, say, £2.20, would be a conversion premium of:

$$\frac{2.50 - 2.20}{2.20} = 0.136 \text{ or } 13.6\%$$

Autonomy, the UK's largest software company, sold £500m of convertible bonds in March 2010. These were five-year bonds (principal to be repaid in March 2015 unless converted to shares before then) issued at a par value of £100, offering a semi-annual coupon of 3.25 per cent per year. The issue was to raise money for acquiring other firms. The five-year bond would be converted into ordinary shares and would have an initial conversion price of £20.6334, a 36 per cent premium to the share price at the time of issue at £15.22. From this information we can calculate the conversion ratio (*see* Exhibit 11.11 for a summary of technical terms):

$$\text{Conversion ratio} = \frac{\text{Nominal (par) value of the bond}}{\text{Conversion price}} = \frac{£100}{£20.6334} = 4.8465 \text{ shares}$$

Each bond carries the right to convert to 4.8465 shares, which is equivalent to paying £20.6334 for each share at the £100 par value of the bond.

At the time of the issue many investors may have looked at the low interest rate on the convertible and said to themselves that although this was greater than the dividend yield on shares (3 per cent) it was less than that on conventional bonds, but offsetting this was the prospect of capital gains made by converting the bonds into shares. If the shares rose to, say, £30 each £100 bond could be converted to 4.8465 shares worth £30 × 4.8465 = £145.395.

Exhibit 11.11 Summary of convertible bond technical jargon

● **Conversion ratio** This gives the number of ordinary shares into which a convertible bond may be converted:

$$\text{Conversion ratio} = \frac{\text{Nominal (par) value of bond}}{\text{Conversion price}}$$

● **Conversion price** This gives the price of each ordinary share obtainable by exchanging a convertible bond:

$$\text{Conversion price} = \frac{\text{Nominal (par) value of bond}}{\text{Number of shares into which bond may be converted}}$$

● **Conversion premium** This gives the difference between the conversion price and the market share price, expressed as a percentage:

$$\text{Conversion premium} = \frac{\text{Conversion price} - \text{Market share price}}{\text{Market share price}} \times 100$$

● **Conversion value** This is the value of a convertible bond if it were converted into ordinary shares at the current share price:

$$\text{Conversion value} = \text{Current share price} \times \text{Conversion ratio}$$

5 Alternatively they may be convertible into preference shares.

The value of a convertible bond (also called an 'equity-linked bond') rises as the value of the underlying ordinary shares increases, but at a lower percentage rate. The value could be analysed as a 'debt portion' (which depends on the discounted value of the coupons) and an 'equity portion' (the right to convert is an equity option). If the share price rises above the conversion price the investor may exercise the option to convert if he/she anticipates that the share price will at least be maintained and the dividend yield is higher than the convertible bond yield. If the share price rise is seen to be temporary the investor may wish to hold on to the bond.

The right to convert may specify a specific date or several specific dates over, say, a four-year period, or any time between two dates. Most convertible bonds are unsecured but as Exhibit 11.12 on Greenhills shows, this is not always the case – a good thing for Hunter Ground.

Exhibit 11.12 Secured convertible debentures

Greenhills

The first AIM-traded company to go into receivership was Greenhills, the restaurant operator. A major investor, Hunter Ground, appointed administrative receivers on 4 December 1996. Hunter Ground held secured convertible debentures from Greenhills worth £506,000.

Source: Investors Chronicle, 20 December 1996, p. 11. Reprinted with kind permission of the Investors Chronicle.

Advantages to the company of convertible bonds

Convertible bonds have the following advantages to the company.

1 *Lower interest than on a similar debenture* The firm can ask investors to accept a lower interest on these debt instruments because the investor values the conversion right. This was a valuable feature for many dot.com companies in the late 1990s. Companies such as Amazon and AOL could pay 5–6 per cent on convertibles – less than half what they would have paid on straight bonds.

2 *The interest is tax deductible* Because convertible bonds are a form of debt the coupon payment can be regarded as a cost of the business and can therefore be used to reduce taxable profit.

3 *Self liquidating* When the share price reaches a level at which conversion is worthwhile the bonds will (normally) be exchanged for shares so the company does not have to find cash to pay off the loan principal – it simply issues more shares. This has obvious cash flow benefits. However, the disadvantage is that the other equity holders may experience a reduction in earnings per share and dilution of voting rights.

4 *Fewer restrictive covenants* The directors have greater operating and financial flexibility than they would with a secured debenture. Investors accept that a convertible is a hybrid between debt and equity finance and do not tend to ask for high-level security, impose strong operating restrictions on managerial action or insist on strict financial ratio boundaries – notwithstanding the case of Greenhills. Many Silicon Valley companies with little more than a web-portal and a brand have used convertibles because of the absence of a need to provide collateral or stick to asset : borrowing ratios.

5 *Underpriced shares* A company which wishes to raise equity finance over the medium term but judges that the stock market is temporarily underpricing its shares may turn to convertible bonds. If the firm does perform as the managers expect and the share price rises, the convertible will be exchanged for equity.

6 *Cheap way to issue shares* Graham and Harvey (2001) found that managers favoured convertibles as an inexpensive way to issue 'delayed' equity. Equity is raised at a later date without the high costs of rights issues etc.

7 *Available finance when straight debt and equity are not available* Some firms locked out of the equity markets (e.g. because of poor recent performance) and the straight debt markets because of high levels of indebtedness may still be able to raise money in the convertible market. Firms use convertible debt 'to attract investors unsure about the riskiness of the company' (Graham and Harvey (2001)).

Advantages to the investor

The advantages of convertible bonds to the investor are as follows.

1 They are able to wait and see how the share price moves before investing in equity.

2 In the near term there is greater security for their principal compared with equity investment, and the annual coupon is usually higher than the dividend yield.

The bonds sold may not give the right to conversion into shares of the issuers, but shares of another company held by the issuer – *see* the cases of Hutchison Whampoa, Telecom Italia and France Telecom in Exhibit 11.13. Note that the term 'exchangeable bond' is probably more appropriate in these cases.

Exhibit 11.13

Brakes applied to convertible bond market

Rebecca Bream

In January Hong Kong conglomerate Hutchison Whampoa sold $2.65bn of bonds exchangeable into shares of Vodafone, the UK mobile phone operator. Hutchison had been gradually divesting its stake in the UK group since completing a $3bn exchangeable bond deal last September.

This was followed at the end of the month by Telecom Italia which sold €2bn of bonds exchangeable into shares of subsidiaries Telecom Italia Mobile and Internet operator Seat.

In February France Telecom sold €3.3bn of bonds exchangeable into shares of Orange, completed at the same time as the mobile unit's IPO, and one of the biggest exchangeable bond deals ever sold in Europe.

Valuing bonds

Bonds, particularly those which are traded in secondary markets such as the London Stock Exchange, are priced according to supply and demand. The main influences on the price of a bond will be the general level of interest rates for securities of that risk level and maturity. If the coupon rate of interest on the par value is less than the current market interest rate the bond will trade at less than the par value of £100 (or €1,000, or €100,000, etc.). Take the case of an irredeemable bond with an annual coupon of 8 per cent. This financial asset offers to any potential purchaser a regular £8 per year for ever (i.e. 8 per cent of the par value of £100). When the bond was first issued general interest rates for this risk class may well have been 8 per cent and so the bond may have been sold at £100. However, interest rates change over time. Suppose that the rate demanded by investors is now 10 per cent. Investors will no longer be willing to pay £100 for an instrument that yields £8 per year. The current market value of the bond will fall to £80 (£8/0.10) because this is the maximum amount needed to pay for similar bonds given the current interest rate of 10 per cent. If the coupon is more than the current market interest rate the market price of the bond will be greater than the nominal (par) value. Thus if market rates are 6 per cent the irredeemable bond will be priced at £133.33 (£8/0.06).

Note that as interest rates fall the price of the bond rises, and vice versa.

The formula relating the price of an irredeemable bond, the coupon and the market rate of interest is:

$$P_D = \frac{i}{k_D}$$

where P_D = price of bond

i = nominal annual interest (the coupon rate × nominal (par) value of the bond)

k_D = market discount rate, annual return required on similar bonds

Also:

$$V_D = \frac{I}{k_D}$$

where V_D = total market value of all of the bonds of this type

I = total annual nominal interest of all the bonds of this type

We may wish to establish the market rate of interest represented by the market price of the bond. For example, if an irredeemable bond offers an annual coupon of 9.5 per cent and is currently trading at £87.50, with the next coupon due in one year, the rate of return is:

$$k_D = \frac{i}{P_D} = \frac{9.5}{87.5} = 0.1086 \text{ or } 10.86\%$$

Redeemable bonds

A purchaser of a redeemable bond buys two types of income promise: first the coupon, second the redemption payment. The amount that an investor will pay depends on the amount these income flows are worth when discounted at the rate of return required on that risk class of debt. The relationships are expressed in the following formulae:

$$P_D = \frac{i_1}{1 + k_D} + \frac{i_2}{(1 + k_D)^2} + \frac{i_3}{(1 + k_D)^3} + \dots + \frac{R_n}{(1 + k_D)^n}$$

and:

$$V_D = \frac{I_1}{1 + k_D} + \frac{I_2}{(1 + k_D)^2} + \frac{I_3}{(1 + k_D)^3} + \dots + \frac{R^*_n}{(1 + k_D)^n}$$

where i_1, i_2 and i_3 = nominal interest per bond in years 1, 2 and 3 up to n years

I_1, I_2 and I_3 = total nominal interest in years 1, 2 and 3 up to n years

R_n and R^*_n = redemption value of a bond, and total redemption of all bonds in year n, the redemption or maturity date

The worked example of Blackaby illustrates the valuation of a bond when the market interest rate is given.

Worked example 11.1 Blackaby plc

Blackaby plc issued a bond with a par value of £100 in September 2012, redeemable in September 2018 at par. The coupon is 8 per cent payable annually in September – first payment in 2013. The facts available from this are:

● the bond might have a par value of £100 but this may not be what investors will pay for it;
● the annual cash payment will be £8 (8 per cent of par);
● in September 2018, £100 will be handed over to the bondholder (in the absence of default).

Question 1

What is the price investors will pay for this bond at the time of issue if the market rate of interest for a security in this risk class is 7 per cent?

Answer

$$P_D = \frac{8}{1 + 0.07} + \frac{8}{(1 + 0.07)^2} + \frac{8}{(1 + 0.07)^3} + ... + \frac{8}{(1 + 0.07)^6} + \frac{100}{(1 + 0.07)^6}$$

P_D = £8 annuity for 6 years @ 7 per cent = 4.7665 × 8 = 38.132

plus $\dfrac{100}{(1 + 0.07)^6}$ = 66.634

£104.766

Question 2

What is the bond's value in the secondary market in September 2015 if interest rates rise by 200 basis points (i.e. for this risk class they are 9 per cent) between 2012 and 2015? (Assume the next coupon payment is in one year.)

Answer

P_D = £8 annuity for 3 years @ 9 per cent = 2.5313 × 8 = 20.25

plus $\dfrac{100}{(1 + 0.09)^3}$ = 77.22

£97.47

Again, note that as interest rates rise the price of bonds falls.

If we need to calculate the rate of return demanded by investors from a particular bond when we know the market price and coupon amounts, we can compute the internal rate of return. For example, Bluebird plc issued a bond many years ago which is due for redemption at par of £100 in three years. The coupon is 6 per cent and the market price is £91. The rate of return now offered in the market by this bond is found by solving for k_D:

$$P_D = \frac{i_1}{1 + k_D} + \frac{i_2}{(1 + k_D)^2} + \frac{R_n + i_3}{(1 + k_D)^3}$$

$$91 = \frac{6}{1 + k_D} + \frac{6}{(1 + k_D)^2} + \frac{106}{(1 + k_D)^3}$$

To solve this the skills learned in calculating internal rates of return in Chapter 2 are required. At an interest rate (k_D) of 9 per cent, the right side of the equation amounts to £92.41. At an interest rate of 10 per cent the right-hand side of the equation amounts to £90.05. Using linear interpolation:

Interest rate	9%	?	10%
Value of discounted cash flows	£92.41	£91	£90.05

$$k_D = 9\% + \frac{92.41 - 91}{92.41 - 90.05} \times (10 - 9) = 9.6\%$$

This is the yield-to-maturity or YTM discussed in the next section.

An Excel spreadsheet version of this calculation is available at www.pearsoned.com/arnold.

The two types of interest yield

There are two types of yield for fixed-interest securities. The **income yield** (also known as the **current yield, flat yield, interest yield** and **running yield**) is the gross (before tax) interest amount divided by the current market price of the bond expressed as a percentage:

$$\frac{\text{Gross interest (coupon)}}{\text{Market price}} \times 100$$

Thus for a holder of Bluebird's bonds the income yield is:

$$\frac{£6}{£91} \times 100 = 6.59\%$$

This is a gross yield. The after-tax yield will be influenced by the investor's tax position.

Net interest yield = Gross yield $(1 - T)$,

where T = the tax rate applicable to the bondholder

The income yield is not the true rate of return available to the investor should he/she buy it because it fails to take into account the capital gain over three years to the expiry of the bond.

At a time when interest rates are higher than 6.59 per cent it is obvious that any potential purchaser of Bluebird bonds in the market will be looking for a return other than from the coupon. That additional return comes in the form of a capital gain over three years of £100 − £91 = £9. A rough estimate of this annual gain is (9/91) ÷ 3 = 3.3 per cent per year. When this is added to the interest yield we have an approximation to the second type of yield, the **yield to maturity** (also called the **redemption yield**). The yield to maturity of a bond is the discount rate such that the present value of all the cash inflows from the bond (interest plus principal) is equal to the bond's current market price. The rough estimate of 9.89 per cent (6.59% + 3.3%) has not taken into account the precise timing of the investor's income flows. When this is adjusted for, the yield to maturity is 9.6 per cent – the internal rate of return calculated above. Thus the yield to maturity includes both coupon payments and the capital gain or loss on maturity.

In the *Financial Times'* bond tables the column headed '**bid yield**' is the yield to maturity given the current bid price (traders quote bid and offer prices, the bid is the price at which market makers will buy from investors, the offer price is what an investor would pay to buy). Examples of these tables are shown later in the chapter, in Exhibit 11.19. It is important to note that many investors sell their bonds before the redemption date. The price received depends on market conditions. If general interest rates have risen over the holding period then a capital loss or a smaller gain than would occur if market interest rates were constant will be experienced, which will have a depressing effect on the rate of return received even though coupons may have been paid during the time the bonds were owned. For example, if an investor bought Bluebird bonds at £91 and sold them one year later when the required rate of return on two-year bonds of this risk level in the market is 10 per cent, instead of receiving the original 9.6 per cent yield to maturity he/she will only achieve a rate of return of 8.86 per cent over the year of holding, viz:

$$\text{Market value of bond after 1 year} = \frac{6}{1 + 0.1} + \frac{106}{(1 + 0.1)^2} = 93.06$$

Thus the return to our investor is:

$$91 = \frac{93.06 + 6}{1 + r} \qquad r = 8.86\%$$

Semi-annual interest

The example of Bluebird given above is based on the assumption of annual interest payments. This makes initial understanding easier and reflects the reality for many types of bond, particularly internationally traded bonds. However, UK companies usually issue domestic sterling bonds with semi-annual interest payments. A bond offering a coupon of 9 per cent would pay £4.50 half-way through the year and the remainder at the end. The rate of return calculation on these bonds is slightly more complicated. For example, Redwing plc has an 11 per cent bond outstanding which pays interest semi-annually. It will be redeemed in two years at £100 and has a current market price of £96, with the next interest payment due in six months. The yield to maturity on this bond is calculated as follows:

Cash flows

Point in time (years)	0.5	1	1.5	2.0	2.0
Cash flow	£5.5	£5.5	£5.5	£5.5	£100

The nominal interest rate over a six-month period is 5.5 per cent (11%/2):

$$96 = \frac{5.50}{1 + k_D/2} + \frac{5.50}{(1 + k_D/2)^2} + \frac{5.50}{(1 + k_D/2)^3} + \frac{5.50}{(1 + k_D/2)^4} + \frac{100}{(1 + k_D/2)^4}$$

At a rate of 6 per cent for $k_D/2$ the right-hand side equals:

$$5.50 \times 4\text{-period annuity @ 6%} = 5.50 \times 3.4651 \qquad = \qquad 19.058$$

$$\text{plus} \quad \frac{100}{(1 + 0.06)^4} \qquad\qquad\qquad\qquad = \qquad \underline{79.209}$$

$$\underline{£98.267}$$

At a rate of 7 per cent for $k_D/2$ the right-hand side equals:

$$5.50 \times 4\text{-period annuity @ 7%} = 5.50 \times 3.3872 \qquad = \qquad 18.630$$

$$\text{plus} \quad \frac{100}{(1 + 0.07)^4} \qquad\qquad\qquad\qquad = \qquad \underline{76.290}$$

$$\underline{£94.920}$$

The IRR of the cash flow equals:

$$6\% + \frac{98.267 - 96}{98.267 - 94.92} \times (7 - 6) = 6.68\%$$

The IRR needs to be converted from a half-yearly cash flow basis to an annual basis:

$$(1 + 0.0668)^2 - 1 = 0.1381 \text{ or } 13.81\%$$

International sources of debt finance

Larger and more creditworthy companies have access to a wider array of finance than small firms. These companies can tap the **Euromarkets** which are informal (unregulated) markets in money held outside the jurisdiction of its country of origin. For example, there is a large market in **Eurodollars**. These are dollar credits (loans) and deposits managed by a bank not resident in the USA. This has the distinct advantage of transactions not being subject to supervision and regulation by the authorities in the USA. So, for example, an Italian firm can borrow dollars from a Spanish bank in the UK and the US regulatory authorities have no control over the transaction. There is a vast quantity of dollars held outside the USA and this money is put to use by borrowers. The same applies to all the major

currencies – the money is lent and borrowed outside its home base and therefore is beyond the reach of the domestic regulators. Today it is not unusual to find an individual holding a dollar account at a UK bank – a **Eurodeposit account** – which pays interest in dollars linked to general dollar rates. This money can be lent to firms wishing to borrow in Eurodollars prepared to pay interest and capital repayments in dollars. There are large markets in **Euro Swiss Francs**, **Eurosterling**, **Euroyen** and many other currencies.[6] The title 'Euro' is misleading as this market is not limited to the European currencies or European banks (and is unconnected with the European single currency, the euro). The title came about because the modern market was started when the former Soviet Union transferred dollars from New York to a Russian-owned bank in Paris at the height of the cold war in 1957. The cable address happened to be EUROBANK. This was long before the currency called the euro was conceived. Nowadays, there is daily **Eurosecurities** business transacted in all of the major financial centres. To add a little precision: '**Eurocurrency**' is short-term (less than one year) deposits and loans outside the jurisdiction of the country in whose currency the deposit/loan is denominated; '**Eurocredit**' is used for the market in medium- and long-term loans in the Euromarkets.

The companies which are large enough to use the Eurosecurities markets are able to put themselves at a competitive advantage *vis-à-vis* smaller firms. There are at least four advantages:

● The finance available in these markets can be at a lower cost in both transaction costs and rates of return.

● There are fewer rules and regulations such as needing to obtain official authorisation to issue or needing to queue to issue, leading to speed, innovation and lower costs.

● There may be the ability to hedge foreign currency movements. For example, if a firm has assets denominated in a foreign currency it can be advantageous to also have liabilities in that same currency to reduce the adverse impact of exchange-rate movements (*see* Chapter 22).

● National markets are often not able to provide the same volume of finance. The borrowing needs of some firms are simply too large for their domestic markets to supply. To avoid being hampered in expansion plans large firms can turn to the international market in finance.

For these internationally recognised firms there are three sources of debt finance:

a the domestic or national market;

b the financial markets of other countries which make themselves open to foreign firms – the **foreign debt market**;

c the Eurosecurities market which is not based in any one country and is not therefore regulated by any country.

Thus, for example, there are three bond markets available to some firms – as shown in **Exhibit 11.14**.

Foreign bonds

A **foreign bond** is a bond denominated in the currency of the country where it is issued when the issuer is a non-resident. For example, in Japan bonds issued by non-Japanese companies denominated in yen are foreign bonds. (The interest and capital payments will be in yen.) Foreign bonds have been given some interesting names: foreign bonds in Tokyo are known as **Samurai bonds**, foreign bonds issued in New York and London are called **Yankees** and **Bulldogs** respectively. The Netherlands allows foreigners to issue Rembrandt bonds and in Spain Matador bonds are traded. Foreign bonds are regulated by the authorities where the bond is issued. These rules can be demanding and an encumbrance to companies needing to act quickly and at low cost. The regulatory authorities have also been criticised for stifling innovation in the financial markets. The growth of the less restricted Eurobond market has put the once dominant foreign bond market in the shade. **Exhibit 11.15** discusses the Kanga bond market; while only one-eighth the size of the Yankee market, it raises significant sums for borrowers.

6 Just to confuse everybody traders in this market often refer to all types of Eurocurrency, from Eurosterling to Euroyen as Eurodollars, and do not reserve the term for US dollars.

Exhibit 11.14 Bond markets

Exhibit 11.15

Hunger for Australian 'kanga' bonds rises

By Peter Smith in Sydney

Borrowers have issued record amounts of Australian kangaroo bonds this year, underlining their desire to diversify their funding.

Issuers have sold A$32.7bn (US$32.2bn) of so-called 'kanga' bonds – which are those raised in Australian dollars by foreign entities – beating the previous full-year high of A$32.4bn recorded during the credit boom of 2006.

The market has become an increasingly valuable source of debt capital for a growing array of international banks and supranational institutions such as the World Bank.

In recent days, Canadian Imperial Bank of Commerce and France's Crédit Agricole have raised A$1.65bn.

Enrico Massi, head of debt capital markets Asia-Pacific at RBC Capital Markets, says issuance could reach nearly A$40bn by the end of 2010.

'Issuers are attracted to Australia because they can diversify their investor base, access domestic Australian investors, and many times, the pricing is competitive to their core benchmark markets. For many issuers, the Australian dollar has become a strategic market to access and develop,' he said.

He adds that investors remain bullish in Australia due to strong economic fundamentals, high relative yields, attractive spreads to benchmark bonds and a currency which hit a 27-year high against its US counterpart when it briefly traded above $0.99.

'Global investors like Australian dollar bonds given the overall package of yields, spreads and currency. At this stage, we don't see any signs of this abating.'

Mark Goddard, executive director of debt capital markets at Australia's Westpac Institutional Bank, says the kangaroo bond market has strengthened in part because Australia is the highest-yielding triple-A rated market in the world.

 Financial Times, 11 October 2010, p. 23.

Eurobonds (international bonds)

Eurobonds are bonds sold outside the jurisdiction of the country of the currency in which the bond is denominated. So, for example, the UK financial regulators have little influence over the Eurobonds denominated in sterling issued in Luxembourg, even though the transactions

(for example interest and capital payments) are in pounds. Bonds issued in US dollars in Paris are outside the jurisdiction of the US authorities. They are medium- to long-term instruments. Eurobonds are not subject to the rules and regulations which are imposed on foreign bonds, such as the requirement to issue a detailed prospectus.[7] More importantly they are not subject to an **interest-withholding tax**. In most countries domestic bonds are subject to a withholding tax by which basic rate income tax is deducted before the investor receives interest. Interest on Eurobonds is paid gross without any tax deducted – which has attractions to investors keen on delaying, avoiding or evading tax. Moreover, Eurobonds are **bearer bonds**, which means that the holders do not have to disclose their identity – all that is required to receive interest and capital is for the holder to have possession of the bond. In contrast, UK domestic bonds are registered, which means that companies and governments are able to identify the owners.

Despite the absence of official regulation, the International Capital Markets Association (ICMA), a self-regulatory body, imposes some restrictions, rules and standardised procedures on Eurobond issue and trading.

Eurobonds are distinct from euro bonds, which are bonds denominated in euros and issued in the eurozone countries. Of course, there have been euro-denominated bonds issued outside the jurisdiction of the authorities in the euro area. These are euro Eurobonds.

The development of the Eurobond (international bond) market

In the 1960s many countries, companies and individuals held surplus dollars outside the USA. They were reluctant to hold these funds in American banks under US jurisdiction. There were various reasons for this. For example, some countries, particularly the former Soviet Union and other communist bloc countries of the cold war era, thought their interests were best served by using the dollars they had on the international markets, away from the powers of the US authorities to freeze or sequestrate (seize) assets. More recently this sort of logic has applied to countries such as Iran. Also in the 1960s the American authorities had some very off-putting tax laws and created a tough regulatory environment in their domestic financial markets. These encouraged investors and borrowers alike to undertake transactions in dollars outside the USA. London's strength as a financial centre, the UK authorities' more relaxed attitude to business, and its position in the global time zones, made it a natural leader in the Euro markets. The first Eurobond was issued in the early 1960s and the market grew modestly through the 1970s and then at a rapid rate in the 1980s. By then the Eurodollar bonds had been joined by bonds denominated in a wide variety of currencies. The market was stimulated not only by the tax and anonymity benefits, which brought a lower cost of finance than for the domestic bonds, but also by the increasing demand from transnational companies and governments needing large sums in alternative currencies and with the potential for innovatory characteristics. It was further boosted by the recycling of dollars from the oil-exporting countries.

In 1979 less than \$20bn worth of bonds were issued in a variety of currencies. The rate of new issuance is now around \$2,000bn a year, with a total amount outstanding (bonds issued but not yet repaid) of over \$24,000bn (see **Exhibit 11.16**). Corporations account for a relatively small proportion of the international bond market. The biggest issuers are the banks. Issues by governments ('sovereign issues') and state agencies in the public sector account for less than one-tenth of issues. Other issuers are international agencies such as the World Bank, the International Bank for Reconstruction and Development, and the European Investment Bank. The two dominant currencies of issue are the US dollar and the euro, with the euro generally more popular than the dollar. Even though the majority of Eurobond trading takes place through London, sterling is not one of the main currencies, and what is more, it tends to be large US and other foreign banks located in London which dominate the market.

Types of Eurobonds

7 Although EU rules mean that a prospectus is required if the bond is marketed at retail (non-professional) investors.

Exhibit 11.16 International bond and notes outstanding and recent issues

Exhibit 11.16 (a) International debt securities (including foreign bonds), amounts outstanding, June 2011, by country of issuer

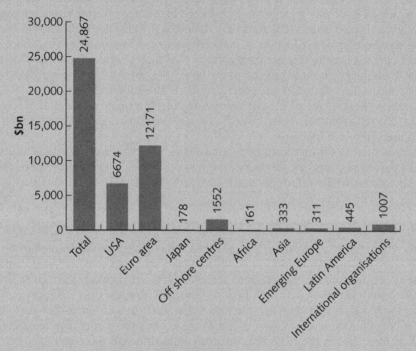

Source: Bank for International Settlement Quarterly Review, September 2011.

Exhibit 11.16 (b) International debt securities (including foreign bonds), amounts outstanding, by type of issuer, currency denomination and type of interest payment

Source: www.bis.org Quarterly Review, September 2011.

The Eurobond market has been extraordinarily innovative in producing bonds with all sorts of coupon payment and capital repayment arrangements (for example, the currency of the coupon changes half-way through the life of the bond, or the interest rate switches from fixed to floating rate at some point). We cannot go into detail here on the rich variety but merely categorise the bonds into broad types.

1 **Straight fixed-rate bond** The coupon remains the same over the life of the bond. These are usually paid annually, in contrast to domestic bond semi-annual coupons. The redemption of these bonds is usually made with a 'bullet' repayment at the end of the bond's life.

2 **Equity related** These take two forms:

 a *Bonds with warrants attached* Warrants are options which give the holder the right to buy some other asset at a given price in the future. An equity warrant, for example, would give the right, but not the obligation, to purchase shares. There are also warrants for commodities such as gold or oil, and for the right to buy additional bonds from the same issuer at the same price and yield as the host bond. Warrants are detachable from the host bond and are securities in their own right, unlike convertibles.

 b *Convertibles* The bondholder has the right (but not the obligation) to convert the bond into ordinary shares at a preset price.

3 **Floating-rate notes (FRNs)** These have a variable coupon reset on a regular basis, usually every three or six months, in relation to a reference rate, such as LIBOR. The size of the spread over LIBOR reflects the perceived risk of the issuer. The typical term for an FRN is about five to 12 years.

Within these broad categories all kinds of 'bells and whistles' (features) can be attached to the bonds, for example **reverse floaters** – the coupon declines as LIBOR rises; **capped bonds** – the interest rate cannot rise above a certain level.

Many bonds have '**call back features**' under which the issuer may buy the bond back after a period of time has elapsed, say five years, at a price specified when the bond was issued. A '**put**' **feature** gives the bondholder the right, but not the obligation, to sell the bond back to the issuer (usually at par value) on designated dates.

The majority of Eurobonds (more than 80 per cent) are rated AAA or AA although some rated below BBB– are issued. Denominations are usually $1,000, $5,000, $10,000, $50,000 or $100,000 (or similar large sums in the currency of issue).

Issuing Eurobonds

With Eurobonds a bank (lead manager or bookrunner or lead underwriter) or group of banks acting for the issuer invite a large number of other banks or other investors to buy some of the bonds.[8] The managing group of banks is responsible for underwriting the issue and it may enlist a number of smaller institutions to use their extensive contacts to sell the bonds (the selling group or syndicate). Exhibit 9.14 in Chapter 9 gave some idea of the relative importance of the Eurobond market to UK-listed firms – in recent years the amount raised on the international market is greater than that raised through domestic debt and equity issues.

Eurobonds are traded on the secondary market through intermediaries acting as market makers. Most Eurobonds are listed on the London or Luxembourg stock exchanges but the market is primarily an over-the-counter one, that is, most transactions take place outside a recognised exchange. Most deals are conducted using the telephone, computers, telex and fax, but there are a number of electronic platforms for trading Eurobonds. The extent to which electronic platforms will replace telephone dealing is as yet unclear. It is not possible to go to a central source for price information. Most issues rarely trade. Those that do are generally private transactions between investor and bond dealer and there is no obligation to inform the public about the deal. **Exhibit 11.17** presents the advantages and disadvantages of Eurobonds.

8 Alternatively in a 'bought deal' the lead manager agrees to buy the entire issue at a specific price and yield. He then tries to sell it on in the market.

Exhibit 11.17 Advantages and drawbacks of Eurobonds as a source of finance for corporations

Advantage

1 Large loans for long periods are available.
2 Often cheaper than domestic bonds. The finance provider receives the interest without tax deduction and retains anonymity and therefore supplies cheaper finance. Economies of scale also reduce costs.
3 Ability to hedge interest rate and exchange-rate risk.
4 The bonds are usually unsecured. The limitations placed on management are less than those for a secure bond.
5 The lower level of regulation allows greater innovation and tailor-made financial instruments.

Drawback

1 Only for the largest companies – minimum realistic issue size is about £50m.
2 Because interest and capital are paid in a foreign currency there is a risk that exchange-rate movements mean more of the home currency is required to buy the foreign currency than was anticipated.
3 The secondary market can be illiquid.

To conclude the discussion of Eurobonds we will consider a few examples and deal with some of the jargon. Exhibit 11.18 describes the first Eurobond from 40 years ago by Autostrade, a company that continues to make use of this financial market.

Exhibit 11.18

Autostrade returns to bond market after 40-year gap

By Charles Batchelor and Ivar Simensen

Autostrade, the Italian motorway operator that launched the Eurobond market in 1963, is to return to the bond market this month after a gap of more than 40 years.

The company yesterday revealed plans for a bond issue worth up to €6.5bn (£4.5bn) to pay off bank loans and finance a 10-year investment programme. It would be by far the largest corporate bond offering in Europe this year – ahead of issues by Britain's Network Rail and Telecom Italia.

'We go to the market once every 40 years,' joked Luca Bettonte, who was born in the year the market started and has been finance director of Autostrade since November.

'This will give us a financial structure more adapted to the needs of the group,' he added.

Autostrade is expected to issue bonds in both euros and sterling following roadshows in continental Europe, the UK and US.

It was in July 1963 that the motorway group issued a $15m (£9m), 15-year bond, creating a market that was to wrest control of non-US bond issues from the American investment banks and cement London's position as an international financial centre.

European banks had been relegated to an underwriting role by the US banks that managed these issues – and hence earned much lower fees.

Siegmund Warburg, founder of SG Warburg – now part of UBS, the Swiss bank group – led negotiations with regulators in the UK and elsewhere to issue bonds that soaked up the large offshore dollar pool created by recurrent US balance of payments deficits.

The fledgling market received a crucial boost just $21^1/_2$ weeks after the Autostrade issue when President John F. Kennedy announced an interest equalisation tax.

The president's aim was to improve the US balance of payments but the result was to increase the cost of US borrowing by European issuers.

The *Financial Times* publishes a table showing a selection of secondary-market bid prices of actively traded international bonds (*see* Exhibit 11.19). This gives the reader some idea of current market conditions and rates of return demanded for bonds of different maturities, currencies and riskiness. The FT has another table, showing similar information for high yield and emerging-market (less financially mature economies, e.g. Argentina) bonds.

Exhibit 11.19

Bonds – Global investment grade

Oct 25	Red date	Coupon	S*	Ratings M*	F*	Bid price	Bid yield	Day's chge yield	Mth's chge yield	Spread vs Govts	
US$											Redemption date April 2012
Morgan Stanley	04/12	6.60	A	A2	A	101.48	3.06	2.24	2.29	2.99	
Household Fin	05/12	7.00	A	A3	AA–	102.77	1.90	0.00	0.35	1.83	
HBOS Treas UK	06/12	5.50	A+	A1	A	101.77	2.59	–0.20	0.68	2.52	Gross (before
Verizon Global	09/12	7.38	A–	A3	A	105.46	0.85	–0.01	0.05	0.73	deduction of tax)
Bank of America	01/13	4.88	A	Baa1	A+	100.36	4.56	–0.31	–0.89	4.44	yield to maturity
Goldman Sachs	07/13	4.75	A	A1	A+	103.39	2.71	–0.35	0.05	2.46	
Misc Capital	07/14	6.13	BBB+	Baa1	–	107.75	3.08	0.00	1.07	2.63	
BNP Paribas	06/15	4.80	A+	Aa3	A+	93.72	6.77	0.00	0.98	6.29	Spread to the
GE Capital	01/16	5.00	AA+	Aa2	–	108.27	2.89	–0.06	0.11	1.86	government bond
Credit Suisse USA	03/16	5.38	A+	Aa1	AA–	106.95	3.63	–0.04	–0.17	2.59	rate (in this case
Swire Pacific	04/18	6.25	A–	A3	A	110.17	4.43	–0.06	0.63	2.80	the US). The extent
Goldman Sachs	02/33	6.13	A	A1	A+	98.71	6.24	–0.11	0.27	3.10	to which the rate
Bell South	10/31	6.88	A–	A2	A	123.32	5.01	0.00	0.12	1.88	of interest (bid
GE Capital	01/39	6.88	AA+	Aa2	–	116.57	5.67	–0.15	–0.01	2.47	yield to maturity or
											redemption yield)
											is greater than that
Euro											on a government
HSBC Fin	06/12	3.38	A	A3	AA–	100.33	2.79	–0.05	–0.02	2.53	bond of the same
Xstrata Fin CA	06/12	4.88	BBB+	Baa2	–	101.58	2.28	–0.17	–0.43	2.01	length of time to
Amer Honda Fin	07/13	6.25	A+	A1	–	107.20	1.94	–0.12	0.06	1.36	maturity (in this
JPMorgan Chase	01/15	5.25	A+	Aa3	AA–	105.56	3.39	–0.16	–0.24	2.59	case 2.63%)
Hutchison Fin 06	09/16	4.63	A–	A3	A–	103.46	3.84	–0.04	0.05	2.60	
Hypo Alpe Bk	10/16	4.25	–	Aa3	–	98.33	4.63	0.02	0.71	3.46	
GE Cap Euro Fdg	01/18	5.58	AA+	Aa2	–	107.30	4.02	–0.08	0.05	2.55	
ENEL	05/24	5.25	A–	A3	A	94.56	5.87	–0.09	0.14	3.51	
											Credit ratings
Yen											
Amer Int	04/12	1.40	A–	Baa1	BBB	98.00	6.17	0.06	2.79	6.03	
Citi Group 15	09/12	1.11	A	A3	A+	99.33	1.89	0.02	0.33	1.77	
ACOM 51	06/13	2.07	BB+	Ba3	A–	98.25	3.22	–0.13	–0.25	3.07	
Deutsche Bahn Fin	12/14	1.65	AA	Aa1	AA	103.36	0.55	–0.01	0.10	0.32	
											Bond price with par
£ Sterling											value set at 100
HSBC Fin	03/12	7.00	A	A3	AA–	101.60	2.96	0.01	0.12	2.35	
Slough Estates	09/15	6.25	–	–	A–	106.70	4.31	0.08	0.28	3.21	
ASIF III	12/18	5.00	A+	A2	A	94.86	5.82	0.01	0.12	3.66	

US $ denominated bonds NY close; all other London close. S* – Standard & Poor's, M* – Moody's, F* – Fitch.

Source: ThomsonReuters

Issuer

Coupon as a percentage of par value

Euro medium-term notes and domestic medium-term notes

By issuing a note a company promises to pay the holders a certain sum on the maturity date, and in many cases a coupon interest in the meantime. These instruments are typically unsecured and may carry floating or fixed interest rates. **Medium-term notes (MTN)** have been sold with a maturity of as little as nine months and as great as 30 years, so the term is a little deceiving. They can be denominated in the domestic currency of the borrower (MTN) or in a foreign currency (**Euro MTN**). MTNs normally pay an interest rate above LIBOR, usually varying between 0.2 per cent and 3 per cent over LIBOR.

An MTN programme stretching over many years can be set up with one set of legal documents. Then, numerous notes can be issued under the programme in future years. A programme allows greater certainty that the firm will be able to issue an MTN when it needs the finance and allows issuers to bypass the costly and time-consuming documentation associated with each stand-alone note (bond). The programme can allow for bonds of various qualities, maturities, currencies or type of interest (fixed or floating). Over the years the market can be tapped at short notice in the most suitable form at that time, e.g. US dollars rather than pounds, or redemption in three years rather than in two. It is possible to sell in small denominations, e.g. $5m, and on a continuous basis, regularly dripping bonds into the market. Banks charge a '**commitment fee**' (around 10 to 15 basis points) for keeping open the option to borrow under an MTN programme, even if the company chooses not to do so in the end. Management fees will also be payable to the syndication of banks organising the MTN facility.

The success of a MTN programme depends on the efficiency of the lead manager and the flexibility of the issuer to match market appetite for lending in particular currencies or maturities with the issuer's demands for funds. The annual cost of running an MTN programme, excluding credit rating agency fees, can be around £100,000. GlaxoSmithKline's current outstanding MTNs are shown at the start of the chapter.

Eurocommercial paper and domestic commercial paper[9]

The issue and purchase of **commercial paper** is one means by which the largest commercial organisations can avoid paying the bank intermediary a middleman fee for linking borrower and lender. Commercial paper promises to the holder a sum of money to be paid in a few days. The lender buys these short-term IOUs, with an average life of about 40 days (normal range 30–90 days, but can be up to 270 days), and effectively lends money to the issuer. Normally these instruments are issued at a discount rather than the borrower being required to pay interest – thus the face value (amount paid on redemption) will be higher than the amount paid for the paper at issuance. Large corporations with temporary surpluses of cash are able to put that money to use by lending it directly to other commercial firms at a higher rate of effective interest than they might have received by depositing the funds in a bank. This source of finance is usually only available to the most respected corporations with the highest credit ratings, as it is usually unsecured lending. Standard & Poor's and Moody's use a different grading system for short-term instruments (e.g. A–1 or Prime–1 are the highest ratings). The main buyers, such as money market mutual funds, are often restricted to having the bulk of their portfolios in the form of 'tier-one' rated issues – top ratings from credit rating agencies. Tier-two and tier-three issues do exist, but the demand is very limited.

While any one issue of commercial paper is short term it is possible to use this market as a medium-term source of finance by '**rolling over**' issues. That is, as one issue matures another one is launched. A **commercial paper programme** (a **revolving underwriting facility**) can be set up by a bank whereby the bank (or a syndicate of banks) underwrites a specified maximum sum for a period of five to seven years. The borrower then draws on this every few weeks or months by the issue of commercial paper to other lenders. If there are no bids for the paper the underwriting bank(s) buys the paper at a specified price. **Eurocommercial paper** is issued and placed outside the jurisdiction of the country in whose currency it is denominated.

9 This topic and the previous one do not sit perfectly in a chapter on long-term finance, but they help to give a more complete view of the Euromarkets.

Project finance

A typical project finance deal is created by an industrial corporation providing some equity capital for a separate legal entity (a 'special-purpose vehicle' (SPV)) to be formed to build and operate a project, for example an oil pipeline, an electricity power plant. The project finance loan is then provided as bank loans or through bond issues direct to the separate entity. The significant feature is that the loan returns are principally tied to the cash flows and fortunes of a particular project rather than being secured against the parent firm's assets. For most ordinary loans the bank looks at the credit standing of the borrower when deciding terms and conditions. For project finance, while the parent company's (or companies') credit standing is a factor, the main focus is on the financial prospects of the project itself.

To make use of project finance the project needs to be easily identifiable and separable from the rest of the company's activities so that its cash flows and assets can offer the lenders some separate security. Project finance has been used across the globe to finance power plants, roads, ports, sewage facilities, telecommunications networks and much more. A few recent examples are given in Exhibit 11.20.

Exhibit 11.20

Project finance has funded . . .

A liquefied natural gas project in Qatar

The biggest project-financed facility was built in Qatar. Qatargas, the state-controlled energy firm, joined with Exxon and raised $7.6bn from 57 investors in 2005 to build a gas freezing and storage plant. The gas is now being shipped to the UK in tankers. Not only did forming a separate project with a state-controlled company reduce political risk (see below) but it also opened doors to lenders in the country.

Developing an oil field

In 2006 Northern Petroleum agreed a €40m project financing facility with Standard Bank to develop a number of onshore oilfields in the Netherlands. Normally a project lender would insist on the sponsoring company or its contractors providing a guarantee that it will be paid back in the event

of failure to complete the project construction. However, Standard Bank agreed that Northern Petroleum has the skills to project manage and to forgo the guarantee. In return the bank received options to buy 3 million shares in Northern Petroleum thus taking some extra reward if the company (project) performs well. (An option gives the right to buy shares at a price already agreed – say £3 when the current share price is £2. If the company does well the share might move to, say, £4 in which case the options become worth at least £1 each – Chapter 21 has more on options.)

A telephone infrastructure

In 2000 Hutchison UK 3G raised £3bn by way of project finance to part-fund the building of the UK's fifth mobile network. This was three-year debt without recourse to shareholders.

This form of finance has grown rapidly over the last 25 years. Globally, about £50bn is lent in this form per year. A major stimulus has been the development of oil prospects. For the UK, the North Sea provided a number of project finance opportunities. Many of the small companies which developed fields and pipelines would not have been able to participate on the strength of their existing cash flow and balance sheet, but they were able to obtain project finance secured on the oil or fees they would later generate.

There is a spectrum of risk sharing in project finance deals. At one extreme there are projects where the parent firm (or firms) accepts the responsibility of guaranteeing that the lenders will be paid in the event of the project producing insufficient cash flows. This is referred to as recourse finance because the lenders are able to seek the 'help' of the parent. At the other extreme, the lenders accept an agreement whereby, if the project is a failure, they will lose money and have no

right of recourse to the parent company. If the project's cash flows are insufficient the lenders only have a claim on the assets of the project itself rather than on the sponsors or developers.

Between these two extremes there might be deals whereby the borrower takes the risk until the completion of the construction phase (for example, provides a completion guarantee) and the lender takes on the risk once the project is in the operational phase. Alternatively, the commercial firm may take some risks such as the risk of cost overruns and the lender takes others such as the risk of a government expropriating the project's assets.

The sums and size of projects are usually large and involve a high degree of complexity and this means high transaction and legal costs. Because of the additional risk to the lenders the interest rates charged tend to be higher than for conventional loans. Whereas a well-known highly credit-worthy firm might pay 20 basis points (0.20 per cent) over LIBOR for a 'normal' parent company loan, the project company might have to pay 200 basis points (2 per cent) above LIBOR.

Advantages of project finance

Project finance has a number of advantages.

1 *Transfer of risk* By making the project a stand-alone investment with its own financing, the parent can gain if it is successful and is somewhat insulated if it is a failure, in that other assets and cash flows may be protected from the effects of project losses. This may lead to a greater willingness to engage in more risky activities, which may benefit both the firm and society. Of course, this benefit is of limited value if there are strong rights of recourse.

2 *Off-balance-sheet financing* The finance is raised on the project's assets and cash flows and therefore is not recorded as debt in the parent company's balance sheet. This sort of off-balance-sheet financing is seen as a useful 'wheeze' or ploy by some managers – for example, gearing limits can be bypassed. However, experienced lenders and shareholders are not so easily fooled by accounting tricks.

3 *Political risk* If the project is in a country prone to political instability, with a tendency towards an anti-transnational business attitude and acts of appropriation, a more cautious way of proceeding may be to set up an arm's length (separate company) relationship with some risk being borne by the banking community, particularly banks in the host country.

4 *Simplifies the banking relationship* In cases where there are a number of parent companies, it can be easier to arrange finance for a separate project entity than to have to deal with each of the parent companies separately.

5 *Managerial incentives* Managers of projects may be given an equity stake in the project if it is set up as a separate enterprise. This can lead to high rewards for exceptional performance.

Sale and leaseback

If a firm owns buildings, land or equipment it may be possible to sell these to another firm (for example a bank, insurance company or specialised leasing firm) and simultaneously agree to lease the property back for a stated period under specific terms. The seller receives cash immediately but is still able to use the asset. However, the seller has created a regular cash flow liability for itself. For example, Dixons, the electrical retailer, raised £59m in 2011 by selling and leasing back a warehouse in Sweden. Tesco financed much of its expansion through sale and leasebacks – *see* Exhibit 11.21 – as do many retailers.

In a number of countries the tax regime propels sale and leaseback transactions. For example, some property owners are unable to use depreciation and other tax allowances (usually because they do not have sufficient taxable profits). The sale of the asset to an organisation looking to reduce taxable profits through the holding of depreciable assets enables both firms to benefit. Furthermore, the original owner's subsequent lease payments are tax deductible.

A further advantage is thought to be the efficiency boost sale and leaseback gives to the firm because managers are made more aware of the value of the assets used in the business. It is thought that when managers see the costs of property ownership in the form of explicit rental

Exhibit 11.21

Leaseback property deals in spotlight

By Daniel Thomas, Rose Jacobs, Claer Barrett, Sarah O'Connor and Simon Mundy

Sale and leaseback property deals are being questioned as legitimate sources of corporate finance as Southern Cross, the struggling care home provider, labours under the high rents imposed by its sales programme five years ago.

During the property boom years, sale and leasebacks – in which companies sell property assets and then rent them back – became increasingly popular as companies realised that their properties could be turned into easy cash in a rising market. However, such deals also involved taking on long-term rental liabilities, and often in complex structures.

The European sale and leaseback market grew from €6.9bn in 2004 to a peak of €46bn by 2007, according to CB Richard Ellis, the property consultancy.

Sale and leaseback deals are often regarded as equivalent to borrowing against the assets of a company, but with the company paying rent rather than interest and without the need to repay the loan. Analysts say this can be more efficient than bank borrowing as long as deals are properly structured and the money is then invested back into the business to cover the new rental costs.

The problems tend to occur when businesses either agree to too high rents or take the money out of the business. Southern Cross used sale and leasebacks to expand but the level of rent it promised to pay when buying businesses and selling their properties left the operating business with little room for manoeuvre. Mergers and acquisitions are a key feature of sale and leaseback activity, with many companies looking to fund purchases through the sale of their real estate assets.

Most of Southern Cross's rents were fixed to rise by about 2.5 per cent each year. When local authorities started to cut fees, it was left with a rent bill rising faster than its revenue.

John Wilson, executive director of corporate strategies at CBRE, says: 'The badly managed businesses will gear themselves to the hilt under high rents and fixed uplifts. But it has been incredibly successful for corporates such as HSBC, which has generated a significant amount of cash flow that was issued to help drive the business. Tesco has funded its European expansion through sale and leasebacks.'

Companies from the UK and Germany have dominated sale and leaseback activity in Europe, although Spanish and Italian banks and retailers also embraced the schemes, peaking with the sale of Santander's headquarters near Madrid to British real estate investors for €1.9bn as part of a wider sell-off of its Spanish real estate assets.

Supermarkets have used sale and leasebacks successfully but 'less is more' have been the watchwords when using property portfolios to leverage finance.

'The vast majority of supermarket estates are still owned freehold but their strategies have been very effective,' said Bryan Laxton, chief executive of Cushman & Wakefield, the property consultancy. Tesco is seen as the leader in the field, having structured joint venture deals with listed property companies including British Land. It has also sold down operational property assets into its own pension fund.

'Sale and leaseback deals have been very helpful in raising big sums for the supermarkets, enabling them to push ahead with expansion plans,' says Chris Blair, head of retail at Savills. 'Crucially, they've managed to retain a high degree of control of the assets, with strict conditions on how much rents can go up by.'

However, some retailers have not been so prudent. 'The reason Woolworths went to the wall was because they did sale and leasebacks on virtually everything. The rents agreed were higher than the market rate, and they were index linked to inflation,' says Mr Laxton.

'When market rents fell, Woolworths' rents still went up. Any chance they might have had of salvaging the business was effectively wrecked as all the asset value had been taken out of the business, and they were clobbered by the effective cost of borrowing.'

Hotels and pub groups have also readily embraced sale and leasebacks with mixed results.

FT *Financial Times*, 5 June 2011, p. 20.

payments moving through their profit and loss account, they become more aware of resources tied up in such assets, and therefore control more tightly the proportion of the firm's capital devoted to them.

A sale and leaseback has the drawback that the asset is no longer owned by the firm and therefore any capital appreciation has to be forgone. Also long lease arrangements of this kind usually provide for the rental payments to increase at regular intervals, such as every three or five years. Companies sometimes find that the leaseback arrangement eliminates the flexibility to move to cheaper premises. There are other factors limiting the use of sale and leaseback as a financial tool. Leasing can involve complex documentation and large legal fees, which often make it uneconomic to arrange leases for less than £20m. There is also a degree of inflexibility: for example, unwinding the transaction if, say, the borrower wanted to move out of the property can be expensive. Another disadvantage is that the property is no longer available to be offered as security for loans.

Santander reversed its sale and leaseback fearing accounting changes that may put the liability on its balance sheet and also so that it has greater control over what it can do with the building, as ell as its desire to show commitment to the communities in which it operates – *see* Exhibit 11.22.

Exhibit 11.22

Santander nears £500m property deal

By Daniel Thomas, Property Correspondent

Santander will buy £500m ($785m) of properties that it occupies across the UK in the first sign of a reversal of the big sale-and-leasebacks transactions of the past decade following accountancy law changes.

The Spanish bank is close to agreeing a deal to buy hundreds of its larger offices and branches for about £500m from Mapeley.

The bank will take back strategically important properties that had been sold to Mapeley for £457m and leased back in an outsourcing agreement made in 2000 by Abbey National. The transaction involved the transfer of most of Abbey's UK occupational portfolio, including 422 freehold properties and 884 leasehold properties.

The transaction is expected to include at least half of the freehold properties that had been sold by the bank, according to Property Week, the trade magazine, although the terms of the deal have not been finalised.

There are a number of reasons behind the move, not least the desire by the bank to own its properties for strategic reasons. It is mainly buying those properties that it wants to occupy in the longer term, including its headquarters in Milton Keynes. It is also expected to include key offices in Glasgow, Bradford, Teesside, Belfast and Sheffield, and successful branches on key high streets.

The decision to buy the properties also in part reflects the recent changes to the accountancy practices that means that leased assets such as property will no longer be kept off balance sheet.

Mark Beddy, a partner at Deloitte, said: 'New leasing changes brings all property on to the balance sheet, regardless of whether it is bought or leased. Sale and leasebacks purely for financial engineering purposes to get it off the balance sheet no longer work under these rules.'

The deal also makes sense for the bank owing to the drop in property prices across the UK. Santander last year acquired Abbey's London headquarters in Euston from British Land for £115m owing to what it saw as an opportunity to acquire the property at a reduced price.

Santander said: 'Santander has been moving towards owning more of the properties in which it operates, as shown by the purchasing of the UK headquarters.

'The deal currently being negotiated with Mapeley is a continuation of this. Santander believes owning the buildings in which it has large strategic operations, is important, not only logistically, but also as it shows our commitment to the communities in which we operate.'

Securitisation

In the strange world of modern finance you sometimes need to ask yourself who ends up with your money when you pay your monthly mortgage, or your credit card bill or the instalment payment on your car. In the old days you would have found that it was the organisation you originally borrowed from and whose name is at the top of the monthly statement. Today you cannot be so sure because there is now a thriving market in repackaged debt. In this market, a mortgage lender, for example, collects together a few thousand mortgage 'claims' it has (the right of the lender to receive regular interest and capital from the borrowers); it then sells those claims in a collective package to other institutions, or participants in the market generally. This permits the replacement of long-term assets with cash (improving liquidity and gearing) which can then be used to generate more mortgages. It may also allow a profit on the difference between the interest on the mortgages and the interest on the bonds. The borrower is often unaware that the mortgage is no longer owned by the original lender and everything appears as it did before, with the mortgage company acting as a collecting agent for the buyer of the mortgages. The mortgage company is usually said to be a seller of **asset-backed securities (ABS)** to other institutions (the 'assets' are the claim on interest and capital) and so this form of finance is often called **asset securitisation**. These asset-backed securities may be bonds sold into a market with many players. Rather than selling the bonds in the mortgage company itself a new company is usually established, called a **'special purpose vehicle'** (**SPV**) or **'special purpose entity'** (**SPE**). This new entity is then given the right to collect the cash flows from the mortgages. It has to pay the mortgage company for this. To make this payment it sells bonds secured against the assets of the SPV (e.g. mortgage claims). By creating an SPV there is a separation of the creditworthiness of the assets involved from the general credit of the company.

> **Asset backed securitisation involves the pooling and repackaging of relatively small, homogeneous and illiquid financial assets into liquid securities.**

The sale of the financial claims can be either 'non-recourse', in which case the buyer of the securities from the mortgage firm or the lender to the SPV (e.g. bond holder) bears the risk of non-payment by the borrowers, or with recourse to the mortgage lender.

Securitisation has even reached the world of rock. Iron Maiden issued a long-dated $30m asset-backed bond securitised on future earnings from royalties. It followed David Bowie's $55m bond securitised on the income from his earlier albums and Rod Stewart's $15.4m securitised loan from Nomura.

Tussauds has securitised ticket and merchandise sales, Keele University has securitised the rental income from student accommodation and Arsenal securitised £260m future ticket sales at the Emirates Stadium. Loans to Hong Kong taxi drivers have been securitised, as have the cash flows from UK funeral fees.

Securitisation is regarded as beneficial to the financial system, because it permits banks and other financial institutions to focus on those aspects of the lending process where they have a competitive edge. Some, for example, have a greater competitive advantage in originating loans than in funding them, so they sell the loans they have created, raising cash to originate more loans. Securitisation was at the heart of the financial crisis when US sub-prime (poor quality) mortgage borrowers failed to repay in substantial numbers. Mortgage-backed bonds of SPVs plummeted in value, the asset-backed bond market froze and the businesses model of lending to households expecting to sell bonds backed with a bunch of mortgages (à la Northern Rock) became untenable as no one would buy the securitised bonds.

Exhibit 11.23 describes the securitisation of Dunkin' Donuts' royalties received from its hundreds of franchises around the world – a steady source of income.

Exhibit 11.23

It's all a question of the right packaging

Richard Beales on fresh ways to isolate a company's income streams and cut its financing costs

In a corporate securitisation, assets and related cash flows are carved out from a business into special purpose entities (SPEs) and repackaged. Debt is then raised against the SPEs alone.

'Securitisation isolates a cash flow and insulates it from extraneous events,' says Ted Yarbrough, head of global securitised products at Citigroup.

Depending on the credit quality and the quantum of borrowing, part or all the debt may be highly rated, and there is sometimes a low-rated or unrated subordinated slice of debt as well. This is not, however, an off-balance sheet financing method – the assets and debt within the SPEs are consolidated in the company's financial statements.

A financing structured this way can achieve higher credit ratings than the business on its own. This partly reflects the structural aspects – for example, the fact that the SPEs can survive a bankruptcy of the umbrella group – and partly the fact that the securities issued are often 'wrapped', or guaranteed, by highly-rated bond insurers such as Ambac, Figic or MBIA in return for a fee.

This is a complex and costly exercise, but can result in much cheaper debt. Once established, a securitisation can be tapped again later if a business grows.

Sometimes securitisation is best suited to part of a business rather than the whole. When applied to an entire business, as with Dunkin' Brands or Domino's, the new financing typically replaces all traditional debt.

While a securitisation does involve financial constraints, they can be fewer and less onerous than with traditional bank and bond debt. Managers would, for example, have greater flexibility to pay dividends or buy back stock.

This reflects the fact that financiers in a securitisation look only to the specific assets and cash flows held within the SPEs. But Eric Hedman, analyst at Standard & Poor's in New York, notes there can be a trade-off in terms of operational flexibility. 'Prior to the securitisation, Dunkin' was an owner operator. Now, the company is no longer the franchisor, there's an SPE. Any new store agreement is for the benefit of the securitisation.' The company's management also does not have sole discretion over advertising spending, for example.

And the Dunkin' Donuts brand is no longer owned by the company. 'The sign on the wall says "Copyright DD IP Holder LLC". That's a bankruptcy-remote SPE set up for the benefit of noteholders [in the securitisation]', Mr Hedman says.

This kind of shift might not suit all managers. But for some executives – particularly those focused on maximising cash returns to shareholders – such considerations can be outweighed by the financial benefits.

Securitised financing

Revenue (eg franchise royalties) → SPEs* ← Owns/Funds → Company ← Other revenues

Priority 1: Int./princ** → Senior noteholders

Priority 2: Int./princ → Subordinated lenders

Priority 3: Excess

Dividends/buybacks → Shareholders

* Special purpose entitles owning franchise agreements, brands etc.
** Often guaranteed by bond insurer in return for additional fee

FT *Financial Times*, 25 July 2007, p. 2.

Islamic banking

Under Islamic Sharia law the payment of *riba*[10] (interest) is prohibited and the receiver of finance must not bear all the risk of failure. Money alone should not create a profit and finance should serve the real economy, not just the financial one. Also investment in alcohol, tobacco, pornography or gambling is not allowed. However, Islam does encourage entrepreneurial activity and the sharing of risk through equity shares. Thus a bank can create profit-sharing products to offer customers. Depositors can be offered a percentage of the bank's profits rather than a set interest rate. Borrowers repay the bank an amount that is related to the profit produced by the project for which the loan was made. One example is **Musharakah**, where a joint enterprise is established by the bank and borrower. Both contribute capital plus management and labour (although some parties, e.g. banks, contribute little other than capital). Profit (loss) is shared in pre-agreed proportions – there is a prohibition against a fixed lump sum for any party. All partners have unlimited liability. Thus for a house purchase the property is purchased by the bank and clients (perhaps 10 per cent of the purchase price). The customer purchases the bank's share gradually, until he is made sole owner after a specified period, usually 25 years. Over the financing period, the bank's share is rented to the customer.

Over 600 banks and financial institutions offer services according to Sharia law. They are most heavily concentrated in the Arabian Gulf countries, Malaysia, Pakistan and Iran. But many conventional banks also offer Sharia products, e.g. HSBC and Lloyds have Islamic mortgages available. Growth has been driven by the rising consciousness in Islamic principles over the last 40 years and the rising wealth of Muslim oil states. What is regarded as compliant with Sharia in one part of the world may not be considered by Islamic scholars to be acceptable in another. Malaysia, for example, tends to be more liberal than Saudi Arabia. The UK has introduced tax,[11] legislative and regulatory changes to encourage Islamic financial services in the City. This has been successful, attracting over US$10bn of funds to London, making it one of the top ten centres. Despite its growth, the volume of Islamic finance is still only around 1 per cent of the size of the conventional finance industry.

Islamic bonds (*sukuk*)

Sukuk (the plural form of the Arabic word *sakk* from which the word cheque is derived) are bonds which conform to Sharia law. Whereas conventional bonds are promises to pay interest and principal, *sukuk* represent part *ownership* of tangible assets, businesses or investments, so the returns are generated by some sort of share of the gain (or loss) made, and the risk is shared. They are administered through a **special-purpose vehicle (SPV)** which issues *sukuk* certificates. These certificates entitle the holder to a rental income or a profit share from the certificate. *Sukuk* may be issued on existing as well as other specific assets that may become available at a future date.

From its inception in 1975, when the Islamic Development Bank and the Dubai Islamic Bank (the first commercial Islamic bank) were established to operate in strict accordance with Sharia law, Islamic finance has made significant progress worldwide, and it was estimated in 2011 that there was more than $100bn of *sukuk* outstanding (and over $1,000bn of Islamic finance, including bank sources). There is some confusion over whether investors can always seize the underlying assets in the event of default on a *sukuk*, or whether the assets are merely placed in a *sukuk* structure to comply with Sharia law. Lawyers and bankers say that the latter is the case, with most sukuk being, in reality, unsecured instruments. They differentiate between 'asset-backed' and 'asset-based' *sukuk*:

- *Asset backed*: there is a true sale between the originator and the SPV that issues the *sukuk*, and *sukuk* holders do not have recourse to the originator. The value of the assets owned by the SPV, and therefore the *sukuk* holders, may vary over time. The majority of sukuk issues are not asset backed.

- *Asset based*: these are closer to conventional debt in that the *sukuk* holders have recourse to the originator if there is a payment shortfall.

10 A strict interpretation of the word riba is usary or excessive interest.

11 For example, stamp duty on a house sale is not paid twice (when the bank buys and when the customer buys from the bank.)

Tesco and Toyota have both issued ringgit *sukuk* in Malaysia. In a further development in November 2009, General Electric (GE) became the first large Western corporation to expand its investor base into this arena with the issuance of its $500m *sukuk*. The assets underlying this *sukuk* are GE's interests in aircraft and rental payments from aircraft leasing.

The term structure of interest rates

Until now we have assumed that the annual interest rate on a debt instrument remained the same regardless of the length of time of the loan. So, if the interest rate on a three-year bond is 7 per cent per year it would be 7 per cent on a five-year bond of the same risk class. However, it is apparent that lenders in the financial markets demand different interest rates on loans of differing lengths of time to maturity – that is, there is a **term structure of the interest rates**. Four of these relationships are shown in **Exhibit 11.24** for lending to the UK, Japanese, German (eurozone) and US governments. Note that default risk remains constant along one of the lines; the reason for the different rates is the time to maturity of the bonds. Thus a one-year German government bond has to offer about 0.5 per cent whereas a 20-year bond offered by the same borrower gives about 3 per cent.

| Exhibit 11.24 | Yield curves for the UK, USA, eurozone and Japanese government bills and bonds |

Source: http//markets.ft.com/markets/bonds 28 October 2011.

An upward-sloping yield curve occurs in most years but occasionally we have a situation where short-term interest rates (lending for, say, one year) exceed those of long-term interest rates (say, a 20-year bond).

Three main hypotheses have been advanced to explain the shape of the yield curve – all three can operate at the same time to influence the yield curve.

a the expectation hypothesis;

b the liquidity-preference hypothesis; and

c the market-segmentation hypothesis.

The expectations hypothesis

The **expectations hypothesis** focuses on the changes in interest rates over time. To understand the expectations hypothesis you need to know what is meant by a '**spot rate of interest**'. The spot rate is an interest rate fixed today on a loan that is made today. So a corporation, Hype plc, might issue one-year bonds at a spot rate of, say, 8 per cent, two-year bonds at a spot rate of 8.995 per cent and three-year bonds at a spot rate of 9.5 per cent. This yield curve for Hype is shown in **Exhibit 11.25**. The interest rates payable by Hype are bound to be greater than for the UK government across the yield curve because of the additional default risk on these corporate bonds.

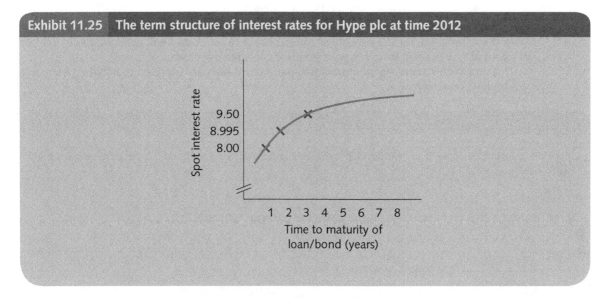

Exhibit 11.25 The term structure of interest rates for Hype plc at time 2012

Spot rates change over time. The market may have allowed Hype to issue one-year bonds yielding 8 per cent at a point in time in 2012 but a year later (time 2013) the one-year spot rate may have changed to become 10 per cent. If investors expect that one-year spot rates will become 10 per cent at time 2013 they will have a theoretical limit on the yield that they require from a two-year bond when viewed from time 2012. Imagine that an investor (lender) wishes to lend £1,000 for a two-year period and is contemplating two alternative approaches:

1 Buy a one-year bond at a spot rate of 8 per cent; after one year has passed the bond will come to maturity. The released funds can then be invested in another one-year bond at a spot rate of 10 per cent, expected to be the going rate for bonds of this risk class at time 2013.

2 Buy a two-year bond at the spot rate at time 2012.

Under the first option the lender will have a sum of £1,188 at the end of two years:

£1,000 (1 + 0.08) = £1,080

followed by £1,080 (1 + 0.1) = £1,188

Given the anticipated change in one-year spot rates to 10 per cent the investor will only buy the two-year bond if it gives the same average annual yield over two years as the first option of a series of one-year bonds. The annual interest required will be:

$£1,000 (1 + k)^2 = £1,188$

$k = \sqrt{(1,188/1,000)} - 1 = 0.08995$ or 8.995 per cent

Thus, it is the expectation of spot interest rates changing which determines the shape of the yield curve according to the expectation hypothesis.

Now consider a downward-sloping yield curve where the spot rate on a one-year instrument is 11 per cent and the expectation is that one-year spot rates will fall to 8 per cent the following year. An investor considering a two-year investment will obtain an annual yield of 9.49 per cent by investing in a series of one-year bonds, viz:

$$£1,000 \ (1.08) \ (1.11) = £1,198.80$$

$$k = \sqrt{(1198.8/1,000)} \ - 1 = 0.0949 \text{ or } 9.49\% \text{ per year}$$

$$\text{or } \sqrt{(1.08)(1.11)} - 1 = 0.0949$$

With this expectation for movements in one-year spot rates, lenders will demand an annual rate of return of 9.49 per cent from two-year bonds of the same risk class.

Thus in circumstances where short-term spot interest rates are expected to fall, the yield curve will be downward sloping.

Worked example 11.2 Spot rates

If the present spot rate for a one-year bond is 5 per cent and for a two-year bond 6.5 per cent, what is the expected one-year spot rate in a year's time?*

Answer

If the two-year rate is set to equal the rate on a series of one-year spot rates then:

$$(1 + 0.05) \ (1 + x) = (1 + 0.065)^2$$

$$x = \frac{(1 + 0.065)^2}{1 + 0.05} - 1 = 0.0802 \text{ or } 8.02\%$$

*In the financial markets it is possible to agree now to lend money in one year's time for, say, a year (or two years or six months, etc.) at a rate of interest agreed at the outset. This is a 'forward'.

The liquidity-preference hypothesis

The expectation hypothesis does not adequately explain why the most common shape of the yield curve is upward sloping. The **liquidity-preference hypothesis** (liquidity premium theory) helps explain the upward slope by pointing out that investors require an extra return for lending on a long-term basis. Lenders demand a premium return on long-term bonds compared with short-term instruments because of the risk of misjudging future interest rates. Putting your money into a ten-year bond on the anticipation of particular levels of interest rates exposes you to the possibility that rates will rise above the rate offered on the bond at some point in its long life. Thus, if five years later interest rates double, say because of a rise in inflation expectations, the market price of the bond will fall substantially, leaving the holder with a large capital loss. On the other hand, by investing in a series of one-year bonds, the investor can take advantage of rising interest rates as they occur. The ten-year bond locks in a fixed rate for the full ten years if held to maturity. Investors prefer short-term bonds so that they can benefit from rising rates and so will accept a lower return on short-dated instruments. The liquidity-preference theory focuses on a different type of risk attaching to long-dated debt instruments other than default risk – a risk related to uncertainty over future interest rates. A suggested reinforcing factor to the upward slope is that borrowers usually prefer long-term debt because of the fear of having to repay short-term debt at inappropriate moments. Thus borrowers increase the supply of long-term debt instruments, adding to the tendency for long-term rates to be higher than short-term rates.

Note that the word liquidity in the title is incorrectly used – but it has stuck so we still use it. Liquidity refers to the speed and ease of the sale of an asset. In the case of long-term bonds (especially government bonds) sale in the secondary market is often as quick and easy for short-term

bonds. The premium for long bonds is compensation for the extra risk of capital loss; 'term premium' might be a better title for the hypothesis.

The market-segmentation hypothesis

The **market segmentation hypothesis** argues that the debt market is not one homogeneous whole, that there are, in fact, a number of sub-markets defined by maturity range. The yield curve is therefore created (or at least influenced) by the supply and demand conditions in each of these sub-markets. For example, banks tend to be active in the short-term end of the market and pension funds to be buyers in the long-dated segment. If banks need to borrow large quantities quickly they will sell some of their short-term instruments, increasing the supply on the market and pushing down the price and raising the yield. On the other hand pension funds may be flush with cash and may buy large quantities of 20-year bonds, helping to temporarily move yields downward at the long end of the market. At other times banks, pension funds and the buying and selling pressures of a multitude of other financial institutions will influence the supply and demand position in the opposite direction. The point is that the players in the different parts of the yield curve tend to be different. This hypothesis helps to explain the often lumpy or humped yield curve.

A final thought on the term structure of interest rates

It is sometimes thought that in circumstances of a steeply rising yield curve it would be advantageous to borrow short term rather than long term. However, this can be a dangerous strategy because long-term debt may be trading at a higher rate of interest because of the expected rise in short-term rates and so when the borrower comes to refinance in, say, a year's time, the short-term interest rate is much higher than the long-term rate and this high rate has to be paid out of the second year's cash flows, which may not be convenient.

Concluding comments

So far this book has taken a fairly detailed look at a variety of ways of raising money by selling shares and has examined the main methods of raising funds through long-term debt. The decision to raise equity or debt finance is neither simple nor straightforward. In the next chapter we consider a wider array of financial sources and types, from leasing to factoring. Knowledge of these will enable the finance manager or other executives to select and structure the different forms of finance to maximise the firm's potential. Topics covered later in the book draw on the knowledge gained in Chapters 10, 11 and 12 to permit informed discussion of such crucial questions as: What is the appropriate mixture of debt and equity? How is the cost of various forms of finance calculated? How can the risk of certain forms of finance (for example a floating-interest-rate term loan) be reduced?

Key points and concepts

- **Debt finance has a number of advantages** for the company:
 - it has a lower cost than equity finance:
 a lower transaction costs;
 b lower rate of return;
 - debt holders generally do not have votes;
 - interest is tax deductible.

- **Drawbacks of debt**:
 - Committing to repayments and interest can be risky for a firm, ultimately the debt-holders can force liquidation to retreive payment;
 - the use of secured assets for borrowing may be an onerous constraint on managerial action;
 - covenants may further restrict managerial action.

- A **bond** is a long-term contract in which the bondholders lend money to a company. A straight 'vanilla' bond pays regular interest plus the capital on the redemption date.

- Debentures are generally more secure than **loan stock** (in the UK).

- A **trust deed** has **affirmative covenants** outlining the nature of the bond contract and **negative (restrictive) covenants** imposing constraints on managerial action to reduce risk for the lenders.

- A **floating rate note (FRN)** is a bond with an interest rate which varies as a benchmark interest rate changes (e.g. LIBOR).

- **Attractive features of bank borrowing**:
 - administrative and legal costs are low;
 - quick;
 - flexibility in troubled times;
 - available to small firms.

- **Factors for a firm to consider with bank borrowing**:

 Costs
 - fixed versus floating;
 - arrangement fees;
 - bargaining on the rate.

 Security
 - asymmetric information;
 - collateral;
 - covenants
 - personal guarantees

- **Repayment arrangements**:

 Some possibilities:
 - grace periods;
 - mortgage style;
 - term loan.

- A **syndicated loan** occurs where a number of banks (or other financial institutions) each contribute a portion of a loan.

- A **credit rating** depends on **a** the likelihood of payments of interest and/or capital not being paid (i.e. default); and **b** the extent to which the lender is protected in the event of a default.

- **Mezzanine debt** and **high-yield bonds** are forms of debt offering a high return with a high risk. They have been particularly useful in the following:
 - management buyouts (MBOs), especially leveraged management buyouts (LBOs);
 - fast-growing companies;
 - leveraged recapitalisation.

- **Convertible bonds** are issued as debt instruments but they also give the holder the right to exchange the bonds at some time in the future into ordinary shares according to some prearranged formula advantages:
 - lower interest than on debentures;
 - interest is tax deductible;

 - self liquidating;
 - few negative covenants;
 - shares might be temporarily underpriced;
 - cheap way to issue shares;
 - an available form of finance when straight debt and equity are not.

- A bond is **priced** according to general market interest rates for risk class and maturity:

 Irredeemable:

 $$P_D = \frac{i}{k_D}$$

 Redeemable:

 $$P_D = \frac{i_1}{1 + k_D} + \frac{i_2}{(1 + k_D)^2} + \frac{i_3}{(1 + k_D)^3}$$
 $$+ \ldots + \frac{R_n}{(1 + k_D)^n}$$

- The **interest (flat) yield** on a bond is:

 $$\frac{\text{Gross interest (coupon)}}{\text{Market price}} \times 100$$

- The **yield to maturity** includes both annual coupon returns and capital gains or losses on maturity.

- The **Euromarkets** are informal (unregulated) markets in money held outside the jurisdiction of the country of origin of the currency.

- A **foreign bond** is a bond denominated in the currency of the country where it is issued when the issuer is a non-resident.

- A **Eurobond** is a bond sold outside the jurisdiction of the country of the currency in which the bond is denominated.

- A **project finance** loan is provided as a bank loan or bond finance to an entity set up separately from the parent corporation to undertake a project. The returns to the lender are tied to the fortunes and cash flows of the project.

- **Sale and leaseback** Assets are sold to financial institutions or another company which releases cash. Simultaneously, the original owner agrees to lease the assets back for a stated period under specified terms.

- **Securitisation** Relatively small, homogeneous and liquid financial assets are pooled and repackaged into liquid securities which are then sold on to other investors to generate cash for the original lender.

- Under **Islamic Sharia law** the payment of interest is prohibited. However, a bank may create profit-sharing products, or a bond may be profit sharing.

- The **term structure of interest rates** describes the manner in which the same default risk class of debt securities provides different rates of return depending on the length of time to maturity. There are three hypotheses relating to the term structure of interest rates:
 - the expectations hypothesis;
 - the liquidity-preference hypothesis;
 - the market-segmentation hypothesis.

References and further reading

To keep up to date and reinforce knowledge gained by reading this chapter I can recommend the following publications: *Financial Times, The Economist, Corporate Finance Magazine,* (London: Euromoney) *Bank of England Quarterly Bulletin, Bank for International Settlements Quarterly Review* (www.bis.org), *The Treasurer* (a monthly journal), *The Treasurer's Handbook* (by the Association of Corporate Treasurers) and *Finance and Leasing Association* (FLA) *Annual Report* (www.fla.org.uk.)

Arnold, G. (2012) *Modern Financial Markets and Institutions.* Harlow: FT Prentice Hall.
 Contains more on banking and money markets.

Arnold, G. and Smith, M. (1999) *The European High Yield Bond Market: Drivers and Impediments.* London: Financial Times Finance Management Report.
 A comprehensive exploration of the potential of the junk bond market in Europe – a history of the US market is also given.

Bharath, S., Dahiya, S., Saunders, A. and Srinivasan, A. (2007) 'So what do I get? The bank's view of lending relationships', *Journal of Financial Economics*, 85, pp. 368–419.
 Strong relationships with clients raise the probability of banks to sell products and make loans.

Brealey, R.A., Cooper, I.A. and Habib, M.A. (2001) 'Using project finance to fund infrastructure investments', in D.H. Chew (ed.) *The New Corporate Finance.* 3rd edn. New York: McGraw Hill Irwin.
 A more detailed treatment of project finance.

Brigham, E.F. (1966) 'An analysis of convertible debentures: Theory and some empirical evidence', *Journal of Finance*, March, pp. 35–54.
 Valuation of convertibles and the major factors influencing price. Evidence that most firms issue convertibles to raise equity finance.

Chava, S. and Roberts, M.R. (2008) 'How does financing impact investment? The role of debt covenants', *Journal of Finance*, LXIII(5), Oct, pp. 2085–121.
 Debt covenants can have a severe impact on borrower company investment after they have been violated.

Chisholm, A.M. (2009) *An Introduction to International Capital Markets.* 2nd edn. Chichester: J. Wiley and Sons.
 Containing four well-written and accessible chapters detailing the bond markets around the world – particularly good on bond valuation calculations.

Debt Management Office, *Quarterly Review.*

Eiteman, D.K., Stonehill, A.I. and Moffett, M.H. (2009) *Multinational Business Finance.* 12th edn. Reading, MA: Addison-Wesley.
 Some useful, easy-to-follow material on international debt markets.

Fabozzi, F.J. (2009) *Bond Markets, Analysis and Strategies.* 7th edn. Harlow: FT Prentice Hall.
 A detailed yet accessible description of bonds with a US bond market focus.

City of London/London Stock Exchange/Oxera (2006) The cost of capital: an international comparison (available from www.londonstockexchange.com). Contains an excellent easy-to-read description of the trading of bonds and costs of listings.

Graham, J.R. and Harvey, C.R. (2001) 'The theory and practice of corporate finance: evidence from the field', *Journal of Financial Economics*, Vol. 60, Issues 2–3, May, pp. 187–243.
 US survey of corporate use of debt.

Hickman, B.G. (1958) 'Corporate bond quality and investor experience', *National Bureau of Economic Research*, 14, Princeton.
 Early research into the returns and default rates on bonds.

Hicks, J.R. (1946) *Value and Capital: An Inquiry into some Fundamental Principles of Economic Theory.* 2nd edn. Oxford: Oxford University Press.
 Liquidity-preference hypothesis to explain the term structure of interest rates.

Howells, P. and Bain, K. (2008) *The Economics of Money, Banking and Finance.* 4th edn. Harlow: Financial Times Prentice Hall.
 A wide-ranging introduction to financial markets, with an economic policy focus.

Lutz, F.A. and Lutz, V.C. (1951) *The Theory of Investment in the Firm.* Princeton, NJ: Princeton University Press.
 Expectations hypothesis of the term structure of interest rates.

Pilbeam, K. (2005) *International Finance*. 3rd edn. London: Macmillan Business.

> An introductory treatment of debt markets.

Saunders, A. and Cornett, M.M. (2007) *Financial Markets and Institutions*. 3rd edn. Boston, MA: McGraw-Hill.

> Contains much more on the US bond markets and on mathematical calculations associated with bond pricing, YTM, etc.

Valdez, S. (2007) *An Introduction to Global Financial Markets*. 5th edn. London: Palgrave Macmillan.

> Easy-to-read background on international bond markets and banking.

Veronesi, P. (2010) *Fixed Income Securities: Valuation, risk and risk management*. New Jersey: John Wiley and Sons.

> A much more detailed look at the bond markets, with a focus on the USA.

Case study recommendations

Please see www.pearsoned.co.uk/arnold for case study synopses

Also see Harvard University: http://hbsp.harvard.edu/product/cases

- Note: Credit rating agencies. Author: William E. Fruhan, (2009). Harvard Business School.

- Yield Curve Basics. Author: Francis Warnock (2006). Darden, University of Pennsylvania. Available at Harvard case study website.

- Rockwood Specialities: High-yield debt issue. Authors: Kevin Kim and Susan Chaplinsky (2004). Darden, University of Pennsylvania. Available at Harvard case study website.

- Parex Banka: Issuing a 200 million bond. Authors: Jordan Mitchell and Basil Kalymon (2007). Richard Ivey School of Business. The University of Western Ontario. Available at Harvard case study website.

- Cypress Semiconductor: 1.25% convertible notes. Author: Robert M. Conroy (2008). Darden, University of Pennsylvania. Available at Harvard case study website.

- Tata Steel Limited: Convertible alternative reference securities. Authors: Vasant Sivaraman and Adithya

Anand (2008). Richard Ivey School of Business. The University of Western Ontario. Available at Harvard case study website.

- BP Amoco (A): Policy statement on the use of project finance. Authors: Benjamin C. Esty and Michael Kane (2010). Harvard Business School. Discusses the pros and cons of project finance.

- BP Amoco (B): Financing the development of the Caspian oil fields. Authors: Benjamin C. Esty and Michael Kane (2010). Harvard Business School. An interest project finance case study.

- Aluminium Bahrain (Alba). The Pot Line 5 Expansion Project. Authors: Benjamin C. Esty, Aldo Sesia, Jr. (2005). Harvard Business School.

- Overview of project finance – 2004 Update (2005). Authors: Benjamin C. Esty and Aldo Sesia, Jr. Harvard Business School.

- Petrolera Zuata. Authors: Benjamin C. Esty and Mathew Mateo Millet (1998). Harvard Business School.

- Poland's A2 Motorway. Authors: Benjamin C. Esty, and Michael Kane (2001). Harvard Business School.

Websites

Association of Corporate Treasurers www.treasurers.org
Bank for International Settlements www.bis.org
Bank of England www.bankofengland.co.uk
The Economist www.economist.com
Financial Times www.ft.com

Fitch ratings www.fitchratings.com
International Capital Market Association www.icma-group.co.uk
Moody's www.moodys.com
Standard & Poor's www.standardandpoors.com

Video presentations

Chief executives and financial directors describe their current policy on raising funds on Cantos.com (www.cantos.com) – this is free to view.

Self-review questions

1 What are the relative advantages and drawbacks of debt and equity finance?

2 Explain the following (related to bonds):
a Par value.
b Trustee.
c Debenture.
d Zero coupon bond.
e Floating-rate note.

3 The inexperienced finance trainee at Mugs-R-Us plc says that he can save the company money on its forthcoming issue of ten-year bonds. 'The rate of return required for bonds of this risk class in the financial markets is 10 per cent and yet I overheard our merchant banking adviser say, "We could issue a bond at a coupon of only 9 per cent." I reckon we could save the company a large sum on the £100m issue.' Do you agree with the trainee's logic?

4 In what circumstances would you recommend borrowing from a bank rather than a capital market bond issue?

5 What are the fundamental considerations to which you would advise a firm to give thought if it were contemplating borrowing from a bank?

6 Is securitisation something to do with anti-criminal precautions? If not, explain what it is and why firms do it.

7 In what ways does the tax regime encourage debt finance rather than equity finance?

8 Why does convertible debt carry a lower coupon than straight debt?

9 What is meant by asymmetric information in the relationship between banker and borrower?

10 What is a syndicated loan and why do banks join so many syndicates?

11 What are the differences between a domestic bond, a Eurobond and a foreign bond?

12 What is the credit rating on a bond and what factors determine it?

13 Why do bond issuers accept restrictive covenants?

14 What are high-yield bonds? What is their role in financing firms?

15 What is a bearer bond?

16 What is a debenture?

17 What is the difference between a fixed-rate and a floating-rate bond?

Questions and problems

MyFinanceLab *Questions with an icon are also available for practice in MyFinanceLab with additional supporting resources.*

Answers to most questions can be found at www.pearsoned.co.uk/Arnold.
Answers to questions marked with an asterisk are to be found only in the Lecturer's Guide.

1 Imagine that the market yield to maturity for three-year bonds in a particular risk class is 12 per cent. You buy a bond in that risk class which offers an annual coupon of 10 per cent for the next three years, with the first payment in one year. The bond will be redeemed at par (£100) in three years.
a How much would you pay for the bond?
b If you paid £105 what yield to maturity would you obtain?

2 A £100 bond with two years to maturity and an annual coupon of 9 per cent is available. (The next coupon is payable in one year.)
a If the market requires a yield to maturity of 9 per cent for a bond of this risk class what will be its market price?
b If the market price is £98, what yield to maturity does it offer?
c If the required yield to maturity on this type of bond changes to 7 per cent, what will the market price change to?

3 a If the government sold a 10-year gilt with a par value of £100 and an (annual) coupon of 9 per cent, what price can be charged if investors require a 9.5 per cent yield to maturity on such bonds?

 b If yields to maturity on bonds of this risk class fall to 8.5 per cent, what could the bonds be sold for?

 c If it were sold for £105, what yield to maturity is the bond offering?

 d What is the flat yield on this bond if it is selling at £105?

An Excel spreadsheet version of these calculations is available at www.pearsoned.com/arnold

4 The price of a bond issued by C & M plc is 85.50 per cent of par value. The bond will pay an annual 8.5 per cent coupon until maturity (the next coupon will be paid in one year). The bond matures in seven years.

 a What will be the market price of the bond if yields to maturity for this risk class fall to 7.5 per cent?

 b What will be the market price of the bond if yields to maturity for this risk class rise to 18 per cent?

5 A zero coupon bond with a par value of £100 matures in five years.

 a What is the price of the bond if the yield to maturity is 5 per cent?

 b What is the price of the bond if the yield to maturity is 10 per cent?

6 Bond 1 has an annual coupon rate of 6 per cent and Bond 2 has an annual coupon of 12 per cent. Both bonds mature in one year and have a par value of £100. If the yield to maturity on bonds of this risk class is 10 per cent at what price will the bonds sell? Assume that the next coupons are due in one year's time.

7* You are considering three alternative investments in bonds. The bonds have different times to maturity, but carry the same default risk. You would like to gain an impression of the extent of price volatility for each given alternative change in future interest rates. The investments are:

 i A two-year bond with an annual coupon of 6 per cent, par value of £100 and the next coupon payment in one year. The current yield to maturity on this bond is 6.5 per cent.

 ii A ten-year bond with an annual coupon of 6 per cent, a par value of £100 and the next coupon payable in one year. The current yield to maturity on this bond is 7.2 per cent.

 iii A 20-year bond with an annual coupon of 6 per cent, a par value of £100 and the next coupon due in one year. The current yield to maturity on this bond is 7.7 per cent.

 a Draw an approximate yield curve.

 b Calculate the market price of each of the bonds.

 c Calculate the market price of the bonds on the assumption that yields to maturity rise by 200 basis points for all bonds.

 d Now calculate the market price of the bonds on the assumption that yields to maturity fall by 200 basis points.

 e Which bond price is the most volatile in circumstances of changing yields to maturity?

 f Explain the liquidity-preference theory of the term structure of yields to maturity.

An Excel spreadsheet version of this calculations is available at www.pearsoned.com/arnold.

8 What are the factors that explain the difference in yields to maturity between long-term and short-term bonds?

9 Find the current yield to maturity on government securities with maturities of one year, five years and ten years in the *Financial Times*. How has the yield curve changed since 2011 as shown in the chapter? What might account for this shift?

10 If the yield to maturity on a two-year zero coupon bond is 13 per cent and the yield to maturity on a one-year zero coupon bond is 10 per cent what is the expected spot rate of one-year bonds in one year's time assuming the expectations hypothesis is applicable?

11 If the yield to maturity on a one-year bond is 8 per cent and the expected spot rate on a one-year bond, beginning in one year's time, is 7 per cent what will be the yield to maturity on a two-year bond under the expectations hypothesis of the term structure of interest rates?

12 In 2006 the term structure of interest rates for UK government securities was downward sloping whereas in many other years it is upward sloping. Explain how these curves come about with reference to the expectations, liquidity and market-segmentation hypotheses.

13 Iris plc borrows £50m at 9.5 per cent from Westlloyds bank for five years. What cash flows will the firm have to find if the interest and principal are paid in the following ways?

 a All interest and capital is paid at the end of the period.

 b Interest only is paid for each of the years (at the year-ends); all principal is paid at the end.

 c £10m of the capital plus annual interest is paid on each anniversary date.

14 What factors should a firm consider when borrowing from a bank?

15 'Convertibles are great because they offer a lower return than straight debt and we just dish out shares rather than having to find cash to redeem the bonds' – executive at Myopic plc. Comment on this statement as though you were a shareholder in Myopic.

16 Lummer plc has issued £60m 15-year 8.5 per cent coupon bonds with a par value of £100. Each bond is convertible into 40 shares of Lummer ordinary shares, which are currently trading at £1.90.
 a What is the conversion price?
 b What is the conversion premium?
 c What is the conversion value of the bond?

17 Explain the following terms and their relevance to debt-finance decision makers:
 a Negative covenant.
 b Conversion premium.
 c Collateral.
 d Grace periods.

18 Outline the main advantages and disadvantages of fixed and floating interest rates from the borrowing company's perspective.

19 (*Examination level*) Flying High plc plans to expand rapidly over the next five years and is considering the following forms of finance to support that expansion.
 a A five-year £10m floating-rate term loan from MidBarc Bank plc at an initial annual interest of 9 per cent.
 b A five-year Eurodollar bond fixed at 8 per cent with a nominal value of US$15m.
 c A £10m convertible bond offering a yield to redemption of 6 per cent and a conversion premium of 15 per cent.

As the financial adviser to the board you have been asked to explain each of these forms of finance and point out the relative advantages and drawbacks. Do this in report form.

20 'We avoid debt finance because of the unacceptable constraint placed on managerial actions.' Explain what this executive means and suggest forms of long-term borrowing which have few constraints.

MyFinanceLab | *Now retake your diagnostic test for Chapter 11 to check your progress and update your study plan.*

Assignments

1 Review the long-term debt instruments used by a company familiar to you. Consider the merits and drawbacks of these and explain alternative long-term debt strategies.

2 Write a report for the senior management of a company you know well explaining your views on the wisdom of using some of the firm's assets in a sale and leaseback transaction.

Visit www.pearsoned.co.uk/arnold to get access to Gradetracker diagnostic tests, podcasts, Excel spreadsheet solutions, *FT* articles, a flashcard revision tool, web links, a searchable glossary and more.

Section 2:

Employee Relations

MANAGEMENT AND EMPLOYMENT RELATIONS

INTRODUCTION

In Chapter 1 we considered in general terms the nature and functions of management concerning industrial relations, and the extent to which management ideologies determine both the climate and practice of employment relations within organisations. These aspects will be examined in greater detail.

The chapter commences with an overview of the employer and management contexts, and this is followed by a discussion of the nature of managerial control over the labour process. We then examine in some detail management styles, ideologies and strategies and how these impact upon employment relations in particular organisational settings within both the public and private sectors. The relationship between personnel management, human resource management and employment relations is then considered at workplace and organisational levels. As the quality of employment relations within smaller firms is to some extent influenced by the advice they receive from employers' associations, the role of the latter within this context is finally examined.

Learning outcomes

When you have read this chapter, you should be able to:

1. Explain the distinction between the terms 'employer' and 'management' and account for the rise of 'managerialism'.

2. Explain the central issues concerning the management of the labour process.

3. Distinguish between management styles, management ideologies and management strategies.

4. Explain the impact of management styles, ideologies and strategies upon industrial relations in both public and private sector organisations.

5. Differentiate between personnel management and human resource management approaches to employment relations within the context of the shift from Fordist to post-Fordist systems.

6. Explain the changing nature of employers' associations.

OF EMPLOYERS AND MANAGEMENT

'Management' and 'employer' are terms assumed, often wrongly, to be synonymous, largely because they are generic categories that overlap with and complement each other. The term 'employer' applies equally to a small business where the owner of the business is the employer of labour (employees), a large company where the employer is equated with the name of that company and its legally registered status ('limited' or 'public limited' company) and large areas of the public sector where the government is either 'direct' employer (as in central government) or indirect employer (as in the National Health Service and education). On the other hand, the term 'management', as defined in Chapter 1, is a process concerned with the functions of planning, co-ordinating, organising, staffing, directing and controlling the various activities and resources of an organisation in order to ensure its efficient operation and to achieve its relevant goals. In larger organisations, professional managers are employed to undertake these functions within their various specialisms (for example, in finance, sales, production, marketing, personnel and human resource management) and, as such, form a distinct employee elite within the organisation.

The managerial occupation

During the eighteenth and early decades of the nineteenth centuries, enterprises tended to be owned and managed by the owners themselves. Owner-managers, in attempting to survive and prosper within a competitive product market, would, according to classical economic theory, seek to minimise labour costs while attempting to maximise the effort and productive capabilities of their employees. To be sure, many employers were highly exploitative of their workforces, as the following example taken from the textile industry illustrates:

> The worst situation is that of those workers who have to compete against a machine that is making its way. The price of the goods which they produce adapts itself to the price of the kindred product of the machine, and as the latter works more cheaply, its human competitor has but the

lowest wages. . . . Of all the workers in competition with machinery, the most ill-used are the hand-loom cotton weavers. They receive the most trifling wages, and, with full work, are not in a position to earn more than ten shillings a week. One class of woven goods after another is annexed by the power-loom, and hand weaving is the last refuge of workers thrown out of employment in other branches, so that the trade is always overcrowded. Hence it comes that, in average seasons, the hand-weaver counts himself fortunate if he can earn six or seven shillings a week, while to reach this sum he must sit at his loom fourteen to eighteen hours a day. (Engels, 1892, pp. 172–3)

On the other hand, many employers sought to treat their workers more humanely within the constraints of competitive markets. Gospel and Palmer (1993) cite the example of Quaker employers, drawing upon research derived from Child (1964).

Self-evaluation activity 2.1

The notion of a 'good employer'
Response on website

In Chapter 1 we considered the unitary perspective which, in its nineteenth-century form, embraced both 'good' and 'bad' employers. The example of the exploitative nature of employers in the textile industry has just been given. In what ways do you think the Quakers as 'good' employers differ from this example?

The rise of managerialism

Watson (1995) defines managerialism as:

> A belief that the people who manage or 'direct' the corporations of modern societies have taken control away from those allegedly separate interests who own wealth. (p. 203)

During the course of the nineteenth and twentieth centuries, many firms became larger and more complex, and with the advent of the joint stock company share ownership became diffuse, eventually giving rise to the formation of a separate category of

employee – the salaried, pofessional manager concerned with the successful running of large, complex business organisations and public bureaucracies. This development represented nothing less than a managerial revolution (Burnham, 1945) through which the specialist knowledge and skills of managerial experts have undermined the dominance of the owners. The managerialist assumptions then are, firstly, that managers, because of their expertise and separation from shareholder interests have greater freedom in running the business either in their own, sectional interests or, in a broader sense, in the interests of the wider community. Secondly, as employees, managers may have a shared, common interest with other employees in the survival of the business, and should the business fail then their situation is no different from that of other employees. Thirdly, as a separate group within the business, managers have the authority to make decisions on behalf of the owners, the consequences of which could conflict with other employee interests. Managers, then, according to the managerialist thesis, comprise a neutral 'buffer zone' between the conflicting interests of capital and labour within the organisation.

Criticisms of managerialism

Self-evaluation activity 2.2

Are managers neutral?
The response is given below

Read the extract in Mini case 2.1 concerning the long-running Liverpool docks dispute, which came to an end in December 1997. To what extent can we criticise the managerialist assumption of manager neutrality?

Mini case 2.1
Liverpool docks dispute

On 25 September 1995, 22 workers employed by the Torside docks company in Liverpool were informed by managers that they would have to work overtime to get a ship ready for sailing. Although the notice was short the dockers had become increasingly used to such demands. What they were not used to was the news

that 'normal overtime arrangements' would not apply. The short notice and the payment arrangements both breached existing agreements between the Mersey Docks and Harbour Company (MDHC), Torside Ltd and the Transport and General Workers Union (TGWU). Taken aback, the dockers decided to discuss the situation with their shop stewards (who were working elsewhere). As the working day finished, the men left the ship and went to the canteen to wait for the stewards. As the first group of five dockers arrived they were met by the Managing Director of the Torside company who sacked them for leaving the ship. Bewildered, they wandered out to meet the others and tell them what had happened. When they in turn went into the canteen they were informed that they should go back to the ship, without their five sacked colleagues, or they would suffer the same fate; they refused to go back on such terms and were sacked.

The next morning the remainder of the Torside workforce gradually heard what had happened and a quick meeting with the stewards was arranged at 8 a.m. Over the previous evening the MDHC Port Stewards had advised the Torside stewards and workforce to go to work and let the senior stewards and the TGWU Docks Officer deal with the sackings via negotiation and the 'normal' grievance procedures. However, the situation was further inflamed by the Managing Director of Torside Ltd, who appeared at the canteen meeting and sacked the entire workforce. On the morning of 27 September the Torside workforce mounted a picket of the Nelson Freight Company (a part-owned subsidiary of MDHC). The Torside men regularly worked side-by-side with dockers from Nelson Freight and the dockers (11 in all) refused to cross the picket line. As a consequence they were sacked by MDHC. The main workforce was now in the Royal Seaforth docks giving the stewards a further day to resolve the dispute. MDHC refused to discuss the issue because they claimed it was an internal dispute at an independent company. Frustrated and angry, the sacked workers informed the Seaforth workforce of their intention to picket the Seaforth docks. On the morning of the 28th the pickets were in place and the Seaforth workforce refused to cross the lines. In response the entire workforce was sacked by MDHC, which proceeded to use casual labour thereafter.

Source: Lavalette and Kennedy, 1996, pp. 1–2

The example of the origins of the Liverpool docks dispute graphically demonstrates that the interests of MDHC management contrast markedly with those of the sacked workforce and that the managerialist assumption of a neutral management buffer is not valid in this case. Watson (1995) suggests counter-arguments to the managerialist thesis and cites research by Nichols (1969) and Pahl and Winkler (1974) in making the following criticisms of managerialism:

- Senior managers tend to internalise profit-related values and priorities and act as long-term profit max-imisers and cost minimisers. Whether or not MDHC management had a hidden agenda to weaken the union, isolate rank-and-file militants and casualise the workforce we may never know for certain, but the cost-minimising strategy of pursuing the em-ployment of a casualised workforce has, from the company's point of view, been successful.
- Research evidence from the USA and other countries (Zeitlin, 1989) supports the assertion that managers' and owners' interests are virtually identical. Main-taining corporate profitability is an aim shared by owners/shareholders and managers alike. Moreover, corporate profits are essential determinants of high managerial income and status and this establishes a 'dependency relationship' between managers and owners in which the owners depend upon man-agerial expertise to generate profits and efficiency-driven cost-minimising strategies and managers depend upon owners for high status and rewards.
- Child (1969) argues that top managers and owners have similar socio-economic origins and back-grounds; correspondingly, they share the same or similar values, attitudes, ideologies and objectives.
- Research by Poole *et al.* (1981) concerning a survey of over 1000 managers suggests that managers do not simply share owner interests or act as agents of cap-ital. Managers' concerns are often more pragmatic than this and are related to their own career and immediate interests. For example, opposition to trade unionism and industrial democracy, Watson suggests, is:

> *less a matter of principled class action (in the interests of the owners) than a matter of defend-ing their own freedom to manoeuvre in their everyday work as is strongly suggested by the evidence that personnel specialists within man-agement hold distinctive attitudes (for or against) in these two areas.* (p. 205)

MANAGEMENT CONTROL AND THE LABOUR PROCESS

The related concepts of 'control' and 'power' are central to our understanding of how the labour process is 'managed'. We are concerned here with the control over the production process in deter-mining how employees within organisations perform their work. The extent to which this control can be exercised depends upon the possession of power. Before examining the ramifications of the debate concerning control of the labour process, we look briefly at the power concept.

The concept of power

Power is a complex concept in its own right and is the subject of broad philosophical and sociological debate. Within the industrial relations arena in-equalities of power sometimes result in conflict, but more often compromise is the order of the day, as we shall see when we consider collective bargaining in Chapter 6. Fox (1985) identifies two strategies that managements could adopt in order to ensure employee compliance. The first is through coercion and the second is through consent. At one extreme, a manager could rely on the exercise of naked power (coercion) to force employees to do his will, while at the other extreme a manager could exercise power in less obvious and direct ways to engineer voluntary compliance with a decision or policy. Many forms of coercive power are derived from dependency relationships. An employer needs workers and uses managers to control that labour, and workers depend upon employers to pay their wages, but, as Fox argues, dependence is rarely one-sided and the important issue is always con-cerned with the balance of power and where it lies. To a certain extent, the balance of power within a unionised context is determined by the perceptions of power which each party – management or union – may have of the other and by assessing which party holds the advantage at a given point in time (Gennard and Judge, 1997, p. 31). In practice, man-agement strategy represents a 'mix' of coercion and consent. The 'mix' usually reveals relatively more coercion towards the bottom of the organisational hierarchy and relatively more consent towards the top.

While coercive power was undoubtedly used by managements and employers in the nineteenth century in order to cajole workers into submitting to certain systems of rules and patterns of behaviour, the more common basis upon which power is exercised by contemporary managements within the employment relationship is consent. In this situation workers regard management's rule as legitimate and offer full consent to it and to the policies and decisions through which it is expressed so that management no longer needs to coerce. By giving full consent, workers 'authorise' management to govern them, 'thereby giving a special significance to the term "authority"'. Management can govern without this authorisation by employing coercion, but it faces at best passive indifference and at worst militant hostility. The value to management of consent is therefore apparent' (Fox, 1985, p. 67).

Self-evaluation activity 2.3

Power bases at the disposal of management
Response on website

Having identified the nature of power by coercion and consent, we are now in a position to consider the different bases of power at the disposal of management. Give examples of each and state which are more relevant to the management of industrial relations today. French and Raven's (1960) analysis of power suggests the following six categories:

1. **Rewards.** Reward power refers to the number of positive incentives that the employee thinks or perceives management has to offer.
2. **Punishment.** Punishment power has to do with the negative things which employees think management can do.
3. **Information.** Information can be a source of power. If employees think that management controls information that employees want, then management has power.
4. **Legitimacy.** Legitimate power as a resource stems from employees feeling that management has a right to make a given request. Legitimate power is normally described as authority and stems from the position or status which a manager has in the organisational hierarchy.
5. **Expertise.** A manager may have expertise within a certain area of his responsibility, or on some topic or

issue. If so, employees may often comply because 'management knows best'.
6. **Referent power.** In some cases an employee will look up to and admire a manager as a person. In this situation the employee may comply with the manager's demands because the employee identifies with the manager and wants to achieve whatever goals and objectives the manager wants to achieve.

The bases of social power managers draw on to exert influence in organisations are therefore dependent upon their access to organisational resources, their location within the communication network and formal organisational structure, who they are trying to influence, their own personal characteristics, the characteristics of the organisation itself and their control over the production and labour process, to which we now turn.

MANAGERIAL CONTROL OF THE LABOUR PROCESS

As we noted earlier, control over the production process in the sense of determining how employees of an organisation perform their work depends on the possession of power that in turn is derived from the differential access to the power bases we have identified. Huczynski and Buchanan (1991) define this type of control as 'the process through which obedience, compliance and conformity to predetermined standards of behaviour are achieved through interpersonal and group processes and is thus a property of the *relationship* between controller and controlled' (p. 595).

Self-evaluation activity 2.4

Examples of management control over the workforce
Response on website

Identify two or three examples of management control over the workforce.

As long ago as 1947, Warner and Low argued that mechanisation and division of labour facilitates management control:

Control problems are simplified on two counts through mechanisation: (1) machines are easier

to control than human beings, and (2) mechanisation tends to disrupt the social solidarity of the workers, who thereby become easier to control than they would if they were to maintain close social relations during working hours . . . these factors tend to increase the subordination of the individual worker to management; from the management's viewpoint they are valuable means of social control over workers. . . . The routinisation of jobs also simplifies control of workers in another way. The individual operative today does not have the feeling of security that the old-time craftsman derived from his special technical abilities. In most cases, today's operative is aware that only a comparatively brief training period protects him in his job from a large number of untrained individuals. The members of the supervisory hierarchy are also well aware of this fact. The psychological effect of this result of the division of labour is to intensify the subordinate position of the individual operative and to make him submit more readily to the limitations of his behaviour required by the supervisory group. (pp. 78, 80, 174)

However, control is rarely one-sided and may be concerned with some issues on which there is consensus between management and employees, and with other issues on which there may be conflict (Child, 1984). Child goes on to argue that:

An increase in control achieved by workers over an issue that is in dispute will be at the expense of the amount of control available to management; and vice versa. Control then takes on a 'win–lose' character. An example might be control over the level of manning in a department. Where there are issues on which the different parties agree, perhaps such as safety, this win–lose character disappears. It is then possible to share control and for an increase in the devolution of control to employees not to mean a loss in control by management. (p. 139)

At the strategic level of the organisation, however, it is management that makes decisions concerning the objectives and policies of the organisation as a whole simply because control over strategic resources such as financial resources resides solely with management. The absence of any input into,

or influence of, the strategic control process on the part of the non-managerial workforce may lead to collective resistance to managerial control over issues such as:

- **the employment contract**, whereby the balance between employee effort or work input contractually required by management and payment contractually offered is mediated through collective bargaining and ultimately through the withdrawal of labour sanction;
- **competitive pressures** faced by many organisations due to global economic factors such as the decline of the Far Eastern 'tiger' economies and over-valued national currencies may oblige managers to exercise more stringent control in an attempt to reduce costs, increase productivity, threaten redundancies and respond more swiftly to market changes.

The labour process debate

Labour process theory has its origins in the work of Marx. Essentially, Marx presents us with a critique of the political economics of capitalism, an economic system which creates two broad social classes: the capitalists, or bourgeoisie, who own and control the means of production, and the working class, or proletariat, who sell their labour power to capitalists in order to survive. Both classes, Marx argues, need each other and are mutually dependent upon each other, but their interests conflict. Capitalists aims to make profits in order to accumulate capital and so make more profits, whereas workers' interests are concerned with increasing wages and improving working conditions. The manager in a capitalist organisation cannot, therefore, depend upon the voluntary and willing co-operation, loyalty and commitment of the workforce and has to seek employee compliance through the exercise of control.

Self-evaluation activity 2.5

Employee compliance
The response is given below

Given that managers cannot rely on a willing workforce and therefore need to exercise control in order to obtain employee compliance, such employee compliance is

not necessarily guaranteed. In other words, there are **limits** to compliance. Suggest examples of situations where employees may regard such compliance as unreasonable.

Compliance in itself presents problems, as Hyman (1980) points out:

> Yet the acceptance of a generalised obligation to follow managerial instruction does not entail that a worker will accept without question every specific order which any manager may issue. There is a logical gap between generalised social values and specific rules in concrete situations. . . . Skilled toolmakers are normally conservative and stolid members of an engineering labour force, unlikely to contest in general terms the right of management to manage; but a supervisor who instructed a toolmaker to sweep the floor would be likely to be told to fuck off. . . . Yet precisely because most workers' customary obedience reflects no more than low-key acquiescence, the limits of obedience are easily tested. . . . There tends to be a 'zone of acceptance' where workers will, for example, normally perform without question tasks which are clearly technically necessary and which come within the customary range of their functions; but as soon as these limits are exceeded, their conformity becomes problematic. (p. 314)

Expressed in a different way, the problem of compliance becomes a 'problem of motivation'. Citing the case of 'Chemco', a large multinational corporation, Nichols (1980) argues that workers' low expectations of work reflects the low trust status of and relatively high levels of control over the workforce. Therefore attempts to change the low expectancy culture by introducing job enrichment and flexibilisation could well fail as workers may regard these changes in terms of replacing one form of control by another, and in any event they have been 'socialised' into accepting this culture and the high levels of compliance that go with it. As Nichols states:

> It is arguable that their [the workers'] problem is not so much that Chemco workers have high expectations of work but rather that they expect so little . . . they do not expect their work to be satisfying and have entered into a grudging bargain with their employers. Part of just one more generation of working class men and women, well used to being denied meaning and control over their lives, like industrial whores they do enough to get enough. 'It's a job' they say. (p. 294)

A further example which demonstrates the limits of compliance concerns air stewardesses and other 'pink-collar' workers such as supermarket checkout staff who must exercise 'emotional labour at work' (Blyton and Turnbull, 1998, 2005). Emotional labour is defined as 'the management of feelings to create a publicly observable facial and bodily display' (Blyton and Turnbull, 2005, p. 75). Since emotional labour involves 'putting on a front' and acting according to the dictates of others over long periods, many workers may experience strain and tensions. A study of supermarket checkout staff reveals that if employees do not exercise emotional labour they are reprimanded by supervisors, using discipline as control: 'We are able to detect when a checkout operator is not smiling or even when she is putting on a false smile . . . we call her into a room and have a chat with her' (ibid., p. 82, citing Ogbonna, 1992).

Labour process theory concerns itself with the imperatives of managerial control and its effects upon workers themselves and the process whereby work becomes deskilled and degraded. The influential work of Braverman (1974) follows the tradition of Marxist critique. His central argument is that the pursuit of capitalist interests has led to a general trend towards deskilling, routinising and mechanising of jobs across the employment spectrum, from manufacturing to retailing and from design to clerical work. Braverman critically evaluates the work of F.W. Taylor in order to support his arguments, and it is his work to which we now turn.

Taylorism and control

The ideas concerning 'scientific management' originated and developed by Taylor (1947) in the late nineteenth and early twentieth centuries became widely disseminated and used by engineers and work study practitioners in Britain, Japan, and, interestingly, in the Soviet Union under Lenin, but had only a limited influence upon the USA (Grint, 1993). For Taylor, the problem of work is the problem of managerial control and the issue for management is to ensure the maximum degree of effort for the minimum amount of reward. The solution, according to Taylor, was to extend the division of labour, separate the conception (thinking) of work from its

execution (doing) and make the workforce less skilled. This would result not only in higher levels of productivity per worker and cheaper labour, but also a more compliant workforce. Having worked as a labourer, clerk and machinist himself, Taylor was well aware of the problems of production at shop-floor level and suggested three reasons for this:

- Management lacked the knowledge to maximise production; their ignorance left them at the mercy of workers' wisdom.
- The workers themselves had a reason for restricting output which included the real fear of underpayment and redundancy.
- The existing payment systems did not include sufficiently sophisticated incentive schemes, where they existed at all.

Taylor blamed management, not the workforce, for these problems and insisted they drop their conventional 'rule of thumb' schemes and use his 'scientific management' techniques. These involved a number of discrete changes which included:

- technical improvements to machinery;
- extension of the division of labour so that each task was fragmented into its smallest constituent units which would be timed and measured;
- a piece-rate system that was individually rather than collectively organised (to avoid encouraging collective action and trade unions) involving accelerating rewards and punishment should the relatively high targets be exceeded or not met; and
- deskilling of jobs to facilitate the employment of cheaper labour and to eliminate the restrictive practices previously used by employees on the basis of their monopoly over knowledge.

Taylorism therefore enabled employers to transfer work which involved planning, design and other 'cerebral' work activities from the shop floor to new production engineering and work study departments. The remaining tasks which were simple, routine and unskilled could then be undertaken by cheap, substitutable and easily available labour. These tasks required little training and, through work study techniques, the input required from workers could be easily and accurately calculated and workers' output could therefore be measured against output targets. Individual workers' output would then be rewarded through payment-by-results incentive schemes. Because tasks were simplified and measurable, worker performance could be easily checked and this facilitated management control.

Braverman and the critique of Taylorism

Braverman makes the assumption that there is a fundamental conflict underlying the relationship between capital and labour, and that the relations between management and workforce and the question of technological change need to be seen in this light. For Braverman, the employment relationship begins when the employer buys the services of an employee in the labour market. In entering into a contract of employment, the employer and employee have only agreed the terms and conditions of the employment relationship. The details of what work employees do, when they do it, and how it is done have to be resolved day by day in the workplace. Braverman argues that, in order to get maximum return on their 'investment' in human labour, employers have to maximise their control over the behaviour of employees, whatever the type of technology currently in use. Moreover, management control systems, according to Braverman, were one aspect of the wider class conflict between capital and labour.

Braverman also argued that the need for management control to cope with uncommitted workers led to the degradation of work skills and workers. He claimed that although science and technology were demanding more education, training and exercise of mental effort, work was increasingly subdivided into routine and easy-to-learn fragments as Taylor had suggested. The need for managers to maintain a disciplined workforce led them into a continuing process in which approaches to control were perpetually refined and intensified. These extensions of management control erode craft skill, reduce workers' independence and reduce the importance of their knowledge of the craft. In addition, workers are excluded from decisions about methods and the pace of work; technology reduces worker skill and discretion; fragmenting tasks, as Taylor recommended, stifles individual development, reduces wages and enhances management status.

Self-evaluation activity 2.6

Illustration of Braverman's thesis
Response on website

Read the following extract about the electrical equipment industry. Does this example illustrate Braverman's thesis?

> Electrical employers transformed the work of making lamps. The jobs were simplified and divided into minute segments with the former skills built into specialised machines. This allowed the companies to cut costs, increase production, and eliminate skilled workers. The craftsmen, who had used their own specialised skills and knowledge to produce the lamps, were replaced by workers, predominantly women, who performed only one special operation and required little training to do the job. (Thompson, 1990, p. 32)

Labour process control and employment relations issues: Fordism and post-Fordism

Management control over the labour process is also an important manifestation of management's assumed right to manage (the exercise of managerial prerogatives). The way management does this is just as much a matter of form, or style, as of content and this is explored further. Initially, however, it is necessary to identify the nature of the dominant control systems which underpin the management of the employment relationship, namely Fordism and post-Fordism.

Summary points

- Owner-managers who were often highly exploitative of labour during the eighteenth and early nineteenth centuries were replaced by the 'managerialism' of the twentieth century as the dominant control ideology and mechanism within the employment relationship.
- 'Managerialism' itself has been criticised, mainly because of its inherent and erroneous assumption

of managerial 'neutrality' which, for example, pervades the HRM literature.
- The concept of power itself and the 'bases of power' model are vital to our understanding of the inequalities inherent within the employment relationship, as is the body of theory concerning managerial control over the labour process which stems from a critique of Taylorism by Braverman.

MANAGEMENT CONTROL SYSTEMS: FROM FORDISM TO POST-FORDISM

The changes in employment relations cannot be seen only as the consequence of a shift in political ideology and economic policy at national level, important though these are. Changes in production technologies such as the shift from mass production (Fordism) to flexible specialisation (post-Fordism) are regarded as crucial in determining the nature of emerging patterns of industrial relations. Ackers *et al.* (1996) cite Kenney and Florida (1993) who:

> use Fordist and post-Fordist neologisms to suggest that unions which are locked within a Fordist paradigm remain reactionary in the face of the new demands of work in what they call 'innovation mediated production', [and] Wickens [1993] argues that just as Fordism created a type of adversarial trade unionism, the new manufacturing system of lean production (or neo/post-Fordist) will favour a more co-operative partnership. (p. 7)

The transition from Fordism to post-Fordism is also accompanied by new ideas about the organisation of work and the notion of flexibility (Procter and Ackroyd, 2001; Boxall and Purcell, 2003; Geary, 2003). Before considering important elements of workplace change, we examine the nature of the 'paradigm shift' from Fordism to post-Fordism.

The emergence of Fordism

Fordism is based on the premise of a linkage between the division of labour and mass markets. As early as the eighteenth century, Adam Smith (1910) realised that the division of labour depends on the desired volume of output which, in turn, depends on

the size of the market. The 'Scientific Management' principles of Taylor (1947) assumed a breakdown of jobs into measurable and relatively unskilled tasks. If a type of technology could be developed to exploit the division of labour in order to maximise production, then markets could be developed to take advantage of the increased production. Henry Ford was among the first to take advantage of this relationship. His name was consequently given to the large-scale, assembly-line industrial system which he developed and others copied. 'Fordism is the name used to designate the system of mass production, tied to the cultivation of mass markets which Henry Ford himself developed' (Hounshell, 1984, p. 34). Fordism, then, concerns manufacturing carried out in large plants, producing mass market materials using assembly-line processes.

The nature of the system

Ford established his first plant at Highland Park, Michigan, in 1913. It made only one product – the Model T Ford car. The model of production worked out by Ford in order to service the potential mass market involved the transfer of traditional skills from workers to specialised machines. By 1914 about 15,000 machines had been installed and company policy was to scrap machines as fast as improved types could replace them. In addition, Ford perfected the flow-line principle of assembly work which meant that

> instead of workers moving between tasks, the flow of parts is achieved as much as possible by machines (conveyors and transporters) so that assembly-line workers are tied to their work position and have no need to move about the workshop. A crucial consequence is that the pace of work is controlled mechanically and not by the workers and supervisors. (Littler and Salaman, 1985, p. 88)

Associated with the new fixed-speed, moving assembly line was an accelerated division of labour and short task-cycle times. Ford pushed job fragmentation to an extreme and records a survey of jobs in his plants:

> The lightest jobs were again classified to discover how many of them required the use of full facilities, and we found 670 could be filled by

legless men, 2637 by one-legged men, two by armless men, 715 by one-armed men and ten by blind men. Therefore out of 7882 kinds of job . . . 4034 did not require full physical capacity. (Ford, 1922, p. 108, cited in Littler and Salaman, 1985, p. 88)

Being associated with scientific management and the diffusion of Taylorist principles, Fordist production systems which depended to a great extent on scientific management became the dominant mode of production within much of British manufacturing industry from the mid-1940s until the late 1970s. The multinational corporation facilitated the spread of Fordist production. For example, Ford established subsidiaries in Britain, Germany, Japan and other countries, as did Ford's main competitor – General Motors. Factories were designed by engineers, invoking the metaphor of large engines comprising cogs and wheels rationally linked together which denies humanity and human emotion. Work was deskilled through task fragmentation and detailed division of labour 'and as workers no longer owned their own means of production, being reliant, as wage slave, on the owner and his management agents, individuals were dehumanised' (Boxall and Purcell, 2003, p. 94).

Self-evaluation activity 2.7
The Ford workplace
Response on website

Mini case 2.2 is an extract from Beynon's *Working for Ford* (1975) which describes the conditions at the former Ford Halewood plant during the late 1960s. After you have read it attempt the question that follows.

Mini case 2.2
Working for Ford

Working in a car plant involves coming to terms with the assembly line. 'The line never stops you are told. Why not? . . . Don't ask. It never stops.' The assembly plant itself is huge and on two levels, with the paint shop on the one floor and the trim and final assembly departments below. The car shell is painted in the paint shop and passed by lift and conveyor to the first station of the trim assembly department. From this point, the body shell is carried up and down the 500-yard length

of the plant until it is finally driven off, tested and stored in the car park. Few men see the cars being driven off the line. While an assembly worker is always dealing with a moving car it is never moving under its own steam. The line stands two feet above floor level and moves the cars monotonously, easily along. Walking the floor of the plant as a stranger, you are deafened by the whine of compressed air spanners, you step gingerly between and upon the knots of connecting air pipes which writhe like snakes in your path and you stare at the moving cars on either side. This is the world of the operator. In and out of the cars, up and over the line, check the line speed and model mix. Your mind restlessly alert, because there's no guarantee that the next car will be the same as the last. But still a blank – you keep trying to blot out what's happening. 'When I'm here my mind's a blank. I make it go blank.' They all say that. They all tell the story about the man who left Ford to work in a sweet factory where he had to divide the reds from the blues, but left because he couldn't take the decision making . . .

The history of the assembly line is a history of conflict over speed-up – the process whereby the pace of work demanded of the operator is systematically increased. This can be obtained in a number of ways, the simplest involving a gradual increase in the speed of the line during a shift. The worker gets suspicious after a bit because he finds he can't make time on the job. He can't get those few stations up the line which allow him a break and half a ciggie now and then. The long-serving stewards and workers at Halewood insist that plant management made frequent use of this type of speed-up in the early days of the plant. Production managers out to make a name for themselves can only do it through figures – through their production and their costs. They abuse their supervision to this end. To service the god of production is also to serve yourself, and in this climate a few dodges are part of the game. (Beynon, 1975, pp. 109, 138–9)

A senior manager
'We are here to make a profit and that's the bottom line. If we don't succeed, we all go down. The assembly line is efficient and the workers know the score. We need close supervision to ensure production targets.'

Source: Beynon, 1975, pp. 109, 138–9

Comment on the nature of workplace industrial relations at the plant.

The limitations of Fordism and the 'neo-Fordist' alternative

There have been a number of criticisms of Fordism which expose its limitations. The nature of these limitations are economic, technological and social, and are now examined:

- The economic limits are basically concerned with the extent to which it is economically viable to continue fragmenting jobs and transferring skills to specialised machinery. As we have seen, mass production depends upon demand, and if that demand is not forthcoming then further specialisation is not economically justifiable. Furthermore, Fordism can only be developed in industries producing standardised products for large markets, and to set up mechanised production lines is enormously expensive.
- Once a Fordist system is established it is quite rigid. In order to alter a product, for example, substantial reinvestment is needed.
- The further subdivision of jobs and labour is dependent upon the further development or transformation of production technology.
- Fordist production systems are relatively easy to copy if sufficient funding is available to set up the plant, and firms in countries in which labour power is expensive find it difficult to compete with those in areas where wages are cheaper. This was a factor involved in the first successes of the Japanese car industry and more recently that of South Korea.
- The limits to the direct control methods of Fordism are set by increasing the costs to the employer of securing the co-operation of the workforce. Generally, in Fordist organisations workers are neither trained to show, nor are rewarded for, initiative, and there is little scope for creative involvement of employees (Salaman, 1984). Workers may not be motivated beyond the prospect of the pay packet, and it is difficult under these circumstances to encourage workers to do more than the bare minimum necessary to get by. Littler and Salaman (1985) provide an account by an American worker (quoted from Douglas, 1980):

 I am – or was – an American autoworker. I built GM cars for 16 years. Then, in March

(1980) I was laid off indefinitely. . . . It was not the worker who determines the quality of the car, but the executives in Detroit and the plant supervisors. The worker who performs a certain task 320 times a day, 5 days a week, knows more about the specifics of this particular job than anyone else. Yet in 16 years, I have never been consulted on how to improve a job qualitatively or quantitatively. There are suggestion programmes but their main concern is always 'how to save the company's money'. The autoworker can only build as good a car as he is instructed or permitted to build. We on the line take our cue from those in head office. If they don't really care about the quality, they can't expect us to either. (p. 40)

According to Sabel (1982), the high point of Fordism is long past but nevertheless, despite the substantial drawbacks, we must also recognise that Fordism had its advantages, particularly for the firm and the consumer in terms of economies of scale. This means that the larger the unit of production, the greater the potential output of goods at cheaper unit costs. In order to take full advantage of these economies, the factory must produce to maximum, or near maximum capacity. This in turn means that there must be a ready market for the goods. The consumer is, therefore, part of this equation, and the consumer also derives benefits from Fordism by being able to afford to buy the goods produced in this way. Those who contend that, despite its limitations, Fordism has not had its day nevertheless concede that there has been a movement from 'traditional' Fordism of the type we have considered, to 'neo' Fordism, which 'is often regarded as representing the alternative production system in which the stultifying rigidities of Fordism were eased apart to allow some degree of flexible production using new technologies to expand the range of products without modifying the tight managerial control structures' (Grint, 1993, p. 296). Neo-Fordism, then, looks at workplace change in relation to the labour process, the introduction of new technologies, automation, new methods of employment and changes in working practices. Horton (1997) describes the neo-Fordist project as being led by technological innovations such as computer-integrated manufacturing systems and electronic offices which in turn 'have led to

reductions in the labour force, employment of more multi-skilled technicians, greater flexibility in production methods and diversification in types of product. At the same time, new working practices and the introduction of participative working groups, such as quality circles, have introduced flexibility into the socio-technical systems in the workplace' (pp. 162–3). Grint (1993), however, sounds a note of caution:

It is not axiomatic either that neo-Fordism should be regarded as a solution to pre-existing problems or that it is prevalent in itself. Even where it does exist . . . there are many who doubt that neo-Fordism is the solution to the problem. For these people the problems lie much deeper than simply at the level of technology and reflect rather the very nature of Fordism as an organisational form, replete with its large-scale and cumbersome bureaucracies, its over-concentrated control structures and its over-centralised decision making. (p. 296)

Post-Fordism

By the 1970s, new ideas about the way work should be organised as a reaction to Taylorism, scientific management and a failing Fordist system began to take root, partly as a result of social changes that had taken place in the 1960s and partly as a result of episodic crises, such as the 'oil crisis' of the mid-1970s, which in turn focused thinking upon competitiveness and productivity.

Post-Fordism represents a movement beyond Fordism, and signifies a qualitative shift in the organisation of production and consumption. As an ideology, post-Fordism is essentially optimistic as it postulates the apparent long-term solution to the assembly-line blues: the breakdown of the assembly line and the introduction of new work technologies are seen as creating opportunities for re-skilling the workforce and offer the prospect of a multi-skilled labour force operating flexibly in a less hierarchical work environment. The assembly line is assumed to be a thing of the past, skill and flexibility levels are increased, teamwork structures are devised and specialised niche markets for high-quality, high-value products and services are sought out. In essence, then, the production changes over

the past few decades associated with post-Fordism can be summarised as:

- changes in product life and product innovation, with shorter flexible runs and a wide range of products on offer;
- changes in stock control, with just-in-time methods removing the need to hold large amounts of costly stock;
- changes in design and marketing, such as the development of niche marketing, in response to an increasingly diverse pattern of consumer demand;
- changes in consumption with increased emphasis upon niche markets, market segmentation and rapidly changing consumer tastes.

Post-Fordism is characteristic of, and incorporates the notion of 'flexible specialisation' which focuses on the move away from mass production to batch production and the manufacture of a wide variety of custom-made goods and services using flexible labour and skilled, adaptable workers. The example in Exhibit 2.1 of the retail sector provides the essence of what post-Fordism represents.

Exhibit 2.1

Post-Fordism: the example of retailing

Since the 1950s retailers have been using computers to transform the distribution system. All mass producers have the problem of forecasting demand. If they produce too little they lose market share. If they produce too much they are left with stocks which are costly to hold or have to be sold at a discount. Retailers face this problem not just for a few products but for thousands. Their answer has been to develop information and supply systems which allow them to order supplies to coincide with demand.

Every evening, Sainsbury's receives details of the sales of all 12,000 lines from each of its shops; these are turned into orders for warehouse deliveries for the coming night, and replacement production for the following day. With computerised control of stocks in the shop, transport networks, automatic loading and unloading in warehouses, Sainsbury's flow-line make-to-order system has conquered the Fordist problem of stocks.

It has also overcome the limits of the mass product. For, in contrast to the discount stores which are confined to a few fast-selling items, Sainsbury's, like the new wave of high street shops, can handle ranges of products geared to segments of the market. Market niching has become the slogan of the high street. Market researchers break down the market by age (youth, young adults, 'grey power'), by household types (dinkies, single-gender couple, one-parent families), by income, occupation, housing and increasingly by locality. They analyse lifestyles, correlating consumption patterns across commodities, from food to clothing and health and holidays.

The point of this new anthropology of consumption is to target both product and shops to particular segments. In modern shops, the emphasis has shifted from the manufacturer's economies of scale to retailer's economies of scope. The economies come from offering an integrated range from which customers can choose their own basket of products. There is also an economy of innovation, for the modern retail system allows new product ideas to be tested in practice, through shop sales, and the successful ones then to be ordered for wider distribution. Innovation has become a leading edge of the new competition. Product life has become shorter, for both fashion goods and consumer durables.

A centrepiece of this new retailing is design. Designers produce the innovations. They shape the lifestyle. They design the shops. With market researchers, they have steered the high street from being retailers of goods to retailers of style. These changes are a response to, and a means of shaping, the shift from mass consumption. Instead of keeping up with the Joneses there has been a move to be different from the Joneses. Many of these differences are vertical, intended to confirm status and class. But some are horizontal, centred around group identities linked to age, or region or ethnicity. Whatever our responses, the revolution in retailing reflects new principles of production, a new pluralism of products and a new importance for innovation. As such it marks a shift to a post-Fordist/postmodernist age.

	Fordist	Post-Fordist
1. Technology	Fixed, dedicated machines	Micro-electronically controlled multi-purpose machines
	Vertically integrated operations	Subcontracting
	Mass production	Batch production
	For a mass consumer market	Diverse, specialised products
2. Products	Relatively cheap	Price variable
	Variable quality	High quality
3. Labour process	Fragmented	Integrated
	Few tasks	Many tasks for versatile workers
	Little discretion	Some autonomy
	Hierarchical authority and technical control	Group control
4. Contracts	Collectively negotiated rate for the job	Payment by individual performance
	Relatively secure	Dual market, secure core; highly insecure periphery

Figure 2.1 Differences between Fordist and post-Fordist systems

Self-evaluation activity 2.8

Differences between Fordism and post-Fordism
The response is given below

Summarise the main differences between Fordism and post-Fordism

Figure 2.1 summarises the main differences between Fordist and post-Fordist systems. It is also important to emphasise that post-Fordism and neo-Fordism may be compared and contrasted apart from the basic distinction between them referred to earlier. For example, both emphasise the importance of flexible production systems to cater speedily for changing market tastes and demand, and to ensure high quality products and services. One important difference, as Horton (1997) puts it, is:

> . . . in how they perceive technology. Neo-Fordists see technology as being used primarily to save labour and improve productivity, and argue that although task structures and modes of management may deviate from conventional Taylorism, they are not significantly different. Neo-Fordism is capitalism's response to the effects of overproduction and saturated domestic markets and the falling rate of profit. It is exploiting new product and labour markets and reconstructing itself, but the classic characteristics of Fordism are still in evidence. (p. 163)

The division between neo-Fordism and post-Fordism extends beyond the workplace to encompass consumer–producer relations, such that neo-Fordism is still premised upon Fordist mass production for international mass markets, whereas post-Fordism implies a large degree of product specialisation for specialised, and often localised, markets.

Summary points: Fordism, neo-Fordism, and post-Fordism

Although, as our analysis revealed, there is some overlap between the three systems, we may attempt to summarise them (following Grint, 1993, p. 297):

- **Fordism** represents the archetypal assembly-line production system with extensive division of labour and isolated workers using limited skills.
- **Neo-Fordism** represents a transitional form in which workers are required to become flexible with the use of multiple skills and multiple tasks.
- **Post-Fordism** occurs when multi-skilled and flexible workers are engaged in production systems which depend on teamworking rather than

isolated individuals, and involve a reduction in the division of labour and some flattening of hierarchical authority, that is, devolved responsibility for decision making. This method of working is also known as flexible specialisation.

STYLES OF MANAGEMENT WITHIN THE EMPLOYMENT RELATIONSHIP

In general terms, 'style', as Legge (1995, p. 31) points out, is simply 'a way of doing something'. As we have seen, managers direct and control labour and the style adopted in enabling them to do so is at its most observable on a day-to-day basis. Gospel and Palmer (1993) suggest that the articulation of a particular management style is best understood within the context of broader ideologies and beliefs held by managements. An ideology is essentially a set of beliefs held by a specific group having the same or similar interests in common, while beliefs refer to those ideas that people hold to be right and true, which provide not only guides and rules for action, but also justifications for actions by which behaviour is made accountable to the self and to others. Beliefs are therefore used as a means of persuasion 'whereby the employer seeks to persuade employees to act in a certain way' (ibid., p. 63). Management style, seen within the context of management ideology and belief systems, has been defined as 'a set of proposals and actions that establishes the organisation's approach to its employees and acts as a reference point for management' (Brewster *et al.*, 1983, p. 62).

The contribution of Fox and Purcell

Fox (1966, 1974) identified three contrasting 'frames of reference', two of which typify management's industrial relations style and are termed unitary and pluralist, while the third, which Fox labels radical, draws upon Marxist theory concerning unequal power relationships and is not considered here. The unitary and pluralist frames of reference or perspectives were considered in Chapter 1, and you should now reread these. Marchington and Parker (1990) argue that there are three essential differences between these two perspectives 'in relation to man-

agement's acceptance and recognition of unions, their views about management prerogatives and employee participation, and in the perceived legitimacy of and reactions to conflict at work' (p. 77). Fox (1974) elaborated on his basic unitary/pluralist dichotomy and identified six variations or subcategories of patterns of industrial relations management that represent combinations of unitary and pluralist perspectives. These are:

- the **traditional** variant where managers and employees both hold unitary frames of reference;
- the **sophisticated modern** where pluralist views are held by managers and employees;
- **sophisticated paternalism** which represents a combination of pluralist employers and unitary employees;
- **classical conflict** representing variants of unitary employers and pluralist employees;
- **continuous challenge**, again representing variants of unitary employers and pluralist employees;
- the **standard modern** 'was the result of ambivalent frames of reference within both management and worker groups; this could occur because of splits within the managerial hierarchy, for example, or as a result of experience, with individual managers' frames of reference varying from one event to another over time' (Marchington and Parker, 1990, p. 78).

Purcell and Sisson (1983) further elaborated upon Fox's categorisation and developed five ideal-typical styles of industrial relations management which are identified below:

Traditionalist, similar to Fox's traditionalist pattern, is characterised by hostile and negative stances to trade unions and a highly exploitative approach to the workforce. This is accompanied by a strong belief in management's right to manage, and that the exercise of its managerial prerogative is legitimate.

Sophisticated paternalist/human relations, differs from Fox's category in that management holds strong unitary views even though there is concern for employee welfare and development. Sophisticated paternalists are similar to traditionalists in that they refuse to recognise or negotiate with trade unions, but will not necessarily use coercive power to keep them out. Rather they would prefer to offer employees incentives such as better pay and

conditions of work and use appropriate recruitment and selection methods in order to provide disincentives to unionisation. Through these methods they aim to encourage employee commitment, loyalty and dependency. Companies identified as typifying this style are Marks & Spencer, Hewlett-Packard, John Lewis Partnership and, before its major restructuring, IBM. Marchington and Parker (1990) argue that 'although most of the enterprises in this category do not recognise unions, their approach to management is substantially different from the traditionalists [and] this group spans the unitary/pluralist distinction, exhibiting elements of both in their management styles' (p. 78).

Sophisticated modern is similar to Fox's category in that pluralist views dominate. There is an acceptance of a trade union presence, even though this might limit the perceived freedom of managerial decision-making. The union presence and voice is seen to contribute in a positive way towards facilitating communication and change and maintaining stability of relationships. There is a strong emphasis upon the development and operation of formal and informal procedures in order to handle and resolve conflicts of interest. Purcell and Sisson (1983) propose two subcategories of the sophisticated modern type. These are:

> **Consulters**: similar to sophisticated paternalist except that unions are recognised. 'The attempt is made to build "constructive" relationships with the trade unions and incorporate them into the organisational fabric. Emphasis is also placed on techniques designed to enhance individual employee commitment to the firm and the need to change (share option schemes, profit sharing, briefing or cascade information systems, joint working parties, quality or productivity circles/councils' (Blyton and Turnbull, 1994, p. 80). Companies tending to approximate to this subcategory are large, fairly successful and have substantial market share, and would include ICI and Cadbury-Schweppes.
>
> **Constitutionalists**: unions have been recognised for some time and are accepted as inevitable. Policies emphasise the need for stability and control. 'Management prerogatives are defended through highly specific collective agreements. The

importance of management control is emphasised with the aim of minimising or neutralising union constraints on both operational (line) and strategic (corporate) management' (ibid., p. 80). Companies most likely to demonstrate characteristics of this subcategory include those single industry companies with mass production technologies selling products within a highly competitive international market. Examples include General Motors and Ford.

Standard modern, where a pragmatic approach to industrial relations is adopted and trade unions are recognised. This is by far the largest group in which industrial relations is considered the responsibility of line or operational management and 'fire-fighting' is often resorted to. The importance attached to industrial relations policies varies from time to time both within and between organisations, and also between different levels within the organisational hierarchy. This type is most commonly manifested in larger multi-product companies that have had a growth history characterised by takeovers and mergers, particularly within heavy engineering and manufacturing. Examples include Rover Cars and Lucas Industries.

Self-evaluation activity 2.9

Relating style to particular cases
Response on website

This exercise is concerned with management styles based on the contributions of Fox and Purcell and Sisson. Consider Mini cases 2.3 and 2.4 and identify the appropriate industrial relations style together with your justification.

Mini case 2.3
Garibaldi supermarket chain

Garibaldi (UK) Ltd is a major supermarket chain with stores predominantly in England and Wales. It is one of the newer supermarkets on the scene that have the policy of 'piling them high and selling them cheap', no frills shopping. Its stores compare in size with those of its competition: Netto, Lidl and Kwiksave. Recruitment is the responsibility of the general

managers of individual stores and staff are expected to function in any area of the store from shelf stacking to checkout work. Competition is fierce and Garibaldi runs a lean operation with an average of ten staff per store. This means that there is a minimum of personnel for any situation, and only at peak times are the relatively few checkouts fully staffed.

Company policies are highly centralised and determined at national level. There is no personnel or human resource department and responsibility for personnel matters lies with the Purchasing Director who has a small secretarial section whose main responsibility in the personnel area is to keep employee records. Apart from 'on site' training for store staff, which is the responsibility of the store manager, there is no formal provision for training and development of employees. Pay levels are determined centrally for full- and part-time staff. Interestingly, the pay of store staff is rather higher than most of the competitor supermarkets which reflects the intensification of work, the flexibility demanded of staff and the fact that checkout work involves the committing to memory of the prices of the relatively limited range of products (there is no bar-coding of products). There is a policy of non-recognition of trade unions. However, Garibaldi's UK management have been advised that, owing to government legislation concerning trade union recognition, this policy will be subject to review in 2003. Procedures concerning grievances, redundancy and equal opportunities do not exist, but these issues are under review. The only formal procedure that operates is the company disciplinary procedure which was introduced after a highly publicised 'unfair dismissal' case.

Mini case 2.4
A division of the Home Office

Manager 1

'For nearly ten years in the Home Office there were two unions. One was the Civil and Public Services Association (CPSA) which became the Civil and Public Services Union (CPSU), which nearly all of the administrative grades belonged to. The other was the National Union of Supervisory Public Servants (NUCPS), which the management grades belonged to. CPSA was the more militant union whilst NUCPS was nigh on dormant. Generally, senior management grudgingly admit to the necessity for unions in the Home Office. Some will argue that it is yet another mechanism by which to monitor bad practice in the office. It is undisputable that the different agendas, when combined in a constructive fashion, do produce a better working environment. . . . In management terms, a union that requests too many meetings over innocuous subjects just wastes valuable time and is not taken as seriously as the union which "picks its battleground", and its moment! In conclusion, unions are a vital element in good industrial relations and provide an essential safety net for staff from target-conscious managers. The union, however, has to acknowledge its responsibilities across the office and should be seen to act responsibly at all times.'

Manager 2

'In a workplace where management liaises with unions, the working environment will only be enriched if, of course, its reps represent the views of its workplace and not their own political views. Sometimes unions can attract individuals who are politically motivated and members feel they are not represented by these people and do not get involved. This is sad. Anyway, unions in my opinion are necessary, people fought vigorously for the right to belong to unions and without them who knows what injustices may have occurred. They still do even with unions present. I would encourage all new staff to join and, if they want to, to get involved.'

Home Office management's approach to trade unions:

1. Encourages trade union membership by including a paragraph in all new entrant letters which recommends they join their recognised trade union.
2. Encourages trade union membership by including a paragraph in the Home Office Staff Handbook which recommends staff join their recognised trade union.
3. Signed a departmental facilities agreement which allows:
 (a) Trade union representatives paid time off in order to undertake trade union activity;
 (b) Trade union representatives access to accommodation, telephones, photocopying, fax, information technology and other facilities;

(c) Staff paid time off to attend trade union meetings;

(d) An organised Whitley joint negotiating structure which allows for regular meetings at a local, departmental and national level between management and trade union representatives on a whole host of issues relating to the pay and conditions of staff.

4. Signed other agreements covering disciplinary matters which allow staff access to trade union representatives whenever they need advice or at any meeting with their manager and trade union representation before, during and after any disciplinary hearings.

5. Signed agreements with the trade unions on issues such as:

(a) promotion/recruitment procedures;

(b) probation procedures;

(c) flexible working hours;

(d) part-time/jobshare arrangements;

(e) sick/special/maternity/paternity leave arrangements;

(f) equal opportunities;

(g) retirement/re-employment;

(h) redundancy arrangements.

There is some evidence to suggest that many organisations adopt a 'mix and match' approach to pluralist and unitarist assumptions (Cully *et al.*, 1999; Kersley *et al.*, 2006). For example, while the sample of managers for the Workplace Employment Relations Survey (WERS1998, 2004) were either neutral (54 per cent) or in favour of union membership (29 per cent) thereby indicating a pluralist orientation, 72 per cent of managers preferred to consult directly with employees than with unions, revealing a unitarist approach (Cully *et al.*, 1999). Kersley *et al.*, 2006 report that managers in 2004 were no more pro-union or anti-union than in 1998. However, management styles and attitudes tend to vary with size of workplace and between private and public sectors (p. 49). In order to test the 'mix and match' approach, a group of the author's students presented a summary of Purcell and Sisson's model to a senior manager of the Tesco supermarket chain whose response is given in Mini case 2.5.

Mini case 2.5
Tesco manager's view of Tesco management style

'Looking at your various models, I would say that Tesco, in the main, uses a "sophisticated modern" approach to the employment relationship in the form of being "consulters". I think we have built a constructive relationship with trade unions and Tesco regard trade unions as a body to work with because they want to and not because they have to. . . . Tesco is a pluralist organisation that works closely with trade unions. There are in a number of stores that I am aware of at least one and sometimes two USDAW representatives who help to handle disputes and other people problems in a fair manner. In terms of the employment relationship the use of trade unions indicates a collective aspect. This is the case. However, we also use individual approaches concerning employees. This means that we can resolve group and individual problems. It also gives us a better chance to train, develop and appraise individuals. In practice this means that Tesco can motivate employees through their management approaches. It also means that employees have a higher commitment to the organisation. This helps to achieve the overall aims and objectives of Tesco as an organisation.'

Commentary: It is clear from this view of Tesco management style that a pluralist (collective) perspective of the employment relationship is taken which recognises the legitimate authority of trade unions as the main employee voice mechanism. However, this exists alongside a more 'individualistic' approach identified by Purcell and Gray (1986) – see below – which is characterised, amongst other things, by a commitment to training, development, appraisals and feedback as part of the day-to-day administration of employees within the organisation.

Individualist and collectivist styles and policies

A further approach devised by Purcell and Gray (1986) and Purcell (1987) identifies two broad categories of approach that overlap with the style categories considered earlier. The first category

represents an individualistic approach to the relationship between employer and employee and relates to 'policies based on the belief in the value of the individual and his or her right to advancement and fulfilment at work' (Purcell and Gray, 1986, p. 213). Employee motivation is encouraged by the development of effective direct communications with individual employees, providing opportunities for personal development and advancement within the organisation; monitoring and evaluating performance; and the devising of rewards that recognise individual effort and performance – and 'with their emphasis on equality of treatment between employees, the trade unions could well be seen as a major constraint on the possibilities of implementing the new principles of effective management' (Gallie *et al.*, 1996, p. 14). Bacon and Storey (1996) also assert that 'the new emphasis upon the individual employee in management strategies suggests that any notion of a standardised group of workers pursuing similar interests has become increasingly difficult to sustain' (p. 43). The individualist approach, then, has the following characteristics:

- The right of employers to offer financial incentives to an employee covered by a collective agreement in order that the employee may accept a personal contract, this right being granted to employers by the Trade Union Reform and Employment Rights Act 1993. In this context, Kessler and Purcell (1995) argue that 'personal contracts represent a reassertion of the managerial prerogative and unilateral control' (p. 339).
- Individualism is often closely associated with certain personnel techniques such as individual performance pay and direct communication with employees which may result in the marginalisation of trade unions within unionised organisations.
- Individualism is closely associated with the ideas of human resource management (HRM) with its emphasis upon developing the talents and capacities of each individual employee and thereby securing the commitment of the employee to the organisation.

Individualism is as much a subject of political rhetoric as it is of HRM. The Conservative White Paper, *People, Jobs and Opportunity* (DoE, 1992) stated that 'there is a new recognition of the role and importance of the individual employee', while Conservative industrial relations legislation has made it easier for employers to adopt individualistic styles and practices. The rhetoric of individualism erroneously assumes that individualism and collectivism are mutually exclusive categories, but it is a compelling argument, the essence of which is captured by Kessler and Purcell (1995):

> The force of the rhetoric of 'new individualism' is not easily challenged. An emphasis on common goals, flexibility and personal performance which allows individuals to achieve commitment to their job and firm is intuitively attractive. Here, management control is achieved via employee commitment – the ultimate dream of the self-managed workforce. The assumption is that what was previously covered by collective regulation is now both unilaterally determined by the employer and focused on or targeted to each employee. The worker is assumed to have neither the interest nor the ability to combine with others, but will strive to maximise his or her own interests which coincide with, or are complementary to, those of the employer. (p. 31)

Individualism and collectivism are not mutually exclusive categories

As we have seen in Chapter 1, the focus of industrial relations is upon collective labour organisations (trade unions and employers' associations) and the institution and process of collective bargaining as determining and regulating the employment contract. Purcell and Gray (1986) define collectivism as 'the recognition by management of the collective interests of groups of employees in the decision-making process' (p. 213). Marchington and Parker (1990) add that this definition 'needs to incorporate not only the structures for employee participation and collective bargaining, but also the approach of management towards these institutions' (p. 80). However, while it is important to define individualism and collectivism, they should not be regarded as dichotomous or mutually exclusive. Examples of both can be found to operate in any one workplace since they concern different aspects of the employment relationship where the employee may be treated both as an individual worker and as

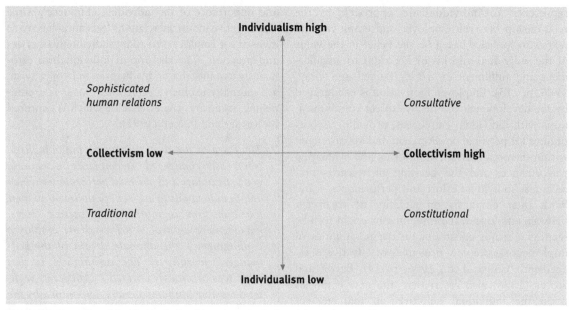

Figure 2.2 Purcell and Gray's typology of management industrial relations styles
Source: Purcell and Gray, 1986. Blackwell Publishing

part of a collective organisation such as a trade union or works council. Essentially, individualism indicates a non-union and/or HRM style approach to employees and includes a cost-minimisation approach to employees, a 'paternalist' stance for employee welfare, and an employee development approach (Storey and Sisson, 1993), while collectivism is concerned with adversarial conflict relations with unions, a partnership/co-operative approach with unions and, less frequently, a non-union but representative stance (Bacon, 2001).

Self-evaluation activity 2.10

Mapping individualism and collectivism
The response is given below

Going back to the typology of management styles based on Purcell and Sisson (1983) and by reference to Figure 2.2, identify which of these are predominantly individualist, which are predominantly collectivist, and which are both equally individualist and collectivist, giving examples of each.

The traditional style is manifested by extremely low scores for both individualism and collectivism. As we have seen with this style, labour is unashamedly exploited and unionism is opposed and often vilified.

Casual labour is often used for labour intensification and cost-minimising purposes. If there is an example of the less unacceptable variant of traditionalism, then it would probably be the high street burger chain of the McDonald's organisation. Sophisticated paternalism/ human relations as described above exists in organisations where individualism is high, and collectivism, which may exist in the form of consultative committees, is low and sometimes non-existent. In addition to the examples of this type already given, other companies identified as typifying this style are to be found in high technology/professional service firms operating on greenfield sites. The consultative and constitutional, as we have seen, are two sophisticated modern styles a nd are contrasted in terms of their sympathy with individualism:

- The consultative style features highly on both collectivist and individualist dimensions and is similar to sophisticated paternalism/human relations, except that unions are recognised. Management attempts both to treat unions almost as partners in order to discuss a whole range of issues and to place great emphasis on securing individual commitment and loyalty through, for example, profit sharing, training and development, joint working parties and team briefing exercises.

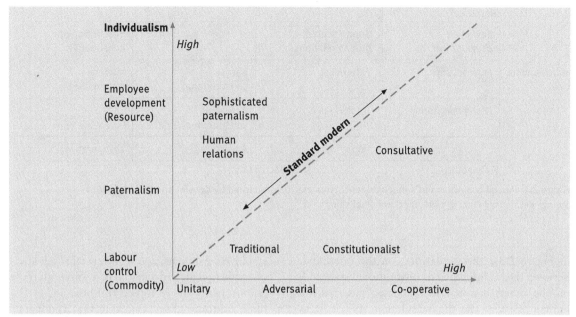

Figure 2.3 Mapping management industrial relations styles
Source: Based on Purcell, 1987

- The constitutional style occurs in organisations where collectivism is high and individualism is low: 'Unions are recognised, but grudgingly as unavoidable rather than welcomed into a constructive dialogue. Management prerogatives are jealously guarded through highly specific collective agreements which are carefully administered and monitored on the shop floor' (Legge, 1995, p. 37).

The fifth style, the standard modern, represents the pragmatic approach as described above, and falls outside the individualism/collectivism matrix. There is no consistent policy concerning union recognition, the union presence either having established itself due to historical factors, or been inherited through company takeover and acquisition. Union bargaining power may be high or low and managerial prerogatives may be in the ascendancy or waning.

The individualism/collectivism dimension was further elaborated by Purcell (1987) and, in relation to the styles already considered, can be depicted as shown in Figure 2.3.

The following points concerning Figure 2.2 need to be emphasised:

- 'High' individualism is concerned with treating employees as a resource with a strong emphasis upon employee training and development.
- 'Low' individualism exists in situations where the employee is treated as an expendable commodity, is highly exploited and is subject to tight control over his or her labour.
- The mid-point represents a situation where the employee's actions are limited by well-intended regulations and actions on the part of the employer.
- 'High' collectivism is concerned with co-operative relationships with employees' collective organisations, whether they be trade unions, staff associations or other collective bodies.
- 'Low' collectivism is characterised by a unitary frame of reference or perspective with no union presence allowed.
- The mid-point between 'high' and 'low' collectivism is often typified by conflict and adversarial relations between employer and collective organisations (normally trade unions).

Legge (1995, 2005) suggests that if the five management styles are superimposed on the graph (see also the Purcell and Ahlstrand (1994) modification

(Resource)				
	Employee development	Sophisticated human relations	??	Sophisticated consultative
Individualism	Paternalism	Paternalist	Bargained constitutional	Modern paternalist
	Cost minimisation	Traditional	Bargained constitutional	??
		None	Adversarial	Co-operative
(Commodity)		**Collectivism**		

Figure 2.4 Purcell and Ahlstrand's management styles matrix as adapted by Kessler and Purcell (1995)
Source: Kessler and Purcell, 1995. Blackwell Publishing

in Figure 2.3), 'the similarities, on the one hand, between the traditional and constitutional style and, on the other, between sophisticated paternalism/ human relations and the consultative style is highlighted' (p. 39). The standard modern style, as Legge also points out, is more difficult to locate 'as, by definition, its appearance changes with circumstances [and probably] is best located as a dotted diagonal line, with the potential to span the range of possibilities' (p. 39).

Purcell and Ahlstrand's revised typology of management styles is shown in the matrix in Figure 2.4 using the individualism/collectivism dimensions as adapted by Kessler and Purcell (1995). As with Purcell's typology, management styles are identified according to the degree of individualism and collectivism they exhibit. Kessler and Purcell point out that some firms may have no real style, 'being essentially opportunistic in reaction to events' (p. 347). This corresponds to the attempted definition of the standard modern style which Purcell and Ahlstrand omit altogether. In relation to the two boxes showing ??, it should be noted that:

• the type of individualistic policies developed by the firm will influence the nature of the collective relationship with a union or other collective body;
• the type of collectivism in action may well influence the nature of the firm's policies towards, and expectations of, individual employees;
• it is highly improbable, however, that a firm with well-established employee development policies representing considerable investment in

employees would engage in and sustain high levels of conflictual and adversarial relations with trade unions, hence the ?? top central box; and
• the ?? bottom right box suggests that a cooperative relationship exists with trade unions but that the policy of the firm is based on cost minimisation, numerical flexibility and the exploitation of labour. The incompatibility of these approaches makes this an unrealistic scenario.

The names of the style categories within the matrix differ slightly from the earlier formulations in Figure 2.3, and for purposes of clarification the following points are made:

• The traditional category remains the same according to the original definition.
• The sophisticated paternalist/human relations also remains the same.
• The sophisticated consultative style of Figure 2.4 is identical to the consultative style of Figure 2.3.
• The bargained constitutional style of Figure 2.4 is identical to the constitutionalist style of Figure 2.3.
• The two categories within Figure 2.4 not specifically mentioned in previous formulations are the paternalist and modern paternalist.

The paternalist projects a welfare and caring image with an emphasis upon loyalty and downward communication. There are fixed grades determined through job evaluation with a high proportion of lower grade employees being women, for whom promotion is a rarity. Everyone knows his or her place within a fixed hierarchy which emphasises stability and order. Conflict is seen as a failure of

communication and unions are avoided. This type is often found in firms within financial and service distribution sectors. The modern paternalist emphasises constructive relationships with trade unions and dissemination of information through a network of collective consultative committees. The image projected is one of caring and concern for employee welfare, but as with the paternalist context there are fixed grades based on job evaluation (allowing input in their determination from union representatives). Pay is average and the overall emphasis is upon stability and order with employees knowing their place. This type is most usually found in stable process industries such as foods and oil.

The style typologies we have considered in this section all stem from Fox's original unitary/pluralist classification. The more recent individualist/collectivist dimensions assist our analysis and understanding of managerial approaches to industrial relations during the course of the twentieth century. During the 1970s the approach of managements to industrial relations veered more towards a greater acceptance of pluralism and collectivism, and there was a detectable trend towards adoption of the sophisticated consultative style. During the 1980s and 1990s we witnessed a reversal of this trend with a move towards the unitary and individualistic approach and towards an approximation of the sophisticated paternalist model on the one hand and towards a cost minimisation approach on the other. However, since 1998 there has, overall, been no further discernible shift towards unitarism amongst organisational and workplace management (Kersley *et al.*, 2006).

Management employment relations styles do not operate independently of other organisational concerns and are clearly related to industrial relations policies and strategies to which we now turn.

MANAGEMENT AND EMPLOYMENT RELATIONS STRATEGIES, POLICIES AND PROCEDURES

Industrial relations strategies and policies are concerned with influencing and directing the employment relationship in the medium to long term. However, the management of industrial relations

has traditionally been low in the order of organisational priorities and smaller firms generally have an unstructured and day-to-day approach to industrial relations management. The Donovan Commission (1968) argued that much of the industrial unrest of the 1960s could be attributed to the inadequate conduct and management of industrial relations at corporate and workplace level, with management at corporate headquarters frequently ignorant or out of touch with what was going on at the workplace. The Commission therefore recommended that corporate industrial relations should be reviewed and appropriate strategies and policies devised and implemented which would reconstruct workplace industrial relations through the operation of positive personnel policies, the formalisation of industrial relations procedures concerning dispute, discipline and grievance handling, the creation of orderly collective bargaining machinery and the formal incorporation of the shop steward within the negotiation process.

The traditional antipathy of British management to the formation and formalisation of effective policies, procedures and practices in industrial relations can be explained in terms of the following:

- Fear of sharing power with trade unions as this may threaten management's decision-making authority and legitimacy:

 > *Even where trade unions are recognised, much managerial time is spent in attempting to preserve management's traditional prerogatives rather than in developing new areas of joint regulation with the trade unions with which it negotiates.* (Farnham and Pimlott, 1995, p. 72)

- Lack of managerial expertise in industrial relations is indicative of a lack of commitment to the management of industrial relations at senior levels. 'Even now, board and senior managerial appointments continue to be dominated by accountants, lawyers and others of the more traditional professional groups' (ibid., p. 72).
- Even though multi-employer industry-wide or national agreements are in decline, 'there is little incentive for line managers to be involved in day-to-day industrial relations' in industries where they operate (ibid., p. 71). Conversely, in

those organisations where industrial relations has been devolved (as, for example, within NHS trust and foundation hospitals), managers may lack the necessary skills required for the efficient and effective management of industrial relations and for dealing with trade unions at plant or operational levels.

- Weaknesses inherent in industrial relations management are often a reflection of poor education and training of British management generally (Handy, 1993) and an absence of expertise and sophistication can lead to production failures, productivity problems and industrial disputes (Nichols, 1986).
- Finally, the low priority accorded to industrial relations on the part of British management is partly due to the consequences of their actions, specifically their failure to secure the active co-operation of the workforce as opposed to mere compliance or enforced consent, and this arises from the fundamental tension that exists, and persists, between employer and employee. Inevitably there is no 'one best way' to manage these conflicts, only different routes to partial failure. It is on this basis that managerial strategy can best be conceptualised 'as the pragmatic choice among alternatives none of which can prove satisfactory' (Blyton and Turnbull, 1994, p. 94, quoting Hyman, 1987, p. 30).

In recent decades managements, particularly within the larger multiple-plant companies, have become more sophisticated in their approaches to industrial relations, mostly where industrial relations policy and practice is incorporated within HRM strategies (see below).

Strategies

In general terms, according to Miller (1993), strategic management is concerned with:

- assessing the organisation's internal competencies and capabilities;
- assessing environmental threats and opportunities;
- deciding the scope of the organisation's activities;
- creating and communicating a strategic vision; and
- managing the process of change in an organisation.

The main purpose of strategy is to influence and direct an organisation as it conducts its activities, and 'may be described as the attempt by those who control an organisation to find ways to position their business and organisational objectives so that they can exploit the planning environment and maximise the future use of the organisation's capital and human assets' (Gennard and Judge, 2005, p. 42, quoting Tyson, 1995). Gennard and Judge consider the main issues concerning strategy (following Johnson and Scholes, 2003).

Firstly, strategy concerns itself with the full range of an organisation's activities.

Secondly, strategy is concerned with the nature of the external environment in which an organisation operates. An environment can be static, where, for example, the product market is stable and decisions are routine and predictable. Many local authorities, for example, have operated in situations where demand for their services was highly predictable and could be met on the basis of fairly accurate estimates of government subsidy together with local revenues. However, sudden changes in the external environment can cause problems. Changes in government funding and alternative methods of raising local income (such as the change from income based on rateable value to other methods such as the council tax) have influenced strategic decisions concerning the efficiency of service provision, which services to retain and which services to 'contract out'. An environment can also be very dynamic, subject to rapid and often unpredictable change, as with organisations operating within the information technology and computing industry. Environments also exhibit varying degrees of complexity where some organisations operate in multiple product markets, which may also be extremely competitive and volatile.

Thirdly, strategy is concerned with the match between the activities of an organisation and its resources. 'These resources can be physical (equipment, buildings) or they can be people. Strategies in respect of physical resources may require decisions about investment or even about the ability to invest. Strategies in respect of people might require decisions about the type of competencies needed for future development and where such resources are to be found' (Gennard and Judge, 1997, p. 92).

Conventional definitions of strategy normally identify and differentiate between different strategic levels. For example, we can distinguish between:

- **first-level or first-order** strategy which deals with the long-term direction of the organisation and the scope of its activities, market positioning and penetration, where to locate, how much to invest, etc.;
- **second-order or business** strategy which is concerned with the operating procedures and relationships between the different parts of the organisation; and
- **third-order or functional** strategy which involves decisions concerning the different functions of the organisation, which includes personnel, HRM and industrial relations functions; devising broad strategies to support business strategy and achieve functional performance objectives.

In relation to these strategic levels, Legge (2005) points out that the assumption inherent in identifying them is that the strategy process is a 'cascade', where the top of the waterfall is the corporate level, and subsequent levels are logically 'downstream' or dependent on directions established at corporate level. Hence, Chandler's (1962) classic dictum that structure – how a firm is organised to achieve its goals: a second-order strategy – follows strategy – the type of business undertaken at present and in the future: a first-order strategy (p. 97).

Employment relations strategy

Employment relations strategies may be defined as 'long-term goals developed by management to preserve or change the procedures, practice or results of employment relations activities over time' (Farnham and Pimlott, 1995, p. 75). The existence of such strategies is based on assumptions that:

- corporate management determine overall strategies to achieve their organisational goals;
- strategic thinking is a prerequisite for organisational success;
- top management have some choice in the matter; and
- choice of industrial relations strategies and policies 'rationally implies they be linked to other objectives and policies' (Thurley and Wood, 1983).

Gennard and Judge (2005) argue that there should be a direct relationship between employment relations strategies and business strategy:

[They] need to be imaginative, innovative and action-oriented. They need to be formulated by a continuing process of analysis to identify what is happening to the business and where it is going. In this context, the relevance of clear business objectives, as expressed through the medium of a mission statement, cannot be overstated. The key is to develop an employee relations strategy which is responsive to the needs of the organisation, which can provide an overall sense of purpose to the employee relations specialist, and which assists employees in understanding where they are going, how they are going to get there, why certain things are happening, and most importantly, the contribution they are expected to make towards achieving the organisational goals. Another key feature is to ensure that the employee relations policies and strategies do not stand alone but integrate with other employment policies and strategies. (pp. 53–54)

It is also important to realise that industrial relations strategy formulation is not only a matter of choice, but also of constraints. Poole (1980) argues that the constraints upon strategy formulation arise from environmental pressures upon the organisation, particularly economic and political. These pressures limit strategic choices and may stifle initiative. Major constraints which Poole identifies stem from the nature of the free enterprise market ideology, which limits managerial discretion by implementing strategies which favour the satisfaction of economic and production needs of the organisation rather than meeting the needs and aspirations of employees (minimising wage costs while maintaining or increasing productivity). Another significant constraint concerns the role of the state in managing the economy which 'through a corporatist political ideology or indirectly through a laissez-faire one, may constrain managerial freedom and initiative at organisational level' (Salamon, 1998, p. 217).

Self-evaluation activity 2.11

Employment relations strategy misfit? The case of Foodgourmet
Response on website

Read Main case 2.1 and attempt the questions which follow.

Main case 2.1
Foodgourmet

Foodgourmet is part of a large, European-owned venture finance conglomerate and is based in Switzerland. It operates in the UK on a single site located on an industrial estate near a major airport in London where it employs 2000 staff. Its primary business is the production of airline in-flight meals. The industry is dominated by a small number of multinational companies operating in highly competitive international markets. The company has been a leading player in the airline food industry since the 1990s and currently employs 22,000 people worldwide and makes 534,000 meals a day for at least 10 international airlines. Its UK factory currently produces meals for a major UK airline During the 2000s, the UK operation had run into severe financial difficulties as a consequence of global recession which affected many airlines. Business picked up somewhat during the early 2000s with an increase in passenger numbers. Unfortunately for Foodgourmet, a considerable proportion of the growing passenger market was in the 'no frills' budget airline market, particularly within the short haul sector where food is not normally offered to passengers. In this environment it had had great difficulty in competing with rival companies in terms of both product quality and price. Despite the improvement in global conditions and an upturn in global demand during the early 2000s Foodgourmet has not actually made a profit since 2000, and several of the company's main airline customers have been in severe financial difficulties thereby increasing the already severe pressure upon airline suppliers. Foodgourmet is perceived by the parent company, which is profitable, to be substantially overstaffed and technically inferior in comparison with its competitors. Because of continuing production problems on the site, its future is less secure than in previous years.

Employment relations issues

The majority of employees on the site (1800) would be classified as blue-collar workers who are largely unskilled. Many of these workers are on temporary flexible contracts but a significant proportion are employed full-time. A large proportion of workers are women and the workforce as a whole is ethnically diverse. In addition, there are approximately 200 other employees (supervisors, managers, administration and food research staff). Staff turnover levels are relatively high amongst temporary workers, as one would expect, despite above average levels of unemployment in the area. The average length of service is just over 10 months. High turnover of staff, according to a confidential 'in house' survey is due to the nature of the work which is highly repetitive, low levels of pay which are set just above the National Minimum Wage, and anti-social hours of work in a continuous shift environment. As a result, employee attachment to the firm is minimal and there is no deep-rooted workplace culture. One trade union is recognised for bargaining purposes – the Transport and General Workers Union (TGWU) represents catering workers and drivers. Relations between employees and management are characterised by relatively low levels of trust and there is little willingness to negotiate agreements that are acceptable to both sides. Indeed, many 'settlements' are merely imposed by local management. This semi-permanent truce means that collective disputes can occur from time to time as in the summer of 2006 which resulted in the sacking of 350 employees after a dispute concerning pay, working conditions and the appointment of part-time workers. Little information is shared between the two sides, and the attitude of most employees towards supervisors and managers is one of suspicion while there is a tendency to distrust anyone who appears to get on with managers. The supervisors believe that they run a tight ship. Managers understand that the supervisors operate 'in a pretty basic and brutal context'. They generally have a poor view of those they supervise, and are highly suspicious of any 'soft' human resource management initiatives. Evidence of mistrust between the different groups is seen in the existence of a high ratio of supervisors to workers and in the elaborate clocking-in procedures.

A changing employment relations strategy?

It is clear that if the firm is to survive it needs to transform its operations dramatically so that it is able to

compete effectively with its international rivals. It needs to replace its outdated manually controlled machinery and processes with cleaner, computer-driven systems. It also needs to become more consumer oriented, enabling it to respond rapidly to changing customer demands. It is expected that the above developments will have far-reaching consequences for staff. The total number employed will have to be reduced by 50 per cent over a two-year period, and the remaining staff retrained to operate the new machinery. Jobs in the future are likely to require a far wider range of separate tasks than is currently the case, to allow the firm to respond more rapidly to short-term customer demands. People will be required who have a higher level of diagnostic and multi-skilling ability than those employed at present. There is also likely to be potential for the introduction of team-working, job rotation and employee involvement programmes, as well as payment of bonuses related to profit levels. Because of the high costs incurred by potential interruptions and the very high costs associated with the possible re-designing of the factory, it is seen as imperative that good employee relations and high trust are fostered and achieved. The current employee relations climate is conducive neither to the introduction of substantial changes nor to the successful management of the proposed revised food preparation processes. The parent company has shown a potential willingness to make available sufficient funds to enable the development of such a strategy. However, because success is heavily dependent on a transformation of the prevailing employee relations climate, future support is conditional upon substantial progress being made in this field.

Tasks

Assume that you have been employed as an HR consultant to make recommendations to the managing director about how the firm might go about achieving its employee relations objectives. Draw up a report using the following guidelines:

1. Assess the employee relations climate and its background by means of a brief SWOT analysis (i.e. identify the chief strengths, weaknesses, opportunities and threats).
2. Identify each of the major stakeholder groups that have an interest in the firm's future. Assess where

differences of interest exist and where there is a common interest on which a high-trust employee relations climate might be built.
3. Draw up a strategy for action in the employee relations field. It is important that you should prioritise your suggestions and take account of any financial implications.

Strategic employment relations management: findings from WERS 2004

The WERS 2004 findings revealed by Kersley *et al.* (2006) indicate that the role played by employment relations managers at workplace level in relation to overall business strategy is patchy indeed. This is understandable given the extensive range of workplaces surveyed and the workplace characteristics considered (a fuller consideration of these factors is provided later in this chapter). Variations in the extent to which employment relations issues play a part in the formulation and exercise of business strategy are influenced by factors such as workplace size, whether the workplace is part of a larger organisation or a 'stand-alone' workplace, size of organisation, the sector in which the workplace operates – public or private – the type of industry and whether trade unions are recognised. Employment relations managers were asked whether their workplace was covered by a formal strategic plan and whether the plan set objectives and identified the means whereby those objectives could be achieved together with the employment relations issues included in the plan. These issues comprised employee development, employee job satisfaction and employee diversity. Overall, 30 per cent of workplaces had no strategic plan at all, but this varied according to sector (50 per cent in construction, hotels and restaurants; 1 per cent in education and public administration), size of firm or workplace (50 per cent) and small independent establishments (50 per cent). With regard to workplaces having a strategic plan embracing **at least one** of the three employment relations issues identified above, 61 per cent of workplaces claimed to have such a plan while 10 per cent of workplaces had a strategic

plan which excluded employment relations issues. Of workplaces having a strategic plan, 87 per cent of these workplaces stated it covered employment relations issues. Strategic plans including employment relations issues were far more prevalent in the public sector (85 per cent) than in the private sector (58 per cent) and were least common in smaller organisations, stand-alone establishments and in manufacturing (10 per cent).

Kersley *et al.* (2006) examine three assumptions **which may guide employers who choose a strategic approach to the management of employees.** These are:

1. That 'employees, as a human resource, can offer the employer a source of sustainable competitive advantage in the production and sale of goods and services' (p. 65) and concerns the role of employee development in business planning. The evidence of WERS 2004 strongly suggests that while employee development (job satisfaction, employee diversity and projected staffing requirements) featured in strategic plans, employee development was not associated with improving or developing the quality of products or services or with marketing strategy and developing new markets. Employment relations elements included in a strategic plan (productivity, labour turnover, absenteeism, workforce training and employee job satisfaction) tended not to be linked to financial targets, returns on investment, total costs or volume of sales. Hence there was no clear link 'between the importance of price or quality factors in the employer's competitive success and the degree to which managers responsible for employment relations matters were involved in preparing the business plan' (p. 65)
2. That 'employers will choose a strategic approach to employment relations when they are engaged in a programme of change which may rely on employee acquiescence or support' (p. 65). This would arguably cast HR managers in the role of 'changemakers' (see below). Here, the evidence from WERS 2004 is more promising, with survey results 'suggesting a robust relationship between recent change initiated by management and the integration of HR with business planning' (p. 67).

3. That 'it pays to adopt a strategic approach to employment relations when there are opportunities to cut labour costs, or where labour costs constitute a relatively high proportion of all costs, since a strategic approach to labour deployment may present opportunities to cut labour costs' (p. 65). Again, WERS 2004 provides ample evidence that strategic HR is associated with the amount of change that management has introduced at the workplace.

In conclusion, the WERS 2004 survey data shows no clear link between strategic HRM and product market strategies, but there is a strong association between HR strategy and management inspired workplace and organisational change. Similarly, there is evidence of HR integration with business strategy in relation to labour costs. However, there is little evidence to suggest that personnel management has become more strategic since the last WERS survey in 1998, and, as Kersley *et al.* (2006) state: 'there has been hardly any change in the proportion of workplaces incorporating employee development in strategic business plans and HR managers are less likely to be involved in the preparation of strategic business plans in 2004 than in 1998' (p. 70).

Summary points

- Typologies of styles of industrial relations management are based upon the basic unitarist/ pluralist distinction of Fox (1966).
- Fox (1974) elaborated upon the basic distinction which in turn was refined by Purcell and Sisson (1983). This typology is the one which is still referred to most frequently in industrial relations texts. The typology comprises:
 - traditionalists;
 - sophisticated paternalists/human relations;
 - sophisticated moderns (consulters/constitutionalists); and
 - standard moderns.
- Purcell and Gray (1986) and Purcell (1987) have positioned management industrial relations styles within the broad categories of 'individualism' and 'collectivism' (which are not mutually exclusive categories).

- The 'individualism/collectivism' dimension was further elaborated upon by Purcell (1987) and Purcell and Ahlstrand (1994).
- During the 1980s and 1990s there was a reversal of the trend towards adopting 'sophisticated consultative' styles of industrial relations management as the 'sophisticated paternalist' (HRM) and 'cost minimisation' approaches gained ground.
- Within a growing number of larger companies industrial relations policies and practices are subsumed under and incorporated within their HRM strategies but overall the situation in 2004 remains unchanged.

METHODS OF MANAGING THE EMPLOYMENT RELATIONSHIP

We now turn our attention to the question of **how** senior management actually manage the employment relationship, with particular reference to personnel management and HRM. The basic traditional methods whereby managers deal with employment relations and personnel matters has been summarised by Gospel and Palmer (1993):

1. Firstly, senior management often depend upon **line management**, who comprise junior and middle managers, to deal with various personnel matters such as recruitment and working with employee representatives. One important advantage in devolving these matters to line management is its familiarity with the immediacy of the work situation and 'being there' to deal with problems as they arise. The tendency to decentralise collective bargaining arrangements and procedures in some organisations in recent years has tended to increase the importance of line management's role in this area. However, undue reliance upon line management has certain disadvantages. Gospel and Palmer (1993, p. 72) point out that:
 - if line managers spend too much time dealing with industrial relations problems, then this 'takes line managers away from their main task which is the management of production';
 - 'different line managers can take different decisions and this can lead to inconsistencies which cause industrial relations problems'; and
 - 'line managers are prone to take a short-term view of personnel matters'.

2. The problems encountered with line management may be minimised, particularly in larger organisations, by the use of **staff specialists** such as personnel managers. We will consider the role of personnel management in the next section, but suffice it to say here that the allocation of responsibility for industrial relations and related matters between staff and line is not clearly defined and changes over time. Gospel and Palmer (1993) point out that:

 > Through the 1960s and 1970s the personnel function grew in power and influence, in part reflecting growing trade union power, increasing legislative intervention, and the institutionalisation of industrial relations. In the 1980s, however, there has been a shift back from managing through the personnel function towards giving line managers more responsibility for personnel matters, especially in such areas as selection, appraisal and training. In more complex areas such as design of pay and benefit systems, many firms are also using specialist external consultants. This sometimes leaves personnel departments with a mixture of more strategic planning functions and lower-level administrative functions. (p. 73)

3. As we have seen in Chapter 1, **employers' associations** play an indirect part in the management of employment relations, and their functions will be considered in greater detail later on.

4. A final method of industrial relations management identified by Gospel and Palmer is through the medium of various forms of **subcontracting** which has become increasingly important in recent years. Subcontracting is a method of employing the labour force indirectly through an agent or subcontractor who also deals with recruiting the workforce, monitoring production and paying workers. Subcontracting arrangements were fairly common in the nineteenth century, particularly in industries such as coal mining, iron manufacture, shipbuilding, cotton and pottery, but declined in importance as competitive and technological pressures increased. There has, however, been a resurgence of subcontracting in

recent years, particularly in clerical, catering and maintenance work, in services provided by the NHS and by local authorities. This development has resulted in many instances in the creation of a so-called 'two-tier workforce' within the public services (see Chapter 5). Gospel and Palmer (1993) point out that:

> Subcontracting has the advantage that labour matters are handed over to someone else, the firm does not need to take on a large staff directly, and it is easier to lay workers off if necessary. It has the disadvantages, however, that organisations using subcontracted labour have less direct control over labour costs and over the effort and compliance of workers. (p. 74)

Subcontracting has often caused a number of disputes including the classic example of that concerning cleaners at Hillingdon Hospital, as related in Mini case 2.6.

Mini case 2.6
Subcontracting at Hillingdon Hospital

A private cleaning company which cut the wages of Asian women cleaners at Hillingdon Hospital in Uxbridge, West London, by up to £30 a week also demanded that they hand over their passports for photocopying to prove that they were legally entitled to work. Many of the women had worked in the hospital for more than 15 years. Yesterday, 56 workers began to picket the hospital after they were sacked for refusing to agree to new terms and conditions, including the salary cuts, reduced payments for weekend working, and cuts in holiday pay. Mal Kiab Bilko said: 'In June when they tried to give us the new contracts they started asking for our passports and photocopying them. It was the timing of it. They were trying to scare people into signing the new contracts.' Pall Mall, the company which employed the women, yesterday said it would not comment on the passport demands. Hillingdon Hospital, which granted the cleaning contract to Pall Mall, has washed its hands of the dispute, saying that the women 'now belong to Pall Mall' and it will not interfere with the working of a 'perfectly reputable company'. The firm is, however, under union attack for allegedly driving down

conditions and forcing other private contractors to follow suit. The women also claimed that Pall Mall had used heavy-handed tactics to persuade the women to sign. The head of Unison's health section said: 'It is outrageous in this day and age that people should be forced to take a £25 to £30 pay cut. Our campaign aim is to point out just what bad employers Pall Mall are.' The union was in dispute with Pall Mall in two other hospitals in England and Scotland.

Source: Adapted from *The Guardian*, 28 November 1995, Maggie O'Kane. Copyright Guardian News & Media Ltd 1995.

Personnel management

In many larger public and private sector organisations the traditional personnel department assumed responsibility for the management of industrial relations amongst other functions, with a minority having dedicated industrial relations departments. Many smaller firms do not have personnel departments and some dispense with personnel managers altogether (Cully *et al.*, 1999). Additionally, as Legge (1995, 2005) points out, there would appear to be a credibility gap affecting personnel management, one of the causes of which must be the lack of consensus concerning the meaning of the term 'personnel management' since there are in existence at least four defining models of the term.

Model one: The normative model

The term 'normative' refers to what 'ought' to be. Personnel management is therefore defined in terms of what it should aspire to. The model is prescriptive, although the definitions actually tend to equate what 'is' with what 'ought to be'. Legge (1995) summarises the approach thus:

> It seems that personnel management is about selecting, developing, rewarding and directing employees in such a way that not only will they achieve satisfaction and 'give of their best' at work, but by so doing enable the employing organisation to achieve its goals. Furthermore, personnel management is the task of all managers, not just of personnel specialists alone. (p. 4)

Model two: The descriptive-functional model

This model defines personnel management in terms of the functions it actually serves rather than what these functions should be and is concerned with the regulation of employment relationships. According to Legge (1995):

> Neither [definition] assumes that the regulation is directed towards some fixed God-given set of organisation goals, but rather implies (or explicitly states) that the goals as well as the means to achieve them are open to negotiation. . . . The existence of different stakeholders within an organisation identifies the necessary function of regulation. If an organisation is to survive, regulation is necessary – and hence is the prime function of personnel management. (p. 5)

Model three: The critical-evaluative model

Legge identifies just one definition – that of Watson (1986) – as being the unique exemplar of this model:

> Personnel management is concerned with assisting those who run work organisations to meet their purpose through the obtaining of the work efforts of human beings, the exploitation of those efforts and the dispensing of those efforts when they are no longer required. Concern may be shown with human welfare, justice or satisfactions but only insofar as this is necessary for controlling interests to be met and, then always at least cost. (Watson, 1986, p. 176)

Watson's definition is critical from a radical (or Marxist) perspective as personnel management is deemed to be exploitative rather than regulatory.

Model four: The descriptive-behavioural model

If personnel management can be defined in terms of what it should do (normative) and what function or functions it actually serves, how do personnel people behave in order to achieve all of this? Definitions based on what personnel specialists actually do 'at best convey an air of disappointment and at worst are positively disparaging, even insulting' (Legge, 1995, p. 6). Drucker's (1961) view of personnel management still holds good:

> Personnel administration . . . is largely a collection of incidental techniques without much internal cohesion. As personnel administration conceives the job of managing workers and work, it is partly a file clerk's job, partly a housekeeping job, partly a social worker's job and partly fire-fighting to head off union trouble or to settle it. . . . The things the personnel administrator is typically responsible for – safety and pension plans, the suggestion system, the employment office and union's grievances – are necessary chores. I doubt though that they should be put together in one department for they are a hodge podge . . . They are neither one function by kinship of skills required to carry out the activities, nor are they one function by being linked together in the work process, by forming a distinct stage in the work of the managers or in the process of the business. (pp. 269–70)

Self-evaluation activity 2.12

Definitions and models of personnel management
Response on website

Given below are two definitions of personnel management. Identify which definition approximates to which model, and justify your decision.

1. Personnel management is a responsibility of all those who manage people, as well as being a description of the work of those who are employed as specialists. It is that part of management which is concerned with people at work and with their relationships within an enterprise. Personnel management aims to achieve both efficiency and justice, neither of which can be pursued successfully without the other. It seeks to bring together and develop into an effective organisation the men and women who make up an enterprise, enabling each to make his or her own best contribution to its success both as an individual and as a member of a working group. It seeks to provide fair terms and conditions of employment, and satisfying work for those employed (IPM, 1963).

2. Personnel management is a series of activities which, firstly, enables working people and their employing organisations to agree about the nature of their working relationship and, secondly, ensures that the agreement is fulfilled (Torrington and Hall, 1987).

Typologies of personnel management

The best-known typology is that of Tyson and Fell (1986). Using a 'low-discretion/high-discretion' continuum and metaphors from the construction industry, they identify three main types:

- '*Clerk of the works*' is mainly concerned with routine matters such as record keeping, preparing letters and documents on instruction, first interviewing of some applicants for employment and welfare matters. The clerk reports to a senior line manager or personnel manager.
- '*Contracts manager*' is most likely to be found in organisations with a strong trade union presence and a traditional industrial relations background. There is involvement in policy making, but not normally of a strategic nature. The main activity is likely to be the making and interpretation of procedures and agreements. In some organisations this type may exercise considerable power and authority which comes from the ability to resolve day-to-day problems, and from intimate knowledge and personal relationships with shop stewards and trade union officers as well as senior line managers.
- '*Architect*' is likely to be extensively involved in policy making as a member of the senior management team and/or to have a seat on the board

of directors. The architect will see himself or herself as 'business manager' first and personnel manager second and will have a broad portfolio which encompasses not just dealing with trade unions but with the organisation's entire human resources. He or she is also likely to be involved in the design of the structure of the organisation. The architect is probably qualified, both academically and vocationally, although he or she may not be a member of the Institute of Personnel and Development, and may well have considerable experience as a line manager or consultant at some stage of his or her career.

As a result of survey and case study work, Storey (1992) proposed an alternative two-dimensional classification based, firstly, upon the extent to which personnel managers intervene in decision making and, secondly, the extent to which the type of intervention which does prevail is strategic or tactical. Figure 2.5 locates the types of personnel management on these dimensions.

Type 1: Advisers

Advisers act as 'internal consultants' and are knowledgeable about current developments but prefer to leave everyday things to line and general managers. The adviser role is compatible with

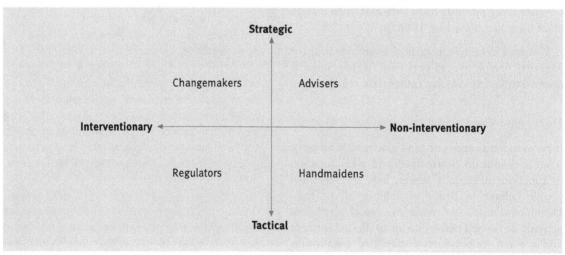

Figure 2.5 Types of personnel management
Source: Based on Storey, 1992

devolved management structures which place more responsibility upon line managers. Advisers arguably have a more strategic focus.

Type 2: Handmaidens

More subservient than advisers, but like the adviser adopts a mainly non-interventionary stance, 'but the kind of contribution made is more of a service provider at the behest of the line' (Storey, 1992, p. 172). Handmaidens act out an imposed role rather than one they want to play and are responsive to customer requirements. The handmaiden role is often the result of organisational restructuring, itself a result of 'prolonged buffeting in the shape of reorganisations, shifts in priorities and culture, budget cuts and similar threats to traditional, and relatively stable, personnel and IR roles' (ibid., p. 172). More specifically, they:

- service the routine requirements of the line;
- fulfil a clerical and welfare function (maintain records for absence, sickness and pay; visiting sick employees); and
- explain rules and regulations and procedures to line managers who are faced with a grievance from a unionised workforce.

The handmaiden role differs from the adviser type in that the service offered is more routine and administrative and more tactical than strategic.

Type 3: Regulators

Regulators are more interventionist in the conduct of managing the employment relationship, but these interventions rarely concern wider strategic policies of the organisation. Storey states (1992, pp. 175–6):

> *In many regards they represent the classic IR manager – responsible for devising, negotiating and defending the procedural and substantive rules which govern employment relations. They are to be found at both company and establishment level. Some of their rule-making activity may appear to have 'strategic' character in that it occasionally involves such 'big' decisions as union recognition and membership or nonmembership of employers' associations. But*

> *these sorts of decisions are rarely recognised as of a corporate strategy nature by senior business managers. . . . In a company or plant where the personnel specialist plays a regulatory role the line manager may feel displaced and upstaged or, in time, readily abdicate managerial responsibility in labour matters to this specialist.*

Type 4: Changemakers

> *This role type denotes the natural location of the human resource manager proper. These personnel specialists make a highly proactive, interventionary and strategic contribution. The orientation is away from bargaining, away from ad hocery, and away from 'humble advice'. It is, in fact, the antithesis of all these. The integration of the different aspects of resourcing, planning, appraising, rewarding and developing and the further integration of all this into the business plan are the characteristic features of this type of personnel approach.* (Storey, 1992, p. 176)

The changemaker role is, however, more ideal than real and may encompass both types of HRM, the 'hard' and the 'soft' (see below).

Self-evaluation activity 2.13

Types of personnel practitioner
This SEA has no commentary

In order to appreciate the nature of Storey's typology, read the four statements given below and identify which of these approximate to the four types of personnel practitioner:

1. 'Personnel is part of the total management system and shares with line managers in running the business – contributing from vision to results, and operating in the forefront of change management. It acts in partnership with line management and provides expert advice on all aspects of manpower management. These include not only traditional personnel areas such as training and employee relations but also the most fundamental issues of company business policy and philosophy.'

2. 'I try to ensure that discussions are between line managers and their opposite numbers on the trade union side. Me and my people are not to be seen as

go-betweens or, still less, as people who make the line managers roll over. The line managers have to have the commitment to the solution. I like to see them getting on with it and I like to keep out of their hair.'

3. 'It is only a few years ago that the production managers here would pass all their IR problems on to us. More than once I have come into this very room [a conference room] to find a plant manager facing a group of stewards whose lads had already walked off the job. As soon as I came through that door the so-called manager would stand up and say "Ah I'm glad you've arrived to sort this out" and then he'd head off out!'

4. 'I basically deal with the production managers and as far as I'm concerned the personnel managers serve them. However, what I do want is definitely more "say" on the types of services offered by the RGMs [regional general managers] and naturally much of this relates to what Personnel are doing. It means I want to look at job descriptions, I want to look at management development . . . yes I really want to know what it is that I am paying for.'

Personnel as contradiction?

The diversity of definitional models reflects the inconsistency and ambiguity of approach adopted by personnel managers to their organisational status and role, and this has resulted in a crisis of credibility. The problem not only concerns the mismatch between the pious aspirations articulated by the normative model and the reality of what personnel managers actually do, but also stems from a chequered history of the profession and the consequences of its role within a capitalist society.

The quality of employment relations and personnel policies and practices is largely a reflection of the quality of British management. If these policies are not particularly successful (as in the case of the Edwardes' era at British Leyland) as a result, for example, of adopting inappropriate strategies or styles, then personnel management often has to shoulder the blame. The following factors help to explain the contradictions inherent within the personnel management function.

Historical

Personnel management had its origins in the larger paternalist firms of the nineteenth century with the emphasis upon employee welfare and well-being. With the advent of the First World War, large numbers of women were employed for the first time in munitions, and the government and other employers recruited personnel or welfare officers, most of whom were also women, in order to deal with recruitment and other labour-related issues. Many firms dispensed with personnel managers and departments as an expensive luxury during the inter-war depression years, but in those firms which retained personnel departments, the gender profile changed and personnel management became increasingly male-dominated as they assumed responsibility for industrial relations matters. The Second World War provided an impetus to the growth of personnel management as once more women were recruited to war-related industries and by 1946 there were around 5000 personnel managers in Britain. However, up to the end of the 1950s personnel management was considered to be a low-status occupation with little professional credibility. Gospel and Palmer (1993) state:

Overall, the majority of personnel managers in Britain lacked formal qualifications and personnel management remained relatively low-status in the management hierarchy. Their role was usually administrative and reactive rather than strategic or proactive and, in dealings with trade unions, much was still left to employers' associations. (p. 75)

During the 1960s and 1970s, with the increasing complexity and volume of individual and collective employment legislation and the higher profiling of employment-related problems and issues, the number of personnel managers increased from 15,000 in the 1960s to 50,000 by the late 1970s. Numbers continue to increase, as does membership of the Institute of Personnel and Development. However, as we have previously noted, many small firms still do not have personnel specialists, and even during the early 1980s more than half of all personnel managers did not belong to the IPM (now Chartered Institute of Personnel and Development, CIPD). Sisson (1995, p. 89) reinforces the point that

'many personnel managers did not see themselves as "professional" in the sense of owing their prime loyalty to the occupation'. Most were 'managers first and personnel people second' (Mackay and Torrington, 1986, pp. 161–2). Other relevant points in recent historical context made by Sisson include:

- Personnel management, as we have already seen, is not a single homogeneous occupation but involves 'a variety of roles and activities which differ from one organisation to another and, perhaps more importantly, from one level to another in the same organisation', and this can be seen in relation to Tyson and Fell's (1986) and Storey's (1992) typologies.
- The 'balkanisation' of personnel management. 'Not only was there a variety of roles and activities, but these tended to be relatively self-contained, with little passage between them. Many of the architects [in relation to Tyson and Fell's typology] came from the ranks of line managers, rather than personnel managers' (p. 89).
- Personnel management was highly structured on gender lines. Women made up the great majority of personnel managers (see the summary of the WERS 2004 survey results below), yet they tended to be employed in lower-level and less well-paid jobs than their male counterparts, which helped to reinforce the 'Cinderella' image of the function as a whole.

Within a capitalist market economy

As Legge (1995) states: 'The fact that personnel specialists oscillate between the "personnel" and "management", between "caring" and "control" aspects of the function, can be attributed to their role in mediating a major contradiction embedded in capitalist systems: the need to achieve both the control *and* consent of employees' (p. 14). The control issue has been dealt with in an earlier section of this chapter. In relation to personnel management, the following issues are relevant:

- Personnel management helps to realise surplus value. 'Surplus value' is a Marxist concept which Giddens (1989) defines thus: 'In the course of the working day, workers produce more than is actually needed by employers to repay the cost

of hiring them. This surplus value is the source of profit, which capitalists are able to put to their own use' (p. 210).
- Personnel managers help to create surplus value by ensuring that control systems are in place. Edwards (1979) identifies three aspects of control relevant to personnel management:
 - direction and specification of work tasks;
 - evaluation, monitoring and assessment of performance; and
 - discipline and reward systems designed to encourage co-operation and compliance.
- As we have seen, control systems often engender employee resistance which takes the form of absenteeism, labour turnover and various forms of industrial action which in turn may impede surplus value and profit. Personnel managers also ameliorate the more adverse consequences of control systems by emphasising the caring/welfare function.
- The personnel manager is therefore a mediator between 'the formally rational criteria of productivity, profit, effectiveness and the rest, [and] the human needs, interests and aspirations of employees' (Watson, 1977, p. 63). This may cause credibility problems as managers oscillate between satisfying the competing demands of 'control' and 'care'.

Within a patriarchal society

A further source of contradiction and ambiguity within the personnel specialism is the legacy of patriarchy. Essentially, patriarchy refers to male dominance, and is 'a set of hierarchical relations between men, and solidarity among them, which enables them to control women. Patriarchy is thus the system of male oppression of women' (Hartmann, 1982, p. 138). Traditionally, because of their role as mothers and carers, women are primarily absorbed in domestic activities and become the 'second sex' because they are excluded from the more 'public' activities in which males are free to engage (de Beauvoir, 1972). The existence of patriarchy has given rise to gender inequalities at work and elsewhere.

Initially, personnel was dominated by women, and up to the 1930s the vast majority of personnel managers were women. The Quaker concern for

employee welfare (often regarded as a female concern) was regarded as low in the order of priorities for most enterprises in the first half of the twentieth century. As Legge (1995) points out:

> This early development of personnel management with female welfare activities in a patriarchal society inevitably meant that the function would carry a legacy as being of low status and unimportance, at least in comparison to central male activities, such as production, finance and so on. . . . It is not surprising, then, that personnel management has an enduring problem of establishing credibility. In its task of managing the contradictions of capitalism, personnel specialists become prey to a series of ambiguities and double-bind situations, from which extraction is difficult, if not to say impossible. In the decade of the enterprise culture and into the 1990s, human resource management is being presented as a model of managing people at work that is more credible than personnel management. (p. 20)

The management of employment relations: survey evidence from WIRS to WERS 1998

Much of the information we have concerning the management of employment relations emanates from the Workplace Industrial Relations Survey (WIRS) series comprising four longitudinally linked national surveys which took place in 1980, 1984, 1990 and 1998 (see Chapter 5 for a general overview of workplace change). The main findings from the 1998 Workplace Employee Relations Survey (WERS 1998) are summarised below (see also Millward et al., 2000):

- The survey confirms the major demographic change concerning the increasing proportion of women in employment relations management – the 'feminisation of personnel' phenomenon referred to earlier in the chapter.
- Also plotted by the survey is the steady rise of the employment relations specialist due mainly to the greater prevalence of specialists in newer workplaces. Millward et al. comment that 'the rise of the ER specialist, and the increased likelihood that they will hold employee relations qualifica-

tions, mark a significant departure in the way that a growing minority of workplaces manage employee relations [and where] . . . the conduct of employee relations is treated as a professional pursuit requiring formal credentials' (p. 81).

- The work content of employment relations specialists has remained remarkably consistent since 1984 with considerable majorities ranging from 61 to 95 per cent dealing with the 'traditional' responsibilities relating to pay and conditions of employment, recruitment/selection, training, payment systems, grievance handling and staffing. However, there has been a slight but perceptible increase in the proportion of non-specialist employee relations managers having functional responsibility for these areas.
- The explosion of HRM titles is in evidence in newer workplaces and in existing ones where there has been a name change from ER specialist to HR manager.
- The survey reveals that within multi-site private sector organisations, board-level representation of employment relations fell from 1984 onwards and fewer head offices were employing ER specialists, thereby revealing a contradiction between the latter trend and the increase in ER workplace specialists.
- Evidence indicates that the job of the ER manager within multi-site organisations has become more complex since 1984 owing to a diffusion of ER practices throughout the organisation and the reduction of facilities enabling ER mangers to perform their tasks.
- These developments affect all sectors, but during the 1990s the public sector was most affected, while the non-unionised private sector was least affected.

With regard to the corporate personnel/ER/HR (PEH) function in multinational and hence multi-site companies, there is much evidence in addition to WERS (Millward et al., 2000) to suggest that there is indeed a decline in the role of PEH at corporate level as a result of decentralisation of organisational structures, and even the decline of collective industrial relations itself (Purcell and Ahlstrand, 1994). However, others would argue that there has been a resurgence of the PEH strategic role in multinational companies (MNCs) associated with the

dynamics of the multi-divisional company – or dominant global M-form company structure and its variant the N-form company (M-form organisations are those organisations having many or multiple divisions; the N-form variant is based around networks) which is based around global information or knowledge economy networks (both types being defined as having structures based on multiple divisions) (Scullion and Starkey, 2000). There is also clear evidence that MNCs are innovators in HR and PEH practice at local as well as national/international level. The popular mantra 'think global, act local' means adapting PEH practice to local circumstances while pushing for performance and market leadership (Boxall and Purcell, 2003). Yet a third approach suggests a 'steady growth' thesis of the PEH function's power and influence arising from the Donovan Report's (1968) recommendation that companies appoint directors responsible for industrial relations (Kelly, 2001). This is reinforced by the work of Kelly and Gennard (2001) whose research indicates that the PEH role continues to be increasingly important in the formulation and implementation of corporate business and HR strategies.

The management of employment relations: survey evidence from WERS 2004

We now turn to the survey evidence culled from WERS 2004 concerning the current dynamics of the management of the employment relationship. Where appropriate, the terms 'personnel management' and 'human resource management' are used, despite some researchers claiming that 'there is little point in discussing the niceties of the difference between personnel management and HRM when, in the US, HRM is just another term for personnel management' (Legge, 2005, p. 3). There is a fuller examination of the personnel and HRM function in the next section of this chapter. WERS 2004 makes a clear distinction between the two functions, as does this book, but in order not to cloud the issue, the term 'employment relations specialist/generalist/manager' will be used when there is no need to distinguish between the two. The main findings are in the form of answers to the following questions:

- *What is the proportion of managers with employment relations responsibilities in UK workplaces?* 90 per cent of managers were 'primarily responsible' for employment relations matters at the workplace, although only 19 per cent of all managers said this was their major job responsibility. However, there was an increase in the proportion of managers with specific employment relations job titles (22 per cent in 2004; 11 per cent in 1998) which reflects the decline in the involvement of general managers in employment relations matters and an increase in functional specialisation within the personnel area. In 2004 there were more human resource managers than personnel managers, a reverse of the situation in 1998. Nevertheless, both HR and personnel managers spent less time on employment relations matters in 2004 as compared with 1998, and this has been a continuing trend since 1984. In workplaces with no HR or personnel managers, general managers have greater responsibility for day-to-day employment relations.

- *Are there more specialist or generalist managers responsible for employment relations matters?* WERS 2004 defines employment relations specialists as 'those whose formal job title was personnel manager, human resource manager, employee relations manager or industrial relations manager *or* who spent more than half their time on employment relations issues' (Kersley *et al.*, 2006, p. 39). In 2004, specialists were found in 28 per cent of workplaces as compared with 17 per cent of workplaces in 1998. Generalists (general managers, financial managers or proprietors) with no specific employment relations related titles and who spent less than half their time on employment relations matters were found in 72 per cent of workplaces in 2004 (83 per cent in 1998). There has, therefore been some increase in specialists and a slight decline in generalists since 1998. The proportion of specialists varied according to type of workplace, size of workplace and the sectoral context. For example, large workplaces were more likely to have specialists, while smaller workplaces that belonged to a larger organisation were more likely to have specialists within the larger organisation rather than at the workplace itself.

Table 2.1 The changing responsibilities of employment relations managers: 1998 and 2004

Type of responsibility	1998	2004	Percentage of workplaces 2004
Rates of pay		Less likely to be responsible for	68
Working hours		Less likely to be responsible for	80
Holiday entitlements		Less likely to be responsible for	62
Pension entitlements		Less likely to be responsible for	37
Recruitment	Common responsibility	Most common responsibility. Unchanged since 1998	94
Training	Common responsibility	Unchanged since 1998	89
Grievances	Common responsibility	Most common responsibility. Unchanged since 1998	95
Disciplinary matters		Most common responsibility	96
Staffing plans	Common responsibility	Unchanged since 1998	90
Equal opportunities	Common responsibility	Less responsibility than in 1998 (90% in 1998)	84
Health and safety	Common responsibility	Unchanged since 1998	88
Performance appraisals	Common responsibility	Unchanged since 1998	88
Employee consultation			90
Responsible for all areas			27

- *To what extent has the employment relations function become feminised?* Survey results indicate that around 75 per cent of HR managers and 66 per cent of personnel managers were women. However, while the proportion of women HR managers increased since 1998, the opposite was true of personnel managers. Women's presence increased in small establishments between 10 and 24 employees (36 per cent in 2004, up from 20 per cent in 1998) and in the construction sector (6 per cent in 2004, up from 1 per cent in 1998). Female specialists were more likely to hold personnel qualifications than men (70 per cent of female specialists compared to 36 per cent of male specialists) and a substantially higher proportion of female specialists were entering the profession with personnel qualifications than their male counterparts. The survey results therefore clearly indicate 'that there is clear evidence that a new cohort of women are "professionalizing" employment relations' (Kersley *et al.*, 2006, p. 75).

- *To what extent have the responsibilities of employment relations managers changed?* The changing responsibilities of employment relations managers are indicated in Table 2.1. Thirteen job duties are listed for 2004 and seven for 1998. Public sector managers were less likely than their private sector counterparts to be responsible for rates of pay, working hours, holiday and pension entitlements and equally responsible for the remaining tasks. Managers in large organisations were more likely to be responsible for recruitment, training, appraisals and employee consultation than managers in smaller organisations.

- *What is the size of the employment relations function?* The size of the employment relations function is partially attributed to size of organisation. Organisations with a relatively centralised structure and where collective bargaining takes place have a larger function than in organisations which are relatively decentralised or have decentralised arrangements where the function may be

smaller or non-existent (Storey and Sisson, 1993). Essentially the question is concerned with how many assistants employment relations managers have, and this varies with size of workplace, with larger workplaces having more assistants, and sector (public sector workplaces having more assistants than private sector workplaces). In 2004 there were more workplaces with no assistants than in 1998, but in those workplaces having some assistance, the function was larger in 2004. The use of Acas and other sources as a means of advice was more widespread in 2004, and this has affected the size of the function to some degree, there being some decline since 1998. The size of HR departments as a whole can also be affected by either outsourcing and/or contracting in HR services such as recruitment, payroll, training and filling temporary positions. In general, however, the size of the employment relations function remained broadly the same in 2004 as in 1998.

- *To what extent are workplace managers autonomous?* 'The increase in the proportion of branch sites with specialists at both the workplace and a higher level, and the decrease in the proportion of workplaces with only a specialist at a higher level suggested an increased decentralisation of the personnel function' (Kersley *et al.*, 2006, p. 42). WERS 2004 results indicate that policies governing holiday or pension entitlements, health and safety, rates of pay, equal opportunities, discipline and grievance were less likely to be determined at local level and more likely to be determined centrally. Policies concerning training, recruitment and performance appraisals were more likely to be followed by local, workplace-based managers. However, few local managers (11 per cent) had a great deal of local autonomy to determine policy and did not, therefore, have to follow a policy on the employment relations issues identified above (and also including working hours, staffing plans, trade union recognition, pay and conditions of employment and payment systems). In general, WERS 2004 results show that 'decentralisation has not been accompanied by greater levels of autonomy for local managers' (ibid., p. 70) and that centralised personnel departments have been increasing their influence on local decision-making

since 1998 thereby reducing the discretion of local managers including specialists. As Kersley *et al.* note, 'The extent of delegation of people management away from personnel departments to line managers and supervisors has continued to be rather limited and has been restricted to issues such as recruitment. The employment relations function seems to be characterised by centralised decision-making and relatively undeveloped monitoring systems' (p. 70).

We now consider the nature of human resource management (HRM) and its relationship to personnel management within the employment relationship.

HUMAN RESOURCE MANAGEMENT AND EMPLOYMENT RELATIONS

HRM arguably incorporates more strategic approaches to managing industrial and employee relations (Farnham, 1997) within larger organisations and in response to changes in product market competition, market structure and technology. HRM and related developments are well documented (Storey, 1992, 1995; Storey and Sisson, 1993; Legge, 1995, 2005). HRM emerged in Britain during the mid-1980s after originating in the United States and could be described as 'the Americanised version of "Japanese" methods' (Storey, 1992, p. 17). Its development has been somewhat haphazard and eclectic, there being no single, consistent approach to HRM in most organisations which have, by their own admission, adopted such practices. The main reason for this, as Storey goes on to argue, is that HRM is subject to different interpretations both theoretically/strategically, and operationally. For example, HRM as we have already noted, is often taken to be synonymous with personnel management; a label change is often considered sufficient, but this merely masks the same old practices and policies. Many organisations go further and attempt to integrate the various personnel management techniques (including elements of industrial relations) in a systematic way (see the summary of WERS 2004 data above). With this in mind, we can identify a general definition and two important HRM categories or models.

Definition

Storey's (1995) definition of HRM is fairly specific in orientation:

> Human resource management is a distinctive approach to employment management which seeks to achieve competitive advantage through the strategic deployment of a highly committed and capable workforce, using an integrated array of cultural, structural and personnel techniques. (p. 5)

On the other hand, Boxall and Purcell (2003) opt for an all-inclusive definition in which the term 'human resource management' is equated with the terms 'employee relations' and 'labour management':

> Human resource management (alternatively 'employee relations' or 'labour management') includes the firm's work systems and its models of employment. It embraces both individual and collective aspects of people management. It is not restricted to any one style or ideology. It engages the energies of both line and specialist managers (where the latter exist) and typically entails a blend of messages for a variety of workforce groups. (p. 23)

The main components of HRM are represented in summary form in Exhibit 2.2. The first element concerns beliefs, assumptions and values about the importance of the human resource above all other factors of production. If the organisation is to be competitive, then the human resource must be developed as a valued asset in order to secure employee commitment, adaptability and continuous improvement. The second element is to do with strategy and the strategic importance of HRM in securing competitive advantage. The third element concerns line management. As we have seen in our discussion of personnel management, line management often assumes greater importance in dealing with operational IR and related issues, and Storey (1995) states:

Exhibit 2.2

The HRM model

1. Beliefs and assumptions
 - That it is the human resource which gives competitive edge.
 - That the aim should be not mere compliance with rules, but employee commitment.
 - That therefore employees should be very carefully selected and developed.
2. Strategic qualities
 - Because of the above factors, HR decisions are of strategic importance.
 - Top management involvement is necessary.
 - HR policies should be integrated into the business strategy – stemming from it and even contributing to it.
3. Critical role of managers
 - Because HR practice is critical to the core activities of the business, it is too important to be left to personnel specialists alone.
 - Line managers need to be closely involved both as deliverers and drivers of the HR policies.
 - Much greater attention is paid to the management of managers themselves.
4. Key levers
 - Managing culture is more important than managing procedures and systems.
 - Integrated action on selection, communication, training, reward and development.
 - Restructuring and job design to allow devolved responsibility and empowerment.

Source: Storey, 1995, p. 6

If human resources are so critical for business success, then HRM is too important to be left to operational personnel specialists. Line managers are seen as crucial to the effective delivery of HRM policies: conducting team briefings, holding performance appraisal interviews, target setting, encouraging quality circles, managing performance-related pay, and so on. (p. 7)

The fourth element concerns key levers used in the implementation of HRM, particularly the emphasis upon the 'management of culture'. Storey notes: 'Corporate culture management has generated much excitement because it is perceived to offer a key to the unlocking of consensus, flexibility and commitment. These are self-evidently prized objectives' (ibid., p. 8).

Within the broad definition of HRM, we have two important subcategories based on Storey's (1987) distinction between 'hard' and 'soft' models which are described below.

The 'hard' model

The 'hard' model emphasises the importance of integrating human resources policies, systems and activities with business strategy, and is a response to internal and external pressures during the 1980s which required organisations to be more competitive nationally and globally and adopt an increasingly market-led stance. These pressures affected both private and public sector organisations and concerned technological change, 'quality' initiatives and customer-oriented services. Organisational changes including mergers and 'rationalisations', decentralising and delayering strategies and the devolution of routine responsibilities to line managers within cost centres reflected a desire to create a performance-oriented culture. It is assumed that personnel policies, systems and practices are consistent with and supportive of business objectives. Specifically, the 'hard' model emphasises:

- that the human resource is no more and no less than a factor of production together with land and capital and is an 'expense' rather than a potential for turning production into wealth;
- that human resources are passive and reactive rather than creative and proactive; and

- that there is an emphasis upon the 'quantitative, calculative and business strategic aspects of managing the headcount in as "rational" a way as for any other economic factor' (Storey, 1987, p. 6).

The 'soft' model

The 'soft' model also stresses the importance of integrating HR policies with business objectives. Specifically, the model has certain assumptions embedded in it (paraphrasing Legge, 1995, p. 36):

- employees are treated as valued assets;
- employees are a source of competitive advantage through their commitment, adaptability and high quality of performance and skills;
- employees are proactive and capable of 'development', worthy of 'trust' and 'collaboration', to be achieved through 'participation' and 'informed choice';
- management generates employee commitment through communication, motivation, and leadership, and
- greater employee commitment will result in improved economic performance and so assist in employee development and training.

Apart from the 'hard' and 'soft' models of HRM, Storey (1992) distinguishes two different HRM approaches identified as 'strong' and 'weak'. The 'strong' approach assumes a distinctive package which encompasses both strategic and operational aspects of HRM, while the 'weak' approach assumes that organisations can get by through changing the name 'personnel' to 'HRM', as with 'old wine in new bottles' (see Figure 2.6).

Self-evaluation activity 2.14

'Strong' commitment: hard or soft?

The response is given below

Given in Exhibit 2.3 is an example of an organisation with a 'strong' commitment and approach to HRM. Indicate whether this is also an example of the 'soft' or 'hard' model.

The example indicates a distinctive 'strong' approach to HRM strategy and practice which is characteristic of the 'soft' model. Moreover, Legge (1995) argues that the

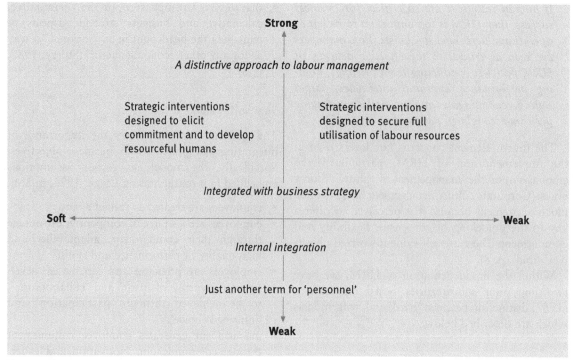

Figure 2.6 Approaches to the management of labour
Source: Storey, 1992, p. 27. Blackwell Publishing

Exhibit 2.3

An organisation with a strong commitment to HRM

1. The firm competes on the basis of product quality and differentiation as well as price.
2. Human resource considerations weigh heavily in corporate strategic decision-making and governance processes. Employee interests are represented through the voice of the human resource staff professionals and/or employee representatives consult and participate with senior executives in decisions that affect human resource policies and employee interests. In either case, employees are treated as legitimate stakeholders in the corporation.
3. Investments in new hardware or physical technology are combined with the investments in human resources and changes in organisational practices required to realise the full potential benefits of these investments.
4. The firm sustains a high level of investment in training, skill development and education, and personnel practices are designed to capture and utilise these skills fully.
5. Compensation and reward systems are internally equitable, competitive and linked to the long-term performance of the firm.
6. Employment continuity and security is an important priority and value to be considered in all corporate decisions and policies.
7. Workplace relations encourage flexibility in the organisation of work, empowerment of employees to solve problems, and high levels of trust among workers, supervisors and managers.
8. Worker rights to representation are acknowledged and respected. Union or other employee representatives are treated as joint partners in designing and overseeing innovations in labour and human resource practices.

Source: Beaumont, 1995, p. 40

'hard' and 'soft' models are not incompatible with each other or mutually exclusive, and many organisations will contain elements of both; it is the combination of the 'strategic' and 'commitment' elements which provides organisations with the opportunity and means to develop competitive strategies based on value added, quality and flexibility rather than on cost alone. It is doubtful, however, whether in practice the take-up of 'soft' HRM is particularly widespread, as Legge (1995) argues:

> [HRM practices and policies] are adopted to drive business values and are modified in the light of changing business objectives and conditions. It is a thinking pragmatism. Insofar that any one model is being implemented, the evidence would suggest more support for the 'hard' rather than the 'soft' model. There is little evidence for the widespread implementation of the long-term developmental 'soft' model, yet it is the latter that is supposed to be distinctly different from the stereotypes of personnel management practice, not the former. Is what we are seeing in reality the implementation of the old-style 'standard modern' personnel management, asserting an opportunistic exercise of managerial prerogative, but dressed up in a 'soft' HRM rhetoric? (p. 47)

HRM and employment relations management in recent historical context

As HRM became, at least in its rhetoric, increasingly dominant during the 1980s and 1990s, so industrial relations rhetoric also began to change. The term 'new realism' was adopted by the media to denote attempts by trade unions to come to terms with the market-led ideology of Thatcherism (liberal individualism) and the decline in union membership. Academics noticed that the old leopard was changing its spots and used the term 'new industrial relations' (NIR) to encompass some of the individualistic concerns of HRM. As Beardwell (1997) asserts:

> It is possible to reconstruct the central problem of industrial relations as being not so much the role of the trade union in the market economy as the role of the individual within the employment relationship, and in this way recast the frame-work of industrial relations so that the traditional collectivism we have been accustomed to is greatly reduced. (p. 7)

The now largely defunct term 'new' industrial relations was topical for a period in the 1990s as a legitimising term used not only to tease out the differences between the 'new' and the 'old' but also to make it more readily assimilated under the HRM banner. Boxall and Purcell (2003) would subscribe to that view as their definition of the subject area of HRM makes perfectly clear. Painting with a broad brush, they contend that HRM incorporates industrial, employment and work relations. In more critical vein, Clark (1997) offered the following interpretation of NIR:

> New industrial relations represents three ideological images propagated by the contemporary state: first the promotion of the managerial prerogative, employee compliance and a low strike level; secondly, a rejection of collective bargaining and trade union recognition as public policy and their replacement with managerially determined regulation and individualism in the employment relationship; thirdly, a prescription for management labour use strategies centred on flexibility and extra-contractual commitment through human resource management. Each image evokes the formative influences of libertarian laissez-faire . . . and rejects influences centred on pluralism, collective bargaining and trade unions. (p. 42)

The above statement by Clark made NIR virtually synonymous with an individualist unitary ideology. In addition, the ideological agenda of government as reflected in the definition above has some basis in practice (see also Chapter 4). The practices that came to be associated with NIR are diverse, although it is possible to identify three distinct patterns of arrangements comprising:

- the 'Japanese model';
- union avoidance and derecognition; and
- the challenge of HRM.

The 'Japanese model'

This is exemplified by the original Toshiba Consumer Products factory set up in Plymouth in 1981 and contains the following elements (Trevor, 1988, pp. 221–42):

- sole bargaining rights for a single trade union;
- a 'no-strike' agreement with binding 'final offer' arbitration as a last resort in disputes of interest;
- a broad-based forum for consultation and employee participation;
- 'single status' conditions of employment; and
- complete freedom on the part of management to organise work.

The proliferation of single-union representation and agreements within 'greenfield' sites since the early 1980s is not a uniquely inspired Japanese phenomenon. As we have seen (Chapter 1), many trade unions such as the former TGWU, in the face of declining membership, had with varying degrees of enthusiasm encouraged such developments. The claimed advantages of a single union are that bargaining and consultation are simplified, that disputes are less likely and that introducing flexible working arrangements is made easier. According to Bevan (1987):

> The fact that agreements are single union, at a stroke, removes many of the potential obstacles to flexibility. Inter-union demarcation lines are a thing of the past and flexibility depends on nothing more than receiving the necessary training to carry out the task required. (p. 9)

WERS 1998 and 2004 point to the decline in multi-unionism against the backdrop of union decline during the period 1990–2004. While more than half of all unionised workplaces had two or more unions present, over half of the unionised workplaces in wholesale and retail, financial services and other community services had a single-union agreement and 43 per cent of all workplaces had single-union representation in 1998, up from 34 per cent in 1990 (Cully *et al.*, 1999; Millward *et al.*, 2000, Kersley *et al.*, 2006). A further impetus to the spread of single unionism is provided by the modest growth of partnership agreements.

Another characteristic of the Japanese model new-style agreements concerns the 'no-strike' clause with dispute resolution in the last resort through 'pendulum arbitration'. Although by the end of 1987 some 28 companies in Britain were known to have strike-free agreements (Oliver and Wilkinson, 1992), Millward (1994) found that these deals were extremely rare in British industry, while WERS 1998 and 2004 barely mentioned them. Millward, for example, states:

> A mere 1 per cent of workplaces with recognised trade unions had pendulum arbitration and in workplaces with a sole union agreement the figure was less than half of 1 per cent. In fact, pendulum arbitration was somewhat more common in multi-union workplaces. It was therefore by no means a distinctive element of 'new-style' agreements, as much of the literature has portrayed. Nor was it especially a feature of younger workplaces or of the industries, regions and trade unions in which the well-documented 'single union deals' have occurred. We concluded that pendulum arbitration was a rare practice, probably not increasing dramatically in its incidence and probably of longer standing than the single union deals of the mid to late 1980s. As a distinctive development in British industrial relations, pendulum arbitration has yet to reach the point of take off. (pp. 123–4)

A third characteristic of the Japanese model of NIR is the company advisory board or company council. These boards, which should be differentiated from the more traditional joint consultative committee, are often regarded as necessary to provide further stability and predictability in workplace industrial relations. The boards comprise elected representatives who are not necessarily shop stewards or trade union members and are chosen by non-union as well as unionised employees, providing a forum for negotiations on pay and conditions where traditional demarcations between consultation and negotiation are eliminated. Companies adopting this system often experience conflicts of interest as a result of the shift of responsibilities from shop stewards to the boards. There can be no doubt that the adoption of the Information and Consultation Directive which is now fully implemented will provide further impetus to the development of representative committees and boards.

A fourth characteristic of the model concerns single-status employment conditions. Based on examining differences between manual and non-manual employees, Millward found that only around one in eight workplaces had equality of employment conditions and that 'workplaces with sole union agreements were no different from the generality of workplaces in this respect' (Millward, 1994, p. 125). By 1998 there appeared to be a significant increase in the proportion of workplaces with single-status

entitlements covering pension schemes, company car or car allowance, private health insurance, four weeks' or more paid annual leave and sick pay in excess of statutory requirements, with 41 per cent of workplaces qualifying (Cully *et al.*, 1999).

A final feature of Japanese-style NIR within the single-union representation context (but not exclusively so) concerned the freedom of management to organise work at the establishment in any way it thought fit.

Union avoidance and derecognition

The second component of NIR concerned the complete and continuing avoidance of trade union involvement. This development is described in more detail in Chapter 3. Millward (1994) in reviewing the situation during the early 1990s stated:

> Union avoidance at new workplaces was far less controversial and thus attracted much less public attention. In many private sector industries, particularly those dominated by small independent firms, the absence of trade unions has always been the common pattern. But as yet we do not know whether union avoidance has become a more common feature of newer workplaces or if the processes of maturation that sometimes led to unionisation have been attenuated. (p. 2)

As we shall see when the issue is discussed in greater detail in Chapter 3, there was growing evidence that trade union derecognition intensified during the early 1990s and support for trade unions weakened amongst employees in unionised organisations (Millward *et al.*, 2000). To a certain extent, while the private sector has witnessed a further weakening of support for unions amongst employees in that sector, WERS 2004 results indicate that the derecognition process has declined dramatically (Kersley *et al.*, 2006).

The impact of human resource management upon the employment relationship

There is, to be sure, a wide gap between the rhetoric of HRM-speak and the reality of the workplace. While at strategic level HRM is often espoused in accommodatory terms, emphasising the treatment of employees as 'assets', fostering a broad-based communications system, and involving employees in the organisation and planning of work, the workplace experience of employees, and in particular unionised employees, sometimes suggests otherwise (see Legge, 1995, 2005, for a fuller discussion). According to the latter perspective, HRM is associated with union derecognition and a systematic attempt to undermine the union role, and to some extent the WIRS and WERS surveys and analysis confirms this view. However, there is one significant caveat here which concerns company *size* and HRM. A large proportion of companies within the *Financial Times* Top 50 recognise trade unions and implement at least some 'industrial relations-friendly' HRM policies focusing on information, consultation and employee involvement. Conversely, going down the size scale, the *smaller* the company the more likely it is to be union-free and, where there is a union presence, the more hostile the employer is to that presence.

Notwithstanding the evidence already presented – and most certainly more empirical evidence is still required – the unavoidable conclusion is that within both unionised companies, and more especially non-unionised companies, employers have at best been only partially successful in developing a positive HRM agenda and developing more sophisticated HR practices. WERS 2004, for example, confirms that sophisticated HR practices are confined mainly to larger workplaces and in the public sector. The reasons for this may lie in the absence of a formal statement of strategy (Hunter and MacInnes, 1994) owing to short-term financial pressures on British managers which prevent them from implementing long-term strategies to develop employee skills and attributes (Sisson, 1993), and to 'widespread managerial incompetence in both technical and organisational matters' (Procter and Ackroyd, 2001).

Implications of these developments for employment relations issues

The developments identified above have affected employment relations issues in the following ways:

- In organisations where HRM is well established and which demonstrate high levels of management involvement and employee commitment, then it is more likely that elements of both

individual, and to a lesser extent collective aspects of employment relations will be incorporated into HRM and be operated relatively successfully, and will manifest themselves as 'high commitment management practices'. High-commitment practices include: the use of personality tests, performance tests, formal off-the-job-training, regular appraisals, group-based team briefings with feedback and participation in problem-solving groups. Within unionised contexts, it has already been established that individual unions are modifying their approaches on both individualistic and collectivist dimensions (Bacon and Storey, 1993, 1996; Boxall and Purcell, 2003; Kessler and Purcell, 2003). Within non-unionised contexts, most UK organisations do not have well-developed HRM (Kersley *et al.*, 2006) but within the sample enterprises which Guest and Hoque (1994) examined, there was a sizeable minority of UK greenfield site operations which did, and whose industrial relations were largely integrated within HRM. The deficiency of HRM

may also be explained by reference to factors other than the absence (or presence) of the collective union voice. In addition, WERS 1998 and to a certain extent WERS 2004 indicate that sophisticated HRM practices are to be found alongside union recognition and workplaces with higher densities of unionisation, and that 'an active and strong union presence is compatible with the broad suite of high commitment management practices' (Cully *et al.*, 1999, p. 111).

- Insofar as collective bargaining is concerned, the evidence of the 1980s and 1990s indicates that, according to Brown (1993):

> the coverage of collective bargaining has contracted substantially, that the scope of bargaining has narrowed, that the depth of union involvement has diminished and that organisational security offered to unions by employers has deteriorated. (p. 195)

Moreover, Millward *et al.* (1992) also demonstrate how much worse off are those employees

Exhibit 2.4

HRM: the rise of human resource managers: a potted history, 1980–98

1. In 1990, 1 per cent of respondents bore the 'human resources' title, but by 1998 7 per cent of managers responsible for workplace employment relations were HR managers, comprising 30 per cent of all employment relations specialists.

2. The increase in HR managers accounts for the increase in specialists between 1990 and 1998. HR managers were not confined to head office in a strategic sense, but were diffused throughout the organisation. The incidence of HR managers increased with workplace size although this is no simple correlative association.

3. Of the very smallest workplaces, for example, there was a disproportionate number of employment relations specialists in 40 per cent of such workplaces. The human resource title was very much in evidence in the privatised services.

4. The growth in HR managers can be partly attributed to the increased penetration of foreign-owned workplaces where HR managers accounted for 64 per cent of employment as compared with 26 per cent in UK-owned workplaces.

5. HR managers were less common in the public sector, where 20 per cent of employment relations specialists were HR managers compared with 35 per cent in the private sector.

6. HR managers are not confined to new workplaces; 32 per cent of employment relations specialists in workplaces aged 10 years or more were HR managers with the corresponding proportion in workplaces aged under 10 years being 29 per cent. Millward *et al.* (2000) conclude that 'it seems likely that human resource managers will become more prevalent if more continuing workplaces change the type of employment relations specialist they employ and new workplaces continue to introduce them' (p. 55).

who do not enjoy the protection of collective bargaining in terms of pay, health and safety, labour turnover, contractual security, compulsory redundancy, grievance procedures consultation, communication and employee representation. Therefore, the erosion of collective bargaining as a result of union substitution practices and/or marginalising the bargaining process has indeed resulted in a deterioration of conditions associated with the employment relationship. The contraction of collective bargaining continued throughout the 1990s and into the 2000s to such an extent that Brown *et al.* (2003) conclude that 'the reality for the vast majority of employees who work in the private sector in Britain is that managements, not trade unions, determine their pay' (p. 204).

- The issue as to whether trade unions and, more recently, HRM have or have not had an impact upon organisational performance has been part of a long-running debate in labour economics. The accumulated evidence summarised by Rose and Woolley (1992) suggests that far from hindering productivity and competition, high levels of unionisation actually encourage it, particularly when associated with well-developed human resource strategies. The assumption, therefore, that encouraging the 'free play' of market forces and discouraging union involvement and representation can somehow result in a more highly competitive and performing organisation, is seriously flawed. The new and often non-unionised labour market, where it has emerged, has in general terms not supported improved organisational competitiveness. Nolan and O'Donnell (2003), in their latest review of the literature, argue that by resisting crude forms of exploitation in production and campaigning for higher wages for their members, 'unions may have a transforming impact on the nature of production and business strategies' (p. 492). With regard to HRM, research by Guest *et al.* (2000) revealed that productivity and financial performance had been improved by extensive use of HR practices. However, as WERS 1998 and WERS 2004 also demonstrate, the application of HR practices has been more prevalent in establishments and workplaces in which there is also a union presence, and the argument therefore shifts as to whether either HR or union presence or both singly and/or in combination have a positive influence upon performance and productivity (Ramsay *et al.*, 2000).

- Finally, the impact of HRM in the public sector, particularly up to the mid-1990s, had been more limited than within the private sector. This view must, however, be qualified by acknowledging, as Bach and Winchester (2003) do, that by the end of the 1980s:
 (a) the privatisation of public corporations removed entire groups of employees from the public sector;
 (b) the introduction of compulsory competitive tendering for many ancillary public services resulted in substantial job losses, a downward pressure on wages and benefits, and more intensive patterns of work; and
 (c) the introduction of controls over public expenditure affected traditional 'comparability' arguments in pay negotiations and replaced this with 'ability to pay' argument in the face of strict cash limits.

Despite these developments, Bach and Winchester (1994) argue that Conservative governments achieved only limited success in encouraging decentralised industrial relations and pay determination in the public services, even though national agreements became more flexible. They go on to conclude that:

> *Advocates of decentralised market-sensitive pay determination will be disappointed to find no evidence that the government intends to withdraw from the active and inconsistent involvement in public sector pay determination that has characterised its predecessors' policies for the last thirty years.* (p. 280)

The changes, the reasons behind them and their impact upon employment relations have helped to create a new climate in which industrial relations operates. They have undoubtedly encouraged managements to take HRM initiatives and adopt human resource strategies geared towards improving employee productivity and commitment and fostering a more harmonious and co-operative employee-oriented organisational culture. However, the HRM rhetoric, as suggested earlier, still belies the reality

in many instances and remains a cause for concern to all parties in the employment relationship.

Are HRM and ER interests truly incompatible and does it matter?

It is likely that those areas of the employment relationship which are more 'individualist' in nature, together with a correspondingly lower priority given to collective and conflictual aspects, are more congruent with HRM and its strategies provided the latter genuinely reconciles the aims of greater employee commitment, investment in long-term training and development and security of employment with a 'pluralist' orientation towards employee representation and all that this entails. However, should employers continue to espouse contradictory values clothed in the rhetoric of HRM (for example, by reiterating the importance of 'quality' and 'customer care' while at the same time precariously cutting costs and 'casualising' the workforce), then the prospects for any reconciliation between the two seem rather poor. This is, of course, particularly true of the British context where strategic HRM is still regarded by some as an ideological movement, the aim of which is to disaggregate labour and marginalise trade unions.

Guest's approach (1989) to this problem is to argue that there is indeed a basic incompatibility between unitarist HRM and the pluralist traditions of British industrial relations, particularly within multi-union 'brownfield' sites. It may seem obvious to argue that a fundamental prerequisite for compatibility/incompatibility is that within an organisational context the two systems should be extant. Where strategic HRM is well developed – and within the British context this is still a relatively rare phenomenon – perhaps on the lines suggested by contingency theory, then industrial relations may well be incorporated within the human resource strategy. Arguably, therefore, compatibility will depend upon the extent to which the collective aspects of the employment relationship are included as a major component of an organisation's human resource strategy. Where, however, the human resource strategy is imposed arbitrarily within a unionised organisation, and where little thought is

given to the industrial relations consequences, then the two systems will be in conflict with each other and even mutually exclude each other. In the UK, the problem of incompatibility arises as the consequence of the latter scenario, where senior managers on the one hand and senior convenors on the other each fear encroachment upon their prerogatives. Senior managers may also perceive themselves as having the upper hand and will take advantage of the weakened position trade unions are in nationally to further weaken them in the workplace. The 'softening-up' process, which includes introducing individualised forms of pay determination, thereby diluting collective bargaining, and excluding unions from other forms of decision making, is seen as a necessary condition for the implementation of 'full-blown' strategic HRM.

There can be little doubt that incorporation of the 'best' elements of an organisation's employment relations system into its HRM strategy is a possible way forward. Given the paucity of such human resource strategies and the piecemeal way HRM policies have been introduced within British organisations, the task remains daunting. The combined HRM/IR strategy must, according to Storey and Sisson (1993) satisfy three criteria:

> *The first of these is that the business strategy must be capable of being translated into operational action plans. Second, it must be made absolutely clear to whom the responsibility for developing the strategy actually belongs: does it rest, for example, at corporate headquarters, the divisional office or at each business unit? Third, some decision has to be taken about the overall thrust of the approach – will it, for example, aspire to match up to one of the 'best practice' models or will it reflect in contingency fashion, the particular needs of the organisation?* (p. 79)

The ongoing conundrum concerning individualism and collectivism in relation to management style (see Kessler and Purcell, 2003), the growing literature in relation to HR strategy (summarised by Boxall and Purcell, 2003), the accommodation of union voice mechanisms (see Chapters 3 and 7), and the extent to which high commitment and performance HR systems, either in concert with a union presence or not, affect performance and productivity (Nolan

and O'Donnell, 2003), will ensure that this discussion and its contradictions will continue to run.

The ongoing debate: the duality of HRM – strategy and well-being

The typologies concerning the role of HR and personnel considered earlier in this chapter (Tyson and Fell, 1986; Storey, 1992) emphasise how the HR function can best contribute towards improved employee and organisational performance by maintaining a clear distinction between strategy and practice. Francis and Keegan (2006) note that in recent years the focus of HRM has changed emphasis, moving towards a 'business partnership model' incorporating the CIPD-driven notion of 'thinking performers' who 'continuously update their professional knowledge and 'add value' to the business by which they are employed' (p. 232). To a certain extent this envisages a shift from 'practice' to 'strategy' – hence the term 'business partner'. The theoretical underpinning which has facilitated the shift in emphasis is based upon the work of Ulrich (1997) and Ulrich and Brocklebank (2005), who identify four key HR roles: *strategic partner; change agent; administrative expert; employee champion*. Here, the 'strategic partner' and 'change agent' roles are strategic in nature (the former being identical to the 'business partner' role which is CIPD's preferred label), while the 'administrative expert' and 'employee champion' roles are largely practical in nature.

Ulrich's model, while lending support to those who advocate a shift from the practical to the strategic, also gives legitimacy to those who argue that the 'employee champion' role is equally as important as the 'strategic partner' role. Indeed, the 'employee champion' role is regarded as crucial to the effective management of the employment relationship as it emphasises the need 'for fair treatment of employees and to treat individuals with dignity' (Francis and Keegan, 2006, p. 234). Dignity and fairness are, to be sure, noble HRM concerns, but the duality of the 'soft' (concern for employees) and the 'hard' (concern for performance and business objectives remain problematic and is reinforced in the research literature concerning the service sector

of the economy with particular reference to the call centre workplace to which we now turn.

RE-FOCUSING UPON THE SERVICE SECTOR: HRM IN PRIVATE SECTOR SERVICES

We have already noted the decline in traditional manufacturing in the UK, the shift from a Fordist to a post-Fordist economy, accompanied by the rise in the service sector of the economy, with the service sector in 2008 accounting for over 80 per cent of employment in the UK. As Legge (2005) comments: 'The stereotypical worker in UK industry is no longer the blue-collar, male, manual factory worker, still the focus of much empirical research on HRM pre-1995, in the guise of empowered/oppressed workers in "lean" "Japanese" car manufacturing plants' (p. 9). Currently, the emphasis is very much upon HRM issues involved in managing service sector employees and the main themes are identified below.

- There are, of course, different types of service work requiring slightly different HR management techniques and skills. Korczynski (2002), amongst others, distinguishes between three categories of service work. The *first* may be labelled the 'service factory' which is prevalent in hospitality services such as fast food outlets where the emphasis is upon uniformity of product delivery with workers acting as intermediaries between product and customer. The *second* is the 'service shop' which comprises both 'front of office' and 'back of office', the former being typified by call or contact centre work (see below). *Finally*, at the top of the service hierarchy, there is a range of professional services known collectively as 'knowledge work' undertaken by 'knowledge workers'. It is the second category – the service shop – that has witnessed the greatest expansion of employment within the service sector as a whole.

- A further relevant notion applicable to the service shop category is that of the 'customer oriented bureaucracy', developed by Frenkel *et al.* (1999), refined by Korczynsky (2002) and based upon Weber's (1964) original conception

of bureaucracy. The idea here is that within a 'rational' organisational bureaucracy, the employee is subject both to formal (managerial) authority and the customer as king. Within private service organisations 'additional demands for cost minimisation *and* delivering customer-oriented service process quality' reinforces employees' dual loyalties (Frenkel *et al.*, 1999, p. 6).

- HRM styles therefore differ according to the category of service work experienced. Within the service factory, the emphasis upon cost minimisation and efficient product delivery as within fast food outlets, some retail chains and some call centres demand variations on the 'hard' variety of HRM and all that entails. Within the service shop or customer-oriented bureaucracy which includes most call centres, a mix of 'hard' and 'soft' HRM is likely where 'HRM then becomes an exercise in combining both 'hard' and 'soft' approaches to walk the tightrope between the Scylla of bureaucratic controls and the Charybdis of necessarily allowing employees some discretion in managing the customer interface' (Legge, 2005, p. 11). Hence, where the employee is subject to strict and close management control via surveillance technology which is typical of most call centres, the 'soft' HRM rhetoric concerning for example 'teamwork', 'involvement', 'customer concern' and so on often belies the reality of working within a closely controlled work environment. Finally, within the 'knowledge work' context, professional knowledge workers are subject to a 'soft', high commitment management (HCM) regime (Legge, 2005).

Given the increased emphasis upon HRM and the employment relationship within both the public, and more importantly the private service sector, we now consider the nature of work and employment relations management within the call centre workplace.

Call centres: the new white-collar factories?

Handy (1995) has argued that the growth of the service economy (also referred to in Chapter 1) has been characterised by an expansion of 'knowledge work' within areas as diverse as local government, libraries, banking and insurance. However, much of this type of work 'requires little more of workers than information transfer' (Warhurst and Thompson, 1998), particularly in the largest growth area of recent years – that of telesales or call centres – and is often characterised by a process 'likely to be governed by scripted interactions, and monitored for deviance by supervisors' (p. 5). The call centre phenomenon is remarkable for its rapid expansion in recent years and warrants further consideration in relation to workplace organisation and the employment relationship (Exhibit 2.5).

The call centre is a relatively recent phenomenon which has changed the complexion of the British (and indeed global) workplace. The growth and application of telecommunications and computerised systems in the field of customer services, sales and information has been nothing short of spectacular during the past 15 years, and in 2005 employed 374,000 people nationwide, including front-line centre agents and operators (87,000) and customer care occupations (287,000) (ONS, 2005). Forecasts for future growth are contradictory, with Datamonitor (2004) forecasting growth to well over 500,000 agent positions by 2008. In contrast, ContactBabel (2007) has predicted that the industry will employ more than a million people by the end of 2009. Areas where call centres are expected to grow are local government and the outsourcing sector.

Call centres (or contact centres as they are also known) integrate computer and telephone technology, designed to provide fast and accurate services to clients, and also to monitor, tape record and measure staff performance. Centres are turning increasingly to 24-hour, seven-day operations as they compete with each other for customers and customer loyalty. Call centres are the consequence of companies across a whole range of services (banking, insurance and other financial services are probably the most visible) focusing more sharply on the needs of individual customers. In order to gain a competitive edge, and in order to offer this level of 'individual' service, the call centre was created to centralise all customer activities:

In today's highly competitive marketplace it is vital that companies build relationships with customers that are lasting and loyal by offering

Exhibit 2.5

Call centres: a selected chronology of events

1998: Call centre to create 2000 jobs

Barclays Bank is to set up a call centre in Sunderland to cope with the rapidly growing demand for its telephone banking service. The centre will open in the first quarter of next year [1999] and is expected to employ 2000 people over the next three years, more than tripling Barclay's telephone banking workforce. Barclaycall, the bank's specialised telephone service, was set up in 1994 and has more than 6 million customers. It employs 650 staff in Coventry, the site of its first call centre, and another 200 at a centre opened in Manchester last year. (*Financial Times*, 27 February 1998, George Graham)

1998: Ear-bashed operatives can find they are working the aural equivalent of Bentham's perfect prison

'I couldn't take it any more – it was driving me mad', says Pete after a year of quickfire phone calls starting and ending with a monotonous compulsory formula – 'Good morning, welcome to Barclaycall, my name is Pete . . . Is there anything else I can help you with? Thank you for calling. Good-bye'. He began to think he would wake up at night screaming that patter. 'I found it all right for most of my time, but at this time of the month, when everyone's just been paid, it was peep, one call, finish that, then peep, another one, all the time.' Pete's worked on sales and service advice for eight-hour shifts, usually with spells of a maximum two hours' phone work. Any 'walkaway' – hanging up to stop calls – was logged and required an explanation. 'There was no problem if you needed walkaway to go to the lavatory, say, but they needed to know how long you were off and why.' Calls are also monitored for quality and length. Calls that drag on mean fewer customers served.

Pete has no criticism of Barclaycall's running of the system. 'There's a career structure and salary rises on performance.' The starting rate of £10,310 rises to £12,129 (with most staff at Pete's call centre on the top rate). The stress of the job in such regulated circumstances becomes hugely increased at the 'cowboy' end of the trade, according to bank unions. According to an officer with the Banking Insurance and Finance Union, 'the worst places are dominated by fear – complain and you're out – and that's where the total control which the computer system allows leads to abuse. People get burned out and they're employing a constant stream of new ones. No one's happy and it's not efficient.'

Professor David Metcalf, of the London School of Economics, warned of the 'Orwellian potential' of such closely monitored work and said LSE studies of 100 call centres showed an eerie parallel with Jeremy Bentham's nineteenth-century 'perfect prison', the Panopticon. 'His principle was complete visibility of all prisoners from a central control centre, and that is what we have here.' (*The Guardian*, 27 February 1998, Martin Wainwright. Copyright Guardian News & Media Ltd 1998.)

1999: Women in teleservices 'frustrated' by routine

First findings from a new European study of work opportunities for women in the fast-growing call centre industry reveal widespread frustration with routine work, frequent reports of employee 'burn-out', training that is too often focused on the product rather than skills development, and limited opportunities for promotion. (IRS, 1999)

2001: Extreme monitoring and lack of breaks top TUC call centre complaints

Extreme monitoring by supervisors and not being allowed to take adequate rest breaks were the top two concerns of call centre workers calling the *It's your Call* hotline, according to a TUC report *Calls for Change*. The report features a 'league table' of complaints from call handlers. One in four complained about extreme monitoring of work and most of these (53 per cent) said they were monitored over when they went to the toilet and the length of time they spent there. Some had to ask permission to go and others complained of being hauled up in front of bosses

to explain why they were going so often. 15.5 per cent said they were not given adequate breaks at work and some of these said they were given no breaks at all even though they were working more than a six-hour shift – against the rules of the Working Time Directive. The report also revealed that call centre workers' salaries amount to only 60 per cent of average earnings. (TUC, 2001)

2002: Call centre recruitment policies are contradictory

Callaghan and Thompson (2002) argue that personnel policies are unsuitable in a call centre context because of the dichotomy between the sort of people that call centre managers 'think' they want and the sort of people more suited to call centre work practices. Only one in seven of job applicants was accepted within the case-study organisation, yet staff turnover was high. Callaghan and Thompson argue that this problem is endemic in the selection process where the focus was on identifying good communicators with 'personality', or 'naturals', but once employed and trained, recruits were 'reprogrammed' and instilled with a sense of conformity, told how to behave and given scripts to follow. The result, unsurprisingly, was high levels of frustration on the part of staff who had been selected for their outgoing personalities, but who found themselves unable to use them. Call centre managers emphasised achieving staff uniformity and hitting target numbers, rather than providing customers with a high-quality service. While managers talked in terms of 'building rapport with the customer', they failed to recognise that this was frequently at odds with their emphasis on hitting numerical targets.

2006: Public sector replicates the private sector

Taylor and Bain (2007) state: 'At least in principle, public sector management could introduce the most advanced technologies and techniques from the private sector . . . In NHS Direct the software (CAS) ultimately incorporated into clinical decision support systems was owned by insurance company Axa Assistance and was chosen because it was perceived as 'safe', 'consistent' and 'directive', enabling rapid call processing. In common with much call centre software based on rigid algorithms that prescribed detailed protocols, CAS minimised employee discretion and maximised speed.' (p. 357)

consistent quality of service and brand values. The call centre is central to this objective. (Customer Service Management, May 1998)

Most call centres are located outside London and the South East. The supply of greenfield sites, coupled with regional grants and lower wages, make migration of large 'tele' operations like British Airways ticket sales and London Electricity enquiries inevitable. Regional accents are also important; studies show that the public perceives the Scottish accent to convey reliability, while other accents such as the Brummie twang may convey criminal tendencies! (Fernie and Metcalfe, 1998).

The call centre workplace

Call centres are far from uniform and have many differentiating features which are summarised in Exhibit 2.6.

The majority of call centres deal with incoming calls; the employee or agent answers the call which is automatically directed or routed to him or her (calls are 'force-fed' where the agent has no control over whether or not to answer a call and as soon as one call is dealt with another is put through) and any relevant information required is computer processed. All time is monitored – whether the agent is actually dealing with calls, in between calls or unavailable for whatever reason. The technology that makes this possible is called 'automatic call distribution' (ACD). The new technology behind the centres enables management to wring every last ounce of productivity out of the workforce. Not a moment is wasted. For outward calls the computer does all the dialling and can detect and automatically drop calls if there is no reply. Sophisticated 'predictive software' allows computer-generated judgements concerning the length of the average call and calculates how many calls it needs to make

Exhibit 2.6

Differentiating features of call centres

1. **In house:** The call centre is part of a larger organisation and handles calls for that organisation only.
2. **Outsourced:** Usually a company in its own right which handles work from a variety of clients. An increasing number of UK companies outsource their work to companies in India and other countries.
3. **Type of work:** Inbound (receive) or outbound (solicit) call handling or a combination of the two.
4. **Degree of service:** Will embrace single function (outbound sales soliciting) or multiple functions such as sales, service, enquiries and technical matters.
5. **Unionisation:** Smaller call centres which are often outsourced are more likely to be union free.
6. **Size:** Call centres vary in size from very small with ten or so handlers to very large with hundreds of handlers, depending upon the nature of the business and the volume of work.
7. **Type of employment:** Non-standard employment is common in call centres, which may employ predominantly agency workers (common in outsourced call centres) who may also be part-time. Many call centres employ a mix of permanent and temporary full-time and part-time handlers.

in order to provide potential customers for the available workforce. Calls, whether outbound or inbound, are completely scripted; the computer prompts the operator through a series of questions to ask a customer. Supervisors can listen in at any time to check whether an employee – who will be expected to deal with several hundred clients a day – is adopting the correct (cheerful) tone and displaying enthusiasm for the job, sometimes referred to as 'emotional labour'.

The monitoring of behaviour and measurement of output, according to some research, at least equals if not exceeds the worst supervisory excesses of the Fordist assembly line. Fernie and Metcalfe (1998) describe the control process in the following terms:

The tyranny of the assembly line is but a Sunday school picnic compared with the control that management can exercise in computer telephony. Indeed, the advertising brochure for a popular call centre is titled TOTAL CONTROL MADE EASY. Critics refer to them as new sweatshops and battery farms. Agents' activities are monitored in real time by the supervisor. Real time screens display status information such as the number of existing calls in queue, how long the oldest call has been waiting, how many agents are on calls and how many are logged out or unavailable. Schedule adherence monitoring allows the supervisor to see whether agents are adhering to what they are scheduled

to be doing at any given moment. There is also, in most centres, the large LED display looking down on agents as a further reminder of their aims; the number of calls waiting to be answered in 6-inch high red letters is a big brother from which no-one can hide. (p. 7)

Fernie and Metcalfe use the analogy of Bentham's Panopticon (mentioned earlier) which Foucault (1979) adopts as a metaphor for the emergent workplace and which describes the sort of supervisory control process within workplaces which is evident in call centres:

All that is needed, then, is to place a supervisor in a central tower and to shut up in each cell . . . a worker. They are like so many cages, so many small theatres, in which each actor is alone, perfectly individualised and constantly visible . . . visibility is a trap. . . . Each individual is securely confined to a cell from which he is seen from the front by the supervisor; but the side walls prevent him from coming into contact with his companions. He is seen but does not see; he is the object of information, never a subject in communication . . . this invisibility is the guarantee of order . . . there are no disorders, no theft, no coalitions, none of those distractions that slow down the rate of work, make it less perfect . . . power should be visible and unverifiable. (p. 53)

The research by Fernie and Metcalf (1998) and others (Arkin, 1997; Baldry *et al.*, 1998; Belt, 1999) provides support for the 'sweatshop' view of call centres as being 'a contemporary version of the 19th century sweatshop or those dark satanic mills' (Knights *et al.*, 1999) or some sort of Orwellian construct. Most of these contributions adopt the Foucauldian perspective, emphasising the disciplinary implications of call centre work and the subservience of employees to the 'electronic panopticon'. Bain and Taylor (1999) provide another description of this type of work:

> *For many employed in the sector, the daily experience is patently of repetitive, intensive and frequently stressful work, based on Taylorist principles, which can result in employee 'burnout'. These pressures are exacerbated through the performance of 'emotional labour'. Individual employee performance is measured and monitored to an unprecedented degree by means of electronic surveillance, augmented by more traditional supervisory methods. Involvement and communication techniques, particularly teamworking, are more concerned with the exercise of managerial control, productivity improvements and social objectives than with any meaningful commitment to developing employee empowerment. Flat organisational structures severely constrain opportunities for promotion and further contribute to the sector's high labour turnover.* (p. 2)

The negative effects of call centre work may be greater for some types of worker than others and be more evident in some types of work situation than others (Deery *et al.*, 2002). It is important to note, however, that not all researchers share the pessimistic views of those cited above espousing what we may collectively label the 'sweatshop view'. An alternative perspective suggests that the relationship between call centre staff and the customer means that the employer is highly dependent on the social skills and emotional labour of staff to ensure that customers are treated well. This implies that the employment relationship has to be managed with care (Frenkel *et al.*, 1998, 1999; Knights *et al.*, 1999; Rose and Wright, 2005) and that management need to balance the requirements of productivity and performance with a concern for customer

satisfaction, focusing upon the quality of interaction between staff and customer. To that end, employers may well utilise the rhetoric, if not the application, of HRM policies in order to emphasise employee commitment and initiative through, for example, 'empowerment' techniques (Rose and Wright, 2005). This alternative perspective, therefore, emphasises a more positive image of call centre work, embracing 'the idea of a semi-professional, empowered worker who uses information technology as an opportunity to tailor services to the client whilst simultaneously using and developing their own skills [and arises] as a consequence of management wanting to customise the product or service to the requirements of the customer' (Simms *et al.*, 1999, p. 6). Frenkel *et al.* (1998, 1999) suggest that this approach, therefore, contains elements associated with professional identity and a knowledge of what the customer needs, and this has to be reconciled with standardised and bureaucratically imposed performance and productivity criteria. The type of organisational model Frenkel *et al.* advocate under these circumstances is called mass customised bureaucracy (MCB). Both the 'sweatshop' and the MCB models have implications for trade union recruitment within call centres (see below).

Self-evaluation activity 2.15

Employment relations in call centres
Response on website

Having read the descriptions of call centres and working conditions within them, try to come to some conclusion about the nature of employment relations within these workplaces.

Is the call centre management regime a threat to union organisation?

The apparently hostile working environment and the fact that workers are not always unhappy with it presents a challenge to those unions seeking to recruit within call centres. Some employers (and the size of employer, the work and the HRM practices adopted vary considerably) adapt personnel policies

to suit the circumstances, often on an ad hoc basis. Flexible and casual working arrangements, a heavy emphasis on teamworking and regular performance reviews are usual methods of binding the employee's interests to those of the company, and for employees there is some degree of stability and certainty in a situation where targets are simple and clearly defined, however difficult they may be to achieve.

At first sight it might be assumed that recruiting employees to the relevant union would be relatively easy as employees are working in close proximity to each other, will have similar interests and will be in constant communication with each other. The reality for most centres is that staff have very little time to communicate with each other and that discussion about collective issues is very difficult, as is identifying an individual to act as workplace representative. Constant monitoring and surveillance prevent agents from giving much, if any, time to union activities. Labour turnover and the extent to which casual staff are employed also hamper union recruitment efforts and activities.

However, the nature of unionisation is patchy, and while union density figures are difficult to ascertain in such a rapidly growing industry there is much to be done to increase the proportion of union members within it. Many of the smaller workplaces are not unionised, while the finance sector is notorious for treating unions with disdain. A senior Amicus-MSF officer (Liverpool branch) contends that: 'Employee relations in call centres are polarised. Where unions are recognised and staff consulted, terms and conditions and the working environment can be very good. However, if not, then working life can be very unpleasant.'

Nevertheless, there are indications that unionisation within the larger call centres is becoming more widespread. The influential annual Incomes Data Services (IDS) survey of pay and conditions in call centres reveals that of the 133 organisations in the survey, 47 per cent recognised a trade union for pay bargaining and a further 5 per cent recognised a union for individual representation only. The increase in recognition since 2000 has been slight but positive. IDS confirms that larger employers are more likely than smaller employers to recognise a union – hence the overall proportion of employees covered by collective bargaining arrangements is around 66 per cent, with a further 8 per cent covered by individual representation. Bain and Taylor (1999) point out that 'in Scotland, for example, just over one half of all employees worked in call centres with either a trade union or staff association' (p. 2). However, within the service sector as a whole, trade union membership has remained constant for the period 2001–6 (Grainger and Crowther 2007). One tendency which we have already noted is that some companies such as Virgin and Barclays have not extended recognition to their call centre operations (although there are signs that Barclays is conceding recognition to its call centres). A review of pay and benefits in call centres (IRS, 1998) within organisations formerly in the public sector reveals that unions had retained recognition in most of the call centres which had opened within the previous three years. However, unions had been excluded from several greenfield sites where alternative employee consultation machinery was in place (London Electricity, Northumbrian Water and Vertex).

In considering a range of union recruitment experiences within call centres, Bain and Taylor (1999, 2002) identify the following approaches.

'Official' union activity, with employer agreement

In instances where the union has an existing agreement with the employer, representatives may gain access to new call centres in order to encourage recruitment. Eagle Star, Abbey National and BT are examples of organisations which permit this type of approach. Occasionally, unions have successfully attempted to recruit and negotiate terms and conditions before the opening of a new call centre within organisations as diverse as First Direct and the Inland Revenue. A more recent development has been the establishment of formal partnership agreements, for example with the Co-operative Bank and Banking, Insurance and Finance Union (BIFU), and Scottish Widows and Amicus-MSF. In addition, as mentioned above, the call centre division of Barclays, Barclaycall, which previously resisted all attempts by Financial and Banking Services Union (UNIFI) to recruit its call centre employees, apparently shifted its stance in early 1999 towards acceptance of a partnership approach which

has provided union access to its Salford, Coventry and Sunderland centres.

Union activity, without employer agreement

In the face of employer resistance and hostility to union recognition within companies such as IBM, Kwik-Fit, BSkyB, Midland Bank (owned by HSBC) and Direct Line, unions have covertly attempted to organise with varying degrees of success. Bain and Taylor (2002) provide examples of tactics union activists have employed to attract new members in hostile environments (see Exhibit 2.7).

Joint union activity

There is evidence of growing co-operation between unions in various sectors concerned with call centre representation. For example, the Finance Sector Direct Staff Forum (FSDF) is a union organisation concerned solely with call centre matters and meets on a regular basis. It comprises the major unions within the sector, such as BIFU and Amicus-MSF, and many staff associations, many of which have affiliated to the TUC. In 1999, BIFU, UNIFI and the NatWest Staff Union made a decision to merge to create a new union (UNIFI) with around 200,000 members. Bain and Taylor (1999) point out that:

> *Whilst it would be starry-eyed idealism to suggest that elements of inter-union rivalry no longer exist, nevertheless, it is clear that the finance unions have made a hard-headed judgement based on the logic of developments in the sector. The result is far-reaching collaboration. The regular meetings provide a constructive forum for the collective discussion of problems and union successes. There can be no doubt that this co-operation is perceived to be of general benefit, perhaps particularly for the smaller unions, and seems likely to encourage further moves towards formal mergers.* (p. 254)

In 2004 UNIFI merged with Amicus which in turn merged with the TGWU in 2007 to form Unite and it remains to be seen whether there will be more concerted action to encourage unionisation in the sector.

Bain and Taylor (2002), in their analysis of the finance sector call centre, demonstrate that despite uneven rates and extent of union presence and

Exhibit 2.7

Recruiting members in hostile environments: the historical experience of UNIFI

At a recent seminar discussing union recruitment, while acknowledging the continuing prioritisation over pay, hours of work, etc., by potential recruits, union activists and officials described particular tactics they had employed to attract new members in hostile environments [Finance Sector Unions (FSU) seminar, Bishop's Stortford, 18 February 1999]. These included consciously targeting non-union members in the course of the union rep carrying out workplace health and safety inspections and audits and taking a strong stand in defence of employees on disciplinary charges. In one call centre no less than three-quarters of the staff were facing disciplinary action and representation in these cases clearly enhanced the union's credibility. In other centres activists have compiled lists of new employees from information supplied by existing union members. Company logos and colours have been successfully and strategically placed on union recruitment material. At other centres special subscription rates have been offered to new staff. Colourful reports testify to the creative and varied methods employed to enhance the unions' profile. In one centre representatives utilised local electronic mail to reach beyond the ranks of existing members. In-workforce activists adopted a philosophy of 'stick your nose in everywhere' leading to a small but no less significant achievement where the union negotiated the relaxation of a strict dress code imposed by the employer.

Source: Bain and Taylor, 2002, p. 252

voice, 'research indicates some growth in both union membership and recognition' (p. 258). This is due partly to the provision of personal services by the unions involved, partly to the diminishing extent of inter-union rivalry and partly as a consequence of union recognition provisions of the ERA 1999 as amended by the ERA 2004.

Targeting recruitment: some successes and failures

Self-evaluation activity 2.16
Organising and servicing approaches
Response on website

In Chapter 3 we identify two approaches which could be adopted by unions in shaping their recruitment strategies – the organising approach and the servicing approach. Briefly summarise these approaches and indicate how these might be applied to the call centre contexts.

Some union successes

- Over 1800 members were recruited by the CWU in two of BT's new call centres at Doncaster and Newcastle. BT has three other unionised call centres, the largest of which is at Warrington employing over 1700 people. The vast majority of new recruits were agency staff who do not work on a BT contract.
- In the finance sector, the First Direct call centre in Leeds was set up in 1989. Of the 3500 staff now employed in First Direct, about one-third have joined BIFU. After initial refusal of recognition, the union secured a collective agreement whereby office representatives have successfully negotiated above-inflation pay deals and fended off performance-related pay in relation to salaries.
- The Norwich Union Direct operation in Shef-field has been open for two years and employs around 350 staff of which 150 are members of Amicus-MSF. Call centre union representatives have access to management and take up issues which arise, including salary levels, rosters and the distribution of overtime. Difficulties for

Amicus-MSF stem from the high staff turnover rate, currently 33 per cent annually, and this raises problems for organisation and continuity of workplace representation.

One problem ultimately resolved

During the late 1990s, Barclays Bank call centres, or Barclaycall centres, presented a difficult problem. At Barclaycall Coventry, Barclay's (then) in-house union UNIFI (now part of Unite) recruited almost half the 300 workers, but only after sustained campaigning and despite the fact that unions were not recognised within Barclaycall.

Prior to the recruitment campaign, and as far as could be ascertained, staff working in the call centre were therefore at a disadvantage in relation to Barclays' mainstream bank employees who were unionised. Recognition had not been granted to Barclaycall employees despite there being a recognition agreement in force for the other employees of the bank. In other respects, staff at Barclaycall Coventry were able to take advantage of the reasonably good facilities that management provided such as a gym and good restaurant and cafeteria facilities. In addition, there were opportunities to take part in local community projects.

On the downside, although there was a consultative committee of sorts, it appeared to be relatively powerless in the absence of a union presence. The challenge for UNIFI was to convince management that unionisation of the workforce would not pose a threat to the management of the employment relationship while at the same time emphasising the important contribution of the union in fighting for the interests of the employees within the call centre with due regard for the wellbeing of the business (see also the UNIFI Annual Report, 1999).

Nevertheless, organising efforts at Barclaycall were rendered more difficult by the following factors:

- there was a 40 per cent yearly staff turnover rate;
- there were no identifiable workplace representatives; and
- Barclays was, at the time, disinterested in 'social partnership' despite union overtures.

However, following a change of policy by top management, Barclays endorsed the 'partnership' model. This development and the greater clout of

the merged finance unions to form UNIFI in 1999 actually facilitated union recognition within Barclaycall itself.

Offshoring and call centres

Offshoring in the service sector is a relatively new phenomenon and the evidence available indicates that it is a growing trend receiving increased media attention (Heckley, 2005). One of the first examples of early UK offshoring is British Airways, which in May 2002 created call centres in India to handle flight booking and processing. Some insurance companies and banks are amongst those companies outsourcing their call centre activities to India and other English speaking countries. Prudential announced its intention to transfer 1000 jobs but agreed to delay this after union pressure for a ban on compulsory redundancies. Norwich Union (parent company Aviva) decided in February 2003 to open a new call centre in India for 1000 employees. Amicus-MSF is involved in resisting these developments, mainly by attempting to secure guarantees of no redundancies. HSBC bank is already processing UK-originated calls in centres in Asia, as is Lloyds TSB. BT is to open two Indian call centres – in Bangalore and Delhi – employing 2200 people by 2004. This development is part of plans which will see BT's UK-based centres drop from around 100 to 31, with the number of call centre workers falling from 16,000 to 14,000. Despite assurances of no permanent UK employees being made redundant, and no compulsory lay-offs amongst agency staff, the union involved (CWU) is suspicious of BT's motives and is resisting the move.

The allure of offshoring for British companies includes the wage bill. Research by Adecco (2003) suggested that British companies would create up to 100,000 call centre jobs in India by 2008. As the wage bill of an up-and-running call centre comprises two-thirds of its operating costs, and with Indian call centre workers earning around £1200 a year – less than one-tenth of the earnings of their British equivalents – companies would be able to reduce their costs substantially. In addition, India has a surplus of skilled and highly educated workers, many of them graduates, who find that the wages in call centres compare extremely favourably or even exceed those wages paid in their chosen occupations.

Apart from the relatively routine call centre operations, Indian advisers are provided with training in accents and briefed on the weather, football scores and even latest TV soap story lines in order to hold conversations with British customers.

As far as future developments are concerned, larger UK companies may well continue to offshore, despite the risks inherent in such moves, such as the distance involved, the control and quality issues and possible political instability. Smaller firms are less likely to take the plunge as the risk of things going wrong tends to increase. Despite the outsourcing trend, which Datamonitor predicts will increase, especially for financial services firms, growth in the UK market will also increase, but less rapidly than hitherto at around 4 per cent annually. Indeed, IDS (2007) found that only 6 per cent of the firms surveyed expected to cut jobs in the next 12 months while 60 per cent had intentions of hiring new staff.

Summary and concluding remarks

The service sector is the largest sector of the economy in both its contribution to output and the proportion of labour it employs. Over 76 per cent of all those in work and over 72 per cent of gross value added in the economy is attributed to the service sector (Heckley, 2005).

Notwithstanding the current state of offshoring, UK call centres have now established themselves as major employers and more people work in call centres than in coal, steel and vehicle production put together. Within these new workplaces, which vary in size, there is strict computer-operated monitoring and supervisory processes and an intensification of work which exceeds that of the traditional assembly line. Despite this, the limited evidence available suggests that call centre workers, or 'agents' are not unhappy with their lot. Suggested reasons for this concern age (a relatively young workforce), response to challenges pertaining to 'customer care', and the benefits of teamworking. Salary levels are also higher than in other parts of the core business (the financial sector, for example). Unionisation is patchy; the problems of organising and recruiting exacerbated by high staff turnover rates and employer union recognition problems. There is

a need for more research on the nature of HRM, union and non-union patterns of organisation within call centres, pay structures and employee attitudes which impinge upon job-related and employment relations contexts. The call centre provides an opportunity to study emerging forms of workplace employment relations which contrast with those in the traditional Fordist, mainly manual, full-time and unionised workplaces.

EMPLOYERS' ASSOCIATIONS

The legal definition of an employers' association is provided in section 122 of the Trade Union and Labour Relations (Consolidation) Act 1992, the essence of which is that:

> *Employers' associations are organisations which consist wholly or mainly of employers or individual owners of undertakings of one or more descriptions and whose principal purposes include the regulation of relations between employers of that description or those descriptions and workers or trade unions.*

This definition implies that employers' associations exist mainly for industrial relations purposes, so it is important to note that non-industrial relations activities concerning commercial matters, for example, feature prominently for most associations.

Their origins

Early employers' associations which formed during the eighteenth century became widespread and fairly influential, and, like trade unions which formed much later in the nineteenth century, were locally based. During this early period there was little effort to co-operate with each other, although individual associations often used to influence rates of pay and some agreed standard wage rates and/or piecework rates. Where there was collaboration, this would be of a commercial and not industrial relations nature. The growth of trade unions in the nineteenth century, however, provided an impetus to the growth of employers' associations as they responded to the threat of organised labour. Many associations became national federations representing employers

in particular industries, examples of which include the Engineering Employers' Federation, the Building Trades Federation and the Shipbuilding Federation. The development of national federations was accompanied during the early twentieth century by a move towards industry-wide bargaining, which became the dominant form of collective bargaining until the 1960s.

During this period, employers, either individually or increasingly through the employers' associations, attempted to counter the growing power of trade unions by adopting oppositionary strategies, which Gospel and Palmer (1993) identify as:

- the use of blackleg or replacement labour in industries such as docks and shipping;
- the use of the so-called 'Document' which 'was a signed undertaking in which a worker accepted, as a condition of employment, that he would leave, or not join, a trade union' (p. 77) and which helped to overcome attempts at unionisation; and
- the use of blacklists of 'militants' compiled by the associations themselves.

During the course of the twentieth century outright opposition to trade unions declined and collective bargaining mechanisms were set up which sought to regulate, jointly with unions, external matters such as pay across the industry, while seeking to minimise union influence within the organisation in an attempt to retain employers' assumed 'right to manage', or managerial prerogative.

Their structure

Employers' associations are heterogeneous in their structure. Gennard and Judge (1997) identify three types. The first is the national federation to which local employers' associations belong, such as the Engineering Employers' Federation (EEF) which comprises 15 independent organisations. The second is the single national body, such as the British Printing Industries Federation (BPIF) 'which is divided into six regions for administrative and representational purposes (until 1982 this was a federated body like the engineers, but a serious national dispute in 1980 caused it to re-invent itself)' (p. 69). The third type is the single association with a

national membership, such as the British Ceramic Federation. Associations are made up of companies of different sizes and the largest of them (the National Farmers' Union is the largest) are organised into autonomous local associations (engineers) or non-autonomous district associations (printers). The number of employers' associations has declined dramatically since the late 1960s, from around 1350 in 1968, to 228 in 1994, to 187 (comprising 94 'listed' and 93 'unlisted') in 2002, and this is indicative of a steady decline in their importance (Certification Office, 2002).

Their traditional functions

1. *Multi-employer bargaining*. A typical response to union demands was for employers within one industry to act collectively. This had the advantage of uniting the strength of the employers against the unions and ensured some degree of uniformity in basic wage rates.
2. *Limiting the scope of collective bargaining*. Although many employers eventually recognised trade unions, they succeeded in limiting the scope of bargaining to industry and external labour market issues, including wages, hours and overtime rates. All issues concerning managerial control within the workplace were left for management itself to determine and included supervision, manning of machines, discipline, hiring and firing and promotion, as the following example of the engineering industry demonstrates:

> In the engineering industry, the protection of managerial prerogatives came to dominate employer association policy and lay behind major confrontations with the unions in 1851–2, 1897–8 and 1922. The skilled engineering workers formed the first central, national union in the UK. In the latter half of the nineteenth century they felt that their traditional craft status and job control was threatened by new technology which enabled once-skilled metal-working jobs to be accomplished by unskilled machine minders. They used their union to demand that the new machine-tools be manned by craftsmen at skilled rates and they resisted the introduction of piecework. On their side, the employers were eager to take advantage of the new technology to increase their control over work and reduce the power of craft groups. They sought to cheapen the labour process by employing less skilled labour and to manage the deskilled work by introducing piecework systems. The battles over managerial prerogative did not occur simply because unions were challenging employers' controls of the labour process, but because employers themselves were tightening and centralising their control of workplace activity. The engineering union lost the confrontation and was forced to sign agreements accepting management's right to operate machines and manage labour as management chose. (Gospel and Palmer, 1993, p. 80)

The above example was typical of what Goodrich (1975) described as the struggle between management and workers over the 'frontier of control'.

3. *Disputes procedures*. In common with the establishment of industry-wide collective bargaining, employers' associations adopted industry-wide disputes procedures as a means of resolving disputes. Only when the procedure was exhausted could constitutional strike action take place.
4. *Industry-wide agreements*. The increase in the number of employers' associations in particular industries not only facilitated the development of employers' federations, but also the establishment of industry-wide bargaining.

Their decline and reasons for it

The dramatic decline in the numbers of employers' associations has been accompanied by some decline in their power and influence, particularly within the industrial relations area. Some of the reasons for this decline lie within the area of collective bargaining, including the following:

- The decline in industry-wide, multi-employer bargaining has meant that employers' associations have become increasingly less attractive to larger organisations in particular, and smaller employers may be reluctant to pay a joining fee if national agreements cannot be sustained. According to the IRS (2002) survey of 50 employers' associations, 28 per cent of them still represent employers in national negotiating forums.

- Larger firms from the 1960s onwards increasingly preferred to negotiate their own agreements independently of employers' associations. This meant that, in effect, industry-agreed wage rates were being undermined so that 'by 1989, only minimum rates of pay and working time remained live issues at national level (for example, in the engineering industry)' (Gennard and Judge, 1997, p. 70).
- Increasingly, larger organisations have their own specialist personnel/HRM departments for managing employment policy and so rely less, or not at all, upon the employers' association for help and advice.
- Some organisations left, or did not join, because of their policy towards trade unions; for example, some organisations may have adopted a 'non-recognition' policy towards trade unions.

Are there exceptions?

Gospel and Druker (1998) examine the electrical contracting industry, which is one of the few cases where multi-employer national bargaining has remained strong (see also Chapter 6). Within engineering, national bargaining is also fairly resilient. For example, the Engineering Construction Industry Association (ECIA) continues to engage in industry-level pay bargaining with trade unions and believes that such arrangements continue to bring benefits for all parties concerned in the particular circumstances of the engineering construction industry (see Mini case 2.7).

Mini case 2.7
The ECIA

The Engineering Construction Industry Association (ECIA) is the principal trade and employer association for the UK engineering construction industry. Its members include many of the largest companies in the world that carry out engineering projects across the globe. Others are much smaller British contractors employing skilled craftspeople on sites all over the UK. Onshore, its members employ around fifty to sixty thousand personnel, including plant designers, planners, project engineers and managers, as well as site workpeople.

The ECIA provides its members with a collective voice to represent their interests on all matters affecting their industry. It is supported by a statutory Industry Training Board and, in partnership with two other employers' associations and three trade unions (Amicus, GMB and Unite), operates the National Agreement through the industry's National Joint Council. Activities of member companies include design and procurement, project management, construction, installation, erection commissioning and decommissioning, dismantling and re-erection, together with the repair and maintenance of power plant; steelwork structures and bridges; steel production and other primary production plant; pipework; process, chemical and petrochemical plant; erection of steel plates, tanks and pressure vehicles; pumps, compressors, switchgear, instrumentation and associated engineering construction activities onsite.

Member firms range in size from those with less than 10 employees to others with more than 3000 and they employ a total of some 60,000 employees (including head office as well as site staff). While the majority of employer members are small and medium-sized enterprises (SMEs), the organisation also covers over 50 multinationals.

Predecessor organisations to the ECIA have operated in the industry since 1918. The ECIA itself was formed in April 1994 through the amalgamation of two associations, the National Engineering Construction Employers' Association (NECEA) and the Oil and Chemical Plant Constructors' Association (OCPCA).

The ECIA is an autonomous organisation whose policies are controlled by a council elected by its members. The association is a member of the CBI and EEF (Engineering Employers' Federation). It is the main employer signatory to the National Agreement for the Engineering Construction Industry (NAECI), and any changes are negotiated through the industry's National Joint Committee (NJC).

The ECIA also represents the interests of member companies within the industry's Engineering Construction Industry Training Board (ECITB) and to government departments, the European Commission, the Health and Safety Executive and the Client's Group. The association's committees, on which many companies are represented, play a 'vital role' in identifying members' interests.

Professional staff based at the association's regional offices aim to provide practical advice and assistance on all employment issues, and to maintain expertise in specific local issues that can be of assistance to members 'before, during and after they undertake work in the particular region'. The association's regional offices

are based in Belfast, Glasgow, Newcastle, Manchester, Sheffield, Oakham and Bristol. The regional staff are backed up by the ECIA's Westminster-based head office staff, including specialists in health and safety, employment and contractual law and other commercial services.

Source: Adapted from IRS, 1998 and www.ecia.co.uk 2008

Their future

Not every employers' association declined in importance, and some larger firms have remained members for reasons other than collective bargaining. For example, a growing number of associations have broadened their advisory services in relation to disciplinary, dismissal and redundancy procedures. These services have become more important to members with the growth in employment legislation since the 1970s concerning unfair dismissal, discrimination on grounds of race and gender, health and safety and equal pay issues. One area in which

employers' associations are featuring more prominently is in representing the views of members to other organisations, including political lobbying (Gennard and Judge, 2002, p. 167). If there is a future for employers' associations, then it lies in the extent to which they diversify their services to accommodate the needs of an increasingly volatile membership. However, with the continuing decline in industry-wide bargaining, it appears unlikely that employers' associations will regain their former importance in respect of their industrial relations functions and that 'employers' associations were a far less important part of the institutional structure of industrial relations in 1990 than they were a decade or more earlier' (Millward *et al.*, 1992, p. 351). The WERS surveys (Millward *et al.*, 2000; Kersley *et al.*, 2006), point to a continuing and sustained decline in the reliance upon the provision of information and advice to members, although it is still an important function (see IRS survey below), and in multi-employer bargaining concerning pay and other terms of employment. The IRS (2002) study of 50 employers' and trade associations confirms at least some of these trends (see Exhibit 2.8).

Exhibit 2.8

Findings from the IRS 2002 survey of 50 employers' and trade associations

- With regard to the provision of free advice, this was still an important function in 2002. The main areas on which advice is provided by a number of employers' associations include: health and safety (45), training and education (45), employment law (35), industrial/employment relations (30), discipline (27), equal opportunities (26), pay (22), employee welfare (20), recruitment (18).
- Lobbying and campaigning is an important role undertaken by employers' associations acting as pressure groups, providing a voice for members. Lobbying and campaigning targets include central government – the most popular with 45 out of the 50 associations acting in this capacity, followed by the European Union (25). Other areas include local government (13), trade unions (8) and the general public (7).
- Concerning the decline of multi-employer bargaining, the main traditional function of employers' associations, only 14 out of 50 associations are actively involved, and even where they are negotiated, many members do not follow the terms of the agreement. Moreover, only seven associations reported that a joint industry board or other third party exists to administer agreements.
- Only 13 of the 50 associations operate a disputes procedure that allows for the interpretation of the multi-employer pay and conditions agreement and disputes outside this agreement. In general, there has been very little change in the numbers of employers making use of the procedure, the main issue of contention over the past year being redundancy and recognition.
- Nearly all associations provide newsletters and other forms of communication for members and 35 have a members-only website. Thirty-nine associations provide networking opportunities via a members-only website.

Although the advent of New Labour has had little impact upon employers' associations so far, most of the IRS survey's panel of associations expected the role of associations or members' perceptions of associations to change over the next four years. One response highlighted the latter:

> Our role has not changed, but the members' perceptions of the importance of that role has increased – due in no small measure to the increased complexity of employment legislation. (IRS, 2002, p. 13)

Summary points

- Four models of personnel management have been identified, and comprise:
 - the normative model;
 - the descriptive functional model;
 - the critical evaluative model; and
 - the descriptive behavioural model.
- In addition, a number of typologies of personnel management have been devised by Tyson and Fell (1986) and Storey (1992). These typologies are not mutually exclusive as they reflect the entire range of personnel practice.
- Personnel management has been dogged by contradictions stemming from different interpretations of the personnel management role (often by practitioners themselves), the historical development of personnel management, the nature of the market economy and assumptions of patriarchy within capitalist society.
- There is a continuing debate concerning the relationship between HRM and ER on the one hand, and HRM and personnel management on the other. With regard to the latter relationship, it could be argued that while there are similarities and differences between the two, HRM has, at least in theory, a stronger strategic orientation than personnel management.
- Accompanying the shift from Fordism to post-Fordism, there has been continuing and consistent growth in both public and private sector services, with implications for the nature of HRM within the sector. The example of the call centre workplace was selected for consideration as call centre employment typifies the nature of much of contemporary service work.

- Employers' associations have declined in both numbers and importance as industry-wide, multi-employer bargaining itself has declined in favour of single-employer bargaining.

RELEVANT WEBSITES

www.cbi.org.uk (Confederation of British Industry) An important site for the organisation representing UK employers. More general in scope than most websites cited in this book with employment relations issues not featuring too prominently.

www.cipd.co.uk (Chartered Institute of Personnel and Development) An extremely useful site for members, but limited access for non-members. The professional association for HR managers.

www.dti.gov.uk (Department of Trade and Industry) A comprehensive and useful site which contains plenty of information relevant to business and employers.

www.berr.gov.uk (Department for Business, Enterprise and Regulatory Reform) The successor to the DTI.

REFERENCES

Ackers, P., Smith, C. and Smith, P. (1996) 'Against all odds? British trade unions in the new workplace', in Ackers, P., Smith, C. and Smith, P. (eds) *The New Workplace and Trade Unionism*. London, Routledge

Adecco (2003) *Best Locations for Contact Centres*. Oxfordshire, Omis Research

Arkin, A. (1997) 'Hold the production line'. *People Management*. February

Bach, S. and Winchester, D. (1994) 'Opting out of pay devolution? The prospects for local pay bargaining in UK public services'. *British Journal of Industrial Relations*, 32, 2, 263–82

Bach, S. and Winchester, D. (2003) 'Industrial relations in the public sector', in Edwards, P. (ed.) *Industrial Relations Theory and Practice*, 2nd edn. Oxford, Blackwell

Bacon, N. (2001) 'Employee relations', in Redman, T. and Wilkinson, A. (eds) *Contemporary Human Resource Management*. Harlow, Financial Times/ Prentice Hall

Bacon, N. and Storey, J. (1993) 'Individualisation of the employment relationship and implications for trade unions'. *Employee Relations*, 15, 1, 5–17

Bacon, N. and Storey, J. (1996) 'Individualism and collectivism and the changing role of trade unions', in Ackers, P., Smith, C. and Smith, P. (eds) *The New Workplace and Trade Unionism*. London, Routledge

Bain, P. and Taylor, P. (1999) '"An assembly line in the head": work and employee relations in the call centre'. *Industrial Relations Journal*, 30, 2, 213–30

Bain, P. and Taylor, P. (2002) 'Union recognition and organisation in call centres'. *Industrial Relations Journal*, 33, 3, 246–61

Baldry, C., Bain, P. and Taylor, P. (1998) 'Bright satanic offices: intensification, control and team Taylorism', in Thompson, P. and Warhurst, C. (eds) *Workplaces of the Future*. London, Macmillan

Beardwell, I.J. (1997) 'How do we know how it really is? An analysis of the new industrial relations', in Beardwell, I.J. (ed.) *Contemporary Industrial Relations: A Critical Analysis*. Oxford, Oxford University Press

Beaumont, P.B. (1995) *The Future of Employment Relations*. London, Sage

Beauvoir, Simone de (1972) *The Second Sex*. Harmondsworth, Penguin

Belt, V. (1999) 'Are call centres the new sweatshops?'. *The Independent*, 3 January

Bevan, W. (1987) 'Creating a no-strike environment: the trade union view'. Paper to Confederation of British Industry Conference, London

Beynon, H. (1975) *Working for Ford*. Wakefield, EP Publishing

Blyton, P. and Turnbull, P. (1994) *The Dynamics of Employee Relations*. London, Macmillan

Blyton, P. and Turnbull, P. (1998) *The Dynamics of Employee Relations*, 2nd edn. London, Macmillan

Blyton, P. and Turnbull, P. (2005) *The Dynamics of Employee Relations*, 3rd edn. London, Macmillan

Boxall, P. and Purcell, T. (2003) *Strategy and Human Resource Management*. Houndmills, Palgrave Macmillan

Braverman, H. (1974) *Labour and Monopoly Capital: The Degradation of Work in the Twentieth Century*. London, Monthly Review Press

Brewster, C., Gill, C. and Richbell, S. (1983) 'Industrial relations policy: a framework for analysis', in Thurley, K. and Wood, S. (eds) *Industrial Relations and Management Strategy*. Cambridge, Cambridge University Press

Brown, W. (1993) 'The contraction of collective bargaining in Britain'. *British Journal of Industrial Relations*, 31, 2, 189–200

Brown, W., Marginson, R. and Walsh, J. (2003) 'The management of pay', in Edwards, P. (ed.) *Industrial Relations Theory and Practice*, 2nd edn. Oxford, Blackwell

Burnham, J. (1945) *The Managerial Revolution*, Harmondsworth, Penguin

Callaghan, G. and Thompson, P. (2002) '"We recruit attitude": the selection and shaping of routine call centre labour'. *Journal of Management Studies*, 39, 2, 233–55

Certification Office (2002) *Annual Report of the Certification Office*. London, HMSO

Chandler, A.D. (1962) *Strategy and Structure: Chapters in the History of the American Industrial Enterprise*. Cambridge, MA, MIT Press

Child, J. (1964) 'Quaker employers and industrial relations'. *Sociological Review*, 12, 3, 293–315

Child, J. (1969) *The Business Enterprise in Modern Society*. London, Harper and Row

Child, J. (1984) *Organisation: A Guide to Problems and Practice*. London, Harper and Row

Clark, I. (1997) 'The state and new industrial relations', in Beardwell, I.J. (ed.) *Contemporary Industrial Relations: A Critical Analysis*. Oxford, Oxford University Press

ContactBabel (2007) *UK Contact Centres in 2007 – The State of the Industry*. Sedgefield

Cully, M., Woodland, S., O'Reilly, A. and Dix, G. (1999) *Britain at Work*. London, Routledge

Datamonitor (2004) *Call Centres in Europe*. London, Datamonitor

Deery, S., Iverson, R. and Walsh, J. (2002) 'Work relationships in call centres; understanding emotional exhaustion and employee withdrawal'. *Journal of Management Studies*, 39, 4, 471–96

DoE (Department of Employment) (1992) *People, Jobs and Opportunity*. London, HMSO

Donovan (1968) *Report of the Royal Commission on Trade Unions and Employers' Associations 1965–1968*, Cmnd 3623. London, HMSO

Douglas, M. (1980) 'Autoworker can only do as well as Head Office permits'. *Albuquerque Journal*, 24 July, A5

Drucker, P. (1961) *The Practice of Management*. London, Mercury Books

Edwards, R. (1979) *Contested Terrain: The Transformation of the Workplace in the Twentieth Century*. London, Heinemann

Engels, F. (1892) 'The condition of the working class in England', in *Marx and Engels on Britain*. Moscow (1953), Foreign Languages Publishing House

Farnham, D. (1997) *Employee Relations in Context*. London, IPD

Farnham, D. and Pimlott, J. (1995) *Understanding Industrial Relations*. London, Cassell

Fernie, S. and Metcalfe, D. (1998) '(Not hanging on the telephone): payment systems in the new sweat shops'. *Centre for Economic Performance*. London, LSE

Ford, H. (1922) *My Life and Work*. New York, Doubleday Page

Foucault, M., (1979) *Discipline and Punish*. Harmondsworth, Penguin/Peregrine Books

Fowler, A. (1987) 'When chief executives discover HRM'. *Personnel Management*, January

Fox, A. (1966) *Industrial Sociology and Industrial Relations*. Royal Commission Research Paper No. 3. London, HMSO

Fox, A. (1974) *Beyond Contract: Work, Power, and Trust Relations*. London, Faber & Faber

Fox, A. (1985) *Man Mismanagement*. London, Hutchinson

Francis, H. and Keegan, A. (2006) 'The changing face of HRM: in search of balance'. *Human Resource Management Journal*, 16, 3, 231–49

French, J.R.P. and Raven, B. (1960) 'The bases of social power', in Cartwright, D. and Zander, A.F. (eds) *Group Dynamics: Research and Theory*. New York, Harper and Row

Frenkel, S., Korczynski, M., Shire, K. and Tam, M. (1998) 'Beyond bureaucracy? Work organisation in call centres'. *The International Journal of Human Resource Management*, 9, 6, 957–79

Frenkel, S., Korczynski, M., Shire, K. and Tam, M. (1999) *On the Front Line: Organisation of Work in the Information Economy*. Ithaca, NY: ILR

Gallie, D., Penn, R. and Rose, M. (eds) (1996) *Trade Unionism in Recession*. Oxford, Oxford University Press

Geary, J.F. (1995) 'Work practices: the structure of work', in Edwards, P. (ed.) *Industrial Relations: Theory and Practice in Britain*. Oxford, Blackwell

Geary, J.F. (2003) 'New forms of work organisation: still limited, still controlled, but still welcome?', in Edwards, P. (ed.) *Industrial Relations Theory and Practice*, 2nd edn. Oxford, Blackwell

Gennard, J. and Judge, G. (1997) *Employee Relations*. London, IPD

Gennard, J. and Judge, G. (2002) *Employee Relations*, 3rd edn. London, CIPD

Gennard, J. and Judge, G. (2005) *Employee Relations*, 4th edn. London, CIPD

Giddens, A. (1989) *Sociology*. Oxford, Polity Press

Goodrich, C.L. (1975) *The Frontier of Control: A Study in British Workshop Politics*. London, Pluto Press

Gospel, H. and Druker, J. (1998) 'The survival of national bargaining in the electrical contracting industry: a deviant case?' *British Journal of Industrial Relations*, 36, 2, 249–67

Gospel, H.F. and Palmer, G. (1993) *British Industrial Relations*. London, Routledge

Grint, K. (1993) *The Sociology of Work*. Oxford, Polity Press

Grainger, H. and Crowther, M. (2007) *Trade Union Membership 2006*. London, ONS

Guest, D. (1989) 'Human resource management: its implications for trade unions and industrial relations', in Storey, J. (ed.) *New Perspectives in Human Resource Management*. London, Routledge

Guest, D. and Hoque, K. (1994) 'The good, the bad and the ugly: employment relations in new non-unionised workplaces'. *Human Resource Management Journal*, 5, 1, 1–14

Guest, D., Michie, J., Sheehan, M., Conway, N. and Metochi, M. (2000) *Human Resource Management and Performance*'. Birkbeck College, University of London School of Management and Organisational Psychology

Handy, C. (1993) *Understanding Organisations*. London, Penguin

Handy, C. (1995) *The Future of Work*. W.H. Smith Contemporary Papers, No. 8

Hartmann, H. (1982) 'Capitalism, patriarchy and job segregation by sex', in Giddens, A. and Held, D. (eds) *Classes, Power and Conflict: Classical and Contemporary Debates*. London, Macmillan

Heckley, G. (2005) 'Offshoring and the labour market: the IT and call centre occupations considered'. *Labour Market Trends* September 2005, 373–85

Horton, S. (1997) 'The employee relations environment', in Farnham, D. (ed.) *Employee Relations in Context*. London, IPD

Hounshell, D.A. (1984) *From the American System to Mass, Production, 1800–1932: The Development of Manufacturing Technology in the United States*. Baltimore, MD, Johns Hopkins University Press

Huczynski, A. and Buchanan, D. (1991) *Organisational Behaviour*. London, Prentice Hall

Hunter, C. and MacInnes, J. (1994) 'Employees and labour flexibility: the evidence from case studies'. *Employment Gazette*, June

Hyman, R. (1980) 'Trade unions, control and resistance', in Esland, G. and Salaman, G. (eds) *The Politics of Work and Occupations*. Milton Keynes, Open University Press

Hyman, R. (1987) 'Strategy or structure? Capital, labour and control'. *Work, Employment and Society*, 1, I, 25–55

IDS (Incomes Data Services) (2007) *Pay and Conditions in Call Centres, 2006*. London, IDS

IPM (1963) 'Statement on personnel management and personnel policies'. *Personnel Management*, March

IRS (1998) 'Back to the future: a new role for employers' associations'. *IRS Employment Trends*, No. 647

IRS (1999) 'Women in teleservices frustrated by routine'. *IRS Employment Trends*, No. 675

IRS (2002) 'Stormy waters ahead for employers' associations?' *IRS Employment Trends*, No. 743

Johnson, G. and Scholes, K. (2003) *Exploring Corporate Strategy*. London, Prentice Hall

Kelly, J. (2001) 'The role of the personnel/HR function in multinational companies'. *Employee Relations*, 23, 6, 536–57

Kelly, J. and Gennard, J. (2001) *Power and Influence in the Boardroom: The Role of the Personnel Director*. London, Routledge

Kenney, M. and Florida, R. (1993) *Beyond Mass Production*. Oxford, Oxford University Press

Kersley, B., Alpin, C., Forth, J., Bryson, A., Bewley, H., Dix, G. and Oxenbridge, S. (2006) *Inside the Workplace: Findings from the 2004 Workplace Employment Relations Survey*. London, Routledge

Kessler, I. and Purcell, J. (1995) 'Individualism and collectivism in theory and practice', in Edwards, P. (ed.) *Industrial Relations: Theory and Practice in Britain*. Oxford, Blackwell

Kessler, I. and Purcell, J. (2003) 'Individualism and collectivism in industrial relations', in Edwards, P. (ed.) *Industrial Relations Theory and Practice*, 2nd edn. Oxford, Blackwell

Knights, D., Calvey, D. and Odih, P. (1999) 'Social managerialism and the time-disciplined subject: quality-quantity conflicts in a call centre'. Paper for the 17th Annual International Labour Process Conference, University of London

Korczynski, M. (2002) *Human Resource Management in the Service Sector*. Basingstoke, Palgrave

Lavalette, M. and Kennedy, J. (1996) *Solidarity on the Waterfront: The Liverpool Docks Lock Out of 1995/96*. Liverpool, Liver Press

Legge, K. (1995) *Human Resource Management: Rhetorics and Realities*. London, Macmillan

Legge, K. (2005) *Human Resource Management: Rhetorics and Realities*, 2nd edn. London, Macmillan

Littler, C.R. and Salaman, G. (1985) 'The design of jobs', in Littler, C.R. (ed.) *The Experience of Work*. Aldershot, Gower

Mackay, L. and Torrington, D. (1986) *The Changing Nature of Personnel Management*. London, IPM

Marchington, M. and Parker, P. (1990) *Changing Patterns of Employee Relations*. London, Harvester Wheatsheaf

Miller, S. (1993) 'The nature of strategic management', in Harrison, R. (ed.) *Human Resource Management, Issues and Strategies*. Wokingham, Addison-Wesley

Millward, N. (1994) *The New Industrial Relations*. London, Policy Studies Institute

Millward, N., Bryson, A. and Forth, J. (2000) *All Change at Work?* London, Routledge

Millward, N., Stevens, M., Smart, D. and Hawes, W.R. (1992) *Workplace Industrial Relations in Transition*. Aldershot, Dartmouth

Nichols, T. (1969) *Ownership, Control and Ideology*. London, Allen and Unwin

Nichols, T. (1980) 'Management, ideology and practice', in Esland, G. and Salaman, G. (eds) *The Politics of Work and Occupations*. Milton Keynes, Open University Press

Nichols, T. (1986) *The British Worker Question*. London, Routledge

Nolan, P. and O'Donnell, K. (2003) 'Industrial relations, HRM and performance', in Edwards, P. (ed.) *Industrial Relations Theory and Practice*, 2nd edn. Oxford, Blackwell

Ogbonna, E. (1992) 'Organisational culture and human resource management: dilemmas and contradictions', in Blyton, P. and Turnbull, P. (eds) *Reassessing Human Resource Management*. London, Sage

Oliver, N. and Wilkinson, B. (1992) *The Japanisation of British Industry*. Oxford, Blackwell

ONS (Office for National Statistics) (2005) *Labour Force Survey*, Spring 2005

Pahl, R.E. and Winkler, J.T. (1974) 'The economic elite', in Stanworth, P. and Giddens, A. (eds) *Elites and Power in British Society*. Cambridge, Cambridge University Press

Poole, M. (1980) 'Management strategies and industrial relations', in Poole, M. and Mansfield, R. (eds) *Managerial Roles in Industrial Relations*. London, Gower

Poole, M., Mansfield, R., Blyton, P. and Frost, P. (1981) *Managers in Focus*. Farnborough, Gower

Procter, S. and Ackroyd, S. (2001) 'Flexibility', in Redman, T. and Wilkinson, A. (eds) *Contemporary Human Resource Management*. Harlow, Financial Times/Prentice Hall

Purcell, J. (1987) 'Mapping management styles in employee relations'. *Journal of Management Studies*, 24, 5, 533–48

Purcell, J. and Ahlstrand, B. (1994) *Human Resource Management in the Multi-Divisional Company*. Aldershot, Dartmouth

Purcell, J. and Gray, A. (1986) 'Corporate personnel departments and the management of industrial relations'. *Journal of Management Studies*, 23, 2, 205–23

Purcell, J. and Sisson, K. (1983) 'Strategies and practice in the management of industrial relations', in Bain, G.S. (ed.) *Industrial Relations in Britain*. Oxford, Blackwell

Ramsay, H., Scholarios, D. and Harley, B. (2000) 'Employees and high performance work systems; testing inside the black box'. *British Journal of Industrial Relations*, 38, 4, 501–31

Rose, E. and Woolley, T. (1992) 'Shifting sands? Trade unions and productivity at Rover Cars'. *Industrial Relations Journal*, 23, 4, 257–67

Rose, E. and Wright, G. (2005) 'Satisfaction and dimensions of control among call centre customer service representatives'. *The International Journal of Human Resource Management*, 16, 1, 136–60

Sabel, C.F. (1982) *Work and Politics: The Division of Labour in Industry*. Cambridge, Cambridge University Press

Salaman, G. (1984) *Working*. London, Ellis Horwood/ Tavistock

Salamon, M. (1998) *Industrial Relations: Theory and Practice*, 3rd edn. London, Prentice Hall

Scullion, H. and Starkey, K. (2000) 'In search of the changing role of the corporate human resource function in the international firm'. *International Journal of Human Resource Management*, 11, 6, 1061–81

Simms, M., Stewart, P., Delbridge, R. and Heery, E. (1999) 'Unionising call centres'. Paper for the 17th Annual International Labour Process Conference, University of London

Sisson, K. (1993) 'In search of HRM'. *British Journal of Industrial Relations*, 31, 2, 201–10

Sisson, K. (1995) 'Human resource management and the personnel function', in Storey, J. (ed.) *Human Resource Management: A Critical Text*. London, Routledge

Smith, A. (1910) *The Wealth of Nations*. London, Dent and Sons (first published 1776)

Storey, J. (1987) *Developments in Human Resource Management: An Interim Report*. Warwick Papers in Industrial Relations, no. 17. Coventry, University of Warwick

Storey, J. (1992) *Developments in the Management of Human Resources*. Oxford, Blackwell

Storey, J. (1995) *Human Resource Management: A Critical Text*. London, Routledge

Storey, J. and Sisson, K. (1993) *Managing Human Resources and Industrial Relations*. Milton Keynes, Open University Press

Taylor, F.W. (1947) *Scientific Management*. New York, Harper and Row

Taylor, P. and Bain, P. (2007) 'Reflections on the call centre: a reply to Gluckman'. *Work, Employment and Society*, 21, 2, 349–62

Terry, M. and Edwards, P.K. (eds) (1988) *Shopfloor Politics and Job Controls*. Oxford, Blackwell

Thompson, P. (1990) *The Nature of Work*. London, Macmillan

Thurley, K. and Wood, S. (eds) (1983) *Industrial Relations and Management Strategy*. Cambridge, Cambridge University Press

Torrington, D. and Hall, L. (1987) *Personnel Management: A New Approach*. London, Prentice Hall

Trevor, M. (1988) 'Toshiba's new British company: competitiveness through innovation'. Unpublished paper, University of Cardiff, Wales

TUC (2001) *It's Your Call*. London, TUC

Tyson, S. (1995) *Human Resource Strategy: Towards a General Theory of Human Resource Management*. London, Pitman

Tyson, S. and Fell, A. (1986) *Evaluating the Personnel Function*. London, Hutchinson

Ulrich, D. (1997) *HR Champions*. Boston, MA, Harvard University Press

Ulrich, D. and Brocklebank, W. (2005) *The HR Value Proposition*. Boston, MA, Harvard University Press

Warhurst, C. and Thompson, P. (1998) 'Hands, hearts and minds: changing work and workers at the end of the century', in Thompson, P. and Warhurst, C. (eds) *Workplaces of the Future*. London, Macmillan

Warner, W. and Low, J.O. (1947) *The Social System of the Modern Factory*. New Haven, Yale University Press

Watson, T.J. (1977) *The Personnel Managers: A Study in the Sociology of Work and Industry*. London, Routledge

Watson, T.J. (1986) *Management, Organisation and Employment Strategy. New Directions in Theory and Practice*. London, Routledge

Watson, T.J. (1995) *Sociology, Work and Industry*. London, Routledge

Weber, M. (1964) *The Theory of Social and Economic Organisation*. New York, Free Press

Wickens, P. (1993) 'Lean production and beyond: the system, its critics and its future'. *Human Resource Management Journal*, 3, 4, 75–90

Zeitlin, M. (1989) *The Large Corporation and Contemporary Classes*. Oxford, Polity Press

TRADE UNIONS AND THE EMPLOYMENT RELATIONSHIP

INTRODUCTION

The main focus of this chapter is upon the collective organisation of employees. Trade unions are still by far the most common form of collective organisation, and these will now be considered in greater detail. The eminent labour historian, Henry Pelling, stated that 'for better or for worse, the structure of present-day British trade unionism can be understood only in terms of its historical development' (1992, p. 1). The chapter therefore begins by tracing the development of trade unions and examining their significance in both historical and contemporary contexts. We then look at trade union structure and government, together with the role of shop stewards, and this is followed by a review of the changing nature of trade unions in the late twentieth and early twenty-first century. Finally, we consider the importance of the role of the TUC and the European context of trade unionism. It should be noted that collective and other forms of representation in non-union settings are examined in Chapter 7.

Learning outcomes

When you have read this chapter, you should be able to:

1. Understand how trade unions have evolved.

2. Identify the functions, role and significance of trade unions in historical and contemporary contexts.

3. Appreciate the importance of trade union structure, government and democracy.

4. Explain the functions and roles of shop stewards.

5. Explain the changing nature of trade unions and the problems faced by them in the twenty-first century.

THE DEVELOPMENT OF BRITISH TRADE UNIONS

We have defined trade unions, outlined their characteristics, aims, objectives and functions in Chapter 1, and it would be useful to review these before reading on. Trade unions in Britain are in a state of continuous evolution with their development spanning three tumultuous centuries. According to Hyman (2003, p. 45), the evolutionary longevity of British trade unionism explains three important and distinctive features associated with unionism:

- 'structural complexity and fragmentation' (variations in size, nature of representation, variety of structure, recruitment patterns etc.);
- 'an ambiguous orientation to political action' (this embraced revolutionary socialism prior to 1926, syndicalism through to political incorporation and 'legitimation' via the Labour Party); and
- 'the potent moral value attached to the principle of "free collective bargaining"'.

Organisational beginnings

Consider the following quote:

Historically, they [trade unions] came into being as a response to capitalism, a form of social and economic organisation where the ownership of the means of production is in private hands, where the object of production is the competitive pursuit of profit in a free market and where the majority, excluded from the ownership of the means of production, are compelled to sell their labour power in order to live. For workers, a reasonably paid, secure job is an essential basis for a decent life. But their wages are a cost to their employers, an important item to be set against profit, and thus to be minimised and dispensed with entirely where labour is insufficiently profitable. Trade unions, therefore, take the stage in order to redress the bargaining imbalance between employer and employee and render the conflict between capital and labour a more equal one, replacing individual competition for jobs by collective organisation as a means to

protect wage levels and the conditions and security of employment. (McIlroy, 1988, p. 1: a modified form of the above quote appears in McIlroy, 1995, p. 2)

McIlroy's quote is instructive for the following reasons. Firstly, trade unionism represents an organisational reaction to the development of capitalism and the process of industrialisation, a dialectical relationship of opposition to, and dependency upon, capitalism. Secondly, the conflict of interest between buyers and sellers of labour power can only be resolved by collective organisation of workers into trade unions engaging in the process of collective bargaining. According to Webb and Webb (1898, p. 173):

Instead of the employer making a series of contracts with isolated individuals, he meets with a collective will and settles, in a single agreement, the principles upon which, for the time being, all workmen of a particular group, or class, or grade will be engaged.

This establishes the 'common rule' of collectively agreed standards (rates of pay, working hours) governing the employment of groups of workers. Thirdly, the need to protect wage levels was guided by the Webbs' doctrines of *supply and demand* and *a living wage*. The doctrine of supply and demand underlined the importance of wage costs being linked to the price of the product or service. However, employers could use this as a justification for reducing wage costs should the product price fall, thereby giving rise to wage-cutting. The doctrine of a living wage was partly a response to endemic wage-reduction strategies of employers and partly due to the resistance of semi-skilled and unskilled workers within the 'new unionism' of the late nineteenth century (see below) to employer wage-cutting.

Self-evaluation activity 3.1

A 'living wage'
Response on website

What, in your opinion, do you think is meant by the term 'a living wage'?

From trade clubs to the 'new unionism'

The first chapter of the Webbs' *History of Trade Unionism, 1866–1920* (1920) provides an interesting description of the origins of trade union organisation in Britain. Trade unions did not grow out of the medieval craft guilds (although some point to a possible association (Hyman, 2003, p. 44)), but can be traced to the local trade clubs of the eighteenth century (Flanders, 1972; Reid, 2005). Whereas the Webbs could point to evidence of temporary associations of wage earners meeting to 'take a social pint of porter together' (1920, p. 23), trade clubs were local associations of skilled craftsmen in many trades whose aims were to protect the wages and status of the craft and their members and to reinforce the tradition of apprenticeship. Some of the trade clubs evolved into what became known as friendly societies which were:

> *societies of skilled tradesmen whose members formed an 'aristocracy of labour' . . . best able to build their organisation on traditions of apprenticeship and the defence of the craft against the unqualified. This they did with the help of a system of friendly benefits. . . . Out of work benefit . . . was most important in preventing men from transgressing the rules of the trade. Accident, sickness, superannuation benefits, even emigration grants, were also provided with the same end in view.* (Flanders, 1972, pp. 12–13)

This 'method of mutual insurance' (a term coined by the Webbs) provided an impetus to the growth of national unions in the latter half of the nineteenth century. All this took place within a national environment uniquely hostile to the development of trade unions. At a time of rapid industrialisation and the emergence of large, unskilled urban workforces, the Combination Acts of 1799 and 1800 ushered in an era of outright repression of trade union activity. Despite this, trade unionism took root, albeit under the guise of friendly societies, and when the Combination Acts were repealed in 1824, workers could organise openly and new unions were formed.

Geographically, trade union development was uneven and intermittent during this period and tended to be localised on an urban or regional basis rather than being focused upon nationally based institutions.

Exhibit 3.1 illustrates the temporary nature and uneven development of unionisation within the rapidly growing coal industry.

The repeal of the Combination Acts and the passing of a new Act in 1825 gave trade unions limited protection, but they remained legally vulnerable. There were many prosecutions and heavy sentences culminating in the most celebrated case of the 'Tolpuddle Martyrs', six agricultural labourers who were sentenced to seven years' transportation in 1834 on the charge of administering 'illegal oaths'. Attempts were made to overcome the problems of local and regional unions and associations, culminating in the establishment of one general union for all workers. There was a rapid rise and decline in 1834 of Robert Owen's Grand National

Exhibit 3.1

The example of the coal industry

A few attempts at organisation had been made in the Scottish and South Wales fields as early as the 1820s, but these proved largely unsuccessful. However, by the 1840s 'county unions' had been formed in the coal mining communities in Durham, Northumberland, Lancashire, Yorkshire and Staffordshire as well as in Scotland. In 1842, delegates from these areas formed a Miners' Association of Great Britain and Ireland, which by 1844 claimed to represent some 70,000 miners, about a third of the total labour force in the industry at that time . . . Union organisation in the mining industry was then set back by economic slump and unsuccessful strikes. By the late 1840s, the Association had all but collapsed, although mining unions survived in several of the coal mining counties.

Source: Martin *et al.*, 1996, p. 43

Consolidated Trades Union. The union failed owing to the cumbersome nature of its organisational structure, limited funds and because the employers in the building trades, where it had most support, retaliated by insisting on their employees signing 'the Document', an undertaking to leave or not to join a trade union.

By the 1850s, many local or regional societies of craftsmen amalgamated to form what became known as new model unions, the first of which was the Amalgamated Society of Engineers (ASE) which was formed in 1851. The case of the ASE is an interesting one and Exhibit 3.2 is an account of how it came into being.

The trend towards amalgamation and national organisation became widespread during the second half of the nineteenth century, which witnessed an unprecedented growth in trade unionism and other representative bodies such as trades councils. A number of factors specific to this period accounted for the growth of trade unions. These include:

- the increasing scale of industry;
- the widening of the market for labour and goods;
- improved transport;
- blurring of occupational boundaries;
- the greater mobility of workers; and
- the growth of employers' associations.

By 1869 membership of unions affiliated to the newly formed Trades Union Congress (TUC) had grown to around 250,000 and by the mid-1870s membership stood at over 500,000. Also during the 1870s, the legal status of trade unions became established through legislation in 1871, 1875 and 1876. The Trade Union Act of 1871, which was amended in 1876, stated that trade unions were no longer unlawful simply because their objectives were 'in restraint of trade'. The Act also gave unions a large measure of freedom from legal proceedings in the conduct of their internal affairs. The Conspiracy and Protection of Property Act of 1875 made collective bargaining and peaceful picketing lawful.

The next phase of development was the most important one because it involved the unionisation of semi- and unskilled workers on a permanent basis and laid the foundations of the modern trade union movement; it became known as the new unionism.

From new unionism to the General Strike

As Reid (2005) points out, until the last quarter of the nineteenth century there had been few signs of the emergence of trade unionism amongst less killed workers, but this was about to change dramatically. The success of the London dockers' strike in 1889 gave an added impetus to union-organising activity in much the same way as the formation of the ASE did earlier. In that year the dockers' union (the forerunner of the Transport and General Workers' Union) and the gas workers' union (the precursor of the General, Municipal, Boilermakers' and Allied Trades Union) were formed. We now look in more detail at the gas industry, which is a notable example of the rise of new unionism.

Mini case 3.1
The gas industry

Hobsbawm (1974) provides an insightful analysis of the explosive growth of unionisation within this nineteenth-century public utility. Space does not permit much detail. We start with a short quote which is followed by summary points.

> *The British gas industry presents a remarkable and extreme example of the rise of trade unionism. Gas workers were – in common with others who were conventionally thought of as 'unskilled' – believed to be incapable of strong and stable trade unionism; and indeed, with short-lived and local exceptions, they had never formed important and lasting organisations before 1889. For 17 years before that date they possessed no traceable unions at all. Yet when in 1889 they demanded concessions which, it was generally held, would raise the industry's wage-bill by one-third, their demands were conceded virtually without a struggle. Moreover, the new unions maintained themselves against subsequent counter-attack. Over a large part of the country, therefore, the industry changed overnight from a wholly unorganised into an exceptionally unionised one; with important effects on its structure and policy. Why did it change? Why did it remain changed? What effects had the rise of the union?* (p. 158)

The following summary points attempt to throw some light upon these questions. For a fuller appreciation of the issues, however, you should read Hobsbawm (1974), Chapter 9.

1. The gas industry was municipally owned and immune from competition. There was no incentive to technological change and labour costs were relatively low. Technical change was therefore sluggish and gas making in the 1880s was substantially similar to what it had been at the beginning of the century. The gas-making process involved carbonisation (the work of making and stoking fires), filling retorts with coal, spreading it and drawing the coke.
2. Stokers and firemen, the key workers in the whole process, had an exceptionally strong bargaining position. But the work was casual, semi-skilled at best, and there were extreme seasonal fluctuations in demand which resulted in pools of surplus labour.

3. 'A considerable impetus was therefore needed to overcome this deadweight of tradition and irregular labour' (p. 162). Gas was an expanding industry and a labour-intensive one, and the labour force had scarcely grown during the 1880s. The impetus for change therefore lay in:
 (a) the intensification of work (increased output using the same number of workers) owing to the expansion of demand for gas;
 (b) increased worker effort for the same wage.
4. By 1888 there were signs of unrest, and in 1889 separate unions were formed in Birmingham, London and Bristol. With the formation of a national union organisation later that year and the dispute which followed, the employers gave way: 'Yet between June and December 1889 most of the important gasworks in the country yielded, hardly even testing the men's strength' (p. 165). The workforce gained important concessions (higher rates of pay; an eight-hour day) and the union consolidated its new-found strength.
5. 'The effect of the union on the industry was striking and wholly beneficial . . . [and] gas embarked on a programme of major technical reorganisation and re-equipment' (p. 166). There is no doubt that the explosion of unionisation in the gas industry shook the employers out of their complacency, but the unions, throughout the remainder of the nineteenth century 'succeeded, even in a period of depression, in safeguarding their status against the machine' (p. 171).

In summary, the history of the unionisation of the gas workers is significant in three respects. Firstly, we are provided with a neat and elegant model of 'trade union explosion': unions, previously almost unknown, become universal overnight. Secondly, gas presents a notable example of an industry which has been modernised almost entirely because of the pressure of labour and the beneficial effects of labour militancy. Finally, gas illustrates the considerable strength of groups of indispensable workers in a situation of technological innovation, especially when this takes place within an already old, well-established and heavily capitalised industry.

The new unionism of unskilled and semi-skilled workers was now firmly established and expanding.

From 1900 to 1914, trade union membership increased from 2 to 4 million, with most of the increase coming after 1910. This period also witnessed the beginnings of non-manual or white-collar unionism amongst teachers, clerks and local authority (municipal) workers.

Political development

An alliance between some trade unions and socialist political groupings emerged in 1900 and became known as the Labour Representation Committee which, in 1906, changed its name to the Labour Party. This political development indirectly influenced legislation during this period (an Education Act, 1907; the Old Age Pensions and Coal Mines [Eight Hours] Acts, 1908; trade boards for fixing legal minimum wages in the 'sweated' trades in 1909 and the National Health Insurance Act of 1912).

The Taff Vale and Osborne judgments

More direct assistance to unions was given by the fledgling Labour Party in relation to decisions made by the law courts against certain unions. One of the most infamous was a judgment given by the House of Lords in the case of the *Taff Vale Railway Company* v *Amalgamated Society of Railway Servants* (1901) which appeared to violate the provisions of the 1871–76 legislation. In this case, the Taff Vale Railway Company sued the union for damages as a result of financial loss through strike action and the verdict was given in favour of the company. The judgment had serious implications for trade unions generally because any strike action would then put union funds at risk. The Trade Disputes Act of 1906 removed this liability and defined the law concerning industrial action until the 1980s. More specifically the Act:

- protected union funds from civil claims for damages;
- legitimised acts done in contemplation or furtherance of a trade dispute so that they were no longer regarded as 'civil conspiracy';
- ended the liability for inducing a breach of contract of employment by persons acting in a trade dispute; and
- made peaceful picketing lawful.

Following this parliamentary success, the political activities of trade unions were next threatened by the Osborne Judgment of 1909 (*Osborne* v *Amalgamated Society of Railway Servants*) in which the House of Lords held that 'it was illegal for a trade union to spend its funds on other purposes than the industrial objects specified in previous Acts' (Flanders, 1972, p. 17). The judgment had serious implications for the Labour Party, which relied heavily on the unions for financial support. Eventually, in 1913, the Trade Union Act reversed the Osborne Judgment and permitted trade unions, with the consent of their members, to set up a separate political fund in order to pursue political objectives.

The only other major piece of legislation affecting trade unions until 1971 was the Trade Disputes and Trade Union Act of 1927, repealed in 1946.

Self-evaluation activity 3.2

Trade union rights

The response is given below

Britain is the only country where trade unions do not have a positive right to strike, organise or to engage in collective bargaining. Why do you think this has come about?

The following quote from Hyman (1995) explains this unique situation:

> *The method by which trade unions and collective bargaining were eventually legalised was not, as in many other countries, by establishing a positive right to organise, to negotiate and to strike, but by defining an area of industrial relations 'immunities'. The key legislative initiatives – the Trade Union Act of 1871, the Conspiracy and Protection of Property Act of 1875 and the Trade Disputes Act of 1906 – were designed to remove the specifically legal obstacles to collective action. But while workers were thus free to organise collectively, the employer was equally free to dismiss a worker for joining a trade union; while unions were entitled to bargain collectively, employers were equally at liberty to refuse to negotiate; and while a union could lawfully call a strike 'in contemplation or furtherance of a trade dispute', striking workers were in breach of their contracts of employment and might therefore be dismissed (or even sued individually for damages). This is in marked contrast to many*

other national labour law regimes, which oblige employers to respect workers' right to unionise, to bargain 'in good faith' with representative unions, and to impose no penalty (beyond withholding pay) on those who legally strike. The absence of statutory regulation, a condition known as voluntarism or collective laissez-faire, was long celebrated as an index of maturity and sophistication. The Royal Commission on Labour in 1894 concluded its lengthy deliberations by insisting that strong organisations of workers and employers, and voluntary agreement between the two parties, offered the most stable and desirable basis for regulating employment. For almost a century thereafter, a major policy commitment of governments of every political complexion was to encourage the institutions and processes of collective self-regulation. (pp. 29–30)

The rise of the shop stewards

Shop stewards are unpaid representatives of trade unions at the workplace and are fairly prominent and widespread within most contemporary unionised work organisations. However, 'there is no evidence that shop stewards achieved any widespread significance much before the First World War' (Coates and Topham, 1988, p. 144). Workplace representation did exist in some nineteenth-century industries such as coal mining and engineering. The first major manifestation of shop steward organisation came with the First World War, a period during which there was considerable co-operation between many unions and government in the interests of prosecuting the war. The policy of co-operation was not accepted so readily by many politically minded workers who regarded employers as profiteering from the war while keeping wages down. There were many unofficial stoppages of work in industries such as munitions, organised by local shop stewards combining to form 'Shop Stewards' Committees', 'Workers' Committees' and the like. These local organisations amalgamated to form the Shop Stewards' Movement (also known as the National Workers' Committee Movement).

The Shop Stewards' Movement articulated the dissatisfaction with wartime conditions and gave political expression to the socialist aims of syndic-alism and workers' control of industry. After a brief interval of optimism spanning a period up to 1920, during which there was a strong belief in the power of the labour movement to change the social order, the great post-war depression gave rise to a harsher reality, and the years up to 1926 were punctuated by a number of national disputes spear-headed by the 'Triple Alliance' of unions representing railwaymen, transport workers and miners. All this activity culminated in the nine-day General Strike, 'the most momentous event in the development of British trade unionism' (Flanders, 1972, p. 19). According to Flanders, the strike demonstrated both the solidarity of the organised workforce and the failure of syndicalism to change society through direct action. The victory of the government, the ongoing depression and falling trade union membership, from a peak of 6.5 million in 1920, signalled a sober reality for both unions and employers.

From the General Strike to 1945

The remainder of the 1920s and 1930s witnessed a more constructive period of industrial relations based on co-operation rather than conflict. It was a time of consolidation and amalgamation for trade unions. The trend towards fewer and larger unions became established, and many of the large unions of today, such as the TGWU, were formed at this time. The unions and the TUC worked more closely with the Labour Party in order to secure change through the ballot box rather than on the picket line. Trade union membership reached its lowest point in 1933, but thereafter membership increased yearly to reach 8 million in 1945 and this tended to reflect, amongst other things, the changed perception of trade unionism as a willing partner in the conduct of national economic and industrial affairs.

Self-evaluation activity 3.3

The development of the trade union movement
Response on website

We have concentrated on the history and development of the trade union movement up to 1945. Identify the main factors which you think account for this development.

Postscript: unions in contemporary perspective: 1945–2008

This brief section summarises some of the main developments affecting trade unions during the second half of the twentieth century. These developments will be considered in more detail either in this chapter or in subsequent chapters to which reference will be made.

- The number of trade unions has continued to decline: in 2002 there were 199 (70 TUC-affiliated) unions, further reducing to 186 in 2006 while in the 1920s there were more than 1300 (see Table 3.3, p. 157).
- Much of this decline can be attributed to mergers and the disappearance of smaller unions.
- Trade union membership rose steadily in 1945 from around 8 million to a peak of 13.289 million in 1979: thereafter, membership fell steadily to 7.801 million in 1997, picked up slightly and levelled at 7.897 in 2001 and 7.779 in 2002. Since 2002 there has been a further slow decline to 7.473 million in 2006 (Certification Office Annual Report, 2007) (year beginning figures; see also Table 3.3).
- During the 1980s and 1990s, non-manual union membership declined only very slowly and now makes up around 50 per cent of total membership, much of this being concentrated within the public sector (see below).
- Since 1979 trade union bargaining power has declined quite substantially for a number of reasons which will be considered in Chapter 6.
- During the 1980s trade union government and democracy were affected by legislation concerning secret ballots, election of union officials and rights of union members (see below).
- Workplace representation and shop steward organisation, despite setbacks in the 1980s, continues to play an integral part in the conduct of industrial relations at workplace level (see below).

Summary points: historical development

- Trade unions developed as a response to the rise of capitalism and the realisation that conflicts of interest between employees and owners could only be resolved collectively.
- During the latter part of the eighteenth and early decades of the nineteenth centuries, trade unions evolved from trade clubs/friendly societies having purely local organisational roots to 'new model' unions of craftsmen, some of which became regionally based.
- The second half of the nineteenth century saw many union amalgamations and moves towards national organisation. In recognition of this trend, the TUC was formed as a national co-ordinating body for affiliated trade unions.
- During this period, unions representing interests of semi-skilled and unskilled workers developed, a phenomenon known as the 'new unionism'. Workplace unionism became more widespread and with it the increased importance of the shop steward.
- After the collapse of the General Strike, there was a period of consolidation with unions and the TUC working closely with the Labour Party.

TRADE UNION STRUCTURE, ORGANISATION AND DEMOCRACY

To a large extent the contemporary structure of British trade unions reflects its uneven development over the years, as described in an earlier section. As we shall see, classification of unions into general categories or types has its problems as Coates and Topham (1988) point out: 'unions come in a wide variety of sizes, shapes and "types": their classification is no longer the simple matter it used to seem' (p. 41). A definition of trade union structure would need to take into consideration the following factors:

- the recruitment patterns to reflect the occupational and skills profile of a union's membership;
- the geographical concentration or dispersion of actual and potential membership; and
- the recruitment strategies adopted by unions.

Trade union organisation and democracy (also referred to as trade union government) is concerned with the internal structure of unions and the extent to which they are representative of their members. It is also concerned with how a union is managed

or administered. Efficient and professional administration is equally as important as the effective and democratic representation of the membership, particularly in the larger, more complex unions with composite memberships.

Trade union structure

As we have mentioned, trade union structure is a fairly complex affair, and for many years there was a reliance upon what has become known as the simple or traditional classification which takes a broadly chronological approach to the issue. The problems with this approach resulted in an alternative approach (although it may also be regarded as complementary) which looks at unions on a continuum ranging from open to closed (Turner, 1962; Hughes, 1968). A third typology considers union structure in terms of recruitment of membership on vertical or horizontal principles. Again, this approach may be seen as complementing rather than supplanting the traditional classification. More recently, it has been argued that structural developments may be explained by reference to strategic issues facing British trade unions (Willman, 2004) and this is explored later in the chapter.

Before we examine these approaches to union structure, it is important to note that:

- trade unions, in common with most other organisations, are dynamic in the sense that they are continually changing (evolving, declining or amalgamating) and are responsive not only to their memberships but also to the wider society, both reactively and proactively; given this propensity for unions to change, then any method of classification is, at best, arbitrary; and
- it is more appropriate to regard the approaches to structure as conceptual constructs, assisting our analysis of trade unions in the 'real' world rather than presenting us with neat categories into which unions can be fitted.

The traditional classification

The traditional classification presents us with a number of ideal types which for our purposes may be regarded as simplified conceptual constructs or abstractions providing a set of characteristics enabling us to identify each union with each type.

The first type is that of the craft union. The craft union is characterised by:

- the principle of recruiting members from a specific skilled trade usually entered through a system of apprenticeship in order for apprentices to qualify as unionised tradesmen;
- the control of the numbers of apprentices entering the trade and the regulation of the length and nature of apprenticeship; and
- the generation of 'fraternity' amongst the members based on a sense of shared skills and similar levels of earnings.

Industrial, technological and other changes have rendered craft unions virtually obsolete. In the face of such changes, the craft union that seeks to preserve its 'pure' form would experience a damaging loss of membership and inevitable extinction. In order to survive, some craft unions have either broadened their membership base or amalgamated to form multi-craft unions. These have proved to be short-term solutions for most craft unions which, at best, have only served temporarily to delay their further decline. Another problem for craft unions in a changing economy was the absence of any political influence within the TUC and Labour Party and the very limited financial services they could offer because of their small membership.

Self-evaluation activity 3.4

Craft bypass
Response on website

Can you think of one example of a craft being bypassed as a result of technological change?

A second category is the industrial union, defined as one which aims to recruit all workers within a particular industry, regardless of occupation. In theory, industrial unionism assumes a more orderly system of trade union organisation (as it does in Germany) and the claimed advantages for industrial unions are based on this assumption. For example:

- an industrial union, being larger than a cluster of occupational/craft unions would represent the united strength of all the industry's workers;

- it eliminates the problem of multi-unionism (more than one union per industry); and
- it simplifies the collective bargaining process.

In practice, however, industrial unionism has not been a successful means of organisation and, in terms of the definition given above, it can be argued that no union today can claim to be exclusively industrial. One example of a union which approximated to this definition was the National Union of Mineworkers (NUM) before the miners' strike of 1985, but even here supervisory grades and colliery managers had a separate union (National Association of Colliery Overmen, Deputies and Shotfirers (NACODS) and the British Association of Colliery Management (BACM) respectively). After 1985, the supremacy of the NUM was challenged by the Nottinghamshire-based Union of Democratic Mineworkers (UDM).

Self-evaluation activity 3.5

Industrial representation
Response on website

Can you think of one other industry which had its workers represented on an industrial basis?

The third category is the general union, which recruits across occupational and industrial boundaries and in theory has no restrictions on potential membership. In practice, however, because of their historical development, the memberships of general unions tend to be focused upon specific industries and occupations. Nevertheless, the main reason for their survival and growth has been their ability to maintain and consolidate membership within their traditional catchment areas and to recruit within non-traditional growth areas. Consider the examples of the Transport and General Workers Union (TGWU) and the GMB, traditionally amongst largest general unions in Britain:

> Both the two largest general unions began life in the late 1880s, organising particular groups of unskilled workers. The main parent of the Transport and General Workers' Union was the Dock, Wharf, Riverside and General Labourers'

Union, and the chief forerunner of the General and Municipal Workers' Union was the National Union of Gasworkers and General Labourers of Great Britain and Ireland. We should note the significance of the phrase 'and general labourers' in the titles of both these pioneering organisations. It tells us that, **from the outset**, these unions deliberately intended that their recruitment should not be restricted to specific industries or occupations. The reason for this is not hard to find; unlike the craftsmen, dockers and gasworkers were in no position to construct a tightly exclusive barrier around their occupations. Because their jobs were casual and relatively unskilled, all 'general labourers' were potential blacklegs threatening effective trade unionism anywhere unless all could be enrolled in the union. Thus the general unions felt it necessary to construct organisations having all the flexibility which other forms of union denied to themselves. It is small wonder that they have flourished and grown to their present dominant size. (Coates and Topham, 1988, p. 47)

Self-evaluation activity 3.6

Advantages and disadvantages of general union structure
Response on website

With the extract from Coates and Topham in mind, attempt to identify some advantages and disadvantages of the general union type.

The general union category is certainly appropriate for the GMB and TGWU, and Table 3.1 (p. 139) demonstrates their supremacy in the membership stakes. Falling membership has provided an impetus for mergers and amalgamations (see below) and this has resulted in increased concentration of membership within the largest unions, of which Amicus and UNISON are probably the best examples to date.

As most contemporary unions do not fit neatly into craft, industrial or general types, other typologies have been used (Salamon, 1998). These include:

1. **The occupational union.** This category comprises unions which organise workers in a particular occupation or occupations which are related to each other. The Union of Shop, Distributive and Allied Workers (USDAW), which recruits its membership from related occupations within the retail sector, is an example.

2. **The white-collar union.** White-collar, or non-manual unions comprise a sector of the trade union movement which has expanded considerably since 1945. They can be regarded as part of the occupational category, but not exclusively so and recruit from a particular non-manual occupation or profession such as the National Union of Teachers (NUT). Apart from unions that concentrate exclusively on white-collar occupations, the large general and quasi-industrial unions often incorporate white-collar sections of their own, such as the Association of Clerical, Technical and Supervisory Staffs (ACTSS) which is part of the TGWU. In addition, some professional associations such as the British Medical Association (BMA) perform some trade union functions, particularly within the area of collective bargaining.

3. **Federations.** Federations of trade unions have arisen as a result of multi-unionism (the existence of several unions within one industry) in a multi-employer context (where there are several employers within the same industry). The need to present a common approach to employers in national industry-wide negotiations made some kind of joint organisation essential. The federation, then, is a rather loose-knit structure which facilitates collective bargaining in an industry with many employers. Federations which have existed in the past include the Confederation of Shipbuilding and Engineering Unions, the National Federation of Building Trade Operatives, and the Printing and Kindred Trades Federation. With the decline of multi-employer bargaining in recent years, the role of federations has also declined. The problems we have identified in relation to the traditional method of classification of unions has resulted in two other main attempts to explain trade union structure which are known as the 'vertical' and 'horizontal' structure and the 'open' and 'closed' structure, which are now briefly considered.

Vertical and horizontal structures

This method of classification assumes that unions are organised along either 'vertical' or 'horizontal' lines. The horizontally organised union recruits from one of several grades of workers across industry boundaries – all managers in a managers' union, all electricians in an electricians' union. This type of union corresponds loosely to craft organisations. The vertical union, on the other hand, aims to recruit all workers, whatever their grade or occupation, with a common industrial background, and therefore corresponds to the industrial union type. These categories are useful in helping to explain, particularly in a historical context, trends and tendencies in union organisation and recruitment and they also reveal the complexity of the existing and changing union organisation in Britain.

Open and closed structures

This method of classification, originated by Turner (1962), adopts a more dynamic approach which assumes that unions are constantly changing in response to changes in their external environments. It also assumes that unions can influence events in a proactive way. A useful way of looking at unions as open structures is provided by open systems theory. The key for viewing organisations as open systems, argues Luthans (1992, p. 532) 'is the recognition of the external environment as a source of significant input. In systems terminology, the boundaries of the organisation are permeable to the external environment (social, legal, technical, economic and political)'.

An open union as an open system actively recruits and/or seeks mergers with other unions in new occupational or industrial sectors and is not able to control entry into a trade or occupation. It is expansionist in orientation, relies on the numerical strength of its membership to provide and reinforce its bargaining power and corresponds more or less to the general union type. A closed union, to all intents and purposes, is a closed system in that it is minimally responsive to changes in its external environment; it 'concentrates on its existing territory, aiming to make that a strongpoint of organisation and bargaining strength' (Coates and Topham, 1988, p. 54). A closed union is analogous to a craft union,

restricting entry to the trade or occupation and adopting an 'exclusive' approach to membership recruitment. The open and closed categories may be regarded as two extremes on an open–closed continuum rather than a dichotomy of mutually exclusive types. At the one extreme we have the completely closed, single-craft or occupational union and, at the other, we have the completely general, open union. The approach is useful because it enables us to assess the extent to which a particular trade union changes over time. During the course of its history, a union may be closed at one time and open at another. For example, the former Amalgamated Society of Engineers (ASE) was a pure craft union and therefore closed. Over time, the union, partly owing to its strong occupational base, transformed itself into the near general unionism of the Amalgamated Engineering Union (AEU) with its engineering, foundry and construction sections. In 1993 the AEU merged with the Electrical, Electronic, Telecommunications and Plumbing Union (EETPU) to form the Amalgamated Engineering Electrical Union (AEEU), making the union even more open. The union has since merged with the Management, Science and Finance Union (MSF) to form a two-divisional organisation called Amicus, comprising Amicus-MSF and Amicus-AEEU. The trend ever since the 1960s has been towards a more open strategy resulting in intense inter-union competition for membership regardless of structural considerations. As aggregate union membership fell during the 1980s and 1990s so the pace of amalgamations and mergers speeded up (see below).

Summary points: trade union structure

We may summarise our consideration of trade union structure as follows:

- The traditional classification of craft, industrial and general categories of union together with the refinements of the occupational and white-collar categories contains serious flaws which have been identified.
- The most significant weakness of the traditional classification worth reinforcing here is that it presents us with a largely static view of structure (the 'snapshot in time' view) and therefore ignores the dynamics of external change and the

	Open	Closed	Vertical	Horizontal
GMB				
UNISON				
NUM				
NUT				

Figure 3.1 Trade union structural types

internal (to the union) pressures which influence a union's policies and decision making.
- The vertical–horizontal analysis of union structure is an improvement upon the traditional classification, but has the disadvantage of placing unions into an 'either/or' category, while the general union may well possess both characteristics.
- The open–closed continuum is, arguably, the most useful as it assumes a dynamic relationship between a union and its complex external environment.

Self-evaluation activity 3.7
Identifying structural types
Response on website

Figure 3.1 is a simple matrix with examples of four trade unions identified in the left-hand column. Simply place a cross in the box or boxes which you think adequately describes the structural type of each of these unions. When you have done this, attempt a brief explanation of your reasoning.

Trade union strategy

One of the main assumptions underlying the identification of structural typologies is the rather determinist one that structure influences union behaviour. In recent years attention has focused upon strategy and the impact of strategic choices made by individual unions and by the union movement as a whole. With regard to membership recruitment, for example, strategy may be focused upon particular areas of potential membership, with unions in the banking and finance sector, for instance, targeting

workers in call centres (Taylor and Bain, 1999). One of the most recent attempts to categorise unions in terms of their strategic interests and identification is that of Hyman (1996) who suggests five types:

- **the exclusive guild**, which safeguards the interests of an occupational elite;
- **the friendly society**, which offers consumer services to individual members, partly as a means of recruitment;
- **the company union**, which co-operates with management on productivity issues;
- **the social partner**, which aims to secure a dialogue with government; and
- **the social movement**, which attracts widespread support by campaigning about popular issues.

It is important to note that the strategies associated with four of these categories (with the exception of the 'exclusive guild' strategy) are also associated with the TUC after its 'relaunch' in 1994 (see below).

Trade union mergers

At the beginning of the twentieth century there were approximately 1300 unions in Britain. By 1989 there were 314 unions, reducing to 268 in 1992 and to 226 in 2001/2 of which 69 are affiliated to the TUC (TUC, 2002). Since 2002 this trend has continued with 186 unions in 2006 (Certification Office Annual Report, 2007). Much of the decline is the result of smaller, craft-oriented unions simply disappearing, while a smaller proportion of the decline in numbers can be attributed to mergers between small and large and medium and large unions. In fact, McIlroy (1995) contended that we had, by the 1980s, entered upon a period of 'merger mania' (p. 18). In retrospect, it is possible to identify certain merger trends and patterns over the past 35 years or so. During the 1970s, the main merger trend was for large unions to take over smaller unions. In the 1980s, the trend for medium sized unions merging with unions of similar size became established while from the late 1980s onwards, the 'super-union' trend became established which was characterised by large unions combining together to form large conglomerates. The term 'merger' is commonly used to include a takeover by a larger union of a smaller union and amalgamation to form a new organisation. As Waddington (2003) points out, mergers raise the

problem of a growing diversity or heterogeneity of membership, which in the case of the main merged unions of UNISON and Amicus, and Amicus and TGWU, for example, 'is associated with attempts to develop new forms of cohesion and articulation among heterogeneous memberships' (p. 224). Examples of mergers since 1980 include:

- Boilermakers with the General and Municipal Workers to form the GMB in 1982.
- National Association of Theatrical, TV and Kine Employees and ABS to form BETA in 1984.
- POEU and CPSA (Posts and Telecommunications section) to form the NCU in 1985.
- Amalgamated Textile Workers to GMB in 1986.
- ASTMS with TASS to form MSF in 1988.
- GMB with APEX (still known as GMB) in 1988.
- Civil Service Union with the Society of Civil and Public Services to form the National Union of Civil and Public Servants in 1988.
- NUR and NUS to form the RMTU in 1990.
- NGA and SOGAT to form the GPMU in 1990.
- BETA and ACTAT to form BECTU in 1990.
- NALGO, NUPE and COHSE to form UNISON (not an acronym) in 1992.
- AEU and EETPU to form AEEU in 1992.
- UCW and NCU to form CWU in 1995.
- IRSF and NUCPS to form PSTCU in 1996 which then through further amalgamation with the Civil and Public Services Association (CPSA) became known as the Public and Commercial Services Union (PCS) in 1998.
- BIFU, UNIFI and NatWest Staff Union to form UNIFI in 1999.
- Engineers and Managers Association (EMA) and the Institution of Professionals, Managers and Specialists (IPMS) to form Prospect.
- AEEU and MSF to form Amicus in 2002.
- Transfer of UNIFI to Amicus in 2004.
- Transfer of Association of Magisterial Officers into the PCS in 2005.
- Amalgamation of Association of University Teachers and NATFHE to form the University and College Lecturers Union, UCU in 2006.
- Merger of AMICUS with TGWU to form UNITE in 2007.

Figure 3.2 depicts the trend in the decline of both numbers of trade unions and trade union membership (the two generally tend to go together) for the period 1976–2006, and Table 3.1 provides

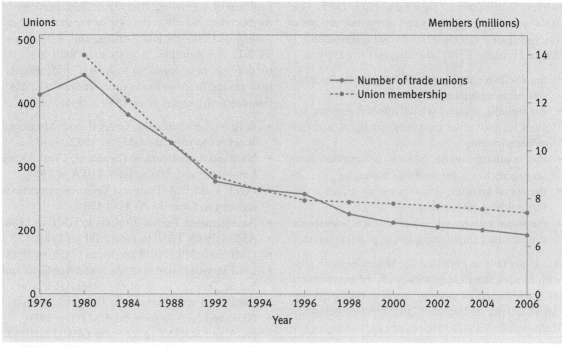

Figure 3.2 Decline in numbers of trade unions and fluctuations in trade union membership: 1976–2006
Source: Labour Market Trends and Certification Officer's reports, various years

membership figures for the 'top ten' unions for 1989, 1996, 1997, 2002 and 2006. It is important to note that there are differences in how the Labour Force Survey (LFS) and the Certification Office report membership, with the latter including the entire UK showing aggregate higher membership levels. For comparative purposes, particularly where back time series go beyond 1989, and as a basis for comparison of more recent data, Certification Office data is used. Where sectoral and occupational membership figures are presented, LFS data is used.

Reasons for merger

Undy *et al.* (1981) analysed union mergers in the 1960s and 1970s and provided a threefold explanation for them. According to Undy *et al.*, there are three reasons for merger. The first is defensive, where a smaller union can escape the problem of its decline through falling membership and faltering finances by merging with a larger union. The second is consolidating, where the larger union reinforces its dominant role within an industry; and the third

is expansionist, where a major union seeks to grow further, often into new industrial and/or occupational sectors as a matter of policy even if it means competing aggressively with a rival union. Mergers may also be prompted by the need to introduce economies of scale, improve organisational efficiency and to enable the merged union to expand into new and existing areas of employment growth (Waddington, 2003).

The accelerated pace of union mergers of the late 1980s and 1990–2000s involving larger organisations may be seen as part of an unplanned process towards rationalisation of the trade union movement, and as a TUC review of 1991 predicted, the merger process has grown 'and will continue to grow over the next ten years' (p. 20). The consequent fall in numbers of unions and growing rate of mergers suggest a greater concentration and heterogeneity of membership within the larger unions, as Table 3.2 indicates. During the 2000s there has been growing activity towards **internationalisation of unions** through the creation of links with UK and overseas unions involving Amicus, TGWU

Table 3.1 Membership of 'top ten' unions: 1989, 1996, 1997, 2002 and 2006

	Top ten unions	Membership (000s) (to nearest 000)
1989	Transport and General Workers' Union	1271
	GMB	823
	National and Local Government Officers' Association	751
	Amalgamated Engineering Union	742
	Manufacturing, Science and Finance Union	653
	National Union of Public Employees	605
	Union of Shop, Distributive and Allied Workers	376
	Electrical, Electronic, Telecommunications and Plumbing Union	367
	Royal College of Nursing of the United Kingdom	286
	Union of Construction, Allied Trades and Technicians	258
1996	UNISON: The Public Service Union	1375
	Transport and General Workers' Union	885
	Amalgamated Engineering and Electrical Union	725
	GMB	718
	Manufacturing, Science and Finance Union	425
	Royal College of Nursing of the United Kingdom	307
	Union of Shop, Distributive and Allied Workers	290
	Communication Workers' Union	275
	National Union of Teachers	271
	National Association of Schoolmasters and Union of Women Teachers	238
1997	UNISON: The Public Service Union	1300
	Transport and General Workers' Union	881
	Amalgamated Engineering and Electrical Union	720
	GMB	710
	Manufacturing, Science and Finance Union	416
	Royal College of Nursing of the United Kingdom	312
	Union of Shop, Distributive and Allied Workers	293
	National Union of Teachers	277
	Communication Workers' Union	274
	National Association of Schoolmasters and Union of Women Teachers	246
2002	UNISON: The Public Service Union	1272
	Amicus	1078
	Transport and General Workers' Union	858
	GMB	683
	Royal College of Nursing	334
	Union of Shop, Distributive and Allied Workers	310
	National Union of Teachers	286
	Communication Workers' Union	284
	Public and Commercial Services Union	267
	National Association of Schoolmasters and Union of Women Teachers	255

Table 3.1 (*cont'd*)

	Top ten unions	Membership (000s) (to nearest 000)
2006	UNISON: The Public Service Union	1310
	Amicus	1160
	Transport and General Workers' Union	807
	GMB	572
	Royal College of Nursing	382
	Union of Shop, Distributive and Allied Workers	340
	National Union of Teachers	331
	National Association of Schoolmasters and Union of Women Teachers	328
	Public and Commercial Services Union	311
	Communication Workers' Union	242

Source: Annual Reports of the Certification Officer, 1990, 1997, 1998, 2002 and 2007

Table 3.2 Trade union distribution by size: 2006

Number of members	Number of unions (listed and unlisted)	Membership (000s)	Number of unions		Membership of all unions	
			%	Cumulative %	%	Cumulative %
Under 100	34	0.7	17.6	17.6	–	–
100–499	40	11.2	20.7	38.3	0.1	0.2
500–999	18	12.5	9.3	47.7	0.2	0.3
1000–2499	25	41.2	13.0	60.6	0.6	0.9
2500–4999	21	76.1	10.9	71.5	1.0	1.9
5000–9999	11	86.1	5.7	77.2	1.2	3.0
10,000–14,999	4	46.5	2.1	79.3	0.6	3.7
15,000–24,999	8	141.4	4.1	83.4	1.9	5.6
25,000–49,999	15	530.1	7.8	91.2	7.1	12.7
50,000–99,999	3	197.4	1.6	92.7	2.6	15.3
100,000–249,999	5	788.5	2.6	95.3	10.6	25.9
250,000 and over	9	5540.6	4.7	100.0	74.1	100.0
Total	193	7473.0	100.0	100.0	100.0	100.0

Source: Certification Officer's Annual Report 2005–2006
Note: Membership data is compiled both by the Certification Officer's Annual Reports and the annual Labour Force Surveys of trade union membership. The Certification Office data covers the membership of all trade unions known to the Certification Officer and since 1975 includes all organisations falling within the definition of a trade union under section 28 of the Trade Union and Labour Relations Act 1974. Details of unions are maintained on an official list. Membership of listed trade unions includes home and overseas members and some people who are self-employed, unemployed or retired. The Labour Force Survey data includes only those trade union members in employment.

and the GMB. Amicus has links with the American union – the United Steelworkers – and it appears likely that the new super-union Unite (formerly Amicus and TGWU) will start the merger process with United Steelworkers during 2007–8. Amicus has a co-operative link up with IG Metall, the German engineering union while the TGWU separately has links with overseas unions such as the SEIU, the US service employees' union. The GMB has recently began working with Solidarity, the Polish union, in an attempt to organise Polish workers in Britain.

Self-evaluation activity 3.8

The birth of UNISON and Amicus-MSF

Response on website

Exhibit 3.3 is a description of the merger that spawned UNISON and the history of Amicus-MSF together with a summary of their membership groupings. The UNISON merger was a unique event in the history of trade union mergers as it involved the amalgamation of three medium to large sized organisations while the Amicus-MSF merger is the culmination of many previous mergers. Read the summary now and attempt the question which follows. (Note that UNISON was the 'newest' union in 1993.)

If you were a member of the UNISON or Amicus-MSF National Executive, what would be your priorities for membership expansion for the next ten years?

Trade union government and democracy

Here we look at how trade unions are internally structured in relation to two areas:

- the management and authority structure (or organisational structure) of unions; and
- the democratic process within unions.

In practice there is considerable overlap between these two areas as much emphasis is placed upon representation of members' interests, and this may naturally impede the efficiency by which decisions are made.

Organisational structure

Despite the heterogeneous nature of British trade unions, we can discern a basic, common structural pattern which includes the following elements:

1. The branch is the first point of contact which a rank-and-file member has with his or her union and 'provides him with an opportunity to participate in the government and administration of the union' (Flanders, 1972, p. 50). The branch may be workplace- or factory-based on a single employer, or it can be based on a particular trade group. Branches vary in size, and within the TGWU, for example, branches range from a minimum of 50 to as many as 5000. They also vary in frequency of meetings: the TGWU stipulates

Exhibit 3.3

UNISON and Amicus-MSF

UNISON is Britain's newest and largest union and remains the largest and most complex merger in British union history (Dempsey and McKevitt, 2001). Its members provide services to the public in both the private and public sectors and it is firmly committed to the public service ethos. Two-thirds of its members are women and UNISON's organisation and constitution reflect the importance of equal opportunities and fair representation. The amalgamation will lead to improvements in an already highly developed system of collective bargaining and workplace representation. The two traditions of party political independence and Labour Party affiliation are maintained through the existence of separate political funds. UNISON came into being on 1 July 1993 through an amalgamation of three partners, the Confederation of Health Service Employees (COHSE) representing around 200,000 health

service staff, the National and Local Government Officers Association (NALGO) representing some 700,000 white-collar staff in a range of public services and the National Union of Public Employees (NUPE) which represented about 600,000 manual staff in the public services. The amalgamation was accomplished after more than three years' intensive negotiation and agreement. Throughout this process, there was widespread consultation with the three unions' members, detailed reports were taken to each union's conferences, and information was provided to the negotiators from educational meetings and research. Arrangements for membership ballots were agreed with the Certification Officer and a motion to amalgamate was put to a secret, individual postal vote of each union's members. The results of the ballots were declared in December 1992. Each union returned a substantial majority in favour of amalgamation. UNISON's membership groups comprise:

- **Local government:** around 800,000 members comprising manual and non-manual workers belong to this group and about 50 per cent of all local government staff are UNISON members.
- **Healthcare:** UNISON has 440,000 members in this group, which includes the NHS. Almost three-quarters of the membership are women, a significant proportion is black, and many work part-time.
- **Electricity:** UNISON has about 20,000 members in the electricity supply industry. About 60 per cent of the membership are women and they work primarily in administration and clerical jobs. There is also some representation in electrical retailing.
- **Gas:** There are approximately 20,000 members in the gas industry covering staff and senior officers, and UNISON is the largest non-manual union.
- **Water:** UNISON is the largest union in the water industry, with around 25,000 members, the majority of whom work for the water companies.
- **Transport:** There are about 5000 transport members who work for Passenger Transport Executives, the British Waterways Board and private and municipal bus companies.
- **Higher education:** Membership is concentrated within non-academic groups.

Amicus-MSF

MSF stands for Manufacturing, Science, Finance and recruits skilled and professional employees in all parts of manufacturing including engineering, electronics, aerospace, cars, chemicals and pharmaceuticals, tobacco and food and drink. MSF also recruits from the finance sector and from the health service and universities etc.

Structure: The basis of the union's work is members in the workplace, which is the foundation of union activities undertaken by workplace representatives elected by members and supported by a network of professional regional officers located throughout the UK. Regional officers are the workplace reps' link to specialist services provided by MSF head office departments such as Communications, Research, Legal and Health and Safety. Work at national level is co-ordinated by national secretaries under the leadership of the General Secretary. The union also has a structure of branches, regional councils and an annual conference. Branches are represented at regional councils and form the basis for the election of delegates to annual conference which is the union's policy-making body. Between annual conferences, the national executive council is responsible for the union's government.

History: MSF was formed in January 1988 when two unions, ASTMS (Association of Scientific, Technical and Managerial Staffs) and TASS (Technical, Administrative and Supervisory Staffs) merged. The membership of the two founding unions complemented each other. TASS members were skilled and professional staff and were employed mainly in the engineering industry, and TASS had its origins in DATA, the Draughtsmen and Allied Technicians' Association. ASTMS had developed into a white-collar union with members in all sectors of industry and services and had itself been created by a merger in 1969. ASTMS had a phenomenal record of growth following its formation and expanded rapidly into new industries and services, particularly the finance and insurance sector.

that branches must meet at least monthly, while others may only meet annually.

The branch provides the opportunity for members to attend its meetings. However, the many studies of membership participation at branch meetings (ranging from the early research of Roberts (1956) to that of Undy and Martin (1984)) indicate that attendance is routinely low and within the 5–10 per cent range. A study of London Transport bus workers (Rose, 1974), a sector where the TGWU branches are based on individual garages, confirms the low attendance figures of previous studies and suggests possible reasons for this including:

- general apathy and disinterest of members;
- work patterns based on shifts;
- male-dominated meetings discourage women members;
- location of meetings;
- perceived domination of branch meetings by cliques of 'activists', and unrepresentative of the membership as a whole.

A more general reason for low branch member participation noted by Hawkins (1981) is 'that for most of them [the members] the union as an institution is not a salient feature of day-to-day life in the workplace. Motivated by instrumental collectivism, they see the union simply as a means of achieving tangible improvements in pay and conditions and as long as it meets their expectations they are not unduly disturbed if the union is led by individuals whose political outlook is at variance with their own' (p. 115).

2. The next level of a trade union's organisational structure is variously called the area, district, division or region. There are formal links between branches at this intermediate level based either on direct representation of each branch or indirectly by, say, the regional membership. The power and influence of the area, district, division or region varies with different unions, but as a general rule, the regional influence may have assumed greater importance with the shift in collective bargaining from industrial to organisational level, particularly within the private sector (including the privatised industries and utilities). The full-time union officer is either appointed by the union or elected by lay members and features prominently at the intermediate level and above. The duties

of officers vary, but the vast majority represent members in formal negotiations at organisational and industry levels. A small proportion has specialist functions in the areas of recruitment, health and safety, research, finance and public relations. The number of officers nationally is relatively small. In 1968, the Donovan Commission estimated that there were about 3000 officers (one for every 3800 members) and according to Kelly and Heery (1994) this number has remained unchanged but with a ratio of one for every 3229 members.

3. The third formal level within the trade union organisational hierarchy is the National Executive Committee (NEC) which is responsible for carrying out the policies agreed at delegate conferences and for the efficient administration of the union between conferences. The delegate conference itself enables branch representatives and other delegates to discuss policy issues and make the decisions to be carried out by the NEC. Conferences vary in size and in frequency of meeting; for some unions, an annual conference will suffice, while others will hold two or even three per year. All members of the NEC, the General Secretary and President are directly elected by the membership, via postal ballot as required by the Trade Union Act (1984) and the Employment Act (1988) as consolidated in the Trade Unions and Labour Relations (Consolidation) Act 1992. NECs generally attempt to ensure adequate representation of the variety of interests and sections within the union, and efforts are being made to encourage greater representation of women and black members on the NEC.

The democratic process

In order to determine the nature of union democracy we need to be aware of the problems associated with the definition of the concept of democracy. (A fuller discussion of the concept is provided in Chapter 6.) There are two main types of democracy, known as direct and representative democracy. The direct form assumes situations whereby everyone has a direct input into the decision-making process – as in the city states of Ancient Greece in which all citizens participated in taking decisions. The early craft unions developed a form of direct democracy

which enabled ordinary members to have access to the unions' meetings and determine decision making. However, in all but the smallest organisations, the direct form of democracy is considered to be unwieldy, impracticable and unworkable, and is irreconcilable with the criteria for administrative efficiency in larger, more complex and bureaucratically structured organisations. The Webbs were the first to point out this paradox and advocated a more practical system of democracy based upon greater representation of members' interests – hence the term representative democracy.

Critics of organisations which purport to be democratic – such as trade unions and political parties – have argued that these organisations, in an attempt to reconcile the demands for democracy on the one hand, and efficiency on the other, are neither particularly democratic nor efficient. Indeed, Michels (1959) asserted that in trade unions, as in other organisations, an 'iron law of oligarchy' operated. Within the trade union context this means, according to McIlroy (1988, 1995), that 'full-time union officials developed a monopoly of expertise – and used their control over resources and the prestige their position gave them to impose their own goals on the members whose ignorance and apathy facilitated this process. Unions were ruled, not by their members, but by small groups of bureaucrats' (p. 158).

In reality, the relationship between the leadership of a trade union and its members is complex. As the example of UNISON demonstrates, the membership of that union is fairly diverse and sectionalised and there are many membership interests to be represented, a process which may be called vertical representation. By the same token, the leadership role within UNISON is both multi-faceted and diffuse and the democratic process additionally implies decision making between various sections of the leadership – a process of horizontal representation. This situation is understandable in UNISON and other large federated unions such as Amicus (now Unite). In the former case there were considerable cultural, organisational and democratic differences between the three constituent unions and to a certain extent these differences still remain (Dempsey and McKevitt, 2001). Studies of trade union democracy reflect the complexities of organisation, sectionalism and diversity of membership interests, and the following points will assist in clarifying the debate:

1. Studies which support the view that at least some **trade unions are inherently oligarchic in nature** include those of Turner (1962) and Edelstein and Warner (1975). Turner provides a threefold classification of union types:

 • the first union type is the **exclusive democracy** whose membership is homogeneous and cohesive with high participation rates, the typical example being the traditional craft unions;

 • the second union type is the **aristocracy** whose membership is more heterogeneous and sectionalised, and in which one group or section has much higher participation rates than the other groups and which consequently dominates the union through full-time officers drawn from that group; and

 • the third union type is the **popular bossdom** whose membership is extremely heterogeneous and largely unskilled or semi-skilled, with very low participation rates, and whose leadership, based on full-time officials, is firmly in control.

 Edelstein and Warner (1975) in their comparative study of union democracy in the USA and Britain argue that oligarchic tendencies within unions have beneficial effects of maintaining unity provided that countervailing interests within the membership are properly organised and represented, thereby preventing any abuse of power on the part of the leadership.

2. Studies which emphasise the **existence of opposition** and therefore of choice for the membership as being a vital element of the democratic process include the classic examination of the TGWU by Goldstein (1952) and the study of the American International Typographical Union (ITU) by Lipset *et al.* (1956). Put simply, if there is no opposition, there is no democracy, bearing in mind the analogy of the one-party state. The nature of the 'opposition' varies from the formalised, seemingly permanent 'party system' of the ITU to more transient groups pursuing short- or medium-term goals as Blackwell's (1990) examination of the Bakers' union indicates. Hawkins (1981) considers the example of the (then) AUEW in this context:

 If an elaborate system of constitutional checks and balances reinforced by the general principle of accountability through the ballot

box, was synonymous with membership control then the AUEW would be a model of democracy. In practice, however, the main result has been the development of a unique system of two-party conflict. Over the last twenty years union elections have been closely contested by two highly organised and ideologically opposed electoral organisations which, having many of the trappings of parties, are worthy of the title. The parties concerned represent respectively the 'establishment' and the 'opposition'. Until the late 1960s the establishment party controlled the main constitutional organs of the union at national level and held the principal offices. Ideologically it has usually been identified with orthodox Labour Party policy. Between 1967 and 1974, however, the more left-wing opposition party (or 'progressives') gained ground by intense campaigning. . . . Their most notable achievement was the capture of the presidency of the union in 1967 by Hugh Scanlon, a former communist who won with communist support. (p. 118)

Other unions such as CPSA, the former NALGO, NUT and UCATT saw the growth of 'rank-and-file' opposition movements, committed to a programme of militant confrontation with employers and the expansion of activist democracy during the 1960s and 1970s.

3. A third area of study considers **size of union and the diversity of membership**. The basic proposition is that as a union grows in size, either by increasing its traditional membership base or by amalgamation, 'the administrative subsystem is likely to become more formalised and bureaucratic, and the representative system will face increased difficulties in ensuring that the differing views of disparate groups are brought to bear on decision making' (Salamon, 1998, p. 140). The recent focus upon trade union renewal and organising (see below) has brought into greater contention the representation of women and other marginalised groups and how their voices can be articulated (Colgan and Ledwith, 2002). Many unions have sought to tackle this problem by decentralising their decision-making and policy formulation processes. A relevant example of how one union

attempted to come to terms with the problem of representing different groups during the 1970s and 1980s is the old 'popular bossdom', the TGWU which we now briefly consider.

From popular bossdom to popular democracy?

When Jack Jones was General Secretary of the TGWU, his vision for the highly centralised, officer-dominated union was to commit it to the 'concept of democratic trade unionism, under rank and file control' (Coates and Topham, 1988, p. 190). Jones himself described the objective in the following way:

> *I am working for a system where not a few trade union officials control the situation but a dedicated, well-trained and intelligent body of trade union members is represented by hundreds of thousands of lay representatives – every one of whom is capable of helping to resolve industrial problems and assisting in collective bargaining and the conclusion of agreements.* (Taylor, 1978, p. 133)

Under Jones, as Heery (1997) points out, 'the union leadership both endorsed and encouraged participation by members in union decision making and activities and promoted self-reliance, such that policy objectives, workplace organisation, collective bargaining and representation rested increasingly in the hands of members themselves and their shop stewards' (p. 177). The research by Undy *et al.* (1981) identifies the reforms undertaken by the TGWU in order to achieve these objectives:

- reducing the power of national trade groups (the centralised 'old guard');
- extending lay participation by encouraging the appointment of shop stewards, decentralising collective bargaining and supporting the ratification of collective agreements by the membership;
- promoting a switch from officer to lay representation;
- decentralising the union's internal financial system, giving regions greater responsibility for financial and administrative decisions; and
- tighter control over appointments to ensure that the strategy of participative unionism was implemented and the culture of the organisation changed.

Self-evaluation activity 3.9

The new unionism of the GMB

Response on website

The 2006 structure of the GMB is described in Main case 3.1, and this is followed by a brief account of the reforms to the union instigated by John Edmonds, its former General Secretary. Read through the passage and attempt the following question (a diagrammatic representation of the GMB structure (as modified in 2006) is provided in Figure 3.3). Comment on the nature of the GMB's democratic structure.

Main case 3.1
The GMB

The GMB is a general union of over 600,000 members. The current General Secretary is Paul Kenny. The structure of the union consists of:

The Branch: The Branch is the basic unit of the union's organisation. Branches consist of all the members of a given area or, in cases where enough members are concentrated in one Branch of industry, it can be industrial or workplace based. Each GMB Branch has its Officers: the Secretary, President, Auditor, Branch Youth Officer and Branch Equality Officer. All Branch Officers are elected every two years. In the workplace there are over 30,000 Shop Stewards and Staff Representatives who are directly elected by the membership. Many workplaces also have a Health and Safety Representative and an Equal Opportunities Officer. Large workplaces often have a senior shop steward known as the Convenor. These people are men and women who are elected by their workmates and are the front-line of the union.

Regions: The GMB keeps in close touch with its members through its nine regional offices and over 60 sub-offices. There are ten regions of approximately equal size of membership and they are responsible for membership servicing. The senior official in each region is the Regional Secretary and is responsible to the regional council for the workings of the union and its officers, staff and administration. The councils are made up of active members of the union who are elected every two years and in turn elect a committee to oversee the business of the region. There are over 300 Regional Organisers in the GMB who are paid, full-time em-

ployees of the union. Their job is to help negotiations and back up our workplace representatives. They are experts in their industries as well as holding experience and knowledge in employment law, pensions and other vital areas of concern to our members.

National Level: Like all trade unions, the GMB belongs to its members. In practical terms this expresses itself through the union's annual Congress. Each year the union brings together around 500 delegates from around the country – any member of the union can put themselves forward as a delegate and seek election in the regional ballot. The Congress, subject to the law, can make any decision on behalf of the union and its policies become the goals for everyone in the organisation.

Central Executive Council: Notwithstanding Congress, the Central Executive Council is the supreme body of the union. The 'CEC' as it is known, meets every two months or so and consists of about 80 members of the union. It is elected by secret ballot of the whole union every four years. For practical reasons its business is run by sub-committees such as Finance, Organisation, Services and Training.

National Office: The senior officials of the union are the General Secretary, and his deputy. Both positions are elected every five years by a secret ballot of the union's 683,000 members giving them enormous democratic credibility to represent working people. They have responsibility for the union's industrial and policy work as well as being the senior executive managers of the GMB.

Sections of the Union: As industry and technology has changed, so too has the nature of work. The blue collar/white collar distinction is disappearing in many industries whilst Human Resource Management has revolutionised working practices for many. In the 1990s the GMB created a new structure to reflect these changes in the economy. Eight Sections were created to cover the whole of the union's membership. So instead of looking at a single company or single employer, we are now able to take a strategic view across a whole sector. Each Section has its own National Committee of lay members elected from within the industry and its own annual Conference. Each Section is headed by a National Secretary and, with the support of National Officers, they lead the negotiations at national level, backed up by Regional Organisers. The Sections include the Apex Partnership which provides

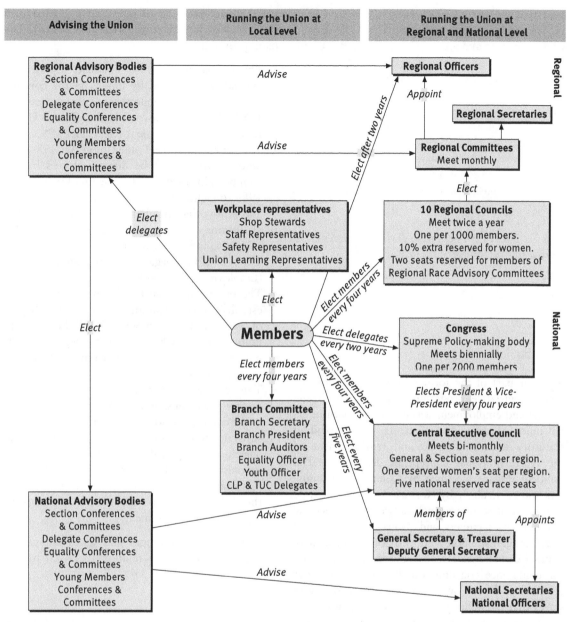

Figure 3.3 Structure of the GMB
Source: www.gmb.org.uk

union representation to administrative, clerical and technical staff at all grades.

The New Agenda: The GMB has led the way in modernising the trade union world. Our New Agenda is based on the premise that our first job is to strive to achieve what it is that our members want from their work. Launched in 1990, the New Agenda stated: 'It is essential that Britain's Unions abandon traditional, reactive stances and set an agenda which confronts the new issues of the 1990s. Britain's performance in the last twenty years has not been impressive. Trade

unions should wish to work together with employers and Government to create a successful industry, a strong economy and a caring, sharing society. Doing so successfully requires that we adjust to the changing contours of the economic and social landscape. The task ahead demands that we take collective bargaining into territory that we have barely explored before.' Since the launch of the New Agenda, which was accepted by the TUC in 1991, trade unions, led by the GMB, have begun to win through on childcare, training packages, employee consultation and many other areas of employment. Perhaps the biggest impact, however, has been the influence on Europe. In 1992 we became the first UK union to open an office in Brussels and in 1994 became the first UK union to sign up to a European Works Council.

Source: GMB, 1998, 2006

Legislation for democracy

A major part of the former Conservative governments' legislative programme dealing with trade unions and employment was concerned with internal union affairs and in particular with providing statutory underpinning to and reinforcement of the representational concept of democracy. The political slogans mouthed by Conservative ministers and particularly by Norman Tebbitt, erstwhile Employment Secretary, such as 'we must return the union to its members and protect the individual member against union tyranny' (Conservative Party Annual Conference 1983) were intended primarily for conference consumption, but also had wider credibility. The Conservatives convinced themselves that the minority of 'activist extremists' was manipulating the majority of the 'passive' membership. McIlroy (1995) argues that 'what has been involved . . . is a qualitative increment to state regulation of trade unionism and a diminution of self-regulation by union members' (p. 42). To be sure, many of the legislative provisions appear to have benefited union members by strengthening their rights in dealing with their own organisation and have ensured a formal, common standard of representation across the union movement. The first New Labour government endorsed the legislation

and had no intention of repealing it (apart from the 'check-off' requirement identified below). The main provisions are:

- The provision of public financial support for expenditure incurred by unions in the conduct of secret ballots and elections (Employment Act 1980) but withdrawn by the Trade Union Reform and Employment Rights Act 1993.
- The provision in the Trade Union Act 1984 that unions' NECs must be directly elected by the membership, extended by the Employment Act 1988 to include the General Secretary, President and non-voting members of the NEC, and that all elections must be conducted by postal ballot subject to independent scrutiny.
- The provision of legal rights for union members (Employment Act 1988).
- The provision in the Employment Act 1988 to establish a new Commissioner for the Rights of Trade Union Members (CROTUM) to help union members who wish to take legal proceedings against their union concerning their new statutory rights.
- The requirement for the employee to provide prior written consent, renewed every three years, to the employer who automatically deducts union subscriptions from earnings (known as the 'check-off'). By 1998, around two-thirds of unionised establishments practised the check-off (Cully *et al.*, 1999). Nevertheless, a campaign by the TUC resulted in the Labour government repealing the requirement.

Some of the advantages and disadvantages of legislated democracy in relation to postal ballots are identified in Exhibit 3.4.

The closed shop: no democracy at the point of entry?

Prior to 1988, the closed shop – defined as 100 per cent union membership (of which there were two types: pre-entry, where the employee joined prior to signing the contract of employment, and post-entry, where the employee joined after signing the contract of employment) – was considered to be an enduring feature of the employment relationship for many employees and employers, albeit highly undemocratic at the point of entry. The employer

Exhibit 3.4

Advantages and disadvantages of legislated union democracy in relation to postal ballots

Arguments for

1. Unions are involved in activities vital to the economy and society and, left to themselves, their decision-making mechanisms are profoundly unsatisfactory. In 1980, more than 40 per cent of General Secretaries were unelected and never had to face the voters.

2. The 'closed shop' inhibits the democratic process by interfering with the freedom of the individual, the right to work, and the efficiency of the enterprise. Those press-ganged into membership are unlikely to become loyal, let alone active members.

3. Participation cannot be improved by cajoling members to attend mass meetings which are open to intimidation and making decisions on the basis of a 'show of hands'. There are risks of manipulation under these circumstances. Workplace ballots are also unsatisfactory if members are not given sufficient privacy when recording votes.

4. The secret postal ballot overcomes these difficulties and it is in the interests of unions to compile a register of members and use the services of an independent scrutiniser.

5. The advantages of the postal ballot outweigh the disadvantages, making the unions more democratic and producing more moderate leadership.

6. Individuals wishing to exert their democratic right not to participate in industrial action require specific protection from union leaders. The Commissioners (CROTUM) are essential to help intimidated members in pursuing their legal rights against unions.

Arguments against

1. Postal ballots produce decreased turnout compared with workplace ballots; there is no evidence that postal ballots produce more moderate leaders.

2. The closed shop is justified by imbalance of power between employer and employee. This argument is somewhat academic as closed shops have virtually ceased to exist.

3. Governments have produced no evidence of intimidation or manipulation, and postal ballots are not necessarily immune to manipulation.

4. Unions' vitality depends upon members acting collectively. Postal balloting can minimise the quality of participation. Members are in a better position to take decisions when they have listened to the arguments. If workers vote in the workplace, they are in a better position to consider collective interests than if they vote as isolated individuals at home.

5. Rights to ignore strike decisions arrived at by state-imposed ballots emphasise that the purpose of legislation is to disorganise and demobilise trade unionism, not make it more democratic.

6. State intervention weakens the roots of democracy in society by restricting the scope of legitimate self-government of social organisations.

Source: Adapted from McIlroy, 1995, pp. 170–2

could not use the criterion of union membership for dismissing employees and in 1988 dismissal owing to union or non-union membership was deemed unfair while in 1990 it became unlawful for employers to refuse to hire workers based on their union membership status. This effectively spelt the demise of the closed shop in Britain, so much so that by 1998 only 2 per cent of workplaces were

identified by WERS 1998 where employees had to be union members to keep their jobs (Cully *et al.*, 1999), contrasted with 23 per cent of workplaces which had a closed shop in operation (Millward and Stevens, 1986). The decline of the closed shop cannot be entirely attributed to the Conservative legislation. Pencavel (2001), for example, argues that the pre-entry closed shop proliferated in the old craft industries such as printing, newspapers, docks and shipping which have been greatly affected by technological change, giving rise to the probability that 'many closed shops would have been swept aside anyway by the onslaught of the new technology' (p. 23).

Summary points

- The number and frequency of trade union mergers has increased in recent decades. Mergers are seen as necessary in order to cope with falling membership and to ensure that the necessary financial and other resources are devoted to implementing recruitment strategies and service provision.
- The typical union representative structure comprises the branch (shop stewards); area, district, divisional and regional departments and sections (full-time officers); a national executive committee and delegates' conference.
- In theory, members' interests are represented within a formal democratic structure which reflects sectional and membership diversity. Studies of union democracy, however, have been critical of union representative structures and, in common with most non-union representative structures, have assumed that:
 - unions, in common with other democratically structured organisations, have a tendency towards oligarchy;
 - the existence of opposition or factionalism is essential for the health and effectiveness of the democratic process; and
 - increasing diversity of union membership creates tensions between the administrative (bureaucratic) and the representative (democratic) subsystems.
- Many unions (such as the GMB) have undergone a certain amount of organisational restructuring in order to encourage broad-based participation in decision making.

TRADE UNION REPRESENTATION AND WORKPLACE ORGANISATION

The main channels for a collective representative voice have shown a considerable decline since the 1980s. The Workplace Employment Relations surveys of 1998 and 2004 (WERS 1998 and WERS 2004) confirmed that this is a continuing trend involving union and non-union forms, particularly in new workplaces. However, as far as actual workplace representatives are concerned, 38 per cent of workplaces employing more than 25 people had union representatives (Kersley *et al.*, 2006), down from 54 per cent in 1984 (Millward *et al.*, 1992). In recent historical context, Terry (2003) reports that the number of shop stewards has declined only fairly gradually since 1978, from 250,000 to 218,000 in 1998. The decline during the 1990s, as Millward *et al.* (2000) point out, was due to the continued decline in union recognition at workplace level. According to Terry (2003) union representatives existed in around 75 per cent of unionised workplaces, with a higher concentration and density within the public services, the privatised utilities and services, in large manufacturing workplaces and less so in finance and banking. In all other sectors, the shop steward phenomenon is an unusual one (Terry, 2003, p. 259). The main decline in 'on-site' representation during the time span of the WIRS series happened in the latter half of the 1980s; between 1984 and 1990 the proportion of union representatives within unionised workplaces fell from 82 per cent to 71 per cent with no further reduction during the 1990s. Millward *et al.* (2000) conclude that 'if unions were losing their organizational strength in the 1990s, then we might have anticipated a continuation in the decline of on-site representation that had begun in the latter half of the 1980s. In fact the evidence from the 1998 [survey] clearly indicates that on-site representation stabilized in the 1990s' (p. 152). However, WERS 2004 report that in 2004, 45 per cent of workplaces with recognised trade unions had an on-site representative from at least one union, down from 55 per cent of workplaces in 1998, but this was compensated for by an increase in access to workplace representatives elsewhere within the larger organisation whereby 21 per cent of union members within recognised workplaces had access to representatives at a site other than their own workplace but within the larger organisation, compared to 14 per cent in 1998.

The role and function of stewards

Employee representatives are elected by fellow employees and, in the case of trade union lay representatives or shop stewards, by union members only, within a specific constituency whose average size is around 29 union members. There is a 'representational weighting' towards the professions, with professional representatives comprising 33 per cent of all union representatives even though they comprise only around 13 per cent of union members (Cully *et al.*, 1999). A further finding was that a higher proportion of union representatives than non-union representatives worked in the professions. The main reason for this degree of 'professional over-representation' may be that professionals generally have more immediate access to communications media than, say, their 'non-professional' counterparts.

Traditionally, many union rulebooks made sparse reference to the definition of a steward's function and responsibilities, although the larger unions and the TUC have recognised for some time that training and education provision is essential if stewards are to perform these functions efficiently on behalf of their members. The concept of role suggests that the steward is in a continuing dynamic relationship with others (his other role set) both within and outside the workplace. Within the workplace, we have an internal role set which comprises:

- Management (personnel, industrial relations, human resource and line management).
- Steward's membership.
- Other shop stewards.

Outside the workplace, the external role set comprises:

- The trade union.
- Shop stewards from other workplaces within the same organisation.
- The full-time union officer.

Within the internal and external role sets (or the role network) there are both formal and informal expectations or perceptions of what the steward should do. In addition, the steward will have his or her own subjective expectations of the role which may, at times, differ from those of the role set. Where different expectations of role behaviour clash, this can result in role conflict.

Self-evaluation activity 3.10

Expectations of the steward's role
Response on website

Provide examples of the sort of expectations the members of a steward's role network may have with regard to the steward's role. Exhibit 3.5 is an example of how UNISON defines the shop steward role.

Exhibit 3.5

The Steward's tasks

Below is an ideal list of tasks a Steward could be asked to undertake. No one Steward could do everything included here, but it will serve as a reference and reminder of what needs to be done.

(a) Recruitment

- finding out who the members and non-members are
- helping keep the members interested in and informed about the union
- trying to get non-members to join the union and
- trying to get members to become Stewards or safety reps

(b) Relations with management

- talking to members about what their problems at work are and discussing how they can best be dealt with
- getting advice and help from senior Stewards or branch officers

- meeting with supervisors/management to sort out members' grievances and problems
- representing members in disciplinary cases
- attending joint consultative meetings with management and Stewards from other unions
- reporting back to members
- ensuring that collective agreements are implemented and kept
- reporting any breaches of agreements to the branch officials or full-time officer
- negotiating and reaching local agreements (this depends on the degree of devolution of local bargaining)
- referring health and safety problems to the Safety Rep. or if there isn't one, raising these issues with management

(c) Representing members

- finding out your members' views on union and work issues
- putting your members' views at relevant meetings such as Stewards' committees (if you have one)
- reporting back from those meetings to members

One of the main requirements of a good Steward is to be accessible to members. This accountability includes representing members' views and interests on the departmental Stewards' committee and branch executive and telling them what has happened. Make sure all your constituents know that you are their Steward – make sure members isolated by where or when they work or the job they do are kept fully informed. Let members know when and where you can be contacted.

(d) Constituency

The constituency is the workplace and should have been defined so that you know whom you are responsible for. If you are not sure, check with other Stewards in your department and agree on an appropriate division of responsibilities.

(e) Negotiation

The vital element in the duties of a Steward is often that of negotiation with management on behalf of members. The link with the rest of the branch structure is still crucially important but is combined with being the first point of contact between member and union in all matters affecting employment. There are limits to your responsibility and authority and the sort of problems you should attempt to solve.

(f) Explaining the union's policies

- finding out UNISON's policies on important issues from UNISON publications, from meetings or from other Stewards/branch officers
- talking to members about these policies
- giving out information/leaflets from the union to your membership
- holding meetings with members

(g) Organisation

- finding out who the branch officers and other reps are
- finding out about how the branch works and how members can take a part in it
- discussing how to improve the organisation of the branch so that it can best help your members

Source: UNISON Stewards' Handbook

Trade union lay representatives: The current situation

During the 1960s and 1970s, the trend towards workplace-based industrial relations, together with the growth in the numbers of shop stewards, became firmly established in a large proportion of manufacturing and public sector establishments and organisations. While some of the factors contributing to this development have been considered in Chapter 1, those specific to the growth in numbers of shop stewards include the following:

- the steady growth in trade union membership and, in particular, of white-collar and public service workers;
- the tendency for trade unions to decentralise their structures, thereby encouraging the involvement of members and shop stewards at the workplace, as exemplified by the TGWU in the previous section of this chapter;
- the introduction of training and education provision for shop stewards under the auspices of the TUC and the Workers' Education Association;
- the acceptance by employers of the recommendations of the Donovan Commission concerning the formalisation of collective bargaining at plant and company level (which also hastened the decline of industry-wide national bargaining in many industries);
- the need for employers to introduce new technology at the workplace, together with payment systems which rewarded local productivity gains, facilitated the development of plant and workplace bargaining and encouraged employer support for workplace union organisation; and
- the role of the state in supporting collective bargaining (active support from Labour governments; passive or grudging support from Conservative governments) and shop steward organisations through health and safety legislation and statutory rights for shop stewards to take time off work in order to perform their duties.

The growth and spread of shop stewards' organisation during the 1970s was not wholly beneficial to managers or to employees. The continuing high level of unofficial disputes involving workplace representatives during this period was problematic and reinforced media perceptions of 'poor' industrial relations and 'militant' shop stewards. Moreover, labour productivity gains were limited (testifying to the failure of local 'productivity bargaining') and wage inflation remained buoyant throughout the period. There was a growing perception amongst employers that workplace bargaining was a hindrance rather than a help and that shop stewards 'had not come up with the goods'. Furthermore, Terry (1995) asserts that:

> Even at their peak, shop steward power and influence were limited and constrained by ideological factors, in particular the decentralisation and relative autonomy of steward organisations and the associated focus of their attention on the short-term bargaining of pay and conditions. This 'narrowness' of activity was in turn reinforced by a continuing managerial refusal to widen the scope of formal bargaining and consultation, in particular to issues of 'managerial relations'. On matters such as work organisation, staffing levels, the speed and intensity of working, managers continued to resist formalisation, being unwilling to concede de jure rights to unions. (p. 211)

The 1980s, 1990s and 2000s

The 1980s witnessed a dramatic decline in trade union membership and with it a decline in the number of shop stewards and an erosion of their power base. To some extent the decline can be attributed to macroeconomic factors such as recession and growth of unemployment, particularly in manufacturing industry. The 1990 WIRS survey (reinforced by the subsequent 1998 and 2004 WERS surveys), covering the period 1984–2004, identifies significant changes (some of which have already been referred to) associated with this trend:

- in establishments in which trade unions are recognised, 38 per cent of them had stewards in 1990 as opposed to 54 per cent in 1984.
- most of the decline in steward representation in private manufacturing took place in those establishments where the proportion of trade union members (or union density) was already low;
- there was a decline in the support given by employers to workplace representation, particularly in the area of shop steward training; and

- the stabilisation in the incidence of on-site union representatives from 1990 onwards (WERS 1998 and 2004).

Other surveys and case study evidence point to the growing 'marginalisation' of shop stewards as managers make changes and take decisions without negotiation, replacing negotiation with consultation and assuming an increasing reliance upon 'direct' forms of communication (Marchington and Parker, 1990). The 'marginalisation thesis' is given further support from case study evidence of unionised Japanese transplants (inwardly investing multinational companies establishing on 'greenfield' sites). Where transplants are unionised, Grant (1997) argues:

> Their approach to employee relations will have generally led to their signing of new-style agreements with a single union. These agreements are based on a spirit and intention which seeks to move industrial relations from a conflictual process to one based on cooperation and trust. In this context, new-style agreements can be seen as attempting to facilitate reductions in 'them and us' (that is in adversarial relations between management and workforce). (p. 209)

However, Grant's analysis of the Japanese manufacturing transplant which he calls 'RENCO' indicates that not only do adversarial relations persist, but also that 'what occurred at RENCO does not suggest that new-style agreements offer trade unions a strategy with which to halt the perceived decline in their influence and power since the early 1980s. Instead, it appears to give credence to the argument that the agreements are symptomatic of, and may even contribute to, this decline' (p. 230).

There is evidence that on-site shop steward representation is becoming progressively ineffective in influencing major outcomes such as negotiating pay and pay differentials and negotiation per se. The enduring ability of union representatives to negotiate effectively to reduce pay differentials (the gap between those on high and low earnings) has finally disappeared (Millward et al., 2000; Kersley et al., 2006). Moreover, in around 50 per cent of workplaces with union representatives, there was no negotiation on any issue, while in 17 per cent there was negotiation on pay alone – a conjunctive

bargaining situation (see Chapter 5). Hence the empirical evidence of WERS 1998 and 2006 suggests that the traditional picture of the convenor being locked in negotiation with local management over a wide range of issues is no longer sustainable. Therefore, the declining effectiveness of steward representation is consistent with other established trends concerning the marginalisation of unions and their representatives, the bypassing of union communication channels, the use of 'negotiation' – where it is used – as a consultative mechanism and the imposition of organisational change without recourse to the use of any form of representation whatsoever.

Shop steward decline and workplace unionism: the growing 'representation gap'

Terry (1995, 2003) attributes the decline of shop steward influence in the 1990s to four sets of factors: economic and industrial changes, the role of the state, new approaches by employers and the contribution of shop-floor unions. These factors have created an ever-widening collective 'representation gap' which is most marked in non-union firms, but which is now becoming increasingly evident in unionised organisations and workplaces.

Economic, industrial and structural

Low levels of unemployment and the relative scarcity of labour, particularly skilled labour, in the 1960s and 1970s resulted in 'tight' labour markets and situations both locally and nationally where the demand for certain types of labour exceeded their supply. This tended to increase both the bargaining power of unions and workplace representatives at shop-floor level, particularly in larger workplaces, and the potential for industrial action. The different circumstances prevailing during the 1980s and 1990s which contributed to the decline in the influence of shop stewards included:

- high levels of unemployment and changes in product markets which weakened bargaining power;
- a decline in the average size of the 'employing' unit and in the number of employees per unit weakened shop steward organisation;

- the displacement effect of new technologies and the introduction of flexible production systems have tended to increase employer control over the work process and the employment relationship; and
- the increase in the incidence of non-standard forms of employment and the outsourcing of employment such as call centre work.

The role of the state

Government policy, including those of the New Labour governments, towards employment relations and market-led initiatives, particularly in the public sector, has been detrimental to shop steward organisation. More specifically:

- much of the legislation concerning industrial action (see Chapter 4) has placed restrictions upon unions and workplace representatives and affected the stability of workplace union organisation;
- the decentralisation and reorganisation of public services has, at least in some sectors such as the National Health Service, restricted local bargaining as a result of 'a managerial desire to exert effective unilateral control over pay and conditions' (Terry, 1995, p. 220);
- the policy of compulsory competitive tendering within local authorities has often resulted in a deterioration in terms and conditions of employment; and
- public sector 'modernisation' programmes, together with public–private funding initiatives and the creation of a two-tier workforce, fragment representation and dilute representational effectiveness.

New approaches by employers

As we have seen in Chapter 2, there has been an increase in employers' bargaining power partly through their greater control of the production process and through increased reliance upon alternative forms of communication and representation which bypassed the traditional trade union representation channels. This, in turn, has 'individualised' the employment relationship and 'marginalised' both shop steward influence and collective bargaining

over non-pay issues. These developments are underpinned by the evolution and increased sophistication of HRM techniques, policies and strategies (see Chapters 2, 6, and 7).

The contribution of workplace union organisation

Terry (1995) states that:

> The events of the 1980s raised serious problems for stewards and their organisations of a qualitatively different kind from those encountered earlier. Rarely did they take the form of allout attack; rather, they reflected a managerial determination to reduce or eliminate steward influence over certain issues, and to construct alternative channels of communication to and from the workforce. Shop stewards were confronted by employers arguing in detail the need not only for job loss but for the rapid introduction of new technology, the development of functional flexibility (multi-skilling), the introduction of new forms of employment (part-time, temporary employees, subcontracting), more intensive working patterns . . . , and other changes associated with a drive for increased labour productivity. Frequently, the need for radical change was driven home by managerial propaganda direct to employees, emphasising the seriousness of the problems faced by the company and the urgency of such change. (p. 222)

In conclusion

The nature of the response of shop stewards and trade unions to these developments is problematic, and is considered in the following section. What is contentious is the effect of what Terry calls 'the growth of a statutory system of employee representation', particularly as far as the implementation of the EU Information and Consultation Directive is concerned, the likely consequence of which could well be a significant increase in non-union forms of representation. The already well-established European Works Council system (see Chapter 6) does not consider national or workplace matters

and appears to have marginal impact upon union representation. The advent of 'social partnership' brings with it representational problems for shop stewards. For example, the partnership approach, which is based on consultation, corporate success and efficiency-driven criteria, suggests a union input based more on expertise than collective interest and therefore begs the question, 'from where is the expertise to come?' (Terry, 2003, p. 280). It is likely that, given these contemporary developments, the steady erosion of the effectiveness of union representational influence at the workplace will continue despite the fact that 'trade union representation remains a reality for substantial proportions of employees and employers in Britain' (Kersley et al., 2006, p. 51).

Self-evaluation activity 3.11

Summarising shop steward organisation
This SEA has no commentary

Identify the factors which contributed to the growth of shop steward organisation in the 1960s and 1970s, and those factors which influenced the decline in shop steward influence during the 1980s, 1990s and 2000s.

TRADE UNIONS: MEMBERSHIP AND RECOGNITION

The 1980s and 1990s and to a lesser extent the 2000s witnessed a serious weakening of the trade union movement nationally, and a persistent and continuing decline in union membership. It is interesting to note that industrial relations texts published during the 1970s (a period of seemingly irreversible membership growth), often did not countenance the possibility that union membership could conceivably decline. In this section we shall attempt to identify the main challenges facing British trade unions with respect to the current situation of membership decline, the issue of recognition and derecognition of trade unions, and the role of the TUC in responding to these and other related issues and problems.

The challenge of trade union membership

The current decline in membership is not unique in the later twentieth and early twenty-first centuries. During the 1920s, for reasons already identified earlier in this chapter, membership fell significantly (see Table 3.3). For the remainder of the period until 1979, and particularly from 1945, membership grew substantially. Trade union membership is no longer in free-fall with the decline slowing considerably in recent years, but it is still very much in evidence as the figures for 2006 suggest (Certification Office Annual Report, 2007; Grainger and Crowther, 2007).

Membership and density: key findings for 2006 from the Labour Force Survey 2007

- The rate of union membership (union density) for employees in the UK fell by 0.6 percentage points to 28.4 per cent in 2006, down from 29.0 per cent in 2005. This was the largest annual percentage point decline since 1998.
- Amongst all those in employment in the UK, union density fell from 26.2 per cent in 2005 to 25.8 per cent in 2006.
- For the third consecutive year, a higher proportion of women than men were trade union members (the difference is statistically significant). Union density among women fell by 0.2 percentage points to 29.7 per cent of employees in 2006, while for men it fell by 0.9 percentage points to 27.2 per cent.
- Of the four nations, Northern Ireland had the highest union density (39.7 per cent of employees). In Wales it was 35.9 per cent, and in Scotland 34.6 per cent. Union density was lowest in England (27.0 per cent).
- Among the English government office regions, the South East had the lowest union density (21.4 per cent) and the North East the highest (38.9 per cent).
- Only one in six (16.6 per cent) private sector employees in the United Kingdom were union members in 2006. Private sector union density fell by 0.6 percentage points, from 17.2 per cent in 2005. Collective agreements covered less

Table 3.3 Trade union membership: 1979–2006

Year	Number of unions at end of year	Total membership at end of year (000s)	Percentage change in membership since previous year
1979	453	13,289	−1.3
1980	438	12,947	−2.6
1981	414	12,106	−6.5
1982	408	11,593	−4.2
1983	394	11,236	−3.1
1984	375	10,994	−2.2
1985	370	10,821	−1.6
1986	335	10,539	−2.6
1987	330	10,475	−0.6
1988	315	10,376	−0.9
1989	309	10,158	−2.1
1990–1	287	9,947 (8,835)	−2.1
1991–2	275	9,585 (8,602)	−3.6
1992–3	268	9,048 (7,310)	−5.6
1993–4	254	8,700 (7,075)	−3.8
1994–5	243	8,278 (6,863)	−4.9
1995–6	238	8,089 (6,709)	−2.3
1996–7	233	7,938 (6,698)	−1.9
1997–8	224	7,801 (6,673)	−1.7
1998–9	224	7,851 (6,705)	0.9
1999–2000	221	7,898 (6,710)	0.9
2000–1	206	7,779 (6,610)	−1.4
2001–2	199	7,751 (6,590)	(neg.)
2002–3	197	7,751 (6,595)	(neg.)
2003–4	195	7,736 (6,556)	−0.2
2004–5	186	7,559 (6,441)	−2.3
2005–6	185	7,473 (n.a.)	−1.1

Note: Membership figures in brackets from 1990–1 onwards refer to the Labour Force Survey/Labour Market Trends/Review series (ONS). The other source is the Certification Office (see note to Table 3.2 concerning statistical discrepancy between ONS and Certification Office).

than one in five private sector employees, while almost one-third (31.7 per cent) worked in a workplace where unions were present.

- Almost three in five (58.8 per cent) public sector employees in the United Kingdom were union members. Public sector union density rose by 0.2 percentage points in 2006. Collective agreement coverage in the public sector was 69.0 per cent, three times greater than in the private sector.

- Trade unions were present in 86.8 per cent of public sector workplaces in the United Kingdom.
- Across all sectors almost half of UK employees (47.1 per cent) were in a workplace where a trade union was present. One-third of UK employees said their pay and conditions were affected by a collective agreement.
- The hourly earnings of union members averaged £12.43 in 2006, 16.6 per cent more than the earnings of non-members (£10.66 per hour).

Membership growth: 1945–79

While aggregate membership grew throughout the period, density of union membership actually declined slightly in most years until 1967. Union density, or density of union membership, is a useful measure as it relates aggregate membership to the size of the labour force nationally, expressed as a percentage. It can also be usefully applied to particular industries or sectors, to an organisation and to a workplace. Union density can therefore be used as a measure of union penetration over a period of time at any, or all, of these levels. The reasons for fluctuations in union density from 1948 to 1967 include the following:

- Those industries with highest union densities (coal, railways) declined in relation to employment (and therefore in relation to aggregate membership) while retaining or increasing measures of density.
- Those industries or sectors where union density was traditionally low, such as financial, banking, insurance, professional, scientific, distribution and leisure services, have expanded and, with one or two exceptions, union membership and density increased.
- The increase in white-collar employment in most manufacturing and service sectors was accompanied by increased white-collar union membership and from 1964 the rate of increase in white-collar membership outstripped the increase in white-collar employment.

Hawkins (1981) has identified a number of factors affecting union growth during this period, and these are now briefly summarised:

1. In general terms, **fluctuations in aggregate membership** could traditionally be explained by upswings and downswings in the economic cycle. During periods of economic expansion, membership would rise and vice versa. However, this 'prosperity theory' of union membership growth is only a partial explanation and does not account for periods of economic decline where membership has not correspondingly declined.
2. More specifically, the **rate of changes in prices and wages or inflation** may exert a positive influence on trade union membership. Hawkins (1981), for example, argues, 'to the extent that unions succeed in negotiating increases in money wages and salaries which keep pace with or exceed the rate of inflation, the lesson is not likely to be lost on non-unionists' (p. 82). However, Bain and Elsheikh (1976) suggest that prices do not have a constant effect on union growth and that once inflation exceeds 4 per cent growth tails off.
3. Concern over the restoring of **pay differentials** and the maintenance of the status of certain occupations, particularly during periods of incomes policy, has acted as a spur to union membership growth. The increase in white-collar union membership may be partially explained by white-collar workers' resentment aroused as a result of compression of differentials between themselves and manual workers.
4. **Unemployment and the threat of unemployment** may, in certain circumstances, have a positive influence upon trade union membership. For example, in the case of white-collar workers, organisational and technological changes may generate fears of redundancy and feelings of job insecurity. This sense of uncertainty, Hawkins (1981) argues, 'may have induced many white-collar staff to join a union for basic self-protection. If they feel threatened by technological and organisational change then at the very least they will see that collective representation could be needed if they are to obtain the best possible severance terms' (pp. 84–5).
5. **Employer recognition of trade unions** is an important determinant of membership growth and decline. The hostility of many employers towards trade unions in past years proved to be a powerful obstacle to the expansion of membership, but during the 1970s more active intervention of governments in encouraging the extension of collective bargaining, reinforced by the statutory recognition procedure established by the Employment Protection Act of 1975, exerted some influence on employers to recognise trade unions.
6. Structural factors such as **size of establishment** tend to have an influence upon union membership and density. Research by Bain and Elsheikh (1976) and the later WIRS surveys confirm that the larger the establishment the greater the union presence and 'voice'. Bain and Elsheikh conclude

that 'the larger the establishment the more interested its employees are likely to be in joining trade unions. For the larger the number of employees the more likely they are to be treated not as individuals but as members of groups, to have their terms and conditions of employment determined by collective rather than individual bargaining' (p. 142).

7. The growth in employment within much of the **public sector** during this period, particularly in the health, education and local authority areas, together with the legal obligation placed upon public corporations to recognise appropriate trade unions and engage in collective bargaining, resulted in increased union membership and density, especially amongst white-collar staffs.

8. Finally, the traditional **reluctance of women** to join trade unions had been gradually replaced by a more receptive attitude towards unionisation, particularly amongst white-collar employees.

In addition to the factors identified above, Pencavel (2001, pp. 9–14) points out that there was considerable *indirect support* for collective bargaining by the state during this period (see Chapter 6), thereby contradicting the view that the regulation of the employment relationship was best left to the parties (unions and employers, for example) concerned. In fact, according to Pencavel, considerable support for collective bargaining was provided by the state as employer within the public sector, with the nationalisation programme immediately after the Second World War creating public corporations that were legally required to recognise unions and to set up collective bargaining machinery. Other state support, which contributed towards a favourable climate for trade unions, included the setting of minimum wages in wage council industries, requiring government contractors to pay union-negotiated wages and discouraging product market competition.

Self-evaluation activity 3.12

Membership decline during the 1980s, 1990s and 2000s

Response on website

We have considered some aspects of industrial relations change in Chapter 1 and more specific issues of relevance to trade unions in this chapter. In relation to membership decline, try to identify the factors you think caused the decline in membership during the 1980s and 1990s. Compare your list with the analysis presented by the GMB, which is summarised on the website.

The nature of membership and 'union voice' decline

Waddington and Whitson (1995) provide a fairly detailed overview of the nature and dimensions of membership decline, the main elements of which are summarised below.

Aggregate unionisation

Although there have been fluctuations in the rate of decline during the 1980s and 1990s, much of the membership gains made during the 1970s had been wiped out by 1987. Moreover, the fall in membership and union density since 1979 represents the longest period of continuous decline recorded.

Male and female unionisation

During the 1970s a large proportion of the increase in total membership was the result of increased unionisation of women. During the 1980s, however, there was a much faster rate of decline in the unionisation of men as compared with that for women, and this trend continued into the 1990s. Waddington and Whitson (1995) assert that 'The decline in employment during this period (1989–92) was almost entirely due to the employment of fewer men. Over the same period the number of men trade union members fell by almost 700,000, and the number of women in membership decreased by about 200,000. In other words, between 1989 and 1991 both potential union membership and actual union membership became relatively more feminised' (p. 159).

Manual and white-collar unionisation

The number of white-collar workers continued to grow during the 1980s and comprised the majority of the total labour force, while manual employment continued to decline. But from 1979 to 1987 there were declines in total membership for both groups, with a much faster rate of decline for manual workers. By 1987, 'white-collar members comprised

48 per cent of total membership, compared to 41 per cent in 1979 and a mere 24 per cent in 1951. After 1987, constant employment density for white-collar workers and further declines among manual workers continued this trend' (ibid., p. 161).

Unionisation by sector

By 1987 public sector trade union members outnumbered those in manufacturing, with union densities of 80 per cent and 60 per cent respectively. Trade union membership declined rapidly in the agriculture, forestry and fishing sectors with resultant falls in density. Union membership grew more slowly than employment in the private services, revealing a decline in union density for this sector. After 1987, union density in manufacturing, agriculture, forestry and fishing, and in construction fell more rapidly than in the non-manufacturing sectors.

Unionisation by industry

In industries where unions are well entrenched (cotton and man-made fibres, printing and publishing, coal mining, gas, electricity, water, post and telecommunications, railways, sea transport and air transport), employment contracted during the 1980s and 1990s. Conversely, in many industries where unionisation is relatively sparse (entertainment and miscellaneous services, distribution, construction, timber and furniture), employment was expanding.

More recent analysis (WERS 1998 and 2004; Machin, 2000; Millward *et al.*, 2000; Pencavel, 2001; Verma *et al.*, 2002; Waddington, 2003; Bryson and Gomez, 2005; Kersley *et al.*, 2006) examines in greater detail the nature of the decline. Machin, by reworking the WERS98 data, concludes that the patterns of decline witnessed during the 1980s continued into the 1990s, with much lower union recognition, membership and density rates in newer establishments being a continuing phenomenon. In addition, the research confirms the continuation of the sectoral pattern, with sharpest falls in membership and union recognition within private manufacturing and to a lesser extent in private services. Furthermore, age of establishment or workplace is associated with aggregate membership and recognition decline, with older workplaces more likely to be unionised than younger ones. Union decline is by no means a UK phenomenon, as Verma *et al.* (2002) point out. It is a global phenomenon and, as such, a global prob-

lem. It would appear that those countries that have adopted neo-liberal approaches and policies are amongst the ones that have witnessed the steepest declines. For example, New Zealand experienced a 56.6 per cent decline in union density between 1980 and 1995, while density in France declined by 65.3 per cent. Both countries compare unfavourably with the UK, where union density declined by 46.1 per cent (all figures from ILO, 1998). Bryson and Gomez (2005) argue that the continuing decline in membership in Britain is a result of the increase in the proportion of employees who have never become members of unions, the so-called 'never membership' phenomenon. Taking data from the *British Social Attitudes Surveys*, Bryson and Gomez estimate that the percentage of employees who had never been union or staff association members rose from 28 to 48 per cent during the period 1983–2001 and they go on to argue that just over 50 per cent of the rise in never-membership is 'due to the compositional change in the workforce in that segments with traditionally high rates of never-membership increased their share of employment' (p. 87). However, 'the biggest single factor determining the probability of never-membership is whether or not an individual is employed in a workplace with a recognised union' (p. 87). The major finding here is that employees in unionised workplaces had a 40 per cent lower probability of never-membership than similar employees in non-unionised workplaces. The WERS 2004 research also confirms that 'the rise in "never membership" among employees in Britain throughout the 1980s and 1990s documented by Bryson and Gomez (2005), appears to have continued into the current decade' (Kersley *et al.*, 2006, p. 87).

In summary, the overall picture is one of decline in both union membership and density since 1979. While there are industrial and sectoral variations in both membership and density, the decline in employment in well-organised industries has been amongst the most persistent of trends during this period. However, Blyton and Turnbull (1998) point out that while the net outcome has been an overall decline in membership levels, unions continue to attract new members. Hence, despite the rise in 'never membership', a picture depicting only a scene of dwindling membership, with employees unwilling to become union members, is, in reality, a gross over-simplification.

Reasons for decline in union membership since 1979

It is generally acknowledged that there are many explanatory factors to be taken into consideration and therefore that no one single-cause explanation of membership decline can suffice (Mason and Bain, 1993). Metcalf (1991, 2005) suggests that union membership and density are determined by a combination of factors including the macroeconomic climate, the composition of jobs and of the workforce, government policy, the attitude and actions of employers, and the position taken by trade unions. A major problem for researchers adopting a multi-causal framework is that of quantification: the extent to which a measurable proportion of membership decline can be attributed to each causal factor or to the interaction of more than one factor. Notwithstanding these and other methodological problems, we can identify a number of reasons for decline (based on Metcalf, 1991, 2005; Waddington and Whitson, 1995; Machin, 2000; WERS 1998 – Millward *et al.*, 2000; Pencavel, 2001; WERS 2004 – Kersley *et al.*, 2006).

Employer policies

Employer policies have been considered in Chapter 2 and briefly in this chapter in relation mainly to union recognition–derecognition and we have noted that:

- during the 1980s employers began to depart from a policy of collaboration with unions to one of bypassing them in favour of direct links with employees and that this could constitute a threat to union density (Beaumont, 1987);
- that the rapidly changing technical and product market environment encouraged at least some employers to seek greater flexibility in the use of labour;
- the advent of HRM conflicted with many of the assumptions of traditional industrial relations; and
- the failure of unions to establish themselves in newly formed workplaces (Millward *et al.*, 2000) is at least partly due to employers' attitudes towards collective bargaining; compared with the pre-1970s' decades, 'the new breed of employers is less altruistic in their dealings with their own employees and this has manifested

itself in the view that unions are irrelevant or, worse, damaging to the enterprise' (Pencavel, 2001, p. 19).

However, Gallie *et al.* (1996) in their study of workplace unionism in a number of organisations argue that 'the evidence adduced for such a profound change in employer strategies is often little more than anecdotal . . . [and that] there was no evidence of widespread anti-unionism among employers and those employers that had unions present emphasised the continuity rather than change in their policies' (p. 14). They go on to argue on the basis of their case evidence that: 'Employers have maintained their relationship with trade unions within the workplace rather than trying to undermine them. The explanation for this is primarily that they consider unions play a valuable role in mediating their relations with the workforce' (p. 19). There is, nevertheless, some tangible survey evidence (Millward *et al.*, 1992; Smith and Morton, 1993) of some employers derecognising trade unions, which may have contributed to some decline in union membership (recognition and derecognition are considered in more detail later on), and of some unions failing to secure recognition at some newer greenfield sites, which may partly explain the absence of membership growth, particularly between 1983 and 1998 and from 1998 to 2004 (Millward *et al.*, 1992, 2000; Kersley *et al.*, 2006).

Business cycle explanations

We have referred to the work of Bain and Elsheikh (1976) in relation to the earlier period of membership growth. Subsequent research in this area (Booth, 1983; Carruth and Disney, 1988; Disney, 1990) tends to support the argument that increases in real wages for a sustained period, as that from 1980 to 1991, may reduce incentives for employees to join trade unions. This is particularly the case with white-collar workers who were motivated to become union members in the 1970s as a result of the narrowing of their pay differentials vis-à-vis manual workers. During the 1980s the white-collar/manual differential steadily increased to such an extent that the incentive to join on the part of white-collar workers was correspondingly reduced. Business cycle explanations also tend to support the argument that as unemployment rises, so trade union membership

falls. During the 1980s and early 1990s, chronically high levels of unemployment 'provide[d] employers with an opportunity to resist unionisation' (Blyton and Turnbull, 1994, p. 108), thereby restricting opportunities for employees to unionise.

There is another economic argument linked to productivity and organisational performance. During the 1980s the issue of the relationship between unions and productivity/performance became highly politicised and to a much greater extent than previously (Pencavel, 2001; Nolan and O'Donnell, 2003). The untested and highly ambiguous assumption that trade unions adversely affect productivity and performance, which received a great deal of publicity during the 1980s, conceivably provided extra ammunition for those employers who were antagonistic towards unions and singled them out as scapegoats for all productivity and performance woes. However, while some small, if not marginal, measure of union decline could be attributed to employers endorsing this untested hypothetical assumption – and current research remains equivocal (Addison and Belfield, 2001) – a consensus could focus upon the results of Pencavel's statistical reworking of selected WERS98 data which concluded that 'average union–non-union differences in labour productivity appear to be negligible [and that] unionism may serve as an agent permitting employees to participate in shaping their work environment without productivity suffering' (p. 36). As a postscript, Metcalf (2005) argues that explanations based on the business cycle 'no longer stand up to scrutiny [as] since 1993 unemployment has fallen continuously and so has union density – the reverse of the key prediction from models based on the economic cycle' (p. 5).

Legislative effects

The impact of industrial relations legislation upon union membership is rather less quantifiable and should be seen within the context of the 'neo-liberal assault' (see Chapter 4) of the Conservative governments, 1980–97 (Waddington, 2003). Freeman and Pelletier (1990) undertook a comprehensive analysis of the effects of labour legislation upon union density for the period 1948–86 and concluded that the unfavourable (to trade unions) legislation of the 1980s adversely affected union density and membership. Notwithstanding the criticisms levelled at

Freeman and Pelletier's analysis and claims, there can be no doubt that, in combination with the other causal factors, the legislation has permitted employers to restrict trade union influence and 'prevent any membership growth during the mid-1980s when employment expanded' (Waddington and Whitson, 1995, p. 167). This is reiterated by Pencavel (2001), who argues that the legal framework of the 1980s gave *new* firms greater flexibility in tailoring employment relations processes and procedures to suit their circumstances without the 'hindrance' of a trade union presence, but more generally it was the abandonment of full employment goals and the 'harsher competitive environment that complemented the new legal setting and produced unionism's decline' (p. 41). Metcalf (2005) also argues that it was not only the legislative changes that had an adverse effect upon union density but also the outlawing of the post-entry closed shop in 1988 and the pre-entry closed shop in 1990. 'This axing of the closed shop then fed through directly into declining density in the 1990s' (p. 6) and also through to the 2000s.

Employment composition

The changing composition of employment during the 1980s and 1990s in relation to trade union membership is marked by:

- a decline in employment where union membership was concentrated;
- an increase in employment where union membership was sparse, scattered or negligible, accompanied by a sectoral shift from manufacturing to services;
- increases in the employment of women from 38 to 40 per cent from 1980 to 1998 in workplaces with 25 or more employees, and increases in the numbers of white-collar workers and part-time workers (WERS 1998 – Millward *et al.*, 2000; Kersley *et al.*, 2006);
- the proliferation of non-standard forms of employment contracts in relation to part-time, temporary, subcontracted and agency employees; and
- the growth of self-employment.

As we have noted, some of these changes were also a feature of the employment pattern during the 1970s, when trade union membership was rising, and so cannot be considered as the only explanation

of the current membership decline. At best, therefore, employment changes account for a proportion of membership decline.

Employees themselves

Falls in union membership, accompanied by a decline in employee voice, suggest that there is a 'withering of support' for union membership amongst the existing workforce and that the reduced support or 'appetite' appears to be the main source of union decline (Millward *et al.*, 2000, pp. 92, 180). This not only affects the private sector but also the public sector, where membership density declined from 80 per cent in 1980 to 62 per cent in 1998 and continued to decline in the 2000s (WERS 1998 and 2004 – Cully *et al.*, 1999; Millward *et al.*, 2000; Kersley *et al.*, 2006). If the 'reduced appetite' explanation is valid, then this could indicate an increasing pay and conditions orientation or 'instrumental' commitment to trade unions on the part of public sector workers. Current research in this area is sparse and recent contributions appear to contradict the reduced appetite explanation, suggesting that improved union representation and a more proactive approach to organising could have a positive effect upon recruitment and membership (Prowse, 2003).

Self-evaluation activity 3.13

Explanations of union membership decline
Response on website

Do you think that these explanations of membership decline are of equal importance?

Derecognition and recognition of trade unions: two sides of the same coin?

The overall incidence of derecognition from 1984 to 2003 has been slight. According to earlier data assembled by Claydon, there were four cases nationally in 1984, with a significant increase to 22 in 1988, an increase which was sustained, albeit with minor fluctuations, in subsequent years. An earlier study (Claydon, 1989) reveals that grade-specific derecognitions, which comprised the highest proportion of derecognitions during the mid-1980s, affected white-collar workers primarily, while later research covering 1989–93 indicates that the incidence of total derecognition involving all grades of employee increased substantially (Claydon, 1997). Even more recent research (Gall and McKay, 1999, 2001) indicates that derecognition cases have declined substantially (see below). What is, perhaps, of greater significance is the distribution of derecognition cases by industry sector from 1984 to 1993. The heaviest and most consistent concentration of cases during this period has been in publishing, paper and print and in petroleum and chemicals; wholesale and retail distribution and engineering featured prominently during 1989–93 and this trend seems to have continued up to 2003.

Against the backdrop of union decline, an underlying trend of persistent decline in union recognition can be discerned, and to this end, WIRS and WERS 1998 and 2004 provide an impressive time series of data dealing with the extent of union presence and recognition in Britain (see Table 3.4a and Table 3.4b).

In commenting upon the data, Machin (2000) confirms that the pronounced decline in recognition was due to a failure to organise in new workplaces throughout the period, noting that there are sectoral differences with the greatest falls in recognition occurring in private manufacturing and in younger workplaces (Millward *et al.*, 2000). However, despite the persistent decline in recognition, Machin's reworking of WIRS and WERS 1998 data demonstrates that derecognition in existing workplaces was relatively infrequent during the 1980–98 period, with 7.5 per cent of panel workplaces derecognising unions. Gall and Mackay's (1999, 2002) review of reported cases of derecognition from 1989 to 2000 reveals that the yearly rate of reported cases of derecognition peaked in the early 1990s – with 79 cases in 1992 – and then declined, with only four cases of total derecognition reported in 1998, six in 1999 and one in 2000.

The derecognition era 1985–2001

The decline in trade union membership, representation and influence which we have commented upon has more ominous implications for trade unions

Table 3.4a Union presence and recognition in Britain: 1980–98 (%)

	1980	1984	1990	1998
Aggregate changes				
Establishments with any union recognised for collective bargaining purposes	64	66	53	42
Workers who are union members	62	58	48	36
Workers covered by collective bargaining	–	71	54	41
Sectoral changes				
Establishments with any union recognised for collective bargaining purposes, private sector manufacturing	65	56	44	30
Establishments with any union recognised for collective bargaining purposes, private sector services	41	44	36	23
Establishments with any union recognised for collective bargaining purposes, public sector services	94	99	87	87

Source: Cully *et al.*, 1999, p. 85; Millward *et al.*, 2000

Table 3.4b Union presence and recognition, 1998 and 2004 (%)

	1998		2004	
	workplaces	employees	workplaces	employees
All workplaces	33	53	27	48
Private sector	20	39	15	32
Public sector	83	91	82	92
Workplace size				
10–24 employees	28	28	18	18
25 or more employees	41	58	39	54

Source: Kersley *et al.*, 2006, p. 120

themselves. Claydon (1997), for example, asserts that since the mid-1980s, 'it has become increasingly apparent that this decline does not simply reflect structural change in the economy and the growth of unemployment, but also the conscious intent of key industrial relations actors, notably the State and employers, to exclude trade unions from control of the employment relationship' (p. 151). The process of exclusion may take one of two forms:

- **marginalisation** of unions, or partial derecognition, where unions are excluded from negotiating over pay and related issues and are confined to negotiating over non-pay issues; or
- **total derecognition**, where unions have no collective negotiation rights whatsoever.

Derecognition may encompass the entire organisation, entailing the withdrawal of collective bargaining rights from all employees. Alternatively,

narrower forms of derecognition may entail either withdrawing bargaining rights from specific grades of employee or withdrawing bargaining rights from all employees at specific plants or workplaces. Whether derecognition is total (or general), or partial may depend upon one or more factors. It may be that the ownership of the business had changed or that there had been changes to the employee relations policies and objectives of a company. Other factors may include the continued depletion of union membership within a company, the move towards other forms of collective agreement such as single-union agreements and a management preference for dealing with employees individually rather than collectively. A survey of 30 British firms undertaken by Brown *et al.* (2001) revealed that the nature of derecognition varied considerably between the surveyed firms, particularly in terms of coverage and scope.

Coverage: In multi-union firms, employers were often selective, the most common practice being to derecognise unions representing managerial staffs, but with some firms this was only the first phase of a staged derecognition strategy ultimately covering all unionised employees, and still other firms would derecognise by function (for example, by derecognising store but not distribution staff).

Scope: Derecognising unions does not mean banishing them from the workplace, since employees have a statutory right to join or not to join a trade union. Derecognising a union for the purpose of negotiating over the entire range of issues, both individual and collective is relatively rare. Some organisations will confine derecognition to collective issues and allow individual representation in disciplinary and grievance cases, while others will confine union activity to consultation on one or more committees. In this sense derecognition is partial for pragmatic reasons and it is clear the extent to which unions have become marginalised in one or more ways (Brown *et al.*, 2001). Claydon (1997) additionally identifies two general approaches to both partial and total derecognition that could be adopted by employers:

1. The first approach Claydon calls 'reactive' in that 'it represents a management response to a weakening of union power brought about largely

by changes in the organisation's industrial relations environment rather than resulting from purposive management action' (p. 169). One important environmental influence upon the propensity to derecognise is existing Conservative legislation which, Smith and Morton (1993, 1994) argue, has weakened trade union power and made unions themselves more susceptible to individualist approaches which undermine collective control over the employment relationship. Claydon points out that 'reactive' approaches are more likely to be appropriate to the weaker unionised and more peripheral areas of the unionised workforce, at least in the first instance.

2. A second approach to derecognition is called 'purposive', 'reflecting a long-term effort by management to eliminate unionised industrial relations' (Claydon, 1997, p. 169). This approach, more strategic than spontaneous, assumes a staged process as mentioned above, directed initially at 'specific groups of workers who are seen as offering least resistance or small groups occupying strategic positions in the production process' (p. 169). The whole process is a gradual one, may take a number of years to complete, and is instigated by larger organisations which have the financial and managerial resources to undertake such an exercise.

Mini case 3.2
The example of Esso

The process of derecognition within the petrochemical industry can be illustrated by reference to the example of Esso's Fawley refinery where a long-term approach involving stage-by-stage targeting of successive groups was adopted by management. The first group to be identified were warehousemen, who were transferred to staff status in 1974 and whose collective bargaining rights were withdrawn. Other groups were then targeted:

on the basis of their size and their strategic position in the production process. Thus instrument fitters were taken out of bargaining in 1979, followed by the boilermakers in 1982. In 1983, management attempted to extend staff status to welders, but at this point, union-led resistance involving industrial

*action (temporarily) put an end to the process. . . .
In 1989 the remaining refinery craftsmen were
transferred to staff status, and in 1993 the process
was completed when the TGWU's bargaining rights
on behalf of 700 process operators at Fawley were
withdrawn. Esso maintained membership check-off
arrangements, and unions retain the right to repres-
ent individual members in discipline and grievance
proceedings. They have, however, ceased to have
a role as collective representatives of the Fawley
workforce. At the same time, moves to end collect-
ive bargaining have been extended to other areas
of Esso's operations. Airport technicians employed
by Esso were transferred to staff status in 1989,
and in 1991 tanker drivers were similarly trans-
ferred and the TGWU derecognised for collective
bargaining.*

Source: Claydon, 1997, p. 164

Self-evaluation activity 3.14

Responses to derecognition

Response on website

How do you think trade unions could respond to the
derecognition threat?

The recognition conundrum

As the number of derecognitions, never high,
diminishes, the number of recognitions in recent
years has increased significantly, resulting in a net
increase of 49,000 workers covered by union recog-
nition agreements between 1997 and 1998 (Gall
and McKay, 2002). The number of recognitions in
2001 reached 264, covering some 85,000 workers
(IRS, 2002a). The growth in the number of recog-
nitions may be explained by the activities of trade
unions, the reactions and responses of employers and
the impact of the recognition procedures contained
within the ERA 1999 (Gall and McKay, 2002).
Since 2001, the number of annual recognition deals
has fluctuated, with no discernible trend up to 2004
when the number of deals stood at 204. However,
in 2005 the number of recognition agreements fell
sharply to 61 (Kersky *et al.*, 2006). More recent evid-
ence concerning recognition is considered below.

Trade union activity is focused upon the TUC re-
launch under the banner of 'new unionism' in 1995
and the subsequent creation of the 'Organising Aca-
demy' in 1997 (see below). According to Gall and
McKay (2002), TUC and union efforts to recruit
new members is paying off, and 'it would be rea-
sonable to suggest that there has been a substantial
increase in the number and extent of recognition
and organising campaigns since the mid 1990s [and
this] has led to more new recognition agreements'
(p. 5). Drawing upon data from employers, unions
and the CAC, Wood *et al.* (2002) conclude that
unions are proactive in seeking to gain members
before approaching employers or 'relying on em-
ployers to initiate discussions' (p. 232), and while
the ERA procedures are used, the main increase in
recognition is voluntary rather than statutory.
However, increases in the *scope* of recognition are
more likely to be union- rather than employer-led
(see below).

Employer reactions to recognition claims, the
evidence suggests (CBI, 1998; Brown *et al.*, 2001;
Wood *et al.*, 2002) means not only that employers
are increasingly compelled to confront recognition
issues, but also that there are difficulties with some
employers in actually conceding recognition claims.
Nevertheless, many employers, if only reluctantly,
accede to the 'business case for trade unionism' and
'overwhelmingly, employers and trade unions have
taken a non-confrontational, voluntary approach
to reaching agreement on recognition in preference
to using the new statutory powers' (IRS, 2002b).

The recognition provisions of the ERA 1999 have
acted as a stimulus to both trade unions and em-
ployers, instilling a sense of urgency and a 'reori-
entation towards existing recognition campaigns'
(Gall and Mckay, 2002, p. 5). Nevertheless, if the
statutory procedure is to be effective, it should
result in changes in behaviour of both unions and
employers, and it may still be too premature to
form any firm conclusions (Wood *et al.*, 2002).

The recognition procedure

Statutory procedures for recognition are not new to
the UK, although the past two attempts are con-
fined to the 1970s. The first statutory procedure

was operated by the now defunct Commission for Industrial Relations (CIR) between 1972 and 1974, while the second was operated by Acas under the 1975 Employment Protection Act and although a considerable number of recognitions were granted, the employers complained that the procedures were biased towards the unions while the unions argued that the procedure was too unwieldy and cumbersome (Wood, 1997). The statutory procedure contained within the ERA 1999, and introduced on 6 June 1999, is the third such attempt to operate a statutory procedure and was designed to deal with the alleged weaknesses of the former attempts. It is described in Exhibit 3.6.

Exhibit 3.6

The procedure for recognition: ERA 1999: introduced June 2000

The procedure applies only where an employer refuses to recognise a trade union and provides the employer and union (the 'social partners') every opportunity at each stage to reach an agreement. For example, once a union has been awarded recognition by the Central Arbitration Committee (CAC), the employer and union are given 30 working days to negotiate their own recognition agreement. It is only if they fail to do so that the specified method of collective bargaining is imposed. Unions are unlikely to make a claim unless they feel reasonably confident of success (see below, main text). Unions usually have 'hit lists' of businesses that they will initially target and are geared up for the process, so employers also need to be prepared for when the campaigning starts in earnest.

1. **Voluntary union recognition (30 working days):** A union makes a formal, written claim for recognition in respect of a specified bargaining unit. The employer then has 10 working days in which to decide whether it will negotiate over recognition or reject it outright. If it decides to negotiate, the employer and union are given a further 20 working days to try to reach an agreement. If an agreement has not been reached, or the employer refuses to negotiate, then the union can refer its claim to the CAC.

2. **Identification of the bargaining unit (30 working days):** Once the CAC has decided the union's claim is admissible, the employer and union have 20 working days to agree a bargaining unit (comprising a definable group such as all hourly paid workers, or those in certain grades, or one particular department across one or more different sites). The union must persuade more than half of those voting to back recognition and the number of votes must represent at least 40 per cent of the bargaining unit. So the union will seek a bargaining unit where this level of support is achievable. If agreement on the bargaining unit cannot be reached, the CAC will decide on the unit within 10 working days. Should employers encourage a large bargaining unit with the aim of diluting the union's influence so that it cannot achieve the requisite level of support in the ballot? (This could backfire and result in the employer having to recognise the union for a wider group of employees.) Or should employers agree a smaller bargaining unit in the hope that support for the union can be contained? (This would give the union a 'foot in the door' from which it could raise a more generalised degree of interest amongst other groups of employees.) Unions are more likely to adopt the incremental approach, if only for the reason that, if they are not successful, they face a three-year moratorium on putting forward another recognition claim for the same bargaining unit.

3. **Campaign and ballot (30 working days):** Once the bargaining unit has been decided and a ballot is due to take place the employer and union have 10 working days to reach an access agreement which establishes the circumstances and times the union can communicate with employees in the bargaining unit to persuade them to vote in favour of recognition. If no agreement is reached during a 20-day access period when both union and employer can campaign for and against recognition respectively, CAC will make the order. The recognition ballot has to be overseen by 'a qualified independent person' such as a solicitor or specified organisation such as the Electoral Reform Society. If the ballot achieves the requisite majority, CAC awards recognition and the process moves to the next stage. If the majority is not achieved the union cannot make another statutory recognition claim for the same bargaining unit for three years.

4. **Setting of bargaining structure (30 working days):** The employer and union have the opportunity, over a period of 30 working days, to negotiate their own collective bargaining structure. If they fail to do so the CAC will impose the specified method of collective bargaining as identified in the procedure.

Can a claim proceed? Before the CAC sets the recognition process in motion it has to be satisfied that the claim is admissible. Situations in which the claim will be thrown out include those where:

- the employer has 20 or fewer employees in the UK;
- the union has previously made an application for union recognition for the same bargaining unit and has been rejected by CAC in the preceding three years;
- the union's membership is less than 10 per cent of the proposed bargaining unit; and
- another trade union is recognised for collective bargaining for any part of the proposed bargaining unit.

The current state of recognition: evidence from WERS 2004 and other research

Some of the new recognition agreements are called partnership agreements (see Chapter 8 for an overview and assessment). The term itself is general enough to subsume any number and type of activity as long as it is, in formal terms, agreeable to the 'partners' and there is equality of power sharing so that unions' and employers' areas of influence are mutually respected. The TGWU, for example, is prepared to endorse partnership agreements where 'partnership is fine so long as the union retains the ability to kick the other in the nuts' (Gall and McKay, 2002, p. 15). Some recognition agreements may not give pride of place to collective bargaining and may permit other non-union forms of representation. This could well reflect employers' intentions to create and retain consultative committees, either as an exclusive forum for non-unionised staff or as an all-inclusive forum, which support collective bargaining as one of several consultative mechanisms. An increase in the number of such committees was expected in advance of the adoption in 2005 of the EU Information and Consultation Directive. A further consequence of the statutory recognition procedures is the greater impetus given to single-union agreements, probably further hastening the decline of multi-union representation.

The IRS 2002 survey of full-recognition deals notes that the great majority of employers and unions have taken a non-confrontational, voluntary rather than statutory approach to reaching agreement on recognition and this is borne out by the evidence: Acas, unlike the CAC, does not play any formal role in determining or adjudicating upon recognition but assists in the voluntary aspects of recognition and in 2001–2, only 49 cases involved the triggering of the statutory recognition process out of some 264 cases completed (Acas, 2002). The IRS (2002a) survey comes up with the following important findings:

- the main sectors of the economy in which recognition deals are occurring are paper and printing (113 cases, comprising 43 per cent of the total), transport and communication (31 cases, 12 per cent of total), general manufacturing (26, 10 per cent), general services (25, 9.5 per cent) and engineering/metals (23, 9 per cent);
- the typical number of employees covered by a new recognition agreement is 65, although the mean figure is 322. The largest agreement is that between the broadcasting and entertainment union BECTU and the real estate company Land Securities Trillium covering 15,000 workers. The smallest deal covered four workers only;
- most employees covered by the new agreements are manual or craft workers (65 per cent), non-manual are in a minority with 18 per cent, while 'mixed' manual–non-manual comprise 18 per cent;
- unions with the best success rates include the print union – GPMU with 36 per cent of the deals covered in the IRS survey, followed by GMB and Amicus;
- the trend in recognition deals is upwards, with the existence of the legal procedure being, arguably, the most important factor in the ability of unions to secure voluntary deals; and

- the **main criticisms** of the legal framework for recognition have focused on:
 - the exclusion of employers with fewer than 21 employees;
 - the narrow range of issues covered by collective bargaining;
 - the criteria for defining the bargaining unit;
 - the general complexity of the procedures;
 - the use of ballots as opposed to membership audit;
 - the availability of employer challenge through judicial review;
 - the exclusion of jurisdiction where recognition already exists; and
 - the thresholds for admissibility and awarding recognition.

More recent research (Gall, 2004; Blanden *et al.*, 2006, Kersley *et al.*, 2006) suggest that while the 1999 recognition procedure has had little direct impact concerning the number of agreements awarded statutorily, the 'indirect impact [of the procedure] on the extent of voluntary recognition appears more extensive with the balance of derecognitions and new recognitions having altered in favour of the latter' (Kersley *et al.*, 2006, p. 117). Both Gall (2004) and Blanden *et al.*, 2006) make more or less the same point in arguing that the majority of new recognition agreements have been secured volunt-

arily, and as Moore (2004) points out, 'the success of the statutory procedure lies in its shadow effect, the conclusion of voluntary agreements in the shadow of the law' (p. 30). Moore also argues that the longer-term effectiveness and objectives of the statutory procedure may well be undermined by a minority of employers and goes on to state perhaps contentiously:

> *The government's aim of fairness at work based upon balancing the rights of employers and workers ignores the reality of workplace relations following decades of employer ascendancy and the fundamental tenet that the employment relationship is unequal. Ultimately this balance of forces means that employers can raise the costs of collective action too high for many workers. The absence of adequate legal redress apparently means that employers can dismiss union activists and are free to state quite openly during CAC ballots that they will consider moving production in the event of union recognition. The deregulation of global markets and the experience of manufacturing communities in the past 20 years mean the threat by a multinational to relocate investment has credibility.* (p. 30)

The more detailed points concerning recognition arising from WERS 2004 as reported by Kersley *et al.* (2006) are summarised below (Exhibit 3.7).

Exhibit 3.7

Recognition findings from WERS 2004

1. Overall, 30 per cent of workplaces recognised at least one trade union for the purposes of negotiating pay and conditions. However, the incidence of union recognition was much higher among larger workplaces than small ones; two-thirds of workplaces with more than 500 employees recognised trade unions compared with just one-fifth of those with between 10 and 24 employees.

2. Union recognition was also positively associated with the size of organisation to which the workplace belonged. Workplaces belonging to organisations with fewer than 100 employees were very unlikely to recognise unions – only 6 per cent. The equivalent figure among workplaces belonging to organisations with 10,000 or more employees was 62 per cent.

3. The recognition of trade unions was almost universal within the public sector workplaces (90 per cent). By contrast, in the private sector only 16 per cent of workplaces recognised unions.

4. Stark contrasts were also apparent between recognition rates in different industry sectors, with universal absence of recognition in hotels and catering establishments. Electricity, gas and water and financial services stood out as the only industry sectors in which recognition was the norm among private sector employees.

Source: Kersley *et al.*, 2006, pp. 118–21

Factors to consider in membership recruitment, recognition and retention

In the light of statutory recognition procedures, the supportive role of the TUC is essential in providing unions, particularly smaller ones, with appropriate guidance and information (see below). Larger unions have a part to play in this respect, as the case of the GMB illustrates (Main case 3.2).

Main case 3.2
Trade union recruitment and recognition: the case of the GMB 1998 and UNISON 2006

The analysis of causes of membership loss undertaken by the GMB also contains survey data concerning the needs of membership and how the union should respond to them. Four broad analytical categories were identified:

(i) **Analysis of reasons for being in the GMB.** The reasons given, in order of importance, include support if a problem arises at work; improved pay and conditions; a belief in trade unionism; GMB industrial benefits; most people at their workplace are union members; GMB membership services; GMB financial services; GMB public campaigning.

(ii) **The support required most at the workplace.** This includes advice and representation on disciplinary and grievance matters; advice and representation on health and safety matters; legal assistance on accidents and problems at work.

(iii) **Bargaining priorities.** These differed between the sexes, women tending to rank equal pay for work of equal value higher than pensions, while men generally place pensions ahead of equal pay. Both sexes rank equal pay in front of other equalities like nursery or crèche facilities and paid paternity leave. The top six bargaining priorities were: improvements in pay; better pensions and retirement rights; equal pay; protection against unfair dismissal; improvements in health and safety; a legal minimum wage.

(iv) **The scope for improvements in workplace support members receive from GMB.** The main observations were:

- most members say that they want more contact with full-time officials. Many members feel that contact with their shop steward or staff representative is already well organised and say the same about contact with their full-time officer;

- three-quarters want more information on union affairs and on pay and conditions negotiations. They also want the GMB to listen more to their views on workplace issues; and

- over two-thirds say they want branch meetings at more convenient times or more appropriate locations.

From survey analysis and other investigations, the GMB report comes up with certain recommendations for action: 'There can be no concealing the need to boost organisation and recruitment and to win recognition in new sites. That must mean steering more resources towards recruitment activities in areas offering the best prospects of success.'

- **Where?** East Anglia, the East Midlands, the South West, Yorkshire and Humberside, and the South East outside Greater London – because those are the parts of the country where most new jobs are expected to appear.

- **Which industries?** The service sector of the economy – public services and private services, notably business areas covered by GMB Commercial Services Section – because that is where recruitment potential is greatest and where most new jobs are being created.

- **Which occupations?** White-collar jobs – especially in the personal and protective occupations and associate professional and technical jobs like nurses, social workers and technicians – rather than craft and skilled manual jobs, because the former are gradually replacing the latter.

- **Which age groups?** Those aged about 30–45 in particular, because their numbers are rising rapidly and there will be four times as many in this age group in five years' time as the numbers of non-students aged below 25. We should use new information technology to encourage young people to become more aware of the world of work and what the GMB does for its members.

- **Men or women?** Increasingly women, because most new jobs are likely to be taken by women.

- **Full-time or part-time jobs?** Increasingly part-time jobs, because they already account for one job in four and this proportion is rising. But probably

not self-employed people because only 10 per cent of them appear to join any union, though special circumstances may apply in the construction industry.

- **Promoting which union services?** Emphasising the terrific deal that the GMB service package represents – support if a problem arises at work, including advice and representation on job security, grievance and disciplinary matters, health and safety issues, training and personal development opportunities and pay, especially equal pay and low pay; specialist legal support; other specialist services including help in improving pensions entitlements and retirement rights and dealing with human resource management initiatives.
- **Championing which issues?** Whichever ones matter most according to the relevant workplace health check but, in general, the top six among most people who join the GMB are: low pay, equal pay, protection against unfair dismissal, better pension and retirement rights, health and safety, and a national minimum wage.
- **How?** In five main ways:
 1. By more workplace contact with members and potential recruits, using the workplace health check system and prioritising officer time.
 2. By establishing GMB organisation on new sites, using the new law that the Labour government is committed to bringing in, obliging employers to recognise a union where the majority of workers want it to represent them.
 3. By acting on the principle of 'follow the work' and winning recognition from major employers who are new to traditional areas of GMB activity, like private contractors to local authorities and new competitors in the energy sector.
 4. By breaking into new recruitment fields, like employment agencies and private residential care homes, with the aim of building genuine partnerships with responsible companies, to the benefit both of employees and employers.
 5. By steering GMB resources towards organisation and recruitment and away from routine administration and low value activities of any kind. The CEC (Central Executive Committee) has already earmarked an initial £0.5 million for a recruitment fighting fund to allow regions to appoint temporary recruiters, and several regional initiatives are going ahead.

Unison: recruitment . . . the challenge for 2010

Recruitment and organisation are the lifeblood of UNISON, as they are of any union. The recruitment campaign, launched in 2006, aims to build a union of 2 million members by 2010. The plans are being finalised for an approach that will galvanise members in branches, regions and service groups. Individuals who join the campaign will take on the task of recruiting 10 new members over 12 months. This comes after a period of recruitment success. UNISON recruited 162,000 new members in 2005 for a net gain of 32,000. And this year (2006) . . . saw the highest monthly membership recruitment on record.

But although membership has been rising, a number of reasons – including competition from other unions, has meant UNISON's density has been declining in key sectors. In some workplaces, fewer than 50% of eligible workers are members of UNISON – and that affects our ability to represent and negotiate for members. The union is growing at 2% a year, but the new strategy raises that to 6% in 2007. The recruitment challenge cannot be separated from UNISON's emphasis on organising as the key to its future: direct involvement in one-to-one recruitment will help members see the value of building a stronger and better organised branch. New research, which looks at the impact of the union's organising and recruiting strategy, confirms that branch development and organising plans and techniques – such as workplace mapping, active recruitment procedures and collaborations with regional staff – are essential building blocks of successful branches.

Yet that organising approach is used by just half of UNISON branches. The NEC calls on branches to:

- Adopt the organising approach to build and revitalise membership and workplace organisation;
- Encourage experienced stewards to attend the One Step Ahead training programme, which equips them with the latest organising and recruitment skills;
- Work with the national union density project team to establish accurate and reliable employer density figures;
- Review and revise facility time agreements to take account of the interests of shift workers, part-time workers and self-organised groups; and
- Access regional pool funds to finance branch organising campaigns, including activist secondments.

Organising success depends on mobilising more activists and using the right recruitment methods. Branches recording high (membership) growth had an active branch development and organising plan including:

- Mapping workplaces;
- A plan to recruit new members;
- Partnership working with regional organising staff and branch development staff;
- Training in recruitment techniques;
- Use of the regional pool for organising activities;
- Regular briefings on recruitment;
- Use of new starters' lists;
- Attending employee induction sessions;
- Allocating a branch budget for recruitment activities;
- Putting recruitment on the branch agenda;
- Using promotional items or incentives.

Source: GMB, 1998; UNISON, 2006

Self-evaluation activity 3.15

Extent to which recruitment aims are achieved
Response on website

To what extent do you think that trade unions in Britain today are able to achieve the recruitment aims established by the GMB and UNISON?

THE FUTURE OF UK TRADE UNIONS

We have identified many aspects of union decline, which, taken together, point to a fairly persistent trend of decline from 1980 onwards. There is nothing to suggest that this trend will either suddenly, or over a short period of time, be thrown into reverse. Probably the best case scenario is to acieve a stabilisation of membership in the mid term as indicated by membership figures for 1998–2006, with marginal increases in membership as more recognition agreements are processed. The initiatives identified in the following pages could undoubtedly have a positive effect on membership, but membership gains can easily be cancelled out by recruitment inertia, employer policies and membership turnover,

to name but a few factors. At the present time, the analogy with attempting to run up a quickly descending escalator would seem to be appropriate for the union movement.

So what can be done? Some light upon this dilemma is shed by a selection of contributions including those of Hyman (2002), Heery (2002), Kelly (2002), O'Grady and Nowak (2004), Wilson (2007) and Willman and Bryson (2007). Kelly contends that unions should take advantage of 'power resources' when negotiating with employers and government. This probably assumes that unions are not using latent bargaining power and other influences to their fullest extent. Secondly, unions should identify and exploit the weaknesses inherent in multinational companies to their own advantage and, finally, collective action from within may not be 'sufficient to defeat powerful opponents' and this may necessitate the support and use of additional resources such as other workers, government, public sector organisations, organised consumers, campaigning groups and social movements. Hyman (2002), on the other hand offers more specific prescriptions and argues that unions in the twenty-first century 'confront old dilemmas, but in new forms' (p. 10). In essence, unions must tackle three issues:

- *Whose* interests do trade unions represent? Relevant constituencies include 'the qualified elite'; the core workforce; peripheral employees and those outside employment.
- *Which* interests of those represented are of primary interest and relevance to trade unions? Interests may include basic collective bargaining over pay and benefits; more rights limiting employers' 'arbitrary authority' by improving employment protection (p. 11); the role of the state and its policies; and interests external to work and union such as environmental, consumer protection and community.
- *How* are interests represented? The main issues are structure of unions and which is the most effective; the organisational capacity of the union, involving a proactive rather than reactive approach to membership and policy generally; the 'complex dialectic between leadership and democracy' (p. 12) in terms of the extent to which union members can influence and shape

priorities and programmes of their unions; and how unions balance 'contradictory modes of action: mobilisation and struggle on the one hand, compromise on the other' (p. 12).

Heery (2002) considers the way ahead in the uneasy and often contradictory relationship between 'partnership' and 'organising' strategies which 'are often presented as alternative options for revitalising British labour' (p. 21). In fact, partnership and organising may be regarded as complementary, constituting a combined union renewal strategy (see below). In the first instance, we look at the pragmatic issue of what unions in general should focus upon for the purpose of recruitment and bringing recognition claims. O' Grady and Nowak point to the creation of the New Unionism Task Group set up by the TUC in 1996 and the subsequent development of the Organising Academy (as described later in the chapter) in 1998 as being influential factors in supporting unions to develop an organising culture, develop existing membership bases and sharpening the appeal of unions to traditionally under-represented groups including women, young workers and workers from black and ethnic minority backgrounds. O'Grady and Nowak (2004) point out that reaching out to under-represented groups has proved to be extremely challenging with the young and ethnic minority groups particularly resistant to recruitment activities and emphasises the need to abandon the 'one size fits all approach' that some unions still cling on to at the expense of making unions more flexible in approach and more attractive to 'atypical' workers. The authors conclude that unions in the UK still need to do much to address membership decline and density, and in particular to 'make a step change in the way they organise; to increase the investment they make in organising; to strategically focus their organising efforts; and to do more to reach out to those workers for whom unions have little appeal or relevance' (p. 162). Wilson's (2007) analysis of union membership and density identifies a number of key issues which 'growing unions are tackling' (p. 29) and offers a less pessimistic scenario than other contributions that have been considered in this chapter, culminating in 'A 9 point plan for growth' summarised below (Exhibit 3.8).

Exhibit 3.8

A nine-point plan for growth

1. A new image for the movement

The fact that most union members are 'professionals' or 'associate professionals' poses difficult questions for the union movement as a whole . . . Most of the union world's typical features (TUC annual Congress, branch structures and terminology such as 'bosses') have not changed in over 100 years despite a radically different union membership profile. Evidence suggests that to be most credible, unions should aim to be seen as calmly persuasive, focus on the practical benefits of membership, be realistic in their campaigning aims and reassert the basic value of collective solidarity . . . There has been a quiet cultural revolution in many unions and the 'brand' should reflect the new culture.

2. Listen to members

Many unions have turned themselves around by an internal shake-up which included paying close attention to what members felt and wanted from their union. Democratic structures are one way in which members' voice can be heard . . . Unions are also using other methods such as, for example, surveys, e-surveys and polling, member panels and group discussion. The Union Modernisation Fund requires unions to have strategic plans and it is striking how many plans now pay explicit attention and devote major resources to member relations.

3. Support activists

Unions have around 250,000 workplace representatives and are becoming more representative of their members. Union Learning Representatives are more likely to be younger, women and black or from ethnic minorities. The newly developing concept of equality reps will also improve reps' profile. Successful unions put great effort into nurturing their activists; supporting them with training, advice, information, giving warm recognition and regular encouragement. Education and training for reps is crucial. TUC Education (unionlearn) trained over 42,000 reps in 2005. Many unions are now seeking agreements to improve their reps' facilities and get better support from management . . .

4. Occupational identity

Retaining and maintaining occupational identity is important, particularly within larger more heterogeneous unions such as general and 'super unions'.

5. Investment in organising

It is essential that unions put more resources into recruiting and organising. Many unions already do this but equally, many do not. There is no adequate model which encapsulates principles and methods of organising, hence 'each union will (should) develop its own appropriate mix of many approaches, all united in the aim of building an active, growing, confident membership' (p. 31).

6. Skills, learning and continuing professional development

'Union members will more than ever need to learn throughout their lives, as technology and work organisation changes' (p. 32). Unions are increasingly offering continuing professional development (CPD) and training as a benefit of membership but the extent to which this type of training is offered is also dependent upon employers investing in such training initiatives.

7. Invest in union management

'Using members' money most effectively means professional management'. This is essential as unions must be seen to be professional managers of people and aspire to the Investors in People (IIP) standard. Many unions have achieved IIP but there are still wide variations between unions in this respect.

8. Equality

Unions should make more efforts to redress inequalities within the workplace, not only in relation to gender, race, age, and disability but also in relation to work conditions, contracts, access to jobs and promotion and pay equality.

9. Unions in society

Traditionally, unions were concerned mainly about jobs and pay rather than wider social issues (the TUC has also traditionally represented the parochial concerns of the trade union movement as a whole). Nevertheless in recent years both the TUC and some larger unions have become involved in wider societal concerns and movements by campaigning, for example, against the BNP and racism, cuts in public services in local communities, lobbying to keep open post offices, combating corporate greed and re-engaging with local communities.

Source: Wilson, 2007

Which areas should unions target for the purpose of increasing membership?

Three sources amongst many – TUC (1999, 2002), IRS (1998, 2002a) and the Labour Force Survey (reported in Grainger, 2006) – identify the areas which are thought to have an influence on trade union membership levels. These are:

- **personal characteristics** of the employee such as gender, ethnicity, age, education, political ideology and area of residence;
- **features of employment** such as occupation, manual or non-manual work, part-time or full-time work, permanence of job, earnings and size of establishment;
- **attitudes to work** such as satisfaction with, and commitment to employment; and
- **macroeconomic conditions**, including the level of employment and the inflation rate.

We have considered some of these factors earlier in the chapter and you should review the appropriate section before reading on. We shall now concentrate upon membership influences identified under the five sub-headings below, but before doing so, it is important to point out that, according to the TUC trends analysis of trade union membership (2002), and the Labour Force Survey (LFS) of 2002, the membership figures for 2002 suggested that trade union membership, apart from minor fluctuations, had stabilised and that trade unions' increased commitment to recruitment was paying off. However, as has been pointed out earlier in this chapter, there has been further marginal membership decline since 2002 (Grainger and Crowther, 2007). Nevertheless, unions are signing up new members in areas where unionisation has been traditionally low and are recruiting more women, part-time and Asian workers (TUC, 2002). Some unions, such as the GMB, are attempting to organise workers in non-traditional occupations where labour is dispersed, where there is no history of unionisation and where employers may be hostile. Examples of atypical occupations as targets for recruitment include lapdancers, minicab drivers and migrant workers (GMB), childcare workers in private nurseries (TGWU) and clergy, mostly drawn from the Church of England (Amicus

MSF). Nevertheless, trade union density remains at a post-war low, the proportion of employees belonging to a union in 2001 being 28.4 per cent (UK figures), having fallen from the 1979 high of 55 per cent.

Men and women (2006 data)

Women traditionally have been less likely than men to join trade unions, although the rate of decline in membership amongst men has been more dramatic: between 1989 and 2001 membership among men fell by around 13 per cent to just below 30 per cent, while the corresponding decline among women has been 4 per cent to 28 per cent. The main reason for this difference is the lower unionisation rate in part-time jobs and the over-representation of women in part-time work. The disproportionately low unionisation rate for women can also be explained with reference to their employment in certain sectors, such as the service sector which has traditionally low density rates, and the fewer opportunities for women to unionise as compared with men (WERS 1998/2004). However, during the period 2003–6, a higher proportion of women than men were trade union members. Union density among women in 2006 fell by 0.2 per cent to 29.7 per cent as compared with 2005, while for male employees it fell by 0.9 per cent to 27.2 per cent.

Age and ethnicity (2006 data)

Unionisation increases rapidly with age. The highest union density recorded for any age group is for employees aged between 40 and 49 years, at 38 per cent. Low rates of unionisation among young employees can be partly explained by the proliferation of part-time and temporary work in sectors which are traditionally under-unionised. Older women employees are less likely to be union members than male employees. Explanations for these variations are tenuous and speculative and await further research. In 2006, a high proportion (45.5 per cent) of union members were aged between 35 and 49, compared with 35.2 per cent of non-members. By contrast, just 1 in 20 (5.3 per cent) union members were aged between 16 and 24, compared with almost one-fifth (18.7 per cent) of non-members.

Almost half (47.6 per cent) of union members had done more than ten years of service compared with only one-fifth (20.7 per cent) of non-members. Approximately 93 per cent of union members were of white ethnic origin and over a quarter (29.6) of union members hold a degree. The majority (69.2 per cent) of union members are in workplaces with 50 employees or more versus 45.8 per cent of non-members.

Overall, black employees are as likely to be in a trade union as the workforce generally with 30 per cent of black, and 29 per cent of white employees. There are, however, gender and ethnic group differences. Afro-Caribbean women have a higher rate of membership than all other female groups at 33 per cent, and black women employees are more likely to be unionised (27 per cent) than black male employees, while mixed, Asian and other ethnic groups have lower densities, varying from 22 to 25 per cent. By ethnicity, Black or Black British employees had the highest union density: 33.1 per cent in 2006 compared to 28.7 per cent for White employees and 24.3 per cent Asian or Asian British employees. Union membership rates were lower among mixed ethnic backgrounds (23.6 per cent) and Chinese or other ethnic groups (18.0 per cent).

Geographical and occupational variations (2006 data)

Table 3.5 shows union density by major occupation and region for all UK employees from autumn 2001 to 2006. Union density of skilled trade occupations has continued to decline – from 30.1 per cent in 2001 to 24.0 per cent in 2006. However, there has been very little change in union density across the other major occupational groups since 2001. With regard to union density by major industry and gender for all UK employees from autumn 1995 to 2006, nearly all of industries have seen a fall in union density over this period.

Sectoral and industrial distribution (2006 data)

Union membership is fairly evenly divided between public and private sectors (LFS includes higher and further education within the public sector). However, union density in the public sector is much

Table 3.5 Union density by region and occupation: 2006

Unionisation in the regions: employees in union and staff associations (%)		Union density by occupation: employees in unions (%)	
South East	22	Managers and senior officials	17
Eastern	23	Professional	47.2
London	25.3	Associate professional/technical	43
South West	24.8	Administrative and secretarial	23.7
East Midlands	26.9	Skilled trades	24
West Midlands	28.4	Personal service	30.5
Yorks and Humberside	28.7	Sales and customer service	12.7
North West	34.4	Process, plant and machine operatives	33.4
North East	38.9	Elementary	20.5
Wales	35.9		
Scotland	34.6		
Northern Ireland	39.7		
England	27		
All employees	29		

Source: Labour Force Survey, Office for National Statistics 2007 (Grainger and Crowther, 2007)

Table 3.6 Union density by industry: 2006

Industry	Percentage of employees in unions		
	All	Private sector	Public sector
Agriculture/forestry/fishing	9	6	–
Mining/quarrying	24	24	–
Manufacturing	22	22	–
Energy and water	49	49	–
Construction	16	12	67
Wholesale and retail trade	11	11	–
Hotels and restaurants	6	5	32
Transport and communication	41	35	73
Financial intermediation	24	24	–
Real estate and business services	10	8	53
Public administration	57	31	59
Education	55	31	59
Health	43	15	60
Other activities	20	9	46

Source: Labour Force Survey, 2007; Grainger and Crowther, 2007

higher (60 per cent) than in the private sector (19 per cent). The gender breakdown of union membership in the two sectors is very different as more men than women work in the private sector. Hence 60 per cent of men belonging to a union are private sector employees, while 66 per cent of women belonging to a union are public sector employees. Union density rates are highest in public administration, education and health, energy and water, and transport, while retail, hotels and catering, agriculture, forestry and fishing, and real estate reveal the lowest densities. Union density among women employees is lower in all industrial sectors apart from financial and business services and hotels and catering (see Table 3.6).

Workplace size, length of service and flexible labour (2006 data)

The larger the establishment, the more likely it is to be unionised. Clearly, it is easier for unions to organise in larger workplaces, and where the workforce is large it is more likely that employees will regard themselves as a collectivity rather than individuals, which will make them more amenable to unionisation (Bain and Elsheikh, 1976). In workplaces with fewer than 25 employees, union density stood at only 15 per cent, compared with 36 per cent among larger establishments (LMT, 2002). The LFS report confirms the direct correlation between union density and length of service. Unionisation rates for employees who have been in their current job for less than one year is 12 per cent, rising to 32 per cent for those who have been in their current job for between five and ten years, and for those in their current job for over 20 years the figure is 60 per cent. The report also provides a breakdown of union membership in different types of 'flexible' employment, including temporary employment, flexitime, job sharing arrangements, term-time working, annualised hours, 4.5-day weeks, nine-day fortnights and zero hours contracts. Temporary work includes fixed term contracts as well as agency temping, casual and seasonal employment, and employees within this category, unsurprisingly, are less likely to be unionised, with 19 per cent union members compared to 30 per cent of employees in permanent jobs. Other forms of flexible working, with the exception of those on zero hours contracts, show relatively high unionisation rates.

Self-evaluation activity 3.16

Recruitment strategies

This SEA has no commentary

From the information provided above, identify those categories of employee on which unions should focus their recruitment strategies.

Recruitment strategies and the 'relaunch' of the TUC

Clearly, the TUC has a crucial role in shaping strategies to counter union decline, recognising the limits to what individual unions can achieve without the assistance and guidance of a concerted overarching strategy. The TUC, of necessity, sought out a new role for itself during the early 1990s, prompted by the weakening of unions as a result of the 'neo-liberal assault' of Thatcherism (Waddington, 2003); continuing employer resistance to unionism in growth sectors of the economy, including attempts by employers to minimise union influence where unions are recognised; the considerable and progressive weakening of links between the union movement and the Labour Party (the 'end of traditionalism' thesis) and restricted access to government. These adverse developments not only encouraged an organisational rejuvenation of the TUC, but also helped to widen and deepen links with the EU in terms of supporting European integration and social policy, and facilitated the development of 'social partnerships' with employers (see Chapter 8). Perhaps the most significant initiative was the adoption of an organising model and strategy to tackle union membership decline, as part of the TUC 'relaunch' and 'new unionism' slogan.

In its analysis of the LFS membership data for 2002, the TUC (2002) asserts, rather optimistically, that 'this latest report shows an encouraging stabilisation in trade union membership in 2001 with the employee unionisation rate remaining at around 30 per cent' (p. 21). The TUC goes on to state:

There are also positive indications that the 'New Unionism' campaign of recent years, focusing on attracting new members (especially among women

and ethnic minority employees) is beginning to bear fruit. Specific examples of this include the increases in union density between 1997 and 1998 among two particular groups of employees – women part-timers and black women. (p. 21)

However the LFS data for 2006 has not borne out the TUC's optimism as Grainger and Crowther (2007) point out: 'The rate of union membership (union density) for employees in the UK fell by 0.6 percentage points to 28.4 per cent in 2006, down from 29.0 per cent in 2005. This was the largest annual percentage point decline since 1998' (p. 1).

The TUC 'relaunch'

In 1994 the TUC reinvented itself by restructuring its administrative and decision-making system and by attempting to generate a 'new ethos and sense of mission' (Heery, 1998). Internally the TUC has reformed its representative machinery which involved:

- The elimination of the standing committees of the General Council and the TUC industry committees while retaining the General Council itself, which meets less frequently, and delegating some of its activities to an Executive Committee and other joint committees.
- The setting up of Task Groups comprising General Council members and other representatives to develop policy on a range of issues 'including stake holding, full employment, representation at work, human resource management, part-time workers and union organising' (Heery, 1998, p. 341).

The TUC also reformed its management practice and structure, which was considered to be unwieldy and bureaucratic, in order to reflect the functioning of the newly created task groups. Heery (1998) states:

There has been a new emphasis on project work across department boundaries; posts have been redesigned and redesignated and their incumbents encouraged to act with greater autonomy; there has been a deliberate attempt to renew the organisation through external appointments; and TUC staff have been granted formal membership

of Task Groups, alongside representatives from affiliates, and encouraged to participate openly in decision making. These developments, in turn, have been supported by greater investment in staff development, including a successful attempt to secure the Investors in People standard. (p. 342)

A further development has been to make the TUC more broadly representative, not only of trade unions but also of labour as a whole. The TUC has attempted to become a more broadly based pressure group reflecting the diversity of employee interests within a 'world of work' context. For example, the broadening of the TUC's constituency included encouraging employees to contact the TUC 'Bad Bosses Hotline' in order to expose employer malpractices and focusing upon hitherto marginal concerns such as gays, young workers and home workers.

The next stage of the TUC relaunch was the inauguration of the TUC's Organising Academy in 1998 which offers training for union officers in recruitment and organising skills. The relaunch not only focuses upon the TUC as an organisation in relation to its internal structure and constituents, but also, in line with its mission statement to adopt a high profile in campaigning nationally, emphasises links external to the labour movement. Heery (1998) identifies four important changes which typify this alliance-building and networking approach:

1. Initiating contacts with political parties other than the Labour Party, by, for example, establishing a presence at the annual conference of all the main parties. There has also been a 'greater emphasis on lobbying members of Parliament in both Houses of Parliament and seeking to identify cross-party support for TUC policy' (p. 343).
2. Strengthening links with the CBI by encouraging reciprocal invitations to both organisations' conferences and establishing contacts with employers' associations, the Association of British Chambers of Commerce, the Institute of Directors, the Institute of Personnel and Development and other bodies. The TUC is also keen to establish and maintain contacts with employers and attempt to influence employer behaviour by, for

example, promoting the idea of 'social partnership' whereby unions co-operate with employers concerning 'the modernisation of British industry on the basis of flexible working and investment in skills' (p. 344).
3. Facilitating contacts with voluntary sector organisations including churches, single-issue campaigning organisations, professional bodies and public agencies and using their specialist knowledge and skills to enrich TUC campaigns. For example, campaigns concerning occupational pensions have embraced organisations such as various pensions bodies, the Consumers' Association, Age Concern and the Police Federation.
4. Developing a new Campaigns and Communications Department to encourage greater professionalism in campaigning on a variety of issues, 'engaging a non-traditional union audience through non-traditional media [such as] the personal finance and women's pages of newspapers like the *Daily Mail* and *Daily Express*, women's magazines and local press and radio' (p. 345). Heery (1998) summarises the TUC relaunch below:

The relaunch of the TUC can be viewed as an attempt both to change trade union methods and to promote a substantive shift in trade union strategy. The changes in methods fall into two broad categories. First, there has been the attempt to promote 'strategic' action by the TUC in which key goals and attainable objectives are identified and a plan is set in train for their realisation. The manifestation of this shift has been the transposition of the TUC's work into a series of campaigns, each conducted through its dedicated Task Group. Second, there has been an emphasis on 'partnership' and the building of supporting coalitions for each campaign, which has been seen in the changed orientation to political parties, employers and third sector organisations. The TUC has become a networking organisation, and in certain respects the relaunch amounts less to the renewal of the labour movement and more to its submersion in a diffuse network of progressive alliances and campaigns. The key substantive change echoes these themes of partnership and coalition, in its

concern to develop an encompassing trade union movement based on recognising and responding to diversity within the workforce. Since the relaunch, the question of union organising has moved to the forefront of TUC policy and has found expression in a dual concern to promote sustained recruitment by member unions and to draw an increasing proportion of women, young, contingent and service-sector workers into trade union membership. (p. 346)

The 'new unionism' and recruitment: 'organising' v 'servicing'

The 'organising' approach, strategy or model, which is described in more detail below, is counterpoised by the 'servicing' model, both of which are intended to reinforce and extend union organisation. The servicing approach, which was initiated by the TUC in 1987, is concerned with providing support and services to union members. The source of such support is external to the workplace and comes typically from full-time union officers and from the union itself, examples of which include a range of financial services packages comprising discounted insurance on holidays, cars, etc., credit card facilities, personal loans and mortgage arrangements, with the object of attracting potential membership. Research undertaken by Waddington and Whitson (1997) and Waddington and Kerr (1999) suggests that the servicing approach used on its own would appear to have had little success in influencing the rate of unionisation, hence the move towards the organising approach (see also Waddington, 2003). The organising approach, the main elements of which are summarised below, complements rather than excludes the servicing approach and seeks to cultivate a proactive culture of organising and recruitment based on the activities of workplace union representatives.

Launched in 1996, the 'new unionism' is based on a number of organising principles which the TUC argues are needed to guide successful organising campaigns. They include:

- **Put organising first:** recruitment and organisation must become the top priority for the whole union movement.

- **Invest real resources:** organising does not come cheap, and only a significant commitment of resources – money and people – to recruitment and organisation can reverse membership decline.

- **Develop a strategic approach:** properly thought-out and resourced organising campaigns which set realistic targets are more likely to deliver results – and boost morale.

- **Cut out wasteful rivalries:** unions must be encouraged to focus on the rise of the non-unionised sector and the threat this poses to the whole union movement.

- **Reflect the diversity of the workforce** and those groups traditionally under-represented in unions.

- **Increase the use of dedicated organisers – and boost their training and status:** the AFL-CIO Organising Institute (USA) and ACTU Organising Works (Australia) programmes have brought new blood into the movement, upskilled the job of organising – and paid for themselves through recruitment success.

- **Build lay representatives' confidence and skills:** investing in building lay representatives' organisation helps strengthen existing bases and frees up full-time officers to organise in new areas.

- **Communication is the key:** imaginative campaigning and use of the mass media are key to getting the union message across to working people.

- **Government sympathy does not guarantee growth:** union membership can continue to slide even where the government in power is sympathetic to union values and, as in Australia, a social partnership accord is in place.

Based on these organising principles, a number of objectives were identified by the new unionism task group. These include promoting organising as top priority together with a shift towards an organising culture; increasing investment of union resources in recruitment and organising; strengthening lay structures and developing new training packages for both lay and full-time organisers; setting up special projects for unions to build their existing bases and break into new areas, winning recognition rights; sharpening unions' appeal to 'new' workers, including women, youth and those at the 'rough

end' of the labour market, through campaigns and the media; promoting debate and disseminating information on successful organising approaches; and assessing the feasibility of launching an organising academy (see right) to train up – mainly young – specialist union organisers.

The TUC has also been informed by research into why people join unions during a period of membership decline (Waddington and Whitson, 1997). The responses to a questionnaire survey of new recruits' reasons for joining a union were placed into one of two broad categories comprising:

- **collective reasons** such as mutual support, improved pay and conditions, peer group pressure and a belief in the principle of union organisation; and
- **individual benefits** including training and education, industrial benefits and professional services, free legal advice and financial services.

Waddington and Whitson found that collective factors are by far the most important reasons why people join trade unions, thereby emphasising the importance of collective forces which underpin union membership and the support amongst new recruits for what are regarded as 'traditional' trade union activities. There is, therefore, little support for the argument that 'individualisation' has dissolved the labour movement since 1979. Indeed, collective reasons for joining a trade union remain as strong as ever, and this is repeated across most industries and occupations. But the fact that employers have found it easy to resist recognition claims, or even an effective union presence, has made unions unavailable to vast numbers of potential members. The lessons to be drawn from this research are that there are two main strategic activities that unions should concentrate on: firstly, deepening recruitment in organised workplaces; and secondly, extending membership in unorganised areas rather than offering financial and other services. Waddington and Whitson's research therefore provides support for the view that trade unions should develop organising strategies rather than concentrate upon 'service' aspects. In adopting organising strategies, the TUC has also been learning from the experiences of unions overseas, particularly Australia and the USA.

The Organising Academy

In 1996 the TUC task group agreed to develop an organisers' academy modelled on the US AFL-CIO's Organising Institute and the Australian 'Organising Works' programme. The TUC gave the Organising Academy the go-ahead in 1997. In commenting upon the rationale for the Academy, the TUC (1998) states:

The Organising Academy stresses that successful organising involves not only recruiting members but building strong sustainable workplace organisation. In this way members can win more power and practical improvements in their working lives – and they are more likely to stay in membership. The old recruitment model, in its extreme form, uses numbers as the main (and sometimes the only) criterion; it makes no allowance for the value of recruiting, say 100 members in a hostile environment compared with 200 in easier recruitment grounds. Nor is any special value attached to using innovative techniques, to making inroads into new jobs or categories of workers, or to putting the brakes on membership throughput. The Academy does not under-estimate the importance of the old adage 'strength through numbers'. The success of many campaigns hinges on winning new members fast and in volume as the best means to achieve real workplace change. What distinguishes the organising model from the old recruitment approach is that organisers aim to achieve success both in numbers and strong organisation. The organising model can deliver numbers plus. This approach underpins our evaluation of organising success and, if we succeed, will help guarantee our future. (p. 15)

Other main features of the Academy include:

- carefully structured arrangements for recruitment, training, coaching, mentoring and placement of predominantly young organisers who will also reflect the gender (at least half the trainees are women) and racial diversity of the workforce the unions aim to attract;
- an active partnership between the national centre and participating unions in shaping, overseeing, managing and delivering the programme;

- a TUC Organising Academy steering group comprising representatives of each sponsoring union – along with appropriate TUC personnel – to oversee all aspects of the initiative;
- recruitment to the programme through an agreed process involving the TUC and participating unions; and
- a rigorous and independent evaluation of the pilot programme.

The US and Australian examples are given in greater detail in Exhibit 3.9.

Concluding comments: is organising working?

The relaunch of the TUC against the backdrop of declining membership, economic recession and, until 1997, right-wing government, 'reinforced by the increased competitive pressures in world markets and the internationalisation of production and corporate organisation' (Kelly, 1998, p. 60), could be regarded not only as a 'modernisation' process but also as a means of accommodating employers by trading benefits to employers (many of whom are hostile to a union presence). One such benefit is co-operation in changing work arrangements and flexibility in return for concessions such as recognition for purposes of collective bargaining; this is the 'social partnership' theme, which is part of the rhetoric of new unionism (Kelly, 1996). Social partnership (see Chapter 8) replaces (or deconstructs) 'traditional' methods since 'the adverse balance of power (in favour of the employer) appears to rule out the feasibility of unions recovering membership and influence by threatening uncooperative employers with sanctions' (Kelly, 1998, p. 59). However, given the 'growing tide of employer hostility' to unions (ibid., p. 63) throughout the 1990s, perhaps despite the efforts of the TUC to renew itself, the appropriateness of union collaboration and social partnership is brought into question. As Kelly suggests: 'It is, after all, difficult for a union to construct a partnership with an employer who would prefer that the union simply did not exist' (ibid., p. 63). Elsewhere, Kelly (1996) argues that militancy often pays off and 'is a better guarantor

of union survival and recovery' than moderation, which yields no significant benefits for the union and increases its dependency upon the employer. This critical view of the employment relationship accords with mobilisation theory (see Chapter 1), with its emphasis upon conflicts of interests within that relationship.

The 'servicing' model of trade unionism (see Figure 3.4) is consistent with the moderate, collaborative and partnership-oriented approach, and is now rejected as a model of recruitment by the TUC. However, the organising model eschews 'traditionalist' terms such as 'militancy', although as Blyton and Turnbull (1998) point out: 'militancy is a method rather than an aim with the emphasis first and foremost on *solidarity* as opposed to *strike* action'. They go on to state:

> *While the servicing union expects its members to ask no more than 'What can the union do **for me**?', the organising union asks 'What can **we** achieve **with** the union?'. The organising union depends upon membership being of value **in itself**: members should be able to identify their own issues, organise to solve their own problems and satisfy their aspirations on a collective basis. If all union members defined their own interests in isolation and then simply looked to 'the union' to service their needs, not only would the costs be prohibitive, but the very basis of organisation and unity would be precarious and ultimately ephemeral. In short, there would be no union.* (p. 137)

Despite certain criticisms of the new unionism campaign and the modernisation of the TUC, the response to the campaign and the relaunch amongst affiliates has been generally positive. The TUC has a new mission, logo and style; its internal structure has been transformed in order to facilitate the refocusing upon its external relationships with government, employers and other significant pressure groups. Above all, its Organising Academy has instilled a more proactive approach to recruitment according to the organising principles identified in Figure 3.4. The TUC, which remains optimistic about the prospects for organising (see Exhibit 3.10) can, with some justification, point to the general stabilisation of union membership during the period 1998–2003, and in particular to the slight

Exhibit 3.9
Lessons from overseas

USA: a recipe for success?

The success of the recruitment campaigns conducted by the American trade union federation, the AFL-CIO, provides hard evidence that the labour movement can organise its way out of decline. Forty years ago American unions represented 35 per cent of the workforce, but that figure has fallen to around 15 per cent. In the face of corporate hostility, changes in the labour market, and a legal framework that is loaded against them, the American trade union movement has begun to reverse decades of sliding membership by conducting a major recruitment drive to attract new workers in emerging industries. The organising drive has targeted workers at the sharp end of the labour market including women, ethnic workers, health care workers, etc. Strategies have included a blitz of nationwide company chains; a sharp rise in the use of specialist union organisers; and high profile popular protests, using the media and improved communication techniques, that draw heavily on community campaign tactics. Using aggressive recruitment techniques and backed by substantial financial resources, the campaign has helped to turn the AFL-CIO into what US magazine *Business Week* has called 'a lean, mean recruiting machine' – the process reversing decades of membership decline. In 1996, for the first time in 30 years, the AFL-CIO reported an increase in membership to 13 million.

Central to the campaign is the commitment to increase the level of investment in organising and recruiting. Working with national unions, regions and locally, the AFL-CIO is helping affiliates restructure so they can organise more effectively, switching funds away from servicing declining membership bases to recruitment in new jobs and industries.

Main aims

A vitally important part of the AFL-CIO's recruitment initiative is the launch of its Organising Institute (OI), which the federation calls 'the engine of the US organising drive'. Set up in 1989, the Institute's stated aims are to:

- highlight the importance of organising within the labour movement
- examine and disseminate information on successful organising approaches
- advise union organising departments on their own strategies
- help unions recruit and train organisers
- coordinate apprenticeships for new organisers.

A key feature of the OI is the partnership approach between the union centre and affiliates in the funding, shaping, resourcing, delivery and evaluation of programmes.

Australia: the 'wisdom of Oz'

Faced with a similar pattern of long-term membership decline, employer hostility, labour market change and anti-union laws, Australian trade unions have also tried to learn from their American counterparts by prioritising organising and recruitment. They have adopted a two-pronged strategy to try to reverse the cycle of decline.

First, the unions undertook a radical reorganisation of their structures through a series of strategic amalgamations. Begun in the late 1980s, the merger programme resulted in 95 per cent of affiliated union members belonging to just 20 Australian Congress of Trade Unions (ACTU) 'super unions'. But the mergers failed to halt membership decline and the key to the survival and growth of the union movement in Australia was a coordinated recruitment campaign, with new young trainee organisers to the fore.

In 1994 ACTU set up its 'Organising Works' programme, under the banner 'Strength in Numbers'. Organising Works is a nine-month traineeship for union activists, involving two weeks of formal residential training and an average of two days per fortnight in the classroom, delivered and assessed by the staff of Organising Works and the Trade Union Training Authority. For the rest of the nine months, trainees receive on-the-job training from officers of their host union, with the expectation that, after graduation, they will be provided with employment from the sponsoring unions in an organising role.

Source: Based on IRS, 1997

Element	Militancy–Organising	Moderation–Servicing
Goals	Ambitious demands (scale and scope) with few concessions	Moderate demands with some or many concessions
Membership resources	Strong reliance on mobilisation of union membership	Strong reliance on employers third parties or law
Institutional resources	Exclusive reliance on collective bargaining	Willingness to experiment with or support non-bargaining institutions
Methods	Frequent threat or use of industrial action	Infrequent threat or use of industrial action
Ideology	Ideology of conflicting interests	Ideology of partnership
Recruitment	Members own the campaign to unionise their workplace	The union is seen as a third party It enters the workplace to increase membership or solve problems
	Members identify their own issues and organise to solve them together	Unions tell members how they can solve their problems
	Mapping the workplace and staff attitudes are crucial; names and information are provided by workers	Relying on the employer to provide a list of the names of workers to the union official
	Initial organising can be done outside work – in workers' homes and other places	Relying on workplace access and employer co-operation
	Establishing initial contacts and finding natural leaders to help recruit	Cold-selling union membership by organisers
	Workers empowered to act for themselves through education and support	Selling the union for services and insurance protection
	An internal organising committee formed and workers encouraged to build the union through one-to-one organising	Relying on full-time officials to recruit and solve problems
	Recruitment and organising are integrated	Recruiting is seen as a separate activity
	Results obtained through sustained efforts – more likely to be permanent	Results are achieved but likely to be short term
	Members share decisions and solve problems together with union leaders	The union is blamed when it cannot get results
	Members make a real contribution to union struggles and identify with the union An attack on the union is an attack on themselves	Members complain when they pay fees and the union does nothing
	The image of the union is positive and active	Organisers resent members not attending meetings or participating
	The union has its own agenda with members involved and it keeps management 'off-balance'	Management acts, while the union reacts and is always on the defensive

Figure 3.4 Servicing and organising recruitment patterns within the framework of 'militancy' and 'moderation'
Source: Adapted from Organising Works, 1995; Blyton and Turnbull, 1998; Kelly, 1998

Exhibit 3.10

Some organising successes: the TUC version

Over the last four years (1998–2002), the TUC has helped train 150 (mainly young) organisers through the Organising Academy, while more individual unions are hiring specialist organisers, setting up organising units and targeting non-union companies in their determination to adapt and survive. There are many lessons to be learnt from this union renaissance of which the main ones are:

- Specialist lead organisers have been crucial, using their planning and organising skills to mount successful campaigns in a range of different settings. The Organising Academy and associated initiatives in individual unions have helped develop a body of organising expertise that was almost certainly lacking in the movement five years ago (1997).
- Building the union on the ground has been done by the workers themselves, with organisers and other 'external' union contacts providing support, expertise and resources. All the campaigns have relied on reps, shop stewards and activists to recruit members, lead worker opinion and, in many cases, plan strategy through organising committees.
- Every campaign has been built on the issues the workers themselves care most about, and unions have often shown great sensitivity about tackling problems without appearing to undermine an industry or employer. Through practical, concrete help, they have shown that collective organisation is the most effective method for winning at work.

But organising is not an easy option. It may be expensive, difficult and time-consuming, and spreading the message in small companies, flexible workforces and high turnover industries requires long-term commitment.

Two success stories

The NUJ

The last two decades have been tough for newspaper journalists as proprietors have torn up recognition agreements with the NUJ, slashed pay rates and given their managers free rein to play the bully boy. But the NUJ is on its way back. Since June 2000, it has clocked up more than 55 new recognition deals (most of them voluntary) and extended the protection of collective bargaining to 5000 newspaper and magazine journalists. And where bosses have dragged their feet, they have more than not simply been putting off the inevitable. The CAC backed the union's case for recognition at the *Bristol Evening Post* earlier this year (2002) – the first crucial victory of the most anti-union regional group, Northcliffe Newspapers. The union has been careful throughout to present recognition not as an end in itself but as a way to claw back the fall in relative earnings. To boost its chances, the NUJ has appointed a new assistant organiser to build up membership in magazines and book publishing and is sponsoring a trainee at the Organising Academy, who will be helping members secure recognition in new media including at Ananova, the first stand-alone, online news service where the NUJ has established chapel organisation.

The ISTC

It is an inspired moment that has since passed into organising folklore: community union ISTC handing out condoms at a night club, to hard-pressed staff at a Scottish computer hardware firm FCI with the message: 'There's more than one form of protection – join a union.'

This was the beginning of a three-year campaign, and it all started when a former ISTC member of the non-union plant contacted the union complaining about the intolerable conditions and management style back in 1998. The union handed the FCI brief to two of its Academy-trained organisers and launched phase one of the campaign – taking the union message to the company's sites and identifying staff who could wage the organising battle from

the inside. They used house calls to track down opinion formers on the shop floor who were interested in becoming activists; they formed the core of a large organising committee, mapping and re-mapping the workplace and systematically approaching non-members. With the union established by the workforce themselves, helped by the ISTC organisers (and sometimes the entire organising team), it was the threat of a major redundancy programme that triggered the final phase of the recognition campaign. The non-union staff forum declared it could not cope, and its entire membership not only joined the ISTC, but urged the 750-strong workforce to do the same as well. And when the union's organisers were bundled out of a car park meeting the very next day, there was another surge in recruitment. Despite management's tough anti-union campaign, the ISTC won the backing of the workforce, gained recognition – and have proved their worth protecting the workforce ever since. When another 150 redundancies were announced in the wake of recognition, the new branch managed to negotiate that down to 90, and reduced the impact of another restructuring by securing the transfer of workers between sites. Membership has continued to rise, currently standing at around 75 per cent, and management style has grown a little less confrontational, while negotiations continue to draw up a full set of procedures for grievance, discipline, equal opportunities, harassment and redundancy.

Source: Adapted from TUC documents, 2002

increases in membership amongst groups who are traditionally resistant to unionisation, especially in the face of sustained employer hostility. A barometer of the future success of organising campaigns will be the extent to which density of unionisation increases in 'non-traditional workplaces', such as call centres which cut across a variety of industry sectors. However, Heery (2002) points out that organising unionism 'remains a minority trend within the British movement' (p. 29), partly owing to resource limitations, to a shortage of trained, committed organisers and to inadequate facilities (Waddington, 2003). Another related issue is the extent to which employees, with the labour market increasingly fragmented and segmented, are able or willing, despite the commitment of organisers, to generate a 'mobilisation consciousness' appropriate to unionising. The organising initiative, while it has clearly secured the endorsement of the union movement, has been subject to fluctuating fortunes. To be sure, the statutory recognition procedures have provided an impetus, but the danger here is of a 'free for all', which ultimately may well be counterproductive to union organisation in the longer term. The measure of the efficacy of organising is the strength of commitment of workplace organisers to motivate employees to join a union, and on this issue it is still too early to judge whether the organising initiative is a success.

TRADE UNIONS, THE TUC AND POLITICS

As we noted in Chapter 1, the industrial and political role of trade unions has declined significantly since 1979. The Conservative governments were committed to trade union reform and to market rather than corporatist solutions to economic problems, and this had implications for the relationship between government, unions and the TUC. We now explore in more detail the nature of this changed relationship.

Access to government

The role and functions of the TUC were briefly described in Chapter 1. We now concentrate upon the extent to which access to government changed during the 1980s and the effect this has had upon the influence of the TUC as a pressure group. Mitchell (1987) provides an interesting and insightful analysis concerning the extent and consequences of TUC access to government, based on an examination of the reports by the General Council of the TUC to each annual conference, during the period 1976–84. Mitchell's analysis has been extended by Marsh (1992). The main conclusions of the analysis are as follows:

- The number of contacts between government and unions did not decrease, but the pattern and quality of those contacts changed significantly as there were fewer meetings, less personal contact and a decline in the number of contacts initiated by government.

- There was a decline in the effectiveness of these contacts as government hostility to the TUC's various policy positions grew more intense and the TUC's influence over the Conservative governments waned.

- The number of tripartite contacts (TUC, CBI and government) became more important to the TUC after 1979. Mitchell (1987) comments that this in itself is not surprising 'as tripartite contacts are institutionalised, not impromptu, and inherently less susceptible to partisan or ideological change than bipartite contacts, as long as tripartite institutions themselves survive' (pp. 514–15).

TUC influence upon government legislation

Prior to 1979 the TUC had considerable influence upon government legislation, but during the 1980s and 1990s TUC influence was minimal, despite the more accommodating strategy adopted by the TUC at the 1983 Annual Conference which subsequently became known as the 'new realism'. There was only one major example of government making a concession to trade unions when it agreed to drop its commitment to 'contracting in' from the 1984 Trade Union Act. We now consider this example in greater detail.

The political funding of trade unions

Prior to the 1984 Act, trade unions' political finance was based on the 1913 Trade Unions Act. This Act established the principle that unions could establish a political fund out of members' subscriptions, provided that any union member who did not want to pay that part of their subscription to the political fund could contract out. The only exception to this was during the period 1927–46 when the government introduced a requirement that those who wished to pay the political levy should

contract in. The difference which contracting-in made to unions' political funds was significant, as Marsh (1992) points out: 'when contracting-out was reintroduced in 1947 those paying the political levy increased from 39 per cent to 60 per cent in eighteen months' (p. 115). Marsh goes on to state:

> *The government's overall strategy in the 1984 Act was clear. They wished to depoliticise the trade union movement; to weaken its link to the Labour Party and force it to concentrate on economic, not political activity. It claimed a mandate for reform, especially as public opinion polls indicated widespread antipathy to the political levy and union political, particularly party political, activity. Soon after the election, Norman Tebbit, the Employment Secretary, announced that the political levy would be reformed so that, once again, contracting-in replaced contracting-out. However, when the Trade Union Bill was published, it didn't include any such provision, rather it contained a redefinition of political objects and a requirement that ballots be held for the continuation of political funds.* (p. 116)

Uncharacteristically, the government had negotiated the issue with the TUC and made the concession to retain contracting-out.

The European dimension

During the 1970s and early 1980s the attitude of the TUC towards the European Community (EC) varied from open hostility to grudging acceptance. From the mid-1980s onwards, there was a more positive and permanent endorsement of Europe, partly because the TUC came to regard the EC (or the European Union as it became known after the Maastricht Treaty of 1992), as a possible alternative means whereby to influence government policy, and partly because the unions and the TUC regarded the Social Charter as a radical programme of reform to extend, protect and promote the rights and interests of workers and which the Labour government finally endorsed in 1997. TUC links with European trade union organisations and the ETUC have also been strengthened. The extent to which the TUC now actively endorses its links with the

EU is illustrated by the following extract taken from a 1997 policy document:

The European agenda will require immediate attention, and the new Government will also need to prepare for the UK's Presidency in the first half of 1998. The TUC looks forward to a new constructive approach to EU matters during the UK Presidency, and indeed during the lifetime of the new Government. A decision on Economic and Monetary Union will need to be taken, on which a referendum will be necessary. The TUC's discussions with fellow trade union organisations in the European Union, the European Commission and other European Governments have reinforced its view that Britain must engage in the debates, and cannot afford to opt out of European developments such as the extension of the competence of the Union to act and the introduction of a single currency. In order to ensure the greatest possible understanding of the issues involved, as well as working towards a national consensus, the TUC has suggested a Task Force on the single currency, involving the CBI and Bank of England as well as the TUC. More generally, the TUC will be playing an active part in the European social partner discussions designed to put the European Union on the road to full employment and, along with its ETUC counterparts, will be urging all governments of the member states to make this a priority and will be pressing for [the adoption of the] Employment Chapter. (TUC, 1997, p. 4)

The TUC, as a supporter of the EU's social policy, was pleased that the Labour government had signed up to the Social Chapter in 1997 (see Chapter 4) and welcomed transposition of the European Works Council Directive and initiatives concerning information and consultation of employees. As an active member of the ETUC, the TUC was playing a significant role in the social dialogue procedure as an EU-supported means for developing directives affecting social policy. Hence, the TUC was playing an important part within the EU tripartite system of 'bargained corporatism', a role that it lacks under the Labour government in the UK, and in addition the TUC has the opportunity to pursue legislative changes resisted by Labour. From 1997 to 2003 the content and transposition of EU directives was

subject to a considerable amount of lobbying by the TUC and CBI. The CBI was successful in deferring the progress of the Information and Consultation Directive while the TUC was urging a more positive approach by government to strengthening the European Work Councils and resisting any derogations which would weaken the Working Time Directives. In the main, however, the TUC has had little influence and involvement in Labour decision making in this and many other respects. Perhaps the elevation of the former General Secretary of the TUC, John Monks, to the presidency of the ETUC will lead to the TUC itself playing a more effective lobbying role both within the EU and in the national arena.

Trade unions and the Labour Party

Since 1979 the relationship between the trade union movement and the Labour Party has been subject to re-evaluation, prompted largely by the transformation of the party that began in 1983 (McIlroy, 1998). The modernisation programme initiated by Blair (see Chapter 4) was, to varying degrees, supported by the major unions and the TUC, exemplified by the TUC's enthusiastic support of 'social partnership' (see Chapter 6) and the 'stakeholder' notion – later abandoned by Labour. However, subsequent policy shifts involving 'partnership with business', developing a flexible labour market and what some saw as a flirtation with the CBI conspired gradually to widen the ideological interests of organised labour and government to such an extent that John Monks, the former General Secretary of the TUC, admitted that trade unions and New Labour were not the 'senior partners of old' (Monks, 1998, p. 126). Unions and the TUC responded with pragmatism to union decline with the new unionism approach, which was concerned not only with 'organising' but also with social market policies and enterprise-level social partnership. It could also be argued that the twin-track approaches of new unionism and social partnership were accommodatory responses to the modernisation and increasingly market-led policies of New Labour as the TUC 'sought to re-brand British trade unions as "part of the solution" to Britain's problems' (Undy, 2002, p. 641). The quid pro quo for unions was the

expectation that New Labour in government would work with the TUC in initiating and supporting substantive improvements to both employment protection and collective aspects of the employment relationship. Procedurally, New Labour eschewed formal partnership with unions at national level for its entire period of government up to 2003 and this, according to Undy (2002), prompted unions to attempt to reinforce their 'traditional' relationship with government which comprised:

- the relatively informal relationship between the TUC as pressure group and the Labour Party; and
- the formal but indirect relationship between individual unions and the Labour Party.

However, the relationship at both levels continued to weaken, particularly in recent years, although it is the second-level relationship that has proved to be the most contentious. With regard to the second level, a majority of unions, and in particular the larger unions, affiliate to the Labour Party. In 1990, for example, the Labour Party had 5.3 million affiliated union members secured through the political levy. However, the relationship between the 'political' and 'industrial relations' functions of unions is complex and often contradictory. Despite the fact that the union share in the Labour Party's finances decreased from 90 per cent in the early 1980s to 50 per cent in 1995 and has declined even further in 2003, unions have been potentially influential within the Labour Party in three ways:

- unions sponsor many Labour Members of Parliament;
- based on the number of affiliated members, union leaders control 50 per cent of the votes at the annual Labour Party conference; and
- unions still have significant say in policy forums and the National Executive Committee of the Labour Party, having 12 of 32 seats on the Executive.

Symptomatic of the decline in influence over government policy is the diminished impact of unions at Labour Party conferences. In 1990 the unions controlled 80 per cent of votes at conference, reducing to 70 per cent in 1994, with the four largest unions alone holding 60 per cent, and then to 50 per cent up to 2003. Between 1997 and 2001 the procedural relationship between the union movement and Labour was at once competitive and co-operative as described above. In terms of substantive outcomes, however, there was much greater dissent and discontent, particularly from 2001 to 2003. The chief areas of contention are:

- **In the field of employment legislation.** While there was support for the recognition procedures and the right to be accompanied in discipline and grievance interviews within the ERA 1999, together with the restoration of trade union rights at GCHQ, there were contentious issues to which the TUC objected, including the substitution of the term 'accompanied' rather than 'represented' in discipline and grievance procedures; the requirement that the union at the 'admissibility' stage of the formal recognition process should demonstrate that it was likely to win support in a subsequent recognition ballot; and the need for the CAC to ensure an imposed bargaining unit was compatible with 'effective management'. These changes had the support of the CBI. Furthermore, the TUC was disappointed with issues arising from the transposition of EU Directives by Labour (see above) which 'systematically minimize the effect of the EU instruments at the stage of transposition into UK law' (Undy, 2002).

- **In relation to privatisation** the main issues focus upon Labour's Private Finance Initiative (PFI) inherited from the Conservatives, the Public Private Partnership (PPP) and the private sector provision of public services (see Chapters 4 and 6). The TUC found it problematic to confront the government on the basis of a long-term campaign and, indeed, to decide how it should approach the government. The line of least resistance was to emphasise the need to protect terms and conditions of all employees affected by these measures (McIlroy, 2000). There have been a number of high-profile controversies concerning the issue, including the part-privatisations of the National Air Traffic Services, London Underground and the National Health Service. The government's commitment to greater private involvement in the Health Service provoked stern opposition from unions such as UNISON and threats by affiliated unions to suspend financial contributions to Labour. Campaigns such as

UNISON's 'Positively Public' have contributed to a growing public awareness of thec implications of PFI and the creation of a 'two-tier workforce' in relation to the transfer of staff to a private sector contractor, thereby widening the rift between government and unions in this area.

It is clear that the relationship between New Labour and the union movement is undergoing a period of difficulty which could not be entirely foreseen in 1997. The successes in terms of procedural and substantive issues and outcomes, such as the stress upon the partnership ideology at workplace level that equated with the 'new unionism', are outweighed in many instances by the raft of unpopular (with the unions) policies identified above, together with the absence of any major involvement by the TUC in government decision making. All of this contributes to the widening ideological gap between New Labour, which has relegated collectivism as a core value, and new unionism, which still accords collectivism a high value.

Self-evaluation activity 3.17

Weakening ties with the unions
Response on website

Why in your opinion do you think the Labour Party has sought to weaken ties with the trade union movement?

Summary and conclusion: rejuvenation, steady state or retirement?

Throughout their history, trade unions have metamorphosed and adapted to change, sometimes reactively, as with their reaction to the failure of the 1926 General Strike, and sometimes proactively, as with some elements of organising and partnership. However, certain enduring characteristics of the union movement have either impeded or hastened change. One important characteristic remains the high degree of organisational fragmentation concerning type, structure and size of unions, as we have seen earlier in the chapter. One consequence of this is that the largest unions mostly formed by mergers

and takeovers after periods of intense union rivalry over membership, and currently representing the vast majority of trade union members, dominate decision making and resource allocation within the TUC. Diversity of political ideology amongst trade union leaderships is a fact of any democratically structured organisation and ensures a measure of competition and conflict concerning strategic decisions affecting a wide range of matters, from European and national government policies down to workplace matters. A change of leadership, therefore, may also mean a change of policy concerning one or more strategic policy issues. During 2002, for example, the election of 'left-wing' union leaders such as Mark Serwotka of PCSU and Andy Gilchrist of the FBU meant that there was likely to be a more polemic relationship between these and other trade unions and the government, as acknowledged by the General Secretary of the TUC: the new leaders 'reflect the impatience I feel sometimes too, that they've not got the relationship with the Labour government on the basis that we want to see' (Brendan Barber, General Secretary of the TUC, quoted in *Financial Times*, 30 January 2003).

The TUC itself remains a loose coalition of affiliated unions whose claim to represent all UK unions is weakened by the fact that a large number of unions are not affiliated. In addition, since 1980 the TUC has all but lost its influence over government decision and policy making while consolidating its role within the EU. An even more daunting prospect amidst employer hostility and government indifference is how to deal with the seemingly intractable and ongoing problem of union decline, both nationally and at the workplace, and which was also a consequence of the neo-liberal offensive of Thatcherism of the 1980s and 1990s. The efficacy of the 'organising' approach has yet to be tested, while partnership initiatives at organisational and workplace level may yet prove to be a transitory phenomenon and possibly to be jettisoned in the same way as other disposables such as the 'third way' and 'stakeholding'. If the UK were to adopt wholesale the Information and Consultation Directive, incorporating fully fledged and effective works councils at workplace level which currently exist in most social market member states, then there would be in all probability no need for formal partnership agreements. This development, coupled

with a reinvigorated workplace 'organising and mobilising' union presence, again at workplace level, together with more clout for European works councils would do much to rejuvenate union organisation and unions themselves.

As was pointed out earlier in the chapter, union decline is a global phenomenon and a number of prescriptions have been mooted to reverse the decline which may apply to more than one country. Part of the solution may reside in a re-examination of the 'who', 'what' and 'how' questions posed by Hyman (2002), referred to earlier in this chapter, and articulated more specifically by Verma *et al.* (2002) in relation to seven areas:

Demand for representation. Charlwood (2002) argues that 40 per cent of non-union employees in the UK would be willing to join a union if they were given a choice to do so. This positive assessment should, arguably, provide an incentive towards increasing and improving organising activities in UK workplaces.

Method of organising. According to Verma *et al* (2002), given the latent demand for union membership, concentrating on organising groups of employees who are dissatisfied with their jobs and see union involvement in purely instrumental terms may not be enough to increase membership. It may well be that unions need to make far more effort with peripheral groups of employees, for example, and to appeal to diverse constituencies of employees with an 'agenda that must reflect the far more differentiated ways in which work connects to life – or in which workers *wish* it to relate' (Hyman, 2002, p. 13). This means looking at individualism and collectivism as mutually inclusive rather than antagonistic, combining also the 'instrumental' (pay conditions, choice, opportunity, flexibility) with the 'affective' (solidarity, commitment).

The retention challenge. Membership turnover or 'churn' means that unions are losing almost as many members (or in many cases more) than they are recruiting. The prescriptions mentioned above may help reduce turnover, but fail to address the problem of membership loss when moving from job to job. One solution mooted is to move towards a system which facilitates lifelong union membership, whereby members are recruited at the start of

their careers and are provided with all services and benefits relevant to particular stages of work and non-work life. The TUC has proposals for lifelong membership of the TUC with a range of benefits etc., which would be supplemented by optional membership of a particular affiliated trade union.

Targeting youth. The TUC and most trade unions acknowledge that there is steeply declining membership amongst young people, particularly within the 18–25 age category and continuing efforts to make trade unions attractive to this age group are being made.

Overcoming employer opposition. Employer opposition is most prevalent amongst small firms within the private sector of the economy.

As far as the future is concerned, Verma *et al.* (2002) identify a number of scenarios applicable to the UK and other countries, including:

- **Continued decline on the basis of past trends.** This scenario is probably the safest to make if present trends are extrapolated to the future, other things being equal, and assuming that unions continue to be 'sclerotic' in adapting to change. At best, unions can hope for a 'downward stabilisation' of membership, although density will continue to decline.
- **Fragmented growth on the basis of existing strengths.** Not a scenario recommended for the UK as the traditional union industrial enclaves continue to decline and existing strengths which reside mainly in the public sector are too concentrated. According to this scenario 'the labour movement could maintain its current base and, with continuous adaptation, become stronger and more effective in some sectors or occupations with little growth or even presence in others' (p. 381).
- **Rejuvenation through crisis.** Taking a longer-term view of history, it is argued that the confluence of certain events such as the Great Depression in the USA and the defeat of Nazism and Fascism at the end of the Second World War bolstered trade union membership – although simple cause–effect is not good methodology and very unreliable as predictor. Multi-causal factor independent variables such as those that account for union decline are even less reliable as predictors.

Table 3.7 Traditional unions into e-unions

	Pre-internet activities of unions	Additional activities after internet
Primary business Delivery of services	Collective bargaining Workplaces Services delivered by reps/leaders Outcomes depend on collective bargain with employer	Individual representation and advice Web Digital AI services Services provided directly to workers
Method of dispute	Strikes	Web communication Cyber picketing
	Pre-internet membership	**Post-internet membership**
Locale	Workplace Members with employer recognition	Differentiated membership Members, subscribers Visitors to website Virtual presence at workplaces
Free-rider problems Internal democracy	Collective bargaining creates incentive to free-ride Elected leaders and bureaucracy	Customised services to members only Decentralised; internet plebiscites Activists operate independently

Source: Diamond and Freeman, 2002. Blackwell Publishing

- **New organisational forms: the cyber union?**
 Unions, as we have mentioned in the British context, have metamorphosed in the past, transforming themselves from local to national, craft to industrial organisations in the nineteenth century, and from manual to professional and then to the emergence of 'super-unions' in the twentieth century. The assumption that unions will change again in the twenty-first century while retaining their organising essence is a reasonable one. Hyman (2002) for example, suggests that in addition to the implications of union modernisation, information technology offers some possibilities of reducing the hierarchical levels while introducing more interactive and open communication and opening the scope more for effective participation in decision making. A 'new' cyber-oriented e-union would be expected to provide individual representation and customised services while continuing to bargain collectively for workers with management. The differences between traditional unionism and e-unionism are identified in Table 3.7.

Whether trade unions reinvent themselves as 'virtual social movements' in cyberspace or elsewhere depends very much upon the nature of the current and potential problems they have to deal with. In any event, the more responsive unions become to the needs of the membership – actual and potential – and the more proactive and inventive unions are in taking up the new opportunities and challenges, the more likely they will survive well into the twenty-first century as rejuvenated and vibrant organisations.

RELEVANT WEBSITES

www.acas.org.uk (The Advisory, Conciliation and Arbitration Service) Useful all-round information.
www.dti.gov.uk/er/emar (Department of Trade and Industry) Up-to-date information on unions and other employment relations matters. Provides access to government statistics website for information on trade union membership, etc. Also details of research, publications, European Union Directives and workplace partnership.

www.etuc.org (European Trades Union Confederation) Provides information on constituent union organisations and other relevant statistics.

www.eurofound.ie (European Foundation for the Improvement of Living and Working Conditions) A very informative website created by the EU which considers policy issues concerning social and work-based matters as well as research and publications at EU, country and sector levels.

www.lrd.org.uk (Labour Research Department) A trade union-oriented research body which researches and regularly publishes across the whole employment relations range. Union members can obtain a password through their union for free access to online material.

www.tuc.org.uk (Trades Union Congress) The website of the TUC provides a wealth of material and information on all aspects of the employment relationship. Contains a good section for students.

www.unions21.org.uk (Unions 21) A website which provides valuable material concerning trade unions and the TUC.

Individual trade unions: website addresses of the larger unions are to be found in the Appendix.

REFERENCES

Acas (2002) *Annual Report 2001–2002*. London, Acas

Addison, J. and Belfield, C. (2001) 'Updating the determinants of firm performance using the 1998 UK Workplace Employee Relations Survey'. *British Journal of Industrial Relations*, 39, 3, 341–66

Bain, G.S. and Elsheikh, F. (1976) *Union Growth and the Business Cycle*. Oxford, Blackwell

Beaumont, P. (1987) *The Decline of Trade Union Organisation*. London, Croom Helm

Blackwell, R. (1990) 'Parties and factions in trade unions'. *Employee Relations*, 12, 1, 12–23

Blanden, J., Machin, S. and Van Reenen, J. (2006) 'Have unions turned the corner? New evidence on recent trends in union recognition in UK firms'. *British Journal of Industrial Relations*, 44, 2, 169–90

Blyton, P. and Turnbull, P. (1994) *The Dynamics of Employee Relations*. London, Macmillan

Blyton, P. and Turnbull, P. (1998) *The Dynamics of Employee Relations*, 2nd edn. London, Macmillan

Booth, A. (1983) 'A reconsideration of trade union growth in the United Kingdom'. *British Journal of Industrial Relations*, 21, 3, 379–91

Brown, W., Deakin, S., Hudson, M. and Pratten, C. (2001) 'The limits of statutory trade union recognition'. *Industrial Relations Journal*, 32, 2, 94–113

Bryson, A. and Gomez, R. (2005) 'Why have workers stopped joining unions? The rise in never-never membership in Britain'. *British Journal of Industrial Relations*, 43, 1, 67–92

Carruth, A. and Disney, R. (1988) 'Where have two million trade union members gone?' *Economica*, 55, 1, 1–19

CBI (1998) *Employment Trends Survey: Measuring Flexibility in the Labour Market*. London, CBI

Certification Office (2007) *Annual Report*. London, Certification Office

Charlwood, A. (2002) 'Why do non-union employees want to unionise?' *British Journal of Industrial Relations*, 40, 3, 463–91

Claydon, T. (1989) 'Union derecognition in Britain during the 1980s'. *British Journal of Industrial Relations*, 27, 2, 214–23

Claydon, T. (1997) 'Union recognition: a re-examination', in Beardwell, I.J. (ed.) *Contemporary Industrial Relations: A Critical Analysis*. Oxford, Oxford University Press

Coates, K. and Topham, T. (1988) *Trade Unions in Britain*. London, Fontana

Colgan, F. and Ledwith, S. (2002) 'Gender and diversity: reshaping union democracy'. *Employee Relations*, 24, 2, 167–89

Cully, M., Woodland, S., O'Reilly, A. and Dix, G. (1999) *Britain at Work*. London, Routledge

Dempsey, M. and McKevitt, P. (2001) 'Unison and the people side of merger'. *Human Resource Management Journal*, 11, 2, 4–16

Diamond, W.J. and Freeman, R.B. (2002) 'Will unionism prosper in cyberspace?' *British Journal of Industrial Relations*, 40, 3, 569–96, Blackwell Publishing

Disney, R. (1990) 'Explanations of the decline in trade union density in Britain: an appraisal'. *British Journal of Industrial Relations*, 28, 2, 165–78

Donovan (1968) *Report of the Royal Commission on Trade Unions and Employers Associations 1965–1968*, Cmnd 3623. London, HMSO

Edelstein, J.D. and Warner, M. (1975) *Comparative Union Democracy*. London, Allen and Unwin

Flanders, A. (1972) *Trade Unions*. London, Hutchinson

Freeman, R. and Pelletier, J. (1990) 'The impact of industrial relations legislation on British trade union density'. *British Journal of Industrial Relations*, 28, 2, 141–64

Gall, G. and McKay, S. (1999) 'Developments in union recognition and derecognition in Britain, 1994–1998'. *British Journal of Industrial Relations*, 37, 4, 601–11

Gall, G. and McKay, S. (2001) 'Facing fairness at work: union perception of employer opposition and response to union recognition'. *Industrial Relations Journal*, 32, 2, 94–113

Gall, G. and McKay, S. (2002) *Trade Union Recognition in Britain; The Dawn of a New Era*. London, LRD

Gall, G. (2004) 'Trade union recognition in Britain 1995–2002: turning a corner? *Industrial Relations Journal*, 35, 3, 249–70

Gallie, D., Rose, M. and Penn, R. (1996) 'The British debate on trade unionism: crisis and continuity', in Gallie, D., Penn, R. and Rose, M. (eds) *Trade Unionism in Recession*. Oxford, Oxford University Press

GMB (1998) *Changing Job Patterns and GMB Recruitment Prospects*. London, GMB

GMB (2002) *A Brief Guide to a Modern Union*. London, GMB

GMB (2006) *How the Union is Structured*. London, GMB

Goldstein, J. (1952) *The Government of a British Trade Union*. London, Allen and Unwin

Grant, D. (1997) 'Japanisation and the new industrial relations', in Beardwell, I.J. (ed.) *Contemporary Industrial Relations: A Critical Approach*. Oxford, Oxford University Press

Grainger, H. (2006) *Trade Union Membership in 2005*. London, ONS

Grainger, H. and Crowther, M. (2007) *Trade Union Membership in 2006*. London, ONS

Hawkins, K. (1981) *Trade Unions*. London, Hutchinson

Heery, E. (1997) 'The new new unionism', in Beardwell, I.J. (ed.) *Contemporary Industrial Relations: A Critical Approach*. Oxford, Oxford University Press

Heery, E. (1998) 'The relaunch of the Trades Union Congress'. *British Journal of Industrial Relations*, 36, 3, 339–60

Heery, E. (2002) 'Partnership v organising: alternative futures for British trade unions'. *Industrial Relations Journal*, 33, 1, 20–35

Hobsbawm, E.J. (1974) *Labouring Men: Studies in the History of Labour*. London, Weidenfeld & Nicolson

Hughes, J. (1968) *Trade Union Structure and Government, Part 1*. Donovan Commission Research Paper no. 5. London, HMSO

Hyman, R. (1995) 'The historical evolution of British industrial relations', in Edwards, P. (ed.) *Industrial Relations: Theory and Practice in Britain*. Oxford, Blackwell

Hyman, R. (1996) 'Changing union identities in Europe', in Leisink, P., Van Leemput, J. and Lilrokx, J. (eds) *The Challenges to Trade Unions in Europe: Innovation or Adaptation*. Cheltenham, Edward Elgar

Hyman, R. (2002) 'The future of unions'. *Just Labour*, 1, 7–15

Hyman, R. (2003) 'The historical evolution of British industrial relations', in Edwards, P. *Industrial Relations Theory and Practice*, 2nd edn. Oxford, Blackwell

ILO (1998) *World Labour Report, 1997–1998*. Geneva, ILO

IRS (1997) 'Organising the unorganised'. *IRS Employment Trends*, November, No. 644

IRS (1998) 'Predicting union membership'. *IRS Employment Trends*, December, No. 667

IRS (2002a) 'Gaining recognition'. *IRS Employment Trends*, February, No. 745

IRS (2002b) 'Part of the union'. *IRS Employment Trends*, November, No. 764

Kelly, J. (1996) 'Union militancy and social partnership', in Ackers, P., Smith, C. and Smith, P. (eds) *The New Workplace and Trade Unionism*. London, Routledge

Kelly, J. (1998) *Rethinking Industrial Relations: Mobilisation, Collectivism and Long Waves*. London, Routledge

Kelly, J. (2002) 'Decline and revival of the international union movement'. *TUC Pamphlet*. London, TUC

Kelly, J. and Heery, E. (1994) *Working for the Union: British Trade Union Officers*. Cambridge, Cambridge University Press

Kersley, B., Alpin, C., Forth, J., Bryson, A., Bewley, H., Dix, G. and Oxenbridge, S. (2006) *Inside the Workplace: Findings from the 2004 Workplace Employment Relations Survey*. London, Routledge

LMT (Labour Market Trends) (2002) 'Trade union membership: an analysis of the data from the Autumn 2001 LFS'. *Labour Market Trends*, July, 343–55

Lipset, S.M., Trow, M.A. and Coleman, J.S. (1956) *Union Democracy*. New York: The Free Press

Luthans, F. (1992) *Organisational Behaviour*. New York, McGraw-Hill

Machin, S. (2000) 'Union decline in Britain'. *British Journal of Industrial Relations*, 30, 4, 631–45

Marchington, M. and Parker, P. (1990) *Changing Patterns of Employee Relations*. Hemel Hempstead, Harvester Wheatsheaf

Marsh, D. (1992) *The New Politics of British Trade Unionism: Union Power and the Thatcher Legacy*. London, Macmillan

Martin, R., Sunley, P. and Wills, J. (1996) *Union Retreat and the Regions: The Shrinking Landscape of Organised Labour*. London, Jessica Kingsley

Mason, B. and Bain, P. (1993) 'The determinants of trade union membership in Britain: a survey of the literature'. *Industrial and Labour Relations Review*, 46, 2, 332–51

McIlroy, J. (1988) *Trade Unions in Britain Today*. Manchester, Manchester University Press

McIlroy, J. (1990) *A History of British Trade Unionism*. Manchester, Manchester University Press

McIlroy, J. (1995) *Trade Unions in Britain Today*, 2nd edn. Manchester, Manchester University Press

McIlroy, J. (1998) 'The enduring alliance? Trade unions and the making of New Labour'. *British Journal of Industrial Relations*, 36, 4, 537–64

McIlroy, J. (2000) 'The new politics of pressure: the Trade Union Congress and New Labour in government'. *Industrial Relations Journal*, 31, 1, 2–16

Metcalf, D. (2005) *British Unions: Resurgence or Perdition?* London, The Work Foundation

Metcalf, D. (1991) 'British unions: dissolution or resurgence?'. *Oxford Review of Economic Policy*, 7, 1, 18–32

Michels, R. (1959) *Political Parties*. Dover, Constable

Millward, N. and Stevens, M. (1986) *British Workplace Industrial Relations 1980–1984*. Aldershot, Gower

Millward, N., Bryson, A. and Forth, J. (2000) *All Change at Work?* London, Routledge

Millward, N., Stevens, M., Smart, D. and Hawes, W.R. (1992) *Workplace Industrial Relations in Transition*. Aldershot, Dartmouth

Mitchell, N. (1987) 'Changing pressure group politics: the case of the TUC, 1976–1984'. *British Journal of Political Science*, 17, 2, 261–74

Monks, J. (1998) 'Trade unions, enterprise and the future', in Sparrow, P.R. and Marchington, M. (eds) *Human Resource Management: The New Agenda*. London, Financial Times/Pitman Publishing

Moore, S. (2004) 'Union mobilisation and counter-mobilisation in the statutory recognition process', in Kelly, J. and Willman, P. (eds) *Union Organisation and Activity*. London, Routledge

Nolan, P. and O'Donnell, K. (2003) 'Industrial relations, HRM and performance', in Edwards, P. (ed.) *Industrial Relations: Theory and Practice*, 2nd edn. Oxford, Blackwell

O'Grady, F. and Nowak, P. (2004) 'Beyond new unionism', in Kelly, J. and Willman, P. (eds) *Union Organisation and Activity*. London, Routledge

Organising Works (1995) *Organising Works*, no. 2. Melbourne, Organising Works

Pelling, H. (1992) *A History of British Trade Unionism*. Harmondsworth, Penguin

Pencavel, J. (2001) 'The surprising retreat of union Britain'. *Stanford Institute for Economic Policy Research*, SIEPR Discussion Paper No. 00-31

Prowse, P. (2003) 'Recruitment and representation amongst nurses in hospital trusts'. Research Paper, University of Bradford School of Management

Reid, A.J. (2005) *United We Stand: A History of Britain's Trade Unions*. London, Penguin Books.

Roberts, B.C. (1956) *Trade Union Government and Administration*. London, Bell

Rose, E. (1974) 'On the nature of work and union involvement: the case of London Busmen'. *Industrial Relations Journal*, 5, 2, 12–23

Salamon, M. (1998) *Industrial Relations: Theory and Practice*, 3rd edn. London, Prentice Hall

Smith, P. and Morton, G. (1993) 'Union exclusion and the decollectivisation of IR in contemporary Britain'. *British Journal of Industrial Relations*, 31, 1, 97–114

Smith, P. and Morton, G. (1994) 'Union exclusion in Britain: next steps'. *Industrial Relations Journal*, 25, 1, 22–35

Taylor, R. (1978) *The Fifth Estate: Britain's Unions in the Seventies*. London, Routledge

Taylor, P. and Bain, P. (1999) 'An assembly line in the head: work and employee relations in the call centre'. *Industrial Relations Journal*, 30, 2, 27–42

Terry, M. (1995) 'Trade unions: shop stewards and the workplace', in Edwards, P. (ed.) *Industrial Relations: Theory and Practice in Britain*. Oxford, Blackwell

Terry, M. (2003) 'Employee representation: the shop stewards and the new legal framework', in Edwards, P. (ed.) *Industrial Relations: Theory and Practice*, 2nd edn, Oxford, Blackwell

TUC (1991) *Annual Report*. London, TUC

TUC (1997) *Annual Report*. London, TUC

TUC (1998) *Focus on Recognition: Trade Union Trends Survey on Union Recognition and Derecognition*. London, TUC

TUC (1999) *Trade Union Trends: Today's Trade Unionists*. London, TUC

TUC (2002) *Annual Report*. London, TUC

Turner, H.A. (1962) *Trade Union Growth, Structure and Policy*. London, Allen and Unwin

Undy, R. (2002) 'New Labour and new unionism, 1997–2001: but is it the same old story?' *Employee Relations*, 24, 6, 638–55

Undy, R. and Martin, R. (1984) *Ballots and Trade Union Democracy*. Oxford, Blackwell

Undy, R., Ellis, W., McCarthy, W. and Halmos, A. (1981) *Change in Trade Unions*. London, Hutchinson

Verma, A., Kochan, T.A. and Wood, S. (2002) 'Union decline and prospects for revival'. *British Journal of Industrial Relations*, 40, 3, 373–84

Waddington, J. (2003) 'Trade union organisation', in Edwards, P. (ed.) *Industrial Relations: Theory and Practice*, 2nd edn. Oxford, Blackwell

Waddington, J. and Kerr, A. (1999) 'Membership retention in the public sector'. *Industrial Relations Journal*, 30, 2, 151–65

Waddington, J. and Whitson, C. (1995) 'Trade unions: growth, structure and policy', in Edwards, P. (ed.) *Industrial Relations: Theory and Practice in Britain*. Oxford, Blackwell

Waddington, J. and Whitson, C. (1997) 'Why do people join unions during a period of membership decline?' *British Journal of Industrial Relations*, 35, 4, 515–46

Webb, S. and Webb, B. (1898) *Industrial Democracy*. London, Longman

Webb, S. and Webb, B. (1920) *The History of Trade Unionism 1866–1920*. London, Longman

WERS (1998) See Cully, M. *et al.* (1998)

WERS (2004) See Kersley, B. *et al.* (2006)

Willman, P. (2004) 'Structuring unions', in Kelly, J. and Willman, P. (eds) *Union Organisation and Activity*. London, Routledge.

Willman, P. and Bryson, A. (2007) *Union Organisation in Great Britain*. London, Centre for Economic Performance, Discussion paper 774, London School of Economics

Wilson, T. (2007) *The Future of Unions*. London, UCU

Wood, S. (1997) *Statutory Union Recognition*. London, IPD

Wood, S., Moore, S. and Willman, P. (2002) 'Third time lucky for statutory union recognition in the UK?' *Industrial Relations Journal*, 33, 3, 215–33

GOVERNMENT POLICY AND EMPLOYMENT RELATIONS

INTRODUCTION

Government is the third and most important 'actor' within the industrial relations 'system' (see Chapter 1). In general terms government may be defined as the political machinery or apparatus within which officials make policies and decisions either as elected representatives or by civil servants. Government can be regarded as both a process involving public policy making to include legislation, policy directives and legislative proposals contained in green and white papers, and a formal structure responsible for the administrative policy-making process. Capitalist societies or states usually (but not always) have governments based on representative multi-party democracy and are termed liberal democracies. In Britain, the ideologies of the two main political parties, particularly when they have been in opposition, have traditionally operated to serve the different and opposing interests of the actors within the industrial relations system but, as we saw in Chapter 1, from 1946 until 1979 parties in government adopted liberal collectivist and corporatist policies which served the interests of both trade unions and employers to varying degrees. However, from 1979 until 1997 the succession of Conservative governments adopted the more radical policies of liberal individualism and neo-laissez-faire (see Chapter 1), with the emphasis upon market forces, and on individualism rather than collectivism. The succeeding New Labour governments chose not to revert to the corporatism of the 1970s, shedding the mantle of 'old Labour' in the process, and veering at times towards the individualism of the Conservatives.

There is some semantic confusion concerning the terms state and government in the industrial relations literature. Gospel and Palmer (1993) declare that 'the state is not synonymous with government' (p. 154) and that the government is part of the state and acts as its representative. A distinction is made, therefore, between government and state, where government is regarded as part of a range of state institutions that include the judiciary, the Civil Service, armed forces and police. While we would accept the validity of this distinction, it is the government of the day, whatever its political complexion, which is the active and only legislator and which therefore plays the most important part in influencing economic, political and social processes and institutions, including, of course, industrial relations. We therefore prefer, wherever possible and appropriate, to use the term 'government' rather than 'state', although occasionally both terms will be used where this is unavoidable.

The traditional role of government and the state in industrial relations embodies the view that government should be non-interventionist. Theoretically, this means that government should remain neutral between employers and employees and should intervene only in order to:

- protect the employment interests of employees when no other means of doing so are available;
- protect the wider interests of society as a whole when these are threatened by particular industrial pressure groups; and

- maintain an even balance of bargaining power between the interests of the buyers and sellers of labour.

While many still subscribe to this view, the approach of government to industrial relations has varied over time. For example, it has been argued that government or the state is most visible and interventionist when 'reforming' industrial relations institutions and processes, the most obvious example being the incremental legislation put into place by the Conservative governments during the period 1980–95 (Howell, 2005). However, at this stage, we need only point out that in reality the government has, and does, intervene in industrial relations in a variety of ways of which the following are examples:

- minimum employment rights and wage levels (minimum wage);
- economic policies, particularly in relation to prices and incomes;
- legislation to regulate the conduct of industrial disputes, collective bargaining and the activities of trade unions;
- conciliation and arbitration in industrial disputes; and
- activities to stimulate and improve the quality of the labour market.

Many of these interventions, which can take the form of statutory legislation and policy guidelines, have been relatively non-controversial as, for example, concerning the role of Acas (see Chapter 1 for an overview of the role of Acas), which is a government agency whose role in the resolution of disputes is still highly valued by trade unions and employers alike. In other areas, however, government intervention can be highly controversial and unpopular with either trade unions or employers. For example, some of the employment legislation of the 1980s and 1990s is widely regarded as being ideologically motivated and contrary to the interests of trade unions.

In this chapter we start by looking briefly at the main theories underpinning the role of government generally and then go on to examine the historical and contemporary role of government as it affected industrial relations during the course of the twentieth century, and particularly during the post-Second World War period. We then go on to consider the effects of both economic policy and incomes policy upon the parties to industrial relations, together with the arguments concerning the desirability of minimum wage legislation. The legislative framework of industrial relations will be examined in some detail, again with regard to the changing role of government as legislator during the 1980s and 1990s, and this is followed by a review of the role and function of government agencies. The industrial relations agenda of the New Labour governments will then be examined and critically assessed, and the chapter ends with a consideration of the European Union, the 'Europeanisation' of employment relations and the impact upon UK industrial relations.

Learning outcomes

When you have read this chapter, you should be able to:

1. Describe the main theories underpinning government policy and account for the traditional and contemporary role of government in employment relations.

2. Trace the development of economic and incomes policy and the impact of these upon employment relations since 1945.

3. Explain the nature of statutory intervention and the role and functions of government agencies.

4. Critically examine the impact of New Labour's employment relations policies.

5. Understand the EU context of policy making and evaluate its impact upon UK employment relations.

THEORETICAL OVERVIEW OF THE ROLE OF GOVERNMENT

As was mentioned in the introduction to this chapter, government in most capitalist societies is based upon representative multi-party democracy, and such societies are termed liberal democracies. There are, however, a number of competing and conflicting perspectives which seek to explain the role of government in liberal democratic societies. We will now consider these perspectives as they are crucial to our understanding of government policies which impact upon industrial relations.

The Marxist perspective

Basically, the Marxist argument is that the distribution of power in capitalist society is a reflection of the relationships of domination and subordination, which are determined primarily by the economic arrangements and mode of production of society. Marx terms this the relations of production, where production is organised socially in ways which have always created classes with opposed interests and unequal resources of power, so that one class will dominate others through economic exploitation. The social class that dominates the economic relations of production will also wield political power over other classes and by doing so maintains and enhances its dominant position in society. Hence the concentration of political power in one class enables that class to dominate others through economic exploitation and the extraction of maximum surplus value from the labour force. According to this analysis, government and the state represented the interests of the dominant capitalist class (also called the bourgeoisie) and were linked to the satisfaction of the economic interests of that dominant class. Thus Marx and Engels (1967) asserted that in capitalist society 'the executive of the modern state is but a committee for managing the common affairs of the whole bourgeoisie' (p. 26).

According to the Marxist analysis, therefore, the state and government in capitalist society are not an impartial referee in the power game, but a vehicle for the realisation of the interests of the bourgeoisie – an agency of class domination which provides the *illusion* of serving the general or national will, while in reality acting as a cloak for class interests. Attempts by the bourgeoisie or dominant capitalist class to cultivate a picture of the state as being above particular group or class interests constitute an ideological strategy to legitimise its own dominant position. The state in turn, through government policies, agencies and institutions, is engaged in a constant exercise to legitimate the existing order. Furthermore, while the economic relations of capitalism give the dominant class control over material forces and political power in society, they are also able to control ideas and beliefs. That is, they possess ideological power, whereby a set of dominant values may be disseminated through major social institutions which justify or legitimise existing socio-economic and political arrangements, and hence their own dominant position. As Marx and Engels (1967) state: 'The ideas of the ruling class are, in every age, the ruling ideas . . . The class which has the means of material production at its disposal has control at the same time over the means of mental production' (p. 28).

Government and the state, according to this analysis, are not neutral but serve the interests of the bourgeoisie and legitimise their dominant position within society. The other classes subject to this degree of domination and exploitation Marx collectively termed the proletariat. The emergent proletariat of the Industrial Revolution soon came to realise that while their interests conflicted with those of the bourgeoisie, individually they were powerless against the employer within the employment relationship and that collective organisation could serve to redress some of the imbalance of power (see Chapter 5).

Self-evaluation activity 4.1

Redressing the power imbalance
Response on website

In what ways, according to a Marxist perspective, do you think the 'proletariat' could redress the power imbalance within the capitalist state?

However, as we have seen (Chapter 3), economism, that is, the pursuit of economic ends, has been

the dominant motivation behind trade union practice, and only rarely has trade union industrial action been geared towards control. The pursuit of financial improvements and better working conditions has been the guiding principle for action, which, while often involving bitter conflicts and protracted disputes, has essentially entailed working within the existing structure of capitalism and not systematically questioning its fundamental assumptions. Economistic trade unionism, then, generates an essentially parochial consciousness, and a collectivism limited in its scope by its lack of independence from the dominant value system of government, ownership and production.

Economistic orientations are reinforced and intensified by the sectionalism inherent in a trade union movement comprising organisations whose individual role is the representation of the interests of workers in specific occupations rather than those of a whole class. This generates what has been termed occupational consciousness, with trade unions – particularly of the craft variety – traditionally being concerned with guarding their status and maintaining differentials in reward in relation to other occupational groups at the expense of any massive class-based assault on capitalism.

In summary, then, the Marxist perspective considers the role of the state and government as serving the interests of the dominant capitalist bourgeoisie class. To the extent that the working class, or proletariat, did not provide the revolutionary opposition spearheaded by the trade union movement, the current Marxist argument is that the state and government have merely incorporated the union movement into the capitalist system by conceding certain economistic demands, thereby attracting criticism that the unions have 'sold out' to capitalism.

Democratic elitism

One of the most influential views of the nature and limits of democracy and government was propounded by Max Weber (1978), one of the 'founding fathers' of sociology, and modified by the economist Joseph Schumpeter (1976). In essence, Weber argued that representative multi-party democracy helps to defend society against both arbitrary decision making on the part of political leaders and

the appropriation of power by bureaucrats. However, in both respects government and other democratic institutions have been less effective than the 'ideal' situation simply because political parties, as with other large institutions and organisations such as large trade unions, develop bureaucratic party machines and structures which threaten the autonomy of government. If a governing party with a large majority is simply able to dictate what is decided, and if the decision-making process is obscured, reducing Parliament to a mere 'talking shop', then the democratic process is much diluted.

In order for democratic systems to be effective, Weber argues that two conditions must be fulfilled. Firstly, there must be parties that represent different interests and have different outlooks. If the policies of competing parties are more or less the same, voters are denied effective choice. Secondly, there must be political leaders who are not caught up in the bureaucratic machinery and who are able to demonstrate leadership within a democratic context. Weber emphasises the importance of leadership within democratic government decision-making contexts, arguing that rule by leadership elites is inevitable and that the best we can hope for is that those elites effectively represent our interests. Multi-party democracy is valued more for the quality of leadership it generates than for the mass participation in politics that it makes possible.

Like Weber, Schumpeter argued that democracy is more important as a method of generating effective and responsible government than as a means of providing significant power for the majority. According to Schumpeter, democracy is the rule of the politician, not the people, and in order to achieve voting support, politicians must nevertheless be at least minimally responsive to the demands and interests of the electorate. Mechanisms of political democracy should be kept largely separate from economic life as the competitive marketplace provides a measure of consumer choice, just as a competitive system of parties provides at least a small measure of political choice.

Democratic elitism may, in part, explain why in liberal democracies any one political party in government at least minimally purports to represent the interests of those sections of the electorate which provide that party with ideological support. However, the electorate generally is portrayed by

democratic elitists as being relatively passive and unenlightened; should, for example, a Labour government enact legislation supportive of workers' rights and trade union interests, it will do so on the assumption that individual citizens can have little or no direct influence on political decision making and would have little motivation to exert such influence. Democratic elitism also assumes that the process and quality of governmental decision making requires the expertise of professionals. The mass of the electorate, it is argued, cannot master the intricacies of the decisions which governments constantly have to take, but civil servants and elected members of representative bodies have the time to acquire specialist knowledge of issues. While 'experts' need to be constrained by the views of those affected by policies they formulate, they can make decisions on an informed basis. Nevertheless, democratic elitists reject the notion that groups representative of the electorate can be active partners or have a dynamic input to governmental decision making.

Pluralism

The pluralist perspective is concerned with the diffusion of power within society, buttressed and safeguarded by a number of important mechanisms and institutions. The pluralist theorists such as Dahl (1961) were strongly influenced by the ideas of Weber and Schumpeter and recognise the existence of elites in modern liberal democracies. Unlike supporters of the Marxist analysis of the capitalist state and the role of government within it, pluralists argue that interests in modern society have become progressively diversified, so that a greater number of groups with particular interests and political demands to be satisfied have come to make their presence felt in the political arena and compete for power. For pluralists, the distinctive feature of a liberal democracy is that it is a political system of 'open' power groups, participating in the power game. The various groups are located in such institutional areas as business, government administration, parliamentary politics, labour, education and culture, and draw their membership from various social strata on the basis of merit and regardless of class, gender and ethnicity.

Liberal democracy, then, is characterised as a system of competing interest groups and elites where no single group is able to secure a monopoly of power and manipulate the system consistently to its exclusive advantage. One important assumption underlying the pluralist analysis is that different interest groups have influence only over a narrow range of issues of concern to themselves and therefore no one group's interests will prevail. This runs contrary to the Marxist emphasis on the prime importance of economic power residing in the hands of a small dominant economic class. According to pluralists, certain developments during the twentieth century strengthened their position and considerably weakened the Marxist analysis. These include:

- the greater role played by government in the economic affairs of the state and the growth of public ownership and nationalisation of public services and industries (now reversed by the privatisations of the 1980s and 1990s and maintained by New Labour);
- the increasing separation of ownership and control in private industry (see Chapter 2); and
- the growth of joint stock companies with an increase in and more diffuse shareholdings. This development was given a major impetus as a result of the privatisations of the 1980s–early 2000s.

Finally, pluralists argue that government policies within liberal democracies are influenced by continual processes of bargaining between numerous groups representing different interests; these competing interests may have some impact upon policy but none of them dominates the actual mechanisms of government. Government is therefore the neutral arbiter of different interests (more like a weather vane subject to the vagaries of wind speed and direction).

Self-evaluation activity 4.2

Summarising pluralism and Marxism
Response on website

Attempt a summary of the pluralist and Marxist perspectives on the role of government.

Concluding comments

Both the Marxist view that government is a tool of capitalism and is therefore ideologically motivated in all it does, and the pluralist perspective that the state is the neutral arbiter deciding between the claims of competing interest groups such as the TUC and CBI may be regarded as simplistic abstractions, and in many instances these conceptions of the role of government do not necessarily correspond to the reality of government decision making within a complex society such as Britain's. We have already pointed out in the introduction to this chapter that the government in Britain has been and can be highly interventionist in all areas and industrial relations is no exception in this regard. Both Marxist and pluralist arguments accept that government intervenes; what is contentious is the nature of that intervention. From a largely pluralist perspective, for example, Gospel and Palmer (1993) state that:

> From the late 1960s . . . industrial relations became more intertwined [than in previous periods] with politics and politics with industrial relations. All recent governments have been concerned to introduce major changes in industrial relations law and practice. Both the TUC and CBI have favoured legislative changes that have provoked opposition from the other side. Fundamental differences in policy towards industrial relations have never been far from the centre of political debate. (p. 154)

Ideally, therefore, government should take the views of both the TUC and the CBI into consideration before acting upon policy decisions or legislating. During the 1960s and 1970s (the era of liberal collectivism and bargained corporatism) various governments, with some exceptions, managed to maintain a balance of power between the competing interest groups of the TUC and CBI within policy forums such as the National Economic Development Council (NEDC) set up by a Conservative government in 1962.

The opposing (Marxist) argument is that the purpose of government intervention is to protect the interests of capital from the encroachments of trade unions upon management's right to manage. Within the context of early 'Thatcherism' Hyman (1984) asserts:

> While Thatcherite anti-unionism is embedded in a visceral ideological hostility, it also reflects an integrated economic analysis. The succession of anti-union laws, the attacks on public welfare, the privatisation of state industries and services, the deliberate creation of mass unemployment, are all logical reflections of a passionate faith in the virtues of competitive capitalism. (p. 222)

Furthermore, government 'non-intervention' cannot be regarded as government neutrality if by not intervening capitalist interests are protected. Edwards (1994), in his analysis of the role of the state, argues that capitalist states in justifying the accumulation of capital (and profits) attempt to legitimise the exploitative nature of the capitalist system of production as manifested within the workplace. Beaumont (1992) and others, however, steer an intermediate path and argue that government neither supports and protects the capitalist mode of production nor is a 'slave' to capitalism. On the other hand, they argue that the state is rarely, if ever, a neutral arbiter of conflicting interests. Neither the Marxist nor the pluralist view may be 'correct', and as Farnham and Pimlott (1995) point out, the economic and social commitments and role of government have actually increased over the past 50 years and 'the pressures for State intervention in industrial relations have been both cumulative and inevitable' (p. 211).

ROLE OF GOVERNMENT IN HISTORICAL CONTEXT TO 1979

The role of government in British employment relations can be divided into five main phases:

1. The period of *laissez-faire* based on the liberal individualist ideology of the nineteenth century.
2. The period of *collective laissez-faire*, prevalent throughout the first half of the twentieth century.
3. The period of *bargained corporatism* of the post-Second World War era from 1945 to 1979.
4. The period of *neo-laissez-faire* of the Conservative governments from 1980 to 1997.
5. The period of *post-laissez-faire* of New Labour, which we consider later in this chapter.

In this section, the first three periods only are considered.

The laissez-faire period

Laissez-faire embodied the principle of non-interference or non-intervention by government during the nineteenth century. This was accompanied by the development of a 'voluntary' system of industrial relations referred to as voluntarism, which is defined as the

> *preference of employers, trade unions and the government to decide of their own free will on matters concerning the regulation of the employment relationship and the conduct of industrial relations.*

Laissez-faire meant that the primacy of free markets, and, in particular, the labour market, determined the process and outcomes of procedures and agreements. Hobsbawm (1974) provides an amusing and illustrative description of the laissez-faire ideology:

> *The orthodoxy of laissez-faire economic liberalism had the force of natural law: a world in which, as in Newtonian physics, prices like water found their natural level; wages, like stones, when unnaturally raised, must come down, and pint-pots did not hold quarts. It was an orthodoxy which made virtually no provision (at least in the all-important field of production) for 'state interference', whose effects, when not directed to 'the sole purpose of disestablishing state interference' must be ruinous.* (p. 260)

Laissez-faire, then, was concerned with the pursuit of self-interest unfettered by any constraints upon the actions of both employees and employers, who were free to enter into individual contracts. This led to the unregulated growth of industry and the factory system together with increasingly intolerable levels of economic exploitation. As was pointed out in Chapter 3, the paradoxical consequence of this was the development of a more organised trade union movement during the latter half of the nineteenth century and a growing collectivist orientation towards regulating the employment relationship.

Collective laissez-faire

The legal doctrines of 'restraint of trade' (see Chapter 2), which prohibited workers organising collectively and taking industrial action, were finally removed and trade unions were finally granted legal immunities. Hyman (2003) states that: 'The method by which trade unions and collective bargaining were eventually legalised was not, as in many countries, by establishing a positive right to organise, to negotiate and to strike, but by defining an area of industrial relations immunities where the effect of the common law [law made by judges] was inhibited' (p. 39). While the Trades Disputes Act 1906 removed the legal impediments to collective bargaining and industrial action (within limits), this Act and subsequent legislation did not give trade unions the legal right to organise workers or to take industrial action. McIlroy (1991) comments that:

> *The legal acceptance of trade unionism, crucially in 1871, 1875 and 1906, did not take the form of a bill of rights, or a developed legal code or a transformation of the judiciary. The armistice the cautious conservative union leaders sought involved no direct assault on the legal framework. Instead the trade unions sought exemption from the common law – not its replacement by a system of positive rights to organise, bargain and strike. If the social, political and economic role of trade unions is fully accepted, then it can be seen that the consequent system of immunities by which unions were granted protection from common law doctrines of restraint of trade, conspiracy and inducement to breach of contract were not 'privileges' which 'placed trade unions above the law'. The system of immunities simply constituted the method by which unions were given basic rights to exist, organise and bargain.* (p. 3)

The government tradition of legal abstentionism, or non-intervention, was therefore not compromised and the principle of voluntarism remained largely intact. There was an acceptance of the principle of collective organisation and bargaining which distinguished this period from the previous one, but the fact that there was no statutory endorsement of collective bargaining and no notion of a legal collective contract made Britain unique in this respect, as other European governments have legislated in this area giving European trade unions the positive collective rights which British trade unions do not have. Governments during this

period have generally been 'reluctant legislators' and, despite acting on the Whitley Report's recommendations (see Chapter 6), legislation on individual employment conditions, for example, has been much weaker in Britain than in other European countries. As Hyman (2003) points out: 'When governments assumed an industrial relations role, this was most often restricted to providing assistance to collective bargainers' (p. 40).

The main areas where government did legislate with regard to the employment relationship included:

- the introduction of health and safety requirements in particular industries or processes;
- the regulation of the employment of women and young persons;
- minimum wage regulation in certain trades; and
- machinery for conciliation and arbitration in industrial disputes.

The importance of this era for the subsequent development of the British industrial relations system cannot be overemphasised. Howell (2005) identifies three important consequences, the first of which was 'that trade unions gained recognition largely *indirectly* through industry bargaining' (p. 84) which established minimum terms and conditions for employment. Industry-wide bargaining persisted well into the 1970s until its collapse a decade later. A second consequence was that the collective laissez-faire era established an emergent industrial relations system in Britain which 'reinforced the ideology of voluntarism' (p. 84) whereby, unlike the legislated system of the United States and many European countries, British trade unions appeared to thrive without direct statutory interventions. This situation, with a few exceptions, persisted until the 1980s. A third effect of this period was the emphasis upon legal immunities granted by the judicial system to trade unions in the absence of any positive statutory trade union rights.

Bargained corporatism: the beginning of the end of voluntarism

'Corporatism' is the term used to describe a society dominated by large organisations whose activities and relations are co-ordinated and planned rather than being determined by competition in the market or by conflict (see also Chapter 1).

Self-evaluation activity 4.3
Becoming a corporatist state
Response on website

Can you think of any trends and developments since 1945 which suggested that Britain was becoming a 'corporatist' state? You can refer back to Chapter 1 if you wish.

The post-war governments built upon the experience of direct intervention in the economy, which became necessary during the Second World War. The period from 1945 until 1979 witnessed a number of fundamental changes in the way government managed the economy, and, with the possible exception of the Conservative government of 1971–4, government policy was fairly consistent in its attempts to achieve a consensus on economic and industrial relations issues. Governments remained committed to free collective bargaining which represented a continuation of the laissez-faire approach that dominated previous periods, but at the same time increasingly favoured direct intervention to regulate incomes in the form of incomes policies (considered later in this chapter) while making concessions to trade unions in other areas of social, industrial and economic policy. This 'trade-off' approach, which involved tripartite decision making within the various quasi-governmental bodies referred to above, became known as bargained corporatism.

The nature of the changes in the way governments managed the economy were both fundamental and complex. Firstly, Keynesian methods of intervention with government managing effective demand – expanding it in a slump and dampening it in an upturn (derisively known at present as the economics of 'boom and bust') – became the new and relatively successful conventional wisdom. One important policy aim was the maintenance of full employment. The guarantee of full employment gradually gave trade unionists greater confidence and increased bargaining power. Pressures to maintain full employment and expand the welfare state resulted in increases in taxation and public

(government) borrowing which in turn produced pressures for increased wages, higher prices and a declining national competitive edge.

Secondly, awareness of declining economic growth rates and the resurgence of wage and price inflation led to attempts from the mid-1960s to introduce prices and incomes policies. The attempted regulation of prices and incomes and to relate pay increases more directly to productivity increases failed primarily because of the decentralised nature of collective bargaining (see Chapter 6), which gave shop stewards considerable power and leeway to bargain over pay and conditions independent of national union leaderships and unfettered by legal constraints.

Thirdly, the failure of state intervention concerning the incomes policies of the 1960s led to a greater emphasis on the reform of industrial relations and trade union structures which resulted in the Donovan Commission Report of 1968 (see Chapters 1 and 6). White papers produced by both the Labour government (*In Place of Strife*) and the Conservative opposition (*Fair Deal at Work*) expressed both parties' intentions to legislate in order to curb industrial action and reform industrial relations. However, none of the legislative proposals contained any provision to put collective bargaining on a legal footing by making collective agreements legally binding, although there was a presumption within the 1971 Industrial Relations Act that collective agreements were presumed to be legally binding upon the parties unless the parties stated their intention to the contrary. The repeal of the Conservative Industrial Relations Act in 1974 restored the status quo ante but the British economy continued to decline during the 1970s.

Fourthly, continued economic decline, rising inflation and a sustained high level and incidence of industrial disputes encouraged a consensus amongst politicians of all major parties that trade unions must be reformed if relative economic decline was not to become absolute and that free collective bargaining was incompatible with full employment and price stability. This encouraged the Wilson and Callaghan governments to introduce the Social Contract, probably the best example of bargained corporatism during the post-war period. In return for the maintenance of full employment, welfare state expenditure and greater state intervention on prices, the trade union leaders would control incomes

growth. The policy of non-intervention or legal abstentionism was put in doubt by the provisions of the Trade Union and Labour Relations Acts (1974, 1976), the Employment Protection Acts (1975, 1978) and the Health and Safety At Work Act (1974) which 'sought to placate the unions and stimulate both employers and unions to introduce many of the procedural and institutional reforms recommended by the Donovan Report – rather than relying on the voluntaristic tradition of prodding and exhortation' (McIlroy, 1991, p. 6).

By 1978 there was more legislation than ever before affecting employment relations either directly or indirectly. It dealt with both 'individual' issues such as unfair dismissal and redundancy, and 'collective' matters concerning union recognition, the closed shop and shop steward facilities. McIlroy (1991) points out that these developments meant that the government 'had carried out a quiet revolution in legal abstention and this, combined with incomes policy, heralded the wake of voluntarism' (p. 7). All this, however, did little to solve the 'union problem'. From 1974 to 1979, unemployment increased to 1.3 million, there were cuts in the welfare state and real living standards fell. By 1978 it became clear that the Social Contract had failed to alleviate Britain's economic problems; it had become a policy of wage restraint aimed at lowering unit labour costs. Indeed this later period, characterised by high levels of industrial conflict, failed incomes policies and 'set-piece battles between the labour movement and the state . . . is understood to represent a failure of industrial relations' (Howell, 2005, p. 119).

Postscript: 1979 and the end of voluntarism

By 1979, therefore, successive attempts to solve Britain's economic and industrial relations problems had failed. The use of legislation to curb trade union activity in some areas and encourage it in others was by now nothing new as witnessed by the 1971 Industrial Relations Act and the 1974–8 legislation. However, the failure of some of this legislation and the economic and industrial relations problems besetting the government, culminating in the so-called 'Winter of Discontent', resulted in electoral defeat and the first Conservative government led by Mrs Thatcher.

Self-evaluation activity 4.4

Summarising

Response on website

Summarise the distinguishing features of both collective laissez-faire and bargained corporatism. (Use one sentence for each.)

ALL CHANGE: NEO-LAISSEZ-FAIRE AND DE-COLLECTIVISATION: 1980–97

The political approach which emerged with the election of the first Thatcher government in 1979 marked a return to laissez-faire individualism in many respects reminiscent of the nineteenth century. The extract in Exhibit 4.1 from Will Hutton's

Exhibit 4.1

1979: The crucial year?

1979 . . . was a crucial year. It was the moment when Conservative England reclaimed its institutions and traditions from the attempt to bend them to a social democratic cause. Labour's weakness had made the 1974 government a dismal affair . . . But Labour's inadequacies were only part of the story . . . More and more businessmen, officials and opinion-formers began to line up behind Mrs Thatcher and her programme. This was partly because the credit boom gave it the illusion of success; but also because the language of free markets, sound money and individual choice had a profound resonance. Mrs Thatcher was speaking for a set of values that had existed long before the post-war consensus.

Sound money and limits on public spending implied no more than a return to the orthodoxies of the 'Treasury view' that Keynes had mocked in the 1930s, while the promotion of competition, free trade and low taxation drew on a tradition that reached back to the eighteenth century. Moreover, the teachings of neo-liberal economics, with the emphasis that the general good can only result from the free interplay of supply and demand, now seemed to be in harmony with the thinking of a straight-talking politician . . . Resources were best allocated where there was more competition; government regulation did stand in the way of market forces; and trade unions did force up the price of labour.

But something deeper was also at work. The British state had not been designed actively to intervene in economic management at either national or local level. The Civil Service tradition that officials should not engage in private sector activity remained strong [and] the accent was still placed on administration rather than intervention; on high policy rather than commercial strategy. So the state had no apparatus for making British industrial policies work and its efforts were undermined by a latent value system always ready to return to an earlier relationship between state, society and economy. Once Keynesianism had been discredited, Mrs Thatcher's job was more to disinter laissez-faire than to reinvent it. The England of Adam Smith, John Stuart Mill and Herbert Spencer had been submerged by the rise of Keynes, the welfare state and the attempt at government direction of the economy, but it had not been extinguished.

Once uncovered, these foundations supported fifteen years of building Conservative hegemony. But the theory was to prove a poor master and the results disappointing . . . Yet the clock cannot be put back – nor should it be. The post-war settlement may have stopped the rot, but it did not solve the basic British problem. Keynesian economics as practised in the UK had its limits. Industrial policy was not a success; incomes policies were an ignominious failure. The welfare state was creaking at the seams, unable to meet the new demands placed upon it. Productivity growth was poor. It is true that income inequality narrowed and wealth became more equitably distributed and that, compared with what went on before and what was to follow, the period can appear like a Golden Age. But even within its own terms it was unsustainable. If Britain cannot go back, to continue on the present path offers little but social polarisation, political authoritarianism and economic weakness.

Source: Hutton, 1995, pp. 52–5

book *The State We're In* seeks to explain why 1979 was such a watershed date, not only for industrial relations but for the whole British economy and society; while Mrs Thatcher's policies were highly retrograde and divisive, there could nevertheless be no return to what, in comparison with the Thatcher years, seemed like the Golden Age of Keynesian economics. The result of these policies had been to create a de-collectivised wasteland by 1997, and as Howell (2005) argues 'even on those scattered islands of collective regulation, overwhelmingly located in older firms, in an ocean of individual industrial relations, trade unions lack effective sanctions, existing largely at the sufferance of employers' (p. 132).

The essential characteristics of the Thatcher and Major years of neo-laissez-faire or the new liberalism were:

- a resurgence of capitalist values (free enterprise, open markets, deregulation, individualism, privatisation) and abandonment of Keynesian 'mixed economy' economics;
- avid pursuit of monetarist supply-side economics;
- a concerted attempt to weaken the fabric of collective bargaining in order to allow market forces much greater impact on pay and conditions of employment; and
- the gradual dismantling of tripartism (Crouch, 2003).

Some of the main features of this period were, firstly, the introduction of government statutory interventions and legislation to reduce the influence and bargaining power of trade unions; a succession of statutes introduced further legal constraints on the freedom of unions to organise and on their ability to use industrial action in the bargaining process. Secondly, the government used high interest rates and financial control of the public sector, rather than incomes policies, to control inflation which helped to sustain the consistently high levels of unemployment. Thirdly, the government introduced legislation which enabled the privatisation of major nationalised industries and services with important industrial relations consequences (see Chapter 6).

In other ways, however, the period of new liberalism significantly reduced the level of intervention consistent with government adherence to the basic policies of both Friedman (1962, 1968) and the Chicago School and Hayek (1978) and the Austrian School of monetarist economics. Measures affecting the employment relationship were justified by government using the argument that existing laws imposed outdated restrictions upon employment opportunities; the effect of many of these measures, however, was to reduce the statutory protection and rights of individual employees. These measures included:

- the reduction of employee rights in relation to unfair dismissal;
- the curtailment of the role and functions of wages councils and their ultimate abolition; and
- the repeal of certain of the protective statutes relating to the employment of women and young persons.

Crouch (1995) summarises the effect of the legislation:

> The post-1979 Conservative governments have had a strong neo-liberal ideology. This has predisposed them: to reject Keynesian demand management and the search for full employment; to oppose policy deals with trade unions that would involve taking action incompatible with neo-liberal principles; and to reject relations with organisations of interests – on both sides of business but especially on the labour side – that interfered with neo-liberal policy priorities. (p. 238)

The Conservative programme

The Conservative programme was thus founded on a combination of the political ideology of laissez-faire individualism or neo-liberalism and the monetarist policy of Hayek and Friedman which provided the intellectual roadmap and blueprint for the main areas of policy affecting industrial relations and which were concerned with:

1. The control and eventual elimination of inflation.
2. The control of public expenditure.
3. The strengthening of market forces.
4. The curbing of trade union power.
5. The abandonment of tripartism.

The control of inflation

The Conservative governments endorsed the argument that the elimination of inflation should be the main economic policy objective which displaced the post-war consensus policy of maintaining full employment. Keynesian-inspired inflation hindered the operation of the free-enterprise market system by encouraging unions to exploit their bargaining power in order to keep wages artificially high. By controlling inflation, the constraints upon the labour and product market (trade unions and employers) could be overcome, and markets would operate more efficiently. The control of inflation (and therefore of prices and incomes) could not be achieved without dismantling many of the controls which inhibited the operation of free markets, imposed by previous 'corporatist' governments. MacInnes (1987) points out that:

> The inertia of too much state control, the lack of commitment to enterprise, the assumption that extra wage demands or profits or public spending could be passed on through higher prices or taxes and mopped up by general inflation; all these would be 'squeezed out' of the system along with inflation. (p. 50)

The attempt to control inflation had not been wholly successful during the period of Conservative government. One important problem as Crouch (2003) argues was the tendency for wages of skilled workers to rise during periods of economic recovery, which was 'largely a result of the neglect of training and other elements of skill provision during recessions, leading to skill shortages which firms seek to resolve through wage rises' (p. 242). The effect of counter-inflationary policies as far as industrial relations was concerned was that government took the TUC and CBI out of the pay determination equation. Both bodies were no longer consulted by government and negotiators were left to their own devices in the knowledge that high unemployment, high interest rates and exchange rates, as market mechanisms, would facilitate pay settlements more in line with government counter-inflation targets.

The control of public expenditure

Closely related to the control of inflation by restricting the supply of money is the problem of controlling public expenditure. Monetarists such as Friedman argue that any effort to control inflation requires a reduction of government deficits (basically, the difference between what a government spends and what it receives in revenue), but whereas Friedman and his associates argue that the main reason for reducing budget deficits is to enhance individual freedom, Minford and the now defunct 'Liverpool School' of monetarism argued that inflation would never be brought under control unless budget deficits are significantly reduced as a matter of priority (Minford, 1985). Conservative governments therefore believed that public expenditure should decline in relation to private expenditure both in order to 'set the market free' and to control inflation. Another related strand of policy was that of tax reductions as an antidote to large pay increases, the assumption being that if workers were paying fewer taxes they would accept lower pay increases.

However, in real terms, public expenditure did not come down until the end of the 1980s, and by the 1990s it had resumed its upward course. Attempts to reduce expenditure through the imposition of 'cash limits' within the public and local authority sectors meant that employers in these sectors had to settle pay claims either above the cash limit or 'ceiling', in which case the excess expenditure had to be met by increased efficiencies or unemployment (or both), or within the limit, which would prevent unemployment but also depress wage increases. If local authorities pursued the latter course, both employers and union representatives could accuse the government of endorsing a public sector pay policy. Indeed, during the 1990s there were more determined efforts by the Major governments to impose a pay ceiling upon the public sector.

The strengthening of market forces

It was the declared intention of the Conservative governments to 'roll back the frontiers of the state' and significantly reduce state intervention in the economy. New liberals were very critical of the general direction of industrial policy since the 1930s, which was characterised by freely available government subsidies, grants and loans, controls on the movement of foreign exchange, on the labour market and employment. All these controls, monetarists

argued, interfered with the 'evolutionary process of the market whereby consumers' interests are served' (Green, 1987, p. 197), and in particular tended to eradicate or distort the price mechanism. The measures put into effect included the following:

- Along with controls on prices and wages, all controls on foreign exchange movements were abolished which gave companies the opportunity to move capital and revenue overseas. This enabled British companies to take advantage of product and labour markets overseas with possible adverse consequences for local labour.
- A new Industry Act did away with the provision for planning agreements and cut public subsidies to industry, including regional aid.
- Enterprise zones, in which firms were to be exempt from tax and 'red tape' constraints, were established in a number of depressed regions even though they were criticised by the right-wing Adam Smith Institute for becoming 'subsidy islands'. The Institute favoured a strategy whereby all small business should be treated as a 'general experimental zone' of the economy.
- The transfer of state-owned assets to the private sector (privatisation) was pursued in order to reduce the size of the public sector, to extend the 'property-owning democracy' by providing windfall gains for small investors, to introduce market forces and restructure industrial relations and to provide the government with a one-off source of revenue which the former Conservative Prime Minister Harold Macmillan criticised as 'selling off the family silver'.
- Withdrawal of the state from the labour market meant the abolition of industry training boards which introduced training opportunities for companies to take advantage of, and which monitored training standards.
- Measures were introduced in order to increase competition within the newly privatised industries, a policy which New Labour governments have since endorsed. Many examples abound, including the deregulation of bus transport and the break-up of British Rail into constituent rail companies.
- The Enterprise Allowance Scheme was introduced in order to encourage unemployed people to become self-employed.

All of these measures had an indirect effect upon industrial relations. The free play of the market mechanism favoured by the Conservative governments also included measures which directly influenced industrial relations and which we will consider in a later section of this chapter.

The curbing of trade union power

New liberals have been severe critics of 'trade union privileges'. Hayek (1984) argued that trade unions contributed to Britain's economic decline and attributed their (in his opinion) unwarranted power to legal privileges, and that the immunity from civil liability, initially granted by the 1906 Trade Disputes Act, is the chief culprit:

> *These legalised powers of the unions have become the biggest obstacle to raising the living standards of the working class as a whole. They are the chief cause of the unnecessarily big differences between the best and worst paid workers. They are the prime source of unemployment. They are the main reason for the decline of the British economy in general.* (p. 52)

Hayek was, of course, a staunch advocate of individualism and the freedom of the individual worker to decide whether he or she wishes the conditions of his or her employment to be determined individually or collectively. Trade unions, Hayek argued, have now become the 'open enemies of the ideal of freedom of association by which they once gained the sympathy of true liberals. Freedom of association means the freedom to decide whether one wants to join an association or not' (p. 61). Hayek, therefore, attached great importance to trade union reform and stated that 'there can be no salvation for Britain until the special privileges granted to trade unions three-quarters of a century ago are revoked' (p. 58). Hayek was writing in the late 1970s, and the Thatcher and Major governments introduced a number of measures purportedly to remove some of the most 'damaging' trade union 'privileges', as we shall see later in the chapter. What is not in doubt is that from being 'centre stage' in tripartite decision making, as far as pre-1979 corporatist government was concerned, trade unions became sidelined and peripheral to the decisions of the Conservative governments.

Kessler and Bayliss (1998) identify five reasons why the new liberals found trade union power objectionable:

1. Unions were too powerful in relation to pay determination: 'They pushed up pay beyond what was compatible with effective performance in the international economy. They protected practices which prevented increases in productivity. They stood out against changes which managers proposed in the interests of efficiency. They usurped managerial authority where they could, especially in the public services' (p. 60).
2. The very existence of trade unions was antithetical to the workings of the 'unfettered' labour market. While, of course, even the Conservative governments would not want to legislate for union derecognition, their very presence contradicted everything new liberalism stood for. It may be reasonably inferred, therefore, that government would not stand in the way of any employer who wished to derecognise unions. Kessler and Bayliss argue that: 'the banning of trade unions at GCHQ [Government Communication Headquarters] Cheltenham in 1984, though brought about for other reasons, showed that the government was prepared to practise what it preached' (p. 60).

Mini case 4.1
The GCHQ affair

From its establishment in 1947, employees at GCHQ were encouraged to join trade unions. In Mrs Thatcher's second term things changed. In January 1984 the Minister for the Civil Service, acting under powers given to him, issued an instruction which changed the terms and conditions of employment of those working at GCHQ. From now on they would be prohibited from being members of a trade union and would only be entitled to belong to a staff association. This body required the approval of the Director of GCHQ and its rules prohibited industrial action and affiliation to other union bodies. At the same time the legal right of GCHQ staff to take a case to industrial tribunal was withdrawn.

The issue was fought through the courts, but GCHQ workers had little chance of victory as in English law there is no positive right to belong to a trade union.

They argued that on broad grounds of *natural justice* there had been no consultation with the unions before the decision was taken. The House of Lords agreed with the view that the unions had a right to be consulted before their members' terms and conditions were drastically revised. But the Law Lords decided that this right was outweighed by the interest of the state in national security – and the government was custodian of that interest. What the government saw as required *was* required by national security. The ban on union membership was, the Law Lords accepted, genuinely motivated by government fears over the national security issue, and it was acting within its legal rights.

The European Court of Human Rights decided that the case was inadmissible as the international convention allows governments to impose non-trade unionism on the army, police force and certain categories of state employee. In November 1988, 25,000 workers took some form of action in support of the 18 remaining trade unionists at GCHQ, another four of whom were threatened with the sack. Despite heroic tenacity on the part of many workers, by 1989 trade unionism had all but been uprooted in GCHQ.

Source: Adapted from McIlroy, 1991, p. 78

In 1997, the New Labour government fulfilled its pledge to restore recognition rights to GCHQ employees.

3. The new liberal Conservative governments swept away consensus politics and the bargained corporatism associated with it in order both to minimise union influence in government decision making and to confine unions' activities to bargaining with employers.
4. Government hostility towards collectivism was reinforced by the idea of putting the individual employee first and the belief that employees should not be coerced into joining unions if they did not wish to do so. 'The coercion to which they were subjected could be removed by putting an end to the closed shop, by limiting picketing and the extent of lawful strike action, and by the introduction of ballots which would enable individuals to assert themselves against the small group of activists who dominated the affairs of unions' (Kessler and Bayliss, 1995, p. 62).
5. There was opposition towards the accumulated legislative protection given to trade unions and

their members during the period of Labour government from 1974 to 1979. As Kessler and Bayliss point out, the Conservative Party manifesto endorsed the party view that unions were dominated by a small minority of 'extremists' and the Labour government had given unions privileges 'without responsibility'. Unions were therefore to be 'cut down to size', as McIlroy (1991) argues:

> Changes in employment legislation dealing with union recognition and the closed shop would enable members to leave trade unions. They would be denied political purchase and their leaders would no longer be consulted by Cabinet or treated to 'beer and sandwiches' by the Prime Minister. Legislation on strikes and picketing would mean that unions would find it harder to deliver. Members would in consequence find membership less attractive. Wider policies such as privatisation would also undermine union power by depriving them of the fertile breeding ground of a complacent monopoly employer. Management would be freer to operate according to the dictates of the market rather than the whims of shop stewards and union leaders. This would be particularly important given the changing pattern of industry. If the blitz on manufacturing industry of the early 1980s had the beneficial side-effect of decimating many of the strongholds of trade unionism, it was vital that the poisonous weed of the old trade unionism should not take root in the new hi-tech industries. A key purpose of legislation was the restriction of trade unionism in the industries of the year 2000. (p. 16)

The abandonment of tripartism

Trade unions, the TUC and, to a large extent, the CBI were sidelined by government as we have noted, together with the other corporatist baggage of tripartite co-operation. When the first Conservative government was elected, there were basically six tripartite channels:

- The National Economic Development Council (NEDC).
- The Manpower Services Commission (MSC).
- The Advisory, Conciliation and Arbitration Service (Acas).
- The Health and Safety Commission.
- The Equal Opportunity Commission (EOC) and the Commission for Racial Equality (CRE) (see Chapter 11).
- The wages councils.

The NEDC was established in 1961 and provided a regular discussion forum for government, unions (TUC) and employers (CBI) in considering both general and specific matters relating to the economy. The administration of these matters was conducted by the National Economic Development Office (NEDO) which provided the three parties with evaluations of issues and statistical data and analysis. The NEDC was not abolished immediately; it was rather a slow death, with government having 'neither industrial policy nor tasks for the union and employer organisations that could provide a serious agenda' (Crouch, 1995, p. 248). The death knell was finally sounded in 1987 and the NEDC was abolished in 1992 after being virtually moribund for the previous five years.

The MSC was formed in 1973 in order to revitalise training and manpower policy, and to take over other Department of Employment functions of manpower forecasting together with the administration of local employment offices and job centres in providing a placement service and employment advice. The first Conservative government significantly reduced its functions, but between 1983 and 1987 the MSC assumed a higher profile by undertaking the controversial task of securing 'changes in the education system that the Department of Education and Science seemed reluctant to pursue' (ibid., p. 249). Basically, this involved the devising of training schemes and the provision of vocational education and even the devising of parts of the school curriculum. While there was an input into the MSC by both TUC and CBI, government largely ignored TUC arguments opposing the policy of securing reductions in the wages of trainees and increases in the pressures on the young unemployed to opt for training rather than unemployment pay. In 1987 the role of the MSC changed again; its functions were diluted, trade union representation was reduced while employer representation increased, and in 1988 the MSC was renamed the Training

Commission and placed under the direct control of the Department of Employment. The Employment Act of 1989 abolished the Commission and replaced it with a Training Agency under the direct control of government; by 1991 the Training Agency itself was abolished to be replaced by a national network of Training and Enterprise Councils (TECs) run by unelected local business leaders, co-opted trade union leaders and senior educational personnel.

Acas lost many of its functions during the 1980s (for an overview of the functions of Acas, see Chapter 1). The Health and Safety Commission continued its work largely unhindered during the period. The various inspectorates were co-ordinated and grouped into a Health and Safety Executive, responsible for the administration of the health and safety regulations backed up by union-appointed workplace safety representatives. Finally, wage councils were the longest standing of the tripartite bodies set up in 1945 to deal with the problem of low pay; it was not until 1986 that there was a serious attempt to abolish the councils which did result in a diminution of their powers, rendering them virtually ineffective until they were finally abolished in 1993. As Crouch (2003) points out, the 1977 New Labour government 'made virtually no changes to this policy of gradually disappearing tripartism' (p. 121).

Self-evaluation activity 4.5

Summarising
Response on website

Summarise the main elements of the new liberal programme as it affected industrial relations.

Concluding comments

The monetarist era is now over, but its legacy remains: the industrial relations map is considerably redrawn since 1979 and, for the time being at least, no substantial change to the legislative framework introduced by the Conservatives was envisaged by the New Labour governments whose agenda we will consider later in the chapter. Given the political ideology of the Conservatives, legislation and policy initiatives reflecting that ideology

were inevitable. All that was considered sacrosanct under the corporatist era was attacked; the 'market' now led and the march towards unleashing its forces would create many casualties in its wake, ranging from the growing number of unemployed to the trade unions suffering from ignominious defeats, as with the National Union of Mineworkers in 1984.

GOVERNMENT ECONOMIC AND INCOMES POLICY: 1945–99

Government economic policy – which we considered briefly in Chapter 1 – has important and fundamental consequences for industrial relations, and may be defined as

the strategy and measures adopted by government to manage the economy as a means of achieving its economic objectives.

In general terms, governments at the macro level are concerned with securing the objectives of:

- full employment;
- price stability (that is, a low rate of inflation);
- economic growth; and
- balance of payments equilibrium.

In practice, given the complexities of the economy and its exposure to international influences, the simultaneous achievement of all these objectives is virtually impossible, so that a degree of prioritising is necessary. Inevitably, political as well as economic considerations will influence this process. Of the economic policy objectives, it is, perhaps, full employment and price stability which have the most immediate impact upon industrial relations, and in view of the fact these two objectives tend to conflict with each other, what is important from an industrial relations viewpoint is where a government puts the emphasis.

Self-evaluation activity 4.6
Economic objectives
The response is given below

The priority accorded to different economic objectives will reflect the ideology of the government of the day. Can you expand on this in general terms? Why do you think that full employment and price stability conflict with each other?

Put simply, governments with a broadly left-wing ideology tend to favour widespread state ownership of the means of production and detailed intervention in the economy as a means of achieving their economic objectives, while governments with a broadly right-wing ideology tend to favour limited state ownership and minimum government intervention in the economy, relying instead on the market mechanism.

Full employment enhances the bargaining power of workers and their unions and thus enables them to force up wages and salaries. Pay increases may lead in turn to price increases and hence to inflation. It follows that unemployment, as we have seen over the past 20 years or so, helps to keep the rate of inflation down. (We examine this in greater detail in this chapter.) It is possible to achieve the aims of full employment and price stability at the same time, but only if government, employers and unions can reach some consensus on a prices and incomes policy – which they have not been able to achieve, at least not for long! It is difficult to achieve such a consensus because such policies, even with a system of bargained corporatism in operation, are difficult to administer: the problem of how to agree a 'norm', how to deal with justified exceptions to the norm, and the means of enforcement is a very complex one. Perhaps the main reason for not arriving at a consensus is because conceptions of what would be a 'fair' prices and incomes policy differ. For example, there is no agreement as to the relative worth of different industries and occupations. There is usually agreement that there should be exceptions, such as the low-paid groups which are 'seriously out of line', or groups where it is in the 'national interest' to encourage growth. But there is always argument as to which groups actually fall into – or outside – these categories. We shall be considering this aspect later.

At the macroeconomic policy level, various general measures can be used by governments operating in mixed economies to achieve their objectives, including fiscal policy (the manipulation of tax rates and government expenditure), monetary policy (the control of the money supply and interest rates), prices and incomes policy (controls on costs and prices), and the management of the exchange rate. These policies are augmented at a more specific level by measures designed to encourage industrial investment, research and development and to protect consumer interest. Fiscal and monetary policies

are the main measures used by governments in Britain since 1945.

Approaches to the management of the economy

We shall look in some detail at three basic approaches to the management of the economy as they affect employment relations (the first two of these were briefly considered in Chapter 1):

• Keynesian demand management;
• monetarism and supply-side economics; and
• the rational expectations model.

Initially, however, it is important to understand what is meant by the inflation phenomenon.

Inflation and deflation

We had a brief look at inflation in Chapter 1 when we described inflation as an increase in prices or the cost of living. One 'explanation' of the cause of inflation is related to the level of demand in the economy, and it is here that the terms deflation and reflation come in. Any policy that results in a fall in the level of demand can be described as a deflationary policy, and anything that leads to a rise in demand as a reflationary policy. It is possible that a reflationary policy may also be inflationary, but this is not always the case. Inflation can be caused by changes in aggregate (total) demand and by changes in aggregate supply.

As far as changes in aggregate supply are concerned, one of the main determinants of the price of a commodity, good or service is the cost of supplying it. An increase in the costs of production often takes the form of increased wage costs brought about by a situation in which groups of workers bid up wages, and this is called cost or wage-push inflation. In the international context these cost increases could be increases in the cost of essential raw materials brought about by producers' cartels flexing their political and economic muscle – such as the rise in price of OPEC (Organisation of Petroleum Exporting Countries) oil in the 1970s. Alternatively, these increases in costs may be attributable to natural causes such as late frosts ruining the coffee bean harvest.

Inflation is also caused by shifts in aggregate demand so that an increase in the aggregate price level can be caused by an increase in aggregate demand. For example, titanium is an essential but rare metal used in the construction of some aircraft and the supply of titanium is fixed for a certain period. If the demand for titanium increases (maybe because the demand for new aircraft is increasing, or different uses have been found for titanium), then the price of titanium will rise because buyers are competing against each other to secure larger proportions of the fixed supply. This relationship between demand and supply affects all commodities and services, including, of course, labour. This type of inflation is called demand-pull. It has been argued that cost-push inflation is the main type that occurred in the 1970s when unions made use of their bargaining strength to push up wages, and employers passed on the additional costs by raising the prices of their products. Demand-pull inflation was in evidence during the credit boom of the 1980s. The control of inflation has been one of the overriding concerns of governments during the post-war period and particularly from the 1960s onwards. The effects of this aspect of government economic policy upon industrial relations are extremely important, as the example in Exhibit 4.2 demonstrates.

We could, therefore, describe the scenario in Exhibit 4.2 as a *deflationary* situation (this is another

Exhibit 4.2

The effects of controlling inflation

This is a hypothetical example relating to the production of widgets in order not to give offence to any particular category of workers or their unions.

As a result of industrial action on the part of the Widgetworkers' Union, wage rates rose in that industry. Note that we are considering wage increases which result not from *demand* pressure in the labour market but from autonomous increases in wage costs (that is, increases in wages which are independent of the state of demand in the labour market). Will this spark off pure *cost-push* inflation? There are several possible outcomes:

- the increased wages could all be offset by increases in labour productivity, such that wage costs did not rise;
- the increase in wage costs could all be paid out of profits, so that profits fell but widget prices did not rise; or,
- if we assume neither of these two things happens, then the result will be that widget prices start to rise.

Suppose that the government senses this, and in an effort to control inflation it introduces policies which increase the amount of tax revenue taken out of the system (assume increases in income tax and or VAT). It therefore succeeds in keeping the level of total spending at its pre-existing level. In other words, aggregate demand is fixed and in such a situation an increase in the price of widgets can only result in one of the following scenarios:

- The amount of widgets purchased falls by exactly the same amount as the price rose, leaving total expenditure on widgets unchanged. In this scenario, the widget workers are 'pricing themselves out of the market'. Demand for their product falls in direct proportion to the increase in price. The demand for widget workers' labour will, therefore, fall as the demand for the product which they produce falls. In all probability, this would lead to unemployment among widget workers.
- The amount of widgets purchased does not fall, but spending on other commodities does fall. In this scenario the demand in other sectors of the economy falls, creating depressed labour markets and possibly unemployment in those sectors. The widget workers have benefited at the expense of workers in other industries and have 'grabbed a larger share of the national cake' for themselves.
- The price of other commodities falls. In this scenario there is a change in relative prices, widgets becoming more expensive relative to other commodities. The overall price level has remained unchanged, however.

The most likely outcome of the widget workers' action is some combination of the first and second scenarios. This represents a fall in the volume of production, accompanied by a rise in unemployment.

meaning of the term *deflation*, which here means a fall in output). Paradoxically, however, what we have here is both a fall in output and employment (deflation) coupled with a rise in the price level (inflation). Thus by restricting aggregate demand in a situation in which cost increases are occurring, the government has produced the worst possible outcome. That is why many post-war governments have – at least until 1979 – preferred to act in an accommodating fashion, allowing the level of aggregate demand to rise so that the same volume of goods can be bought at the new higher prices. By allowing demand to rise they prevent the fall in sales – and therefore the fall in output and employment – that would otherwise have occurred. If the government acts in this consensual fashion it is evidence that, even though it may be capable of restricting demand, it is unwilling to do so, preferring the evil of inflation to what it regards as the greater social evil of unemployment.

However, such a policy may encourage inflation in the longer term, because the widget workers by their action appear to have gained increases in wages without suffering any fall in employment. This will have a 'demonstration effect' on workers in other industries who will also push for wage increases which, if granted, will result in increases in the price of those commodities. Inflation therefore proceeds and, as it does, people develop expectations that the government will continue to act in an accommodating fashion by allowing demand to rise. Thus, cost inflation and demand inflation reinforce one another.

The control of inflation, whichever economic policy is adopted, affects prices and incomes; governments influenced by Keynesian economics used incomes policies in their attempts to control cost or wage-push inflation and hence indirectly curb collective bargaining. The unemployment effects of monetarist anti-inflation policy has led to a decline in trade union membership and a weakening of trade union bargaining power. It is for these reasons that the relationship between inflation, unemployment and incomes is examined in greater depth later on.

Keynesian demand management

Keynesian demand management strategies, as we have noted earlier, dominated macroeconomic

policy from the 1950s through to the late 1970s. The simple precept of Keynesian economics is that it is the role of the government to manage aggregate demand, through budgetary and fiscal measures, in order to ensure a level of economic activity which maintains full employment.

Self-evaluation activity 4.7

The Keynesian model
This SEA has no commentary

The Keynesian model was summarised in Chapter 1. Reread the relevant section and then summarise the approach in your own words.

Here, we shall look at those aspects which Keynesian economists and policy makers consider most relevant to industrial relations, namely, the nature of demand, the determinants of aggregate demand and the manipulation of aggregate demand. But first we build upon the Keynesian model we introduced in Chapter 1. The basic model derives from a theoretical view of the economy as a circular flow of income. The simple economy (see Figure 4.1) comprises two economic units – firms and households, and also comprises two flows:

- 'real' flows of goods and services (the continuous line); and
- money flows of income and expenditure (the dotted line) in the opposite direction.

With reference to Figure 4.1, firms pay incomes to households in the form of wages, rent, interest and profits in return for the use of labour services, land and capital owned by households. Households in turn spend their income on goods and services produced by firms. The real economy is rather more complex, and in the Keynesian model it is the level of aggregate demand which is responsible for determining the values of most other variables in the macroeconomic system. As we have seen, aggregate demand influences the rate of inflation; it will also influence the level of output, the level of employment, and hence of unemployment, the level of investment, of savings, the rate of growth, spending on imports and so on. Using our basic 'firms' and 'households' dichotomy we can represent this figuratively (see Figure 4.2).

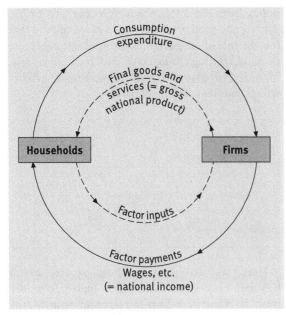

Figure 4.1 The circular flow of income

as payment for goods and services and back again to households as payment for the factor services (labour, capital, etc.) which were used in production.

- The economy is said to be in equilibrium when spending which has 'leaked out' of the system or withdrawals in the form of savings, spending on imports and tax payments, is matched by an exactly equal volume of injections – investment, government spending and export sales.

Self-evaluation activity 4.8

Effects on employment
Response on website

According to the model, what would be the effect on employment of a reduction in the amount of income in the circular flow, for example, as a result of increased taxation?

The level of demand in the economy determines the volume of production, investment and so on; but what determines the level of aggregate demand itself? Crucial to the Keynesian paradigm is the concept of macroeconomic equilibrium:

- Spending is assumed to flow around the economy in a circular fashion – from households to firms

The manipulation of aggregate demand

The final element of the Keynesian model is perhaps the most obvious, and is concerned with the extent to which the level of aggregate demand can be manipulated by the government. We saw in Chapter 1 how government can reduce people's disposable income and therefore their ability to spend through

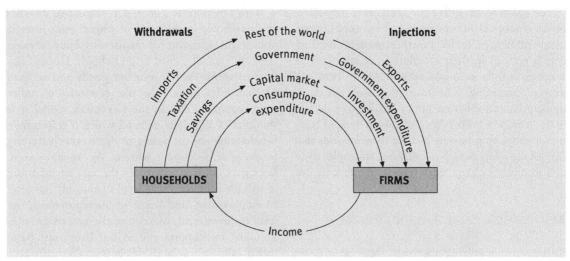

Figure 4.2 Dynamics of circular flow

higher taxation. On the other hand, an increase in government spending, say on education, roads and pensions, will increase incomes of teachers, road builders and pensioners and therefore lead to an increase in spending. The following terms are important when considering government expenditure:

- The overall level of government spending relative to its revenue from taxation is known as its **budget stance**.
- If government spending exceeds government tax revenue, this is said to be a **budget deficit** as the government takes out of the economy (in the form of taxation) less than it puts back (in the form of government spending). Such a budget is sometimes described as reflationary.
- When government spending equals total tax revenue, this is said to be a **balanced budget**, and when tax revenues exceed government spending, the budget is in surplus. A budget surplus is described as deflationary in the sense that it reduces aggregate demand.

Self-evaluation activity 4.9

Maintaining full employment

The response is given below

As we have seen, the maintenance of full employment was a key objective for governments in the post-war period up to the late 1970s. Describe how this was done, using some of the terms introduced above.

It was seen as the accepted task of governments, whatever their political persuasion, to use budgetary measures to stimulate or deflate the economy as circumstances required, in order to keep the level of unemployment as low as possible without causing cost-push inflation. If the level of unemployment began to rise, and economic activity declined, the government would stimulate demand either by reducing taxation or by increasing government (public) expenditure. If necessary, the government would borrow in order to do so. Prior to 1939, a budget deficit was considered the road to economic and financial disaster. In Keynesian economics, deficit budgeting became an acceptable method of ensuring relative prosperity, steady economic growth and very low levels of unemployment. By the 1970s, governments were finding it increasingly difficult to maintain full employment, cope with increasing and

escalating budget deficits and contain inflation. What began to emerge in the late 1970s was a high-taxation economy, with rising public expenditure, increasing trade union power, and the phenomenon known as stagflation – sharply rising prices (inflation) and unemployment at the same time. Many economists and politicians began to have doubts about the validity of Keynesian demand management, and this heralded a new approach by the first Conservative administration.

Monetarism and supply-side economics

We looked at monetarism briefly in Chapter 1. Here we shall consider monetarism in relation to inflation and unemployment and the 'supply-side' economics to which it is related. A definition of monetarism (Pass and Lowes, 1998) would comprise the following:

> *Monetarism is a body of analysis relating to the influence of MONEY in the functioning of the economy. The theory emphasises the importance of the need for a 'balanced' relationship between the amount of money available to finance purchases of goods and services, on the one hand, and the ability of the economy to produce such goods and services, on the other.* (p. 92)

The theory provides an explanation of inflation centred on excessive increases in the money supply. Simply defined, money supply is that amount of money in circulation in the economy at any given point in time. The size of the money supply is an important determinant of the level of spending in an economy and its control is a particular concern of monetary policy. However, the monetary authorities have a problem because, given the number of possible definitions of the money supply (see Figure 4.3), it is difficult for them to decide which is the most appropriate money supply category to target for control purposes.

In the 1980s, the UK government, as part of its medium-term financial strategy, set 'target bands' for the growth of initially sterling M3 and later M0. Towards the end of the period of Conservative government, formal targeting of the money supply

Initials	Definition	Amount £bn July 1996
	'Narrow' money (money held predominantly for spending)	
	Bank notes and coin in circulation	22
M0	Currency plus banks' till money and operational balances at Bank of England	24
M1	M0 plus UK private sector bank deposits	325
M2	M1 plus UK private sector deposits in banks and building societies	452
	'Broad' money (money held for spending and/or as a store of value)	
M3	M1 plus UK private sector time bank deposits and UK public sector sterling deposits	537
M4	M3 plus net building society deposits	652
M5	M4 plus UK private sector holdings of money market instruments (e.g. Treasury Bills plus national savings)	682

Figure 4.3 Money supply definitions

had been abandoned, although the authorities continued to 'monitor' M0, together with M4 as 'indicators' of general monetary conditions in the economy. One of the main contentions of monetarism is that inflation stems from the excessive growth of the money supply.

Self-evaluation activity 4.10

Inflation according to monetarists
Response on website

What type of inflation do you think monetarists have in mind?

Monetarists also argue that if the government spends more than it receives in taxes (there is a budget deficit), increasing the public sector borrowing requirement (defined as the excess of government expenditure over tax receipts, requiring the government to make good the difference by borrowing money from the banking system (Treasury Bills) or from the general public (long-dated bonds)) to finance the shortfall, then the increase in the money supply which results from financing the increase in the public sector borrowing requirement will increase the rate of inflation. The 'pure' quantity theory of money ($MV = PT$ – see Exhibit 4.3) suggests that the ultimate cause of inflation is excessive monetary creation (that is 'too much money chasing too little output') – thus it is seen as a source of demand-pull inflation.

Monetarists suggest that 'cost-push' is not a truly independent theory of inflation – it has to be 'financed' by money supply increases. For example, assume a given stock of money and given levels of output and prices. Assume now that costs increase (for example, higher wage rates) and this causes suppliers to put up prices. Monetarists argue that this increase in prices will not turn into an inflationary process (that is, a persistent tendency for prices to rise) unless the money supply is increased. The given stock of money will buy fewer goods at the higher price level and real demand will fall; but if the government increases the money supply – as Keynesians recommend – then this enables the same volume of goods to be purchased at the higher price level. If this process continues, cost-push inflation is validated.

Exhibit 4.3

The quantity theory of money

This theory posits a direct relationship between the money supply and the general price level in an economy. The basic identity underlying the quantity theory was first developed by Irving Fisher (1911). The Fisher equation states that:

$$MV = PT$$

where M is the money stock; V is the velocity of circulation of money (the average number of times each pound or dollar changes hands in financing transactions during a year); P is the general price level; and T is the number of transactions or the total amount of goods and services supplied.

Monetarists therefore argue that it is the responsibility of government to:

- maintain 'sound money' by pursuing a fixed level of money supply increase, departing from it only with great caution;
- reduce government borrowing; and
- reduce the overall level of government spending.

The financing of government spending through taxation or by borrowing from the public is not 'sound money' and has, according to monetarists, undesirable side effects even if this does not contribute to an increase in the money supply. Some of these undesirable consequences include the disincentive effect of raising taxes; reducing people's ability to purchase goods and services which leads to a fall in consumption and eventually in society's welfare. A further undesirable consequence is that the money which the government borrows could have otherwise been spent on consumption, or they may be funds which could otherwise have been lent to some other sector, such as private industry. 'Sound money' is supposed to keep inflation down and the goals identified above are intended to ensure that the government does not itself inject unnecessary money into the economy.

Monetarists go on to argue that if the monetary system is well regulated and controlled, the rest of the economy can safely be left to self-regulating market forces. This approach may mean high unemployment in the short term, but in the longer term it will lead to improved productivity and competitiveness and thus to sustained economic growth.

Monetarist views on the determinants of unemployment

Unlike Keynesian economists, monetarists are not committed to the maintenance of full employment if this interferes with the workings of markets. They believe that real wage and employment levels are determined in the labour market and that the market is in equilibrium. They distinguish between short-run and long-run equilibrium. Short-run equilibrium is a situation in which expectations are incorrect and hence are unfulfilled, whereas in long-run equilibrium the expectations of all the parties involved are correct anticipations of future events. The suppliers of labour (the unions, say) will be interested in the real wage. At the same time firms will take on labour only as long as the wage they have to pay is less than the value of what that labour can produce. In other words, they also will be interested in the real wage (the money wage relative to the money value of the extra output that the labour can produce).

Monetarists believe that this real wage is flexible in the long run and that this flexibility will ensure full employment (or rather, no involuntary unemployment) in a market equilibrium situation. Any registered unemployment that remains will be 'natural' since the economy will be at the 'natural level' of unemployment.

The natural level of unemployment explained

Assume that the government undertakes expansionary policies designed to reduce the level of unemployment. The effect will be first of all to increase demand in the market for goods and services, pushing up prices. The demand for labour, therefore, increases because each employee becomes more productive in the sense that the *value* of the goods which they produce per hour will rise. The disequilibrium situation in the labour market caused by the increased demand for labour causes money wages to rise and this results in an expansion of labour supply as more individuals opt voluntarily for labour rather than leisure. Thus employment levels increase, along with money wages and prices.

Note, however, that this short-run effect will occur only if workers can be fooled into supplying more labour by an increase in money wages alone, in a situation in which real wages remain unchanged, prices and wages having increased at the same rate. Workers in this case are said to suffer from money illusion. In the longer run, however, they realise that increased prices have completely offset the increase in money wages and they therefore revert to their former behaviour. Those who have recently entered employment drop out again, preferring leisure to labour at this real wage. This fall in the supply of labour results in labour shortages and consequently a further rise in money wages. This increase in money wages, which may also be a temporary increase in real wages, leads to a fall in demand for labour, the net result being that the economy falls back to the natural level of unemployment.

Supply-side economics and the 'rational expectations' hypothesis

Closely linked with monetarism, supply-side economics emerged during the 1970s, and policies based on supply-side economics were aimed at improving the competitive efficiency of markets, particularly the labour market. Not only had inflation to be 'squeezed out' of the economy by monetary discipline, but also the economy had to be freed from obstacles inhibiting the efficient working of the market mechanisms.

Self-evaluation activity 4.11
Obstacles to the market
Response on website

What do you think are the main obstacles to 'the efficient working of market mechanisms'?

However, supply-side economists also advocate a range of positive measures to improve the efficiency of product and labour markets such as:

- increased competition between producers;
- better education and training of the labour force; and
- the introduction of new technologies.

Rational expectations

In the Depression years of the 1930s, Keynes argued that demand should be increased in order to reduce unemployment. The classical economists (those who came before Keynes) resisted, arguing in favour of balanced budgets and action to reduce wages. In the post-war era Keynesian economics dominated and became the 'conventional wisdom', but during the mid-1970s the conventional wisdom was under attack and by 1980 Keynesian economics was in the wilderness. New-style monetarism is the absolute negation of the Keynesian belief that demand management was capable of raising output and reducing unemployment. The first part of the attack on Keynesianism came with the so-called 'crowding out' hypothesis (discussed earlier) whereby it was argued that the government was incapable of raising demand because any increase in government spending would displace an equivalent amount of private investment spending. This hypothesis lost support by the mid-1980s and was replaced by a much more sophisticated and damaging critique of Keynesian views.

The new critique (also related to supply-side economics) was based on the rational expectations hypothesis (REH) and gave new impetus to the debate about the causes of unemployment. The debate itself was called the real wage debate which concerned the question of whether unemployment was the result of real wages being too high. Had workers priced themselves out of jobs and would

unemployment fall if workers accepted lower real wages? Would an expansion of demand engineered by the government succeed in reducing unemployment or would it merely lead to wage inflation without any impact on employment levels?

What is REH?

REH suggests that firms and individuals predict future events without bias and with full access to relevant information at the time the decision is to be made. Only 'new' information will have an effect on expectations or behaviour. Expectations play an important part in pay determination and bargaining, whereby each side (employers and employees) have to anticipate future events such as the rate of inflation; by doing this, employment would be based on real wages at all times. The rational expectations model is perhaps more applicable to 'perfect' markets and is rather less successful when applied to modern 'real world' macroeconomic problems. The controversy which surrounded this seemingly innocuous hypothesis is based on the view that when REH is combined with a certain view of the labour market it appears to offer a theoretical justification for the sort of policy stance which right-wing governments like to adopt. That is, REH provides radical right-wing governments with a justification for abandoning any sort of reflationary actions to reduce unemployment since it forms a vital part of an analysis which concludes that such reflationary policies are ineffective and damaging. If REH is true, and if the labour market works in ways that monetarists believe, then expansionary (Keynesian) fiscal and monetary policies cannot alleviate unemployment. Reflation brings inflation without any increase in real output. Demand management, in a Keynesian sense, is dead and the way is open for 'supply-side' policies – 'making markets work better'.

Monetarism and Keynesianism: summary and conclusion

As we have noted, Keynesianism became the economic conventional wisdom with its largely optimistic outlook, as Dunnett (1998) points out:

The message of Keynesianism was one of hope; governments could spend their way out of a recession and thereby eliminate the scourge of unemployment. There is absolutely no doubt that the Keynesian medicine worked. And it was easy for Keynesianism to win the hearts and minds of the people, for the medicine was pleasant to take. Just inject more spending into the economy and prosperity will follow with no nasty side effects – or so it seemed at the time. (p. 61)

During the 1960s and 1970s inflation was becoming a major concern, and the Keynesian prescription in the form of deflation accompanied by a slowdown in economic growth and a rise in the level of unemployment, was rather more unpalatable. The treatment was painful but largely ineffective. Critics argued that the existence of both unemployment and inflation demonstrated the inability of Keynesian economics to deal with these 'twin evils', and it was under these circumstances that the monetarists started to gain intellectual and ideological support. The government policy of increasing public spending was, of course, criticised by monetarists and had, according to Dunnett (1998), four main consequences:

- It became increasingly costly and difficult for government to service the increasingly burdensome national debt.
- Increasing public borrowing had 'crowded out' private sector investment and had therefore hindered the growth of the private sector.
- Increasing government expenditure led to monetary expansion and therefore to inflation which resulted in the raising of inflationary expectations amongst both employees and employers which in turn made the reduction of monetary expansion more difficult to achieve.
- The increasingly active role of the state in supporting both individuals, through generous state benefit payments for example, and firms, from 'bailing out' of financial trouble through to providing generous regional incentives, had led to a decline in traditional values of self-advancement and self-help and 'this moral degeneration had manifested itself at the personal level in a belief that the individual had the right to be maintained by the state (the "nanny state"), and at

the company level by the belief that the state should cushion the firm from the unpleasant effects of market forces' (p. 62).

From the late 1970s to the mid-1980s, monetarism held sway. But towards the end of that decade disillusion with monetarist policy, because of its apparent failure to control aggregate demand by controlling the money supply, resulted in the displacement of monetarism by specific supply-side policies, some of which were based on the rational expectations model.

Incomes policy

Inflation, arguably, is fuelled by expectations of unions and firms. Unions expect that an increase in wage rates will not result in a decline in demand for its labour as increased wage costs will be passed on to the consumer in the form of higher prices. The employer expects that as a result of increased costs, which have been passed on to customers in the form of higher prices, the demand for the firm's product will not fall because there will be an increase in purchasing power and because the firm's competitors are also announcing similar price increases. These expectations could be dampened in the longer term by deflationary demand management policies, but this was deemed to be politically and socially unacceptable during the Keynesian post-war period. The alternative policy option would be to introduce a period of pay restraint; these incomes policies were an important part of government counter-inflation policy up until 1979.

The rationale for incomes policies (also called prices and incomes policies, as some governments sought to place some curbs on prices as part of a two-pronged strategy for reducing inflation) was that if wage costs could be held down in the short run, this would bring down the rate of inflation. This would, in turn, reduce the expected rate of inflation and hence the wage increases negotiated in the following time period would be more modest, the hoped-for result being the progressive reduction in the rate of inflation consistent with full employment, price stability and economic growth.

Incomes policies have proved to be fairly complex and varied, ranging from statutory to voluntary and involving price constraints and a whole complex of administrative bodies such as the old

Prices and Incomes Board. There are six broad types of incomes policy:

1. Efforts to inform or influence 'public opinion' on the need for restraint. These may influence the general level of expectations concerning wages and prices.
2. Implementation of more formal guidelines for restraint on a voluntary or mandatory basis.
3. Attempts to restrain cost pressures in specific sectors, especially 'key sectors' such as the public sector where wage and price decisions are highly visible.
4. Short-term government intervention to freeze or severely restrain wage and price increases, either to buy time or influence inflation expectations.
5. The operation of a longer-term co-ordinated system of income determination with or without government involvement.
6. 'Institutional engineering', including the long-term reform of bargaining structures to lessen the pressure from competitive wage bargaining; labour market policies to improve mobility and ease inflationary bottlenecks; and reform of the legal framework to control strikes, improve mediation and arbitration, or limit union power.

The last type (6) is, perhaps, not immediately identifiable as a form of incomes policy, but its objectives are those normally identified and associated with incomes policy. The first four types of policy are typical of the various forms of incomes policy adopted in Britain during the 1960s and 1970s, while the sixth is identified with the type of policy pursued during the 1980s and 1990s. The fifth type, the operation of a longer-term system of pay restraint, has never been successfully achieved in Britain, although the 'Social Contract' of the 1970s had some short-term success, the policy being largely administered by the parties themselves.

Elements of an incomes policy

There are two main elements to an incomes policy. Firstly, there are the rules which guide or constrain the behaviour of parties, that is the norm and the criteria for any exceptions to the norm. Secondly, there are the mechanisms of compliance; that is, the enforcement policies and procedures and the administrative machinery, if any, through which the policy is managed and/or enforced – the main

choice is between voluntary and statutory or mandatory policies (as we identified above) – and the extent to which statutory policies are backed up by appropriate sanctions. Whatever the objectives and type of policy, there are three basic criteria which should be observed:

- the rules and the administrative machinery should make economic sense and have some sort of economic rationale;
- the objectives and rules must be simple enough to be easily understood; and
- policies, if they are to be in place for any length of time, must be flexible enough to encompass broadly accepted notions of fairness; this is particularly important if the policy is to achieve any kind of consensus about its operation.

Most incomes policies include, as an essential component, some sort of 'norm' for pay increases. The most straightforward is an outright pay 'freeze' which, however, lacks flexibility and is difficult to sustain in the long term. Most incomes policies specify a wage 'target', 'guiding light', or 'norm' together with a list of exceptions. In Britain, norms have been set in relation to the underlying increase in productivity in the economy, or in relation to the rate of inflation. The problem of how the norm should be 'stated' is important, and in the past it has been expressed as a percentage, a percentage with lower and/or upper limits, as a flat rate, as a combined flat rate and percentage, and as 'averages' and 'ceilings'.

Self-evaluation activity 4.12

The norm
The response is given below

1. What do you think are the possible side effects of expressing the norm as a percentage?
2. What do you think is the main problem of expressing the norm as an average?

1. Percentages and flat rates can both have awkward side effects. It is argued, for example, that flat-rate increases depress or 'squeeze' differentials, although there are associated problems concerning how differentials are measured. Percentage increases, on the other hand, will consistently increase the gap between lower and higher paid workers. The combination of a flat rate and a percentage norm, as in the

Conservative government's counter-inflation policy (1971–3) represented an attempt to balance these problems.
2. The obvious problem with the norm as an average is that some people have to get less than the average in order that others might exceed it. In any event, what usually happens is that the norm becomes the standard and gains by the exceptional cases are not offset by 'losses' elsewhere. In other words, the norm becomes the minimum.

With most incomes policies, particularly of the statutory type, there are exceptions to them. Any attempt to restrain the growth of incomes in the longer term must provide for a range of exceptions broad enough to allow for some flexibility and the correction of anomalies. However, the range should not be so broad as to undermine the objectives of the policy in the first place. One of the most comprehensive statements of exceptions was that provided under the Labour government's 1965 incomes policy which allowed four exceptions to the 3–3.5 per cent norm. These comprised:

- **the low paid:** where there was a general recognition that existing levels of remuneration were too low to maintain a reasonable standard of living;
- **productivity:** where the employees concerned had made a direct contribution towards increasing productivity;
- **comparability:** where there was widespread recognition that certain groups had fallen seriously out of line with the level of remuneration for similar work; and
- **manpower shortages:** where it was essential in the national interest to secure a change in the distribution of manpower and a pay increase was necessary for the purpose.

Self-evaluation activity 4.13

The exceptions
Response on website

Can you think of any likely problems concerning the application of these exceptions?

Securing compliance with incomes policies

Because of the inherent difficulties with policies which attempt to restrain pay in a formal, statutory way, governments have often opted for voluntary incomes policies. They are 'voluntary' in the sense that no legislation has been placed on the statute book, though governments have attempted to ensure compliance with these policies by a variety of means. During the 1970s this took the form of tripartite agreements between government, TUC and CBI. However, since neither the CBI nor the TUC had any power to compel their members to abide by the agreements, the effectiveness of the agreements depended to a large extent on the degree to which a consensus existed about the desirability of wage and price restraint. Within the British context, there is often insufficient consensus for agreements to have much effect. Hence, consensus and compliance can only be achieved and maintained if the policy is acceptable to all parties, based on the perceived need for, and fairness of, the policy in the first place (for example, that the policy covers all forms of income, including prices and profits).

The main problem with statutory policies is what action to take when particular groups refuse to comply. With most of the UK's statutory policies there has been some form of third party agency or institution, typical of the corporatist approach, such as the National Board for Prices and Incomes in 1964–70, to whom the government can refer borderline cases or claims for exception. Referral decisions of this nature have not always been perceived as fair, with powerful groups receiving more favourable treatment than less powerful ones. The same argument applies if the policy includes penal sanctions, but with all the attendant problems of the use of courts in industrial relations. As a result, where sanctions have been imposed to support an incomes policy, they have been directed primarily at employers rather than employees and trade unions. Overall, however, there has been a marked tendency to avoid direct prosecution. Under phases 3 and 4 of the Social Contract (1977–9), for example, the government threatened sanctions against firms in breach of the policy in the form of the loss of export credit guarantees and the removal of government contracts, rather than directly prosecuting those firms.

Administrative machinery and incomes policy: chronological details

A feature of British incomes policies has been the variety of different types of administrative machinery set up either to advise the government or to administer the policy. These have included the Council on Prices, Productivity and Incomes – also known as the 'Three Wise Men' (1957) – and the National Incomes Commission (1962). The first to play a fully active role in the operation of a comprehensive incomes policy was the National Board for Prices and Incomes (or Prices and Incomes Board) which was established as an advisory and consultative body to help administer the Labour incomes policy of 1965–9. Later bodies included the Pay Board (1972), the Price Commission (1973), and the Standing Commission on Pay Comparability (1974–9). Details of post-war incomes policies are given in Table 4.1.

Why have incomes policies had limited success?

Since 1947 there have been over 30 attempts to institute an incomes policy of one sort or another (see Table 4.1 for details of the main ones), and none of them has lasted for more than two years. The reason for this is that there are too many institutional and political constraints upon the long-term effectiveness of incomes policies.

Self-evaluation activity 4.14

Institutional and political constraints
Response on website

Can you identify some of these institutional and political constraints?

The success of an incomes policy may also be determined by the extent to which that policy reduces the rate of price inflation (and inflation generally). For this purpose it is not sufficient merely to compare the rate of inflation in those years when the policy was in operation with those years when it was not, since incomes policies have only been introduced when the inflation rate was high. What is needed is an analysis to estimate what the rate of inflation would have been in the

Table 4.1 Post-war UK incomes policies: 1948–2008

Year	Type of policy	Co-ordinating bodies
1948–50: Labour	'No increase of individual money incomes'	National Arbitration Tribunal
1956: Conservative	'Price plateau' policy	Council on Prices, Productivity and Incomes: 'Three Wise Men'
1961–2: Conservative	'Pay pause' followed by 'guiding light' norm of 2.5%	National Incomes Commission
1965: Labour	3.5% norm with exceptions	National Board for Prices and Incomes (NBPI)
1966: Labour	Six months' incomes standstill Six months' 'severe restraint' with 'nil norm'	NBPI
1968–9: Labour	3.5% 'ceiling' with exceptions for justified productivity agreements (no cash limit)	NBPI
1969: Labour	2.5–4.5% voluntary norm with exceptions for productivity	NBPI (abolished by Conservatives, 1970)
1970: Conservative	Public sector pay restraint (N-1)	No overseeing body
1972–3: Conservative	Stage 1: complete freeze on pay, prices, dividends and rents Stage 2: £1 a week plus 4% up to a maximum of £250 per year Stage 3: 7% maximum or £2.25 a week up to £350 per year. Plus 40p for each 1% increase in RPI	Pay Board Price Commission
1974: Labour	TUC and government agreement to limit increases to cost of living (RPI)	
1975–6: Labour	£6 per week, and nothing for those earning over £8500 per year	Social Contract Phase 1
1976–7: Labour	5% increases with minimum of £2.50 and maximum of £4 per week	Social Contract Phase 2
1977: Labour	Unilateral government imposition of 10% plus 'self-financing productivity agreements'. TUC acquiescence	Social Contract Phase 3
1978–9: Labour	Government-imposed 5% limit. No TUC support and exceptions for productivity	Social Contract Phase 4
1980s and 1990s: Conservative	Severe financial constraints on public sector pay. 1992–3, maximum permitted increase was 1.5%. For 1993 onwards, a freeze on public sector pay, but 2.5% permitted No formal pay policy, however	
1997–2008: New Labour	Continued pay restraint in public sector (e.g. Gordon Brown's dictat to public sector employees, 2007) but no formal pay policy	

absence of incomes policy and compare this with the rate of inflation that actually occurred with the policy in operation. The difference between the two could then be ascribed to the effects of incomes policy. The Phillips curve has been used to illustrate this possibility.

Phillips's analysis, published in 1958, was concerned with the rate of change of money wages and the level of unemployment. Phillips found that as a result of his analysis there appeared to be a fairly stable relationship between the level of unemployment and the rate of wage inflation in Britain. If we look at Figure 4.4, we see that a fall in unemployment from A to B due to an increase in aggregate demand brings about an increase in the rate of money wages from C to D, reflecting employers' greater willingness to grant wage increases as the demand for their product expands. By contrast, rising unemployment and falling demand leads to a slowing down in the rate of increase in money wages. The 'curve' suggests, then, that there is a 'trade-off' between unemployment and demand-pull inflation. We can see, therefore, that if the level of unemployment is, say, 1 per cent, the Phillips curve model predicts that the rate of inflation will be 7 per cent.

We can use this as a way of measuring the effectiveness of incomes policies in moderating the rate of inflation. If, for example, in a particular year in which an incomes policy was in operation, the

average level of unemployment were 2 per cent, we could predict from the Phillips curve that the rate of wage inflation would be 3 per cent. If the actual rate of wage inflation was, say, only 2.5 per cent, then the difference between the two could be the result of the moderating influences of the policy. In other words, the policy would have succeeded in reducing the rate of wage inflation by 0.5 per cent.

While there has been strong empirical support for the Phillips curve relationship in the past, in recent decades unemployment and inflation have tended to co-exist. This has led to attempts to reformulate the Phillips curve by Friedman and other monetarists who argue that there is no trade-off between inflation and unemployment. For them (for reasons which are outside the remit of this book), the Phillips curve is vertical and incomes policy is unnecessary as the economy will always return to the natural level of unemployment.

Summary points

- Prices and incomes policy is concerned with controlling inflation by *directly* attempting to halt or slow down the inflationary spiral of price–wage rises. The basic rationale for an incomes policy is that whereas deflationary monetary and fiscal policies can only control inflation by increasing the rate of unemployment, a

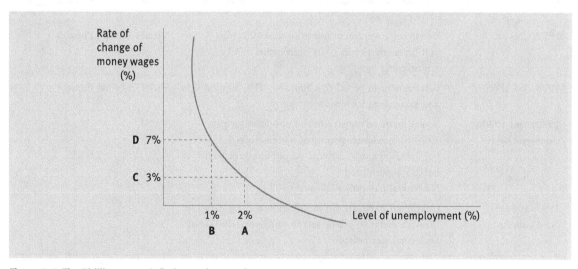

Figure 4.4 The Phillips curve: inflation and unemployment
Source: Phillips, 1958. Blackwell Publishing

prices and incomes policy, if applied rigorously, can check inflation and maintain high levels of employment.

- An incomes policy can be operated on a voluntary or statutory (compulsory) basis. In the former case, an appeal is made to the collective responsibilities of firms not to increase their prices 'unduly' and for trade unions to 'moderate' their demands for wage increases. These exhortations have often proved to be too vague and have been given short shrift by the parties concerned.

- A statutory policy has greater chance of success, particularly in the very short term as in the case of a 'pause' or 'freeze', and also in the medium term (the British experience suggests two years) if it is backed by strong penalties for non-compliance.

- Typical elements of the statutory approach include:
 - an initial, brief (six months to a year) standstill or freeze on all prices, wages, dividend, etc. increases; and
 - a following period (usually phased to allow for a progressive relaxation of controls), in which either general 'norms' are laid down for permitted wages and prices, for example by limiting them to say, 3 per cent per annum; or, more specifically, the establishment of formulas for linking permitted price and wage increases to, for example in the case of a wage rise, increases in productivity.

- The introduction of pay formulas and the creation of exceptional cases requires the establishment of some regulatory body (such as the NBPI) to ensure that the proposed price and wage increases are indeed justified.

- Supporters of a prices and incomes policy (usually Keynesian economists) see it as a useful way of 'defusing' inflationary expectations, thereby removing the danger of accelerating inflation rates. Opponents (usually monetarists) argue that such a policy would interfere with the operation of market forces.

The national minimum wage

The UK minimum hourly wage for adults was set at £5.52 from October 2007. At present and in addition to the adult rate there are two other national minimum wage (NMW) rates covering the 18–22 and 16–17 age categories, the former category set at £4.60 and the latter at £3.40, both from October 2007. The 16–17 NMW age category was introduced only recently. Until 1999 the UK did not have a comprehensive statutory NMW, although statutory minimum wages were set in certain low paying sectors, firstly by the trade boards and then by the wages councils between 1909 and 1993, when the wages councils were abolished (the only exception to this being the Agricultural Wages Board which sets minimum rates for farm workers). The wages councils began to be dismantled in the 1980s; they were viewed by the Conservative government as being riddled with anomalies and an unnecessary interference with the workings of the 'free' market. At the same time, the Labour Party adopted a policy of introducing a statutory NMW to replace the wages councils. Both political parties agreed that wages councils were no longer appropriate to a modern economy ('by the time they were abolished there was a Council setting minimum wages in the Ostrich and Fancy Feather and Artificial Flower industry but none in the private security industry' (Lourie, 1997, p. 4)).

The opposition of Conservative governments to the idea of a NMW are based upon the economic premises of monetarism discussed previously. Essentially, using the assumption of the competitive labour market, wage levels will be determined by factors such as inflation and unemployment in such a way that the supply of, and demand for, labour correspond to set a 'labour market clearing wage'. The introduction of a NMW set above the market-clearing rate, it is argued, would depress the demand for labour, which in turn would result in job losses. There would also be a 'knock-on' effect exerting upward pressure on all levels of pay. In contrast to this argument is the one more synonymous with Keynesian economic policy which assumes that the market is not 'perfectly competitive' and that distortions to the market can only be overcome by government intervention through, amongst other measures, the introduction of a NMW. Supporters of this argument suggest that there are no inevitable consequences of the introduction of a NMW and increases in unemployment and inflation.

Shortly after the election of a Labour government in 1997, the Low Pay Commission (LPC) was set up with a brief to:

- recommend the initial level at which the national minimum wage might be introduced;
- make recommendations on lower rates or exemptions for those aged 16–25; and
- consider and report on any matters referred to it by ministers.

The report of the LPC made 24 recommendations, most of which were accepted by the government, but with the following modifications:

- that the rate for young people is 20p lower than that proposed by the LPC;
- that workers aged 21 will be covered by the 'development rate' (see Exhibit 4.4), though the LPC recommended that this should apply only to 18–20 year olds; and

Exhibit 4.4

The LPC recommendations

Defining the wage

1. The NMW should apply to the gross amount of those earnings that are defined as included in its scope. The amount should be calculated before tax, NI and other appropriate authorised deductions are made.
2. Incentive payments should be included in the earnings that count towards the NMW. All pieceworkers must, whatever the piece rate set and output achieved, be paid no less than the NMW on average for the pay reference period.
3. Homeworkers and others paid by output, rather than by time, must be paid at least the NMW on average for the pay reference period.
4. Incentive payments should only count in the pay period in which they are received, which may not necessarily be the period in which they are earned.
5. Any service charge or centrally organised system of distributing tips and gratuities whereby workers receive their share through the payroll, such as the 'tronc', should be included in the NMW.
6. Cash tips paid directly by customers to staff should be excluded from calculation of the NMW.
7. Premium payments for overtime and shifts should be excluded from the definition of earnings for the NMW . . . only standard pay for overtime and shift hours should be counted.
8. Allowances and supplements should be excluded from the definition of the NMW.
9. With the exception of accommodation, benefits should be excluded from the calculation of the NMW.
10. An 'offset' should be allowed where accommodation is provided as a benefit-in-kind . . . but should be phased out in the longer term.
11. The actual working time definition should define what constitutes working time for the purposes of the NMW. The NMW should also apply to all working time when a worker is required by the employer to be at the place of work and available for work, even if no work is available for certain periods.
12. For hours when workers are paid to sleep on the work premises, workers and employers should agree their allowance, as they do now. But workers should be entitled to the NMW for all times when they are awake and required to be available for work.
13. The pay reference period over which eligible earnings may be averaged for the NMW should be the normal pay period, as agreed between worker and employer, up to a maximum of one calendar month.

Training and development

14. All those aged 16 and 17 should be exempt from the NMW.
15. All those on apprenticeships should be exempt from the NMW.

16. A minimum development rate should be available for 18–20 year olds.
17. A development rate for those aged 21 or over should be available for a maximum of six months for workers beginning a new job with a new employer and who are receiving accredited training.

Choosing the rate

18. We advise that the appropriate rate for the NMW should be £3.70 per hour in June 2000. Consistent with introducing the rate at an earlier date and our aim to proceed with prudence, however, we recommend that the initial rate of £3.60 per hour should be introduced in April 1999.
19. We recommend that an initial development rate of £3.20 per hour should be introduced in April 1999. Our advice is that the appropriate development rate in June 2000 should be £3.30 per hour.

Implementing and enforcing

20. The NMW should commence in April 1999.
21. Employers should be obliged to display on pay slips both the NMW and details to enable workers to confirm readily whether they have received the statutory minimum.
22. An existing government agency should be asked to take on the responsibility of verifying employers' compliance with the NMW.
23. Employers should be encouraged to display details of the NMW prominently in the workplace.
24. There should be a review of the NMW, in the first instance, within two years of its introduction, to examine its initial impact and to assess its future level, definition and possible exceptions.

Source: Low Pay Commission, 1998

- that no undertaking be given that the full rate will be automatically increased.

The LPC's role was initially limited; its main task post-NMW was to monitor the impact of the NMW with a view to any future uprating or variation of the NMW level(s). The LPC now has a broader remit which includes reviewing the effectiveness of the NMW within and between industry sectors, commissioning research projects dealing with the impact of the NMW and producing annual reports providing 'snapshots' of its work.

The National Minimum Wage Act 1998

The Act provided for the introduction of the NMW in April 1999 covering every region of the UK and all sectors of the economy. Agriculture, however, remains outside the scope of the legislation, although agricultural wage boards will continue to fix statutory minimum wage rates for agricultural workers. The Act closely follows the recommendations of the LPC (with the exceptions noted earlier) and its main points are:

- The introduction of a statutory NMW at the rate of £3.60 an hour before deductions (£3.00 an hour for 18–21 year olds and £3.20 an hour for accredited trainees aged 22 or over in the first six months of a new job with a new employer), in April 1999. Regulations under the Act may vary the rate from time to time.
- The Act applies to all 'workers' over school-leaving age in the UK other than 'voluntary workers'. It also excludes servicemen and women, prisoners and sharefishermen and women, and Regulations under the Act exclude 16 and 17 year olds and those on formal apprenticeships.
- The Act also applies to homeworkers and agency temps without contracts which make them 'workers', civil servants, parliamentary staff, merchant seamen and women, and the Act may be extended to offshore workers and others whom it does not expressly exclude.

- The Act rules out the possibility of providing a modified rate of the NMW for, or of excluding, workers according to the region, sector, size of business or occupation in which they work or, if they are over 25, on the basis of their age.
- Regulations under the Act will prescribe how to calculate a worker's hourly rate of remuneration for the purposes of determining if that is at least the NMW.
- The Act places duties on employers to pay their workers no less than the NMW, to give them a NMW statement and to keep records. In addition to their rights to receive at least the NMW and a NMW statement, the Act also gives workers a right of access to records, a right not to suffer detriment in certain circumstances and, if they are employees, a right not to be unfairly dismissed in the same circumstances.
- Workers may enforce their right to be paid at least the NMW by complaining to an employment tribunal of an unauthorised deduction from their wages or by bringing a civil action for breach of contract. Their other rights under the Act are enforceable before employment tribunals only.
- The other enforcement mechanisms under the Act are a range of powers exercisable by enforcement officers, who will come from an existing government agency, and six new criminal offences, each punishable by a fine of up to £5000.
- In any civil proceedings to recover the difference between what a person has been paid and the NMW, the presumption will be that the person was paid less than the NMW and that he or she qualifies for the NMW. The burden of proof will therefore be upon the employer, who will need to prove otherwise.

Economic, social and regional impact of the NMW

At the outset it was possible to make some generalisations by extrapolating from the initial set statutory level of £3.60. With regard to the workforce, it is clear that women workers and particularly those employed on a part-time basis would benefit from the NMW. For example, the adult and development rates covered around 1.4 million female employees and 1.3 million part-time workers. In 2006, the NMW covered approximately 1.25 million jobs

(LPC, 2007) In its report the LPC (1998) identified those sectors which would experience the greatest changes, in terms of coverage of employees affected, as a result of the NMW, including:

- **Retail:** Around 500,000 employees, mainly in smaller stores were covered.
- **Hospitality:** 340,000 workers affected, around 20 per cent of whom were under 21 and so were covered by the development rate.
- **Cleaning and security:** 900,000 workers received the NMW.
- **Social care:** Private nursing and residential homes were affected, with some 80,000 employees in receipt of the NMW.
- **Clothing and footwear:** Around 40,000 workers were affected.

In terms of labour costs, the LPC estimated that the NMW would increase the national wage bill by 0.6 per cent. However, Philpott (1997) argues that the indirect impact of the NMW, via the restoration of pay differentials, would be greater, particularly in sectors – such as the public sector – with flat pay structures and a concentration of pay rates just above the minima. Some employers, whose main cost is the increase in the wage bill, may devise strategies to mitigate any such increase by cutting back on labour-related costs such as fringe benefits and training. Later evidence reported by Rubery and Edwards (2003) suggests that the NMW has had some impact in reducing wage inequality, but this appears marginal. Nevertheless there is what Rubery and Edwards call a 'clear pay spike at the NMW level suggesting that wages are being concentrated at this point and hence that there has been an equalisation of pay and that differential effects have been small' (p. 465). The impact of the NMW on prices depends upon the ability of employers to pass on increased labour costs in increased prices and the degree of competition in the markets in which they operate. Low-wage sectors tend to be in very competitive markets and this may inhibit the impact on inflation. Garrard and Martin (1996) estimated that a NMW of £3.80 accompanied by a restoration of pay differentials would increase the inflation rate (other things being equal) by 1.1 per cent. However, by 2004 it became clear that such estimates of higher inflation rates due to the inception of the NMW have been

exaggerated. In research conducted for the Work Foundation, Coats (2007) argues that the NMW has been 'on a consistent upward trajectory since its introduction in 1999, with particularly significant increases since 2003' (p. 5), with women, and particularly women working part-time, being the most significant beneficiaries. One of the most important measures of the impact of the NMW is by means of its '**bite**', which is defined 'as the ratio of the adult minimum wage to the median hourly wage' (LPC, 2007, p. xi). The LPC reveals that the bite has grown from 47.6 per cent of median earnings in 1999 to 53 per cent in 2006. Moreover, the minimum wage increases have outstripped average earnings growth for 2005 and 2006, but with the increase in price inflation during 2007, the NMW grew less in real terms than had been expected (LPC, 2007).

The effects of a minimum wage on employment depend critically on its level. As we have pointed out, standard economic theory suggests that if the cost of labour increases, the demand for it must fall. Simulations of the impact of a NMW on employment through macroeconomic models of the economy yield a wide range of results, depending on the assumptions made by the modellers. Fernie and Metcalf (1996) summarise available simulations which suggest employment losses associated with a NMW set at half male median earnings ranging from 9000 to 259,000 with an average of around 80,000. Machin (1997) in a review of the employment effects of minimum wage setting in wages councils' industries concluded that:

> *Evidence from the past experience of minimum wages in Britain suggests the employment effects then were moderate or non-existent. One should be somewhat cautious about generalising this to the case of a national minimum wage but, nevertheless, the previous experience of minimum wages in Britain was not detrimental to jobs and unemployment.* (p. 152)

The current and previous NMW levels do not necessarily mean that employers, despite CBI reservations, would inevitably react by cutting jobs, particularly as employment growth is determined by a variety of factors. The existence of a NMW in other countries such as the USA has not prevented them experiencing rapid job growth over the longer term and indeed the LPC (2007) points out that employment in low pay areas has remained at consistently high levels since the inception of the NMW and Coats (2007) concludes that 'there is no strong evidence of a negative effect on employment following the introduction and subsequent uprating of the NMW [and] there is no contradiction between a rising NMW and the retention of a high level of labour market flexibility' (p. 6). The LPC also stresses that as a result of the ongoing influx of migrant workers into the UK since EU enlargement in 2004, estimated at some half a million (LPC, 2007), many such workers have found employment in low-paid occupations such as agriculture, food processing and packaging and this has, according to LPC evidence, proved beneficial to the UK economy, notwithstanding that some of these workers are vulnerable to exploitation by unscrupulous employers and 'gang masters'.

In terms of social justice the NMW can be regarded as one component of New Labour's social policy. More specifically, the NMW has slowed, further widening the gap between the lowest and the highest paid (chief executives of large corporations are not included in the latter category), alleviating some in-work poverty but barely improving work incentives. The impact of the NMW across the regions of the UK varies owing to different employment structures and other local factors. For example, the LPC estimated that around 14 per cent of the employed workforce (130,000 employees) in the North East, which has the lowest level of average full-time earnings in Britain, are affected. In addition, around 13 per cent of employees (130,000) in Wales are covered, particularly in the hospitality and tourism sectors, while in London and the South East 400,000 workers are eligible. Finally, four areas can be identified directly concerning industrial relations where there has been some 'NMW effect'. These are:

Pay differentials: In many organisations pay structures, particularly at the lower end, are relatively tight. The introduction of the NMW has in some cases led to the consolidation of pay into fewer pay bands, despite opposition from a few trade unions and managers eager to encourage employees to take on more responsibilities through greater work flexibilisation and intensification.

The 'going rate': There is no perceptible 'NMW effect' upon re-establishing the importance of the 'going rate'. The 'going rate' is that amount the employer should be prepared to pay as a result of comparisons with levels of wages paid in other organisations. Since the NMW attempts to create a minimum 'wage floor', employers may be discouraged from offering wages below the rate for similar jobs in other organisations as this may 'squeeze' differentials and result in union opposition. Nevertheless, in recent years, many employers have, in typical HRM style, been able to persuade their employees that pay increases should be determined more by the success of the individual company (e.g. profit-sharing) than by any external factors such as the inflation rate or pay increases elsewhere. It is, therefore, probable that the more substantial the annual increase in the NMW, the more likely it is to reinforce 'going rate' comparisons. However, this assumes a much higher NMW level than the 2007 level of £5.52.

Pay structures: Pay structures have changed significantly in recent years, with a move away from basic rates to more incentive payments, bonuses and fringe benefits (such as pension contributions). As the NMW is set as an hourly rate, some employers have been encouraged to consolidate incentive payments into that rate.

Contracted-out services: The main impetus behind the explosion in contracting out non-core services since the 1980s has come from the fact that such services (typically, cleaning, catering and security) can be provided more cheaply in this way as employees tend to be paid less. However, the introduction of the NMW has not significantly eroded let alone removed this cost differential.

International comparisons

Other countries having a statutory minimum wage include France, Luxembourg, the Netherlands, Portugal, Spain and the USA. Most other developed nations have some form of minimum wage. Belgium and Greece, for example, have a national minimum wage set by legally binding collective agreement, while Japan and Canada have statutory minimum wages which vary from sector to sector and from region to region. In Germany, Italy and the Scandinavian countries, national industrial relations systems provide for legally binding, industry-level collective agreements which set minimum wages across almost all sectors of the economy. Research dealing with the economic impact of European minimum wages concludes that there is scant evidence that minimum wages have any particular effect on employment levels in Europe (Dolado et al., 1996). The authors point out:

> The evidence on the employment effects of minimum wages is very mixed. We have found evidence that higher minimum wages reduced employment in some cases (particularly for young workers) and raised it for others (particularly for total employment). But it is surprisingly hard to find strong evidence of any adverse employment effects of minimum wages in situations where many commentators are firmly convinced (rightly or wrongly) that the job losses exist: France in the 1980s is a good example of this. As the employment effects of minimum wages on the youth labour market do seem to be worse, there is a strong case for having a lower minimum wage for young workers. We should emphasise that none of our results suggests that the effects (good or bad) on the economy of current levels of minimum wages are particularly large. The presence or absence of a minimum wage will not be the difference between economic success and failure. (p. 31)

Table 4.2 provides a comparison of key features of European minimum wage systems, and a more detailed overview of the NMW structure in the USA and France is given in Exhibit 4.5.

Policing the minimum wage

Policing or enforcement of the NMW is the responsibility of the Inland Revenue, which responds to all complaints made about employers suspected of not paying the NMW. The enforcement approach is via a confidential helpline and a network of 16 teams of six NMW compliance officers per team, located throughout the country. There are five key aspects of the compliance team's work, which are:

- responding to all complaints from workers and third parties, referred by the helpline, that the minimum wage has not been paid;

Table 4.2 Selected countries with a statutory minimum wage (SMW): 2007
1 January 2005–1 January 2007

Name and coverage	How SMW established	Updating mechanisms	Linkage to consumer prices	Current monthly rates	Other government intervention
Belgium	*Revenue minimum mensuel moyen garanti* (RMMMG) applies to employees aged 21 outside scope of agreed industry minima. Reduced youth rates. Covers c. 8% of workforce. Excludes apprentices, trainees, sheltered workshops	By legally binding national collective agreement (No. 43 for adults, No. 50 for youth rates)	RMMMG, like all pay, is index-linked to consumer prices. Rates increased when central agreement renegotiated, usually every 2 years	1258.91 euros in 2006 comprising 39% of average earnings. Rates reduced by 6% for each year under 21. Includes regulatory contractual bonuses	Collectively agreed sectoral minima may be extended to non-signatory parties by royal decree; c. 85% private sector covered by industry or company CAs
France	*Salaire minimum interprofessionnel de croissance* (SMIC) applies to private/semi-public employees aged 18 outside scope of agreed industry minima. Reduced youth/trainee rates. Covers 11.2% workforce. Disabled covered by separate regulations	By statute	SMIC is index-linked to consumer prices. Also reviewed annually by National Collective Bargaining Board	1254.28 euros in 2006 comprising 49% of average earnings. 16/17 year olds receive 89–90% full rate. Includes all reg. contractual bonuses	Collectively agreed sectoral minima may be extended to non-signatory parties by Ministry of Labour. Covers c. 80% of private sector workforce
Greece	Binding legal minimum wage rates (depending on marital status service) for wage and salary earners in private and public sectors. Covers est. 10% of wage earners	As part of national collective agreement	Rates increased when central agreement renegotiated every 1–2 years, most recently in 2000	625.97 euros in 2006 comprising 41% of average earnings	Collectively agreed minima can be extended to non-signatory parties by Ministry of Labour
Luxembourg	*Salaire social minimum* (SSM) applies to private sector employees aged 18 outside scope of agreed industry minima. Reduced youth rates. Covers 15% of workforce	By statute	Index-linked to consumer prices. Parliament reviews biennially in line with economic and pay growth	1570.28 euros in 2007 comprising 42% of average earnings	Collectively agreed sectoral minima can be extended. Majority of workforce covered by co/sector CAs
Netherlands	*Minimumloon* covers employees aged 23 outside scope of agreed industry minima. Reduced youth rates. Covers 200,000 (3.7% of workforce including part-timers and some home workers)	By statute	Link with collectively agreed wage rate index abolished in 1991. Government usually increases annually	1300.80 euros in 2007 comprising 44% of average earnings. Includes all reg. contractual bonuses. Youth rates 30–85% of full rate	Collectively agreed sectoral minima can be extended to non-signatory parties. CAs cover c. 70% of private sector workforce

Table 4.2 (*cont'd*)

Name and coverage	How SMW established	Updating mechanisms	Linkage to consumer prices	Current monthly rates	Other government intervention
Portugal	*Remuneração mínima mensal garantida* (RMMG) covers employees aged 18. Reduced rates for youth, trainees under 25. Covers c. 6.9% of workforce. Disabled under separate regulations	By statute	Updated annually by law after tripartite consultation, taking into account economic growth, inflation and productivity	403.00 euros in 2007 comprising 57% of average earnings. Includes regular pay elements. Youths 75% of full rate, trainees under 25, 80%	Collectively agreed minima can be extended to non-signatory parties. Covers c. 80% of private sector workforce
Spain	*Salario mínimo interprofesional* (SMI) covers employees aged 18. Reduced youth rates. Covers 500,000. Apprentices excluded (rates specified in CAs usually 70–90% of SMI)	By statute	Updated annually by law after tripartite consultation, taking forecast inflation and economic performance into account	570 euros in 2007 comprising 34% of average earnings	Extension of collectively agreed rates possible but rarely occurs
Bulgaria				92.30 euros in 2007	
Croatia				282.23 euros in 2005	
Czech Republic				284.38 euros in 2006	
Hungary				240.14 euros in 2007	
Ireland				1438.67 euros in 2007	
Poland				233.01 euros in 2006	
Romania				115.06 euros in 2007	
Turkey				302.61 euros in 2007	
UK (for comparison)				1380.54 euros in 2006	

Note: Belgium and Greece are included, even though the SMW originates in a national agreement in both cases.

Exhibit 4.5

Minimum wage systems in the USA and France

USA

The USA has had a federal minimum wage since the passage of the Fair Labor Standards Act (FLSA) in 1938. Many individual states also set their own minimum wage level which is, in some cases, higher than the federal rate. The federal rate in 1997 was $5.15 an hour. Overtime pay at a rate not less than 1.5 times regular rates of pay is required after 40 hours of work a week. There is no formula for increasing the minimum wage: every increase requires a bill amending the FLSA to be passed by Congress and signed into law by the President. The FLSA applies to enterprises that have employees who are engaged in interstate commerce, producing goods for interstate commerce, or handling, selling or working on goods or materials that have been moved in or produced for interstate commerce. For most firms, an annual dollar volume of business test of $500,000 applies (those enterprises under this dollar amount are not covered).

The following are covered by the Act regardless of their dollar volume of business: hospitals, institutions primarily engaged in the care of the sick, aged, mentally ill or disabled who reside on the premises; schools for children who are mentally or physically disabled or gifted; preschools, elementary and secondary schools and institutions of higher education; and federal, state and local government agencies.

Some groups of employees are exempt from the federal minimum wage. These include executive, administrative and professional employees, employees of certain seasonal amusement and recreational establishments and employees engaged in newspaper delivery. Employees under 20 years of age may be paid a minimum wage of not less than $4.25 an hour during the first 90 consecutive calendar days of employment with an employer. Employers may not displace any employee to hire someone at the youth minimum rate. Employers may pay employees on a piece-rate basis, as long as they receive at least the equivalent of the required minimum hourly wage rate.

France

The French introduced a statutory minimum wage, known as the SMIG (*Salaire Minimum Interprofessionnel Garanti*) by an Act in 1950. This was an hourly rate designed to cover the basic needs of a single unskilled worker as assessed by special survey. A subsequent Act in 1952 linked the SMIG to changes in the cost of living, which protected the minimum wage against inflation but failed to ensure that it kept pace with the general level of wages. In 1970 an Act replaced the SMIG with the SMIC (*Salaire Minimum Interprofessionnel de Croissance*) with a view to guaranteeing the lowest paid workers a share in economic growth. SMIC is a basic hourly rate applicable throughout industry, the service sector and agriculture. It takes into account regular bonuses, tips and the value of board and lodging where provided. The monthly rate was increased to 1254.28 euros in 2006 comprising 49 per cent of average earnings. There are lower rates for young workers. There are three principles governing the revision of the SMIC:

1. Protection against inflation: as soon as the retail price index (RPI) shows a rise of 2 per cent since the last increase, the SMIC must be increased by 2 per cent on the first day of the following month.
2. Those on the SMIC must share in the nation's economic growth: the government can at any time raise the SMIC by more than the RPI would merit, for example at a time of particularly rapid rises in general wage levels.
3. The SMIC must be revised annually. A committee (the *Commission Nationale de la Negociation Collective*) made up of relevant government ministers, an equal number of representatives of the Employers' Confederation and the main trade unions, and the Chairman of the Social Section of the Conseil d'État examines the level of the SMIC each year in the light of reports on the country's economic situation and recommends any changes. The Council of Ministers takes the final decision.

Ministry of Labour inspectors (*Inspecteurs du Travail*) carry out random checks to ensure that employers comply with the law and investigate complaints.

Exhibit 4.6

NMW arrears: some 'real life' examples

Case one: A complaint was received from a former worker of a mortgage advice company because she had worked some weekends and had not been paid. The employer had kept no records and denied that weekends had been worked. Evidence was gathered that supported the worker's claim and the employer eventually agreed to pay the wage arrears identified as being paid below the minimum wage as a result of the legislation.

Case two: A part-time car driver and car cleaner was paid £50 per week for working 16 hours. When enquiries were made of the employer he confirmed this was the case, saying that he was unaware of the existence of a minimum wage.

Case three: Six workers who had been employed as sales representatives for a building hardware retailer complained that they had not been paid for all the hours they worked. The employer was not able to produce any records of pay for hours worked and was keen to pay the arrears identified without recourse to employment tribunal.

Source: Low Pay Commission, 2007, pp. 20–2

- carrying out inspections of employer's records to check employers are meeting their obligations to pay the minimum wage;
- helping employers understand their obligations under minimum wage law;
- securing pay arrears (see Exhibit 4.6); and
- regularly presenting cases to employment tribunals on behalf of workers.

Alongside the helpline is the Central Information Unit, which collates statistical data concerning enforcement performance and helps to publicise the NMW to a variety of organisations such as Citizen's Advice Bureaux, trade unions, large employer groups, community and voluntary organisations. From 1999 to 2003 the helpline handled over 7500 complaints about non-payment of the minimum wage and up to £10 million in pay arrears for workers, with £5 million arrears identified in 2001–2 alone, an increase of almost £2 million on the previous year (Rubery and Edwards, 2003, pp. 461–2). In the period 2005–6 there were over 2100 complaints about non-payment of the NMW, an increase of 7 per cent over 2003–4. The Inland Revenue/ HMRC conducted 4900 investigations into minimum wage underpayment in 2005–6 (LPC, 2007). However, the figures may be distorted as a relatively few large cases, in terms of arrears or workers, can have a major impact on the results. Nevertheless,

these figures do indicate that, contrary to more optimistic views, minimum wage arrears is an important issue which the government feels compelled to act upon, with support from the TUC. Table 4.3 indicates the number of complaints and enforcement issues for the period 2003–6.

Developments in enforcing the NMW

In 2005, the government announced a strategy of targeted enforcement in the low-paying sectors, the aim of which 'is to improve compliance by raising the profile of the minimum wage in each sector in turn and by addressing sector-specific minimum wage concerns, followed by an enforcement drive, encouraging workers paid below the minimum wage to come forward' (LPC, 2007, p. 229). One such sector-specific campaign took place in the hairdressing sector. Of the 629 compliance cases registered, 504 were investigated and concluded. Of these, around half of the employers were found to be non-compliant, with arrears of £380,000 identified for 491 workers, most of whom were women. Findings of research commissioned by the LPC (Croucher and White, 2007) within the hairdressing sector 'suggest that the campaign has been a modest success, but that total overall awareness of the minimum wage among both employers and staff (particularly trainees) in this

Table 4.3 National Minimum Wage: Enquiries and complaints to the Inland Revenue/HMRC, and enforcement action taken, 2003–6

	2003/4	2004/5	2005/6	April to September 2006
Enquiries received by the helpline	53,226	57,773	61,355	25,044
Complaints of underpayment	1,969	1,910	2,100	968
Visits to employers	5,541	5,155	4,904	1,712
Enforcement notices issued	45	32	81	35
Penalty notices issued	3	0	1	0
Value of underpayments identified	£2.5 million	£3.8 million	£3.3 million	£1.4 million

Source: DTI, HMRC, UK, 2003–6

sector remains patchy. The second sector chosen by the DTI in 2006 for targeting was the childcare sector, which employs a significant proportion of women, and this is ongoing. The LPC also recommended that sectors such as agriculture and food processing that employ a substantial number of migrant workers should be targeted. The evidence concerning exploitation of migrant workers is according to the LPC 'compelling . . . [and] needs to be addressed as a priority'. The LPC report goes on to state: 'Therefore we recommend that the Government, as part of its enforcement programme, choose a low-paying sector to target in 2007/08 that has a high concentration of migrant workers' (ibid., p. 230).

GOVERNMENT AS LEGISLATOR

Before 1980, and particularly during the 1950s and to a lesser extent the 1960s, there was very little legislation which had a direct impact upon industrial relations. Kahn-Freund (1954), a prominent labour law specialist, commented of this period:

There is, perhaps, no major country in the world in which the law has played a less significant role in shaping of these relations than in Great Britain and in which today the law and legal profession have less to do with labour relations . . . British industrial relations have, in the main, developed by way of industrial autonomy. This notion of autonomy is fundamental . . . it means that employers and employees have formulated

their own codes of conduct and devised their own machinery for enforcing them. (p. 44)

Contrast this with the 1980s and 1990s. McIlroy (1991) comments of this period:

Since 1979 Britain's trade unions have been hit by wave after wave of trade union legislation. Not a year has passed without new proposals being aired, new bills being introduced into Parliament, new Acts receiving the Royal Assent. The trade union problem has scarcely been declared to have been solved by Conservative politicians before a new Green Paper proposing further measures to deal with it is up and running. After the great Acts of 1980, 1982 and 1984 had apparently, at least in Conservative eyes, dealt with the important abuses once and for all, we have had further important statutes in 1988, 1989 and 1990 dealing with new problems – as well as a host of ancillary measures and still more promised. Britain has moved from a system of industrial relations whose legal framework was minimal to one where law progressively reaches into every nook and cranny of relations between employers and trade unions. (p. 1)

Before 1980, then, and particularly before 1970, legislation on strikes and picketing, for example, aimed to keep the law out of industrial relations and gave trade unionists a great degree of freedom to withdraw their labour. Employers and unions were expected to deal with matters concerning the employment relationship through collective bargaining within only a minimal framework. Terms

and conditions of employment and the procedure for their agreement were jointly regulated through collective bargaining by employers and trade unions, not by Parliament and the courts. This is the system which was characterised by voluntarism, collective laissez-faire, state abstentionism and statutory non-intervention, terms which refer to the same phenomenon. It is through the significant pieces of legislation of 1871, 1875 and 1906 that trade unions gradually became exempt from the common law rather than having to operate within a framework of positive rights to organise, bargain and strike. Unions were granted immunities by which they were given protection from common law doctrines of restraint of trade, conspiracy and inducement to breach of contract. This did not prevent individuals taking unions to court over various issues and in cases such as *Rookes* v *Barnard* (1964) the courts sought to limit the immunities of trade unions which were invariably restored by statutory intervention. The situation changed dramatically from 1980 onwards.

Functions of labour law

Kahn-Freund (1977) has suggested that the law has three distinct functions which affect industrial relations to varying degrees. These are:

- **The auxiliary function:** whereby the law can support the autonomous system of collective bargaining by providing norms and sanctions to stimulate the bargaining process itself. It can also strengthen the operation of collective bargaining by promoting the observance of concluded agreements.
- **The regulatory function:** whereby the law can provide a code of substantive rules to govern the terms and conditions of employment. These would be designed to supplement the substantive rules provided by the parties themselves.
- **The restrictive function:** whereby the law can provide the 'rules of the game' of what is allowed and what is forbidden in the conduct of industrial hostilities. This, Kahn-Freund argues, is necessary in order to protect the parties from each other, and to protect the interests of the community at large.

The essence of Kahn-Freund's argument is that compared with other industrialised countries, Britain in the 1960s had experienced minimal intervention in relation to these functions. He suggests that this peculiarly British experience can be attributable to, firstly, a steadfast and determined refusal to use the direct sanctions of the law to assist either the collective bargaining process or the operation of concluded agreements. Secondly, an almost complete failure to provide anything even remotely deserving the name of a 'code of rules' governing the mutual rights and duties of employers and employees in their individual relationship. Thirdly, and much the most conspicuous characteristic, was the conflict between the traditions of the common law as interpreted by judges and the needs of society as interpreted by Parliament. As a result of this conflict, all the statutes concerned with trade unions and labour relations were negative. Their main purpose had been to remove obstacles which the courts had erected (such as restraint of trade and conspiracy), which threatened to impede the operation of industrial relations. In other words, the law had created 'negative' immunities rather than 'positive' rights.

Self-evaluation activity 4.15

Functions of labour law

Response on website

To what extent do you think these functions have been developed in Britain during the 30 or so years since Kahn-Freund put forward these ideas?

The extent of employment legislation until 1979

As we have already indicated, there had been relatively little legislation directly affecting the conduct of industrial relations – with the major exception of the 1971 Industrial Relations Act. Legislation concerning aspects of the individual's relationship with his or her employer did, of course, exist, and the volume of this grew during the 1970s. Long-standing examples include safety regulations applied in most industries and statutory bodies such as wages

councils which regulated pay in some industries and occupations. But, basically, employees' rights were derived primarily from their contracts of employment, while the law, particularly prior to 1970, made little attempt to regulate collective labour relations except to give trade unions immunity from civil actions for damages.

A chronology of legislation affecting industrial relations and trade unions from 1721 until 1979 in relation to Kahn-Freund's three functions is given in Table 4.4. Note that the list is selective with the main statutes and cases identified, although individual employment law cases are not identified at all as they would be far too numerous to detail.

As we can see from the cases and legislation in Table 4.4, the traditional emphasis by governments on 'voluntarism' did not imply or preclude the complete absence of statutory intervention. Action

Table 4.4 The law and industrial relations, 1721–1979

Date	Legislation or case	Description
1721	*Journeymen Tailors of Cambridge*	Judges declared trade unionism a criminal conspiracy
1797	Unlawful Oaths Act	With the Combination Acts this made all collective agreements enhancing wages or conditions criminal and trade unionism illegal
1799	Combination Act	See above
1800	Combination Act	See above
1813	Statute of Artificers (Repeal) Act	Abolished some of the powers of magistrates to fix wages in favour of freedom of contract
1823	Master and Servant Act	Updated earlier legislation making breach of contract a criminal offence for *the employee*
1824	Combination of Workmen Act	Repealed Combination Acts and granted unions limited legality. But they were still liable to criminal offences when striking/picketing
1825	Combination Laws Repeal Act	As above
1859	Molestation of Workmen Act	Limited unions' criminal liabilities
1867	*Hornby* v *Close*	Judges declared union rules to be unenforceable
1871	Criminal Law Amendment Act	Gave unions greater protection against the criminal law and restraint of trade – granted them a limited civil status
1871	Trade Union Act	As above
1872	*R* v *Bunn*	Restricted policy of acceptance of unions by making strikes common law conspiracies and still criminal offences
1875	Conspiracy and Protection of Property Act	Reversed *Bunn*'s case: protected strikes against criminal conspiracy if 'in contemplation or furtherance of a trade dispute'
1875	Repeal of Master and Servant Legislation	
1901	*Quinn* v *Leathem*	The judges developed *civil law* liability for conspiracy, opening unions to attacks the 1875 Act had sought to minimise by excluding the criminal law

Table 4.4 (*cont'd*)

Date	Legislation or case	Description
1901	*Taff Vale*	Landmark decision which allowed the new civil law remedies to be pursued against unions as legal persons
1906	Trade Disputes Act	Reversed *Taff Vale* and protected unions from civil law liabilities such as conspiracy and including breach of contract in contemplation or furtherance of a trade dispute
1910	*Osborne Judgment*	House of Lords limited trade union political activities on birth of Labour Party
1913	Trade Union Act	Reversed *Osborne* decision and introduced balloting for political funds and right to 'opt out'
1924	*Reynolds* v *Shipping*	The courts went some way to accepting trade unionism as a legitimate social activity and recognising boycotting and closed shop
1927	Trade Disputes and Trade Union Act	After General Strike, it limited picketing and secondary action, stopped civil service unions affiliating to TUC and changed 'opting out' of political levy to 'opting in'
1942	*Crofter*	Further acceptance by judges of trade union purposes
1946	Trade Disputes and Trade Union Act	Repealed the Act of 1927
1964	*Rookes* v *Barnard*	House of Lords judgment which opened trade unionists to tort of intimidation
1965	Trade Disputes Act	Protected trade unionists from *Rookes* v *Barnard*
1965	Prices and Incomes Act	Criminal enforcement of incomes policy
1969	*In Place of Strife*	Labour government unsuccessfully sought to legislate to control industrial action
1970	Equal Pay Act	Attempt to end pay discrimination against women
1971	Industrial Relations Act	Comprehensive Conservative legislation to restrict strikes and picketing, etc.
1972	Counter Inflation Act	Criminal offence to breach incomes policy
1974	Trade Union and Labour Relations Act	Repealed Industrial Relations Act. Legislated in firmer form the immunities in the 1965 Act
1975	Employment Protection Act	Extended the floor of rights for individual workers and also dealt with union recognition and rights for officials
1975	Sex Discrimination Act	Legislated against discrimination at work
1976	Trade Union and Labour Relations (Amendment) Act	Strengthened position on dismissal and union membership
1976	Race Relations Act	Legislated against discrimination at work
1978	Employment Protection (Consolidation) Act	1974–9 legislation consolidated

to legalise fundamental trade union activities through the granting of immunities in the face of common law liabilities was part of the essential nature of the voluntary system. The auxiliary function of legislation, which included the supporting and supplementing of collective bargaining (such as the wages councils to support low-income groups), the establishment of health and safety standards and the protection of individual employees within the employment relationship, was regarded as being consistent with the tradition of voluntarism. From 1979, as Dickens and Hall (2003) point out, it was 'the nature and function of the legislation enacted which has transformed the legal environment in which relations between employers, employees and trade unions are conducted . . . and which constituted a decisive shift away from voluntarism' (p. 127). We now turn to the post-1979 legislation.

Post-1979 legislation

The period of continuous Conservative government from 1979 was characterised by frequent, often controversial changes to the framework of labour law. The sequence of 'step-by-step' legislation significantly increased the extent of legal regulation to which industrial relations is subject and, according to Dickens and Hall (2003), 'the period has seen the final death of voluntarism, under which law was essentially an adjunct to an autonomous, self-regulated system of industrial relations' (p. 127). The legislation has been motivated, in the view of Wedderburn (1986), by a need to dilute trade union power, to emphasise individualist rather than collectivist values, and to reinforce employer prerogative. The ideologically inspired reasons for the legislation have already been referred to in the context of the influence of the Hayek school of monetarism.

The legislation is concerned with three broad areas which we now consider in more detail:

- the relationship between employer and employee;
- the relationship between employer and union; and
- the relationship between the union and its membership.

The relationship between employer and employee

As part of the strategy for focusing upon the individual employee and asserting the primacy of market forces, the Conservative governments aimed to reduce or even remove employees' statutory rights where these hitherto had constrained the labour market as a result of the protective legislation of the 1960s and 1970s, and so encourage 'flexibility' of labour within a climate in which entrepreneurial initiatives could flourish. It was felt that the scales in the employment relationship were too heavily weighted in favour of the employee and that the employer was faced with unnecessarily high labour costs and a heavy burden of 'red tape'. Government was therefore committed to a programme of 'deregulation' within the labour market, although in some areas employment rights were actually increased in order to meet certain EU requirements (even though Britain had 'opted out' of the Social Chapter). Nevertheless, at the end of the Conservative period of government in 1997, employees retained most of the statutory rights that the 1960s and 1970s legislation had granted them, and some areas, for example those concerning sex and race discrimination, remained virtually unaffected by deregulation. Deregulation even had some positive benefits, as Dickens and Hall (2003) point out:

Employees benefited from the enactment of individual employment rights in that many sought and gained redress at industrial tribunals in circumstances where previously none would have been available. Arbitrary 'hire and fire' approaches to discipline were curbed; 'due process' and corrective procedures were instituted. Those losing their jobs through no fault of their own are compensated. Pay structures have been revised and de-sexed with the use and threat of equal pay actions providing a lever to reform. The gender pay gap has narrowed. Discrimination legislation has curbed the most overt discriminatory practices, especially in recruitment; has indicated how less overt, taken for granted, practices can be discriminatory; and has given a push to the development of equal opportunity policies. Maternity rights facilitate mothers' interaction with the labour market. (p. 135)

The adverse impact of deregulatory measures upon employees, however, more than cancel out the benefits referred to above. Some of these include:

- Adverse effects upon women employees as a result of the abolition of wages councils in 1994, which at the time covered around 2.5 million workers who were mainly women.
- Many part-time workers and, to a lesser extent, full-time workers were excluded from the protections offered concerning unfair dismissal as a result of the hours and length of service qualifications (see Chapter 13); deregulation removed certain legal safeguards from employees who were not unionised or covered by collective bargaining.
- Generally, employment protection rights were curtailed and some protections were abolished altogether; by 1997 the employment relationship remained relatively unregulated by law, hence there was 'little left to deregulate' (ibid., p. 137).

The relationship between employer and union

The relationship between employer and union changed considerably during the 1980s and 1990s. The legislation influenced this process in two ways: firstly, collective bargaining was severely undermined as a result of the legislation promoting the rights of the individual and, secondly, the scope for unions taking industrial action was considerably curtailed.

The undermining of collective bargaining

Since 1979 collective bargaining has been undermined by the repeal of the legislative supports for collective bargaining, compulsory trade union membership and trade union recognition granted by the legislation of the 1970s, and in particular by the Employment Protection Acts. The Conservative governments also sought to protect the interests of non-unionists by the incremental legal undermining of the closed shop and the eventual abolition of the 'pre-entry' closed shop in 1990, making it unlawful for employers to refuse job applicants on the grounds that they were not union members. Furthermore, the 1993 Trade Union Reform and Employment Rights Act considerably modified the 'check-off' arrangements whereby most union members had union subscriptions deducted from pay by the employer who then gave them to the union. This measure, together with other measures such as ballot financing, threatens the financial viability of unions. All in all, as Dickens and Hall (1995) suggest, there has been a legislative shift to individualist relations as witnessed by a decline in the proportion of workers covered by collective agreements and the decline in trade union membership itself (see Chapter 3). The absence of any legislative obstacle in the way of employers wishing to derecognise unions has not only encouraged the spread of non-unionism, but also more individualist managerial approaches as typified by some forms of HRM. Dickens and Hall conclude:

> Overall, we can see that at a time when sectoral and labour-market change increased the unions' need for positive legal support to aid organisation, such support was removed. At a time when unions are weakened by recession and declining membership, their economic and organisational security is reduced by legislative change. In a context where some employers are questioning the appropriateness or functional value of collective bargaining, some of the tactics which in the past have been part of the unions' legitimate armoury of persuasion have been made unlawful, and non-unionism is increasingly supported by law. (p. 279)

Curtailment of industrial action

This is examined in greater detail in Chapter 8 and is summarised only here. The legislation has restricted the scope for taking 'lawful' industrial action in the following ways:

- the withdrawal of immunities from specific types of industrial action, for example, picketing away from pickets' own workplace was made unlawful (Employment Act 1980);
- restricting the areas subject to industrial action by redefining 'lawful' industrial action: lawful industrial action can only be taken 'in contemplation or furtherance of a trade dispute';
- unions became liable for taking 'unlawful' industrial action, whereas previously individuals who were organising the action were liable;
- lawful industrial action became subject to progressively stringent balloting requirements; and

- the range of potential litigants was extended from employers, to union members who had complaints about balloting procedures (1988), to members of the public who are adversely affected by industrial action.

The relationship between the union and its membership

The main concern of the legislation in this area has been to provide for the introduction of secret ballots by unions in union elections. For example, the 1984 Trade Union Act required secret ballots every five years in order to elect union executive councils and this was extended to the election of all union general secretaries and presidents in 1988. Government concern about balloting requirements extended not only to industrial action but also to unions' political funds which became subject to 'review' ballots every ten years (1984).

A summary of the legislation concerning the collective nature of employer–union and union–membership relationships is given below. For an overview and details of the legislation concerning the employer and individual employee, please refer to the separate chapters dealing with this (Chapters 10, 11 and 12). In addition, the provisions in the legislation which deal with industrial action are dealt with in detail in Chapter 8.

A summary of the legislation concerning employer–union and union–membership relationships

The 1980 Employment Act

The Act focused mainly upon industrial action, picketing and the closed shop.

(a) **Industrial action**

The Employment Act introduced a distinction between *primary* and *secondary* industrial action for the first time in British law. **Before 1980**, any industrial action was immune from civil action provided it related to *someone's* trade dispute – not necessarily your own. **After 1980**, immunity was removed unless:

- the purpose of the secondary action was to interfere directly with the flow of goods or services to or from the employer in dispute;

- its purpose was to interfere directly with the flow of goods of an 'associated employer' and the goods or services were in substitution for those normally supplied to or by the employer in dispute.

Any employer who considered that action was being taken 'unlawfully' could start legal proceedings against individuals (but not against the trade union until measures were introduced in the 1982 Employment Act) who were 'inducing' the action. This was normally against the person organising the strike (for example, the General Secretary or national officer of the relevant union). The employer could seek an injunction stopping the action and could sue the individual named for damages.

(b) **Picketing**

Peaceful picketing for a trade dispute had been lawful since the 1906 Trades Disputes Act. The 1980 Employment Act restricted this right to picket by laying down new rules on where and when workers can 'lawfully' picket. Any picketing outside these limits is unlawful and employers can take legal action to stop it. **Before 1980**, therefore, picketing was lawful virtually anywhere providing it was in furtherance of a trade dispute. **After 1980**, immunity from prosecution for picketing was removed unless:

- employees are picketing their own place of work; or

- they are union officials joining members they represent in lawful picketing; or

- they are dismissed workers of the company concerned.

(c) **The closed shop**

The closed shop was the result of agreement between an employer and the relevant trade union whereby 100 per cent union membership was enforced on signing the contract of employment. However, **before 1980**, specific exceptions did apply:

- an individual could be expelled from, or refused admission to, a trade union where a closed shop operated; and

- an employee could refuse to join a trade union only on the 'grounds of religion' which prevented him or her from joining any union.

After 1980, an individual could not be 'unreasonably' expelled from or refused

admission to a union where a closed shop was in operation. If an individual were to be 'unreasonably' expelled, the Employment Appeal Tribunal could order the union to contribute to a compensation award. Furthermore, the statutory religious conscience clause has been widened to include objections on other grounds of conscience or deeply held personal belief concerning union membership. In addition, non-union members at the time any new closed shop agreements came into force are now exempt from compulsion to join the trade union concerned.

The 1982 Employment Act

The 1982 Employment Act introduced a new definition of a 'trade dispute', new limitations on trade union immunity, and further restrictions on the closed shop.

(a) **New definition of a trade dispute**

Strikes are only immune from legal action if they fall inside the legal definition of a 'trade dispute'. The 1982 Act substantially reduced the protection by changing and narrowing the definition of a trade dispute. **Before 1982**, a trade dispute was defined as any dispute 'connected with' terms and conditions, discipline, dismissals or bargaining machinery, whether between 'employers and workers' or 'workers and workers'. **After 1982**, for industrial action to be lawful the dispute must now relate 'wholly or mainly' to the issues identified above, but with the following exclusions:

- disputes which are merely 'connected with' rather than related 'wholly or mainly' to the issues previously identified;
- disputes between 'workers and workers';
- disputes which are not between an employer and that employer's own employees; and
- international action unless it directly affects the terms and conditions of the UK workers taking action.

(b) **New limitations on trade union immunity**

Individuals could invariably be prosecuted if they stepped outside the area of immunity, but union funds have been protected since the 1906 Trade Disputes Act so that **before 1982**, no action was possible against the union (as opposed to individual members) for what its members

did, whether they acted officially or unofficially, legally or illegally. **After 1982**, unions can now be sued for damages and their funds sequestrated where 'unlawful' industrial action organised by their officials is 'authorised or endorsed' by a responsible person or body within the union. The upper limit for damages which can be awarded against unions is £250,000 for unions with over 100,000 members.

(c) **Further restrictions on the closed shop**

Before 1982, a worker could be 'fairly' dismissed for refusing to become a union member in a closed shop situation as a result of an agreement between employer and union (except for non-union workers in closed shop agreements concluded after 1980 who were exempted from compulsion to join a union as a result of the 1980 Employment Act). **After 1982**:

- it is unfair for an employer to sack a non-unionist where there is a closed shop unless this closed shop (now renamed union membership agreement) has been 'approved' in a ballot during the preceding five years. In this ballot, 80 per cent of the employees covered, or 85 per cent of those voting must vote in favour of the union membership agreement;
- damages are substantial for individuals who complain to industrial tribunals about their dismissals and the complaint is upheld, with a minimum basic award of £2000; and
- the union can be 'joined' as a party (in addition to employers) in the dismissal case and the tribunal can award compensation against the union instead of or as well as the employer.

The 1984 Trade Union Act

The 1984 Trade Union Act was concerned with reforming trade union structure with the aim of making trade unions more accountable to their members together with further restrictions upon industrial action. The main provisions of the Act concerned the legal requirements for union elections, legal requirements for industrial action ballots, and legal requirements for political fund ballots.

(a) **Union elections**

Before 1984, unions decided their own form of democratic participation and their own rules

and methods of voting. **After 1984,** unions have had to change their rules and procedures to comply with the law. Voting members of union executive councils must be elected by secret ballot every five years from a members' register.

(b) **Industrial action ballots**

Before 1984, industrial action and its various forms was decided upon by union members in a variety of ways such as mass meetings, secret ballot, or by spontaneous reaction to events. **After 1984,** it became unlawful to take industrial action without a ballot. Hence for unions to retain immunity from being sued a secret ballot approving industrial action must be held, and members must be informed that by taking part in the ballot and voting for industrial action they would be breaking their contracts of employment.

(c) **Political fund ballots**

Before 1984, unions could have political funds and engage in political activity. **After 1984,** unions must hold a political fund secret ballot every ten years, and should a union lose a political fund ballot, it would not be able to hold a political fund or engage in political activities.

The 1988 Employment Act

There were four main provisions concerning the 1988 Employment Act. These were the removal of a union's right to discipline members who fail to take industrial action, further restrictions on union membership agreements, further legal requirements for union elections and the introduction of a Commissioner for the Rights of Trade Union Members.

(a) **Membership discipline**

Before the 1988 Act unions could discipline members for ignoring a call for industrial action after a ballot in favour of such action. **After 1988,** it became unlawful for unions to discipline members for ignoring a call for industrial action after a ballot in favour of such action. If a union member is disciplined by the union, he or she can take his or her case to industrial tribunal and be compensated. Moreover, union members now had a right to seek court orders to restrain unballoted industrial action.

(b) **Membership agreements**

Before the 1988 Act:

- industrial action could be taken in an effort to create or maintain a 100 per cent union membership agreement; and
- dismissals for non-membership of a union could be lawful provided it was within an 'approved' union membership agreement context as laid down by the 1982 Act in which 85 per cent of members had voted in favour of a union membership agreement.

After the 1988 Act:

- it became unlawful to undertake industrial action designed to create or maintain a 100 per cent union membership agreement; and
- all dismissals for non-membership of a union are unlawful even where there is an 'approved' union membership agreement.

(c) **Union elections**

Before 1988, voting members of union executive councils had to be elected every five years from a members' register. **After the 1988 Act** union general secretaries and presidents are subject to the same electoral arrangements and term of office requirements as voting members of the executive council and all ballots must now be postal.

(d) **Commissioner for the Rights of Trade Union Members (CROTUM)**

Before 1988, trade unions conducted their own internal enquiries into complaints of malpractice from members. **After the 1988 Act** the appointment of Commissioner was made, with the power to assist union members taking or contemplating legal action against their union for any breach of the law concerning union elections, industrial action, political fund ballots and union accounts.

The 1990 Employment Act

The 1990 Employment Act contains four major provisions concerning the pre-entry closed shop, further restrictions on secondary industrial action and unofficial industrial action and an extension of the role of CROTUM.

(a) **Abolition of pre-entry closed shop**

Before 1990, a minority of closed shop agreements (traditionally within some crafts such as printing and within engineering) stipulated that an individual had to be accepted as a union

member before starting work in a job covered by such an agreement. **After the 1990 Act** a worker cannot be refused a job on the grounds of non-membership or membership of a union. This effectively abolishes the pre-entry closed shop.

(b) **Further restrictions on secondary industrial action**

Before the 1990 Act there was immunity from civil action for inducing industrial action by workers at the premises of an 'associated employer' (a separate firm related to the actual firm in dispute) of an employer in dispute, or at the associated employer's customers or suppliers, if certain conditions were met. **After 1990**, it became unlawful to induce industrial action by workers of an employer not party to a trade dispute, except where such action meets the lawful picketing requirements.

(c) **Severe restrictions on unofficial action**

Before 1990:

- those taking unofficial action did not need to ballot before taking such industrial action and the union was not liable for such action; and
- employers could dismiss strikers taking unofficial action, but, in order to avoid unfair dismissal claims, employers had to dismiss all those taking such action and not rehire any dismissed worker for at least three months.

After 1990:

- unions became automatically liable for all industrial action, including unofficial action, unless the union concerned has taken specific measures to 'repudiate' the action;
- employers could select for dismissal any employees taking unofficial action and those employees have no right to claim unfair dismissal; and
- any industrial action, whether official or balloted upon or not, is deemed unlawful where it is called in support of workers dismissed for taking unofficial action.

(d) **An extension of the role of CROTUM**

Before 1990, CROTUM could assist union members taking or considering taking legal action against their union for any breach of the law concerning union elections, industrial action, etc. **After the 1990 Act** the Commissioner could

be named as a party to an action against unions, and could also assist in legal proceedings over complaints about union rulebooks.

The Trade Union and Labour Relations (Consolidation) Act 1992

This Act consolidated all existing provisions concerning collective labour law and trade union law provision.

The 1993 Trade Union Reform and Employment Rights Act (TURER)

The last major piece of Conservative legislation concerning the collective aspects of the employment relationship again focuses upon industrial action. The Act also creates the Commissioner for Protection Against Unlawful Industrial Action. There are also measures concerning the payment of union subscriptions.

(a) **More restrictions on industrial action**

- **Before 1993**, separate ballots for industrial action were required for each workplace involved (Employment Act 1988), and balloting could take place at the workplace without the union being required to give notice of the ballot to the employer.
- **After the 1993 Act** a trade union now has to ensure that the ballot is conducted by post in order to have immunity from any legal repercussion. In addition, the union must give the employer concerned seven days' notice of the ballot. Further, the union must give the employer seven days' notice prior to calling industrial action, assuming that a majority of those balloted voted in favour of taking industrial action.

(b) **Creation of Commissioner for Protection Against Unlawful Industrial Action**

After the 1993 Act any individual who as a result of unlawful industrial action is likely to be prevented from receiving goods and services can apply to the High Court for an order to prevent further industrial action. The post of Commissioner for Protection Against Unlawful Industrial Action was set up in order to assist members of the public with legal advice and representation, thereby enabling them to stop unlawful industrial action via the High Court.

(c) **Payment of union subscriptions and union membership**

Before the 1993 Act:

- in common with other organisations, union members were required to provide their authorisation for the check-off once only. (The 'check-off' system allowed employers to deduct union subscriptions from employees' pay.) Union members could then terminate their authorisation as and when they saw fit; and
- as a result of the long-standing Bridlington Agreements, unions were discouraged from 'poaching', and therefore had some measure of control over their membership.

After 1993:

- union members must now give their written consent every three years if they wish to pay their union subscriptions by the 'check-off' system; and
- unions cannot take any disciplinary action against a member who leaves his or her union, nor can a union refuse membership to a member of another union who wishes to join that union.

In conclusion

It is highly unlikely that there will be a return to the largely autonomous voluntarist system which characterised government approaches to employment relations up to 1979. In addition to the Employment Relations Act 1999, there have been a number of other measures which have added to employment protection (see Chapters 10, 11 and 12), including the Employment Act 2002. However, the framework established by the Conservative governments is likely to remain intact, for the foreseeable future at least.

NEW LABOUR POLICIES AND LEGISLATION: 1997–2008 – NEO-LIBERALISM OR THIRD WAY?

The ideological direction of the 'New' Labour government elected in May 1997 remains problematic, although Smith and Morton (2001) maintain that in some areas New Labour has 'taken over New Right Conservative policy' (p. 121) and is essentially neo-liberal. In order to distinguish itself from previous Conservative administrations a loosely defined 'third way' was identified incorporating the notion of 'stakeholding' and 'partnership', and embodied the notions of inclusiveness, fairness and social solidarity 'in contrast to atomism, individualism and exclusive concern with profitability allegedly characterising Thatcherism (Howell, 2005, p. 177). During the first New Labour period of government, financial 'prudence', relying to some extent upon the 'supply-side' economics practised by previous Conservative administrations, appeared to be one of the cornerstones of economic policy. New Labour had no plans to increase public expenditure during the first two years in office, and any increases in spending, at least initially, would be accounted for by increases in indirect and corporate taxation. The overriding concern of the first New Labour government was to sustain the steady pattern of economic growth inherited from the previous government, although growth targets were being revised downwards as a result of the global turbulence in money markets prompted by the downturn in the Far Eastern, South American and Russian economies during the mid to late 1990s. The control of inflation so as not to undermine business confidence was also a major policy aim; low inflation was seen as a precondition for long-term economic growth. The 1997 manifesto proposals included:

- more efficient use of public expenditure, in partnership with the private sector where necessary, and adhering to planned public spending for at least two years of a New Labour government;
- fair taxes to encourage work and reward effort;
- encouraging small businesses and local economic growth; and
- reducing long-term unemployment.

In addition, and in contrast to the previous Conservative governments of the 1980s and 1990s, New Labour believed that to be economically successful Britain must harness the talents of the workforce to the full, that economic success is dependent upon partnership and not confrontation between employees and employers, and that the way to achieve this is 'through trust, consultation, teamworking

and offering people real security' (DTI, 1998). By 2003, the reality belied the rhetoric.

There is some doubt that the New Labour governments' approach to the economy and to employment issues varies substantially from that of the *new liberal* or *neo-liberal* stance of its predecessors, and the degree to which it does differ in offering a coherent 'third way', by claiming to combine social justice with economic efficiency, has now been subject to further debate and analysis (Howell, 2005; Smith and Morton, 2006). By 2003, for example, evidence of government handling of the firefighters' dispute of 2002–3 suggested a growing polarisation of interests between government and organised labour. Moreover, continuing disgruntlement amongst trade unions within the public sector services arising from New Labour's public services reform agenda, Public Private Partnerships (PPP) and Public Finance Initiative (PFI) together with 'modernisation' of such services and ongoing exhortations concerning public sector pay during 2007 and 2008 has led to a further distancing between unions and government. The following sections look at the policy developments and employment relations legislation of the New Labour governments from 1997 to 2008.

The evidence from 1997 to 2008

In its election manifesto directed at the business community, *New Opportunities for Business*, it was stressed that Labour would not bring about a 'blanket repeal of the main elements – on ballots, picketing and industrial action – of the 1980s employment and industrial relations legislation' (DTI, 1998). A Labour government would help to create a 'fair and flexible labour market' through the development of 'an adaptable, flexible and skilled workforce' and through the establishment of partnerships in industry. A Labour government would not 'be held to ransom by the unions . . . [and] unions will get no special favours under a Labour government' (Tony Blair, *The Sun*, 12 April 1997). It was clear that there would be no return to the corporatist days of the 1960s and 1970s or to the days of 'beer and sandwiches' at 10 Downing Street; business leaders rather than trade union leaders were to be invited to see the Prime Minister

in the first instance. Nevertheless, national trade union leaders were invited to join a range of advisory bodies such as the newly formed Low Pay Commission, the 'welfare to work' programme concerned mainly with the long-term unemployed, a body to examine obstacles to competitiveness, and a standing committee on preparing for European economic and monetary union. One of the first decisions by the New Labour government was to restore trade union recognition at the government's communications centre in Cheltenham (GCHQ) which was seen as a welcome indication of a more receptive mood by government towards trade unions.

New Labour, in opposition, had committed itself to developing a programme of employment relations reform which had three objectives:

- to encourage greater adaptability at work;
- to deepen the sense of partnership between employers and employees; and
- to achieve 'fairness at work'.

To this end, a Department of Trade and Industry minister made it clear that:

> These three objectives are interlinked and none can be achieved in isolation . . . We believe every individual should have the right to decent minimum standards of fairness at work which are enforceable by law. It is not merely a moral right but makes sound economic sense. Our primary aim is to bring a sensible and fair balance to the world of work between the rights and responsibilities of employers and employees. (Ian McCartney at the 'Unions 21' Conference, November 1997)

We now turn to the *Fairness at Work* white paper (1998) as this contains the most comprehensive overview of New Labour's employment relations philosophy during Blair's first government. This was followed by the Employment Relations Act 1999 (ERA 1999) which implemented the white paper proposals in stages.

Fairness at Work and the Employment Relations Act 1999

> There will be no going back. The days of strikes without ballots, mass picketing, closed shops and secondary action are over. Even after the

changes we propose, Britain will have the most lightly regulated labour market of any leading economy in the world. (Tony Blair, 1998)

The above quote from the white paper *Fairness at Work* expresses some elements of the government's political ideology relevant to employment relations. What is particularly clear and unambiguous is the rejection of corporatism and the implicit perseverance with previous Conservative policies and legislation. For trade unions, the most important Labour pledge was the promise of legislation which would provide them with the legal right to recognition. The recognition proposals of the Act and their consequences were detailed in Chapter 3. The outcome of discussions held with both the TUC and CBI resulted in recognition proposals contained in the *Fairness at Work* white paper of May 1998, and this was followed by the Employment Relations Act of 1999. Predictably, the CBI had reservations about the whole idea, arguing that recognition legislation would have adverse effects on business, and suggesting specific amendments, including:

- proof by trade unions that they enjoyed at least 40 per cent support from relevant employees in a bargaining unit before a recognition ballot could be heard;
- exemption from recognition proposals for small companies;

- acceptance that individual employees should be free to agree their own terms and conditions with their employers even if they worked in units covered by union recognition;
- a ban on strikes concerning recognition; and
- a right for employers to call a union recognition ballot where 50 per cent of employees demonstrated that they wanted one.

Most importantly, the CBI was convinced that 'it had secured an assurance from 10 Downing Street that companies need not have to recognise trade unions for collective bargaining purposes unless they secured the consent of 50 per cent plus one of those employed in the proposed bargaining unit and entitled to vote, and not just a majority of those who actually voted in the ballot as the TUC had maintained' (Taylor, 1998, p. 297). The TUC argued that few, if any, workplaces would manage to secure recognition rights if the CBI position were upheld.

The Employment Relations Act (ERA) 1999

The legislation (see Exhibit 4.7), based upon the white paper proposals as outlined above, represented an attempt to modernise employment relations in Britain with the aim of promoting a new culture of 'partnership' at work. Taken together

Exhibit 4.7

The Employment Relations Act: an overview

The ERA 1999 sets out the main provisions of the government's *Fairness at Work* white paper. The main changes are:

Individual rights (see also Chapter 10)

The qualifying period for unfair dismissal is reduced from two years to one with effect from 1 June 1999, and the maximum unfair dismissal compensatory award is raised from £12,000 to £50,000 from 25 October 1999 and is index-linked from that date. Employees on fixed term contracts are no longer able to agree with an employer to waive their unfair dismissal rights (but can still waive their redundancy rights).

Employees taking lawful industrial action have the right not to be unfairly dismissed, irrespective of their length of service. For the employee to be protected, the dismissal must occur within eight weeks from the start of the industrial action. The employer's right to dismiss employees for participating in 'unofficial' industrial action remains.

Where an employee has been invited to a disciplinary or grievance hearing, he or she is entitled to be accompanied by one companion who may be a trade union official or colleague of choice. That person can address the

meeting and consult with the employee during the hearing, but will not be able to answer questions on behalf of the employee.

Employment protection rights are also extended to workers other than employees by means of Regulations, in response to the growing number of 'atypical' workers.

Family rights

As part of New Labour's family-friendly agenda, the Act creates new rights relating to parental and maternity leave. Final Regulations implementing the EU Parental Leave Directive came into force on 15 December 1999. According to the Directive, employees who have 'responsibility for a child' are entitled to 13 weeks' unpaid leave if they satisfy the one-year qualifying period.

Pregnant employees benefit in full from the changes in maternity leave regulations from spring 2000. The ordinary leave period is increased from 14 to 18 weeks and employees may choose the date on which this period is to start. The Regulations lower the qualifying period of service for the entitlement to extended maternity leave of up to 40 weeks from two years to one. There is now compulsory maternity leave of 2 weeks following childbirth. An employee who exercises her right to ordinary maternity leave is entitled to the benefit of all the terms and conditions of her employment during her absence, other than those entitling her to remuneration.

There is a new right to a reasonable amount of time off during working hours for reasons related to a dependant, such as to make arrangements for the provision of care for a dependant who is ill or injured.

Collective rights (see also Chapter 3 for more detail)

The Act sets out a new regime for the recognition of trade unions by employers and the rights that trade unions can enjoy once recognised. Although encouraging a voluntary approach, the Act allows for compulsory recognition for collective bargaining purposes under certain circumstances. One or more unions can obtain an order from CAC that it or they be recognised. This new right will depend on various detailed procedures being followed and will only affect those employers with at least 21 employees. The union will have to demonstrate that it has the support of at least 40 per cent of the relevant workforce and a majority of those voting. A ballot may be avoided if the majority of workers are members of the union and there is no industrial relations or other reason why recognition should not be awarded automatically. The CAC may also specify a legally enforceable method by which the parties should conduct collective bargaining if the parties are unable to agree a method themselves.

Once recognised, trade unions have the right to be consulted under the usual statutory rights concerning redundancy programmes, health and safety issues and transfers of undertakings as well as matters they have agreed in a collective bargain. A union recognised under the statutory procedure will in some circumstances also have the right to be consulted on training.

with the signing of the social protocol and adoption of the Social Chapter as part of the Maastricht Treaty, endorsement of the EU Working Time Directive and implementation of the £3.60 national minimum wage, it would have been reasonable to argue at the time that there was potential for a distinct shift in the 'balance of power' in favour of employees – a move welcomed as long overdue by many unions. However, it was also argued that far from being radical and revolutionary the legislative provisions were cautious and unambitious and that 'the government did not alter its [white paper] proposals significantly in response to criticism from unions as to their inadequacy from the perspective of promoting and strengthening workers' collective organisation or individual rights' (Smith and Morton, 2001, p. 123). The legislative provisions were the result of extensive consultation with the TUC and CBI which inevitably, given New Labour's new-found 'employer friendliness', led to a 'watering down' of some clauses which the CBI found contentious. Concessions to employers ranged

from the adoption of similar procedures for dere-cognising unions as for recognising them, to the small firms exemption, which excludes organisations with fewer than 21 employees from statutory union recognition. An IRS (1999b) survey of employers' reactions to the white paper proposals and legislative provisions suggests that, despite criticisms made by the CBI and Institute of Directors:

> *What is surprising from our mini-case studies is not how much, but how little the legislation will impact on companies as a whole. This lends support to the view that the Fairness at Work legislation will act as something of a minimum 'safety net' rather than bringing about major change in the majority of workplaces. In the area of improved individual rights, for instance, many employers already have written disciplinary and grievance procedures which entitle employees to some form of representation. On the subject of union recognition, 44 of the UK's 50 largest companies already recognise unions for collective bargaining purposes. And many firms currently operate some family-friendly policies, including provision for maternity, paternity and emergency leave . . . In many organisations, Fairness at Work will thus not undermine management in the way some commentators fear. Our mini-case studies suggest that while there will be an increase in time-consuming bureaucracy, the autonomy of management in strategic decision making will not be challenged.* (p. 26)

Other points arising from the IRS survey concerning the implications of the legislation upon industrial relations include:

- the employer view that the legislation is unlikely to change the course of British industrial relations or the employment relations structures in organisations in any drastic way;
- that many larger companies have consultative machinery such as company councils or joint consultative committees for resolving workplace issues and, given their relative popularity, it is almost certain that, in the event of unions being recognised for collective bargaining, these consultative forums will be retained; and

- the view that the core objectives of *Fairness at Work* in terms of promoting both social partnership (see Chapter 8) and greater employee commitment and productivity 'are unlikely to be achieved'; the legislation is unlikely, on its own, to create cultural change or 'create the conditions conducive to the kind of cultural change the government would like to see'.

The IRS report concludes:

> *Employer responses to Fairness at Work – in terms of individual firms and their represent-atives such as the CBI and IoD – perhaps reflect how dramatically the industrial relations landscape has changed since 1979. Any attempt to legislate against the power of employers is seen as turning the clock back to the 'bad old days' of the corporatist 1970s. Companies, it seems are suspicious of regulation, intervention and the 'nanny state', and – in an age of direct consultation, flatter management structures and financial participation – some perceive unions as being less and less relevant to the real needs of employees. If the long-term success of Fairness at Work rests in part on the attitudes of employers, the omens are not looking good at this early stage. Labour may believe it can dismantle parts of the Conservative industrial relations architecture through legislation, but addressing its apparently embedded cultural legacy will be more of a challenge.* (p. 28)

Self-evaluation activity 4.16

Practical consequences of ERA 1999
The response is given below

What do you think are the practical consequences of ERA 1999 for employers?

As can be seen, the Act covered much ground, and much of the detail is contained in subsequent regulations which have now been implemented. Employers without recognised unions need to assess their approach to employee consultation and involvement if union support is likely to be significant and to consider agreeing to recognition where it might otherwise be imposed. Employment handbooks and procedures should be updated to take account of the new parental leave, domestic incidents and maternity provisions,

and the right to be accompanied to disciplinary and grievance procedures. The lifting of the ceiling to £50,000 and subsequently to £52,600 concerning unfair dismissal compensation has, on balance, provided enough incentive not to be complacent. Managers need to realise that bad disciplinary decisions will be costly, and the cheap (and all too easy) option of a cost-effective compromise agreement following a termination without procedures will be a thing of the past as ensured by the Employment Act 2002.

The national minimum wage 1999

The national minimum wage, which came into effect in 1999, constitutes a wage floor that removes the gross exploitation of many employees such as casual and part-time workers. However, the relatively low level at which the wage was set and the continuing low level (£5.52 in 2007 and a lower rate for 18–21 year olds called the development rate) has incurred the continuing opposition of the TUC, which has always campaigned to establish a much higher rates and an automatic uprating of the wage. A fuller discussion of the national minimum wage is to be found in an earlier part of this chapter.

Employment protection

The first Blair government opted in to the Social Chapter of the European Union, and many of the new employment protection rights since 1997 have been the result of a transposition of relevant European Union Directives into UK law (see below), either within the ERA 1999, the Employment Act 2002 or by Regulations. A summary of these employment protection rights up to and including 2008 is given in Exhibit 4.8 (see also Chapter 10).

In addition, the government made some concessions to the CBI regarding the Information and Consultation Directive (see Chapter 6) and to the 'two-tier' workforce in local government (see below).

Employment Act 2002 and other related developments

The Employment Act 2002 is described in greater detail in Chapter 10. In essence the Act concerns itself with the revision of disputes procedures, incorporating disciplinary and grievance procedures the statutory versions of which are already in place; reforms to the employment tribunal system; and more generous provision regarding parental leave and payments. Provisions concerning maternity/paternity/adoption leave and pay, dispute resolution, equal pay questionnaires, union learning representatives, dismissal procedures, fixed term and flexible working and tribunal reform have all been implemented.

Employment Relations Act 2004

The Employment Relations Act (ERA 2004) is probably the last major piece of employment relations legislation of New Labour's third term in office. The Act is the outcome of a review of the ERA 1999 and the main provisions are:

- revised trade union recognition (and derecognition) procedure;
- provisions concerning industrial action;
- provisions to make funds available for trade union modernisation;
- a power to make regulations to introduce information and consultation in the workplace by implementing the EC Directive on Information and Consultation.

As of 2008, these regulations are now in force.

Amendments to the **statutory union recognition procedure** include providing improved access for trade unions to a workforce. On accepting a union's recognition application, the CAC will appoint a qualified and independent person acting on behalf of a union in order to distribute material by post to workers. The Act imposes additional duties on employers on being informed of a ballot and also imposes sanctions and remedies against unfair practices by both employers and trade unions in relation to recognition and derecognition ballots. The Act also introduces measures to tackle intimidation of workers during recognition and derecognition ballots by introducing rules which define improper campaigning activity by employers and unions and by clarifying what 'reasonable access' unions have to the workers in a bargaining unit.

With regard to **industrial action**, the Act contains provisions to increase the protections against dis-

Exhibit 4.8

Employment protection rights: 1997–2008 (for legislation preceding 1997 see Chapter 10)

Existing rights have been improved upon and new ones introduced:

1. National minimum wage
2. Right to be accompanied in grievance and disciplinary hearings
3. Working time
4. Urgent family leave
5. Parental leave
6. Part-time workers' right to equal treatment
7. Protection and equal treatment for fixed-term contract workers
8. Public interest disclosure ('whistle-blower') protection
9. Paid paternity leave
10. Paid time off for union representatives
11. Adoption leave
12. Right to request a flexible working arrangement
13. Equal pay questionnaire
14. Maternity leave
15. Reform of the Transfer of Undertakings (Protection of Employment) Regulations
16. Reform of the ERA 1999
17. Anti-discrimination measures
18. Extension of Working Time Regulations
19. Employment tribunal reforms
20. Dispute resolution – new ACAS code on disciplinary and grievance procedures and minimum statutory disputes procedures
21. Commission for Equality and Human Rights 2007
22. Changes to sex discrimination regulations, widening harassment definition
23. Additional paternity leave 2008
24. Protection for vulnerable agency workers 2008

missal of employees taking official, lawfully organised industrial action by extending the 'protected period' from 8 to 12 weeks thereby putting into practice the relevant Warwick Agreement commitment (see below).

The 'Warwick Agreement' 2004 and the Trade Union Freedom Bill 2006

The Warwick Agreement was concluded at Warwick University in July 2004 between the government and unions concerning labour employment relations policy and trade union legislation. Exhibit 4.9 provides relevant details together with the basic provisions of the Trade Union Freedom Bill.

Public sector reform

While reforms to employment rights attracted varying degrees of approval, it is in the area of public sector reform and 'modernisation' that the second Blair government has encountered considerable opposition from the TUC and others. This is despite substantial increases in public expenditure arising from the second public spending review 2001–4 which reversed the first Blair government's parsimony in adhering to the Conservative public spending guidelines. The reform of public services has been central to New Labour's agenda for a variety of reasons, incorporating the government argument that state intervention and investment

Exhibit 4.9

The Warwick Agreement, July 2004 and the Trade Union Freedom Bill, 2006

The Warwick Agreement

The deal, struck at Warwick, attempted to pacify discontented elements within the union movement and government, thereby averting the threat of mass disaffiliation from the party by the unions, and helped secure union support for Labour in the 2005 election. The meeting took the form of a 'policy forum' which is designed to discuss policy issues outside the main party conference. The outcome of the forum's deliberations was a series of agreements across a range of issues concerning pensions, public services and manufacturing, etc. A number of commitments were made by government, although many were in the form of policy reviews. Initially the unions were satisfied with the outcome, but subsequent slow progress on the part of government led the TUC to pass a motion at its 2005 Conference which called for a trade union freedom private member's bill in the wake of the dispute between Gate Gourmet and its catering staff at Heathrow Airport which would secure better protection for workers amid a climate of deregulation.

The government made the following commitments:

- A women at work commission was promised to investigate unequal pay.
- A pledge to eradicate a two-tier workforce in the public sector that saw privately employed workers paid less.
- Changes to be made to the PFI to guarantee greater equality when choosing between PFI investment and conventional public spending.
- Agreement to protect pensions for workers moving from one employer to another and for employees having a 50 per cent representation among trustees managing pension schemes with pensions being formally included within the collective bargaining process.
- Support for a new EU agency workers directive and the introduction of sector forums in low-paid areas.
- Workers on strike would not be allowed to be dismissed until 12 weeks after the start of the dispute, instead of eight weeks.

Trade Union Freedom Bill campaign

The Fairness at Work Composite resolution adopted at the TUC Conference 2005 called on the General Council to support a Trade Union Freedom Bill. The Bill marks the centenary of the Trade Disputes Act 1906 which first introduced the UK system for immunities from tortuous liability for unions when organising industrial action. The Bill was introduced as a private member's bill in 2006. The three main areas of legal reform are:

- Improved protection from dismissal and more effective remedies for workers taking part in official industrial action.
- Simplification of the complex regulations on notices and ballots which restrict the ability of unions to organise industrial action where a clear majority of members have voted in support.
- Modernisation of what constitutes a trade dispute, enabling limited forms of supportive action, thereby ensuring that UK industrial action laws reflect changes in the UK labour market, including increased contracting out and enabling unions to respond where employers take steps to outsource work during the course of a dispute with a view to breaking a strike.

in the public sector are integral to enhanced competitiveness in world markets. This line of reasoning has a number of strands, as identified by Bach (2002):

- the emphasis upon a 'strong' interventionist state with an increase in regulatory and audit activity (Kirk and Wall, 2002) has involved the use of performance management systems and new

inspectors to 'direct and monitor performance against a plethora of centrally defined targets' (Bach, 2002, p. 326);

- regulation rather than ownership is the important criterion to ensure improved delivery of services which logically should involve a 'mixed economy' approach, utilising the private sector to provide some public services, as exists within many EU economies; and

- a strong 'networking' approach involving trade unions and private organisations in discussions about public sector modernisation: specific issues include establishing networks to increase patient involvement in the NHS.

While there is broad consensus amongst trade unions concerning the aims of government policy, there remains considerable opposition to the means and methods proposed and employed to finance public services and the role of the private sector in their provision under the banner of 'Public Private Partnerships'. The 'modernisation', or reform of education, health and social care, education and the emergency services has continued to be an overriding issue during the government's third term and has had important implications for employment relations in a number of crucial areas such as the reform of pay systems and changes in working practices and skill mixes. Bach *et al.* (2005) point out that:

> *these changes are occurring within a context of reinforced systems of employment performance management, which in turn are linked to an emphasis on output targets, business performance indicators and 'league tables' . . . At the same time, the rhetoric of modernisation also often extols the benefits of new, less conflict prone, relationships between employers and trade unions under the 'partnership' paradigm in which employee involvement and participation is mainstreamed into decision making.* (p. 629)

The separate issue of pay determination within the public sector is also problematic and is considered in Chapter 5.

Private sector involvement and the Private Finance Initiative (PFI)

The first Blair government continued with its predecessor's privatisation policies, endorsing the view that improvements in the quality and efficiency of service provision would ensue even if this resulted in job losses and deterioration of conditions of service for those employed by the newly privatised companies. The partial privatisation of the National Air Traffic Service and the initial refusal to renationalise Railtrack after its poor management record confirmed this policy – although subsequently Railtrack collapsed and the government in this exceptional case was compelled to renationalise. Furthermore, New Labour accepted the PFI policy of the Conservatives aimed at utilising private sector funds to finance public sector capital expenditure without increasing the public sector borrowing requirement. The PFI policy was introduced in 1992 and Exhibit 4.10 provides an explanation of its workings.

There are a number of objections to PFI which are central to the employment relationship within the public sector. The first objection concerns the 'value for money' issue which now assumes precedence over public spending and borrowing concerns. As a result of the stance taken by the ASB (Accounting Standards Board) there has been an increase in documentation and consultancy fees due to lengthier negotiations and an increased rate of return demanded by SPVs. Both these factors have led to an increase in costs, which have fuelled the debate as to whether PFI really does represent 'value for money'. Secondly, the TUC and trade unions generally have viewed PFI as an antecedent of privatisation and expressed concern about the consequences that this development would have upon union membership and influence. Thirdly, there has been concern about the impact on terms and conditions of employment of workers transferred to private sector employers as part of the PFI process, that those workers not covered by TUPE Regulations would, upon transfer to the private sector, experience inferior pay and working conditions compared with those they enjoyed in the public sector. This has prompted unions such as UNISON to mount campaigns to highlight the problem and to publicise the creation of the so-called 'two-tier' workforce. However, in a rather surprising move which to some extent placated the unions but at the same time aggravated 'business leaders' (*Financial Times*, 14 February 2003), the government endorsed a code of practice covering all workers

Exhibit 4.10

PFI explained

Under PFI the private sector enterprise (referred to as the 'operator') usually undertakes to design, build, finance and operate a property in order to provide the required service demanded by the public sector body (referred to as the 'purchaser') responsible for the ultimate delivery of the service. For larger contracts the private sector side of the partnership can be a Special Purpose Vehicle (SPV), which is a consortium of companies involved in construction, finance and other disciplines relevant to the particular public sector project. The policy of privatisation was regarded as an important step towards restoring the private sector's role within the economy. PFI, however, has swung the pendulum back even further. Instead of being a provider of services, a streamlined public sector has transferred many of its functions to private companies. The state now contracts out both construction of capital assets and the provision of services to a new breed of organisation, enabling the constructors to become both operators and builders of new facilities such as schools and hospitals. McKendrick and McCabe (1997) argue that the main aims of PFI are:

- accelerating investment in the infrastructure through providing access to private capital;
- improving the way in which facilities are designed and procured;
- enabling a better balance between capital and current spending; and
- constraining public expenditure in favour of private sector expenditure.

 Most public sector departments have used PFI to improve and upgrade their infrastructure, including health (Norfolk and Norwich General Hospital), prisons (Fazakerley, Liverpool), education (Avery Hill student village), culture (Royal Armouries Museum) and defence (Defence Helicopter Flying School). Since coming into power in 1997, New Labour has endorsed the idea with enthusiasm, so much so that it is almost impossible to detect any policy difference from the previous Conservative government.

transferred as a result of PFI within the local authority context. These workers are now to enjoy 'fair and reasonable' terms and conditions 'which are, overall, no less favourable' than those of their colleagues who were working for the public sector and were simply transferred. The Transfer of Undertakings (Protection of Employment) Regulations 2006 introduced new requirements concerning contracting out and in (see Chapter 12).

Conclusion

Apart from a renewed commitment to the European Union and its social policy objectives which are ongoing (see the following section which deals with European Union social policy), the establishment of a statutory minimum wage and the Employment Relations Act define the extent of New Labour's intervention within the employment relations arena

during its first term of government. During the second Blair government, despite further legislation considered above, a great deal of ambiguity regarding its political ideology vis-à-vis employment relations remained. New Labour apparently sought to placate employers by attempting to strike a balance between employment protection on the one hand, and employer prerogative on the other (Dickens and Hall, 2003). Sensitivity to the concerns of employers manifests itself in the modest national minimum wage levels from 1999 to 2004, the modest proposals for trade union recognition (see Chapter 3) and the rejection of TUC proposals for improving the ERA 1999, as evidenced by the white paper (2003) review of the ERA 1999 (which subsequently gave rise to the ERA 2004).

Commenting on the review of the Employment Relations Act, Brendan Barber the TUC General Secretary said: 'While there are some useful

*advances in this White Paper that will make a real difference to people at work, unions will find the government's rejection of many TUC proposals extremely disappointing. The government would be unwise to ignore the real anger in unions today. Our call for people at work to be represented by a union when a majority back it, irrespective of the size of the business, is a basic human right. Our call for an end to rigged votes in recognition ballots where abstentions count the same as votes against is a simple matter of democracy. Our call to end the right of employers to sack staff after eight weeks on strike would enshrine the basic human right to withdraw your labour. Of course we welcome the measures that will help people at work and the technical improvements in employment law and union recognition procedures, **but on balance the White Paper has been too influenced by business lobbying.'**
(TUC Press Release, 27 February 2003)*

New Labour continues to heed CBI views concerning the impact of regulation upon business performance and the effect of this upon employment costs. The government acknowledgement that the 'regulatory burden' is a sensitive employer issue may explain 'light touch' regulation and commitment to 'soft touch' legislation and codes of practice. These amount to relatively little in practice. Examples are employer-friendly amendments to the Working Time Directive, which reduce the record-keeping requirements on employers enabling employees to 'opt out' of the statutory 48-hour limit (Dickens and Hall, 2003), and in the area of equality where government rejected EOC proposals for the introduction of mandatory employer pay reviews. Within the area of individual employment protection, while there have been some improvements prompted by EU Directives, progress has been slower than in many other EU countries, and at best could be described as 'constrained expansion' (Dickens, 2002), which is better than no expansion at all. However, the verdict of Smith and Morton (2001) is less kind:

> *The devil in Labour's employment law programme is its commitment to a particular form of employer domination of the employment relationship. From this flows its support for a minimalist regulation of the employment relationship and hostility to the politics and practice*

of trade unionism conceived as the mobilisation of workers' collective power. Devilish details flow from devilish values. (p. 135)

This view reinforces the argument that New Labour employment relations policies are geared more towards continuity with the policies of previous Conservative governments than with promoting radical change. To be sure, the first Blair government put an end to the overt hostility between the labour movement and government; trade unions and the TUC were encouraged to endorse the new 'social partnership' culture (subsequently ignored by government) in which they had a theoretical and rhetorical part to play, together with the CBI and employers whom Labour courted so fervently before and after being elected into government. The balance of power between employers and employees in the workplace even where unions are recognised hardly changed as a result of legislative developments; employers are likely to remain in the ascendancy and continue to dominate the employment relations agenda for the foreseeable future (Kessler and Bayliss, 1998; IRS, 1999a; Smith and Morton, 2001; Dickens and Hall, 2003). This view is also reinforced by TUC suspicion of the government's motives in resisting, with reservations and qualifications, the (then) draft EU Information and Consultation Directive (see Chapter 6) which eventually made works councils mandatory for firms with 50 workers or more. The draft directive was resisted by government on the grounds that its implementation would impede the scope for employers to decide what was the most appropriate system of information and consultation for their organisation. But the logical position for government to adopt 'would have been to be supportive of the draft directive. Information and consultation is an essential part of a partnership arrangement between employers and employees' (Gennard, 2002, p. 593). In that context, John Monks, the former TUC General Secretary, has stated that 'the employers are more afraid of this [works councils] than they are of trade union recognition because they think it will be a Trojan horse for unions to get into every company' (*The Guardian*, 24 May 1999).

New Labour's third term has been characterised by 'more of the same' with rigid adherence to public sector reform, few concessions to organised labour

and a dogged pursuance of minimalist employment protection rights based on a grudging acceptance of EC Directives and hostility and scepticism towards the European model of a regulated labour market (Smith and Morton, 2006). The Warwick Agreement, 2004 made little progress and did not satisfy the TUC, which wanted more government commitments to follow up the changes agreed at Warwick. Smith and Morton (2006) conclude from their review of nine years of New Labour that:

> *In nine years of government, New Labour has developed a distinctive form of neoliberalism in which Conservative legislation on trade unions and industrial action has been integrated within a more subtle discourse of social partnership and collective and individual rights . . . The UK remains in open disregard of international standards on workers' rights to organise and take industrial action . . . The statutory recognition procedure enshrines their [unions,] illegitimacy . . . [and] are only to be accorded limited rights under strict conditions . . . Partnership agreements entrench employers' power . . . [and] the new information and consultation procedures create a potential framework for the incorporation of labour within the market imperatives of employing organisations.* (p. 414)

In similar vein, Howell (2005) concludes:

> *While the industrial relations institutions currently being constructed by New Labour differ in some respects from those of its Conservative predecessor, they are fundamentally convergent with the decollectivist thrust of the third system of industrial relations characterising the Conservative period of office. New Labour legislation has grafted a framework of greater legal regulation of social relations onto Conservative reforms, while not challenging the decollectivist architecture of the Conservative era. Both the Conservative and New Labour employment relations policies largely reject collective regulation.* (p. 193)

It appears, therefore, that continuity with the neo-liberal ideology of 1979–97 rather than change has characterised government policy towards employment relations during the period 1997–2008, and we would still agree with Kessler and Bayliss (1998), who argued some years ago that the 'present balance of forces' in which employers are dominant will remain: 'the unions may retreat no further, but employers will remain firmly in the ascendancy' (p. 301).

THE EUROPEAN UNION AND EMPLOYMENT RELATIONS

There can be no doubt that the influence of the European Union upon member states through its institutions, 'social partners', treaty provisions and directives has assumed much greater importance during the 1990s than in previous decades as a result of moves towards a common currency and eventual political union, together with attempts to co-ordinate social and economic policy across a whole range of substantive and procedural issues. Our main concern here is with the 'social' dimension of EU policy – the term 'social' being used in treaty provisions and directives to include employment and employment relations matters. In order to understand the process of social policy making it is necessary to consider the main policy-making institutions and decision-making processes of the EU insofar as they impinge upon employment relations issues. Before doing so, it is important to note that there are two main methods that are employed by the EU in its attempts to develop an 'integrated' system of European employment relations (Hall, 1992, 1994). These are:

- the adoption of regulatory measures, usually in the form of directives aiming to 'harmonise' or align more closely the laws and practices of member states or to regulate transnational employment relations matters; and
- the use of 'procedural' initiatives 'such as the promotion of "social dialogue" between European-level employer and trade union organisations and their inclusion into a network of sectoral or advisory bodies which feed into the Commission's policy development work' (Hall, 1994, p. 284).

The process of policy and decision making within the European Commission is far from smooth. The Council of Ministers which is responsible for decision making has often curtailed the wider ambitions of

the Commission within the social policy field. Moreover, the presidency of the Council of Ministers, which is held on a six-monthly rotating basis by a member state government, can exert a major influence upon the direction of EC social policy. The pace and direction of social policy can also be heavily influenced by certain key member states (France, Germany and the UK) which can either encourage or impede its development – the UK Conservative governments of the 1980s and 1990s for example, blocked a range of proposed directives within the Council leading to an 'impasse' over EC labour law initiatives (Hall, 1994), while the West German government under Brandt adopted a more facilitative and proactive approach to policy making during the 1960s. To a certain extent, policy making has become a more complex affair in recent years as a result of the enlargement of the European Union.

The institutions of the EU relevant to social policy making

All EU policy and decision making involves four main institutions. These are the European Commission, the Council of Ministers, the European Parliament (EP) and the European Court of Justice (ECJ). Other institutions relevant to social policy generation comprise the Social Partners representing national union and management/employers' bodies and the Economic and Social Committee.

The European Commission is the principal body for initiating policy, and will comprise 38 Commissioners, provisionally one from each of the 18 smaller member states and two each from the ten larger ones. Each Commissioner has responsibility for one administrative department, known as a Directorate-General and for one set of issues. Hence, there is a Commissioner for Social Affairs who is responsible for 'employment, industrial relations and social affairs'. The most important function of the Commission is to initiate policy to form the basis of European legislation. Other functions include:

- The responsibility for ensuring that the provisions of the various treaties (such as the Treaty of Rome), policy and legislative decisions are actually put into effect and that member states comply with these.

- The responsibility to act as 'power broker' should there be disagreement between member states within the Council of Ministers in order to reach a compromise.
- The responsibility to take action against member states should they fail to fulfil a treaty obligation by bringing the matter before the ECJ.

The Council of the European Union (Council of Ministers and the European Council) is the most important law-making institution. Membership of the Council varies according to what is being discussed, and there are a number of constituent bodies, each of which will consider particular issues. The Social Affairs Council, for example, is responsible for all employment relations issues; it comprises Employment Ministers (or equivalent) from each of the 28 member states and makes decisions on draft proposals put forward by the Commission.

The European Parliament (EP) comprises 732 (maximum from 2004 according to the Treaty of Nice) representatives who are Members of the European Parliament (MEPs), elected by universal suffrage. Each member state has an allocation of MEPs proportionate to its population, with Germany having the greatest number of seats (99) and Luxembourg and Malta having the least (six and five respectively). The EP, unlike national parliaments, has limited power and influence, although subsequent to the Maastricht and Amsterdam Treaties it acquired limited powers of veto which now extend to many social policy areas. The traditional functions of the EP include:

- a consultative role: the Council of Ministers must consult with the EP on all aspects of EU legislation;
- a supervisory role with power to dismiss the European Commission on passing a vote of no confidence (such action was taken successfully for the first time in 1999); and
- the power to reject the entire draft annual budget of the EU by majority vote, enabling individual modifications to be negotiated.

The European Court of Justice comprises 28 judges, one from each member state, and deals with two categories of cases. Firstly, it makes decisions concerning whether member states have complied with their treaty obligations; it also monitors the legality

of the acts of the Council of Ministers and of the Commission. Secondly, it makes judgments on cases originating within individual member states concerning the interpretation of EU directives and legislation. For example, cases involving sex discrimination can be referred to the ECJ if they are not resolved to the satisfaction of one party by the judicial system of a member state. The ECJ will make preliminary judgments or rulings which are ultimately binding upon member states.

The Social Partners

The main Social Partners are the European Trade Union Confederation (ETUC) and the Union of Industrial and Employers' Confederations of Europe (UNICE). These were described in Chapter 1. In addition to these, another employers' organisation, the European Centre of Public Enterprises (CEEP), representing public sector employer interests, plays a less significant part in social policy determination. The Commission's aim 'to develop the dialogue between management and labour at European level which could, if the two sides consider it desirable, lead to relations based on agreement' (Article 118b, Single European Act 1987) has been only partially successful. The 'dialogue' was intended to result in social policy initiatives upon which the Social Partners could agree. While there were some successes, the interests and values of the ETUC and UNICE, whereby the former is more receptive to social policy developments and interventions and the latter is predisposed to oppose such initiatives, were not conducive in helping to create a climate of co-operation. Moreover, the aim of developing Europe-wide collective bargaining machinery with the Social Partners being the major actors has encountered serious problems and obstacles apart from the ideological incompatibility of the Partners. Some of these problems are identified by Leat (1999) citing Schulten (1996):

- There are no institutional or organisational underpinnings and machinery, and no political mandate which would enable the Partners to negotiate at this level.
- Political interests of the actors are still predominantly national and relatively narrowly focused.

- European-level bargaining ideally requires the commitment of member states to political union, thereby subordinating national interests to those of the European state.

Nevertheless, the Maastricht Treaty and the Treaty of Amsterdam give much greater prominence to the roles of the Social Partners in consultation and negotiation of collective agreements in areas of social policy (see Exhibit 4.11).

Economic and Social Committee

The Economic and Social Committee comprises representatives from those involved in the main areas of social and economic activity such as businesses, employees, professional organisations and agriculture. Membership composition is in proportion to the size of the member states. The Committee has a right to be consulted and also provides advice on economic and social matters.

EU law, treaties and social policy

EU law is in two parts; primary law comprises legal provisions contained in treaties and related documents which define the obligations of the parties, while secondary law contains legal provisions derived from primary law which are incorporated into regulations, directives, decisions, recommendations and opinions.

Regulations are rarely used but are directly applicable to and binding upon member states. Regulations do not require any intervention from the member state to give them legal force. Regulations take precedence over and supersede national law.

Directives are also binding upon member states, but require member states to take some action in order to incorporate them into legislation. Directives usually have an implementation date. For example, the UK endorsed the European Works Council Directive and the date for UK implementation was 31 December 1999. This means that a directive becomes law for member states by a certain date and is part of the EU legal framework.

Decisions are made by the Council and occasionally by the Commission and are binding on those parties to whom they are addressed.

Exhibit 4.11

The legislative process in Europe

There are four different routes by which EU proposals on employment issues can become law. These are:

The consultation procedure: a proposal is submitted to the Council of Ministers by the Commission. Following consultation of the European Parliament and the Economic and Social Committee, the Council may adopt the proposal on a unanimous vote.

The co-operation procedure: here the Council adopts a 'common position', by qualified majority voting, which is then put forward to the European Parliament for a second reading. The European Parliament then either approves or takes no decision on the common position; either of these positions leads to the automatic adoption of the proposal by the Council. Alternatively, it can reject the proposal – in which case the Council can adopt it only on a unanimous vote – or it may propose amendments, which will lead to a new proposal by the Commission. Adoption by the Council is by qualified majority voting.

The co-decision procedure: the European Parliament has a right to veto proposals where a common position has been reached by the Council. This right was established by the Treaty of European Union, which came into force on 1 November 1993, and was reinforced by the Treaty of Amsterdam.

The Social Partners: can reach an agreement under the social policy Protocol and Agreement (Social Chapter) annexed to the Treaty of European Union. The Commission is required to consult the Partners on social legislation, as well as the content of the measure, before a proposal is submitted. The UK's 'opt-out' of the Social Chapter has meant that it has not been covered by legislation adopted via this route. However, as a result of the Labour government's decision to sign up to the social policy Agreement, the UK is formally covered under the relevant provisions of the Treaty of Amsterdam (1999).

The employers' and trade unions' representatives that comprise the Social Partners should forward an opinion or recommendation on the proposal to the Commission. If they wish to negotiate, they have nine months to reach agreement, though this may be extended by a joint decision of the Commission and the Partners. Agreement resulting from this process can be implemented either 'in accordance with the procedures and practices specific to management and labour of the member states' or, where requested by the Social Partners, by a Council decision on a proposal by the Commission. The issue concerned determines whether the Council's decision can be taken by qualified majority voting or only on a unanimous vote.

Where the Partners cannot reach agreement, or either side refuses to discuss the subject matter, then the Commission may submit a proposal to proceed under either the co-operation or consultation procedure. For example, following the refusal by the private sector employers to engage in negotiations, the Commission has advanced its own proposal on national-level employee information and consultation.

When adopted at European level, the two key ways EU employment measures are incorporated into UK law are by the passing of a new statute or by the introduction of regulations.

Source: Based on IRS, 1999a

Recommendations and opinions are not legally binding, and together with resolutions, solemn declarations and codes of practice have a moral rather than a legal imperative. The Community Charter of Fundamental Social Rights for Workers (known as the Social Charter) is one such example.

Treaties and the social policy framework

The treaties governing the establishment and continuing development of the EU have also established certain social policy initiatives and frameworks. However, social policy has been dogged by the

debate between advocates of the 'free market' and those who consider intervention is necessary for the social well-being and protection of individuals and groups within the labour market and the employment relationship.

The Treaty of Rome 1957, created a customs union and common market and gave the European Economic Community (EEC), as it was then known, a distinct legal personality. Certain 'articles' within the Treaty established the basic principles of social policy as then conceived. These are:

- equal pay between women and men (Article 119);
- free movement of labour (Article 48 and others); and
- help with relocation and retraining of individuals affected by the integration of Community countries into a common market. Article 123 'provided the basis for the creation of the European Social Fund (ESF) which has been the main mechanism for achieving improved employment opportunities and enhancing geographic and occupational mobility' (Leat, 1999, p. 231).

The period up to 1985 saw the enlargement of the EEC and a number of directives on workers' rights concerning redundancies and equal opportunities. There was little consensus on other issues, the most notable being the Fifth Directive concerning employee participation and information (see Chapter 8). The era of Conservative governments from 1979 ensured that, as a result of persistent blocking of directives, very little progress was made on the social policy front. The period since 1985, notable in its earlier years for the appointment of the social interventionist Jacques Delors as President of the European Commission, saw a number of important developments in, and a more systematic approach to, social policy which would enable member states, with or without the co-operation of the UK, to apply the directives under, for example, the Social Charter Action Programme of 1989.

The Single European Act (SEA) 1987

The Act introduced institutional changes in order to establish the basis for the single European market by the end of 1992. It also introduced qualified majority voting within the Council of Ministers in order to speed up decision making on measures necessary to achieve the single market. Article 118(b) opened the possibility for European-level social dialogue between the Social Partners; this had no immediate impact on the development of free-standing agreements, but was followed later by the Agreement on Social Policy under the Maastricht Treaty. The creation of a single market provided the impetus for the development of social policy.

The Social Charter

The proposed establishment of the single market involving the removal of physical barriers to trade implied an intensification of competition between firms and attempts on the part of employers to reduce labour costs by moving investment to other member states with lower labour costs and relatively deregulated labour markets – a practice which became known as social dumping. Fear of worsening employment relations and deterioration of conditions of employment as a result of social dumping and other factors led the Commission to propose a Community Charter of Fundamental Social Rights for Workers (Social Charter), as summarised in Exhibit 4.12, which laid down minimum conditions and rights which should be incorporated into the employment legislation of member states. The Social Charter proposals were acceptable to all member states with the exception of the UK. Since the Charter proposals required a unanimous vote amongst Council members, the UK had effectively vetoed the Charter, which consequently was not legally binding upon member states, remaining a 'statement of intent'. The Charter was supported by a Social Action Programme (SAP) which contained 47 proposals, including 17 draft directives, ten of which concerned health and safety issues. The SAP excluded some important areas such as specifying minimum pay levels, the right to strike, the right of freedom of association which includes the right to join a trade union or employers' association, and imposing or constraining the process and status of collective bargaining. The UK veto therefore considerably weakened the impact of the Social Charter and the accompanying SAP but nevertheless it formed the basis of a draft Social Chapter of the Maastricht Treaty, 1991.

Exhibit 4.12

The Social Charter: a summary

The proposals enshrining the rights of all EU citizens are:

- the freedom of movement for workers and self-employed persons across all countries of the EU;
- adequate protections for employment and remuneration;
- improvement of living and working conditions;
- adequate social protection and social security;
- freedom of association – including the right to join or not to join trade unions;
- adequate and continuing vocational and job training;
- equality of treatment for men and women;
- information, consultation and participation of workers on key workplace issues;
- health, protection and safety at the workplace;
- protection of children and adolescents at work;
- the access of elderly persons to labour markets; and
- the access of disabled persons to labour markets.

The Maastricht Treaty 1992

Also known as the Treaty of European Union, the Treaty established the European Union and introduced a number of major changes in the scope for regulating social and employment policy across the community of member states. During negotiations in 1991 leading up to the Treaty, attempts were made to amend Articles 117–122 (the 'social' clauses of the Treaty of Rome as amended by the Single European Act) in order to facilitate and broaden the scope of decision making on employment matters, and to allow for greater qualified majority voting on employment-related matters. The UK government's refusal to co-operate with and agree to a revised Treaty that contained the draft Social Chapter – the infamous 'opt-out' – compelled the other (then) 11 member states to find an alternative solution which was annexed to the Treaty under a mechanism known as the Social Policy Protocol and Agreement (see below).

The Social Policy Protocol and Agreement

This provides a legal mechanism for implementing social policy, giving employers and unions the right to negotiate binding European framework agreements. The Protocol stated that member states (with the exception then of the UK) wished to continue developing social policy in line with the 1989 Social Charter and had therefore adopted an Agreement to this end. The Protocol authorises member states to make use of the institutions, procedures and mechanisms of the Maastricht Treaty in order to give effect to the Agreement. The Protocol thus enshrined the UK 'opt-out', while the Agreement constitutes the so-called Social Chapter. The agreement on social policy attached to the Social Protocol provides for qualified majority voting (QMV) by member states in the following areas:

- working conditions;
- information and consultation of employees;
- equal opportunities between men and women; and
- integration of people excluded from the labour market.

Proposals may be blocked where a sufficient number of member states form a blocking majority under QMV rules (26 out of 77 votes). Policy areas where unanimity is still required include:

- social security and protection of employees;
- protection of employees whose contract is terminated;
- collective representation;

- conditions of employment for third world country nationals legally resident in the EU; and
- financial provision for job creation schemes.

Policy areas outside the scope of the EU are: pay; the right of association; the right to strike; and the right to impose lockouts. The Social Policy Agreement gives a wide role to the EU-level Social Partners. Where the Commission wishes to propose a measure, it is required to consult the Partners, firstly, on the need for action at European level and, secondly, on whether it should be introduced by legislation or by collective agreement. Where the Partners choose to negotiate a collective agreement this must be done within nine months and it then passes to the Council for adoption as a directive without alteration.

The Treaty of Amsterdam

The Treaty of Amsterdam (1999), to which the UK under New Labour is party, provides a legal framework for the EU to pursue objectives and take action in a number of social and employment areas that were not possible before. The main provisions affecting employment relations, and which incorporate revised Articles 118 and 119, include:

- The incorporation of the Social Policy Protocol and Agreement (see above) in the main text of the Treaty with Article 118 providing the legal basis for EU action.
- The introduction into the Treaty of a specific Chapter on employment issues (the Employment Chapter) which for the first time requires governments to co-ordinate their strategies for creating employment and promoting a skilled, trained and adaptable workforce. It also requires the member states to produce an annual report on the employment situation in the EU, detailing the effectiveness of actions taken.
- A renewed commitment to take action to 'combat discrimination based on sex, racial or ethnic origin, religion or belief, disability, age or sexual orientation' under a new Article 6a which enables the Council unanimously to take such action.
- A renewed obligation upon each member state, under the new Article 119, to ensure that the principle of equal pay and equal pay for equal value is applied (see Chapter 11).

The Treaty of Nice 2003

The Nice summit (2000) gave rise to yet another Charter, that of Fundamental Rights of the European Union, which, while separate from the Social Charter, incorporates similar rights and will enable individuals to refer to the Charter in the determination of legal cases arising from national and EU contexts. The Charter is summarised in Exhibit 4.13. The Treaty of Nice came into force in 2003. It dealt mostly with reforming the EU institutions so that the Union could function efficiently after its enlargement to 25 member states.

The Reform Treaty Agreement, Brussels 2007

EU leaders agreed on a mandate for an Intergovernmental Conference to draw up the Reform Treaty at the end of 2007 with a view to implementation by 2009. The new text will make the Charter of Fundamental Rights legally binding. The UK, however, decided to opt out of the Charter. The Reform Treaty is the EU's response to the negative outcome of the French and Dutch referenda on the European Constitution in 2005.

New Labour's European agenda

The election of the Labour government signalled a more positive approach towards the EU. As we have already noted, a most significant development in the UK's relationship with the EU was the decision to end the 'opt-out' from the Social Chapter of the Maastricht Treaty, accept the Employment Chapter of the Amsterdam Treaty and in due course the Charter of Fundamental Rights agreed at the Nice Summit in 2000. However, the UK, for the time being at least, has chosen to 'opt out' of the Fundamental Rights Charter. The transposition into UK domestic legislation of the various EU Directives (see below) is having and will have important consequences for employers, trade unions and individual employees, particularly as Britain traditionally had considerably less legal regulation in the areas of employment and social policy than most other member states. The government, in line with the majority of member states, now endorses the concept of a social market economy which aims to

Exhibit 4.13

Charter of Fundamental Rights of the European Union

The Charter includes the following Articles relevant to the employment relationship. For a more detailed description, consult the website www.europa.eu.int

Article 12: Freedom of assembly and of association

Includes the implied right of everyone to form and join trade unions.

Article 21: Non-discrimination

Any discrimination based on any ground such as sex, race, colour, ethnic or social origin, genetic features, language, religion or belief, political or any other opinion, membership of a national minority, property, birth, disability, age, or sexual orientation shall be prohibited.

Article 23: Equality between men and women

Equality between men and women must be ensured in all areas, including employment, work and pay. The principle of equality shall not prevent the maintenance or adoption of measures providing for specific advantages in favour of the under-represented sex.

Article 27: Workers' right to information and consultation within the undertaking

Workers or their representatives must, at the appropriate levels, be guaranteed information and consultation in good time in the cases and under the conditions provided for by Community law and national laws and practices.

Article 28: Right of collective bargaining and collective action

Workers and employers, or their respective organisations, have, in accordance with Community law and national laws and practices, the right to negotiate and conclude collective agreements at the appropriate levels and, in cases of conflicts of interest, to take collective action to defend their interests, including strike action.

Article 30: Protection in the event of unjustified dismissal

Every worker has the right to protection against unjustified dismissal, in accordance with Community law and national laws and practices.

Article 31: Fair and just working conditions

Every worker has the right to working conditions which respect his or her health, safety and dignity. Every worker has the right to limitation of maximum working hours, to daily and weekly rest periods and to an annual period of paid leave.

Article 33: Family and professional life

The family shall enjoy legal, economic and social protection. To reconcile family and professional life, everyone shall have the right to protection from dismissal for a reason connected to maternity and the right to paid maternity leave and to parental leave following the birth or adoption of a child.

provide sustainable economic growth 'underpinned by a social dimension characterised by a commitment to a strong welfare state, a partnership between government, employers and workers, and minimum standards at work' (IRS, 1997). However, the government also has reservations concerning any social regulation that might add to the cost burdens of industry and which would impair business competitiveness. The expectation is, therefore, that the government has not, and will not adopt Directives indiscriminately, and will temper its enthusiasm for the social market with a concern for economic efficiency.

Some significant Directives adopted by New Labour include (see Chapter 11 for an up-to-date and comprehensive overview):

Posted Workers Directive: this aims to ensure fair competition and provide minimum standards of employment for workers temporarily moved to another EU member state. All member states, including the UK, implemented the Directive by 24 September 1999.

Parental Leave Directive: gives parents the right to three months' unpaid time off work. The Directive had to be implemented in the UK by 15 December 1999; the Employment Relations Act 1999 together with separate regulations gave effect to the Directive.

European Works Councils: companies with more than 1000 employees in the participating states and at least 150 workers in each of two or more of these countries must set up a European Works Council or another appropriate procedure to inform and consult employees on key organisational issues. The UK gave effect to the Directive by the end of December 1999.

Directive on part-time work: this provides for equal treatment of part-timers with full-time employees, except where 'justified by objective reasons'. The UK implemented the Directive on 1 July 2000.

Directive on the burden of proof in sex discrimination cases: this places a greater onus on the employer to prove that discrimination did not take place in such cases. The Directive was implemented in the UK on 12 October 2001.

Part-time workers; fixed-term work: the Social Partners had been negotiating on the use of fixed-term contracts since March 1988. The ensuing Directive was transposed on 1 October 2001.

Working Time Directive: sets maximum 48 working hours per week and was transposed by the UK on 17 December 1999. Certain 'excluded' sectors, such as road, rail, air and sea, are now covered.

Directive on Information and Consultation of workers: employers are required to inform and consult employees on specific issues concerning the organisation, including its activities and economic and financial situation. The Directive was adopted in 2002 and in the UK a phased implementation is proposed, dependent on the size of the employer, starting from March 2005 and with completion by 2008.

Young Workers Directive: protection for young or adolescent workers, above minimum school leaving age but below 18, not to be employed for more than 40 hours a week (8 hours a day). Implemented in UK on 6 April 2003.

Working Time Directive – excluded sector amendments: now to include those employed in road, rail, sea, inland waterway and lake transport, sea fishing and 'other work at sea' and the activities of doctors in training. Changes operational from 1 August 2003.

Acquired Rights Amendment Directive: allows for the inclusion of pensions within TUPE. UK. Implemented January 2004.

Race Directive: covers discrimination on grounds of race or ethnic origin and required changes to the Race Relations Act 1976. Changes implemented on 19 July 2003.

Equal Treatment Framework Directive: covers discrimination on grounds of religion or belief, disability, age and sexual orientation based on proposals in government consultation document *Towards Equality and Diversity* (2001–2). Implementation of proposals for religion or belief and sexual orientation by 2 December 2003; and for age and disability, 2 December 2006.

Temporary Agency Workers Directive: providing for the same treatment of agency workers compared with permanent workers. The consultation period ended on 18 October 2002. No set date for implementation.

Takeover Directive (draft): to guarantee employee consultation regarding informing and consulting workers and shareholders on takeover bids. No set date for implementation.

Summary points

- EU social policy is influenced by the political complexion of member state governments and the nature of the presidency of the Council of Ministers.
- Social policy decision making originates from proposals by the European Commission. The main decision-making bodies are the Council of Ministers, the European Parliament and the European Court of Justice, together with the Social Partners and the Economic and Social Committee.
- The legal instruments which put social policy into effect comprise regulations, directives and decisions. Instruments which are not legally binding include recommendations, opinions, resolutions and codes of practice.
- The procedures giving legal effect to proposals on directives, etc. at supranational level consist of the consultative procedure, the co-operation procedure, the co-decision procedure and agreements made by the Social Partners.
- The main Acts and treaties which govern social and economic policy are the Treaty of Rome; the Single European Act (which gave rise to the Social Charter); the Maastricht Treaty (which contains the original Social Chapter and Social Policy Protocol and Agreement); the Treaty of Amsterdam (which incorporates the 'new' Social Chapter endorsed by the UK), and the Nice Summit which agreed the Charter of Fundamental Rights.
- A more positive approach towards the EU on the part of the UK government has led to the adoption of a number of directives which are in the process of being implemented by incorporation either into new legislation such as the Employment Relations Act or by separate Regulations.

RELEVANT WEBSITES

www.acas.org.uk (Advisory, Conciliation and Arbitration Service) Provides information not only on disputes resolution but also on government initiatives in the area of general employment relations.

www.dti.gov.uk/er (Department of Trade and Industry) Contains a plethora of detail on government initiatives and policy.

www.berr.gov.uk (Department for Business, Enterprise and Regulatory Reform) The successor to the DTI.

www.eurofound.ie (European Foundation for the Improvement of Living and Working Conditions) Contains information on research projects directed and commissioned by the EU across a range of issues.

www.europa.eu.int (European Union On-Line) Full of factual information about the European Union, its institutions, legislative procedures and employment relations.

www.lowpay.gov.uk (Low Pay Commission) Annual reports on the operation of the national minimum wage.

www.statistics.gov.uk (Office for National Statistics) A wide variety of topics, including the labour force and the economy.

REFERENCES

Bach, S. (2002) 'Annual review article, 2001'. *British Journal of Industrial Relations*, 40, 2, 319–39

Bach, S., Kessler, I. and White, G. (2005) 'Employment relations and public sector "modernisation" under Labour'. *Personnel Review*, 34, 6, 629–33

Beaumont, P.B. (1992) *Public Sector Industrial Relations*. London, Routledge

Coats, D. (2007) *The National Minimum Wage: Retrospect and Prospect*. London, The Work Foundation

Crouch, C. (2003) 'The state: economic management and incomes policy', in Edwards, P. (ed.) *Industrial Relations Theory and Practice*, 2nd edn. Oxford, Blackwell

Croucher, R. and White, G. (2007) *Awareness of the Minimum Wage in the Hairdressing Industry: An evaluation of the DTI/HMRC Targeted Campaign*. Research Report for the Low Pay Commission, University of Middlesex Business School and University of Greenwich Work and Employment Research Unit. London, Low Pay Commission

Dahl, R. (1961) *Who Governs? Democracy and Power in an American City*. London, Yale University Press

Dickens, L. (2002) 'Individual statutory employment rights since 1997: constrained expansion'. *Employee Relations*, 24, 6, 619–37

Dickens, L. and Hall, M. (1995) 'The state: Labour law and industrial relations', in Edwards, P. (ed.) *Industrial Relations: Theory and Practice in Britain*. Oxford, Blackwell

Dickens, L. and Hall, M. (2003) 'Labour law and industrial relations; a new settlement?', in Edwards, P. (ed.) *Industrial Relations Theory and Practice*, 2nd edn. Oxford, Blackwell

Dolado, J., Kramarz, F., Machin, S., Manning, A., Margolis, D. and Teulings, C. (1996) 'The economic impact of minimum wages in Europe'. *Economic Policy*, No. 23, 57–71

Donovan Commission (1968) *Report of the Royal Commission on Trade Unions and Employers' Associations 1965–1968*, Cmnd 3623. London, HMSO

DTI (Department for Trade and Industry) (1998) *Fairness at Work*, Cm 2968. London, HMSO

Dunnett, A. (1998) *Understanding the Economy: An Introduction to Macroeconomics*. London, Longman

Edwards, P.K. (1994) 'Discipline and the creation of order', in Sisson, K. (ed.) *Personnel Management*, 2nd edn. Oxford, Blackwell

Farnham, D. and Pimlott, J. (1995) *Understanding Industrial Relations*. London, Cassell

Fernie, S. and Metcalf, M. (1996) *Low Pay and Minimum Wages: The British Evidence*. LSE: Centre for Economic Performance

Fisher, I. (1911) *The Purchasing Power of Money*. New York, Macmillan

Friedman, M. (1962) *Capitalism and Freedom*. Chicago, University of Chicago Press

Friedman, M. (1968) 'The role of monetary policy'. *American Economic Review*, 58, March, 1–17

Garrard, A. and Martin, W. (1996) *Labour's Economics: Can Mr Blair do it?* London, UBS Global Research

Gennard, J. (2002) 'Employee relations and public policy developments, 1997–2001'. *Employee Relations*, 24, 6, 581–94

Gospel, H. and Palmer, G. (1993) *British Industrial Relations*. London, Routledge

Green, D.G. (1987) *The New Right: The Counter-revolution in Political, Economic and Social Thought*. Brighton, Wheatsheaf Books

Hall, M. (1992) 'Behind the European Works Council Directives: the European Commission's legislative strategy'. *British Journal of Industrial Relations*, 30, 4, 547–66

Hall, M. (1994) 'Industrial relations and the social dimension', in Hyman, R. and Ferner, A. (eds) *New Frontiers in European Industrial Relations*. Oxford, Blackwell

Hayek, F.A. (1978) *The Road to Serfdom*. London, Routledge

Hayek, F.A. (1984) *1980s' Unemployment and the Unions*. Hobart Paper 87. London, IEA

Hobsbawm, E.J. (1974) *Labouring Men: Studies in the History of Labour*. London, Weidenfeld & Nicolson

Howell, C. (2005) *Trade Unions and the State*. Woodstock, Princeton University Press

Hutton, W. (1995) *The State We're In*. London, Jonathan Cape

Hyman, R. (1984) *Strikes*. London, Fontana

Hyman, R. (2003) 'The historical evolution of British industrial relations', in Edwards, P. (ed.) *Industrial Relations Theory and Practice*, 2nd edn. Oxford, Blackwell

IRS (1997) 'Labour's European agenda'. *IRS Employment Review*, No. 639

IRS (1999a) 'Employment law update: What's next from Brussels?'. *IRS Employment Review*, No. 671

IRS (1999b) 'New ground rules for employment relations'. *IRS Employment Review*, No. 674

Kahn-Freund, O. (1954) 'The legal framework', in Flanders, A. and Clegg, H.A. (eds) *The System of Industrial Relations in Great Britain*. Oxford, Blackwell

Kahn-Freund, O. (1977) *Labour and the Law*. London, Stevens

Kessler, S. and Bayliss, F. (1995) *Contemporary British Industrial Relations*. London, Macmillan

Kessler, S. and Bayliss, F. (1998) *Contemporary British Industrial Relations*, 2nd edn. London, Macmillan

Kirk, R. and Wall, A. (2002) 'The private finance initiative'. *Public Management Review*, 1, 4, 529–47

Leat, M. (1999) 'The European Union', in Hollinshead, G., Nicholls, P. and Tailby, S. (eds) *Employee Relations*. London, Financial Times/Pitman Publishing

Lourie, J. (1997) *National Minimum Wage Bill*. Research Paper 97/133. House of Commons

Low Pay Commission (1998) *The National Minimum Wage: First Report of the Low Pay Commission*. Cmnd 3976, London, HMSO

Low Pay Commission (2002) *National Minimum Wage Annual Report (2002)*. www.lowpay.gov.uk

Low Pay Commission (2007) *National Minimum Wage Annual Report (2007)*. www.lowpay.gov.uk

Machin, S. (1997) 'A national minimum wage: who would be affected and the effect on employment', in Philpot, J. (ed.) *Implementing a National Minimum Wage*. London, Employment Policy Institute

MacInnes, J. (1987) *Thatcherism at Work*. Milton Keynes, Open University Press

Marx, K. and Engels, F. (1967) *The Communist Manifesto*. London, Penguin

McKendrick, J. and McCabe, W. (1997) 'An observer's tale: Stonehaven Community Hospital'. *Public Money and Management*. 17, 3, 17–20

McIlroy, J. (1991) *The Permanent Revolution? Conservative Law and the Trade Unions*. Nottingham, Spokesman

Minford, P. (1985) *Unemployment, Cause and Cure*, 2nd edn. Oxford, Blackwell

Pass, C. and Lowes, B. (1998) *Collins Dictionary of Economics*. Glasgow, HarperCollins

Phillips, A.W. (1958) 'The relation between unemployment and the rate of change of money wage rates in the United Kingdom, 1816–1957'. *Economics*, 25, 283–99

Philpott, J. (ed.) (1997) *Implementing a National Minimum Wage in the UK: Key Issues for the Low Pay Commission*. London, Economic Policy Institute

Rubery, J. and Edwards, P. (2003) 'Low pay and the national minimum wage', in Edwards, P. (ed.) *Industrial Relations Theory and Practice*, 2nd edn. Oxford, Blackwell

Schulten, T. (1996) 'European Works Councils: prospects of a new system of European industrial relations'. *European Journal of Industrial Relations*, 2, 3, 303–24

Schumpeter, J. (1976) *Capitalism, Socialism and Democracy*. London, Allen and Unwin

Smith, P. and Morton, G. (2001) 'New Labour's reform of Britain's employment law: the devil is not only in the detail but in the values and policy too'. *British Journal of Industrial Relations*, 39, 1, 119–38

Smith, P. and Morton, G. (2006) 'Nine years of New Labour: neoliberalism and workers' rights'. *British Journal of Industrial Relations*, 44, 3, 401–20

Taylor, R. (1998) 'Review article 1997'. *British Journal of Industrial Relations*, 36, 2, 293–331

TUC (2002) 'TUC welcomes government's £10m crackdown on scrooge bosses', Press Release (September)

Weber, M. (1978) *Economy and Society: An Outline of Interpretive Sociology*. Berkeley, University of California Press

Wedderburn, K. (1986) *The Worker and the Law*. London, Penguin

White Paper (1969) *In Place of Strife*. London, HMSO

White Paper (1970) *Fair Deal at Work*. London, HMSO

EMPLOYEE PARTICIPATION, PARTNERSHIP AND INVOLVEMENT

INTRODUCTION

The term 'employee voice' has been used in the wider context associated with trade union decline in Britain during the 1980s and 1990s as in: 'Have employees lost their voice?' (Millward *et al.*, 2000, ch. 4). It incorporates the formal mechanisms of employee participation and both the formal and informal activities of workplace representatives on the one hand, and direct means of communication on the other. Employee voice channels are also found in non-union organisations and workplaces, although not to the same extent as in unionised workplaces. In this chapter we use 'employee voice' not as a concept per se but as a 'catch-all' term used to cover a wide range of processes and structures which allow and even empower employees, directly or indirectly, to contribute to decision making within the organisation.

Employee participation is concerned with the representation of worker interests within the organisation's decision-making process, the emphasis being upon representation and formality. In this book, and this chapter particularly, a clear distinction is made between employee participation on the one hand, and employee involvement on the other. It is necessary to make this distinction because, contrary to some views, there is in practice no staged process from involvement to participation which employers adopt in order to secure worker representation in the decision-making process, although ideally and normatively employers should practice both. More importantly, it is erroneous to extend the term employee or worker participation to practices which are more appropriately labelled 'involvement'. As a theoretical construct, the involvement–participation continuum has its uses, as we shall see. Indeed, we argue that most employers shy away from formal machinery which facilitates 'employee voice' and at best they are 'reluctant participators'.

'Partnership', 'social partnership' and 'partnership agreements' are relatively recent terms which have entered the lexicon of employment relations. Social partnership is characteristic of northern European countries such as Germany, Austria, the Netherlands and Scandinavia and denotes mostly formal arrangements and structures of negotiation and joint consultation between unions and employers at national, sectoral and workplace levels. At workplace level, probably the most salient example of partnership based on consensus is the works council, considered in greater detail later in the chapter. Despite the rhetoric of partnership which was manifested in the approach of the first New Labour government, the concept, as Terry (2003) points out, does not sit easily within the UK context in the absence of a legislative framework of the type that exists in some European nations, and without the requisite degree of 'shared commitment to commercial success, the balance between change (flexibility) and security, and the emphasis on dialogue and expertise' (p. 279). Nevertheless, the TUC endorsed the concept at national and organisational levels and encouraged the formation of partnership agreements between employers, unions and employees.

Within most work organisations in Britain, structures and mechanisms of formal employee participation do not feature very prominently. Apart from the machinery of collective bargaining and the 'pseudo' participation which often characterises joint consultative committees (see below), employees, more often than not, are unable to give voice to their collective interests through formal participative structures such as works councils, a situation exacerbated by the anti-collectivist ideology of 1980s' Thatcherism. Within the employment relationship in Britain, industrial action, as an expression of collective concern and power of employees, is often the only means of facilitating the bargaining process in order to achieve a favourable outcome to negotiations. The absence of democratic structures in many work organisations is at odds with the liberal democratic structures which exist within the wider European context, and is a problem which, arguably, should be addressed. Apart from adopting the European Works Council Directive, much more could have been done by the first Blair government through, for example, the introduction of legislation providing a statutory right to collective representation for all employees, possibly on the lines of the national works council system which operates in many EU countries. While formal participatory structures may not eliminate industrial action, the establishment of a general framework for informing and consulting employees might encourage employers and employee representatives to work 'in a spirit of co-operation' rather than conflict (EU Directive on worker information and consultation, 2001, partially implemented in 2005 and fully implemented by 2008).

Employee participation, according to Farnham (1997), is one of four policy choices open to managements in determining their industrial relations strategies 'including how work relations are structured, how work is organised and what emphasis they [management] should adopt in managing people at work' (p. 354). The other three choices are:

- worker subordination via managerial prerogative (see Chapter 2);
- union incorporation via collective bargaining (see Chapter 5); and
- employee commitment via employee involvement practices.

There is no satisfactory definition of participation partly because of the numerous and varied practices which are labelled 'participation', partly because there are normative and ideological connotations, and partly because there are semantic problems with 'participation' and related terms such as industrial democracy and employee involvement. At the most general level, participation can be unsatisfactorily defined as **the extent to which employees and their representatives should and do enter into joint decision making with management and its representatives**. This definition says nothing about the extent or depth of participation, the motives of the parties concerned, the degree of influence the parties exert upon one another, or the organisational structures most appropriate to the participation process.

Space does not permit a lengthy examination of these issues (see Hyman and Mason, 1995; Marchington and Parker, 1990; and Harley *et al.*, 2005, for a detailed analysis of these and other topics) and we shall confine ourselves to considering briefly the important terms relevant to participation before looking at the distinction between employee involvement (EI) and employee participation. We then go on to look at the extent of employee participation initiatives in Britain and why they have not been particularly successful. The relatively successful type of employee participation based upon the German system of 'co-determination' is considered in greater detail before dealing finally with European Works Councils. We then look at the empirical work which traces the extent of employee voice in the UK using the results of the Workplace Employment Relations Surveys for 1998 (Cully *et al.*, 1999) and 2004 (Kersley *et al.*, 2006). Finally we look at the extent of the partnership ethos in Britain and the success or otherwise of partnership agreements concluded to date.

Learning outcomes

When you have read this chapter, you should be able to:

1. Understand the nature and scope of employee participation and related terms.

2. Distinguish between 'employee involvement' and 'employee participation' and identify the main types of employee participation practised in Britain.

3. Explain the workings of the 'co-determination' system and the role and functions of European Works Councils.

4. Identify the extent of employee voice mechanisms in the UK.

5. Assess the degree of success or otherwise of social partnership and partnership agreements.

6. Explain the nature of employee involvement.

THE NATURE AND CONTEXT OF EMPLOYEE PARTICIPATION

There are two distinct approaches which have shaped participatory organisational structures in Western Europe during the post-Second World War period. The first approach concerns the rise of 'managerialism' (see Chapter 2) and the resurrection of managerial prerogatives during the 1980s together with the dominance of HRM practices. This approach considers employee influence in terms of 'involvement' in order to achieve certain organisational goals. The decision-making agenda, particularly concerning strategic issues, is set by management, as are the organisational goals and values to which employees are meant to be committed. While employees are denied influence over management decisions, Hyman and Mason (1995) assert that:

> In responding to the urgency of . . . market uncertainties and signals few employers can afford to be deflected by employee objections or encumbered by constitutional obstacles constructed by their unions. HRM seeks to find a solution to this conundrum by involving employees in task-based activities, but also alerting them to the precarious nature of paid work in a dynamic market environment through systems of communication and information provision.

> It might also be argued that HRM can serve to reduce or eliminate the potential of trade unions to materially interfere with management decision making processes or outcomes. (p. 6)

This, approach, therefore, emphasises employee involvement (EI) concerning job- and task-based decisions rather than operational and strategic managerial decisions. The second approach incorporates the strategy evidenced in most European Union countries and views participation as an employee right to question and influence organisational decision making. This has resulted in formalised structures of participation underpinned by legislation and based on representative democracy.

Self-evaluation activity 6.1

Main parties to employee participation
The response is given below

Identify the main parties concerned with employee participation together with the interests of each in the participatory process.

The main parties concerned are labour, employers and the democratic state. All three have different interests attributed to them of a largely ideological nature concerning the participatory process. These are considered in turn.

1. Employee interests

According to Hyman and Mason (1995), writers in the radical tradition contend that employees have little or no formal influence at work within a capitalist society. They argue for total democratisation of the workplace which implies, in a Marxist sense, partial or complete control over the means of production as a precondition. Instead of 'employee or worker participation', radical theorists prefer to use the term industrial democracy, and in situations where workers have total control over the means of production (that is, in socialist states), workers' control. Industrial democracy as a concept is concerned with both direct and indirect representation. In the former situation, employees represent themselves individually, and directly influence and jointly determine decisions with management (management being assumed to be just as necessary a function within such organisations as within conventional organisations) without intermediaries or representatives. By definition, this can take place only within smaller organisations, the main examples of which are worker co-operatives. In the latter situation, employee representatives make decisions on behalf of their constituents, and it is here that we have the industrial equivalent of parliamentary democracy.

However, there is some debate as to what actually constitutes 'true' industrial democracy: should it, for example, be regarded as an ongoing process of 'encroaching control', whereby trade unions progressively gain experience of managerial functions and responsibilities through the extension of collective bargaining (see Chapter 5); or should it involve trade unions and/or employees appropriating and supplanting economic and political control of industrial organisations? Also, if industrial democracy is to emulate parliamentary democracy, there should be provision for the 'opposition' to become the 'government'. Moreover, in capitalist societies this analogy is inappropriate because the 'opposition' of employees and their unions is a permanent one, and despite degrees of joint decision making, the more apposite analogy would be that of the one-party state.

2. Employer interests

Writers in what Hyman and Mason (1995) call the conservative tradition are associated with employers' interests and managerial needs 'to direct and control the labour of subordinates under conditions which can be alienating, insecure and poorly rewarded materially and motivationally' (p. 9). This does not preclude enhancing the motivational content of work, stressing employee involvement in task-related activities and management exercises in raising employee performance, as long as these produce positive outcomes for employers and contribute towards the economic success of the organisation. Most employers in Britain have not been proactive in matters of participation. The main reasons for this state of affairs include the following:

- The need, perceived or real, to **reinforce and confirm the legitimacy of managerial power and decision making**, particularly within a unitarist framework (see Chapter 2).
- The need to **manage and contain conflict in the interests of preserving harmonious relationships**; this, again, is part of the unitary ideology of management. Union avoidance is a major strategy; we may call this the push strategy, which involves pushing against trade unions and their activists. Another major strategy is the desire on the part of some employers to create an organisational environment in which employees do not feel the need for outside protection; this can be termed a pull strategy, which involves pulling employees towards employers by offering certain inducements such as rewarding individual effort and employee shareholding schemes. Ramsay (1977) has argued that there are certain patterns or 'cycles' which can be discerned over time (called the cycles of control thesis). During periods of economic growth and prosperity which have traditionally been accompanied by increased levels of trade union activity, Ramsay argues that employer efforts to harness greater employee involvement are intensified as the 'union threat' increases. Conversely, during periods of recession or economic stagnation, employer interest in involvement techniques wanes as trade union activity wanes. While Ramsay's argument would appear to be more applicable to the post-war period prior to 1979, it has been criticised by others such as Ackers et al. (1996) and Marchington (2005), who argue that employee involvement techniques are introduced by employers for a variety of reasons apart from cyclical ones. They argue that during the 1980s and 1990s the greater demands upon companies generally to compete in, and respond effectively to, the increasingly stringent requirements of both national and global product markets has put

employee involvement and HRM much higher on the managerial agenda. Moreover, Ramsey's cycles analysis 'failed to predict the growth of direct participation since the 1980s [but] still helps to explain why indirect participation has declined as trade union power has reduced' (Marchington, 2005, p. 35)

- The need to **maintain, sustain and increase productivity** and to pursue **motivational objectives** has been of perennial concern to employers ever since F.W. Taylor's (1947) work on 'scientific management' and the growth of Fordist production systems enabled workers to maximise their incomes through increased productivity (see Chapters 2 and 5). This was followed by the subsequent growth of the 'human relations' and 'neo-human relations' streams of management thought (encapsulated in the work of Argyris (1964), Herzberg (1974), Likert (1961) and McGregor (1960), to name but a few), which emphasised that greater motivation, higher levels of job satisfaction, appropriate leadership styles and effective teamworking could contribute to greater employee well-being and facilitate employee integration into the production process. Again, as Blyton and Turnbull (1998) point out:

> *The human relations [and neo-human relations] view is consistent with a managerial orientation which is strongly unitarist in perspective. More than this, however, management's advocacy of certain types of participation represents an acknowledgement that employee commitment needs to be actively secured rather than passively assumed, and that involving employees in decision making is a means of achieving this. Management's support for [some forms of] participation is also an acknowledgement of the potential contribution of employee knowledge to the management of the organisation – in particular tapping valuable worker experience regarding the way work tasks are organised and performed. More generally this management orientation is an acknowledgement that many employees seek not only financial recompense from work but also a more extensive engagement with the institution in which they spend a large proportion of their waking hours.* (p. 222)

- The need for **enterprise consciousness** among employees, according to Hyman and Mason (1995) 'echoes unitarist human relations principles [and]

can be found within contemporary constructions of "human resource management"' (p. 11). Practices, which more accurately can be described as 'employee involvement', include team briefings, quality circles, *kaizen*-oriented activities and cascading communications.

3. The democratic state

Democratic institutions can only survive and prosper within a democratic state, but even so, apart from political democracy, fully democratic institutions and organisations are relatively rare, most often confined in Britain to membership organisations which are largely voluntary, and to trade unions and related associations. We examined the role of government and the state in Chapter 4. In Britain and the United States, government has been relatively abstentionist in the industrial relations arena, but rarely neutral: Labour governments before 1980 have tended to enact protective and enabling legislation favouring collective organisation often within a corporatist framework, while Conservative governments tended to favour employers and their organisations. Overall, before 1979, governments became more actively involved if the balance of power favoured one party over another. They often (but not always) acted upon recommendations of major government commissions such as the Whitley Commission in 1917, which established negotiating committees at national level, and the Donovan Commission in 1968, which confirmed the value of collective bargaining entered into freely by the parties concerned and underlined the view that collective bargaining between independent unions and employers constituted the most appropriate form of 'industrial democracy' within a pluralist society. The only government commission dealing specifically with employee participation and industrial democracy, the Bullock Commission which reported in 1977, produced recommendations which were not taken up by any subsequent government. Government inaction in the employee participation area contrasts sharply with the experience of other European countries, particularly those within the European Union, where legislation has been enacted to promote representative structures of participation, which in the case of Germany applies to the vast majority of organisations in both the public and private sectors.

The 1980–97 period of Conservative governments was, as we have seen (Chapter 4), one of regulation and restriction of trade union powers but witnessed two

fairly modest measures incorporating the introduction of tax incentives for companies operating employee share ownership and profit-related pay schemes and the introduction of a requirement for companies to report on employee participation initiatives in their annual reports. The New Labour governments spanning the period 1997–2007 introduced the following initiatives:

- Clearer obligations on employers to consult on collective redundancies and transfer of undertakings in both unionised and non-unionised organisations.
- The implementation in 1999 of the European Directive on European Works Councils (1994).
- Implementation of the Information and Consultation Directive (2002).
- Funding for training of managers and employee representatives to facilitate partnerships at work.

Employee participation: an overview

We have already noted that there is considerable semantic confusion concerning the term 'employee participation'. We could, for example, opt for the all-embracing definition put forward by Wall and Lischeron (1977) as the 'influence in decision making exerted through a process of interaction between workers and managers' (p. 38). For our purposes, this definition is too general as it incorporates 'employee involvement', and also raises questions concerning complexities and variations in practice as pointed out by Blyton and Turnbull (1994, 1998). For example, there are issues relating to the:

- **depth of participation** concerning the extent to which employees or their representatives influence the final decision. This can range from *minimal* (little or no involvement) to *moderate* as with joint consultation, decision making, collective bargaining and works councils, to *dominant* as with worker co-operatives;

- **range or scope** of decisions which are open to participation. This is determined by the willingness of the parties, particularly management, to broaden the scope (as with *co-operative bargaining*), the structure and size of the organisation and whether participation is required by legislation;
- **forms of participation structure**, of which there are many, ranging from suggestion schemes to board-level representation; there may be *formal* and *informal* mechanisms and activities, and *direct* or *indirect* methods;
- **levels at which participation takes place**; ranging from unit, or department to workplace where it is usually *direct*, often *informal*, and *task- or work-based*; and
- **purpose and outcomes of participatory activity**, which may be merely to communicate and inform employees of a decision that has already been made (sometimes referred to as *pseudo participation*).

We are now in a position to place participation within the whole range of activities whereby employees may be able to influence managerial decisions. Blyton and Turnbull (1998), for example, have devised the model shown in Figure 6.1 which they call 'a continuum of employee participation'. Although useful in helping us to place different types of involvement and participation, it omits the other variables that we looked at above. The following headings incorporate the essential characteristics of involvement and participation which extend from 'no involvement' to 'full employee control' and which are identified in Figure 6.2 (we choose some, but not all of the above variables):

A. Values and ideology (attitudes and approaches to power and the employment relationship)
B. Definitions of involvement/participation
C. Forms of involvement/participation
D. Levels of decision making.

Figure 6.1 Blyton and Turnbull's continuum of employee participation
Source: Blyton, P. and Turnbull, P., *The Dynamics of Employee Relations*, 2nd edn, 1998, Macmillan reproduced with permission of Palgrave Macmillan.

Values/ideology	Definitions	Forms of participation/ involvement	Levels of decision making
1. **Unitary view:** the enforcement and legitimisation of clear, hierarchical command in the interests of economic efficiency	1. No involvement or participation, apart from enjoying the economic benefits of the enterprise	1. Formal hierarchy and downward communication between management and shop floor	1. Possibly social and welfare (health and safety, recreational facilities, pension funds, etc.)
2. **Integrative:** the harmonisation of management/workforce objectives under the 'human relations' leadership of management. Strong but primitive HRM orientation	2. A process whereby the employee can and/or does individually exert some control over decision making concerning the task and/or job. Typical 'employee involvement' techniques	2. Direct individual and group involvement through job enlargement, job enrichment, flexibility arrangements, team briefings, 'kaizen' arrangements, suggestion schemes. Some profit-sharing. The role of collective representation, where it exists, is minimised	2. Personnel and HRM: hiring and firing, apprenticeship, manning levels, etc.
3. **Distributive and pluralist:** the progressive or more sudden transfer of power from management to employee on a 'power-sharing' basis but where management retains ultimate control	3. A process whereby employees exert collective influence over decision making and the labour process	3. Genuine 'employee participation'. Indirect collective participation either through: (a) trade unions and collective bargaining; or, (b) new forms of representation such as worker directors and works councils	3. Shared economic control or co-determination within the enterprise: (a) over technical matters such as methods of production; and (b) over business methods such as pricing, marketing, product choice and design, etc.
4. **Complete democratisation** of enterprises. New, democratic organisational forms	4. A process whereby employees exert full collective control over all decision making and the labour process	4. (a) Direct democracy in smaller enterprises such as producer co-operatives (b) Indirect democracy in larger enterprises within a system of 'workers' control or 'self-management'	4. (a) Employee decision making at all levels in co-operatives within capitalist society (b) Supra-enterprise policy making (economic decisions at regional and national levels) within a 'socialist' society

Figure 6.2 Positioning employee participation

The framework in Figure 6.2 incorporates many of the factors and characteristics that you may have considered. It demonstrates the theoretical logic of progression from one type of involvement or participation to another, and in this sense represents a more detailed continuum than that of Blyton and Turnbull. However, the evidence for such a progression either within capitalist or erstwhile socialist countries is slender indeed. It should also be pointed out that many of these examples are ephemeral as, for example, Yugoslav 'self-management', employee

directors in British Steel and the Post Office, and the three large industrial co-operatives in Britain during the early 1970s (such as the Triumph Meriden co-operative). What Figure 6.2 does, however, is place employee participation firmly in the third category, with the main examples of collective bargaining and other forms of worker representation such as the German 'co-determination' example being relatively enduring features, especially when compared with most other forms of involvement and the 'industrial democracy' examples of the fourth category.

Employee involvement and employee participation contrasted

Having identified employee participation (EP) within the continuum detailed in Figure 6.1, we can now distinguish quite clearly between EI and EP. In this respect, the definitions of both EP and EI provided by Hyman and Mason (1995) are quite adequate for our purposes. They define EP as:

state initiatives which promote the collective rights of employees to be represented in organisational decision making, or to the consequences of the efforts of employees themselves to establish collective representation in corporate decisions, possibly in the face of employer resistance. This definition would include collective bargaining over terms and conditions of employment. (p. 21)

EI is defined as:

practices and policies which emanate from management and sympathisers of free market commercial activity and which purport to provide employees with the opportunity to influence and where appropriate take part in the decision making on matters which affect them. (p. 21)

EI, then, is usually instigated and controlled by management often, but not always, espousing a unitary ideology concerning the employment relationship. Management sets the agenda which is consistent with requirements for a flexible and adaptable workforce within a competitive product market. Information disseminated by management concerning the enterprise as a whole is normally not subject to any decision-making input from employees, although employees are expected to respond positively towards it. Employee decision making, as we have already noted earlier in this chapter, is normally confined to task-based activities.

Self-evaluation activity 6.2

Main characteristics of employee participation
This SEA has no commentary

We have identified the main characteristics of employee involvement. Attempt a short paragraph, similar to the one above, which describes the main characteristics of employee participation, and compare your efforts with what is included in Figure 6.3.

Employee participation	Employee involvement
Mainly pluralist	*Mainly unitarist*
1. Inspired by government and/or workforce with some control delegated to workers	1. Inspired and controlled by management
2. Aims to harness collective employee inputs through market regulation	2. Oriented towards encouraging individual employee inputs through market regulation
3. Collective representation	3. Directed to responsibilities of individual employees
4. Management and organisational hierarchies chain of command broken	4. Management and organisational structures flatter but hierarchies undisturbed
5. Active involvement of employee representatives	5. Employees are often passive recipients of information and decisions already made
6. Decision making at higher organisational levels	6. Decisions tend to be task-based
7. Plurality of interests recognised and machinery for their resolution provided	7. Assumes common interests between employer and employees
8. Aims to distribute strategic influence beyond management	8. Aims to concentrate strategic influence among management

Figure 6.3 Essentials of EP and EI
Source: Based on Hyman and Mason, 1995, p. 25

Rationale, approaches and initiatives of EP

Rationale

As we have seen, employee participation usually emerges from a collective employee interest, supported by political ideas, parties and governments receptive to such ideas and practices. Employers, on the other hand, have usually resisted participatory ideas and practices. Hyman and Mason (1995) provide an example of employer prejudice to the participation proposals of the Bullock Committee of Inquiry on Industrial Democracy (1977):

> Tensions between the contrasting interests of employers and labour became evident in the UK during the late 1970s: during this period, political expediency to mobilise union support was articulated by a strong (if patchy) union impetus towards participative arrangements which were capable of propelling employee interests beyond the areas bounded by collective bargaining alone. Together these movements manifested in proposals for worker directors, planning agreements and joint representative councils. The most ambitious of these initiatives was undoubtedly the attempt to introduce a participative framework based on worker directors using the formula of a unitary board composed of equal numbers of shareholder and union appointees supplemented by a minority of 'neutral' directors. These proposals, made by a majority of members sitting on the Bullock Committee established by the Labour government, were subsequently frustrated by internal divisions in the union movement, a lack of political will by the then ruling but tottering government, and the concerted opposition of employers and Conservative politicians toward threatened erosion of managerial decision making and hierarchical prerogatives. In brief, the confrontational stances implicit in traditional voluntaristic industrial relations as expressed in a preference for collective bargaining were unable, ideologically or practically, to accommodate the joint concessions required by the parties for the adoption of alternative participative arrangements. The subsequent emergence and realisation of the 'Thatcherite' enterprise economy effectively removed any formal government policy attachment toward collective participation in the UK during the 1980s and early 1990s. (pp. 29–30)

Factors external to the organisation of work strengthened the rationale for employee participation during the 1960s and 1970s. For example, it was felt that rising levels of educational attainment would result in more critical questioning of the assumptions underlying everyday organisations and institutions and possibly lead to their restructuring on democratic lines. An increasingly intellectually sophisticated population would no longer accept the societal status quo unquestioningly, and as Salamon (1998) states: 'The period saw the demise of the "deferential society" and the rise of the "democratic imperative": that is those who will be substantially affected by decisions made by social and political institutions must be involved in the making of those decisions' (p. 358). Pressures for greater participation were also evident in order to counter the alienating tendencies of Fordist production systems and this gave rise to various experiments in 'autonomous working groups', particularly in Norway and Sweden.

The British Labour governments of the 1960s and 1970s supported limited intervention to establish formal systems of employee participation, although it was not until the formation of the Bullock Committee itself that any serious attempt to establish a statutory national framework for employee participation became apparent: a White Paper published in 1978 recommended setting up Joint Representative Committees 'which, in organisations of over 2000 employees could instigate a ballot of employees to secure one-third employee representation on the board' (Salamon, 1998, p. 359). The Bullock Committee recommendations and the subsequent White Paper were not acted upon, and a change of government in 1979 ensured that they never would be. There were two significant attempts to introduce worker directors, into the British Steel Corporation in 1967 and the Post Office in 1977, but these 'experiments' were relatively short-lived and there were various problems with them.

While national initiatives for employee participation petered out in Britain during the 1980s and early 1990s, government support for collective

participation remained strong in individual European countries and within the European Union. Hyman and Mason (1995) identify the following conditions necessary for participation to thrive:

- A supportive political environment, enabling 'a balance of worker and employer influence through collective participation' to be achieved through supportive legislation.
- The important influence of stable social democratic governments, such as those in pre-1980 Germany (then West Germany) and Sweden. In the case of Germany, the ascendancy to power of the Christian Democrats under the Chancellorship of Kohl made no difference to the consensus between government, unions and employers in maintaining the statutory system of employee participation, or 'co-determination'.
- The maintenance of broad political consensus concerning the concept and practice of participation, seen as necessary 'for the regulation of an otherwise undisciplined labour market' (p. 30).
- Stability, encouraged through a 'sharing of responsibility for company performance by the individuals involved' and the belief that 'open confrontation between representatives of capital and labour is not necessarily the most beneficial approach to meet the longer-term interests of either party' (p. 30).

Approaches

Self-evaluation activity 6.3
Approaches to participation
The response is given below

Can you think of at least three approaches to participation which are practised in Britain and other European countries?

We can identify six approaches to participation (which, with the exception of collective bargaining, are described more fully in this chapter):

1. **Collective bargaining**: Collective bargaining has been considered in Chapter 5, where it was argued that a broadening of the scope of bargaining from conjunctive to co-operative, or from distributive to integrative, would provide employees in unionised organisations with the appropriate means to participate in major areas of decision making. In this context, partnership agreements are important (see below).
2. **Collective employee share schemes**: These are schemes which encourage the accumulation of wealth through the collective ownership and administration of company shares 'which would offer institutional influence to union shareholders similar to that enjoyed by pension funds and other collective bodies' (Hyman and Mason, 1995, p. 37).
3. **Works councils**: These are found in most European countries and while their structures vary both between and within countries, they are wholly representative bodies comprising employees and sometimes employer representatives who have both a right to receive company information concerning its policies and activities and a right to be consulted on issues prior to their implementation. Works councils often operate in both the public and private sectors of industry.
4. **Representation on company boards**: Organisations which operate formally constituted works councils will also have higher-level representational bodies such as 'management' or 'supervisory' boards with roughly equal representation and, higher still, employee representation on company boards. Management boards meet less frequently than works councils and consider matters of longer-term and strategic importance. Their function is to monitor and sometimes help formulate company policy and strategy over a wide range of issues. Decisions made at this level are referred upwards to the company board on which a minority of employee representatives sit.
5. **Joint Consultative Committees (JCCs)**: Joint consultation between employers and employees is concerned with the discussion of issues and 'matters of joint concern which are not the subject of negotiation with trade unions' (Donovan, 1968, p. 15). Management tends to determine the issues for discussion and reserves the right to decide the final outcome without 'subjecting it to joint agreement with employees or their representatives' (Salamon, 1998, p. 233). The forum for such discussions is known as the Joint Consultative Committee.
6. **European Works Councils**: Not to be confused with company works councils, European Works Councils (EWCs) were formed as a result of the 1994 European Works Council Directive of the European Union. The Directive provides for EWCs to be set up

in any multinational organisation employing at least 1000 employees where there are at least 150 employees in each of two member states. An EWC meets once a year to discuss strategic aspects of the company's activities including the structure, finance and economic policies of the company, production, sales and employment issues, introduction of new working methods or production processes, transfers of production, mergers, closures and redundancies.

Initiatives

The main initiatives in Europe have come from individual governments and the European Union itself. We confine ourselves here to the role of the European Union in encouraging the adoption and spread of employee representation systems. As long ago as 1970, before Britain's entry into the European Economic Community (as it was called then) in 1973, proposals for a 'European Company' with employee representation on a 'two-tier' board and works council were under discussion by the Central Council of Ministers. These discussions were based on the so-called draft Fifth Directive

introduced in 1972 dealing with company law, which included proposals for employee representation. The discussions were suspended amidst disagreement in 1982, and it was not until 1989 that a European Company Statute was introduced which included plans for employee participation compatible with the Fifth Directive (Hyman and Mason, 1995).

Brief history of the Fifth Directive

The Directive (see Exhibit 6.1) required that in companies employing more than 500 people there should be management board representation. Owing to opposition from employers and Conservative politicians in Britain, the draft directive was not ratified, and in 1983 the requirements were watered down: EU member states were invited to introduce employee participation either through management/ supervisory board representation, or through works councils.

After the Fifth Directive

With the advent of the Single European Market, further proposals for employee participation were put forward in 1989 within the Statute for the European Company. These proposals had originally

Exhibit 6.1

What the Fifth Directive says

The original version of 1972 would have guaranteed a measure of employee participation in certain circumstances. It would have required limited companies with 500 or more employees to set up a two-tier board system with supervisory and management functions. The supervisory board with minority employee representation would have had the right to nominate and dismiss members of the management board. The management board would have been required to submit a report every three months on the state of company affairs to the supervisory board. The authorisation of the supervisory board would have been needed for the closure or transfer of the company or substantial parts of it, for substantial curtailment or extension of the company's activities, for substantial changes of organisation within the company and for the establishment or termination of long-term co-operation with other companies.

The original proposal was watered down in 1975 and again in 1983, thus allowing for a more nebulous form of participation and a higher employment threshold level of 1000 employees or more. These later provisions 'represent considerable relaxation as compared to the earlier proposals and leave a great deal of latitude to Member States in the choice of management systems' (Vandamme, 1986, p. 143). However, the Commission's (and the European Parliament's) perseverance has not been rewarded, and in face of opposition from UNICE (the European employers' organisation) and the British Conservative government, negotiations dragged on aimlessly.

Source: Bridgford and Stirling, 1994, p. 144

been put forward as a draft Regulation in 1970, then amended in 1975 and put to rest in 1982. This memorandum is even more defensive than the reconstituted Fifth Directive and no further action has been taken.

In 1980, the Vredeling Directive (named after the European Commissioner responsible for social affairs at the time) was introduced. It required public limited companies with complex structures, such as multinational companies, and with more than 100 employees to provide employees' representatives at local level with regular information concerning company-wide matters including its economic and financial position, its employment situation, its production and investment plans and its plans for introducing new working methods. Companies were also required to consult employee representatives when planning decisions might be detrimental to employees' interests; such decisions could involve closures, mergers and the like. If companies refused to provide such information, member states could impose penalties on the offenders, and employee representatives would also be entitled to seek more company information if that provided was deemed to be insufficient. Again, as a result of opposition, the Commission produced an amended version in 1983 which increased the threshold to 1000 employees, reduced the frequency with which information should be given, and restricted the type of information to be given.

As we saw in Chapter 4, the Community Charter of Fundamental Social Rights for Workers (signed by all member states except Britain in 1989 and commonly known as the Social Charter) emphasised the importance of information, consultation and participation of workers in companies or groups of companies with subsidiaries in two or more member states. Further decisions affecting employee rights were made at the inter-governmental conference in Maastricht in 1991 which resulted in the Treaty of European Union (known as the Maastricht Treaty). The treaty contained the so-called Social Chapter, which Britain initially refused to sign under the Conservatives but which was endorsed by the New Labour government in 1998. The Social Chapter provides for 12 fundamental rights to workers. These have been translated into practical proposals for government action within the so-called Action Plan, and numbers

17 and 18 deal generally with rights to information, consultation and participation in decision making. The proposals for information disclosure and consultation closely follow the Vredeling Directive outlined above. In December 1990 the Commission produced a Directive on European Works Councils. We now go on to consider three forms of participation in greater detail. These are:

- joint consultation and JCCs;
- works councils, supervisory boards and employee directors;
- European Works Councils.

The Information and Consultation Directive (2002), fully implemented in 2008, is intended to complement the information and consultation requirements of the other European Union Directives considered above. The detail of this Directive and the UK Regulations stemming from it, are considered later in this chapter.

JOINT CONSULTATION AND JCCS

JCCs were recommended by Whitley in 1917 as a means of involving employees in management decision making and controlling 'militant' trade unionism. Notwithstanding the general definition of JCCs given above, empirical evidence and theoretical contributions provide a more complex picture of their role and function. There is debate concerning the extent to which JCCs are institutional examples of either employee involvement or employee participation. As we shall see, the answer is 'a bit of both', bearing in mind the relationship which joint consultation has with collective bargaining and the ideological perspectives of the parties to the employment relationship. Joint consultation takes place mainly at the higher organisational and the lower establishment levels within both the public and private sectors of industry and in multinational and national enterprises (including inwardly investing companies). The popularity of joint consultation and JCCs since their introduction in the early twentieth century has waxed and waned; they enjoyed greater popularity during the two high-consensus world war periods, and are well established in the public sector. There was

some decline in joint consultation during the 1950s and 1960s, due partly to the trend towards 'domestic' bargaining (see Chapter 5) but overall, during the post-Second World War period, although the number of JCCs has gradually declined, the picture is one of overall stability. This is particularly so in the period since the 1980s, which also evidences a trend towards consultation in non-union organisations or organisations where unions are not recognised.

Joint consultation: involvement or participation . . . or both?

Self-evaluation activity 6.4

Joint consultation types

The response is given below

Read the description of the three types of joint consultation and indicate whether they are examples of EI or EP.

Three approaches to joint consultation have been identified (Farnham and Pimlott, 1995), known as pseudo consultation, classical consultation and integrative consultation.

Pseudo consultation is basically downward communication within the JCC, where management informs employee representatives of decisions already taken. Employees and employee representatives are not empowered to influence management decisions. Pseudo consultation or 'information giving' is practised more commonly in organisations which are union-free or where unions are particularly weak and 'as a method of industrial relations, it merely seeks to maintain management's right to manage, neither to challenge it nor to legitimise managerial authority' (p. 52).

Classical consultation involves employee representatives discussing and considering matters which directly affect the workforce or sections of it. Employee representatives within such JCCs may be able to influence events before the final decision is taken by management. Farnham and Pimlott identify four characteristics of this type of joint consultation:

- matters of common interest to employees and employer are dealt with, with the exception of terms and conditions of employment which could be contentious;

- joint consultative machinery is separate from collective bargaining machinery;
- it is the responsibility of management to take and implement decisions arising from the consultative process; and
- the consultation process involves all employees, unionised and non-unionised and including supervisory and managerial staff.

Integrative consultation extends the range of issues subject to consultation, again of common concern to employers and employees, and can include matters such as introduction of new technology and other aspects of change, productivity and flexible working. The aim of the exercise is to arrive at a joint decision concerning problems arising from these matters, and is more similar to integrative or co-operative bargaining than to classical consultation or distributive bargaining. This type of joint consultation should reinforce rather than supplant collective bargaining (see below).

In looking at these three types of joint consultation, we could argue that pseudo consultation does not provide for any form of EI or EP. Employees are considered passive recipients of selective management information. Management makes the final decision at the end of the classical consultation process, but employee representatives get the opportunity to provide opinions and comments within a two-way communication process. This type of consultation process is more indicative of EI than EP. EP features prominently within the integrative consultation process for reasons given above.

A refinement to the above typology is provided by Marchington (1987) who identified four different models or 'faces of consultation'. These are the non-union model, the competitive model, the adjunct model and the marginal model.

The **non-union model** is virtually identical to the pseudo consultation approach and aims to prevent workplace union organisation. Non-union JCCs are talking shops in which management sets the agenda. Employee representatives are informed of developments and are expected to endorse management thinking. The **competitive model** is somewhat similar to the classical consultation approach whereby in unionised organisations collective bargaining is seen as the 'competitor': the purpose of JCCs is to reduce the influence of collective bargaining by

considering strategic issues and problems concerning, for example, the company's market position. Management is represented by senior line managers and non-managerial employees by a combination of shop stewards and other worker representatives. The **adjunct model** is similar to the integrative approach and the emphasis within JCCs is upon joint problem-solving concerning high-level, strategic information such as market prospects, business plans, quality and customer relations. Farnham and Pimlott (1995) add:

> *Managerial representation is provided by senior line management and members from the personnel team, with the workforce represented by shop stewards. The process is one of mutual influence between the management and union representatives. Within it, advance information provided to the members and management allows the union representatives to meet before the JCC takes place. This is to make the formal meetings more effective.* (p. 418)

This model is regarded as the 'best practice' model for pluralist management whereby both parties have a desire for the JCC to succeed. Finally, the **marginal model** is very low-key and JCCs consider relatively trivial matters concerning welfare and other peripheral issues.

Joint consultation and collective bargaining

In examining the developments in collective bargaining in Britain over the past 30 or so years (see Chapter 5), we noted that its scope had narrowed and its coverage had declined. Nevertheless, collective bargaining remains the single most important process of determining pay and working conditions for millions of employees. Clegg (1985) consistently argued that collective bargaining establishes the role of trade unions, within a system of industrial governance, with trade unions being a permanent 'opposition' which prevents the development of autocracy in industry. In this sense, while collective bargaining remains central to trade union mobilisation, its adversarial essence should not be diluted by other less adversarial, opposing and, by implication, inferior forms of involvement/participation

such as joint consultation. Others, such as Marchington and Parker (1990, echoing Terry, 1986), argue that collective bargaining has been 'undermined by a resurgence and upgrading of JCCs [and that] its role [has been] progressively reduced to form without content' (p. 37). There are, therefore, two opposing views concerning the role of joint consultation in relation to collective bargaining. These are:

- **The upgrading or revitalisation perspective** whose proponents (Terry, 1983; Batstone, 1984; Edwards, 1985) argue that managements have been introducing or upgrading their JCCs in order to deal with issues which were traditionally within the province of collective bargaining. These revitalised JCCs concern themselves with important strategic decisions of the plant or company and by doing so reduce the influence of shop stewards and other union officials within the collective bargaining process. To be sure, the JCCs will have shop steward representatives, who, from the standpoint of management, will gain a closer understanding of company problems and therefore come to accept the logic of management solutions. In this way, many of the issues previously dealt with by collective bargaining can be settled by consultative arrangements. Moreover, 'it is further assumed that managements are successful in their pursuit of such a strategy to the extent that they feel no need to confront trade unions "head on" via policies of a more aggressive nature' (Marchington and Parker, 1990, p. 40).

- **The downgrading or marginalisation perspective** whose supporters (Cressey *et al.*, 1985; MacInnes, 1985) argue that consultation has been downgraded, becoming marginal to the regulation of affairs in the workplace. JCCs deal with trivia to the point where one of the parties decides that there is no point in continuing with the dialogue. Moreover, committee members may 'find they have more pressing priorities which take precedence over their attendance at the JCC, and eventually someone not only forgets to organise a meeting, others forget they have even forgotten' (Marchington and Parker, 1990, p. 40).

Marchington and Armstrong (1986) proposed a third perspective:

in which consultation operates as an adjunct to negotiation (collective bargaining), as complementary to each other rather than working as competing processes in the regulation of workplace affairs. Negotiation is used for the determination of wages and working conditions, whereas consultation acts as a sounding board, helps to lubricate relationships, and generally fills the gaps needed to administer employee relations. (p. 41)

This perspective conforms to the adjunct model which we considered in the previous section. Nevertheless, as Hyman and Mason (1995) assert, putting this unresolved debate to one side, JCCs are 'highly appropriate': firstly, where collective bargaining is centralised at industry or company level 'hence creating a need for a discussion forum at local level' (p. 125); secondly, in large organisations where there is often a lack of communication channels between management and employees; and, thirdly, 'where companies are seeking to reduce the importance of collective bargaining, and JCCs offer a viable alternative' (p. 125).

It should also be borne in mind that JCCs are not, of course, confined to unionised establishments and 'constitute the most common form of representative voice in workplaces where there are no union members' (Kersley *et al.*, 2006, p. 126). However, the proportion of JCCs in non-union establishments is relatively small and they do not adequately fill the representation gap consequent upon the decline in union membership and collective bargaining. At best, JCCs could, and some probably do, provide trade unions with the opportunity to engage formally with managers in the absence of collective bargaining machinery as a poor substitute for collective negotiation. It has also been argued that statutory support for employee consultation as a result of the full implementation in 2008 of the Information and Consultation Directive (2002) would be potentially beneficial by facilitating union activity in this area (Heery *et al.*, 2004).

Joint consultation and JCCs: some empirical evidence

The WIRS, WERS 1998 and WERS 2004 survey findings (Millward *et al.*, 1992; Cully *et al.*, 1999;

Millward *et al.*, 2000; Kersley *et al.*, 2006) remain the most authoritative. Table 6.1 provides data from 1980 to 1998 and Table 6.2 presents findings for 2004. While both tables are not strictly comparable as different items and weightings are used and the workplace size category of 10–24 employees is used for the first time in the 2004 survey, general trends can be discerned for the period 1998–2004. The findings for 1980–98 are given first.

The findings for the period 1980–98 concern JCCs at both workplace and higher organisational levels. With reference to Table 6.1, the surveys show that the overall incidence of workplace JCCs has been fairly stable since 1990 with 29 per cent of workplaces having a JCC on site. However, it is useful to draw a distinction between JCCs as 'window dressing' and those that are 'functioning consultative committees' (that is, those that meet at least once every three months). With regard to the latter category, there has been a long-term decline in their incidence from 30 per cent in 1980 to 23 per cent in 1998, affecting all sizes of establishments in all sectors of the economy, although it should be noted that the decline affected the public sector from 1990 to 1998 only.

The data also indicate that JCCs were much more prevalent in workplaces where unions were recognised than in workplaces where there was no recognised union, with the former category witnessing a decline accounted for by the decline in public sector JCCs amongst other factors. In workplaces with no recognised union, the picture is one of stability with JCC incidence varying by only three percentage points. Within private sector workplaces where unions are recognised, the decline in JCC incidence is steeper (35 per cent in 1980 to 24 per cent in 1998). Within industries, there were changes in the JCC incidence with JCCs becoming more common in private sector transport and communications and declining within the health services and energy. A further finding of significance is that JCCs are not as permanent an institution as might have been supposed, with 12 per cent of continuing workplaces abandoning their JCCs while 17 per cent established JCCs between 1990 and 1998. Two further findings concerning the incidence of JCCs are relevant:

- in workplaces with no recognised union, the existence of a fully functioning JCC did not

Table 6.1 Incidence of workplace joint consultative committees by broad sector and by union recognition: 1980–1998

	1980 (%)	1984 (%)	1990 (%)	1998 (%)
Any consultative committee				
All establishments	34	34	29	29
Functioning consultative committee				
All establishments	30	31	26	23
Size of establishment				
25–49 employees	21	21	18	14
50–99 employees	29	32	31	25
100–199 employees	39	47	37	32
200–499 employees	60	54	43	49
500 or more employees	66	70	61	58
Private sector	26	24	18	20
Private manufacturing and extraction	32	26	21	24
Private services	22	23	17	18
Public sector	39	42	45	32
Unions recognised	37	36	34	30
No recognised union	17	20	17	18
Private sector only				
Unions recognised	35	29	21	24
No recognised unions	16	20	17	18

Source: Millward *et al.*, 2000, p. 109

increase the prospects for trade union recognition; and

- in workplaces that derecognised trade unions, 'the [subsequent] decline in employee voice . . . is not being offset by the introduction of consultative committees as alternative channels of representation' (Millward *et al.*, 2000, p. 111).

WERS 1998 also looked at the operation of JCCs in terms of influence over managerial decision making. Around one-third of managers for the period 1990–98 rated their consultative committee as very influential. In relation to higher-level consultative committees operating in organisations with several workplaces, the incidence of these increased during the period 1990–98 with 56 per cent of workplaces belonging to a larger organisation reporting a higher-level committee, up from 48 per cent in

1990. The increase in the number of such committees is at least partly due to the (then pending) impact of the transposition of the European Works Council Directive in 1999.

The findings for the period 1998–2004 generally provide a similar picture to that of the preceding period. Data for 2004 are given in Table 6.2.

The main WERS 2004 findings are summarised below.

- JCCs were present in 14 per cent of workplaces, being a normal occurrence in workplaces with 200 or more employees, but there were hardly any present in small workplaces with fewer than 25 employees. JCCs were more common in public sector than in private sector workplaces.
- Since 1998, the incidence of JCCs has declined, particularly in workplaces with fewer than

Table 6.2 Workplace characteristics of joint consultative committees 2004

	Workplace-level committee (%)	Higher-level committee only (%)	No committee (%)
All workplaces	14	25	62
Workplace size			
10–24 employees	4	26	70
25–49 employees	16	24	59
50–99 employees	26	27	47
100–199 employees	47	16	37
200–499 employees	59	13	28
500 or more employees	73	9	18
Organisation status			
Stand-alone workplace	6	–	94
Part of a larger organisation	18	36	46
Organisation size			
10–99 employees	5	1	94
100–999 employees	18	29	53
1000–9999 employees	22	44	35
10,000 or more employees	21	50	30
Sector of ownership			
Private	11	20	69
Public	28	46	26
Industry			
Manufacturing	21	4	75
Electricity, gas and water	52	35	14
Construction	8	5	87
Wholesale and retail	11	31	58
Hotels and restaurants	4	28	68
Transport and communication	16	29	55
Financial services	5	57	38
Other business services	10	16	74
Public administration	42	40	18
Education	30	31	40
Health and social work	13	25	62
Other community services	14	23	62

Source: Kersley *et al.*, 2006, p. 127

100 employees from 17 per cent in 1998 to 10 per cent in 2004. The decline was particularly marked in workplaces that did not recognise trade unions (14 per cent in 1998 to cognise trade unions (14 per cent in 1998 to 8 per cent in 2004). In larger workplaces with 100 or more employees the decline was marginal (56 per cent in 1998 and 54 per cent in 2004).

- There were higher-level or 'multi-issue' JCCs at regional, divisional or head office level for 25 per cent of workplaces which did not have a JCC at workplace level (27 per cent in 1998). The withdrawal of workplace JCCs accelerated during the 1998–2004 period with 62 per cent of workplaces not covered by a JCC in 2004 compared with 53 per cent in 1998.

The conclusions that we can arrive at concerning JCCs in Britain during the past 35 years or so are, firstly, that while functioning JCCs remain a relatively important feature of industrial relations in many companies and workplaces, both within the private and public sectors, there has been a further decline in their incidence and representative voice during the 1990s and early 2000s. Secondly, given the variations in size and sector of establishments and workplaces, there appears to be greater informality in the operation of JCCs in the smaller service-based sectors; a more sophisticated and formalised approach in the declining but relatively larger manufacturing and public sectors where trade unions are generally stronger; and pressures for greater formalisation of communication and participatory structures, particularly in transnational organisations more sensitive to EU policies, directives and legislation.

Summary points

- The two main approaches which have influenced participatory structures within the European Union are, firstly, EI, which is concerned with job- and task-based decisions, and, secondly, EP, which provides employees with the means to influence organisational decision making.
- Employee interests within the decision-making process may theoretically extend to industrial democracy which challenges employer rights to manage, while employer interests are directed towards maintaining and reinforcing the legitimacy of managerial power and decision making.
- Government initiatives to introduce a statutory form of EP in Britain came to nothing with the shelving of the Bullock Committee Report in 1979. This contrasts sharply with the experience of many EU countries where legislation has been

introduced, and the European Commission itself which has encouraged participative structures to be developed in the EU member states.
- Approaches to participation include:
 - collective bargaining;
 - collective employee share schemes;
 - works councils;
 - employee representation on company boards;
 - joint consultative committees; and
 - European Works Councils.
- JCCs are still fairly common in Britain, but there are reservations concerning the extent to which they are truly participative.

CO-DETERMINATION AND WORKS COUNCILS

We now consider works councils and management boards (including employee directors) within the formalised context typical of many European countries. As we have seen, works councils within the European Union often have statutory underpinnings and are formal structures having written constitutions dealing with election of representatives, frequency of meetings, issues for discussion and so on. There has been considerable opposition in Britain to the adoption of works councils on the European model. Employers have resisted them owing to their perceived threat to managerial authority and prerogatives, while unions are worried about the possible dilution of union representative functions and influence should non-union employees become council members, and the possible consequences of making unpopular decisions affecting the unionised workforce. However, there have been employer-led initiatives in situations where the union presence is weak or non-existent ('company councils' or 'employee councils' being examples), or where trade unions have been derecognised as in the privatised Northumbrian Water. Some Japanese inwardly investing companies such as Nissan have introduced company councils within either a union-free environment or where single-union deals have been negotiated. The Information and Consultation Directive 2002, now fully implemented and considered further in this chapter, imposes a more general duty to consult with employees within the UK.

The German system of co-determination

The German system of co-determination (*Mitbestimmung*) is generally regarded as the 'best practice' model for employee participation in Europe. It comprises an employee-only works council (*Betriebsrat*) at workplace, company or group level, and employee representation on the supervisory/management boards (*Aufsichtsrat*) of companies. Works councils are underpinned by legislation but not mandatory (Van Ruysseveldt and Visser, 1996). There is no formal involvement by trade unions in the activities of the works council, but employers and works councils must co-operate with both unions and employers' organisations. Trade unions do, however, have representation rights at supervisory board level under the 1976 Co-determination Act, which applies to large companies. It is also quite common for the chairperson of a works council to have a seat on the supervisory board, establishing a direct link between these bodies. The works council system applies to all private sector companies with more than five employees, while the supervisory board system applies to private sector companies with more than 500 employees. Parallel legislation provides for works councils in the public sector. The co-determination model (see below for different interpretations) is characterised by a high degree of formalisation and legal regulation, and for this reason the relationship between employer and employees at enterprise level is often described as 'institutionalised co-operation' (Van Ruysseveldt and Visser, 1996).

The term 'works council', as Frege (2002) points out, has been subject to differing interpretations and is best understood within the context of co-determination. A number of models of co-determination have been devised, some of which are useful for possible application to the UK (Frege, 2002). These are outlined below:

1. The *democratisation/integration model* defines co-determination as 'the institutionalisation of social processes which allows for the positive integration of all participants' (Furstenberg, 1981, p. 31). It is a form of corporate governance underpinned by legislation.
2. The *surrogate/compensation model* sees co-determination as providing workers' rights not based on ownership but on legitimate democratic grounds.
3. The *counterpower/conflict model* regards co-determination as a means to restrict management power and control.
4. The *social control model* is a Marxist argument that co-determination supports the subordination of the working class and hides the real conflict of interest between workers and employers.
5. The *partnership model* sees co-determination as 'a participatory process leading to high trust, co-operation and compromise which are regarded as positive outcomes and not as a selling out to management' (Frege, 2002, p. 225).

Self-evaluation activity 6.5

Model applicability

This SEA has no commentary

In view of the transposition of the Information and Consultation Directive, which model would you select as being the most appropriate to the UK context (bear in mind that many of the models overlap).

Arguments for having works councils

Frege (2002) points out that many German academics put forward strong arguments for the co-determination and works council system. One strong argument is that co-determination improves the quality of local or workplace employment relations and the functioning of the organisation's internal labour market, thereby having a positive impact upon the company's economic performance. More specific arguments concerning the influence of works councils upon intra-organisation employment relations include:

1. The works council provides an employee voice for all employees, and not only trade union members, which reduces labour turnover and hence hiring and training costs.
2. The works council increases trust and co-operation between employer and employee. Employers know that they cannot get rid of works councils and therefore concentrate upon establishing co-operative methods of working.

3. Works councils increase the flow of information between management and workforce resulting in a greater equality of information exchange which in turn results in a more informed decision-making process and facilitates new and improved solutions.
4. The presence of works councils may well induce the diffusion of 'best practice' throughout the organisation in terms, for example, of improving production methods and working practices through the introduction of new technology and lessening the prospect of resistance to change.
5. Works councils can help improve quality of product and/or service.

Works council representation

The works council is the core of the German co-determination model (see Exhibit 6.2).

Works councils, as employee-only bodies, are directly elected by the workforce for an individual establishment (*Betrieb*). An 'establishment' could mean a company if it is small enough, an individual plant within a multi-plant company, one department store within a chain, or a distinct works on a single site characterised by several types of operation. Where a company comprises several establishments,

each with its own works council, a works council for the company as a whole can be formed from delegates of existing works councils. Similarly, if the company is part of a group or consortium, a group (or combine) works council can be set up.

Works council size

Where the establishment has five to 20 employees, only one representative may be elected. Five members may be elected in establishments with 51–150 employees, 15 members where there are 1001–2000 employees, and 31 members for workforces between 7001 and 9000 employees. In establishments having more than 9000 employees, two more members can be added for each additional 3000 employees. All manual and non-manual employees, together with trainees, are eligible for membership. The company's management board, owners and executives are ineligible for works council membership. Membership is dominated by DGB-affiliated trade unionists (DGB is equivalent to the TUC): in the 1994 elections, for example, DGB candidates won two-thirds of all seats, and accounted for three-quarters of all works council chairs, a success rate repeated in subsequent elections. The number of non-union works council members rose from 17 per

Exhibit 6.2

Historical development of co-determination

The idea of worker representation through works councils was first raised by the revolutionary Constitutional Assembly in Frankfurt in 1848 and was included in its draft constitution for a democratic German republic. By the end of the First World War a powerful, radical works council movement had developed which saw itself as the political basis of a post-war socialist order. Works councils became an important part of the structure of the Weimar Republic (1919–33). The councils in the Republic were incorporated into the liberal-democratic constitution and were legally authorised to represent workers and consult with employers. Collective bargaining was reserved for unions, operating at sectoral and national levels, while councils were bound to observe and implement agreements. This dual system of industrial relations, established in the Weimar Republic, continued nationally in West Germany after the Second World War. However, the trade unions initially opposed the early legislation (1951 and 1952) establishing works councils as the councils were perceived to be anti-union, did not provide sufficient rights for workers and threatened to weaken unions at plant level. It was only after collective bargaining was consolidated at industry level in the early 1960s that unions began to see works councils as legitimate devices for worker representation. Works council rights were considerably strengthened by the Social Democratic government under Willy Brandt in 1972, and it is this legislation, as amended by the Conservative–Liberal coalition in the 1980s, which governs the current structure and powers of works councils.

cent in the mid-1970s to 25 per cent in the late 1990s. Coverage of the labour force by works councils is limited by two main factors. Firstly, around a quarter of the labour force work in establishments that are too small to meet the size threshold, or are excluded because of the nature of their activities, or are in the public sector (which has its own arrangements). Secondly, while works councils are underpinned by legislation, they are not mandatory. Even so, around two-thirds of private sector employees work in establishments with a works council.

Their representative status, duties, rights and powers

Works councillors are elected for four years. In establishments with more than 300 employees, the employer may release a certain number of council members, on full pay, for works council activities. Members have a right to vocational and other training relevant to their duties, and are protected against dismissal, apart from offences relating to gross misconduct, while in office. Works councils are required to co-operate with the employer 'for the good of the employees and the establishment' (1972 Act), and cannot take industrial action, although informal sanctions do exist and act as a counter to employers' ability to grant or withhold a variety of concessions. The general statutory duties of works councils include:

- compliance with the law, with collective agreements and with works agreements for the benefit of employees;
- making recommendations to the employer on action to benefit employees and the establishment;
- promoting the rehabilitation and integration of people with disabilities, older workers and foreign workers; and
- calling meetings of employees at least four times a year, to which the employer is invited.

The rights of works councils range from information dissemination through participation in decisions, to joint decision making. The main rights are:

- **The right to be heard,** by which councils have a right to express opinions on issues as well as to initiate proposals in some areas.

- **The right to information:** works councils have a general right to be informed concerning any issues relevant to management decision making.
- **The right to consultation** where employers seek the views of works councils before making decisions.
- **The right to co-determination** whereby the employer cannot proceed with a course of action without the agreement of the works council on issues which are subject to joint determination.

The co-determination rights are the most important as they cover social policy issues such as payment methods and systems, bonus rates, piecework rates, premiums and performance-related pay, work and holiday schedules, overtime, reduced working hours and the 'humanisation' of work. Other issues about which works councils must be consulted include:

1. *Job design and the work environment*: Works councils must be informed of and consulted about changes to work arrangements and processes, changes to factory/plant and premises, and must be given the scope to make suggestions or express reservations. Works councils have a right of co-determination (joint decision making) concerning the consequences of these changes and of mitigating their effects.
2. *Personnel matters*: Councils do exercise considerable influence over personnel management on matters which in Britain would be considered within the realm of managerial prerogative. Their influence therefore extends to major aspects of workplace relations and the internal labour market. Specifically, the rights concerning personnel include:
 - *Personnel planning* where there is a right to information and to make recommendations on the planning process itself, staff changes or movements and vocational training.
 - *Recruitment* whereby works councils can ask for vacancies to be advertised internally before external recruitment begins; failure to do this may lead to the council withholding consent to an appointment. Application forms require council approval as do guidelines for selection, transfer, regrading or dismissal of employees.

- *Engagement, transfer and regrading* where, in establishments with more than 20 employees, the council must be informed about any engagement and movement of staff and shown any application or selection documents. The council can refuse to approve proposals concerning these matters if the employer breaches any agreed guidelines.
- *Individual dismissal* where all dismissals must be notified, with the reasons for the dismissal, to the works council which has a statutory right to object. Any dismissal which is not notified is null and void.

3. *Financial and business matters*: In all companies having more than 100 permanent employees a subcommittee of the works council (the Economic Committee) can be formed to deal specifically with information given by the employer concerning the state of the business. Employers are required to give information on the financial state of the business supported by appropriate documentation as long as business confidentiality is not compromised. The information includes the economic and financial situation of the company, the product and market situation, investment, production and rationalisation plans, including new working methods, and reduction in activities, closures or transfer of operations. Employers in companies with more than 1000 employees must also inform employees individually, every three months in writing, concerning the state of the business. In firms with more than 20 employees, information can be presented verbally.

4. *Redundancies*: In companies with 20 or more employees, the employer must inform and consult the works council concerning any change to the business resulting in redundancies and must seek an agreement with the council about these changes. Works councils also have a right to negotiate levels of financial compensation for redundant employees.

5. *Works councils and trade unions*: German trade unions do not have a formal right to workplace representation and workplace bargaining is not recognised in the sense that it is in Britain. To be sure, shop stewards do exist, but mainly to provide lines of communication to the national union concerning pay claims. Since works councils are prevented from taking industrial action, shop stewards often take responsibility for co-ordinating official and unofficial strikes at plant level (although it has to be said that workplace-based disputes are rare occurrences). In practice, shop stewards work closely with works councils, reflecting the fact that a large proportion of councillors are union members.

Employee representation at board level

Participation at board level occurs within the two-tier board structure set up by the 1965 Joint Stock Companies Act. The structure comprises a supervisory board and a management board. The management board is responsible for conducting the business operations of a company, represents the enterprise legally, and is formally the employer. The supervisory board is legally required to appoint the management board or managing directors, depending on the type of organisation, and to oversee its activities. Employee representatives sit on the supervisory board which meets between two and four times a year. Only joint stock companies are required to have two boards as a matter of course. Other types of company are required to create a two-tier structure only if they are large enough to qualify for inclusion in one of the co-determination systems.

Supervisory board duties and rights

The supervisory board has a general right to request information from the management board on all aspects of the business, and this right also applies to individual members seeking information provided the request is supported by another member. Both supervisory boards and works councils are covered by confidentiality requirements. Information which must be provided as a matter of course includes:

- proposed corporate policies and other basic issues concerning the management of the enterprise;
- the profitability of the business, especially the return on equity;
- the general progress of the business; and
- operations which might be of considerable importance to the profitability or liquidity of the business.

Forms of board-level participation

There are three forms of board-level participation. The first form covers joint stock and limited liability companies with more than 2000 employees under the provisions of the 1976 Co-determination Act, now extended to cover the former East Germany. In these companies the supervisory board comprises equal numbers of shareholder and employee members, with the size of the board varying according to company size. Some seats on the board are reserved for trade union representatives (if there is a trade union presence in the company), and the remaining seats are allocated to employees, with a guarantee of at least one seat for each of the manual, non-manual and managerial categories. Election is usually direct, by employee groups in enterprises with up to 8000 employees, and by electoral college in larger firms. The most important single activity of the supervisory board is to elect the management board, with the chair of the former board having a casting vote. From the union perspective, the 50–50 composition of the supervisory board is compromised by the presence of managerial staff on the employees' side who often support the shareholders' view on important issues. The board also elects a 'Labour Director' (sometimes against the wishes of the employee representatives) to the management board who oversees personnel and HRM matters.

The second type of supervisory board exists in enterprises with more than 1000 employees working in the coal, iron and steel industries under the co-determination legislation of 1951 and 1956. Here, as in the previous example, the board consists of an equal number of employee and shareholder representatives, but in contrast to the previous example, the chair of the board must be a neutral member, and the 'Labour Director' is appointed subject to the approval of the employee representatives. However, the number of boards and companies has fallen within these industrial sectors as, in common with other European and North American economies, the numbers employed in coal, iron and steel industries have declined, as have the industries themselves.

Supervisory boards in companies with 500–2000 employees constitute the third type whereby, under the 1952 Works Constitution Act (the predecessor to the 1972 Act), one-third of supervisory board members must be employee representatives. In other respects, the functions of the supervisory boards within these companies are identical with the first and second types we have considered.

Works councils: conclusions and prospects

The 'best practice' German model is not without its critics. Strauss (1979) raises two important issues which are more than academic. The first issue is whether the prescriptions for participation match the realities of the participation process; the second issue is concerned with 'who benefits'? Are there, for example, positive benefits and outcomes such as higher productivity, increased employee satisfaction and fewer grievances for the parties involved in the co-determination process? Trade unions have often criticised the effectiveness of works councils by claiming that information provided by employers is insufficient and inadequate, and may arrive too late for any useful employee input. These issues affect all countries which have introduced works council arrangements (see Exhibit 6.3) and as Bridgford and Stirling (1994) comment: 'In certain countries, doubts about employee participation are so manifest that legislation has been introduced (in France and Belgium, for example), in order to remedy the situation' (p. 140). In Germany itself, there have been criticisms that trade unions as organisations are unrepresented at works council level, and that the works councils are not permitted to discuss issues which unions consider as being central to the employment relationship, such as pay and the introduction of new technology. Most important in the German case is the prohibition of strike action under the Works Constitution Act 1952 which states that 'acts of industrial warfare between the employer and the works council shall be unlawful'. Perceptions of works councils and their effectiveness vary from organisation to organisation and by industry sector. For example, Bridgford and Stirling cite research reported in Berghahn and Karsten (1987) which identifies six 'perceptual categories' of works council (see also earlier arguments concerning advantages of works councils) These are:

- the works council which is respected but has an ambiguous position between workers and management;

Exhibit 6.3

Some national works council systems

As in the UK, specific legislation providing for information and consultation of employees exists in areas covered by EU Directives – collective redundancies, transfers of undertakings, and health and safety. However, the right to be informed and consulted on an ongoing basis about more general company matters is a pivotal part of the role of works councils in many countries. All member countries of the EU, except the UK and Ireland, have legislated for the provision of information and consultation systems. The works council or equivalent is the most commonly used, but their nature and their ability to impact upon management decision making differs from country to country. In most countries all companies or establishments over a certain size in terms of numbers of employees are required to set up a works council or similar body. In many member states the size of works council increases with the total number of employees. All member states have rules to protect confidential information. In general, works council members are bound by confidentiality requirements where the employer considers information to be commercially sensitive, and employers may be allowed to withhold information where disclosure would harm the company. In some member states such as France, Sweden and Italy, trade unions have a guaranteed involvement in works councils. In France and Germany there is a clear separation between the consultative and negotiating roles of trade unions.

The Netherlands: Has a system of information and consultation rights that applies to companies employing more than 50 people. The rights cover issues such as financial and employment situations, work organisation, information technology, mergers, closures, investment systems, recruitment and changes to the company's structure. Co-determination rights also exist in areas such as redundancies, recruitment, promotions, training, job evaluation, working time and holidays. In relation to productivity as compared with the UK, hourly productivity was 25 per cent and 26 per cent higher in the Netherlands for 1991 and 2001 respectively.

Austria: Information and consultation rights apply in companies with more than five employees and cover issues such as the financial and employment situation of the company, on which consultation must take place a minimum of four times a year. In addition, where a change to the business is planned, consultation must take place. As in the case of Germany, co-determination rights exist on such issues as rest breaks, daily working time, payment systems, recruitment of temporary workers, social plans for redundancy, and training and retraining. Austria's labour productivity figures per hour worked were 10 per cent above the UK's for 1992, rising to 16 per cent in 2001.

Finland: Information and consultation rights apply to companies employing more than 30 employees (20 if collective redundancies are proposed). The rights cover matters such as financial information (twice a year or immediately if changes are proposed), employment and training. Co-determination rights exist concerning changes that affect the workforce and proposed job cuts. Finland's productivity per hour was 8 per cent above that of the UK in 2001.

- the works council which is firm in its representation of workers' interests and is respected by the employer;
- the works council which is co-operative but acts as a countervailing power;
- the works council which is an organ of management;
- the isolated works council; and
- the ignored works council.

Notwithstanding these criticisms, other evidence (Heller, 1986) suggests that employees do exercise some influence over management decision making at enterprise level and that 'the existence of formal rules (within the German context) makes a substantial difference in promoting the actual participation of employees' (p. 82). In many cases, employee participation in decision making is reinforced by the presence of works councillors on supervisory

boards, although there is a danger that the loyalties of trade union and other employee representatives on such boards may be divided between the interests of the enterprise and its management and the interests of the employees whom they represent.

Frege (2002) concludes that, despite the challenges of German unification and European integration, the works council institution has not been weakened since the late 1980s and, if anything, councils are increasingly being included as 'comanagers' in new areas of decision making such as technological and organisational restructuring. The government-appointed Co-determination Commission issued its report on Germany's system of board-level determination (whereby both employee and shareholder representatives sit on the supervisory boards of large companies) in December 2006 (IRS, 2007). The report gives a generally positive evaluation of board-level co-determination, finding that it is not a barrier to the success of German companies and not fundamentally rejected by managers. This finding is also confirmed by Fitzroy and Kraft (2005), whose empirical research in a number of German companies concludes that co-determination provides no obstacle to productivity and may, indeed, enhance it. The report recommends a number of changes aimed at improving, but not fundamentally reforming, co-determination, such as: allowing scope for flexibility (e.g. on the size of the supervisory board) and simplification at enterprise level, by agreement; including the employees of foreign subsidiaries on the supervisory boards of German companies, through voluntary negotiation; and addressing some perceived inconsistencies in existing law. However, given that the commission's recommendations were not unanimously agreed, their prospects of adoption are uncertain.

Empirical evidence, therefore, suggests that works councils, and the co-determination system generally, remain a stable institution and that there is somewhat of a revival of interest in them, partly due to their importance being reinforced by the Information and Consultation Directive, 2002 (which we consider below in relation to the UK) and to the decentralising tendencies evident within European employment relations systems.

EUROPEAN WORKS COUNCILS

Introduction and background

The European Works Councils Directive was approved by the Council of Ministers in September 1994, under the terms of the Maastricht Treaty, from which the UK initially 'opted out' but has now, under New Labour, 'opted in'. The EWC Directive 'represented one of the most far-reaching and controversial industrial relations measures ever passed into European law' (AEEU, 1997). With many companies now operating on a transnational scale, the Directive sought to ensure that employees in large and medium-sized multinational organisations are properly informed and consulted about the enterprise's progress and prospects. All EU member states, with the exception of the UK, had to transpose the Directive into national legislation by September 1996. Initial (EU) estimates suggested that the EWC Directive would affect up to 2000 enterprises or groups, with between 10,000 and 15,000 subsidiaries, and that 'upwards of 40,000 EWC representatives could be participating in 5000 meetings every year' (AEEU, 1997). Research by Wortmann and Dorrenbacher (1994) indicated that 1500 large European firms would be affected, covering 5 million employees within the EU. However, Hall et al. (1995) suggested a more conservative estimate of 860 EU-based companies being affected, with 100–140 of them being UK firms.

A clause in the Directive (known as Article 13) provides for voluntary agreements, reached before September 1996, to continue in operation after the deadline for implementation. Trade unions and many companies have used this clause to press ahead with negotiations on voluntary EWC agreements and, according to an EU analysis (1996), over 100 companies had reached EWC agreements by January 1996. By 2002, over 600 EWCs in multinational companies within the European Economic Area had been established (Gilman and Marginson, 2002), and by 2004, with European Union enlargement, nearly 800 EWCs were established with around 1432, or 65 per cent of eligible companies yet to set up EWCs (eurofond 2007). The European Foundation for the Improvement of Living and

Working conditions website www.eurofound.ie provides up-to-date information concerning details of agreements concluded.

What the Directive said

The aim of the Directive was to ensure that the opinions of employees are considered and included in the decision-making procedures of central management and 'to improve the right to information and consultation of employees in Community-scale undertakings . . . and groups of undertakings' (Article 1). Article 2 of the Directive defines consultation as 'the exchange of views and the establishment of dialogue between employees' representatives and central management or any more appropriate level of management'.

The enterprises affected by the Directive are, firstly, 'community-scale undertakings', defined in Article 2 as 'an undertaking with at least 1000 employees within all the states covered by the Directive and at least 150 employees in two or more of the countries', and secondly, 'community-scale groups of undertakings', defined as groups with at least 1000 employees within EU countries which have two or more group undertakings in different countries within the EU with at least 150 employees. For example, a Dutch group consisting of a Dutch subsidiary employing 1100 people, and a separate French subsidiary employing 150 people would be covered by the Directive. The Directive also applies to undertakings and groups with headquarters outside the EU, provided they meet the workforce size thresholds.

The Directive allows for the level at which an EWC is established to be determined through negotiation. Generally, EWCs are likely to be established at group level in the controlling undertaking, a controlling undertaking being defined as one which can exert a 'dominant influence' over another by virtue of, for instance, ownership, financial participation or other criteria. The negotiating partners could also agree to create EWCs along product lines, or have a group-level EWC plus several others covering different sectors of the business. The responsibility for 'creating the conditions and means necessary' for the setting up of an EWC lies with the enterprise's central management team.

The procedure for creating an EWC comprises three main stages:

- **Stage one** of the procedure may be initiated by either the management team or at the request of at least 100 employees or their representatives from more than one of the 17 states covered. Trade unions are already using these provisions to initiate negotiations.
- **Stage two** involves the formation of a Special Negotiating Body (SNB) comprising between three and 17 members, with at least one coming from each of the member states in which the company has operations, in proportion to the number of employees. The composition of SNBs can include employee and trade union officials, and advisory 'experts' such as lawyers and economists.
- **Stage three** requires central management to open negotiations with the SNB with a view to reaching a written agreement on an EWC.

There are four possible outcomes to the negotiations between the SNB and central management. The first option is that the SNB decides not to proceed with negotiations, or to terminate negotiations in progress on a two-thirds majority vote. This option is not likely to be pursued by union representatives. The second option is the drawing up of a written agreement to establish an EWC arrangement, and covers the following issues:

- the undertakings or establishments covered;
- the composition of the EWC, the number of members, the allocation of seats and the term of office;
- the EWC's functions and the procedure for information and consultation;
- the venue, frequency and duration of meetings; and
- the duration of the agreement and the procedure for its renegotiation.

The agreement to establish an information and consultation procedure instead of an EWC is a third option which was included in the Directive after some employers had argued that an EWC was unnecessary because other methods for consulting and informing their workforces were in place. If, after three years, no agreement is reached, option four allows for the safety-net provisions laid out in

the annex to the Directive to apply. These provisions are known as subsidiary requirements, which also come into play if management refuses to start negotiations within six months of a request to do so. Subsidiary requirements lay down what are effectively minimum standards concerning EWC roles and activities.

The subsidiary requirements

The subsidiary requirements provide that an EWC be established on the basis of standard rules governing its competence, composition and procedures. The competence of the EWC is limited to those matters which concern the enterprise as a whole or those which concern operations in at least two EU countries. The composition of the EWC ranges from three to 30 members (who must be employees of the enterprise) elected or appointed by and from the existing employee representatives or, where there are no such representatives, by the entire body of employees. The election and appointment of EWC members must be carried out in accordance with national practice and legislation, and EWC seats are allocated on the same numerical basis as laid down for the SNB. If size warrants, the EWC may elect a 'select committee' with a maximum of three members. The EWC will have the right to meet central management annually to be informed and consulted about:

- the structure of the enterprise and its economic and financial situation;
- the probable development of the business and of production and sales;
- the employment situation and probable trend;
- investments; and
- substantial changes concerning organisation, new working methods or production processes, transfers of production, mergers, cutbacks or closures of undertakings, establishments or important parts thereof, or collective redundancies.

The select committee or, where none exists, the full EWC, has the right to be informed and to meet with management concerning measures significantly affecting employee's interests (see last bullet point above). These meetings should take place as soon as possible on the basis of a report drawn up by

management, on which the EWC may put forward an opinion. The EWC can adopt its own rules of procedure. For example, prior to any meeting with central management, the EWC, or the select committee, is entitled to meet without management being present. EWC members must inform employee representatives in the enterprise's various establishments of the content of the information and consultation procedures to be carried out. The EWC may be assisted in this by experts of its own choice. In addition, the operating costs, including the cost of organising meetings, interpretation and the accommodation and travelling expenses of members of the EWC and select committee are to be met by central management unless otherwise agreed. Finally, four years after an EWC is established under the subsidiary requirements, it must decide whether to open negotiations with the management for an agreement covering a company-specific EWC arrangement or to continue to operate on the basis of the subsidiary requirements.

The initial UK opt-out

As a result of the Conservative government's opt-out from the Social Chapter of the Maastricht Treaty, Britain was excluded from coverage of the EWC Directive and was not forced to comply with its terms.

Self-evaluation activity 6.6

Consequences of the UK opt-out
Response on website

What do you think were the consequences of the opt-out for British employees and companies?

Voluntary agreements

Before the original deadline of 22 September 1996 (the date the EWC Directive was to come into force), there was nothing to prevent voluntary EWC agreements being concluded, and these would remain in effect after that date (Article 13). By 1996 over 100 UK companies had reached such agreements. The voluntary agreement approach found favour with employers' organisations such as the CBI and the

EEF, but the danger of Article 13 agreements is that they are not fully protected by the law and there have been 'pre-emptive agreements proposed and signed that have sought to marginalise trade union representation' (Cressey, 1998, p. 73). Marks & Spencer and BP both sought to get management appointees as representatives, and this exposed them to challenge in the courts. The reasoning behind this was that if trade unions or employee representatives representing at least 100 employees in more than one member state felt that a voluntary agreement failed to meet criteria laid down in Article 13, they could, once the Directive came into force, ask for an SNB to be constituted in accordance with Article 5. If a company refused to set up an SNB on the grounds that it already had a voluntary agreement in line with Article 13, the matter could be referred to the courts.

Progress to date

Undoubtedly the principal development as far as the UK is concerned was the transposition and implementation by December 1999/January 2000 of the 'extension' Directive applying the original 1994 Directive, although some relatively minor amendments were made by a number of other member states. This mainly required the adoption of measures by the UK which had set out its transposition timetable involving:

- the use of Regulations under s 2(2) of the European Communities Act 1972;
- the launch of a consultation exercise towards the end of 1998;
- the submission of draft Regulations to Parliament before the 1999 summer recess; and
- the entering into force of the Regulations on 15 December 1999 and 17 January 2000.

The extension of the EWC Directive brought in at least another 125 UK-based multinationals within its scope (on top of the 114 companies already covered), plus some 175 multinationals based elsewhere. These groups had until 15 December 1999 to reach a voluntary 'Article 13-type' agreement before the legislation took effect. Before the process of transposing the extension Directive was completed, the original Directive had to be reviewed by

the Commission who could propose 'suitable amendments to the Council where necessary'.

Those multinationals covered by the original Directive which *did not* conclude voluntary Article 13 EWC agreements before the 22 September 1996 deadline were compelled to set up SNBs under the procedures of Article 5 of the Directive (as transposed in national law), with a view to concluding EWC agreements under Article 6. By June 1998, 21 months after the first SNB requests could potentially have been submitted by employees or their representatives, the number of Article 5/6 deals appeared low, amounting to no more than 45 examples out of those 700–800 companies (see the example of Cadbury, an Article 5/6 deal, in Exhibit 6.4) covered by the original Directive and without an Article 13 agreement (IRS, 1998). With regard to EWC agreements providing for information and consultation on transfers of production, mergers, closures and cutbacks, the European Parliament adopted a resolution in 2000 in which it called for the EWC Directive to be strengthened so as to ensure that information and consultation over restructuring is clearly provided for in formal terms.

As part of the process towards the 'Europeanisation' of employment relations, contact, liaison and co-operation is developing not only between trade unions organising in the various European operations of multinational companies, but also through direct contacts with EWCs, as Carley (2002) points out:

It is in this area that EWCs appear to have developed a role in the Europeanisation of bargaining within multinationals, facilitating an exchange of information on working conditions, working hours, employment practice and sometimes pay between employee representatives from different countries. This information is relevant to local and national-level negotiations within the enterprise. (p. 4)

Debate concerning the wider EWC role in European-level bargaining is largely speculative. However, a fundamental stage within that process should take into consideration the factors which influence choices made by management and employee representatives in concluding agreements establishing EWCs (Gilman and Marginson, 2002). These include:

Exhibit 6.4

An EWC agreement

Cadbury Confectionery Stream
European Employee Information and Consultation Forum
19/02/97

PRINCIPLES

This is an agreement between the Cadbury Schweppes Confectionery Stream group of companies in Europe, and its employee representatives on the provision of consultation and information sharing on transnational matters affecting employees within the Stream in Europe. The management and the representatives agree to co-operate in a spirit of constructive dialogue and exchange of ideas. By the provision of information and discussion, both agree to actively participate in the Forum. Members of the Forum are committed to acting in the best interests of the Stream and its employees. In general it is agreed that employee communications and involvement are best served within each of the Stream businesses and close to the workplace. The Forum shall not undermine existing consultative or information sharing channels at local level.

MEMBERSHIP AND REPRESENTATION
Covered by the Agreement

Stream	Country	No. Reps
Basset GmbH	Germany	–
Cadbury Ltd	UK	2
Cadbury Dulciora (including Chocolates Hueso Dulciora and Dulces Hispania)	Spain	1
Cadbury Faam BV	Netherlands	–
Cadbury France SA	France	1
Cadbury Ireland Limited (including Trebor Ireland Ltd)	Ireland	3
Cadbury Portugal – Produtos de Confeitaria LDA	Portugal	–
Piasten Schokladenfabrik Hofmann GmbH & Co KG	Germany	1
Trebor Bassett Group	UK	2
Central functions of Cadbury Schweppes Group and Stream Offices		1

REPRESENTATIVE ELIGIBILITY

Any current active employee of a Confectionery Stream business in the qualifying country can be nominated to attend the Forum subject to national law and local rules of eligibility. Employee representatives are elected to serve at the Forum meetings on the basis of nomination by Works Councils where relevant, or by secret ballot. Employee representatives are appointed to the Forum for four years. The appropriate members of management will attend the Forum according to the agenda items to be discussed. These will be from senior management such as MD, Regional MD, Business unit heads or functional heads as appropriate. In addition it will be usual for senior personnel management from the business units to be in attendance.

MEETINGS AND AGENDA

Forum meetings will take place annually. The duration of the meeting should provide a reasonable amount of time to conduct all business. Items on the agenda will be derived from the following list: the structure of the business; the economic and financial situation; the probable development of the business; employment trends; future trends; production and sales; substantial organisation changes; introduction of new working methods and production processes; transfers of production; mergers, cutbacks and closures; collective redundancies; health and safety; equal opportunities; environmental issues; capital expenditure; access for education and training for employees.

Source: Adapted from www.eurofound.ie (accessed 6 January 2003)

- a 'statutory model' effect whereby, scope for negotiations notwithstanding, agreements tend to conform with the provisions of the Directive's statutory model;
- a 'learning effect' under which innovatory features of earlier agreements are diffused to later agreements;
- a 'country effect' whereby, in their main features, EWCs resemble the national arrangements for employee information and consultation of the country in which an MNC is headquartered; and
- a 'sector effect', whereby in important respects EWCs within a given sector resemble each other, possibly through the impact of the respective trade unions or European industry federations of trade unions.

A number of factors may influence the conduct of management and employee representative negotiators. These include:

- company-specific factors such as the nature of the business and employment relations arrangements;
- the terms of the Directive itself, including its provisions;
- different systems of industrial relations and employee representation arrangements found in the countries in which multinational corporations operating in the European Economic Area are headquartered; and
- the sector in which the companies concerned are located.

Gilman and Marginson conclude that there is indeed a multiplicity of factors which constrain the management and employee representatives in negotiating on the provisions of EWC agreements, with the influence of both country and sector factors significant. This seems to contradict the view of a homogenous 'Europeanisation' process and 'reflects a more general process of "converging divergences" under which growing divergence in industrial relations arrangements and practice within national systems is occurring alongside increased cross border convergence of practices within given sectors' (Gilman and Marginson, 2002, p. 50).

In 2007, The European Economic and Social Committee (EESC) called for a revision of the European Works Councils (EWCs) Directive (Directive 94/45/EC), citing three key issues:

- Firstly the EESC stressed the need to eliminate the discrepancies that exist in the definitions of information and consultation between this and subsequent Directives (the Directive supplementing the statute for a European company with regard to the involvement of employees (Directive 2001/86/EC), the Directive establishing a framework for informing and consulting employees (Directive 2002/14/EC), and the Directive supplementing the statute for a European cooperative society with regard to the involvement of employees (2003/72/EC).
- Secondly, the need to increase proportionally the number of worker representatives on the special negotiating bodies (SNBs) and European works councils (EWCs), given the enlargement of the EU (the Directive having set membership at a maximum of 17) was emphasised.
- Finally the recognition of the right of national and European trade unions to belong to SNBs and EWCs (as they are permitted under the Directives on the involvement of employees in the SE and SCE) should be granted.

If implemented, these proposals would give weight to the argument that EWCs could provide greater opportunities for employees through their representatives to extend their voice and what relatively limited influence they have over company-wide strategic issues.

Concluding remarks

The growth in the number of EWCs should facilitate the greater spread of information and consultation across transnational companies. However, the extent to which such practices are successful depends upon the degree to which managements are willing to broaden out the range of issues for discussion in accordance with trade union aspirations. In practice, different objectives have been sought from the Directive at EU level, with management bodies such as UNICE trying to limit discussion and scope while trade unions have sought to widen the net. Another important issue concerns certain procedural aspects. Cressey (1998) contends that:

There has been and will continue to be a series of negotiations in companies about whether they

have adequate procedures concerning exemptions from the legislation and the ways to adapt to the directive. There will be variation across nations and a variety of processes put in place. In this sense the actual constitution of what is acceptable information, consultation and related participatory forms is still to be decided. (p. 78)

In a more positive vein, an effective EWC should provide managements with the opportunity to communicate corporate strategy, to allow discussion of change, to encourage international contact and to encourage an identity among staff of 'belonging' to an international company. Trade unions and employee representatives may regard EWCs as being useful as they gain access to company information which enables comparisons to be made which in turn facilitates their bargaining activities. A study by Marginson *et al.* (1999) of 386 voluntary agreements made by groups and undertakings *before* the EWC Directive came into force in 1996, involving one-third of the 1200 multinational companies covered by the Directive, concluded that the Directive itself has provided a major impetus to European-level negotiations between the management of multinational companies and employee representatives. These 'Article 13' agreements have given rise to many active EWCs which 'have the potential to develop and sustain new and effective forms of employee-interest representation at European level' (IRS, 1998). However, the conventional view of EWCs as labour-friendly institutions does not preclude their value to employers as 'employer-friendly tools of HRM' (Timming, 2007) or as a means of reinforcing managerial authority and control within the broader participatory context.

Summary points

- The German system of 'co-determination' remains the most visible and important national example of EP in Europe.
- The co-determination system comprises:
 - works councils; and
 - a two-tier board structure consisting of a supervisory and a management board.
- European Works Councils (EWCs) are company-wide bodies which conform to the requirements of the EWC Directive of 1994 and affect

'community-scale undertakings' and 'community-scale groups of undertakings'.
- The UK initially opted out of the Social Chapter and so was excluded from coverage of the EWC Directive. The UK's subsequent endorsement of the Social Chapter meant that the UK transposed the Directive during December 1999/January 2000.

EMPLOYEE VOICE, INFORMATION AND CONSULTATION OF EMPLOYEES AND PARTNERSHIP

Here we consider certain aspects of 'employee voice' with particular reference to the Information and Consultation of Employees Regulations (ICE), and partnership approaches. The term 'employee voice', as was pointed out in the introduction to this chapter, has entered the employment relations lexicon as a general term to include all varieties of participation, involvement and information-sharing within unionised and non-unionised contexts. The term itself is meaningless unless it is associated with a particular voice mechanism such as participation and/or involvement practices as, for example, demonstrated by Millward *et al.* (2000). In relation to the UK, there is, as we have seen in Chapter 3, a considerable amount of literature and research devoted to the decline in union representation, membership and influence during the 1980s, 1990s and into the 2000s (for example with regard to the case of joint consultative committees in unionised organisations). At the same time there has been an increase in the use of communication channels by employers, particularly regarding regular meetings between senior managers and workforce, and briefing groups. A crucial issue addressed by WERS 1998 and WERS 2004 (Cully *et al.*, 1999; Millward *et al.*, 2000; Kersley *et al.*, 2006) relates to the effectiveness of voice mechanisms from the employees' perspective. This reveals that with regard to assessments of how managers responded to employee concerns and suggestions there was a positive association with non-union or direct communication channels, but perceptions of fairness and fair treatment were positively associated with union channels of communication and a well-established union

Table 6.3 Percentages of workplaces having union and non-union voice arrangements: 1984–98

	1984	1990	1998
Type of voice arrangements (5 items)			
Union only	24	14	9
Union and non-union	42	39	33
Non-union only	16	28	40
Voice, but nature not reported	2	–	–
No voice	16	19	17
Type of voice arrangement (7 items)			
Union only	–	11	6
Union and non-union	–	42	37
Non-union only	–	33	46
Voice, but nature not reported	–	–	–
No voice	–	14	11

Source: Millward *et al.*, 2000, p. 122

presence. This, in turn, has implications for employment relations, government policy and union survival. No forms of direct involvement of the types considered in Chapter 7 were positively associated with fairness. As Millward *et al.* (2000) conclude:

> If 'fairness at work' is to remain one of the criteria by which labour market policy is judged (Department of Trade and Industry 1998), then the continuing decline of union representation must be a cause of concern. No amount of 'direct participation' – management dominated arrangements which were showed to be less durable than union representation – can be expected to encourage fair treatment for employees at work. (p. 230)

Millward *et al.* (2000) identify seven types of voice mechanism which have been dealt with in this book. These are:

1. one or more recognised trade unions (see Chapter 3);
2. a functioning consultative committee with representatives chosen through union channels (this chapter);
3. a functioning consultative committee with representatives not chosen through union channels (this chapter);
4. regular meetings between senior management and workforce (this chapter);

5. briefing groups (this chapter);
6. problem-solving groups (this chapter); and
7. non-union employee representatives.

Table 6.3 provides a summary of union and non-union voice arrangements, 1984–98.

In relation to the EU Information and Consultation Directive and Regulations

As mentioned earlier in the chapter, receptiveness on the part of UK governments to formalised systems of employee participation, such as those based on the co-determination and works council structures, has been lukewarm at best. The UK did, however, agree to adopt the EU Information and Consultation Directive of 2002 in stages from 2005, when the Directive became the Information and Consultation of Employees Regulations (ICE), to 2008. Details are provided in Exhibit 6.5.

Responses of government, TUC and CBI to the Directive

Currently, UK law provides for the information and/or consultation of employees or their representatives in the areas of collective redundancies (Chapter 12), transfers of undertakings (Chapter 12),

Exhibit 6.5

What the Information and Consultation Directive says

Directive 2002/14/EC of the European Parliament and of the Council

Object

The purpose of the Directive is to establish a general framework setting out minimum requirements for the right to information and consultation of employees in undertakings or establishments within the Community. The Information and Consultation of Employees Regulations came into force on 6 April 2005, for organisations employing more than 150 people in the UK. From 6 April 2007, coverage was extended to organisations employing 100 or more employees; and from 6 April 2008 to those employing 50 or more. The Regulations are designed to ensure that employees have the right to be informed and consulted on a regular basis about issues in the organisation for which they work. They apply to 'undertakings' – defined as public or private organisations 'carrying out an economic activity, whether or not operating for gain'.

The requirements outlined in the Regulations do not automatically apply to every undertaking. Employers can initiate the process themselves, or an employee request must be made by at least 10 per cent of employees (the 'trigger mechanism' in the organisation (subject to a minimum of 15 employees and a maximum of 2500 employees). Where there is a pre-existing information and consultation agreement in place (PEA), any request for new arrangements needs to be endorsed by at least 40 per cent of the workforce for negotiations to proceed.

Standard provisions based on the Information and Consultation of Employees Directive apply as a default in situations where no agreement is reached on information and consultation arrangements as a result of a request for negotiations. These require the employer to inform employee representatives about the organisation's activities and economic situation, and consult them on employment issues and major changes in work organisation or employees' contractual relations.

Scope

The Directive applies to undertakings employing at least 50 employees in any one Member State, or establishments employing at least 20 employees in any one Member State.

Practical arrangements and coverage

It is up to Member States to determine the practical arrangements for exercising the right to information and consultation at the appropriate level. Information and consultation covers:

(a) information on the recent and probable development of the undertaking's or establishment's activities and economic situation;

(b) information and consultation on the situation, structure and probable development of employment and threat to employment (possible redundancy); and

(c) information and consultation on decisions likely to lead to substantial changes in work organisation or contractual relations including those covered by legislation concerning collective redundancies and transfers of undertakings.

Consultation must take place with appropriate timing, method and content, at the relevant level of management and representation depending on the subject under discussion, on the basis of the information supplied by the employer, and in such a way as to enable employees' representatives to meet the employer and obtain a reasoned response to any opinion they may formulate. In addition, consultation should take place with a view to reaching

agreement on decisions within the employer's powers concerning substantial changes in work organisation or in contractual relations, including collective redundancies and transfers of undertakings.

Other provisions

The Directive contains provisions on the protection of employee representatives, enforcement and sanctions, the handling of confidential information and the relationship with other employment legislation.

Source: www.dti.gov.uk (accessed 18 January 2003); IRS Employment Review, 2006

collective bargaining (Chapter 5), occupational pensions, European Works Councils and the European Company Statute. UK developments in this area have been erratic and piecemeal, and progress has been hindered additionally by the conflicting interests of unions and the TUC on the one hand and of employers and the CBI on the other. However, the Information and Consultation Directive imposes a general requirement that member states adopt appropriate structures to facilitate and enhance consultation and information-sharing, which, for the majority of EU states are already in place in the form of legislated-for works councils and other co-determination systems. Within the UK there was until recently (2008), as we have noted previously, no such comprehensive framework concerning information and consultation and, arguably, the tradition of voluntarism in industrial relations and the ideological interests already noted to have militated against such a development. Notwithstanding this, the second Blair government had transposed the Directive in 2005, and to that end made its preliminary position clear in its report entitled: 'High performance workplaces: The role of employee involvement in a modern economy' (DTI, 2002).

Self-evaluation activity 6.7

The government's position

The response is given below

Is it possible to gauge from the title of the government report the voice mechanism(s) it may favour?

The report emphasises the business case for information and consultation, but only in the context of encouraging 'high performance workplaces' (HPWs). HPWs are characterised by 'high levels of employee involvement

and regard' (DTI, 2002, p. 11), valuing and motivating employees; adopting a joint approach to solving business problems involving everyone in the process; recognising the different rights, responsibilities and interests of different groups and individuals; implementing change through involving, consulting and informing all stakeholders in the business; helping to improve work/life balance; and, in some cases, coming to agreement whereby flexibility and employment security are traded. Clearly, then, information and consultation are regarded by government as one means of securing HPWs.

The report cites WERS 1998 in claiming that a wide diversity of practices exist aimed at 'involving people more closely in the workplace' (ibid., p. 16), but fails to mention one of its significant conclusions concerning employee voice: that no matter how much management-initiated involvement practices proliferate and are emphasised, employee perceptions of fairness in relation to decision making depend heavily upon union recognition and representation. There is, therefore, a clear emphasis upon involvement rather than participation and an overriding concern for the business case which ignores fairness and full participation in decision making. The main message of the report, however, is that there should not be a single model which is applicable to all organisations, but rather a diversity of approaches without legislative compulsion: 'Individual organisations should be able to develop their own arrangements tailored to their particular circumstances through voluntary agreements' (ibid., p. 18). This would apply particularly to small to medium-sized enterprises (SMEs):

It is particularly important in the case of small and medium sized enterprises that legislation should only be imposed where absolutely necessary. This is why the Government opposed any reduction in the 50-employee threshold in the Information

and Consultation Directive, and obtained deroga-
tions enabling us to delay applying the legislation
to firms with less than 150 employees for up to
3 years (to March 2008). Once fully implemented,
the Directive will only apply to 1% of companies in
the UK – though 75% of employees stand to benefit.
(ibid., p. 25)

In response to the discussion document, the TUC presented its own submission and, to its credit, this is more of an academic document and therefore both more critical and more considered than the government document (TUC, 2002). While the TUC paper agrees with the main contention of the government paper (henceforth 'DTI') that there is no simple formula for high performance, there are a number of criticisms, some of omission, that it makes. Firstly, there is little causal analysis in DTI as to *why* a positive attitude to employee involvement contributes to performance, much of the analysis residing within the HR literature to which little or no reference is made by DTI. The TUC report on the other hand cites numerous studies in support of straightforward arguments relating involvement positively with business gains. Secondly, the TUC rejects any notion advanced by many in the personnel profession that an exclusive focus on individual employee involvement is a recipe for success, together with the argument that the sole purpose of information and consultation is to align workers' aspirations with the goals of the business, which is essentially a 'unitarist' perspective. While there is evidence that direct participation or involvement can improve company performance, it is indirect (employee) participation that provides the best means for ensuring information-sharing and hence performance; it is, therefore, the 'collective voice to build commitment and trust [that is] likely to raise organisational performance' (TUC-CBI, 2001, para. 34). Hence the notion that direct and indirect participation conflict or mutually exclude each other is profoundly mistaken. Indeed, much research points to the probability that direct participation is more likely where there is a recognised union and some form of works council (TUC, 2002, p. 4), that direct and indirect involvement/ participation are mutually reinforcing and can make important contributions to building HPWs.

Thirdly, given that handling information and the consultative process are learnt skills, often through experience as much as through instruction, the TUC posits the question: are Britain's senior managers up to the job, given the argument that it is the quality of management that, at least in part, accounts for the poor productivity record of British firms and the 'productivity gap' between British and European, US and Far Eastern companies? Fourthly, the UK corporate governance model based on the 'shareholder economy' could mean that involving employees in corporate decision making is a risky investment. The model also points to the relative weakness of other stakeholders in the organisation such as employees themselves. Most European countries, on the other hand, have a family of institutions (such as sectoral and/or regional collective bargaining machinery, arrangements for co-determination and social partner involvement in welfare and training systems) giving a well-established voice to all stakeholders. Fifthly, the TUC recommends a Code of Practice (not mentioned in DTI or the Directive) to make specific reference to subjects on which consultation should take place, and has produced a wide-ranging list:

- organisational changes;
- introduction of new working methods and production processes;
- transfers of production;
- mergers;
- cut-backs or closures of undertakings or establishments;
- collective redundancies;
- grievance and disciplinary procedures;
- pensions;
- payment systems;
- equal opportunities;
- training and workforce development;
- working hours and holidays;
- flexible working arrangements;
- environmental issues; and
- health and safety.

Sixthly, there should be a distinction drawn between consultation on the one hand and collective bargaining on the other at appropriate levels of representation. These functions should be kept separate as they are in most EU countries where formally legislated-for works councils exist. However,

the paper identifies three practices which would be possible by agreement. These include:

- information and consultation via recognised unions with supplementary arrangements for non-union groups of employees, who must also be provided for by law, following judgements in the European Court of Justice on the UK Regulations implementing the Directive on Collective Redundancies and Transfers;
- an information and consultation body made up of representatives from unionised groups appointed by recognised unions and elected representatives from other non-union groups; and
- an information and consultation body for which elections are held for all seats. This is the most common current selection practice for JCCs.

Seventhly, the TUC has a preference for the Directive to apply to undertakings of at least 50 employees on grounds of ensuring equal treatment for employees within multi-establishment undertakings and providing for consultation with higher-level management who are more likely to be responsible for decision making. This understanding would also be more in keeping with the existing pattern of consultation arrangements within the UK and would also facilitate a 'single channel plus' or 'supplemented single channel' approach whereby union representatives in undertakings which recognise unions would be consulted primarily with other representatives consulted complementarily. Furthermore, within the UK context, the most viable approach to implementing the Directive would combine minimum standards with flexibility by:

- establishing a general duty on employers to carry out the necessary information and consultation procedures as directed by the Directive, where requested by employees;
- allowing employers and employees to determine the practical arrangements for information and consultation via negotiated agreements;
- in the absence of agreed information and consultation arrangements, enabling employees to seek the establishment of the necessary arrangements via some form of trigger mechanism; and
- making provision for a statutory fall-back framework to be enforced on employers who are unwilling to introduce the necessary information and consultation arrangements by agreement.

However, the TUC also argues that the government should try to promote information and consultation in small and medium-sized establishments (SMEs) and regrets the small firms' exclusion permitted by the Directive as small firms usually do not recognise unions and experience the vast majority of employment protection violations. The report goes on to argue:

> Giving workers a voice in their workplace will encourage workplace resolution of individual disputes. Such an approach is needed in the workplaces where the problems are greatest – small businesses. (p. 27)

Unlike the TUC, the CBI's position was more hostile to the Directive, although its website does not give much away to date, merely the statement:

> CBI is deeply disappointed by the agreement of this dossier. Nonetheless the current text contains some useful flexibilities that will help limit its damaging impact. We will be pressing the Government to make full use of them during the implementation process. (www.cbi.org, accessed 18 January 2003)

With regard to the impact of ICE both generally and upon employers and employees now the regulations have been fully implemented, it is necessary to await further research findings post-2008, and in particular the results of the next WERS survey (possibly WERS 2010). Interim findings such as those of Hall (2006) are provisional and are based upon limited case study evidence and it should be noted that 'employers need not act unless 10 per cent of their employees trigger statutory procedures intended to lead to negotiated agreements. Voluntary, 'pre-existing agreements' (PEAs) may effectively pre-empt the use of the Regulations' procedures' (Hall, 2006, p. 457). The extent of adoption of ICE by employers has been fairly limited to date (2008) and there has been a considerable reluctance on the part of employers to adopt PEAs. Moreover, 'as suggested by a number of interviewees, many employers see no need to institute such agreements or may be reluctant to do so' (Hall, 2006, p. 470), and there has been relatively sparse evidence of employees and trade unions using the 'trigger mechanism' to initiate statutory negotiations (see Exhibit 6.5) and indeed, according to research by IRS (2006) and

Employee Participation, Partnership and Involvement **493**

Hall (2006), only around 3 per cent of employers expect their employees to initiate or 'trigger' negotiations. Notwithstanding initial reluctance on the part of employers, employees and trade unions to adopt ICE, there may, as Hall suggests, be grounds for optimism as surveys such as IRS (2006) reveal that some employers at least were making future provisions for adoption of the Regulations.

In relation to partnership

Definitions of partnership remain unsatisfactory and unclear, having different meanings and levels of analysis (Tailby and Winchester, 2000; Heery, 2002). The TUC has a headline definition: 'Partnership means a grown-up relationship between bosses and workers', while the DTI partnership website has a longer but more amorphous definition:

> *Partnership at work refers to the relationship between employers, employees and their representatives. Partnership is about developing better employment relationships at all levels, helping to build trust in the workplace, the sharing of information and working together to solve business problems.* (www.dti.gov.uk/partnershipfund/index.html, accessed 18 January 2003)

The main pressure groups such as the TUC, CBI and Institute of Directors have, then, provided different interpretations of partnership, defining the term for their own ends (Ackers and Payne, 1998; Undy, 1999). The CIPD (Chartered Institute of Personnel and Development) views partnership as having 'more to do with an approach to the relationship between employers and employees individually, than it has to do with trade unions' (IPD, 1997). It is, therefore possible to define partnership in either pluralist or unitary terms (see Chapter 2), with the TUC view of partnership, for example (see below), being appropriately pluralist in nature. The Involvement and Participation Association (www.partnership-at-work.com, accessed 18 January 2003) has been instrumental in providing a definition of partnership that is more workable than most, and which has been endorsed by a number of large enterprises and some trade unions (see below). Heery (2002) identifies four levels at which partnership

operates. Firstly, at European level it can denote union involvement in the negotiation of framework agreements concerning, for example, parental leave and part-time work. Secondly, at national level, the TUC may be regarded as a partner in economic and social management. Thirdly, at sectoral level, the TUC works with a range of employer and management organisations in order to negotiate 'framework agreements' guaranteeing minimum employment standards. Finally, at company level social partnership can involve the negotiation of partnership agreements, normally between unions and management with the intention of creating a more harmonious and co-operative set of relationships within the organisation. Heery points out that, given the decentralised nature of UK employment relations, it is the growing numbers of partnership agreements that are the focus of attention.

Clearly, the two parties to the partnership agreement – trade unions and employers – will have both mutual and differing reasons for forming the agreement. For example, unions would hope to capitalise on the recognition procedures of the ERA 1999 by using partnership as a vehicle for the promotion of wider collective representation and collective bargaining while simultaneously sharing with management the concern for promoting performance and productivity in order to secure employment security. Hence unions would make certain concessions in return for enhanced employment protection, while employers would also make concessions in order to improve performance and productivity. As John Monks, the former General Secretary of the TUC, stated:

> *There is increasing evidence that partnership delivers. For employees it provides greater job security in satisfying, good quality jobs with access to training and influence over work organization. For employers the benefits include better quality decision-making and outcomes achieved by involving the whole workforce. A reduction in the amount of time spent on grievances and a more committed staff with a flexible approach to work.* (TUC, 2001, p. 2)

The TUC rejects the view that partnership constitutes 'concession bargaining' or 'cosying up' to employers, or failing properly to defend the interests

of members. Rather, the TUC argues that partnership is about *real* joint decision making and problem solving, about unions having more influence over employer behaviour and workers exercising greater control over their immediate working environment. Partnership, according to the TUC, depends on good employment relations and is more than traditional collective bargaining. The partnership agenda covers issues such as business strategy and how an organisation can meet the challenges of changing markets, technologies and customer requirements. It also embraces the development of a shared approach to training and the introduction of new forms of work. Partnership supplements and reinforces collective bargaining through greater openness and has a clear focus on issues affecting the quality of working life. The 'six principles of partnership' which the TUC endorses are:

- shared commitment to the success of the enterprise;
- recognition of legitimate interests;
- commitment to employment security;
- focus on the quality of working life;
- openness; and
- adding value.

Self-evaluation activity 6.8

Benefits to management
The response is given below

Identify the benefits to management/employer of partnership agreements.

Partnership at organisational level now involves working with rather than against employers, and as such requires management to accept the logic of some form of representation and communication through trade unions, this being the quid pro quo of the consultative style of management (Purcell, 1987) considered in Chapter 2. Apart from providing decisions with a degree of legitimacy they would otherwise not have, other alleged benefits to management include cost-effectiveness of communicating via representatives rather than individually, the value accrued to upward communication from staff and the stability such a relationship provides to managing employees (IRS, 1998).

History and background to partnership

The Involvement and Participation Association (IPA) was formed in 1896 in order to promote the idea of partnership and to bring together management and trade union representatives, hence the concept and practice of partnership per se is nothing new, despite the use of the terms 'social partners' and 'social partnership' during the 1980s and 1990s. Two long-standing examples of partnership are the multiple retailer the John Lewis Partnership, where individual employees are regarded as partners and receive a substantial share of the company's profits, and ICI, the chemical company, where partnership comprises an all-embracing joint consultation system with trade unions dating back to 1926. The IPA, then, has sought to disseminate best practice, provide guidance and advice and has established an underpinning set of partnership principles and practices (Martinez Lucio and Stuart, 2002).

During the 1980s a partnership dialogue was initiated by trade unions as part of the 'new realism' initiative (see Chapter 3). This focused upon challenges facing British industry and the need for a positive trade union response, which would include the development of a joint approach with employers to create economic success, improving quality, performance, cost and price competitiveness. It would also include considering issues such as training, investment, research and development, work restructuring, equal opportunities and health and safety. Partnership would also benefit from new forums for information and consultation such as works councils and an approach which stresses both 'individualism' (involvement and communication) and 'collectivism' (representative participation). In 1992 a joint statement of intent by employer and union representatives under the auspices of the IPA was issued which emphasised the following:

1. The parties to agree joint aims such as a joint commitment to the success of the organisation, a recognition to jointly build trust and a joint declaration recognising the legitimacy of the role of each party.
2. The areas where the parties need to rethink their approach. Management is asked to do more to ensure employment security, share the results of

success with all who contribute to it and recognise the employee's right to be informed, consulted and represented. Unions are asked to promote job flexibility, to recognise that union and non-union members have a right to representation, giving up the right to single channel representation, and to accept management attempts to involve individual employees.

3. A summary of the benefits of the new approach enabling discussion on a range of subjects not featuring prominently in collective bargaining in the UK in the past, such as quality through improvement, training, education, investment, communication, equal opportunity, corporate values, company success, environment and health and safety.

4. Possibilities for representation channels or forums were to broaden the existing collective bargaining framework to include subjects of wider policy and the introduction of 'new' institutions such as works councils where a wide agenda of issues could be discussed by employers and employee representatives.

The TUC, as we have seen, has also developed its interest in partnership as a way of renewing and extending the role of organised labour within the workplace and moving beyond the traditions and legacies of adversarial employment relations. In 1999 it developed its six partnership principles and then went on to form its own partnership consultancy and training body – the Partnership Institute – which aims to encourage the formation of partnership practices.

With the election of the first Blair government in 1997 there was an increased emphasis and impetus given to partnership as part of its 'modernisation' agenda. This was expressed in the white paper *Fairness at Work*, which stated: 'This White Paper is part of the Government's programme to replace the notion of conflict between employers and employees with the promotion of partnership' (DTI, 1998, p. 1). The substitution of conflict for partnership is problematic in itself since, on the one hand, collective voice and representation are undermined and de-emphasised, while on the other, many of the partnership policies advocated by government in the public sector generally and the National Health Service in particular 'are concerned with new forms of individual-oriented human resource management practices and workplace strategies and not simply union-oriented ones' (Martinez Lucio and Stuart, 2002). The government's partnership agenda has been given substance via the DTI with the creation of the Partnership at Work Fund, 'an essential part of the Government's non-legislative approach to improve industrial relations in order to secure productivity improvements' (DTI, 2002, p. 12). The Fund, which encourages and finances joint working on matters such as involvement, bullying and the quality of working life, provides up to £50,000 of matched finance for each partnership project, and additional funding during 2002 was provided to support the planned expansion of the Fund. There were 49 Fund 'winners' in 2002, of which Barclays is an example (see Main case 6.1).

Main case 6.1
Partnership at Barclays

Setting the scene
During the 1990s, employment relations at Barclays was characterised by a sequence of strikes and other industrial action. Strike action threatened the bank's plans for restructuring, which meant streamlining its functions and making staff redundant. Moreover, industrial action was unwelcome publicity for the bank, which was experiencing public dissatisfaction with branch closures. The catalyst for the move towards partnership relations was a series of branch strikes in 1997 over an unpopular performance-related pay scheme. The new management in the employee relations department realised that if the union, UNIFI, were to be brought into mainstream decision making, conflict would be better managed and disagreements could be resolved outside the public glare. For its part, UNIFI, the finance union, was also looking for a change. In pre-partnership times the union was left out of decision making and only informed of decisions that had already been made, and the only leverage UNIFI had in influencing decision making was industrial action or the threat of industrial action. As an alternative means of dealing with the employment relationship, UNIFI now argued that partnership meant that the union would not be

contained by management and it could have a say before decisions were taken. Partnership provided an alternative to strike action, which had never been popular with the union membership, and also offered new membership recruitment opportunities.

The agreement

Following lengthy discussions at the partnership steering committee during the late 1990s, the ensuing agreement produced a three-year pay and benefits deal, and a commitment to improving relations between the bank and UNIFI, working together to rebuild trust and respect as the basis for future relationships through co-operation and joint problem solving. Six principles of partnership were agreed to cement this new vision of employment relations:

1. To secure and promote the long-term success of Barclays.
2. To promote the interests of employees, customers and shareholders.
3. To ensure that Barclays meets customer expectations by having people with the right skills in the right place at the right cost.
4. To facilitate the management of change.
5. To ensure employees are managed fairly and professionally.
6. To promote equality of treatment and opportunity for all, valuing diversity.

The bank agreed to help the union influence the implementation of business strategy and plans, to facilitate UNIFI's role to promote the interests of its members, and to improve training, coaching and careers guidance for staff. In exchange, UNIFI endorsed the importance of co-operation with managers to develop shared agendas to promote the long-term success of the business. Whereas UNIFI traditionally rarely thought about the business case in negotiations, the partnership agreement commits the union to recognising business goals and objectives. As a result of a ballot, the agreement was accepted on a 20 per cent turnout.

To support the initiative, the bank established a partnership steering group to monitor progress and to recommend improvements to the new relationship. The steering group included senior figures from both sides, as well as lay representatives. In addition, nine joint working parties, with elected and jointly trained

representatives, were set up to examine company-wide issues such as change management, flexible working, performance management, pay, union facilities and representation, health and safety, equality and diversity, IT and job evaluation. The bank has also agreed to train 300 line managers and union staff representatives in partnership working (beginning in September 2002) in order to prevent it being regarded purely as a board-level initiative.

Outcomes of the Agreement

Working in partnership has had three key outcomes of particular significance to UNIFI. These concern culture, terms and conditions, and union organisation.

A new culture of employment relations

A successful bid in the second round of the DTI Partnership at Work Fund has resulted in a new leadership development programme for managers and union representatives, designed to encourage new ways of working based on trust. Part of this initiative involved a rolling programme of workshops across Barclays' various business units. The workshops focused upon:

- Developing a shared understanding of the business and its drivers, including the importance of diversity, work–life balance etc.
- Putting the partnership principles in local context.
- Putting partnership in the context of effective change.
- Building self-confidence and confidence in each other.
- Personal skills, for example, in the area of conflict resolution and communications.

'In the longer term, the aim is to integrate these workshops into the organisation's existing learning and development offering, which is centred upon the Barclays' University (the home for all learning and development for all employees). This step will help embed partnership with UNIFI even further into the Barclays' culture' (DTI, 2002).

New terms and conditions

Two three-year pay deals, the most recent signed in 2002, signalling the end of annual pay bargaining negotiations, included a new performance pay system, harmonised terms and conditions, and private healthcare. In addition to a pre-existing agreement called

'HR Policies and Procedures for Managing Change' that provided a generous package in the event of redundancies, the bank has also agreed to give affected members of staff six months' notice, during which time they are paid to look for alternative work, provide career counselling, a job-swap scheme, retraining assistance and an augmented pension. The agreement of these was an important precursor to signing the partnership agreement, which the workforce endorsed with an overwhelming majority in a secret ballot in April 1999.

Union organisation

Partnership has brought a new system of union representation and extended recognition to new parts of the bank (in December 2002, six union representatives were seconded specifically to trade union recruitment for one month). Voluntary union representation at a local level is now formalised by a growing network of over 120 jointly accredited UNIFI lay representatives and six full-time health and safety representatives. Representatives also receive extensive training in discipline and grievance, union recruitment and the law, which conform to an agreed role profile. Representatives are also allocated appropriate resources and two days a month to handle union business.

Challenges

- Union officials now have to consider both a business case and employee welfare in joint decision making. Part of the deal is that the union must also take ownership for controversial decisions.
- The union has a duty to communicate with its members on joint decisions, without undermining the trust of the bank in relation to confidential information or by appearing to be 'in bed with the boss'.
- The legitimacy of the union relies on its ability to convince members and non-members that their collective strength has a continuing impact on the nature of relations between bank and union.
- The credibility of the union relies on its ability to set and influence the business agenda and be prepared to exercise its power.
- Partnership has been slow to filter down the corporate hierarchy, particularly through the layers of line management and it has yet to be embedded throughout the company.

Self-evaluation activity 6.9

How successful is the Barclays partnership agreement?
Response on website

Based on your reading of the Barclays case, comment on the success or otherwise of the partnership agreement.

Issues and dilemmas: partnership as 'Janus-faced'?

Partnership agreements are varied and diverse, reflecting the specific needs and priorities of organisation, employees and unions. Often they are unwieldy compromises, which may not be in the long-term interests of either party. Here we consider in greater detail, through the research of Bacon and Storey (2000) and Oxenbridge and Brown (2002), the problem of *ambiguity* which is expressed in the two contrasting views of the partnership relationship (the term 'Janus-faced' is also appropriate, Janus being a Roman god who, as guardian of doorways and gates, is represented with two faces looking simultaneously forwards and backwards). The two contrasting views are essentially concerned with either the belief that partnerships represent a lifeline to unions after years of marginalisation, providing them with a legitimate voice in the wide-ranging affairs and issues of the organisations involved, or the argument that partnership agreements actually weaken unions and threaten and undermine workplace unionism. These views, as we have seen, are also ideological positions held by unions on the one hand and some employers on the other, often expressed in oppositional terms of 'collectivism v individualism' and 'pluralism v unitarism' (see Chapter 2). They also point to the motives of employers in pursuing partnership. As such, this dilemma raises more hypothetical questions and contentions than it answers. Such questions include:

- Does the adoption of a partnership agreement/arrangement signify a major change in management style including re-engaging with trade unions?
- Do partnership agreements require management to devise long-term strategies for managing the employment relationship?

- Do partnership agreements provide employers with the excuse for short-termism?
- Do partnership arrangements encourage the pursuit of 'individualism' of the type exercised in non-union firms at the expense of 'collective representation'?
- Or do new agreements manifest a mix and match of unitarism and pluralism where the two complement each other?

As a result of researching a number of large organisations such as Ford, Unilever, Cadbury-Schweppes and Royal Mail, Bacon and Storey (2000) arrive at the following conclusions. Firstly, there was little evidence that the agreements secured would provide stability in the longer term; hence partnership or 'framework' agreements may only be useful as 'stop-gaps' and short-term expediency. Secondly, while the motives of employers in securing agreements may have been to shift the emphasis in employment relations management more towards individualism, any further motives amongst management to marginalise or even derecognise unions were not realised. In fact, agreements were made for highly pragmatic reasons in some organisations, 'even where unions were aggressively sidelined' (ibid., p. 423). Thirdly, there was no real evidence that firms were seeking genuine joint determination over any issue; indeed there was greater interest in attempting to overcome union resistance to management plans despite agreements emphasising joint approaches. Nevertheless, such agreements are not to be regarded as 'hollow shells', as some of them did 'in the main re-establish a role for trade unions and offered forums to establish joint rules and procedures, although the agreements were firmly management-driven' (ibid., p. 424).

Research by Oxenbridge and Brown (2002) in 11 case-study organisations, spanning a range of industry sectors, examined the motives and benefits to the parties (see above), the content of partnership arrangements and relationships, together with strategies of control vis-à-vis trade unions. With regard to arrangements and relationships, one major issue is whether union bargaining rights are enhanced or weakened by partnership agreements. It was found that, overall, the bargaining agenda was limited and negotiation over substantive issues restricted, with some firms providing unions with relatively extensive recognition rights while others within the service sector allowed only minimal rights. The situation concerning representation and consultation was equally varied, involving senior managers and full-time union officers in some organisations, and workplace representatives and management in other, mainly production organisations. Companies with consultative structures such as JCCs and works councils tended to be union-dominated but recognised the need for non-union representation, while others had no or minimal consultative machinery.

In relation to control strategies, Oxenbridge and Brown (2002) found that the less formal the partnership arrangements, the more extensive were union rights. However, many firms used strategies to monitor unions after the partnership agreement was concluded. These include:

- Negotiating agreements or changes to existing agreements which explicitly limited union rights and activity in the workplace.
- Refusing to deal with 'difficult' trade union officials, and dealing only with officials perceived to be compliant.
- Endeavouring to reduce the number of unions the company dealt with.
- Taking steps to reduce union control over communication and consultative structures and increase management control of both (p. 267).

Oxenbridge and Brown conclude that managements had various and varying reasons for entering into partnership agreements, and may use agreements as vehicles for either encouraging or inhibiting collective bargaining and representation, more usually the latter.

Concluding comments

The evidence to date is still patchy and inconclusive and research in the area is relatively uncritical (Kelly, 2001). Arguably, for partnerships to prosper and yield benefits to employer and unions/employees, there should be a long-term commitment by managers to working closely with unions (Bacon, 2001). Should this commitment be lacking, then partnerships are unlikely to be successful as managers may well take an opportunistic view of the costs and benefits of partnership to the organisation. A central

assumption held by government and the CBI is that partnership is a model of co-operation in which adversarial industrial relations has no place and unions are required to be compliant. The TUC envisages a more proactive relationship with management, with unions being active partners in joint consultation and decision making. Whatever assumption is made, a crucial issue is whether partnership agreements will deliver benefits and returns to both parties, and if these benefits do not materialise, or if costs outweigh benefits, then enthusiasm for partnership may well subside.

Summary points

- While there has been a decline in union voice since 1980 there has been an increase in the use of communication channels by employers, particularly regarding regular meetings between senior managers and workforce, and briefing groups.
- Perceptions of fairness and fair treatment are positively associated with union channels of communication and a well-established union presence.
- The Information and Consultation Directive which is to be phased in from 2005 will provide a legislative basis for union and non-union representation within larger organisations.
- Definitions of partnership vary, as do the type of partnership agreement, with some ambiguity in how the parties interpret them in theory and in practice.
- The 'six principles of partnership' which the TUC endorses are:
 - shared commitment to the success of the enterprise;
 - recognition of legitimate interests;
 - commitment to employment security;
 - focus on the quality of working life;
 - openness; and
 - adding value.
- Research suggests that a crucial issue for the long-term viability of partnership is whether partnership agreements will deliver benefits and returns to both parties, and if these benefits do not materialise, or if costs outweigh benefits, then enthusiasm for partnership may wane.

EMPLOYEE INVOLVEMENT

Earlier in this chapter, we distinguished between employee participation and involvement. Whereas employee participation stresses collective representation of employees in joint decision making, employee involvement (EI) has an individualist focus and is part and parcel of 'soft' HRM approaches to managing the employment relationship, usually, but not necessarily, associated with a union-free environment in larger organisations. In recent years there has been a tendency for some academic researchers to combine both EI and EP and deal with them as one fused concept and set of practices and label it as 'EIP' (Harley *et al.*, 2005; Cox *et al.*, 2006). However, dealing with EIP in this way can gloss over and obfuscate the very real differences between the two, and the approach taken in this chapter continues to treat them, with some justification, as separate but related concepts.

Within a union-free environment EI is initiated and driven by employers, partly for union substitution purposes. EI is also used by managers in both unionised and non-unionised organisations and workplaces to change employee attitudes and behaviour in order to secure greater commitment and raise employee output within a 'high performance' work system environment. Although the term 'employee involvement' first began to appear in the management literature during the late 1970s, and became a familiar part of management vocabulary in Britain during the 1980s, the concept dates back to the 1920s with the inception of the 'human relations' school of management and then during the 1950s and 1960s was associated with ideas concerning job enlargement, job enrichment and job design. During the 1980s, EI was increasingly utilised within an HRM context and framework, reinforced by the dissemination of Japanese management methods with which it is still associated. The forms and methods of EI tend to change, or at least change emphasis and labels, with a high turnover in usage. For example, the more formal method of *quality circles* has largely been replaced by a more all-embracing *total quality management* (TQM) concept entailing a process of 'continuous improvement' based on the Deming-inspired and Japanese adopted 'philosophy' of *kaizen* (see Exhibit 6.6).

Exhibit 6.6

Kaizen

'For many, *kaizen* is the distinguishing feature between Japanese and Western organisations and the belief in the possibility and desirability of continuous improvement has been held out as underpinning Japanese production methods.' The emphasis on continuous improvement derives from Buddhism because 'the idea of perfection is far more present in this way of thinking than in that of the West. It is associated with a pessimism which is typically Buddhist and which is grounded on the fact that one knows one will never get there – in contrast to the optimism of the Westerner who can reach his goal because he is happy with less' (Kolm, 1985, p. 20). The assumption here is that there is no limit to possible improvement.

Eliminating waste in Japanese companies through *kaizen* involves an attempt to harness the mental as well as the manual skills of shopfloor workers. 'Individuals are encouraged to make suggestions – through quality circles, suggestion schemes and so on – as to how savings can be made. Such participation is not mandatory, though failure to make suggestions will result in criticism and may mean smaller bonuses' (Oliver and Wilkinson, 1992, p. 35).

Kaizen allowed managers to access workers' knowledge of the production process. Garrahan and Stewart (1992) noted that workers have suggested changes which have led to the speeding up of work. They also acknowledge that through *kaizen* workers learn how to participate in the Nissan way of working in a way which is acceptable to their employers. In addition to this, it is important to note that the legitimacy of *kaizen* has been maintained as projects are not narrowly defined or directed towards improvements in the labour process or other areas which directly affect the accumulation of profit.

Employee involvement in practice

The Workplace Industrial Relations surveys of 1980, 1984, 1990, WERS 1998, and WERS 2004 together with other research conducted for the Department of Employment by Marchington *et al.* (1992), reveal the extent of EI practices in British workplaces – both union and non-union. The later surveys report significant growth since the early 1980s 'to the extent that it is now common parlance of most senior managers' (Marchington, 1995, p. 283). The findings of both WERS 1998 and WERS 2004 indicate that 'new' management practices concerned with and related to employee involvement schemes are fairly widespread in many of the workplaces surveyed. Although no comparisons as yet have been made with earlier data, we can safely assume that the growth in EI practices has been maintained. Table 6.4, derived from WERS 1998 data, identifies 16 frequently discussed management practices and employee involvement schemes together with the proportion of workplaces operating them. The table does not distinguish between sector, employment size and the type of union presence. The survey also found that over half of workplaces operated five or more of the 16 practices and that there are definite groupings of practices commonly used. For example, training, teamworking, supervisors trained in employee relations matters and problem-solving groups are all associated with one another.

A more optimistic picture of the extent of EI is provided by the IRS (2002) survey of 52 organisations. The more common methods used by these organisations include:

- **notice boards:** used by 96 per cent of organisations – the simplest way to communicate;
- **company intranet and emails:** 88 per cent of organisations use an intranet and 85 per cent use email to convey information to employees. This medium is also used for 'upward' communication;
- **team briefings/meetings:** used by almost 90 per cent of organisations;

Table 6.4 New management practices and employee involvement schemes

	Percentage of workplaces
Most employees work in formally designated teams	65
Workplace operates a system of team briefing for groups of employees	61
Most non-managerial employees have performance formally appraised	56
Staff attitude survey conducted in last 5 years	45
Problem-solving groups (e.g. quality circles)	42
Single status between managers and non-managerial employees	41
Regular meetings of entire workforce	37
Profit-sharing scheme operated for non-managerial employees	30
Workplace operates a just-in-time system of inventory control	29
Workplace-level joint consultative committee	28
Most supervisors trained in employee relations skills	27
Attitudinal test used before making appointments	22
Employee share ownership scheme for non-managerial employees	15
Guaranteed job security or no compulsory redundancies policy	14
Most employees receive minimum of five days' training per year	12
Individual performance-related pay scheme for non-managerial employees	11

Source: WERS 1998; First Findings
Note: Base all workplaces with 25 or more employees based on responses from 1926 managers

- **company journal or newspaper:** 77 per cent of organisations use this method, representing a decline from 92 per cent in 1999;
- **attitude surveys:** undertaken annually, these are used by 73 per cent of organisations;
- **employee reports:** still one of the most unpopular methods, used by 35 per cent of organisations; and
- **video presentations:** the least popular method with 19 per cent of organisations.

Kersley *et al.* (2006) consider direct communication methods as the essence of EI (as is the case in this chapter) and these are considered in due course. The incidence of all forms of direct communications noted in WERS 1998 had increased by 2004 as the WERS 2004 findings indicate (Table 6.5). Other forms of direct communications not included in the 1998 survey comprised meetings between senior managers and the entire workforce, team briefings, employee surveys, e-mail, any written two-way communication, notice boards, intranet and any downward communication and were reported in WERS 2004. It should also be

noted from Table 6.5 that public sector and larger workplaces registered higher incidences of EI arrangements.

Table 6.6 provides a snapshot of EI practices for the period 1993–2002, according to the IRS EI surveys, 2002 being the last of such surveys. The 2002 survey report concludes that the passing of the EU Information and Consultation Directive, now phased in to cover all organisations/enterprises with at least 50 employees by 2008, should provide the impetus for employers before that date to implement, use and update the various EI practices referred to, and that 'employee relations and employee commitment and motivation are the areas most likely to benefit from employee involvement initiatives' (IRS, 2002, p. 14).

Types of employee involvement practices

Hyman and Mason (1995) identify four categories of EI comprising:

Table 6.5 Direct communication arrangements by sector

Year Sector	1998 (%) Private sector	1998 (%) Public sector	1998 (%) All workplaces	2004 (%) Private sector	2004 (%) Public sector	2004 (%) All workplaces
Face-to-face meetings						
Meetings between senior managers and the whole workforce	–	–	–	77	89	79
Team briefings	–	–	–	68	81	71
Any face-to-face meetings	82	96	85	90	97	91
Written two-way communications						
Employee surveys	–	–	–	37	66	42
E-mail	–	–	–	36	48	38
Suggestion schemes	29	35	31	30	30	30
Any written two-way communication	–	–	–	62	84	66
Downward communication						
Notice boards	–	–	–	72	86	74
Systematic use of management chain	46	75	52	60	81	64
Regular newsletters	35	59	40	41	63	45
Intranet	–	–	–	31	48	34
Any downward communication	–	–	–	80	97	83

Source: Kersley *et al.*, 2006, p. 135

- downward communication to individual employees;
- downward communication to groups of employees;
- upward communication for individual employees; and
- upward communication for groups of employees.

Table 6.6 identifies these processes for selected methods of EI and the goal(s) to be achieved.

Downward communication from managers to employees is used to inform and 'educate' employees so that they are more likely to endorse management initiatives and plans. Methods used include briefing groups and team briefing, and other forms of structured and less formal communication such as employee reports, house journals or company newspapers. Downward communication is also justified if it is successful in concentrating employee attention on product market and 'quality' issues. Using Hyman and Mason's comprehensive classification, the following types of EI are identified in Table 6.7.

Downward communication to individual employees

Self-evaluation activity 6.10

Provide examples of written downward communications

The response is given below

If you work within an organisation, identify examples of written downward communications used in your

Table 6.6 Employee involvement over time: 1993–2002

Survey year	1993	1996	1999	2002
Survey sample	62	26	49	52
Organisations recognising a trade union	82%	88%	59%	67%
Rationale for introducing employee involvement initiatives	Builds and reinforces the bond between employees and organisation, enhances employee commitment	To engender a greater commitment to, and identification with, the goals of the business and to increase employee participation	Better working relationships to enhance wider corporate performance	To create sense of ownership in employees, and to ensure that employees understand the strategic direction of the business and their role in achieving success
Main employee involvement methods (% of respondents using)	Company newspaper (85%); health and safety committee (79%); team briefings (79%); collective bargaining (69%)	Team meetings (81%); company journal (81%); team briefings (81%); collective bargaining (77%)	Team meetings (92%); company journal (92%); team briefings (86%); email communications (82%)	Noticeboards (96%); team meetings (90%); company intranet (86%); team briefings (87%)
Effect of employee involvement initiatives on trade unions (% of those recognising at least one union)	Strengthened (14%); weakened (35%); no effect (51%)	Strengthened (24%); weakened (32%); no effect (44%)	Strengthened (16%); weakened (33%); no effect (52%)	Strengthened (44%); weakened (15%); no effect (41%)
Whether initiatives had been specifically designed to weaken role of trade union	Yes in a fifth of organisations	Yes in two organisations	Yes in five organisations	Yes in six organisations
Major barriers to employee involvement	Senior managers (20%); middle management (23%); supervisors (7%); trade unions (6%)	Senior managers (21%); middle managers (14%); supervisors (21%); trade unions (5%)	Senior managers (4%); middle managers (8%); supervisors (5%); trade unions (11%)	Senior managers (7%); middle managers (2%); supervisors (2%); trade unions (7%)
Key areas benefiting from employee involvement	Employee job satisfaction, productivity, effective decision making	Quality, employee job satisfaction, employee commitment	Commitment/ motivation, employee relations, quality	Employee relations, management decision making

Source: Based on IRS, 2002

Table 6.7 Employee involvement processes

Methods	Communication	
	Flow	**Goal**
Group		
Briefing groups	Downward	Team communication
Chair's forums	Downward	Information dissemination
Semi-autonomous work groups	Upward	Group responsibility
Quality circles	Upward	Quality ethos, diagnostic improvements
Individual		
Counselling/mentoring	Upward	Employee welfare/development
Appraisal and development	Upward	Career development
Suggestion schemes	Upward	Diagnostic improvements

Source: Hyman and Mason, 1995, p. 77

organisation. If you do not work in an organisation, contact a large organisation within your area in order to get this information.

Concentrating on written information, the following are examples of the more commonly used methods:

- *Employee handbooks* are sometimes issued to employees on joining the organisation but many organisations neglect to do this. The contents of handbooks vary but, provided they are updated regularly, the handbooks provide useful information on the organisation and its background, its objectives and purpose, its products or services, how the organisation operates, the main conditions of employment and employee benefits, and the 'rules' of the organisation including summaries of the main procedures such as grievances, discipline, redundancy and equal opportunities.
- *Employee reports* are provided by many larger organisations on an annual basis to employees, and provide up-to-date information on the company's activities concerning sales, production, financial, investment, sales, projections of company performance in the longer term, and other company-relevant material. By having this information in a readable, easily understood form, employees are better able to understand the company's sources of income, investment and expenditure, and with information presented to employees in a systematic, fair and easily understood manner, greater trust can

be engendered between management and its workforce (Farnham, 2000).

- *Notice boards, letters, bulletins and briefing notes* are all fairly common, especially in larger organisations. Notice boards are an accessible and cheap method of providing current information, while letters may convey information concerning a single topic sent directly to employees. Regular bulletins and briefing notes are aimed mainly, but not exclusively, at middle and junior managers in order to update them on important matters.
- *Newsletters and house journals* have become widespread throughout Europe and are often used in conjunction with each other. They can be useful sources of information provided the issues are relevant and the material is produced in an interesting, professional fashion. It is, however, debatable as to whether this approach achieves its informational goals or whether management have adequately thought through the aims of written forms of communication. Hyman and Mason (1995), citing a survey of 102 publications from the UK's 1000 largest companies undertaken by Spurr (1990), argue that, as only a handful of items (24 out of some 4000 different news topics) were contributed by employees, it is questionable whether 'written, essentially downward communication methods might be considered a meaningful form of involvement' (p. 35).

Downward communication to groups of employees

There are two main methods used to communicate downwards to groups and they are identified below. The nature of the communication is predominantly oral, and the degree of interaction between management and employees varies depending upon the size of group, the nature and purpose of the communication and to whom it is directed.

Meetings/forums

These may take the form of departmental meetings, the purpose of which is to enable departmental heads to convey information from senior management to staff on a regular and largely informal basis (although written agendas and minutes may be used). Another form of meeting is the mass meeting, which is formalised, fairly infrequent and allows senior management to address all staff on specific topics at a particular location. Important announcements may be made and there is limited opportunity for discussion.

Team briefings

Group methods of downward communication have been popularised by team briefings which 'reflect the unitarist approach to employee involvement, placing great emphasis on "cascading information down the line", from executive management through to the shop floor' (Hyman and Mason, 1995, p. 79). Team briefings are used to:

- inform employees of high-level or strategic decisions;
- communicate general information concerning company goals and performance, together with other matters; and
- explain the reasons for decisions concerning aspects of change, for example, changes to production technology and how these affect local work arrangements, the work group and the department(s) concerned.

Team briefings therefore have a 'local flavour' and teams are composed of colleagues who normally work in close proximity to each other. The number of team members varies from about four to 16, and teams have a 'leader' or 'coach' who may be the supervisor. Briefing meetings are held regularly

on a monthly or bi-monthly basis and ideally should be brief (no more than 30 minutes). Typically, a briefing meeting comprises each manager or supervisor (the 'leader' or 'coach') meeting his or her team face to face on a regular basis. Information is cascaded downwards and is directly relevant to 'performance indicators'; targets are identified, progress reports made and 'points of action' developed.

The aims of team briefings as far as the organisation is concerned are, firstly, to provide line managers and supervisors with a greater part to play in day-to-day employee relations and 'help make this level of management feel an integral and strategically important part of the organisation' (ibid., p. 79) and, secondly, to increase the level of employee commitment at workplace level. Securing employee commitment within the team-briefing context is regarded as desirable, if not necessary, in order to:

- decrease misunderstanding between management and employees;
- increase employee acceptance of organisational and technological change by explaining to them the reasons for these changes; and
- 'to improve upward communication in the long term, by making employees feel that they have the knowledge about the organisation that allows them to contribute positively to its decision making processes' (ibid., p. 79).

The system is designed to ensure that all employees from executive management down to the shop or office floor are fully informed of matters that affect their work. Gennard and Judge (1997) describe the system in the following way:

Leaders of each briefing session prepare their own briefs, consisting of information relevant and task-related to the employees in the group. The brief is then supplemented with information which has been passed down from higher levels of management. Any employee's questions raised which cannot be answered at the time are answered in written form within a few days. Briefers from senior management levels are usually encouraged to sit in at briefings being given by more junior managers, while line managers are encouraged to be available to brief the shop floor employees. Although team briefing is not a consultative process and is basically one-way,

question-and-answer sessions do take place to clarify understanding. Feedback from employees is very important just as professional managers will explain management's view to the employees in a regular and open way, using examples appropriate to each work group. (p. 129)

Team briefing in theory may be regarded as a 'panacea', but in practice there may be a number of problems and pitfalls. For example, how are team briefings to be set up within a workplace which operates on a continuous shift-working basis, when employees are working all the time except for their rest breaks? Marchington and Parker (1990) identify a number of problems in one of their case study firms, Foodpack, a large food manufacturing company. Mini case 6.1 explores teamworking problems in a food packaging company and Mini case 6.2 within a bank environment.

Mini case 6.1
Team briefing at Foodpack

Although the ground had been well prepared, the Personnel Manager was under no illusion that the team briefing offered a panacea for all the company's ills, and he was sensitive to its potential pitfalls. At the time of the launch he said: 'People can soon realise that they're being brought together and told a lot of crap. Also, they may develop into bitching sessions . . . You have got to remember that this audience is not used to receiving information. But it is equally important not to talk down to the shop floor, only to talk in relevant language.'

There was a mixed reception from employees to the team briefing activities and on the positive side the researchers conclude: 'Clearly, therefore, team briefing seems to have had a direct, if minor effect on activity and also on attitudes to the company.' Less positively, 'departments such as baking and engineering were less convinced about the value of the sessions'. The bakers' foremen address their groups every month, but this 'gets squeezed in when there is a breakdown or at any other convenient moment, such as when we change commodities'. Because of the continuous nature of the process, and the extensive shift arrangements for this group of operators, it was not always possible for these supervisors to attend their brief by the

Production Manager. One of these also indicated the difficulty he faced in trying to interest his staff, since much of the information is about 'market performance, management changes, company acquisitions, not just about Foodpack. That kind of information interests some, but not others . . . nine out of ten here are only interested if it affects their pockets.'

The engineers were also dubious about the benefits of more information of the type they had been given, and one of them described his feelings in this way: 'Whilst it gives you more interest in what is going on, I'm not dying to know. I'm not won over myself. I haven't bought shares or anything, though I might do when I've got a bit of money.' Proponents of new realism and an enterprise culture would do well to recognise that such a calculative orientation to work is not unusual on the shop floor. There are always likely to be problems in maintaining team briefing in an environment where workloads are highly variable over the course of the year, particularly during peak periods when continuity of production is paramount.

Source: Marchington and Parker, 1990, pp. 147–9

Mini case 6.2
Barkers Bank

Team briefing was introduced for the most popular and pressing of reasons, primarily to facilitate change (overcome resistance) and to tie in with the bank's strategy and longer-term objectives. As the bank was relocating, redundancies were inevitable, so it was essential that an effective structure of communication was in place. The briefing process emphasised the role of the line manager who would be 'chief facilitator' as an alternative channel of communication to the traditional union one. Managers themselves became 'team leaders'. Briefings lasted between 15 and 30 minutes and took place after the main brief was received from head office.

One problem with briefing was the difficulty of communicating change positively in a climate of uncertainty. If staff were not told, this would cause suspicion and apprehension, and if staff were told, it would be in such vague terms that it merely served to reinforce fears. The position of managers was ambiguous, not only to staff but also to the managers themselves, and the nature of this 'role ambiguity' resulted

in inconsistencies of approach as managers were not always able to deal with issues or queries raised by staff, either because of disagreements or because they did not have the answers.

Upward communication involves the use of what Hyman and Mason (1995) call 'diagnostic techniques' which aim at using employee knowledge of the process of production and other technological and organisational issues to 'maximise a zero-defects standard in production' (p. 81). This approach focuses upon the individual employee and the work group and includes the categories identified below.

Upward communication for individual employees

Three main techniques are in common use. These are attitude surveys, suggestion schemes and appraisal schemes.

Attitude surveys

These satisfy management's need to obtain the views and opinions of employees on issues of mutual importance. The feedback obtained should be acted upon rather than stored in personnel files to gather dust. Reasons for conducting attitude surveys include the need to diagnose any problems within the organisation; the assessment of the consequences of organisational change; the measurement of employee attitudes before and after the change programme; the provision of feedback on management policies, actions and plans; and the identification of issues which concern employees collectively.

Suggestion schemes

These have a long tradition in Britain, and may be considered to be the oldest form of EI, the first formal scheme of its type being introduced in the 1880s in the Scottish shipbuilding industry. Traditionally, suggestion schemes have been used to minimise costs, but more recently, particularly in Japanese companies, they have been used to encourage employee commitment and self-motivation. Employees are encouraged to contribute ideas concerning the improvement of working methods, cutting costs of production and improving other aspects of the organisation's activities. Ideas which are accepted are financially rewarded.

Appraisal and development schemes

Appraisal schemes have grown in popularity and are often linked with the total quality management approach. Coverage of appraisal schemes, once confined to managerial grades, is now increasingly extended to other non-manual and even manual grades. In essence, the appraisal process involves both the appraisee (the person to be appraised) and the appraiser (usually the immediate manager or supervisor) in a yearly assessment of past performance, the setting of goals for the next year and monitoring the extent to which these goals have been achieved. The 'development' aspect is concerned with allocating resources to the employee in order to enable him or her to achieve the agreed goals. While it is outside the scope of this book to consider appraisal schemes in any detail, it is important to note that there are a number of problems associated with them, a few of which are now identified:

- If the scheme is not properly resourced, then employees may not have the opportunity to improve their performance through the provision of training and educational facilities and may therefore regard appraisal as a means of reinforcing management control.

- If appraisal is linked to performance-related pay, then this can create tensions within the appraiser–appraisee relationship. For example, if promotion opportunities and pay are subject to performance appraisal, then the open relationship may be compromised by the reluctance of the appraisee to be frank about weaknesses, and the appraiser may be reluctant to provide too positive an assessment of performance.

- The complexity of many appraisal and development schemes requires, ideally, thorough training of both appraisers and appraisees in order to ensure that schemes are fully effective.

Upward communication for groups of employees

The purpose of 'upward communication' techniques and approaches is to exploit employees' knowledge and expertise of their jobs, particularly through the mechanisms of small groups and teams. The main approaches briefly considered here, teamworking and quality circles, are 'quality driven' and are geared towards improved methods of production and service delivery within a context which encourages co-operative relationships and change. The evolving

'philosophy' which is used to justify these approaches is known as total quality management (TQM) based on Deming's notion (1981) of total quality control (TQC) adopted in Japan and then exported to western economies.

TQC and TQM

> *Production, not quality control must have primary responsibility for quality; and everybody, including top management, must participate in project-by-project quality improvement.* (Shonberger, 1982, p. 82)

TQC concepts are based on the work of the American management scientist W.E. Deming. Shunned by the USA, his ideas were enthusiastically taken up in Japan, where he is regarded as the father of Japanese quality control. (A prize named after him, the annual Deming prize, is awarded to the Japanese manufacturer exhibiting the most impressive quality performance.) The main TQC concepts and categories are identified in Table 6.8.

Production responsibility means assigning the primary responsibility for quality to production personnel thereby removing it from the quality control department. The initiative for this must come from the top of the organisational hierarchy. The *rate* of quality improvement can be accelerated by implementing items from TQC categories 2–5 (as shown in Table 6.8). As far as goals are concerned, the *habit of continuous improvement* is directed towards perfection, which involves measurement of quality performance and the striving for perfect conformance to specifications (zero defects). Quality depends upon the integrated efforts of marketing, design engineering, purchasing, manufacturing engineering, production and service departments, and supports a quality strategy which presumes that ever-better quality will forever increase market share and the total market as well. The other categories and concepts listed support the TQC philosophy of continuous improvement. Within the TQC scheme of things, quality circles are just one of the 18 TQC concepts listed in Table 6.8. But as they became increasingly popular in Britain and the USA, we consider them briefly below.

TQM has become the more acceptable term in western economies, but the basic ideas are the same as those underpinning TQC. Essentially, TQM endorses the guiding philosophy and goal of

Table 6.8 Total quality control: concepts and categories

TQC category	TQC concept
1. Organisation	Production responsibility
2. Goals	Habit of improvement
	Perfection
3. Basic principles	Process control
	Easy-to-see quality
	Insistence on compliance
	Line stop
	Correcting one's own errors
	100 per cent check
	Project-by-project improvement
4. Facilitating concepts	QC as facilitator
	Small lot sizes
	Housekeeping
	Daily machine checking
5. Techniques and aids	Exposure of problems
	Foolproof devices
	Analysis tools
	QC circles

Source: Schonberger, 1982, p. 51. Reprinted with the permission of The Free Press, a Division of Simon & Schuster Adult Publishing Group, from JAPANESE MANUFACTURING TECHNIQUES: Nine Hidden Lessons in Simplicity, by Richard J. Schonberger. Copyright © 1982 by Richard J. Schonberger. All rights reserved.

continuous improvement (*kaizen*) and places considerable emphasis upon increasing employee work responsibilities, reorganising work and increasing employee involvement in problem-solving activities in order to achieve that goal. There is the same emphasis upon inter-departmental co-operation and integration in order to facilitate quality improvement where it matters, that is, by the production and service workers.

Teamworking and semi-autonomous working groups

This is a form of task-based involvement which focuses upon 'whole jobs' and is concerned with enlarging and extending the range and scope of tasks

which comprise the job. The basic ideas behind teamworking date back to the 1960s when Herzberg *et al.* (1959) of the managerialist 'neo' human relations school developed the techniques of job enlargement and job enrichment, the former concentrating upon increasing the range and diversity of tasks making up a job, and the latter upon introducing more elements of responsibility into work tasks. These techniques became integrated into a system of working which incorporated so-called principles of job design. Job design has been used to encourage group working, not only by enlarging and enriching jobs, but also by developing new 'user-friendly' production technologies as alternatives to Fordist assembly-line technology which, under certain circumstances, enable semi-autonomous work groups to make the product (cars, for example) 'on site'. In such situations, workers have considerable discretion, autonomy and responsibility over pace of work, how much to produce and when to produce, thereby maximising their EI potential. The 'experiments' in work group autonomy had very limited success in Britain and were dominated by 'high profile' examples mainly in Scandinavia.

Teamwork in teams of varying size from around seven upwards is now considered as incorporating both semi-autonomous working groups and the more prescriptive enlargement and enrichment approaches, and is often referred to as 'flexible specialisation'. Teamwork requires considerable investment in training, with benefits of improved employee commitment, morale and motivation. Geary (1994) in describing the range of teamworking techniques comments:

> In its most advanced form, team working refers to the granting of autonomy to workers by management to design and prepare work schedules, to monitor and control their own work tasks and methods, to be more or less self-managing . . . At the other end of the spectrum, management may merely wish employees of comparable skill to rotate between different tasks on a production line or the integration of maintenance personnel to service a particular group of machines. (p. 37)

Quality circles

The quality circle (QC) is a Japanese development dating from around 1962. QCs comprise small voluntary groups of workers, both operatives and specialists such as engineers in the same circle. One of the main activities of QCs is concerned with the use of problem-solving techniques such as brainstorming, problem identification, data collection and analysis and presentation skills in order to reduce waste, improve performance and quality, increase competitiveness, promote self-development and group identity and to encourage communications. In addition, 'morale-enhancing ideas – softball leagues, vending machines, repainting the lunchroom, and so on – are legitimate topics for QC discussion, and motivational benefits are expected to derive from the employee interaction and involvement that takes place in circles' (Shonberger, 1982, p. 185). Members are also trained in the use of simple statistical analysis in order to improve quality and meet quality objectives.

QCs flourished initially in the US where they 'sprouted . . . like dandelions in a spring lawn' (ibid., p. 181), and then became popular for a time in Britain during the 1980s. However, it is important to emphasise that circles are low on the priority list of important things to get accomplished and their impact as a method of employee involvement in western countries is relatively limited. Shonberger, for example, points out:

> It is a mistake to think of QCs – for all their morale and motivation advantages – as a ticket to achieving the quality levels that have been attained by the Japanese. In fact, QC circles founded on such a premise could do more harm than good in that they might delay for several years the introduction of a real quality control programme. (p. 185)

The success of QCs in Britain depends upon whether, as in Japan, they are regarded as an integral part of an organisation-wide quality management programme. Indeed, many circles have foundered because they were regarded as a panacea for certain organisational problems, or introduced as one more management 'fad'. The introduction of quality circles in Ford UK as a result of its doomed but well intentioned 'After Japan' initiative is a case in point. McKinlay and Starkey (1992) argue that 'the dismal failure of the labour relations element of the campaign was directly attributable to Ford's attempts to impose quality circles as a structural

remedy for relatively poor productivity and quality, rather than introducing them as mechanisms for mobilising employee commitment to company goals' (p. 116).

A survey of manufacturing practices in a number of companies undertaken by Oliver and Wilkinson (1992) concluded that quality circles were the least favourably rated and the least successful. The reasons for this, they suggest, are:

> That quality circles were one of the first elements of Japanese practice to be emulated by British companies, so that there has been more chance for the 'honeymoon effect' to wear off . . . [and that] quality circles have been seen by many companies as a relatively low investment innovation and consequently have failed to attract the necessary commitment, being treated merely as 'bolt-on' accessories. (pp. 162–3)

The problems associated with quality circles, therefore, include the effects of transposing a Japanese-derived 'culture-bound' concept and method used successfully in Japanese companies into a western organisational context with no quality ethos and no traditions of group-based quality management. Another problem with QCs concerns their introduction into unionised organisations where, as in the Ford example (Exhibit 6.7, below), opposition may be encountered. Union opposition may be based upon perceptions of incompatibility between the essentially 'collective' orientation of industrial relations and the 'individualistic' preoccupations of HRM practices where QCs belong to the latter category.

Employee involvement: concluding comments

The take-up of EI has been fairly comprehensive and widespread in a growing number of organisations as the WIRS surveys and WERS 1998/2004 suggest. Although EI can and has been regarded as a major union substitution practice, this is only one reason why managers have adopted it. A substantial number of larger unionised companies have integrated EI into their existing union channels without compromising the role of union representatives or altering collective methods of communication. Other companies use EI practices as an integral part of a wider HRM strategy geared towards increasing employee identification with, and commitment to, the organisation and are at least partially successful in this. However, yet other organisations, perhaps in a majority, have adopted EI as a 'fad', as with many other new management practices such as 'empowerment', and as we may expect, there is little integration of EI within HRM strategy. Within these and other organisations, EI may not work effectively in

Exhibit 6.7

Quality circles at Ford

The 'After Japan' campaign was a programme of productivity and quality improvement, a major part of which involved the introduction of quality circles to the shop floor of Ford's European car plants. The company invested substantial sums of money in the programme, which included the training of circle leaders and members in techniques of problem solving and analysis. Three people were appointed to coordinate the programme at company level, and plant managers were responsible for circle activities in their plants. There was a short pilot project, after which quality circles were launched across all plants in the UK. There was little consultation with unions or lower levels of management, as senior management considered quality circles to be a 'minor change for the better'. In the six months or so following their introduction, some successes were documented (for example, a 2.5 per cent saving in scrap at the Bridgend engine plant). However, union resistance was mounting, and in 1981, the trade unions withdrew their support from the programme. According to Guthrie's (1987) analysis, the programme was a 'resounding failure' in terms of its aims of improving work attitude and generating net cost savings.

Source: Oliver and Wilkinson, 1992, p. 169

practice as line managers may 'lack the enthusiasm and commitment . . . and many employers have committed insufficient time and resources to training supervisors to deliver EI at the workplace' (Marchington, 1995, p. 301). However, the implementation of the EU Information and Consultation Directive is likely to encourage organisations and enterprises to devise and incorporate effective EI approaches as part of their ongoing HR strategies although evidence of this since its full implementation in 2008 is still sparse.

A more fundamental criticism is posited by, for example, Hyman and Mason (1995), who argue that EI has had little or no effect upon the extent to which employees have influence within their organisations because:

- evidence that employees influence organisational decisions and other corporate matters is extremely limited. EI is confined either to immediate work and task issues or to facilitating communications;
- EI is concerned with securing employee commitment. With greater emphasis upon involvement practices, 'there is a danger that collective means to influence employer and managerial decisions will become further eroded' (p. 192); and
- EI is associated 'functionally and operationally' with employee flexibility and labour market deregulation 'which raises further doubts about the capability of involvement to serve as a vehicle for the expression of employee interests' (p. 192).

We conclude, therefore, that the impact of EI upon the employee has been marginal. In Britain employees, particularly in non-union organisations, are subject to management-initiated and -directed involvement as the main, if not the sole, means of communication and information and for employees in these and other organisations, the EU Information and Consultation Directive now fully implemented is likely to encourage a greater proliferation of EI practices although research to date is inconclusive.

RELEVANT WEBSITES

www.dti.gov.uk (Department of Trade and Industry) Provides useful information and statistics concerning small and medium-sized enterprises (SMEs), together with information relating to its Small Business Service.

www.berr.gov.uk (Department for Business Enterprise and Regulatory Reform) The successor to the DTI.

www.eurofound.ie (European Foundation for the Improvement of Living and Working Conditions) Information concerning social partnership, European Works Councils, consultation and information.

www.partnership-at-work.com (Partnership at Work) An excellent site for all aspects of partnership.

www.tuc.org.uk/partnership (Trades Union Congress) Good for exploring the TUC's position on partnership and information and consultation.

REFERENCES

Ackers, P. and Payne, J. (1998) 'British trade unions and social partnership: rhetoric, reality and strategy'. *International Journal of Human Resource Management*, 9, 3, 529–50

Ackers, P., Smith, C. and Smith, P. (1996) *The New Workplace and Trade Unionism: Critical Perspectives on Work and Organisation*. London, Routledge

AEEU (1997) *European Works Councils*. London, AEEU

Argyris, C. (1964) *Integrating the Individual and the Organisation*. New York, Wiley

Bacon, N. (2001) 'Employee relations', in Redman, T. and Wilkinson, A. (eds) *Contemporary Human Resource Management*. Harlow, Financial Times/Prentice Hall

Bacon, N. and Storey, J. (2000) 'New employee relations strategies in Britain: towards individualism or partnership?' *British Journal of Industrial Relations*, 38, 3, 407–27

Batstone, E. (1984) *Working Order*. Oxford, Blackwell

Berghahn, V.R. and Karsten, D. (1987) *Industrial Relations in West Germany*. Oxford, Berg

Blyton, P. and Turnbull, P. (1994) *The Dynamics of Employee Relations*. London, Macmillan

Blyton, P. and Turnbull, P. (1998) *The Dynamics of Employee Relations*, 2nd edn. London, Macmillan

Bridgford, J. and Stirling, J. (1994) *Employee Relations in Europe*. Oxford, Blackwell

Bullock Report (1977) *Report of the Committee of Inquiry on Industrial Democracy*, Cmnd 6706. London, HMSO

Carley, M. (2002) *Bargaining at European Level? Joint Texts Negotiated by European Works Councils.* Dublin, European Foundation for the Improvement of Living and Working Conditions

Clegg, H.A. (1985) 'Trade unions as an opposition which can never become a government', in McCarthy, W.E.J. (ed.) *Trade Unions.* Harmondsworth, Pelican

Cox, A., Zagelmeyer, S. and Marchington, M. 'Embedding employee participation and involvement at work'. *Human Resource Management Journal*, 16, 3, 250–67

Cressey, P. (1998) 'European works councils in practice'. *Human Resource Management Journal*, 8, 1, 67–79

Cressey, P., Eldridge, J. and MacInnes, J. (1985) *Just Managing.* Milton Keynes, Open University Press

Cully, M., Woodland, S., O'Reilly, A. and Dix, G. (1999) *Britain at Work.* London, Routledge

Deming, W. (1981) 'What top management must do'. *Business Week*, July, 19–21

Donovan (1968) Report of the Royal Commission on Trade Unions and Employers' Associations 1965–1968, Cmnd 3623. London, HMSO

DTI (Department of Trade and Industry) (1998) *Fairness at Work*, Cm 2968. London, HMSO

DTI (Department of Trade and Industry) (2002) 'High performance workplaces: the role of employee involvement in a modern economy. A discussion paper'. London, DTI

Edwards, P. (1985) 'Managing labour relations through the recession'. *Employee Relations*, 7, 2, 3–7

European Foundation for the Improvement of Living and Working Conditions (EUROFOND) (2007a) *Foundation Research on European Works Councils, 1994–2006.* Eurofond, Luxembourg

European Foundation for the Improvement of Living and Working Conditions (EUROFOND) (2007b) *Industrial Relations Developments in Europe.* Eurofond, Luxembourg

Farnham, D. (1997) *Employee Relations in Context.* London, IPD

Farnham, D. (2000) *Employee Relations in Context*, 2nd edn. London, CIPD

Farnham, D. and Pimmlott, J. (1995) *Understanding Industrial Relations.* London, Cassell

Fitzroy, F. and Kraft, K. 'Co-determination, efficiency and productivity'. *British Journal of Industrial Relations*, 43, 2, 233–47

Frege, C.M. (2002) 'German works councils: a critical assessment'. *British Journal of Industrial Relations*, 40, 2, 221–48

Furstenberg, F. (1981) 'Zur Methodologie der Mitbestimmungsforschung', in Diefenbacher, H. and Nutzinger, H.G. (eds) *Mitbestimmung.* Frankfurt, Campus

Garrahan, P. and Stewart, P. (1991) 'Nothing new about Nissan', in Law, C. (ed.) *Restructuring the Automobile Industry.* London, Routledge

Geary, J.E. (1994) 'Task participation: employees' participation enabled or constrained?', in Sisson, K. (ed.) *Personnel Management.* Oxford, Blackwell

Gennard, J. and Judge, G. (1997) *Employee Relations.* London, IPD

Gilman, M. and Marginson, P. (2002) 'Negotiating European Works Councils: contours or constrained choice'. *Industrial Relations Journal*, 33, 1, 36–51

Guthrie, G. (1987) 'After Japan and beyond'. *Production Engineer*, May, 29–31

Hall, M., Carley, M., Gold, M., Marginson, P., and Sisson, K. (1995) *European Works Councils: Planning for the Directive.* London, IRS

Hall, M. (2006) 'A cool response to the ICE regulations? Employer and trade union approaches to the new legal framework for information and consultation'. *Industrial Relations Journal*, 37, 5, 456–72

Harley, B., Hyman, J. and Thompson, P. (2005) *Participation and Democracy at Work: Essays in Honour of Harvey Ramsay.* London, Palgrave Macmillan

Heery, E. (2002) 'Partnership v organising: alternative futures for British trade unionism'. *Industrial Relations Journal*, 33, 1, 20–35

Heery, E., Healy, G. and Taylor, P. (2004) 'Representation at work: themes and issues', in Healy, G., Heery, E., Taylor, P. and Brown, W. (2004) *The Future of Worker Representation.* Basingstoke, Palgrave Macmillan

Heller, F.A. (1986) 'Does formal policy or law as used in Europe contribute to improved employee information and participation?', in Vandamme, J. (ed.) *Employee Consultation and Information in Multinational Corporations.* Beckenham, Croom Helm

Herzberg, F. (1974) *Work and the Nature of Man*. London, Staples Press

Herzberg, F., Mausner, B. and Synderman, B. (1959) *The Motivation to Work*. London, Granada

Hyman, J. and Mason, B. (1995) *Managing Employee Involvement and Participation*. London, Sage

IPD (1997) *Employment Relations into the 20th Century*. London, IPD

IRS (1998) 'Works councils more prevalent than expected'. *IRS Employment Trends*, No. 664

IRS (2002) 'Employee involvement'. *IRS Employment Trends*, No. 763

IRS (2006) *Employment Review*, No. 859

IRS (2007) 'Germany: co-determination review'. *European Employment Review*, No. 397

Kelly, J. (2001) 'Social partnership agreements: who gains, who loses?' *Candid*, magazine of the GMB London Region, 5 July

Kersley, B., Alpin, C., Forth, J., Bryson, A., Bewley, H., Dix, G. and Oxenbridge, S. (2006) *Inside the Workplace: Findings from the 2004 Workplace Employment Relations Survey*. London, Routledge

Kolm, S.C. (1985) 'Must one be a Buddhist to grow? An analysis of the cultural basis of Japanese productivity', in Koslowski, P. (ed.) *Economics and Philosophy*. Tubingen, J.C.B. Morh

Likert, R. (1961) *New Patterns of Management*. New York, McGraw-Hill

MacInnes, J. (1985) 'Conjuring up consultation'. *British Journal of Industrial Relations*, 23, 1, 93–113

Marchington, M. (1987) 'A review and critique of research on developments in joint consultation'. *British Journal of Industrial Relations*, 25, 3, 339–52

Marchington, M. and Armstrong, R. (1986) 'The nature of the new joint consultation'. *Industrial Relations Journal*, 17, 2, 158–70

Marchington, M. and Parker, P. (1990) *Changing Patterns of Employee Relations*. Hemel Hempstead, Harvester Wheatsheaf

Marchington, M., Goodman, J., Wilkinson, A. and Ackers, P. (1992) *New Developments in Employee Involvement*. Research Series No. 2, Sheffield, Department of Employment

Marchington, M. (1995) 'Involvement and participation', in Storey, J. (ed.) *Human Resource Management: A Critical Text*. London, Routledge

Marchington, M. (2005) 'Employee involvement: patterns and explanations', in Harley, B., Hyman, J. and Thompson, P. (2005) *Participation and Democracy at Work: Essays in Honour of Harvey Ramsay*. London, Palgrave Macmillan

Marginson, P., Gilman, M., Jacobi, O. and Krieger, H. (1999) *Negotiating European Works Councils: An Analysis of Agreements Under Article 13*. London, The Stationery Office

Martinez Lucio, M. and Stuart, M. (2002) 'Assessing partnership: the prospects for and challenges of, modernisation'. *Employee Relations*, 24, 3, 252–61

McGregor, P. (1960) *The Human Side of Enterprise*. New York, McGraw-Hill

McKinlay, A. and Starkey, K. (1992) 'Competitive strategies and organisational change', in Salaman, G. (ed.) *Human Resource Strategies*. London, Sage

Millward, N., Smart, D., Stevens, M. and Hawes, W.R. (1992) *Workplace Industrial Relations in Transition*. Aldershot, Dartmouth

Millward, N., Bryson, A. and Forth, J. (2000) *All Change at Work*. London, Routledge

Oliver, N. and Wilkinson, B. (1992) *The Japanisation of British Industry*. Oxford, Blackwell

Oxenbridge, S. and Brown, W. (2002) 'Two faces of partnership? An assessment of partnership and co-operative employer/trade union relationships'. *Employee Relations*, 24, 3, 262–76

Purcell, J. (1987) 'Mapping management styles in employee relations'. *Journal of Management Studies*, 24, 5, 533–48

Ramsay, H. (1977) 'Cycles of control: worker participation in sociological and historical perspective'. *Sociology*, 11, 3, 481–506

Salamon, M. (1998) *Industrial Relations: Theory and Practice*. London, Prentice Hall

Shonberger, R.J. (1982) *Japanese Manufacturing Techniques*. London, Macmillan

Spurr, I. (1990) 'Are house journals just hot air?' *Involvement and Participation*, 607, 14–17

Strauss, G. (1979) 'Workers' participation symposium introduction'. *Industrial Relations*, 18, 3, 247–61

Tailby, S. and Winchester, D. (2000) 'Management and trade unions: towards social partnership?', in Bach, S. and Sisson, K. (eds) *Personnel Management: A Comprehensive Guide to Theory and Practice*. Oxford, Blackwell

Taylor, F.W. (1947) *Scientific Management*. New York, Harper and Row

Terry, M. (1983) 'Shop stewards through expansion and recession'. *Industrial Relations Journal*, 14, 3, 49–58

Terry, M. (1986) 'How do we know if shop stewards are getting weaker?' *British Journal of Industrial Relations*, 24, 2, 169–80

Terry, M. (2003) 'Employee representation', in Edwards, P. (ed.) *Industrial Relations Theory and Practice*, 2nd edn. Oxford, Blackwell

Timming, A.R. (2007) 'Euoropean Works Councils and the dark side of managing worker voice'. *Human Resource Management Journal*, 17, 3, 248–64

TUC (2001) *Partners for Progress: Winning at Work*. London, TUC

TUC (2002) TUC Submission on the Government's Discussion Document 'High Performance Workplaces', www.tuc.org.uk/law/tuc

TUC-CBI (2001) *The UK Productivity Challenge*. London, TUC-CBI

Undy, R. (1999) 'Annual review article: New Labour's "industrial relations settlement" the Third way?'. *British Journal of Industrial Relations*, 37, 2, 315–36

Vandamme, J. (ed.) (1986) *Employee Consultation and Information in Multinational Corporations*. Beckenham, Croom Helm

Van Ruysseveldt, J. and Visser, J. (1996) *Industrial Relations in Europe: Traditions and Transitions*. London, Sage

Wall, T.D. and Lischeron, J.A. (1977) *Worker Participation*. Maidenhead, McGraw-Hill

WERS (2004) See Kersley, B. *et al.*, 2006

WERS (1998) See Cully, M. *et al.* (1998)

Whitley, J.H. (1918) *Relations between Employees and Employed, Reports 1916–1918*. London, HMSO

WIRS (1990) See Millward, N. *et al.* (1992)

Wortman, M. and Dorrenbacher, C. (1994) 'An assessment of the qualitative impact of the proposed directive on European Works Councils'. Berlin, fast eV

COLLECTIVE DISPUTES AND THEIR RESOLUTION

INTRODUCTION

Some writers argue that there has been a re-emergence of interest in conflict, this becoming, for whatever reason, more 'fashionable' in recent years (Danford and Stewart, 2003). However, in 'mature', democratic and pluralist societies, the potential for conflict in its many manifestations will always exist. The pluralist perspective legitimises conflict as a means whereby different interests may be articulated and resolved through normal democratic mechanisms. Moreover, it could be argued that democratic and participative processes within the wider society exist to ensure that conflicts do not pose a threat to the dominant class-based interests within the wider society. This argument, which provides the rationale for this chapter, is reinforced by Coser (1956) who asserts that employers and employees, as parties to conflict, engage in a process that neither side can win. The situation described by Coser is analogous to a 'game', which is played according to certain 'rules'. In this way, conflict becomes institutionalised in terms of an agreed set of rules and procedures endorsed by both parties. In similar vein, Dahrendorf (1959) argues that the legitimisation of trade unions by employers and the state constituted a major step towards industrial democracy and institutionalisation of industrial conflict. Manifestations of this phenomenon included:

- the consolidation of collective bargaining within a framework of agreed-upon rules and procedures thereby regulating and resolving conflicts between the parties;
- the implementation of institutionalised mechanisms for arbitrating and mediating between parties in dispute;
- the establishment of formal representation of employees' interests; and
- the tendency towards an institutionalisation of employee participation such as the national works councils established in many EU member states.

Within the employment relationship in Britain, industrial action, as an expression of collective concern and power of employees, is often the only means of facilitating the bargaining process in order to achieve a favourable outcome to negotiations.

As we noted in Chapter 1, the inequalities inherent in the social class structure of society and in the distribution of wealth and income are reflected in the inequalities in income, power and control relationships between managers and workers within the workplace. These inequalities manifest themselves in various forms of industrial conflict, some of which are overt, while others are hidden. The study of the employment relationship is partly concerned with analysing the causes and consequences of industrial conflict and the effectiveness of methods of conflict resolution by reference to its most overt forms – the strike and other types of overt industrial action.

We start by defining and identifying different types of industrial action before concentrating on the strike and the causes of strikes. We then go on to consider the pattern of strike activity in

Britain in recent years. The extent to which the legislation of the last three decades has affected the nature and scope of industrial action will then be examined. Finally, collective disputes resolution and management is considered.

Learning objectives

When you have read this chapter, you should be able to:

1. Define industrial action.

2. Identify the main causes of industrial action.

3. Explain the basic patterns of strike activity in Britain from 1946 to 2001 in terms of duration and frequency of disputes, and number of worker days lost.

4. Assess the extent to which the recent legislation has affected industrial action.

5. Identify the appropriate means of collective conflict management and its resolution.

DEFINITION AND TYPES OF INDUSTRIAL ACTION

Self-evaluation activity 8.1

Range of behaviours associated with industrial conflict
The response is given below

The following statement by Kornhauser *et al.* (1954) adequately sets the scene. What do you think is the 'total range of behaviour' to which Kornhauser *et al.* refer?

> *Complete work stoppages and outbreaks of violence due to industrial disputes are certainly the most dramatic expressions of industrial conflict. For the general public they are also the most disturbing. In the minds of many industrial conflict has come to mean strikes . . . But a true understanding of industrial strife . . . demands consideration of related, less spectacular manifestations as well. It may even be suggested that the general object of study is not the labour dispute, the strike or the lockout, but the total range of behaviour and attitudes that express opposition and divergent orientations between industrial owners and managers on the one hand and working people and their organisations on the other. (p. 17)*

The statement by Kornhauser suggests that there are many types of industrial action, and the range of industrial action is suggested by Kerr (1964):

> *Its means of expression are as unlimited as the ingenuity of man. The strike is the most common and most visible expression. But conflict with the employer may also take the form of peaceful bargaining and grievance handling, of boycotts, of political action, of restriction of output, of sabotage, of absenteeism or of personnel turnover. Several of these forms, such as sabotage, restriction of output, absenteeism, and turnover, may take place on an individual as well as on an organised basis and constitute alternatives to collective action. Even the strike is of many varieties. It may involve all the workers or only key men. It may take the form of refusal to work overtime or to perform a certain process. It may even involve such rigid adherence to the rules that output is stifled. (p. 27)*

Industrial action may be defined as stoppages of work, instigated both collectively and individually by employees or trade unions on the one hand, or more rarely by management on the other. The various forms of collective industrial action can now be described briefly:

- **The strike:** a situation where workers collectively withdraw their labour from the work situation for varying periods of time.
- **The lockout:** a situation where the employer refuses to allow workers to gain access to their workplaces and a stoppage of work results.

- **The go-slow:** a situation where workers who are in dispute with their employer decide literally to 'slow down' the pace of work.
- **The work to rule or contract:** observing contracts of employment to the letter; interpreting procedures, job specifications and the content of collective agreements in their fine detail, and getting management to issue precise instructions concerning issues such as health and safety procedures.
- **The removal of overtime:** a situation where workers decide not to work any overtime hours thereby working only those hours specified in the contract of employment with a view to slowing production.
- **The work-in and sit-in:** situations where workers continue to work and to 'occupy' the place of work, often as a protest against company closures, while refusing management access to the production process.

The strike, being the most overt form of industrial action, is also the most popular and demonstrative manifestation of the collective solidarity of a unionised workforce. The other, often less popular forms of industrial action identified above are taken *either* as action preceding a strike, and if that action is successful a strike will then be unnecessary, *or* as action which is just as important as a strike and which may even be preferred to strike action because it is cheaper to the union (no strike pay) and may not be regarded as a breach of contract (even though employees could be subject to disciplinary action). Non-strike industrial action was more popular during the 1960s partly because employees in buoyant labour markets receiving relatively high pay during periods of 'full' employment were not prepared to sacrifice pay for strike action, and partly because these forms of industrial action were more effective in securing pay increases and other concessions from management (Hyman, 1984). During the 1970s and 1980s there was a decline in these forms of industrial action, as research by Brown (1981), Edwards (1995) and the WIRS and WERS 1998/2004 demonstrate. The suggested reasons for the decline include the weakening of the effectiveness of workplace union organisation which made it more difficult to co-ordinate such action, together with the increasing propensity for managements to resist and

sustain production during times of non-strike activity. Manifestations of individual industrial action include:

- **Labour turnover:** one of the most direct ways of reacting to the deprivations within the work situation is to leave the job.
- **Absenteeism:** grievances or dissatisfactions felt by individuals may manifest themselves in higher rates of absenteeism.
- **Pilfering and fiddling:** part of a 'counter-culture' set up by workers in the work situation which represents a challenge and opposition to the dominant interests and values of the employer.
- **Sabotage:** 'the deliberate disruption of work flows within an organisation or the undermining of the conditions whereby dominant management purposes are readily achieved' (Watson, 2008, p. 306).

The distinction between organised and unorganised conflict has been used to categorise workers' responses to work situations which cause dissatisfaction or deprivation. Unorganised conflict represents situations whereby workers respond to the 'oppressive situation in the only way open to them as *individuals*: by withdrawal from the source of discontent, or, in the case of certain forms of individual sabotage or indiscipline, by reacting against the immediate manifestation of oppression' (Hyman, 1984, p. 56). Unorganised conflict is mainly spontaneous, rarely calculative and the manifestations of conflict are mainly individual, although some forms of spontaneous unofficial collective strike action could be placed in this category. Organised conflict, on the other hand, is more likely to be collective and to 'form part of a conscious strategy to change the situation which is identified as the source of discontent' (ibid., p. 56). The legal definition of industrial action or 'trade dispute' is contained in the Trade Union and Labour Relations (Consolidation) Act (TULRCA) 1992, s. 218 and is:

any dispute between employers and workers, or between workers and workers which is connected with one or more of the following matters:

(a) terms and conditions of employment, or the physical conditions in which any workers are required to work

(b) *engagement or non-engagement, or termination or suspension of employment or the duties of employment of one or more workers*

(c) *allocation of work or the duties of employment between workers or groups of workers*

(d) *matters of discipline*

(e) *the membership or non-membership of a trade union on the part of a worker*

(f) *facilities for officials of trade unions; and*

(g) *machinery for negotiation or consultation, and other procedures, relating to any of the foregoing matters, including the recognition by employers or employers' associations of the right of a trade union to represent workers in any such negotiation or consultation or in the carrying out of such procedures.*

The legal definition is used mainly to determine whether the industrial action or trade dispute is lawful or unlawful according to certain criteria laid down in the legislation and which we shall consider later in this chapter. As Farnham (1997) argues:

The state takes an active role in regulating industrial conflict. If the state cannot achieve industrial

peace by persuasion, argument or third party intervention, it provides certain legal backstops to contain and constrain what it defines to be legitimate industrial action. These are aimed at protecting those damaged by industrial action, keeping the sanctions within acceptable constitutional bounds and discouraging what the state defines as politically destabilising employee relations conflict. (p. 366)

Self-evaluation activity 8.2

Motives for taking industrial action
Response on website

Identify what the main motives for taking industrial action might be.

A framework which can be used to analyse industrial conflict in both its individual and collective manifestations in the widest possible range of employment situations is provided by Watson (1995, pp. 294–6) and is summarised in Exhibit 8.1.

Exhibit 8.1

A framework for the analysis of industrial conflict

1. In a world where valued resources are scarce, people form coalitions of interest to help in the pursuit or defence of interests with regard to these resources.

2. Over time, some groups win out over others in the competition for scarce resources and attempt to consolidate their advantage through their control of institutions and through the propagation of ideologies.

3. Industrial capitalism emerged as 'bourgeois' groups became successful in pursuing their interests in certain societies, but the advantages which accrue from their use of such formally rational means as bureaucracy, technical division of labour, wage labour, advanced technology and the rest are constantly threatened. The threat comes not only from challenges on the part of less privileged groups but also as a result of various contradictory tendencies in the industrial capitalist system itself.

4. The relationship between the employer and employee centres on an *implicit contract*. This is an agreement between unequal parties in which the employee, in the light of his or her particular motives, expectations and interests, attempts to make the best deal possible, given his or her personal resources (skill, knowledge, physique, wealth, etc.). The bargain which is struck involves a certain relationship (in part explicit but largely, owing to its indeterminacy, implicit) between the employee inputs of effort, impairment and surrender of autonomy and employee rewards of cash payment and fringe benefits, job satisfactions, social rewards, security, power status, career potential.

5. The bargain is essentially unstable, especially as a result of the market context in which it is made. Market viability on the part of the employer creates a constant pressure to minimise costs – this in turn leading to

pressure to either cut the rewards or increase the efforts of the employee – either way to the employees' disadvantage. However, employees are bound to defend themselves, especially since they buy the goods and services on the same market. Paradoxically, the advertising and marketing efforts of employing organisations create a pressure on their employees to increase, or at least hold stable, their rewards (employees and customers being ultimately the same people).

6. To increase efficiency or market viability, employers introduce various organisational and technological changes, but any such change, however minor it may seem, potentially invites opposition from employees whose implicit contracts may be seen to be threatened. This may be because of a tendency to reduce 'rewards' like job satisfaction or the opportunity to use craft skills or because of a tendency to call for increased employee 'inputs' in the form of increased effort or a further reduction in the amount of autonomy which the employee has at work. Potential conflict, we can see, arises with practically any kind of managerial initiative in employment situations.

7. Both to improve their market position and to defend themselves, employees tend to form various coalitions of interest to present the kind of group challenge which is necessary to have any effect in the face of the greater power of the employer. Thus we get, within the employing organisations, trade union organisation, 'professional' group mobilisation and 'informal' office and shop floor groupings. All of these present challenges to the managerial prerogative.

8. In every workplace there is a constantly renegotiated agreement about what goes on and what rewards accrue. Only a fraction of this negotiating process is formal and much of the agreement is tacit. External conditions are never constant and therefore there are always threats to the stability of arrangements. The underlying conflicts of interest between employer and employee may become overt and apparent at any time and will tend to centre on two main issues: the amount of material rewards available to the employee and the extent of control over employees conceded to the employer.

9. We can say that a grievance situation arises whenever a particular implicit contract is perceived to go out of balance. The grievance may lead to any of a range of employee reactions, from striking to absenteeism and from obstructive behaviour to resigning. A grievance can be settled or accommodated not only by a return to the prior status quo but by a rebalancing of the implicit contract in a new form; an increase in cash being agreed to compensate for a loss in autonomy resulting from technical change, for example.

Source: Adapted from Watson, 1995, pp. 294–6

STRIKES AND THEIR CAUSES

'A strike has been defined as a **temporary stoppage of work by a group of employees in order to express a grievance or enforce a demand**' (Hyman, 1984, p. 17). Within the context of this definition, the term *temporary* makes it clear that workers intend to return to their jobs when the strike is over. The term *stoppage of work* distinguishes the strike from other forms of industrial action undertaken by a *group* of employees thereby emphasising its collective nature. The strike is also a calculative act, which is specifically designed to express grievances, to seek a solution to problems and to apply pressure to enforce demands. The Office for National Statistics

(ONS), which is the central institution for the collection and collation of strike data in Britain, has its own definition of strikes for statistical purposes as being: **all stoppages of work due to industrial disputes involving ten or more workers and lasting for at least one day**. Where the total days lost exceed 100 working days, a strike is included in the ONS data even if it fails to count under the criteria of its own definition. Whether this measure is an accurate reflection of strikes in British industry is difficult to judge. Brown (1981), for example, estimates that since Britain has historically been particularly affected by short and small-scale stoppages, especially in the manufacturing sector of the economy, as many as half the actual strikes may

be excluded from the statistics in any one year. It has been more conventional to assume that the statistics covered around 66 per cent of the total number of strikes and 95 per cent of the days lost. The disparity really relates to the ease with which long stoppages are recorded and the difficulty of accounting for the 'lightning strikes' that existed and persisted in particular industries such as car manufacturing.

The main types of strike

Before looking at the actual causes and reasons given for taking industrial action in the form of strikes, it is important to note that six main types of strike have been identified, but it should also be noted that these categories are not mutually exclusive:

1. *The trial of strength*: has become 'the classic stereotype of the industrial dispute – the only sort which is ever likely to make the history books' (Hyman, 1984). These strikes tended to be long-drawn-out affairs involving considerable costs to employers, the workforce and the unions concerned, invoking the metaphor of industrial relations as 'trench warfare'. These protracted disputes have, historically, comprised a small minority of stoppages within a given period.
2. *The demonstration stoppage*: Hyman contends that 'the great majority of strikes fall in the category of demonstrations in force' (p. 24). The stoppage is often spontaneous although the underlying causes of this type of strike may be of long standing. Hyman adds: 'The spontaneous or demonstration strike is usually both small in scale and quickly settled. It is true that such strikes sometimes spread . . . and occasionally they prove unexpectedly protracted . . . but these cases are very unusual' (p. 24).
3. *The official strike*: is one where a union 'officially' supports its members according to the union rules governing the conduct of disputes.
4. *The constitutional strike*: is one which takes place *after* all relevant procedures have been exhausted and the parties acknowledge that they have failed to agree.
5. *The unofficial strike*: is one which has not been recognised by the union leadership. Traditionally, unofficial strikes tended to be spontaneous,

informal, short in duration and involving relatively few people. During the 1960s and 1970s, the vast majority of strikes in any one year were recorded by the Department of Employment as being unofficial simply because the large majority of disputes were over before the unions which might have had members involved had even heard of them, 'the matters at issue having been settled by direct negotiation between management and workers concerned' (Turner, 1969, p. 22). In recent years, the number of unofficial disputes has declined significantly.

6. *The unconstitutional strike*: is one which takes place *before* all relevant procedures have been exhausted.

Self-evaluation activity 8.3
Decline in unofficial strikes
Response on website

Why do you think the number of unofficial strikes has declined in recent years?

Main case 8.1
Anatomy of a strike and its causes:
1 The Thatcher legacy

The Magnet dispute

Magnet is a British subsidiary of the American conglomerate Berisford International and manufactures kitchen storage cupboards and worktops. Its Darlington factory has been at the centre of Britain's longest-running strike. In August 1996, 350 of Magnet's Darlington workers stopped work over pay; they voted decisively, via their four unions, for an entirely legal, official stoppage. Early that September, the company resolved the dispute by sacking the 350 strikers, and they have since been replaced by non-unionised workers, and that, as far as Berisford is concerned, is the whole story. These days, its official press releases refer to bringing 'the legacy of the 1996 dispute to an end', or at most, to 'a small legacy of a picket line outside the Darlington factory'. Its spokesperson adds: 'The jobs at Darlington have been filled. There never has been any question of reinstatement.'

The picketing rituals at Magnet have long turned automatic. Besides the shouting and staring (and drivers looking down at their steering wheels), there is

the coffee-fetching, the stacking and unstacking of firewood, the tabloid rustling in quiet moments – and there are a lot of those. But the slow, old-fashioned quality of all this is deceptive. The Magnet strike is encrusted with allegations and counter-allegations: strikers harassed by private detectives, workers harassed by strikers, petrol poured over picket's caravans, nails poured under the wheels of delivery.

After two decades of legislation to make them rarer, modern strikes tend to be like this: bitter, fought at the fringes of the law, neither side really recognising the other as legitimate at all. The Magnet dispute seems to echo the Liverpool dockers strike and the 1993 stoppage at Timex in Dundee. However, the backdrop to the dispute has changed somewhat, and although the 'New' Labour government is not noted for its support of employees against chief executives, its white paper *Fairness at Work* (1998) suggests that Magnet-style industrial relations have had their day. The white paper proposals for reinforcing the individual and collective rights of employees has made the dispute a potential test case and a symbol to represent the old, soon-to-be-outdated way of doing things. In particular the proposal to change the law in line with the government's belief 'that in general those dismissed for taking part in lawfully organised official industrial action should have the right to complain to a tribunal of unfair dismissal' (p. 45) should deter employers from taking extreme measures against employees.

Roots of the dispute

Until the 1980s, the Magnet factory was a recognisably pre-Thatcherite enterprise: 'You could walk out when the coffee wasn't hot enough' said a long-term employee, only half-joking. Then, in 1989, there was a management buy-out just in time for the recession. As the market for houses shrank, so did the demand for kitchens to put in them and by 1993, with no dividend paid to shareholders for four years, Magnet decided to take drastic action. The workers would have to take a pay cut.

Pay cuts varied from between £5 and £50 a week. The best-paid employee received only £260; the vote for a strike was overwhelming. Before the strike commenced, the company abandoned the pay cuts. In return, the unions agreed that wages would be frozen for three years. A senior convenor and leader of the strike committee said: 'The company was not making money and we all agreed to help out.' It seemed that the idea of

'partnership' which New Labour currently supports, existed in embryonic form at Magnet. But a sourness lingered. Shop floor 'perks' such as time off for bereavement began to disappear. In 1994, Berisford International bought Magnet and, as the business pages of newspapers approvingly noted, 'outlets were closed' and 'the workforce was cut back'. Darlington veterans muttered about the 'worst management of the lot'.

Berisford was not, in reality, a 'partnership' business, but a more common sort of employer. Before buying Magnet, it had traded in commodities and sugar refining, lost a lot of money in American property, and tried and failed to take over Clark's shoes. By 1996, Magnet was profitable again and the pay freeze was due to end. The unions asked for a 3 per cent pay increase. The management agreed to give the money to three-fifths of the workforce; the rest, better paid and longer serving, would get 'improvements' to shifts and overtime and a 'productivity bonus'. By the end of August the pickets were out on the grass and *The Northern Echo* was already using the word 'deadlock'. By March 1998, the pickets were still active even though 52 of the original 350 strikers went back to work before Magnet's deadline to do so – the 12th day of the strike – expired. The remainder have challenged their sacking with pickets of Magnet's showrooms, shouting in shareholders meetings, a march through Darlington, and collaboration with a number of external interested parties. There have been competing claims concerning the extent to which the factory has been profitable; while the Magnet management claim that profits have risen by 25 per cent, the strikers claim that fewer trucks are entering the gates with lesser loads. Such warring claims seem the sum of the dispute these days. Javelin PR put out their triumphant management faxes; the pickets count number plates, and watch the forklifts beep and slalom behind the gates. Specially installed security cameras peer at each picket. Just as the strikers stare at the factory instead of working in it, so the management watch the strikers instead of negotiating with them.

Self-evaluation activity 8.4

Causes of the Magnet dispute
This SEA has no commentary

Identify the main causes of the Magnet strike, then compare your list with the causes given below.

Main case 8.2
Anatomy of a strike and its causes: 2 The Blair legacy

The firefighters' dispute 2002–3

Since the late 1970s firefighters' pay increases have been determined by a formula linking the pay of a fully qualified firefighter to the earnings of the top quarter of adult male manual workers. This formula has led to a 20 per cent increase in firefighters' pay since 1997 and was strongly defended by the Fire Brigades Union (FBU) until 2001. Andy Gilchrist, General Secretary of the FBU, said in the July 2000 issue of the FBU's *Fire Fighter* magazine that 'our wages remain ahead of other essential public sector workers precisely because we have maintained the formula'. Negotiations on pay and conditions of service for fire brigade personnel are conducted in the National Joint Council for Local Authorities' Fire Brigades. This is a voluntary organisation covering England, Wales, Scotland and Northern Ireland on which employing authorities, through the Local Government Association and the Convention of Scottish Local Authorities, and the Fire Authority of Northern Ireland are represented, together with the FBU.

Negotiations begin

The negotiating process began in May 2002 and the FBU lodged a claim for a 40 per cent pay increase for firefighters. The employers responded by indicating that any significant pay increase had to be matched by modernisation of the fire service. The employers offered the FBU an unconditional interim 4 per cent pay increase from 7 November 2002 in advance of any agreement on a new pay formula. The employers also invited the FBU to join them in asking for an independent review (subsequently called the Bain Report Review) into firefighters' pay and conditions. This was rejected and in September 2002 the FBU issued a strike ballot. On 18 October 2002 the FBU announced support from its membership for strike action in pursuit of its claim for £30,000 for firefighters and control room staff.

The employers' initial offer and the Bain Report

The initial employers' offer was for an immediate 4 per cent pay increase linked to talks about reforming working practice plus, another 7 per cent from November 2003 if all reforms had been agreed. This offer was made on 12 November, and according to the employers, the full offer amounted to 11.3 per cent

over two years at a time when inflation stood at 2.1 per cent. The offer was based on the recommendations of the independent review by Sir George Bain.

Run-up to Bain

In July 2002, during negotiations with the FBU, the UK employers proposed a joint approach to government to establish an independent review. The FBU refused, so the employers approached the government alone. In early September, after negotiations within the Joint National Council broke down, the government decided it would be helpful to establish an independent review. The Bain Review was launched on 20 September and its remit was to review current issues surrounding the fire service fairly and objectively and make recommendations accordingly. The Review published an interim position paper on 11 November and this was followed by the final Report, published on 17 December 2002.

UK firefighters set to walk out as talks fail
The first firefighters' strike in more than 20 years looks certain to go ahead on Wednesday after government told employers that there was no more money on the table and talks with unions collapsed. Barring a last minute pay deal which few in Whitehall expect, ancient army Green Goddess fire engines will take to the streets . . . when more than 50,000 firefighters are due to walk out. Calling the strike 'unjustified, dangerous and wrong', Tony Blair insisted that modernisation of the fire service had to go hand in hand with higher pay. Whitehall officials told employers no additional funding was available to improve on the recommendations from Sir George Bain, who has reviewed firefighters' pay, for an 11 per cent pay rise linked to changes in working practices. A senior representative on the employers' side said that when he saw the Bain Review's position paper, he knew the strike would take place, given the FBU's demand for a no-strings pay increase of 40 per cent. The Treasury is refusing to sanction the extra money, fearing that an overly generous award could trigger a wave of claims across the public sector. Mr Gilchrist (FBU leader) called the pay offer 'derisory and insulting' and he accused 'dark forces' in the Labour government of trying to provoke a strike rather than pay a fair wage. After Wednesday's 49-hour walkout the union plans a series of three eight-day stoppages

on November 22, December 4, and December 16. Several employers confirmed they had received strong indications from ministers that, while the government would back the Bain Review's recommendations, it would not offer any more – curtailing employers' freedom to offer more than an extra percentage point or so given their tight finances. (Adams *et al.* 2002)

What the Bain Report said

The main theme of the Report is that the fire service needs to be changed from top to bottom and every aspect of its work needs to be reformed. The focus needs to change from dealing with fire incidence to greater emphasis on fire prevention together with a modern, flexible, risk-based approach to allocating resources. The Bain Report is confident that, given the scope for reform, the move to a modern fire service would pay for itself over time and that in addition more lives will be saved and property losses reduced and communities will be more secure as a result. The main points the Report makes are:

- There has been a lack of leadership throughout the fire service at political, institutional and operational levels.
- There must be a new policy-making body, led by ministers, to set a clear framework of what the government requires from the service and the ways in which it should be modernised.
- A new system is needed that deploys resources to deal with most likely risks of fire in the most cost-effective way, based on risk assessment.
- New primary legislation is needed to put the fire service on a proper, modern basis.
- The review does not recommend regionalisation of the fire service but does recommend that fire authorities should increasingly collaborate where increased efficiencies and economies could result.
- New policy structure needs to be complemented by new institutions within the fire service – the Fire Service College must become the focus for the intellectual leadership of the service and the Fire Service Inspectorate should become a major engine of change and should help drive through the reforms proposed.
- There is a need for a new collective group to be engaged in policy work, bringing together Chief Fire Officers and central and local government.

- An improved programme of HR management should be put in place as a matter of high priority.
- A new pay structure should be based around an Integrated Personnel Development Scheme (IPDS) with the need to encourage mobility and flexibility. The system should be competence-based. The Report's findings indicate that there is no case for significant increases in pay based on the existing pay system. The employers' offer is based on the Bain recommendations.
- Comprehensive modernisation of the current pensions scheme is required.
- The Grey Book (conditions of service) needs to be amended so managers are free to manage others locally, such as flexible shift systems, part-time working and different crewing trends at different times of day. The Appointments and Promotions Regulations should be replaced by a core set of national requirements. The Discipline Regulations should be replaced with a system based on ACAS Code of Practice and the current negotiating machinery should be replaced. Non-compulsory redundancies may be necessary.

Reactions to Bain

The employers: In favour of the Bain recommendations: 'The LGA believes the Bain recommendations form the basis of delivering the changes required as long as all parties, Government, fire and local authorities and the staff play their full part' (LGA, 2003).

The FBU: Major objections concerning pay: 'Despite claims that Bain was acting independently, the recommendation of a 4% increase payable effective [from] November 2002 was exactly the rate of rise previously offered by the Fire Service Employers when negotiations officially broke down in September, and which led to the ballot for strike action being conducted by the FBU'; and modernisation, which is viewed as cost-cutting exercises involving 'further reductions in firefighter and control staff numbers' (FBU, 2003).

Academic commentary: The FBU website contains a condemnatory commentary on Bain by Seifert (2003a). This states that the final Report confirms the views expressed by the FBU that the Report is not independent of government, it usurps the views of employers, 'embraces the more extreme reforming instincts of members of the government', and its

rhetoric is couched in managerialist terms as is its ideology. The Report's authors have a narrow vision which focuses upon 'costs' and 'cost-effectiveness' rather than safety and quality of service. Its view of pay is parsimonious and it parrots government policy relating to, inter alia, 'affordability'. There is a paucity of evidence presented to substantiate the Report's pay recommendations which 'mimic government thinking elsewhere in the public sector' (p. 2). Seifert concludes that the government missed an opportunity 'to use the goodwill, professional knowledge and dedication of public sector workers as the starting point for reforms. By embracing crude private sector models of employment – specifically Taylorisation through deskilling – alongside discredited ideas of efficiency – see the case for the privatisation of the railways for example – the report and the government have signed the warrant which may end the most successful provision of fire protection and safety in Europe' (p. 3).

Subsequent developments

1. **Modernisation:** As far as 'modernisation' is concerned – a catch-all term used by government to justify the introduction of cost-effective measures justified by job cuts, new or modified pay structures, de-centred decision making and arguably a 'managerialist' ideology – the FBU (2003) maintains, albeit by adopting a different interpretation of the term, that 'modernisation is ongoing and receives the general support of the FBU. Indeed, we have pioneered new approaches to fire cover, fire safety and fire prevention whilst arguing for the increased funding necessary to upgrade training and equipment. We are happy to co-operate with necessary changes to training and skill acquisition as well as the more flexible use of resources in order to further improve the service given to the public. Our only caveat is that change be agreed with our members, not imposed by employers or unelected managers' (Andy Gilchrist, FBU, 2003).

2. **Government intervention:** Between September and December 2002, the government intervened on three occasions between the FBU and the employers. The most serious intervention came after tentative agreement was reached, including a staged increase in pay amounting to 16 per cent by November 2003. Intervention in the form of the Office of the Deputy Prime Minister 'effectively blocked this opportunity to make progress' (FBU, 2003). Contrary to the

government's argument, the employers confirmed that the proposals in the draft agreement were fully costed and all figures were available to the government throughout the talks.

The last offer and perhaps the final one

A further offer by the employers was received by the FBU on 18 March 2003 and included a five-stage pay process with a 16 per cent increase by July 2004 and from that point increases in pay for 2005 and 2006 in line with a pay formula yet to be decided. The Executive Council of the FBU agreed to recommend the offer to the membership. A recall of Annual Conference on 19 March 2003 recommended that the membership reject the offer, which it proceeded to do. Professor Frank Burchill suggested some amendments, which have been rejected by the government and employers. The dispute finally ended on 12 June 2003. A compromise 16 per cent pay deal tied to limited changes in working practices was accepted by a 3 to 1 margin at a special conference in Glasgow.

Source: Based on Bain Report, 2002; FBU, 2003; LGA, 2003; Seifert, 2003a, 2003b – websites accessed 23 March 2003; 25 April 2003

Self-evaluation activity 8.5

Differing perspectives on the conduct of the firefighters' dispute
This SEA has no commentary

Read the three annotated views relating to the conduct of the parties involved in the firefighters' dispute. Which of these do you think is the most valid? Justify your choice.

View 1 (Seifert, 2003b)

The local authority employers 'continue to dance to the tune of public sector policy dogma' which believes that private sector service provision is more efficient than what the public sector can produce and is therefore more akin to nineteenth-century free market dogma. The employers' offer has to be seen in the context of delegated business units making decisions without reference to central authority, and free of collective union voice: 'Such

is the thinking behind "foundation" hospitals, Best Value in local government, education reforms and, of course, the "modernising" agenda for the fire service.' The offer bypasses existing collective bargaining machinery at local and national level and seeks to impose operational and employment decisions upon the firefighters. The current National Joint Committee (NJC) will be replaced by a 'working group representing all fire service stakeholders' but we do not know who will select them. Associated with this is the government Ad Hoc Forum functioning outside the NJC which influences the agreement. Seifert goes on to say:

> So where does the decision-making power lie? With whom is the FBU negotiating? Why does central government intervene so actively in a dispute between independent employers and an independent union? Why should either side be bound by the secret ruminations of something with such a Kafkaesque name as Ad Hoc Forum? At the end of this the employers are so unable to decide for themselves that the government insists that implementation will be audited to make sure that the new local leaders of the fire service are doing their job properly. These appear to be the same senior managers entrusted with the entire future of the service, unworried by bargaining with the unions, unaccountable to local communities, and eventually answerable only to the board of directors of the highly modern FirePlc. (Seifert, 2003b, p. 2)

View 2 (Metcalf, 2003)

The employers are incompetent and divided and they are bargaining with an intransigent union and this has always been a recipe for disaster. There is a lack of bargaining experience as the firefighters' pay has been determined by a formula agreed in the late 1970s and 'this lack of experience in bargaining is well evidenced by the cack-handed, stupid way the parties have conducted themselves in this dispute'. The FBU conjured the 40 per cent claim apparently 'out of thin air' but came down to 16 per cent as soon as 'Gordon Brown said "boo" to the union'. The employers are worse as they went 'cap in hand' to the Treasury with uncosted proposals asking the Chancellor to sign a blank

cheque. This boils down to a lack of HR expertise: 'are there any HR professionals in the employers' negotiating team? If so, what on earth is their role? If not, the employers should get some in now.' The four principles that should determine public sector pay – comparability, recruitment, retention and productivity (couched in the buzzwords of 'modernisation'; 'flexibility' and 'restructuring') give different responses to the 'right settlement'. Metcalf goes on to assert: 'Assuming collective bargaining is to continue we cannot be put through this shambles again. There should be compulsory arbitration using final offer [pendulum] arbitration.'

View 3 (Burchill, 2003)

The independent chairman of the NJC, Frank Burchill, counters Metcalf concerning the latter's assertion that there are no HR professionals in the employers' negotiating team. The team is serviced by the Employers' Organisation which provides advice in negotiations across local government. In addition, the General Secretary and Deputy General Secretary of the TUC were involved. Burchill states that there is no shortage of HR and industrial relations experts willing to give advice and comment, and 'none of this fits with his [Metcalf's] picture of "incompetent, divided employers", "intransigent union", "lack of experience in bargaining", "cack-handed, stupid behaviour of the parties" and so on. The negotiators on both sides are highly intelligent people trying to reconcile conflicting interests . . . ideal outcomes are easier to perceive than achieve.'

Causes of strikes in general

Strikes have not been spread evenly throughout the labour force. For example, from 1966 to 1970 the number of days lost through strikes, relative to the size of workforce in particular industries, was greatest in the docks industry, followed by the car industry, shipbuilding and coal mining. These are some of the traditional, strike-prone industries which tended to distort the strike picture during the 1960s and 1970s. A number of explanations have been put forward in order to account for this distortion, and these are identified below.

Community integration

Kerr and Siegel (1954), in a study of strikes in 11 countries, found that miners, dockers and seamen had the highest strike records. They argue that community integration is the key to explaining the level of strike activity in these occupations. They also point out that miners, dockers and seamen tended to live in occupational communities which are relatively isolated and insulated from the wider society. In such communities, a consciousness of kind develops which involves a strong awareness of shared grievances, a close emotional commitment to trade unionism and a high level of working-class solidarity. Shared grievances and worker solidarity, set in the context of a close-knit community, tend to make strike action more likely. However, Kerr and Siegel's argument does not appear to have much empirical validity today, as most of the traditional industries around which occupational communities were based have declined and the communities themselves have fragmented. This is particularly the case in Britain with regard to the coal, shipbuilding and steel industries, all of which have experienced dramatic decline in their work-forces and hence a decline in trade union membership and density.

Technological determinism

A second traditional explanation for variation in strike activity emphasises the role of technology, and has been used to explain the traditionally high frequency of strikes in the car industry. The work of Blauner (1964) was used to demonstrate that there was a direct correlation between the type of technology used in the production process and worker 'alienation'. Basically, Blauner hypothesised that assembly-line technology produces high levels of alienation amongst assembly-line workers and this leads to the development of hostile relations between workers and management. Strikes, as an expression of industrial conflict, will therefore be more likely in industries employing this type of production technology. Blauner's explanation has been criticised on a number of counts, not least for the assumption that there is an inevitability about the relationship between technology as determining behaviour and attitudes amongst workers. More fundamentally, Hyman (1984) points out that

explanations based on Blauner's assumptions do not account for variations in strike activity within the same industries in different countries and posits the question: 'Why does the strike record for the British motor industry contrast so markedly with the comparative harmony in Germany or Japan, when the technology of car assembly is internationally uniform?' Research by Gallie (1978, 1988), and the early WIRS analyses (Daniel and Millward, 1983) do not lend support to Blauner's hypothesis, as technology is but one factor amongst many which may predispose workers to take strike or any other type of industrial action. The example of the 2002–3 firefighters' dispute, which commenced as a pay dispute but became embroiled in 'modernisation' – changing working practices based on technology and flexibility – and the possible threat of redundancies, is a case in point (see Main case 8.2). Similarly, the postal workers dispute with Royal Mail in 2007 involved pay and 'modernisation' as key issues.

Negotiating procedures

A third explanation for variation in strike activity deals with the effectiveness of the negotiating machinery available for resolving disputes. An early study by Ross and Hartman (1960) compared strike activity levels in 15 countries from 1900 to 1956. The study concluded that strikes are least likely to occur when there are well-established industry and organisational procedures for consultation and negotiation. If procedures exist whereby grievances can be speedily formulated and efficiently channelled into negotiating machinery, strikes are less likely to result. This view was supported by findings within the Devlin Report (1965), a government-sponsored investigation into the British docks industry. Devlin argued that a major reason for the high level of strikes in the industry (apart from casualisation of dock labour) was the ineffectiveness and cumbersome nature of the machinery for resolving disputes.

Strikers' definition of the situation

Hyman (1984) provides a critique of the above explanations for variations in strike levels between different industries. He contends that these explanations largely ignore the strikers' definition of

the situation. For example, workers in one industry may define strikes as a last resort, while those in another may see strikes as a routine and even natural part of industrial life. Hyman argues further that workers do not simply react to production technology or negotiating machinery and predictably strike or not strike as the case might be; they define their work situation and the act of striking in a particular way. Hyman does not deny that factors such as production technology can influence behaviour, but maintains that they are translated into action via the meanings given to them by the workforce. Thus an explanation of the strike-prone British car industry and the relatively strike-free situation in the same industry in Japan and Germany requires a knowledge of the meanings and definitions workers give to industrial life.

Causes of strikes in particular

Table 8.1 shows stoppages, the number of workers involved and working days lost by main cause of dispute for the selected years 1998, 2001 and 2006. Table 8.2 provides a time series of working days lost by main cause of dispute for alternate years 1991–9 and then from 2001 to 2006. The biggest single cause of strikes has traditionally been disputes over wages. In 2006, 73 per cent of working days lost were due to disputes over pay

and accounted for 68 per cent of all stoppages. Issues causing disputes concerning pay are fairly varied and can include union demands for pay increases and bonuses, the restoration of pay differentials, rates for particular jobs and conditions in which the work is undertaken, guaranteed payments, changing payment systems and re-grading affecting pay, 'perks' and fringe benefits and reductions in earnings. Disputes concerning redundancy are the second most important causal category comprising 22 per cent of days lost and 13 per cent of all stoppages. The other causal categories listed are less significant. Working conditions and supervision accounted for 2 per cent and 3 per cent; dismissal and disciplinary measures accounted for 1 per cent and 3 per cent; manning and working allocation for 1 per cent and 3 per cent for working days lost and all stoppages respectively.

The proportion of days lost owing to pay disputes increased in 2006 compared with 2005, with redundancy increasing most significantly. It is important to note that, as Table 8.2 indicates, there are considerable fluctuations from year to year with totals being distorted by larger strikes. Nevertheless, the trend from 1991 to 1999, with the exception of 1996, is downwards, with totals for 2000 and 2001 showing some increase. The figures for the following years also fluctuate by cause as with 2002 for wages and 2006 for fringe benefits. It is also important to note that one or two large disputes can distort any

Table 8.1 Stoppages, workers involved and working days lost by main cause: 1998, 2001 and 2006

Cause	Stoppages			Workers involved (000s)			Working days lost (000s)		
	1998	2001	2006	1998	2001	2006	1998	2001	2006
Pay: wage rates and earnings levels	61	63	101	40.6	50.0	44.6	146.8	140.5	77.1
Pay: extra wage and fringe benefits	12	6	7	6.1	1.5	562.5	18.1	2.6	475.1
Duration and pattern of hours worked	5	10	9	1.4	7.3	1.2	2.2	13.2	4.1
Redundancy questions	19	24	20	19.9	23.8	96.1	54.5	88.1	166.7
Trade union matters	6	3	7	1.7	0.7	1.3	1.9	5.8	2.3
Working conditions and supervision	13	11	5	4.1	38.4	1.5	13.8	172.9	15.7
Staffing and work allocation	31	46	4	6.2	41.6	4.7	16.2	79.0	5.0
Dismissal and other disciplinary measures	19	31	5	12.6	16.7	1.4	28.0	23.0	8.5

Source: LMT, 1999, 2002; Hale, 2007a

Table 8.2 Working days lost by main cause in all industries and services, various years: 1991–2006 (000s)

	1991	1993	1995	1997	1999	2001	2002	2003	2004	2005	2006
Wage rates and earnings	306	145	119	103	159	141	1039	280	759	87	77
Extra wage and fringe benefits	3	5	83	26	8	2.6	137	140	3	8	475
Duration and pattern of hours worked	16	34	39	7	5	13.2	3	63	19	7	4
Redundancy questions	248	391	72	69	35	88.1	15	5	107	17	167
Trade union matters	4	4	3	2	2	5.8	5	0	11	6	2
Working conditions and supervision	66	3	1	8	15	173	110	2	0	9	16
Staffing and work allocation	62	62	88	18	6	79	10	7	5	22	5
Dismissal and other disciplinary matters	56	6	18	4	14	23	7	2	1	2	9
All causes	761	649	415	235	242	525	1323	499	905	157	755

Source: LMT, 2002, p. 598; Hale, 2007a

discernible general trend 'and can make comparisons over time difficult. Indeed, the increase in working days lost due to disputes over redundancies (in 2006) has resulted from one stoppage in the public administration sector' (Hale, 2007a, p. 28).

PATTERNS OF STRIKE ACTIVITY IN THE POST-WAR PERIOD

In order to understand the pattern of strike activity, it is necessary to describe the main measures of strikes used in compiling the strike data collected by the Office for National Statistics (ONS). Tables and analyses of the data appear in the monthly statistical journal *Labour Market Trends* up to December 2006 and the *Economic and Labour Market Review* from January 2007 onwards. Until September 1996 the raw data was collected from the Employment Service local office network, some public sector organisations, newspapers and other sources, but since 1996 information has been collected directly from the employer or trade union involved after the Office for National Statistics has been notified of a dispute from press reports. All reported data must conform to the official definition of stoppages. The main measures used are working days lost, number of stoppages and workers involved. We now look at these measures, but first of all, a

more detailed description of the ONS definition of stoppages is given (we looked at this briefly in the previous section). The descriptions given are adapted from the *Economic and Labour Market Review* (June 2007, pp. 35–6).

Definition of stoppages

The statistics cover stoppages of work in progress in the UK during a year caused by labour disputes between employers and workers, or between workers and other workers, connected with terms and conditions of employment. The statistics exclude disputes that do not result in a stoppage of work. Stoppages involving fewer than ten workers or lasting less than one day are also excluded unless the total number of working days lost in the dispute is 100 or more. Stoppages over issues not directly linked to terms and conditions between workers and employers are omitted, although in most years this is insignificant. The statistics include 'lockouts', that is where an employer prevents their employees from working by refusing entry to the place of work, and 'unlawful', that is, unlawfully organised strikes. However, no distinction is made between a 'strike' and a 'lockout' or between 'lawful' and 'unlawful' stoppages. This is mainly because of the practical difficulty in deciding into which category

a particular stoppage falls. It was for similar reasons that a distinction between 'official' and 'unofficial' disputes was no longer made after 1981.

Main measures of strikes

Working days lost

In measuring the number of working days lost, account is taken only of the time lost in the *basic working week*. Overtime and weekend working are excluded and no allowance is made for absence from work. Where strikes last less than the basic working day, the hours lost are converted to full-day equivalents, as are days lost by part-time workers. The number of working days lost in a stoppage reflects the actual number of workers involved at each point in the stoppage. The calculation is arrived at by multiplying the duration of the stoppage by the total number of workers involved in the stoppage.

Number of stoppages

There are difficulties in ensuring complete recording of stoppages, in particular for short disputes lasting only a day or so, or involving only a few workers. Because of this recording difficulty and the cut-off applied, the number of working days lost is considered to be a better indicator of the impact of labour disputes than the number of recorded stoppages.

Workers involved

The figures for workers involved are for workers both *directly* and *indirectly* involved at the establishment where the dispute occurred. Workers indirectly involved are those who are not themselves parties to the dispute but are laid off because of the dispute. However, the statistics exclude workers at other sites who are indirectly affected. Workers involved in more than one stoppage during the year are counted in the statistics for each stoppage in which they take part. Part-time workers are counted as whole units. Given in Exhibit 8.2 is the method by which the number of workers involved at any time in the stoppage are recorded.

Britain's strike pattern

Self-evaluation activity 8.6

Identifying patterns and trends
The response is given in the text below

Examine the strike statistics in Table 8.3 and attempt to identify any patterns or trends in relation to the three variables described above (working days lost, number of stoppages and workers involved). What conclusion can you arrive at with regard to larger stoppages involving the loss of 100,000 working days or more from 1977?

Exhibit 8.2

Recording numbers involved in stoppages

The statistics try to record the number of workers that are involved at any time in the stoppage. For example, consider a three-day strike where there are 200 workers involved on the first day; 300 on the second day, of whom 100 were involved for the first time; and 200 on the third day, of whom 50 were involved for the first time. The total number of workers involved in the dispute is 350 – the sum of all those involved on the first day, and those joining for the first time on subsequent days. However, the number of workers taking strike action for the first time cannot always be easily ascertained. In such cases the statistics record the highest number involved at any one time (300 in the above example). Take another example, where there are 200 workers involved in a stoppage on each of days one, two and three. It may be necessary to assume that there was a total of 200 workers involved, although it is possible, but unlikely, that as many as 600 workers could have been involved. For this reason, the statistics may underestimate the number of workers involved in a dispute. However the estimate of the number of working days lost is unaffected by this consideration.

Source: Economic and Labour Market Trends 2007, p. 35

Table 8.3 Stoppages in progress, United Kingdom: 1946–2006

Year	Working days lost (000s)	Workers involved (000s)	Stoppages	Stoppages involving loss of 100,000 working days or more
Annual averages				
1946–52	1,888	444	1,698	
1953–59	3,950	790	2,340	
1960–68	3,189	1,451	2,372	
1969–73	12,497	1,581	2,974	
1974–79	12,178	1,653	2,412	
Annual figures				
1977	10,142	1,166	2,737	12
1978	9,405	1,041	2,498	7
1979	29,474	4,608	2,125	15
1980	11,964	834	1,348	5
1981	4,266	1,513	1,344	7
1982	5,313	2,103	1,538	7
1983	3,754	574	1,364	6
1984	27,135	1,464	1,221	11
1985	6,402	791	903	4
1986	1,920	720	1,074	2
1987	3,546	887	1,016	3
1988	3,702	790	781	8
1989	4,128	727	701	6
1990	1,903	298	630	3
1991	761	176	369	1
1992	528	148	253	–
1993	649	385	211	2
1994	278	107	205	–
1995	415	174	235	–
1996	1,303	364	244	2
1997	235	130	216	–
1998	282	93	166	–
1999	242	141	205	–
2000	499	183	212	1
2001	525	180	194	1
2002	1,323	943	146	nr
2003	499	151	133	nr
2004	905	151	130	nr
2005	157	93	116	nr
2006	755	713	158	nr

Source: LMT, 2002; *Economic and Labour Market Review* 2007 time series

Main trends in the pattern of strike activity

The main trends prior to 2002 are summarised and adapted from Waddington (2003) and are as follows:

- During the late **1940s and early 1950s** there were, in relative terms, fewer strikes than in many subsequent periods on all three measures of strikes. Wages and issues of trade union principle were the main causes of stoppages.
- During the early **1950s onwards** there were a number of large national strikes which occurred for the first time since 1926 in industries such as engineering, shipbuilding, printing and dock working with pay and trade union principles being the main causes.
- During the **1960s** there was a substantial increase in the number of small strikes in the car industry and related sectors reflecting a growth in unofficial shop-floor disputes, while at the same time there was a continuation of the larger national disputes and 'this produced a peak of strike numbers in 1970 when 3906 strikes were recorded' (Edwards, 1995, p. 439). Docks, motor vehicles, shipbuilding, aircraft, non-electrical engineering, electrical engineering, locomotives and iron and steel accounted for half of non-coal stoppages and around 75 per cent of days lost and workers involved. Overall, however, up to 1968 the increase in the total number of strikes as compared to the previous period was slight.
- During the **1970s** the numbers of strikes began to fall slightly, but again the picture is distorted by the presence of large disputes which kept the numbers of workers involved and working days lost on the high side. As Table 8.3 indicates, there were several large disputes from 1977 to 1979, including stoppages in engineering and public sector disputes, culminating in the 'Winter of Discontent'.
- During the **1980s** all the main measures of strikes recorded falls, albeit with fluctuations. The large number of working days lost in 1984 is attributed to the coal strike of that year.
- During the **1990s and early 2000s** there were further substantial falls on all three indices and the number of large disputes fell significantly although there were some increases in 2002 and early 2003.

- For the period **up to 2006** 'the rates for the UK as a whole show the same pattern of general decline with occasional peaks that can be seen on the working days lost series' (Hale, 2007a).

For the period **1977–2006**, we can illustrate the extent to which large disputes distort the underlying trends by pointing to the high number of days lost in 1979 and 1984. This was also evident in 1997 when two disputes and stoppages in transport manufacturing accounted for some 22 per cent of working days lost. Tables 8.1 and 8.2 show a substantial decline in strike activity in the 1990s, while Table 8.3 shows that the number of strikes has been on a general downward trend throughout the last 20 years. Turning to working days lost, we see a similar downward trend but with some increases from 2000 onwards. Interestingly, the 234,700 working days lost in 1997 (equivalent to 10 days lost per 1000 employees) was the lowest on record for strike rates. The longer-term trend in strike activity, taking the base year as 1980, remains downward and it is still too premature to comment on recent years' statistics which may indicate an end to this trend.

However, a report in IRS (2002) is less circumspect and points to the upsurge in industrial disputes during the early part of 2002 (see Exhibit 8.3). Its analysis is speculative rather than academic in nature and is based on the apparent deterioration in relationships between government and unions. Much of the industrial action has taken place within the privatised rail network where there are wide variations in pay between different companies and between drivers and other staff. Safety has often been compromised and this factor has been an ongoing source of dispute between guards and their employers. Labour market factors, such as the shortage of train drivers, has strengthened the bargaining power of this particular group, and unions have had the upper hand in negotiations. Many of the threatened and actual disputes in 2007/8 are taking place within the public sector, the most notable being in public services and Royal Mail. However, it is premature to argue that the 'upsurge' in industrial action represents the beginnings of a longer-term upward trend, but it is nevertheless significant, particularly as it may be a reflection, in part at least, of the deterioration in relationship

between the Labour government and the unions (see Chapters 3 and 4). The industrial action itself has affected relatively few sectors and there has not been a general trend, although underlying tensions within the public sector, the eruption of the fire-fighters' dispute, the ongoing strife in the railway network and pay negotiations affecting local government workers made 2003 a livelier prospect.

Snapshot for 2006

The 2006 total of 754,500 working days lost through labour disputes is significantly higher than the 2005 (157,400) total. The 2006 total is also higher than the average number of working days lost per year in the 1990s (660,000) but lower than the average for both the 1980s (7.2 million) and the 1970s (12.9 million). Hale (2007a) also points out that:

> The 158 stoppages total in 2006 is higher than the 2005 and 2004 totals of 116 and 130 respectively. There were three stoppages beginning in 2005 which continued into 2006. The number of stoppages has fallen sharply since the 1980s, when the average number was 1,129. The average number in the 1990s was 273. There were 713,300 workers involved in labour disputes during 2006; this compares with 92,600 in 2005. The number of workers involved is higher than the average number involved in the 1990s (201,600) but below the average in the 1980s (1,040,300). (p. 25)

On the whole, industrial action was fairly localised in 2006. However, one dispute involving the University and College Union and the Universities and Colleges Employers Association featured prominently (see Exhibit 8.3).

Exhibit 8.3

The lecturers' dispute, 2006

One of the most prominent disputes of 2006, lasting for some four months, was, at times, acrimonious, with the parties holding deeply entrenched stances, seemingly unbridgeable, for the duration of the dispute. The dispute, some argue, was the bitter manifestation of years of festering pay discontent as lecturers fell behind comparable professions in the pay stakes. It has been argued that political differences between the two lecturers' unions impeded progress toward resolution of the dispute. The parties involved were NATFHE (National Association of Teachers in Further and Higher Education) and the Association of University Teachers (AUT) for the lecturers. Both NATFHE and the AUT merged during the latter weeks of the dispute to become the University and College Union (UCU). The negotiating body for the university employers, the second party to the dispute is the University and Colleges Employers' Association (UCEA).

The claim and the rationale for it

The joint NATFHE and AUT pay claim was a 23 per cent pay increase over three years. The rationale underlying the claim went something like this:

> As you are doubtless aware, university staff have become increasingly overworked and underpaid over the last two decades. In the last twenty years, salaries have fallen in value by around 40%. Since 1976, our workloads have increased by around 140%. No other profession in the UK has endured anything like this. Academics spend on average four vital earning years in postgraduate studies before they can apply for academic jobs. Most now endure years of short-term contracts, start on lower salaries and their earnings at the peak of their careers are lower than any other profession, including teachers, doctors, lawyers and other highly skilled professionals. This has a huge impact on the career expectations and on the lives of academic staff. It is hardly surprising that many leave the profession and those who stay are increasingly demoralised as workloads increase and they see no reward in pay. We have waited twenty years for university Vice Chancellors (VCs) to

address this and they have consistently claimed that they would like to increase our pay if only they had the money to do so. The VCs have received the biggest injection of new funding for a generation. Universities are receiving more than £3.5 billion over the next three years in new funding, much of it levied through top-up fees. When VCs lobbied for these fees, they claimed they wanted to spend that money on our pay. They told the Minister for Higher Education that at least a third of the new money should go on staff pay and conditions. But VCs are now refusing to spend this new money on pay. (UCU official: www.uvcu.org.uk – now deleted)

In response to the AUT/NATFHE claim of 23 per cent over three years, the UCEA offered 6 per cent over two years. The lecturers' unions rejected the offer and industrial action commenced on 8 March. Briefly, the industrial action comprised:

- A one-day strike on Tuesday 7 March 2006.
- Boycott of assessment.
- Boycotts of staff appraisal.
- Boycotts of call-out arrangements.
- Boycotts of cover for absent colleagues.

The dispute and the industrial action continued throughout March and April, but after further negotiation in April, the university employers made a 'final offer' in early May of 12.6 per cent over three years which AUT/NATFHE rejected. The dispute became more acrimonious, with Vice Chancellors in some universities threatening to deduct lectures' pay and some universities actually docking at least 10 per cent of pay. Towards the end of May, UCEA made a revised offer of 13.1 per cent which was initially rejected by the newly formed UCU, but after talks at the TUC both parties agreed the 13.1 per cent offer in early June after some minor concessions by UCEA but subject to a ballot of UCU members. For many union members this was seen as a hasty and unexpected settlement prompted by the politics of two unions merging, the deal being largely an outcome of decisions made by senior AUT officials, almost certainly with a view to gaining or maintaining organisational advantage in the post-merger union. Nevertheless, there was a majority of UCU members in favour of the deal which was implemented during the course of 2006.

The evidence from WERS 1998 and WERS 2004

The WIRS/WERS 1998/2004 series spans 24 years from 1980 to 2004 with a further WERS being planned for 2008/9. Reliable data concerning industrial action within workplaces therefore includes the earlier period when industrial action was more prominent and widespread than during the latter period. It is, unsurprising that the WIRS/WERS 1998/2004 data reflects the trend reported in successive ONS publications such as *Labour Market Trends* (LMT) and *Economic and Labour Market Review* (ELMR), the successor to LMT from January 2007 (see Table 8.4). Between 1980 and 1990 the decline in industrial action at workplace level was due largely to a reduction in non-strike action, with strike action being as common in 1990 as it was in 1980. During the 1990s both non-strike and strike action declined, with the former affecting 3 per cent of unionised workplaces in 1998 (9 per

cent in 1990), and the latter affecting 2 per cent of unionised workplaces in 1998 (16 per cent in 1990). At sectoral level, industrial action features more prominently within the public than in the private sector, but overall, by 1998, all forms of collective industrial action had virtually disappeared in all but a few workplaces.

Distribution of strike activity by industry sector

Self-evaluation activity 8.7

Identifying trends

The response is given in the text below

As we have seen, certain industries have been more strike-prone than others. Table 8.5 shows working days lost per 1000 employees in mining, manufacturing and services sectors for the period 1977–2004. What trend or trends can you identify?

Table 8.4 Industrial action in workplaces with recognised unions: 1980–2004

	1980 (%)	1984 (%)	1990 (%)	1998 (%)	2004 (%)
All workplaces					
None	75	69	80	93	91
Non-strike action only	10	8	4	2	2
Strike action only	9	11	11	1	2
Both strike and non-strike action threatened or taken	7	11	5	4	5
Private sector manufacturing					
None	62	70	88	95	na
Non-strike action only	11	14	10	5	na
Strike action only	15	9	*	0	na
Both strike and non-strike action	12	7	3	0	na
Private sector services					
None	89	85	93	97	na
Non-strike action only	5	4	1	1	na
Strike action only	5	8	1	2	na
Both strike and non-strike action	1	3	5	1	na
All Private Sector					
None				97	97
Non-strike action only				1	1
Strike action only				0	0
Both strike and non-strike action threatened or taken				3	3
Public sector					
None	73	61	67	90	87
Non-strike action only	12	7	4	1	5
Strike action only	8	14	23	4	8
Both strike and non-strike action	8	17	6	9	16

Source: Millward *et al.*, 2000, p. 178; Kersley *et al.*, 2006, p. 209

The distribution of strikes between the three sectors of mining, manufacturing and services has changed since 1960. Edwards (1995) comments: 'The most dramatic trend was a rise in the role of services, which were virtually strike-free during the early 1960s, and by the late 1980s they accounted for a fifth of all strikes' (p. 441).

The 'working days lost per 1000 employees' measure is the standard method that has been used to convert working days lost into a strike rate that

takes account of the size of the labour force. This also enables comparisons to be made across industries and regions that differ in size. Since the number of employee jobs has not changed dramatically over the last 20 years, the rates for the UK show the same pattern of general decline and occasional peaks that can be seen in the working days lost measure. Between 1982 and 1993 the mining, energy and water supply industries had the highest rate in each year except 1989, when there was a

Table 8.5 Working days lost per 1000 employees, United Kingdom: 1977–2006

Year	Mining, energy and water	Manufacturing	Services	All industries and services
1977	251	1,101	124	448
1978	372	1,135	77	413
1979	232	3,347	422	1,272
1980	259	1,691	42	520
1981	374	396	117	195
1982	649	352	211	248
1983	2,212	345	39	178
1984	38,425	529	114	1,278
1985	7518	183	86	299
1986	293	220	46	90
1987	482	124	181	164
1988	536	339	116	166
1989	165	156	199	182
1990	245	228	44	83
1991	87	52	30	34
1992	97	23	24	24
1993	91	28	31	30
1994	2	15	13	13
1995	6	17	20	19
1996	8	24	70	58
1997	9	21	8	10
1998	1	8	13	12
1999	–	14	7	10
2000	17	13	20	20
2001	141	11	22	20
2002	1	6	62	51
2003	2	18	20	19
2004	29	6	41	34
2005	34	5	6	6
2006	74	6	32	28

Source: LMT, 1999, p. 304, 2002, p. 594; ELMR, 2007a, p. 28

large strike in the public administration sector. Up until the late 1980s the rate for the manufacturing industries had been significantly higher than that of the service sector. However, over the 1990s, the rates have been fairly similar with the exception of 1996, when the service sector rate was almost three times the rate for the manufacturing sector. During 2000 and 2001, the rate of working days lost increased in services and in mining, energy and water. According to WERS 2004 the incidence of industrial action in 2004 was similar to that in 1998 (see Table 8.4). Action short of a strike took place in relatively few workplaces with 61 per cent of workplaces (representing 2 per cent of all establishments) experiencing industrial action reporting non-strike action such as 'working to rule' (28 per cent), 'overtime bans'/'restrictions initiated by employers (28 per cent), 'go slows' 13 per cent and

'blacking of work' (3 per cent). Collective disputes, as in previous years' were most common among workplaces in the public sector, particularly within Public Administration and Education, and WERS 2004 establishes a positive association between the incidence of industrial action and the level of union membership in the workplace:

> *Among public sector workplaces where less than half of the employees were union members, only one in twenty (4 per cent) had experienced industrial action, compared with one in ten (11 per cent) where membership density was between 50 and 89 per cent and one quarter where at least 90 per cent of employees were union members.* (Kersley et al., 2006, p. 209)

There was no association between union membership and the incidence of industrial action within the private sector, however.

International comparisons

It is useful to compare the UK strike rate with those of other countries in order to establish whether other countries display similar trends to those in the UK. We could argue, for example, that as there are similar trends between countries, then economic factors may constitute the most likely explanation for decline in strike activity, since most of the EU countries have experienced high rates of unemployment and similar economic conditions. In historical terms, we could explain the similarity in trends by reference to 'long wave' theory (see below). In the British context the claims of the previous Conservative governments that the reduction in strike activity was the result of its industrial relations legislation are largely unfounded, given similar strike patterns in other EU countries where there has been little or no such legislation.

An analysis of strike data for EU and Organisation for Economic Co-operation and Development (OECD) countries for the period (Hale, 2007a) reveals some similarities and some variations in strike activity both within the EU and OECD countries as shown in Table 8.6. In 2001, the UK had the 11th lowest strike rate (defined as the number of working days lost due to labour disputes per 1000 employees) in the OECD, the same ranking as in 2000. As we have already seen, the UK strike rate doubled between 1999 and 2000 and then remained at that level for 2001, and this is also a feature within the EU and OECD. The OECD average strike rate of 29 days in 2001 is the lowest in the Labour Market Trends series and the lowest since 1983, but it should be noted that this statistic is slightly distorted by the high US figure. Notwithstanding this, the UK strike rate has been below both OECD and EU averages since 1991, with the exception of 1996. More specifically, the average UK strike rate for the period 1997–2001 was 52 per cent lower than the previous five-year period (1992–6) with equivalent falls for the OECD and EU being 45 per cent and 23 per cent respectively.

With regard to the 2005 data (Hale, 2007a), Table 8.6 shows the number of working days lost through labour disputes per 1000 employees (the strike rate) over the ten-year period 1996 to 2005 for each of the OECD and EU countries, where figures are available. This shows that the UK strike rate decreased by 82 per cent in 2005, ranking it 12th highest out of 27. In 2004, the UK ranked 22nd lowest out of 29. For comparison, on the same basis in 2005, the UK ranked 15th lowest out of the 27 countries where figures were available. Over the OECD as a whole, 13 countries saw their strike rate fall in 2005 and eight showed a rise, the most significant of which was Finland, increasing from a rate of 21 in 2004 to 322 in 2005. The OECD average strike rate of 29 days in 2005 showed a decrease from 31 (revised) in 2004. (Hale, 2007a, pp. 23–4). Figure 8.1 shows the strike rates in 2005 for the 19 EU countries that supplied data, with the UK having the eighth highest rate. Luxembourg, Austria, Sweden, Estonia, Hungary, Latvia, Malta, Poland and Slovakia all had an average strike rate of zero for 2005. France, Belgium and Cyprus did not supply figures and so have been excluded. Figure 8.2 displays the UK strike rate against the EU average for each year from 1996 to 2005. The UK strike rate has been significantly below the EU average since 1996. Within the EU, Germany and Luxembourg have shown low strike rates over the latest 10-year period, while Spain continues its trend of high strike rates, with an average of 62 in 2005, second only to Finland. Generally, it can be seen from the statistics, where available, that the strike rate in the new EU member countries is low (Hale, 2007a).

Table 8.6 Working days lost per 1000 employees, selected EU and OECD countries

Average	1992–6	1997–2001	1992–2001	2001–5
United Kingdom	24	21	22	26
(UK ranking)	6	8	7	12th out of 27 in 2006
Austria	2	1	2	80
Belgium	38	21	29	na
Denmark	46	292	172	36
Finland	170	58	112	91
France	97	73	84	34
Germany	17	1	9	4
Ireland	110	86	96	30
Italy	172	62	116	120
Luxembourg	13	1	6	0
Netherlands	30	5	17	12
Portugal	30	19	24	15
Spain	385	178	271	189
Sweden	54	6	30	34
EU 14 average	84	46	64	53
Cyprus				na
Estonia				na
Latvia				0
Lithuania				na
Malta				9
Hungary				2
Poland				1
Slovakia				na
Australia	107	69	87	62
Canada	174	192	183	208
Iceland	556	571	564	401
Japan	2	1	2	1
New Zealand	54	19	36	19
Norway	121	78	98	80
Switzerland	1	3	2	4
Turkey	175	28	95	20
USA	54	17	31	36
OECD average	61	47	54	42

Source: LMT, 2003; Hale, 2007b

International definitions of strikes differ

A significant problem in collating international strike data is that definitions of strikes and other measurement criteria differ from country to country, as Table 8.7 indicates. Most countries rely on voluntary notification of disputes to a national or local government department, backed by media reports.

No country within the OECD aims to record the full effects of stoppages, neither are other forms of action such as work-to-rule and overtime bans included. There are differences in the criteria that determine inclusion in statistics. Most countries exclude small stoppages, the threshold being defined in terms of the numbers involved, the length of the dispute, the number of days lost or a combination

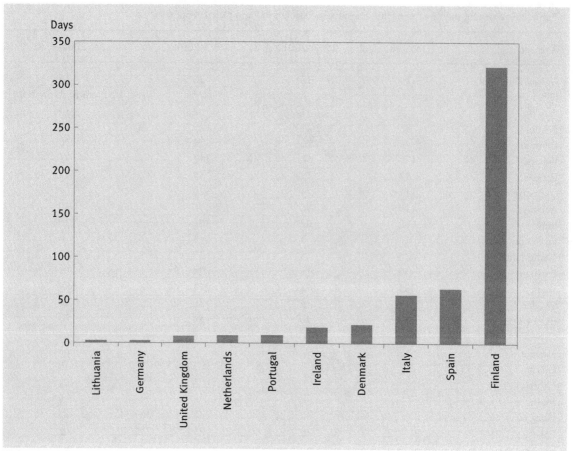

Figure 8.1 European Union strike rate: 2005 (individual countries)
Note 1 Excludes France, Belgium and Cyprus.
Note 2 Luxembourg, Austria, Sweden, Estonia, Hungary, Latvia, Malta, Poland and Slovakia had a strike rate of zero in 2005.
Source: ELMR, 2007, 1, 4, p. 25

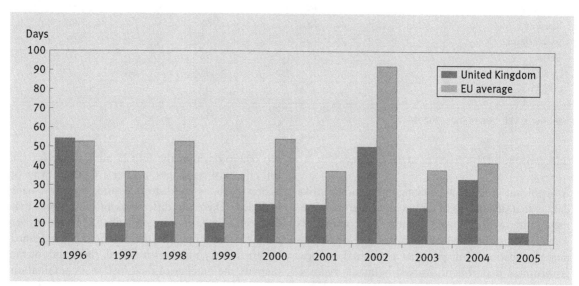

Figure 8.2 Annual strike rates: 1996–2005, EU and United Kingdom (ten new EU members induded from 2004)
Source: ELMR, 2007, 1, 4, p. 25

Table 8.7 Labour disputes: comparison of coverage and methodology

Country	Minimum criteria for inclusion in statistics	Are political stoppages included?	Are indirectly affected workers included?	Sources and notes
United Kingdom	Ten workers involved and of one-day duration unless 100 workdays not worked	No	Yes	Office for National Statistics collects information initially from press reports and then contacts employers and unions directly
Australia	Ten workdays not worked	Yes	Yes	Information gathered from Industrial Relations Department, employers, unions and press
Austria	No restrictions on size	Yes	No	Trade unions provide information
Belgium	No restriction on size. Excluding public sector stoppages	Yes	No	Questionnaires to employees following police or media coverage
Canada	Half-day duration plus 10 workdays not worked	Yes	No	Reports from Canada Manpower Centres, provincial Labour Departments' conciliation services and press
Denmark	100 workdays not worked. By employers' organisations	Yes	Yes	Voluntary reports submitted annually
Finland	One-hour duration	Yes	Yes	Principally returns from employers (90%); some reports from employees and press
France	One workday not worked. Excluding agriculture	Yes	Yes	Labour inspectors' reports
Germany	Ten workers involved and one-day duration unless 100 workdays not worked. Excluding public administration. From 1993 data covers entire FRG; earlier data covers West Germany only	Yes	No	Compulsory notification by employers to local employment offices
Iceland	Restrictions on size	Not known	No	No information

Country				
Ireland	Ten workdays not worked or one-day duration	Yes	Yes	Reports from Department of Enterprise and Employment, Department of Social Welfare and press
Italy	No restrictions on size	Yes	No	No information
Japan	Half-day duration. Excluding unofficial disputes	Yes	No	Legal requirement to report to Labour Relations Commission
Luxembourg	No information	Not known	Not known	No information
Netherlands	No restrictions on size	Yes	Yes	Questionnaires to employers following a strike. National Dutch Press Bureau collects relevant news items on a contractual basis for Statistics Netherlands
New Zealand	Ten workdays not worked. Before 1988 excluding public sector stoppages	Yes	Yes	Information initially from press reports, employee and employer organisations and labour inspectors and subsequently from employer report forms
Norway	One-day duration	Yes	No	Employers' reports to the Ministry of Labour and Government Administration and press
Portugal	Strikes only. No restriction on size. Excluding general strikes at national level; excluding public administration	Yes	No	Legal obligation on trade unions to notify Ministry of Labour and Social Security
Spain	Strikes only before 1990. One-hour duration. Before 1989, excluding civil service	Yes	No	Legal obligation on party instigating strike to notify competent labour authority
Sweden	Eight hours not worked	Yes	No	Information gathered following press reports
Switzerland	One-day duration	Yes	No	Federal Office for Industry, Crafts, Occupations and Employment requests returns from employers and unions following press reports
Turkey	No restriction on size. Excluding energy services and most public services; excluding general strikes	No	Yes	Legal obligation on part of trade unions to notify Regional Directorates of Labour
United States	One-day or one-shift duration and 1000 workers involved	No	Yes	Reports from press, employers, unions and agencies involved

of all or some of these. Any difference in thresholds affects the number of days lost that are recorded. The USA and Denmark have particularly high thresholds, making comparison difficult. The USA, for example, includes only those disputes involving more than 1000 workers. Some countries exclude the effects of disputes in certain industrial sectors. Portugal, for example, omits public sector strikes and general strikes while Japan excludes days lost in unofficial disputes. Political stoppages are excluded for the UK, USA and Turkey. The inclusion or omission of those workers indirectly involved in a stoppage (those who are unable to work because others at their workplace are on strike) varies between countries. Half the countries listed in Table 8.7, including Australia, Belgium, France, the Netherlands, New Zealand, the UK and the USA, attempt to include them while Germany, Canada, Italy and Japan exclude them. This results in the latter category of countries recording a lower number of working days lost than those countries in the former category.

Explaining the strike trends

Edwards (1995) notes that there are five likely explanations for falling strike rates in the UK or indeed falling strike rates generally. These are:

- economic conditions;
- the shift of employment away from strike-prone industries and sectors;
- legal restrictions;
- improved means of dispute resolution; and
- 'better industrial relations'.

Economic conditions

Citing evidence from Davies (1979) for the period 1966–75, Edwards found that 'unemployment reduced the number [of disputes], but that it was not the high level of unemployment, but increases in the level of unemployment which reduced strikes' (p. 446). In addition, it was also found that high levels of inflation tended to encourage strikes as concern with maintaining real income grew. By the same token, lower and declining inflation levels generally reduced employee expectations of higher pay increases.

Move away from strike-prone industries

As we noted earlier, many of the traditional strike-prone industries have declined both absolutely and in terms of numbers of employees. This in turn has reduced the bargaining power of trade unions representing workers in those industries. Nowhere is this more so than in the coal industry, which was one of the most strike-prone industries. Edwards (1995) comments:

> We may take its [the coal industry's] actual number of strikes per employee and calculate the number of strikes that it would have experienced had it stayed at the same size that it had in 1971 and in 1981. During the period 1986–1990, there would have been over 300 more strikes per annum on the 1971 employment level, and around 200 more on the 1981 level. This would have increased the number of strikes in Britain as a whole by two-fifths and a quarter respectively. (p. 446)

Role of the law

The employment relations legislation of the 1980s and 1990s has restricted the definition of what constitutes lawful industrial action and has made it more difficult for workers to take industrial action as a result of balloting procedures and threats concerning the use of injunctions by employers. Research by Edwards (1992) suggests that there is no clear-cut relationship between the cumulative effects of legislative developments and industrial action. In attempting to 'measure the impact of the law once the effects of the labour market forces and structure of the economy have been taken into account, no consistent results for worker involvement or days lost have emerged, though the number of stoppages seems to have been reduced' (p. 446). The results, therefore, appear to be inconclusive, and there is, moreover, no evidence to suggest that the legislation has made workers less willing to take industrial action, but 'as part of a complex of other changes [the legislation] has indirectly shaped assumptions about the desirability and efficacy of action (p. 447)'.

Disputes and balloting procedures

According to Edwards (1995), the trend towards formalisation of procedures, including disputes

procedures, occurred during the 1970s, and so would have had little impact upon strike incidence or working days lost during the 1980s and 1990s. Strike ballots have been legally required since 1984; evidence of ballots determining the outcome of a dispute is flimsy. This is partly because many strikes are of particularly short duration, with a high proportion lasting less than one day, and take place without a ballot being conducted. While this action is 'unlawful', these 'lightning' disputes are difficult to enforce and the law to all intents and purposes is irrelevant. Referring to research by Kessler and Bayliss (1995), who examined ACAS records containing data on strikes taken as a result of ballots, Edwards (1995) estimates that at least 60 per cent of strikes may take place without ballots in any one year and so we may only be generalising on the basis of the remainder of balloted strikes (40 per cent) and those disputes which were subjected to ballots but did not result in strike action; as Edwards puts it: 'the question is not whether some disputes are now settled without strikes but whether more ballots are now held, and whether the percentage of cases settled without a strike has increased' (p. 447).

'Better industrial relations'

This depends upon the nature or climate of industrial relations in the first place, and is a subjective as well as a relative evaluation. The climate and quality of industrial relations within an organisation is determined by many factors such as management style, union presence or absence, density of unionisation, technology, markets, skill requirements and so on. In similar fashion to Handy's typology of organisational culture (1993), 'good' or 'bad' industrial relations may be influenced by the nature of the power and control relationships between employer and employees such as the reassertion of managerial prerogatives over the past 20 years; the nature of the roles played by management and individual managers which incorporates management style and ideology (see Chapter 2); the task culture and production process which includes technological changes and flexibilisation (see Chapter 5) and the extent to which individuals share the organisational goals, emphasising 'commitment', 'involvement', 'trust' and 'co-operation'. In general terms, if the

industrial relations climate is 'poor', assuming a state of 'bad' industrial relations, then the greater the propensity for industrial action and strikes. Conversely, 'good' industrial relations would suggest industrial harmony rather than conflict. However, the deterministic nature of this simplistic cause–effect relationship belies a more complex interaction of factors.

Self-evaluation activity 8.8
The effects of Thatcherism
Response on website

If Thatcherism resulted in a deterioration in the general quality and climate of industrial relations, why did the number of strikes, workers involved and working days lost decline?

Long wave theory: a caveat

Kelly (1998) criticises industrial relations textbooks for being 'highly contemporary in their focus . . . the lack of adequate historical analysis opens up the danger of constructing future trends by simply projecting the recent past'. Essentially, long wave theory concerning strikes (developed initially by Kondratieff, 1979) looks at economic upswings and downswings over a period from around 1870 to 1974 within an international context. The basic conclusion from the research into strikes and long wave theory reported by Kelly is that towards the end of the Kondratieff upswings of 1869–75, 1910–20 and 1968–74 there were major strike waves which also coincided with periods of trade union growth; lesser strike waves can be detected towards the end of the Kondratieff downswings of 1889–93 and 1935–48. However, we argue that notwithstanding the validity of long wave theory, industrial relations textbooks should concentrate upon recent and contemporary data and trends while at the same time acknowledging the contribution of long wave theory (and mobilisation theory). Extrapolation from recent trends is a hazardous undertaking, especially if those trends are considered in isolation from the broader historical context. Unfortunately, space does not permit an examination

of these issues which, as Kelly admits, remain contentious and problematic (1998, p. 107).

Summary points

- Industrial action is defined as work stoppages instigated either by management or trade union, and includes strikes, lockouts, go-slows, overtime bans, work-ins and sit-ins.
- Industrial action/conflict may be both individual and collective, organised and unorganised.
- The legal definition of industrial action (TULRCA) is necessary to determine whether industrial action is either lawful or unlawful.
- The main types of strike identified in the literature include:
 - the trial of strength;
 - the demonstration stoppage;
 - the official strike;
 - the unofficial strike;
 - the constitutional strike; and
 - the unconstitutional strike.
- Causes of strikes include the general categories of:
 - community integration;
 - technological determinism;
 - negotiating procedures; and
 - strikers' definition of the situation.
- More specific causes of strikes include:
 - pay;
 - hours of work;
 - redundancy;
 - trade union matters;
 - working conditions;
 - staffing; and
 - dismissal and disciplinary measures.
- Strike patterns are analysed using measures of:
 - working days lost;
 - number of stoppages; and
 - number of workers involved.
- Strike patterns and trends in the UK may be explained by:
 - economic conditions;
 - shift of employment from strike-prone industries;
 - legal restrictions;
 - improved means of dispute resolution; and
 - 'better industrial relations'.

STRIKES AND THE LAW

We now look in greater detail at the legislation concerning industrial action enacted by successive governments during the past 30 years or so and which was considered in general terms in Chapter 4. The legislation restricted the definition of what constitutes lawful industrial action and narrowed the immunities which trade unions had gained under the 1906 Trades Disputes Act. Before looking at the specific provisions of the legislation, which we examine chronologically in order to demonstrate the incremental progression of the various statutory provisions concerning industrial action, we consider briefly the situation that existed before 1980. McIlroy (1991) provides a clear and concise account which is reproduced in Exhibit 8.4.

The legislation examined

Employment Act 1980

Picketing
Concern about picketing as a result of the 'Winter of Discontent' was expressed in the Conservative Party manifesto and in the white paper which preceded the 1980 Act. Particular attention was paid to the 'secondary picketing' phenomenon (picketing of employers not directly involved in disputes and picketing affecting the general public and the violence and intimidation which accompanied picketing generally). The government wanted to limit the scale and scope of picketing which would limit action to the workplace directly involved. Secondary picketing, therefore, became unlawful and the regulation of picketing would be a matter for the police and the criminal law. Specifically the Act contained the following provisions:

- workers to be protected when picketing at or near their own place of work, limiting pickets to the site on which they worked;
- there were provisions for mobile workers (such as lorry drivers) and workers whose location made picketing impracticable (such as oil rigs);
- there were protections for union officials and dismissed workers; and
- although not part of the Act, the Code of Practice on Picketing (1980) emphasised that picket

Exhibit 8.4

The situation before 1980

If you go on strike then you are usually breaking your contract of employment. The courts have also found that a range of other industrial action . . . involves employees in breaking their contracts of employment. An employer often has little to gain financially by suing employees for breach of contract, apart from the unhelpful impact this is likely to have on future industrial relations. However, there is a civil wrong developed by the courts termed *inducement to breach of contract*. If employers could show the courts that it was the *union* that instigated, influenced or supported the industrial action then they might be able to convince the courts that the union was inducing the workers to break their contracts of employment.

In many cases judges were willing to do this and grant a legal order, an *injunction* instructing the union to call off the action. If the union did not do this it would be *in contempt of court* and could be fined large sums of money or eventually have its assets *sequestrated*. The courts also developed other civil wrongs – conspiracy, intimidation, and interference with contracts – which they used against union activities.

The position was made more difficult by the practice of the courts of issuing *interim injunctions*. An employer could within a matter of days secure a preliminary hearing of the case. The judge was only concerned as to whether, on the face of it, the employer had an arguable case, not whether it could be proved to the hilt, and whether looking at all the circumstances, the judge felt that it was more convenient to freeze the situation and restore the *status quo* by ordering the union to call off the industrial action until the full trial took place.

In the vast majority of cases the courts found for the employers, ignoring the problems this caused for unions and members who had to wait six months or a year before they could bring their bargaining power fully to bear on the employer. Of course, in most cases, the employers never returned to court for the full trial. The use of the interim injunction adequately met their purposes.

All of this meant, quite simply, that strikes and most forms of industrial action were unlawful. Trade unions, therefore, pressed parliament to *immunise* them from the impact of this judge-made law. If they were to carry out their functions of protecting their members, then they needed *specific immunities* from, for example, the civil wrong or tort of inducing breach of contract. Parliament decided unions would be protected where the industrial action is **'in contemplation or furtherance of a trade dispute'** (Trade Disputes Act, 1906). A *trade dispute* was defined quite widely as a dispute between employers and workers, which was related to, or connected with one or more of a long list of industrial matters. The list covered such issues as terms and conditions of employment, engagement, or dismissal of employees, allocation of work, discipline procedures and so forth.

If the industrial action fell within this definition of a trade dispute, then it was protected – or at least the trade unions were over the first hurdle. If the action did not fall within this definition, then the workers and their trade unions were in trouble. They then possessed no immunity and could be sued for committing one of the civil wrongs – most commonly inducement to breach of contract.

A major aim of the 1980 Act was to limit the immunities trade unionists possessed when taking industrial action.

Source: McIlroy, 1991, p. 41

numbers should not exceed six at any entrance to a workplace, that pickets should not seek to halt essential supplies and that 'everyone has a right to decide for himself whether he will cross a picket line'.

Secondary action

The government now wanted to deal with the secondary boycott, the situation where workers taking industrial action requested workers employed by other employers such as customers, suppliers,

contractors or transport workers, not to handle their product for the duration of the dispute. These forms of secondary action had been protected by the Trade Union and Labour Relations Act but were now restricted. The two main, rather complex provisions which defined secondary action are as follows:

1. Where workers, stewards or union officers induce a group of workers to break their contracts with their employer who is not himself a party to the dispute; or where workers, stewards or union officers interfere with the performance of contracts of employment or induce others or threaten to induce others to interfere with it.
2. If as a result of inducement to break or interfere with contracts of employment, a party to a commercial contract has been induced to break it, or its performance has been interfered with or threats to do so have been made.

For example, if workers on strike ask drivers not to remove finished goods from their plant and the drivers agree, thereby breaking their contract by refusing their employer's orders, and as a result their employer is in breach of his commercial contract with the struck employer then, on the face of it, there will be secondary action within the Act.

In summary, pure secondary action such as solidarity strikes where there was no contractual relationship between those involved in the primary strike and those seeking to help them was not protected and therefore unlawful (for example, miners taking action to support railway workers). Only secondary action where there was a contractual relationship between the primary and secondary employers would be lawful, and even then only within constraints. The provisions governing secondary action have proved complex and subject to a variety of interpretations.

The Employment Act 1982

Definition of trade disputes
The Act tightened up the definition of a trade dispute in three respects:

1. *Workers and their employer*: Before 1982 a trade dispute meant a dispute between employers and workers. The Act now changed this to workers and their employer. This would mean that in cases where trade unionists, in order to ensure basic terms and conditions were maintained, took industrial action against an employer *whose own employees were not taking action*, the dispute would not be protected.
2. *Workers and workers*: Before the 1982 Act disputes which to some extent involved conflicts between different groups of workers over, for example, demarcation, or the introduction of new technology, fell within the definition of a trade dispute. This type of action is now unlawful and the words *workers and workers* which appeared in the pre-1982 definition are omitted.
3. *Wholly or mainly*: Before the 1982 Act the definition of a trade dispute stated that the dispute taking place must simply *be connected with* one or more of:
 - terms and conditions of employment or the physical conditions in which workers are required to work;
 - engagement or non-engagement, or termination or suspension of employment or the duties of employment, of one or more workers;
 - allocation of work or the duties of employment as between workers or groups of workers;
 - matters of discipline;
 - the membership or non-membership of a trade union on the part of a worker;
 - facilities for officials of trade unions; and
 - machinery for negotiation or consultation, and other procedures, relating to any of the foregoing matters, including the recognition by employers or employers' associations of the right of a trade union to represent workers in any such negotiation or consultation or in the carrying out of such procedures.

The 1982 Act deleted *connected with* and replaced those words with *relate wholly or mainly* to one or more of these matters. This meant that where there were mixed elements in a dispute such as political factors as well as employment-related factors and where the political factors dominated, then there would be no protection by immunity. The intention here was to ensure that disputes are industrial and not 'political'.

Disputes outside the UK
Before the 1982 Act, the definition of a trade dispute stated: 'There is a trade dispute . . . even

though it relates to matters outside Great Britain.' The Act made it unlawful for workers in Britain to take industrial action to support workers in dispute in other countries – unless the workers in Britain were likely to be affected by the outcome of the dispute taking place abroad in relation to one of the matters listed in the definition of a trade dispute.

Union liability; authorised/endorsed action; damages against unions

Industrial action was now more likely to be unlawful than in the past. The next step was to ensure that the union was financially responsible for unlawful industrial action. The Act changed the law so that trade unions could be sued in their own name for any action which fell outside the definition of a trade dispute or specific immunities. The union would be liable whenever unlawful industrial action was authorised or endorsed by a responsible person such as the union executive, anyone with power under the rule book to endorse or authorise the action, executive officers of the union or any other employed official of the union. The industrial action would not be regarded as 'authorised' or 'endorsed' if, for example, the union executive or executive officers repudiated the action.

The Act also set limits on the damages which could be awarded against unions in any one legal action. The limits are:

- £10,000 for unions with fewer than 5000 members;
- £15,000 for unions with between 5000 and 25,000 members;
- £125,000 for unions with between 25,000 and 100,000 members;
- £250,000 for unions with more than 100,000 members.

Dismissal of strikers

Under common law, employers could treat workers' action in going on strike as a repudiation of their contracts warranting dismissal. The Act permitted an employer to selectively re-engage strikers provided that more than three months had elapsed since the date of the worker's dismissal. If an employer follows this procedure other strikers dismissed and not reengaged will have no right to a tribunal hearing. This provision thus strengthened the employers'

position in a strike situation and undermined workers' rights.

Self-evaluation activity 8.9

Lessons that could be learnt from the Messenger dispute in historical context
Response on website

Mini case 8.1 is an account of the dispute between *Messenger* free newspapers and the National Graphical Association in 1983. What lessons could employers and unions learn from this dispute?

Mini case 8.1

The Messenger dispute: an historic case

Eddie Shah ran a small group which published five *Messenger* free newspapers in the Lancashire and Cheshire area. He had problems with the National Graphical Association and when he opened a new typesetting plant at Bury he tried to exclude the union. The dismissal of six NGA members at the *Stockport Messenger* led the union to mount pickets at Bury and more importantly at Shah's Warrington plant to which most of the work done by NGA members had been transferred. For the NGA, the closed shop, control of membership and control of technology in the growing free sheet sector of the industry were key issues. They therefore asked all other NGA members not to work on, and all advertisers not to use the Messenger group's papers. This meant that for Eddie Shah his business was at stake.

In October 1983, Shah obtained injunctions against the print union and against the NUJ whose members had been asked not to handle copy. The two injunctions issued against the NGA under the 1980 and 1982 Acts ordered a halt to secondary picketing at Shah's Bury and Warrington plants and the withdrawal of NGA instructions to members to boycott Messenger newspapers which under s. 14 of the 1982 Act constituted pressure to enforce 100 per cent membership. The NGA ignored the orders and, on 17 November 1983, the High Court found the NGA in contempt of court. A £50,000 fine was increased by a further £100,000 on 25 November as mass picketing of Shah's Warrington depot intensified and the judge also ordered the sequestration of the union's assets. In

December the NGA was fined a further half a million pounds. An NGA strike in Fleet Street at the end of November produced further legal action by the Newspaper Proprietor's Association.

Source: McIlroy, 1991, pp. 69–73

According to Evans (1987), the number of injunctions sought by employers between May 1984 and April 1987 totalled 80, of which 11 concerned picketing, 16 concerned secondary action and 47 related to pre-strike ballots. A survey by Labour Research in 1987 reveals that from 1987 to 1988, there were 18 instances of legal action instigated by employers, seven of which concerned picketing and five of which concerned balloting. A further survey for Labour Research (1994) revealed that while the number of cases declined in 1992 and 1993, there was a marked increase in 1994 with 12 out of the 13 cases concerning changes to balloting arrangements as a result of the 1993 Act.

The Trade Union Act 1984

Ballots prior to industrial action

The balloting provisions apply not only to strikes but also to other industrial action, and state that the immunities protecting unions in taking lawful industrial action would continue to apply provided that unions adopt the following procedures:

- There had to be a ballot of all those whom the union reasonably believes will be called on to take part in the strike or other industrial action.
- The ballot must be secret, involve marking a paper and be conducted by post. The ballot could be conducted at the workplace if held immediately before, after, or during working hours.
- The ballot must be held not more than 28 days before the action begins or not more than 28 days before the action is authorised or endorsed where the union supported previously unofficial action. In other words, if a ballot was held, but strike action was delayed for more than 28 days because of continuing negotiation or because of the restraining effect of an injunction, another ballot would have to be held.
- The question on the ballot papers requires a straight 'yes' or 'no' about willingness to take industrial action, and must explicitly state that

taking industrial action will involve a breach of employment contracts.
- The resulting action will only be protected by immunity if there is a straight majority in favour of the action. But there will then be no obligation on a union to support industrial action and no legal protection for members taking action against dismissal by their employer.

If the above procedures are not followed, then the Act gave a right to employers, customers and suppliers affected by the industrial action to take action for an injunction and damages.

The Employment Act 1988

Ballots on industrial action

The Act introduced three important changes to the 1984 Act:

1. **Union members.** The 1984 Act provided that unions would lose their immunity against legal action if they induced workers to take industrial action in breach of their contracts of employment without a ballot. The right to take legal action in these circumstances was given only to employers. The 1988 Act extended this right to union members. This was seen by government as extending the rights of the individual and increasing pressure on the union.
2. **Strike-breaking.** Unions sometimes took disciplinary action against members who worked normally during a strike or other industrial action, did the work of strikers, refused to pay a levy or cross picket lines. The Act now introduced a right not to be unjustifiably disciplined, and gave members the right to take a case to industrial tribunal where they had:
 - not joined in or supported a strike or industrial action even if it was official;
 - made allegations that the union or its officers acted contrary to union rules or broke agreements; and
 - brought legal proceedings against the union.
3. **Separate ballots.** Where a ballot involved unions at different workplaces they could simply be counted to produce an overall result. Under the 1988 Act, this situation would prevail where all members involved share a 'common distinguishing factor' (where, for example, all those voting

in the ballot represent all the union members in a particular grade or occupation employed by that employer). In all other instances there would be separate ballots for each workplace.

The Employment Act 1990

The main proposals concerning industrial action are based on the green paper *Unofficial Action and the Law* and include limits on secondary action, unofficial industrial action and dismissal of strikers.

Secondary action

The 1980 Act had given workers some protective immunity concerning taking industrial action to prevent or disrupt the flow of goods or services to or from a supplier or customer of the employer in dispute providing certain requirements were met. The 1990 Act removes immunity from all forms of secondary action so that workers at a struck plant seeking to get workers at the plant of a customer or supplier not to handle delivery would be open to legal action for damages, as would any union authorising or supporting the action. This applies not only to those working under a contract of employment but also to independent contractors, freelance workers and the self-employed working under a contract of services.

Unofficial action

Provisions of the Act make unions responsible for the actions of anyone empowered by the rules to authorise or endorse industrial action whether they be the union executive committee, general secretary or president, any other committee of the union, any official of the union including lay shop stewards as well as paid officers. Responsibility and legal liability for the actions of all union personnel will apply, and a union cannot evade responsibility for the actions of its officials or other activists by changing its rules. The only way a union can escape being deemed to have authorised or endorsed industrial action is if it specifically repudiates the action.

Dismissal of strikers

Where industrial action is unofficial, the normal rules on dismissal identified in the Employment Act 1982 are relaxed. The main provisions are as follows:

- Any workers taking part in unofficial action such as the leaders or shop stewards may be selected out for dismissal and will have no right to take a case to industrial tribunal.
- Any industrial action in support of those selectively dismissed in unofficial action will be unprotected by the immunities and will be open to legal action by any employers or other persons affected.
- Action will not be deemed unofficial and covered by these provisions if all those taking part are non-trade unionists.

Trade Union Reform and Employment Rights Act 1993

The Act tightened up the provisions dealing with strikes in the following ways:

- All strike ballots had to be postal, thereby putting to an end the practice of workplace ballots established in 1984.
- Unions are required to provide employers with written notice of their intent to ballot members on industrial action at least seven days before commencement of the ballot, together with sample papers of the ballot at least three days before the start of the ballot.
- A union must ensure that it provides the employer with details of the ballot result and the names of those involved in the ballot.
- Strike ballots which involve 50 or more members must be independently scrutinised.
- A union must give the employer at least seven days' written notice of its intention to take official industrial action.
- Any individual who is deprived of goods or services as a result of unlawful industrial action can bring proceedings before the High Court in order to restrain the unlawful act; such individuals can also apply to the new Commissioner for protection against unlawful industrial action for help and advice.

Employment Relations Act 1999

The Act makes substantial changes to the law in relation to the way legal action is conducted and the treatment of employees involved in disputes. The main changes are:

1. The simplification of ballots on industrial action. Where both parties agree, it will be possible to extend the 28-day period within which action must be taken before a ballot elapses to a maximum of eight weeks. This, it is hoped, will encourage further negotiation without the threat of legal action concerning ballot and notice provisions.

2. Those taking strike action will be offered greater protection from being dismissed. It is now 'automatically unfair' to dismiss an employee taking lawful industrial action for eight weeks (see also Chapter 12). Dismissal will then be fair only if the employer has taken 'all reasonable steps' to resolve the dispute.

3. While trade unions are no longer required to give employers a list of their members' names when an industrial action ballot or strike is held, they must still provide the employer with information concerning the group of employees to be balloted or asked to take strike action.

Employment Relations Act 2004

The Act contains the following provisions:

- Provisions to increase the protections against the dismissal of employees taking official, lawfully organised industrial action by extending the 'protected period' from 8 to 12 weeks;

- Exempting 'lock-out' days from the 12 week protected period;

- Specifically in relation to the above, **Section 26** amends the protections for striking employees in section 238A of the 1992 Act by changing the length and scope of the protected period currently specified in the section. It does this by extending the period from 8 to 12 weeks and by providing for 'locked-out' days to be disregarded when determining the length of the period. As a result of the amendments made by this section, the period will in effect end when 84 days have passed since the start of the action on which no lock-out has occurred. This means, for example, that where a lock-out occurred on two days, the total period of protection becomes 86 days.

- Defining more closely the actions which employers and unions should undertake when taking reasonable procedural steps to resolve industrial disputes, specifically subsection (2) sets out the first matter, which is whether the conciliation or mediation meetings have been attended, on behalf of the employer and union, by an 'appropriate person'. Under subsection (6), an appropriate person is, in the case of the employer, a person who has the authority to settle the matter on behalf of the employer or a person authorised by such a person to make recommendations to him or her with regard to the settlement of the matter. In the case of the union, an 'appropriate person' is a person responsible for handling the matter subject to the conciliation or mediation on behalf of the union.

- Measures to simplify the law on industrial action ballots and ballot notices.

The legislation: summary and concluding comments

Self-evaluation activity 8.10

Union immunities and industrial action
Response on website

Before we assess the legislation on industrial action, attempt the following exercise that demonstrates the current position on trade union immunities concerning industrial action and which will assist you in reviewing that legislation. You should answer 'yes' or 'no' to the following questions:

In the event of strike action taking place:

1. Does the action constitute an inducement to breach, interfere with, conspiracy to break, or threat to break, a contract of employment?

2. Is the action taken in contemplation or furtherance of a trade dispute?

3. Is the dispute a trade dispute within the legal definition, that is:
 (a) between worker and employer
 (b) with workers or ex-workers of the employer
 (c) in relation to a matter specified by law
 (d) wholly or mainly connected with (c)?

4. Is the origin of the dispute within the UK?

5. Is the action primary action at the place of the original dispute?

6. Are pickets limited to the workplace of the original dispute and restricted in numbers?

7. Has a secret postal ballot been held in which a majority of those involved in the action have voted in favour of the action?

8. Has seven days' notice of the ballot and seven days' notice of the action been given to the employer?
9. Has the employer access to independent scrutiny of the strike ballot?
10. Have people involved in the strike ballot been identified?

The legislation dealing with strikes and industrial action in all the aspects described above is quite different now from what it was in 1979. As we have seen, strike activity is substantially lower than it was in the 1960s and 1970s and in 1997, for example, the DfEE recorded the lowest ever incidence of strikes since records began. We also considered some explanations attempting to account for this trend and concluded that government legislation could not, of itself, account for the declining trend. The apparent willingness of some employers to resort to litigation, while headline-provoking, tends to conceal the fact that most employers did not use the legislation, possibly for fear of prejudicing years of efforts and achievements in order to promote a constructive industrial relations climate and because 'normally the employer's aim is to stop industrial action rather than obtain damages' (Dickens and Hall, 2003).

However, it could be argued that the legislation governing strike and pre-strike activity, particularly with regard to balloting provisions, has resulted in changes which have influenced the negotiating behaviour of both parties. Balloting provisions have been accepted as a matter of routine by many union negotiators, despite initial opposition from unions and some employers. In the event of negotiations breaking down and subsequent industrial action being contemplated, ballots must be held. A very high proportion of ballots taken nationally (around 90 per cent in any one year) are decisively in favour of industrial action, and this tends to confer greater legitimacy upon the union's negotiating position than previous (now unlawful) practices, involving a 'show of hands' or site meetings, for demonstrating support for industrial action could provide. No longer can an 'active minority' be accused of orchestrating and manipulating industrial action for its own ends. In many cases, therefore, the legitimacy of the 'majority vote' in secret postal ballots may provide the impetus to further negotiation and resolution of the dispute without recourse to

industrial action or the involvement of 'third parties' such as Acas.

Progressive restrictions on unions' legal immunities, together with changes in picketing arrangements and curbs upon secondary action are more difficult to assess. Many of the 'high profile' disputes of the 1980s (such as the *Messenger* and *News International* disputes) demonstrated some employers' almost obsessive enthusiasm in resorting to court injunctions and other legal actions. On the other hand, disputes such as the miners' strike, even though it took place in the early years of the legislative onslaught, demonstrated the extent to which the new constraints on secondary action and picketing could be flouted. It may be, as Kessler and Bayliss (1998) suggest, that the low and declining level of industrial action in recent years has meant:

> *that there have not been enough occasions on which the law might be tested for its practical significance to have emerged [and] if there were an upsurge in strike activity in the future, the significance of the changed legal framework might turn out to be greater than at present appears.* (p. 252)

Moreover, the law has had relatively little impact upon the incidence of 'unofficial' disputes which are deemed 'unlawful'. A significant proportion of unofficial stoppages are of very short duration (often less than a day and so do not fall within the official DfEE definition of stoppages), and are normally settled by negotiation at local level. There is little evidence that the provisions of the 1990 Employment Act concerning 'unofficial' strikes and the facility for employers to dismiss the 'leaders' of them have actually been used by employers; to do so would certainly be detrimental to 'good' industrial relations practice. The first Blair government accepted that dismissal of strikers taking lawful industrial action and the requirement to provide employers with the names of union members being balloted are unfair. The Employment Relations Act 1999 gave employees unfair dismissal rights for taking part in lawful industrial action and simplified the law and the Code of Practice on industrial action ballots and notice and, in particular, removed the provision concerning naming of union members. The TUC, not surprisingly, wanted the government to go further and is pressing for change in its response to the Government's review of

the Employment Relations Act. As early as 1998, however, the TUC made its reservations known to the Government:

> The length of the Code [of Practice] illustrates the complexity of the framework of law on industrial action. The detailed obligations on unions provide enormous scope for employers to challenge any proposed industrial action. The test applied to applications for injunctions means that action can be halted on an allegation that there has been some infringement of the law, which is subsequently proved to be unfounded. This exacerbates disputes and we believe the emphasis should be on seeking a speedy resolution to the matter. As well as the unfairness of mischievous challenges to ballots, the TUC is concerned that unions can find themselves exposed to claims for damages even when every attempt has been made to comply with the obligations and it was understood that the action was lawful. Where an employer challenges the validity of the ballot after the action has taken place and shows that some aspect of the balloting requirements has not been met, then the union could face substantial claims for damages even though the action was considered to be lawful at the time. We would urge the Government to examine aspects of the current legislation with a view to removing the anomalies whereby employers can frustrate the expressed wishes of a majority voting in industrial action ballots by resorting to legal technicalities. (1998, p. 12)

We have argued, therefore, that government legislation is one (but certainly not the main) reason for the decline in UK strike activity. As long as the incidence of strike action remains low, the impact of legislation upon such activity would seem to be slight at best, and 'legal changes were part of a much wider range of developments affecting strike activity' (Dickens and Hall, 2003).

RESOLUTION OF COLLECTIVE DISPUTES

Within a unionised workplace or organisation, most procedural and substantive issues are resolved through the collective bargaining process (see Chapters 5 and 10). When negotiations break down, there are two main methods of resolution commonly adopted. The first method entails the use of a collective disputes procedure which typically identifies a number of stages but which is not used as a mechanism for preventing collective disputes. Rather, the procedure may help in facilitating fair treatment in the handling of disagreements and assist the parties towards resolution. Some procedures provide for third party intervention from outside the workplace or establishment affected by the collective dispute thus enabling the dispute to be referred to Acas (the preferred third party) or to another independent mediator or arbitrator.

Collective disputes procedures: the evidence from WERS 2004

A significant minority of workplaces (43 per cent) had formal procedures in place for dealing with collective disputes, slightly down on the WERS 1998 figure of 47 per cent. Table 8.8 shows the distribution of collective disputes procedures by a number of workplace characteristics.

As Table 8.8 indicates, the larger the workplace, the more likely that collective disputes procedures exist. Hence, 38 per cent of workplaces with between 10 and 24 employees and 74 per cent of workplaces with at least 500 employees had procedures in place and therefore a slight majority of employees overall (58 per cent) were covered by such procedures. The proportion of all collective disputes procedures and the percentage of employees covered by them was predictably higher in public sector workplaces (77 per cent) than in private sector workplaces (36 per cent), 'and were more prevalent in workplaces having a recognised union (78 per cent) than in workplaces without recognition (29 per cent)' (Kersley et al., 2006, p. 212). The vast majority of collective disputes procedures covered all non-managerial employees and most procedures provided for the main substantive causal issues underlying most disputes, namely pay and conditions (86 per cent); health and safety (84 per cent); work and organisation (82 per cent) and redundancy (72 per cent). With regard to referral to a third party for conciliation and/or mediation, a majority of workplaces having collective disputes procedures (63 per cent) contained provisions to referral, mainly to Acas.

Table 8.8 Collective disputes by selected workplace characteristics: 2004

	Proportion of workplaces having collective disputes procedures (%)	Proportion of employees covered by collective disputes procedures (%)
All workplaces	43	58
Workplace size		
10–24 employees	38	37
25–49 employees	46	45
50–99 employees	52	52
100–199 employees	61	61
200–499 employees	61	63
500 or more employees	74	79
All workplaces with 25 or more employees	51	62
Organisation status		
Stand-alone workplace	28	39
Part of a larger organisation	51	63
Organisation size		
10–19 employees	28	30
100–999 employees	44	45
1000–9999 employees	53	66
10,000 employees or more	63	76
Sector of ownership		
Private	36	48
Public	77	84

Source: Kersley *et al.*, 2006, p. 213

Acas and collective disputes

The Advisory, Conciliation and Arbitration Service (Acas) was established in 1974 as the Conciliation and Arbitration Service (CAS) whose terms of reference were to provide conciliation and mediation as a means of avoiding and resolving disputes. Its statutory functions were broadened in 1993 to include the general duty of improving industrial relations in relation to the settlement of trade disputes and in 1999 reference to the settlement of trade disputes was removed (Employment Relations Act 1999). The role of Acas, therefore, is much wider than originally conceived, and while collective disputes resolution and prevention remains an important function, its contemporary activities 'are better understood as fitting into a wider paradigm which includes dispute resolution but equally promotes strategies for improved workplace relationships and conflict prevention' (Dix and Oxenbridge, 2004, p. 512).

The disputes resolution role of Acas

The collective conciliation function is the one most commonly deployed, but it should be borne in mind that Acas cannot compel the parties to a collective dispute to come together and also cannot impose a settlement upon the parties to the collective dispute. It is, of course, important for employers and employee representatives to resolve problems before resorting to collective conciliation and before a

costly collective dispute may emerge. To that end Acas can assist in promoting solutions via workshops and working parties whereby employers and employee representatives can work together to explore underlying problems and then strive to implement practical solutions. In using the assistance of Acas, the chances of employers and employee representatives avoiding potential conflict are, therefore, much reduced. If, however, despite the efforts of Acas, the parties cannot agree on joint methods to resolve outstanding issues through collective bargaining and/or joint regulation, and a seemingly intractable collective dispute, perhaps involving some form of industrial action ensues, then the conciliation option may well be a last resort.

Initiating conciliation and the conciliation process itself

Acas is normally involved in collective dispute cases where the workplace and/or organisation operates a formal procedure for dealing with collective disputes and where Acas is referred to within the procedure. Many cases are initiated as a result of a joint approach from employer and employee representatives and cases may also be initiated by either employer or trade union (see Table 8.9).

As employers and employee representative parties expect Acas to fulfil a number of different roles, a number of 'roles and qualities' expected of the conciliation approach have been identified (Dix and Oxenbridge, 2004) and the most important of these are identified below.

1. *The presence of an intermediary.* The conciliation process is primarily geared towards avoiding industrial action and while both parties to the dispute would want to avoid industrial action,

it is likely that the positions of the two parties would be firmly entrenched and that there would be little further dialogue between them. Nevertheless the parties would reasonably require the third party involvement of an intermediary to assist in resuming the dialogue and provide 'a chance to change the dynamics of the situation, allowing parties to air their frustration or anger in a "safe", less confrontational environment' (Dix and Oxenbridge, 2004, p. 517). In order to facilitate this climate, the conciliator is required to be impartial, trustworthy and confidential to both parties, allowing only authorised communication to either side, and demonstrating patience, listening skills and an ability to establish rapport with the parties.

2. *Acting as 'messenger'.* As Dix and Oxenbridge assert, conciliator as messenger fulfils the traditional role expectations of the conciliator by the parties. The conveyance of information between the parties where the conciliator acts as a 'go-between' is also combined with a more proactive conciliatory role of 'using tactics to shed new light on proposals by, for example, hinting at how far the opposing side might be prepared to move and allowing parties to calmly reassess their own position' (Dix and Oxenbridge, 2004, p. 517).

3. *Providing an informed, independent perspective.* The conciliator must be seen by both parties to be independent, informed and able to offer unbiased views. The parties are likely to request views on the strength of their respective cases which could encourage them to consider any deficiencies in their arguments.

4. *Generating new options and pointing out the consequences of failure to agree.* At this stage the

Table 8.9 Collective conciliation requests: 2004–6

Year	Total received	Employer	Trade union	Joint	Acas
2005/06	952	159	294	400	99
2004/05	1123	164	339	470	150
2003/04	1245	172	348	581	144

Source: Acas Annual Report 2006

Table 8.10 Collective conciliation cases by outcome

Year	Total cases	Completed	Successful	Unsuccessful	Withdrawn
2006/07	835	802	758 (94.5%)	44	33
2005/06	936	904	830 (91.8%)	74	32
2004/05	1024	985	946 (96.4%)	39	39
2003/04	1271	1232	1149 (93.3%)	83	39

Source: *Acas Annual Report*, 2007

conciliator may make suggestions and contribute new ideas, possibly based upon the experience of the conciliator and knowledge of the industrial sector of the dispute 'perhaps couched in "what if" scenarios' (p. 518). The role of the conciliator, having made progress thus far, would include pointing out the consequences of failure to reach a resolution.

5. *Conciliation styles.* Research by Dix (2000) suggests that the parties discern varying styles which conciliators may adopt. At one extreme, there is the conciliator as messenger who did not provide any views and acted merely as 'go-between'. At the other extreme the conciliator adopts a 'proactive' style, presenting new ideas and bringing novel perspectives to bear upon the collective dispute. In practice, conciliators will take a contingency approach and adopt different styles depending upon for example, the varying stages of the conciliation process. Dix and Oxenbridge (2004) also point out:

> The overwhelming preference expressed by the parties was for a proactive approach as it gave parties the confidence that the conciliator will try all avenues to achieve an acceptable outcome. Parties felt that a proactive approach was consistent with impartiality if it was clear that the conciliator's actions – testing either party's stance, giving their own view, suggesting possible ways forward and so on – were based on an objective and even-handed assessment. (p. 519)

Conciliation outcomes

Acas identifies four outcomes of the conciliation process:

- 'an actual settlement';
- 'progress made towards a settlement';
- 'referred to arbitration';
- 'no resolution'.

Acas statistics regard a case as 'successful' if any of the first three outcomes identified above is achieved. According to this criterion, a very large number of cases are reported by Acas as successful, with percentages of completed cases varying within the 90–100 per cent category (see Table 8.10).

When a settlement is in sight, a joint agreement will be sought by the conciliator in the form of a document stating the details of what was agreed and signed by the parties. The agreement commits the parties to self-enforce the settlement but Acas has no statutory power to impose the settlement.

The process of mediation

Where a settlement is not reached via the conciliation route, mediation can be arranged by Acas. Mediation is a rarely used mechanism for dispute resolution in the UK (see Table 8.11), but when it is used, Acas is not involved in the mediation process it organises, this being delegated to an independent mediator or Board of Mediation. Each side makes its case in writing, with the parties then presenting evidence. The mediator then makes formal but non-binding recommendations and proposals which are used to prompt a settlement. The settlement cannot be imposed by a third party and the parties to the dispute are at liberty to accept or reject the mediator's proposals.

The arbitration process

Arbitration, where the parties to a collective dispute appoint an arbitrator agreed by them to evaluate

Table 8.11 Cases referred to arbitration and dispute mediation: 2003–7

	2003/4	2004/5	2005/6	2006/7
Single arbitrator	62	51	55	44
Board of Arbitration	1	0	0	0
Single mediator	6	6	2	2
Board of Mediation	0	1	0	0
Police Arbitration Tribunal	0	0	0	1
Total	69	58	57	47

Source: Acas Annual Report, 2007

the dispute and arrive at a decision which is mutually acceptable and which provides the basis of a solution to the dispute, is used fairly infrequently (see Table 8.11) in instances where either negotiation or conciliation have failed to resolve the dispute. Arbitration awards are not legally binding but, as with collective bargaining agreements, binding in honour only. In 2007, around 30 per cent of issues referred to arbitration concerned pay and 26 per cent concerned other pay and conditions of employment. The use of a single arbitrator is by far the most popular recourse by the parties to the dispute, as Table 8.11 indicates. The alternative to the single arbitrator is the Board of Arbitration which is an unpopular choice for the parties, probably because it is too formalised with a chairman and two representatives from employer and trade union. Arbitration is a little used means of last resort mainly because of objections to the process by both employers and trade unions and it appears likely that it will be relatively little used in the future as in the past. Moreover, Gennard and Judge (2005) point out that the parties are guided by pragmatic approaches to arbitration:

> [Trade unions] are in the bargaining business and are suspicious of anything that impedes their ability to gain by whatever means the best possible deal for their members . . . However, a major reason in employers' reluctance to resort more readily to arbitration is the reputation of the arbitration process itself – that the employer cannot retain control of events and must accept whatever the arbitrator may award, and that

> the arbitrator will 'split the difference' between the parties. Arbitration is first and foremost a process which transfers the ultimate responsibility for certain key business decisions from management to a third party. This is in contrast to collective bargaining, conciliation and mediation in which each side retains considerable authority over events. (p. 175)

Concluding comments

Collective industrial disputes which include activity short of a strike together with many unreported and unrecorded instances of collective discontent remain a significant feature of the UK employment relations landscape. To be sure, the decline in the level of strike activity in recent decades may indicate that organised collective conflict generally is at an historically low level but this is no indicator of the extent of latent conflict and the potential for such conflict to occur within a capitalist society (Hyman, 1984; Smith and Morton, 2006) The causes of the decline in overt collective conflict in the form of strikes have been well documented earlier in the chapter, and for the UK these include the nature of the restrictive legislation concerning strikes as well as the other causal factors common to most developed societies in a global context. The significance of industrial action internationally has also been referred to in this chapter, and it is, therefore, unsurprising that organised collective conflict remains, and probably will remain, a manifestation of the nature of employment relations systems for some time to come.

RELEVANT WEBSITES

www.cipd.org.uk (Chartered Institute of Personnel and Development) Useful for members for access to 'People Management' online.

www.dti.gov.uk/er (Department of Trade and Industry) Access to strike data via *Labour Market Trends*.

www.berr.gov.uk (Department for Business, Enterprise and Regulatory Reform) The successor to the DTI.

www.lga.gov.uk (The Local Government Association) Useful for employer perspective on fire dispute.

www.tuc.org.uk (Trades Union Congress) Good student resources and links to other websites.

REFERENCES

Acas (2007) *Annual Report 2007*. London, Acas

Adams, C., Turner, D. and Odell, M. (2002) *Financial Times*, FT.com site, accessed 13 November

Bain Report (2002) 'The future of the Fire Service'. www.irfs.org.uk

Blauner, R. (1964) *Alienation and Freedom*. Chicago, Chicago University Press

Brown, W.A. (ed.) (1981) *The Changing Contours of British Industrial Relations*. London, Heinemann

Burchill, F. (2003) 'Firefighters' dispute negotiators are no fools'. *People Management*, April, 22

Coser, L.A. (1956) *The Functions of Social Conflict*. London, Routledge and Kegan Paul

Dahrendorf, R. (1959) *Class and Class Conflict in Industrial Society*. London, Routledge and Kegan Paul

Danford, A. and Stewart, P. (2003) 'The rediscovery of conflict', in Hollinshead, G., Nicholls, P. and Tailby, S. (eds) *Employee Relations*. Harlow, Financial Times/ Prentice Hall

Daniel, W.W. and Millward, N. (1983) *Workplace Industrial Relations in Britain*. Aldershot, Gower

Davies, R.J. (1979) 'Economic activity, incomes policy and strikes'. *British Journal of Industrial Relations*, 17, 2, 205–23

Devlin (1965) *Final Report of the Committee of Inquiry Under the Rt Hon. Lord Devlin into Certain Matters Concerning the Port Transport Industry*, Cmnd 2734. London, HMSO

Dickens, L. and Hall, M. (2003) 'Labour law and industrial relations: a new settlement', in Edwards, P. (ed.) *Industrial Relations Theory and Practice*, 2nd edn. Oxford, Blackwell

Dix, G. (2000) 'Operating with style: the work of the ACAS conciliator in individual employment rights cases', in Towers, B. and Brown, W. (eds), *Employment Relations in Britain: 25 Years of ACAS*. Blackwell, London

Dix, G. and Oxenbridge, S. (2004) 'Coming to the table with Acas: from conflict to co-operation'. *Employee Relations*, 26, 5, 510–30

ELMR (Economic and Labour Market Review) (2007a, 2007b) see Hale, P. (2007a, 2007b)

Edwards, P.K. (1992) 'Industrial conflict'. *British Journal of Industrial Relations*, 30, 3, 361–404

Edwards, P. (1995) 'Strikes and industrial conflict', in Edwards, P. (ed.) *Industrial Relations: Theory and Practice in Britain*. Oxford, Blackwell

Evans, S. (1987) 'The use of injunctions in industrial disputes'. *British Journal of Industrial Relations*, 25, 3, 419–35

Farnham, D. (1997) *Employee Relations in Context*. London, IPD

Fire Brigades Union (2003) 'Modernisation: the facts from the Fire Brigades Union'. www.fbu.org.uk/pay2003

Gallie, D. (1978) *In Search of the New Working Class: Automation and Social Integration in the Capitalist Enterprise*. Cambridge, Cambridge University Press

Gallie, D. (1988) *Employment in Britain*. Oxford, Blackwell

Gennard, J. and Judge, G. (2005) *Employee Relations*, 4th edn. London, CIPD

Hale, P. (2007a) 'Labour disputes in 2006'. *Economic and Labour Market Review*, 1, 6, 25–36

Hale, P. (2007b) 'International comparisons of labour disputes'. *Economic and Labour Market Review*, 1, 4, 23–31

Handy, C.B. (1993) *Understanding Organisations*. London, Penguin

Hyman, R. (1984) *Strikes*. London, Fontana

Kerr, C. and Siegel, A. (1954) 'The inter-industry propensity to strike', in Kornhauser, A., Dubin, R. and Ross, A.M. (eds) *Industrial Conflict*. New York, McGraw-Hill

Kersley, B., Alpin, C., Forth, J., Bryson, A., Bewley, H., Dix, G. and Oxenbridge, S. (2006) *Inside the*

Workplace: Findings from the 2004 Workplace Employment Relations Survey. London, Routledge

Kessler, S. and Bayliss, F. (1995) *Contemporary British Industrial Relations*. Basingstoke, Macmillan

Kessler, S. and Bayliss, F. (1998) *Contemporary British Industrial Relations*, 2nd edn. Basingstoke, Macmillan

Kondratieff, N.D. (1979) 'The long waves in economic life'. *Economic Review*, 2, 4, 519–62 (first published in 1926)

Kornhauser, A., Dubin, R. and Ross, A.M. (eds) (1954) *Industrial Conflict*. New York, McGraw-Hill

LMT (Labour Market Trends) (1999) 'Labour disputes in 1998'. *Labour Market Trends*, June, 299–311

LMT (Labour Market Trends) (2002) 'Labour disputes in 2001'. *Labour Market Trends*, November, 589–603

LMT (Labour Market Trends) (2003) 'International comparison of labour disputes in 2000'. *Labour Market Trends*, January, 19–27

Labour Research Department (1987) 'Legal action instigated by employers'. October, 26

Labour Research Department (1991) 'Employers and litigation'. October, 31

Local Government Authority (2003) 'Commentary on the Bain Report'. www.lga.gov.uk

McIlroy, J. (1991) *The Permanent Revolution? Conservative Law and the Trade Unions*. Nottingham, Spokesman

Metcalf, D. (2003) 'A plague on both your houses'. *People Management*, March, 24–6

Millward, N., Bryson, A. and Forth, J. (2000) *All Change at Work*. London, Routledge

Ross, A.M. and Hartman, P.T. (1960) *Changing Patterns of Industrial Conflict*. New York, Wiley

Seifert, R. (2003a) 'Comments on the full Bain Report'. www.fbu.org.uk

Seifert, R. (2003b); 'Comments on the employers' offer of the 6th March 2003 in the 2002/2003 fire dispute'. www.fbu.org.uk

Smith, P. and Morton, G. (2006) 'Nine years of New Labour: neoliberalism and workers' rights'. *British Journal of Industrial Relations*, 44, 3, 401–20

TUC (1998) *Response to Fairness at Work*. London, TUC

Turner, H.A. (1969) *Is Britain Really Strike-Prone?* Cambridge, Cambridge University Press

Waddington, J. (2003) 'Trade union organisation', in Edwards, P. (ed.) *Industrial Relations Theory and Practice*, 2nd edn. Oxford, Blackwell

Watson, T.J. (1995) *Sociology, Work and Industry*. London, Routledge

Watson, T.J. (2008) *Sociology, Work and Industry*. London, Routledge

WERS (2004) See Kersley, B. *et al.* 2006

WIRS (1980) See Daniel, W.W. and Millward, N. (1983)

Section 3:

Organisational Behaviour

APPROACHES TO ORGANISATION AND MANAGEMENT

Organisational behaviour is a discursive subject and much has been written about it. The study of organisations and management has therefore to proceed on a broad front. It is the comparative study of the different approaches that will yield benefits to the manager. The study of organisations, their structure and management is important for the manager. Identification of major trends in management and organisational behaviour, and the work of leading writers, provide a perspective on concepts and ideas discussed in more detail in other chapters.

Learning outcomes

After completing this chapter you should be able to:

- identify major trends in the development of organisational behaviour and management thinking;
- contrast main features of different approaches to organisation and management;
- evaluate the relevance of these different approaches to the present-day management of organisations;
- explain the relationships between management theory and practice;
- assess the value of the study of different approaches to organisation and management;
- recognise the relationship between the development of theory, behaviour in organisations and management practice;
- establish a basis for consideration of aspects of organisational behaviour discussed in subsequent chapters.

Critical reflection

'It is often claimed that what leading writers say is an important part of the study of management and organisational behaviour. Others say that all these different ideas are little more than short-term fads and have little practical value.'

What do you think? What role does management theory have in helping us solve problems we face in our organisational lives today?

THEORY OF MANAGEMENT

A central part of the study of organisation and management is the development of management thinking and what might be termed management theory. The application of theory brings about change in actual behaviour. Managers reading the work of leading writers on the subject might see in their ideas and conclusions a message about how they should behave. This will influence their attitudes towards management practice.

The study of management theory is important for the following reasons:

- It helps to view the interrelationships between the development of theory, behaviour in organisations and management practice.
- An understanding of the development of management thinking helps in understanding principles underlying the process of management.
- Knowledge of the history helps in understanding the nature of management and organisational behaviour and reasons for the attention given to main topic areas.
- Many of the earlier ideas are of continuing importance to the manager and later ideas on management tend to incorporate earlier ideas and conclusions.
- Management theories are interpretive and evolve in line with changes in the organisational environment.

As *McGregor* puts it:

Every managerial act rests on assumptions, generalizations, and hypotheses – that is to say, on theory. Our assumptions are frequently implicit, sometimes quite unconscious, often conflicting; nevertheless, they determine our predictions that if we do a, b will occur. Theory and practice are inseparable.[1]

Miner makes the point that the more that is known about organisations and their methods of operation, the better the chances of dealing effectively with them. Understanding may be more advanced than prediction, but both provide the opportunity to influence or to manage the future. Theory provides a sound basis for action.[2] However, if action is to be effective, the theory must be adequate and appropriate to the task and to improved organisational performance. It must be a 'good' theory.

DEVELOPMENTS IN MANAGEMENT AND ORGANISATIONAL BEHAVIOUR

It is helpful, therefore, to trace major developments in management and organisational behaviour and what has led to the concentration of attention on such topics as motivation, groups, leadership, structure, and organisation development.[3]

Writing on organisation and management, in some form or another, can be traced back thousands of years.[4] Also, *Shafritz* makes an interesting observation about the contribution of William Shakespeare (1564–1616):

While William Shakespeare's contribution to literature and the development of the English language have long been acknowledged and thoroughly documented, his contribution to the theory of management and administration have been all but ignored. This is a surprising oversight when you consider that many of his plays deal with issues of personnel management and organizational behavior.[5]

However, the systematic development of management thinking is viewed, generally, as dating from the end of the nineteenth century with the emergence of large industrial organisations and the ensuing problems associated with their structure and management.[6] In order to help identify main trends in the development of organisational behaviour and management theory, it is usual to categorise the work of writers into various 'approaches', based on their views of organisations, their structure and management. Although a rather simplistic process, it does provide a framework in which to help direct study and focus attention on the progression of ideas concerned with improving organisational performance.

Figure 2.1 Main approaches to organisation, structure and management

CLASSICAL → HUMAN RELATIONS → SYSTEMS → CONTINGENCY

Emphasis on purpose, formal structure, hierarchy of management, technical requirements, and common principles of organisation.	Attention to social factors at work, groups, leadership, the informal organisation, and behaviour of people.	The integration of the classical and human relations approaches. Importance of the socio-technical system. The organisation within its external environment.	No one best design of organisation. Form of structure, management, and 'success' of the organisation dependent upon a range of situational variables.

A framework of analysis

There are, however, many ways of categorising these various approaches. For example, *Skipton* attempts a classification of 11 main schools of management theory.[7] Whatever form of categorisation is adopted, it is possible to identify a number of other approaches, or at least sub-divisions of approaches, and cross-grouping among the various approaches. The choice of a particular categorisation is therefore largely at the discretion of the observer.

The following analysis will revolve around a framework based on four main approaches, shown in Figure 2.1:

- classical – including scientific management and bureaucracy;
- human relations – including neo-human relations;
- systems;
- contingency.

Attention is also drawn to other 'approaches' or ideas, including:

- decision-making;
- social action;
- postmodernism.

See Figure 2.4 on page 63.

THE CLASSICAL APPROACH

The **classical** writers thought of the organisation in terms of its purpose and formal structure. They placed emphasis on the planning of work, the technical requirements of the organisation, principles of management, and the assumption of rational and logical behaviour. The analysis of organisation in this manner is associated with work carried out initially in the early part of the last century, by such writers as Taylor, Fayol, Urwick, Mooney and Reiley, and Brech. Such writers were laying the foundation for a comprehensive theory of management.

A clear understanding of the purpose of an organisation is seen as essential to understanding how the organisation works and how its methods of working can be improved. Identification of general objectives would lead to the clarification of purposes and responsibilities at all levels of the organisation and to the most effective structure. Attention is given to the division of work, the clear definition of duties and responsibilities, and maintaining specialisation and co-ordination. Emphasis is on a hierarchy of management and formal organisational relationships.

Sets of principles

The classical writers (also variously known as the formal or scientific management writers – although scientific management is really only a part of the classical approach) were concerned with improving the organisation structure as a means of increasing efficiency. They emphasised the importance of principles for the design of a logical structure of organisation. Their writings were in a normative style and they saw these principles as a set of 'rules' offering general solutions to common problems of organisation and management.

Most classical writers had their own set of principles but among the most publicised are those of *Fayol* and *Urwick* (*see* Chapters 11 and 14). Fayol recognised there was no limit to the principles of management but in his writing advocated 14.[8] Urwick originally specified eight principles, but these were revised to ten in his later writing.[9]

Mooney and Reiley set out a number of common principles which relate to all types of organisations. They place particular attention on:

- **the principle of co-ordination** – the need for people to act together with unity of action, the exercise of authority and the need for discipline;
- **the scalar principle** – the hierarchy of organisation, the grading of duties and the process of delegation; and
- **the functional principle** – specialisation and the distinction between different kinds of duties.[10]

Brech attempts to provide a practical approach to organisation structure based on tried general principles as opposed to the concentration on specific cases or complex generalisations of little value to the practising manager. He sets out the various functions in the organisation and the definition of formal organisational relationships.[11] Although clearly a strong supporter of the formal approach in some of his views such as, for example, on the principle of span of control, Brech is less definite than other classical writers and recognises a degree of flexibility according to the particular situation.

Brech does place great emphasis, however, on the need for written definition of responsibilities and the value of job descriptions as an aid to effective organisation and delegation. This work builds on the ideas of earlier writers, such as Urwick, and therefore provides a comprehensive view of the classical approach to organisation and management.

Evaluation of the classical approach

The classical writers have been criticised generally for not taking sufficient account of personality factors and for creating an organisation structure in which people can exercise only limited control over their work environment. The idea of sets of principles to guide managerial action has also been subject to much criticism. For example, *Simon* writes:

> Organisational design is not unlike architectural design. It involves creating large, complex systems having multiple goals. It is illusory to suppose that good designs can be created by using the so-called principles of classical organisation theory.[12]

Research studies have also expressed doubt about the effectiveness of these principles when applied in practice.[13] However, the classical approach prompted the start of a more systematic view of management and attempted to provide some common principles applicable to all organisations. These principles are still of relevance in that they offer a useful starting point in attempting to analyse the effectiveness of the design of organisation structure. The application of these principles must take full account of:

- the particular situational variables of each individual organisation; and
- the psychological and social factors relating to members of the organisation.

Major sub-groupings

Two major 'sub-groupings' of the classical approach are:

1 **scientific management**, and
2 bureaucracy.

SCIENTIFIC MANAGEMENT

Many of the classical writers were concerned with the improvement of management as a means of increasing productivity. At this time emphasis was on the problem of obtaining increased productivity from individual workers through the technical structuring of the work organisation and the provision of monetary incentives as the motivator for higher levels of output. A major contributor to this approach was *F. W. Taylor* (1856–1917), the 'father' of scientific management.[14] Taylor believed that in the same way that there is a best machine for each job, so there is a best working method by which people should undertake their jobs. He considered that all work processes could be analysed into discrete tasks and that by scientific method it was possible to find the 'one best way' to perform each task. Each job was broken down into component parts, each part timed and the parts rearranged into the most efficient method of working.

Principles to guide management

Taylor was a believer in the rational–economic needs concept of motivation. He believed that if management acted on his ideas, work would become more satisfying and profitable for all concerned. Workers would be motivated by obtaining the highest possible wages through working in the most efficient and productive way. Taylor was concerned with finding more efficient methods and procedures for co-ordination and control of work. He set out a number of principles to guide management. These principles are usually summarised as:

- the development of a true science for each person's work;
- the scientific selection, training and development of the workers;
- co-operation with the workers to ensure work is carried out in the prescribed way;
- the division of work and responsibility between management and the workers.

In his famous studies at the Bethlehem Steel Corporation, Taylor, who was appointed as a management consultant, applied his ideas on scientific management to the handling of pig iron. A group of 75 men were loading an average of $12\frac{1}{2}$ tons per man per day. Taylor selected a Dutch labourer, called Schmidt, whom he reported to be a 'high-priced' man with a reputation for placing a high value on money, and a man of limited mental ability. By following detailed instructions on when to pick up the pig iron and walk, and when to sit and rest, and with no back talk, Schmidt increased his output to $47\frac{1}{2}$ tons per day. He maintained this level of output throughout the three years of the study. In return Schmidt received a 60 per cent increase in wages compared with what was paid to the other men.

One by one other men were selected and trained to handle pig iron at the rate of $47\frac{1}{2}$ tons per day and in return they received 60 per cent more wages. Taylor drew attention to the need for the scientific selection of the workers. When the other labourers in the group were trained in the same method, only one in eight was physically capable of the effort of loading $47\frac{1}{2}$ tons per day, although there was a noticeable increase in their level of output.

Reactions against scientific management

There were strong criticisms of, and reaction against, scientific management methods from the workers who found the work boring and requiring little skill. Despite these criticisms Taylor attempted to expand the implementation of his ideas in the Bethlehem Steel Corporation. However, fears of mass redundancies persuaded the management to request Taylor to moderate his activities. Yet Taylor's belief in his methods was so strong that he would not accept management's interference and eventually they dispensed with his services.

Scientific management was applied for a time in other countries with similar criticisms and hostile reactions. The ideas of scientific management were also adopted in the American Watertown Arsenal despite the lingering doubts of the controller. He was not convinced about the benefits of paying bonuses based on methods which reduced time taken to complete a job; also the workers reacted unfavourably to time and motion studies and he was fearful of a strike. The controller eventually gave way, however, and the scientific management approach was adopted – to be followed almost immediately by a strike of moulding workers. The strike at Watertown Arsenal led to an investigation of Taylor's methods by a House of Representatives Committee which reported in 1912.

The conclusion of the committee was that scientific management did provide some useful techniques and offered valuable organisational suggestions, but gave production managers a dangerously high level of uncontrolled power. The studies at Watertown Arsenal were resumed but the unions retained an underlying hostility towards scientific management. A subsequent attitude survey among the workers revealed a broad level of resentment and hostility, by both union and non-union members, to scientific management methods. As a result of this report the Senate banned Taylor's methods of time study in defence establishments.

Taylorism as management control

There has also been considerable interest in 'Taylorism' as representing a system of management control over workers. Taylor placed emphasis on the content of a 'fair day's work' and on optimising the level of workers' productivity. A major obstacle to this objective was 'systematic soldiering' and what Taylor saw as the deliberate attempt by workers to promote their best interests and to keep employers ignorant of how fast work, especially piece-rate work, could be carried out.

According to *Braverman*, scientific management starts from the capitalist point of view and method of production, and the adaptation of labour to the needs of capital. Taylor's work was more concerned with the organisation of labour than with the development of technology. A distinctive feature of Taylor's thought was the concept of management control.[15] Braverman suggests Taylor's conclusion was that workers should be controlled not only by the giving of orders and maintenance of discipline but also by removing from them any decisions about the manner in which their work was to be carried out. By division of labour, and by dictating precise stages and methods for every aspect of work performance, management could gain control of the actual process of work. The rationalisation of production processes and division of labour tends to result in the de-skilling of work and this may be a main strategy of the employer.[16]

Cloke and Goldsmith also suggest that Taylor was the leading promoter of the idea that managers should design and control the work process scientifically in order to guarantee maximum efficiency. He believed in multiple layers of management to supervise the work process and in rigid, detailed control of the workforce.

Taylor's theories justified managerial control over the production process and removed decision making from employees and from owners as well. The increasingly authoritative operational role of management diminished the direct involvement of owners in day-to-day decision making. Managers saw this as an opportunity to solidify their power and adopted Taylor's ideas wholesale. In the process, they affirmed efficiency over collaboration, quantity over quality, and cost controls over customer service.[17]

Critical reflection

'Despite the strong criticisms of scienic management, in the right circumstances the underlying principles still have relevance and much to offer business organisations today. It is just that many commentators appear reluctant to openly admit that this is the case.'

What are your views? Where could scientific management be applied for the best overall effect?

RELEVANCE OF SCIENTIFIC MANAGEMENT

While Taylor's work is often criticised today it should be remembered that he was writing at a time of industrial reorganisation and the emergence of large, complex organisations with new forms of technology. Taylor's main concern was with the efficiency of both workers and management. He believed his methods of scientific management would lead to improved management–labour relations and contribute to improved industrial efficiency and prosperity.

Taylor adopted an instrumental view of human behaviour together with the application of standard procedures of work. Workers were regarded as rational, economic beings motivated directly by monetary incentives linked to the level of work output. Workers were viewed as isolated individuals and more as units of production to be handled almost in the same way as machines. Hence, scientific management is often referred to as a machine theory model.

Taylor's work continues to evoke much comment and extreme points of view. For example, *Rose* suggests:

> *It is difficult to discuss the 'contribution' of F. W. Taylor to the systematic study of industrial behaviour in an even-tempered way. The sheer silliness from a modern perspective of many of his ideas, and barbarities they led to when applied in industry, encourage ridicule and denunciation.*[18]

The theme of inefficiency

Rose argues that Taylor's diagnosis of the industrial situation was based on the simple theme of inefficiency. Among his criticisms are that Taylor selected the best workers for his experiments and assumed that workers who were not good at one particular task would be best at some other task. There is, however, no certainty of this in practice. Taylor regarded workers from an engineering viewpoint and as machines, but the one best way of performing a task is not always the best method for every worker.

The reduction of physical movement to find the one best way is not always beneficial and some 'wasteful' movements are essential to the overall rhythm of work. Rose also argues that the concept of a fair day's pay for a fair day's work is not purely a technical matter. It is also a notion of social equity and not in keeping with a scientific approach. *Drucker*, however, claims:

> *Frederick Winslow Taylor may prove a more useful prophet for our times than we yet recognize . . . Taylor's greatest impact may still be ahead . . . the under-developed and developing countries are now reaching the stage where they need Taylor and 'scientific management' . . . But the need to study Taylor anew and apply him may be the greatest in the developed countries.*[19]

According to Drucker, the central theme of Taylor's work was not inefficiency but the need to substitute industrial warfare by industrial harmony. Taylor sought to do this through:

- higher wages from increased output;
- the removal of physical strain from doing work the wrong way;
- development of the workers and the opportunity for them to undertake tasks they were capable of doing; and
- elimination of the 'boss' and the duty of management to help workers.

Drucker also suggests that Taylor's idea of functional foremen can be related to what is now known as matrix organisation (matrix organisation is discussed in Chapter 14). Support for Drucker's views appears to come from *Locke* who asserts that much of the criticism of Taylor is based on a misunderstanding of the precepts and that many of his ideas are accepted by present-day managers.[20]

Impetus to management thinking

Whatever the opinions on scientific management, Taylor and his disciples have left to modern management the legacy of such practices as work study, organisation and methods,

payment by results, management by exception and production control. The development of mass assembly line work ('Fordism'), which was invented by Henry Ford in 1913 and which dominated production methods in Western economies, can be seen to have many common links with the ideas of scientific management.[21] The concept of Six Sigma, which is discussed in Chapter 20, can also be related to Taylor's quest for 'systematic management'. For example, in his book on the future of management, *Hamel* makes the following observation:

> *One can imagine Taylor looking down from his well-ordered heaven and smiling fondly at the Six Sigma acolytes who continue to spread his gospel. (His only surprise might be that 21st-century managers are still obsessing over the same problems that occupied his inventive mind a hundred years earlier.)*[22]

The principles of Taylor's scientific approach to management appear still to have relevance today. We can see examples of Taylorism alive and well, and management practices based on the philosophy of his ideas. As an example, Figure 2.2 shows a 'Hanger Insertion

Figure 2.2	Hanger Insertion Programme: an example of scientific management

KEY IDEAS

Hanger Insertion

- The new programme involving the process of hanging merchandise on hangers efficiently and effectively.

The purposes of this new programme:

- To assist the stores in better customer service – by having the merchandise ready to go on the floor, saving space in the stockroom, and creating customer goodwill.
- To increase the units per hour produced.
- To perform the job duties as efficiently and effectively as possible.

TECHNIQUES

- Keep the necessary items needed in your range. All supplies should be within arm's reach. For example, place the trash bin next to you, have your hanger supply near you. You should not need to take any steps.

- For ANY prepack, Unpack merchandise in the prepack or unpack enough of the prepack in the amount to be placed on the trolley, tearing the plastic off of the entire group.
 Lay the merchandise out on the unpack table, and if applies, unfold each piece, removing tissue, etc.
 Insert the hangers and hang the *entire group* of merchandise at once.

- When removing hangers from the merchandise, have the merchandise in a group on the unpack table; remove these hangers working from the front to the back.

- When inserting hangers, as a group, insert working from the back to the front of the group on the unpack table. Hang pieces as a group.

- If merchandise is bulky, Leave merchandise folded, **remove all of the plastic at once**, insert hangers for merchandise unpacked, hang all pieces on the trolley, then remove at the same time all excess plastic, clips, etc.

- When possible, it is more efficient to remove all the plastic at once after the merchandise is hung.

- When hanging pants, skirts, etc., slip the hanger over both sides of the piece of merchandise and push metal clips down at the same time. This will alleviate additional steps.

- When pants are in plastic and hangers have to be removed, hang them first, take pants off hangers, lay on table, throw away plastic, insert hangers.

- When having to button pants, skirts, etc., take the top of the button through the hole first. This makes the process flow easier and more efficient.

- Put your supply of hangers in the cover of a tote and place on the table next to you.

Programme' for a large American department store. Large hotel organisations often make use of standard recipes and performance standard manuals and it is common for housekeeping staff to have a prescribed layout for each room, with training based on detailed procedures and the one best way. Staff may be expected to clean a given number of rooms per shift with financial incentives for additional rooms. The strict routine, uniformity, clearly specified tasks, detailed checklists and close control in fast-food restaurants such as McDonald's also suggest close links with scientific management.

Whatever else Taylor did, at least he gave a major impetus to the development of management thinking and the later development of organisational behaviour. For example, *Crainer and Dearlove* suggest that although Taylor's theories are now largely outdated, they still had a profound impact throughout the world and his mark can be seen on much of the subsequent management literature.[23] And *Stern* goes a stage further:

> The 'scientific management' of Frederick Taylor . . . shaped the first coherent school of thought with application to the industrialised world. He was our first professional guru and Taylorism – with its twin goals of productivity and efficiency – still influences management thinking 100 years on.[24]

It is difficult to argue against the general line of Taylor's principles but they are subject to misuse. What is important is the context and manner in which such principles are put into effect. There is arguably one best way *technically* to perform a job, particularly, for example, with factory assembly line production. However, account needs to be taken of human behaviour. People tend to have their preferred way of working and the need for variety and more interesting or challenging tasks. Provided work is carried out safely and to a satisfactory standard and completed on time, to what extent should management *insist* on the 'one best way'?

It seems that Taylor did not so much ignore (as is often suggested) but was more *unaware* of the complexity of human behaviour in organisations and the importance of the individual's feelings and sentiments, group working, managerial behaviour and the work environment. However, we now have greater knowledge about social effects within the work organisation and about the value of money, incentives, motivation, and job satisfaction and performance.

BUREAUCRACY

A form of structure to be found in many large-scale organisations is **bureaucracy**. Its importance in the development of organisation theory means that it is often regarded as a subdivision under the classical heading and studied as a separate approach to management and the organisation of work. The ideas and principles of the classical writers were derived mainly from practical experience. Writers on bureaucracy, however, tend to take a more theoretical view.

Weber, a German sociologist, showed particular concern for what he called 'bureaucratic structures', although his work in this area came almost as a side issue to his main study on power and authority.[25] He suggested that 'the decisive reason for the advance of bureaucratic organization has always been its purely technical superiority over any other form of organization'. Weber pointed out that the definition of tasks and responsibilities within the structure of management gave rise to a permanent administration and standardisation of work procedures notwithstanding changes in the actual holders of office.

The term 'bureaucracy' has common connotations with criticism of red tape and rigidity, though in the study of organisations and management it is important that the term is seen not necessarily in a deprecative sense but as applying to certain structural features of formal organisations. Weber analysed bureaucracies not empirically but as an 'ideal type' derived from the most characteristic bureaucratic features of all known organisations. He saw the development of bureaucracies as a means of introducing order and rationality into social life.

Main characteristics of bureaucracies

Weber did not actually define bureaucracy but did attempt to identify the main characteristics of this type of organisation. He emphasised the importance of administration based on expertise (rules of experts) and administration based on discipline (rules of officials).

- The tasks of the organisation are allocated as official duties among the various positions.
- There is an implied clear-cut division of labour and a high level of specialisation.
- A hierarchical authority applies to the organisation of offices and positions.
- Uniformity of decisions and actions is achieved through formally established systems of rules and regulations. Together with a structure of authority, this enables the co-ordination of various activities within the organisation.
- An impersonal orientation is expected from officials in their dealings with clients and other officials. This is designed to result in rational judgements by officials in the performance of their duties.
- Employment by the organisation is based on technical qualifications and constitutes a lifelong career for the officials.[26]

The four main features of bureaucracy are summarised by *Stewart* as specialisation, hierarchy of authority, system of rules and impersonality.

- **Specialisation** applies more to the job than to the person undertaking the job. This makes for continuity because the job usually continues if the present job-holder leaves.
- **Hierarchy of authority** makes for a sharp distinction between administrators and the administered or between management and workers. Within the management ranks there are clearly defined levels of authority. This detailed and precise stratification is particularly marked in the armed forces and in the civil service.
- **System of rules** aims to provide for an efficient and impersonal operation. The system of rules is generally stable, although some rules may be changed or modified with time. Knowledge of the rules is a requisite of holding a job in a bureaucracy.
- **Impersonality** means that allocation of privileges and the exercise of authority should not be arbitrary, but in accordance with the laid-down system of rules. In more highly developed bureaucracies there tend to be carefully defined procedures for appealing against certain types of decisions. Stewart sees the characteristic of impersonality as the feature of bureaucracy which most distinguishes it from other types of organisations. A bureaucracy should not only be impersonal but be seen to be impersonal.[27]

CRITICISMS OF BUREAUCRACY

Weber's concept of bureaucracy has a number of disadvantages and has been subject to severe criticism.

- The over-emphasis on rules and procedures, record keeping and paperwork may become more important in its own right than as a means to an end.
- Officials may develop a dependence upon bureaucratic status, symbols and rules.
- Initiative may be stifled and when a situation is not covered by a complete set of rules or procedures there may be a lack of flexibility or adaptation to changing circumstances.
- Position and responsibilities in the organisation can lead to officious bureaucratic behaviour. There may also be a tendency to conceal administrative procedures from outsiders.
- Impersonal relations can lead to stereotyped behaviour and a lack of responsiveness to individual incidents or problems.

Restriction of psychological growth

One of the strongest critics of bureaucratic organisation, and the demands it makes on the worker, is *Argyris*.[28] He claims that bureaucracies restrict the psychological growth of the

individual and cause feelings of failure, frustration and conflict. Argyris suggests that the organisational environment should provide a significant degree of individual responsibility and self-control; commitment to the goals of the organisation; productiveness and work; and an opportunity for individuals to apply their full abilities.

When these ideas are related to the main features of bureaucracy discussed above, such as specialisation, hierarchy of authority, system of rules and impersonality, it is perhaps easy to see the basis of Argyris' criticism.

A similar criticism is made by *Caulkin* who refers to the impersonal structure of bureaucracy as constructed round the post rather than the person and the ease with which it can be swung behind unsocial or even pathological ends.

> *The overemphasis on process rather than purpose, fragmented responsibilities and hierarchical control means that it's all too easy for individuals to neglect the larger purposes to which their small effort is being put.*[29]

EVALUATION OF BUREAUCRACY

The growth of bureaucracy has come about through the increasing size and complexity of organisations and the associated demand for effective administration. The work of the classical writers has given emphasis to the careful design and planning of organisation structure and the definition of individual duties and responsibilities. Effective organisation is based on structure and delegation through different layers of the hierarchy. Greater specialisation and the application of expertise and technical knowledge have highlighted the need for laid down procedures.

Bureaucracy is founded on a formal, clearly defined and hierarchical structure. However, with rapid changes in the external environment, de-layering of organisations, empowerment and greater attention to meeting the needs of customers, there is an increasing need to organise for flexibility. *Peters and Waterman* found that excellent American companies achieved quick action just because their organisations were fluid and had intensive networks of informal and open communications.[30] By contrast, the crisis IBM experienced in the 1980s/ 1990s over the market for personal computers is explained at least in part by its top-heavy corporate structure, cumbersome organisation and dinosaur-like bureaucracy.[31]

According to *Cloke and Goldsmith*, management and bureaucracy can be thought of as flip sides of the same coin. The elements of bureaucracy generate organisational hierarchy and management, while managers generate a need for bureaucracy.

> *Bureaucracies provide a safe haven where managers can hide from responsibility and avoid being held accountable for errors of judgement or problems they created or failed to solve. In return, managers are able to use bureaucratic rules to stifle self-management and compel employees to follow their direction . . . Yet bureaucratic systems can be broken down and transformed into human-scale interactions. We have seen countless managers recreate themselves as leaders and facilitators, employees reinvent themselves as responsible self-managing team members, and bureaucracies transform into responsive, human-scale organizations. Alternatives to organizational hierarchy are both practical and possible.*[32]

Organisational solutions

As organisations face increasing global competitiveness and complex demands of the information and technological age, the need arises for alternative forms of corporate structure and systems. *Ridderstrale* points out that in the past century the hallmark of a large company was hierarchy, which rests on principles at odds with the new strategic requirements. 'Bureaucracies allowed people with knowledge to control ignorant workers. Now, new structures are needed as knowledge spreads.' Ridderstrale suggests four specific ways in which

high-performing organisations have responded to increasingly complex knowledge systems by developing organisational solutions which depart from the traditional bureaucratic model:

- more decentralised and flatter structures in order that quick decisions can be taken near to where the critical knowledge resides. Flatter structures can be achieved by increasing the span of control and reducing layers from the top or removing layers of middle management;
- the use of more than a single structure in order that knowledge may be assembled across the boundaries of a traditional organisation chart. If people have less permanent places in the hierarchy they are more readily able to move across functional and geographical borders;
- converting companies into learning organisations and giving every employee the same level of familiarity with personnel and capabilities. Successful companies develop a detailed inventory of core competencies. In order fully to exploit current knowledge, managers need to know what the company knows;
- the broader sharing of expertise and knowledge, which may be located in the periphery where little formal authority resides. Managers need to share principles to ensure co-ordination and to encourage 'lowest common denominators' and the development of 'tribal' qualities through shared ownership and rewards, common norms, culture and values.[33]

Public sector organisations

In the case of public sector organisations, in particular, there is a demand for uniformity of treatment, regularity of procedures and public accountability for their operations. This leads to adherence to specified rules and procedures and to the keeping of detailed records. In their actual dealings with public sector organisations people often call for what amounts to increased bureaucracy, even though they may not use that term. The demands for equal treatment, for a standard set of regulations that apply to everyone, and that decisions should not be left to the discretion of individual managers are in effect demands for bureaucracy.

Green argues that, although bureaucracies are becoming less and less the first-choice format for organisational shape, there is still a place for bureaucracy in parts of most organisations and especially public sector organisations such as local authorities and universities. The use and implementation of tried and tested rules and procedures help to ensure essential values and ethics, and that necessary functions are run on a consistent and fair basis.[34] New forms of information technology such as electronic transactions processed from home or public access terminals are likely to change processes of government service delivery, administrative workloads and the nature of bureaucracy.[35]

Relevance today

By their very nature, bureaucracies are likely to attract criticism. For example, there appears to be a particular dilemma for management in personal service industries. The underlying characteristics of bureaucracy would seem to restrict personal service delivery which requires a flexible approach, responsiveness to individual requirements and the need for initiative and inventiveness.[36] Much of this criticism is valid, but much also appears unfair.

Stewart suggests that more organisations today contain mainly or a considerable number of professionals. Such organisations will still have bureaucratic features although there is more reliance on professional discretion and self-regulation than on control through rules and regulations.[37] However, despite new forms of organisation which have emerged, many writers suggest that bureaucracy is still relevant today as a major form of organisation structure.[38]

Critical reflection

'Despite the frequent criticisms of bureaucratic structures, it is difficult to envisage how large-scale organisations, especially within the public sector, could function effectively without exhibiting at least some of the features of a bureaucracy. Demands for alternative forms of structure are unrealistic.'

How would you attempt to justify the benefits of bureaucratic structures?

STRUCTURALISM

Sometimes Weber's work is associated with the ideas of writers such as Karl Marx under the sub-heading of the **structuralism** approach, which is a synthesis of the classical (or formal) school and the human relations (or informal) school.[39] A major line of thought was that the earlier approaches were incomplete and lacked adequate theoretical assumptions and background. The structuralism approach provides a radical perspective of social and organisational behaviour.[40] Greater attention should be given to the relationship between the formal and informal aspects of the organisation, and the study of conflict between the needs of the individual and the organisation, and between workers and management. (See also the discussion on conflict in Chapter 3.) Structuralism is sometimes associated as part of a broader human relations approach, which is discussed below.

THE HUMAN RELATIONS APPROACH

The main emphasis of the classical writers was on structure and the formal organisation, but during the 1920s, the years of the Great Depression, greater attention began to be paid to the social factors at work and to the behaviour of employees within an organisation – that is, to **human relations**.

The Hawthorne experiments

The turning point in the development of the human relations movement ('behavioural' and 'informal' are alternative headings sometimes given to this approach) came with the famous experiments at the Hawthorne plant of the Western Electric Company near Chicago, America (1924–32) and the subsequent publication of the research findings.[41] Among the people who wrote about the Hawthorne experiments was Elton Mayo (1880–1949), who is often quoted as having been a leader of the researchers. However, there appears to be some doubt as to the extent to which Mayo was actually involved in conducting the experiments and his exact contribution to the human relations movement.[42]

There were four main phases to the Hawthorne experiments:

■ the illumination experiments;
■ the relay assembly test room;
■ the interviewing programme;
■ the bank wiring observation room.

The illumination experiments

The original investigation was conducted on the lines of the classical approach and was concerned, in typical scientific management style, with the effects of the intensity of lighting upon the workers' productivity. The workers were divided into two groups, an experimental group and a control group. The results of these tests were inconclusive as production in the experimental group varied with no apparent relationship to the level of lighting, but actually

increased when conditions were made much worse. Production also increased in the control group although the lighting remained unchanged. The level of production was influenced, clearly, by factors other than changes in physical conditions of work. This prompted a series of other experiments investigating factors of worker productivity.

The relay assembly test room

In the relay assembly test room the work was boring and repetitive. It involved assembling telephone relays by putting together a number of small parts. Six women workers were transferred from their normal departments to a separate area. The researchers selected two assemblers who were friends with each other. They then chose three other assemblers and a layout operator. The experiment was divided into 13 periods during which the workers were subjected to a series of planned and controlled changes to their conditions of work, such as hours of work, rest pauses and provision of refreshments. The general environmental conditions of the test room were similar to those of the normal assembly line.

During the experiment the observer adopted a friendly manner, consulting the workers, listening to their complaints and keeping them informed of the experiment. Following all but one of the changes (when operators complained too many breaks made them lose their work rhythm) there was a continuous increase in the level of production. The researchers formed the conclusion that the extra attention given to the workers, and the apparent interest in them shown by management, were the main reasons for the higher productivity. This has become famous as the 'Hawthorne Effect'.

The interviewing programme

Another significant phase of the experiments was the interviewing programme. The lighting experiment and the relay assembly test room drew attention to the form of supervision as a contributory factor to the workers' level of production. In an attempt to find out more about the workers' feelings towards their supervisors and their general conditions of work, a large interviewing programme was introduced. More than 20,000 interviews were conducted before the work was ended because of the depression.

Initially, the interviewers approached their task with a set of prepared questions, relating mainly to how the workers felt about their jobs. However, this method produced only limited information. The workers regarded a number of the questions as irrelevant; also they wanted to talk about issues other than just supervision and immediate working conditions. As a result, the style of interviewing was changed to become more non-directive and open-ended. There was no set list of questions and the workers were free to talk about any aspect of their work. The interviewers set out to be friendly and sympathetic. They adopted an impartial, non-judgemental approach and concentrated on listening.

Using this approach, the interviewers found out far more about the workers' true feelings and attitudes. They gained information not just about supervision and working conditions but also about the company itself, management, work group relations and matters outside of work such as family life and views on society in general. Many workers appeared to welcome the opportunity to have someone to talk to about their feelings and problems and to be able to 'let off steam' in a friendly atmosphere. The interviewing programme was significant in giving an impetus to present-day human resource management and the use of counselling interviews, and highlighting the need for management to listen to workers' feelings and problems. Being a good listener is arguably even more important for managers in today's work organisations and it is a skill which needs to be encouraged and developed.[43]

The bank wiring observation room

Another experiment involved the observation of a group of 14 men working in the bank wiring room. It was noted that the men formed their own informal organisation with sub-groups or cliques, and with natural leaders emerging with the consent of the members. The group developed its own pattern of informal social relations and 'norms' of what constituted 'proper' behaviour. Despite a financial incentive scheme where the workers could receive

more money the more work produced, the group decided on a level of output well below the level they were capable of producing.

Group pressures on individual workers were stronger than financial incentives offered by management. The group believed that if they increased their output, management would raise the standard level of piece rates. The importance of group 'norms' and informal social relations are discussed in Chapter 8.

EVALUATION OF THE HUMAN RELATIONS APPROACH

The human relations approach has been subjected to severe criticism. The Hawthorne experiments have been criticised, for example, on methodology and on failure of the investigators to take sufficient account of environmental factors – although much of this criticism is with the value of hindsight. The human relations writers have been criticised generally for the adoption of a management perspective, their 'unitary frame of reference' and their over-simplified theories.[44]

Other criticisms of the human relations approach are that it is insufficiently scientific and that it takes too narrow a view. It ignores the role of the organisation itself in how society operates.

Sex power differential

There are a number of interpretations of the results of the Hawthorne experiments, including the possible implications of the 'sex power differential' between the two groups. In the relay assembly room where output increased, the group was all female, while in the bank wiring room where output was restricted, the group was all male. The workers in the relay assembly test room were all young unmarried women. All except one were living at home with traditional families of immigrant background. In the work environment of the factory the women had been subjected to frequent contact with male supervisors and therefore 'the sex power hierarchies in the home and in the factory were congruent'. It is suggested, therefore, that it was only to be expected that the women agreed readily to participate with management in the relay assembly test room experiment.[45]

Importance of the Hawthorne experiments

Whatever the interpretation of the results of the Hawthorne experiments, they did generate new ideas concerning the importance of work groups and leadership, communications, output restrictions, motivation and job design. They placed emphasis on the importance of personnel management and gave impetus to the work of the human relations writers. The Hawthorne experiments undoubtedly marked a significant step forward in providing further insight into human behaviour at work and the development of management thinking. The Hawthorne experiments are regarded as one of the most important of all social science investigations and are recognised as probably the single most important foundation of the human relations approach to management and the development of organisational behaviour.

In a review of humane approaches to management, *Crainer* asserts: 'The Hawthorne Studies were important because they showed that views of how managers behaved were a vital aspect of motivation and improved performance. Also, the research revealed the importance of informal work groups.'[46]

Humanisation of the work organisation

Whereas supporters of the classical approach sought to increase production by rationalisation of the work organisation, the human relations movement has led to ideas on increasing production by humanising the work organisation. The classical approach adopted more of a

managerial perspective, while the human relations approach strove for a greater understanding of people's psychological and social needs at work as well as improving the process of management. It is usually regarded as the first major approach to organisation and management to show concern for industrial sociology.

The human relations approach recognised the importance of the informal organisation which will always be present within the formal structure. This informal organisation will influence the motivation of employees who will view the organisation for which they work through the values and attitudes of their colleagues. Their view of the organisation determines their approach to work and the extent of their motivation to work well or otherwise.

Human relations writers demonstrated that people go to work to satisfy a complexity of needs and not simply for monetary reward. They emphasised the importance of the wider social needs of individuals and gave recognition to the work organisation as a social organisation and the importance of the group, and group values and norms, in influencing individual behaviour at work. It has been commented that the classical school was concerned about 'organisations without people' and the human relations school about 'people without organisations'.

Critical reflection

'The human relations approach to organisations and management makes all the right sounds with an emphasis on humane behaviour, considerate management and recognition of the informal organisation. However, it is more about what people would like to believe and lacks credibility and substance.'

To what extent do the criticisms and shortcomings of the human relations approach detract from its potential benefits?

NEO-HUMAN RELATIONS

Certainly there were shortcomings in the human relations approach and assumptions which evolved from such studies as the Hawthorne experiments were not necessarily supported by empirical evidence. For example, the contention that a satisfied worker is a productive worker was not always found to be valid. However, the results of the Hawthorne experiments and the subsequent attention given to the social organisation and to theories of individual motivation gave rise to the work of those writers in the 1950s and 1960s who adopted a more psychological orientation. New ideas on management theory arose and a major focus of concern was the personal adjustment of the individual within the work organisation and the effects of group relationships and leadership styles. This group of writers is often (and more correctly) categorised separately under the heading of '**neo-human relations**'. The works of these writers are examined in more detail in Chapter 7 and Chapter 12 but are summarised broadly here.

The work of Maslow

A major impetus for the neo-human relations approach was the work of *Maslow* who, in 1943, put forward a theoretical framework of individual personality development and motivation based on a hierarchy of human needs.[47] The hierarchy ranges through five levels from, at the lowest level, physiological needs, through safety needs, love needs and esteem needs, to the need for self-actualisation at the highest level. Individuals advance up the hierarchy only as each lower-level need is satisfied. Although Maslow did not originally intend this need hierarchy to be applied necessarily to the work situation it has, nevertheless, had a significant impact on management approaches to motivation and the design of work organisation to meet individual needs. The work of Maslow provides a link with the earlier human relations approach.

Some leading contributors

Among the best-known contributors to the neo-human relations approach are *Herzberg* and *McGregor*. Herzberg isolated two different sets of factors affecting motivation and satisfaction at work. One set of factors comprises those which, if absent, cause dissatisfaction. These are 'hygiene' or 'maintenance' factors which are concerned basically with job environment. However, to motivate workers to give of their best, proper attention must be given to a different set of factors, the 'motivators' or 'growth' factors. These are concerned with job content.[48]

McGregor argued that the style of management adopted is a function of the manager's attitudes towards human nature and behaviour at work. He put forward two suppositions called Theory X and Theory Y which are based on popular assumptions about work and people.[49]

Other major contributors to the neo-human relations approach are *Likert*, whose work includes research into different systems of management;[50] *McClelland*, with ideas on achievement motivation;[51] and *Argyris*, who considered the effects of the formal organisation on the individual and psychological growth in the process of self-actualisation.[52] Argyris' major contributions include his work on organisational learning and on effective leadership.[53]

The neo-human relations approach has generated a large amount of writing and research not only from original propounders but also from others seeking to establish the validity, or otherwise, of their ideas. This has led to continuing attention being given to such matters as organisation structuring, group dynamics, job satisfaction, communication and participation, leadership styles and motivation. It has also led to greater attention to the importance of interpersonal interactions, the causes of conflict and recognition of 'employee relations' problems.

THE SYSTEMS APPROACH

More recently, attention has been focused on the analysis of organisations as 'systems' with a number of interrelated sub-systems. The classical approach emphasised the technical requirements of the organisation and its needs – 'organisations without people'; the human relations approaches emphasised the psychological and social aspects, and the consideration of human needs – 'people without organisations'.

The **systems approach** attempts to reconcile these two earlier approaches and the work of the formal and the informal writers. Attention is focused on the total work organisation and the interrelationships of structure and behaviour, and the range of variables within the organisation. This approach can be contrasted with a view of the organisation as separate parts. The systems approach encourages managers to view the organisation both as a whole and as part of a larger environment. The idea is that any part of an organisation's activities affects all other parts.

Systems theory

Systems theory is not new and has been used in the natural and physical sciences for a number of years. One of the founders of this approach was the biologist *Ludwig von Bertalanffy* who used the term 'systems theory' in an article published in 1951 and who is generally credited with having developed the outline of General Systems Theory.[54] The systems approach to organisation has arisen, at least in part, therefore, from the work of biologists, and *Miller and Rice* have likened the commercial and industrial organisation to the biological organism.[55]

Using a General Systems Theory (GST) approach, *Boulding* classified nine levels of systems of increasing complexity according to the state of development and knowledge about each level.[56] Organisations are complex social systems and are more open to change than lower-level simple dynamic or cybernetic systems. Boulding felt there were large gaps in both theoretical and empirical knowledge of the human level and the social organisations level of

systems, although some progress has now been made with recent theories of organisational behaviour.

The business organisation as an open system

The business organisation is an open system. There is continual interaction with the broader external environment of which it is part. The systems approach views the organisation within its total environment and emphasises the importance of multiple channels of interaction. Criticisms of earlier approaches to organisation are based in part on the attempt to study the activities and problems of the organisation solely in terms of the internal environment. The view of the organisation as an open system is examined in Chapter 3.

The systems approach views the organisation as a whole and involves the study of the organisation in terms of the relationship between technical and social variables within the system. Changes in one part, technical or social, will affect other parts and thus the whole system.

Longwall coal-mining study

The idea of socio-technical systems arose from the work of *Trist* and others, of the Tavistock Institute of Human Relations, in their study of the effects of changing technology in the coal-mining industry in the 1940s.[57] The increasing use of mechanisation and the introduction of coal-cutters and mechanical conveyors enabled coal to be extracted on a 'longwall' method.

Shift working was introduced, with each shift specialising in one stage of the operation – preparation, cutting or loading. However, the new method meant a change in the previous system of working where a small, self-selecting group of miners worked together, as an independent team, on one part of the coalface – the 'single place' or 'shortwall' method.

Technological change had brought about changes in the social groupings of the miners. It disrupted the integration of small groups and the psychological and sociological properties of the old method of working. There was a lack of co-operation between different shifts and within each shift, an increase in absenteeism, scapegoating and signs of greater social stress. The 'longwall' method was socially disruptive and did not prove as economically efficient as it could have been with the new technology.

The researchers saw the need for a socio-technical approach in which an appropriate social system could be developed in keeping with the new technical system. The result was the 'composite longwall' method with more responsibility to the team as a whole and shifts carrying out composite tasks, the reintroduction of multiskilled roles and a reduction in specialisation. The composite method was psychologically and socially more rewarding and economically more efficient than the 'longwall' method.

The socio-technical system

The concept of the organisation as a 'socio-technical' system directs attention to the transformation or conversion process itself, to the series of activities through which the organisation attempts to achieve its objectives. The **socio-technical system** is concerned with the interactions between the psychological and social factors and the needs and demands of the human part of the organisation, and its structural and technological requirements.

Recognition of the socio-technical approach is of particular importance today. People must be considered as at least an equal priority along with investment in technology. For example, *Lane et al.* point out that major technological change has brought about dramatic changes in worker behaviour and requirements. It is people who unlock the benefits and opportunities of information communication technology.[58]

Technology determinism

The concept of socio-technical systems provides a link between the systems approach and a sub-division, sometimes adopted – the **technology approach**. Writers under the technology

heading attempt to restrict generalisations about organisations and management and emphasise the effects of varying technologies on organisation structure, work groups and individual performance and job satisfaction. This is in contrast with the socio-technical approach which did not regard technology, *per se*, as a determinant of behaviour.

Under the heading of the technology approach could be included the work of such writers as *Walker and Guest* (effects of the assembly line production method on employee behaviour);[59] *Sayles* (relationship between technology and the nature of work groups);[60] and *Blauner* (problems of 'alienation' in relation to different work technologies).[61] Chapter 16 examines technology and organisations.

THE CONTINGENCY APPROACH

The classical approach suggested one best form of structure and placed emphasis on general sets of principles while the human relations approach gave little attention at all to structure. In contrast the **contingency approach** showed renewed concern with the importance of structure as a significant influence on organisational performance. The contingency approach, which can be seen as an extension of the systems approach, highlights possible means of differentiating among alternative forms of organisation structures and systems of management. There is no one optimum state. For example, the structure of the organisation and its 'success' are dependent, that is contingent upon, the nature of tasks with which it is designed to deal and the nature of environmental influences.

The most appropriate structure and system of management is therefore dependent upon the contingencies of the situation for each particular organisation. The contingency approach implies that organisation theory should not seek to suggest one best way to structure or manage organisations but should provide insights into the situational and contextual factors which influence management decisions. Contingency models of organisation and management are discussed in Chapter 15.

A summary of management theory and some links with other chapters is set out in Figure 2.3.

OTHER APPROACHES TO THE STUDY OF ORGANISATIONS

The four-fold framework of classical, human relations, systems and contingency approaches provides a helpful, although rather simplistic, categorisation. The study of organisations, their structure and management is a broad field of inquiry. Depending on the views and preferences of the writer, other possible main approaches include decision-making and social action.

THE DECISION-MAKING APPROACH

The systems approach involves the isolation of those functions most directly concerned with the achievement of objectives and the identification of main decision areas or sub-systems. Viewing the organisation as a system emphasises the need for good information and channels of communication in order to assist effective decision-making in the organisation. Recognition of the need for decision-making and the attainment of goals draws attention to a sub-division of the systems approach, or a separate category, that of the **decision-making (decision theory) approach**. Here the focus of attention is on managerial decision-making and how organisations process and use information in making decisions.

Successful management lies in responding to internal and external change. This involves the clarification of objectives, the specification of problems and the search for and implementation of solutions. The organisation is seen as an information-processing network with numerous decision points. An understanding of how decisions are made helps in understanding behaviour in the organisation. Decision-making writers seek to explain the mechanisms by which conflict is resolved and choices are made.

Figure 2.3 Concept map of management theory

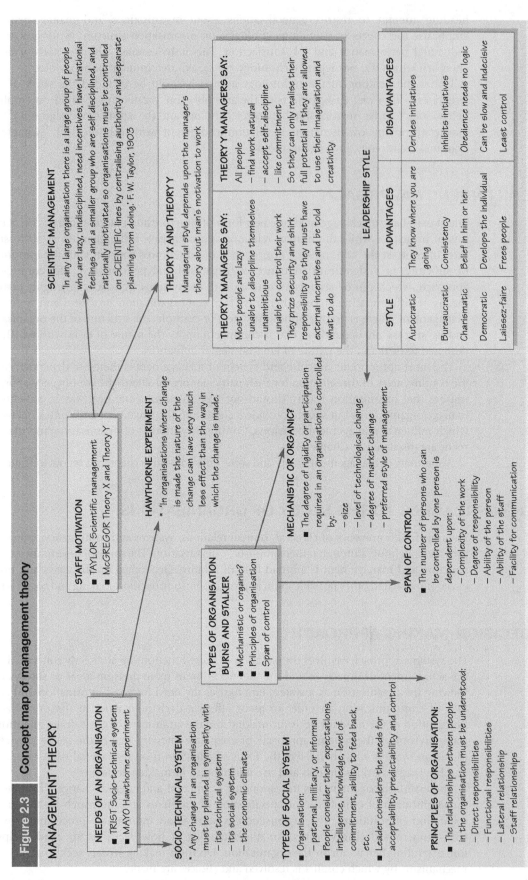

MANAGEMENT THEORY

NEEDS OF AN ORGANISATION
- TRIST Socio-technical system
- MAYO Hawthorne experiment

SOCIO-TECHNICAL SYSTEM
* Any change in an organisation must be planned in sympathy with
 - its technical system
 - its social system
 - the economic climate

TYPES OF SOCIAL SYSTEM
- Organisation:
 - paternal, military, or informal
- People consider their expectations, intelligence, knowledge, level of commitment, ability to feed back, etc.
- Leader considers the needs for acceptability, predictability and control

PRINCIPLES OF ORGANISATION:
- The relationships between people in the organisation must be understood:
 - Direct responsibilities
 - Functional responsibilities
 - Lateral relationship
 - Staff relationships

STAFF MOTIVATION
- TAYLOR Scientific management
- McGREGOR Theory X and Theory Y

HAWTHORNE EXPERIMENT
* "In organisations where change is made the nature of the change can have very much less effect than the way in which the change is made."

TYPES OF ORGANISATION BURNS AND STALKER
- Mechanistic or organic?
- Principles of organisation
- Span of control

MECHANISTIC OR ORGANIC?
- The degree of rigidity or participation required in an organisation is controlled by:
 - size
 - level of technological change
 - degree of market change
 - preferred style of management

SPAN OF CONTROL
- The number of persons who can be controlled by one person is dependent upon:
 - Complexity of the work
 - Degree of responsibility
 - Ability of the person
 - Ability of the staff
 - Facility for communication

SCIENTIFIC MANAGEMENT
"In any large organisation there is a large group of people who are lazy, undisciplined, need incentives, have irrational feelings and a smaller group who are self disciplined, and rationally motivated so organisations must be controlled on SCIENTIFIC lines by centralising authority and separate planning from doing.' F. W. Taylor, 1903

THEORY X AND THEORY Y
Managerial style depends upon the manager's theory about man's motivation to work

THEORY X MANAGERS SAY:
Most people are lazy
- unable to discipline themselves
- unambitious
- unable to control their work
They prize security and shirk responsibility so they must have external incentives and be told what to do

THEORY Y MANAGERS SAY:
All people
- find work natural
- accept self-discipline
- like commitment
So they can only realise their full potential if they are allowed to use their imagination and creativity

LEADERSHIP STYLE

STYLE	ADVANTAGES	DISADVANTAGES
Autocratic	They know where you are going	Derides initiatives
Bureaucratic	Consistency	Inhibits initiatives
Charismatic	Belief in him or her	Obedience needs no logic
Democratic	Develops the individual	Can be slow and indecisive
Laissez-faire	Frees people	Least control

Some leading writers

Leading writers on the decision-making approach include *Barnard, Simon* and *Cyert and March*. The scope of the decision-making approach, however, is wide and it is possible to identify contributions from engineers, mathematicians and operational research specialists in addition to the work of economists, psychologists and writers on management and organisation.

Barnard stressed the need for co-operative action in organisations. He believed that people's ability to communicate, and their commitment and contribution to the achievement of a common purpose, were necessary for the existence of a co-operative system.[62] These ideas were developed further by Simon. He sees management as meaning decision-making and his concern is with how decisions are made and how decision-making can be improved. Simon is critical of the implication of man as completely rational and proposes a model of 'administrative man' who, unlike 'economic man', 'satisfices' rather than maximises. Administrative decision-making is the achievement of satisfactory rather than optimal results in solving problems.[63]

Economic models of decision-making, based on the assumption of rational behaviour in choosing from known alternatives in order to maximise objectives, can be contrasted with behavioural models based not so much on maximisation of objectives as on short-term expediency where a choice is made to avoid conflict and to stay within limiting constraints. Managers are more concerned with avoiding uncertainties than with the prediction of uncertainties.[64]

SOCIAL ACTION

Social action represents a contribution from sociologists to the study of organisations. Social action writers attempt to view the organisation from the standpoint of individual members (actors) who will each have their own goals and interpretation of their work situation in terms of the satisfaction sought and the meaning that work has for them. The goals of the individual, and the means selected and actions taken to achieve these goals, are affected by the individual's perception of the situation. Social action looks to the individual's own definition of the situation as a basis for explaining behaviour. Conflict of interests is seen as normal behaviour and part of organisational life.

According to *Silverman*, 'The action approach . . . does not, in itself, provide a theory of organisations. It is instead best understood as a method of analysing social relations within organisations.'[65]

Criticisms of earlier approaches

A main thrust of social action is the criticism of earlier approaches to organisation and management and of what is claimed to be their failure to provide a satisfactory basis for the explanation or prediction of individual behaviour. For example, criticism is directed at approaches which focused on the goals and needs of the organisation rather than on considerations of the effectiveness of an organisation in meeting the needs of its individual members.

The human relations approaches have been criticised because of their focus on generalised theories of good management, group psychology and the suggestion of needs common to all individuals at work. The technology approach has been criticised for attributing feelings of alienation to the nature of technology and the status of work groups rather than an analysis which focused on concern for the individual's expectations of, and reactions to, work. The systems approach has been criticised for failure to examine the orientation of individual members to the organisation, the different expectations people have of their work or ways in which the environment influences expectations of work.

Unitary or pluralistic view

Important contributors to a social action approach include *Goldthorpe* (industrial attitudes and behaviour patterns of manual workers)[66] and *Fox*. In a research paper written for the

Royal Commission on Trade Unions and Employers' Associations (the Donovan Report), Fox suggests two major ways of perceiving an industrial organisation – a 'unitary' approach and a 'pluralistic' approach.[67]

With the unitary approach the organisation is viewed as a team with a common source of loyalty, one focus of effort and one accepted leader. The pluralistic approach views the organisation as made up of competing sub-groups with their own loyalties, goals and leaders. These competing sub-groups are almost certain to come into conflict. The unitary and pluralistic perspectives of the organisation are also referred to in Chapter 3 and Chapter 13.

Action theory

A theory of human behaviour from an 'action approach' is presented by *Bowey*.[68] She suggests that action theory, systems theory and contingency theory are not necessarily incompatible approaches to the understanding of behaviour in organisations. It would be possible to take the best parts of the different approaches and combine them into a theory that would model empirical behaviour and also facilitate the analysis of large numbers of people in organisations. Bowey goes on to present such a theory as a particular form of an action theory approach. According to Bowey, action theory is not capable of dealing with the analysis of the behaviour of a large number of people in organisations. Her theory is based, therefore, on three essential principles of action theory, augmented by four additional concepts taken from systems theory.

The three essential principles of action theory can be summarised as below:

- Sociology is concerned not just with behaviour but with 'meaningful action'.
- Particular meanings persist through reaffirmation in actions.
- Actions can also lead to changes in meanings.

Bowey suggests that these three principles apply mainly to explanations of individual, or small-scale, behaviour. She gives four additional concepts, taken from systems theory, on which analysis of large-scale behaviour can be based. These concepts are redefined in accordance with an action approach.

- **Role.** This is needed for the analysis of behaviour in organisations. It explains the similar action of different people in similar situations within the organisation and the expectations held by other people.
- **Relationships.** This is needed to explain the patterns of interaction among people and the behaviours displayed towards one another.
- **Structure.** The relationships among members of an organisation give rise to patterns of action which can be identified as a 'transitory social structure'. The social factors, and non-social factors such as payment systems, methods of production and physical layout, together form the behavioural structure.
- **Process.** Human behaviour can be analysed in terms of processes, defined as 'continuous interdependent sequences of actions'. The concept of process is necessary to account for the manner in which organisations exhibit changes in structure.

The three principles of action theory, together with the four additional concepts from systems theory, provide an action approach to the analysis of behaviour in organisations. Bowey goes on to illustrate her theory with case studies of five different types of organisations, all in the restaurant industry.

A NUMBER OF APPROACHES

We can now see that within the broad four-fold classification of classical, human relations, systems and contingency approaches it is possible to identify a number of other approaches or at least sub-divisions of approaches, although there is no consensus on the categorisation of these different approaches or on the identification of the various contributors to one

particular approach. So far we have established a possible nine-fold classification: classical (including scientific management); bureaucracy; human relations; neo-human relations; systems; technology; contingency; decision-making; and social action – and if structuralism is included, we have a ten-fold classification. This classification could be extended still further. For example, another more recent categorisation sometimes identified as a separate approach is management science – with emphasis on quantitative analysis, mathematical models, operational research and computer technology (*see* Figure 2.4).

| Figure 2.4 | An outline of developments of approaches to organisation and management |

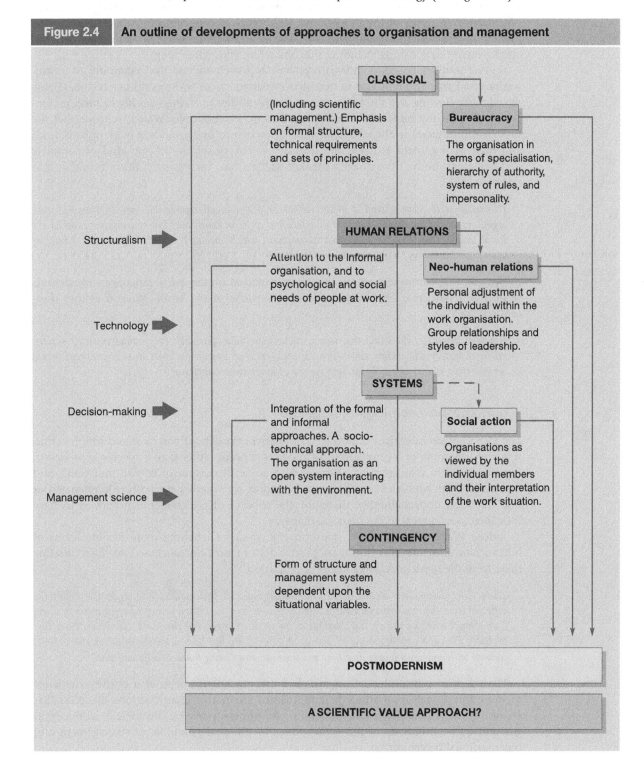

POSTMODERNISM

The work of contemporary writers discussed above together with the achievements of practitioners such as Alfred P. Sloan Jr (1875–1966, Chief Executive and Honorary Chairman of General Motors) gave rise to the so-called 'modern organisation'.[69] With the development of the information and technological age a more recent view of organisations and management is the idea of **postmodernism**. In the 1990s, writers such as *Clegg* described the postmodern organisation in terms of the influence of technological determinism, structural flexibility, premised on niches, multiskilled jobs marked by a lack of demarcation, and more complex employment relationships including subcontracting and networking.[70]

Postmodernism rejects a rational systems approach to our understanding of organisations and management and to accepted explanations of society and behaviour. Highly flexible, free-flowing and fluid structures with the ability to change quickly to meet present demands form the basis of the new organisation. For example, *Watson* suggests that the modernism inherent in the systems-control approach to understanding work organisations and their management is naïve and unrealistic. The possibility of any kind of complete and coherent body of management knowledge has increasingly been brought into question.

> *To enable us to move toward a more realistic or pragmatically reasonable way of 'framing' work organisation and its management, a shift has first to be made in our deeper assumptions about the social world. These are the modernist assumptions which inevitably underpin the whole edifice of work organisation and management thinking.*[71]

By contrast, postmodernism places greater attention on the use of language and attempts to portray a particular set of assumptions or versions of the 'truth'. Watson defines postmodernism as:

> *A way of looking at the world that rejects attempts to build systematic (or 'foundationalist') explanations of history and society and which, instead, concentrates on the ways in which human beings 'invent' their words, especially through the use of language or 'discourse'.*[72]

A generalised sociological concept

The idea of postmodernism is, however, not easy to explain fully in clear and simple terms. It is arguably more of a generalised sociological concept rather than a specific approach to organisation and management. There is even some discussion of two connotations, and theories or philosophies of the concept depending on whether the term is hyphenated or not.[73] Perhaps understandably, therefore, the concept of postmodernism appears to have little interest or appeal to the practical manager.

Indeed Watson, for example, questions the value of labelling more flexible forms of bureaucratic structure and culture as postmodern or post-bureaucratic and differentiating these from the modernist bureaucratic organisation.

> *There is no postmodern or post-bureaucratic organisational form available to us that is essentially different from the modernist bureaucratic organisation. We are indeed seeing different mixes of direct and indirect management control attempts as the world changes. But the world was always changing. Probably from the very beginning of industrialisation there has been a mixing of direct and indirect controls with emphases in one direction and then the other being made at different times.*[74]

Nevertheless, postmodernist organisation can arguably be seen as a healthy challenge to more traditional approaches. It puts forward alternative interpretations of rationality, credibility and ambiguity, and a thoughtful critical perspective on disorders in work organisations, and reminds us of the complexities in our understanding of management and organisational behaviour.

Critical reflection

'The idea of postmodernist organisation can be likened to the "Emperor's new clothes". In reality it is too theoretical and too vague, and lacks any real adaptive value for the practical manager.'

How would you attempt to challenge this assertion? What is your own opinion of postmodernism?

RELEVANCE TO MANAGEMENT AND ORGANISATIONAL BEHAVIOUR

The different possible categorisations are not necessarily a bad thing; they illustrate the discursive and complex nature of management. The possible sub-divisions and cross-groupings help illustrate the many factors relevant to the study and practice of management and organisational behaviour. Discussion on the various categorisations of approaches and the identification of individual writers within a particular approach can provide a useful insight into the subject.

Positive advantages

Whatever form of categorisation is adopted, the division of writers on organisation and management into various approaches offers a number of positive advantages.

- It is helpful to students in the arrangement and study of their material.
- It provides a setting in which to view the field of management and to consider the contribution of individual writers.
- It traces the major lines of argument developed by writers seeking to advise practising managers on how they might improve performance.
- It provides a framework in which the principles enunciated can be set and against which comparisons with management practice can be made.
- It helps in organisational analysis and in the identification of problem areas. For example, is the problem one of structure, of human relations or of the socio-technical process?
- It enables the manager to take from the different approaches those ideas which best suit the particular requirements of the job. For example, in dealing with a problem of structure, the ideas of the classical writers or of contingency theory might be adopted. When there is a problem relating to human resource management, ideas from the human relations movement might be of most value. If the problem is one of environmental influence, insights from the systems approach might prove most helpful. For problems of a more quantitative nature, ideas from the decision-making approach or from management science might be applicable.

Caveats to be noted

There are, however, a number of important caveats that should be noted.

- The various approaches represent a progression of ideas, each building on from the other and adding to it. Together they provide a pattern of complementary studies into the development of management thinking. The different approaches are not in competition with each other and no one approach should be viewed as if it were the only approach, replacing or superseding earlier contributions. Many ideas of earlier writers are still of relevance today and of continuing importance in modern management practice.
- Any categorisation of individual writers into specific approaches is inevitably somewhat arbitrary and not all writers can be neatly arranged in this manner. This is only to be

expected. Such writers are expounding their current thoughts and ideas in keeping with the continual development of management theory and changes in management practice. The comment made about some management writers that they are saying different things at different times might therefore be taken more as a compliment than as a criticism.

■ Even when there is agreement on the nature of the contribution from different writers, the actual division into varying approaches may take a number of forms. In other words, while there might be acceptance of the need for a framework, there is no agreement on its shape. Different authors have adopted different formats in which to set out the developments in management thinking.

■ Some of the literature categorises management thinkers into divisions called 'schools'. The use of this term suggests a clarity of distinction between each division and a uniformity of beliefs within each division. This is perhaps an exaggeration. The distinction between these so-called schools is not clear-cut and there is not necessarily a consistency of thinking among the various contributors in each division. The term 'approaches' to management is more indicative of the obscure lines between the different categorisations and, paradoxically, it is the suggestion of vagueness that, arguably, makes it a more appropriate term to use.

> *Of course, management theories have often been the subject of discourse and criticism. Some critics see organisational philosophies as management fads that will be replaced by new ones as other theories are proposed. That may well be the case, but it is good for management theories to evolve, because organisations change, the environment changes, and as a result, management practices and techniques change . . . Theories provide us with valuable insights into how we can be more understanding, influential and ultimately more successful in managing organisations and the turbulent dynamic environments in which they operate . . . you of course, may have a different view!*
>
> Jacqueline McLean[75]

The importance of cultural contexts

A major criticism of the attempt to define generalised models of management theory is the assumption of national culture. In a review of management theory and practice, *Heller* contrasts British and American thinking with methods employed by the Japanese. In the 1960s, Western managements showed a total lack of curiosity about competition from Japan; British and European managers were still obsessed by the American example. The Japanese built hugely on what they had borrowed from the USA. However, the Japanese also practised and perfected what management scientists often only preached.[76]

Although British management has failed to live up to Japanese standards, professional standards among managers in Britain have improved greatly over the past 25 years. The potential of a widening Europe and the Japanese penchant for locating more plants in Britain provide the best reasons for brighter prospects.

Schneider and Barsoux draw attention to how the different theories on how to organise all reflect societal concerns of the times as well as the cultural backgrounds of the individuals. Different approaches reflect different cultural assumptions regarding, for example, human nature and the importance of task and relationships.[77]

Cheng, Sculli and Chan also question the universality of theories of management and organisational behaviour on the grounds that they have not adequately addressed the factor of culture. 'Traditionally, the greatest aspiration of researchers is to discover objective, universalistic principles of behaviour. The tacit assumption behind this is that these principles may be discovered without reference to cultural contexts.' They conclude that while there may be some universality to organisation structures, for example the need for some form of hierarchy whatever its shape may be, different national cultures frequently give those structures different meanings.[78]

TOWARDS A SCIENTIFIC VALUE APPROACH?

It might arguably be that the study of organisations, their structure and management is moving towards a more scientific approach. Management science can assist managers in the analysis of complex problems that are subject to quantitative constraints and in the optimisation of decisions in such problems. It may also assist in the establishment of broad theory.

> It is obvious from even a cursory glance at the history of management science that science and technology are considered to be key instruments in solving workplace problems and in controlling workplaces . . . While Taylorist scientific management may have its academic critics, management science is thriving. It is itself a large business, providing employment for management consultants whose sole concern is solving workplace problems of other corporations.[79]

Balance between philosophy and science

Miner, however, suggests that although the degree of commitment to the scientific value system is increasing, as yet there is insufficient research to move the field entirely into science, completely divorced from philosophy. At present management theory is clearly in the 'schools' phase. As discussed earlier, it is possible to argue over the use of the term 'schools'. However, whatever terminology is used, and whatever the state of our knowledge, the message from Miner is clear:

> . . . schools of management thought are very much a reality, and the management student who approaches the field without at least a minimal understanding of them does so at some risk.[80]

Whatever the moves towards a more scientific approach, many operational problems in organisations relate to the nature of human behaviour and the people–organisation relationship and do not lend themselves to the application of a scientific answer. For example, according to *Handy*:

> If there were such a thing as Management Science, presumably there would be scientific laws and rules. I was to be grievously disappointed. I read endless hypotheses that tried to explain why people and organisations behaved the way they did but no proof . . . Managing a business, or any organisation, I came to see was more practical art than applied science.[81]

BENEFITS TO THE MANAGER

Whatever the balance between philosophy and science, a knowledge and understanding of management theory will help with the complexities of management in modern work organisations.

According to *Crainer*, management is active, not theoretical. But management is nothing without ideas.

> Ideas drive management as surely as the immediate problems which land on managers' desks or which arrive via their email. Decisions have to be based on ideas, as well as instinct. Without ideas managers flit desperately from crisis to crisis. They cannot know where they are going, why they are doing something or what they will achieve, without the fuel of ideas.[82]

Crainer also suggests that as one idea after another fails to translate into sustainable practice, there is a growing disillusionment with the pedlars of managerial wisdom.

> Yet, the desire for instant solutions which tackle all managerial problems in one fell swoop remains strong . . . Amid the hard sell, the quick fixes and organisational placebos, it is true to say that there is little that's original. But, without gurus, managers would lose a rich source of inspiration, information and controversy.[83]

Reporting on a 12-year study of the knowledge and use of management concepts in technical organisations, *Flores and Utley* suggest that a look back at the theories and principles that have been taught in the past could give an indication of the success of any new approach and help prepare today's and tomorrow's managers for the future.[84] And *Stern* has this to say:

> *Management thinkers still have a lot to tell us. You don't have to believe everything they say, but they may at least offer stimulation; they might provoke senior managers into abandoning complacency and trying to see problems in a new light.*[85]

There is undoubtedly much scepticism about, and criticism of, management gurus. For example, in a cynical and provocative feature in *The Times*, *Billen* suggests that the tide is turning against the gurus and their gobbledegook.

> *In the past two decades, management theory, once rejected in Britain by both management and unions, has been deliberately imposed on almost every aspect of commercial and public life . . . It would be a brave new world without such gobbledegook in it but – to use a management theorist's phrase – an empowered one, too. Managers would be chosen not for their ability to bandy jargon with their superiors but for their empathy, pragmatism, experience and decisiveness with their staff.*[86]

Whatever the value of management theory, clearly no single approach to organisation and management provides all the answers. It is the comparative study of different approaches which will yield benefits to the manager. There is, of course, no shortage of new ideas on organisational behaviour and management thinking. To what extent, however, do these ideas lead to improved organisational performance? *Ghoshal et al.* suggest that:

> *There is much truth in the saying that every living practitioner is prisoner to the ideas of a dead theorist. Immunized by their daily confrontation with the 'real world' corporate managers typically exhibit a healthy distrust of theory that has, in general, served them well.*[87]

There are no definitive or final solutions to the problems of organisations. The nature of work organisations and the environment in which they operate is becoming increasingly complex and subject to continual change. However, at least we do understand more about the dynamics of management and organisational behaviour as a basis for the analysis of human behaviour in organisations.[88] *Stern* suggests that 'Management is both science and art, and the trick of it lies in separating the good ideas from the bad, knowing when to be scientific and when to be artful.'[89]

There are, then, many aspects to management. There are no simple solutions, no one best way to manage. However, the study of organisations, their structure and management is still important for the manager and remains an indispensable part of the job.

Critical reflection

'The historical study of different approaches to organisation and management and the development of organisation theory have no practical relevance for today's managers. It is really no more than a luxury for students and the time could be spent better on the study of more important topic areas.'

*How would you present a **counter** argument?*

SYNOPSIS

■ The study of organisational behaviour has to proceed on a broad front. A central part of this study is the development of management thinking and what might be termed management theory. In order to help identify main trends in the development of organisational behaviour, it is usual to categorise the work of leading writers into various 'approaches' based on their views of organisations, their structure and management. This provides a simplistic framework on which to direct study and focus attention.

■ The classical writers placed emphasis on purpose and structure, on the technical requirements of the organisation, and on the assumption of rational and logical behaviour. The human relations writers emphasised the importance of the informal organisation and the psychological and social needs of people at work. The systems approach focuses attention on the interactions between technical and social variables. The organisation is seen in continual interaction with the external environment. Contingency theory highlights possible means of differentiating between alternative forms of structures and systems of management.

■ This four-fold categorisation provides a useful starting point for the identification of main trends in the development of management thinking. Within this framework, however, it is possible to identify a number of other approaches or sub-divisions of approaches. The decision-making approach emphasises the need for good information and channels of communication. Social action writers attempt to view the organisation from the position of individual members who will each have their own interpretation of the work situation in terms of the satisfaction sought and the meaning that work has for them.

■ With the development of the information and technological age the need arises for alternative forms of corporate structure and systems. A more recent view is the idea of postmodernism. This rejects a rational systems approach to our understanding of organisations and management, and to accepted explanations of society and behaviour. Postmodernism is arguably more of a generalised sociological concept rather than a specific approach to organisation and management. Nevertheless, postmodernist organisation can arguably be seen as a healthy challenge to more traditional approaches and reminds us of the complexities in our understanding of management and organisational behaviour.

■ Whatever form of categorisation is adopted, the division of writers on organisation and management into various approaches offers a number of advantages. It helps in organisational analysis and the identification of problem areas. It enables the manager to take from the different approaches those ideas that suit best the particular requirements of the job. There are, however, a number of caveats that should also be noted, including the significance of cultural contexts.

■ It might be that the study of organisations is moving towards a more scientific value approach. However, whatever the balance between philosophy and science, a knowledge of management theory will help with the complexities of management in modern work organisations. There is much scepticism and criticism of management gurus but the study of organisation theory is an indispensable part of the job. Ideas are as important to management decisions as is instinct. It is necessary to view the interrelationships among the development of theory, behaviour in organisations and management practice.

REVIEW AND DISCUSSION QUESTIONS

1. Assess critically the relevance of scientific management to present-day organisations. Illustrate your answer with reference to your own organisation.

2. To what extent is there anything positive to be said for bureaucratic structures? Select a large-scale organisation of your choice and suggest ways in which it displays characteristics of a bureaucracy.

3. What are the main conclusions that can be drawn from the Hawthorne experiments? Discuss critically the relevance of these experiments for management and organisational behaviour today.

4. Summarise the main features of the neo-human relations approach to organisation and management. How does it differ from other approaches?

5. Evaluate the application of the systems approach to the analysis of work organisations. Suggest an example of a work situation in which the systems approach might be appropriate.

6. Contrast approaches to improving organisational performance based on attention to technical and structural requirements with those based on concern for psychological and social factors.

7. Explain what is meant by a social action approach. Assess critically the practical relevance of 'action theory'.

8. Identify, and outline briefly, major trends in management theory since the beginning of this century. Debate critically the extent to which the ideas of management gurus have any practical relevance or benefits for managers.

The story of the middleman

Stefan Stern

Reports of the death of middle management were not merely exaggerated, they were wrong. Yes, organisations have de-layered. Yes, the current 'white-collar' recession is having a big impact on the middle tier of professionals within businesses. But middle managers have not been abolished. They are still here, hard at work.

That is one reason that the book *The Truth About Middle Managers* by Paul Osterman is welcome. It attempts to take a serious look at the reality of middle management. The author has made a sincere attempt to shed more light on this under-analysed cadre of managers. Sincere but also, regrettably, flawed. The author defines his terms clearly enough. 'Senior management makes the decisions that set the organisation's course, whereas middle management interprets and executes those decisions,' he writes. Based on his research, Osterman tests some of the common assumptions made about middle managers.

It is not true, he argues, that middle managers are sinking into a pit of despair as their numbers fall and job insecurity rises. In fact, in the US at any rate, there are more managers than ever. They are 'less secure, but more in demand'. Nor is it true, Osterman asserts, that middle managers are alienated from their work and have little commitment to what they do. 'Middle managers are the glue that holds organisations together,' he writes.

> Middle managers very much enjoy what they do and have what I term a strong craft commitment to their work. But it is also true they have lost their loyalty to their firm. As organisations have divested themselves of managerial levels, core managerial responsibilities have been pushed down to middle management. Middle managers are now the negotiators between different interests and are making key decisions about trade-offs.

That is certainly true, as is his other observation,

> In the past the nature of the firm was stable, whereas today it is constantly being reshaped. The continuous organisational turmoil that ensues creates an environment that seems chaotic and out of control from the perspective of middle management.

So why has he come up with some relatively sunny conclusions?

A key part of the research for this book involved in-depth interviews with 50 middle managers from two separate organisations, a bank and a high-tech company. But these interviews were conducted in 2004 and 2005. How were your prospects back then? A lot better than today, we can assume. Second, who were these managers? Osterman explains: 'The middle managers were chosen randomly from a list provided by the human resources staff in each organisation.' Did HR allow any malcontents, whingers and otherwise less-than-upbeat people to be interviewed? It seems unlikely. So we must be sceptical – insecurity is real, not imagined, and disillusionment is widespread. As one of his witnesses said, even then, 'I think if you asked people if they had a choice today whether they'd take a job or take the [redundancy] package, you'd get a fair number of people whose hands would be raised for the package – mine included.'

Source: Stern, S. 'The Story of the Middleman', *Financial Times*, 25 February 2009. Copyright © 2009 The Financial Times Limited, reproduced with permission.

Discussion questions

1 This article describes some research into management and organisational behaviour. Explain which of the approaches to organisational behaviour outlined in the chapter you think Osterman takes, and why.

2 What does the article tell us about the problems associated with researching organisational behaviour? How can such problems be minimised or avoided?

ASSIGNMENT

a Answer each question 'mostly agree' or 'mostly disagree'. Assume that you are trying to learn something about yourself. Do not assume that your answer will be shown to a prospective employer.

	Mostly agree	*Mostly disagree*
1 I value stability in my job.	☐	☐
2 I like a predictable organisation.	☐	☐
3 The best job for me would be one in which the future is uncertain.	☐	☐
4 The army would be a nice place to work.	☐	☐
5 Rules, policies and procedures tend to frustrate me.	☐	☐
6 I would enjoy working for a company that employed 85,000 people worldwide.	☐	☐
7 Being self-employed would involve more risk than I'm willing to take.	☐	☐
8 Before accepting a job, I would like to see an exact job description.	☐	☐
9 I would prefer a job as a freelance house painter to one as a clerk for the Department of Motor Vehicles.	☐	☐
10 Seniority should be as important as performance in determining pay increases and promotion.	☐	☐
11 It would give me a feeling of pride to work for the largest and most successful company in its field.	☐	☐
12 Given a choice, I would prefer to make £30,000 per year as a vice-president in a small company to £40,000 as a staff specialist in a large company.	☐	☐
13 I would regard wearing an employee badge with a number on it as a degrading experience.	☐	☐
14 Parking spaces in a company lot should be assigned on the basis of job level.	☐	☐
15 If an accountant works for a large organisation, he or she cannot be a true professional.	☐	☐
16 Before accepting a job (given a choice), I would want to make sure that the company had a very fine programme of employee benefits.	☐	☐
17 A company will probably not be successful unless it establishes a clear set of rules and procedures.	☐	☐
18 Regular working hours and holidays are more important to me than finding thrills on the job.	☐	☐
19 You should respect people according to their rank.	☐	☐
20 Rules are meant to be broken.	☐	☐

Source: Adapted from DuBrin, A. J. *Human Relations: A Job-Oriented Approach*, Reston Publishing/Prentice Hall (1978), pp. 296–7. Copyright © 1978. Reproduced with permission from Pearson Education Inc.

b You should then consider and discuss the further information supplied by your tutor.

PERSONAL AWARENESS AND SKILLS EXERCISE

Objectives

Completing this exercise should help you to enhance the following skills:

- Demonstrate your knowledge and understanding of scientific management techniques.
- Write an objective set of instructions for undertaking a simple piece of work.

Exercise

Using the example from Figure 2.2 as a model, you are required to develop a *detailed* programme using scientific management techniques for any *two* of the following simple domestic tasks:

- booking an airline ticket;
- cooking a simple meal (for example spaghetti bolognese);
- bathing a small child;
- rearranging 100 CDs in some form of order, 10 to each shelf;
- washing up after a small dinner party;
- renewing your passport.

Discussion

- What are the potential upsides and downsides of removing operator discretion in this way?
- Explain with supporting reasons those tasks or activities that you believe are particularly suited to a scientific management approach.
- How do you feel about carrying out routine tasks on an ongoing basis over which you are given little personal discretion?

CASE STUDY

Dell Computers: the world at your fingertips

Breaking the mould

The growth of the home personal computer (PC) market is one of the most remarkable success stories of the last quarter century. If you own a home PC or an electronic notebook and you live in the United States, then there is a one in three possibility that it arrived on your doorstep packed in boxes labelled 'Dell'. Whilst Dell has a smaller proportion of the PC market outside the USA (it is locked in close competition with its nearest rival, Hewlett-Packard, which overtook Dell to become the biggest seller of PCs in late 2008) there remains a strong possibility that your new PC was assembled in Limerick, Penang or Xiamen. Any of these is a very long way from the bedroom of a campus dormitory at the University of Texas at Austin, which is where Michael Dell began to build and sell computers directly to customers in 1984 before dropping out of college to run his business full-time.

Michael Dell transformed a business run from his bedroom at university to one of the leading companies in the IT market.

In 1984, building a PC from components was still a specialised activity, and while some people were able to assemble their own equipment in order to save money and get precisely what they wanted, the majority of domestic customers bought ready-made products from retailers. The distribution channel for the industry usually contained five components: supplier (of components, chips, software etc.), manufacturer, distributor, retailer and customer. Michael Dell's idea was to sell direct, and at the same time allow customers to have a PC partly tailored to their personal requirements by choosing options from a list of components and specifications which he would then assemble to order. This move eliminated two of the five elements of the distribution channel (the distributors and the retailers) leaving only three players: the suppliers, Dell and the customer.[90]

The opportunity to develop this new approach into a successful business was made possible by the coalescence of three trends: increased levels of consumer confidence and knowledge about the product itself; better and faster software which enabled first the phone-based and then the internet-based ordering system to run effectively; and finally technological and manufacturing advances which enabled Dell to lower the price of a PC to a level where it clearly became good value for money. Whilst Dell supplied both business and individual customers, it was in the home PC market that the approach had particular success. Each computer was assembled to order, with components purchased from suppliers as they were required, so Dell was able to identify and respond to customer preferences and industry trends very quickly, and without a significant amount of capital being tied up in inventory or stock (the value of which would be declining rapidly as new and better products emerged). The system had the added advantage that customers pre-paid for the goods, thus placing Dell on a firm financial footing from the outset.

While this approach to the manufacture of consumer goods is by no means unique (the 'lean manufacturing' approach is widely used in the car industry for example) and other players in the IT market adopted it, Dell was able to make it work more successfully than its competitors. The basic business model transferred readily to the internet, where the process of 'mass customisation' can be managed even more effectively on-line.[91] Dell's growth at the turn of the century took it worldwide, and it was placed first in a ranking of the 'Most Admired Companies' by *Fortune* magazine in February 2005.[92] Dell has also won accolades for ethical standards of corporate behaviour.

Not all plain sailing

The brand image which helped put Dell at the top of Fortune's list in 2005 depended very heavily on its ability to pull together both its own efforts and those of other organisations (i.e. component manufacturers, transport and logistics organisations, delivery companies etc.), often in far-flung regions of the world, to put together a package which offered both reliability and value for money for its customers. As we have seen, its original strength was in its ability to cut out the 'middle man' and deliver that package quickly and cheaply. But the IT business is both highly competitive and a dizzyingly fast-moving environment; and in the early years of the 21st century Dell had to rebalance the content of its package. The area where the Dell operation proved most vulnerable was that of customer service and technical support. In the more traditional world of retail outlets, customers were able to discuss purchases and return faulty equipment or seek support at a store. Such a network of customer support was absent from the Dell model.

Initially Dell outsourced customer support (along with delivery), but as expectations about after-sales service rose, its call centre support lagged behind these expectations resulting in some very public criticism,[93] not least of which was in the form of a long-running critical blog by dissatisfied customer and journalist Jeff Jarvis.[94] Dell brought its technical support centres back in-house; two were based in Canada, but mostly they were 'offshored' (but not 'outsourced') to the Philippines, Malaysia and India, where Dell opened new Business Centres in 2007.[95] It also launched its own blog[96] as a means of capturing and responding to customer complaints. In July 2006, Dell's share price dropped substantially after a profit warning was issued following the decision to make a major investment in customer support systems.[97] The task then facing Dell's management was to persuade investors that the proposed plan would result in a long-term improvement of the company's ability to stay ahead of the game and ultimately deliver a good return on investment.

Why was this move necessary? To a large extent, the very success of Dell at the cheaper end of the market meant that similar low-cost operators ceased to be a major competitive threat by the end of the 1990s. However, as home computers became big business for more up-market companies and those which had previously focused on business customers, Dell found itself competing directly with the very companies it had side-stepped in the 1990s: Hewlett-Packard, Lenovo (the Chinese company which bought the IBM computer manufacturing arm in 2005) and even Sony. These organisations were not only able to provide high-quality, reliable products, but also had much stronger customer service support. This revealed a strategic weakness in Dell's operation and forced it to raise its game not only in terms of the computing power it delivers, but also in terms of its after-sales service.

The soul of Dell

Dell is keen to balance business performance with responsible operations; the overall general philosophy is described by the company as 'The Soul of Dell'[98] and the Code of Conduct reflects its ambitions to

> conduct business the Dell Way – the right way, which is 'Winning with Integrity'. Simply put, we want all members of our team, along with our shareholders, customers, suppliers and other stakeholders, to understand that they can believe what we say and trust what we do.[99]

Feedback from the workforce as well as customers is clearly critical to the success of Dell, and the workforce is encouraged to get involved in the process through its 'Tell Dell' system.

> There is change happening all across Dell, creating a revolution in how we interact and drive for business results. Processes are changing, attitudes are shifting, objectives are being aligned, careers are being enhanced and people are listening. Closely. At the core of it is Tell Dell. The Tell Dell survey program has been continually refined over the past several years from being a good informational instrument to its current use as a critical analytic and diagnostic tool for making Dell a better place to work and a stronger company. Part of the Winning Culture philosophy is to engage directly with our employees, the way we do with our customers. As managers at Dell, it is critical that we support our Winning Culture by working to deliver an unbeatable employee experience each and every day.
>
> Ro Parra and Joe Marengi, Senior Vice Presidents of Americas.[100]

Talking to Hyderabad

This case study is being written on a Dell computer. It was ordered from the front room of a terraced house in the south of England at about 10pm one March evening. Within minutes, I had an email from Sunita at the Hyderabad Customer Experience Centre to say she would be tracking my order to completion and giving me updates on its progress. I could look at the progress it was making by following events on the website, which told me that the components were on their way to Limerick, then that the PC had been assembled, then that it had been dispatched to the distribution hub where it was joined by the chosen accessories. I could see when it crossed from Ireland to the UK and when it had reached the local distribution centre, and finally Sunita phoned me to announce the delivery day and time about one week after the order was placed.

She rang again to ensure that it had arrived and was operating to my satisfaction. When I mentioned that the cooling fan seemed rather noisy, she logged a call to the technical support team (also in India) and I found myself, phone in one hand, screwdriver in the other, involved in what can only be described as the postmodern experience of running a diagnostic test on my PC, with Sunita's colleague talking me through the process of opening the operating unit, dismantling the fan and checking the nature of the fault. As a result, a local engineer was dispatched with a replacement component. Within ten days the whole operation was complete to both my and Sunita's satisfaction, and we said our farewells.

Your tasks

1 Analyse the organisational choices that Dell has made using two of the four main analytical models that are presented in Figure 2.1. Which approach do you think is more appropriate and why?

2 What are the main organisational challenges which Dell faces in order to 'conduct business the Dell Way?' What are the implications for line managers and supervisors of creating a corporate culture based on the Dell Way?

3 Dell is using technologically sophisticated methods to collect 'soft' data about its performance from both customers (Direct2Dell) and staff (Tell Dell). Evaluate these initiatives, and discuss the value of such information in relation to 'hard' data (such as sales figures, share price etc.) as a management tool.

4 Critically review the concept of postmodernism as a means of understanding the nature of highly diverse (in terms of geography, technology, organisation, technical specialisation and culture) organisations such as Dell.

Notes and references

1 McGregor, D. *The Human Side of Enterprise*, Penguin (1987), p. 6.

2 Miner, J. B. *Theories of Organizational Behaviour*, Dryden Press (1980).

3 See, for example, Mullins, L. J. 'Approaches to Management', *Management Accounting*, vol. 57, no. 4, April 1979, pp. 15–18, and Mullins, L. J. 'Some Further Approaches to Management Theory',

Management Accounting, vol. 58, no. 3, March 1980, pp. 30–3.

4 See, for example, George, C. S. *The History of Management Thought*, second edition, Prentice Hall (1972).

5 Shafritz, J. M. *Shakespeare on Management*, Carol Publishing Group (1992), p. xi.

6 For a review of management thinking see, for example, Sheldrake, J. *Management Theory: From Taylorism to Japanization*, International Thomson Business Press (1996). See also Flores, G. N. and Utley, D. R. 'Management Concepts in Use – a 12-Year Perspective', *Engineering Management Journal*, vol. 12, no. 3, September 2000, pp. 11–17.

7 Skipton, M. D. 'Management and the Organisation', *Management Research News*, vol. 5, no. 3, 1983, pp. 9–15.

8 Fayol, H. *General and Industrial Management*, Pitman (1949). See also Gray, I. *Henri Fayol's General and Industrial Management*, Pitman (1988).

9 Urwick, L. *Notes on the Theory of Organization*, American Management Association (1952).

10 Mooney, J. D. and Reiley, A. C. *The Principles of Organization*, Harper and Bros (1939); revised by Mooney, J. D., Harper & Row (1947).

11 Brech, E. F. L. *Organisation: The Framework of Management*, second edition, Longman (1965).

12 Simon, H. A. *Administrative Behaviour*, third edition, Free Press (1976), p. xxii.

13 Woodward, J. *Industrial Organization: Theory and Practice*, second edition, Oxford University Press (1980).

14 Taylor, F. W. *Scientific Management*, Harper & Row (1947). Comprises 'Shop Management' (1903), 'Principles of Scientific Management' (1911) and Taylor's testimony to the House of Representatives' Special Committee (1912).

15 Braverman, H. *Labor and Monopoly Capital*, Monthly Review Press (1974).

16 For a study of employers' labour relations policies, including comments on the work of Braverman, see Gospel, H. F. and Littler, C. R. (eds) *Managerial Strategies and Industrial Relations*, Heinemann Educational Books (1983).

17 Cloke, K. and Goldsmith, J. *The End of Management and the Rise of Organizational Democracy*, Jossey-Bass (2002), p. 27.

18 Rose, M. *Industrial Behaviour*, Penguin (1978), p. 31. See also Rose, M. *Industrial Behaviour*, second edition, Penguin (1988), ch. 2.

19 Drucker, P. F. 'The Coming Rediscovery of Scientific Management', *The Conference Board Record*, vol. 13, June 1976, pp. 23–7; reprinted in Drucker, P. F. *Towards the Next Economics and Other Essays*, Heinemann (1981).

20 Locke, E. A. 'The Ideas of Frederick W. Taylor: An Evaluation', *Academy of Management Review*, vol. 7, no. 1, January 1982, pp. 14–24.

21 For a discussion on 'Fordism', see, for example, Fincham, R. and Rhodes, P. S. *The Individual, Work and Organization*, second edition, Weidenfeld and Nicolson (1992).

22 Hamel, G. *The Future of Management*, Harvard Business School Press (2007), p. 13.

23 Crainer, S. and Dearlove, D. *Financial Times Handbook of Management*, second edition, Financial Times Prentice Hall (2001).

24 Stern, S. 'Guru Guide', *Management Today*, October 2001, pp. 83–4.

25 Weber, M. *The Theory of Social and Economic Organization*, Collier Macmillan (1964).

26 Blau, P. M. and Scott, W. R. *Formal Organizations*, Routledge and Kegan Paul (1966).

27 Stewart, R. *The Reality of Management*, third edition, Butterworth-Heinemann (1999).

28 Argyris, C. *Integrating the Individual and the Organization*, John Wiley & Sons (1964).

29 Caulkin, S. 'Faceless Corridors of Power', *Management Today*, January 1988, p. 65.

30 Peters, T. J. and Waterman, R. H. *In Search of Excellence*, Harper & Row (1982).

31 Tibballs, G. *Business Blunders*, Robinson Publishing (1999).

32 Cloke, K. and Goldsmith, J. *The End of Management and the Rise of Organizational Democracy*, Jossey-Bass (2002), pp. 92–4.

33 Ridderstrale, J. 'Business Moves Beyond Bureaucracy', in Pickford, J. (ed.) *Financial Times Mastering Management 2.0*, Financial Times Prentice Hall (2001), pp. 217–20.

34 Green, J. 'Is Bureaucracy Dead? Don't Be So Sure', *Chartered Secretary*, January 1997, pp. 18–19.

35 See, for example, Waller, P. 'Bureaucracy Takes New Form', *Professional Manager*, May 1998, p. 6.

36 See Mullins, L. J. *Hospitality Management and Organisational Behaviour*, fourth edition, Longman (2001).

37 Stewart, R. *The Reality of Management*, third edition, Butterworth-Heinemann (1999).

38 See, for example, Wilson, F. A. *Organizational Behaviour: A Critical Introduction*, Oxford University Press (1999).

39 For example, see Etzioni, A. *Modern Organizations*, Prentice Hall (1964), p. 41.

40 See, for example, Aktouf, O. 'Management and Theories of Organizations in the 1990s: Towards a Critical Radical Humanism?', *Academy of Management Review*, vol. 17, no. 3, 1992, pp. 407–31.

41 There are many versions of the Hawthorne experiments. Among the most thorough accounts is Roethlisberger, F. J. and Dickson, W. J. *Management and the Worker*, Harvard University Press (1939). See also Landsberger, H. A. *Hawthorne Revisited*, Cornell University Press, Ithaca (1958).

42 See, for example, Rose, M. *Industrial Behaviour*, second edition, Penguin (1988).

43 See, for example, Buggy, C. 'Are You Really Listening?', *Professional Manager*, July 2000, pp. 20–2.

44 Silverman, D. *The Theory of Organisations*, Heinemann (1970).

45 Stead, B. A. *Women in Management*, Prentice Hall (1978), p. 190.

46 Crainer, S. *Key Management Ideas: Thinkers That Changed the Management World*, third edition, Financial Times Prentice Hall (1998), p. 111.

47 Maslow, A. H. 'A Theory of Human Motivation', *Psychological Review*, vol. 50, no. 4, July 1943, pp. 370–96.

48 Herzberg, F. W., Mausner, B. and Snyderman, B. B. *The Motivation to Work*, second edition, Chapman and Hall (1959).

49 McGregor, D. *The Human Side of Enterprise*, Penguin (1987).

50 Likert, R. *New Patterns of Management*, McGraw-Hill (1961). See also Likert, R. *The Human Organization*, McGraw-Hill (1967); Likert, R. and Likert, J. G. *New Ways of Managing Conflict*, McGraw-Hill (1976).

51 McClelland, D. C. *Human Motivation*, Cambridge University Press (1988).

52 Argyris, C. *Understanding Organizational Behavior*, Tavistock Publications (1960) and *Integrating the Individual and the Organization*, Wiley (1964).

53 See, for example, Caulkin, S. 'Chris Argyris', *Management Today*, October 1997, pp. 58–9.

54 Bertalanffy, L. von 'Problems of General Systems Theory: A New Approach to the Unity of Science', *Human Biology*, vol. 23, no. 4, December 1951, pp. 302–12.

55 Miller, E. J. and Rice, A. K. *Systems of Organization*, Tavistock Publications (1967).

56 Boulding, K. 'General Systems Theory – The Skeleton of Science', *Management Science*, vol. 2, no. 3, April 1956, pp. 197–208.

57 Trist, E. L., Higgin, G. W., Murray, H. and Pollock, A. B. *Organizational Choice*, Tavistock Publications (1963).

58 Lane, T., Snow, D. and Labrow, P. 'Learning to Succeed with ICT', *The British Journal of Administrative Management*, May/June 2000, pp. 14–15.

59 Walker, C. R. and Guest, R. H. *The Man on the Assembly Line*, Harvard University Press (1952). See also Walker, C. R., Guest, R. H. and Turner, A. N. *The Foreman on the Assembly Line*, Harvard University Press (1956).

60 Sayles, L. R. *Behaviour of Industrial Work Groups*, Wiley (1958).

61 Blauner, R. *Alienation and Freedom*, University of Chicago Press (1964).

62 Barnard, C. *The Functions of the Executive*, Oxford University Press (1938).

63 Simon, H. A. *The New Science of Management Decision*, revised edition, Prentice Hall (1977).

64 Cyert, R. M. and March, J. G. *A Behavioural Theory of the Firm*, second edition, Blackwell (1992).

65 Silverman, D. *The Theory of Organisations*, Heinemann (1970), p. 147.

66 Goldthorpe, J. H., Lockwood, D., Bechhofer, F. and Platt, J. *The Affluent Worker*, Cambridge University Press (1968).

67 Fox, A. *Industrial Sociology and Industrial Relations*, HMSO (1966).

68 Bowey, A. M. *The Sociology of Organisations*, Hodder & Stoughton (1976).

69 For further information see Crainer, S. *Key Management Ideas: Thinkers That Changed the Management World*, third edition, Financial Times Prentice Hall (1998).

70 Clegg, S. R. *Modern Organizations: Organization Studies in the Postmodern World*, Sage (1990).

71 Watson, T. J. *Organising and Managing Work*, Financial Times Prentice Hall (2002), p. 51.

72 Ibid., p. 50.

73 See, for example, Legge, K. *Human Resource Management: Rhetorics and Realities*, Macmillan Business (1995).

74 Watson, T. J. *Organising and Managing Work*, Financial Times Prentice Hall (2002), p. 254.

75 McLean, J. 'Management Techniques and Theories', *Manager, The British Journal of Administrative Management*, August/September 2005, p. 17.

76 Heller, R. 'The Change Managers', *Management Today: 25th Anniversary Issue*, 1991, pp. 12–16.

77 Schneider, S. C. and Barsoux, J. *Managing Across Cultures*, second edition, Financial Times Prentice Hall (2003).

78 Cheng, T., Sculli, D. and Chan, F. 'Relationship Dominance – Rethinking Management Theories from the Perspective of Methodological Relationalism', *Journal of Managerial Psychology*, vol. 16, no. 2, 2001, pp. 97–105.

79 Bradley, H., Erickson, M., Stephenson, C. and Williams, S. *Myths at Work*, Polity Press (2000), pp. 96–7.

80 Miner, J. B. *Management Theory*, Macmillan (1971), p. 145. See also Miner, J. B. *Theories of Organizational Behaviour*, Holt, Rinehart and Winston (1980), ch. 1.

81 Handy, C. *Myself and Other More Important Matters*, William Heinemann (2006), p. 61.

82 Crainer, S. *Key Management Ideas: Thinkers That Changed the Management World*, third edition, Financial Times Prentice Hall (1998), p. xi.

83 Crainer, S. 'The Rise of Guru Scepticism', *Management Today*, March 1997, pp. 48–52.

84 Flores, G. N. and Utley, D. R. 'Management Concepts in Use – a 12-year Perspective', *Engineering Management Journal*, vol. 12, no. 3, September 2000, pp. 11–17.

85 Stern, S. 'Guru Guide', *Management Today*, October 2001, p. 87.

86 Billen, A. 'Goodbye to Glib Gurus and Their Gobbledegook', *The Times*, 9 March 2009.

87 Ghoshal, S., Barlett, C. A. and Moran, P. 'Value Creation: The New Millennium Management Manifesto', in Chowdhury, S. (ed.) *Management 21C*, Financial Times Prentice Hall (2000), p. 122.

88 See, for example, Klein, S. M. and Ritti, R. R. *Understanding Organizational Behavior*, second edition, Kent Publishing (1984), ch. 1.

89 Stern, S. 'The Next Big Thing', *Management Today*, April 2007, p. 50.

90 Kraemer, K. Dedrick, J. and Yamashiro, S. 'Refining and Extending the Business Model with Information Technology: Dell Computer Corporation', *The Information Society*, vol. 16, 2000, pp. 5–21.

91 Visit any of the Dell direct order websites to see how this operates; in the UK the address is www.dell.co.uk. The corporate address with wider company information is at www.dell.com.

92 *Fortune*, 22 February 2005.

93 Lee, L. 'Dell: Facing Up to Past Mistakes', *Business Week On-line*, 19 June 2006, www.businessweek.com (accessed 28 July 2009).

94 Jeff Jarvis' blog is at www.buzzmachine.com.

95 Dell Corporate website, Community pages (accessed 28 July 2009).

96 Now called Direct2Dell and accessible via http://en.community.dell.com/.

97 Allison, K. and Nuttall, C. 'Dell Shares Tumble After Warning Over Sales', FT on-line, 21 July 2006.

98 'The Soul of Dell' can be found at the Dell website, (accessed 28 July 2009).

99 Dell's 'Code of Conduct', also at the Dell website (accessed 28 July 2009).

100 'Tell Dell' is described in the recruitment pages of the Dell website (accessed 28 July 2009).

THE NATURE OF LEADERSHIP

An essential part of the process of management is co-ordinating the activities of people and guiding their efforts towards the goals and objectives of the organisation. This involves the process of leadership and the choice of an appropriate form of behaviour and action. Leadership is a central feature of organisational performance. The manager needs to understand the nature of leadership influence, factors that determine relationships with other people and the effectiveness of the leadership relationship.

Learning outcomes

After completing this chapter you should be able to:

- explain the meaning and importance of leadership in work organisations;
- contrast main approaches to, and studies of, leadership;
- examine leadership as an aspect of behaviour, and different styles of leadership;
- explore contingency theories of leadership;
- evaluate the nature and main components of transformational leadership and inspirational leadership;
- explain the leadership relationship and the exercise of leadership power and influence;
- review the variables which determine effective leadership and development.

Critical reflection

'Leadership is all about determination, personality and innate ability at the right time for a particular competitive situation. Many effective business leaders have no formal academic qualifications and each has their own individual leadership style.'

Does this suggest that successful leaders are more likely born to be so rather than trained? What benefit do you expect to achieve from an academic study of leadership?

THE MEANING OF LEADERSHIP

There are many ways of looking at **leadership** and many interpretations of its meaning. Leadership might be interpreted in simple terms, such as 'getting others to follow' or 'getting people to do things willingly', or interpreted more specifically, for example as 'the use of authority in decision-making'. It may be exercised as an attribute of position or because of personal knowledge or wisdom. Leadership might be based on a function of personality or it can be seen as a behavioural category. It may also be viewed in terms of the role of the leaders and their ability to achieve effective performance from others. Leadership can also be discussed in terms of a form of persuasion or power relationship.

From a comprehensive review of leadership theory and research, *Bass* concludes that: 'There are almost as many different definitions of leadership as there are persons who have attempted to define the concept.'[1] According to *Crainer* there are over 400 definitions of leadership and 'it is a veritable minefield of misunderstanding and difference through which theorists and practitioners must tread warily'.[2] It is difficult, therefore, to generalise about leadership, but essentially it is a **relationship through which one person influences the behaviour or actions of other people**. This means that the process of leadership cannot be separated from the activities of groups and effective teambuilding.

Changing nature of the work organisation

The changing nature of work organisations involves moving away from an emphasis on getting results by the close control of the workforce and towards an environment of coaching, support and empowerment. This places an ever growing importance on leadership. The leader–follower relationship is reciprocal and effective leadership is a two-way process that influences both individual and organisational performance. Leadership is related to motivation and interpersonal behaviour.[3] A major report from the Advanced Institute of Management Research refers to the dual role of leadership.

> Leaders both motivate employees and design effective organisations. There are two broad conceptions of what leaders do – they motivate their followers and they design organisational contexts to enable their followers to function effectively.[4]

Teamwork and inspiration

Leadership today is increasingly associated not with command and control but with the concept of teamwork, getting along with other people, inspiration and creating a vision with which others can identify. According to *Levine*, leaders need to focus on moving people and organisations forward by increasing the competency of staff and the co-operation of teams in order to improve the organisation. A leader's job is constantly to challenge the bureaucracy that smothers individual enthusiasm and the desire to contribute to an organisation. Leaders in the new millennium will create an environment that encourages the development of skills, learning and openness so that those on their team can participate in the deployment of financial and human resources.[5] A CBI report makes the point that 'Effective leaders, who can inspire their people to realise their personal and collective potential, are often the deciding factor between a company being good at what it does and achieving greatness.'[6]

LEADERSHIP OR MANAGEMENT?

What is the relationship between leadership and management? Although the two terms are often used interchangeably, management is more usually viewed as getting things done through other people in order to achieve stated organisational objectives (*see* Chapter 11).

Management is regarded as relating to people working within a structured organisation and with prescribed roles. To people outside the organisation the manager might not necessarily be seen in a leadership role. The emphasis of leadership is on interpersonal behaviour in a broader context. It is often associated with the willing and enthusiastic behaviour of followers. **Leadership does not necessarily take place within the hierarchical structure of the organisation. It occurs at different levels and can be manifested in different ways.** Many people operate as leaders without their role ever being clearly established or defined. For example, *Belbin* suggests that

> there is a clear implication that leadership is not part of the job but a quality that can be brought to a job . . . The work that leadership encompasses in the context clearly is not assigned but comes about spontaneously.[7]

Attitudes and relations with others

There are other differences between leadership and management. *Zaleznik* explores difference in attitudes towards goals, conceptions of work, relations with others, self-perception and development.

- Managers tend to adopt impersonal or passive attitudes towards goals. Leaders adopt a more personal and active attitude towards goals.
- In order to get people to accept solutions, the manager needs continually to co-ordinate and balance in order to compromise conflicting values. The leader creates excitement in work and develops choices that give substance to images that excite people.
- In their relationships with other people, managers maintain a low level of emotional involvement. Leaders have empathy with other people and give attention to what events and actions mean.
- Managers see themselves more as conservators and regulators of the existing order of affairs with which they identify and from which they gain rewards. Leaders work in, but do not belong to, the organisation. Their sense of identity does not depend upon membership or work roles and they search out opportunities for change.[8]

The 7-S organisational framework

The differences between leadership and management have been applied by *Watson* to the 7-S organisational framework, discussed in Chapter 20. Watson suggests that whereas managers tend towards reliance on strategy, structure and systems, leaders have an inherent inclination for utilisation of the 'soft' Ss of style, staff, skills and superordinate (or shared) goals. Watson also suggests, although cautiously, that 7-S management could be seen as the province of leaders. Managers will not ordinarily be capable of achieving sufficient mastery of all seven factors to attain a consistently high level of organisational performance.[9]

Leading versus managing

Summarising the views of scholars who have attempted to differentiate between leading and managing, *Kent* draws attention to the following characteristics:

- managers do things right; leaders do the right things;
- managing is an authority relationship; leading is an influence relationship; and
- managing creates stability; leading creates change.

Kent suggests that although the ideas are provocative and stimulating they provide a basis for a deeper understanding of the dynamics behind the two processes.[10]

A close relationship

Despite a continuing debate on differences between management and leadership, there is a close relationship between them and it is not easy to separate them as distinct activities.

Today, there appears an increasing tendency to emphasise the interrelationship between management and leadership and to see them more as synonymous.

> *I have never been fond of distinguishing between leadership and management: they overlap and you need both qualities.*[11]

> *Increasingly, management and leadership are being seen as inextricably linked. It is one thing for a leader to propound a grand vision, but this is redundant unless the vision is managed so it becomes real achievement.*[12]

Many methods of management training can also be used as a means of measuring leadership style. For example, the Leadership Grid® (discussed in Chapter 12) was until recently known as the Managerial Grid®.

The debate between Leadership and Management is well rehearsed, and usually produces shades of two perspectives, presented here as extremes: A hierarchical relationship with Leadership at the top; Leadership and Management equal in status, but at opposite ends of a continuum. Frankly, there is little evidence to support one view over the other. But there is overwhelming evidence that people like the idea of being a 'leader'. Indeed this may be the reason why the debate still rages, as it fulfils a need for differentiation.

Ray Moorcroft[13]

Critical reflection

'In universities, many lecturers inspire students and are viewed as leaders but not usually as managers. In sport, we frequently hear talk about great leaders who are not managers of the team. There appears to be a clear and accepted distinction between leadership and management.'

Why do you think this distinction does not appear to apply in the same way within business organisations? How do you distinguish between leadership and management?

APPROACHES TO LEADERSHIP

Due to its complex and variable nature there are many alternative ways of analysing leadership. It is helpful, therefore, to have some framework in which to consider different approaches to study of the subject.

One way is to examine managerial leadership in terms of:

- the qualities or traits approach;
- the functional or group approach, including action-centred leadership;
- leadership as a behavioural category;
- styles of leadership;
- contingency theories;
- transitional or transformational leadership; and
- inspirational or visionary leadership. (*See* Figure 10.1.)

THE QUALITIES OR TRAITS APPROACH

The first approach assumes that leaders are born and not made. Leadership consists of certain inherited characteristics, or personality traits, which distinguish leaders from their followers: the so-called Great Person theory of leadership. The **qualities approach** focuses attention on the man or woman in the job and not on the job itself. It suggests that attention is given to the selection of leaders rather than to training for leadership.

Figure 10.1	A framework for the study of managerial leadership

QUALITIES OR TRAITS APPROACH

Assumes leaders are born and not made. Leadership consists
of certain inherited characteristics or personality traits.
Focuses attention on the person in the job and not on the job itself.

THE FUNCTIONAL or GROUP APPROACH

Attention is focused on the functions and responsibilities of leadership,
what the leader actually does and the nature of the group.
Assumes leadership skills can be learned and developed.

LEADERSHIP AS A BEHAVIOURAL CATEGORY

The kinds of behaviour of people in leadership positions and the
influence on group performance. Draws attention to range of
possible managerial behaviour and importance of leadership style.

STYLES OF LEADERSHIP

The way in which the functions of leadership are carried out and the
behaviour adopted by managers towards subordinate staff.
Concerned with the effects of leadership on those being led.

THE SITUATIONAL APPROACH AND CONTINGENCY MODELS

The importance of the situation. Interactions between the variables
involved in the leadership situation and patterns of behaviour.
Belief that there is no single style of leadership appropriate to all situations.

TRANSFORMATIONAL LEADERSHIP

A process of engendering motivation and commitment, creating a vision
for transforming the performance of the organisation, and appealing to the
higher ideals and values of followers.

INSPIRATIONAL LEADERSHIP

Based on the personal qualities or charisma of the leader and
the manner in which the leadership influence is
exercised.

Drucker (writing originally in 1955) makes the point that:

Leadership is of utmost importance. Indeed there is no substitute for it. But leadership cannot be created or promoted. It cannot be taught or learned.[14]

There have been many research studies into the common traits of leadership. For example, *Bass* reports on numerous studies of traits of leadership from 1904 to 1970 including those relating to personal characteristics such as chronological age, physical appearance (including a positive correlation between height and weight), speech, capacity, achievement, participation, responsibility and status. A conclusion, perhaps not surprisingly, suggests that although personality is a factor in differentiating leadership it is not a matter of the mere possession of some combination of traits. Leaders acquire status through a working relationship with members of a group.[15]

Attempts at identifying common personality, or physical and mental, characteristics of different 'good' or 'successful' leaders have met with little success.[16] Investigations have identified lists of traits that tend to be overlapping, contradictory or with little correlation for most features. It is noticeable that 'individuality' or 'originality' usually features in the list. This itself suggests that there is little in common between specific personality traits of different leaders. It is perhaps possible therefore to identify general characteristics of leadership ability, such as self-confidence, initiative, intelligence and belief in one's actions, but research into this area has revealed little more than this.

Limitations of the traits approach

There are three further limitations with this approach.

- First, there is bound to be some subjective judgement in determining who is regarded as a 'good' or 'successful' leader. (This can make for an interesting class discussion.)
- Second, the lists of possible traits tend to be very long and there is not always agreement on the most important.
- Third, it ignores the situational factors.

Even if it were possible to identify an agreed list of more specific qualities, this would provide little explanation of the nature of leadership. It would do little to help in the development and training of future leaders. Although there is still limited interest in the qualities, or traits, approach, attention has been directed more to other approaches to leadership. The qualities or traits approach gives rise to the questions of whether leaders are born or made and whether leadership is an art or a science. The important point, however, is that **these are not mutually exclusive alternatives**. Even if there are certain inborn qualities that make for a good leader, these natural talents need encouragement and development. Even if leadership is something of an art, it still requires the application of special skills and techniques.

THE FUNCTIONAL (OR GROUP) APPROACH

This approach to leadership focuses attention not on the personality of the leader, nor on the man or woman in the job, *per se*, but on the **functions of leadership**. Leadership is always present in any group engaged in a task. The functional approach views leadership in terms of how the leader's behaviour affects, and is affected by, the group of followers. This approach concentrates on the nature of the group, the followers or subordinates. It focuses on the content of leadership. Greater attention can be given to the successful training of leaders and to the means of improving the leaders' performance by concentrating on the functions which will lead to effective performance by the work group.

The functional approach believes that the skills of leadership can be learned, developed and perfected. In contrast to the view of Drucker (referred to above), *Kotter* makes the point that successful companies do not wait for leaders to come along. 'They actively seek out

people with leadership potential and expose them to career experiences designed to develop that potential. Indeed, with careful selection, nurturing and encouragement, dozens of people can play important leadership roles in a business organisation.'[17] A similar point is made by *Whitehead*:

> *There has been a dramatic change in how management thinkers regard leadership today. Leaders are not born, they say, but made. And the good news is everyone can do it. You don't have to be promoted to a management position. You can be a leader whatever job you do. You don't have to be the boss to be a leader.*[18]

ACTION-CENTRED LEADERSHIP

A general theory on the functional approach is associated with the work of *John Adair* and his ideas on **action-centred leadership** which focuses on what leaders actually *do*.[19] The effectiveness of the leader is dependent upon meeting three areas of need within the work group: the need to achieve the common **task**, the need for **team maintenance**, and the **individual needs** of group members. Adair symbolises these needs by three overlapping circles (*see* Figure 10.2).

Figure 10.2	Interaction of needs within the group

Source: Adair, J. *Action-Centred Leadership*, Gower Press (1979), p. 10. Reproduced with permission from John Adair.

Task needs involve:
- achieving the objectives of the work group;
- defining group tasks;
- planning the work;
- allocation of resources;
- organisation of duties and responsibilities;
- controlling quality and checking performance;
- reviewing progress.

Team maintenance needs involve:
- maintaining morale and building team spirit;
- the cohesiveness of the group as a working unit;

- setting standards and maintaining discipline;
- systems of communication within the group;
- training the group;
- appointment of sub-leaders.

Individual needs involve:
- meeting the needs of the individual members of the group;
- attending to personal problems;
- giving praise and status;
- reconciling conflicts between group needs and needs of the individual;
- training the individual.

The action by the leader in any one area of need will affect one or both of the other areas of need. The ideal position is where complete integration of the three areas of need is achieved. Adair draws attention to the value of the three overlapping circles in emphasising the essential unity of leadership: a single action can be multi-functional in that it touches all three areas. The three-circle approach used by Adair also serves to illustrate the close relationship between leadership and management. The list of leadership functions can be connected with Henri Fayol's classic list of common management activities[20] (discussed in Chapter 11). Building the team and satisfying individual needs would include leadership. Achieving the common task clearly involves the process of management.

LEADERSHIP AS A BEHAVIOURAL CATEGORY

This approach draws attention to the kinds of behaviour of people in leadership situations. One of the most extensive research studies on behavioural categories of leadership was the Ohio State Leadership Studies undertaken by the Bureau of Business Research at Ohio State University. The focus was on the effects of leadership styles on group performance. Results indicated two major dimensions of leadership behaviour, labelled 'consideration' and 'initiating structure'.[21]

- **Consideration** reflects the extent to which the leader establishes trust, mutual respect and rapport with the group and shows concern, warmth, support and consideration for subordinates. This dimension is associated with two-way communication, participation and the human relations approach to leadership.
- **Initiating structure** reflects the extent to which the leader defines and structures group interactions towards attainment of formal goals and organises group activities. This dimension is associated with efforts to achieve organisational goals.

Consideration and initiating structure can be seen as the same as maintenance function (building and maintaining the group as a working unit and relationships among group members) and task function (accomplishment of specific tasks of the groups and achievement of goals) that were discussed in Chapter 9. Consideration and initiating structure were found to be uncorrelated and independent dimensions. Leadership behaviour could, therefore, be shown on two separate axes. A high-consideration, high-structure style appears to be generally more effective in terms of subordinate satisfaction and group performance, but the evidence is not conclusive and much seems to depend upon situational factors. However, later findings suggest that the best leadership style entails high levels of both people-centred and task-centred dimensions.[22]

Employee or production-centred supervisors

Another major research study was carried out at the University of Michigan Institute for Social Research at the same time as the Ohio State studies. Effective supervisors (measured along dimensions of group morale, productivity and cost reduction) appeared to display four common characteristics:

Figure 10.3	Two major dimensions of managerial leadership

Group interaction analysis	Task functions	Maintenance functions
Ohio State leadership study	Initiating structure	Consideration
University of Michigan study	Production-centred supervision	Employee-centred supervision
McGregor, assumptions about people and work	Theory X	Theory Y
Blake and McCanse, Leadership Grid®	Concern for production	Concern for people

- delegation of authority and avoidance of close supervision;
- an interest and concern in their subordinates as individuals;
- participative problem-solving; and
- high standards of performance.

Likert, who has summarised the findings of the University of Michigan studies, used the terms **employee-centred** and **production-centred** supervisors.[23] These terms are similar to the dimensions of consideration and structure. The first three of these supervisory characteristics are examples of consideration. The fourth characteristic exemplifies structure. Like consideration and structure, employee-centred and production-centred supervision need to be balanced. Likert concluded that employee-centred supervisors who get best results tend to recognise that one of their main responsibilities is production. Both the Ohio State and the University of Michigan studies appear to support the idea that there is no single behavioural category of leadership that is superior. There are many types of leadership behaviour and their effectiveness depends upon the variables in any given situation.

Major dimensions of managerial leadership

Despite the many types of actual leadership behaviour, we have seen that there appears to be general agreement on two major dimensions of managerial leadership. This can be extended to include the works of McGregor and of Blake and McCanse, discussed as part of managerial behaviour in Chapter 12 (*see* Figure 10.3).

STYLES OF LEADERSHIP

Attention to leadership as a behavioural category has drawn attention to the importance of leadership style. In the work situation it has become increasingly clear that managers can no longer rely solely on the use of their position in the hierarchical structure as a means of exercising the functions of leadership. In order to get the best results from subordinates the manager must also have regard for the need to encourage high morale, a spirit of involvement and co-operation, and a willingness to work. This gives rise to consideration of the style of leadership and provides another heading under which to analyse leadership behaviour.

Leadership style is the way in which the functions of leadership are carried out, the way in which the manager typically behaves towards members of the group.

The attention given to leadership style is based on the assumption that subordinates are more likely to work effectively for managers who adopt a certain style of leadership than for managers who adopt alternative styles. Attention to the manager's style of leadership has

come about because of a greater understanding of the needs and expectations of people at work. It has also been influenced by such factors as:

- increasing business competitiveness and recognition of efficient use of human resources;
- changes in the value-system of society;
- broader standards of education and training;
- advances in scientific and technical knowledge;
- changes in the nature of work organisation;
- pressure for a greater social responsibility towards employees, for example through schemes of participation in decision-making and work/life balance; and
- government legislation, for example in the areas of employment protection, and the influence of the European Union.

All of these factors have combined to create resistance against purely autocratic styles of leadership.

Broad framework of leadership style

There are many dimensions to leadership and many possible ways of describing leadership style, such as dictatorial, unitary, bureaucratic, benevolent, charismatic, consultative, participative and abdicatorial. With so many potential descriptions of leadership styles it is useful to have a broad framework in which to focus attention and study. The style of managerial leadership towards subordinate staff and the focus of power can therefore be considered within a simplified three-fold heading.

- The **authoritarian (autocratic) style** is where the focus of power is with the manager and all interactions within the group move towards the manager. The manager alone exercises decision-making and authority for determining policy, procedures for achieving goals, work tasks and relationships, control of rewards or punishments.
- The **democratic style** is where the focus of power is more with the group as a whole and there is greater interaction within the group. The leadership functions are shared with members of the group and the manager is more part of a team. The group members have a greater say in decision-making, determination of policy, implementation of systems and procedures.
- A **laissez-faire (genuine) style** is where the manager observes that members of the group are working well on their own. The manager consciously makes a decision to pass the focus of power to members, to allow them freedom of action 'to do as they think best', and not to interfere; but is readily available if help is needed. There is often confusion over this style of leadership behaviour. The word 'genuine' is emphasised because this is to be contrasted with the manager who could not care, who deliberately keeps away from the trouble spots and does not want to get involved. The manager just lets members of the group get on with the work in hand. Members are left to face decisions that rightly belong with the manager. This is more a non-style of leadership or it could perhaps be labelled as abdication.

CONTINUUM OF LEADERSHIP BEHAVIOUR

One of the best-known works on leadership style is that by *Tannenbaum and Schmidt* (*see* Figure 10.4).[24] Originally written in 1958 and updated in 1973, their work suggests a continuum of possible leadership behaviour available to a manager and along which various styles of leadership may be placed. The continuum presents a range of action related to the degree of authority used by the manager and to the area of freedom available to non-managers in arriving at decisions. The Tannenbaum and Schmidt continuum can be related to McGregor's supposition of Theory X and Theory Y (discussed in Chapter 12). Boss-centred leadership is towards Theory X and subordinate-centred leadership is towards Theory Y.

| Figure 10.4 | Continuum of manager–non-manager behaviour |

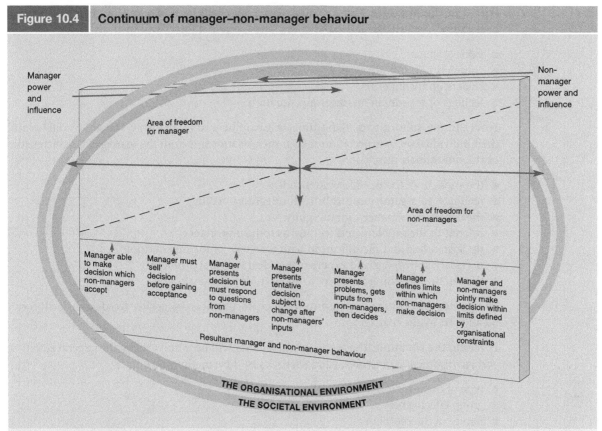

Four main styles of leadership

Moving along the continuum, the manager may be characterised according to the degree of control that is maintained. Neither extreme of the continuum is absolute as there is always some limitation on authority and on freedom. This approach can be seen as identifying four main styles of leadership by the manager: tells, sells, consults, joins.

- **Tells**. The manager identifies a problem, makes a decision and announces this to subordinates, expecting them to implement it without an opportunity for participation.
- **Sells**. The manager still makes a decision but recognises the possibility of some resistance from those faced with the decision and attempts to persuade subordinates to accept it.
- **Consults**. The manager identifies the problem but does not make a decision until the problem is presented to the group, and the manager has listened to the advice and solutions suggested by subordinates.
- **Joins**. The manager defines the problem and the limits within which the decision must be made and then passes to the group, with the manager as a member, the right to make decisions.

Three main forces

Tannenbaum and Schmidt suggest that there are three factors, or forces, of particular importance in deciding what types of leadership are practicable and desirable. These are: forces in the manager, forces in the subordinate and forces in the situation.

Forces in the manager. The manager's behaviour will be influenced by their personality, background, knowledge and experiences. These internal forces will include:

- value-systems
- confidence in subordinates
- leadership inclinations
- feelings of security in an uncertain situation.

Forces in the subordinate. Subordinates are influenced by many personality variables and their individual set of expectations about their relationship with the manager. Characteristics of the subordinate are:

- the strength of the need for independence
- readiness to assume responsibility for decision-making
- the degree of tolerance for ambiguity
- interest in the problem and feelings as to its importance
- understanding and identification with the goals of the organisation
- necessary knowledge and experience to deal with the problem
- the extent of learning to expect to share in decision-making.

The greater the positive response to these characteristics, the greater freedom of action can be allowed by the manager.

Forces in the situation. The manager's behaviour will be influenced by the general situation and environmental pressures. Characteristics in the situation include:

- type of organisation
- group effectiveness
- nature of the problem
- pressure of time.

Tannenbaum and Schmidt conclude that successful leaders are keenly aware of those forces which are most relevant to their behaviour at a particular time. They are able to behave appropriately in terms of their understanding of themselves, the individuals and the group, the organisation, and environmental influences. Successful managers are both perceptive and flexible. Forces lying outside the organisation are also included. Tannenbaum and Schmidt suggest a new continuum of patterns of leadership behaviour in which the total area of freedom shared between managers and non-managers is redefined constantly by interactions between them and the forces in the environment.

Critical reflection

'The Tannenbaum and Schmidt continuum is probably the single most important and relevant study of leadership. Successful managers clearly need to be both consistent in personality and behaviour, yet adaptable to the three forces that continually influence their leadership style and decision-making along the various points of the continuum.'

To what extent can you argue against this assertion? What do you think is the single most important study of leadership?

CONTINGENCY THEORIES OF LEADERSHIP

The continuum of leadership behaviour draws attention to forces in the situation as one of the main forces influencing the nature of managerial behaviour. The **situational approach** emphasises the situation as the dominant feature in considering the characteristics of effective leadership. There are, however, limitations to the situational approach. There are

people who possess the appropriate knowledge and skills and appear to be the most suitable leaders in a given situation, but who do not emerge as effective leaders. Another limitation is that it does not explain fully the interpersonal behaviour or the different styles of leadership and their effect on members of the group. Finally, in the work organisation, it is not usually practicable to allow the situation continually to determine who should act as the leader.

Despite the limitations of the situational approach, situational factors are important in considering the characteristics of leadership. More recent studies focus on the interactions between the variables involved in a leadership situation and patterns of leadership behaviour, and provide another general approach to the study of leadership – contingency theory. Contingency theories are based on the belief that there is no single style of leadership appropriate to all situations. Major contingency models of leadership include:

- **Favourability of leadership situation** – Fiedler
- **Quality and acceptance of leader's decision** – Vroom and Yetton and Vroom and Jago
- **Path–goal theory** – House, and House and Dessler
- **Readiness level of followers** – Hersey and Blanchard.

FIEDLER'S CONTINGENCY MODEL

One of the first leader–situation models was developed by *Fiedler* in his contingency theory of leadership effectiveness.[25] Fiedler's contingency model was based on studies of a wide range of group situations and concentrated on the relationship between leadership and organisational performance. In order to measure the attitudes of the leader, Fiedler developed a 'least preferred co-worker' (LPC) scale. This measures the rating given by leaders about the person with whom they could work least well. The questionnaire contains up to 20 items. Examples of items in the LPC scale are pleasant/unpleasant, friendly/unfriendly, helpful/frustrating, distant/close, co-operative/unco-operative, boring/interesting, self-assured/hesitant, open/guarded.

Each item is given a single ranking of between one and eight points, with eight points indicating the most favourable rating. For example:

Pleasant	:	:	:	:	:	:	:	:	Unpleasant
	8	7	6	5	4	3	2	1	

The LPC score is the sum of the numerical ratings on all the items for the 'least preferred co-worker'. The original interpretation of the LPC scale was that the leader with a high LPC score derived most satisfaction from interpersonal relationships and, when relationships with subordinates need to be improved, is motivated to act in a supportive, considerate manner. The leader with a low LPC score derived most satisfaction from performance of the task and achieving objectives. Establishing good relationships with subordinates is a secondary motivation. It was thought that high LPC scores would be associated with effective performance by the group. However, the interpretation of LPC has changed a number of times and there is still uncertainty about its actual meaning.

Favourability of leadership situation

Fiedler suggests that leadership behaviour is dependent upon the favourability of the leadership situation. There are three major variables which determine the favourability of the situation and which affect the leader's role and influence:

- **Leader–member relations** – the degree to which the leader is trusted and liked by group members, and their willingness to follow the leader's guidance.

Figure 10.5 | **Correlations between leader's LPC scores and group effectiveness**

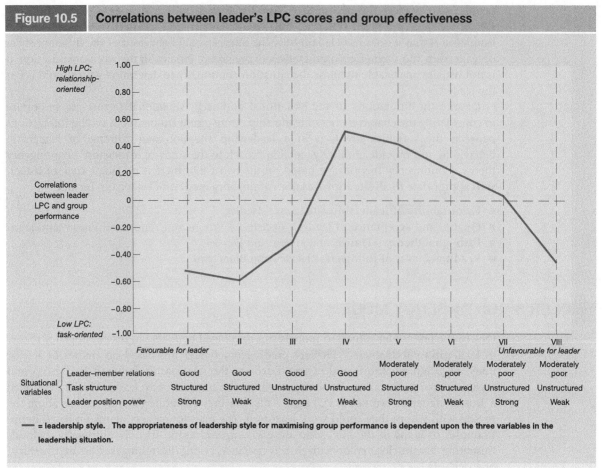

Situational variables		I	II	III	IV	V	VI	VII	VIII
	Leader–member relations	Good	Good	Good	Good	Moderately poor	Moderately poor	Moderately poor	Moderately poor
	Task structure	Structured	Structured	Unstructured	Unstructured	Structured	Structured	Unstructured	Unstructured
	Leader position power	Strong	Weak	Strong	Weak	Strong	Weak	Strong	Weak

— = leadership style. **The appropriateness of leadership style for maximising group performance is dependent upon the three variables in the leadership situation.**

Source: Adapted from Fielder, F. E. *A Theory of Leadership Effectiveness*, McGraw-Hill (1967), p. 146. Reproduced with permission from Fred E. Fielder.

- **The task structure** – the degree to which the task is clearly defined for the group and the extent to which it can be carried out by detailed instructions or standard procedures.
- **Position power** – the power of the leader by virtue of position in the organisation, and the degree to which the leader can exercise authority to influence (for example) rewards and punishments, or promotions and demotions.

From these three variables, Fiedler constructed eight combinations of group–task situations through which to relate leadership style (*see* Figure 10.5).

When the situation is

- **very favourable** (good leader–member relations, structured task, strong position power), or
- **very unfavourable** (poor leader–member relations, unstructured task, weak position power),
- then a **task-oriented leader** (low LPC score) with a directive, controlling style will be more effective.

When the situation is

- **moderately favourable** and the variables are mixed, then the leader with an interpersonal relationship orientation (high LPC score) and a **participative approach** will be more effective.

Fiedler is suggesting, therefore, that leadership style will vary as the favourability of the leadership situation varies.

Organisational variables

Fiedler's work has been subject to much debate and criticism but it does provide a further dimension to the study of leadership.[26] It brings into consideration the organisational variables that affect leadership effectiveness and suggests that in given situations a task-oriented, or structured, style of leadership is most appropriate. The 'best' styles of leadership will be dependent upon the variable factors in the leadership situation.

Fiedler argues that leadership effectiveness may be improved by changing the leadership situation. Position power, task structure and leader–member relations can be changed to make the situation more compatible with the characteristics of the leader. Leaders with a low LPC score could be placed in a leadership situation that is very favourable or very unfavourable. Leaders with a high LPC score could be placed in a leadership situation that is of moderate favourability.

VROOM AND YETTON CONTINGENCY MODEL

Another contingency model of leadership is provided by *Vroom and Yetton*.[27] They base their analysis on two main aspects of a leader's decision: its quality and its acceptance.

- **Decision quality**, or rationality, is the effect that the decision has on group performance.
- **Decision acceptance** refers to the motivation and commitment of group members in implementing the decision.

 A third consideration is

- the amount of **time required** to make the decision.

 The Vroom and Yetton model suggests five main management decision styles:

- **Autocratic**
 A.I: Leader solves the problem or makes the decision alone using information available at the time.
 A.II: Leader obtains information from subordinates but then decides on solution alone.

- **Consultative**
 C.I: The problem is shared with relevant subordinates, individually. The leader then makes the decision that may or may not reflect the influence of subordinates.
 C.II: The problem is shared with subordinates as a group. The leader then makes the decision that may or may not reflect the influence of subordinates.

- **Group**
 G.II: The problem is shared with subordinates as a group. The leader acts as chairperson rather than an advocate. Together the leader and subordinates generate and evaluate alternatives and attempt to reach group consensus on a solution.

Decision rules

Vroom and Yetton suggest seven decision rules to help the manager discover the most appropriate leadership style in a given situation. The first three rules protect the **quality of decisions**.

1 Is there a quality requirement such that one solution is likely to be more rational than another?
2 Is there sufficient information to make a high-quality decision?
3 Is the problem structured?

The last four rules protect the **acceptance of decisions**.

4 Is acceptance of the decision by subordinates critical to effective implementation?

5 If you were to make the decision yourself, is it reasonably certain that it would be accepted by subordinates?

6 Do subordinates share the organisational goals to be obtained in solving the problem?

7 Is conflict among subordinates likely in preferred solutions?

These rules indicate decision styles that the manager should **avoid** in a given situation and indicate the use of others. Decision tree charts can be produced to help in the application of the rules and to relate the situation to the appropriate leadership style.

THE VROOM AND JAGO REVISED DECISION MODEL

In a revised version of the original model, *Vroom and Jago* retain the five main decision-making styles but incorporate a larger number – 12 – of contingency variables.[28] The new model specifies that any of the five decision styles may be effective in given situations. The contingency variables relate to:

- quality requirement;
- commitment requirement;
- leader information;
- problem structure;
- commitment probability;
- goal congruence;
- subordinate conflict;
- subordinate information;
- time constraint;
- geographical dispersion;
- motivation time; and
- motivation development.

Unlike the Vroom and Yetton model that requires a definite yes/no answer, ten of these situational variables are answered on a five-point scale. For example, to the question 'How important is subordinate commitment to the decision?', the manager selects one of the following responses: no importance; low importance; average importance; high importance; critical importance.

Use of decision trees

Vroom and Jago developed four decision trees relating to a generic type of managerial problem:

- an individual-level problem with time constraints;
- an individual-level problem in which the manager wishes to develop an employee's decision-making ability;
- a group-level problem in which the manager wishes to develop employees' decision-making abilities; and
- a time-driven group problem.

The manager selects one of the trees and moves along the branches by answering the questions at each decision point. This leads to one of the five described decision-making styles.

PATH–GOAL THEORY

A third contingency model of leadership is the **path–goal theory**, the main work on which has been undertaken by *House*,[29] and by *House and Dessler*.[30] The model is based on the belief that the individual's motivation is dependent upon expectations that increased effort to

achieve an improved level of performance will be successful, and expectations that improved performance will be instrumental in obtaining positive rewards and avoiding negative outcomes. This is the 'expectancy' theory of motivation, which was discussed in Chapter 7.

Main types of leadership behaviour

The path–goal theory of leadership suggests that the performance of subordinates is affected by the extent to which the manager satisfies their expectations. Path–goal theory holds that subordinates will see leadership behaviour as a motivating influence to the extent that it means:

- satisfaction of their needs is dependent upon effective performance; and
- the necessary direction, guidance, training and support, which would otherwise be lacking, is provided.

House identifies four main types of leadership behaviour:

- **Directive leadership** involves letting subordinates know exactly what is expected of them and giving specific directions. Subordinates are expected to follow rules and regulations. This type of behaviour is similar to 'initiating structure' in the Ohio State Leadership Studies.
- **Supportive leadership** involves a friendly and approachable manner and displaying concern for the needs and welfare of subordinates. This type of behaviour is similar to 'consideration' in the Ohio State Leadership Studies.
- **Participative leadership** involves consulting with subordinates and the evaluation of their opinions and suggestions before the manager makes the decision.
- **Achievement-oriented leadership** involves setting challenging goals for subordinates, seeking improvement in their performance and showing confidence in subordinates' ability to perform well.

Path–goal theory suggests that the different types of behaviour can be practised by the same person at different times in varying situations. By using one of the four styles of leadership behaviour the manager attempts to influence subordinates' perceptions and motivation, and smooth the path to their goals (*see* Figure 10.6).

Two main situational factors

Leadership behaviour is determined by two main situational factors: the personal characteristics of subordinates and the nature of the task.

Figure 10.6 Representation of the path–goal theory of leadership

■ **The personal characteristics of subordinates** determine how they will react to the manager's behaviour and the extent to which they see such behaviour as an immediate or potential source of need satisfaction.

■ **The nature of the task** relates to the extent that it is routine and structured or non-routine and unstructured.

For example, when a task is highly structured, the goals readily apparent and subordinates are confident, then attempts to further explain the job or to give directions are likely to be viewed as unacceptable behaviour. However, when a task is highly unstructured, the nature of the goals is not clear and subordinates lack experience, then a more directive style of leadership behaviour is likely to be welcomed by subordinates. Effective leadership behaviour is based, therefore, on both the willingness of the manager to help subordinates and the needs of subordinates for help. Leadership behaviour will be motivational to the extent that it provides necessary direction, guidance and support, helps clarify path–goal relationships and removes any obstacles which hinder attainment of goals.

READINESS OF THE FOLLOWERS OR GROUP

A major variable in the style of leadership adopted by the manager is the nature of subordinate staff. This view is developed by *Hersey and Blanchard* who present a form of situational leadership based on the 'readiness' level of the people the leader is attempting to influence. Readiness is the extent to which followers have the ability and willingness to accomplish a specific task. It is not a personal characteristic of the individual but how ready the individual is to perform a particular task.[31]

Readiness (R) is divided into a continuum of four levels: R1 (low), R2 and R3 (moderate) and R4 (high).

■ **R1 – low follower readiness** – refers to followers who are both *unable and unwilling* and who lack commitment and motivation; or who are *unable and insecure*.

■ **R2 – low to moderate follower readiness** – refers to followers who are *unable but willing* and who lack ability but are motivated to make an effort; or who are *unable but confident*.

■ **R3 – moderate to high follower readiness** – refers to followers who are *able but unwilling*, and who have the ability to perform but are unwilling to apply their ability; or who are *able but insecure*.

■ **R4 – high follower readiness** – refers to followers who are both *able and willing* and who have the **ability** and commitment to perform; or who are *able and confident*.

Task behaviour and relationship behaviour

For each of the four levels of maturity, the appropriate style of leadership is a combination of task behaviour and relationship behaviour.

■ **Task behaviour** is the extent to which the leader provides directions for the actions of followers, sets goals for them and defines their roles and how to undertake them.

■ **Relationship behaviour** is the extent to which the leader engages in two-way communication with followers, listens to them and provides support and encouragement.

From the combination of task behaviour and relationship behaviour derive four leadership styles (S): telling (S1), selling (S2), participating (S3) and delegating (S4). The appropriate leadership style corresponds with the readiness of the followers (*see* Figure 10.7).

■ **S1 – telling** – emphasises high amounts of guidance (task behaviour) but limited supportive (relationship) behaviour. This style is most appropriate for *low follower readiness* (R1).

■ **S2 – selling** – emphasises high amounts of both directive (task) and relationship behaviours. This style is most appropriate for *low to moderate follower readiness* (R2).

Figure 10.7	Situational Leadership® model

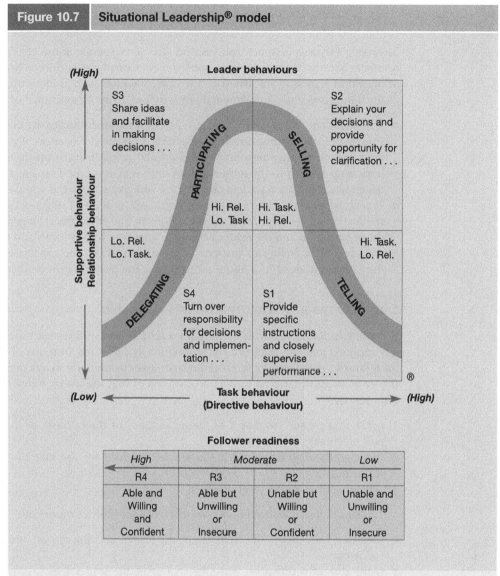

- **S3 – participating** – emphasises a high amount of two-way communication and supportive (relationship) behaviour but low amounts of guidance (task behaviour). This style is most appropriate for *moderate to high follower readiness* (R3).
- **S4 – delegating** – emphasises little direction or support with low levels of both task and relationship behaviours. This style is most appropriate for *high follower readiness* (R4).

Development of subordinates

Hersey and Blanchard suggest that the key to using situational leadership is that any leader behaviour may be more or less effective according to the readiness of the person the leader is attempting to influence. The model draws attention to the importance of developing the ability, confidence and commitment of subordinates. The manager should help subordinates to develop in readiness to the extent that they are able and willing to go. This development should take place by adjusting leadership behaviour through the four styles of telling, selling, participating and delegating.

TRANSFORMATIONAL LEADERSHIP

Increasing business competitiveness and the need for the most effective use of human resources has resulted in writers on management focusing attention on how leaders revitalise or transform organisations. Based on the work of writers such as *Burns* this has given rise to a distinction between two fundamental forms of leadership: transactional or transformational.[32]

- **Transactional leadership** is based on legitimate authority within the bureaucratic structure of the organisation. The emphasis is on the clarification of goals and objectives, work task and outcomes, and organisational rewards and punishments. Transactional leadership appeals to the self-interest of followers. It is based on a relationship of mutual dependence and an exchange process of 'I will give you this, if you do that.'
- **Transformational leadership**, by contrast, is a process of engendering higher levels of motivation and commitment among followers. The emphasis is on generating a vision for the organisation and the leader's ability to appeal to higher ideals and values of followers, and creating a feeling of justice, loyalty and trust. In the organisational sense, transformational leadership is about transforming the performance or fortunes of a business.

Components of transformational leadership

According to *Bass*, the transformational leader motivates followers to do more than originally expected and the extent of transformation is measured in terms of the leader's effects on followers. Applying the ideas of Burns to organisational management, Bass proposed a theory of transformational leadership that argues that the leader transforms and motivates followers by:

1 generating greater awareness of the importance of the purpose of the organisation and task outcomes;
2 inducing them to transcend their own self-interests for the sake of the organisation or team; and
3 activating their higher-level needs.[33]

Transformational leadership is comprised of four basic components:

- **idealised influence** – the charisma of the leader, and the respect and admiration of the followers;
- **inspirational motivation** – the behaviour of the leader which provides meaning and challenge to the work of the followers;
- **intellectual stimulation** – leaders who solicit new and novel approaches for the performance of work and creative problem solutions from followers; and
- **individualised consideration** – leaders who listen and give special concern to the growth and developmental needs of the followers.[34]

Yukl provides a set of guidelines for transformational leadership:

- **Articulate a clear and appealing vision** of what the organisation could accomplish or become to help people understand the purpose, objectives and priorities of the organisation, and to help guide the actions and decisions of members.
- **Explain how the vision can be attained** and establish a clear link between the vision and a credible conventional yet straightforward strategy for attaining it.
- **Act confident and optimistic** about likely success, demonstrate self-confidence and conviction, and emphasise positive aspects of the vision rather than the obstacles and dangers.
- **Express confidence in followers** and their ability to carry out the strategy for accomplishing the vision, especially when the task is difficult or dangerous, or when members lack confidence in themselves.

■ **Use dramatic, symbolic actions to emphasise key values** and demonstrate leadership behaviour through dramatic, highly visible actions including risking personal loss, self-sacrifice or acting unconventionally.

■ **Lead by example** by recognising actions speak louder than words, through exemplary behaviour in day-to-day interactions with subordinates and by demonstrating consistency in daily behaviour.[35]

INSPIRATIONAL OR VISIONARY LEADERSHIP

Many writers see transformational leadership as the same thing as charismatic, visionary or inspirational leadership. *Kreitner et al.* refer to charismatic leadership as transforming employees to pursue organisational goals over self-interests:

> *Charismatic leaders transform followers by creating changes in their goals, values, needs, beliefs, and aspirations. They accomplish this transformation by appealing to followers' self-concepts – namely, their values and personal identity.*[36]

Writers such as Burns and Bass identified leaders by their actions and the impact those actions have on other people.

Successful transformational leaders are usually identified in terms of providing a strong vision and sense of mission, arousing strong emotions in followers and a sense of identification with the leader. As mentioned at the start of this chapter, leadership today is increasingly associated with the concept of creating a vision with which others can identify, getting along with other people and the concept of inspiration. This might be considered as part of transformational leadership or arguably it has given rise to a new approach to leadership – that of **inspirational** or **visionary leadership**. Inspirational leadership is not concerned so much with the theory of leadership but more with the skills of motivating and inspiring people.

The importance of vision

Effective transformational leaders are those who inspire people and create a vision for the organisation and its future direction. According to *Whitehead*:

> *The big word now associated with leadership is vision. The ability to see the bigger picture. To take the long-term view. What the ultimate objectives of the organisation are and how people can work together to achieve them . . . Perhaps the most important attribute is that a good leader inspires people by creating a climate where it is OK for people to make mistakes and learn from them, rather than what happened in the past which was to blame and punish them. Leading from this position, they gain a higher level of commitment from their people than mere compliance.*[37]

Kahan sees visionary leadership as transformative. It involves greatness, penetrating the ordinary, and requires total involvement. Among the qualities visionary leaders cultivate are imagination, engagement, tangible results and penetrating self-reflection. They engage society with its competitive, divergent viewpoints. Visionary leadership is ultimately about increasing performance but also with the rewards of tangible results to your membership and deep personal satisfaction.[38]

> *Leadership is not about the leader, it is about how he or she builds the confidence of everyone else. Leaders are responsible for both the big structures that serve as the cornerstone of confidence, and for the human touches that shape a positive emotional climate to inspire and motivate people . . . Leaders deliver confidence by espousing high standards in their messages, exemplifying these standards in the conduct they model and establishing formal mechanisms to provide a structure for acting on those standards.*[39]

'Charisma and the ability truly to inspire and move loyal followers in the desired direction is one of the most controversial and elusive leadership qualities.'

Do you believe charismatic leadership brings about improved individual and organisational performance? Can you relate personal experience(s) of charismatic leadership that has truly inspired? Do you possess charisma?

Personal qualities or charisma

Leadership may be based on the personal qualities, or charisma, of the leader and the manner in which influence is exercised. The concept of charismatic or inspirational leadership is not new and has been applied in the organisational context by writers such as Max Weber (1864–1920).[40] The importance of charisma for effective leadership today is emphasised by *Conger*, who also believes that many of the traits that make a successful leader can be taught, including charisma.

> *Now the big question is whether you are born with charisma or whether you can develop it. I believe you can develop elements of it. For example, you can take courses to improve your speaking skills. You can learn to stage events that send powerful messages. You can learn to think more critically about the status quo and its shortcomings. You can do more on a daily basis to motivate your team. What you simply cannot learn is how to be passionate about what you do. You have to discover that for yourself, and passion is a big part of what drives a charismatic leader. It is also what motivates and inspires those who work for the charismatic leader.*[41]

Is charisma enough?

However, the extent to which charismatic or inspirational leadership helps bring about improvement in organisational performance is open to much debate. *Conger* also draws attention to the danger that the leader's vision, dynamism and inspirational nature are highly attractive to followers, which leads to a natural dependence. Staff see this extraordinary figure as a model to be emulated and the leader's abilities become the yardstick by which they measure their own performance. This is a potential source of leadership derailment. Dependence makes the followers more susceptible to deception.[42]

Dearlove draws attention to the increasing focus on leaders as real people managing in a consensus-seeking manner. 'While traditional views of leadership tend eventually to concentrate on vision and charisma, the message now seems to be that charisma is no longer enough to carry leaders through.'[43] *Bloomfield* also refers to the cult of the individual, supposedly charismatic leader and the danger that this leads businesses into deep water far more often than the application of rational leadership. Too often the charismatic leader, aided and abetted by the language of current management fashion, attempts to 'inspire', to delight with their vision and to produce a mission statement of where the business might be – at the expense of real substance.[44]

Adair argues that to be a truly inspirational leader one must understand the spirit within. All people have the potential for greatness. The inspirational leader connects with the led, appreciates the capabilities of others and through trust will unlock the powers in others. Adair refers to 'the inspired moment' – a recognition and seizure of a brief window of opportunity that can act as a powerful catalyst that inspires both the leader and the led.[45]

Need for visionary leadership

Many writers are calling for leaders at all levels with vision and who can inspire with passion and emotion, as well as deliver bottom-line results. For example, during the American

presidential election of 2008 there was considerable debate over the comparative appeal between the experience of Hillary Clinton and the charisma of Barack Obama.

In her discussion of the creation of the democratic enterprise (organisations that can flourish economically and can also be places of excitement and stimulation, fulfilment and tranquillity), *Gratton* maintains that it is the creation of a shared purpose and the role of the leadership team that are most vital. The role of the leader as visionary is fundamental to creating the broad philosophical context of democracy and as the architect of shared purpose.[46]

Referring to the work of Goffee and Jones, *Witzel* suggests: 'Leadership is one of the most vital and yet elusive ingredients in modern business. Leaders provide vision, direction, inspiration, give the business a sense of purpose and at the same time act as a moral compass.'[47] *Goffee and Jones* point out that the need for visionary leadership is becoming increasingly important. Traditional business hierarchies gave managers and workers a sense of their own position and what was expected of them. Now, as these hierarchies break down, it is leaders themselves who must fill the void, helping subordinates to understand their place and purpose. Personal leadership is beginning to replace organisational structure.[48]

> *What sets great leaders apart is their ability to engage those around them in a shared vision of the future. By making the right decisions, they demonstrate their commitment to turning that vision into reality; and by doing so successfully, they instil in others the confidence to trust in their leadership.*
>
> Sir Bryan Nicholson[49]

The inspirational gap

According to a survey by the Chartered Management Institute, the power to inspire is rated highest among desirable leadership qualities. A detailed survey of almost 1,500 practising managers in a broad cross-section of organisations found that the key characteristic that leaders should ideally possess, inspiration, was identified by 55 per cent of managers. However, most leaders appeared to lack this characteristic, with only 11 per cent of respondents saying they experienced this in reality.[50]

The survey from the Chartered Management Institute highlighted a significant 'inspirational gap' in leadership across UK organisations. The Department of Trade and Industry undertook a research project to explore how to start closing this critical leadership inspiration gap.[51] 'It is now accepted that for the UK to maintain its competitiveness there is a growing need for companies to adopt strategies that will enable a greater level of innovation and the provision of higher value and services.' The report is based on a study of 568 followers at different management levels working in a wide variety of organisations. It confirms that today's workforce is more diverse, informed and sophisticated than ever before. Ultimately people are still looking for something different and better in organisational leadership.

Key conclusions of the report include:

■ For the past 30 years there have been increasing amounts of data to suggest that leadership has a lot more to do with inspiration and vision than with straightforward technical competence. Leadership is now recognised as a transferable skill, and it can be developed by continued learning and development throughout a person's career.

■ Managers demand visionary leaders who win not only results but also the trust and respect of their teams. It is the relationship between people that results in action.

■ In order to keep followers motivated and committed in an era of unrelenting change, leaders must be able to create organisation cultures that foster not only performance but also a sense of pride and fun.

A summary of leadership and management is set out in the concept map in Figure 10.8.

Figure 10.8 Concept map of leadership and management

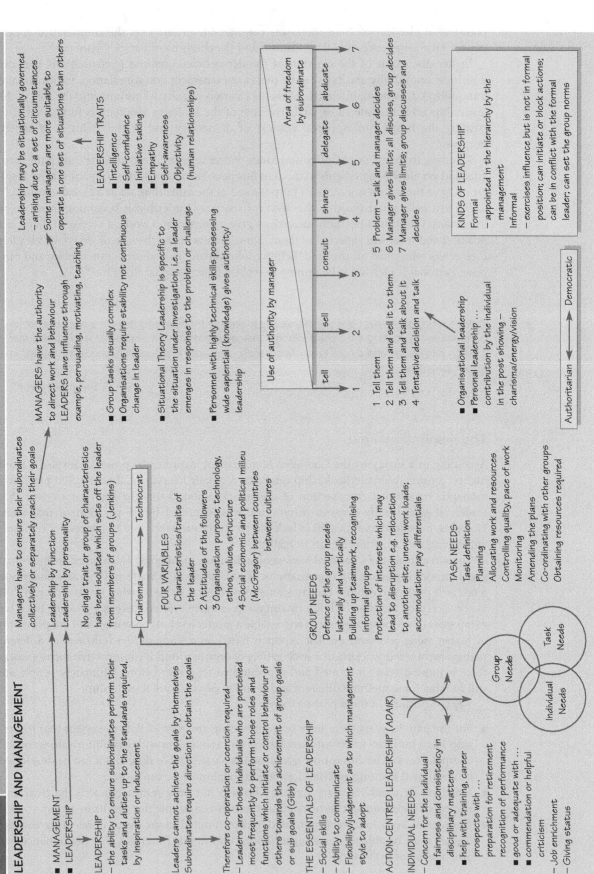

LEADERSHIP AND INNOVATION

A 2005 report by the Advanced Institute of Management Research in co-operation with the Chartered Management Institute draws attention to the impact of leadership on innovation.[52] The report refers to the dual role of leaders, first as motivators, inspiring people to transcend the ordinary, and second as architects, designing an organisational environment that enables employees to be innovative. 'The impact of leadership on innovation goes well beyond the motivating effect of the inspirational or charismatic leader. Leaders also affect innovation through organisational design and must create appropriate organisational environments to suit the different innovation processes.' The primary challenges for organisational leaders in promoting innovation are to:

- recognise and develop appropriate leadership for the different stages of the innovation process; and
- create organisational contexts that support complete innovation processes of different degrees of novelty.

Conceptual framework

The report distinguishes between leaders who primarily motivate through transformational actions – a 'motivational' perspective – and those who take a more transactional approach and emphasise the co-ordination of organisational tasks – a 'structuralist' perspective. In order to address the question of how leadership affects innovation within organisations, the report proposes a conceptual framework that reflects the complex interaction among leadership, the organisational context and innovation (Figure 10.9).

Figure 10.9	The 'leadership for innovation' conceptual framework

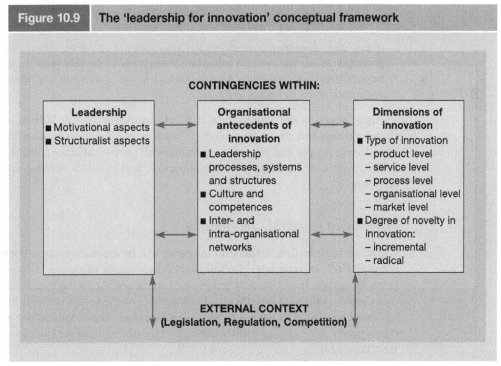

Source: From Munshi, N. *et al. Leading for Innovation: The Impact of Leadership on Innovation*, Advanced Institute of Management Research (AIM) (2005), Figure 5, p. 18. Reproduced with thanks to AIM fellows and scholars: A. Munshi, A. Oke, P. Puranam, M. Stafylarakis, S. Towells, K. Moeslein and A. Neely.

There is, however, a need for being mindful that leadership:

- can manifest itself at all levels in the organisation, not just the top;
- need not be concentrated in the person of a single leader but may act through distributed leadership systems; and
- sets the organisational context for followers' activities both through motivation and the administrative co-ordination of systems that support innovation.

THE LEADERSHIP RELATIONSHIP

Whatever the perceived approach to leadership, the most important point is the nature of the leadership relationship and the manner in which the leader influences the behaviour and actions of other people. Leadership is a dynamic form of behaviour and there are a number of variables that affect the leadership relationship. For example, *Bass* reviews leadership influence in terms of persuasion, a power relation, an instrument of goal achievement, an emerging effect of interaction and the initiation of structure.[53] Four major variables are identified by *McGregor* as:

- the characteristics of the leader;
- the attitude, needs and other personal characteristics of the followers;
- the nature of the organisation, such as its purpose, its structure, and the tasks to be performed; and
- the social, economic and political environment.

McGregor concludes that 'leadership is not a property of the individual, but a complex relationship among these variables'.[54]

According to *Kouzes and Posner*, 'credibility is the foundation of leadership'. From extensive research in over 30 countries and response to the question of what people 'look for and admire in a leader, in a person whose direction they would willingly follow', people have consistently replied that they want

> leaders who exemplify four qualities: they want them to be honest, forward-looking, inspiring and competent. In our research our respondents strongly agree that they want leaders with integrity and trustworthiness, with vision and a sense of direction, with enthusiasm and passion, and with expertise and a track record for getting things done.[55]

Fullan refers to the importance of relationship building as a basic component of the change process and effective leadership: 'Leaders must be consummate relationship builders with diverse people and groups – especially with people different from themselves. Effective leaders constantly foster purposeful interaction and problem solving, and are wary of easy consensus.'[56]

Power and leadership influence

Within an organisation, leadership influence will be dependent upon the type of power that the leader can exercise over the followers. The exercise of power is a social process which helps to explain how different people can influence the behaviour/actions of others. Five main sources of power upon which the influence of the leader is based have been identified by *French and Raven* as reward power, coercive power, legitimate power, referent power and expert power.[57] We shall consider these in terms of the manager (as a leader) and subordinate relationship.

- **Reward power** is based on the subordinate's *perception* that the leader has the ability and resources to obtain rewards for those who comply with directives; for example, pay,

promotion, praise, recognition, increased responsibilities, allocation and arrangement of work, granting of privileges.

- **Coercive power** is based on fear and the subordinate's *perception* that the leader has the ability to punish or to bring about undesirable outcomes for those who do not comply with directives; for example, withholding pay rises, promotion or privileges; allocation of undesirable duties or responsibilities; withdrawal of friendship or support; formal reprimands or possibly dismissal. This is in effect the opposite of reward power.
- **Legitimate power** is based on the subordinate's *perception* that the leader has a right to exercise influence because of the leader's role or position in the organisation. Legitimate power is based on authority, for example that of managers and supervisors within the hierarchical structure of an organisation. Legitimate power is therefore 'position' power because it is based on the role of the leader in the organisation, and not on the nature of the personal relationship with others.
- **Referent power** is based on the subordinate's *identification* with the leader. The leader exercises influence because of perceived attractiveness, personal characteristics, reputation or what is called 'charisma'. For example, a particular manager may not be in a position to reward or punish certain subordinates, but may still exercise power over the subordinates because the manager commands their respect or esteem.
- **Expert power** is based on the subordinate's *perception* of the leader as someone who is competent and who has some special knowledge or expertise in a given area. Expert power is based on credibility and clear evidence of knowledge or expertise; for example, the expert knowledge of 'functional' specialists such as the human resources manager, management accountant or systems analyst. The expert power is usually limited to narrow, well-defined areas or specialisms.

Subordinates' perception of influence

It is important to note that these sources of power are based on the subordinates' perception of the influence of the leader, whether it is real or not. For example, if a leader has the ability to control rewards and punishments but subordinates do not believe this, then in effect the leader has no reward or coercive power. Similarly, if subordinates in a line department believe a manager in a (different) staff department has executive authority over them then even if, *de facto*, that manager has no such authority there is still a perceived legitimate power.

French and Raven point out that the five sources of power are interrelated and the use of one type of power (for example, coercive) may affect the ability to use another type of power (for example, referent). Furthermore, the same person may exercise different types of power, in particular circumstances and at different times.

Other sources of power

Finlay suggests that in addition to the five sources of power identified by French and Raven can be added:

- **personal power**, supported and trusted by their colleagues and subordinates; and
- **connection power**, which results from personal and professional access to key people and information.[58]

Yukl suggests that a further relevant source of power is **control over information**.[59]

You have to look at leadership through the eyes of the followers and you have to live the message. What I have learned is that people become motivated when you guide them to the source of their own power and when you make heroes out of employees who personify what you want to see in the organisation.

Anita Roddick[60]

Power, responsibility and wisdom

Lloyd suggests that the way we think about leadership is a contributory factor to the leadership crisis. Leadership has traditionally been associated with those who have power and there is a need to re-examine the core relationship between power and responsibility. Rather than gaining and keeping power for ourselves, more emphasis should be given to unifying consideration of the two concepts together with greater attention to the subject of wisdom.

> *The new agenda moves us from that narrow focus to a much broader concept of leadership that is more concerned with how power is used, i.e. in whose interest power is used. This explicitly recognises that the use of power is deeply values driven . . . We need to give much greater attention to the values agenda by exploring wisdom, then seeing that emphasis reflected as wise leadership.*[61]

Critical reflection

'Despite the vast amount of writing on the subject by both academics and practising managers, it is extremely difficult to give a precise and agreed meaning of leadership. Nor is there agreement on one best model or style of leadership, or how leadership potential can best be developed.'

Do you find this confusing and a hindrance to your studies? What do you believe are the essential and distinctive characteristics that make for an effective leader?

LEADERSHIP EFFECTIVENESS

Goleman reports that the most effective executives use a collection of distinct leadership styles, each in the right measure, at just the right time. Although the authoritative style of leadership can be occasionally overbearing, it was found to be most effective and can motivate and inspire commitment to the goals of the organisation. The affiliative style has potential to create harmony within teams and can be used in conjunction with the authoritative style. The democratic approach was seen as positive, and encourages input from staff and helps build consensus through participation. The coaching style, although the least frequently used, can help staff identify their strengths and encourage long-term development goals. The study concludes that the most effective leaders rely on more than one leadership style, and were able to master a mixture of authoritative, democratic, affiliative and coaching styles. Leaders with the best results use most of the styles in a given week – seamlessly and in different measure – depending on the business situation.[62]

Goleman also reminds us that whatever a leader is wanting to achieve it is all done with people and from his recent research identifies six leadership styles. Each style springs from different components of emotional intelligence, and help build commitment and improve the emotional climate. (Emotional intelligence was discussed in Chapter 4.) They are:

1 **Visionary** – provides long-term vision
2 **Coaching** – develops people long-term
3 **Affiliative** – creates harmony in work
4 **Democratic** – commitment through consultation
5 **Pace-setter** – pushes to accomplish tasks
6 **Commanding** – demands compliance.

Goleman cautions that the last two styles are easily misused. The more of all these styles deployed the better; research suggests that mastery of four or more fosters improved performance and a better working environment.[63]

Variables affecting leadership effectiveness

Clearly, there is no one 'best' form of leadership that will result in the maintenance of morale among group members and high work performance. Three main aspects to be considered in determining the most appropriate style of leadership are the manager, the group and the work environment. However, there are many variables that underlie the effectiveness of leadership in work organisations. More specifically, these include the following:

- the characteristics of the manager, personality, attitudes, abilities, value-system, and the personal credibility of the manager;
- the type of power of the manager and the basis of the leadership relationship;
- the characteristics of the followers: diversity, their needs and expectations, attitudes, knowledge, confidence and experience, and their motivation and commitment;
- the relationship between the manager and the group, and among members of the group;
- the type and nature of the organisation, organisation culture, and different stages in innovation and development;
- the nature of the tasks to be achieved, the extent to which structured or routine;
- the technology, systems of communication and methods of work organisation;
- organisation structure and systems of management;
- the type of problem and the nature of the manager's decisions;
- the nature and influence of the external environment;
- the social structure and informal organisation, and the psychological contract;
- the influence of national culture.

The shadow of leadership

Leadership is clearly a major feature of effective teamwork. Good leaders surround themselves with talented and capable members of staff, and then in their behaviour and actions serve as a role model. *McCabe* suggests that leaders who want to transform their performance and the effectiveness of the team should look at how their own shadow could be getting in the way. Leaders focus on what they see as important and they are typically quite unconscious of the unintended but massive impact they are having on their colleagues, teams and clients. All leaders cast a shadow and whatever a particular leadership style, the shadow will affect others and can compromise people's engagement at work and business effectiveness. Leaders need to be fully aware of the shadow they cast and the impact they have on others.

> *To be successful, leaders today have to find ways to engage people's ideas, energy and inspiration and this means they will have to build much stronger relationships – and what will prevent such relationships from occurring is their shadow.*[64]

Authority without arrogance

The turbulent and uncertain economic situation of recent times has resulted in many commentators drawing attention to the expectations for clear, decisive and authoritative leadership. For example, *Masson* refers to the leadership attribute of self-assurance, being authentic and comfortable with whom you are. What leaders need is an acute self-awareness and to avoid arrogance.

> *That self-assurance needs to come with an honest assessment of oneself. The whole idea of perfection in leadership is outdated and unhelpful, and leaders who don't open themselves to feedback, and don't reflect on their own behavior, come across as arrogant. Part of being 'authentic' is being open to vulnerability and admitting to one's mistakes.*[65]

Reeves and Knell suggest that being a successful leader is less about who you are or what you do than about what you know. This includes four pieces of knowledge: where the organisation is heading; what is going on; who they are; and how to build a strong team. Leaders

in the most successful organisations are authoritative but their secret is that they use their authority without arrogance. Successful leaders

- build a 'culture of discipline' and are about getting things done, controlling costs and marshalling resources;
- keep in touch with how people are feeling. They don't waste time worrying if everyone is happy but understand the emotional temperament of the organisation and emotional responses from people;
- know where they are strong but also know their weaknesses and display a fierce humility;
- are motivated by what they build, such as great teams and talent people, rather than what they get;
- have a clear sense of where the organisation is going, but very often this is the result of collective decision-making in a talent team.[66]

CROSS-CULTURAL DIMENSIONS OF LEADERSHIP

In Chapter 1 we referred to cross-cultural dimensions of organisational behaviour, identifying some potentially important differences in attitudes and behaviour between different cultural groups. In particular, it was suggested that people's perceptions of authority, independence and uncertain situations could vary according to cultural background and experience. One might reasonably surmise therefore that the topic of leadership will be subject to cultural variation. There has been a consistent view expressed within the leadership literature that another major variable influencing choice of leadership style may be national culture. *McGregor* concluded for example that the social, economic and political environment affected the leadership relationship, together with the attitudes and needs of 'followers'.[67]

Tannenbaum and Schmidt identify leaders' own value-systems as factors that influence their chosen style. They also highlight subordinates' – or non-managers' – needs for independence and tolerance of ambiguity as relevant variables in the choice of style.[68] These factors vary according to the cultural context in which the leadership relationship takes place. One should be wary of stereotyping the behaviour of leaders or subordinates, and many myths appear to have grown around notions of 'orderly' German, 'undisciplined' Italian and even 'obstructive' British workers. However, there are reasons to suggest that there may indeed be national cultural differences that are relevant to an understanding of leadership.

Culture as a contingent factor in leadership?

The contribution of contingency approaches to understanding leadership suggest that contrasting types and styles of leadership may be more or less appropriate in different situations. *Tayeb* draws attention to cross-cultural leadership and points out that in a global business landscape, national culture affects leadership styles and behaviours. It is clear that people living in different parts of the world have different expectations from those in a leadership position. The way in which employees perceive their leaders, as employee-oriented or task-oriented, appears to vary from culture to culture.[69]

Global Leadership and Organisational Behaviour Effectiveness (GLOBE)

Project GLOBE, the full name of which is the Global Leadership and Organisational Behaviour Effectiveness research programme, is a very large-scale research project which sought to identify those leader behaviours and attributes which would be accepted and therefore effective in all societies and, contrastingly, those which would only be accepted and effective in some cultural contexts. This study was conducted by an international team of researchers led by *Robert House* and encompassed 62 countries across the world, including some which had not always featured in cross-cultural study – for example newly capitalist

states in Eastern Europe. The GLOBE study commenced in 1991 and has led to a series of publications in the early 21st century.[70]

The GLOBE study conceived leadership as essentially reciprocal, in that leadership must be endorsed by followers, which endorsement, the authors claim, will be subject to cultural variation. At the same time, leaders will themselves have been immersed in a particular culture and consequently influenced by the norms and values surrounding leadership within that culture.

The results, according to the GLOBE researchers, are some significant variations in leadership style, attributes and behaviour. In the GLOBE study, charismatic and team-oriented leaders were shown to be globally endorsed – and hence universally effective. Leaders who displayed high levels of trust, integrity and vision were supported by subordinates in all societies.

It was also found that there were so-called universal impediments to success; for example *self-protective* leaders characterised by malevolence and 'face-saving' were viewed negatively by subordinates in all cultures.

There were, finally, some aspects of leadership which varied between societies. In common with Hofstede (see Chapter 1) the GLOBE study identifies clusters of societies with important points of commonality. To take one example, in a situation which might imply a directive style of leadership, subordinates in the 'Anglo' cluster of societies (in effect the main English-speaking countries) would prefer some degree of informality on the part of the leader and as much of a participative style as the situation allowed.

The GLOBE study recognises that strategic organisational contingencies such as the sector an organisation operates in will affect leadership style and behaviour; however, the GLOBE researchers concluded that such factors would be moderated by the national cultural context. Leader effectiveness will be influenced by the interaction between leaders and subordinates, which is dependent on the nature of power relations within the particular culture, and organisational contingencies applying in all societies.

LEADERSHIP DEVELOPMENT

Education and training in management needs to emphasise not only interpersonal skills but also a flexibility of approach, diagnostic ability and the realisation that the most effective form of leadership behaviour is a product of the total leadership situation. According to Investors in People, leadership development is not just a corporate issue:

> *The ability to create and communicate a clear vision, and motivate people to deliver it, is as important to the small entrepreneur as to the leader of 1000 people. All organisations should be identifying the managers they will need in a few years' time and developing them. All top managers should be planning their succession and supporting the people who will step into their shoes when it's time to move on.*[71]

A leadership culture

Melville-Ross refers to the importance of developing leadership skills in everyone, not just those at the top. Even people in the most junior positions can play a leadership role. It is about the dissemination of ideas, taking the initiative and encouraging others to see it that way. For this to happen, you need an open leadership culture that runs right through the organisation. People are encouraged to take personal responsibility and are not afraid to speak up with ideas or take risks. However, Melville-Ross acknowledges that there is still a long way to go before this type of behaviour becomes the norm in UK industry.

> *A lot of organisations do still have this hierarchical approach where the boss knows best and there will be hell to pay if you don't do it their way. It is still deeply ingrained. It is even more of a problem in the public sector where it is difficult to create very imaginative, flexible, quick-on-their feet leaders because there are so many accountabilities – and that encourages public sector people to behave in a more buttoned up way.*[72]

Figure 10.10	The leadership 'jigsaw'

VISION – Do you:
1 Work hard at communicating your vision for the organisation to all staff at all levels?
2 Understand that your vision must appeal to your staff at both an emotional and practical level if they are to join you on your journey?
3 Understand the culture and values of your organisation and their impact on its future development?
4 Recognise blind alleys?

MOTIVATION – Do you:
1 Understand that every member has a different set of motivational stimuli?
2 Explain your decisions in terms of their benefit to the organisation and its members?
3 Celebrate and reward individual and team achievements?
4 Prefer to offer carrots, rather than wield sticks?

EXAMPLE – Do you:
1 Match your words with your actions?
2 Take full responsibility for organisational problems, even if you were not directly responsible?
3 Occasionally muck in when your staff are under pressure at work?
4 Regularly consider what you see in the bathroom mirror?

EMPOWERMENT – Do you:
1 Believe that people generally respond well when given greater responsibility for their own performance?
2 Allocate sufficient resources to training and development?
3 Get a buzz when staff set and achieve their own goals?
4 Realise that the organisation would still function if you were not there?

RELATIONSHIPS – Do you:
1 Work hard at countering a 'them and us' culture within your organisation?
2 Set clear codes of acceptable conduct and take action against breaches of them?
3 Stress that everyone contributes to the success of the team(s) they belong to?
4 Admit when you make a mistake?

COMMUNICATIONS – Do you:
1 Use your influence to encourage two-way communications at all levels in your organisation?
2 Encourage personal contact rather than written, mechanical or technological alternatives?
3 Encourage a diversity of opinion and constructive criticism?
4 Walk the talk?

Source: Cutler, A. 'A Good Fit Is Essential', *Professional Manager*, vol. 15, no. 3, May 2005, p. 38. Reproduced with permission from Chartered Management Institute and Alan Cutler.

The leadership jigsaw

Cutler has designed a 'jigsaw' of best practice. There are six interlinking pieces: vision, example, relationships, motivation, empowerment and communications as a guide to the measurement and development of leadership skills. Cutler believes that leadership is not such a difficult role if condensed to these essential elements and has devised a set of questions to help aspiring leaders to find out if they have all the necessary pieces of the jigsaw (*see* Figure 10.10).[73]

Seven principles for developing leaders

Referring to his action-centred leadership model (discussed earlier in this chapter), *Adair* identifies seven key principles of leadership development that can be applied successfully in different kinds of organisations in both the public and private sectors.

1 **Development of a strategy for leadership development** for each of the three levels of leadership – operational, strategic and team.

2 **Selection** of those with high potential for becoming effective leaders.
3 **Training for leadership** that implies instruction with a specific end in view. Identify your business training needs in the leadership context and assign them priorities.
4 **Career development** through giving a person the right job at the right time. People grow as leaders through the actual practice of leading.
5 **Line managers as leadership developers** by developing the individual's potential and sharing their knowledge of leadership.
6 **Corporate culture** that is valued at all levels and should encourage a climate of self-development in leadership.
7 **The chief executive** who should be leading from the front and who owns the problem of growing leaders.

The seven principles are complementary and are likely to have a synergetic effect if applied as a whole. Although a simple framework, Adair maintains the seven principles form the first coherent and effective approach for growing leaders.[74]

> We are not born as leaders, but we are born with the potential to become a leader. This potential has to be worked on and we have to go through a learning experience to equip us to become leaders. Sometimes the potential is realised and sometimes it is not. Opportunities play a part in this; the best organisations seem to grow their own leaders. The best, the very good and the excellent do give priority to developing leaders.
>
> John Adair[75]

NO ONE BEST FORM OF LEADERSHIP

We have seen that there are many alternative forms and styles of managerial leadership. Within an organisation different individuals may fulfil the functions of leadership and there are many different styles of leadership. A potential danger with the contingency approach is that the manager may appear to lack consistency in leadership style. However, although subordinates may reasonably expect some degree of consistency from the manager in approaching the same type of problem with the same style, this is not to say that different types of problems should be approached in the same manner. Subordinates would ordinarily expect a different style of managerial leadership according to the contingencies of the situation.

The right leader for the right situation

A good manager will clearly recognise that different styles of leadership are called for in different situations. As an obvious and (hopefully) extreme example, emergency situations such as a major fire in a building demand an assertive, directive style of action. As *Rajan* also points out: 'Of course, different leadership styles are needed to cope with different situations: for example, the autocratic style makes sense when an organisation is in deep trouble and needs to achieve a rapid turn-around. That style would be counter-productive when the organisation is in a growth situation.'[76] And *Stern* maintains that although in more carefree times business gurus exalted leaders who admitted to frailty, this is not so any more. The task of sustaining growth in a sluggish market calls for driven, leather-skinned bosses. Instead of touchy-feely management the quality of 'mental toughness' is needed to help elite performers to prevail.[77]

Different types of leadership may also be most appropriate at different stages in the development of a business organisation. Leadership can also vary between public and private sectors and depend upon the size of the organisation. A primary challenge for organisational leaders in promoting innovation is:

> *Recognise and develop appropriate leadership for the different stages of the innovation process. How leaders are selected, supported, evaluated, motivated and developed is likely to differ depending upon*

the stage of the innovation process they are responsible for. For instance, transformational leadership skills may be more useful in early-stage innovation activity, such as R & D and product development, but transactional leadership skills are also essential to the smooth functioning of commercialisation.[78]

LEADERS OF THE FUTURE

Gratton points out that while we are part of organisations shaped by technology that created the patents, ideas and innovations that brought success, the past will not bring sustainable competitive advantage for the future. To do this we have to build the potential of people in our organisations, the knowledge they bring and their commitment and enthusiasm. Building human potential demands a new agenda, a new set of challenges for leaders and a redefined set of managerial capabilities. This new agenda creates a set of expectations of the leaders. Gratton sets out four expectations as the message for leaders.

- **Expectation 1: dream collectively** – create a time and a process for you and your colleagues to dream about the future; create enthusiasm and excitement and a vision for the future; view the present as a pathway to the future; allow people to work independently but within the frame of the general direction; and work to identify and co-ordinate the major themes for action.
- **Expectation 2: balance the short term with the longer term** – think in the past, the present and the future; be aware of the human scale of change and create plans of action that reflect human time scales and a capacity in human potential; build a vision for the future that engages people and allows them to understand their future role.
- **Expectation 3: build an organisation that values people** – treat people with respect and have their ideas taken seriously and allow them to believe they can make a difference; be aware of the need to create communication channels with employees; demonstrate a commitment to people; treat people with politeness, respect and dignity and create a strong role model for others to follow.
- **Expectation 4: understand the reality of the organisation** – create a deep, shared understanding of the current state of the business, and examine the metaphor of the organisation; put the building of a highly committed workforce at the centre of strategy; build a model of your organisation around high levels of trust, commitment and inspiration; develop an understanding of process fairness and justice, and understand employees' perceptions of integrity, consistency and pride.[79]

New skills and competencies

Bennis hails the arrival of new leadership and suggests that 'the leaders of the future will have to cast off the heavy burden of command and control, hierarchically based leadership'. Leaders will have to learn an entirely new set of skills and four competencies will determine the success of new leadership.

1 **The new leader understands and practises the power of appreciation** – as a generalisation most organisations are woefully neglectful of bestowing acknowledgement or appreciation, yet it is one of the most powerful motivators, especially for knowledge workers.
2 **The new leader keeps reminding people of what is important** – organisations drift into entropy and bureaucratisation of imagination when they forget what's important. Reminding people of what is important can give meaning and value to work, and collective focused energy.
3 **The new leader generates and sustains trust** – the terms of the new social contract of work have changed and no one can depend on lifelong loyalty or commitment to any organisation. Trust has powerful connotations and the ingredients are a combination of competencies, constancy, caring, fairness, candour and, most of all, authenticity.

4 **The new leader and the led are intimate allies** – new leadership is all about great leaders being made by great groups and by organisations that create the social architecture of respect and dignity, and great leadership brings that about. Without each other, the leader and the led are culturally impoverished.

> *The post-bureaucratic organization requires a new kind of alliance between leaders and the led. Today's organizations are evolving into federations, networks, clusters, cross-functional teams, temporary systems, ad hoc task forces, lattices, modules, matrices – almost anything but pyramids with their obsolete top–down leadership. The new leader will encourage healthy dissent and value those followers courageous enough to say no. It will go to the leader who exults in cultural differences and knows that diversity is the best hope for long-term survival and success. This does not mark the end of leadership. Rather the need for a new, far more subtle and indirect form of influence for leaders to be effective.*[80]

In his discussion on the future of management, *Hamel* argues the point that in any constitutional democracy success does not depend upon brilliant leadership. If democracies are more resilient than large companies it is not because they are better led. In a democracy, the pace of change depends only tangentially on the vision and moral courage of those in power. 'The real challenge, then, isn't to hire or grow great leaders, but to build companies that can thrive with less-than-perfect leaders.'[81]

Critical reflection

'There is much commentary on the need for less hierarchical structures and for a changed culture of leadership based on skills and competencies throughout the organisation as a whole.'

But how realistic is this? What does such a changed culture actually entail and how can leadership potential best be developed? And what do you see as the future of leadership?

SYNOPSIS

■ There are many ways of looking at leadership and many interpretations of its meaning, but essentially it is a relationship through which one person influences the behaviour or actions of other people. The leader–follower relationship is reciprocal and effective leadership is a two-way process. Leadership is related to motivation, the process of communication, the activities of groups and the process of empowerment. The changing nature of business organisations has placed increasing importance on leadership.

■ There is arguably a close relationship between leadership and management, especially in work organisations, and a tendency to see them as synonymous. However, there is much to suggest that there are differences between the two and it does not follow that every leader is a manager. Leadership occurs at many different levels and in many different ways. It

may be viewed in more general terms, with emphasis on interpersonal behaviour in a broader context.

■ Due to its complex nature there are many alternative ways of analysing leadership. Leadership may be examined in terms of the qualities or traits approach; the functional or group approach; as a behavioural category; styles of leadership; through the situational approach and contingency models; the distinction between transactional or transformational leadership; and inspirational or visionary leadership.

■ Contingency theories draw attention to the interactions between the variables involved in a leadership situation and patterns of leadership behaviour. The most appropriate form of leadership is dependent upon the variables in a particular leadership situation. Different contingency theories have concentrated on different

situational variables. These include favourability of the leadership situation, decision acceptance and decision quality, path–goal theory, and the 'readiness' of followers.

■ The attention given to transformational leadership and the importance of charisma has given rise to an increasing focus on the concept of leaders creating a vision with which others can identify and inspiring followers to improve organisational performance. There is, however, doubt about the extent to which leaders possess these personal qualities. Leadership is a dynamic form of behaviour and the leader's influence is dependent upon the type of power exercised over other people. Another major influence on leadership behaviour may be national culture.

■ Attention needs to be given to the criteria for leadership effectiveness and to leadership development. Leaders of the future will face new expectations and will need to learn new sets of skills. There are many variables that underlie the effectiveness of leadership, including dimensions of national culture. There is no one best form or style of leadership. The most successful form of leadership behaviour is a product of the total leadership situation. Leaders of the future will need to work within less hierarchical based systems of command and control.

REVIEW AND DISCUSSION QUESTIONS

1 Explain clearly what you understand by the meaning of leadership. How would you distinguish leadership from management?

2 Distinguish between different approaches to the study of leadership and discuss critically what you see as the relevance today of each of these approaches.

3 Using the Tannenbaum and Schmidt continuum, identify, with reasons, your preferred style of leadership. Give an example of a situation in which you might need to adopt an alternative style of leadership.

4 What do you understand by leader–situation models of leadership? Assess the practical value to the manager of: (i) Fiedler's contingency model of leadership effectiveness; and (ii) Hersey and Blanchard's readiness of the followers or group situational model.

5 Discuss the main sources of power and leadership influence. Give a practical example of each of these main sources of power and influence within your own organisation.

6 Explain clearly the nature and main features of transformational leadership. Give your own examples of people you would regard as transformational leaders. Discuss critically the relevance of personality and charisma for effective leadership.

7 If you were a consultant on leadership, what areas of needs would you include in designing a leadership development programme for managers in a large work organisation? Justify your ideas.

8 Discuss the main situational variables that are likely to influence the most appropriate form of managerial leadership behaviour. Detail three work situations in which a different style of leadership is likely to be most effective.

MANAGEMENT IN THE NEWS

Managing the mood is crucial

Stefan Stern

'Moaning is not a management task,' Rupert Stadler, chief executive of the German carmaker Audi, told this newspaper this month. 'We can all join in the moaning, or we can make a virtue out of the plight. I am rather doing the latter.' Mr Stadler is choosing to accentuate the positive. After all, who wants to be led by a pessimist? Jeffrey Immelt, chief executive of General Electric, keeps his darker thoughts to himself while maintaining a public breeziness. As he told the Harvard Business School conference last October: 'You can't sit there in front of over 300,000 people and say: "I don't know what to do!" You have to say: "We're gonna nail this one, and here's why!"'

Management in the news – continued

Leaders have to be resilient. At the moment the bad news is coming not in single spies, but in battalions. Tough trading conditions test character as much as business acumen. Your physical and emotional response to these challenges is just as important as the decisions you actually take, because employees are more sensitive to mood than leaders often realise. And moods are contagious. Research carried out at New York University and the University of Michigan found that in 70 different teams, people working together in meetings ended up sharing moods – whether good or bad – within two hours. And bad moods spread faster than good ones. In their 2001 Harvard Business Review article 'Primal Leadership', Daniel Goleman, Richard Boyatzis and Annie McKie argued that one of the key duties of leadership is to manage your emotions with care. 'Moods that start at the top tend to move the fastest because everyone watches the boss,' they wrote. 'They take their emotional cues from him. Even when the boss isn't highly visible his attitude affects the mood of his direct reports, and a domino effect ripples throughout the company.'

Leaders risk reverting to earlier, less skilful versions of themselves under pressure. They can slip into a default mode of frantic busyness, which to colleagues may look a lot like panic. They can find themselves instinctively adopting a crude command and control management style, even though they know this might not be the best way to deal with an intelligent, questioning (but anxious) workforce. Instead leaders should be trying to create a greater sense of safety. There are four things they can do to achieve this.

- First, they must take prompt and considered action in the face of any crisis.
- Second, leaders need to communicate honestly and consistently.
- Third, leaders have to make an emotional connection with the workforce. This is not a time to be remote or aloof. That will only add to the sense of uncertainty.
- Lastly, leaders need to inspire. A 'call to arms' can work if it follows on from the sort of confidence-boosting measures described above. But it will fall flat if the leader has failed to make a strong connection with his colleagues, and they are too fearful to be able to buy into it.

So yes, the way leaders behave matters. Temperament and character can help stop a bad situation from getting worse. But markets are tough, and recovery seems a long way off. Mr Stadler is going to need all his optimism.

Source: Stern, S. 'Managing the Mood Is Crucial', *Financial Times*, 23 March 2009. Copyright © 2009 The Financial Times Limited, reproduced with permission.

Discussion questions

1 What does this article tell us about the qualities or traits needed to be a good leader?

2 Analyse the article using Hersey and Blanchard's situational leadership model. Which of the four 'situations' is described? What skills would you add to those suggested in the article to enable managers to lead effectively in these circumstances?

ASSIGNMENT 1

a Think of:

 (i) one of the 'best' leaders, *and*

 (ii) one of the 'worst' leaders that you have experienced, preferably in a work situation.

b Identify and list those specific qualities, or lack of them, which were characteristic of *each* leader. Where possible, draw up your list under three broad headings of:

 (i) personal attributes – for example, appearance, mannerisms, intelligence;

 (ii) social relationships – for example, approachability, understanding, interests;

 (iii) task performance – for example, knowledge, empowerment, discipline.

c Give a brief description of an actual situation that illustrates the behaviour/actions of *each* leader and the results of such behaviour/action. Keep your answer balanced. Try to be as objective as possible and avoid personal bias.

d Draw up your *own* list, with brief supporting descriptions, of the main characteristics you would expect to be exhibited by a successful leader. Be prepared to justify your lists and descriptions in class discussion.

ASSIGNMENT 2

Your leadership style

For each of the following ten pairs of statements, divide five points between the two according to your beliefs, perceptions of yourself, or according to which of the two statements characterises you better. The five points may be divided between the A and B statements in any way you wish with the constraint that only whole positive integers may be used (i.e. you may not split the points equally between the two). Weigh your choices between the two according to the one that better characterises you or your beliefs.

1. A As leader I have a primary mission of maintaining stability. _____
 B As leader I have a primary mission of change. _____

2. A As leader I must cause events. _____
 B As leader I must facilitate events. _____

3. A I am concerned that my followers are rewarded equitably for their work. _____
 B I am concerned about what my followers want in life. _____

4. A My preference is to think long-range: What might be. _____
 B My preference is to think short-range: What is realistic. _____

5. A As leader I spend considerable energy in managing separate but related goals. _____
 B As leader I spend considerable energy in arousing hopes, expectations, and aspiration among my followers. _____

6. A While not in a formal classroom sense, I believe that a significant part of my leadership is that of a teacher. _____
 B I believe that a significant part of my leadership is that of a facilitator. _____

7. A As leader I must engage with followers at an equal level of morality. _____
 B As leader I must represent a higher morality. _____

8. A I enjoy stimulating followers to want to do more. _____
 B I enjoy rewarding followers for a job well done. _____

9. A Leadership should be practical. _____
 B Leadership should be inspirational. _____

10. A What power I have to influence others comes primarily from my ability to get people to identify with me and my ideas. _____
 B What power I have to influence others comes primarily from my status and position. _____

Details of scoring and interpretation will be provided by your tutor.

PERSONAL AWARENESS AND SKILLS EXERCISE

Objectives

Completing this exercise should help you to enhance the following skills:

- Evaluate your leadership skills;
- Review attributes associated with leadership;
- Advance your self-knowledge of teamwork and leadership.

Exercise

Evaluate your skills – Self-knowledge is crucial for evaluating achievements and potential. Below is a list of attributes associated with leadership. Read through these statements and evaluate the leadership skills demonstrated by your team and those that you display. Score yourself from one to ten for each attribute or put ticks or crosses in the boxes. Use this information to consider areas where you or your team could develop.

→

Personal awareness and skills exercise – continued

1 Demonstrating initiative, delivering operational excellence, implementing decisions and delivering results

I reinforce people's determination to do the right thing. ☐
I have a strong work ethic. ☐
I do things right the first time. ☐
I stay focused on priorities and recognise when to delegate tasks. ☐
I stretch myself to meet the values of others and myself simultaneously. ☐
I demonstrate values by tangible and visible actions. ☐
I choose service over self-interest. ☐
I act with integrity. ☐

2 Drawing groups together, enjoying team management and placing importance on the development of others

I reward and recognise team members daily. ☐
I use analogy to simplify conceptual ideas. ☐
I connect and integrate values into the working operation of the organisation. ☐
I clarify future direction in terms that make sense. ☐
I reduce strategic plans to simple ideas which can be easily communicated. ☐
I communicate effectively with internal and external stakeholders. ☐
I target communication to the needs of the audience in pace, level and method of delivery. ☐
I break complex targets down into digestible pieces. ☐

3 Offering support, demonstrating active listening and encouraging others to achieve objectives

I demonstrate trust in others to perform effectively. ☐
I recognise that leadership is a process of upward as well as downward influence. ☐
I inspire excitement with my communication style. ☐
I encourage hard-hitting debate and dialogue. ☐
I display stature and presence to gain commitment and loyalty. ☐
I put aside personal ambition for the sake of the whole. ☐
I take time to connect with each team member. ☐
I set clear goals and success criteria, allowing people to use their initiative. ☐

4 Demonstrating decisiveness, offering inspiration and eliciting respect by touching hearts, not just minds

I take pride in winning as a team, not just individually. ☐
I foster the development of a common vision. ☐
I appear consistently enthusiastic and inspirational about the vision. ☐
I build the capacity of the next generation of leaders by investing in the team. ☐
I hold myself accountable, without blaming others. ☐
I hold myself accountable with the clear understanding that ethical standards must never be compromised. ☐
I manage the ambiguity of leadership and power. ☐
I find a sense of continuity through others. ☐

Source: The Path to Leadership: Developing a Sustainable Model within Organisations, CBI (in association with Harvey Nash), September 2005. Reproduced with permission from CBI and Caspian Publishing Ltd.

Discussion

■ How difficult was it for you to complete this exercise?
■ Are there specific attributes in which you believe you are particularly strong or weak?
■ What benefits have you gained from this exercise and what new have you learned about yourself?

Being Apple: Steve Jobs

Steve Jobs is currently CEO of Apple and one of the world's best-known business leaders. The many biographies of Jobs on the internet[82] agree on the basic details. He was born in 1955 in California. In 1976, he and Steve Wozniak founded the Apple Computer Company. The next year saw the launch of the company's second computer – the Apple II – whose success established Apple as one of the main brands in the fledgling personal computer (PC) industry. Apple went public in 1980 and by 1983 Jobs was looking for an experienced corporate manager to oversee the company's continuing expansion; he hired John Sculley from Pepsi Cola. In 1984, Apple launched the Macintosh,[83] whose innovative design was surely one of the key steps forward in the development of today's user-friendly PCs.

In 1985, Jobs fell out with the Apple board and with Sculley and resigned from the company. He went on to found the computer company NeXT, whose workstation products were seen as innovative and influential, but which were too expensive for mass market success. By the early 1990s, NeXT was concentrating on software rather than hardware, and Apple was experiencing significant financial problems as the PC market started to mature. In 1996, Apple bought NeXT and installed Jobs as interim CEO in 1997. Jobs was back and set about some radical surgery to improve Apple's profitability. The technology that arrived with the NeXT purchase allowed a new operating system to be developed and Jobs was closely associated with the development and launch of the brightly-coloured and inspirational iMac in 1998.

The 'i' prefix was adopted by Apple for a series of further innovations as its renaissance under Jobs continued, including the launch in 2001 of the spectacularly successful iPod music player and the iTunes service to support it. This success has provided the company with a whole new set of strategic options in music and entertainment. Then came the the the iPhone in 2007 and the Macbook Air, produced from an A4 envelope at its launch in 2008.[84] Steve Jobs, however, is not someone to concentrate his efforts on just a single industry. In 1986, he bought a computer graphics operation from Lucasfilm and renamed it Pixar, which became one of the leading players in computer animation. In partnership with Disney it produced a stream of immensely successful animation movies from *Toy Story* (1995) to the surprising, multi-award-winning box-office hit *Wall-e* (2008) whose character Eve owes

Where would they be without him? Apple's way of doing business has been strongly influenced by its charismatic founder Steve Jobs.

more than a little to Apple design principles. In 2006, Disney and Pixar merged, leaving Jobs as a significant shareholder in Disney and a member of the Disney board.

Cool entrepreneurship

At one level, Steve Jobs can be seen as one of the group of successful young men who made the information revolution happen over the last three decades. These new entrepreneurs didn't fit the traditional model of the buttoned-down businessman – they weren't always academically successful (like Michael Dell, Jobs dropped out of college), they dressed casually and thought unconventionally. While they may differ greatly in leadership style and manner, they share a dedicated, driven, even obsessive approach to work coupled to a strong vision of the change they want to create. There has always, however, been something distinctive about the Apple way of doing things, resulting in the fierce loyalty that often inspires Apple users. As one commentator put it:

Lodged in the DNA of Silicon Valley, there is a rebel gene known as Apple Computer. Most of the other ingredients are the generally uniform, inoffensive elements you would expect to find in the soul of an engineer . . . The Apple gene comes from an altogether different place. Its essence is one part design flair, two parts marketing hype. It carries elements of risk-taking and inventiveness. It is closely intertwined with the technical drive that pervades Silicon Valley and is the source of occasional startling originality, yet the technology is always subservient to

something else. If Apple's genetic make-up stands apart, it owes much to Steve Jobs.[85]

Evidence that Apple is centred on the personality of its leader is plentiful. Jobs supplies the inspiration and vision and is the company's face. When there is a key new product to launch, it is usually the CEO who reveals it to the world, having been personally involved in whatever it took to bring the product into being. As a recent report observed, his keynote speeches at Apple conferences are 'more like rock concerts than corporate events',[86] with Jobs centre stage.

What is it about Steve Jobs' leadership that commands such attention? He values pure creativity very highly, but in the thousands of words written about him on the internet, adjectives such as 'tolerant' or 'easygoing' do not feature very often. The words 'passionate, charming, inspirational, abrasive'[87] are much more representative, with many expressing much stronger views. Jobs seems to be someone who sets himself very high standards and then demands the same of everyone around him. This can lead to disappointment, frustration, anger and – on occasion – harsh treatment of those who are seen as having let him and the company down. Jobs provided an insight into this mentality in an interview in 1995 with the Smithsonian Institution:[88]

I always considered part of my job was to keep the quality level of people in the organizations I work with very high. That's what I consider one of the few things I actually can contribute individually . . . to instil in the organization the goal of only having 'A' players. . . . the difference between the worst taxi cab driver and the best taxi cab driver to get you crosstown Manhattan might be two to one. The best one will get you there in fifteen minutes, the worst one will get you there in a half an hour. . . . In the field that I'm in the difference between the best person and the worst person is about a hundred to one or more. The difference between a good software person and a great software person is fifty to one. . . . Therefore, I have found, not just in software, but in everything I've done it really pays to go after the best people in the world. It's painful when you have some people who are not the best people in the world and you have to get rid of them; but I found that my job has sometimes exactly been that: to get rid of some people who didn't measure up and I've always tried to do it in a humane way. But nonetheless it has to be done and it is never fun.

Although Jobs became and remained wealthy over most of his career, his motivation seems not to centre on money. His annual salary as Apple's CEO is famously set at $1. What drives him is innovation: he is the man who wants 'to put a ding in the universe'.[89] This means not purely technical innovation, but the ability to imagine products that are revolutionary in their impact on everyday life. Design and marketing have been integral to the Apple appeal, resulting in some truly transformative (and very successful) products like the Macintosh and the iPod, but also many that did not really connect commercially. This demanding agenda has had its costs, both for the company and for Jobs personally. Business strategy commentators sometimes observe that the real money is to be made by changing the way a business works, not by pure innovation.

Technical innovation will earn you lots of adoring fans (think Apple). Business-model innovation will earn you lots of money (think Dell) . . . If your cool new thing doesn't generate enough money to cover costs and make a profit, it isn't innovation. It's art.[90]

If wealth is the scorecard, then Steve Jobs, who is at 178 on the 2009 Forbes list of the world's richest people, doesn't come close to Bill Gates at number one or Michael Dell at 25.[91] The overall impression though is that this is not the point for Jobs; changing the world is more important than building the biggest pile of money.

The succession problem

The comparison with Bill Gates leads to another issue that often crops up for organisations that are dominated by a strong and charismatic leader: that of succession. A recent business news article[92] pointed out that Microsoft had recently gone to some lengths to plan for Bill Gates' gradual retirement from the company. Gates' role had been split into two, with a successor lined up within the company for each part. The pre-announced two-year transition was intended to reassure the markets about the future for a post-Gates Microsoft. At Apple, things weren't so clear. In August 2004, Jobs underwent surgery for a rare form of pancreatic cancer. He survived and was back at work after just one month; and amidst much speculation he took a further six months of medical leave in 2009. His brush with mortality caused many to wonder about Apple's prospects without him, although Jobs himself seems sanguine;

Remembering that I'll be dead soon is the most important tool I've ever encountered to help me make the big choices in life.[93]

Nevertheless, this remains an important question for the company. A quote from venture capitalist Michael Moritz sums up Jobs' importance to Apple:

Steve is an utterly remarkable man – one of the most interesting, original and creative businessmen of the last 50 years. His achievements at both Apple and Pixar over the last ten years put paid to the doubters who say that no individual can change the course of a company or industry – let alone two companies or industries.[94]

Apple has never done things in a conventional way and it may be that asking about succession planning is

missing the point about the way the organisation is run. As a leader, Steve Jobs' charismatic and demanding presence has pervaded Apple and made it what it is today. The question must now be faced: is it impossible to replace the magic of Steve Jobs, or is he 'awesome, but not the entire company'?[95]

Your tasks

1 How and to what extent does Steve Jobs' career illuminate the difference between management and leadership?

2 How can Steve Jobs' leadership style be analysed? To what extent does the evidence so far conform to the Burns model of transformational leadership?

3 Jobs' career has been in two industries that are characterised by rapid market change, fast technological development and considerable turbulence. Critically examine the extent to which these situational factors bear upon the leadership style that Jobs has shown over the years.

Notes and references

1 Bass, B. M. *Handbook of Leadership: Theory, Research and Managerial Applications*, third edition, The Free Press (1990), p. 11.

2 Crainer, S. 'Have the Corporate Superheroes Had Their Day?', *Professional Manager*, March 1995, pp. 8–12.

3 See, for example, Adair, J. *Leadership and Motivation*, Kogan Page (2006).

4 'Leadership for Innovation', Advanced Institute of Management Research, 2005.

5 Levine, S. R. 'The Value-Based Edu-Leader', in Chowdhury, S. (ed.) *Management 21C*, Financial Times Prentice Hall (2000), p. 90.

6 CBI 'The Path to Leadership: Developing a Sustainable Model within Organisations', Caspian Publishing (2005), p. 4.

7 Belbin, R. M. *Changing the Way We Work*, Butterworth-Heinemann (1997), p. 98.

8 Zaleznik, A. 'Managers and Leaders: Are They Different?', *Harvard Business Review*, May–June 1977, pp. 67–78.

9 Watson, C. M. 'Leadership, Management and the Seven Keys', *Business Horizons*, March–April 1983, pp. 8–13.

10 Kent, T. W. 'Leading and Managing: It Takes Two to Tango', *Management Decision*, vol. 43, no. 7/8, 2005, pp. 1010–1017

11 Fullan, M. *Leading in a Culture of Change*, Jossey-Bass (2001), p. 2.

12 Dearlove, D. 'Reinventing Leadership', in Crainer, S. and Dearlove, D. (eds) *Financial Times Handbook of Management*, second edition, Financial Times Prentice Hall (2001), p. 538.

13 Moorcroft, R. 'To Lead or to Manage? That Is the Question', *Manager, The British Journal of Administrative Management*, November 2005, p. 4.

14 Drucker, P. F. *The Practice of Management*, Heinemann Professional (1989), p. 156.

15 Bass, B. M. *Handbook of Leadership: Theory, Research and Managerial Applications*, third edition, The Free Press (1990).

16 See, for example, Bryman, A. 'Leadership in Organisations', in Clegg, S. Hardy, C. and Nord, W. (eds) *Managing Organsations: Current Issues*, Sage (1999), pp. 26–62.

17 Kotter, J. P. 'What Leaders Really Do', *Harvard Business Review*, May–June 1990, p. 103.

18 Whitehead, M. 'Everyone's a Leader Now', *Supply Management*, 25 April 2002, pp. 22–4.

19 Adair, J. *Action-Centred Leadership*, Gower Press (1979). See also Adair, J. *The Skills of Leadership*, Gower Press (1984).

20 Adair, J. *Leadership and Motivation*, Kogan Page (2006).

21 Fleishman, E. A. 'Leadership Climate, Human Relations Training and Supervisory Behavior', in Fleishman, E. A. and Bass, A. R. *Studies in Personnel and Industrial Psychology*, third edition, Dorsey (1974).

22 Bryman, A. 'Leadership in Organisations', in Clegg, S. Hardy, C. and Nord, W. (eds) *Managing Organisations: Current Issues*, Sage (1999), pp. 26–62.

23 Likert, R. *New Patterns of Management*, McGraw-Hill (1961).

24 Tannenbaum, R. and Schmidt, W. H. 'How to Choose a Leadership Pattern', *Harvard Business Review*, May–June 1973, pp. 162–75, 178–80.

25 Fiedler, F. E. *A Theory of Leadership Effectiveness*, McGraw-Hill (1967).

26 See, for example, Yukl, G. *Leadership in Organizations*, fifth edition, Prentice Hall (2002).

27 Vroom, V. H. and Yetton, P. W. *Leadership and Decision-Making*, University of Pittsburgh Press (1973).

28 Vroom, V. H. and Jago, A. G. *The New Leadership: Managing Participation in Organizations*, Prentice-Hall (1988).

29 House, R. J. 'A Path–Goal Theory of Leadership Effectiveness', *Administrative Science Quarterly*, vol. 16, September 1971, pp. 321–38.

30 House, R. J. and Dessler, G. 'The Path–Goal Theory of Leadership', in Hunt, J. G. and Larson, L. L. (eds) *Contingency Approaches to Leadership*, Southern Illinois University Press (1974).

31 Hersey, P. and Blanchard, K. H. *Management of Organizational Behavior: Utilizing Human Resources*, sixth edition, Prentice-Hall (1993).

32 Burns, J. M. *Leadership*, Harper & Row (1978).

33 Bass, B. M. *Leadership and Performance Beyond Expectations*, Free Press (1985).

34 Bass, B. M. and Avolio, B. J. *Improving Organizational Performance Through Transformational Leadership*, Sage Publications (1994).

35 Yukl, G. *Leadership in Organizations*, sixth edition, Pearson Prentice Hall (2006).

36 Kreitner, R., Kinicki, A. and Buelens, M. *Organizational Behaviour*, First European edition, McGraw-Hill (1999), p. 487.

37 Whitehead, M. 'Everyone's a Leader Now', *Supply Management*, 25, April 2002, pp. 22–4.

38 Kahan, S. 'Visionary Leadership', *The Great Washington Society of Association Executives*, www.leader-values.com (accessed 28 January 2006).

39 Kanter, R. M. *Confidence: Leadership and the Psychology of Turnarounds*, Random House (2004), pp. 325–6.

40 Weber, M. *The Theory of Social and Economic Organization*, Oxford University Press (1947).

41 Conger, J. 'Charisma and How to Grow It', *Management Today*, December 1999, pp. 78–81.

42 Conger, J. 'The Danger of Delusion', *Financial Times*, 29 November 2002.

43 Dearlove, D. 'Reinventing Leadership', in Crainer, S. and Dearlove, D. (eds) *Financial Times Handbook of Management*, second edition, Financial Times Prentice Hall (2001), p. 538.

44 Bloomfield, S. 'Charismatic Leaders are Passé', *Professional Manager*, vol. 12, no. 1, January 2003, p. 37.

45 Adair, J. *The Inspirational Leader: How to Motivate, Encourage and Achieve Success*, Kogan Page (2003).

46 Gratton, L. *The Democratic Enterprise*, Financial Times Prentice Hall (2004).

47 Witzel, M. 'Book Review: A Rewarding Read if You Want to Lead', www.ft.com (accessed 31 January 2006).

48 Goffee, R. and Jones, G. *Why Should Anyone Be Led By You?*, Harvard Business School Press (2006).

49 Nicholson, (Sir) B. 'In My Opinion', *Management Today*, January 2006, p. 10.

50 Horne, M. and Jones, D. S. *Leadership: The Challenge for All?*, Chartered Management Institute (2001).

51 'Inspired Leadership: Insights into People Who Inspire Exceptional Performance', Department of Trade and Industry, August 2004.

52 Munshi, N. *et al.* 'Leading for Innovation: The Impact of Leadership on Innovation', Advanced Institute of Management Research, September 2005.

53 Bass, B. M. *Handbook of Leadership: Theory, Research and Managerial Applications*, third edition, The Free Press (1990), p. 11.

54 McGregor, D. *The Human Side of Enterprise*, Penguin (1987), p. 182.

55 Kouzes, J. M. and Posner, B. Z. 'The Janusian Leader', in Chowdhury, S. (ed.) *Management 21C*, Financial Times Prentice Hall (2000), p. 18.

56 Fullan, M. *Leading in a Culture of Change*, Jossey-Bass (2001), p. 5.

57 French, J. R. P. and Raven, B. 'The Bases of Social Power', in Cartwright, D. and Zander, A. F. (eds) *Group Dynamics: Research and Theory*, third edition, Harper and Row (1968).

58 Finlay, P. *Strategic Management: An Introduction to Business and Corporate Strategy*, Financial Times Prentice Hall (2000), p. 103.

59 Yukl, G. *Leadership in Organizations*, sixth edition, Pearson Prentice Hall (2006).

60 Roddick, A. *Body and Soul*, Ebury Press (1991), p. 214.

61 Lloyd, B. 'Balancing Power with Responsibility and Wisdom', *Professional Manager*, vol. 17, no. 3, May 2008, p. 37.

62 Goleman, D. 'Leadership That Gets Results', *Harvard Business Review*, vol. 78, no. 2, March–April 2000, pp. 78–90.

63 Goleman, D. reported in 'Leaders in London: Fifth Annual International Leadership Summit', *Manager: The British Journal of Administrative Management*, Winter 2009, pp. 17–21.

64 McCabe, B. 'The Disabling Shadow of Leadership', *Manager, British Journal of Administrative Management*, April/May 2005, pp. 16–17.

65 Masson, L. 'Leading through Turbulent Times', *Chartered Secretary*, June 2008, p. 16.

66 Reeves, R., and Knell, J. 'Your Mini MBA', *Management Today*, March 2009, pp. 60–4.

67 McGregor, D, *The Human Side of Enterprise*, Penguin (1987).

68 Tannenbaum, R. and Schmidt, W. H. 'How to Choose a Leadership Pattern', *Harvard Business Review*, May–June 1973, pp. 162–75, 178–80.

69 Tayeb, M. 'Cross-Cultural Leadership', in CBI, *The Path to Leadership: Developing a Sustainable Model within Organisations*, Caspian Publishing (2005), pp. 14–20.

70 House, R. J., Hanges, P. J., Javidan, M., Dorfman, P. J. and Gupta, V. (eds) *Culture, Leadership and Organisations: The GLOBE Study of 62 Societies*, Sage (2004).

71 Investors in People UK *The Leadership and Management Model* (2003), p. 3.

72 Melville-Ross, T. 'A Leadership Culture Has to Run Right Through an Organisation', *Professional Manager*, vol. 16, no. 1, January 2007, pp. 18–21.

73 Cutler, A. 'A Good Fit Is Essential', *Professional Manager*, vol. 14, no. 3, May 2005, p. 38.

74 Adair, J. *How to Grow Leaders*, Kogan Page (2005).

75 'A Conversation with John Adair', *Manager: The British Journal of Administrative Management*, April/May 2007, p. 20.

76 Rajan, A. 'Meaning of Leadership in 2002', *Professional Manager*, March 2002, p. 33.

77 Stern, S. 'If You Think You're Hard Enough', *Management Today*, March 2003, pp. 46–51.

78 'Leadership for Innovation', Advanced Institute of Management Research, March 2005.

79 Gratton, L. *Living Strategy: Putting People at the Heart of Corporate Purpose*, Financial Times Prentice Hall (2000).

80 Bennis, W. 'The New Leadership', in Crainer, S. and Dearlove, D. (eds) *Financial Times Handbook of Management*, second edition, Financial Times Prentice Hall (2001), pp. 546–50.

81 Hamel, G. with Breen, B. *The Future of Management*, Harvard Business School Press (2007), p. 169.

82 See, for example, the selection at http://www.answers.com/topic/steve-jobs.

83 Those around in that year may recall the iconic Orwellian '1984' television advert which cost $1.5m, was directed by Ridley Scott, aired only once in the USA during the 1984 Superbowl, and made advertising history with its implied critique of IBM. If you missed it, then you can view it on YouTube, or at www.apple-history.com.

84 Recordings of the unveilings can be viewed on YouTube, www.youtube.com.

85 Waters, R. 'Apple Bites Back', *Financial Times*, 10 June 2005.

86 Naughton, J. and Mathiason, N. 'Will Jobs' Departure Cut Apple to the Core?', *Observer Business and Media*, 30 July 2006.

87 Waters, R. 'Apple Bites Back', *Financial Times*, 10 June 2005.

88 'Oral and Video Histories: Steve Jobs', http://americanhistory.si.edu/collections/comphist/sj1.html, interview dated 20 April 1995.

89 http://www.quotationsbook.com/quotes/215/view and many others.

90 Hawn, C. 'If He's So Smart . . . Steve Jobs, Apple and the Limits to Innovation', *Fast Company Magazine*, January 2004, at http://www.fastcompany.com/magazine/78/jobs.html.

91 See http://www.forbes.com/2009/03/11/worlds-richest-people-billionaires-2009-billionaires_land.html.

92 Naughton, J. and Mathiason, N. 'Will Jobs' Departure Cut Apple to the Core?', *Observer Business and Media*, 30 July 2006.

93 Shiels, M. 'Steve Jobs a National Treasure', BBC news website, 15 January 2009 (accessed 23 July 2009).

94 Quoted in Waters, R. 'Apple Bites Back', *Financial Times*, 10 June 2005.

95 Shiels, M. 'Steve Jobs a National Treasure', BBC news website, 15 January 2009 (accessed 23 July 2009).

ACADEMIC VIEWPOINT

Below you will find the title and abstract of a recent article in an academic journal which explores a topic relevant to the chapters in Part 3.

Baruch, Y. and Jenkins, S. 'Swearing at Work and Permissive Leadership Culture', *Leadership and Organizational Development Journal*, vol. 28, no. 6, 2006, pp. 492–507.

Abstract

Purpose: The purpose of this paper is to examine the use of expletives and swearing in the workplace. It proposes to challenge leadership style and to suggest ideas for management best practice.

Design/methodology/approach: Case studies and qualitative analysis were applied, methods that fit well for this sensitive topic.

Findings: This paper identifies the relevance, and even the importance, of using non-conventional and sometimes uncivil language in the workplace.

Research limitations/implications: Sample size and representativeness present limitations.

Practical implications: There is a need for leaders to apply, under certain circumstances, a permissive leadership culture. This paper advises leaders on how it may lead to positive consequences.

Originality/value: The paper is an original contribution to an area where research is scarce. A certain originality element stems from the fact that, focusing on swearing language, the paper found it necessary to use swear words (avoiding usage of the explicit form); bearing in mind the purpose of the paper, the paper hopes that this will not cause offence to the readership of the journal.

Commentary

Academic discussion of topics such as communication in relation to group dynamics, workplace culture and leadership style tend to focus on formal behaviours. However, the reality of many work environments (and indeed the fictionalised depiction of the workplace in film and on television) is often characterised by informality and 'colourful' language including swearing. There is often an assumption that swearing and bad language are negative behaviours. This interesting paper challenges that assumption, and suggests that there are different **types** of swearing, some of which may be positive in effect. It also reveals some interesting characteristics of language use in terms of gender and culture; and it concludes with some important observations about the role of managers with regard to 'industrial language'.

N.B. The article itself contains a small number (12) of annotated expletives to illustrate points.

The article might prompt you to consider the following questions.

- What does the information in the article tell us about the importance of the 'informal' aspects of group and team behaviour?

- How can the study of workplace language, including swearing, enhance our understanding of the nature of managerial leadership?

- What light do studies of this sort shed on problems experienced by team members and team leaders who are not part of a dominant organisational culture?

- How far do you think the idea of a workplace 'language policy', initiated by managers, is feasible?

The Eden Project

If a single word can be used to sum up the achievements of Tim Smit, that word might be 'regeneration'. To turn one derelict, neglected corner of south-west England into a successful tourist business attracting millions of visitors is a remarkable achievement; but to do it twice is simply astonishing. Yet this is precisely what Smit has done; and in the Eden Project we can see the nature of this achievement through a blend of visionary and innovative leadership combined with a strong sense of the value of teamwork.

Before Eden

Cornwall is one of several parts of the UK which suffered economic decline during the later 20th century. Its industrial heritage has all but disappeared in the wake of globalisation and the shifting nature of the industrial world landscape. The last tin mine closed in 1998, and the ruined mine towers are witness to what was once the largest tin-mining industry in the world. The production of china clay remains one of Cornwall's oldest current industries, but that too is in decline and job losses in this sector continue to be announced. The fishing business is contracting, and traditional agricultural and horticultural production, mainly vegetables and flower bulbs, is being challenged by similar, year-round levels of production in developing countries. Cornwall as a county has, for some years, been in receipt of European Union Objective One funding destined to assist with economic regeneration in Europe's poorest regions. This level of relative poverty is probably something which many of the tourists who visit Cornwall's beautiful landscapes, historic properties and wild coastland do not generally see; and indeed tourism has become one of the largest single income-generating business sectors in the area. Whilst there are some strong indications that the Cornish economy might be revitalised by the arrival of new, knowledge-based industries which are supported by technological developments, tourism remains at the heart of the county's economy.[1]

In 1990, in a project which would contribute substantially to Cornwall's reputation as a tourist destination, John Willis, Tim Smit and John Nelson began to restore the long-derelict gardens surrounding the stately home and seat of the Tremayne family at Heligan, near Mevagissey. The story of this garden, its dereliction after the start of the Great War of 1914, its rediscovery following a storm in 1990 and its

The Eden Project is the realisation of one man's extraordinary vision through powerful teamwork and global co-operation.

Source: Tamsyn Williams/The Eden Project

restoration, in part as a memorial to the gardeners who would have died in the war, is one of enormous poignancy and beauty.[2] For Smit, an archaeology and anthropology graduate who had also developed a love of gardens, it was a project which enabled him to use many of his professional skills, and the garden itself has become one of England's most loved,[3] and a major attraction for Cornwall.

However, while Heligan is horticultural archaeology and the gardens today are, in essence, a living museum of 19th-century estate gardening, the Eden Project was a very different type of restoration, and one which drew upon Smit's additional skills as a rock music producer and showman. What Smit was restoring in his second major project was land; and the vision and purpose behind the Eden Project looks to the future rather than the past.

Ten things to do with a disused clay pit . . .

Photographs of what was to become the Eden Project prior to the arrival of Tim and his team reveal the extent of the transformation. In the mid 1990s the worked-out Bodelva china clay pit near St Austell looked very much like what many believed it to be: a derelict, polluted and worthless piece of land stripped of fertile soil – essentially a 34-acre puddle. The statistics behind its transformation into one of the most spectacular tourist attractions in the country are mind-boggling. The first task, in 1998 when the project began, was to landscape the site, and shift 1.8 million tons of earth to reduce the pit side gradients, a task which took twelve dumper trucks and eight bulldozers six months. During the first

two months of work, it rained almost continuously which resulted in 43 million gallons of water draining into the clay-lined pit.[4] This was both a problem and an opportunity; the problem was to design a drainage system which would prevent the whole site turning into a soggy bog during the average English summer; but the opportunity was to demonstrate one of the founding principles of sustainability, and use the run-off water to service the site. The system designed to meet this purpose collects, on average, 22 litres a second, and almost half the water needed to run the project (including plant watering, a 22-metre waterfall in the tropical biome and the numerous toilets!) is 'grey' water, in other words that which can be harvested from the site itself. Over 85,000 tonnes of soil, made from waste products and other organic material, were needed to turn the clay-lined puddle into the fertile ground in which over a million plants of 5,000 and more species could grow, to create a series of global gardens.

The two original 'biomes', spectacular greenhouses which re-create a humid tropical environment and warm temperate climate respectively, are perhaps what most visitors remember about the project, although more than half the site is actually open-air. The Humid Tropics biome was confirmed, in 2004, by the *Guinness Book of Records* as the largest conservatory in the world at 240 metres by 100 metres by 55 metres high, enclosing 15,590 square metres. It houses 'the biggest jungle in captivity' and contains plants native to the tropical areas of the world including Malaysia, West Africa and South America as well as islands like the Seychelles. The Warm Temperate biome covers 6,540 square metres, and replicates a mediterranean climate housing plants which represent those which grow between 30° and 40° north and south of the equator. A recent addition to the buildings on site is 'The Core', the Project's education centre, the roof of which is constructed on the same mathematical principle (the Fibonacci sequence of interwoven spirals) which appears in nature in many plant formations, and which appears to be the way in which some plants pack the maximum number of seeds, spines or leaves into the smallest possible area.[5]

If you build it, they will come

The Annual Report of 2005 stated that, to that date, the Eden Project (which is a wholly owned subsidiary of the Eden Trust, a registered charity) had cost £120m to build. The money has been raised from a variety of sources including grant funding such as that from the UK government's millennium project fund; and further funding is being sought from the National Lottery to finance additional building. Together with commercial loans, the grant money is used for capital investment on the site and educational or conservation projects in

other parts of the world. Running costs in 2007/8 were £20m, and revenue comes from both the commercial activities of the Project and gifts or donations.[6] The money is used to run the operation, maintain the asset base and service the commercial loans; so although as a charity it does not make a profit, it does have to run at commercially successful levels. Visitors are the major source of revenue. In its first year of operation it attracted twice the number of visitors estimated in the business plan, and over 7 million in its first five years of operation. Visitor numbers appear to be stabilising at about 1.2 million a year. But what exactly do people come to see?

Tim Smit's vision for Eden is far from being that of just another garden. He is, as we have noted, not a horticulturalist, but an archaeologist, anthropologist and former rock show organiser. The purpose of Eden is essentially to educate people about the environment and the relationship of humanity with the plant world, but to do so in such a way as to set a conservation and sustainability example which is, above all things, spectacular fun. The 2007–8 Annual Review explains this purpose thus:

> *The Eden Project exists to explore our dependence on the natural world; rebuilding connections of understanding that have faded from many people's lives. We use the living collection of plants as a canvas on which to tell stories that illustrate our dependence on plants and resources, that we are part of nature not apart from it, and that by working with the grain of nature we can develop more resilient individuals, communities and societies to face the challenges of the 21st Century.*[7]

The Project identifies three essential elements in its approach to this task;

- educational programmes; this includes the design of the site, and all the events which happen there, many of which are connected with schools and colleges or seek to convey important social messages.[8] Current programmes include 'Gardens for Life' which co-ordinates school gardening and educational activities involving 25,000 children at 400 participating schools in the UK, Kenya and India; and the 'Mud Between Your Toes' experience which aims to reconnect children with nature and the environment.
- operational practice; Eden believes the way it runs the site should be an inspiration and example to both commercial corporations and public bodies; this is part of its aim to develop the notion of Social Enterprise, 'Where the twin needs of good citizenship and the rigour of sound commerce meet'.[9] A good illustration of this is its 'waste neutral' initiative.
- Eden as convenor and agent for change; this aspect involves using the Eden venue to host major events

that facilitate dialogue and debate about significant environmental matters. For example, in May 2007 it hosted a conference of business and community leaders as part of the Prince of Wales Business Summit on Climate Change; and it has developed the Post-Mining Alliance which focuses on the problems of managing the environmental legacy of former mining areas like Bodelva itself.

The educational purpose which underlies the Project shows that this is, indeed, far more than just another garden.

Eden's education programmes present the need for environmental care to the widest possible public audience through celebrating what nature gives us – the focus is unashamedly on love and awe rather than guilt and fear, weaving expertise in horticulture, arts, media, science, technology, education and commerce in order to raise awareness and inspire people to action.[10]

The achievement of this objective requires both focused and decisive leadership, but also powerful teamwork.

Taking a lead

The television series *Gardeners of Eden*[11] which presented a year in the life of the Eden Project gives some insight into both the nature of Tim Smit's leadership style and the range of activities undertaken by the different teams required to run the Project. It also shows some of the very human problems associated with such an enterprise, including conflicts of interest between the Project's main purpose and some of the professional teams whose tasks are to contribute to that objective.

Smit generally dresses casually and has the slightly scruffy air of someone who is not accustomed to spend much of his working day in an office or behind a desk. In a *Guardian* article prior to a major lecture at the RSA, the interviewer noted some of Smit's key qualities.

Smit's secret, if there is one, seems to be that he can bring people of very different disciplines and skills together, get them to brainstorm and collaborate, and come up with the extraordinary. The Eden Project, he says, has attracted locals by the score, but also high-flying artists, businessmen, architects, scientists, engineers, educationalists, horticulturalists and ecologists from all over Britain. 'It feels like a renaissance organisation,' says one woman who left a senior management job to work there as a director and has been amazed both at what gets done and the way it works. 'It's attracted a critical mass of people, and there's this passionate belief, right through the project, that it belongs to everyone who works there, that it's a team thing. I guess it demonstrates that you can have an organisation that is highly effective financially, environmentally and socially. It's a kind of experiment to show that you can work in different ways.'

A local woman who has been with Eden since the start is more succinct. 'It's the most equal place I've known,' she says.

'This is a stage for change,' says Smit, who admits that Eden can seem like a sect to outsiders. 'Many people have made life choices to come here. Most could earn five times as much elsewhere. But I'm aware that if you want to effect real change, and we do, that you must not own it. You have got to make sure that it's owned by more than one person.'[12]

Smit is described as optimistic and positive, with a mission to make people think differently. He is concerned to challenge dogma from all sides, and is happy to question the views of committed environmentalists like José Bové as well as those of traditionalists. Although educational, he is convinced that the Eden Project need not be stuffy or seek to preach; above all fun, excitement and spectacle are integral to the educational process. This lays him open to the accusation that it is no more than a 'green theme park'; and indeed his desire to make the project a centre for spectacle and display brings him into conflict with the horticulturalists on the site. In the year of filming, it was clear that the two managers of the biomes deeply resented the disturbance and damage done to their plants by teams of electricians hired to lay lighting cables in and around the buildings to support some of the spectacles and events which are planned. A third curator-in-waiting is frustrated that the project to build the dry tropics biome which is planned to house his extensive cactus and succulent collection has been put back by several years, leapfrogged by the project to build the 'Core' education centre.

Smit is also very 'hands-on' in the sense that he is both integral to many of the special events (for instance the Rainforest Conference organised in September 2005) but is equally prepared to help selling tickets and guiding visitors on the peak season 'tricky days', peak visitor days on which staff who do not normally work with visitors are encouraged to follow his example and pitch in to help keep the operation moving.[13]

Working in Paradise

By 2008, the Project had grown to be a major local employer with 450 staff on the payroll, and 150 or more additional regular volunteer workers who are drafted in to help with (mostly) peak seasonal activities such as horticulture and visitor operations. The workforce is focused into a number of 'Eden Teams', the main one being the **Destination Team**. This team includes the **Green Team** of horticultural curators and other experts who manage the biomes and the planting, but in addition the people who run events and exhibitions as well as the retail and catering operations. This team is very much the 'front of house', as the

gardeners work in the public eye during the day. However, as the programme shows, they also work outside opening hours, often at night, to carry out certain potentially hazardous activities, such as lopping unstable branches from trees in the rainforest. It is also clear from the series that there can be significant differences of opinion and interest between the Green Team and Smit. This came to the fore when Smit planned the first major winter event, the 'Time of Gifts' festival. This was partly an attempt to increase winter visitor numbers to the site, but required special construction (of an ice rink) and lighting in order to accommodate a variety of story-telling activities in the biomes, as well as 'light-and-magic' processions and shows. The whole event clearly opened something of a rift between members of the 'green' team and Smit since many felt that their values were being compromised and the whole Project was becoming a sort of Disneyland. One curator told the BBC crew that the events not only did physical damage, but also damaged the morale of staff. Not only were curators upset, but the catering and housekeeping staff were also very concerned by the heavy demands (not least of which was having to learn to skate!) which would be made, and Smit is seen running a fairly fraught staff meeting with Destination personnel in an attempt to encourage them and gain extra commitment. When the event was successful, the staff were thrown a celebratory party, but nevertheless some of the Green Team were absent in protest. Smit explains his view about this conflict of interests:

I'm not into horticulture; my role isn't horticulture. My job is to fizz people into getting excited about horticulture, which is a very, very different activity. And actually, the certainties that horticulturalists want are exactly the sort of thing I want to shake up.[14]

While the Destination Team is clearly the face of the Eden Project, other teams include: the **Foundation Team** who work with supporters of the Project and also look outwards to develop education and other scientific and technological projects; the **Marketing Team** and the **Communications Team** who run an in-house publishing company as well as more traditional communications activities including the website;[15] the **Development Team** which is involved with major projects such as building and includes people from partner organisations such as architects and construction companies; the **Finance Team**, who ensure the project is economically viable and fully accountable to its various stakeholders; the **Creative Team** which develops and produces events, including the regular concerts, many of which feature major pop and rock artists; and the **Organisational Development Team** who 'look after our people' and are essentially concerned to link the processes and operations and build the Eden culture. Eden also includes the public as their **Visiting Team**, in other words the paying customers whose interaction with the project is vital to its continuation.

Between them Tim Smit and the Eden Project teams have been tremendously successful in both business and educational terms. Not only has a vision been realised in terms of the physical development of the site, but the benefits include an estimated increased incremental value to the Cornish economy of £1.2m in 2007–8.[16] It has created over 400 jobs, and the majority of staff were recruited locally. But above all, it has provided millions of people with a memorable and exciting experience which almost all would recommend to others.

Your tasks

In the television programme, Smit explains part of his management philosophy thus:

It is essential for me to like everybody I work with, which is not a very professional thing if you were doing an MBA; you employ people on their merits and their CVs. Bugger that for a game of darts! If I'm going to get out of bed in the morning to do something like this, I want to walk through that door really looking forward to seeing everybody that's there. And you know what? I have the tremendous privilege of that being so.

■ Using frameworks and concepts from the chapters on work groups and teams, critically review this approach to the creation of work teams and organisations. What are the strengths and the risks of taking such a view about the people who work for you?

■ Analyse Tim Smit's leadership style in the light of appropriate theories. Does it help or hinder his leadership that, as chief executive of a project about plants, he is 'not a horticulturalist'?

■ To what extent do you think that the non-profit-making nature of this organisation enhances the sense of collaboration and teamwork between various groups of the workforce?

■ Tim Smit now lectures all sorts of both commercial and non-commercial organisational leaders about management. Analyse the extent to which his approach might be transferable to both profit-making organisations and public sector ones, whose stakeholder groups are very different from those at Eden.

Notes and references

1 Smale, W. 'How Cornwall's Economy Is Fighting Back', BBC News website, 2006 http://news.bbc.co.uk (accessed 4 August 2009).
2 Smit, T. *The Lost Gardens of Heligan*, Orion Books (2000) (first published 1997).
3 Visit the Lost Gardens of Heligan website at www.heligan.com to get a feel for this glorious garden.
4 The Eden Project Guide 2004/5.
5 For instance pine cones, sunflower heads, pineapples and many cacti show this pattern.
6 Eden Project Annual Review 2007–8 available for download from the Eden Project website, www.edenproject.com (accessed 4 August 2009).
7 Eden Project Annual Review 2007–8, p. 1.
8 Eden, for instance, ran an 'Africa Calling' concert during the 2005 'Live8' day which featured a host of bands and internationally known artists from many parts of Africa.
9 Eden Project Annual Report to 27 March 2005, p. 7.
10 Eden Project Annual Review 2007–8, p. 3.
11 BBC DVD 2005 *The Eden Project: The Gardeners of Eden*, published by the BBC, covers part of the years 2004/5.
12 Vidal, J. 'Shaping the Future', *The Guardian*, 6 October 2004, available from the Guardian website at http://society.guardian.co.uk/print/0,,5031884-111982,00.html (accessed 4 August 2009).
13 BBC DVD 2005 *The Eden Project: The Gardeners of Eden*.
14 Ibid.
15 Including a webcam: see http://www.bbc.co.uk/cornwall/content/webcams/eden_webcam.shtml.
16 Eden Project Annual Review 2007–8, p. 6.

4

INDIVIDUAL DIFFERENCES AND DIVERSITY[1]

Individual differences can foster creativity, enjoyment and satisfaction at work but can also be the root of conflict and frustration. Our unique bundle of different attributes and characteristics shapes our values and what we plan to give and what we expect to receive from working. People are not homogeneous, and individual differences are the basis of diversity. Effective managers need to steer a course that matches the needs and expectations of the individual with the requirements of the organisation.

Learning outcomes

After completing this chapter you should be able to:

■ focus on valuing individual differences and factors affecting behaviour and performance;

■ apply key issues of personality studies to the work organisation;

■ explain the nature of ability and emotional intelligence;

■ detail the nature and significance of attitudes to the workplace;

■ assess the value of psychometric tests and assessments;

■ explore the nature and importance of diversity management;

■ identify dimensions of diversity and evaluate the business case for diversity.

Critical reflection

'Organisations can achieve nothing without the efforts of their individual members. Whatever the nature of an organisation's products or services, relationships at work and interactions among its members are at least equally important.'

To what extent do you agree that success at managing individual differences is the real key to organisational effectiveness?

THE RECOGNITION OF INDIVIDUALITY

As mentioned in Chapter 1, organisations are made up of their individual members. The individual is a central feature of organisational behaviour, whether acting in isolation or as part of a group, in response to expectations of the organisation, or as a result of the influences of the external environment. Where the needs of the individual and the demands of the organisation are incompatible, this can result in frustration and conflict. It is the task of management to integrate the individual and the organisation and to provide a working environment that permits the satisfaction of individual needs as well as the attainment of organisational goals.

Managing relationships at work has always been a key skill, but the speed at which organisations and the external environment are undergoing change places increasing pressure on individuals at work. The effective management of people requires not only an understanding of the individual employees but also recognition of the culture of the organisation. What is expected and accepted in one organisation may not be the same in another. For instance, creativity and individuality may be encouraged in one business but undermined by bureaucracy in another.

A discussion of individual behaviour in organisations is therefore riddled with complexity and contradictions. Managers are required to be competent at selecting the individuals who will be valuable to the organisation. They need to be observant about the individuals who are performing well and have the potential to develop within the organisation. They also need to be able to value individual difference and be sensitive to contrasting needs. Finally managers need to know themselves and understand their uniqueness and the impact their personality has on others.

Individual differences and change

Sensitivity to individual needs and differences, especially in terms of their resilience, becomes particularly significant when organisations embark on change initiatives. Even when the change appears to be relatively straightforward, the reality is likely to be messy and complex. When organisations are working through change and when change appears to be externally imposed, the management of people takes on a different dimension in terms of the sensitivity required. In this situation there is an implicit requirement of changes in attitudes and beliefs. Such changes may lead to new mindsets, new attitudes and new perceptions that enable people to cope and adjust to the different world. At these times effective management is vital; managers will be expected to understand the strains that their employees feel during times of change, but at the same time be able to deal with their own stress levels.

HOW DO INDIVIDUALS DIFFER?

Our sense of self is shaped by our inherited characteristics and by influences in our social environment. The process of growing up – such as the impact of our early family life and the country in which we live – has a significant part to play in our identity. Most social scientists would agree that both inherited and environmental factors are important in our development, and it is the way in which these factors interact which is the key to our adult personality. However, scientists differ with regard to the weight they place on these factors – some believing that our personality is heavily influenced by our inherited characteristics and will never change, others believing the reverse.

But first, what are the differences among individuals? These include:

- ethnic origin
- physique
- gender

- early family experiences
- social and cultural factors
- national culture
- motivation
- attitudes
- personality traits and types
- intelligence and abilities
- perception.

Some of these characteristics are shared with others, for example individuals who are from the same ethnic group or who have the same ability levels or who share similar physical attributes such as short-sightedness. But our uniqueness stems from the dynamic ways in which these inherited and environmental factors combine and interact. The ways in which it is possible to differentiate between individuals include an understanding of personality, the heart of individual differences and the importance and functions of attitudes. This is explored in this chapter. An understanding of the ways in which people learn is fundamental to an appreciation of individual differences and is considered in Chapter 5. The process of perception and communications is examined in Chapter 6. All contribute to a greater understanding of self and others.

PERSONALITY

Personality may be viewed as consisting of stable characteristics that explain why a person behaves in a particular way. So, for instance, independence, conscientiousness, agreeableness and self-control would be examples of these personality characteristics. However, it is only when we see/hear/observe a person that we can gain an understanding of their personality. For example, a person who is independent may show that characteristic by displaying a strong sense of self-sufficiency. We would expect him or her to take the initiative and not to depend on other people. Furthermore, if the characteristic is 'stable' we can rely on this being a consistent part of the person's behaviour. We would be surprised if the person one day demonstrated autonomy and initiative and the next withdrew and delayed any decisions. We anticipate that individuals are generally consistent in the way in which they respond to situations.

There are times when we might be surprised by somebody's behaviour and we may feel they are 'acting out of character'. Of course this would be known only if we had an understanding of their 'typical behaviour' in the first place. Individuals may exaggerate or suppress certain personality traits, for example if they are under stress or influenced by drink/drugs. It is self-evident that managers need to learn the art of 'reading' people's behaviour in order to manage relationships effectively.

NOMOTHETIC AND IDIOGRAPHIC APPROACHES

Broadly speaking, personality studies can be divided into two main approaches, labelled as nomothetic and idiographic.

The **nomothetic approach** is a measurable and specific perspective that looks at the identification of traits and personality as a collection of characteristics. These characteristics are ones that can be described, identified and measured and therefore can be subjected to observation and tests. This perspective is especially helpful for managers when they are involved in the selection, training and development of individuals. Nomothetic approaches tend to view environmental and social influences as minimal and view personality as consistent, largely inherited and resistant to change. Although they would not diminish the difficulties that measuring personality brings, nomothetic approaches would claim that it is possible to measure and predict the ways in which personality types would behave given certain circumstances.

Nomothetic researchers closely align themselves to studies that are 'scientific' in a positivistic sense. (The term positivism refers to the branch of science that is exclusively based on the objective collection of observable data – data that are beyond question.) Such an approach transfers methods used in natural sciences to the social world. Some psychologists are interested in describing and measuring characteristics and comparing individuals' scores. Does this person exhibit more or less than 'average' of this particular trait? Being able to predict behaviour is a major aim and outcome of this approach.

The **idiographic approach** is a holistic and dynamic perspective which insists that managers take into account a 'whole' understanding of the individual at work. This may also require going beyond the study of pure psychology to an understanding of the societal context in which the person lives. These are called idiographic approaches and are particularly pertinent in understanding motivation, career development and team relationships.

Idiographic approaches are concerned with understanding the uniqueness of individuals and the development of the self-concept. They regard personality development as a process that is open to change. They regard individuals as responding to the environment and people around them and see the dynamics of the interactions as playing a critical part in shaping personality. The measurement of traits is seen as largely inappropriate in that one person's responses may not be comparable to another's. They suggest that personality assessment is not a valid method of understanding the unique ways in which a person understands and responds to the world. The depth and richness of a person's personality cannot be revealed in superficial paper-and-pencil questionnaires. Furthermore, the categories defined by psychologists are too narrow in scope and depth.

Theory and the world of work

The application of theory to the world of work is not always easy and some find the process confusing when theory does not match with their experiences. Psychological investigations emphasise the complexity and variety of individual behaviour and insist that simple answers and explanations are generally inadequate. The study of personality provides an excellent example of some of the complexities involved in applying psychological theory in practice.

Consider two individuals who share similar characteristics. They are both 24 years old and have lived in the same area; both have a first-class honours degree in pharmacy and they have identical personality assessment profiles. However, we would still predict differences with regard to their attitude and performance in the workplace. In addition, differences would be predicted in the ways they interact with others. If one of the pharmacists was male and/or African, a further set of assumptions might be made. It is not only the features themselves which identify individuals as being different, it is also their interaction which leads to a unique pattern of behaviour. The complexities of the process pose a number of questions that interest psychologists and evoke different responses (*see* Tables 4.1 and 4.2).

Figure 4.1 identifies the links between the dynamics of personality and life's experiences.

Table 4.1	The role of early experiences – what is its impact?
Environment is significant	**Inherited characteristics are significant**
Approach taken by idiographic approaches	*Approach taken by nomothetic theorists*
The personalities of the two pharmacists described above are the culmination of experiences. Their personalities have been shaped by the people around them from their very earliest years. Early family life – the relationship between family members, the size of the family, the rewards and punishments exercised by parents – would have had an influence on the type of person each is now. In other words, the environment and early learning experiences have significantly contributed to their personality development.	The pharmacists inherited a genetic make-up which would remain core and would be resistant to change. Early experiences, while they may shape the person to a certain extent, do not alter the inherited make-up. Intelligence, physical appearances, physiological reactions are 'wired' in from birth – the 'core' of the individual is a 'given'.

Table 4.2	Is it possible to 'measure' an individual's personality?
No, personality is unique	**Yes, there are identifiable traits**
Approach taken by idiographic approaches	*Approach taken by nomothetic theorists*
Idiographic approaches do not believe it is possible to put personal characteristics to the test. Our very uniqueness makes comparisons difficult, if not impossible. Is it appropriate to consider the 'strength' of a trait? Our pharmacists may not always reveal their true 'self' – at times circumstances may force them to 'mask' their preferred ways of behaving. Our pharmacists may not reliably report on their own behaviour or there may be a real difference between what they say and what others see. Critics of questionnaires believe answering 'set' questions is 'forcing' responses to questions that may not be relevant. Instead it may be more appropriate to use open-ended techniques. This ensures that individuals use their own definitions and allows for greater understanding about their motivations and causes of behaviour.	Identifying an individual's personality typically refers to distinguishing traits or types. Personality traits are usually identified by what people do, the behaviour they exhibit, e.g. sociable. Psychologists have designed questionnaires which ask people to respond to a series of questions. They assert that asking a person to report on the way they feel or behave is a legitimate way of assessing personality. These self-reporting questionnaires would then be subject to quantitative methods. It is therefore possible to quantify the strength of a person's trait and to enable comparisons to be made with others. Such information then becomes a basis for prediction. For example, if a person has a high score on extraversion, it would be possible to predict the way in which the individual might behave in a given situation.

Figure 4.1	To what extent does our personality remain constant?

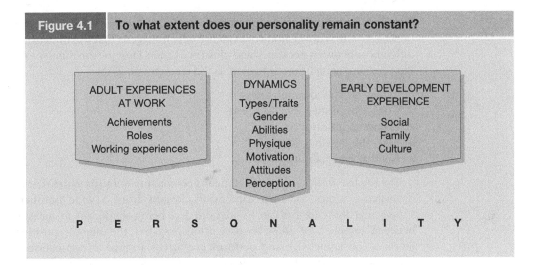

Uniqueness and similarities

Tables 4.1 and 4.2 focus on two major issues of prime importance in the study of personality. First, is personality a constant throughout our lifetime, which remains resistant to change and circumstances? Second, to what extent can we measure and compare individuals on the basis of their personality? This second question assumes that it is possible to distinguish personality characteristics in the first place. Trying to make sense of the nature of personality has resulted in a prolific number of theories, with some psychologists focusing solely on the unique make-up of individuals, others drawing comparisons between individuals or looking for broad similarities in aspirations and goals. Table 4.3 charts these differences as series of 'levels'.

In a work context we tend to be more interested in understanding 'what' an individual's personality is rather than why it is as it is. Furthermore, it is important to understand how various personality characteristics relate to performance at work. The nomothetic approach explores the 'what' of personality and the idiographic approach enriches our understanding of 'why'.

Table 4.3	Different levels of personality research
Level	**Psychologists' research interests**
LEVEL 3 ☺ ☺ ☺ ☺ ☺ ☺ ☺ ☺ ☺ ☺ ☺ ☺ Universal human features	Common human aspirations
LEVEL 2 ☺ ☺ ☺ ☺ ☺ ☺ ☺ ☺ Some shared features – gender; ability	Identification, measurements, comparison (nomothetic)
LEVEL 1 ☺ Unique combination of features	'Self' – unique interaction with the world (idiographic)

NOMOTHETIC PERSONALITY THEORIES

The big five

The identification of personality traits has been a dominant subject of research in the UK and the USA. There is now a body of evidence which suggests that five dimensions capture distinct differences between people. These clusters of traits (not personality types) are known as the Big Five[2] and sometimes expressed in the acronym OCEAN:

- Openness/closed-mindedness
- Conscientiousness/heedlessness
- Extraversion/introversion
- Agreeableness/hostility
- Neuroticism/stability

The big five form the basis of standard personality questionnaires that determine positive or negative scores for each dimension. Results from a wide number of studies have shown that these factors can be identified as being significant in measuring the variation between people.[3] Of these, conscientiousness has the highest positive link with high levels of job knowledge and performance across a range of occupations.[4] However, some researchers are critical of the descriptors used.[5] *Bentall* suggests they are 'tainted by the investigators' values' and continues: 'I suspect that most people will have a pretty clear idea of where they would like to find themselves on the dimensions of neuroticism, extraversion, openness, agreeableness and conscientiousness.' He questions the ethical and political nature of the scales.[6] The relationship between personality and work performance is also questioned by *Robertson* who suggests that the only two of the five dimensions linked consistently with high levels of performance are conscientiousness and emotional stability.[7]

Despite these reservations, the strength and value of the Big Five model has been extolled in a review by *Lord and Rust*. They conclude that:

Indeed, the five factor model has become the linchpin that holds personality assessment together, at least within the work context. Without it, how would we generalize with confidence from the validity of one work-based instrument to that of another? Furthermore, the model links the study of assessment instruments within the HR field to research in personality and related areas carried out within clinical and mainstream psychology fields in which the Big Five have also become dominant.[8]

Individual Differences and Diversity **653**

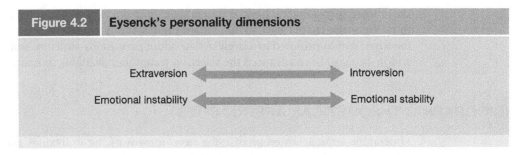

Figure 4.2	Eysenck's personality dimensions

Extraversion ⟷ Introversion

Emotional instability ⟷ Emotional stability

Eysenck

Hans Eysenck believed that personality was largely inherited and that we are born with differing physiological tendencies. He identified two major individual differences – *see* Figure 4.2. Eysenck's approach was influenced by the positivistic tradition with his research findings grounded in robust research. His aim was to produce objective evidence of personality differences using large samples of the population.[9] The two dimensions define four distinct personality types:

- stable extraverts (sanguine) with traits such as being talkative, responsive, easygoing, lively, carefree;
- unstable extraverts (choleric) with traits such as being impulsive, changeable, excitable, restless;
- stable introverts (phlegmatic) with traits such as being calm, even-tempered, peaceful, thoughtful,
- unstable introverts (melancholic) with traits such as being anxious, moody, reserved, pessimistic.

Individuals in Eysenck's theory could, therefore, be one of four main personality types. The type would lead to a predisposition of traits that would, itself, lead to the likelihood of certain behaviours. For instance, a person typed as an extravert would predictably talk over things with someone to help them think it through, while an introvert would prefer to mull it over before talking about the issue. Eysenck developed an instrument to measure personality type called EPQ (Eysenck's Personality Questionnaire).

Supporting research evidence

Although Eysenck's theory appears simplistic, it has an impressive amount of supporting research evidence. His approach has immediate appeal to managers in organisations who are concerned with predicting the future behaviour of their employees, either for selection or promotion. Given the evidence that personality is a useful predictor of behaviour, it is not surprising that the use of psychometric tests has grown substantially over the past decade and that the majority of large companies use occupational tests.[10] (Further information about testing is given later in this chapter.)

Cattell

Cattell's work resembles Eysenck's in the methods used to study personality. He used quantitative, objective techniques in order to analyse his data and followed traditional scientific procedures in order to understand the basic dimensions of personality.[11] He identified two main types of personality traits:

- **surface traits** – that seem to cluster together consistently and are observable in behaviour such as assertiveness;
- **source traits** – such as self-discipline that can only be inferred and seem to underlie and determine the traits which are likely to 'surface' into behaviour.

Unlike Eysenck, Cattell did not 'type' individuals but used 'traits' as his main personality descriptor. They also differed with regard to the determinants of personality: Eysenck viewed

the inherited physiological basis as the main determinant, whereas Cattell was more interested in taking social factors into account when understanding an individual's personality. Both theorists have contributed to a lively debate about personality structure and its measurement and in doing so have advanced the selection techniques available to managers.[12]

IDIOGRAPHIC THEORETICAL APPROACHES

Idiographic approaches emphasise the development of the individual and of individuals' views of themselves – their self-concept. Supporters of idiographic approaches are critical of the nomothetic approach that attempts to categorise individuals on the basis of group data. They argue that the techniques used to collate the group data are questionable and the outcome inappropriate to an understanding of personality. For the idiographic researchers, personality is expressed through the experiences and development of the individual. It cannot be understood outside a social context and has to be studied in the light of individuals' own perceptions of their world.

Idiographic researchers would always take into account the social circumstances of the person and in particular the relationships with others, family life and social conditions. In early childhood strong personal relationships and unconditional love are essential for later fulfilment and psychological growth. *Carl Rogers'* theory claims that personality is embedded within personal relationships. The process of becoming an adult requires the ability to give and receive unconditional regard – the warmth and respect for the *person*, who they *are*, regardless of how they behave.[13] The phrase 'the looking-glass self' was first discussed by *Cooley* – by this he meant that we come to know ourselves through our relationship with others and their reactions to us.[14]

Gurus in idiographic approaches

Erikson

Erik Erikson's theory is a good example of the idiographic approach. He viewed personality development as continuing throughout life. He was interested in the effect of experiences on the development of the self-concept and how different individuals resolved personal conflicts.[15] He recognised the importance of early childhood in establishing certain basic concepts of trust, autonomy and initiative, but also claimed that all stages of life produce different tensions and conflicts.

For Erikson, there are eight distinct stages of life, each of which produces different tensions and conflicts that have to be resolved (*see* Table 4.4). Successful resolution of these conflicts produces a healthy personality, whereas difficulties in earlier stages may produce problems later on. Erikson's theory not only makes considerable sense in terms of face validity (i.e. the

Table 4.4	Erikson's eight stages of personality development			
Stage 1	Trust	v	Mistrust	1st year
Stage 2	Autonomy	v	Doubt	2–3 years
Stage 3	Initiative	v	Guilt	4–5 years
Stage 4	Industry	v	Inferiority	6–11 years
Stage 5	Identity	v	Role confusion	12–18 years
Stage 6	Intimacy	v	Isolation	Young adult
Stage 7	Generativity	v	Self-absorption	Middle age
Stage 8	Integrity	v	Despair	Old age

Source: Adapted from Erikson, E. H. *Identity and the Life Cycle*, Norton (1980), worksheet table appendix. Copyright © 1980 by W. W. Norton & Company, Inc. Copyright © 1959 by International Universities Press, Inc. Reproduced with permission from W. W. Norton & Company Inc.

'it feels right' factor), it also links with other research indicating that managers' motivations and goals change with age (see *Hunt*, who identified nine different career/life stages).[16]

COMPLEMENTARY APPROACHES

Some researchers do not fit easily into either of the two broad approaches of nomothetic or idiographic and have their own theories and models of personality development, for example the work of Carl Jung and the cognitive approach of George Kelly.

Jung

Carl Jung's theory is of particular significance in that it bridges the psychoanalytic approach (of writers such as Sigmund Freud) with modern approaches of personality test design. His theory identifies life energy as concerned with hopes and goals of the future and not just of the past. Jung describes three levels of personality:

- a conscious level (daily reality);
- an unconscious level (contains our unique complexes);
- a collective unconscious level (store of universal and evolutionary experiences).

Jung identified four universal aspects of everyone's personality that he referred to as archetypes; for example he claimed we all strive for self-actualisation; have a darker self; have both masculine and feminine qualities; and have a persona – a role we can play.[17]

The Myers–Briggs Type Indicator® (MBTI®)

Jung is probably best known for his constructs that form the foundation for the MBTI personality indicator. The **Myers–Briggs Type Indicator (MBTI)** assessment tool was designed by *Isabel Briggs Myers* and *Katherine Briggs* who applied the rigours of systematic testing to Jung's personality functions and attitudes.[18] Jung identified differences between individuals in terms of their libidinal energy that could flow outwards to the external world (extravert) or inwards to their inner world (introvert). Personality differences would also be manifest through differing cognitive functions of thinking, feeling, sensation and intuition. The Myers–Briggs assessment added a further dimension of style of living. The personality types are shown in Figure 4.3.

The MBTI tool has promoted considerable research interest, particularly with regard to the correlation between personality type, occupations and management style – *see* Table 4.5. The Myers–Briggs assessment asserts that people tend to be attracted to and have the most satisfaction in work that allows them to express and use their psychological type preferences. Such a match enables them to handle their tasks more effectively and generates more energy. Confidence is a likely outcome of this process. The Myers–Briggs instrument is an affirmatory tool and knowledge gained through using the MBTI assessment can lead to recognition and respect for differences between people and appreciation for the value such differences bring.[19]

Table 4.5	Leadership types and the Myers–Briggs types		
ISTJ Salt of the earth	**ISFJ** Behind-the-scenes leader	**INFJ** Oracle for people	**INTJ** Designer of the future
ISTP Walking encyclopedia	**ISFP** Gentle spirit	**INFP** Values crusader	**INTP** Blueprinter of ideas
ESTP Self-starter	**ESFP** Everyone's friend	**ENFP** Spark of energy	**ENTP** Classic entrepreneur
ESTJ Take-charge leader	**ESFJ** Servant leader	**ENFJ** Values spokesperson	**ENTJ** Grand scale organiser

Figure 4.3	The Myers–Briggs Type Indicator® (MBTI®) assessment tool showing characteristics frequently associated with particular personality types

	Sensing types		Intuitive types	
Introverts	**ISTJ** Quiet, serious, earn success by thoroughness and dependability. Practical, matter-of-fact, realistic and responsible. Decide logically what should be done and work towards it steadily, regardless of distractions. Take pleasure in making everything orderly and organised – their work, their home, their life. Value traditions and loyalty.	**ISFJ** Quiet, friendly, responsible, and conscientious. Committed and steady in meeting their obligations. Thorough, painstaking and accurate. Loyal, considerate, notice and remember specifics about people who are important to them, concerned with how others feel. Strive to create an orderly and harmonious environment at work and at home.	**INFJ** Seek meaning and connection in ideas, relationships and material possessions. Want to understand what motivates people and are insightful about others. Conscientious and committed to their firm values. Develop a clear vision about how best to serve the common good. Organised and decisive in implementing their vision.	**INTJ** Have original minds and great drive for implementing their ideas and achieving their goals. Quickly see patterns in external events and develop long-range explanatory perspectives. When committed, organise a job and carry it through. Sceptical and independent, have high standards of competence and performance – for themselves and others.
	ISTP Tolerant and flexible, quiet observers until a problem appears, then act quickly to find workable solutions. Analyse what makes things work and readily get through large amounts of data to isolate the core of practical problems. Interested in cause and effect, organise facts using logical principles, value efficiency.	**ISFP** Quiet, friendly, sensitive and kind. Enjoy the present moment, what's going on around them. Like to have their own space and to work within their own time frame. Loyal and commited to their values and to people who are important to them. Dislike disagreements and conflicts, do not force their opinions or values on others.	**INFP** Idealistic, loyal to their values and to people who are important to them. Want an external life that is congruent with their values. Curious, quick to see possibilities, can be catalysts for implementing ideas. Seek to understand people and to help them fulfil their potential. Adaptable, flexible and accepting unless a value is threatened.	**INTP** Seek to develop logical explanations for everything that interests them. Theoretical and abstract, interested more in ideas than in social interaction. Quiet, contained, flexible and adaptable. Have unusual ability to focus in depth to solve problems in their area of interest. Sceptical, sometimes critical, always analytical.
Extraverts	**ESTP** Flexible and tolerant, they take a pragmatic approach focused on immediate results. Theories and conceptual explanations bore them – they want to act energetically to solve the problem. Focus on the here-and-now, spontaneous, enjoy each moment that they can be active with others. Enjoy material comforts and style. Learn best through doing.	**ESFP** Outgoing, friendly and accepting. Exuberant lovers of life, people and material comforts. Enjoy working with others to make things happen. Bring common sense and a realistic approach to their work, and make work fun. Flexible and spontaneous, adapt readily to new people and environments. Learn best by trying a new skill with other people.	**ENFP** Warmly enthusiastic and imaginative. See life as full of possibilities. Make connections between events and information very quickly, and confidently proceed based on the patterns they see. Want a lot of affirmation from others, and readily give appreciation and support. Spontaneous and flexible, often rely on their ability to improvise and their verbal fluency.	**ENTP** Quick, ingenious, stimulating, alert and outspoken. Resourceful in solving new and challenging problems. Adept at generating conceptual possibilities and then analysing them strategically. Good at reading other people. Bored by routine, will seldom do the same thing the same way, apt to turn to one new interest after another.
	ESTJ Practical, realistic, matter-of-fact. Decisive, quickly move to implement decisions. Organise projects and people to get things done, focus on getting results in the most efficient way possible. Take care of routine details. Have a clear set of logical standards, systematically follow them and want others to also. Forceful in implementing their plans.	**ESFJ** Warm-hearted, conscientious and cooperative. Want harmony in their environment, work with determination to establish it. Like to work with others to complete tasks accurately and on time. Loyal, follow through even in small matters. Notice what others need in their day-to-day lives and try to provide it. Want to be appreciated for who they are and for what they contribute.	**ENFJ** Warm, empathetic, responsive and responsible. Highly attuned to the emotions, needs and motivations of others. Find potential in everyone, want to help others fulfil their potential. May act as catalysts for individual and group growth. Loyal, responsive to praise and criticism. Sociable, facilitate others in a group, and provide inspiring leadership.	**ENTJ** Frank, decisive, assume leadership readily. Quickly see illogical and inefficient procedures and policies, develop and implement comprehensive systems to solve organisational problems. Enjoy long-term planning and goal setting. Usually well informed, well read, enjoy expanding their knowledge and passing it on to others. Forceful in presenting their ideas.

Source: Modified and reproduced by special permission of the publisher, CPP, Inc., Mountain View, CA 94043 from the *Introduction to Type®*, *Sixth Edition* booklet by Isabel Briggs Myers, revised by Linda K. Kirby and Katharine D. Myers. Copyright © 1998 by Peter B. Myers and Katharine D. Myers, All rights reserved. Further reproduction is prohibited without the publisher's written consent. Introduction to Type® is a registered trademark of the MBTI Trust, Inc. in the United States and other countries.

Critical reflection

'The MBTI assessment tool has been in and out of fashion over the years and there is constant debate about its continuing relevance and usefulness.'

What value do you believe the MBTI assessment has as a tool for measuring people's personality type? Can you give a specific example of where it might be used with advantage?

Kelly's personal construct theory

Kelly's theory of personal constructs does not just consider personality development; it considers the whole person in terms of their perceptions, attitudes and goals. For Kelly, personality is the individual's way of construing and experimenting with their world. Kelly was critical of separating the study of personality apart from the 'whole' person:

> *The castrating effect of separating personality off as a mini-psychology in its own right is perhaps best seen in the curiously named study of 'individual differences', which in fact turns out to be the study of group sameness. As a result we have focused on the establishment of general dimensions, at some point along which all individuals can be placed, rather than on a study of the dimensions which each individual develops in order to organise his own world.*[20]

For Kelly it was critical to take data from one individual person (idiography) and to employ a technique that could cope with the qualitative nature of the data to be collected. He developed the Repertory Grid that was able to measure an individual's construct of the world. Kelly was thus able to employ a clear and valid measure within an idiographic approach. This was an important advance in idiographic techniques and the repertory technique has become increasingly important as a research tool. It enables the person to use their own constructions of the world but in such a way that they are comparable and measurable.

APPLICATIONS WITHIN THE WORK ORGANISATION

Recruitment and selection

It would be rare for organisations not to take the personality of a candidate into consideration at a selection interview. For some organisations, personality is a major criterion for selection or rejection. The hospitality industry, for example, is replete with research studies demonstrating the potency of personality.[21] So, how do organisations assess a candidate's personality?

The interview remains the most usual method of selection, but there is an increasing use of objective psychometric measures. Such growth in psychometric testing is significant and a number of studies have demonstrated its growing popularity.[22] Concern has been expressed about the use and misuse of psychological instruments and there is a continuing debate within psychological circles with regard to the validity of these measures[23] – that is, do they actually measure what they claim to measure? Testing is discussed in detail later in this chapter. There are controversies and sensitivities surrounding the use of any psychological test, but tests of typical performance are especially problematic in certain circumstances. As *Anastasi* has stated:

> *The construction and use of personality inventories are beset with special difficulties over and above common problems encountered in all psychological testing. The question of faking and malingering is far more acute in personality measurement than in aptitude testing.*[24]

Critics have accused consultants and practitioners of inappropriate use of personality assessments and claim low validity between non-work-related personality assessments and work performance.[25] *Goss* suggests that the use of personality assessments not only is an infringement of the individual's privacy but also leads to unfortunate organisational consequences, with 'cloning' as an outcome. Such techniques can be perceived as a form of social engineering and an insidious form of organisational control.[26] Aware of these problems, the British Psychological Society has produced guidelines and codes of practice for users of psychometric tests. Furthermore, evidence is emerging to show that where personality questionnaires have been specifically designed and related to work characteristics, prediction and validity scores are much higher.[27]

Personal development and teamworking

Personality questionnaires can be particularly valuable if individuals complete them for their personal development or if they are used within team-building and development programmes. Here, they can initiate discussion about individual differences, the importance of diversity in teamworking and the strengths that each personality type can bring to the working situation. The notion of judgement is therefore out of the equation. Personality questionnaires can thus be a valuable diagnostic tool at the start of a coaching session or as a preliminary to a team-building process – an audit of strengths and weaknesses. At these times a discussion can be held to look at a balanced team with complementary personalities, skills and abilities. This could be followed by group training exercises designed to develop strengths and balance the weaknesses of the team. An effective team at work should be aware of the division of their strengths and weaknesses.

> *None of us is perfect; but a group of people, whose strengths and talents complement each other, can be.*[28]

Personality and social expectations

Although personality may be a powerful determinant of a manager's effectiveness, account must also be taken of the social rules and expectations within the workplace. People learn the behaviour that is expected of them and may mask their true preferences. For instance, an introverted academic lecturer may prefer to be reflective and have time to think but will be required to 'perform' in front of 200 undergraduate students and be expected to respond immediately to questions. We can respond in ways that are not 'true to type' and we may be required to take on roles at work that may run counter to our preferences. We have to learn coping strategies and adaptive skills, but for some people stress may result. Furthermore, different temperaments may be rewarded at different times depending on whether they are going through a period of growth or retrenchment. Whereas a manager may be recognised for exciting promotional activity and product development in one situation, other personality characteristics may be needed if there is a period of slow-down and attention to detail and costs. *Gray* contends that researchers will never to able to solve and develop accurate, valid and reliable performance measures. 'Many jobs or critical aspects of them, cannot be quantified. Performance measures are often justifiably subjective, vague and contradictory.'[29]

EMOTIONS AT WORK

Until recently workplaces were seen as rational, logical places where emotions were excluded or seen in a negative light. *Hochschild*'s[30] research describes the way in which some jobs require a display of certain emotions, especially those in the service industries, where customer care is inextricably linked with making people feel good. Such work has been labelled

Table 4.6	A sequence of work emotions, thought and behaviour

- Jane is asked to carry out a difficult project, usually given only to more experienced colleagues. She feels valued, flattered and trusted – also a little worried.
- While working hard on the project her emotions range from excitement and elation to fear and frustration.
- She completes the task well and feels proud and relieved.
- Jane tells her boss and shows her completed work.
- Boss gives no thanks or praise and picks out a trivial error.
- Jane then feels resentful and angry and thinks that she will never again 'put herself out' for her boss. Also feels exploited.
- Thinks about looking for another job.
- Doesn't volunteer to do additional tasks any more.
- Starts to feel sad and disappointed.
- Updates her CV and regularly starts looking at job advertisements.

Source: Briner, R. 'Feeling and Smiling', *The Psychologist*, vol. 12, no. 1, January 1999, pp. 16–19. Reproduced with permission from the British Psychological Society.

as emotional labour and distinguishes between surface acting – displaying emotion without experiencing it – and deep acting – involving thinking, visualising to induce the emotion in the situation. Briner challenges psychologists to broaden research to throw light on the complexities of emotions in the workplace. He notes that organisations specify the emotions they would like their employees to feel in the mission statements and in more subtle ways in terms of the rewards and career enhancements people receive when they display appropriate emotions. However, he suggests that little is known about the incidence of emotion at work and the part it plays in work behaviours. The illustration shown in Table 4.6, although simplistic, plots a possible sequence of events and the power of rewards (or not) and psychological well-being (or not).

Stress at work

The significance of stress at work has been discussed in Chapter 3. Personality is a contributing factor in the understanding of stress. Stress is a complex topic. It is individually defined and is intrinsically tied into an individual's perceptual system. Everyone has a range of comfort within which they can feel steady and safe. Stress occurs when the individual feels that they are working outside of that comfort zone. Individuals will differ when they feel discomfort. The effects of stress will differ too; for some, the incidence of stress may energise and activate but for others it may immobilise.

The costs of stress at individual, organisational and national levels are well known. *Cooper* has indicated the high incidence of stress throughout organisations, irrespective of seniority. He suggests that every job has its own stress fingerprint.[31] Stress is a term that is commonly used and misused; some individuals may say that they are 'stressed out' at the slightest amount of pressure and tension. It also contains a perverse sense of status; for instance, a librarian complained bitterly that her role was regarded as having low stress, implying that jobs given a 'high stress' position also ranked high in prestige.

TYPE A AND TYPE B PERSONALITIES

Two polar sets of behaviour that link with personality and health have been identified by medical students *Friedman and Rosenman*, who identified recurring patterns of personality in patients suffering from premature heart disease.[32] Individuals with a **Type A personality** are excessively competitive and thrive on hard work and long hours. They work under moderate to high levels of stress and exhibit characteristics such as:

- a high need for achievement;
- extreme competitiveness;
- impatience with obstacles to the completion of tasks;
- aggressiveness;
- a tendency to move and speak rapidly;
- an aversion to idleness;
- restlessness and urgency about time.

Individuals with a **Type B personality** are considered to exhibit the opposite characteristics from Type A. They may still have high levels of drive and ambition but are more relaxed, work at a steady pace and do not exhibit a sense of time urgency.

According to Friedman and Rosenman, Type A personalities are far more vulnerable to heart attacks than Type B personalities. Individuals who have a personality classified as Type A are more likely to suffer from heart disease under severe stress than individuals with a Type B personality.[33] Research also supports the link between stress and Type A personality.[34]

Type A people and team performance

Gratton reports on what happens when Type A people, for whom time urgency is crucial, get to work together with less time-urgent people. Type A people are likely to pay a great deal of attention to the passage of time, constantly check the time remaining and see time as their enemy. Typically they will be very efficient in their use of time, and will use deadlines to prioritise tasks and increase their work pace. Type A people have the potential to keep things moving and active but can have a detrimental impact.[35] A study by *Waller et al.*[36] found that where teams were responsible for completing creative tasks, Type A time-urgent people tended to impose strict, linear schedules on members and this reduced the innovative performance of the team.

> ### Critical reflection
>
> 'Whatever the skills, experience or qualifications of an individual, personality is arguably the most important criterion at selection interview and in their subsequent relationships with other people at work.'
>
> *What do you think? How large a part does personality play in influencing a person's aptitude for a job?*

ABILITY

Individuals vary with regard to their mental abilities and the extent to which they apply them at work, and different occupations require different skills, competencies and abilities. The 'happy' scenario is one where a match occurs between the individual's abilities and their occupation, but reality suggests that this is not always the case. The extremes include employees bored rigid with a simple task who become careless and make a succession of mistakes, and the employees who have been promoted beyond their capability. The result could be stress either for the individuals unable to cope or for their colleagues who are picking up the debris left behind.

In a similar vein to the studies of personality, different schools of thought have emerged with regard to the study of abilities. Similar debates to the ones that surround the study of personality have also swirled around the research on intelligence.

- Is intelligence inherited? Is it constant throughout life? Is it dependent upon our life's experiences, our culture, our education, etc.?
- What is the nature of intelligence? Can it be measured and how?

Is intelligence inherited?

The **nativists** believe that intelligence is mostly inherited (nature), while the **empiricists** believe that our environment shapes our behaviour and mental abilities (nurture). *Howe*[37] summarises recent convincing evidence to lend support to the empiricists. He cites evidence from early intervention programmes such as Head Start initiatives to show that intervention can have an impact on IQ. He concludes: 'The empirical findings provide no support for the pessimistic conclusion that low intelligence and the problems associated with it are inevitable and unalterable.'

The political implications of research into the nature of intelligence are striking. Some of the earliest theories influenced the educational philosophy of England and Wales, including how children were selected for different types of secondary education and the kind of help that should be given to children with special needs.

The nature of intelligence

Arguments have raged within psychologists' circles as to the nature of intelligence. Is it dependent on a general overall factor that will have an overarching effect on specific activities? Or are specific activities independent of each other? In other words, if a child shows a high level of ability at mathematics, is this dependent on an overall high general ability? General ability can be seen as a kind of powerhouse that releases some of its energy into the child's ability at mathematics. (For other children it may act as a limiting factor.) *Spearman*[38] proposed a two-factor theory of intelligence and suggested that every intellectual task involves a level of mental agility – a general factor (g) – plus specific abilities (s). This idea, developed by *Vernon*,[39] resulted in a model that placed abilities in a hierarchy (*see* Figure 4.4). Abilities at the lower end of the hierarchy are more likely to correlate, hence if a child has a good vocabulary, they are more likely to have abilities in reading and comprehension too.

Thurstone[40] claimed seven primary mental abilities that can be separately measured resulting in a profile of scores:

- spatial ability
- perceptual speed

Figure 4.4	A hierarchy of abilities

General ability (*g*) (powerhouse)

Specific ability, e.g. verbal educational ability — *Major factors* — Spatial and mechanical ability

Specific ability, e.g. verbal reasoning — *Minor factors* — Mechanical reasoning

Specific ability, e.g. vocabulary test — *Specific operational skills* — Dexterity test

Source: Adapted from Vernon, P. E. *The Structure of Human Abilities*, Methuen and Co. (1950). Reproduced with permission from Taylor and Francis.

- numerical reasoning
- verbal reasoning
- memory
- verbal fluency
- inductive reasoning.

Intelligence – one or many?

Guilford[41] criticised theories that aimed to simplify intelligence into a small number of factors. He devised a model that identified 120 different abilities (*see* Figure 4.5) and suggested that intellectual ability requires individuals to think in one of three dimensions:

- **Content.** What must the individual think about (for example, meaning of words or numbers)?
- **Operation.** What kind of thinking is the individual required to do (for example, recognising items, solving a problem, evaluating an outcome)?
- **Product.** What kind of outcome or answer is required (for example, classifying or reordering items)?

Guilford also expressed concern about the convergent nature of tests that required a single solution or answer. He suggested that tests should also be looking at an individual's ability to produce divergent answers.

Multiple intelligences

Gardner[42] felt that intelligent behaviour that could be observed in everyday life was excluded from these earlier studies. He believed that the simplification of intelligence in terms of an

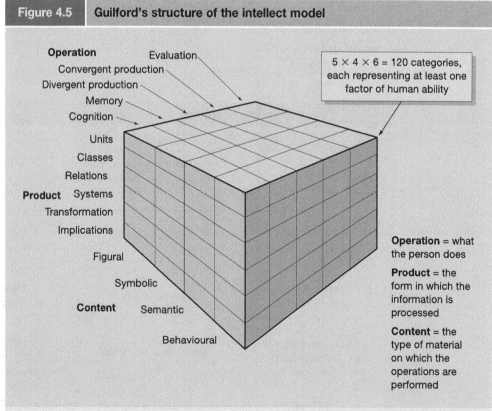

Figure 4.5 Guilford's structure of the intellect model

Source: From Guilford, J. P. 'Three Faces of Intellect', *American Psychologist*, vol. 14, pp. 469–79. Reproduced with permission from APA.

IQ measure was unrealistic and failed to take into account the full range of intelligent activity. He suggested there was a multiple of intelligences and categorised them into six varieties (all of which could be further divided):

Verbal Mathematical	Akin to the factors described in earlier theories
Spatial capacity	Ability shown by artists and architects
Kinaesthetic	Abilities of a physical nature
Musical	Abilities of musicianship
Personal intelligences	Interpersonal – skills with other people Intrapersonal – knowing oneself

EMOTIONAL INTELLIGENCE (EI)

A development of some of Gardner's ideas was made by *Goleman* who in 1955 published his ground-breaking work on EI (or EQ, for Emotional Quotient). Goleman agreed that the classical view of intelligence was too narrow. He felt that the emotional qualities of individuals should be considered. These, he felt, played a vital role in the application of intelligence in everyday life. He identified the key characteristics as:

> *abilities such as being able to motivate oneself and persist in the face of frustrations; to control impulse and delay gratification; to regulate one's moods and keep distress from swamping the ability to think; to empathise and to hope.*[43]

Emotional intelligence is the sum of a range of interpersonal skills that form the public persona. EI has received considerable attention over the last few years as the concept has been identified as a key aspect of managing people effectively. *Goleman* argues for a more empathetic style of management and suggests that EI predicts top performance and accounts for more than 85 per cent of outstanding performance in top leaders.[44] The Hay Group, working with Goleman, have identified 18 specific competencies that make up the four components of emotional intelligence and have produced an inventory designed to measure emotional competence (*see* Figure 4.6). The Emotional Competence Inventory defines EI as 'The capacity for recognising our own feelings and those of others, for motivating ourselves and for managing emotions within ourselves and with others.'[45]

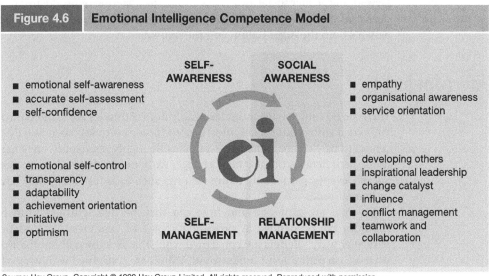

Figure 4.6	Emotional Intelligence Competence Model

SELF-AWARENESS
- emotional self-awareness
- accurate self-assessment
- self-confidence

SOCIAL AWARENESS
- empathy
- organisational awareness
- service orientation

SELF-MANAGEMENT
- emotional self-control
- transparency
- adaptability
- achievement orientation
- initiative
- optimism

RELATIONSHIP MANAGEMENT
- developing others
- inspirational leadership
- change catalyst
- influence
- conflict management
- teamwork and collaboration

Significance of emotional intelligence

Recognising and understanding the implications of emotions and being able accurately to self-assess one's inner resources, abilities and limits are key to becoming an emotionally intelligent leader. Being able to read emotional currents is an important skill for managers to develop and employ. It requires them to know and understand the individuals within their teams and the way in which the individuals relate and interact.

Recent research from the Chartered Management Institute identifies EI as one of the key skills managers and leaders will need in the coming decade.[46] According to *Landale* it should really be no surprise to find EQ so much in demand.

> *After all, we work in structures which are much flatter than ever. We have to be much faster on our feet with both colleagues and clients and, whatever the team structure, there is increasing proximity for us to build the relationships we need – fast. In this context EQ is the glue that holds people and teams together.*[47]

Developing EI

Landale refers to the importance of empathy in EI which both involves how a person self-manages and addresses how to engage with the emotions of others, and suggests a six-step process for developing EI.

- Know what you feel.
- Know why you feel it.
- Acknowledge the emotion and know how to manage it.
- Know how to motivate yourself and make yourself feel better.
- Recognise the emotions of other people and develop empathy.
- Express your feelings appropriately and manage relationships.

> *There seems little doubt that managers and leaders who have trained up in EQ have far more initiative in dealing with organizational life than those who don't. Stress will always exist at work, but EQ gives people the tools and ways of thinking to manage it to their advantage.*[48]

A number of steps in raising emotional intelligence are also suggested by *Garrett*, including ensuring staff are managing their interpersonal relationships before a problem arises, focusing first on leaders and creating an EQ culture for the organisation about itself and the companies it deals with.[49] According to *Dann*, becoming highly self-aware allows an individual to recognise inner and outer conflict and develop more proactive self-management. Developing greater social awareness allows the fostering of productive relations and a greater degree of engagement between employees and management. A manager with a high EQ benefits both the organisation and the individual.[50]

ATTITUDES

There are no limits to the attitudes people hold. Attitudes are learned throughout life and are embodied within our socialisation process. Some attitudes (such as religious beliefs) may be central to us – a core construct – and may be highly resistant to any change, whereas other, more peripheral attitudes may change with new information or personal experiences. Specific events, particularly traumatic ones such as redundancy, may have a dramatic effect on our attitudes.

So what are **attitudes** and how can they be distinguished from beliefs and values? Attitudes can be defined as providing a state of 'readiness' or tendency to respond in a particular way.[51] **Beliefs** are concerned with what is known about the world; they centre on what 'is', on reality as it is understood. **Values** are concerned with what 'should' be and what is desirable.

Gross suggests that 'to convert a belief into an attitude, a "value" ingredient is needed which, by definition, is to do with an individual's sense of what is desirable, good, valuable, worthwhile and so on'. Gross has suggested that whereas 'adults may have thousands of beliefs, they may have only hundreds of attitudes and a few dozen values'.[52] *Hofstede* defines values as a 'broad tendency to prefer certain states of affairs over others'.[53]

The functions of attitudes

Katz has suggested that attitudes and motives are interlinked and, depending on an individual's motives, attitudes can serve four main functions:

- **Knowledge.** One of the major functions is to provide a basis for the interpretation and classification of new information. Attitudes provide a knowledge base and a framework within which new information can be placed.
- **Expressive.** Attitudes become a means of expression. They enable individuals to indicate to others the values that they hold and thus to express their self-concept and adopt or internalise the values of a group.
- **Instrumental.** Held attitudes maximise rewards and minimise sanctions. Hence, attitudes towards other people (or objects) might be held because of past positive (or negative) experiences. Behaviour or knowledge that has resulted in the satisfaction of needs is thus more likely to result in a favourable attitude.
- **Ego-defensive.** Attitudes may be held in order to protect the ego from an undesirable truth or reality.[54]

Prediction of behaviour

Is it possible to predict behaviour if we know an individual's attitude? Research suggests the answer is 'no' – what we say and what we do may be very different. Such evidence indicates that attitudes can be revealed not only in behaviour but also by the individual's thoughts (although these may not be revealed in public) and by feelings, the strength of which demonstrates the extent to which the attitude is a core or peripheral construct.

A classic study by *La Piere* illustrates this point. Visiting American hotels and restaurants with a Chinese couple, La Piere found no sign of prejudiced attitudes in the face-to-face situation, but there were marked racist attitudes in the follow-up attitude survey. He found complete contradictions between public and private attitudes.[55]

These findings have important implications for the study of attitudes and reveal two important issues for the psychologist and manager.

1 Attitudes cannot be seen; they can only be inferred.
Given that the attitudes employees hold are important for morale and the effectiveness of organisations, it is important that there is confidence in the measurement techniques used to assess the strength of attitudes. As attitudes are inferred, heavy reliance is placed therefore on the accuracy of assessment. Although there are a number of techniques that could be used to measure attitudes, the two most common are **direct observation** and **self-reporting techniques**.

All of us observe others and assess attitudes on the basis of communication style (both verbal and non-verbal) and behaviour. This is an example of an informal approach – unsystematic, spontaneous and based on our understanding of social cues. We may be wrong in our judgement. Students who turn up late for classes, slouch on their seat and do not ask questions may still hold very positive attitudes towards the subject. Managers may also be erroneous in their assumptions and beliefs about their colleagues (both subordinates and superiors). Their beliefs may never have been tested out – merely assumed to be correct.

Serious mistakes can be made when dealing with people across different cultures. For instance, eye contact in Western countries is normally associated with confidence, politeness

and attentiveness, but in some African countries it may be seen as rude and disrespectful. Bulgarians nod when they mean 'no' and shake their heads when they mean 'yes', while the Greeks nod upwards or raise their eyebrows for 'no' and shake the head side to side or tilt it to say 'yes'. A lack of 'cultural literacy' can lead to incorrect assumptions, poor relationships and a failure to make useful business connections.[56]

Organisations that assess their employees' attitudes by using attitude questionnaires (self-reporting techniques) are attempting systematically to gauge and measure these assumptions. Attitude questionnaires are time-consuming to design and administer. The questions asked, their relevance, style and length are all important variables in the validity of the questionnaire. So, too, is the honest completion of questionnaires. Making public people's private attitudes may also have its dangers as expectations of change may be envisaged. If these do not occur, disappointment and low morale may be the result.[57] (See also the discussion on the Johari window in Chapter 9.)

2 Attitudes are often shared within organisations and as such are embodied in the culture of organisations.

Classic research has shown the influence of the wider community in the formation of orientations towards work. Differences in class/orientation may elicit a range of loyalties and possibly produce opposing perceptions of commitment, loyalty and co-operation. Attitudes are not just individually formed but arise out of interaction with others. They are often 'locked-in', often regarded as obvious, mere common sense, and are so much taken for granted that they may be overlooked. Sharing the belief system of others also has affective outcomes. If people feel that they belong and are included, it enables them to feel good about working in an organisation. If, however, people do not feel part of the organisation – if they feel that they do not share the dominant attitudes and beliefs – negative emotional consequences are likely to result.

Researchers of organisational culture suggest that it is the shared perceptions of daily practices that are at the core of organisational cultures.[58] 'The reality of everyday life is taken for granted as reality.'[59] (Organisational culture is explored in more detail in Chapter 19.) Implications of the unquestioning nature of the 'reality' of what can or cannot be done can lead to individuals becoming 'culturally blinkered'. Insitutionalised attitudes result. Major problems arise when these attitudes are formed on the basis of stereotypes and prejudice, as was evidenced in the Stephen Lawrence Inquiry into the murder of a black teenager stabbed to death in London in April 1993:

> *Unwitting racism can arise because of lack of understanding, ignorance or mistaken beliefs. It can arise from well intentioned but patronising words or actions. It can arise from unfamiliarity with the behaviour or cultural traditions of people or families from minority ethnic communities. It can arise from racist stereotyping of black people as potential criminals or troublemakers. Often this arises out of uncritical self-understanding born out of an inflexible police ethos of the 'traditional' way of doing things. Furthermore such attitudes can thrive in a tightly knit community, so that there can be a collective failure to detect and to outlaw this breed of racism. The police canteen can too easily be its breeding ground.[60]*

Attitudes are not just created within organisations. Attitudes inherent within wider society are reinforced or reshaped by the organisation.

Employee attitude surveys

Attitude surveys or questionnaires are used by many organisations as a way of attempting to gauge the attitudinal climate of the organisation and monitor the views of members of staff. The Chartered Management Institute defines an employee attitude survey as:

> *A planned procedure which enables an organisation to obtain the opinions of its employees on a particular issue or on the organisation itself, so as to take account of them in the planning process or make changes beneficial to the organisation and individuals alike.*

Table 4.7	An example of an attitude questionnaire					

Please tick one box that most closely represents how you feel about each statement	Strongly disagree			Strongly agree	
	1	2	3	4	5
I believe in what OrgCo is trying to achieve	☐	☐	☐	☐	☐
I enjoy discussing OrgCo with people who do not work here	☐	☐	☐	☐	☐
I know how my job contributes to OrgCo's aims and objectives	☐	☐	☐	☐	☐
Good and bad news about what is happening at OrgCo is communicated regularly	☐	☐	☐	☐	☐
My values and those of the organisation are very similar	☐	☐	☐	☐	☐
Right now, staying with OrgCo is a matter of necessity as much as desire	☐	☐	☐	☐	☐
I am constantly interrupted in my work	☐	☐	☐	☐	☐
I enjoy my job	☐	☐	☐	☐	☐
I am encouraged to seek out new training opportunities	☐	☐	☐	☐	☐
My manager discusses with me ways in which I can improve my work performance	☐	☐	☐	☐	☐
OrgCo is serious about removing barriers to ensure equality of opportunity	☐	☐	☐	☐	☐
Staff at OrgCo regularly help and support each other at work	☐	☐	☐	☐	☐
I lack direction from my manager	☐	☐	☐	☐	☐
When things do not go well in our team/department we learn from the experience	☐	☐	☐	☐	☐
Communication within my team is positive and effective	☐	☐	☐	☐	☐
Taking everything into account I have a high level of job satisfaction with my team	☐	☐	☐	☐	☐

Surveys can encourage employee involvement, allow management to be more aware of employees' opinions, and provide effective communications or a sounding board. However, surveys require significant time and costs to administer and evaluate, and may generate suspicion from staff about 'hidden agendas' of the survey. The frequency should be no more than every 18 months and it is important to report results of the survey and plans of action to all employees.[61]

The usual method of measurement is by adopting a five-point 'Likert scale' (as in the example shown in Table 4.7) that reflects the comparative strength of the attitude.[62]

ATTITUDE CHANGE

The permanency of attitudes clearly has implications for attitudinal change. At the beginning of the previous section it was pointed out that whereas peripheral attitudes may easily change with new information or experiences, central attitudes tied into other cognitive systems may be much more difficult to shift.

Theories on attitude change stress the importance of **balance** and **consistency** in our psyche. *Heider*, for example, suggests that not only would we find it uncomfortable to hold two conflicting attitudes, but to do so would motivate us to change one of the attitudes in order to reach a balanced state.[63]

Cognitive dissonance is the term given to the discomfort felt when we act in a way that is inconsistent with our true beliefs. It suggests that we are motivated to reduce its impact.[64]

The process of attitude change is dependent on a number of key factors, the most important being:

- why an attitude is held in the first place;
- why it should change;
- what the benefits are and to whom;
- what the outcomes are if it does not change.

Considerable research has demonstrated the importance of the following variables in a programme of attitude change:

- the persuader's characteristics;
- presentation of issues;
- audience characteristics;
- group influences;
- outcome of attitude change (reward or punishment).

The last decade has produced tumultuous change for employees and their managers. It would be rare indeed to find an organisation that has not experienced some degree of change in structure, product, processes, philosophy, culture or ownership. The way in which these changes are implemented can have a dramatic impact on the attitudes of staff.

Critical reflection

'Changing people's behaviour is comparatively easy but changes to personality or attitudes are far more difficult. And a change in behaviour does not necessarily mean a change in personality or attitudes.'

So should we simply concentrate on how to change behaviour and ignore the study of personality and attitudes?

TESTING AND ASSESSMENT

Much has been written about the value of selection tests and questionnaires and they are subject to a number of criticisms. It should be noted that the word 'test' is often taken to refer to measures of intelligence, achievement and developed abilities, and aptitude for particular tasks. Measures of interests, social attitudes, emotional stability or traits of personality are usually referred to as questionnaires or profiles, or similar. Answers are regarded as common or uncommon, typical or untypical, rather than right or wrong, good or bad. The word 'test' is therefore usually avoided in such measures, as in, for example, the Cattell 16PF Questionnaire.

The early tests of intelligence have evolved into a large psychological business. Most people will have taken a **psychometric test** of one kind or another by the time they are an adult in employment. Tests may be administered at school or college, or as part of the selection assessment process at work. The use of tests is widespread and growing. They are perceived to be useful as an objective discriminating tool, but they are not without controversies and sensitivities.

Tests are divided broadly by the British Psychological Society into the following:

1 **Tests of typical performance.** These assess an individual's typical responses to given situations. Answers are not right or wrong but identify choices, preferences and strength of feelings. Personality assessments and interest inventories are examples of such tests.
2 **Tests of maximum performance.** These assess an individual's ability to perform effectively under standard conditions. Performance on these tests, which include ability and aptitude tests, can be judged as right or wrong. Ability tests come in many different forms and may test a **general intellectual functioning** or a **specific ability** (such as verbal reasoning, numerical reasoning, etc.).

Alice Heim (cited in *Anastasia*) developed a series of general ability tests – AH series – which is widely used to assess general ability. These test three key areas: verbal, numerical and diagrammatical reasoning. For example, an individual would be asked questions similar to the following:

Which one of the five words on the right bears a similar relation to each of the two words on the left?

		A	**B**	**C**	**D**	**E**
sensible	noise	sound	judgement	tone	silly	sensitive

Modern Occupational Skills Tests are an example of specific ability tests and measure a range of clerical and administrative skills: verbal checking, technical checking, numerical estimation, etc. They claim to be an aid in the selection of administrative staff. Their tests are short and can be used singly or together as a battery of tests. The individual would be asked questions similar to the following:

The two figures on the left have a feature in common. One, and one only, of the figures on the right lacks this feature. Which is it?

Some tests are designed to be given individually whereas others are suitable for administering within a group situation. However, there are certain minimum features and standards of conditions that distinguish psychological tests from other forms of informal assessments; tests are essentially 'an objective and standardised measure of a sample of behaviour'.[65]

Features of psychometric tests

Psychometric tests have certain standard features:

1 Tests will comprise a standard task or a set of questions with a standard means of obtaining the score.
2 A technical manual will explain what the test is measuring, how it was constructed, and the procedures for administering, scoring and interpreting the test.
3 Details of the test's validity (whether the test measures what it claims to measure) and reliability (the test's ability to measure consistently) will also be shown in the manual along with the inferences that can be drawn from the data.

For a test to be considered as a psychological instrument it must be **objective, standardised, reliable, valid** and **discriminating** (*but not discriminatory*). The selection and choice of the test should be based on a number of other key features such as its acceptability, practicality, time, costs and perceived and actual added value.

Personality questionnaires

The practical value of personality 'tests' has long been subject to much debate. According, for example, to *Barrett*:

A dismal history has been recorded by personality tests. There have been a few scattered successes with some modern techniques, but on the whole the typical personality questionnaire, test, or inventory has not proved to be useful. In many of them, the 'right' answers (which exist despite the naive disclaimer that there are no right answers) are so obvious that everyone comes out a model of healthy adjustment. But even if all applicants were to answer each question with complete candor, the value of their answers for predicting success would still be in doubt because the complexities of human personality are as yet poorly understood.[66]

The use and limitations of tests

All tests have limitations. Tests can sample behaviour only at one particular moment in time. The information they provide is dependent upon good testing practice and will only add evidence to the decision-making process. Tests will not provide the answer. Some individuals are very nervous and may not perform at their best and indeed some may feel indignant that they are obliged to take a test at all.

Great skill is required, therefore, in the administering of tests or questionnaires and in the interpretation of results. This would probably entail the services of a consultant psychologist, trained to the British Psychological Society (BPS) standard. A suitable physical environment is also important. The possible reaction of candidates must be considered. Some might find any form of 'test' something of an ordeal or regard it as an unpleasantness. A major concern with the majority of tests is the doubts about validity and lack of statistically proven reliability.

Despite the continuing debate about their value, it does appear that an increasing number of organisations are using psychometric measures (to measure characteristics such as personality and ability) as part of their recruitment and selection procedures. However, a major consideration in the controversy about the use of psychometric tests is how to avoid any cultural bias. There are still widespread doubts and criticisms about the use and value of personality tests, and continuing debate about their value in predicting performance at work.[67]

Even when psychometric tests *are* used, they should not be used in isolation but as part of a comprehensive selection process and applied in appropriate circumstances to supplement the interview, never as a substitute for it. It is also important to ensure adequate feedback to candidates in the process.

The reasons for using psychological tests may be summarised as follows:

1 They make decisions about people
 - more systematic
 - more precise.
2 They predict future performance and reduce uncertainty.
3 They provide more accurate descriptions of people and their behaviour. Precise definitions and measured variables lead to further studies and improve understanding of the relationship between tests and performance. But:
 - tests should be seen as an additional source of information only;
 - tests may be expensive and time-consuming;
 - without proper professional practice, they can be misused and results abused;
 - they may be seen as an intrusion;
 - they may be regarded as inappropriate;
 - practice may have an effect on test results.

DIVERSITY MANAGEMENT

The concept of diversity

An integral and essential feature of individual differences is the concept of diversity. We have seen from the discussion above that people are not homogeneous. **Diversity** focuses on the multiplicity of differences among people – on the variety of people as heterogeneous groupings. Individual differences are the basis of diversity.

For *Kandola and Fullerton*, diversity is defined as follows:

The basic concept of managing diversity accepts that the workforce consists of a diverse population of people. The diversity consists of visible and non-visible differences which will include sex, age, background, race, disability, personality and workstyle. It is founded on the premise that harnessing these differences will create a productive environment in which everybody feels valued, where their talents are being fully utilised, and in which organisational goals are met.[68]

Individual differences and diversity have long been recognised as important for effective team performance but in recent years greater attention has been given to the management of diversity. Reasons for this include:

- demographic changes in the workforce;
- wider customer base;
- equal employment opportunities legislation;
- a shortage of higher-level skills;
- programmes of affirmative action and positive discrimination;
- increasing number of women and part-time workers entering the workforce;
- changing social attitudes;
- a more global environment and increasing internationalisation.

However, valuing differences is easier said than done. It means relating and working with people who hold different perspectives and views, bringing different qualities to the workplace, having different aspirations and having different customs and traditions. Differences are challenging; they question people's views, perceptions and attitudes and require individuals to see things from a different frame of reference. Managing diversity does not mean that managers champion their own values and try to shift other people's values to conform and match their own!

The Chartered Management Institute provides the following description of diversity:

The concept of diversity encompasses any sort of difference between individuals. These could be differences in ethnic origin, age, gender, disability, family status, education, social or cultural background, personality or attitudes – in fact, anything which may affect workplace relationships and achievements. The management of diversity involves the implementation of strategies through which a network of varied individuals are integrated into a dynamic workforce.[69]

In addition to the above it is possible to identify a number of 'secondary' learned characteristics that a person acquires and modifies throughout life and over which the individual has relatively more influence. These include:

- religious beliefs
- sexual orientation
- work experience
- personal style
- income
- geographical location.

Devolution and regionalisation

Alterations to the identity that individuals hold have also been apparent over the last decade. Devolution and regionalisation have increased and paradoxically so too has the trend towards greater integration into multinational groupings (in terms of both company mergers and political agendas). A complex range of possible identities and affiliations results.

Consider a Scottish national living in the United States, working for a Japanese company and directing European markets: such a manager will have a diverse set of allegiances which may in turn affect motivation and morale. The growth of the portfolio worker and contract worker may result in an employment relationship that is short-term, instrumental and driven by outcomes and performance. Loyalty to the organisation and commitment to mission

statements do not enter into such a partnership. The rise of consumerism in and out of the workplace has led to greater understanding and expectations of 'rights' and redress of perceived injustice. It is not only morally and socially acceptable to treat all people fairly in the workplace; legislation insists that managers do so.

From equal opportunities to managing diversity

Equal opportunities relates to legislation intended to outlaw discrimination. The government is committed to protect individuals at work against discrimination in employment on the basis of gender, disability, race, religion, sexual orientation or age. Encouraging a diverse workforce is high on the government's agenda and the reluctant employer is having their hand forced by statutory obligations. Although diversity in the workplace relates to treating everyone equally, it complements and further develops initiatives on equal opportunities. Future demographic patterns present new challenges for managers.

> *Diversity management goes beyond what is required by legislation designed to promote equal opportunities and prevent discrimination. It comprises an approach which recognises and values differences and aims to make positive use of the unique talents and perspectives within the workforce. The focus is on individuals rather than minority groups.*[70]

Among those who believe that equal opportunities policies and training, though important, are not by themselves enough to secure the positive value of individual contributions is *Guirdham*. Only where an organisation has fully embraced diversity, trained its staff accordingly and inculcated its principles in every way will the barriers to good work communications between subgroups be lowered.

> *Some organisations 'champion' diversity, valuing the positive contribution that diverse individuals can bring, others tolerate it, merely following equal opportunities precepts, and others again treat it as a problem. These different policies and practices significantly affect the climate in which men and women, people of different ethnicities and so on conduct their work-based interactions.*[71]

All these changes amount to a picture in which the white, Protestant male will no longer dominate. Instead, we can anticipate a complex pattern where, ideally, individual differences will be valued and celebrated and, at the very least, equal opportunities practice will be observed. Personal qualities and characteristics that may have been downgraded, ignored or regarded as nuisance factors will be perceived as adding value. In the longer term, an effective policy on diversity should arguably eliminate the need for affirmative action or positive discrimination.

THE BUSINESS CASE FOR DIVERSITY

As businesses become increasingly global it is even more important for managers to have a sound understanding of diverse countries and workforces. According to ACAS, the business case for diversity – that a more diverse employee base will attract a more diverse customer base and increase sales, improve performance etc. – is a well-argued one.[72]

Organisations that embrace difference and diversity as opposed to those which are merely compliant will, it is claimed, succeed in a fiercely competitive climate. For example, as J. M. Barry Gibson, (then) Chief Executive of Littlewoods, has stated:

> *The fact is that if we effectively exclude women, ethnic minorities and disabled people we are fishing in a smaller pool for the best possible talent. As a service organisation, we ought to reflect the style, taste and opinions of our consumers, who of course represent sexes, all colours and creeds, all ages and disabilities. The main point is that cultural diversity will strengthen the quality of the company and will make us much more outward-looking.*[73]

A joint report from the CBI and TUC, supported by the Equality and Human Rights Commission, suggests that promoting diversity in the workplace and employing people solely on the basis of their ability can bring many real business benefits. These include:

■ increasing employee satisfaction, which helps attract new staff and retain those already there, reduces recruitment costs, and can increase productivity;

■ understanding better how the company's diverse customers think and what drives their spending habits, or how they access markets they have not previously been able to tap into so effectively;

■ finding enough workers to fill skills gaps in areas with tight labour markets, where there are not enough 'obvious candidates' for the vacancies they have.

The report also makes clear that diversity can be improved through positive action – such as encouraging applications from types of people who have not in the past applied for jobs, additional training, providing support networks or adapting work practices – but not positive discrimination.[74]

Embracing individual differences

As part of the creative process within organisations, *Hill* refers to the need to embrace individual differences while pursuing collective identity and goals.

The creative process demands a mix of diverse individuals. For the collective to benefit from this diversity by drawing on each individual's talents there needs to be a process that allows for varied perspectives, priorities and styles. The only way these voices can be expressed and heard is to treat people fairly, which means to treat people differently . . . If member diversity is to be acknowledged and differences of opinion encouraged, the collective must develop a culture of trust in which members will want to support one another.[75]

Positive and negative propositions

A report from the Chartered Institute of Personnel and Development refers to a central theme of diversity as 'valuing everyone as individuals' and suggests there is an increasing volume of evidence of a convincing link between valuing people and value creation in business. Diversity programmes require cultural and organisational changes that are difficult to manage. However, the benefits of a diverse workforce include customer focus, innovation, creativity and learning, business process improvement and the financial bottom line.

There is no denying the mounting empirical and anecdotal evidence that good diversity management can lead to improved business performance where the business contexts and market conditions are taken into account appropriately. Conversely, poorly developed and poorly matched diversity practice can be detrimental to business, creating without gain, raising expectations without delivery, and increasing cost without benefit.[76]

The report introduces the idea of measuring diversity and suggests the adoption of a balanced scorecard approach to integrate diversity into business strategy and operational activities. The scorecard puts forward eight propositions that take into account both the positive and negative forces of diversity.

Positive forces of diversity are those that:

■ promote cost-effective employment relations;
■ enhance customer relations;
■ enhance creativity, flexibility and innovation;
■ promote sustainable development and business advantage.

Negative forces of diversity are:

■ diminishing cultural relatedness;
■ the need for financial support to support flexibility;
■ the jeopardising of workplace harmony;
■ possible conflict between organisational slack and tight fit.

Diversity and management recruitment

The Institute for Employment Studies, in conjunction with the Chartered Management Institute, emphasises the importance of diversity as a strategic priority for retaining and developing key people in an organisation. They draw attention to the different career ambitions of managers from under-represented groups and state that, if organisations want management talent at the top, recruitment approaches must recognise that managers from different ethnic groups are attracted by different benefits. For example, compared with other ethnic groups, black managers were more likely to cite good progression opportunities; Asian managers more likely to cite working for a good employer; managers from mixed background to cite challenging work; white managers and black managers more likely to mention better work/life balance.[77]

Diversity action plans

Management of diversity requires an effective action checklist and plan. As an example, The Office for National Statistics (ONS) has produced a comprehensive and detailed Equality Scheme 2008–2011 which includes reference to ONS as an employer; equality impact assessments; and governance, monitoring, reporting and reviewing. This is shown as Figure 4.7.

Figure 4.7	ONS Equality Scheme

ONS EQUALITY SCHEME 2008–2011

'ONS is committed to valuing diversity and promoting equality in the way it does business as a statistics office and as an employer. We aspire to demonstrating best practice in the way we do this beyond merely meeting our statutory equality duties.

As an employer, our vision is that ONS will be regarded as an employer of choice and will be recognised as a great place to work and thrive for all, regardless of age, disability, gender and gender identity, ethnicity, religion, sexual identity and work-life balance needs. At the same time, we believe equality and diversity are everyone's business regardless of background.

While progress has been made, in particular through the valuable contributions made by ONS's diversity networks and champions, this scheme recognises that there is more to be done to build a culture and environment in which all members of our workforce recognise that diversity is valued.'

Key points of the Equality Scheme include:

- This equality scheme is both a description of how ONS plans to meet its statutory equality duties as a public authority and a commitment to achieving best practice in promoting equality and eliminating discrimination and harassment
- It is a single comprehensive scheme with the intention of promoting equality in its widest sense, in relation to age, disability, ethnicity, gender and gender identity, religion/belief, sexual identity and work/life balance
- Promoting equality is core to the expectations ONS staff should have of ONS as an employer, and in the expectations ONS has of its workforce

Detailed equality and diversity action plans, outcomes and outputs are set out for each of the following areas.

1. Diversity Governance and Measurement	2. ONS as an Employer
3. ONS Public Functions	4. Race Equality
5. Gender Equality	6. Disability Equality
7. Sexual Orientation	8. Religion or Belief
9. Age	10. Work/life Balance

Source: Office for National Statistics. Crown Copyright material is reproduced under terms of the Click-Use Licence.

Figure 4.8 Concept map of diversity at work

DIVERSITY AT WORK

* DIMENSIONS OF DIVERSITY
* THE CASE FOR ACTIVELY MANAGING DIVERSITY
* SOME APPROACHES TO MANAGING DIVERSITY

THE CASE FOR ACTIVELY MANAGING WORKPLACE DIVERSITY

* THE BUSINESS CASE
* THE ETHICAL CASE
* THE LEGAL CASE

DIMENSIONS OF DIVERSITY

Diversity includes, but is not limited to, a person's:

Gender
Age
Ethnic origin
Physical abilities
Educational qualifications
Practical skills level
Educational background
Sexual orientation
Religious beliefs
Work experience
Physical characteristics
Upbringing as a child
Geographic location
Family circumstances
Income source
Language(s) spoken
Physical appearance
Personality
Learning ability
Ancestry
Accent

Everyone in the population will possess these dimensions of diversity, but in the employment situation some dimensions will assume greater relevance and importance

MANAGING DIVERSITY – TEN PRACTICAL IDEAS

1 Test assumptions about people before acting on them
2 Ensure that organisational policies related to discipline and grievance are clearly understood
3 For all employees, but particularly new recruits, make sure that written and unwritten diversity policies are understood and acted upon
4 Maintain open channels of communication to try to locate possible issues before they become problems
5 Learn how to understand the views of all staff members and encourage open approaches
6 Be prepared to listen to varying methods of solving work-based problems
7 Learn about and have regard to any strongly-held beliefs (such as religious observances, food, relationships) that are held by individuals
8 Acknowledge all contributions to improving working environments and processes from whatever the source
9 Know your own cultural diversity biases – and work at not letting them affect the workplace
10 Take care that any workplace based social events can be enjoyed by all workers – especially relevant (but not restricted) to those with physical disability

ETHICS

The ethical case rests on the belief that 'people should be valued for reasons related to business as well as for moral and social reasons' (Chartered Institute of Personnel and Development)

Within this lies an organisation's formal policies on

■ Corporate Social Responsibility (CSR)
■ Equality and diversity
■ Discipline and grievance
■ Subcontractor employment practices

Increasingly, where an organisation is part of a supply chain, other members of that chain will require formal monitoring and control of these policies

BUSINESS

A workforce drawn from a range of backgrounds working in a diversity-sensitive organisation can:

– provide a wide range of skills beneficial to the organisation, some of which may be very scarce
– help the organisation develop creative ways of solving intractable problems
– provide better access to multicultural and gender markets
– assist an organisation develop a good image with employees, customers and other stakeholders leading to:
 * enhanced employee satisfaction
 * better employee retention
 * improved customer loyalty

LEGAL

In an ideal world universal acceptance of diversity would be the norm. But differences lead to prejudice, and in the workplace these can result in:

■ Inappropriate behaviour towards others
■ Unwarranted direct and indirect discrimination
■ Lack of opportunity for improved pay levels and/or promotion prospects
■ Provision of lower service levels
■ Bullying and harassment

For particularly bad situations, legislation lays down requirements aimed at providing better standards of treatment. Topics addressed by legislation include, as examples only:

– Gender
– Race
– Disability
– Age

Organisations and individuals risk fines and loss of reputation for non-compliance

Diversity works

Our Diversity Initiatives at Hilton Hotels Corporation are designed to produce quantifiable and qualitative results which go beyond just establishing and maintaining a diverse workforce. We have incorporated diversity principles into all aspects of our business operations: employment, training and mentoring, marketing, community support, and management performance measurements.

While successful diversity programming can result in receiving awards, plaques and trophies (which look nice on our walls), at Hilton we're concerned with much more than an accumulation of hardware. Our achievements in diversity programming, and the priority we place on it, go to the very heart, soul and spirit of our organization . . . who we are, and what we stand for.

Yes, we welcome and appreciate acknowledgements of our diversity accomplishments; and we'll find room for more plaques and trophies recognizing our good work. But far beyond the pride that goes with such recognition is our commitment to the belief that our Diversity Initiatives enhance our competitiveness and strengthen the business value of our corporation; for those reasons, we take pride in the fact that, at Hilton Hotels Corporation . . . 'diversity works'.

Stephen F. Bollenbach, President and CEO[78]

A summary of diversity at work is set out in the concept map in Figure 4.8.

Critical reflection

'Despite all the rhetoric and claimed advantages of diversity, it is still more about the benefits to business rather than moral or social concerns. In any case, in reality it is little more than another form of political correctness and viewed with scepticism by the majority of the ordinary workforce.'

How would you respond to such a claim?

DIVERSITY TRAINING

More than ever, effective organisational performance demands an understanding of, and response to, diversity. This necessitates a work climate that respects individual differences and treats all members of staff with dignity and mutual respect. Diversity training will not be effective unless there is active support from the top and it is recognised as a company-wide initiative and part of the core value of the organisation.

Organisations need to manage diversity in a manner that benefits the well-being of all members of staff. Training should involve:

- increasing the awareness and value of diversity;
- education in understanding the culture and values of members of a diverse workforce;
- the ability to communicate effectively with all members of staff – and also customers and suppliers;
- developing the skills of effective diversity management;
- addressing biases, prejudices and stereotypes.

Business in the Community (BITC) is one of the agencies that help businesses to embrace a culture of inclusiveness by helping them to look at the competitive case for diversity. Current activities focus on labour market discrimination, religious beliefs, sexual orientation, and general diversity and equality.[79] As another example, ACAS draws attention to managing disability and to the importance of line managers' contribution to organisational culture and managing performance. Training managers in effective people management skills and developing a culture of inclusion are crucial.[80] Attention to top management is also required. *Arkin* suggests that in company headquarters the chances are that the people

will be overwhelmingly white, male, able-bodied and of a certain age. There is little joined-up thinking between activities under the diversity agenda and the nurturing of top talent.[81]

The effective management of diversity will also entail a review of organisational processes and the execution of work. For example, not everyone

- shares the same work ethic or seeks the same goals and objectives;
- responds in the same way to working in a bureaucratic structure;
- works better in a self-managed group or with a more participative style of management;
- will fit the same psychometric profile;
- is motivated in the same way; or
- reacts the same way to different forms of control.

Diversity management requires time and effort and may well have a high financial cost. There is a general feeling that badly managed initiatives do more harm than good. Managing diversity requires a company-wide philosophy and commitment, a change to organisational culture and supportive systems of management and training.

Diversity and stereotyping

Diversity also challenges many traditional stereotypes (discussed in Chapter 6). Stereotyping infers that people within a particular perceived category are assumed to share the same traits or characteristics. Stereotypes are a means of making simplified judgements of other people instead of coping with a range of individual stimuli. Stereotyping attributes to all individuals the characteristics or tendencies of the categorisation as a whole. An important feature of managing diversity is an awareness of, and training in, overcoming inaccurate stereotyped perceptions and attributions. A greater understanding of cultural differences in non-verbal communications and body language will help improve interpersonal relationships.

> *There have been instances in my life, both at home and at work, when people have felt I'm a little crazy because I am pushy, outspoken, energetic, competitive, enthusiastic, driven and strong. Crazy, because that's not what's expected of an Asian woman. Crazy because it's not what the majority of people are like. And crazy, because they think they know me better than I know myself.*
>
> Saira Khan – star of *The Apprentice* television series[82]

Managers' attitudes, values and beliefs

If they are to be successful in managing diversity, managers need to have greater reserves of emotional intelligence (discussed earlier in this chapter). In turn this suggests that managers need to have an awareness of, and be able to get in touch with, their own attitudes, values and beliefs – what they are and where they come from. *Clements and Jones* recognise that the process can be uncomfortable:

> *A model of good diversity training will recognize that when people engage in an exploration of their attitudes, values, beliefs and prejudices, this may be an uncomfortable process. Some will find out things about themselves that will cause them emotional pain, and often the tension in learners will relate to how they should respond.*[83]

TOP PERFORMING ORGANISATIONS

An increasing number of public and private organisations appear to recognise the business case for diversity. The government department for Business, Enterprise and Regulatory Reform (BERR), created on the disbanding of the Department of Trade and Industry, is among top public sector performers. In the private sector, Lloyds TSB has been praised for its approach.

BERR diversity statement

'Promoting Equality, Valuing Diversity'

The BERR Operating Committee and Management Board agreed the Department's revised diversity strategy in September 2008. This is the second diversity strategy and builds on the success of the earlier 2006–8 strategy. The 2008–11 strategy reflects the cross-government diversity and equality priorities set by the Cabinet Office and aims to tackle those issues identified as key by staff and stakeholders.

Proposed actions are based on a number of key themes and pressure points for the Department that needed to be addressed in relation to:

- representation of women, ethnic minorities and disabled staff in senior levels
- changing behaviour to create an inclusive culture
- building on strong leadership and accountability for diversity
- talent management – bringing in and bringing on people from different backgrounds
- mainstreaming diversity and equality considerations in management, operations and in policy development.[84]

Lloyds TSB diversity programme

Lloyds TSB provides strong organisational commitment to diversity. The Board and Group Executive Committee agree the diversity programme and also oversee its delivery. This, coupled with a clear plan of action, has enabled Lloyds TSB to achieve a considerable improvement in performance.

Lloyds TSB participates in benchmarking exercises run by national campaigns covering the main diversity strands. The benchmarks independently assess performance, track progress over time and also compare performance against other organisations. This kind of external evaluation is extremely important and helps Lloyds TSB to maintain momentum and continue to strive to retain their leading edge status.

Lloyds TSB is currently ranked the number one organisation in the UK for gender, race, disability and sexual orientation equality. Its policies and practices are recognised as amongst the best and the strategy is underpinned by focus on these key actions:

1 **Diversity metrics** – all aspects of the workforce are monitored, analysed and reported on by diversity demographic. Progress is measured against aspirational goals and diversity interventions in place are measured for effectiveness using key performance indicators.

2 **Employee research** – extensive quantitative and qualitative research is carried out with staff to ensure that strategies put in place address their specific needs. In addition, ongoing consultation with employees provides feedback on how well the strategy is working.

3 **Training and development** – training is available for all staff to raise awareness of diversity issues and to give them the tools to manage difference. Development workshops for specific groups are also available, which inspire and motivate attendees to take control of their personal and career development.

4 **Top level commitment** – as well as agreeing and committing to the delivery of the diversity programme the Group Executive Committee and the Board monitor progress and require regular updates. In addition, Lloyds TSB Executives demonstrate their commitment to valuing diversity by communicating key messages to all staff about the strategy; progress, challenges and successes.[85]

Source: Lloyds TSB Equality and Diversity Team.

> *Managing diversity well potentially benefits an organisation in the areas of social responsibility, cost, resource acquisition, marketing, creativity, problem solving and organisational flexibility. To gain these benefits, however, the organisation must create a climate that values diversity and where each employee has an equal chance to contribute and succeed.*
>
> A. M. Francesco and B. A. Gold *International Organisational Behavior*[86]

CRITICISMS AND LIMITATIONS

Despite the potential benefits from managing diversity, there are a number of criticisms and perceived limitations. According to ACAS, to date an understanding of diversity and its implementation remains the domain of larger organisations with an HR department. A large proportion of smaller organisations tend to focus on how to treat employees fairly within the law.[87] There are concerns over increasing legislation and government initiatives aimed at 'forcing' further advancements in equal opportunities. There is a general feeling that badly managed initiatives do more harm than good.

Whilst acknowledging that the positive management of diversity aims to promote an inclusive culture in which individuals are valued and respected, the Chartered Management Institute points out that diversity management should not be mistaken for equal opportunities or be merely a question of legal compliance. Managers should avoid handling diversity issues insensitively; invading employees' privacy; failure to consult and gain commitment throughout the organisation; or falling into an 'us' and 'them' mentality.[88]

Individuality and groups

Social interaction is a natural feature of human behaviour and group working is a major feature of organisational life. Strong and cohesive groups can have beneficial effects for the organisation but there are potential disadvantages. There is arguably a potential conflict with workforce diversity because of the need to consider staff both as individuals and also as members of a group. The greater the compatibility of its members and the more homogeneous the group, the greater the danger of the group developing its own subculture. Members may display a critical attitude towards people outside the group or members of other groups. Encouraging individuality and at the same time expecting group co-operation and teamwork are potential triggers for tension.

Concern for moral and social issues

A major concern with the increasing attention to diversity is that too much attention is given to the advantages for business rather than to broader moral or social issues and the ethical arguments for equality of treatment.

In arguing the case for combining heterogeneity and homogeneity, *Nordström and Ridderstråle* suggest that although quite often people talk favourably about diversity since it supposedly promotes a better atmosphere and equality, the typical manager is persuaded to change the mix of people at the company for economic reasons. 'The competitive reality is that organisations that are bogged down in issues of race, gender, age, sexual preferences, look and so on, will slip deeper down in the mire.'[89]

Kirton and Greene believe that the 'business case' should be broadened to include wider issues of social justice and social responsibility.[90] *Liff and Cameron* argue that organisational culture needs to shift radically to win the 'hearts and minds rather than just achieve reluctant compliance'. In their article, which uses women as their illustration, they assert that there are real dangers in conventional equality measures. Focusing on women as having special problems requiring special treatment results in resentment and defensive attitudes from

managers. They believe that one of the first essential stages to enact change is to consider the organisational culture and the way in which it could move to an equality culture.[91]

However, *Lucas* points out that:

> One of the key messages the experts want to get across is that paying attention to diversity isn't just a moral obligation, it's a business imperative. Workers in organisations where diversity is valued generally feel more engaged with their employer and are more likely to stay on board. The organisation will build a reputation as an 'enlightened' employer, and will be able to attract the best people at a time when talent is at a premium. The business can also draw on the expertise of its diverse workforce to create new and improved products and services which will help them get ahead in competitive, global markets.[92]

DIVERSITY, GENDER AND ORGANISATIONS

One of the most significant and important aspects of managing diversity is that of gender equality, and the participation of men and women in the workforce.[93] One of our initial perceptions and classifications of another individual is usually the identification of their gender.

- How does this perception affect our behaviour?
- What difference does it make if our work group is predominantly male or female?
- Do women and men have different experiences at work?
- If organisations are rational and neutral institutions – why should gender make a difference?
- Does it matter that many classic theories have been based on research carried out on men, by male researchers?
- What has been the influence of diversity policies on work behaviour and on the position of women in organisations?

Emotions, politics and gender

Emotions and politics surround the issue of gender. *Alvesson and Due Billing* suggest that some people may be over-sensitive to gender and interpret any negative comment as if it is symbolic of an act of discrimination. Likewise under-sensitivity may also occur and organisations may remain gender blind to everyday instances of bias and distortion. Although not easy, achieving the right balance (neither overwhelming nor rejecting the pervasiveness of gender) is an important skill in managing men and women at work.[94]

Contradictions and confusion

Gender research is replete with contradictions and confusions. Although there is a body of evidence to confirm the position, status and (lack of) power of women in organisations – aspects that can be measured and quantified – such clarity is blurred when it comes to understanding the subjective and qualitative aspects of working life. It is not helpful to view all men or all women as homogeneous groups. There may be as many differences within each gender as between the two genders. Social class, race and age will affect attitudes, beliefs and values and may impinge upon different understandings of gender. Although earlier organisational research could be criticised as having been conducted by men largely investigating male behaviour, so too much of the research on women has been dominated by white middle-class women assuming their values are those that should be upheld.

Perhaps the most positive approach to take is for an organisation to acknowledge the changing working pattern of all employees and to consider the best working practices for managing a diverse workforce as a whole. This should not be done mechanically but by analysis of the organisation and its workforce. Organisations need to analyse, consciously debate and question their unwritten assumptions and expectations in order to reveal

prejudices inherent in the culture of their organisations. Analysis of the way in which culture is expressed in all its trivial detail would lead to an understanding of perceptions and attitudes. Until a full analysis is completed it remains doubtful whether more egalitarian practices will develop.

IBM – united by diversity

When IBM decided men and women should be paid equally for doing the same job, and should have equal responsibilities and career opportunities, it made headline news. Not surprisingly – it was in 1935. This early recognition of the importance of an inclusive workplace laid the foundation for today's focus on diversity, where every employee is encouraged to perform at their best, and where different opinions are both welcomed and appreciated.

IBM Corporation[95]

Critical reflection

'We know that every person is an individual in their own right, but many theories and models of organisational behaviour still appear to apply to people in general. Rather than looking at similarities among people, we should be more concerned with the study of differences among individuals.'

What are your views? What do you believe is the value of theories or models of organisational behaviour?

SYNOPSIS

■ Organisations are made up of their individual members and the individual is a central feature of organisational behaviour. A distinguishing factor of successful managers is the recognition of individual differences and their ability to bring out the best in the people who work with and report to them. A discussion of individual behaviour is riddled with complexity and contradictions. Managing relationships well depends on an understanding and awareness of members of staff and of their talents, abilities, interests and motives.

■ A significant difference among individuals is in terms of their personality – those stable characteristics that explain why a person behaves in a particular way. Differences between individuals can be the source of problems and conflict. Personality clashes may occur; differences of attitudes and values may lead to polarisation and discrimination. Although psychologists do not agree in terms of the relative importance of certain factors, there is much to be gained from both nomothetic and idiographic approaches.

■ Personality is a major consideration for recruitment selection or rejection. The identification of personality traits has been a dominant subject of research. There is now a body of evidence that suggests five main

dimensions: openness/closed-mindedness, conscientiousness, extraversion/introversion, agreeableness and neuroticism/stability (OCEAN). Account must also be taken of social rules and expectations within the workplace. Two polar sets of characteristics linked with work behaviour, health and stress are Type A and Type B personalities.

■ Individuals vary with regard to their mental abilities and application. Different occupations require different skills, competencies and abilities. Arguments rage over the nature of intelligence; whether it is dependent on a general overall factor or specific independent activites, and the extent to which it is inherited. Emotional intelligence (or EQ) is the sum of a range of interpersonal skills that form the public persona and has received considerable attention over the last few years. However, tests are not a panacea and can, if used inappropriately, lead to a sense of false security.

■ There are no limits to the attitudes people hold. Attitudes and motives are interlinked and serve a number of important functions. Assessment of attitudes is vital in selecting potential employees and future managers. Given the difficulties of attitude measurement and doubts associated with predicting

behaviour, such assessment is fraught with problems. Attitudes can take on a permanency that is maintained by the culture of the organisation and thus be very resistant to change. Psychometric tests and questionnaires may help to identify individual characteristics but they are subject to limitations.

■ An understanding of diversity, which complements and further develops initiatives on equal opportunities, demands a work climate that respects individual differences and treats all members of staff with dignity and mutual respect. Diversity challenges many traditional stereotypes and one particular aspect is the management of gender equality. An increasing number of organisations appear to recognise the business case for diversity as part of the inclusive and creative process but there a number of potential criticisms including concern for moral and social issues.

REVIEW AND DISCUSSION QUESTIONS

1 What do you see as the main issues relating to the effective management of individuals at work?

2 Discuss the major ways in which individual differences are demonstrated at work.

3 You are required to interview one person from your work or study group to produce an assessment of their personality. What questions will you ask and how accurate do you feel your assessment will be?

4 Why are attitudes difficult to measure and change? Design a simple questionnaire to administer to your colleagues on attitudes towards stress at work.

5 To what extent do you see a clear differentiation between equal opportunities and the effective management of diversity?

6 How would you plan and implement a training programme intended to overcome inaccurate stereotyped perceptions and attributes?

7 Discuss critically the contention that too much attention is given to the advantages for business from the management of diversity rather than to broader moral or social issues.

8 Prepare a discussion document on your experiences of organisational behaviour and gender equality at work.

MANAGEMENT IN THE NEWS

The Apprentice, week nine

Michael Ball

Week nine of *The Apprentice*, broadcast by the BBC on 20 May, saw Ben 'I've got a scholarship to Sandhurst' Clarke finally dismissed from the show. The decision came as quite a shock to the other contestants and probably most viewers. Why did Sir Alan Sugar fire Clarke? He was no more culpable than his teammates for the loss in the latest task. Maybe Sugar was taking into account Clarke's previous behaviour on the show. Was he too arrogant? He took the art of self-acclaim to a new high. Maybe it was because of Clarke's habit of aggressively blaming everybody else in the boardroom for the things that had gone wrong. Or was it because of his annoying habit of shouting 'Can I just finish'?

Strangely, it appears these were not factors in Sugar's decision. At 22, Clarke was the youngest of the show's candidates. Maybe Sir Alan Sugar considered he was too young. Certainly, in his exit interviews, Clarke seemed to put his dismissal down to being 'too young' and 'too inexperienced'. Having chosen to try and gain employment via a reality TV show, Clarke does not have the benefit of protection against the potentially discriminatory reason for his exit. In the real employment world the number of age discrimination cases is taking off. The employment tribunal statistics for the period April 2007 to March 2008 show 2,949 age discrimination claims compared with only 972 in 2006/2007, a three-fold increase, and the number of claims has continued to rise.

Being inexperienced, rather than too young, can legitimately mean candidates will be out of their depth in a new position. However, employers should take care when setting out their reasons for selection. It is not just older workers that can claim protection under

→

Management in the news – continued

the age discrimination laws – younger workers are also protected and any employer who turns down candidates just because of their age could find itself in trouble. A recent tribunal decision shows the risks that employers face. In Thomas v Eight Members Club and Killip (ET/2202603/2007), a 19-year-old was rejected after a four-month probationary period. The employer alleged that the decision was based not on her age but on the fact that she had made mistakes during the probation period; but the tribunal found evidence suggesting the employer had considered there might not have been a problem if she had been a few years older. It concluded that the club had discriminated against the employee and awarded her £1,500 for injury to feelings.

This highlights the danger of employers making assumptions about experience, age and capability. Employers may want candidates to have a defined number of years' experience but this type of specification will rule out candidates from certain age groups and may be challenged. An employer may state that at least five years' experience is required. But would three years' experience of an exceptional nature with a market-leading competitor be sufficient to give the candidate the ability to do the job?

Employers should establish from the outset what specifications are justified to guard against challenges to the process. The only way to do this is to analyse the person and job specification. Identifying the key talents required for the job, rather than the years of experience it needs, will draw the focus away from issues of age discrimination and stereotypical assumptions.

Source: Ball, M. '*The Apprentice*, Week Nine', *People Management Online*, 27 May 2009. Reproduced by permission of People Management magazine (www.peoplemanagement.co.uk) and the author.

Discussion questions

1 What does the article tell us about the relative importance of personality, ability and experience in the selection process?

2 Explain which of the three you think is the best predictor of job performance, and why.

3 Critically review the likely impact which age discrimination legislation and the increasing number of tribunal cases might have on managerial attitudes to workplace diversity more generally.

ASSIGNMENT

1 On your own, read the publisher's notice from the *Seattle Times*, USA, 27 March 2007.

2 What is your immediate, personal reaction to the notice?

3 Form into small groups with your colleagues and compare your more considered reactions including different cultural approaches and interpretation of the Fair Housing Act by the *Seattle Times*. What conclusions do you draw?

4 To what extent do you think such a notice would be appropriate in the UK and/or any other country?

PUBLISHER'S NOTICE:
Recent amendment of the Federal Fair Housing Act suggests that we caution advertisers against real estate advertising that may be interpreted as discriminatory. The Fair Housing Act makes it illegal to advertise any preference, limitation, or otherwise encourage discrimination because of race, color, religion, sex, national origin, handicap, or familial status. Also, local laws forbidding discrimination in real estate ads not only repeat the federal categories but add prohibitions against discrimination based on age, parental status, sexual orientation, political ideology, or a renter's qualification for rent subsidy support.

To avoid both civil and criminal liability, obvious words should be avoided that connote any of the forbidden categories. Other words not so obvious have been interpreted liberally by the courts to violate the categories.

The Seattle Times Co. makes a substantial good faith effort to help advertisers reduce their risk of liability. For example, the following terms may, in the context of an ad, be considered in violation of federal, state or local laws and, if so, would be unacceptable in real estate advertising in either The Seattle Times or the Post-intelligencer.

Adult
Bachelor
Couple
Mature
No Children
One Person
Retired*
Sex (may be OK in advertising for roommates)
Single
Two People

Christian
Executive (such as 'large executive home')
Exclusive
Handicap ('not suitable for')
Integrated
Membership Approval
Mentally Ill
Religious
Religious Landmark (near St. Mark's)
Older Persons*
Senior Citizens*
Physically Fit Person (ideal for)
Private (private community – no; private drive – OK)

Race
Restricted
Senior Discount*
This list is by no means complete. If you have any questions about our policy on this matter, please contact us at the Seattle Times.

*Housing for the elderly may be exempt from the Fair Housing Act, if specific criteria have been met. A letter from the advertiser stating that the requirements of the Federal Fair Housing Act have been met in one of the following ways must be on file prior to publication.

The dwelling or housing community must either (1) be designed and operated to assist elderly persons under a state or federal program, (2) be occupied solely by persons 62 years of age or older, or (3) have at least 80 percent of its occupied units occupied by at least one person 55 years of age or older per unit AND have significant facilities and services designed to meet the physical and social needs of older persons.

Retirement communities would qualify as housing for older persons exempt from the Fair Housing Act.

Source: *Seattle Times*, 27 March 2007.

PERSONAL AWARENESS AND SKILLS EXERCISE

Objectives

Completing this exercise should help you to enhance the following skills:

■ Explore the meaning, dimensions and impact of diversity.
■ Develop greater empathy towards other people.
■ Reflect on your attitudes and behaviours towards individual differences.

Exercise

For each of the following ten statements you are required to indicate *honestly and fully* the extent to which you:

1 Believe in managing diversity for moral and social reasons.
2 Are happy mixing with people from different cultures.
3 Resist stereotyping or profiling individuals into general categories of people.
4 Show patience and understanding when dealing with people whose English language is limited.
5 Accept that positive discrimination can sometimes be fully justified.
6 View diversity as distinctly different from political correctness.
7 Enjoy learning about different cultures and values.
8 Believe that diversity enriches the working lives of all employees.
9 Feel comfortable working closely with a colleague who has a different sexual orientation.
10 Are prepared to take orders from someone much younger or much older than yourself, or from the opposite gender.

Discussion

After completing the questionnaire, pair with a colleague – where possible with a different ethnicity, culture, gender or age group – and compare and discuss critically both sets of responses.

■ What does this exercise say about your awareness of, and adaptability, to diversity?
■ To what extent were you surprised by the responses or comments from your colleague?
■ What conclusions have you drawn from this exercise?

CASE STUDY

B&Q: the business case for diversity

B&Q is the UK's largest home improvement chain of stores, selling materials and equipment for the home and domestic gardening market. The founders, Richard Block and David Quayle, opened their first store in Southampton in 1969, then in 1980 the company was acquired by FW Woolworth and in 1982 it became part of Paternoster the former name for the Kingfisher Group, which is currently Europe's leading home improvement retail group. In addition to B&Q in the UK and Ireland, Kingfisher also owns Brico Depot with stores in France, Spain and Poland, Castorama with stores in France, Poland and Russia, Screwfix in the UK, Koctas in Turkey and B&Q China. It also has a 21% stake in Hornbach, Germany's leading DIY warehouse retailer. B&Q UK's headquarters remain in Hampshire.

In 1996, the Kingfisher group opened a B&Q store in Taiwan and in 1999 it moved into mainland China: the outlet opened in Shanghai on the eighth day of the eighth month (a lucky day according to Chinese tradition) of 2001 was the largest B&Q store in the world. The Kingfisher group now runs 48 Chinese stores, including one of the world's largest, B&Q Beijing, which also sells furniture and furnishing materials. The nature of the Chinese property market has also made it viable for the company to offer a fitting and decorating service for customers moving into newly built apartments, thereby expanding its business opportunities through a strategy of vertical integration.[96]

In 2009 B&Q employed around 34,000 people nationwide in 330 stores across the UK. Despite being affected by the drop in the housing market during 2007–9, the organisation is currently planning to double its profits by 2012. It proposes to do this by re-focussing on its core values, which place a strong emphasis on its people.[97]

B&Q and the 'demographic time bomb'

For some decades, population statistics have shown that the UK population is ageing, and the impact of this so-called 'demographic time bomb' began to generate particular concerns during the late 1980s. Some businesses, like B&Q, took a critical look at their current employment practices as a result of predicted shortages in certain parts of the labour market, and the consequent fear of intensified competition between employers for younger workers. This was particularly important for a growing company like B&Q, which might find its expansion plans would be seriously harmed by labour shortages. In 1989, therefore, B&Q

Is diversity in the workplace simply political correctness? B&Q recognised the value of diversity after a new store staffed by over-50s outperformed its other stores.

Source: Courtesy of B&Q plc

management reviewed its workforce, and noted that not only did it have a predominantly young age profile (the majority of staff were aged 16–26), but staff turnover costs were particularly high in the 18-to-20-year-old category. They also noted positive customer feedback about their older staff, who appeared to deliver better customer service, partly because of their own knowledge of DIY.

The company management decided to tackle the problem by challenging widely held views about the disadvantages and problems of employing older workers. Initially, the B&Q Board expressed some concerns about the proposal to target older people in the labour market and were naturally cautious about unproven claims of their effectiveness. 'In 1990 it seemed to make good common sense to employ older people but a number of stereotypes and issues were raised. Answers were needed to explode these myths.'[98]

The concerns and myths about older workers reflected findings in other studies on the subject such as that reported in 1993 to the Institute of Personnel Management (now the CIPD).[99] These included both positive and negative features: for instance, older workers were seen as more reliable, loyal, conscientious

and hard-working than younger ones; at the same time they were viewed as less adaptable, especially to new technology, as well as being less able and less motivated to learn or be trained. Other studies have shown that stereotypical views about older workers tend to cluster under general headings of poor performance (including those related to assumptions about age-related physical impairment), absenteeism and turnover.[100] There were also concerns about the relationship between younger and older workers, and particularly those between young managers and older staff members.

B&Q managers decided that it would be important to collect some hard evidence if they were to gain the backing of the business owners. In 1989 they opened a new store in Macclesfield, staffed wholly by workers over 50. The experiment was monitored by a research team from Warwick University, who carried out a study to benchmark the Macclesfield store's performance against a selection of four similar stores during its first year of operation. The results were significant: the Warwick team reported that the Macclesfield store had higher profits, substantially reduced staff turnover, over a third less absenteeism and almost two-thirds less 'shrinkage' (loss to stock as the result of damage or pilfering by staff and customers).[101] Many of the Board's concerns had clearly been put to rest; the business case for diversifying the workforce had been supported by the evidence. B&Q therefore began to adopt a positive approach towards the recruitment and employment of an age-diverse workforce. This was more than ten years before legislation on the subject came into operation in the UK. Further research in 1995 confirmed the initial results, leading the company to reaffirm its initial commitment to increasing the age diversity of its workforce. There were clear indications that the policy is about good business in all senses of the word. In 2000 the company became one of the founding members of the Employers Forum on Age (EFA),[102] an independent group of over 200 UK employers that sets out to campaign for and support the cause of employing an age-diverse workforce.

Diversity at B&Q: the growing agenda
Having been successful with its approach to employing the over-50s, B&Q also recognises the value of a broader approach to diversity. The company website includes substantial information about its current approach to social responsibility, including respect for the diversity of people.

> We believe that a diverse workforce creates a mix of talents that makes us a successful business. We want B&Q to be a 'great place to work and shop'. It is our policy to implement procedures to eliminate discrimination and promote equality of opportunity in employment so that age, gender, colour, ethnic or national origin, culture, religion, disability, marital status, political affiliation or sexual orientation are not barriers for anybody who wants to work and shop at B&Q.[103]

The B&Q board takes an active interest in the diversity strategy and B&Q employs an Engagement and Diversity Advisor to lead the programme for the company. The strategy includes a strong commitment to cultural diversity, and to people with disabilities. The company reflects all this in its advertising and publicity material as well as its personnel and management policies, thus making diversity an important part of the business's brand values and public image.

The disability policy was formulated in 1998, and, like the age policy, it links the importance of understanding and integrating disability issues into the business strategy. The twin goals are to remove barriers that make working and shopping at B&Q difficult for disabled people. Similarly, the cultural diversity strategy at B&Q goes beyond simple compliance measures to ensure that the company does not breach the law. In 2001 the company discovered that over 1,000 of its staff were bilingual, and that between them they spoke over 60 languages other than English, including British Sign Language. Employees are actively encouraged to use languages other than English where this can help to understand and respond to customer needs, and many wear language badges to indicate this. The company produces a cultural diversity information pack for use in stores, together with a calendar of religious and cultural festivals which not only helps staff to understand customers but assists managers with work scheduling.

What next for B&Q?
The economic downturn and the particular problems in the UK housing market during 2007–9 have clearly had a major impact on the home improvement sector generally. However, B&Q CEO remains upbeat about the company's strategic plan to double its profits by 2012.[104] The key to B&Qs strategy is its people; real staff featured heavily in the spring 2009 television advertising campaign and the company is refining and enhancing its communication strategy with a bi-monthly employee magazine, regular short films to communicate the business progress to store staff and the CEO's blog. It is investing in training through five in-house 'academies' which aim to ensure all staff have both knowledge and confidence about all key areas of business, from practical DIY skills to understanding finance. And since the company has recently won a prestigious international Gallup Great Workplace Award for the third year running, this investment may just deliver the goods.[105]

Your tasks

1 Why did B&Q adopt its present approach to diversity? How far do you agree or disagree with these reasons for its action, and why?

2 Review B&Q's approach in the light of theories about personality. Which of the theoretical approaches do you think might best explain the company's approach to its staff and customers?

3 How might the B&Q approach to diversity encourage individuals (both staff and customers) to contribute to the organisation's performance?

4 B&Q operates in a very specific sector: retail home improvement building and gardening materials and equipment. Would its approach to diversity translate to other types of organisation, for example an on-line or telephone retail insurance company (for example selling motor, travel or home insurance), a car maker, or a state-run school or hospital?

Notes and references

1 We wish gratefully to acknowledge Linda Carter, the original author of this chapter and the joint author in the eighth edition of this text.

2 McCrae, R. R. and Costa, P. T. 'More Reasons to Adopt the Five-Factor Model', *American Psychologist*, vol. 44, no. 2, 1989, pp. 451–2.

3 Bayne, R. 'The Big Five versus the Myers-Briggs', *The Psychologist*, January 1994, pp. 14–17.

4 Barrick, M. R. and Mount, M. K. 'The Big Five Personality Dimensions and Job Performance: A Meta-Analysis', *Personnel Psychology*, Spring 1991, pp. 1–26.

5 Mount, M. K., Barrick, M. R. and Strauss, J. P. 'Validity of Observer Ratings of the Big Five Personality Factors', *Journal of Applied Psychology*, April 1994, p. 272.

6 Bentall, R. P. 'Personality Traits May Be Alive, They May Even Be Well, But Are They Really Useful?', *The Psychologist*, July 1993, p. 307.

7 Robertson, I. 'Undue Diligence', *People Management*, no. 22, November 2001, pp. 42–3.

8 Lord, W. and Rust, J. 'The Big Five Revisited: Where Are We Now? A Brief Review of the Relevance of the Big Five for Occupational Assessment', *Selection and Development Review*, vol. 19, no. 4, August 2003, pp. 15–18.

9 Eysenck, H. J. *Eysenck on Extraversion*, Crosby Lockwood Staples (1973).

10 Mabey, B. 'The Majority of Large Companies Use Occupational Tests', *Guidance and Assessment Review*, vol. 5, no. 3, 1989.

11 Personality tests have been debated by: Bartram, D. 'Addressing the Abuse of Personality Tests', *Personnel Management*, April 1991, pp. 34–9; and Fletcher, C. 'Personality Tests: The Great Debate', *Personnel Management*, September 1991, pp. 38–42.

12 Howarth, E. 'A Source of Independent Variation: Convergence and Divergence in the Work of Cattell and Eysenck', in Dreger, R. M. (ed.) *Multivariate Personality Research*, Claiton (1972).

13 Rogers, C. *A Way of Being*, Houghton Mifflin (1980).

14 Cooley, C. 'The Social Self', in Parsons, T., Shils, E., Naegele, K. D. and Pitts, J. R. (eds) *Theories of Society*, The Free Press, New York (1965).

15 Erikson, E. H. *Identity and the Life Cycle*, Norton (1980).

16 Hunt, J. W. *Managing People at Work: A Manager's Guide to Behaviour in Organisations*, third edition, McGraw-Hill (1992).

17 Jung, C. G. *Analytical Psychology: Its Theory and Practice*, Routledge and Kegan Paul (1968). See also Jacobi, J. *Psychology of C. G. Jung*, seventh edition, Routledge and Kegan Paul (1968).

18 Myers, I. B. *Introduction to Type*, sixth edition, Consulting Psychologists Press (1998); and Myers, K. D. and Kirby, L. K. *Introduction to Type Dynamics and Development*, second edition, Consulting Psychologists Press (2000).

19 Hirsh, S. K. and Kise, J. *Introduction to Type and Coaching: A Dynamic Guide for Individual Development*, Consulting Psychologists Press (1994).

20 Kelly's theory as described by Bannister, D. and Fansella, F., in *Inquiring Mind: The Theory of Personal Constructs*, Penguin (1971), pp. 50–1.

21 Stone, G. 'Personality and Effective Hospitality Management', paper presented at the International Association of Hotel Management Schools Symposium, Leeds Polytechnic, Autumn 1988; and Worsfold, P. A. 'Personality Profile of the Hotel Manager', *International Journal of Hospitality Management*, vol. 8, no. 1, 1989, pp. 55–62.

22 Bartram, D. 'Addressing the Abuse of Psychological Tests', *Personnel Management*, April 1991, pp. 34–9; Newell, S. and Shackleton, V. 'Management Selection: A Comparative Survey of Methods Used in Top British and French Companies', *Journal of Occupational Psychology*, vol. 64, 1991, p. 23.

23 Kline, P. 'The Big Five and Beyond', conference paper given at the British Psychological Society Occupational Psychology Conference, University of Warwick, January 1995.

24 Anastasi, A. *Psychological Testing*, Macmillan (1988), p. 560.

25 Blinkhorn, S. and Johnson, C. 'The Insignificance of Personality Testing', *Nature*, 348, 1990, pp. 671–2.

26 Goss, D. *Principles of Human Resource Management*, Routledge (1994).

27 Gibbons, P., Baron, H., Nyfield, G. and Robertson, I. 'The Managerial Performance and Competences',

conference paper given at the British Psychological Society Occupational Psychology Conference, University of Warwick, January 1995.

28 Platt, S. with Piepe, R. and Smythe, J. *'Teams': A Game to Develop Group Skills*, Gower (1988).

29 Gray, M. J. 'Personality and Performance', *Selection and Development Review*, vol. 19, no. 1, February 2003, p. 4.

30 Hochschild, A. R. *The Managed Heart: Commercialization of Human Feeling*, University of California Press (1983).

31 Cooper, C. 'Papering Over the Cracks: Individual Strategies or Organizational Intervention in Dealing with Stress at Work', conference paper given at the British Psychological Society Occupational Psychology conference, University of Warwick, January 1995.

32 Friedman, M. and Rosenman, R. *Type A Behavior and Your Heart*, Knopf (1974).

33 Rosenmann, R., Friedman, F. and Straus, R. 'A Predictive Study of CHD', *Journal of the American Medical Association*, vol. 89, 1964, pp. 15–22; and Warr, P. and Wall, T. *Work and Well Being*, Penguin (1975).

34 See, for example, Jex, S. M., Adams, G. A., Elacqua, T. C. and Bachrach, D. G. 'Type "A" as a Moderator of Stressors and Job Complexity: A Comparison of Achievement Strivings and Impatience-Irritability', *Journal of Applied Psychology*, vol. 32, no. 5, 2002, pp. 977–96.

35 Gratton, L., *Hot Spots*, Financial Times Prentice Hall (2007).

36 Ibid., p. 83.

37 Howe, M. J. A. 'Can IQ Change?', *The Psychologist*, February 1998, pp. 69–72.

38 Spearman, C. *The Abilities of Man*, Macmillan (1927).

39 Vernon, P. E. *The Structure of Human Abilities*, Methuen and Co. (1950).

40 Thurstone, L. L. 'Primary Mental Abilities', *Psychometric Monographs*, no. 1, 1938.

41 Guilford, J. P. 'Three Faces of Intellect', *American Psychologist*, vol. 14, pp. 469–79.

42 Gardner, H. *Frames of Mind*, second edition, Fontana (1993).

43 Goleman, D. *Emotional Intelligence*, Bloomsbury (1996), p. 34.

44 Goleman, D. *Working with Emotional Intelligence*, Bantam Books, New York (1998).

45 Boyatzis, R., Goleman, D. and Hay/McBer, *Emotional Competence Inventory Feedback Report*, Hay Group (1999).

46 'Management Futures: The World in 2018', Chartered Management Institute, March 2008.

47 Landale, A. 'Must Have EQ', *Manager: The British Journal of Administrative Management*, February/March 2007, pp. 24–5.

48 Ibid.

49 Garrett, A. 'Crash Course in Raising Emotional Intelligence', *Management Today*, August 2005, p. 16.

50 Dann, J. 'Managing Your Emotions', *Professional Manager*, vol. 17, no. 4, July 2008, pp. 32–4.

51 Ribeaux, P. and Poppleton, S. E. *Psychology and Work*, Macmillan (1978).

52 Gross, R. D. *Psychology: The Science of Mind and Behaviour*, Edward Arnold (1987).

53 Hofstede, G. *Culture's Consequences: International Differences in Work-Related Values*, Sage (1980).

54 Katz, D. 'The Functional Approach to the Study of Attitudes', *Public Opinion Quarterly*, issue 21, 1960, pp. 163–204.

55 La Piere, R. T. 'Attitudes versus Action', *Social Forces*, issue 13, 1934, pp. 230–7.

56 Gidoomal, R., Mahtani, D. and Porter, D. *The British and How to Deal With Them*, Middlesex University Press (2001).

57 Sykes, A. J. M. 'The Effect of a Supervisory Training Course in Changing Supervisors' Perceptions and Expectations of the Role of Management', *Human Relations*, 15, 1962, pp. 227–43.

58 Hofstede, G., Nevijan, B., Dhayu, D. D. and Sanders, G. 'Measuring Organisational Cultures: A Qualitative and Quantitative Study across 20 Cases', *Administrative Science Quarterly*, vol. 35, 1990, pp. 286–316.

59 Berger, P. L. and Luckmann, T. *The Social Construction of Reality*, Penguin (1966), p. 37.

60 MacPherson, Sir William *The Stephen Lawrence Inquiry*, The Stationery Office, February 1999, Section 6.17.

61 'Undertaking Employee Attitude Surveys' Checklist 078, Chartered Management Institute, February 2007.

62 Likert, R. 'A Technique for the Measurement of Attitudes', *Archives of Psychology*, vol. 22, no. 1, 1932, pp. 1–55.

63 Heider, F. 'Attitudes and Cognitive Organization', *Journal of Psychology*, vol. 21, 1946, pp. 107–12.

64 Festinger, L. A. *A Theory of Cognitive Dissonance*, Row, Peterson and Co. (1957); reissued by Stanford University Press and Tavistock Publications (1962).

65 Anastasia, A. *Psychological Testing*, Macmillan Publishing (1988), p. 23.

66 Barrett, R. S. 'Guide to Using Psychological Tests', in Fleishman, E. A. (ed.) *Studies in Personnel and Industrial Psychology*, revised edition, Dorsey Press (1967), p. 58.

67 See, for example, Furnham, A. *The Psychology of Behaviour at Work*, Psychology Press (1997); and Wilson, C. 'Tough Choices', *Manager: The British Journal of Administrative Management*, May/June 1999, pp. 10–12.

68 Kandola, R. and Fullerton, J. *Managing the Mosaic Diversity in Action*, IPD (1994), p. 19.

69 'Implementing a Diversity Management Programme' Checklist 152, Chartered Management Institute, January 2008.

70 Ibid.

71 Guirdham, M. *Interactive Behaviour at Work*, third edition, Financial Times Prentice Hall (2002), p. 67.

72 'Back to Basics: Acas' Experience of Equality and Diversity in the Workplace', ACAS Policy Discussion Paper no. 5, November 2006.

73 'Littlewoods: Increasing Diversity, Increasing Profits', *Equal Opportunities Review*, no. 81, September/October 1998, pp. 20–7.

74 'Talent not Tokenism: The Business Benefits of Workforce Diversity', CBI and TUC, June 2008.

75 Hill, L. A. 'Leadership as Collective Genius', in Chowdhury, S. (ed.) *Management 21C*, Financial Times Prentice Hall (2000), p. 53.

76 'Managing Diversity: Linking Theory and Practice to Business Performance', CIPD, May 2005.

77 'Management Recruitment: Understanding Routes to Greater Diversity', Chartered Management Institute, June 2008.

78 From http://hiltonworldwide.hilton.com (accessed 1 March 2006).

79 Information on BITC can be found at http://www.bitc.org.uk.

80 ACAS 'Managing Diversity', *Employment Relations Matters*, issue 3, Spring 2005.

81 Arkin, A. 'Hidden Talents' *People Management*, vol. 11, no. 14, 14 July 2005, p. 26.

82 Khan, S. *P.U.S.H. for Success*, Vermilion (2006), p. 230.

83 Clements, P. and Jones, J. *The Diversity Training Handbook*, Kogan Page (2002), p. 45.

84 www.berr.gov.uk (accessed 3 March 2009).

85 Information kindly provided by Lloyds TSB Equality and Diversity Team.

86 Francesco, A. M. and Gold, B. A. *International Organizational Behavior*, Prentice Hall (1998), p. 236.

87 'Back to Basics: Acas Experience of Equality and Diversity in the Workplace', ACAS Policy Discussion Paper no. 5, November 2006.

88 'Implementing a Diversity Management Programme' Checklist 152, Chartered Management Institute, January 2008.

89 Nordström, K. and Ridderstråle, J., 'Funky Inc.,' in Crainer, S. and Dearlove, D. (eds), *Financial Times Handbook of Management*, second edition, Financial Times Prentice Hall (2001), p. 63.

90 Kirton, G. and Greene, A.-M. *The Dynamics of Managing Diversity*, Butterworth Heinemann (2000).

91 Liff, S. and Cameron, I. 'Changing Equality Cultures to Move Beyond Women's Problems', *Gender, Work and Organization*, vol. 4, no. 1, January 1997, pp. 35–46.

92 Lucas, E. 'Making Inclusivity a Reality', *Professional Manager*, vol. 16, no. 4, July 2007, pp. 32–5.

93 See, for example, 'What's Keeping Women out of the Top Jobs?', *Social Agenda*, The European Commission, no. 16, February 2008, pp. 7–10.

94 Alvesson, M. and Due Billing, Y. *Understanding Gender and Organization*, Sage (1997).

95 *IBM in the UK 2005*, IBM Corporation, 2005, p. 41.

96 From the B&Q website: www.diy.com/diy/jsp/ bq/templates/content_lookup.jsp?content=/ aboutbandq/2004/company_information/ history_brief.jsp&menu=aboutbandq.

97 Talk at Portsmouth University Business School by CEO Euan Sutherland, 9 July 2009.

98 B&Q 'Is Age a Barrier to Employment? Equality + Diversity: Achieving a Balanced Workforce', http://www. diy.com/diy/jsp/aboutbandq/2004/social_responsibility/ pdfs/age_policy.pdf (accessed 28 July 2009).

99 Warr, P. and Pennington, J. *Views about Age Discrimination and Older Workers*, Institute of Personnel Management (1993).

100 Stoney, C. and Roberts, M. 'The Case for the Older Worker at Tesco: An Examination of Attitudes, Assumptions and Attributes', Carleton University School of Public Policy and Administration Working Paper no. 53, 2003.

101 B&Q op. cit.

102 The Employers Forum on Age can be found at www.efa.org.uk.

103 B&Q Statement of Social Responsibility, www.diy.com (accessed 28 July 2009).

104 Talk at Portsmouth University Business School by CEO Euan Sutherland, 9 July 2009.

105 Gallup Great Workplace Award, http://www.gallup.com/ consulting/ (accessed 28 July 2009).

6 PERCEPTION AND COMMUNICATION[1]

Perceived reality, not actual reality, is the key to understanding behaviour. How we perceive others and ourselves is at the root of our actions and intentions. Understanding the perceptual process and being aware of its complexities can help develop insights about ourselves and may help in reading others. The words we use, the way we look and the body language we display communicate our view of the world. The importance of perception and communications in guiding our behaviour needs to be understood for effective relationships with others.

Learning outcomes

After completing this chapter you should be able to:

- explain the nature of the perceptual process and selectivity and attention;
- detail internal and external factors that provide meaning to the individual;
- examine the organisation and arrangement of stimuli, and perceptual illusions;
- explain the importance of selection and attention, and organisation and judgement;
- identify problems and difficulties in perceiving other people and non-verbal communications;
- evaluate the relevance of neuro-linguistic programming and transactional analysis;
- review the importance of an understanding of perception and communication.

Critical reflection

'Many people do not consciously think about the person with whom they are interacting. They translate their model of the world from their own perceptions and assume that others are working from the same model. There is no way managers can cope with so many individual perspectives so they might just as well rely on their own judgement.'

What are your views?

THE PERCEPTUAL PROCESS

The significance of individual differences is particularly apparent when focusing on the process of **perception**. We all see things in different ways. We all have our own, unique picture or image of how we see the 'real' world and this is a complex and dynamic process. We do not passively receive information from the world; we analyse and judge it. We may place significance on some information and regard other information as worthless; and we may be influenced by our expectations so that we 'see' what we expect to see or 'hear' what we expect to hear. Although general theories of perception were first proposed during the last century, the importance of understanding the perceptual process is arguably even more significant today. Perception is the root of all organisational behaviour; any situation can be analysed in terms of its perceptual connotations. Consider, for instance, the following situation.

A member of the management team has sent an email to team leaders asking them to provide statistics of overtime worked within their section during the past six months and projections for the next six months. Mixed reactions could result:

- One team leader may see it as a reasonable and welcome request to provide information which will help lead to improved staffing levels.
- Another team leader may see it as an unreasonable demand, intended only to enable management to exercise closer supervision and control over the activities of the section.
- A third team leader may have no objection to providing the information but be suspicious that it may lead to possible intrusion into the running of the section.
- A fourth team leader may see it as a positive action by management to investigate ways of reducing costs and improving efficiency throughout the organisation.

Each of the section heads perceives the email communication differently based on their own experiences. Their perceived reality and understanding of the situation provokes differing reactions.

In addition, there are likely to be mixed reactions to the use of email as the means of communication in this instance.

Individuality

We are all unique; there is only one Laurie Mullins and there is only one of you. We all have our own 'world', our own way of looking at and understanding our environment and the people within it. A situation may be the same but the interpretation of that situation by two individuals may be vastly different. For instance, listening to a podcast may be riveting to one person but a boring way to spend 20 minutes to another. One person may see a product as user-friendly but another person may feel that it is far too simplistic and basic. The physical properties may be identical, but they are perceived quite differently because each individual has imposed upon the object/environment/person their own interpretations, their own judgement and evaluation.

A possible framework for the study of perception and communication is set out in Figure 6.1.

SELECTIVITY IN ATTENTION AND PERCEPTION

It is not possible to have an understanding of perception without taking into account its sensory basis. We are not able to attend to everything in our environment; our sensory systems have limits. The physical limits therefore insist that we are selective in our attention

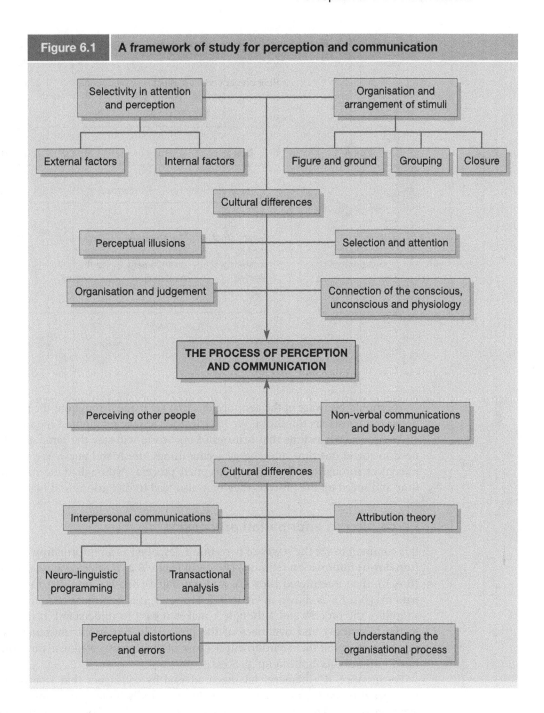

Figure 6.1 A framework of study for perception and communication

and perception. Early pioneer work by psychologists has resulted in an understanding of universal laws that underlie the perceptual process. It seems that we cannot help but search for meaning and understanding in our environment. The way in which we categorise and organise this sensory information is based on a range of factors including the present situation, our emotional state and any experiences of the same or a similar event.

Some information may be considered highly important to us and may result in immediate action or speech; in other instances, the information may be simply 'parked' or assimilated in other ideas and thoughts. The link between perception and memory processes becomes obvious. Some of our 'parked' material may be forgotten or, indeed, changed and reconstructed over time.[2]

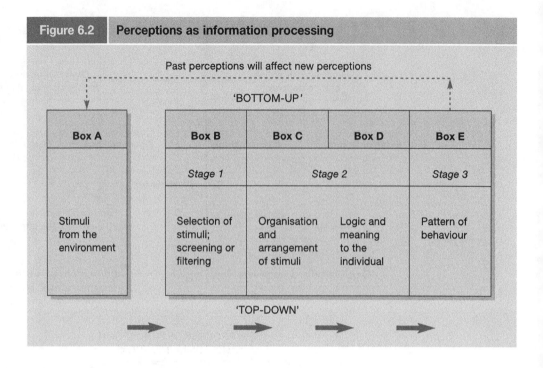

Figure 6.2 Perceptions as information processing

We should be aware of the assumptions that are made throughout the perceptual process, below our conscious threshold. We have learned to take for granted certain constants in our environment. We assume that features of our world will stay the same and thus we do not need to spend our time and energy seeing things afresh and anew. We make a number of inferences throughout the entire perceptual process. Although these inferences may save time and speed up the process, they may also lead to distortions and inaccuracies.

Perception as information processing

It is common to see the stages of perception described as an information-processing system: (top-down) information (stimuli) (Box A in Figure 6.2) is selected at one end of the process (Box B), then interpreted (Box C), and translated (Box D), resulting in action or thought patterns (Box E), as shown in Figure 6.2. However, it is important to note that such a model simplifies the process and although it makes it easy to understand, it does not do justice to the complexity and dynamics of the process. In certain circumstances, we may select information out of the environment because of the way we categorise the world. The dotted line illustrates this 'bottom-up' process.

For instance, if a manager has been advised by colleagues that a particular trainee has managerial potential, the manager may be specifically looking for confirmation that those views are correct. This process has been known as 'top-down' because the cognitive processes are influencing the perceptual readiness of the individual to select certain information. This emphasises the active nature of the perceptual process. We do not passively digest the information from our senses, but we actively attend and indeed, at times, seek out certain information. (See also the discussion on self-fulfilling prophecy later in this chapter.)

Meaning to the individual

The process of perception explains the manner in which information (stimuli) from the environment around us is selected and organised to provide meaning for the individual. Perception is the mental function of giving significance to stimuli such as shapes, colours, movement, taste, sounds, touch, smells, pain, pressures and feelings. Perception gives rise to individual behavioural responses to particular situations.

Figure 6.3

Despite the fact that a group of people may 'physically see' the same thing, they each have their own version of what is seen – their perceived view of reality. Consider, for example, the image (published by W. E. Hill in *Puck*, 6 November 1915) shown in Figure 6.3. What do you see? Do you see a young, attractive, well-dressed woman? Or do you see an older, poor woman? Or can you now see both? **And who can say with certainty that there is just the one, 'correct' answer?**

Internal and external factors

The first stage in the process of perception is selection and attention. Why do we attend to certain stimuli and not to others? There are two important factors to consider in this discussion: first, internal factors relating to the state of the individual; second, the environment and influences external to the individual. The process of perceptual selection is based, therefore, on both internal and external factors.

INTERNAL FACTORS

Our sensory systems have limits – we are not able to see for 'miles and miles' or hear very low- or very high-pitched sounds. All our senses have specialist nerves that respond differently to the forms of energy that are received. For instance, our eyes receive and convert light waves into electrical signals that are transmitted to the visual cortex of the brain and translated into meaning.

Our sensory system is geared to respond to changes in the environment. This has particular implications for the way in which we perceive the world and it explains why we are able to

ignore the humming of the central heating system but notice instantly a telephone ringing. The term used to describe the way in which we disregard the familiar is 'habituation'.

Sensory limits or thresholds

As individuals we may differ in terms of our sensory limits or thresholds. Without eye glasses some people would not be able to read a car's number plate at the distance required for safety. People differ not only in their absolute thresholds but also in their ability to discriminate between stimuli. For instance, it may not be possible for the untrained to distinguish between different types of wine but this would be an everyday event for the trained sommelier. We are able to learn to discriminate and are able to train our senses to recognise small differences between stimuli. It is also possible for us to adapt to unnatural environments and learn to cope.[3]

We may also differ in terms of the amount of sensory information we need to reach our own comfortable equilibrium. Some individuals would find loud music at a party or gig uncomfortable and unpleasant, whereas for others the intensity of the music is part of the total enjoyment. Likewise, if we are deprived of sensory information for too long this can lead to feelings of discomfort and fatigue. Indeed, research has shown that if the brain is deprived of sensory information then it will manufacture its own and subjects will hallucinate.[4] It is possible to conclude therefore that the perceptual process is rooted to the sensory limitations of the individual.

Psychological factors

Psychological factors will also affect what is perceived. These internal factors, such as personality, learning and motives, will give rise to an inclination to perceive certain stimuli with a readiness to respond in certain ways. This has been called an individual's perceptual set (*see* Figure 6.4).

Differences in the ways individuals acquire information have been used as one of four scales in the Myers–Briggs Type Indicator (discussed in Chapter 4). They distinguish individuals who 'tend to accept and work with what is given in the here-and-now, and thus become realistic and practical' (sensing types) from others who go beyond the information from the senses and look at the possible patterns, meanings and relationships. These 'intuitive types' 'grow expert at seeing new possibilities and new ways of doing things'. Myers and Briggs stress the value of both types and emphasise the importance of complementary skills and variety in any successful enterprise or relationship.[5]

Figure 6.4	Factors affecting an individual's perceptual set

Personality and perception have also been examined in the classic experiments by *Witkin et al.* on field dependence/independence. Field-dependent individuals were found to be reliant on the context of the stimuli, the cues given in the situation, whereas field-independent subjects relied mainly on their internal bodily cues and less on the environment. These experiments led Witkin to generalise to other settings outside the psychological laboratory and to suggest that individuals use, and need, different information from the environment to make sense of their world.[6]

The needs of an individual

The needs of an individual will affect their perceptions. For example, a manager deeply engrossed in preparing an urgent report may screen out ringing telephones, the sound of computers, people talking and furniture being moved in the next office, but will respond readily to the smell of coffee brewing. The most desirable and urgent needs will almost certainly affect an individual perceptual process. Members of a church choir might well form a perception of the minister quite different from that of a parishioner seeking comfort after the recent death of a close relative.

The 'Pollyanna Principle' claims that pleasant stimuli will be processed more quickly and remembered more precisely than unpleasant stimuli. However, it must be noted that intense internal drives may lead to perceptual distortions of situations (or people) and an unwillingness to absorb certain painful information. This will be considered later in this chapter.

Learning from experiences has a critical effect throughout all the stages of the perceptual process. It will affect the stimuli perceived in the first instance, and then the ways in which those stimuli are understood and processed, and finally the response which is given. For example, it is likely that a maintenance engineer visiting a school for the first time will notice different things about it than will a teacher attending an interview or a child arriving on the first day. The learning gained from experiences colours what is seen and processed.

Critical reflection

'Popular sports, film or television celebrities often appear to have a far greater impact on perception, communications and behaviour than any textbook, manager or training course.'

Why do you think this is the case and to what extent does this apply to you? Is it necessarily a bad thing?

CULTURAL DIFFERENCES

There are many ways of describing **culture** but the following definition from *Schein* helps relate culture to diversity and perception.

> *A pattern of basic assumptions – invented, discovered or developed by a given group as it learns to cope with its problems of external adaptation and internal integration – that has worked well enough to be considered valuable and therefore to be taught to new members as the correct way to perceive, think and feel in relation to these problems.*[7]

The ways in which people interact are also subject to cultural differences and such differences may be misconstrued. Embarrassment and discomfort can occur when emotional lines are broken. This was demonstrated in an American study that researched the experience of Japanese students visiting the USA for the first time. The researchers felt that the Japanese

students faced considerable challenges in adapting to the new culture. Some of the surprises that the students reported related to social interaction:

Casual visits and frequent phone calls at midnight to the host room-mate were a new experience to them. The sight of opposite-sex partners holding hands or kissing in public places also surprised them . . . That males do cooking and shopping in the household or by themselves, that fathers would play with children, and that there was frequent intimacy displayed between couples were all never-heard-of in their own experiences at home.[8]

The ways in which words are used and the assumptions made about shared understanding are dependent upon an individual's culture and upbringing. In cultures where it is 'normal' to explain all details clearly, explicitly and directly (such as the USA), other cultures may find the 'spelling out' of all the details unnecessary and embarrassing. In France, ambiguity and subtlety are expected and much is communicated by what is **not** said. *Hall* distinguished low-context cultures (direct, explicit communication) from high-context cultures (meaning assumed and non-verbal signs significant).[9]

Those organizations that can create a culture that challenges unhelpful perceptual processes (stemming, say, from ignorance, prejudice or arrogance) will, in our view, be more able to absorb new information and respond intelligently to change. Broadening our mind, however, is much easier said than done. To understand why this is so, it is worth looking at influences on our perceptual processes. At the most fundamental level lie our values and beliefs. These also colour what we see and how we interpret events. Given this, it is important we reflect on how our own values influence the decisions we make.[10]

McCrum refers to a joke circulated on the Web by disaffected UN staff. A worldwide survey was conducted by the UN. The only question asked was: 'Would you please give your honest opinion about solutions to the food shortage in the rest of the world?' The survey was a failure. In Africa they didn't know what 'food' meant; in India they didn't know what 'honest' meant; in Europe they didn't know what 'shortage' meant; in China they didn't know what 'opinion' meant; in the Middle East they didn't know what 'solution' meant; in South America they didn't know what 'please' meant; and in the USA they didn't know what 'the rest of the world' meant.[11]

Cultural differences often lead to stereotypical views. For example, *Stewart-Allen* discusses a common mindset about Americans:

American business people seem to suffer from a long-standing image problem abroad. The stereotypical view is that they are loud and impatient with a 'bigger is better' attitude; they lecture others about how to do business the American way and are insular in outlook.

However, a more accurate assumption is that Americans lack international exposure.[12] Stereotyping is discussed later in this chapter.

Diversity Resource Handbook

Portsmouth Hospitals NHS Trust has produced a comprehensive 'Diversity Resource Handbook' that recognises the diversities of traditions, cultures and religious needs within a multi-ethnic and multicultural society. The booklet is intended to provide practical advice and guidelines for the delivery of a sensitive service to the diverse community they serve. The booklet sets out advice on race, religious and cultural awareness; multicultural requirements; major world religions; interpreting and translating; sexual orientation and gender; aids to communication; and useful contacts.

Diversity Resource Handbook – continued

Myths and realities

There are many different myths concerning people from ethnic minorities. A few of these myths are listed below:

- People from ethnic backgrounds 'look after themselves adequately' and therefore do not require much outside help.
- Elderly people from ethnic minorities are generally looked after by their own families.
- Black staff are the most suited to administer treatment of ethnic minority clients.

Awareness in a multicultural society – some guidelines

- Be aware that in some communities it may not be the custom to shake hands, especially among women. A woman may feel uncomfortable or may not wish to be in a room with a man who is not a relative. An act of comfort, for example putting an arm around a person, may cause embarrassment or offence.
- Be sensitive to the difficulties that may be caused for ethnic minorities by using jargon and slang. Using colloquialisms or terms of endearment may cause offence: for example, 'love', 'dear' or 'darling'.
- Appreciate cultural differences in body language: for example, looking away instead of maintaining eye contact is not necessarily a sign of dishonesty or disrespect. In some communities it may be the opposite.
- Ask for the individual's personal and family name. Don't ask someone what his or her Christian name or surname is.
- Just because someone responds to questions in English they may not fully understand what is being said.
- Don't underestimate the influence of your own cultural background on your unconscious perceptions and behaviours.

Source: From Portsmouth Hospitals NHS Trust *Diversity Resource Handbook*. Courtesy of Florise Elliott, Diversity Advisor. Reproduced with permission.

The importance of language

Our language plays an important role in the way we perceive the world. Our language not only labels and distinguishes the environment for us but also structures and guides our thinking patterns. Even if we are proficient skiers, we do not have many words we can use to describe the different texture of snow; we would be reliant on using layers of adjectives. The Inuit, however, have 13 words for snow in their language. Our language is part of the culture we experience and learn to take for granted. Culture differences are relevant because they emphasise the impact of social learning on the perception of people and their surroundings.

So, language not only reflects our experience but also shapes whether and what we experience. It influences our relationships with others and with the environment. Consider a situation where a student is using a library in a UK university for the first time. The student is from South Asia where the word 'please' is incorporated in the verb and in intonation; a separate word is not used. When the student requests help, the assistant may consider the student rude because they did not use the word 'please'. By causing offence the student has quite innocently affected the library assistant's perceptions.

Much is also communicated in how words are said and in the silences between words.

In the UK speech is suggestive and idiomatic speech is common:

'Make no bones about it' (means get straight to the point)
'Sent to Coventry' (means to be socially isolated).

And action is implied rather than always stated:

> 'I hope you won't mind if I' (means 'I am going to')
> 'I'm afraid I really can't see my way to . . .' (means 'no').

Conversational pitfalls

A well-known quotation, attributed to George Bernard Shaw, is:

> *'England and America are two countries divided by a common language.'*

From frequent visits to America, the author can give numerous personal testimonies to this, including these actual words: 'I am just going to the trunk (boot of the car) to get my purse (handbag), fanny bag (bum bag) and money wallet (purse).'

McCrum gives some examples of conversational pitfalls:[13]

Australia	talking disparagingly about Aboriginal people
China	human rights; Tibet, Taiwan; sex; religion; bureaucracy
Far East	confusing Japanese, Chinese or Korean in any combination
Greece, S.Cyprus	asking for Turkish coffee
India	poverty; sex; dowry deaths
Ireland	referring to Great Britain as the 'Mainland'; talking about 'the British Isles' to include Ireland; asking why they use euros rather than pounds sterling
Latin America	talking about 'Americans' to mean just North America
Mexico	nepotism
The Netherlands	calling the country 'Holland' (inaccurate and offensive to people not from the Holland provinces)
New Zealand	using the term 'Mainland' for either North or South islands; mis-pronouncing Maori place-names
Northern Ireland	asking people whether they're Catholic or Protestant
Russia	corruption, contract killings, etc.
South Africa	banging on about apartheid (it ended some time ago)
Spain	criticism of bullfighting
US South	the Confederate flag

Source: McCrum, M. *Going Dutch in Beijing*, Profile Books (2007) pp. 44–5. Reproduced with permission from Profile Books Ltd.

EXTERNAL FACTORS

The knowledge of, familiarity with, or expectations about a given situation or previous experiences will influence perception. External factors refer to the nature and characteristics of the stimuli. There is usually a tendency to give more attention to stimuli which are, for example,

- large
- moving
- intense
- loud
- bright
- novel
- repeated
- in strong contrast to their background.

Any number of these factors may be present at a given time or in a given situation. The use of these stimuli is a key feature in the design of advertising. (Think of your own examples.) It is the **total pattern** of the stimuli together with the **context** in which they occur that influence perception. For example, it is usually a novel or unfamiliar stimulus that is more noticeable, but a person is more likely to perceive the familiar face of a friend among a group of people all dressed in the same-style uniform (*see* Figure 6.5).[14]

Figure 6.5	Is everybody happy?

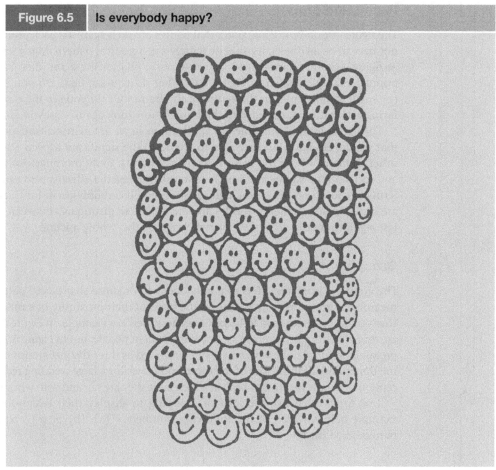

Source: Block, J. R. and Yuker, H. E. *Can You Believe Your Eyes?*, Robson Books (2002), p. 163.

We are all familiar with the expression 'what on earth is that doing here?'. The sight of a fork-lift truck on the factory floor of a manufacturing organisation is likely to be perceived quite differently from one in the corridor of a university. Consider another example: the sight of a jet ski (left temporarily by someone moving house) in the garage of a person known to be scared of water is likely to elicit such a remark. Yet the sight of numerous jet skis on the beach is likely to pass without comment. The word 'terminal' is likely to be perceived differently in the context of: (i) a hospital, (ii) an airport or (iii) a computer firm. Consumer psychologists and marketing experts apply these perceptual principles with extraordinary success for some of their products.

ORGANISATION AND ARRANGEMENT OF STIMULI

The Gestalt School of Psychology led by Max Wertheimer claimed that the process of perception is innately organised and patterned. It described the process as one that has built-in field effects. In other words, the brain can act like a dynamic, physical field in which interaction among elements is an intrinsic part. The Gestalt School produced a series of principles, which are still readily applicable today. Some of the most significant include the following:

- figure and ground
- grouping
- closure.

Figure and ground

The figure–ground principle states that figures are seen against a background. The figure does not have to be an object; it could be merely a geometrical pattern. Many textiles are perceived as figure–ground relationships. Figure–ground relationships are often reversible, as in the popular example shown in Figure 6.6. What do you see first? Do you see a white chalice (or small stand shape) in the centre of the frame? Or do you see the dark profiles of twins facing each other on the edge of the frame? Now look again. Can you see the other shape?

The figure–ground principle has applications in all occupational situations. It is important that employees know and are able to attend to the significant aspects (the figure) and treat other elements of the job as context (background). Early training sessions aim to identify and focus on the significant aspects of a task. Managerial effectiveness can also be judged in terms of chosen priorities (the figure). Stress could certainly occur for those employees who are uncertain about their priorities and are unable to distinguish between the significant and less significant tasks. They feel overwhelmed by the 'whole' picture.

Grouping

The grouping principle refers to the tendency to organise shapes and patterns instantly into meaningful groupings or patterns on the basis of their proximity or similarity. Parts that are close in time or space tend to be perceived together. For example, in Figure 6.7 (a), the workers are more likely to be perceived as nine independent people, but in Figure 6.7(b), because of the proximity principle, the workers may be perceived as three distinct groups of people. Consider the importance of the layout of the room and tables for a large wedding reception and the perception of people in terms of both at which table they are sat, and with whom they are grouped!

Taxi firms often use the idea of grouping to display their telephone number. In the example below, which of the following numbers – (a), (b) or (c) – is most likely to be remembered easily?

Figure 6.6

Figure 6.7

(a) (b)

(a) 347 474 (b) 347474 (c) 34 74 74

Similar parts tend to be seen together as forming a familiar group.

In the following example there is a tendency to see alternate lines of characters – crosses and noughts (or circles). This is because the horizontal similarity is usually greater than the vertical similarity. However, if the page is turned sideways the figure may be perceived as alternate noughts and crosses in each line.

× × × × × × × ×
○ ○ ○ ○ ○ ○ ○ ○
× × × × × × × ×
○ ○ ○ ○ ○ ○ ○ ○

It is also interesting to note that when asked to describe this pattern many people refer to alternate lines of noughts and crosses – rather than crosses and noughts.

There is also an example here of the impact of cultural differences, mentioned earlier. The author undertook a teaching exchange in the USA and gave this exercise to a class of American students. Almost without exception the students described the horizontal pattern correctly as alternate rows of crosses and noughts (or zeros). The explanation appears to be that Americans do not know the game as 'noughts and crosses' but refer to it as 'tic-tac-toe'.

Closure

There is also a tendency to complete an incomplete figure – to fill in the gaps (mentally) and to perceive the figure as a whole. This creates an overall and meaningful image for the individual rather than an unconnected series of lines or blobs.

In the example in Figure 6.8[15] most people are likely to see the blobs as either the letter B or the number 13, possibly depending on whether at the time they had been more concerned with written material or dealing in numbers. However, for some people, the figure may be described in terms of just a series of 11 discrete blobs or perceived as some other (to them) meaningful pattern/object. According to Gestalt theory, perceptual organisation is instant and spontaneous. We cannot stop ourselves making meaningful assumptions about our environment. The Gestaltists emphasised the ways in which the elements interact and claimed that the new pattern or structure perceived had a character of its own, hence the famous phrase 'the whole is more than the sum of its parts'.

Figure 6.8

Source: King, R. A. *Introduction to Psychology*, third edition, McGraw-Hill (1996).
Reproduced with permission from the author, Professor Richard King.

PERCEPTUAL ILLUSIONS

Here are some examples to help you judge your perceptive skills. In Figure 6.9 try reading aloud the four words.

Figure 6.9	
	M – A – C – D – O – N – A – L – D
	M – A – C – P – H – E – R – S – O – N
	M – A – C – D – O – U – G – A – L – L
	M – A – C – H – I – N – E – R – Y

It is possible that you find yourself 'caught' in a perceptual set that means that you tend to pronounce 'machinery' as 'MacHinery as if it too were a Scottish surname.

In Figure 6.10, which of the centre blue circles is the larger – A or B?

Figure 6.10

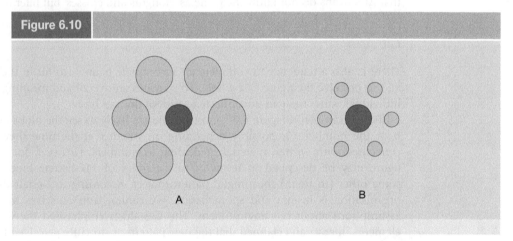

A B

Although you may have guessed that the two centre circles are in fact the same size, the circle on the right (B) may well **appear** larger because it is framed by smaller circles. The centre circle on the left (A) may well **appear** smaller because it is framed by larger circles.

In Figure 6.11 try saying the *colour* of the word, *not* the word itself.

Figure 6.11

BLUE	GREY	YELLOW	MAUVE
BLACK	ORANGE	GREEN	RED
WHITE	PURPLE	BLUE	BROWN

The physiological nature of perception has already been discussed briefly but it is of relevance here in the discussion of illusions. Why does the circle on the right in Figure 6.10 look bigger? Why is it difficult to say the colour, not the word? These examples demonstrate the way our brain can be fooled. Indeed, we make assumptions about our world that go beyond the pure sensations our brain receives.

Beyond reality

Perception goes beyond the sensory information and converts patterns to a three-dimensional reality that we understand. This conversion process, as we can see, is easily tricked. We may not be aware of the inferences we are making as they are part of our conditioning and learning. The Stroop experiment illustrates this perfectly.[16] (See Assignment 1 at the end of this chapter.)

An illustration of the way in which we react automatically to stimuli is the illusion of the impossible triangle (*see* Figure 6.12).

Figure 6.12

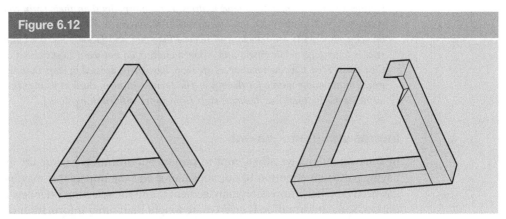

Source. Gregory, R. L. *Odd Perceptions*, Methuen (1900), p. 71. Reprinted by permission of the publishers, Routledge, a division of Taylor & Francis Ltd.

Even when we know the triangle is impossible we still cannot stop ourselves from completing the triangle and attempting to make it meaningful. We thus go beyond what is given and make assumptions about the world, which in certain instances are wildly incorrect. Psychologists and designers may make positive use of these assumptions to project positive images of a product or the environment. For instance, colours may be used to induce certain atmospheres in buildings; designs of wallpaper or texture of curtains may be used to create feelings of spaciousness or cosiness. Packaging of products may tempt us to see something as bigger or perhaps more precious.

SELECTION AND ATTENTION

What information do we select and why? The social situation consists of both verbal and non-verbal signals. The non-verbal signals include:

- bodily contact
- proximity
- orientation
- head nods
- facial expression
- gestures
- posture
- direction of gaze
- dress and appearance
- non-verbal aspects of speech.

Verbal and non-verbal signals are co-ordinated into regular sequences, often without the awareness of the parties. The mirroring of actions has been researched and is called 'postural echoing'.[17] There is considerable evidence to indicate that each person is constantly influencing the other and being influenced.[18]

Cook has suggested that in any social encounter there are two kinds of information that can be distinguished:

- **static information** – information which will not change during the encounter – for example colour, gender, height and age; and

■ **dynamic information** – information which is subject to change – for example mood, posture, gestures and expression.[19]

Culture and socialisation

The meanings we ascribe to these non-verbal signals are rooted in our culture and early socialisation. Thus it is no surprise that there are significant differences in the way we perceive such signals. For instance, dress codes differ in degrees of formality. *Schneider and Barsoux* summarise some interesting cultural differences:

> *Northern European managers tend to dress more informally than their Latin counterparts. At conferences, it is not unlikely for the Scandinavian managers to be wearing casual clothing, while their French counterparts are reluctant to remove their ties and jackets. For the Latin managers, personal style is important, while Anglo and Asian managers do not want to stand out or attract attention in their dress. French women managers are more likely to be dressed in ways that Anglo women managers might think inappropriate for the office. The French, in turn, think it strange that American businesswomen dress in 'man-like' business suits (sometimes with running shoes).[20]*

Impression management

In some situations we all attempt to project our attitudes, personality and competence by paying particular attention to our appearance and the impact this may have on others. This has been labelled 'impression management'[21] and the selection interview is an obvious illustration. Some information is given more weight than other information when an impression is formed. It would seem that there are central traits that are more important than others in determining our perceptions.

One of these central traits is the degree of warmth or coldness shown by an individual.[22] The timing of information also seems to be critical in the impressions we form. For example, information heard first tends to be resistant to later contradictory information. In other words, the saying 'first impressions count' is supported by research and is called **'the primacy effect'**.[23] It has also been shown that a negative first impression is more resistant to change than a positive one.[24] However, if there is a break in time we are more likely to remember the most recent information – **'the recency effect'**.

ORGANISATION AND JUDGEMENT

The way in which we organise and make judgements about what we have perceived is to a large extent based on our previous experiences and learning. It is also important at this point to be aware of the inferences and assumptions we make which go beyond the information given. We may not always be aware of our pre-set assumptions but they will guide the way in which we interpret the behaviour of others. There has been much research into the impact of implicit personality theory.[25] In the same way that we make assumptions about the world of objects and go beyond the information provided, we also make critical inferences about people's characteristics and possible likely behaviours.

A manager might well know more about the 'type of person' A – a member of staff who has become or was already a good friend, who is seen in a variety of social situations and with whom there is a close relationship – than about B – another member of staff, in the same section as A and undertaking similar duties, but with whom there is only a formal work relationship and a limited social acquaintance. These differences in relationship, information and interaction might well influence the manager's perception if asked, for example, to evaluate the work performance of A and B.

Judgement of other people can also be influenced by perceptions of such stimuli as:

■ role or status;
■ occupation;

- physical factors and appearance; and
- non-verbal communication and body language (discussed later in this chapter).

Physical characteristics and appearance

In a discussion on managing people and management style, *Green* raises the question of how managers make judgements on those for whom they are responsible including positive and negative messages.

> *In my personal research people have admitted, under pressure, that certain physical characteristics tend to convey a positive or negative message. For example, some people find red hair, earrings for men, certain scents and odours, someone too tall or too short; a disability; a member of a particular ethnic group and countless other items as negative . . . Similarly there will be positive factors such as appropriate hairstyle or dress for the occasion . . . which may influence in a positive way.*[26]

A person may tend to organise perception of another person in terms of the 'whole' mental picture of that person. Perceptual judgement is influenced by reference to related characteristics associated with the person and the attempt to place that person in a complete environment.

Perception and height

In one experiment, an unknown visitor was introduced by the course director to 110 American students, divided into five equal groups.[27] The visitor was described differently to each group as:

1 Mr England, a student from Cambridge;
2 Mr England, demonstrator in psychology from Cambridge;
3 Mr England, lecturer in psychology from Cambridge;
4 Dr England, senior lecturer from Cambridge;
5 Professor England from Cambridge.

After being introduced to each group, the visitor left. Each group of students was then asked to estimate his height to the nearest half inch. They were also asked to estimate the height of the course director after he too had left the room. The mean estimated height of the course director, who had the same status for all groups, did not change significantly among groups. However, the estimated height of the visitor varied with perceived status: as ascribed academic status increased, so did the estimate of height (*see* Table 6.1).

Table 6.1	Estimated height according to ascribed academic status	
Group	**Ascribed academic status**	**Average estimated height**
1	Student	5′ 9.9″
2	Demonstrator	5′ 10.14″
3	Lecturer	5′ 10.9″
4	Senior lecturer	5′ 11.6″
5	Professor	6′ 0.3″

Source: Adapted from Wilson, P. R. 'Perceptual Distortion of Height as a Function of Ascribed Academic Status', *Journal of Social Psychology*, no. 74, 1968, pp. 97–102. Copyright © 1968 by Taylor & Francis Informa UK Ltd. Permission conveyed through the Copyright Clearance Center, Inc.

Several popular surveys and newspaper articles appear to support the suggestion that tall men are more likely to be successful professionally, have better promotion prospects and earn higher salaries than short men. (We leave you to make your own judgement about this claim!)

An interesting example is the appointment (June 2009) of the new speaker of the House of Commons, John Bercow, who is 5′ 6″ in height. This appointment prompted newspaper articles about 'heightism' and perceptions about the 'shorter man'.[28]

'We often mask what we really feel, act in ways that cover our true emotions and speak words that we don't really mean – so in our dealings with other people we need to look beyond what is seen and heard and delve beneath the surface.'

How do you think we can best judge the true beliefs and intentions of other people?

CONNECTION OF THE CONSCIOUS, UNCONSCIOUS AND PHYSIOLOGY

Perceptual processes demonstrate the integration of our conscious self, our unconscious self and our physiology.

- **Conscious self** – this means our immediate awareness of what is around us. The state of mind we are in when we are making decisions to act and the meaning we place on the world.
- **Unconscious self** – this relates to the way we carry out tasks with no active thinking taking place; the way we habitually do things automatically – our autopilot. These habits allow the conscious mind to be free to assess new and novel decisions. Habits are very important to us as we do not want to think about everything we do, but habits can get in the way when we want to change habits.
- **Physiology** – the interconnectedness with physiology has already been explained and there is growing evidence for using research identifying the mind–body connections. *Spitzer* explains that:

 The human brain contains in the order of 100 billion (10^{11}) neurons and each neuron has up to 10 thousand connections of which less than ten are to the same neuron, such that each neuron is connected with a thousand other neurons. So there are approximately 100 trillion connections (10^{14}).[29]

Each thought and activity corresponds to a pattern of neuron activity – so by repeating the same thought or action we strengthen the associated neural connection. Thus automatically connecting the conscious and unconscious mind with physiology, each aspect influences the other and our emotions operate in all.

Framing

The term framing is used to explain how we interpret particular circumstances. Rather like a picture frame, we place into the frame our particular perspective, focus and colour on things. So if we are feeling happy our experience is being 'framed' in a positive way. What is in the 'frame' will depend on what is filtered in or out. Whether we look at a difficult situation as a 'problem' or as an opportunity, or whether we see a mistake as a terrible failure or as a learning moment, will depend on how we have 'framed' the experience. If we are in a good mood we may only filter in messages from our environment that confirm our happy state, we may create an inner dialogue in which our inner voice is reaffirming why we are feeling so content. We may also be visualising a situation in which we are successful and these thoughts are establishing neural pathways. Helping people to reframe situations can be part of the coaching process (*see* Chapter 5).

Appreciative inquiry

A reframing technique that has been used to positive effect in leading change has been the approach of appreciative inquiry. This technique, initially introduced by Cooperrider, Srivastva and colleagues[30] in the 1980s, created a theory called appreciative inquiry that

proposed a constructive perspective on change. They started with the proposition that everybody sees the world through their own set of personal 'filters' and that sharing these could be helpful – thus differences should be valued. For every organisation, team or individual something works well, which is worth building on and extending. That which we understand to be reality arises from what we focus on and reality is created in the moment.

They emphasised the importance of language as the way we create our reality and that we can therefore use it to create many realities. Asking questions of an organisation, the group, the individual means they are influenced in some way and that people have more confidence to progress to the future when they take with them what has been most helpful and of value from the past. It is important to value difference because we see the world through our own set of personal filters that is often different from a shared set of reality. So, in their approach, teams of people are faced with a different frame, a different mindset in which to analyse and evaluate change.

Hammond[31] describes the different steps to solving an organisational problem:

Traditional problem-solving approach	Appreciative inquiry approach
■ 'felt need' – identification of problem	■ appreciating/valuing the best of 'what is'
■ analysis of causes	■ envisioning 'what might be'
■ analysis of possible solutions	■ dialoguing 'what should be'
■ action planning	■ innovating 'what will be'

PERCEIVING OTHER PEOPLE

There are a number of well-documented problems that arise when perceiving other people. Many of these problems occur because of our limitations in selecting and attending to information. This selectivity may occur because:

■ we already know what we are looking for and are therefore 'set' to receive only the information which confirms our initial thoughts; or

■ previous training and experience have led us to short-cut and see only a certain range of behaviours; or

■ we may group features together and make assumptions about their similarities.

The Gestalt principles apply equally well to the perception of people as to the perception of objects. Thus we can see, for example, that if people live in the same geographical area, assumptions may be made about not only their wealth and type of accommodation but also their attitudes, their political views and even their type of personality.

> To interact effectively (present ourselves and communicate appropriately, influence others, work with them in relationships and groups or lead them) we must have a grasp of what others are thinking and feeling, including their motives, beliefs, attitudes and intentions. In social perception, accuracy and differentiation are essential but difficult. Achieving them may be linked to the complexity of a person's system of cognitive constructs.
>
> Maureen Guirdham[32]

Is it any wonder that conflicts and differences of opinion occur when we perceive others? The way we see others, the habits we have formed, the associations we have made and the assumptions we make lead us to make errors and distortions when we are perceiving others. The focus of the following section is to examine the perception of people and to consider the impact this has on the management and development of people at work.

The principles and examples of perceptual differences explained earlier apply to the way we perceive others. Some examples might be as follows:

■ **Grouping** – the way in which a manager may think of a number of staff – for example, either working in close proximity; or with some common feature such as all IT technicians, all

graduate trainees or all black workers; as a homogeneous group rather than a collection of individuals, each with their own separate identity and characteristics.

- **Figure and ground** – a manager may notice a new recruit and set them apart from the group because of particular characteristics such as age, appearance or physical features.
- **Closure** – the degree to which unanimity is perceived and decisions made or action taken in the belief that there is full agreement with staff when, in fact, a number of staff may be opposed to the decision or action.

A manager's perception of the workforce will influence attitudes in dealing with people and the style of managerial behaviour adopted. The way in which managers approach the performance of their jobs and the behaviour they display towards subordinate staff are likely to be conditioned by predispositions about people, human nature and work. An example of this is the style of management adopted on the basis of McGregor's Theory X and Theory Y suppositions, discussed in Chapter 12. In making judgements about other people it is important to try to perceive their underlying intent and motivation, not *just* the resultant behaviour or actions.

The perception of people's performance can be affected by the organisation of stimuli. In employment interviews, for example, interviewers are susceptible to contrast effects and the perception of a candidate is influenced by the rating given to immediately preceding candidates. Average candidates may be rated highly if they follow people with low qualifications, but rated lower when following people with higher qualifications.[33]

Testing assumptions

Recognising the assumptions held and testing these out requires a heightened level of critical reflection. Many leadership and management development courses start with a 'self-awareness and diagnostic' module intended to help their participants understand and recognise their style and preferences and the impact their style has on others. Courses which take a more challenging stance will encourage managers to question their existing frames of mind and challenge them constantly to re-evaluate their purpose, strategies and action. Such courses take an action inquiry approach and Testing Out Leadership courses typically start with an awareness of self.

Testing out assumptions[34]

Action inquiry: widening our attention

Making unconscious assumptions can limit learning. Failure is perhaps the most common way we become aware that they are only assumptions – at least the erroneous ones – not facts, as we may have previously believed. The later in life we wait to discover our erroneous assumptions in this manner, the more painful the consequences of the failure – divorce, jobloss, etc.

We cannot be aware of all our assumptions and cannot help but act out of our assumptions, but it is profoundly important that we learn to test our assumptions in the midst of action. By doing so we create a climate in which others:

1 in the organisation become more aware that they too are making assumptions;

2 become more willing to help us test our own assumptions (sometimes even before we are aware that we are making assumptions);

3 gradually become more willing to test their own assumptions as well.

Once formed, assumptions can blind us to the need for inquiry. We therefore need to behave in a way that reveals the unknown in the midst of action. Cultivating ongoing self-awareness and consciousness is an essential part of action inquiry and self or organisational

→

Testing out assumptions – continued

transformation – a lifetime practice. Acting in such a way and being visibly committed to such a course of action places you in a stronger position to influence others to do the same.

Our attention, perceptions and actions are limited by our untested assumptions.

- Our attention does not register a great deal of what occurs – it is selective and limited by our frame of attention at any given time.

- Our language, mindsets, frame of reference tend to highlight and emphasise some aspects of our experience and dispose us to see things in a certain way – personal bias.

- Our actions generate much of what we know but we are often unaware of how our actions skew what we know by the impact they have on others and their response.

- Data we have about the world are ordinarily about the past rather than the present, are drastically unsystematic and incomplete and rarely tested for validity on the spot. Scientific method can only disconfirm not confirm a proposition. We often therefore rely on assumptions to simplify matters.

Not all assumptions will be tested or tested well. Many assumptions will be tested and generate learning, subsequent success and higher morale, while minimising failure and accompanying lower morale. An organisation that cultivates courageous, intelligent, competent testing of assumptions will have an enormous competitive advantage over those in the same field which do not.

Figure 6.13	Cycle of perception and behaviour

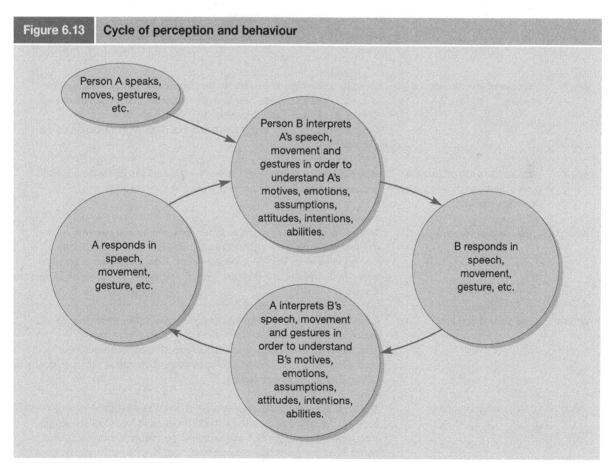

Source: From Guirdham, M. *Interactive Behaviour at Work*, third edition, Financial Times Prentice Hall (2002), p. 162. Reproduced with permission from Pearson Education Ltd.

712 Business Studies 1 Volume 2

The dynamics of interpersonal perception

Unlike with the perception of an object that just exists, when you perceive another individual they will react to you and be affected by your behaviour – the dynamics are all-important. This interaction is illustrated in the following quotation:

> *You are a pain in the neck and to stop you giving me a pain in the neck I protect my neck by tightening my neck muscles, which gives me the pain in the neck you are.*[35]

The interaction of individuals thus provides an additional layer of interpretation and complexity. The cue that we may attend to, the expectation we may have, the assumptions we may make, the response pattern that occurs, leave more scope for errors and distortions. We are not only perceiving the stimulus (that is, the other person), we are also processing their reactions to us at the same time that they are processing our reactions to them.

Thus person perception differs from the perception of objects because:

■ it is a continually dynamic and changing process; and
■ the perceiver is a part of this process who will influence and be influenced by the other people in the situation (*see* Figure 6.13).[36]

Setting and environment

Person perception will also be affected by the setting, and the environment may play a critical part in establishing rapport. For example, next time you are involved in a formal meeting, for example, attending an in-house development centre, consider the following factors that will all influence the perceptual process.

Why?	Purpose of and motives for meeting	Likely to be an important event for the participant, may be a catalyst for promotion and may signal new and relevant development opportunities. Chance to be visible and demonstrate skills and abilities. Opportunity to network with other managers. Thus high emotional cost to participant.
Who?	Status/role/age/gender/ethnic group/appearance/personality/interests/attitudes	How participant prepares for the event will be influenced by factors listed opposite and previous history and encounters of all parties.
When?	Time, date of meeting	The timing of the event might be particularly affected by events outside of the workplace. So if the participant has dependants or responsibilities, the timing of this event may become significant. If the participant is asked to attend in the middle of a religious festival, then again the relevance of time is critical.
Where?	Environment/culture	Organisations will often stage development events away from the 'normal' workplace in an attempt to bring about objectivity and neutrality. How the event is staged, the amount of structure and formality, how feedback is given, the demonstration of power and control will be evidence of the culture of the organisation.
How?	Past experience/rapport	The experience of the development event will in part be influenced by the expectations of the participant. If this is the second development centre, then experiences of the first will colour the perceptions; if this is the first centre, then the participant may be influenced by previous experiences of similar events (selection event) or by stories from previous attendees.

NON-VERBAL COMMUNICATION AND BODY LANGUAGE

We have referred previously in this chapter to the significance of non-verbal communication and body language. This includes inferences drawn from posture, gestures, touch, invasions of personal space, extent of eye contact, tone of voice or facial expression. People are the only animals that speak, laugh and weep. Actions are more cogent than speech and humans rely heavily on body language to convey their true feelings and meanings.[37] It is interesting to note how emotions are woven creatively into email messages. Using keyboard signs in new combinations has led to a new e-language – to signal pleasure :), or unhappiness :–c, or send a rose –{---@ encapsulate feelings as well as words. The growth of this practice has led to an upsurge of web pages replete with examples.

According to *Mehrabian*, in our face-to-face communication with other people the messages about our feelings and attitudes come only 7 per cent from the words we use, 38 per cent from our voice and 55 per cent from body language, including facial expressions. Significantly, when body language such as gestures and tone of voice conflicts with the words, greater emphasis is likely to be placed on the non-verbal message.[38]

Although actual percentages may vary, there appears to be general support for this contention. According to *Pivcevic*: 'It is commonly agreed that 80 per cent of communication is non-verbal; it is carried in your posture and gestures, and in the tone, pace and energy behind what you say.'[39] *McGuire* suggests that when verbal and non-verbal messages are in conflict, 'Accepted wisdom from the experts is that the non-verbal signals should be the ones to rely on, and that what is not said is frequently louder than what is said, revealing attitudes and feelings in a way words can't express.'[40]

James suggests that in a sense, we are all experts on body language already and this is part of the survival instinct:

> Even in a 'safe' environment like an office or meeting room you will feel a pull on your gaze each time someone new enters the room. And whether you want to or not, you will start to form opinions about a person in as little as three seconds. You can try to be fair and objective in your evaluation, but you will have little choice. This is an area where the subconscious mind bullies the conscious into submission. Like, dislike, trust, love or lust can all be promoted in as long as it takes to clear your throat. In fact most of these responses will be based on your perception of how the person looks.[41]

In our perceptions and judgement of others it is important therefore to watch and take careful note of their non-verbal communication. Managers should also be aware of the subconscious message that their own body language conveys to members of staff. For example, *Kennett* points out that we take signals from our leaders and if managers are exhibiting signs of anxiety their body language and critical talk will amplify employees' susceptibility to stress.[42] However, although body language may be a guide to personality, errors can easily arise if too much is inferred from a single message rather than a related cluster of actions. Consider the simple action of a handshake and the extent to which this can provide a meaningful insight into personality. Does a firm handshake by itself necessarily indicate friendship and confidence? And is a limp handshake a sign of shyness or lack of engagement with the other person? According to *Fletcher*: 'You won't learn to interpret people's body language accurately, and use your own to maximum effect, without working at it. If you consciously spend half an hour a day analysing people's subconscious movements, you'll soon learn how to do it – almost unconsciously.'[43] However, as *Mann* points out, with a little knowledge about the subject it is all too easy to become body conscious. Posture and gesture can unmask deceivers, but it would be dangerous to assume that everyone who avoids eye contact or rubs their nose is a fibber.[44]

According to *Akehurst* the advice to anyone trying to spot a liar is simple. 'Close your eyes. Don't look at them. Listen to what they are saying. Non-verbal cues are very misleading and we use too many stereotypes.'[45]

The reality is that body language is not a precise science. One gesture can be interpreted in several ways. It may give a possible indication of a particular meaning but by itself

cannot be interrupted with any certainty. Crossing your arms is often taken as a sign of defensiveness but could equally mean that the person is cold or finds this a comfortable position.[46]

Despite these limitations, it is essential that managers have an understanding of non-verbal communication and body language and are fully cognisant of the possible messages they are giving out.

Cultural differences

There are many cultural variations in non-verbal communications, the extent of physical contact and differences in the way body language is perceived and interpreted. Italians and South Americans tend to show their feelings through intense body language, while the Japanese tend to hide their feelings and have largely eliminated overt body language from interpersonal communication. When talking to another person, the British tend to look away spasmodically, but Norwegians typically look people steadily in the eyes without altering their gaze. In South Korea, women refrain from shaking hands. The Japanese often have a weak handshake whereas in Britain a firm handshake is encouraged. When the Dutch point a forefinger at their temples this is likely to be a sign of congratulations for a good idea, but with other cultures the gesture has a less complimentary implication.

In many European countries it is customary to greet people with three or four kisses on the cheek and pulling the head away may be taken as a sign of impoliteness. All cultures have specific values related to personal space and 'comfort zone'. Arabs tend to stand very close when speaking to another person but most Americans when introduced to a new person will, after shaking hands, move backwards a couple of steps to place a comfortable space between themselves and the person they have just met.[47] One reason why Americans tend to speak loudly is that their sense of personal space is twice that of the British.

> *All things are not what they seem. The ability to work out what is really happening with a person is simple – not easy, but simple. It's about matching what you see and hear to the environment in which it all happens and drawing possible conclusions. Most people, however, only see the things they think they are seeing.*[48]

A concept map of interacting with other people is set out in Figure 6.14.

Critical reflection

'There are so many forms of non-verbal communication cues, either intentional or unintentional, that can be interpreted in a number of ways. There are also wide variations in cultural norms that influence the essential meaning and context of interactions. Attempting to make valid inferences from body language is of little real value and its use should be discouraged.'

How would you argue against this assertion?

INTERPERSONAL COMMUNICATIONS

It is difficult to consider the process of interpersonal perception without commenting on how people communicate. Communication and perception are inextricably bound. How we communicate to our colleagues, boss, subordinates, friends and partners will depend on our perception of them, on our 'history' with them, on their emotional state.

Fitzherbert draws an interesting comparison between magic, perception and communication.

Figure 6.14 **Concept map of interacting with people**

INTERACTING WITH PEOPLE

- DEFINITION
- FACTORS CONTRIBUTING TO RAPPORT

FACTORS
- Proxemics
- Orientation
- Environmental characteristics
- Non-verbal signs
- Other spoken communication
- Dominance roles and rituals

DEFINITION
- An interview is a conversation with a purpose usually 1:1
 Tx – THE TRANSMITTER OF THE COMMUNICATION
 Rx – THE RECEIVER OF THE COMM'N
 (there may be many Rxs)

'PURPOSE-LESS CONVERSATION'
- a form of 'social grooming' e.g. about the weather
- often with casual or unknown contacts 'Good morning, how are you?'
- ritualisation of everyday contact prior to important communications (not to do this in the UK is often considered impolite)

PROXEMICS
The closeness of the Tx to the Rx(s)
- Consider closeness but be aware of cultural differences and taboos, especially between strangers
- With closeness note mirroring of body movements

Including touching the Rx

ORIENTATION
Relative positions
- Side-by-side can imply friendliness, intimacy, helpfulness, etc.
- Face-to-face can imply competition, confrontation, etc.
- Territorially – on whose ground will the interview/meeting take place? (theirs/yours 'neutral?')

ENVIRONMENTAL CHARACTERISTICS
- In a large space, Rxs group ... to hear better?
- In a small space Rxs separate ... maintain personal space?
- Furniture, e.g. tables ... could form psychological barriers
- No furnishings ... Rx feels exposed and vulnerable
- Ambient noise too high may hinder communication flow
- Distances too great
- Atmospheric conditions (heating/lighting/ventilation)

GRAMMATICAL GIMMICKS
Superfluous and meaningless e.g.
- 'you know'
- 'whatever'
- 'I mean'
- 'really'
- and also grunts, snorts, etc.

DOMINANCE ROLES AND RITUALS
Rituals of greetings and farewells
- handshake, kiss, hug, bow, salute, curtsy, raised hat, etc.

BETWEEN SEXES
- strokes, holds, pats ... friendly
- hits ... less friendly
- handshake – ritual touching for reassurance

NON-VERBAL SIGNALS
GAZE direct mutual gaze implies intimacy emotions perceived from eyes e.g. anger, pleasure, surprise

GESTURES position of fingers/hands/arms – the same gesture may have different meanings across cultures

MOUTH a smile encourages and reassures
- communicates emotional state
- controlled or uncontrolled

hands – fingers open, closed, fist formed
fingers – relaxed, pointed ...
limbs – open or closed
hands – moving or positioned

TOUCH

EYEBROWS raised rapidly – greeting, flirting, etc.
furrowed – puzzled, angry, etc.

CLOTHES indicate something of a person's values, status and authority, or just bodily adornment

TONE soft/friendly – loud/assertive (of voice)
pitch, stress and timing imply mood and emphasis

HEAD MOVEMENTS – nods, shakes and tilts indicative of emotional states or moods

may imply ...
- aggressive intent
- defensive reaction
- submissive attitude etc.

POSTURE lean forward – confidentially, intimacy, etc.
lean back – relaxed, easy, less concerned, etc.

Source: Copyright © 2008 The Virtual Learning Materials Workshop. Reproduced with permission.

Magicians are acutely aware that the moment people see, hear, feel, taste or smell anything it automatically triggers a range of expectations and perceptions in their minds. In effect, it opens up a 'file' in their brain that tells them what they already know about the subject and rejects anything that doesn't fit. Magicians build their communication and effects around the expectations and perceptions they trigger.

Clarity and impact aside, communication will be effective only if you can convince the audience about what you are telling them or showing them. Fitzherbert sets out twenty rules of perception and communication, shown in Figure 6.15.[49]

Importance of feedback

Feedback is a vital ingredient of the communication process. We may misjudge the receiver and regard our communication as unsuccessful, but unless we have some feedback from the other party we may never know whether what we have said or done was received in the way it was intended. The feedback may reaffirm our perceptions of the person or it may force us to review our perceptions. In our dealings with more senior staff the process of communication can be of special significance, including non-verbal communication, posture and tone.[50]

Two major approaches to, and ways of explaining, interpersonal communications are neuro-linguistic programming and transactional analysis.

Figure 6.15	Twenty rules of perception and communication

ENGAGEMENT	ATTENTION	IMPACT	CONVICTION
1 The framework for any communication is determined by the **expectations and perceptions** that you **trigger**	**5** Concentrated attention requires a **single point of focus**	**12** The senses offer **five different ways** into the brain	**17** To be convincing you, yourself, must **be convinced**
2 Expectations and perceptions can be reinforced or diminished by **prestige, atmosphere and environment** and **desire**	**6** Attention **tracks from left to right**, then settles at the left	**13 Firsts and lasts** are remembered	**18** Doubts are reduced by **openness**, but may be increased by **over-stressing**
3 Communication can only register effectively when it builds on **what the audience already knows**	**7** The audience will look where you **look**, where you **point**, where you **tell them** to look	**14 Negatives impede** communication as they need unscrambling before the meaning can be interpreted	**19** People put more reliance on something they have **worked out for themselves**
4 The brain filters out most information it receives, leaving only what it considers important	**8 Curiosity, movement, sound, contrast** and **anything that is new or different** are friends *and* foes. Each has the potential to seize attention	**15 Over-familiarity** leads to 'invisibility'	**20** People's reactions are influenced by those of their **peers**
	9 The **wider environment** can often add to or detract from your message	**16** Sustained impact depends on transferring information **to long-term memory**	
	10 Every element of your **content** will either **add to or detract** from your message		
	11 Attention is sustained by variation, which **shortens mental time**		

Source: Nick Fitzherbert, www.fitzherbert.co.uk. Reproduced with permission.

NEURO-LINGUISTIC PROGRAMMING (NLP)

NLP emerged in the early 1970s as an offshoot of psychotherapy, psychology and hypnotherapy and as such appears to offer lots of different things to different people. A popular definition of **NLP** is in terms of a model of interpersonal communication concerned with the relationship between successful patterns of behaviour and subjective experiences that underlie them. John Grinder and Richard Bandler, the co-founders of NLP saw it as a means of helping to provide people with better, fuller and richer lives.[51] It is an approach that aims to enhance the effectiveness of interpersonal communications and facilitate learning and personal development. The name originates from the three disciplines which all have a part to play when people are communicating with others: neurology, linguistics and programming.

- **Neurology** – the nervous system, and processes linking body and mind.
- **Linguistics** – the study of words and how these are understood and communicated.
- **Programming** – refers to behaviours and strategies used by individuals.

The broad nature of NLP has led to a variety of different definitions according to the interpretation of the individual.

Shapiro describes NLP in terms of:

a process where communication and psychotherapy come together. It is about understanding the way we use our senses – sight, hearing, touch, smell and taste – to experience what's going in the world and learn to understand that not everyone is the same. It is about developing more tolerance and changing things that aren't going the way you want them to go in your life.[52]

The definition from the British Board of NLP is:

The study of human experiences, communication, thinking, language and behaviour. NLP is about noticing conscious and unconscious behavioural patterns. It's about duplicating excellence and modeling how we communicate to ourselves and others.[53]

Originally Grinder and Bandler studied notable therapists at work with their clients. The aim was to identify 'rules' or models that could be used by other therapists to help them improve their performance. The focus was on one-to-one communication and self-management. The application of NLP shifted from therapy situations to work organisations, with clear messages for communicating and managing others. NLP emphasises the significance of the perceptual process and the way in which information is subjectively filtered and interpreted. These interpretations are influenced by others and the world in which we live. Gradually individuals learn to respond and their reactions and strategies become programmed, locked in, automatic.

Awareness and change

At its heart NLP concerns awareness and change. Initially knowing and monitoring one's own behaviour and being able consciously to choose different reactions are fundamental to the process. Selecting from a range of verbal and non-verbal behaviours ensures control happens and changes 'automatic' reactions into consciously chosen programmes. Many different approaches and techniques are incorporated into NLP. Some concern mirroring and matching the micro skills of communication in terms of body movements, breathing patterns or voice tempo. Others concern the positive thinking required in goal-setting 'outcome thinking' and the personal resources required in its achievement.

NLP has attracted considerable interest in recent years and there are a number of passionate devotees. There are numerous courses and seminars intended to demonstrate to participants how they can learn the skills to change themselves for improved personal or professional effectiveness and a greater enjoyment from life. It is also a popular approach to coaching (discussed in Chapter 5). Paul McKenna, the well-known television hypnotist, is a registered NLP practitioner and makes use of NLP principles in his courses on life training, including for example helping people to lose weight.

Some of the ideas of NLP have been incorporated in other bodies of knowledge on communication. So, for example, *McCann* bases his communication work on the findings of Grinder and Bandler to produce a technique called psychoverbal communication.[54] *Stone* reports on the value of NLP as central to the ability in influencing others, especially concerning establishing rapport in order to understand the opinions, insights or motivations of others, and in the way you communicate and the outcomes you want to achieve.[55]

Another feature of NLP is 'anchors' that we all have. Anchors are 'triggers' that help keep habits in place and put us in a certain state of mind.[56]

Anchors can be visual, like people, clothes and cars. They can be auditory, like a particular piece of music, an advertising jingle or the voice of a dear friend. They can be kinaesthetic, like the feel of your favourite clothes, sitting in your armchair or the warmth of a hot bath. They can be olfactory or gustatory, like the smell of a hospital (why do they all smell the same?) or the taste of coffee or chocolate (Lindt!). Words can be anchors because they evoke ideas; your name is a powerful anchor for your identity. Anchors evoke emotional states and most of the time we do not notice the anchors, only the states. Some anchors are neutral. Some put us into good states. Others put us into bad states.[57]

TRANSACTIONAL ANALYSIS (TA)

Transactional analysis is one of the most popular ways of explaining the dynamics of interpersonal communication. Originally developed by *Eric Berne*, it is a model of people and relationships that encompasses personality, perception and communication.[58] Although Berne used it initially as a method of psychotherapy, it has been convincingly used by organisations as a training and development programme.

TA has two basic underlying assumptions:

- All the events and feelings that we have ever experienced are stored within us and can be replayed, so we can re-experience the events and the feelings of all our past years.
- Personality is made up of three ego states that are revealed in distinct ways of behaving. The ego states manifest themselves in gesture, tone of voice and action, almost as if they are different people within us and they converse with each other in 'transactions' either overtly or covertly.

Berne identified and labelled the ego states as follows, each with their own system of communication and language:

- **Adult ego state** – behaviour that concerns our thought processes and the processing of facts and information. In this state we may be objective, rational, reasonable – seeking information and receiving facts.
- **Parent ego state** – behaviour that concerns the attitudes, feelings and behaviour incorporated from external sources, primarily our parents. This state refers to feelings about right and wrong and how to care for other people.
- **Child ego state** – behaviour that demonstrates the feelings we remember as a child. This state may be associated with having fun, playing, impulsiveness, rebelliousness, spontaneous behaviour and emotional responses.

Berne believed these transactions, that take place in face-to-face exchanges and verbal communication, form the core of human relationships. He claimed that the three ego states exist simultaneously within each individual, although at any particular time any one state may dominate the other two. All people are said to behave in each of these states at different times. We may be unaware which ego state we are operating in and may shift from one to another.

Preferred ego state

We all have a preferred ego state which we may revert to: some individuals may continually advise and criticise others (the constant Parents); some may analyse, live only with facts and

distrust feelings (the constant Adult); some operate with strong feelings all the time, consumed with anger or constantly clowning (the constant Child). Berne emphasised that the states should not be judged as superior or inferior but as different. Analysis of ego states may reveal why communication breaks down or why individuals may feel manipulated or used.

Berne insists that it is possible to identify the ego state from the words, voice, gestures, and attitude of the person communicating. For example, it would be possible to discern the ego state of a manager if they said the following:

'Pass me the file on the latest sales figures.'
'How do you think we could improve our safety record?'
(Adult ego state)

'Let me help you with that – I can see you are struggling.'
'Look, this is the way it should be done; how many more times do I have to tell you?'
(Parent ego state)

'Great, it's Friday. Who's coming to the pub for a quick half?'
'That's a terrific idea – let's go for it!'
(Child ego state)

Complementary or crossed reaction

A dialogue can be analysed in terms not only of the ego state but also whether the transaction produced a **complementary reaction** or a **crossed reaction**. Complementary means that the ego state was an expected and preferred response. So, for instance, if we look at the first statement, 'Pass me the file on the latest sales figures', the subordinate could respond: 'Certainly – I have it here' (Adult ego state) or 'Can't you look for it yourself? I only gave it to you an hour ago' (Parent ego state).

The first response was complementary whereas the second was a crossed transaction. Sometimes it may be important to 'cross' a transaction. Take the example 'Let me help you with that – I can see you are struggling' (Parent ego state). The manager may have a habit of always helping in a condescending way, making the subordinate resentful. If the subordinate meekly accepts the help with a thankful reply, this will only reinforce the manager's perception and attitude, whereas if the subordinate were to respond with 'I can manage perfectly well. Why did you think I was struggling?', it might encourage the manager to respond from the Adult ego state and thus move their ego position.

Understanding of human behaviour

Knowledge of TA can be of benefit to employees who are dealing with potentially difficult situations. In the majority of work situations the Adult–Adult transactions are likely to be the norm. Where work colleagues perceive and respond by adopting the Adult ego state, such a transaction is more likely to encourage a rational, problem-solving approach and reduce the possibility of emotional conflict.

If only the world of work was always of the rational logical kind! Communications at work as elsewhere are sometimes unclear and confused, and can leave the individual with 'bad feelings' and uncertainty. Berne describes a further dysfunctional transaction, which can occur when a message is sent to two ego states at the same time. For instance, an individual may say 'I passed that article to you last week, have you read it yet?' This appears to be an Adult-to-Adult transaction and yet the tone of voice or the facial expressions might **imply** a second ego state is involved. The underlying message says, 'Haven't you even read that yet . . . you know how busy I am and yet I had time to read it!' The critical Parent is addressing the Child ego state. In such 'ulterior transactions' the social message is typically Adult to Adult and the ulterior, psychological message is directed either Parent–Child or Child–Parent.

Given the incidence of stress in the workplace, analysis of communication may be one way of understanding such conflict. By focusing on the interactions occurring within the

workplace, TA can aid the understanding of human behaviour. It can help to improve communication skills by assisting in interpreting a person's ego state and which form of state is likely to produce the most appropriate response. This should lead to an improvement in both customer relations and management–subordinate relations. Therefore TA can be seen as a valuable tool to aid our understanding of social situations and the games that people play both in and outside work organisations.[59]

Critical reflection

'Neuro-linguistic programming and transactional analysis may appear to have some value when discussed in the classroom but are too theoretic and abstract for the practical manager.'

Is there any way in which you can realistically see a manager known to you making use of either of these concepts to improve interpersonal communications?

ATTRIBUTION THEORY

It seems, therefore, that part of the process of perceiving other people is to attribute characteristics to them. We judge their behaviour and their intentions on past knowledge and in comparison with other people we know. It is our way of making sense of their behaviour. This is known as **attribution theory**. Attribution is the process by which people interpret the perceived causes of behaviour. The initiator of attribution theory is generally recognised as *Heider*, who suggests that behaviour is determined by a combination of **perceived** internal forces and external forces.[60]

■ **Internal forces** relate to personal attributes such as ability, skill, amount of effort or fatigue.
■ **External forces** relate to environmental factors such as organisational rules and policies, the manner of superiors, or the weather.

Behaviour at work may be explained by the locus of control, that is whether the individual perceives outcomes as controlled by themselves or by external factors. Judgements made about other people will also be influenced strongly by whether the cause is seen as internal or external.

Basic criteria in making attributions

In making attributions and determining whether an internal or external attribution is chosen, *Kelley* suggests three basic criteria: distinctiveness, consensus and consistency.[61]

■ **Distinctiveness**. How distinctive or different was the behaviour or action in this particular task or situation compared with behaviour or action in other tasks or situations?
■ **Consensus**. Is the behaviour or action different from, or in keeping with, that displayed by most other people in the same situation?
■ **Consistency**. Is the behaviour or action associated with an enduring personality or motivational characteristic over time, or an unusual one-off situation caused by external factors?

Kelley hypothesised that people attribute behaviour to internal forces or personal factors when they perceive **low distinctiveness**, **low consensus** and **high consistency**. Behaviour is attributed to external forces or environmental factors when people perceived **high distinctiveness**, **high consensus** and **low consistency** (*see* Figure 6.16).

An example of these criteria related to a student who fails a mid-sessional examination in a particular subject is given in Table 6.2.

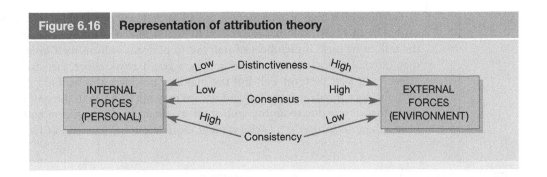

Figure 6.16	Representation of attribution theory

Table 6.2	Example of criteria in making attributions		
	Distinctiveness	**Consensus**	**Consistency**
Internal attribution	Student fails all mid-sessional examinations	Student is the only one to fail	Student also fails final examination
External attribution	Student gains high marks in other mid-sessional examinations	All students in the class get low marks	Student obtains a good mark in final examination

Source: Adapted from Mitchell, T. R. *People in Organisations*, second edition, McGraw-Hill (1982), p. 104. Reproduced with permission from the McGraw-Hill Companies.

An additional consideration in the evaluation of task performance within an organisational setting is whether the cause of behaviour was due to 'stable' or 'unstable' factors:

- **stable factors** are ability, or the ease or difficulty of the task;
- **unstable factors** are the exertion of effort, or luck.[62]

The combination of internal and external attributions, and stable and unstable characteristics, results in four possible interpretations of a person's task performance (*see* Table 6.3).

Table 6.3	Classification of possible attributions for performance	
	Internal attributions	**External attributions**
Stable factors	ABILITY	TASK DIFFICULTY
Unstable factors	EFFORT	LUCK

Implications of attribution theory

Employees with an internal control orientation are more likely to believe that they can influence their level of performance through their own abilities, skills or efforts. Employees with an external control orientation are more likely to believe that their level of performance is determined by external factors beyond their influence.

Studies appear to support the idea that staff with an internal control orientation are generally more satisfied with their jobs, are more likely to be in managerial positions and are more satisfied with a participatory style of management than staff with an external control orientation.[63] As a generalisation it might be implied that internally controlled managers are more effective than those who are externally controlled. However, this does not appear to be always the case.[64]

People with a high achievement motivation may perceive that successful performance is caused by their own internal forces and their ability and effort rather than by the nature of the task or by luck. If members of staff fail to perform well on their tasks they may believe that external factors are the cause and as a result may reduce the level of future effort. However, if staff perform well but the manager perceives this as due to an easy task or to luck, the appropriate recognition and reward may not be given. If the staff perceive that good performance was due to ability and/or effort, the lack of recognition and reward may well have a demotivating effect. (Achievement motivation is discussed in Chapter 7.)

PERCEPTUAL DISTORTIONS AND ERRORS

We have seen that differences in perception result in different people seeing different things and attaching different meanings to the same stimuli. Every person sees things in their own way and as perceptions become a person's reality this can lead to misunderstandings. The accuracy of interpersonal perception and the judgements made about other people are influenced by:

- the nature of the relationship between the perceiver and the other person;
- the amount of information available to the perceiver and the order in which information is received;
- the nature and extent of interaction between the two people.

There are five main features that can create particular difficulties and give rise to perceptual problems, bias or distortions in our dealings with other people. These are:

- stereotyping
- the halo effect
- perceptual defence
- projection
- self-fulfilling prophecy.

These problems with people perception arise because of the selectivity which exists in the perceptual process. We do not enjoy living in a world where uncertainty abounds and our perceptual system works to minimise our energy consumption. We do not have to start every day afresh – we have our store of memories and experiences to guide us. The paradox is that this process is also our downfall. Errors and bias are inherent in such a system. Although exhortations can be made for us to become more aware of our own biases and to take more time in making judgements, we are working against our normal quick-fire perceptual system.

STEREOTYPING

This is the tendency to ascribe positive or negative characteristics to a person on the basis of a general categorisation and perceived similarities. The perception of that person may be based more on certain expected characteristics than on the recognition of that person as an individual. It is a form of typecasting. **Stereotyping** is a means of simplifying the process of perception, making sense of the world and making judgements of other people instead of dealing with a range of complex and alternative stimuli. It occurs when an individual is judged on the basis of the group to which it is perceived that person belongs. When we see all people belonging to a particular group as having the same characteristics, we are stereo-typing individuals. Pre-judgements are therefore made about an individual without ever really knowing whether such judgements are accurate; they may be wildly wrong.

Examples of common stereotyping may be based on:

- **nationality**, for example all Germans are orderly and industrious, all Australians like cricket;
- **occupation**, for example all accountants are boring, all librarians are serious and undemonstrative;

- **age**, for example all young people are unreliable, no old person wants to consider new ideas;
- **physical**, for example all people with red hair have a fiery temperament; all fat people are lazy;
- **education**, for example all graduates are intelligent;
- **social**, for example all unemployed people are lazy; immigrants do not want to learn English;
- **politics**, for example all Labour voters favour strong trade unions, all Conservative voters support privatisation.

(See also the discussion of social identity theory in Chapter 8.)

Social implications

Although stereotyping condenses the amount of information that we need to know and thus enables us to cope with a vast information flow, the consequences of attributing incorrect characteristics are extremely negative. Stereotyping can lead to bias and a failure to try and really understand other people.[65]

Stereotyping infers that all people within a particular perceived category are assumed to share the same traits or characteristics. A significant social implication of stereotyping is therefore the perception held about particular groups of people based on, for example, gender, race, disability, sexual orientation, age, or religious belief.

A major danger of stereotyping is that it can block out accurate perception of the individual or individual situation. Stereotyping may lead to potential situations of prejudice or discrimination. An example might be the perception of people with HIV or AIDS.[66] Stereotyping may work either negatively or favourably for a particular group of people. For example, a sizeable number of employers still appear to maintain negative and inaccurate stereotypes about the capabilities and training of older workers. However, some firms, such as B&Q, the home-improvement chain, have a policy of staffing certain stores with people over 50 years of age. (See the Case Study at the end of Chapter 4.)

THE HALO EFFECT

The **halo effect** is the process by which the perception of a person is formulated on the basis of a single favourable or unfavourable trait or impression. The halo effect tends to shut out other relevant characteristics of that person. Some examples might be as follows:

- A candidate for employment who arrives punctually, is smart in appearance and friendly may well influence the perception of the selectors, who then place less emphasis on the candidate's technical ability, qualifications or experience for the job.
- A new member of staff who performs well in a first major assignment may be perceived as a likely person for promotion, even though that assignment is not typical of the usual duties the member of staff is expected to undertake.
- A single trait, such as good attendance and timekeeping, may become the main emphasis for judgement of overall competence and performance rather than other considerations such as the quantity, quality and accuracy of work.

A particular danger with the halo effect is that where quick judgements are made on the basis of readily available stimuli, the perceiver may become 'perceptually blind' to subsequent stimuli at variance with the original perception and (often subconsciously) notice only those characteristics that support the original judgement. See also the self-fulfilling prophecy, discussed below.

The rusty halo effect

The process may also work in reverse: the **rusty halo effect**. This is where general judgements about a person are formulated from the perception of a negative characteristic. For example,

a candidate is seen arriving late for an interview. There may be a very good reason for this and it may be completely out of character. But on the basis of that one particular event the person may be perceived as a poor timekeeper and unreliable. Another example may be a new member of staff who performs poorly in a first major assignment. This may have been due to an unusual set of circumstances and not typical behaviour, but the person may still be perceived as a bad appointment.

PERCEPTUAL DEFENCE

Perceptual defence is the tendency to avoid or screen out certain stimuli that are perceptually disturbing or threatening. People may tend to select information that is supportive of their point of view and choose not to acknowledge contrary information. For example, a manager who has decided recently to promote a member of staff against the advice of colleagues may select only favourable information which supports that decision and ignore less favourable information which questions that decision.

PROJECTION

Attributing, or projecting, one's own feelings, motives or characteristics to other people is a further distortion which can occur in the perception of other people. Judgements of other people may be more favourable when they have characteristics largely in common with, and easily recognised by, the perceiver. **Projection** may also result in people exaggerating undesirable traits in others that they fail to recognise in themselves.

Perception is distorted by feelings and emotions. Projection may be used as a means of attempting to externalise difficult or uncomfortable feelings. For example, a manager who is concerned about possible redundancy may perceive other managers to be even more concerned. People have a tendency to perceive others less favourably by projecting certain of their own feelings or characteristics on to them. As another example, supervisors may complain that their manager did not work hard enough to secure additional resources for the department when in fact the supervisors failed to provide the manager with all the relevant information and statistics. However, projection may also be used to externalise positive feelings onto other members of staff by attempting to create an overstated and unrealistic level of expectations and performance.

Discussed by Freud in his description of defence mechanisms, projection is a way in which we protect ourselves from acknowledging that we may possess undesirable traits and assign them in exaggerated amounts to other people. For instance, a manager who considers all subordinates as insincere may be projecting one of the manager's own characteristics. Perception of 'self' and how people see and think of themselves, and evaluate themselves, are discussed in Chapter 9.

SELF-FULFILLING PROPHECY

A common feature of social interaction is the concept of the **self-fulfilling prophecy** (sometimes known as the Pygmalion effect), a term that is usually attributed to *Merton.*[67] The essence of the prophecy is that simply because it has been made, this will cause it to happen. People strive to validate their perceptions irrespective of the actual reality. People's beliefs or expectations influence their actions and behaviour in such a way as to make the beliefs or expectations more likely to come true. If staff believe a rumour (prophecy) that there will be no promotions or bonuses for the foreseeable future, they are likely to behave in such a way that their performance would not justify promotion or bonuses (even if the rumour were not true).

Rosenthal and Jacobson undertook a study of American school students in which psychological tests were claimed to predict levels of achievement. The researchers informed teachers

that certain named students had been identified as 'fast developers' when, in reality, students were assigned at random to both the high-potential and control groups. At the end of the academic year those students designated with high potential achieved noticeably greater increased IQ scores and reading ability than the control group of students.[68] In the organisational setting, a study by *Word et al.* produced evidence that black candidates in job interviews received fewer supportive non-verbal signs from white interviewers than white candidates. As a result the black candidates gave less confident answers to questions and were given a poorer rating.[69]

The expectation of managers has a powerful influence on the behaviour and performance of staff. If a manager expects only minimal performance from staff, they are not likely to perform to the best of their abilities. Therefore, managers need to establish an organisational framework and supportive culture that reinforces positive performance expectations at all levels of the organisation. Staff should also be encouraged to have high self-expectations of performance through working towards common goals.

UNDERSTANDING THE ORGANISATIONAL PROCESS

The process of perception has been outlined as selective and subjective: we perceive the world in our own terms and expect the world to 'fit' into our constructs. Throughout our development we have learned to distinguish what is important and significant (figure) from information that is additional and contextual (ground). This process is repeated when we join new organisations or take a new job within the same organisation. Fitting into the organisation involves selecting information that is necessary from that which is less significant. At times, the process can be distorted and we can also be 'tricked' into seeing the world in particular ways.

Although some organisations may discriminate, stereotyped perceptions are not always calculated: they are often made automatically and without conscious thought – in much the same way as we may be tricked by visual illusions. In fact, perceptual illusions are a very appropriate way of understanding the organisational setting, including for example the processes affecting women. The 'Ames Room' is relevant for this purpose.[70] This is a room of an irregular size with one of the far corners at a greater distance than the other, although the room is arranged and decorated so that it gives the appearance of being rectangular. If two people of the same size stand in diagonally opposite corners, one in the furthest corner and the other in the near corner, a visual illusion occurs whereby our perception of depth is 'tricked' to see the furthest away looking dramatically smaller (*see* Figure 6.17).

The culture of the organisation

By analogy it is possible to see the room as representing the culture of the organisation surrounded by beliefs and traditions, rather like pictures on the wall. They seem reasonable, logical and appropriate. The individual standing at the furthest corner of the room could, for example, be seen as the female, the nearer the male. Both people are in the room surrounded by the culture, but one, the male, is nearer and more visible. He is perceived differently and advantageously, whereas the woman is perceived in a relatively inconsequential way. If the woman stays at the back of the room in an ancillary position or leaves the room altogether, she is reinforcing the beliefs around the walls.

Some women, however, do become managers and these exceptional women would then join the male corner and would seem to become larger and more visible. However, the perceptual distortion is complete because the lone woman could legitimately be viewed as a 'trick', as an illusion. For the males, their position fits and they have only to prove their merit for a management post and not that they are different from the norm. Their success will feed back into the system and reaffirm the beliefs that are held.

For any organisation to be effective it is imperative that the staff are competent to do their work and satisfy the 'psychological contract' (discussed in Chapter 1). One part of the role

Figure 6.17 The Ames Room

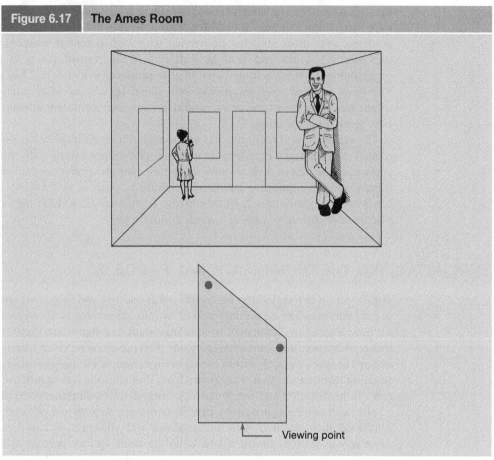

Viewing point

Source: Hicks, L. 'Gender and Culture: A Study of the Attitudes Displayed by Managers in the Hotel World', unpublished doctoral thesis, University of Surrey, 1991, p. 303.

of managers is to select and train those people whom they predict will perform successfully on the job, and then to monitor and assess their competence for promotion. Accordingly, it clearly seems important for managers to be aware of their own prejudices and assumptions. By opening channels and encouraging and developing all staff, trust might be fed back into the system from which equity could begin and stereotypes might end.

Critical reflection

'It is not unreasonable to argue that there is no such thing as reality – only the individual's perception or interpretation of reality. Yet, managers require an understanding of perception in order to help interpret the behaviour and intentions of other people.'

If you were a manager how would you hope to avoid organisational problems that result from perceptual differences?

SYNOPSIS

■ The process of perception connects our physiology with our conscious thoughts and actions as well as our unconscious habits and assumptions. By understanding how we see the world and sharing our thoughts with others, we share the same social world. Although we all see the world through our own 'coloured spectacles', by understanding others' perspectives and by widening our understanding of how others may see the world,

depth and variety is encouraged and problems of bias and distortion become minimised. Perception is the root of all organisational behaviour and any situation can be analysed in terms of its perceptual connotations.

■ For managers, an understanding of perception is essential to ensure that they are aware of the problems that can arise from the process of attention and selectivity. The process of perception is innately organised and patterned in order to provide meaning for the individual and is based on both internal and external factors. It is important to recognise the importance of cultural differences and the use of language. The organisation and arrangement of stimuli is influenced by three important factors: figure and ground, grouping and closure.

■ It is important to be aware of potential perceptual illusions. Part of the process of perceiving other people is to attribute characteristics to them. We judge their behaviour and intentions on past knowledge and in comparison with other people. Perception gives rise to individual behavioural responses in given situations. The principles of perceptual differences reflect the way we perceive other people and are the source of many organisational problems. In the work situation, the process of perception and selection of stimuli can influence a manager's relationship with other staff.

■ The ways in which we organise and make judgements about what we have perceived are to a large extent based on previous experiences and learning. It is also important to be aware that there are inferences and assumptions that go beyond the information given. Judgements of other people can also be influenced by such stimuli as role or status, occupation, physical factors and appearance, non-verbal communications and body language. The social situation consists of both verbal and non-verbal signals. It is necessary to be aware of cultural differences in non-verbal communications.

■ The importance of communication and the way we interact with others cannot be overestimated, as our well-being and morale can be affected by the nature of these social experiences. Communication and perception are inextricably bound. Two major approaches to interpersonal communications are neuro-linguistic programming (NLP), which can illuminate areas of understanding and help to improve communication skills, and transactional analysis (TA), which is a theory that encompasses personality, perception and communication.

■ Part of the process of perceiving other people is to attribute characteristics to them. Attribution is the process by which people interpret the perceived causes of behaviour. There are a number of potential difficulties and errors that arise with interpersonal perception including stereotyping, the halo effect, perceptual defence, projection and self-fulfilling prophecy. The perceptual process is selective and subjective. In the work situation, perceptual differences reflect the way we perceive other people. It is important to understand the organisational process.

REVIEW AND DISCUSSION QUESTIONS

1 Explain fully why the study of perception is important in the study of management and organisational behaviour.

2 Discuss those factors that affect selection and attention in the process of perception. Give your own examples of the importance of cultural differences and the use of language.

3 Identify clearly the most significant principles that influence the organisation and arrangement of stimuli. Provide your own example of each of these principles.

4 Explain the main distortions or errors that can occur in perceiving other people and support your answer with practical examples.

5 Discuss critically the amount of attention that you believe should be given to non-verbal communications and body language.

6 What do *you* see as the practical benefits of (i) neuro-linguistic programming (NLP); and (ii) transactional analysis (TA)?

7 Explain the principles of attribution theory and its importance to, and implications for, management. Apply the principles to your *own* working life.

8 Give your own examples of what you believe are the main causes and implications of perceptual distortions and errors.

MANAGEMENT IN THE NEWS

How to be happy in life: let out your anger

Amelia Hill

Conventional advice about keeping a stiff upper lip and staying cool can damage your career and lower your satisfaction in life, according to new research. If you want to be promoted and attain true happiness, you should get angry. According to the Harvard Study of Adult Development, a piece of research that has tracked the lives of 824 men and women since 1965, those who repress their frustration are at least three times more likely to admit they had hit a glass ceiling in their careers and have disappointing personal lives. On the other hand, the study found, those who learned to harness and channel their anger were far more likely to be professionally well-established, as well as enjoying emotional and physical intimacy with their friends and family.

Professor George Vaillant, a psychiatrist at Harvard Medical School, has spent the last 44 years as director of the Study of Adult Development, based at the Harvard University Health Service. 'People think of anger as a terribly dangerous emotion and are encouraged to practise "positive thinking", but we find that approach is self-defeating and ultimately a damaging denial of dreadful reality,' he said. 'Negative emotions such as fear and anger are inborn and are of tremendous importance. Negative emotions are often crucial for survival: careful experiments such as ours have documented that negative emotions narrow and focus attention so we can concentrate on the trees instead of the forest.'

Vaillant criticises the boom in anti-anger, mood-stabilising drugs and the growing market for anger-management counselling and classes. He believes that, while uncontrolled exhibitions of anger are destructive, learning to positively channel our anger serves a vital role in our well-being. Internalising the emotion can cause depression, health problems and communication difficulties. 'Psychologists, having dealt for generations with damaged psyches, should now be engaged in the psychological equivalent of reverse engineering,' he said. 'We all feel anger, but individuals who learn how to express their anger while avoiding the explosive and self-destructive consequences of unbridled fury have achieved something incredibly powerful in terms of overall emotional growth and mental health. If we can define

and harness those skills, we can use them to achieve great things.'

Dr Carol Tavris, a social psychologist and author of *Anger: The Misunderstood Emotion*, agrees. She believes properly expressed anger can help to clarify relationship problems and also clinch business deals, fuel political agendas and give people a sense of control during uncertain times. Dr James Averill, a University of Massachusetts Amherst psychologist, believes anger has a bad name because it is erroneously associated with violence. In a study of everyday anger, Averill found that angry episodes helped strengthen relationships about half the time and only lead to violence in less than 10% of cases. 'Anger can be used to aid intimate relationships, work interactions and political expression,' said Averill. 'When you look at everyday episodes of anger, as opposed to those that have more dramatic outcomes, the results are usually positive.'

The philosopher and author Alain de Botton agrees that anger is a misunderstood emotion. 'Though philosophers have traditionally been concerned with the pursuit of happiness,' he said, 'the stubborn recurrence of anger means the development of a workable approach to it must surely outstrip the value of any utopian quest for happiness.'

Source: Adapted from Hill, A. 'How to Be Happy in Life: Let Out Your Anger', *Observer*, 1 March 2009. Copyright Guardian News & Media Ltd. 2009. Reproduced with permission.

Discussion questions

1 Using the 'cycle of perception and behaviour' model shown in Figure 6.13, examine how the expression of anger by one person might have a positive effect on the communication process as the article suggests.

2 What particular problems might the expression of anger (either verbally or using non-verbal signals) cause in a culturally diverse environment?

3 What can the article tell us about the wider role of emotions at work? Should managers control displays of emotion such as anger in both themselves and their staff? Give reasons for your answer.

ASSIGNMENT 1

Stroop – illustrative experiment

(This is a development of Figure 6.11 and provides a further opportunity to review possible perceptual illusion.)

a Write two vertical lists of 20 colour names in felt tip pen. For the first list, use the correct colour pen for the colour word you are writing (for example, blue pen for the word blue). Repeat some of the colours but place them in random order.

b For the second list, use different colour pens for the colour word (for example, use a red pen for the word blue).

c Now ask a colleague to read out loud the colour that the word is written in (not the word itself). Compare the amount of time it takes your colleague to read out the two lists. The second list probably not only took longer but had more mistakes and more hesitations.

William Stroop, who first conducted this experiment, noted that the task interferes with expected behaviour. It is difficult to stop yourself from reading the word (the result of our early learning), which in this case directly impairs performance.

ASSIGNMENT 2

Form small groups and then undertake, individually, the following exercise.

COMMUNICATION

1. Read everything before you do anything.
2. Put your name in the upper right-hand corner of the paper, in the space provided.
3. Circle the word 'name' in the second sentence, above.
4. Draw five small squares in the upper left-hand corner of this paper.
5. Put an X in each of the five small squares you have drawn.
6. Put a circle around each of those five small squares above.
7. Sign your name, under and to the left of the title above.
8. Draw a circle, in pen, around sentences 6 and 7 above.
9. Multiply 70 × 30 and write the result on the reverse side.
10. Draw a circle around the word 'paper' in sentence 4, above.
11. Please now call out your first name, loudly.
12. If you feel that you have carefully followed these directions, call out, loudly: 'I have carefully followed directions!'
13. Add 107 and 278, and write the sum on the reverse, immediately under the first figure that you wrote there.
14. Circle that figure on the reverse.
15. In a normal voice, count aloud from 1–10.
16. If no one else has said it, say now, 'I am the leader!'
17. Now that you have read all of the foregoing, very carefully, please complete ONLY sentences 1 and 2.

What conclusions do you draw from this exercise?

PERSONAL AWARENESS AND SKILLS EXERCISE

Objectives

Completing this exercise should help you to enhance the following skills:

■ Distinguish between facts and assumptions or inferences.
■ Examine the basis upon which you make judgements.
■ Review the nature of your communication and decision-making processes.

Exercise

After reading the following story you are required to:

1 Read the 15 statements about the story and check each to indicate whether you consider it to be true, false or?

'T' means that the statement is definitely true on the basis of the information presented in the story.
'F' means that it is definitely false.
'?' means that it may be either true or false and that you cannot be certain of which on the basis of the information presented in the story. If any part of a statement is doubtful, mark it '?'.

Answer each statement in turn. You may refer to the story as often as needed but do not go back to change any answer later and do not re-read any statements after you have answered them.

2 After you have checked all 15 statements, work in small groups of three to five and discuss your individual answers. How much agreement is there among members of your group? *Do not change any of your first individual answers. However, if as a result of your group discussion you would now give a different answer to any of the statements, note this alongside your original answer.*

The story

A businessman had just turned off the lights in the store when a man appeared and demanded money. The owner opened a cash register. The contents of the cash register were scooped up and the man sped away. A member of the police force was notified promptly.

Statements about the story

1 A man appeared after the owner had turned off his store lights.	T	F	?
2 The robber was a man.	T	F	?
3 The man who appeared did not demand money.	T	F	?
4 The man who opened the cash register was the owner.	T	F	?
5 The storeowner scooped up the contents of the cash register and ran away.	T	F	?
6 Someone opened a cash register.	T	F	?
7 After the man who demanded the money scooped up the contents of the cash register, he ran away.	T	F	?
8 While the cash register contained money, the story does not state how much.	T	F	?
9 The robber demanded money of the owner.	T	F	?
10 A businessman had just turned off the lights when a man appeared in the store.	T	F	?
11 It was broad daylight when the man appeared.	T	F	?
12 The man who appeared opened the cash register.	T	F	?
13 No one demanded money.	T	F	?
14 The story concerns a series of events in which only three persons are referred to: the owner of the store, a man who demanded money and a member of the police force.	T	F	?
15 The following events occurred: someone demanded money, a cash register was opened, its contents were scooped up and a man dashed out of the store.	T	F	?

Source: From Hanley, W. V. *Communications and Interpersonal Relations, Texts and Cases*, sixth edition, Irwin (1992), p. 213.

Discussion

■ How would you explain differences in individual perceptions of the same statement?
■ On what basis did members of your group give different answers and how did their perception of the statements about the story differ?
■ To what extent can you be absolutely certain about anything?

Behavioural economics

So, you have an assignment due tomorrow, 2,000 words, deadline 1600. Have you written it yet? Maybe a paragraph or two? But you've got lots of notes, a heap of books from the library, a few articles downloaded from Google Scholar and some ideas, but you just haven't quite got them down on paper yet. And you've known about this deadline for, what, two weeks? A month? More. . . . ? Still, no worries; twenty-four hours to go. But first you need some more coffee – and, drat! The milk has run out so a quick trip to the corner store. And perhaps you can just read this text message. And then you can get on with it. Honestly. If you are 'Human', the chances are you may recognise at least part of this scenario. The good news is that almost everybody else does. The less good news is that you will probably do it again. It's painful, it's frustrating, but it's true. Luckily, a few recent and highly readable studies by behavioural economists can give you an insight into why, and how it can be avoided.

Reason and irrationality
The basis for these ideas is the link between perception, thought and behaviour, and particularly our behaviour in terms of the economic decisions and choices people make in their everyday life. Many of these choices are personal; how much to pay for a coffee at Waterloo railway station, where to rent or buy a house, how much to put into a pension plan or why you should be the first to order your food when you go out to dinner with a group of friends.[71] However, the principles shed light on the perception–thought–behaviour process, which is equally important in organisational contexts. Some choices and decisions are specifically related to management and organisational behaviour: matters of pay, reward, performance, honesty and discrimination. In the cases discussed, the decisions people make appear to be both irrational, but entirely understandable. This was the starting point for Dan Ariely, who explains that behavioural economics is a relatively new field that links economics and psychology; it focuses on judgement and decision-making and seeks to identify the causes of 'irrational' behaviour. Moreover, he considers that:

> we are not only irrational, but predictably irrational –
> that our irrationality happens in the same way, again
> and again. Whether we are acting as consumers,
> businesspeople or policy makers . . . Moreover, these
> irrational behaviors of ours are neither random nor

Behavioural economics explores the links between perception, thought and behaviour, particularly in terms of the economic choices people make in their everyday lives.

> senseless, They are systematic, and since we repeat them
> again and again, predictable.[72]

Social and market norms
Much of Ariely's research has been experimental, and one set of experiments offers an insight into the nature of the effort reward bargain. Do we work harder when we are paid? Not necessarily. The experiment which revealed this involved three groups of participants who were asked to carry out a simple repetitive task of clicking and dragging circles across a computer screen using a mouse. The system counted how many circles were moved in the 5 minutes given for the task. Some groups were paid well for participating; others paid less well and yet others asked to take part as a favour. As anticipated, the well paid worked harder than the poorly paid (by about 50%); but the unpaid outperformed both. Why? Ariely's conclusion was that different norms had been applied – social ones rather than market ones – and that in many circumstances social norms are more effective motivators.

Does this mean organisations can use social norms as well as market norms to encourage effort? A group of lawyers was shown to be content to offer <u>free</u> legal advice to needy retired clients, but not at all likely to offer the same service for a reduced fee. Here social norms were powerful where market norms actually had a deterrent effect. Indeed, further experiments showed that even the mention of money could drive out social norms and change behaviour. The psychological technique of 'priming' (the creation of a certain set of expectations, indirectly, prior to some kind of activity) was used to introduce the *idea* of market norms to some people but not others, although nobody was actually

going to be paid for taking part this time. Some participants were primed to think about money via a sentence unscrambling task before attempting a difficult visual puzzle (the sentences they were given used words like salary), and others were given neutral sentences. The behaviour of the primed participants during the puzzle element was notably different:

> They were more selfish and self-reliant; they wanted to spend more time alone; they were more likely to select tasks that required individual input rather than teamwork; . . . Indeed, just thinking about money makes us behave as most economists believe we behave – and less like the social animals we are in our daily lives.[73]

Moreover, it seems that once we have switched over from social to market norms in our thinking, it is very difficult for us to switch back. The social relationship may have been irretrievably ruined.[74] Obviously, the vast majority of work organisations rely on market norms to a significant extent, and rarely more so than when people are paid for performance. The link between pay and performance seems logical, and much managerial work involves performance measurement and judgement with the aim of improving performance. For instance, when salaries were replaced by piecework in a car windscreen repair business (workers were paid per windscreen re-fit, and required to correct any mistakes they made without extra pay) productivity improved and errors were reduced.[75] However, the problem for advocates of this type of incentive scheme is that performance in most jobs is not as easily measured as it is in the windscreen repair business; and workers will generally adjust their behaviour to achieve the measured targets regardless of the overall result.

> It's simply too difficult for managers to work out the details of what should be done, and to judge whether what should be done is being done. The frustrations of working life are a direct result of that struggle.[76]

All you need is Nudge

An example of the application of behavioural economics shows how people can be encouraged, rather than forced, to behave in ways which are seen to be beneficial (to themselves, to their communities, the environment etc.) and deals with the age-old problem of why we can't seem to do things that we know are good for us or 'right'. We lack self-control, especially when costs are felt immediately but the pay-off doesn't arrive for some time. This is why dieting is hard but chatting on Facebook is easy. We tend to defer changes to our behaviour and are over-optimistic about our

future behaviour; our diets always start tomorrow and will be spectacularly effective. But it seems that we can be 'nudged' to change our *future* behaviour in a way that makes it stick. For instance, Thaler and Sunstein report on the success of the 'Save More Tomorrow' plan as a means of encouraging people to contribute more sensibly to pension schemes. Instead of requiring people to contribute more of their pay today, they were asked to commit to increasing their savings in the future. The savings plan deducted the money from their salaries, and the increased deductions were timed to coincide with pay raises.

> By synchronising pay raises and savings increases, participants never see their take-home amounts go down, and they don't view their increased retirement contributions as losses.[77]

The scheme enlisted the power of four key behavioural responses to perceived factors. The 'painful' part was deferred; there was never a perception of 'loss', in this case of spending power; the system was easy and the default contributions were the increasing ones; and the power of inertia meant that opting out of the increases was more effort than staying in. The combined effects meant that the 'nudge' was effective, even though there was no obligation to continue with the increases.

Now, about that essay

A further practical example of this is the website created by Yale Economics professor Dean Karlan called 'stickK.com' which is described as a 'commitment store', and which is based on two key principles of behavioural economics:

1 People don't always do what they claim they want to do.
2 Incentives get people to do things.[78]

The process is described by Thaler and Sunstein:

> An individual puts up money and agrees to accomplish a goal by a certain date. He also specifies how to verify that he has met his goal. For example he might agree to a weigh-in at a doctor's office . . . (if the goal is to lose weight). If the person reaches his goal, he gets his money back. If he fails, the money goes to charity.[79]

So, back to that essay. Only 20 hours to go and still only 426 words. If only you'd written 250 words a day for the last 10 days, you'd be polishing off the references and making it look nice by now! So, next time you get an assignment, how about you and your mates visit stickK.com?

Your tasks

1 Discuss and plan an experiment like the 'circle-dragging' one carried out by Ariely which you could use to see if you find the same differences in motivation resulting from the use of 'social' and 'market' norms.

2 To what extent should managers appeal to 'social norms' when planning the work of their staff? What are the benefits and what are the dangers?

3 Consider the idea of 'priming'. Explain how this might fit into the cycle of perception and behaviour illustrated in Figure 6.13. How might a manager, either consciously or unconsciously, 'prime' others to receive their communications in different ways?

4 What can we learn from the ideas behind the 'Save More Tomorrow' scheme or 'stickK.com' about how to help people to change both their perceptions and behaviour at work in such a way as to improve personal effectiveness?

Notes and references

1 We wish gratefully to acknowledge Linda Carter, the joint author of this chapter in earlier editions.

2 Bartlett, F. C. *Remembering Cambridge*, Cambridge University Press (1932).

3 Kohler, I. 'The Formation and Transformation of the Visual World', *Psychological Issues*, vol. 3, 1964, pp. 28–46, 116–33.

4 Bexton, W., Heron, W. and Scott, T. 'Effects of Decreased Variation in the Sensory Environment', *Canadian Journal of Psychology*, vol. 8, 1954, pp. 70–6.

5 Myers, I. B. *Introduction to Type*, Oxford Psychologists Press (1987).

6 Witkin, H. A., Lewis, H. B., Hertzman, M., Machover, K., Meissner, P. P. and Wapner, S. S. *Personality Through Perception*, Harper & Row (1954).

7 Schein, E. H. *Organizational Culture and Leadership*, Jossey Bass (1992), p. 9.

8 Ling, C. and Masako, I. 'Intercultural Communication and Cultural Learning: The Experience of Visiting Japanese Students in the US', *The Howard Journal of Communications*, vol. 14, 2003, pp. 75–96.

9 Hall, E. T. 'The Silent Language of Overseas Business', *Harvard Business Review*, vol. 38, no. 3, 1960, pp. 85–7.

10 Dainty, P. and Anderson, M. 'Mindset for Managers', in Chowdhury, S. (ed.) *Management 21C*, Financial Times Prentice Hall (2000), pp. 109–10.

11 McCrum, M. *Going Dutch in Beijing*, Profile Books (2007), p. vii.

12 Stewart-Allen, A. L. 'Changing the Mindset about Americans', *Professional Manager*, vol. 15, no. 5, September 2006, p. 37.

13 McCrum, M. *Going Dutch in Beijing*, Profile Books (2007), pp. 44–5.

14 Block, J. R. and Yuker, H. E. *Can You Believe Your Eyes?*, Robson Books (2002).

15 Morgan, C. T. and King, R. A. *Introduction to Psychology*, third edition, McGraw-Hill (1966), p. 343.

16 Stroop, J. R. 'Studies of Interference in Serial Verbal Reactions', *Journal of Experimental Psychology*, vol. 4, no. 18, 1935, pp. 643–62; and Penrose, L. S. and Penrose, R.

'Impossible Objects: A Special Type of Illusion', *British Journal of Psychology*, part 1, February 1958.

17 Kendon, A. 'Some Functions of Gaze Direction in Social Interaction', *Acta Psychologica*, vol. 26, 1967, pp. 22–63.

18 Mehrabian, A. *Nonverbal Communication*, Aldine Atherton (1972).

19 Cook, M. *Interpersonal Perception*, Penguin (1971).

20 Schneider, S. C. and Barsoux, J. *Managing Across Cultures*, second edition, Financial Times Prentice Hall (2003), p. 29.

21 Goffman, E. *The Presentation of Self in Everyday Life*, Penguin (1971).

22 Asch, S. E. 'Forming Impressions on Personality', *Journal of Abnormal and Social Psychology*, vol. 41, 1946, pp. 258–90.

23 Miller, N. and Campbell, D. T. 'Recency and Primacy in Persuasion as a Function of the Timing of Speeches and Measurements', *Journal of Abnormal and Social Psychology*, vol. 59, 1959, pp. 1–9.

24 Hodges, B. 'Effect of Volume on Relative Weighting in Impression Formation', *Journal of Personality and Social Psychology*, vol. 30, 1974, pp. 378–81.

25 Gahagan, J. *Interpersonal and Group Behaviour*, Methuen (1975).

26 Green, J. 'When Was Your Management Style Last Applauded?', *Chartered Secretary*, December 1998, p. 28.

27 Wilson, P. R. 'Perceptual Distortion of Height as a Function of Ascribed Academic Status', *Journal of Social Psychology*, no. 74, 1968, pp. 97–102.

28 See, for example, Leitch, L. 'The Big Problem that Short Men Face', *The Times*, 24 June 2009.

29 Spitzer, M. 'Brain Research and Learning over the Life Cycle in Personalising Education', OECD (2006).

30 Cooperrider, D. L. and Srivastva, S. 'An Invitation to Organizational Wisdom and Executive Courage', in Srivastva, I. S. and Cooperrider, D. L. (eds) *Organizational Wisdom and Executive Courage*, New Lexington Press (1998).

31 Hammond, S. A. *The Thin Book of Appreciative Inquiry*, second edition, Thin Book Publishing Company, (1998).

32 Guirdham, M. *Interactive Behaviour at Work*, third edition, Financial Times Prentice Hall (2002), p. 161.

33 Wexley, K. N., Yukl, G. A., Kovacs, S. Z. and Sanders, R. E. 'Importance of Contrast Effects in Employment Interviews', *Journal of Applied Psychology*, vol. 56, 1972, pp. 45–8.

34 Torbert, W. R. *Managing the Corporate Dream*, McGraw-Hill (1987). See also Breakthrough Consultancy, www.breakthrough.ie.

35 Laing, R. D. *Knots*, Penguin (1971), p. 30.

36 Guirdham, M. *Interactive Behaviour at Work*, third edition, Financial Times Prentice Hall (2002).

37 See, for example, Torrington, D. *Face-to-Face in Management*, Prentice Hall (1982).

38 Mehrabian, A. *Tactics of Social Influence*, Prentice Hall (1970).

39 Pivcevic, P. 'Taming the Boss', *Management Today*, March 1999, p. 70.

40 McGuire, T. 'Don't Just Listen', *Chartered Secretary*, September 1998, p. 24.

41 James, J. *Body Talk at Work*, Judy Piatkus (2001), p. 3.

42 Kennett, M. 'First-Class Coach', *Management Today*, May 2008, p. 68.

43 Fletcher, W. 'Let Your Body Do The Talking', *Management Today*, March 2000, p. 30.

44 Mann, S. 'Message in a Body', *Professional Manager*, November 2000, pp. 32–3; and Ribbens, G. and Thompson, R. *Understanding Body Language in a Week*, Institute of Management and Hodder & Stoughton (2000).

45 Akehurst, L. in Morrish, J. 'Spot the Liar', *Management Today*, October 2006, pp. 46–51.

46 See, for example, James, J. *The Body Language Bible*, Vermillon (2008).

47 For other examples of cultural differences, see Schneider, S. C. and Barsoux, J. *Managing Across Cultures*, second edition, Financial Times Prentice Hall (2003).

48 Pease, A. and Pease, B. *The Definitive Book of Body Language*, Orion Books Limited (2005), p. 2.

49 'Nick Fitzherbert Applies the Rules of Magic to Coaching People in Communication Skills', www.fitzherbert.co.uk. See also Fitzherbert, N. 'Magic Tricks in Communication', *Professional Manager*, vol. 14, no. 5, September 2005, pp. 32–3.

50 See, for example, Pivcevic, P. 'Taming the Boss', *Management Today*, March 1999, pp. 68–72.

51 Bandler, R., Grinder, J., Dilts, R. and Delozier, J. *Neuro Linguistic Programming Volume I: The Study of the Structure of Subject Experience*, Meta Publications (1980).

52 Shapiro, M. 'Getting Your Brain in Gear', *Professional Manager*, vol. 16, no. 5, September 2007, pp. 26–9.

53 From www.bbnlp.com (accessed 13 February 2009).

54 McCann, D. *How to Influence Others at Work*, second edition, Butterworth Heinemann (1993).

55 Stone, K. 'Influential People', *Manager: The British Journal of Administrative Management*, June/July 2005, pp. 22–3.

56 Shapiro, M. 'Getting Your Brain in Gear', *Professional Manager*, vol. 16, no. 5, September 2007, pp. 26–9.

57 O'Connor, J. and Lages, A. *Coaching with NLP*, Element (2004), pp. 114–15.

58 Berne, E. *Games People Play*, Penguin (1966).

59 For a summary of NLP, TA, and other thoughts on business psychology, see Butcher, D. 'Buyer's Guide to Business Psychology', *Management Today*, May 2005, pp. 54–7.

60 Heider, F. *The Psychology of Interpersonal Relations*, John Wiley & Sons (1958).

61 Kelley, H. H. 'The Process of Causal Attribution', *American Psychologist*, February 1973, pp. 107–28.

62 Bartunek, J. M. 'Why Did You Do That? Attribution Theory in Organizations', *Business Horizons*, September–October 1981, pp. 66–71.

63 Mitchell, T. R., Smyser, C. M. and Weed, S. E. 'Locus of Control: Supervision and Work Satisfaction', *Academy of Management Journal*, September 1975, pp. 623–31.

64 Durand, D. E. and Nord, W. R. 'Perceived Leader Behaviour as a Function of Personality Characteristics of Supervisors and Subordinates', *Academy of Management Journal*, September 1976, pp. 427–38.

65 See, for example, Stewart-Allen, A. L. 'Changing the Mindset about Americans', *Professional Manager*, vol. 15, no. 5, September 2006, p. 37.

66 Goss, D. and Adam-Smith, D. *Organizing AIDS*, Taylor & Francis (1995).

67 Merton, R. K. *Social Theory and Social Structure*, Free Press (1957).

68 Rosenthal, R. and Jacobson, L. *Pygmalion in the Classroom*, Holt, Rinehart and Winston (1968).

69 Word, C. O., Zanna, M. P. and Cooper, J. 'The Nonverbal Mediation of Self-Fulfilling Prophecies in Interracial Interaction', *Journal of Experimental Social Psychology*, vol. 10, no. 1, 1974, pp. 109–20.

70 Ames, A. 'Visual Perception and the Rotating Trapezoidal Window', *Psychological Monographs*, vol. 65, no. 7, 1951.

71 Ariely, D. *Predictably Irrational; The Hidden Forces that Shape Our Decisions*, Harper Collins (2008), Chapter 13.

72 Ibid., p. xx.

73 Ibid., p. 75.

74 The first of the 2009 Reith Lectures by Prof. Michael Sandel 'Markets and Morals' makes similar points; available as a podcast and transcript from the BBC website, http://www.bbc.co.uk/programmes/b00729d9.

75 Harford, T. *The Logic of Life*, Little, Brown (2008).

76 Ibid., p. 102.

77 Thaler, R., and Sunstein, C. *Nudge: Improving Decisions about Health, Wealth and Happiness*, Yale University Press (2008), p. 113.

78 See the 'About Us' section of the website at www.stickK.com.

79 Thaler and Sunstein op. cit., p. 231.

7 WORK MOTIVATION AND JOB SATISFACTION

The relationship between the organisation and its members is influenced by what motivates them to work and the rewards and fulfilment they derive from it. The nature of the work organisation, styles of leadership and the design and content of jobs can have a significant effect on the satisfaction of staff and their levels of performance. The manager needs to know how best to elicit the co-operation of staff and direct their efforts to achieving the goals and objectives of the organisation.

Learning outcomes

After completing this chapter you should be able to:

- explain the meaning and underlying concept of motivation;
- detail main types of needs and expectations of people at work;
- explain frustration-induced behaviour and possible reactions to frustration at work;
- examine main theories of motivation and evaluate their relevance to particular work situations;
- review the meaning, nature and dimensions of job satisfaction;
- assess broader influences on motivation and job satisfaction;
- evaluate the relationship between motivation, job satisfaction and work performance.

Critical reflection

'Some writers argue that people do not lack motivation, only the right triggers to motivate them. Some claim that motivation can only come from within and attempts from other people to motivate you have little lasting influence.'

What are your views? In your own words, what motivates you most?

THE MEANING OF MOTIVATION

The study of **motivation** is concerned, basically, with why people behave in a certain way. The basic underlying question is 'Why do people do what they do?' In general terms, motivation can be described as the direction and persistence of action. It is concerned with why people choose a particular course of action in preference to others, and why they continue with a chosen action, often over a long period and in the face of difficulties and problems.[1]

From a review of motivation theory, *Mitchell* identifies four common characteristics which underlie the definition of motivation:[2]

- **Motivation is typified as an individual phenomenon.** Every person is unique and all the major theories of motivation allow for this uniqueness to be demonstrated in one way or another.
- **Motivation is described, usually, as intentional.** Motivation is assumed to be under the worker's control, and behaviours that are influenced by motivation, such as effort expended, are seen as choices of action.
- **Motivation is multifaceted.** The two factors of greatest importance are: (i) what gets people activated (arousal); and (ii) the force of an individual to engage in desired behaviour (direction or choice of behaviour).
- **The purpose of motivational theories is to predict behaviour.** Motivation is not the behaviour itself and it is not performance. Motivation concerns action and the internal and external forces which influence a person's choice of action.

On the basis of these characteristics, Mitchell defines motivation as 'the degree to which an individual wants and chooses to engage in certain specified behaviours'.

A fuller definition is given by the Chartered Management Institute:

Motivation is the creation of stimuli, incentives and working environments that enable people to perform to the best of their ability. The heart of motivation is to give people what they really want most from work. In return managers should expect more in the form of productivity, quality and service.[3]

Underlying concept of motivation

The underlying concept of motivation is some driving force within individuals by which they attempt to achieve some goal in order to fulfil some need or expectation. This concept gives rise to the basic motivational model, which is illustrated in Figure 7.1. People's behaviour is

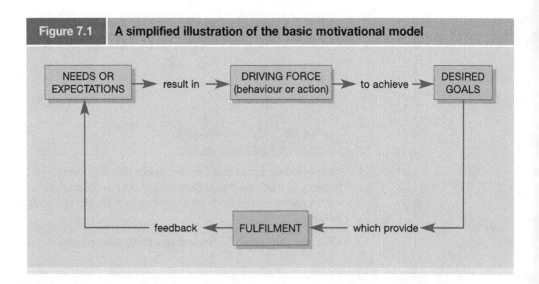

| Figure 7.1 | A simplified illustration of the basic motivational model |

determined by what motivates them. Their performance is a product of both ability level and motivation.

$$Performance = function\ (ability \times motivation)$$

Kreitner et al. suggest that although motivation is a necessary contributor for job performance, it is not the only one. Along with ability, motivation is also a combination of level of skill, knowledge about how to complete the task, feelings and emotions, and facilitating and inhibiting conditions not under the individual's control.[4] However, what is clearly evident is that if the manager is to improve the work of the organisation, attention must be given to the level of motivation of its members. The manager must also encourage staff to direct their efforts (their driving force) towards the successful attainment of the goals and objectives of the organisation.

NEEDS AND EXPECTATIONS AT WORK

But what is this driving force and what is it that people really want from work? What are people's needs and expectations and how do they influence behaviour and performance at work? Motivation is a complex subject, it is a very personal thing, and it is influenced by many variables. *Farren* reminds us of the 12 human needs that have been around since the beginning of recorded history: family, health and well-being, work/career, economic, learning, home/shelter, social relationships, spirituality, community, leisure, mobility, and environment/safety. 'Work and private life in the new millennium will continue to revolve around the 12 human needs.'[5]

The various needs and expectations at work can be categorised in a number of ways – for example the simple divisions into physiological and social motives or into extrinsic and intrinsic motivation.

- **Extrinsic motivation** is related to 'tangible' rewards such as salary and fringe benefits, security, promotion, contract of service, the work environment and conditions of work. Such tangible rewards are often determined at the organisational level and may be largely outside the control of individual managers.
- **Intrinsic motivation** is related to 'psychological' rewards such as the opportunity to use one's ability, a sense of challenge and achievement, receiving appreciation, positive recognition and being treated in a caring and considerate manner. The psychological rewards are those that can usually be determined by the actions and behaviour of individual managers.[6]

Higher set of motivational needs

According to *Kets de Vries*, the best-performing companies possess a set of values that creates the right conditions for high performance; he questions whether in such best companies there is something more going on that touches upon a deeper layer of human functioning, causing people to make an extra effort. The emphasis is on widening choice that enables people to choose more freely, instead of being led by forces of which they are unaware; and it is a motivational needs system on which such choice is based. Kets de Vries suggests that in addition to the motivation needs system for physiological needs, sensual and enjoyment needs, and the need to respond to threatening situations, companies that get the best out of their people are characterised by a system based on a higher set of motivational needs:

- **attachment/affiliation** – concerning the need for engagement and sharing, a feeling of community and a sense of belonging to the company; and
- **exploration/assertion** – concerning the ability to play and work, a sense of fun and enjoyment, the need for self-assertion and the ability to choose.[7]

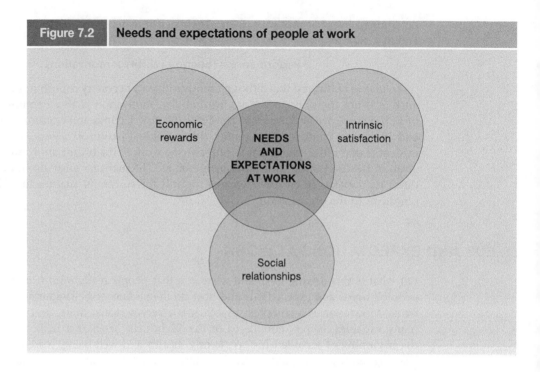

Figure 7.2 Needs and expectations of people at work

A three-fold classification

Given the complex and variable nature of needs and expectations, the following is a simplistic but useful, broad three-fold classification as a starting point for reviewing the motivation to work (*see* Figure 7.2):

- **Economic rewards** – such as pay, fringe benefits, pension rights, material goods and security. This is an **instrumental** orientation to work and concerned with 'other things'.
- **Intrinsic satisfaction** – derived from the nature of the work itself, interest in the job, and personal growth and development. This is a **personal** orientation to work and concerned with 'oneself'.
- **Social relationships** – such as friendships, group working and the desire for affiliation, status and dependency. This is a **relational** orientation to work and concerned with 'other people'.

A person's motivation, job satisfaction and work performance will be determined by the comparative strength of these sets of needs and expectations and the extent to which they are fulfilled. For example, some people may make a deliberate choice to forgo intrinsic satisfaction and social relationships (particularly in the short term or in the earlier years of their working life) in return for high economic rewards. Other people are happy to accept comparatively lower economic rewards in favour of a job that has high intrinsic satisfaction and/or social relationships. Social relationships would appear to be an important feature for many people, especially, for example, for those working in the hospitality industry where interactions with other people and the importance of supportive working relationships and good teamwork can be strong motivators at work.[8]

MONEY AS A MOTIVATOR

Earlier writers, such as F. W. Taylor, believed in economic needs motivation. Workers would be motivated by obtaining the highest possible wages through working in the most efficient and productive way. Performance was limited by physiological fatigue. For Taylor, motivation

was a comparatively simple issue – what the workers wanted from their employers more than anything else was high wages. This approach is the **rational–economic concept of motivation**. The ideas of F. W. Taylor and his 'rational–economic needs' concept of motivation (discussed in Chapter 2) and subsequent approaches to motivation at work have fuelled the continuing debate about financial rewards as a motivator and their influence on productivity.

Where there is little pleasure in the work itself or the job offers little opportunity for career advancement, personal challenge or growth, many people may appear to be motivated primarily, if not exclusively, by money. Weaver suggests that for many hourly workers in the hospitality industry, such as dishwashing, waiting or housekeeping staff, the work does not change much among different companies and there is little attachment to a particular company. For such staff, *Weaver* proposes a 'Theory M' programme of motivation based on direct cash rewards for above-average performance. A percentage base is calculated from the average performance of workers on the staff.[9] Yet we frequently see pronouncements from prominent business figures that motivation is about much more than money.

> *Work is about letting people know they are important, their hard work and efforts matter, and they're doing a good job. And this kind of recognition, in fact, can sometimes be more important than money.*
>
> Gary Kusin, CEO, FedEx Kinko's[10]

The short answer appears to be that for the vast majority of people, money is clearly important and a motivator at work **but** to what extent and **how** important depends upon their personal circumstances and the other satisfactions they derive from work. The bottom line is surely the extent to which money motivates people to work **well** and to the best of their abilities. Although pay may still make people tick, there are now a number of other important influences on motivation. For many people, the feeling of being recognised and valued appears more important than money in motivating them to stay in a particular job. (See the discussion of Herzberg's two-factor theory of motivation later in this chapter.)

BROADER INTRINSIC MOTIVATION

Popular press reports appear to indicate that many people are increasingly motivated by broader concerns such as their work/life balance (discussed in Chapter 3), opportunities for flexible working, career advancement and personal development and growth, and a feeling of identification with the values of the organisation. The motivation to work is also influenced by the changing nature of the work environment and the concept of the 'psychological contract', which was discussed in Chapter 1.

> *If your staff do something good, tell them. And then tell them again. And again. Keep it up. Put it in writing. Send them a memo – something they can keep. Put it in the company newsletter. Add a note to their file. Whatever, but make it widely known they did good. This is a quick and cheap method of praising and motivating your team and it lets everyone know you are monitoring, praising, motivating.*[11]

As *Grayson and Hodges* point out, historically loyalty was bought and employers offered gradual progression up the hierarchy, a decent salary and job security in return for a hard day's work. 'Increasingly, motivation is based on values rather than purely on financial reward.'[12]

However, according to *Gratton* finding intrinsically motivating tasks is not easy.

Finding tasks and experiences that are intrinsically motivating sounds relatively straightforward but in fact it requires a heightened awareness of who we are. Without this emotional self-awareness we have no capacity to judge whether the tasks available to us could be intrinsically motivating . . . Finding intrinsically motivating tasks also requires the companies of which we are members to communicate the tasks available and to encourage volunteering.[13]

Waller refers to the importance today of identity and that work inevitably plays a key role on shaping identity. Waller questions how much of ourselves do we put into our job. He points out that not long ago, a job was something you did to put bread on the table but nowadays (global financial situation apart) people in a cushy job with a decent salary, paid holiday, pension, health care and a well-stocked sandwich trolley will jack it all in, saying 'It's not really me'. If people are getting absorbed by their work-life, they expect their job to help them to discover and develop themselves.[14]

Critical reflection

'It's all very well talking about a contented workforce, praise and recognition but at times of high unemployment, rapid change or uncertainty a secure job, increased training and steady income are the true motivators. In the real world money is the most potent need and strongest motivator.'

Can you argue convincingly against this contention?

FRUSTRATION-INDUCED BEHAVIOUR

What happens if a person's motivational driving force is blocked and they are unable to satisfy their needs and expectations, and what is the likely effect on their work performance? There are two possible sets of outcomes: constructive behaviour or frustration (*see* Figure 7.3).

Constructive behaviour

Constructive behaviour is a positive reaction to the blockage of a desired goal and can take two main forms: problem-solving or restructuring.

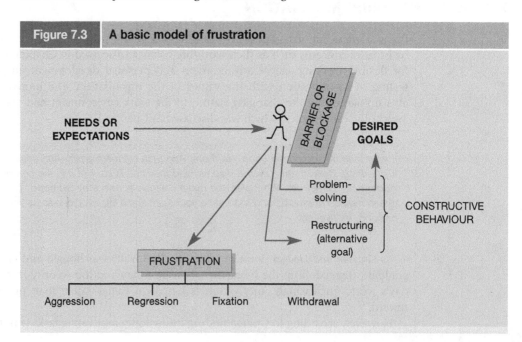

| Figure 7.3 | A basic model of frustration |

- **Problem-solving** is the removal of the barrier – for example finding an alternative means of undertaking a task, repairing a damaged machine or bypassing an unco-operative superior.
- **Restructuring**, or compromise, is the substitution of an alternative goal, although such a goal may be of a lower or different order – for example taking an additional part-time job because of failure to be promoted to a higher grade, or reassessing the work/life balance.

Note: Even if a person engages in constructive behaviour in response to a barrier or blockage, it could be said that the person was 'frustrated', if only mildly or in the short term, in an attempt to satisfy a desired goal. However, the term 'frustration' is usually interpreted as applying to **negative responses** to a barrier or blockage which prevents satisfaction of a desired goal.

Frustration (negative responses)

Frustration is a negative response to the blockage of a desired goal and results in a defensive form of behaviour. There are many possible reactions to frustration caused by the failure to achieve a desired goal. These can be summarised under four broad headings: aggression, regression, fixation and withdrawal.[15] However, these categories are not mutually exclusive. Most forms of frustration-induced behaviour at work are a combination of aggression, regression and fixation.

Aggression is a physical or verbal attack on some person or object, for example striking a supervisor, rage or abusive language, destruction of equipment or documents, or malicious gossip about a superior. This form of behaviour may be directed against the person or object that is perceived as the source of frustration, that is the actual barrier or blocking agent. However, where such a direct attack cannot be made, because, for example, the source of frustration is not clear or not specific, or where the source is feared, as with a powerful superior, aggression may be displaced towards some other person or object.

With **displaced aggression** the person may find an easier, safer person or object as a scapegoat for the outlet of frustration – for example picking arguments with colleagues, being short-tempered with subordinates, shouting at the cleaners or kicking the waste-paper bin. A more constructive form of displaced aggression is working off frustrated feelings through demanding physical work or sport, or perhaps by shouting/cursing when alone or in the company of an understanding colleague.

Regression is reverting to a childish or more primitive form of behaviour – for example sulking, crying, tantrums or kicking a broken machine or piece of equipment.

Fixation is persisting in a form of behaviour which has no adaptive value and continuing to repeat actions which have no positive results – for example the inability to accept change or new ideas, repeatedly trying a door that is clearly locked or a machine which clearly will not work, or insisting on applying for promotion even though not qualified for the job.

Withdrawal is apathy, giving up or resignation – for example arriving at work late and leaving early, sickness and absenteeism, refusal to accept responsibility, avoiding decision-making, passing work over to colleagues or leaving the job altogether.

Factors influencing frustration

Among the factors which determine an individual's reaction to frustration are the:

- level and potency of need (*see*, for example, Maslow's theory of motivation, discussed below);
- degree of attachment to the desired goal;
- strength of motivation;
- perceived nature of the barrier or blocking agent; and
- personality characteristics of the individual.

It is important that managers attempt to reduce potential frustration, for example through:

- effective recruitment, selection and socialisation;
- training and development;
- job design and work organisation;
- equitable HRM policies;
- recognition and rewards;
- effective communications;
- participative styles of management;
- attempting to understand the individual's perception of the situation.

Proper attention to motivation and to the needs and expectations of people at work will help overcome boredom and frustration-induced behaviour.

THEORIES OF MOTIVATION

There are many competing theories that attempt to explain the nature of motivation. These theories may all be at least partially true and help to explain the behaviour of certain people at certain times. The issue of motivation is often most acute for younger people starting on their career, for people at mid-career positions or for those who find limited opportunities for promotion or further advancement. For employers there may be difficulties in motivating staff both in the longer term and in the short run. It is because of the complexity of motivation and the fact that there is no ready-made solution or single answer to what motivates people to work well that the different theories are important to the manager. They show there are many motives that influence people's behaviour and performance. Collectively, the different theories provide a framework within which to direct attention to the problem of how best to motivate staff to work willingly and effectively.

Criticisms and reservations

It is important to emphasise, however, that these various theories are not conclusive. They all have their critics (this is particularly true of the content theories of motivation) or have been subject to alternative findings that purport to contradict original ideas. Many of these theories were not intended initially to have the significance that some writers have subsequently placed upon them. It is always easy to quote an example that appears to contradict any generalised observation on what motivates people to work. Despite these reservations the different theories provide a basis for study and discussion, and for review of the most effective motivational style (*see* Figure 7.4).

> *You don't motivate individuals. You provide them with an environment to be self-motivated. It is a personal decision, but it's management's job to provide the right environment.*
>
> Kathy Schofield, Director of Human Resources, HFC Bank[16]

The manager, therefore, must judge the relevance of these different theories, how best to draw upon them, and how they might effectively be applied in particular work situations. The manager should be aware of at least the main theories of motivation.

Content theories and process theories

The usual approach to the study of motivation is through an understanding of internal cognitive processes – that is, what people feel and how they think. This understanding should help the manager to predict likely behaviour of staff in given situations. These different cognitive theories of motivation are usually divided into two contrasting approaches: content theories and process theories.

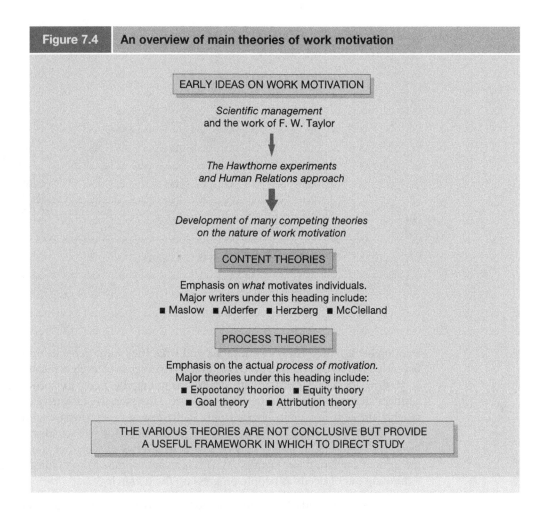

| Figure 7.4 | **An overview of main theories of work motivation** |

EARLY IDEAS ON WORK MOTIVATION

*Scientific management
and the work of F. W. Taylor*

*The Hawthorne experiments
and Human Relations approach*

*Development of many competing theories
on the nature of work motivation*

CONTENT THEORIES

Emphasis on *what* motivates individuals.
Major writers under this heading include:
■ Maslow ■ Alderfer ■ Herzberg ■ McClelland

PROCESS THEORIES

Emphasis on the actual *process of motivation.*
Major theories under this heading include:
■ Expectancy theories ■ Equity theory
■ Goal theory ■ Attribution theory

THE VARIOUS THEORIES ARE NOT CONCLUSIVE BUT PROVIDE
A USEFUL FRAMEWORK IN WHICH TO DIRECT STUDY

■ **Content theories** attempt to explain those specific things that actually motivate the individual at work. These theories are concerned with identifying people's needs and their relative strengths, and the goals they pursue in order to satisfy these needs. Content theories place emphasis on the nature of needs and **what motivates**.

■ **Process theories** attempt to identify the relationship among the dynamic variables that make up motivation. These theories are concerned more with how behaviour is initiated, directed and sustained. Process theories place emphasis on the **actual process of motivation**. These theories are discussed later in this chapter.

CONTENT THEORIES OF MOTIVATION

Major content theories of motivation include:

■ Maslow's hierarchy of needs model;
■ Alderfer's modified need hierarchy model;
■ Herzberg's two-factor theory;
■ McClelland's achievement motivation theory.

MASLOW'S HIERARCHY OF NEEDS THEORY

A useful starting point is the work of *Maslow* and his theory of individual development and motivation, published originally in 1943.[17] Maslow's basic proposition is that people are

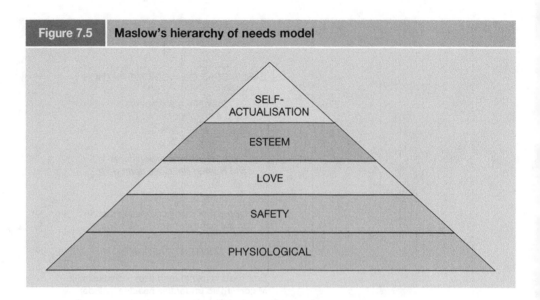

Figure 7.5 Maslow's hierarchy of needs model

wanting beings, they always want more, and what they want depends on what they already have. He suggests that human needs are arranged in a series of levels, a hierarchy of importance.

Maslow identified eight innate needs, including the need to know and understand, aesthetic needs and the need for transcendence. However, the hierarchy is usually shown as ranging through five main levels, from, at the lowest level, physiological needs, through safety needs, love needs and esteem needs, to the need for self-actualisation at the highest level. The **hierarchy of needs** may be shown as a series of steps but is usually displayed in the form of a pyramid (*see* Figure 7.5). This is an appropriate form of illustration as it implies a thinning out of needs as people progress up the hierarchy.

■ **Physiological needs**. These include homeostasis (the body's automatic efforts to retain normal functioning) such as satisfaction of hunger and thirst, the need for oxygen and to maintain temperature regulation. Also sleep, sensory pleasures, activity, maternal behaviour and, arguably, sexual desire.
■ **Safety needs**. These include safety and security, freedom from pain or threat of physical attack, protection from danger or deprivation, the need for predictability and orderliness.
■ **Love needs** (often referred to as social needs). These include affection, sense of belonging, social activities, friendships, and both the giving and receiving of love.
■ **Esteem needs** (sometimes referred to as ego needs). These include both self-respect and the esteem of others. Self-respect involves the desire for confidence, strength, independence and freedom, and achievement. Esteem of others involves reputation or prestige, status, recognition, attention and appreciation.
■ **Self-actualisation needs**. This is the development and realisation of one's full potential. Maslow sees this as 'What humans can be, they must be' or 'becoming everything that one is capable of becoming'. Self-actualisation needs are not necessarily a creative urge and may take many forms which vary widely from one individual to another.

Once a lower need has been satisfied, it no longer acts as a strong motivator. The needs of the next higher level in the hierarchy demand satisfaction and become the motivating influence. Only unsatisfied needs motivate a person. Thus Maslow asserts that *'a satisfied need is no longer a motivator'*.

Not necessarily a fixed order

Although Maslow suggests that most people have these basic needs in about the order indicated, he also makes it clear that the hierarchy is not necessarily a fixed order. There will be

a number of exceptions to the order indicated. For some people there will be a reversal of the hierarchy, for example:

- Self-esteem may seem to be more important than love to some people. This is the most common reversal of the hierarchy. It is often based on the belief that the person most loved is strong, confident or inspires respect. People seeking love try to put on a show of aggressive, confident behaviour. They are not really seeking self-esteem as an end in itself but for the sake of love needs.
- For some innately creative people the drive for creativity and self-actualisation may arise despite lack of satisfaction of more basic needs.
- Higher-level needs may be lost in some people who will continue to be satisfied at lower levels only: for example, a person who has experienced chronic unemployment.
- Some people who have been deprived of love in early childhood may experience the permanent loss of love needs.
- A need which has continued to be satisfied over a long period of time may be undervalued. For example, people who have never suffered from chronic hunger may tend to underestimate its effects, and regard food as rather an unimportant thing. Where people are dominated by a higher-level need this may assume greater importance than more basic needs.
- People with high ideals or values may become martyrs and give up everything else for the sake of their beliefs.

Maslow claims that the hierarchy is relatively universal among different cultures, but he recognises that there are differences in an individual's motivational content in a particular culture.

Degrees of satisfaction

Maslow points out that a false impression may be given that a need must be satisfied fully before a subsequent need arises. **He suggests that a more realistic description is in terms of decreasing percentages of satisfaction along levels of the hierarchy.** For example, arbitrary figures for the average person may be: satisfied 85 per cent in physiological needs; 70 per cent in safety needs; 50 per cent in love needs; 40 per cent in esteem needs; and 10 per cent in self-actualisation needs. There is a gradual emergence of a higher-level need as lower-level needs become more satisfied. The relative importance of these needs changes during the psychological development of the individual. Maslow subsequently modified his views by noting that satisfaction of self-actualisation needs by growth-motivated individuals can actually enhance these needs rather than reduce them. Furthermore, he accepted that some higher-level needs may still emerge after long deprivation of lower-level needs rather than only after their satisfaction.

Evaluation of Maslow's theory

Based on Maslow's theory, once lower-level needs have been satisfied (say at the physiological and safety levels), giving more of the same does not provide motivation. Individuals advance up the hierarchy as each lower-level need becomes satisfied. Therefore, to provide motivation for a change in behaviour, the manager must direct attention to the next higher level of needs (in this case, love or social needs) that seek satisfaction.

Applications to the work situation

There are a number of problems in relating Maslow's theory to the work situation. These include the following:

- People do not necessarily satisfy their needs, especially higher-level needs, just through the work situation; they satisfy them through other areas of their life as well. Therefore the manager would need to have a complete understanding of people's private and social lives, not just their behaviour at work.

- There is doubt about the time that elapses between the satisfaction of a lower-level need and the emergence of a higher-level need.
- Individual differences mean that people place different values on the same need. For example, some people prefer what they might see as the comparative safety of working in a bureaucratic organisation to a more highly paid and higher status position, but with less job security, in a different organisation.
- Some rewards or outcomes at work satisfy more than one need. Higher salary or promotion, for example, can be applied to all levels of the hierarchy.
- Even for people within the same level of the hierarchy, the motivating factors will not be the same. There are many different ways in which people may seek satisfaction of, for example, their esteem needs.
- Maslow viewed satisfaction as the main motivational outcome of behaviour. But job satisfaction does not necessarily lead to improved work performance.

A useful basis for evaluation

Although Maslow did not originally intend that the need hierarchy should necessarily be applied to the work situation, it remains popular as a theory of motivation at work. Despite criticisms and doubts about its limitations, the theory has had a significant impact on management approaches to motivation and the design of organisations to meet individual needs. It is a convenient framework for viewing the different needs and expectations that people have, where they are in the hierarchy, and the different motivators that might be applied to people at different levels. The work of Maslow has drawn attention to a number of motivators and stimulated study and research. The need hierarchy model provides a useful base for the evaluation of motivation at work. For example, *Steers and Porter* suggest a list of general rewards and organisational factors used to satisfy different needs (*see* Table 7.1).[18]

Saunders contends that despite the time that has elapsed, Maslow's theory remains watertight.

> *When prehistoric man first took shelter in a cave and lit a fire, he was satisfying his lowest – physiological and safety needs. When a Buddhist achieves a state of nirvana, she is satisfying the fifth and highest – self-actualisation . . . The cave these days might be a three-bedroom semi with garden and*

Table 7.1	Applying Maslow's need hierarchy	
Needs levels	**General rewards**	**Organisational factors**
1 Physiological	Food, water, sex, sleep	a Pay b Pleasant working conditions c Cafeteria
2 Safety	Safety, security, stability, protection	a Safe working conditions b Company benefits c Job security
3 Social	Love, affection, belongingness	a Cohesive work group b Friendly supervision c Professional associations
4 Esteem	Self-esteem, self-respect, prestige, status	a Social recognition b Job title c High-status job d Feedback from the job itself
5 Self-actualisation	Growth, advancement, creativity	a Challenging job b Opportunities for creativity c Achievement in work d Advancement in the organisation

Source: Steers, R. M. and Porter, L. W. *Motivation and Work Behaviour*, fifth edition, McGraw-Hill (1991), p. 35. Reproduced with permission from the McGraw-Hill Companies.

off-street parking, but the fact remains that once we've got enough to feed, clothe and house our fami-lies money is a low-level motivator for most people. The dash for cash is soon replaced by the desire for recognition, status and ultimately (although Maslow reckoned that a lot of us never get this far) the need to express yourself through your work.[19]

Critical reflection

'John Adair points out that presenting Maslow's hierarchy as a pyramid model gives the impression that the greatest needs are in the lower levels. Adair suggests that the pyramid should be inverted as physiological needs, for example, are limited but there are fewer limitations the further up you go.'[20]

How would you best explain and present Maslow's hierarchy of human needs?

ALDERFER'S MODIFIED NEED HIERARCHY MODEL

A modified need hierarchy model has been presented by *Alderfer*.[21] This model condenses Maslow's five levels of need into only three levels based on the core needs of existence, relatedness and growth (ERG theory) (*see* Table 7.2 on p. 267).

■ **Existence needs** are concerned with sustaining human existence and survival and cover physiological and safety needs of a material nature.
■ **Relatedness needs** are concerned with relationships to the social environment and cover love or belonging, affiliation and meaningful interpersonal relationships of a safety or esteem nature.
■ **Growth needs** are concerned with the development of potential and cover self-esteem and self-actualisation.

A continuum of needs

Like Maslow, Alderfer suggests that individuals progress through the hierarchy from existence needs to relatedness needs to growth needs as the lower-level needs become satisfied. However, Alderfer suggests these needs are more a continuum than hierarchical levels. More than one need may be activated at the same time. Individuals may also progress down the hierarchy. There is a frustration–regression process. For example, if an individual is continually frustrated in attempting to satisfy growth needs, relatedness needs may reassume most importance. The lower-level needs become the main focus of the individual's efforts.

Alderfer proposed a number of basic propositions relating to the three need relationships. Some of these propositions followed Maslow's theory, some were the reverse of the theory. A number of studies were undertaken to test these propositions across different samples of people in different types of organisations. Results from the studies were mixed. For example, the proposition that the less existence needs are satisfied the more they will be desired received constant support from all six samples. However, the proposition that satisfaction of existence needs activates desire for relatedness needs was not supported in any of the six samples.

Satisfaction of needs

Unlike Maslow's theory, the results of Alderfer's work suggest that lower-level needs do not have to be satisfied before a higher-level need emerges as a motivating influence. The results, however, do support the idea that lower-level needs decrease in strength as they become satisfied. ERG theory states that an individual is motivated to satisfy one or more basic sets

of needs. Therefore if a person's needs at a particular level are blocked, attention should be focused on the satisfaction of needs at the other levels. For example, if a subordinate's growth needs are blocked because the job does not allow sufficient opportunity for personal development, the manager should attempt to provide greater opportunities for the subordinate to satisfy existence and relatedness needs.

HERZBERG'S TWO-FACTOR THEORY

Herzberg's original study consisted of interviews with 203 accountants and engineers, chosen because of their growing importance in the business world, from different industries in the Pittsburgh area of America.[22] He used the critical incident method. Subjects were asked to relate times when they felt exceptionally good or exceptionally bad about their present job or any previous job. They were asked to give reasons and a description of the sequence of events giving rise to that feeling. Responses to the interviews were generally consistent and revealed that there were two different sets of factors affecting motivation and work. **This led to the two-factor theory of motivation and job satisfaction.**

Hygiene and motivating factors

One set of factors are those which, if absent, cause dissatisfaction. These factors are related to job context, they are concerned with job environment and extrinsic to the job itself. These factors are the '**hygiene**' or '**maintenance**' **factors** ('hygiene' being used as analogous to the medical term meaning preventive and environmental). They serve to prevent dissatisfaction. The other set of factors are those that, if present, serve to motivate the individual to superior effort and performance. These factors are related to job content of the work itself. They are the '**motivators**' or **growth factors**. The strength of these factors will affect feelings of satisfaction or no satisfaction, but not dissatisfaction. **The opposite of dissatisfaction is not satisfaction but, simply, no dissatisfaction** (*see* Figure 7.6).

The hygiene factors can be related roughly to Maslow's lower-level needs and the motivators to Maslow's higher-level needs (*see* Table 7.2). To motivate workers to give of their best, the manager must give proper attention to the motivators or growth factors. Herzberg emphasises that hygiene factors are not a 'second-class citizen system'. They are as important as the motivators, but for different reasons. Hygiene factors are necessary to avoid unpleasantness at work and to deny unfair treatment. 'Management should never deny people proper treatment at work.' The motivators relate to what people are allowed to do and the quality of human experience at work. They are the variables which actually motivate people. The work of Herzberg indicates that it is more likely good performance leads to job satisfaction rather than the reverse.

Evaluation of Herzberg's work

Herzberg's theory is, however, a source of frequent debate. There have been many other studies to test the theory. The conclusions have been mixed. Some studies provide support for the theory. However, it has also been attacked by a number of writers. There are two common general criticisms of Herzberg's theory. One is that the theory has only limited application to 'manual' workers. The other is that the theory is 'methodologically bound'.

It is often claimed that the theory applies least to people with largely unskilled jobs or whose work is uninteresting, repetitive and monotonous, and limited in scope. Yet these are the people who often present management with the biggest problem of motivation. Some workers do not seem greatly interested in the job content of their work or with the motivators or growth factors.

A second, general criticism concerns methodology. It is claimed that the critical incident method, and the description of events giving rise to good or bad feelings, influences the

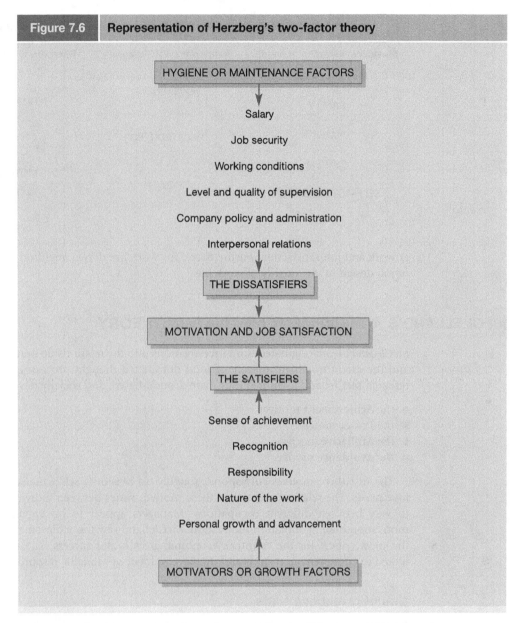

Figure 7.6 Representation of Herzberg's two-factor theory

results. People are more likely to attribute satisfying incidents at work, that is the motivators, as a favourable reflection on their own performance. The dissatisfying incidents, that is, the hygiene factors, are more likely to be attributed to external influences and the efforts of other people. Descriptions from the respondents had to be interpreted by the interviewers. This gives rise to the difficulty of distinguishing clearly between the different dimensions and to the risk of possible interviewer bias.

Despite such criticisms, there is still evidence of support for the continuing relevance of the theory. According to *Crainer and Dearlove*:

Herzberg's work has had a considerable effect on the rewards and remuneration packages offered by corporations. Increasingly, there is a trend towards 'cafeteria' benefits in which people can choose from a range of options. In effect, they can select the elements they recognise as providing their own motivation to work. Similarly, the current emphasis on self-development, career management and self-managed learning can be seen as having evolved from Herzberg's insights.[23]

Whatever the validity of the two-factor theory, much of the criticism is with the benefit of hindsight, and Herzberg did at least attempt an empirical approach to the study of motivation

Table 7.2	Linking Maslow's, Alderfer's and Herzberg's theories of motivation		
Maslow's hierarchy of needs	**Alderfer's ERG theory**	**Herzberg's two-factor theory**	
PHYSIOLOGICAL	EXISTENCE	HYGIENE FACTORS	
SAFETY			
LOVE	RELATEDNESS		
ESTEEM	GROWTH	MOTIVATORS	
SELF-ACTUALISATION			

at work and job satisfaction. Furthermore, his work has drawn attention to the importance of job design in the 'quality of work life'.

McCLELLAND'S ACHIEVEMENT MOTIVATION THEORY

McClelland's work originated from investigations into the relationship between hunger needs and the extent to which imagery of food dominated thought processes. From subsequent research McClelland identified four main arousal-based, and socially developed, motives:

- the **Achievement** motive;
- the **Power** motive;
- the **Affiliative** motive;
- the **Avoidance** motive.[24]

The first three motives correspond, roughly, to Maslow's self-actualisation, esteem and love needs. The relative intensity of these motives varies between individuals. It also tends to vary between different occupations. Managers appear to be higher in achievement motivation than in affiliation motivation. McClelland saw the achievement need (n-Ach) as the most critical for the country's economic growth and success. The need to achieve is linked to entrepreneurial spirit and the development of available resources.

Use of projective tests

Research studies by McClelland use a series of projective 'tests' – Thematic Apperception Tests (TATs) – to gauge an individual's motivation. For example, individuals are shown a number of pictures in which some activity is depicted. Respondents are asked to look briefly (10–15 seconds) at the pictures and then to describe what they think is happening, what the people in the picture are thinking and what events have led to the situation depicted.[25] An example of a picture used in a projective test is given in Assignment 2 at the end of this chapter. The descriptions are used as a basis for analysing the strength of the individual's motives.

People with high achievement needs

Despite the apparent subjective nature of the judgements, research studies tend to support the validity of TAT as an indicator of the need for achievement.[26] McClelland has, over years of empirical research, identified four characteristics of people with a strong achievement need (n-Ach): a preference for moderate task difficulty, a preference for personal responsibility for performance, the need for feedback, and innovativeness.

- They prefer **moderate task difficulty** and goals as an achievement incentive. This provides the best opportunity of proving they can do better. If the task is too difficult or too risky, it would reduce the chances of success and of gaining need satisfaction. If the course of action is too easy or too safe, there is little challenge in accomplishing the task and little satisfaction from success.
- They prefer **personal responsibility for performance**. They like to attain success through the focus of their own abilities and efforts rather than by teamwork or chance factors outside their control. Personal satisfaction is derived from the accomplishment of the task and recognition need not come from other people.
- They have the need for **clear and unambiguous feedback** on how well they are performing. A knowledge of results within a reasonable time is necessary for self-evaluation. Feedback enables them to determine success or failure in the accomplishment of their goals and to derive satisfaction from their activities.
- They are **more innovative**. As they always seek moderately challenging tasks they tend always to be moving on to something a little more challenging. In seeking short cuts they are more likely to cheat. There is a constant search for variety and for information to find new ways of doing things. They are more restless and avoid routine and also tend to travel more.

Characteristics of achievement motivation

The extent of achievement motivation varies between individuals. Some people rate very highly in achievement motivation. They are challenged by opportunities and work hard to achieve a goal. Money is not an incentive but may serve as a means of giving feedback on performance. High achievers seem unlikely to remain long with an organisation that does not pay them well for good performance. Money may seem to be important to high achievers, but they value it more as symbolising successful task performance and goal achievement.

McClelland's research has attempted to understand the characteristics of high achievers. He suggests that n-Ach is not hereditary but results from environmental influences and he has investigated the possibility of training people to develop a greater motivation to achieve.[27]

McClelland suggests four steps in attempting to develop achievement drive:

- Striving to attain feedback on performance. Reinforcement of success serves to strengthen the desire to attain higher performance.
- Developing models of achievement by seeking to emulate people who have performed well.
- Attempting to modify their self-image and to see themselves as needing challenges and success.
- Controlling day-dreaming and thinking about themselves in more positive terms.

McClelland was concerned with economic growth in underdeveloped countries. He has designed training programmes intended to increase the achievement motivation and entrepreneurial activity of managers.

McClelland and Burnham has also suggested that as effective managers need to be successful leaders and to influence other people, they should possess a high need for power.[28] However, the effective manager also scores high on inhibition. Power is directed more towards the organisation and concern for group goals and is exercised on behalf of other people. This is 'socialised' power. It is distinguished from 'personalised' power that is characterised by satisfaction from exercising dominance over other people, and personal aggrandisement.

PROCESS THEORIES OF MOTIVATION

Process theories, or extrinsic theories, attempt to identify the relationships among the dynamic variables that make up motivation and the actions required to influence behaviour and actions. They provide a further contribution to our understanding of the complex nature of work motivation. Many of the process theories cannot be linked to a single writer, but major approaches and leading writers under this heading include:

Figure 7.7 Expectancy theory: the motivational link

- expectancy-based models – Vroom, and Porter and Lawler;
- equity theory – Adams;
- goal theory – Locke;
- attribution theory – Heider and Kelley (discussed in Chapter 6).

Expectancy theories of motivation

The underlying basis of **expectancy theory** is that people are influenced by the expected results of their actions. Motivation is a function of the relationship between:

1 effort expended and perceived level of performance; and
2 the expectation that rewards (desired outcomes) will be related to performance.

There must also be:

3 the expectation that rewards (desired outcomes) are available.

These relationships determine the strength of the 'motivational link' (*see* Figure 7.7).

Performance therefore depends upon the perceived expectation regarding effort expended and achieving the desired outcome. For example, the desire for promotion will result in high performance only if the person believes there is a strong expectation that this will lead to promotion. If, however, the person believes promotion to be based solely on age and length of service, there is no motivation to achieve high performance. A person's behaviour reflects a conscious choice between the comparative evaluation of alternative behaviours. **The choice of behaviour is based on the expectancy of the most favourable consequences.**

Expectancy theory is a generic theory of motivation and cannot be linked to a single individual writer. There are a number of versions and some of the models are rather complex. More recent approaches to expectancy theory have been associated with the work of Vroom and of Porter and Lawler.

VROOM'S EXPECTANCY THEORY

Vroom was the first person to propose an expectancy theory aimed specifically at work motivation.[29] His model is based on three key variables: **valence, instrumentality** and **expectancy** (VIE theory or expectancy/valence theory). The theory is founded on the idea that people prefer certain outcomes from their behaviour over others. They anticipate feelings of satisfaction should the preferred outcome be achieved.

Valence

The feeling about specific outcomes is termed **valence. This is the attractiveness of, or preference for, a particular outcome to the individual.** Vroom distinguishes valence from value. A person may desire an object but then gain little satisfaction from obtaining it. Alternatively, a person may strive to avoid an object but find, subsequently, that it provides satisfaction. **Valence is the anticipated satisfaction from an outcome.** This may differ substantially from value, which is the actual satisfaction provided by an outcome.

The valences of certain outcomes may be derived in their own right, but more usually they are derived from the other outcomes to which they are expected to lead. An obvious example is money. Some people may see money as having an intrinsic worth and derive satisfaction from the actual accumulation of wealth. Most people, however, see money in terms of the many satisfying outcomes to which it can lead.

Instrumentality

The valence of outcomes derives, therefore, from their instrumentality. This leads to a distinction between first-level outcomes and second-level outcomes.

- **The first-level outcomes are performance-related.** They refer to the quantity of output or to the comparative level of performance. Some people may seek to perform well 'for its own sake' and without thought to expected consequences of their actions. Usually, however, performance outcomes acquire valence because of the expectation that they will lead to other outcomes as an anticipated source of satisfaction – second-level outcomes.
- **The second-level outcomes are need-related.** They are derived through achievement of first-level outcomes – that is, through achieving high performance. Many need-related outcomes are dependent upon actual performance rather than effort expended. People generally receive rewards for what they have achieved rather than for effort alone or through trying hard.

On the basis of Vroom's expectancy theory it is possible to depict a general model of behaviour (*see* Figure 7.8).

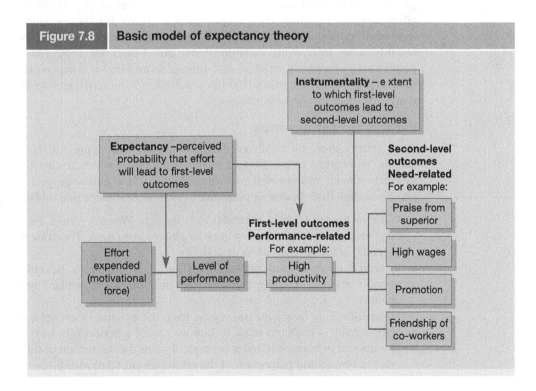

| Figure 7.8 | Basic model of expectancy theory |

Expectancy

When a person chooses between alternative behaviours which have uncertain outcomes, the choice is affected not only by the preference for a particular outcome but also by the probability that such an outcome will be achieved. People develop a **perception** of the degree of probability that the choice of a particular action will actually lead to the desired outcome. This is **expectancy**. It is the relationship between a chosen course of action and its predicted outcome. Expectancy relates effort expended to the achievement of first-level outcomes. Its value ranges between 0, indicating zero probability that an action will be followed by the outcome, and 1, indicating certainty that an action will result in the outcome.

Motivational force

The combination of valence and expectancy determines the person's motivation for a given form of behaviour. This is the **motivational force**. The force of an action is unaffected by outcomes which have no valence or by outcomes that are regarded as unlikely to result from a course of action. Expressed as an equation, motivation (M) is the sum of the products of the valences of all outcomes (V), times the strength of expectancies that action will result in achieving these outcomes (E). Therefore, if either, or both, valence or expectancy is zero, then motivation is zero. The choice between alternative behaviours is indicated by the highest attractiveness score.

$$M = \sum^{n} E \cdot V$$

There are likely to be a number of outcomes expected for a given action. Therefore, the measure of $E \cdot V$ is summed across the total number of possible outcomes to arrive at a single figure indicating the attractiveness for the contemplated choice of behaviour.

THE PORTER AND LAWLER EXPECTANCY MODEL

Vroom's expectancy/valence theory has been developed by *Porter and Lawler*.[30] Their model goes beyond motivational force and considers performance as a whole. They point out that effort expended (motivational force) does not lead directly to performance. It is mediated by individual abilities and traits, and by the person's role perceptions. They also introduce rewards as an intervening variable. Porter and Lawler see motivation, satisfaction and performance as separate variables and attempt to explain the complex relationships among them. Their model recognises that job satisfaction is more dependent upon performance, than performance is upon satisfaction.

Explanation of relationships

These relationships are expressed diagrammatically (*see* Figure 7.9) rather than mathematically. In contrast to the human relations approach which tended to assume that job satisfaction leads to improved performance, Porter and Lawler suggest that satisfaction is an effect rather than a cause of performance. It is performance that leads to job satisfaction.

- **Value of reward** (Box 1) is similar to valence in Vroom's model. People desire various outcomes (rewards) which they hope to achieve from work. The value placed on a reward depends on the strength of its desirability.
- **Perceived effort–reward probability** (Box 2) is similar to expectancy. It refers to a person's expectation that certain outcomes (rewards) are dependent upon a given amount of effort.
- **Effort** (Box 3) is how hard the person tries, the amount of energy a person exerts on a given activity. It does not relate to how successful a person is in carrying out an activity. The amount of energy exerted is dependent upon the interaction of the input variables of value of reward and perception of the effort–reward relationship.

Figure 7.9	The Porter and Lawler motivation model

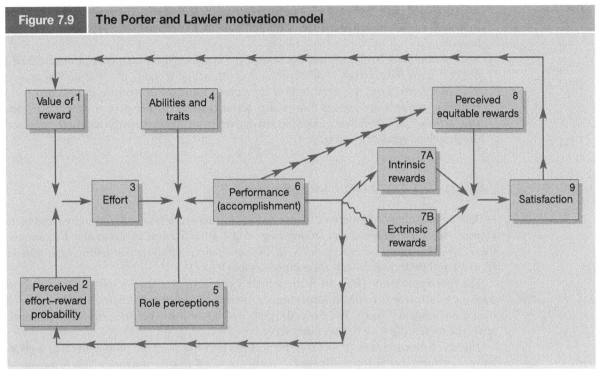

- **Abilities and traits** (Box 4). Porter and Lawler suggest that effort does not lead directly to performance but is influenced by individual characteristics. Factors such as intelligence, skills, knowledge, training and personality affect the ability to perform a given activity.

- **Role perceptions** (Box 5) refer to the way in which individuals view their work and the role they should adopt. This influences the type of effort exerted. Role perceptions will influence the direction and level of action which is believed to be necessary for effective performance.

- **Performance** (Box 6) depends not only on the amount of effort exerted but also on the intervening influences of the person's abilities and traits, and their role perceptions. If the person lacks the right ability or personality, or has an inaccurate role perception of what is required, then the exertion of a large amount of energy may still result in a low level of performance or task accomplishment.

- **Rewards** (Boxes 7A and 7B) are desirable outcomes. Intrinsic rewards derive from the individuals themselves and include a sense of achievement, a feeling of responsibility and recognition (for example Herzberg's motivators). Extrinsic rewards derive from the organisation and the actions of others and include salary, working conditions and supervision (for example Herzberg's hygiene factors). The relationship between performance and intrinsic rewards is shown as a jagged line. This is because the extent of the relationship depends upon the nature of the job. If the design of the job permits variety and challenge, so that people feel able to reward themselves for good performance, there is a direct relationship. Where job design does not involve variety and challenge, there is no direct relationship between good performance and intrinsic rewards. The wavy line between performance and extrinsic rewards indicates that such rewards do not often provide a direct link to performance.

- **Perceived equitable rewards** (Box 8). This is the level of rewards people feel they should fairly receive for a given standard of performance. Most people have an implicit perception about the level of rewards they should receive commensurate with the requirements and demands of the job, and the contribution expected of them. Self-rating of performance links directly with the perceived equitable reward variable. Higher levels of self-rated performance

are associated with higher levels of expected equitable rewards. The heavily arrowed line indicates a relationship from the self-rated part of performance to perceived equitable rewards.

- **Satisfaction** (Box 9). This is not the same as motivation. It is an attitude, an individual's internal state. Satisfaction is determined by both actual rewards received and perceived level of rewards from the organisation for a given standard of performance. If perceived equitable rewards are greater than actual rewards received, the person experiences dissatisfaction. The experience of satisfaction derives from actual rewards that meet or exceed the perceived equitable rewards.

LAWLER'S REVISED EXPECTANCY MODEL

Following the original Porter and Lawler model, further work was undertaken by *Lawler* (*see* Figure 7.10).[31] He suggests that in deciding on the attractiveness of alternative behaviours, there are two types of expectancies to be considered: effort–performance expectancies (E → P) and performance–outcome expectancies (P → O).

The **first expectancy (E → P)** is the person's perception of the probability that a given amount of effort will result in achieving an intended level of performance. It is measured on a scale between 0 and 1. The closer the perceived relationship between effort and performance, the higher the E → P expectancy score.

The **second expectancy (P → O)** is the person's perception of the probability that a given level of performance will actually lead to particular need-related outcomes. This is measured also on a scale between 0 and 1. The closer the perceived relationship between performance and outcome, the higher the P → O expectancy score.

Motivational force to perform

The multiplicative combination of the two types of expectancies, E → P and the sum of the products P → O, determines expectancy. The motivational force to perform (effort

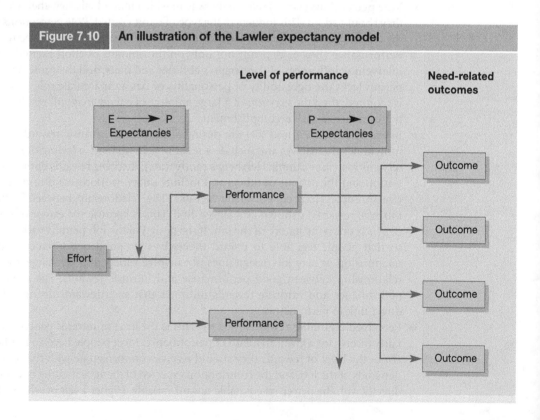

Figure 7.10 An illustration of the Lawler expectancy model

expended) is determined by multiplying $E \rightarrow P$ and $P \rightarrow O$ by the strength of outcome valence (V).

$$E(Effort) = (E \rightarrow P) \times \sum [(P \rightarrow O)V]$$

The distinction between the two types of expectancies arises because they are determined by different conditions. $E \rightarrow P$ expectancy is determined in part by the person's ability and self-confidence, past experience and the difficulty of the task. $P \rightarrow O$ expectancy is determined by the attractiveness of the outcomes and the belief about who controls the outcomes, the person him/herself or other people.

IMPLICATIONS FOR MANAGERS OF EXPECTANCY THEORIES

There are a number of versions of expectancy theory. The main elements tend to be very similar, however, and this suggests the development of a generally accepted approach. Expectancy models are not always easy to understand, or to apply. There are many variables which affect behaviour at work. A problem can arise in attempting to include a large number of variables or in identifying those variables which are most appropriate in particular situations.

Expectancy theory does, however, draw attention to the complexities of work motivation. It provides further information in helping to explain the nature of behaviour and motivation in the work situation, and helps to identify problems in performance. Expectancy theory indicates that managers should give attention to a number of factors, including the following:

■ Use rewards appropriate in terms of individual performance. Outcomes with high valence should be used as an incentive for improved performance.

■ Attempt to establish clear relationships between effort–performance and rewards, as perceived by the individual.

■ Establish clear procedures for the evaluation of individual levels of performance.

■ Pay attention to intervening variables such as abilities and traits, role perceptions, organisational procedures and support facilities, which, although not necessarily direct motivational factors, may still affect performance.

■ Minimise undesirable outcomes which may be perceived to result from a high level of performance, such as industrial accidents or sanctions from co-workers, or to result despite a high level of performance, such as short-time working or layoffs.

Porter and Lawler also emphasise that the expectancy model is just a model and that expectancy theory applies only to behaviours which are under the voluntary control of the individual. The two general types of choices over which individuals have voluntary control of work performance in organisations are:

1 the amount of effort and energy expended; and
2 the manner in which they go about performing their work.

> *There is always a choice about the way you do your work, even if there is not a choice about the work itself. You always have a choice about the attitude you bring to the job.*
>
> World famous Pike Place Fish Market, Seattle[32]

Critical reflection

'Expectancy theories of motivation appear to make sense in the classroom and form the basis of an interesting academic debate, but it is unlikely the practising manager will be impressed or take much notice.'

What do you think? How would you explain the potential benefits of expectancy theory to a sceptical manager?

EQUITY THEORY OF MOTIVATION

One of the major variables of satisfaction in the Porter and Lawler expectancy model is perceived equitable rewards. This leads to consideration of another process theory of motivation – **equity theory**. Applied to the work situation, equity theory is usually associated with the work of *Adams*.[33]

Equity theory focuses on people's feelings of how fairly they have been treated in comparison with the treatment received by others. It is based on exchange theory. Social relationships involve an exchange process. For example, a person may expect promotion as an outcome of a high level of contribution (input) in helping to achieve an important organisational objective. People also compare their own position with that of others. They determine the perceived equity of their own position. Their feelings about the equity of the exchange are affected by the treatment they receive when compared with what happens to other people. Most exchanges involve a number of inputs and outcomes. According to equity theory, people place a weighting on these various inputs and outcomes according to how they perceive their importance. When there is an unequal comparison of ratios the person experiences a sense of **inequity**.

Behaviour as a consequence of inequity

A feeling of inequity causes tension, which is an unpleasant experience. The presence of inequity therefore motivates the person to remove or to reduce the level of tension and the perceived inequity. The magnitude of perceived inequity determines the level of tension. The level of tension created determines the strength of motivation. Adams identifies six broad types of possible behaviour as consequences of inequity (*see* Figure 7.11):

■ **Changes to inputs**. A person may increase or decrease the level of their inputs, for example through the amount or quality of work, absenteeism, or working additional hours without pay.

Figure 7.11	An illustration of Adams's equity theory of motivation

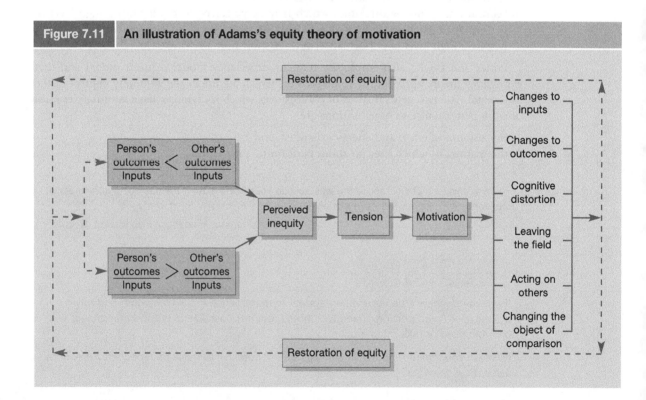

- **Changes to outcomes**. A person may attempt to change outcomes such as pay, working conditions, status and recognition, without changes to inputs.
- **Cognitive distortion of inputs and outcomes**. In contrast to actual changes, people may distort, cognitively, their inputs or outcomes to achieve the same results. Adams suggests that although it is difficult for people to distort facts about themselves, it is possible, within limits, to distort the utility of those facts: for example, the belief about how hard they are really working, the relevance of a particular qualification, or what they can or cannot obtain with a given level of pay.
- **Leaving the field**. A person may try to find a new situation with a more favourable balance, for example by absenteeism, request for a transfer, resigning from a job or from the organisation altogether.
- **Acting on others**. A person may attempt to bring about changes in others, for example to lower their inputs or accept greater outcomes. Or the person may cognitively distort the inputs and outcomes of others. Alternatively, a person may try to force others to leave the field.
- **Changing the object of comparison**. This involves changing the reference group with whom comparison is made. For example, where another person with a previously similar outcome–input ratio receives greater outcomes without any apparent increase in contribution, that other person may be perceived as now belonging to a different level in the organisation structure. The comparison need not necessarily be made with people who have the same inputs and outcomes. The important thing is a similar ratio of outcomes to inputs.

Under the control of the manager

The manager may seek to remove or reduce tension and perceived inequity among staff by influencing these types of behaviour – for example by attempting to change a person's inputs or encouraging a different object of comparison. People measure and compare their total inputs and outcomes so, for example, a working parent may prefer greater flexibility in working hours in return for lower monetary rewards. However, there are likely to be only two courses of action under the direct control of the manager. Outcomes can be changed by, for example, increased pay, additional perks or improved working conditions, or by instigating a person leaving the field through transfer, resignation or, as an extreme measure, dismissal. It is important to remember that equity theory is about the perceived ratio of inputs to outputs and these perceptions may not reflect the reality of the situation.

The ultimatum game

The **ultimatum game** is an economic behavioural game that can arguably be related to the concept of equity theory.[34] Two participants, A and B, are given the opportunity to split a given sum of money between them. The game is played anonymously and once only. One person (A) has to decide to make a one-time, take it or leave it, offer to B (ultimatum). If the other person (B) agrees to the division, both A and B keep their share of the money. However, if the offer is rejected neither person receives anything. Experiments indicate that if A offers around 50% of the money then B will accept the offer. But if A offers a noticeably lesser amount than 50%, B will typically refuse the offer in which case neither participant receives anything. One might expect B to accept because even a lesser amount, whatever the offer, is better than nothing. Can you see how this might be related to perceptions of equity theory? Viewers of the ITV1 television quiz programme *Divided*, in which contestants have to agree how to divide a cash prize, may see a similarity with the ultimatum game.

GOAL THEORY

Another theory usually considered under the heading of motivation to work is **goal theory**, or the theory of goal-setting (*see* Figure 7.12). This theory is based mainly on the work of

Figure 7.12 An illustration of Locke's theory of goal-setting

Locke.[35] The basic premise of goal theory is that people's goals or intentions play an important part in determining behaviour. Locke accepts the importance of perceived value, as indicated in expectancy theories of motivation, and suggests that these values give rise to the experience of emotions and desires. People strive to achieve goals in order to satisfy their emotions and desires. Goals guide people's responses and actions. Goals direct work behaviour and performance and lead to certain consequences or feedback. *Locke* subsequently pointed out that 'goal-setting is more appropriately viewed as a motivational technique rather than as a formal theory of motivation'.[36]

Goal-setting and performance

The combination of goal difficulty and the extent of the person's commitment to achieving the goal regulates the level of effort expended. People with specific quantitative goals, such as a defined level of performance or a given deadline for completion of a task, will perform better than people with no set goal or only a vague goal such as 'do the best you can'. People who have difficult goals will perform better than people with easier goals.

Gratton refers to 'stretch goals' which are ambitious, highly targeted opportunities for breakthrough improvements in performance. These goals should stem from critical success indicators and come from deep discussions within the company, and from collaboration within and across task forces, and lead to the development of activities and tactics to achieve the goals.[37] People lacking positive motivation at work may also help gain improved results and a better sense of achievement by setting themselves specific goals and identifying tasks directly related to their work and measurable targets of time and performance.

Practical implications for the manager

Goal theory has a number of practical implications for the manager:

■ Individuals lacking in motivation often do not have clear goals. Specific performance goals should systematically be identified and set in order to direct behaviour and maintain motivation.

■ Goals should be set at a challenging but realistic level. Difficult goals lead to higher performance. However, if goals are set at too high a level or are regarded as impossible to achieve, this can lead to stress and performance will suffer, especially over a longer period.

■ Complete, accurate and timely feedback and knowledge of results is usually associated with high performance. Feedback provides a means of checking progress on goal attainment and forms the basis for any revision of goals.

■ Goals can be determined either by a superior or by individuals themselves. Goals set by other people are more likely to be accepted when there is participation. Employee participation in the setting of goals may lead to higher performance.

Much of the theory of goal-setting can be related to the system of management by objectives (discussed in Chapter 12). MBO is often viewed as an application of goal-setting, although it was devised originally before the development of goal-setting theory. However it is viewed, the theory of goal-setting provides a useful approach to work motivation and performance. And *Hannagan* goes so far as to suggest: 'At present goal-setting is one of the most influential theories of work motivation applicable to all cultures.'[38]

ATTRIBUTION THEORY

A more recent approach to the study of motivation is attribution theory. Attribution is the process by which people interpret the perceived causes of behaviour. This was discussed in Chapter 6.

RELEVANCE TODAY FOR THE MANAGER

Given that most major theories of motivation date back many years it is inevitable that questions will be raised about their relevance today. *Reis and Pena* question whether motivating people to work in the 21st century with theories conceived during the past hundred years is likely to be feasible. They conclude that the core message is that managers should reconsider the outdated motivational patterns utilised to maintain role performance in organisations and adopt a fresh motivation formula for the 21st century based on friendship, work and respect.[39]

However, we have seen from the discussions above that there still appears to be general support for the theories – and, perhaps ironically, particularly for the early theories of Maslow, Herzberg and McClelland. A Chartered Management Institute checklist maintains that these theories are still valid today. 'A basic understanding of their main principles will provide the background for building a climate of honesty, openness and trust.'[40] From a 12-year study of the use of management concepts in technical organisations, *Flores and Utley* found the work of Maslow and McGregor the most popular motivational theories and also refer to the relationship between Maslow and Herzberg and the successful implementation of quality systems.[41]

Whatever the relevance of the different theories of motivation, to what extent do individuals have control over their own level of motivation or how much is dependent upon the leadership they encounter? *Adair* reassesses the theories of Maslow and Herzberg in terms of action-centred leadership, which is discussed in Chapter 10. Adair also argues that the extent to which you can motivate anyone else is limited and refers to the fifty-fifty rule of motivation, that is:

> *Fifty percent of motivation comes from within a person and 50% from his or her environment, especially from the leadership encountered there. The fifty-fifty rule in motivation does not claim to indentify the different proportions in the equation exactly. It is more like a rough and ready rule of thumb. In effect it says no more than a substantial part of motivation lies with a person while a substantial part lies, so to speak, outside and beyond control.*[42]

ORGANISATIONAL BEHAVIOUR MODIFICATION

Another possible approach to motivation is that of **organisational behaviour modification (OBMod)**. This is the application of learning principles to influence organisational

behaviour. In particular it can be seen as a form of Skinner's operant conditioning, or reinforcement theory, discussed in Chapter 5. Reinforcement is a feature of the behaviourism approach and shaped by environmental influences. The reward for a particular form of behaviour is likely to result in the reinforcement of that behaviour. A negative outcome or lack of acknowledgement for the behaviour is likely to mean that the behaviour will stop. *Luthans and Kreitner* suggest that OBMod 'represents a merging of behavioral learning theory on the one hand and organizational behavior theory on the other'.[43]

According to Luthans and Kreitner, a major premise of OBMod is that positive consequence management is much more effective than negative consequence management. Organisations that encourage the members to learn and undertake desired behaviours and not to undertake undesired behaviours follow five main steps:

1 **Identify** the observable, objective and measurable behaviours relevant to the desired organisational performance.
2 **Measure** the frequency with which those behaviours actually occur under normal conditions. Provide baseline performance data as a point of reference to compare with changes in step 5.
3 **Determine** the antecedents of the behaviours, the reinforcements to encourage patterns of behaviour and the consequences that follow from those behaviours.
4 **Develop** an intervention strategy for change in order to strengthen desirable behaviours and weaken undesirable behaviours, through the use of operant conditioning and reinforcement theory including punishment if necessary.
5 **Measure and evaluate** systematically (using the same measure as in step 2) the extent to which the frequency of desired behaviours and undesired behaviours have changed, and improvements in organisational performance.

Applications of OBMod

To what extent can OBMod be applied effectively to improve motivation and performance in work organisations? OBMod works best for behaviours that are specific, objective and countable. There have been a number of studies in the United States that indicate positive results in behaviours that improved performance in reducing errors, attendance and punctuality, health and safety and customer service.[44] In a study of a Russian textile factory, following the OBMod approach, workers were subjected to two forms of intervention – extrinsic rewards and social rewards. The extrinsic rewards provided valued American products, such as clothing, music tapes and hard-to-get foods, for improved performance. Social rewards such as attention, recognition and praise from supervisors were for performing specified actions such as checking looms, undertaking repairs and helping others. Both the extrinsic and social interventions led to highly significant increases in performance. This contrasted with a previous participative job design approach that involved asking workers for ideas for improving performance and enriching their jobs that did not work. The researchers suggest cultural issues and the workers' past experiences may explain the failure of the participative intervention strategy, and that the OBMod approach has wider application.[45]

Although there appear to be a number of supporters in America, in the UK it is a controversial concept. Critics claim that OBMod is not an accepted theory of motivation and that there are too many individual differences for people to be treated as subjects of operant conditioning. OBMod is concerned only with shaping. There is the added criticism of a 'Big Brother' approach with excessive management manipulation and control over employees, more in line with scientific management (recall the discussion in Chapter 2). This in turn could also have the added disadvantage of discouraging individual initiative and adaptability to change circumstances. Workers subject to OBMod programmes may tend to ignore those aspects of voluntary behaviours, such as social support or assistance to colleagues, that are not subject to direct reward and reinforcement.

THE MOTIVATION OF KNOWLEDGE WORKERS

Recent advantages in telecommunications and in scientific and technological knowledge have led to greater emphasis on the knowledge and expertise of staff and the importance of creativity. *Tampoe* suggests that at the core of the new industrial trend are the 'knowledge workers' – those employees who apply their theoretical and practical understanding of a specific area of knowledge to produce outcomes of a commercial, social or personal value. The performance of knowledge workers should be judged on both the cleverness of ideas and the utility and commercial value of their applied knowledge. Creativity is necessary and needs to be encouraged but should be bounded by commercial realism. This presents management with a new challenge of how to motivate the knowledge workers.[46]

Tampoe suggests that the personal motivation of knowledge workers is based on the value they place on the rewards they expect to earn at work. In addition to the individual's own motivation, the performance of knowledge workers is dependent upon four key characteristics (*see* Figure 7.13):

- task competence;
- peer and management support;
- task and role clarity; and
- corporate awareness.

The challenge to management is to ensure the effectiveness of the four key variables and to recognise the need for staff to supervise and manage themselves and the wider rewards expected by knowledge workers.

A climate of creativity

Lucas draws attention to skills shortages as one of the biggest challenges facing employers in the new millennium. In order to attract and keep talented individuals, the so-called knowledge workers, organisations cannot rely simply on a pay rise or cash bonus but have to be more creative about the way they structure remuneration packages. Individual performance-related pay is still the most widely used reward strategy, but attention is also given to employee share ownership, competence-related pay and team reward – and also to non-cash incentives such as gift vouchers. However, Lucas points out that employees, especially high flyers, rank challenging and interesting work and freedom higher on their motivational list than money

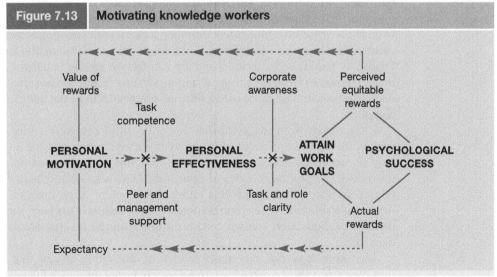

| Figure 7.13 | Motivating knowledge workers |

Source: Tampoe, M. 'Knowledge Workers: The New Management Challenge', *Professional Manager*, Institute of Management, November 1994, p. 13. Reproduced with permission from Chartered Management Institute.

and performance-related pay. 'Research suggests that most organisations haven't recognised the need to identify and tap into their employees' personal motivators.'[47]

A report from the Chartered Institute of Personnel and Development draws attention to the management of knowledge workers, highlighting the importance of autonomy, challenging work and sharing in the creation of organisational values. With the development of new technology it is important to motivate employees to capture, share and transfer knowledge.[48]

Whitmore suggests that in order to create a climate for creativity among employees, recognition must be given to the importance of two human needs that rise above all others and exist independent of race, creed and culture – the need for self-belief and the development of emotional intelligence; and the ever-present need that every human being has for a sense of meaning and purpose in their lives.

> *Self-belief and meaningful work are the fundamental bedrocks that underlie business performance. Of course, pay and conditions are important too, but we know that. It is these two others that are barely recognised . . . but business leaders ignore them at their peril.*[49]

CROSS-CULTURAL DIMENSIONS OF MOTIVATION

Whatever the popularity of different theories of motivation, doubts are raised about their universality on the ground that they have not adequately addressed the factor of culture.[50] Are theories of motivation universally applicable or are there meaningful differences in motivation at work, or in life more generally, in different societies? Many readers may feel able to recognise perceived variations in extrinsic, intrinsic and relational aspects of motivation as a result of experience of foreign cultures. Do similarities in workplace attitudes and behaviour outweigh differences? A number of writers have questioned whether motivational theories and models originating in one culture are amenable to transference to other parts of the world. *Francesco and Gold* devote a substantial proportion of a discussion of motivation to examining the extent to which American motivation theories are applicable outside the United States.

When discussing Maslow's contribution to this topic and, in particular, the concept of a hierarchy of needs, Francesco and Gold suggest: 'In an international context the circumstances and values of a particular culture can influence the ordering and importance of needs. The values of individualism and collectivism can make the hierarchy more or less relevant.'[51] In evaluating McClelland's work, Francesco and Gold question whether the meaning of an underlying concept, in this case achievement, can even be understood worldwide in the sense it was intended: 'Another concern with Learning Needs Theory is that the concept of achievement is difficult, if not impossible, to translate into languages other than English.'[52] A study of motivation and job satisfaction among hotel workers in Brazil found that a number of Herzberg's hygiene and motivating factors did not affect job satisfaction or dissatisfaction. A main cause of this difference appeared to be the influence of organisational culture.[53]

It has already been suggested that one criticism of content theories of motivation centres on its relative applicability in different circumstances, and the suggestion that there may be variations across cultures falls within this line of reasoning. However, perhaps less obviously, process theories of motivation have also been criticised for being culture-bound. As they focus on process rather than content, such theories may appear to be more applicable in diverse cultural contexts. Nonetheless it has been suggested that process theories of motivation contain certain inbuilt assumptions that are themselves culturally derived.

Adler reminds us that expectancy models of motivation assume that individuals believe that they can, to some extent, control their environment and influence their fate. If, as in the cases of more fatalistic cultures such as China, people do not have the same sense of

internal attribution, the expectancy model may have less force and therefore less applicability. When Adams's equity theory is applied across the world, differences in interpretation have been recorded.[54] *Chen* suggests that while individualistic cultures place a high regard on equity, collectivist cultures value equality more than equity. Again we see here the possibility that while a theory of motivation may be essentially valid in principle, it is legitimate to think about the ways in which national culture can intervene in terms of its interpretation in different societies.[55]

> ### Critical reflection
>
> 'Motivation and job satisfaction are very subjective and affected by many variables including cultural influences, unknown domestic situations and personal relationships outside of work. Generalised management models cannot meet all individual circumstances and are therefore a complete waste of your study time.'
>
> *To what extent do you agree?*

JOB SATISFACTION

The meaning and nature of job satisfaction

Attempting to understand the nature of job satisfaction and its effects on work performance is not easy. Job satisfaction is a complex and multifaceted concept, which can mean different things to different people. It is usually linked with motivation, but the nature of this relationship is not clear. Satisfaction is not the same as motivation. **Job satisfaction** is more of an attitude, an internal state. It could, for example, be associated with a personal feeling of achievement, either quantitative or qualitative.

It is often suggested that job satisfaction is necessary in order to achieve a high level of motivation and performance. However, although the level of job satisfaction may well affect strength of motivation, this is not always the case. The relationship between job satisfaction and performance is an issue of continuing debate and controversy. One view, associated with the early human relations approach, is that satisfaction leads to performance. An alternative view is that performance leads to satisfaction. *Reeves* draws attention to the relationship between accomplishment at work and the need to 'work harder'.

> *All this busy-ness and stress is creating more heat than light. It is a sign not of work being too hard but too shallow. Human nature is driven by a desire to accomplish things, and so the fewer opportunities for accomplishment a job contains, the more likely we are to fill the void by tearing around in a frenzy in an effort to persuade ourselves and others that our work has a purpose, that it is important.[56]*

Dimensions of job satisfaction

There is some doubt whether job satisfaction consists of a single dimension or a number of separate dimensions. Some workers may be satisfied with certain aspects of their work and dissatisfied with other aspects. Job satisfaction is itself a complex concept and difficult to measure objectively. The level of job satisfaction is affected by a wide range of variables relating to individual, social, cultural, organisational and environmental factors.

- **Individual factors** include personality, education and qualifications, intelligence and abilities, age, marital status, orientation to work.
- **Social factors** include relationships with co-workers, group working and norms, opportunities for interaction, informal organisation.
- **Cultural factors** include underlying attitudes, beliefs and values.

- **Organisational factors** include nature and size, formal structure, HR policies and proce-dures, employee relations, nature of the work, technology and work organisation, super-vision and styles of leadership, management systems, working conditions.
- **Environmental factors** include economic, social, technical and governmental influences.

These different factors all affect the job satisfaction of certain individuals in a given set of circumstances but not necessarily in others. For example in times of economic depression and fears of high unemployment, job security is likely to be the prominent concern for many members of staff. According to the FreshMinds survey discussed in Chapter 3, when it comes to job satisfaction it pays to be older. Apparently 100 per cent of older boomers (born between 1946 and 1963) are satisfied with their job, but only 66 per cent of Generation Y (typified by travel first, then a career) feel the same way. And Generation Y want more at work such as gym membership and sabbaticals.[57]

A survey by the Chartered Management Institute found that organisational culture and values emerged as very strong motivational drivers, and a manager's relationship with their line manager had a powerful impact on job satisfaction and related measures.[58]

Five contractual areas

Mumford examines job satisfaction in two ways:

1 in terms of the fit between what the organisation requires and what the employee is seeking; and
2 in terms of the fit between what the employee is seeking and what they are actually receiving.

On the basis of various schools of thought on job satisfaction, Mumford identifies five contractual areas by which this organisational/employee relationship can be examined: the knowledge contract, the psychological contract, the efficiency/reward contract, the ethical contract and the task structure contract (*see* Table 7.3).[59]

Table 7.3	Five contractual areas relating to job satisfaction	
	The firm	**The employee**
The knowledge contract	Needs a certain level of skill and knowledge in its employees if it is to function efficiently	Wishes the skills and knowledge they bring with them to be used and developed
The psychological contract	Needs employees who are motivated to look after its interests	Seeks to further interests private to self, e.g. to secure: achievement, recognition, responsibility, status
The efficiency/rewards contract	Needs to implement generalised output, quality standards and reward systems	Seeks a personal, equitable effort–reward bargain and controls, including supervisory ones, which are perceived as acceptable
The ethical (social value) contract	Needs employees who will accept the firm's ethos and values	Seeks to work for an employer whose values do not contravene their own
The task structure contract	Needs employees who will accept technical and other constraints which produce task specificity or task differentiation	Seeks a set of tasks which meets their requirements for task differentiation, e.g. which incorporate variety, interests, targets, feedback, task identity and autonomy

Source: Mumford, E. 'Job Satisfaction: A Method of Analysis', *Personnel Review*, vol. 20, no. 3, p. 14, 1991. Copyright © Emerald Group Publishing Limited. All Rights Reserved. Reproduced with permission.

The work environment

An increasingly important issue affecting job satisfaction and efficiency is the nature of the work environment and workplace facilities. *Handy* argues that an inspired workplace will result in inspired workers and draws attention to the importance for work performance of the atmosphere, quality and style of buildings and offices.[60]

A 2003 study by the Chartered Management Institute reports on UK managers' attitudes to and experiences of their physical working environment. The study was undertaken among a random sample of 4,000 managers across all levels and sectors and size of organisation. Topics addressed included hours worked, commuting and travel, flexible working, the existing and preferred layout of offices and the use of new technologies. Concerns were expressed about the need for more quiet areas, under-equipped meeting rooms, lack of adequate meeting space, and their offices not making a good impression on clients and visitors. Nearly half of those surveyed would relinquish one week's annual leave for a better office, and sizeable numbers would forgo £1,000 in salary or private medical insurance for a significantly upgraded workspace. And even if the role, salary and benefits were no better, 45 per cent would contemplate changing companies in return for an improved work environment.[61]

> More than any other element, fun is the secret of Virgin's success. I am aware that the idea of business being fun and creative goes right against the grain of convention, and it's certainly not how they teach it at some of those business schools, where business means hard grind and lots of 'discounted cash flows' and 'net present values' . . . For us, our employees matter most. It just seems common sense to me that, if you start off with a happy, well motivated workforce, you're much more likely to have happy customers. And in due course the resulting profits will make your shareholders happy.
>
> Richard Branson[62]

According to *De Vita*, well-being at work pays because employees who are happy and healthy take fewer days off sick, are more productive and more likely to stay with their organisation. The starting point to supporting and promoting well-being in the workplace has to be good people management and effective work organisation. Good line management is the most important of the characteristics of a high-quality workplace that has high levels of commitment and low absence rates.[63]

Flexible working arrangements

An increasingly significant aspect of motivation and job satisfaction is flexible working. According to CIPD, 'This relates to an organisation's working arrangements in terms of working time, working location and the pattern of working.'[64] Moves towards greater flexibility may afford opportunities for employees to have more freedom and control over their working arrangements and have noticeable effects on their job satisfaction and performance. Flexible working arrangements are discussed in Chapter 15.

Broader approaches

Broader approaches to job satisfaction aim to give the person improved empowerment and job enrichment through greater autonomy and authority over the planning, execution and control of their work. It focuses attention on intrinsic satisfaction. Job enrichment increases the complexity of the work. It should provide the person with a more meaningful and challenging job and offer greater opportunities for psychological growth.

The main methods of achieving job enrichment include the following:

■ permitting workers greater freedom and control over the scheduling and pacing of their work as opposed to machine pacing;

- allowing workers to undertake a full task cycle, build or assemble a complete product or component, or deliver a complete service;
- providing workers with tasks or jobs which challenge their abilities and make fuller use of their training, expertise and skills;
- giving workers greater freedom to work in self-managing teams with greater responsibility for monitoring their own performance and the minimum of direct supervision; and
- providing workers with the opportunity to have greater direct contact with clients, consumers or users of the product or service.

In an organisation, empowerment means that each staff member is responsible for creating that organisation's culture. There aren't many motivating forces more potent than giving your staff an opportunity to exercise and express their idealism.

Anita Roddick[65]

ALIENATION AT WORK

One main approach to job satisfaction is in terms of frustration and alienation at work. Job satisfaction can be seen as the obverse of frustration at work (discussed earlier in this chapter). **Alienation** refers to the detachment of the person from their work role. The concept of alienation at work is associated originally with the views of *Marx*.[66] He saw the division of labour in pursuit of profit, and exploitation by employers, as a denial of the workers' need for self-expression. Workers become estranged from the product of their work. Work no longer provided a satisfying experience in itself, but represented a means of satisfying other external demands. The concept of alienation has been extended by *Blauner*.[67] He describes alienation in terms of four dimensions: powerlessness, meaninglessness, isolation and self-estrangement.

- **Powerlessness** denotes the workers' lack of control over management policy, immediate work processes, or conditions of employment.
- **Meaninglessness** stems from standardisation and division of labour. It denotes the inability to see the purpose of work done or to identify with the total production process or finished product.
- **Isolation** is not belonging to an integrated work group or to the social work organisation and not being guided by group norms of behaviour.
- **Self-estrangement** is the failure to see work as an end in itself or as a central life issue. Workers experience a depersonalised detachment and work is seen solely as a means to an end.

In recent years attention to job satisfaction has also become more closely associated with broader approaches to improved job design and work organisation, and the quality of working life movement, and with stress and the work/life balance (discussed in Chapter 3).

A concept map of job satisfaction is set out in Figure 7.14.

A COMPREHENSIVE MODEL OF JOB ENRICHMENT

Attempts to improve intrinsic motivation must not only include considerations of job characteristics but also take account of individual differences and attributes, and people's orientation to work. A popular and comprehensive model of job enrichment has been developed by *Hackman and Oldham* (*see* Figure 7.15).[68] The model views job enrichment

Figure 7.14 | **Concept map of job satisfaction**

JOB SATISFACTION

- FACTORS AFFECTING JOB SATISFACTION
- DOES JOB SATISFACTION MATTER?
- IMPROVING JOB SATISFACTION

IMPROVING JOB SATISFACTION
Job satisfaction can be increased by
- CAREFUL SELECTION
- SETTING APPROPRIATE OBJECTIVES
- PLANNING THE DEVELOPMENT OF EMPLOYEES
- KEEPING EMPLOYEES INFORMED
- RECOGNISING ACHIEVEMENTS

CAREFUL SELECTION
Enhanced job satisfaction can come from careful selection of:
- employees as they enter the organisation
- tasks and employees who match them

SETTING APPROPRIATE OBJECTIVES
Appropriate objectives include
- Targets that challenge the employee, but do not overstretch him or her
- Those that are appropriate to the organisation's needs and match the employee's interests

RECOGNISING ACHIEVEMENTS
Job satisfaction is much enhanced where performance is recognised by:
- Performance-related pay
- Non-financial recognition
 - certificates
 - employee-of-the-month awards
 - simple verbal thanks
- Competitions, prizes and awards

KEEPING EMPLOYEES INFORMED
Job satisfaction needs effective communications about:
- The tasks which have to be done
- The performance against targets
- Departmental and organisational changes which may affect jobs

PLANNING THE DEVELOPMENT OF EMPLOYEES
Some dimensions which can be implemented by most managers are:
- Careful design of jobs so that they contain an element of development
- Delegating and empowering where possible and appropriate
- Arranging project-type activities
- Arranging formal training when this is needed

DOES JOB SATISFACTION MATTER?
- ETHICAL VIEW
- ECONOMIC VIEW
- BEHAVIOURAL VIEW

ECONOMIC VIEW
How does improving job satisfaction benefit the organisation?
- Improved productivity
 - quality of output
 - quantity of output
- Better employee co-operation
- Reduced downtimes
- Fewer accidents
- Reduced
 - lateness
 - absenteeism
 - training costs
- Fewer
 - complaints
 - grievances
- Lower employee turnover

BEHAVIOURAL VIEW
Improved job satisfaction can reduce
- Social problems
- Boredom/monotony
- Physical strain
- Mental stress

FACTORS ASSOCIATED WITH HIGH JOB SATISFACTION
- Variety of meaningful tasks
- Unobtrusive supervision
- Greater responsibility
- Self-pacing
- Chances for self-development
- Feedback on performance

These aspects are closely associated with Herzberg's 'Motivators'

FACTORS ASSOCIATED WITH LOW JOB SATISFACTION
- Unclear targets/objectives
- Poor organisational communications
- Insecurity
- Lack of reward (both monetary and intangible rewards)

ETHICAL VIEW
JOB SATISFACTION is a natural output of work NOT an input to higher efficiency

LOW LEVEL/HIGH LEVEL

MASLOW'S HIERARCHY OF NEEDS
Self-fulfilment – creativity
Ego needs – self-esteem status
Social needs – belonging
Safety needs – protection
Physiological needs – food, shelter

Figure 7.15 A job characteristics model of work motivation

Source: Hackman, J. R. and Oldham, G. R. *Work Redesign*, Addison-Wesley Publishing Company, Inc. (1980), Figure 4.6, p. 90. Reproduced with permission from Pearson Education, Inc.

in terms of increasing five core job dimensions: skill variety, task identity, task significance, autonomy and feedback. These core job characteristics create three psychological states:

■ experienced meaningfulness of the work;
■ experienced responsibility for the outcomes of the work; and
■ knowledge of the actual results of the work activities.

Five core dimensions

The five core job dimensions can be summarised as follows:

■ **skill variety** – the extent to which a job entails different activities and involves a range of skills and talents;
■ **task identity** – the extent to which a job involves completion of a whole piece of work with a visible outcome;
■ **task significance** – the extent to which a job has a meaningful impact on other people, either inside or outside the organisation;
■ **autonomy** – the extent to which a job provides freedom, independence and discretion in planning the work and determining how to undertake it;
■ **feedback** – the extent to which work activities result in direct and clear information on the effectiveness of job performance.

An example of a job with little enrichment could be that of a production assembly line worker or a kitchen porter, where all five core characteristics are likely to score low. An example of an enriched job could be that of a parish priest who draws upon a wide range of social skills and talents, who can usually identify with the whole task and whose job has clear and important meaning and significance. There is a very high level of autonomy and likely to be direct and clear feedback.

Motivating potential score

From these five core job dimensions, Hackman and Oldham have developed an equation which gives a single index of a person's job profile. By answering a questionnaire – the Job Diagnostic Survey (JDS) – and by giving a score (between 1 and 7) to each job dimension, the person can calculate an overall measure of job enrichment, called the motivating potential score (MPS).

Examples of questions from the JDS are:

■ How much variety is there in your job?
■ To what extent does your job involve doing a whole and identifiable piece of work?
■ In general, how significant or important is your job?
■ How much autonomy is there in your job?
■ To what extent does doing the job itself provide you with information about your work performance?

$$MPS = \frac{\{\text{Skill variety} + \text{Task identity} + \text{Task significance}\}}{3} \times \text{Autonomy} \times \text{Feedback}$$

The first three job dimensions of skill variety, task identity and task significance are averaged, since it is the combination of these dimensions which contributes to experienced meaningfulness of work. The remaining two job dimensions, autonomy and feedback, stand on their own. Since scores for skill variety, task identity and task significance are additive, this means that the absence of one dimension can be partially offset by the presence of the other dimensions. However, if either autonomy or feedback is absent then, because of the multiplicative relationship, the MPS would be zero. The job would offer no potential to motivate the person.

Empirical support for the model

Empirical support for the model is mixed. From their studies, Hackman and Oldham claim that people with enriched jobs and high score levels on the Job Diagnostic Survey experienced more satisfaction and internal motivation. The core job dimensions of skill variety, task identity and task significance combined to predict the level of experienced meaningfulness of the work. The core dimensions of autonomy and feedback did not relate so clearly to experienced responsibility and knowledge of results. Some of the other dimensions were as good, or better, in predicting these psychological conditions. In general, however, the results of their studies showed that jobs that scored high on the core dimensions were associated with high levels of personal and work outcomes.

Luthans et al. report on evidence from a number of studies of American workers that the job design approach leads to improvement in motivation and performance, but also that the approach did not work in the Russian factory study discussed earlier in this chapter.[69]

In a study of a sample of six hotels (with between 35 and 65 bedrooms) in Great Yarmouth, *Lee-Ross* undertook an examination of the reliability of the JDS among seasonal workers. From an analysis of 163 questionnaires, Lee-Ross concludes that in general, reliability scores were compatible with those of Hackman and Oldham. The JDS appears to hold just as well for hotel workers as for workers in other industries.[70]

Based on integrating Hackman and Oldham's job characteristics model with Maslow's hierarchy of needs, *Roe et al.* propose a general model of work motivation, tested with Bulgarian, Hungarian and Dutch workers. The model indicates that situational characteristics lead to critical psychological factors, inducing two main motivational factors – **job involvement** and **organisational commitment** – which in turn lead to two proximal outcomes of work motivation – **effort** and **job satisfaction** – which affect **performance, stress** and **tendency to leave the organisation**. Although there were some differences that draw attention to cultural variables, there was also a large degree of similarity in results across the three countries.[71]

CONTEXTUAL FACTORS IN JOB DESIGN

The different methods of job design are not necessarily separate approaches. They are inter-related and there is some overlapping among them. For example, goal-setting is sometimes viewed as another approach to job design. Goal-setting involves building goals, feedback and incentives into the structure of the job. In addition, there are many other associated (contextual) factors which affect job design, including, for example: organisational culture, structure, systems of management and style of leadership, trade unions, HR policies and procedures, communications, group norms, ergonomics, the management of change, and the working environment.

The potential benefits of improved job design are unlikely to be realised if attention is focused on the content of jobs alone. Of equal, if not more, importance is the process by which redesign is carried out. This has led to recognition of the importance of management style and, increasingly, of organisation culture.[72] Central to improving the quality of work-ing life is a participative, open style of management involving employees in decisions that affect them, including the design or choice of technology. Management should attempt to develop a relationship of trust among all members and sections of the organisation and a meaningful partnership approach with trade unions.

Theories of work motivation and job satisfaction have influenced management systems and styles of leadership, and developments in HR policies and procedures. The human resource management function is centred on people's needs while working in an organisa-tion and ways in which their work promotes or frustrates the fulfilment of these needs.[73] The practice of modern human resource management is directed towards providing conditions under which people work willingly and effectively, and contribute to the success of the organisation. This involves concern for employee motivation and job satisfaction.

Critical reflection

'Individuals have a variety of changing, and often conflicting, needs and expectations which they attempt to satisfy in a number of ways at different times.'

What are the most powerful influences on your own work motivation and job satisfaction? How do you think these will change in five years' time?

SYNOPSIS

■ The study of motivation is concerned, basically, with why people behave in a certain way. The underlying concept of motivation is some driving force within individuals by which they attempt to achieve some goal in order to fulfil some need or expectation. Individuals have a variety of changing, and often competing, needs and expectations which they attempt to satisfy in a number of ways. If a person's motivational driving force is blocked and they are unable to satisfy their needs and expectations, this may result either in constructive, problem-solving behaviour or in frustration-induced behaviour.

■ There are many competing theories that attempt to explain motivation at work. The different theories may be divided into two contrasting groups: content theories and process theories. Content theories place emphasis on what motivates and are concerned with identifying people's needs and their relative strengths, and the goals they pursue in order to satisfy these needs. Main content theories include Maslow's hierarchy of needs model, Alderfer's modified need hierarchy model, Herzberg's two-factor theory and McClelland's achieve-ment motivation theory.

■ Process theories place emphasis on the actual process of motivation. These theories are concerned with the relationships among the dynamic variables that make up motivation, and with how behaviour is initiated, directed and sustained. Many of the process

theories cannot be linked to a single writer, but major approaches under this heading include expectancy-based models, equity theory, goal theory and attribution theory. Another possible approach to motivation is organisational behaviour modification (OBMod).

■ These different theories are not conclusive. However, it is because of the complexity of motivation that these different theories are important to the manager, and many writers still expound their relevance today. They help demonstrate the many motives that influence people's behaviour at work. They provide a framework within which to direct attention for how best to motivate and reward staff to work willingly and effectively. One major doubt concerning the different theories of motivation is about their universality, on the grounds that they do not adequately address the factor of culture.

■ Attempting to understand the nature of job satisfaction and links with work performance is not easy. Although the level of job satisfaction may well affect the strength of motivation, this is not always the case. Job satisfaction is more of an internal state and could be associated, for example, with a feeling of personal achievement. Job satisfaction is a complex concept and difficult to measure objectively. The level of job satisfaction is affected by a wide range of individual, social, organisational and cultural variables.

■ Broader approaches to satisfaction aim to give the person improved empowerment and job enrichment through greater autonomy and control over their work. Attention has also been given to a comprehensive model of job enrichment and five core dimensions. Moves towards greater flexibility may have noticeable effects on job satisfaction and performance of staff. Despite many theories and studies there are still doubts as to how best to manage an organisation so that staff have both high job satisfaction and productivity. Account must also be taken of contextual factors, including management style and culture, and developments in human resource management.

REVIEW AND DISCUSSION QUESTIONS

1 Explain what you understand by the underlying concept of motivation. Summarise the main needs and expectations to be taken into account in considering the motivation of people at work.

2 What do you understand by frustration-induced behaviour? Give a practical example, preferably from your work experience, of each of the main forms of this behaviour.

3 Critically assess the practical value of Maslow's hierarchy of needs model to improving the motivation of people at work. Give examples of the extent to which the theory could meaningfully be applied to staff in your own organisation.

4 Debate critically the validity of the contention that the motivation for staff to work well depends on more than a high salary and good working conditions.

5 Explain your understanding of expectancy-based theories of motivation. Use a simple diagram to help explain an expectancy theory of your choice. What implications do expectancy theories of motivation have for the manager?

6 Give detailed practical examples of situations in which each of the following theories of motivation might be appropriate: (i) achievement motivation; (ii) equity theory; (iii) goal theory.

7 What exactly do you understand by job satisfaction? What are the main dimensions of job satisfaction? Give specific examples of causes of both job satisfaction and job dissatisfaction that you have experienced.

8 Evaluate critically the relationship between motivation, job satisfaction and effective work performance. Give reasons in support of your views.

Top marks for the best employee awards

FT

Rhymer Rigby

Employee of the month (or the week, or the year) awards have a bad image. They are popularly associated with low-paid, low-status service sector jobs – a dollop of worthless recognition on top of an already low-value package. Implemented properly, they can be a valuable form of recognition that motivates staff, especially in today's reward-constrained climate. Handled wrongly, however, they can backfire and foster cynicism.

Stephen Carella, a team leader at Kwik-Fit Financial Services, an insurance intermediary, was its Employee of the Year 2008. 'It was a goal I'd set myself at the start of the year,' he explains. Once he had won six employee of the month awards, he knew he was in with a good chance. He adds: 'It's a great incentive and what really motivated me is the recognition you get. It's a fantastic thing to put on your CV.' Mr Carella was presented with his award at a dinner for 100 of the company's top performers and their partners at Edinburgh's Balmoral Hotel. He also received a cash prize of £10,000. 'It was,' he says, 'the best night of my life.'

The scheme, explains Brendan Devine, KFFS group managing director, has been running for four years and is part of a complex structure of recognition. Each department has an employee of the month award, which accords privileges such as free food in the staff bistro, gym membership and parking. From these are drawn quarterly qualifiers who could make it on to a shortlist for employee of the year. 'It's part of an overall strategy to identify who top performers are,' says Mr Devine, adding that at the dinner, the 34 departmental winners of the annual title also receive awards and £1,000. 'In a way, the recognition is the most important part though – [the] reward goes beyond your pay packet.'

Ben Williams, a corporate psychologist, says such schemes can be valuable but cautions that they must be implemented properly. He says: 'By and large they're a good thing and encourage beliefs and behaviours the company might want to promote such as high sales or great customer care. In industries where people move round, they can encourage them to stay.' However, he says: 'You need to avoid a celebrity-like cult of the individual. Teams need to be considered together. If everyone's a high performer, it can be divisive to only reward the single highest performer.'

There is also the vexed question of recognition versus material reward. The key is getting the underlying corporate culture right. If it is wrong, says Williams, 'recipients can be made to look obsequious sycophants,

Employee award schemes can be a valuable form of recognising the contributions of employees but if handled badly can backfire and foster cynicism. How can employers strike the right balance in both deciding what to do and what to avoid?

like swots at school'. Still, no matter what you do, there will always be groups that are damning about such recognition: 'That's one of the reasons to give cash rewards – you get buy-in from the cynical brigade.'

But for all the organisations that take these considerations on board, there are still plenty that do not. 'I was the best-performing employee of the quarter,' says one salesman at another company, 'and I went up on stage and was given a £20 M&S voucher – which makes you feel a bit like a monkey performing for bananas.' He spent his voucher on strawberries and a few months later he won employee of the year. Soon after he left the company.

Source: Rigby, R. 'Top Marks for the Best Employee Award', *Financial Times*, 11 May 2009. Copyright © 2009 The Financial Times Limited, reproduced with permission.

Discussion questions

1 What evidence is there in the article that employee award schemes can help meet the needs and expectations of people at work outlined in Figure 7.2?

2 Explain which two motivation theories you think are most useful for a manager who is planning an employee award scheme both to decide what to include in the scheme and what to avoid.

ASSIGNMENT 1

a List, as far as possible in rank order, the specific needs and expectations that are most important **to you as an individual**. (Do *not* include basic physiological needs such as to satisfy thirst or hunger, or a *minimal* standard of accommodation.)

b Explain, briefly, to what extent these needs and expectations are met currently by your present work situation and/or to what extent you anticipate they will be met by your future career ambitions.

c Think of any work experience that you have had – even a short-term, vacation or part-time job. Briefly describe those aspects of the job and/or experiences that:

(i) motivated you to work well and to the best of your ability; and

(ii) had a demotivating influence on your behaviour and performance.

Be prepared to share your feelings and comments as part of a class discussion.

ASSIGNMENT 2

a Write a brief description of what you think is happening to the people in the picture and what you think will happen to them in the future.

b After you have written your description, compare your response with those of your colleagues.

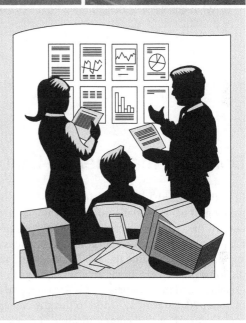

PERSONAL AWARENESS AND SKILLS EXERCISE

Objectives

Completing this exercise should help you to enhance the following skills:

- Analyse and review what determines motivation to work.
- Reflect upon your perceptions about the motives of other people.
- Take account of individual needs and expectations at work.

Exercise

1 First, undertake Assignment 1 and bear in mind your responses to the assignment. *Exchange accounts with a partner before proceeding further*.

2 Now assume you are the newly appointed general manager of a privately owned 50-room seaside hotel with restaurant. You have been brought in as a trouble shooter and at interview you were informed there is serious concern about the generally poor level of work performance, that morale is low and there is a disturbing high level of staff turnover.

■ Detail fully the likely actions you would take to help overcome the present situation.

■ Indicate clearly the priorities you would have in mind.

■ Make clear any necessary, reasonable assumptions.

■ Explain how you might draw upon those theories/studies you consider relevant.

3 Write, fully and honestly, the extent to which there is disparity between your own motives and, based on the above, motivating other people. How would you explain and rationalise differences?

4 Compare and discuss critically accounts with your partner, and be prepared to explain and justify your views.

Discussion

■ How far did you avoid generalisations about what motivates other people?

■ What assumptions did you make about the work ethic of staff at the hotel?

■ To what extent where you able to distance your own motivations?

■ What conclusions do you draw from this exercise?

CASE STUDY

Don't get mad, get on-line!

In 2005 the word 'blog', meaning an on-line journal or web log which is regularly updated by the author, entered the Oxford English Dictionary for the first time. Figures collected by internet monitoring organisations suggest that by the time the word made it into the dictionary there were about 30 million blogs in existence, and the numbers were increasing at the rate of about 70,000 per day.[74] Add to this the emergence of social networking and communication sites such as Facebook and Twitter and there has never been such a wide range of possible ways to launch personal thoughts into a waiting cyberworld. Not all are about work, but the fact that life in the office or workplace is a significant part of many people's lives means that many blogs, posts and tweets include references to work, bosses, colleagues and customers alongside other normal daily experiences, opinions about news events and so on. A number of blogs are specifically about work, and these are the ones which tend to hit the headlines, usually when an employee gets into trouble for airing their opinions about the organisation they work for in the blogosphere.

Why do individuals blog about work? At one level, blogging is no different from gossip. Many bloggers expect to have small audiences, possibly of like-minded

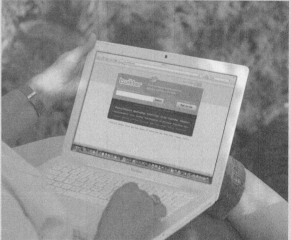

Is it acceptable to blog, post or tweet about your company? Social networking and communication sites provide a wide range of ways to share personal thoughts in a public venue resulting in organisational responses that can range from accepting to creative to hostile.

people who have similar experiences to discuss; the content of blogs may be much like the discussions with colleagues that are routinely held in the round the water cooler or coffee machine, or with friends in a pub or

bar after work. Most blogs include opportunities for email and on-line discussion, and so become a lively mix of intimate diary items and chatroom-style comments. For some authors the aim is to give an insight into their working life, perhaps discussing a type of job which many people know about but few really understand. In the UK, at least one chief police constable and a number of ambulance service workers are known to blog primarily about their work.[75] However, many see it as a way of letting off steam about aspects of their work which enrage them, be it the organisation, their individual managers, their annoying colleagues or – as often – the absurd behaviour of members of the general public and customers in particular.[76] This can make blogging a particularly risky activity, at least if the blogger wishes to keep their job.

Careless blogging can get you dooced

In 2004 Ellen Simonetti hit the headlines[77] when she was sacked by her employer, the American Delta Airlines, essentially for identifying them as the company about which she was blogging on her 'Queen of the Sky' website. The offence which got her sacked was not the blog itself, but the fact that by posting photographs of herself draped across the seats of an aircraft in her uniform (pictures which were described by the company as 'inappropriate') she identified the organisation itself, and therefore was considered to have brought it into disrepute. In January 2005, in a similar British case, Joe Gordon, an employee of Waterstone's bookshop in Edinburgh of 11 years' standing, was dismissed for gross misconduct[78] after 'bringing the company into disrepute' by complaining about his 'evil boss' at the fictionalised but nevertheless sufficiently recognisable bookstore 'Bastardones' in his blog 'The Wolamaloo Gazette'.[79]

The term 'doocing' has since been used to describe the phenomenon of being sacked for blogging, a fate which also befell Catherine Sanderson or 'La Petite Anglaise' who was dismissed from the Parisian branch of British accounting firm Dixon Wilson in July 2006 for committing the 'real and serious' offence of blogging mischievously but anonymously about her boss and colleagues.[80] As with Simonetti, it was when she posted photographs of herself on the site that the company decided that she, and therefore it, could be identified, and that it had to act against its employee. Market Sentinel offers an internet monitoring service (much like that of a press agency) to companies who want to know what is being posted about them, and be alerted to potential threats posed to their brand image in cyberspace. This too can result in disciplinary action as 13 cabin crew at Virgin Atlantic discovered to their cost when they were dismissed for posting derogatory comments about Virgin customers on Facebook.[81]

Learning to love bloggers

Not every organisation has reacted with hostility to bloggers. The chief constable and the ambulance workers mentioned above are at least tolerated and at best supported by their employers (the chief constable's blog is hosted by the North Wales Police website). The same was also true for Robert Scoble, at Microsoft, whose blog (Scobleizer) not only turned him into a cyber-celebrity, but also acted to help humanise the previously monolithic corporate face of the company.[82] Other organisations have actively embraced blog culture, and sought to use it to their advantage, mainly to aid recruitment. Dell, the US computer giant, has also created its own blog (Direct2Dell) as a means of engaging with customer criticism. An increasing number of organisations have recognised the impossibility of controlling employees' private blogs, but have offered guidance and codes of practice for their workforce as a means of setting out company policy and thereby setting boundaries of acceptable behaviour. IBM, for example has developed a set of eleven guidelines for its staff, some of which are summarised below:[83]

- Know and follow IBM's Business Conduct Guidelines.
- IBMers are personally responsible for their posts.
- You must make it clear that you are speaking for yourself and not on behalf of IBM.
- Respect copyright, fair use and financial disclosure laws.
- Don't provide IBM's or another's confidential or other proprietary information.
- Don't use ethnic slurs, personal insults, obscenity etc.; and show proper consideration for others' privacy and topics that may be considered objectionable or inflammatory such as politics and religion.
- Don't pick fights, be the first to correct your own mistakes and don't alter previous posts without indicating that you have done so.
- Try to add value. Provide worthwhile information and perspective.

A great many organisations have seized the opportunity to communicate with staff, customers, members and others via website-based blogs.

Organisational consequences: possibilities and challenges

IBM's approach, the development of guidelines for employees, is increasingly being seen as the way forward for organisations which are concerned about blogging. It prevents them from appearing heavy-handed, avoids the adverse publicity that can sometimes be stirred up by a sacking, and might also preclude legal challenges, for instance on the grounds of unfair dismissal, or as an attempt to curtail freedom of

speech. Simonetti, Gordon and Sanderson all challenged their dismissals using employment tribunals or their equivalents, opening the question of the validity of dismissal for blogging. The existence of company guidelines which have clearly been breached by a blogger is likely to support an employer's case for dismissal.

The UK Chartered Institute of Personnel and Development considers that there are occasions when blogging might be easily identifiable as a disciplinary offence but would not necessarily support a dismissal; for instance, the abuse of company equipment and time by workers 'blogging or tweeting on the job' might not be deemed to warrant dismissal by an employment tribunal unless the post additionally caused harm to the organisation's reputation and interests.[84] On the other hand, disclosure of confidential information might well breach company data protection policies; and dismissal for libellous or defamatory comments might stand up to the test of a tribunal. The spectre of cyber-bullying is another concern, since social networking sites like Facebook have the potential for defamatory and libellous comments and even illicit recordings to be posted for circulation to a specified group. Similarly, it seems possible that if employees are using blogs to air their work grievances rather than using the more normal (and in the UK statutorily required) grievance procedures, then they might well be risking fair dismissal. However, it is also worth considering how far disgruntled employees' blogs indicate that organisational grievance procedures or other employee feedback mechanisms (such as attitude surveys) are not operating very successfully and that important information about employee morale and job dissatisfaction is being overlooked.

Finally it might also be necessary to consider how far blogs are acceptable as a form of whistleblowing, and whether employees who use blogs in this way would be protected by relevant legislation such as the Public Interest Disclosure Act (PIDA) of 1998 in the UK. The PIDA extends protection to whistleblowers, but normally on the basis that they have already exhausted internal organisational methods of raising their concerns before going public. Here again, blogs might be of enormous value to senior managers within an organisation whose ability to monitor the reality of working life in relation to aims regarding (for example) employee morale or issues of corporate social responsibility is limited.

The last word should perhaps go to an anonymous blogger who reported to *Personnel Today* magazine:

Blogging – with its potential audience of millions, is an easy way to exercise my creativity and make my views heard. I'm dissatisfied with my job and unhappy with the way recent restructuring and management decisions have led to low morale, although I do not have an 'evil boss' like the Waterstone's employee. Most of my work-related moans on my blog are minor, everyday niggles about annoying colleagues or the dull nature of my employment, but I am not afraid to occasionally pull out the big guns over issues I feel passionately about.[85]

Your tasks

1 Using a basic model of expectancy theory such as that in Figure 7.8 or one of goal-setting theory such as Locke's (Figure 7.12) assess the various motivational forces which might be operating when employees blog about their employer.

2 It seems that for some people, blogging about work can be viewed as a form of frustration-induced behaviour. Critically review the process of blogging as a method of expressing job dissatisfaction. How do you think managers should respond to cases of work-related blogging by frustrated employees?

3 Organisational responses to employee blogs or Facebook posts outlined in the case might be categorised as either hostile (sack and sue); accepting (control and monitor); or creative (encourage and use). For each of these approaches, identify some basic guidelines for handling cases such as those of Simonetti, Gordon and Sanderson, bearing in mind the motivational effects that your proposals might have on both bloggers and other employees.

Notes and references

1 Krech, D., Crutchfield, R. S. and Ballachey, E. L. *Individual in Society*, McGraw-Hill (1962).

2 Mitchell, T. R. 'Motivation: New Directions for Theory, Research, and Practice', *Academy of Management Review*, vol. 7, no. 1, January 1982, pp. 80–8.

3 'Motivating Your Staff in a Time of Change', Checklist 068, Chartered Management Institute, March 2006.

4 Kreitner, R., Kinicki, A. and Buelens, M. *Organizational Behaviour*, first European edition, McGraw-Hill (1999).

5 Farren, C. 'Mastery: The Critical Advantage', in Chowdhury, S. (ed.) *Management 21C*, Financial Times Prentice Hall (2000), p. 95.

6 See, for example, Rudolph, P. A. and Kleiner, B. H. 'The Art of Motivating Employees', *Journal of Managerial Psychology*, vol. 4, no. 5, 1989, pp. i–iv.

7 Kets de Vries, M. 'Beyond Sloan: trust is at the core of corporate values' in Pickford, J. (ed.) *Financial Times Mastering Management 2.0*, Financial Times Prentice Hall (2001), pp. 267–70.

8 For a fuller discussion, see Mullins, L. J. *Hospitality Management and Organisational Behaviour*, fourth edition, Longman (2001).

9 Weaver, T. 'Theory M: Motivating with Money', *Cornell HRA Quarterly*, vol. 29, no. 3, November 1988, pp. 40–5.

10 Kusin, G. 'A 360-Degree Spin', *Hemisphere United*, October 2005, p. 76.

11 Templar, R. *The Rules of Management*, Pearson Prentice Hall (2005), p. 66.

12 Grayson, D. and Hodges, A. *Everybody's Business: Managing Risks and Opportunities in Today's Global Society*, Financial Times (2001), p. 76.

13 Gratton, L. *Hot Spots*, Financial Times Prentice Hall (2007), p. 133.

14 Waller, D. 'Are You What You Do?', *Management Today*, October 2008, pp. 42–6.

15 See, for example, Brown, J. A. C. *The Social Psychology of Industry*, Penguin (1954 and 1986).

16 Cited in Crainer, S. 'Re-engineering the Carrot', *Management Today*, December 1995, p. 66.

17 Maslow, A. H. 'A Theory of Human Motivation', *Psychological Review*, 50, July 1943, pp. 370–96 and Maslow, A. H. *Motivation and Personality*, third edition, Harper and Row (1987).

18 Steers, R. M. and Porter, L. W. *Motivation and Work Behaviour*, fifth edition, McGraw-Hill (1991).

19 Saunders, A. 'Keep Staff Sweet', *Management Today*, June 2003, p. 75.

20 Adair, J. *Leadership and Motivation*, Kogan Page (2006).

21 Alderfer, C. P. *Existence, Relatedness and Growth*, Collier Macmillan (1972).

22 Herzberg, F., Mausner, B. and Snyderman, B. B. *The Motivation to Work*, second edition, Chapman and Hall (1959).

23 Crainer, S. and Dearlove, D. (eds) *Financial Times Handbook of Management*, second edition, Financial Times Prentice Hall (2001), p. 361.

24 McClelland, D. C. *Human Motivation*, Cambridge University Press (1988).

25 For examples of pictures, see Osland, J. S., Kolb, D. A. and Rubin, I. M. *Organizational Behaviour: An Experimental Approach*, seventh edition, Prentice Hall (2001).

26 See, for example, Spangler, W. D. 'Validity of Questionnaire and TAT Measures of Need for Achievement: Two Meta-Analyses', *Psychological Bulletin*, July 1992, pp. 140–54.

27 McClelland, D. C. 'Business Drive and National Achievement', *Harvard Business Review*, vol. 40, July–August 1962, pp. 99–112.

28 McClelland, D. C. and Burnham, D. H. 'Power Is the Great Motivation', *Harvard Business Review*, vol. 54, March–April 1976, pp. 100–10.

29 Vroom, V. H. *Work and Motivation*, Wiley (1964); also published by Krieger (1982).

30 Porter, L. W. and Lawler, E. E. *Managerial Attitudes and Performance*, Irwin (1968).

31 Lawler, E. E. *Motivation in Work Organizations*, Brooks/Cole (1973).

32 Lundin, S., Paul, H. and Christensen, J. *Fish: A Remarkable Way to Boost Morale and Improve Results*, Hyperion Press (2001), p. 37.

33 Adams, J. S. 'Injustice in Social Exchange', in Berkowitz, L. (ed.) *Advances in Experimental and Social Psychology*, Academic Press (1965). Abridged in Steers, R. M. and Porter, L. W. *Motivation and Work Behavior*, second edition, McGraw-Hill (1979), pp. 107–24.

34 Werner, G., Schmittberger, R. and Schwarze, B. 'An Experimental Analysis of Ultimatum Bargaining', *Journal of Economic Behavior and Organization*, vol. 3, no. 4, December 1982, pp. 367–88.

35 Locke, E. A. 'Towards a Theory of Task Motivation and Incentives', *Organizational Behavior and Human Performance*, vol. 3, 1968, pp. 157–89.

36 Locke, E. A. 'Personal Attitudes and Motivation', *Annual Review of Psychology*, vol. 26, 1975, pp. 457–80.

37 Gratton, L. *Living Strategy: Putting People at the Heart of Corporate Purpose*, Financial Times Prentice Hall (2000), p. 193.

38 Hannagan, T. *Management*, fourth edition, Financial Times Prentice Hall (2005), p. 363.

39 Reis, D. and Pena, L. 'Reengineering the Motivation to Work', *Management Decision*, vol. 39, no. 8, 2001, pp. 666–75.

40 'Motivating Your Staff in a Time of Change', *Management Checklist 068*, Chartered Management Institute, March 2006.

41 Flores, G. N. and Utley, R. 'Management Concepts in Use – a 12-Year Perspective', *Engineering Management Journal*, vol. 12, no. 3, September 2000, pp. 11–17.

42 Adair, J. *Leadership and Motivation*, Kogan Page (2006), p. 38.

43 Luthans, F. and Kreitner, R. *Organisational Behavior Modification and Beyond*, second edition, Scott Foresman (1985), p. 36.

44 Stajkovic, A. D. and Luthans, F. 'Differential Effects of Incentive Motivators on Work Performance', *Academy of Management Journal*, vol. 44, no. 3, 2001, pp. 580–90.

45 Luthans, F., Stajkovic, A., Luthans, B. C. and Luthans, K. W. 'Applying Behavioral Management in Eastern Europe', *European Management Journal*, vol. 16, no. 4, August 1998, pp. 466–74.

46 Tampoe, M. 'Knowledge Workers – The New Management Challenge', *Professional Manager*, November 1994, pp. 12–13.

47 Lucas, E. 'Turning On the Knowledge Workers', *Professional Manager*, May 1999, pp. 10–12.

48 'Managing Knowledge Workers: The HR Dimension', Chartered Institute of Personnel and Development, January 2002.

49 Whitmore, Sir J. 'Breaking Down the Barriers to Management Creativity', *Manager, The British Journal of Administrative Management*, May/June 2002, pp. 24–6.

50 See, for example, Cheng, T., Sculli, D. and Chan, F. S. 'Relationship Dominance – Rethinking Management Theories from the Perspective of Methodological Relationalism', *Journal of Managerial Psychology*, vol. 16, no. 2, 2001, pp. 97–105.

51 Francesco, A. M. and Gold, B. A. *International Organizational Behavior*, second edition, Pearson Prentice Hall (2005), p. 126.

52 Ibid., p. 129.

53 Sledge, S., Miles, A. K. and Coppage, S. 'What Role Does Culture Play? A Look at Motivation and Job Satisfaction among Hotel Workers in Brazil', *International Journal of Human Resource Management*, vol. 19, no. 2, September 2008, pp. 1667–82.

54 Adler, N. J. *International Aspects of Organizational Behaviour*, third edition, South Western College Publishing (1997).

55 Chen, C. C. 'New Trends in Reward Allocation Preferences: A Sino-US Comparison', *The Academy of Management Journal*, vol. 38, no. 2, 1995, pp. 402–28.

56 Reeves, R. 'Reality Bites', *Management Today*, May 2003, p. 37.

57 Stern, S. 'My Generation' *Management Today*, March 2008, pp. 40–6.

58 Worrall, L. and Cooper, C. 'The Quality of Working Life 2007', Chartered Management Institute, October 2007.

59 Mumford, E. 'Job Satisfaction: A Method of Analysis', *Personal Review*, vol. 20, no. 3, 1991, pp. 11–19.

60 Handy, C. 'Boring Workplace, Boring Worker', *Management Today*, November 1997, p. 29.

61 'The Workplace Survey', Chartered Management Institute, March 2003; Myerson, J. 'Workspace Heaven?', *Management Today*, June 2003, pp. 53–61.

62 Branson, R. *Losing My Virginity*, Virgin Publishing (1998), pp. 431, 444.

63 De Vita, E. 'Best Fit', *Management Today*, September 2008, pp. 54–8.

64 'Flexible Working: The Implementation Challenge', CIPD, October 2005, p. 6.

65 Roddick, A. *Business As Unusual*, Thorsons (2000), p. 70.

66 Marx, K. 'The Notion of Alienation', in Coser, L. A. and Rosenburg, B. *Sociological Theory*, Collier Macmillan (1969), pp. 505–10.

67 Blauner, R. *Alienation and Freedom*, University of Chicago Press (1964).

68 Hackman, J. R. and Oldham, G. R. *Work Redesign*, Addison-Wesley (1980).

69 Luthans, F., Stajkovic, A., Luthans, B. C. and Luthans, K. W. 'Applying Behavioral Management in Eastern Europe', *European Management Journal*, vol. 16, no. 4, August 1998, pp. 466–74.

70 Lee-Ross, D. 'The Reliability and Rationale of Hackman and Oldham's Job Diagnostic Survey and Job Characteristics Model among Seasonal Hotel Workers', *International Journal of Hospitality Management*, 17, 1998, pp. 391–406.

71 Roe, R. A., Zinovieva, I. L., Dienes, E. and Ten Horn, L. A. 'A Comparison of Work Motivation in Bulgaria, Hungary and the Netherlands: Test of a Model', *Applied Psychology: An International Review*, vol. 49, 2000, pp. 658–87.

72 See, for example, Cartwright, J. *Cultural Transformation*, Financial Times Prentice Hall (1999).

73 See, for example, Torrington, D., Hall, L. and Taylor, S. *Human Resource Management*, sixth edition, Financial Times Prentice Hall (2005).

74 Personnel Today 'Blogging: Waste of Time or Corporate Tool?', published 21 March 2006 and available at www.personneltoday.com (accessed 28 July 2009).

75 The Chief Constable of North Wales at http://www.north-wales.police.uk/portal/blogs/ and two blogs by members of the London Ambulance service, Random Acts of Reality (www.randomreality.blogware.com) and Nee Naw (www.neenaw.co.uk).

76 E.g. waiterrant.net for those in the restaurant trade.

77 BBC News website 'US Blogger Fired by Her Airline', http://news.bbc.co.uk, dated 3 November 2004 (accessed 28 July 2009).

78 Personnel Today 'Don't Blog Your Way into Trouble', published 17 January 2005 and available at www.personneltoday.com (accessed 28 July 2009).

79 The Wolamaloo Gazette, www.wolamaloo.org.uk.

80 Smith-Spark, L. 'How to Blog and Keep Your Job', BBC news website, http://news.bbc.co.uk 20 July 2006 (accessed 28 July 2009).

81 BBC News website 'Crew Sacked over Facebook Posts', 31 October 2008.

82 Watkins, D. 'How Big Business Barged In On the Bloggers', *The Guardian*, 20 March 2006.

83 For the full guidelines and discussion about how they should be managed, visit http://www.snellspace.com/IBM_Blogging_Policy_and_Guidelines.pdf.

84 Spencer, S. 'Illegal Blogging', *People Management*, 27 January 2005.

85 Personnel Today 'Don't Blog Your Way Into Trouble', published 17 January 2005 and available at www.personneltoday.com.

ACADEMIC VIEWPOINT

Below you will find the title and abstract of a recent article in an academic journal which explores a topic relevant to the chapters in Part 2.

Inkpen, A. 'Knowledge Transfer and International Joint Ventures: The Case of NUMMI and General Motors', *Strategic Management Journal*, vol. 29, 2008, pp. 447–53.

Abstract

Using a case study of NUMMI, a joint venture between General Motors (GM) and Toyota, this research note examines alliances and knowledge transfer with a focus on the organizational processes used to transfer knowledge. The results suggest two possible explanations for the knowledge transfer outcome. The primary explanation is that the systematic implementation of knowledge transfer mechanisms can overcome the stickiness and causal ambiguity of new knowledge. A second explanation is that creating successful knowledge transfer should be viewed from a change management perspective in which trial and error learning experiences and experimentation support the transfer outcome.

Commentary

Ideas about organisational learning and knowledge transfer are gaining increasing significance in a world where tacit knowledge (the everyday assumptions, habits and experiences which individuals acquire during the experience of work) often holds the key to effective performance or improvements in organisational processes. The article describes a specific experiment designed to promote knowledge transfer of the 'Toyota Production System' (TPS) into General Motors (GM) which began in 1984. The joint venture site, a disused GM manufacturing plant in Fremont, California, allowed Toyota access to experience of managing an American workforce and gave GM the opportunity to study successful Japanese manufacturing processes at close hand. The experience is described, and the problems of the initial phase (to about 1990) might seem to suggest that in the short term the experiment was unsuccessful. However, it is also made clear that senior management commitment from 1992 onwards resulted in a better organised process, and the development of an effective network of TPS-experienced managers within GM. This network supported the creation of a systematic knowledge transfer process that ultimately enhanced GM's performance.

The article might prompt you to consider the following questions.

- What was the nature of the initial problems encountered by the Fremont experienced managers when attempting to transfer their new knowledge back into GM?

- The article explains how the creation of a specific set of activities by the Technical Liaison Office helped to improve the knowledge transfer process. How did these activities contribute to its effectiveness?

- What are the implications of the article's findings for the social aspects of managing knowledge transfer within an organisation?

- Does knowledge transfer always have to take so long? Can anything be learned from the article which would help an organisation speed up the process?

<table>
<tr><td>PART 2
CASE STUDY</td><td>Philanthropy: the resurgence of personal
social responsibility?</td></tr>
</table>

PART 2 CASE STUDY

Philanthropy: the resurgence of personal social responsibility?

Something rather spectacular happened on 26 June 2006: Warren Buffet, the world's second wealthiest man, announced that he intended to give 85 per cent of his fortune to the Bill and Melinda Gates Foundation. There, it will join the billions that Bill Gates, the world's wealthiest man, has already pledged, to make an enormous sum of money to support good works around the world. A few months earlier, the late Anita Roddick, who founded and built up Body Shop International, had announced her intention to give away half of her fortune. Philanthropy has long been a noble and admirable part of the capitalist tradition and now seems to be back in the news.

Why is this sort of philanthropy of interest to students of organisational behaviour? Several reasons can be suggested:

- Firstly, of course, the wealth that is given away is often the result of setting up and running an organisation that successfully fulfils its purpose over a long period: the profits that flow to the owner result from customers choosing and paying for its output.
- Also, the generosity of wealthy individuals makes an interesting contrast with the more familiar concept of 'corporate social responsibility', which sometimes involves donations of company, rather than personal money.
- The charitable foundations, together with their external relationships, are of interest in their own right.

The word philanthropy is derived from the Greek and is defined as 'love of humankind; the disposition or effort to promote the happiness of and well-being of one's fellow-people.[1] The practice of philanthropy was well-established before that of capitalism of course, but the early stages of the growth of the American economy saw a significant surge in the social custom of philanthropy. Although it may have been no part of their aim, the names of some of America's most significant philanthropists are as well-known for their giving as for the business careers that made the money. Two celebrated examples from the same era provide a view of the way a philanthropic life can be lived.

From Carnegie and Rockefeller to Bill and Melinda Gates

Andrew Carnegie (1835–1919) was born in Dunfermline, Scotland. He was the son of a weaver and

Source: Adrian Wyld/AP/Press Association Images

Bill Gates and his wife set up the Bill and Melinda Gates Foundation with part of the personal fortune he had earned from the success of Microsoft.

the family emigrated to the United States in 1848. Like many at that time, Carnegie started work at the age of 13 doing a number of jobs until 1865, when he started his own business. This was to become the foundation of the steel industry in Pittsburgh and the origin of Carnegie's fortune. At the turn of the new century, Carnegie sold the business for $480m and spent the rest of his life devoted to his philanthropic interests. These were diverse, but centred around the theme of the provision of public libraries and education.[2] Over his life, Carnegie gave away more than $350m (multiply by about twenty for today's values). Some of the quotes attributed to him[3] show the combination of hard-nosed business acumen and the strong sense of social duty that characterises this type of philanthropist:

And while the law of competition may be sometimes hard for the individual, it is best for the race, because it ensures the survival of the fittest in every department.

Surplus wealth is a sacred trust which its possessor is bound to administer in his lifetime for the good of the community.

I would as soon leave my son a curse as the almighty dollar.

As will be seen, similar sentiments and values continue to motivate today's philanthropists. John D. Rockefeller (1839–1937) was born in the United States to a farming family. In his business career, he founded and developed the Standard Oil Company, which became the leading force in the fast-growing oil industry. At the age of 57, Rockefeller decided that he should step aside from the day-to-day leadership of Standard Oil and devote himself to philanthropy. This had been important to him from his early life, but also because of his religious convictions and his approach to finance:

> *I believe it is every man's religious duty to get all he can honestly and to give all he can.*

Like Carnegie, his philanthropic interests centred on education, with substantial donations to found and develop universities and research institutes, as well as the establishment of trusts and foundations for the improvement of education at all levels. Over his life, he gave away some $540m.[4] Again, some of the quotes attributed to the man[5] show a mixture of hard-headedness and generosity that is far from sentimental:

> *Charity is injurious unless it helps the recipient to become independent of it.*

> *I believe that every right implies a responsibility; every opportunity, an obligation; every possession, a duty.*

The emerging philanthropists of the twenty-first century have often made their money through businesses that were not even heard of in the lifetimes of Carnegie and Rockefeller. Bill Gates, for example, is one of the founders of the enormously successful Microsoft Corporation, whose information products are about as far from steel and oil as can be imagined. This case is mainly concerned with the Bill and Melinda Gates Foundation (BMGF), which was established in 1994 with an initial gift of about $94m from the two founders.[6] It grew rapidly from 1999 to a value of $29.2bn by 2005, by which time a cumulative total of $10.2bn had been awarded. In 2006, it had 270 employees in three offices (Seattle, Washington and Delhi).

The organisation is organised around its three main priorities, which are: global development; global health; and US programmes. In a letter published on the Foundation's website,[7] Bill and Melinda Gates explain their aims in respect of global health, pointing out that health is fundamental to economic development:

> *When health takes hold, life improves by all measures. Conversely, poor health aggravates poverty, poverty deepens disease, and nations trapped in this spiral will not escape without the world's help. In Africa, the cost of malaria in terms of treatment and lost productivity is estimated to be $12 billion a year. The continent's gross domestic product could be $100 billion higher today if malaria had been eliminated in the 1960s. And if HIV infection rates continue at their present levels, the world will likely see 45 million new infections by 2010 and lose nearly 70 million people by 2020. That's 70 million of the most productive members of society – health workers, educators, and parents.*

> *Therefore, the foundation's Global Health program works to ensure that lifesaving advances in health are created and shared with those who need them most. Our primary focus areas are HIV/AIDS, TB, malaria, child survival and childhood immunization, and maternal and reproductive health.*

> *To begin, we invest heavily in research to help discover new and better products, particularly vaccines. The foundation also supports work to develop products that can be manufactured and distributed. Then, once a product is developed, we work to make sure that there are systems in place to adopt and sustain these new drugs as they become available. The foundation is a major supporter of the Global Alliance for Vaccines and Immunization (GAVI). This alliance has provided basic immunizations to over 8 million children who would not otherwise have been immunized. As a result, GAVI has already saved an estimated 500,000 children's lives.*

In the world of business, as opposed to philanthropic foundations, there has been growing interest in recent years in the subject of corporate governance: what the business is aiming to do and how it can be sure that its actions are consistent with those aims. It has been common for wealthy individuals to adopt a corporate format in making good works happen, often by setting up and then directing a dedicated foundation to look after both the strategic and operational aspects of the task. This seems to acknowledge the benefits of the corporate approach in terms of efficiency and the ability to recruit and apply specialist skills, while still retaining control by the founder or the founding family. It is also easy to appreciate how focused and effective such an organisation can be in pursuing the goals of the founder, and to acknowledge the possibility that an effective philanthropic foundation may be at least as effective as, say, a government or international agency.

As will already be clear, some of the world's philanthropic foundations have multinational corporation-sized (even government-sized) budgets, meaning that the issue of governance is rightly of some concern to the society within which these organisations operate. One does not need to be a fan of James Bond movies to appreciate that very rich individuals using their wealth to pursue their private aims is not in itself guaranteed to be in the general interest.

In fact, foundations often go to some lengths to communicate their values and aims publicly. BMGF has adopted two key values:

- All lives – no matter where they are being led – have equal value.
- To whom much has been given, much is expected.

These values are the basis for fifteen principles that guide BMGF in its operations:[8]

- This is a family foundation driven by the interests and passions of the Gates family.
- Philanthropy plays an important but limited role.
- Science and technology have great potential to improve lives around the world.
- We are funders and shapers – we rely on others to act and implement.
- Our focus is clear – and limited – and prioritizes some of the most neglected issues.
- We identify a specific point of intervention and apply our efforts against a theory of change.
- We take risks, make big bets, and move with urgency. We are in it for the long haul.
- We advocate – vigorously but responsibly – in our areas of focus.
- We must be humble and mindful in our actions and words. We seek and heed the counsel of outside voices.
- We treat our grantees as valued partners, and we treat the ultimate beneficiaries of our work with respect.
- Delivering results with the resources we have been given is of the utmost importance – and we seek and share information about those results.
- We demand ethical behaviour of ourselves.
- We treat each other as valued colleagues.
- Meeting our mission – to increase opportunity and equity for those most in need – requires great stewardship of the money we have available.
- We leave room for growth and change.

As can be seen, these principles relate to the foundation in its external dealings (with other agencies, for example, with the public in general or with its 'grantees', i.e. recipients of aid), but also in its internal relationships (ethical behaviour, respect and professional standards). BMGF is also committed in these principles to communicating clearly what it is aiming to do and what it has achieved.

Something of the founder's sense of responsibility was evident in the comments that Bill Gates made at the announcement of Warren Buffet's donation to the Foundation. Gates joked that there was something more scary about the possibility of making a mistake with Buffet's money than with his own.[9] These are not sentiments that politicians are often heard to express, making an interesting contrast with the mainstream government-funded approach to social projects that has come to dominate the past fifty years.

Warren Buffet and Anita Roddick

Warren Buffet's fortune was made through the Berkshire Hathaway organisation, which for many years has been

The world's most generous man? In 2006 Warren Buffet, the world's second wealthiest man, promised to give 85 per cent of his fortune to support good works around the world.

Source: Seth Wenig/AP/Press Association Images

very successful in providing investment management services for its clients. Buffet himself is famously moderate in his lifestyle, with a liking for a diet of burgers and Cherry Coke. His extraordinary wealth was recently augmented by his firm decision not to get involved in the late-90s dotcom boom and subsequent bust: his policy has always been to concentrate on business fundamentals and to invest for the long term. He also has a long-standing reputation for pithy quotes and one attributed remark seemed to sum up the chaos caused by the collapse of rapid stock market growth and the series of corporate scandals that followed:

It's only when the tide goes out that you can see who's been swimming without their trunks on.

From remarks made by Buffet at the announcement of his association with the Gates Foundation,[10] it seems clear that he had been thinking about an involvement in philanthropy for some time. Some of his motivation is bound up with the American tradition of philanthropy by wealthy individuals, including the notion that there is something problematic ('almost un-American' as he put it[11]) about the idea that huge wealth should result from accidents of birth. Children should be left wealthy enough to do anything, but not enough to do nothing. He had also become very impressed by the approach taken by BMGF and by Bill and Melinda themselves: the announcement coincided with that of the succession plans for Gates' leadership of Microsoft, which will allow Gates to devote more time

to the Foundation. Buffet has become a trustee of the Foundation and jokingly promised at the launch not to assess Gates' efforts more than once a day. At the same meeting, both men acknowledged the inspirational value that the news of the donation could have: one questioner suggested that the success of organisations like BMGF could do much to improve public confidence in charitable donation in general and perhaps increase the willingness of a far wider spectrum of people to give.

The decision by the UK entrepreneur Anita Roddick to join the ranks of business-based philanthropists added some interesting features to the discussion. Roddick was something of a business celebrity for much of her career, having founded and built up the very successful Body Shop International, a business whose market appeal was always strongly centred on the values of its founder. Its campaigns against animal testing of cosmetics and in favour of fair trade, for example, became prominent during the 1990s. Explaining that she did not want to die rich, Roddick announced at the end of 2005 that she intended to give away half her £100m fortune, much of which resulted from the sale of her business to L'Oréal. This extraordinarily generous act does not register very far up the world league table of philanthropy, but nonetheless represents a significant step for the UK.

Anita Roddick had often been sharply critical of some aspects of business life in the UK, especially where she had assessed attitudes as being selfish and short-termist. But, in her view, the rich have to look after the poor, and 'I don't think in our society we have any understanding of that.'

Anita Roddick, founder of the Body Shop, who built a business based on caring values, gave half of her wealth away.

A BBC article[12] commented at the time that personal philanthropy was less prominent in the UK than in America, possibly because people in the UK regard it as a government responsibility to look after the poor, with projects financed from general taxation and with additional contributions from companies under the heading of 'corporate social responsibility'. This is not to suggest that government programmes and corporate donations are by any means unimportant in the United States, but rather to emphasise how unusual personal philanthropy has been in the UK. The article suggested that personal philanthropy might be assuming greater prominence in the UK because of a growing belief that the state is no longer providing an adequate safety net. Whatever the truth of this suggestion, the prospect of more significant philanthropic foundations in the UK will raise some interesting questions of how public and private agencies can learn to work together in identifying priorities and designing programmes of action to address social problems.

Corporate versus personal philanthropy

Many large businesses in the UK have made significant donations to charity from corporate funds, which may be partly motivated by a desire for approval from some stakeholder groups. However, alongside the well-known company names have been some large donations from less prominent companies. One report in 2006,[13] for example, suggested that TCI, a leading hedge fund business, had become one of the most generous UK donors to charity, despite the very limited public awareness of the hedge fund sector among the UK public. TCI seems to have been designed by its founder to generate funds for charity in this way, but other corporate donations are made from company profits. As such, corporate philanthropy – and corporate social responsibility in general – has come in for criticism from some quarters, on the basis that it amounts to acts of generosity using other people's money (specifically, that of the shareholders, who own the company). The economist Milton Friedman has been forcefully suggesting for some decades that business should get on with the business of business: making money for its owners through successfully marketing products and services within the law. From this point of view, donations to charity by individuals making choices about their own funds are more desirable than acts of corporate generosity using other people's funds. In reality, public opinion seems to be sympathetic towards the idea of corporate donations to charity, whatever scepticism may sometimes be expressed about motives. However, from any reasonable point of view, there remains an important difference between giving personally and approving corporate gifts: the difference, perhaps, between signing your own and a company cheque.

Source: Jean/Empics Entertainment/Press Association Images

At a BMGF conference, Bill Gates alluded to the celebrated work of Adam Smith, the Scottish economist who first explained the general benefits of free markets in identifying and providing for needs effectively and efficiently. From these ideas have come the modern economies that provided the context in which organisations like Microsoft, Berkshire Hathaway and Body Shop International can generate large amounts of wealth, mainly through providing products and services that are attractive enough to cause people to choose to spend their own money on them. In short, this is the main reason why recent generations have in most cases been richer than their predecessors. The tradition of philanthropy on the part of wealthy individuals is by no means contrary to the desirability of free and fierce competition: rather, wealth generation and philanthropy can only go hand in hand.

What is perhaps less well known about Adam Smith is his significant contribution to moral philosophy. Perhaps the way to bring this discussion to a close is with a quote from the beginning of Adam Smith's *Theory of Moral Sentiments*, which was highlighted by Bill Gates in explaining the basic importance of philanthropy:

> *How selfish soever man may be supposed, there are evidently some principles in his nature which interest him in the fortune of others and render their happiness necessary to him though he derives nothing from it except the pleasure of seeing it.*

Philanthropic foundations are organisations that are interesting in their own right, in respect of the origin of their funds, in their interaction with other types of organisation and, of course, in the effects they have on the societies within which they operate.

Your tasks

- Philanthropic foundations have often been set up to concentrate efforts in addressing particular types of need (improving educational facilities, for example). How are these organisations likely to perform as learning organisations and why?

- Considering the BMGF's statement of principles included in the case, how effective is this organisation likely to be in attracting and harnessing a diverse range of talents and experience among its employees and partners?

- To some extent, philanthropic foundations are engaged in the same types of social projects as government agencies. How might approaches to employee motivation differ between the two types of organisation? What could either type of organisation usefully learn from the other?

Notes and references

1 New Shorter Oxford English Dictionary (1993).
2 http://www.carnegie.org/sub/about/biography.html (accessed 30 July 2009).
3 http://www.brainyquote.com/quotes/authors/a/andrew_carnegie.html (accessed 30 July 2009).
4 http://archive.rockefeller.edu/bio/jdrsr.php (accessed 30 July 2009).
5 http://www.brainyquote.com/quotes/authors/j/john_d_rockefeller.html (accessed 30 July 2009).
6 http://www.gatesfoundation.org/AboutUs/QuickFacts/Timeline/default.htm (accessed 30 July 2009).
7 http://www.gatesfoundation.org/AboutUs/OurValues/GatesLetter.htm (accessed 30 July 2009).
8 http://www.gatesfoundation.org/AboutUs/OurValues/GuidingPrinciples.htm (accessed 30 July 2009).
9 http://www.telegraph.co.uk/news/main.jhtml?xml=/news/2006/06/27/wrich27.xml (accessed 30 July 2009).
10 See video clips at http://www.gatesfoundation.org/AboutUs/RelatedInfo/Discussion-060626.htm (accessed 30 July 2009).
11 http://www.telegraph.co.uk/news/main.jhtml?xml=/news/2006/06/27/wrich27.xml (accessed 30 July 2009).
12 http://news.bbc.co.uk/1/hi/business/4524046.stm (accessed 30 July 2009).
13 http://news.bbc.co.uk/1/hi/business/5123244.stm (accessed 30 July 2009).

17 ORGANISATIONAL CONTROL AND POWER

An underlying feature of organisational behaviour is the concept of control and power. Control systems exist in all spheres of the operations of the organisation and are a necessary part of the process of management. Work organisations are complex systems of social relationships, status and power, and attention should be given to the manager–subordinate relationships. The manager needs to understand the nature of power and control in order to improve work behaviour and organisational performance.

Learning outcomes

After completing this chapter you should be able to:

- explain the nature and importance of control in work organisations, and the essential elements in a management control system;
- detail different forms of control and characteristics of an effective control system;
- explain the nature of power and management control, and review perspectives of organisational power;
- assess the nature and impact of financial and accounting systems of control;
- explore the concept of empowerment and the manager–subordinate relationship;
- examine the process of delegation, and the benefits and art of delegation;
- recognise the human and social factors that influence people's patterns of behaviour.

Critical reflection

'The controversial nature of control means that some writers prefer to use alternative terms such as monitoring or evaluating. But whatever term is used, the process of maintaining order is an integral part of the individual and organisational relationship, and a necessary feature of regulating work behaviour and effective management.'

Do you agree? What term would you favour for this process, and why?

THE CONTROVERSIAL NATURE OF CONTROL

In the discussion on the role of the manager (Chapter 11) attention was drawn to the motivation of staff and the importance of direction and control over the performance of other people's work. By their very nature, control systems are concerned with the regulation of behaviour. This concern for the regulation of behaviour and improvement in performance raises questions as to the ethical nature of control. (Ethical behaviour in business is discussed in Chapter 18.) Unfortunately 'control' often has an emotive connotation and is interpreted in a negative manner to suggest direction or command by the giving of orders. People may be suspicious of control systems and see them as emphasising punishment, an indication of authoritarian management, and a means of exerting pressure and maintaining discipline. Some writers seem to take this view, and even to suggest that organisational control is exploitation of employees.[1]

This, however, is clearly too narrow an interpretation. There is far more to control than simply a means of restricting behaviour or the exercise of authority over others. Control is not only a function of the formal organisation and a hierarchical structure of authority, it is also a feature of organisational behaviour and a function of interpersonal influence.[2] *Tannenbaum*, for example, sees control as an inherent characteristic of the nature of organisations. The process of control is at the centre of the exchange between the benefits that the individual derives from membership of an organisation and the costs of such benefits.

> *Organization implies control. A social organization is an ordered arrangement of individual human interactions. Control processes help circumscribe idiosyncratic behaviors and keep them conformant to the rational plan of the organization. Organizations require a certain amount of conformity as well as the integration of diverse activities. It is the function of control to bring about conformance to organizational requirements and achievement of the ultimate purposes of the organization.*[3]

Control is, therefore, a general concept that is applied to both individual behaviour and organisational performance. Nevertheless, we should note, for example, the comments by *Drummond* who in a critical discussion about mechanistic thinking in organisations makes the point: 'Common sense suggests that control is preferable to anarchy, and more control is preferable to less. While such assumptions are not necessarily wrong, they are not universally correct either.'[4]

Child suggests that although control is an essential process of management, it is strangely neglected by many writers on organisation. Among possible reasons for this is that

> *control has a sinister ring to it, associated in people's minds with power and manipulation. As a result, there may be some reluctance among many business school writers to discuss control, in order to avoid embarrassment for their sponsors in positions of corporate power. The claim that it is a purely technical process, concerning feedback on accounting and operations, also amounts to a desensitizing of the subject.*[5]

Individual behaviour

Most people show an ambivalence towards control. While they may not wish to have them applied by other people to their own performance they recognise the need for, and usefulness of, control systems. Under certain conditions, however, people may actually desire control. *Lawler* gives three reasons why employees might want to be subject to a control system:

- to give feedback about task performance;
- to provide some degree of structure of tasks, definition of how the tasks are to be carried out, and how performance will be measured; and
- where reward systems, for example pay, are based on performance.[6]

Control can stand for reliability, order and stability. Whenever a person inquires 'I would like to know how well I am doing', this in effect can be seen as asking for control. Members of staff want to know what is expected of them and how well they are performing. This places emphasis on the exchange of information, and feedback and comparison of actual results

against planned targets. Control is a basis for training needs, for the motivation to achieve standards and for the development of individuals.[7]

According to *Tulgan*, 'control' (together with timing and customisation) is one of the three factors that should guide rewards and incentives in the workplace of the future. 'It is critical to make very clear to individual contributors exactly what performance – what results, within what guidelines, parameters and deadlines – the organisation needs, and will therefore reward.'[8]

However, as *Wilson* reminds us, individuals are not just passive objects of control: 'They may accept, deny, react, reshape, rethink, acquiesce, rebel, or conform and create themselves within constraints imposed on them.'[9] And in a discussion of management processes in the new century, *Lorange* notes that the control process will also change dramatically:

> Perhaps the name 'control' will no longer exist, given the behaviourally dysfunctional overtones that tend to come with it. We shall, however, still use it here as a convenient term of reference, and remember that the content behind the phenomenon will be dramatically different.[10]

Organisational performance

At the organisational level, management need to exercise 'control' over the behaviour and actions of staff in order to ensure a satisfactory level of performance. Managerial control systems are a means of checking progress to determine whether the objectives of the organisation are being achieved. According to *Zimmermann* an organisation without control is impossible.

> Every organization has control systems that co-ordinate the exercise of decision rights that are dispersed among individuals. Control systems also serve another important function in the organization. They measure how effectively decisions have been translated into results. This second feature of control systems relates to the goal achievement of the company. In this perspective, control systems are about influencing the behavior of individuals in the interest of the corporation. Both functions are closely interlinked.[11]

Control completes the cycle of managerial activities. It involves the planning and organisation of work functions, and guiding and regulating the activities of staff. Control provides a check on the execution of work and on the success or failure of the operations of the organisation. The whole purpose of management control is the improvement in performance at both the individual and organisational level (*see* Figure 17.1). Lack of adequate supervision

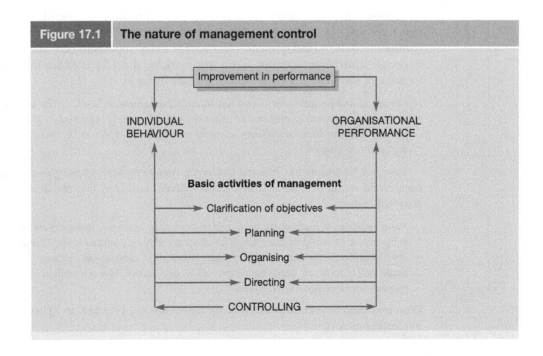

Figure 17.1 The nature of management control

and control, or of an effective risk-management system, are major features of poor organisational performance and can even lead to the collapse of a company.[12] A major international report undertaken by Proudfoot Consulting found that poor management in terms of inadequate planning and control and insufficient day-to-day supervision of work is still the largest single reason for lost productivity.[13]

EXPRESSION OF MANAGERIAL BEHAVIOUR

While the need for some form of control is constant, the extent and manner of control is variable. The exercise of control is an expression of management systems and styles of behaviour. As mentioned in Chapter 11, what is really important is what control is intended to achieve and the manner in which it is exercised.

One view of control is based on the classical approach and traditional assumptions of organisation and management. Control is viewed as an essential feature of formal organisation and a hierarchical structure of authority. It may also be recalled that the idea of 'Taylorism' and scientific management (discussed in Chapter 2) can be seen as representing a form of close management control over workers and the actual process of work and production system. As a consequence of their status and position within the hierarchical structure, managers have control over the flow of information that mainly moves down the organisation through vertical lines of communication.

By contrast, the human relations approach places emphasis on the social organisation, and the importance of groups and informal relationships. Control is seen more as a feature of interpersonal influence and takes place within a network of interaction and communications. Control should not be seen therefore only in the sense that it suggests close and constant supervision or as an organisational constraint on freedom of action by the individual.

The contingency approach takes the view that the most appropriate structure and system of management depend upon the particular situation. The nature of management control is an organisational variable. Recall the discussion on the organisational setting (Chapter 3) and consider likely variations in the extent and nature of management control among a range of diverse organisations.

Environment of consultation and communication

In previous chapters we have discussed the general movement towards flatter organisation structures and the increasing importance of an integrating rather than a hierarchical or controlling style of management. The message today appears to be that control must never outweigh leadership. 'Control is the hallmark of the Old World while leadership is a measure of the New.'[14] A similar point is made by *Lucas*:

> *Command and control is out. Consultation and communication is in . . . The idea of a leader as an autocratic, domineering, opinionated character is fast becoming outmoded in industry. It just doesn't fit with the new knowledge-driven economy where people expect to be consulted not commanded, nurtured not nannied.*[15]

However, according to *Cloke and Goldsmith*, many employees have grown up in hierarchical organisations and become accustomed to external authority and the dead weight of organisational history.

> *Many employees actually prefer being told what to do by autocratic managers and are willing to accept being treated like children in exchange for irresponsibility and reduced stress. They are willing to blindly obey hierarchical authority and keep silent before their superiors in exchange for job security. It is easier by far to be an unthinking drone who obeys orders from above than a self-managing team member who is responsible for results.*[16]

(You may wish to remind yourself of the discussion on Theory X and Theory Y management in Chapter 12.)

ELEMENTS OF AN ORGANISATIONAL CONTROL SYSTEM

Whatever the nature of control and whatever form it takes there are five essential elements in an organisational control system (*see* Figure 17.2):

- planning what is desired;
- establishing standards of performance;
- monitoring actual performance;
- comparing actual achievement against the planned target; and
- rectifying and taking corrective action.

1 **Planning what is desired** involves clarification of the aims to be achieved. It is important that people understand exactly what *should* happen and what is required of them. This requires that objectives and targets are specified clearly, particularly key activities, and wherever possible given some measurable attribute. Planning provides the framework against which the process of control takes place.

2 Related to planning is the **establishment of defined standards of performance**. This requires realistic measurements by which the degree and quality of goal achievement can be determined. Whenever possible these measurements should be stated in quantitative terms. Planning and measurement are prerequisites of control. Without them there can be no control. Objectives and targets, and standards of performance, should be stated clearly and communicated to those concerned, and to those who are subject to the operation of the control system.

3 The third aspect of control is the need for a means of monitoring actual performance. This requires feedback and a system of reporting information that is accurate, relevant and timely, and in a form that enables management to highlight deviations from the planned standard of performance. Feedback also provides the basis for decisions to adjust the control system, for example the need to revise the original plan. Feedback should relate to both the desired end-results and the means designed to achieve them.

4 Next, it is necessary **to compare actual performance against planned targets**. This requires a means of interpreting and evaluating information in order to give details of progress, reveal deviations and identify probable causes. This information should be fed back to those concerned to let them know how well they are getting on.

Figure 17.2	The five essential stages of organisational control

5 The final element of a management control system is the **taking of corrective action to rectify** the situation that has led to the failure to achieve objectives or targets, or other forms of deviations identified. This requires consideration of what can be done to improve performance. It requires the authority to take appropriate action to correct the situation, to review the operation of the control system and to make any necessary adjustments to objectives and targets or to the standards of performance.

> ### Critical reflection
>
> 'Criticism by certain writers of management control is totally misplaced. Control is an indispensable and welcomed process of the work organisation. Although they may not always admit it openly, most members of staff prefer to know exactly what they are expected to do and how to behave, and to receive regular management review and feedback on their performance.'
>
> *How would you attempt to present a counter argument?*

FORMS OF CONTROL

Control is far-reaching; it can serve a number of functions and can be manifested in a number of forms. For example, controls can be concerned with:

- observance of legislation and recommended codes of practice;
- policies and procedures, standing orders;
- the structure of the organisation and role relationships;
- type of production system or use of technology;
- systems that focus on the measurement of inputs, outputs, processes or the behaviour of people;
- general results or specific actions;
- the measurement and performance of day-to-day operational activities – this calls for more specific standards of performance and speedy corrective action;
- recruitment and selection, socialisation, training and development;
- an evaluation of overall performance of the organisation as a whole or with major parts of it. This requires broadly based standards of performance and remedies for corrective action. Total quality control, concerned with all areas of the organisation, can be seen as part of total quality management programmes (*see* Chapter 20).

According to *McKenna*, codes of conduct (discussed in Chapter 18) can constitute another form of control:

> *Developing and distributing a code of conduct is a form of control that sets out the rules of behaviour and values with which an organisation's senior managers expect their subordinates will conform. Such a code will only be accepted if subordinates observe that managers at all levels live this code in their actions, beliefs and involvement in collective learning.*[17]

Control in the public sector

Public sector organisations have political purposes and are concerned with service to and the well-being of the community. However, in recent years there has been a vigorous policy of privatisation and creating freedom from direct state control and the transfer of business undertakings to private hands. At the same time, there has been increased government pressure to ensure cost-effectiveness, investment by private sector involvement, and efficiency and economy in their operations. The demand for uniformity of treatment and public accountability for their operations results in high levels of statutory controls, legislation and

ministerial guidance. In the case of local government, for example, there is the added consideration of the relationship between elected members and permanent officers.

Despite the apparent relaxation of authority and transfer of power from central government there is evidence that public sector managers are under increasing political pressure. The demand for strategic management in the public sector has resulted in a greater emphasis on performance output measures with indicators of both a qualitative and quantitative nature. *Shovelton* draws attention to the increasing importance of accountability as one of the foundations of public services. Public sector organisations need to demonstrate shareholder value, fair treatment of employees and high environmental standards to a range of stakeholders, and public services face a difficult challenge in providing 'more' or 'better' or 'clearer' accountability.[18] In the case of local government there is also much publicity directed to the accountability of senior management and the effectiveness of control systems, especially, for example, with high-profile social services cases.[19]

Technology and control systems

From a further analysis of the data collected from Woodward's south Essex study of 100 manufacturing firms (discussed in Chapter 15), clear links emerged between the original classification of technology and the above categorisation of managerial control systems (*see* Table 17.1).

Unit and small batch production firms tended to have unitary and mainly personal controls (A1). Process production firms tended to have unitary and mainly impersonal controls (A2). The similarities in some organisational characteristics between unit production firms and process firms identified in Woodward's south Essex study could be explained by the fact that in both groups unitary control systems predominated.

Table 17.1	Relationship between control system and classification of technology			
	Control system A1 (%)	Control system B1 (%)	Control system B2 (%)	Control system A2 (%)
Unit and small batch production	75	25	–	–
Large batch and mass production	15	35	40	10
Process production	–	–	5	95
Total firms	28	21	18	33

Source: Woodward, J. *Industrial Organization: Theory and Practice*, second edition, Oxford University Press (1980), p. xxi. Reproduced with permission from Oxford University Press.

In the case of large batch and mass production firms, those with predominantly personal controls (B1) had similar organisational characteristics to unit firms and those with predominantly mechanical controls (B2) had an organisation structure similar to process firms.

From the analysis, Reeves and Woodward suggest that control systems may be the underlying variable that links organisational behaviour and technology. The classification of control systems they propose might provide a better means of predicting certain facets of organisational behaviour than the classification of technology.[20]

Wilson points out that technology is not just about devices and machines but also about social relations that encourage some form of interaction. Technology is a human, political and social activity. 'The locus of control cannot always be moved from workers to managers during technical change nor from managers to workers. Control ultimately does lie with management, though workers may resist it.'[21]

Information technology

In previous chapters we have referred to the impact of developments in information technology and these developments will also have a significant impact on management control systems. Processes of communication are increasingly linked to computer systems with the rapid transmission of more information to more people including immediate access to other national or international offices. Information technology and office automation are changing the nature of the workplace and the way in which people work. For example, advances in telecommunications have resulted in a significant growth in teleworking, with staff working from home with a computer network, telephone and fax. This has many potential advantages but also raises questions of self-motivation, security and systems of management control.

Nordström and Ridderstråle suggest that with increasing use of IT, control will not disappear but become more indirect. Information systems will be used to increase control by measuring more things, new things at multiple levels, and at a greater frequency than before. To a certain extent this is a substitute for the loss of hierarchy control resulting from the introduction of new structures.[22] Another interesting situation arising from the increasing use of information technology is the legal position on organisations monitoring staff emails and internet usage.[23] A more detailed discussion on technology, work and organisational behaviour is included in Chapter 16.

Critical reflection

'Technology is the ultimate determinant of the design of an effective control system whether for mass production systems, virtual team or remote working, personal surveillance or working from home. There is not less control today, only different forms of control.'

What are your views? How has technology influenced the nature of control over your behaviour at work?

STRATEGIES OF CONTROL IN ORGANISATIONS

Six significant strategies of control in organisations are explained by *Child* (*see* Figure 17.3):

1 personal centralised control;
2 bureaucratic control;
3 output control;
4 control through electronic surveillance;
5 HRM control; and
6 cultural control.[24]

Personal centralised controls

This approach is often found in small owner-managed organisations and is characterised by the centralisation of decision-making and initiative around a leadership figure. Control consists largely of personal inspection to see that decisions are carried out, and the leader may spend a high proportion of time supervising the work personally. Once the organisation grows large enough to employ someone to undertake detailed supervision of everyday tasks, the locus of decision-making and close supervision will tend to become separated. The authority of the leader will usually rest upon the rights of ownership, special personal qualities (charisma) or technical expertise.

Bureaucratic control

This approach to control is familiar in public sector organisations and in many other types of large organisations. It is based on the specification of how members should behave

Figure 17.3	Strategies of organisation control

1 Personal centralised control
 1.1 direct supervision of people's activities
 1.2 centralised decision-taking
 1.3 personal leadership: founded upon ownership rights, charisma, and/or technical expertise
 1.4 reward and punishments reinforcing conformity to personal authority

2 Bureaucratic control
 2.1 breaking down of task into easily definable elements
 2.2 formally specified methods, procedures and rules applied to the conduct of tasks
 2.3 budgetary and standard cost-variance accounting controls
 2.4 technology designed to limit variation in conduct of tasks, with respect to pace, sequence and possibly physical methods*
 2.5 routine decision-taking delegated within prescribed limits
 2.6 reward and punishment systems reinforcing conformity to procedures and rules

3 Output control
 3.1 jobs and units designed with responsibility for complete outputs
 3.2 specification of output standards and targets
 3.3 use of 'responsibility accounting' systems
 3.4 delegation of decisions on operational matters: semi-autonomy
 3.5 reward and punishment linked to attainment of output targets

4 Control through electronic surveillance
 4.1 speed and quality of work recorded and assessed remotely via information and communication technology (ICT)
 4.2 employee's performance assessed against that of other employees and trends
 4.3 such monitoring of performance used to reward and discipline employees

5 HRM control
 5.1 use of selection methods to ensure that new recruits 'fit' the profile of attitude, behaviour, and capabilities desired by management
 5.2 training and development designed to reinforce this desired profile
 5.3 assessment procedures and reward systems used to encourage conformity

6 Cultural control
 6.1 development of employees' personal identification with management goals
 6.2 strong emphasis on the collective and mutually supportive character of the organisation – e.g. analogy with the 'family'
 6.3 employment characterised by security of tenure and progression within the organisation
 6.4 semi-autonomous working: few formal controls

*Some authorities distinguish this as a separate control strategy. For example, Richard Edwards (1979), *Contested Terrain: The Transformation of the Workplace in the Twentieth Century*, New York, Basic Books.

Source: Child, J. *Organization: Contemporary Principles and Practice*, Blackwell Publishing (2005), p. 121. Reproduced with permission from Wiley-Blackwell.

and carry out their work. There is an attempt to ensure predictability through formal job descriptions and procedures, the breaking down of tasks into constituent elements, and the specification of standard methods for the performance of tasks. Reward and punishment systems can be designed to reinforce this control strategy. Compliance can be rewarded by upgrading, improved status, favourable employment benefits and job security. Bureaucratic control will make use of accounting control systems such as budgetary control and standard cost variances. The bureaucratic strategy also permits delegation without loss of control. Managers can delegate routine decision-making within formally prescribed limits of discretion.

Output control

This approach relies upon the ability to identify specific tasks having a measurable output or criterion of overall achievement – for example, an end-product, a part manufactured to agreed standards, batch production or a sub-assembly. Rewards and sanctions can be related to performance levels expressed in output terms. Output control strategy is aimed at facilitating the delegation of operational decision-making without the need for bureaucratic controls or relying on close personal supervision. Once output standards have been agreed, subordinates can work with a 'semi-autonomous' relationship to management, free from detailed control over how tasks are carried out. Output control may be difficult to apply to certain activities, such as the legal department of a business organisation. Although it may be difficult to establish suitable and agreed measures of output, and it may be difficult for management to codify the activities involved, output control may be more appropriate than the application of a bureaucratic control strategy.

Control through electronic surveillance

The essence of control is that the speed and quality of work is recorded and assessed remotely through the use of ICT without reliance on personal supervision. Control data are precise rather than impressionistic and subject to management bias. Monitoring of performance can be used readily as the basis for reward and discipline. Control through electronic surveillance is applied to many types and levels of activity. A common example is call centres although customer service representatives dislike the pressure from this form of control and the objectivity of relying on electronically produced statistics is subject to challenge.

HRM control

HRM procedures can be used both to develop people at work and to control their behaviour and performance. They enhance the contribution to the achievement of organisational goals and objectives. Systematic selection techniques are designed to ensure new recruits fit the profile and technical competencies required by management. Performance evaluation and appraisal provide feedback to both management and employees. Appraisals should provide the basis for reward and for an assessment of the need for further training or development. If training and development programmes are attuned to the needs of employees and the requirements of their jobs this should contribute to better performance.

Cultural control

This approach has been identified with moves away from conventional forms of organisation and is based on maintaining control through internalised compliance rather than external constraint. The basis of cultural control is the acceptance and willing compliance with the requirements of management and belief of the organisation. A major example is the cultural control that tends to be exemplified by larger Japanese corporations, although this is subject to criticism of compulsory sociability. Although a strong corporate culture is intended to provide an alternative to control, in practice strenuous efforts are usually made to ensure employees conform to the culture. Provided members have the necessary skills and ability they can be given wide freedom of action in deciding how to undertake their responsibilities. Cultural control, combined with personal autonomy, has long been associated with the professions. Despite criticisms of cultural control it is in tune with the increasing number of professional and knowledge workers, and is consistent with self-managing units or teams working with only limited formal controls.

CHARACTERISTICS OF AN EFFECTIVE CONTROL SYSTEM

Whatever the nature or form of control there are a number of characteristic features of an effective control system. Control systems can have positive as well as negative effects. It is important therefore that they are designed and implemented in a constructive and rewarding way.

Although they do not readily admit it, most people probably prefer some degree of control over their lives because it gives them some stability and contributes to their general welfare and safety. Nevertheless, the negative connotation of control still exists and is amplified by the ways in which controls have been traditionally set, implemented, and used in formal organizations.

F. Luthans, *Organizational Behavior*[25]

According to *Hicks and Gullett*, 'Control systems should be understandable and economical, be related to decision centres, register variations quickly, be selective, remain flexible and point to corrective action.'[26] Developing the suggestion of Hicks and Gullett, we can identify a number of important characteristics of an effective control system.

- For a control system to be meaningful, **it must be understood by those involved in its operation**. The purpose of the control system and the information it provides must be fully comprehensible to those who have to act on the results. The level of sophistication of a control system should be related to the nature of the activities involved and to the technical competence of the staff. Information must be presented in a suitable form. If information is presented in a way which people do not understand they are likely to disregard it, and the full potential of the control system will not be realised.

- Controls should **conform with the structure of the organisation and be related to decision centres responsible for performance**. Information should be supplied to those managers who have the responsibility for specified areas of activity and who are capable of using this information to evaluate the degree of success in achievement of objectives. The information should enable managers to control their area of responsibility, and should be presented in a form that shows clearly when corrective action is necessary.

- An effective control system should **report deviations from the desired standard of performance as quickly as possible**. Ideally, indications of likely deviations should be discovered before they actually occur. It is important for deviations from the plan to be reported in good time so that corrective action to remedy the situation can be undertaken promptly. For example, information that the budget is likely to be overspent or under-spent should arrive in sufficient time to enable the manager to do something about it and avoid drastic last-minute action.

- The control system should **draw attention to the critical activities important to the success of the organisation**. An unnecessary number of controls over comparatively unimportant activities are uneconomic and time-consuming; they can have a demoralising effect on staff and may possibly result in lack of attention to the key control points. Certain control points are more important than others. Careful control must be maintained in key result areas and in those activities that are crucial to the success of the organisation. For example, a restaurant manager would need to have information on the number of orders taken at different times, and the number and type of meals provided, in order to deploy staff in the most effective manner.

- To be effective, **a control system must be flexible**. It must yield information that is not influenced by changes in other factors unconnected to the purpose of the control system. For example, a control system established five years ago, which specifies that reports to top management should be made whenever expenditure exceeds the budget by more than £x, is unlikely to be effective if no account has been taken of the effects of inflation. Also, if the same amount is applied in all cases, high-spending departments may be subject to excessive control and low-spending departments not monitored closely enough.

- The control system should be **consistent with the objective of the activity to which it relates**. In addition to locating deviations from the planned standard of performance, the control system should be sophisticated enough to indicate ways in which performance can be improved. For example, in the field of social services it may not be sufficient just to know that expenditure has been kept within the budget. It would be more helpful to know in what areas expenditure has been incurred. It might be that the highest share of

expenditure has gone to those who may be more knowledgeable of their rights and the procedures involved, than those who may arguably be in greater financial need. The control system should therefore address itself to causes of deviations rather than to symptoms.

- Controls may point to a number of possible problem areas for corrective action. Management will need to investigate these possibilities and **determine the most appropriate form of corrective action** to deal with the causes of the deviation and solve the problems identified.
- Control systems should themselves **be subject to a continual review** to ensure they are effective and appropriate in terms of the results they produce. They should not be too costly or elaborate, but should satisfy the characteristic features suggested above.

POWER AND MANAGEMENT CONTROL

Work organisations are not only systems of hierarchical structure, they are also systems of intricate social relationships, status and power. **Power** is a complex and dynamic concept and difficult to define easily. **At a broad level, power can be interpreted in terms of control or influence over the behaviour of other people with or without their consent.** Sometimes power is interpreted in terms of the *extent* of the influence which can actually be exercised over other people, and sometimes it is taken to include influence over objects or things as well as people. In exploring the nature of organising work, *Knights and Willmott* suggest that 'Power is often associated with coercive and repressive features of social life. It is the means through which a ruling class, political elite or managerial group controls subordinate strata within a society or an organisation.'[27]

Robbins and Judge suggests that as power may exist but not be used it implies a potential that need not be actualised to be effective. Power is therefore a capacity or a potential. The most important aspect of power is probably dependency. 'A person can have power over you only if he or she controls something you desire.'[28]

Power is an inherent feature of work organisations and is often the underlying reality behind the decision-making process. It is central to the framework of order and system of command through which the work and activities of the organisation are carried out, for example through the operation of bureaucratic structures and the implementation of policies, rules and procedures. Lack of power and influence, and office politics, are among the main sources of managerial stress within organisations. The view of power as of functional importance is in keeping with a unitary approach to organisation. Management control is the predominant means by which the activities of staff are guided towards the achievement of organisational goals. The exercise of power is that which comes from a position of formal authority within the management structure of the organisation and which legitimises control over subordinate staff.

Power, involvement and compliance

From a comparative analysis of complex organisations, *Etzioni* provides a classification of organisational relationships based on structures of control and the use of power resources as a means of ensuring compliance among members.[29] The Etzioni typology involves three dimensions: power, involvement, and the identification of kinds of power with kinds of involvement. **Compliance** is the relationship between the kinds of power applied by the organisation to control its members and the kinds of involvement developed by members of the organisation.

Power differs according to the means by which members of the organisation comply.

- **Coercive power** relies on the use of threats, or physical sanctions or force, for example, controlling the need for food or comfort.
- **Remunerative power** involves the manipulation of material resources and rewards, for example, through salaries and wages.
- **Normative power** relies on the allocation and the manipulation of symbolic rewards, for example, esteem and prestige.

Involvement is the degree of commitment by members to the organisation.

■ **Alienative involvement** occurs where members are involved against their wishes. There is a strong negative orientation towards the organisation.
■ **Calculative involvement** occurs where attachment to the organisation is motivated by extrinsic rewards. There is either a negative orientation or a low positive orientation towards the organisation.
■ **Moral involvement** is based on the individual's belief in, and value placed on, the goals of the organisation. There is high positive orientation towards the organisation.

Matching power with involvement

When considered together, nine logical types of organisational relationships and compliance result from this typology (*see* Figure 17.4). Based on this analysis, Etzioni suggests that a particular kind of power usually goes with a particular kind of involvement:

■ coercive power with alienative involvement – relationship 1 (typified, for example, by prisons);
■ remunerative power with calculative involvement – relationship 5 (typified, for example, by business firms);
■ normative power with moral involvement – relationship 9 (typified, for example, by churches).

The matching of these kinds of power and involvement is congruent with each other and represents the most common form of compliance in organisations. The other six types of organisational relationships are incongruent. Etzioni suggests that organisations with congruent compliance structures will be more effective than organisations with incongruent structures.

Figure 17.4 | **Organisational relationships and compliance**

PERSPECTIVES OF ORGANISATIONAL POWER

There are many potential sources of power which enable members of an organisation to further their own interests and which provide a means of resolving conflicts. Sources of organisational power include, for example, structure, formal authority, rules and regulations, standing orders, control of the decision-making process, control of resources and technology, control of information or knowledge, trade unions and staff organisations, age coupled with experience, gender and the informal organisation.

Gender and power

You may recall the suggestion of the sex power differential as part of the evaluation of the Hawthorne experiments, discussed in Chapter 2.

An example of gender and power is given by the Equality and Human Rights Commission who report on a survey on women in positions of power and influence. The survey found a glaring example of the lack of women in senior positions of power, including those in the civil service, top management, senior positions in the judiciary, directors of FTSE companies, Members of Parliament, and senior appointments in local authorities, the armed forces and the police force.

> *Britain cannot as an economy afford to go on asking people to fit their families around the demands of ever-more intense '24/7' global competition, and marginalizing or rejecting workers who fail to fit into traditional and inflexible working arrangements. Only when we get this right will we see women as well as men making it into positions of real power and influence.*[30]

Different levels of power

Power can also be viewed in terms of the different levels at which it is constituted. *Fincham* looks at organisational power in terms of three types or levels of analysis: processual, institutional and organisational.[31]

- At the **processual level** power originates in the process of daily interaction. The level of analysis is that of lateral relations between management interest groups and the basis of explanation is strategic. Processual power focuses on the 'micro-politics' of organisational life. It stresses power as negotiation and bargaining, and the 'enactment' of rules and how resources are employed in the power game.
- At the **institutional level** managerial power is seen as resting on external social and economic structures that create beliefs about the inevitability of managerial authority. Power is explained as being 'mandated' to the organisation. When managers seek to exercise power they can draw on a set of institutionally produced rules such as cultural beliefs about the right to manage.
- The **organisational level** stresses the organisation's own power system and the hierarchy as a means of reproducing power. Dominant beliefs, values and knowledge shape organisational priorities and solutions or reflect the interests of particular groups or functions. Those in authority select others to sustain the existing power structure. Organisational hierarchies transmit power between the institutional interests and the rules and resources governing action.

Organisational sources of power

Pfeffer has identified a number of critical ways in which individuals or groups may acquire power in organisations when viewed as social entities:

- **providing resources** – for example money, prestige, legitimacy, rewards and sanctions, and expertise that create a dependency on the part of other people;
- **coping with uncertainty** – the ability to permit the rationalisation of organisational activity, for example through standard operating procedures, or to reduce uncertainty or unpredictability;
- **being irreplaceable** – having exclusive training, knowledge or expertise that cannot readily be acquired by others, or through the use of or lack of adequate documentation or specialised language and symbols;
- **affecting decision processes** – the ability to affect some part of the decision process, for example by the basic values and objectives used in making the decision, or by controlling alternative choices;
- **by consensus** – the extent to which individuals share a common perspective, set of values or definition of the situation, or consensus concerning knowledge and technology.[32]

PLURALISTIC APPROACHES TO POWER

In Chapter 10 we discussed a classification by *French and Raven* of social power based on a broader perception of leadership influence.[32] French and Raven identified five main sources of power:

- reward power;
- coercive power;
- legitimate power;
- referent power;
- expert power.

Power, however, arises not only from sources of structure or formal position within the organisation but from interpersonal sources such as the personality, characteristics and talents of individual members of the organisation. For example, in Chapter 10 we also discussed charisma, or personal power, as a feature of transformational leadership. We can also distinguish between **legitimate (organisational) power**, which derives from a person's position within the formal structure of the organisation and the managerial hierarchy of command, and **personal (informal) power**, which derives from the individual and is in the eye of the beholders who believe that person has the ability to influence other people or events and to make things happen.

The exercise of power is, then, a social process that derives from a multiplicity of sources and situations.[34] This suggests a more pluralistic approach and recognises power as a major organisational variable. Many different groups and individuals have the ability to influence the behaviour and actions of other people, and in a number of different ways. This is not a new concept, however. In the 1920s the renowned management writer Mary Parker Follett focused on a human behaviour aspect, rejected the notion of domination and the exercise of power over other people, and argued for developing power with others in the organisation to make things happen. Effective control over work processes and social relationships would be achieved through group power and co-operative management. Follett advocated the replacement of personal power with the authority of task or function, and successful management based on the 'law of the situation'.[35]

Network of social relationships

Organisations function on the basis of networks of interdependent activities. Certain jobs or work relationships enable people to exercise a level of power in excess of their formal position within the structure of the organisation. A classic example is someone, perhaps a personal assistant or office manager, who fulfils the role of gatekeeper to the boss. There is an inherent danger with this type of role relationship that the boss may become too dependent upon the gatekeeper. Undertaking the responsibilities delegated by the boss and maintaining control can lead to the gatekeeper's misuse of their role and to an abuse of power. Another example is with information technology problems where comparatively junior members of staff with particular technical expertise may have a way of ignoring the normal chain of command.

Many people within organisations also have the ability to grant or withhold 'favours' within the formal or the informal interpretation of their job role – for example, secretaries, caretakers, security staff and telephonists. Staff may exercise negative power – that is, 'the capacity to stop things happening, to delay them, to distort or disrupt them'.[36] A common example could be the secretary who screens and intercepts messages to the boss, delays arranging appointments and filters mail. Negative power is not necessarily related proportionately to position and may often be exercised easily by people at lower levels of the hierarchical structure.

Another example is given by *Green* who refers to the negative power that can be held by comparatively junior staff. The person who sorts and distributes the incoming mail has

the opportunity to use negative power by the delay or disruption of items for reasons that may be entirely personal.[37] A reality of organisational life is the vagaries of social relationships including office politics, and also the grapevine and gossip. Although it is a difficult topic to pin down, *Mann* refers to the key role that gossip plays in power relationships and knowledge production in organisations and maintains that 'There is an undeniable relationship between knowledge and power which lies at the root of gossiping.'[38]

Motivational need for power and control

Power can be a positive source of motivation for some people (see the discussion on achievement motivation in Chapter 7). There is often a fine line between the motivation to achieve personal dominance and the use of social power. It has to be acknowledged, however, that there are clearly some managers who positively strive for and enjoy the exercise of power over other people. They seek to maintain absolute control over subordinates and the activities of their department/section, and welcome the feeling of being indispensable. The possession of power is an ultimate ego satisfaction and such managers do not seem unduly concerned if as a result they are unpopular with, or lack the respect of, their colleagues or subordinate staff.

Kirwan-Taylor discusses control freaks who exist in every office and are capable of making everyone's life a misery. Control freaks try to dominate the environment by establishing order on what they perceive as chaos and attempting to control how other people think and behave. At one end of the spectrum are motivated and organised employees and at the other end obsessional, temperamental bullies. Sometimes, however, being a control freak is considered a positive attribute and key to success. Although control freaks function to a high standard, few people can bear to work with them.[39]

Critical reflection

'It is a very poor manager who relies on the exercise of formal power, position within the organisation structure, and rules and procedures. A high level of control is self-defeating as it is likely to produce a negative response, increase internal conflict and restrict the freedom and initiative of the individual.'

What do you think? How would you prepare a counter argument?

THE BALANCE BETWEEN ORDER AND FLEXIBILITY

Stewart refers to the classic dilemma that underlies the nature of control: finding the right balance for present conditions between order and flexibility. This involves the trade-off between trying to improve predictability of people's actions against the desirability of encouraging individual and local responsiveness to changing situations. The organisation may need a 'tight–loose' structure with certain departments or areas of work closely controlled ('tight') while other departments or areas of work should be left fluid and flexible ('loose').[40]

Three main forms of control

According to Stewart, 'control can – and should – be exercised in different ways'. She identifies three main forms of control:

- **Direct control by orders, direct supervision and rules and regulations**. Direct controls may be necessary, and more readily acceptable, in a crisis situation and during training. But in organisations where people expect to participate in decision-making, such forms of control may be unacceptable. Rules and regulations which are not accepted as reasonable,

or at least not unreasonable, will offer some people a challenge to use their ingenuity in finding ways round them.

- **Control through standardisation and specialisation**. This is achieved through clear definition of the inputs to a job, the methods to be used and the required outputs. Such bureaucratic control makes clear the parameters within which one can act and paradoxically makes decentralisation easier. Provided the parameters are not unduly restrictive they can increase the sense of freedom. For example, within clearly defined limits which ensure that one retail chain store looks like another, individual managers may have freedom to do the job as they wish.

- **Control through influencing the way that people think about what they should do**. This is often the most effective method of exercising control. It may be achieved through selective recruitment of people who seem likely to share a similar approach, through the training and socialisation of people into thinking the organisation's way, and through peer pressure. Where an organisation has a very strong culture, people who do not fit in, or learn to adapt, are likely to be pushed out, even though they may appear to leave of their own volition.

Stewart also refers to a second, related dilemma of finding the appropriate balance between centralisation, as a means of exercising control, and decentralisation. (Centralisation and decentralisation were discussed in Chapter 14.)

BEHAVIOURAL FACTORS IN CONTROL SYSTEMS

We have seen that control systems can help fulfil people's needs at work and their presence may be welcomed by some members of staff. Often, however, control systems are perceived as a threat to the need satisfaction of the individual. Control over behaviour is resented and there is a dislike of those responsible for the operation of the control system. **Control systems provide an interface between human behaviour and the process of management.**

> *The broad objective of the control function is to effectively employ all the resources committed to an organization's operations. However, the fact that non-human resources depend on human effort for their utilization makes control, in the final analysis, the regulation of human performance.*
> C. Reeser and M. Loper, *Management: The Key to Organizational Effectiveness*[41]

Control often provokes an emotional response from those affected by it. It should be recognised, therefore, that the activities of a management control system raise important considerations of the human factor and of the management of people. The effectiveness of management control systems will depend upon both their design and operation, and the attitudes of staff and the way they respond to them. The manner in which control is exercised and the perception of staff will have a significant effect on the level of organisational performance.

Overcoming resistance to management control

Even when control systems are well designed and operated there is often strong resistance, and attempted non-compliance, from those affected by them. Control systems are bound to be viewed with a certain amount of suspicion and possible resentment by members of staff. Therefore, if they are to be successful in leading to improved performance and organisational effectiveness, they require attention to factors that influence human behaviour.

No form of control is absolute and organisations can achieve their objectives only through the efforts of their members. There are a number of factors, discussed in other chapters, that can affect the successful implementation of management control systems, including the following.

- **Consultation and participation**. If staff are committed personally to particular objectives they are more likely to direct themselves and to exercise self-control over their level of performance. Staff should understand, and accept, the purpose and nature of control systems.
- **Motivation**. People are influenced by the expected results of their actions. Motivation is a function of the relationship between effort expended and perceived level of performance, and the expectation that reward will be related to performance. Recognition given for a satisfactory level of attainment coupled with a suitable reward system, as integral parts of control, can do much to motivate staff and encourage improved performance.
- **Organisation structure**. The structure of an organisation and its pattern of management can affect the implementation of control systems. Organisations with a mechanistic structure are more readily suited to the operation and implementation of traditional systems of control. In organic structures the effectiveness of control is more dependent upon individual involvement and commitment to the aims of the organisation. Traditional systems of control are therefore less suited to organisations with an organic structure.
- **Groups and the informal organisation**. Membership of a harmonious and effective work group can be a source of motivation and job satisfaction. Socialisation can help create a feeling of commitment to the group and reduce the need for formal management control. With the development of autonomous work groups, members have greater freedom and wider discretion over the planning, execution and control of their own work. Informal group 'norms' and peer pressure can be one of the most powerful forms of control. In order to maintain co-operation and commitment of staff the manager must continually review at both the individual and group level the operation of the control system and the progress made in achieving objectives.
- **Leadership style and systems of management**. The style of managerial leadership is a function of the manager's attitudes towards people, and assumptions about human nature and behaviour – for example McGregor's Theory X and Theory Y. The central principle of Theory X is direction and control through a centralised system of organisation and the exercise of authority. By contrast, Theory Y is based on the principle of the integration of individual and organisational goals, and the exercise of self-direction and self-control in the service of objectives to which they are committed. The character of control processes is one of the organisational variables identified in Likert's four-fold model of management systems. In System 1 (exploitive authoritative) the major concern with performance of the control function is at the top hierarchical level in the organisation and concentrated in top management. In System 4 (participative group) concern for performance of control functions is spread throughout the organisation, review and control functions are carried out at all levels, and the formal and informal organisation share the same goals.

FINANCIAL AND ACCOUNTING SYSTEMS OF CONTROL

Management control systems are frequently thought of in terms of financial and accounting systems. The reasons for this are easy to understand.

- The stewardship of financial resources is of vital concern to the majority of organisations. In both private enterprise and public sector organisations there is an increasing need to demonstrate value for money expended. Control systems are often geared to highlight easily identifiable performance of sales, costs and profits.
- Organisational aims, objectives and targets are often expressed in financial terms and measured in terms of profitability. Results are measured and reported in financial terms.
- Money is quantifiable and is a precise unit of measurement. It is easily understood, and is often used as a common denominator and as a basis for comparison.
- Financial limits are easy to apply as a measure of control and easy to relate to. For example, the need for control is an integral part of the process of delegation or empowerment. This

control may easily be applied where, for example, a manager gives a subordinate the authority, without prior reference, to incur expenditure on certain items up to a given financial cost limit.

It is understandable, therefore, that so much attention is given to financial and accounting systems of measurement and control. Managers rely on accurate information systems as a basis of control and this information is frequently expressed in financial terms. However, accounting statements focus on only a limited area of activity. 'Thanks to the need for objectivity, everything in accounting statements is inward looking, concentrating on costs and based on the concept of capital maintenance.'[42]

Strategic control and financial control

Management control, however, embraces far more than just financial or accounting considerations. It is concerned with the whole process of management: with the extent to which organisational aims are achieved and with improvement in performance. Control includes considerations of such factors as production, inventory, quality, judgement, consumer satisfaction, market share, social responsibilities and the human factor and management of people. For example, *Goldsmith and Clutterbuck* point out that high-performance companies keep their operating businesses in line with a mixture of both strategic and financial control. Most high-performance companies give strategic control equal or near-equal priority to financial control.[43]

Design and application of systems

In their discussion of the role of accounting systems in organisational control, it is interesting to note the words of *Berry, Broadbent and Otley*:

> Accounting systems provide a fundamental way of handling high levels of complexity by the imposition of a set of standard operating procedures; this provides a major strength of accounting as a control system. However, weaknesses also stem from the imposition of standard systems in complex situations because inventive human minds find ways of reporting desired results through the manipulation of the system rather than by behaving in expected ways.[44]

This wording appears to imply that the accounting system is the arbiter of correct behaviour and that people are to 'blame' for their failure to act in the way imposed by accounting systems (and presumably by the accountants who designed them).

Budgetary control and human behaviour

Accounting control systems such as internal audit, management by exception and budgetary control tend to operate in a negative way and to report only on the unfavourable, or on favourable variances which may have adverse consequences, for example less spent than budgeted. 'Success' for the accounting staff may be equated with the 'failure' of other staff. As a result there is no specific recognition from management. There is only a limited sense of achievement or self-esteem for favourable performance or where no corrective action is required. There is little, if any, positive motivation.

As *Hannagan* points out, budgeting involves participation of managers and workforce representatives, and by its nature is the responsibility of people.

> Budgeting by its nature necessitates the authorisation and delegation of budget activities between individual managers and other personnel. This principle is known as 'control by responsibility' – it makes an individual responsible for the whole or part of a particular budget. It is designed so that the targets set can be achieved – if the machine groups achieve their targets the production department concerned achieves its target, and so on.[45]

There is, of course, nothing wrong with the use of accounting systems of control such as internal auditing, management by exception and budgetary control. What needs to be

considered is the manner in which these controls and techniques are applied and the differences in use as a result of the attitudes adopted and the motives felt to be important. Control systems can have positive as well as negative effects. Financial and accounting control systems, as with other forms of control, should be designed and implemented in a constructive and rewarding way. To do this, they must take account of individual, social and organisational factors that determine people's patterns of behaviour.

THE CONCEPT OF EMPOWERMENT

Discussion on the balance between order and flexibility, and control versus autonomy, draws attention to the importance of empowerment. Despite the general movement towards less mechanistic structures and the role of managers as facilitators, there appears to be some reluctance especially among top managers to dilute or weaken hierarchical control. A study of major UK businesses suggests that there are mixed reactions to the new wave of management thinking. While the prospect of empowerment can hold attractions for the individual employee, many managers are keen to maintain control over the destiny, roles and responsibilities of others. Beneath the trappings of the facilitate-and-empower philosophy the command-and-control system often lives on.[46] However, in a discussion on modern leadership and management, *Gretton* makes the point that 'Today's leaders understand that you have to give up control to get results. That's what all the talk of empowerment is about.'[47]

The meaning of empowerment

Empowerment is generally explained in terms of allowing employees greater freedom, autonomy and self-control over their work, and responsibility for decision-making. However, there are differences in the meaning and interpretation of the term. *Wilkinson* refers to problems with the existing prescriptive literature on empowerment. The term 'empowerment' can be seen as flexible and even elastic, and has been used very loosely by both practitioners and academics. Wilkinson suggests that it is important to see empowerment in a wider context. It needs to be recognised that it has different forms and should be analysed in the context of broader organisational practice.[48]

The concept of empowerment also gives rise to a number of questions and doubts. For example, how does it differ in any meaningful way from other earlier forms of employee involvement? Is the primary concern of empowerment getting the most out of the workforce? Is empowerment just another somewhat more fanciful term for delegation? Some writers see the two as quite separate concepts while other writers suggest empowerment is a more proactive form of delegation.

According to *Mills and Friesen*, 'Empowerment can be succinctly defined as the authority of subordinates to decide and act.'

> It describes a management style. The term is often confused with delegation but, if strictly defined, empowerment goes much further in granting subordinates authority to decide and act. Indeed, within a context of broad limits defined by executives, empowered individuals may even become self-managing.[49]

Empowerment and delegation

Attempting to distinguish clearly between empowerment and delegation is not easy. However, there appears to be general agreement that empowerment describes a management style and the granting of genuine additional power to other members of staff. Empowerment is viewed as the more embracing process. Arguably, it is the process of empowerment that gives rise to the act of delegation. According to *Tulgan*, for example, 'The key to empowerment is effective delegation; giving individual contributors ownership of tangible results.'[50]

At the individual (or personal) level, **delegation** is the process of entrusting authority and responsibility to others throughout the various levels of the organisation. It is the

authorisation to undertake activities that would otherwise be carried out by someone in a more senior position. Downsizing and de-layering have arguably limited the opportunities for delegation, although this may be offset by demands for greater flexibility and empowerment. In any event, delegation is still an essential process of management. As *Crainer* points out, in the age of empowerment, the ability to delegate effectively is critical.

> *Delegation has always been recognised as a key ingredient of successful management and leadership. But, in the 1980s delegation underwent a crisis of confidence . . . The 1990s saw a shift in attitudes. No longer was delegation an occasional managerial indulgence. Instead it became a necessity. This has continued to be the case.*[51]

Extreme forms of behaviour

The concept of delegation may appear to be straightforward. However, anyone with experience of a work situation is likely to be aware of the importance of delegation and the consequences of badly managed delegation. Successful delegation is a social skill. Where managers lack this skill, or do not have a sufficient awareness of people-perception, there are two extreme forms of behaviour that can result.

- At one extreme is the almost total lack of meaningful delegation. Subordinate staff are only permitted to operate within closely defined and often routine areas of work, with detailed supervision. Staff are treated as if they are incapable of thinking for themselves and given little or no opportunity to exercise initiative or responsibility.
- At the other extreme there can be an excessive zeal for so-called delegation when a manager leaves subordinates to their own resources, often with only minimal guidance or training, and expects them to take the consequences for their own actions or decisions. These 'super-delegators' misuse the practice of delegation and are often like the Artful Dodger, and somehow contrive not to be around when difficult situations arise. Such a form of behaviour is not delegation; it is an abdication of the manager's responsibility.

Either of these two extreme forms of behaviour can be frustrating and potentially stressful for subordinate staff, and unlikely to lead to improved organisational effectiveness. The nature of delegation can have a significant effect on the morale, motivation and work performance of staff. In all but the smallest organisation the only way to get work done effectively is through delegation, but even such an important practice as delegation can be misused or over-applied.

THE MANAGER–SUBORDINATE RELATIONSHIP

Delegation is not just the arbitrary shedding of work. It is not just the issuing and following of orders or carrying out of specified tasks in accordance with detailed instructions. Within the formal structure of the organisation, delegation creates a special manager–subordinate relationship. It is founded on the concept of:

- authority;
- responsibility; and
- accountability (ultimate responsibility).

> *Delegation means the conferring of a specified authority by a higher authority. In its essence it involves a dual responsibility. The one to whom authority is delegated becomes responsible to the superior for doing the job, but the superior remains responsible for getting the job done. This principle of delegation is the centre of all processes in formal organization.*
>
> J. D. Mooney, *The Principles of Organization*[52]

- **Authority** is the right to take action or make decisions that the manager would otherwise have done. Authority legitimises the exercise of empowerment within the structure and

rules of the organisation. It enables the subordinate to issue valid instructions for others to follow.

- **Responsibility** involves an obligation by the subordinate to perform certain duties or make certain decisions and having to accept possible reprimand from the manager for unsatisfactory performance. The meaning of the term 'responsibility' is, however, subject to possible confusion: although delegation embraces both authority and responsibility, effective delegation is not abdication of responsibility.
- **Accountability** is interpreted as meaning ultimate responsibility and cannot be delegated. Managers have to accept 'responsibility' for the control of their staff, for the performance of all duties allocated to their department/section within the structure of the organisation, and for the standard of results achieved. That is, 'the buck stops here'.

The manager is in turn responsible to higher management. This is the essence of the nature of the 'dual responsibility' of delegation. The manager is answerable to a superior and cannot shift responsibility back to subordinates. The responsibility of the superior for the acts of subordinates is absolute.[53] In order to help clarify the significance of 'dual responsibility' in delegation, it might be better expressed as:

The subordinate is responsible to the manager for doing the job, while the manager is responsible for seeing that the job gets done. The manager is accountable to a superior for the actions of subordinates.

Authority commensurate with responsibility

Delegation, therefore, embraces both authority and responsibility. It is not practical to delegate one without the other (*see* Figure 17.5). Responsibility must be supported by authority and by the power to influence the areas of performance for which the subordinate is to be held responsible. Authority can be delegated readily, but many problems of delegation stem from failure to delegate sufficient authority to enable subordinates to fulfil their responsibilities. For example, if a section head is held responsible to a departmental manager for the performance of junior staff but is not empowered (given authority) to influence their selection and appointment, their motivation, the allocation of their duties, their training and development, or their sanctions and rewards, then the section leader can hardly be

| Figure 17.5 | The basis of delegation |

held responsible for unsatisfactory performance of the junior staff. To hold subordinates responsible for certain areas of performance without also conferring on them the necessary authority within the structure of the organisation to take action and make decisions within the limits of that responsibility is an abuse of delegation.

The manager should accept the blame as the person **accountable** for the performance of the department/section, and obligated to see that the task was completed satisfactorily. It is necessary to maintain the organisational hierarchy and structure of command. Managers should protect and support subordinate staff and accept, personally, any reprimand for unsatisfactory performance. It is then up to managers to sort out things in their own department/section, to counsel members of staff concerned and to review their system of delegation.

Critical reflection

'The idea of empowerment and helping people accept a feeling of ownership and personal responsibility for their actions and to exercise a high level of self-control is all right in theory. But as I am held accountable for the performance of staff in my department and have to accept any adverse consequences of their behaviour it is only right that I should exercise close control and supervision over them.'

What is your point of view?

BENEFITS OF DELEGATION

It is a principle of delegation that decisions should be made at the lowest level in the organisation compatible with efficiency. It is a question of opportunity cost. If decisions are made at a higher level than necessary they are being made at greater cost than necessary. Delegation is therefore a matter of sound economics as well as good organisation. Properly handled, delegation offers many potential benefits to both managers and staff. Delegation should lead to the optimum use of human resources and improved organisational performance. Studies of successful organisations lend support to the advantages to be gained from effective delegation.[54]

Best use of time

Time is one of the most valuable, but limited, resources and it is important that the manager utilises time to the maximum advantage. Delegation leaves the manager free to make profitable use of time, to concentrate on the more important tasks and to spend more time in managing and less in doing. This should enable the manager to be more accessible for consultation and improve the process of communications.

Training and development

Delegation provides a means of training and development, and of testing the subordinate's suitability for promotion. It can be used as a means of assessing the likely performance of a subordinate at a higher level of authority and responsibility. Delegation thereby helps to avoid the 'Peter Principle' – that is, 'in a hierarchy every employee tends to rise to his level of incompetence' (discussed in Chapter 1). If managers have trained competent subordinates this will not only aid organisational progress but should also enhance their own prospects for further advancement.

Strength of the workforce

Delegation should lead to an improvement in the strength of the workforce. It should give subordinates greater scope for action and opportunities to develop their aptitudes and

abilities. Delegation is a form of participation and can lead to improved morale by increasing motivation and job satisfaction. If empowerment focuses attention on 'motivators' or 'growth' factors it can help satisfy the employee's higher-level needs. Delegation creates a climate in which subordinates can become more involved in the planning and decision-making processes of the organisation.

REASONS FOR LACK OF DELEGATION

With so many good reasons for delegation, why is it that managers often fail to delegate or do not delegate successfully? Delegation is influenced by the manager's perception of subordinate staff. It is also influenced by the subordinate's perception of the manager's reasons for delegation. Failure to delegate often results from the manager's fear.

- The manager may fear that the subordinate is not capable of doing a sufficiently good job. Also, the manager may fear being blamed for the subordinate's mistakes.
- Conversely, the manager may fear that the subordinate will do too good a job and show the manager in a bad light.

The manager should, of course, remember that the task of management is to get work done through the efforts of other people. If the subordinate does a particularly good job this should reflect favourably on the manager.

Assumptions about human nature

A reluctance to delegate might arise from the manager's belief in, and set of assumptions about, human nature and behaviour (discussed in Chapter 12).[55] The Theory X manager believes that people have an inherent dislike of work, wish to avoid responsibility, and must be coerced, controlled, directed and threatened with punishment in order to achieve results. Such a manager is likely, therefore, to be interested in only limited schemes of delegation, within clearly defined limits and with an easy system of reward and punishment.

The Theory Y manager believes that people find work a natural and rewarding activity, they learn to accept and to seek responsibility, and they will respond positively to opportunities for personal growth and to sympathetic leadership. Such a manager is more likely to be interested in wider schemes of delegation based on consultation with subordinates, and with responsibility willingly accepted out of personal commitment.

Trust and empowerment

An essential ingredient of effective management is the ability to put your trust in others and to let go some of the workload. Empowerment is also a matter of confidence and trust – both in subordinates and the manager's own performance and system of delegation. In allowing freedom of action to subordinates within agreed terms of reference and the limits of authority, managers must accept that subordinates may undertake delegated activities in a different manner from themselves. This is at the basis of the true nature of trust. However, learning to put trust in other people is one of the most difficult aspects of successful delegation for many managers, and some never learn it.

As *Stewart* points out, managers who think about what can be done only in terms of what they can do, cannot be effective. Managing is not a solo activity.

> *Managers must learn to accept their dependence upon people. A key part of being a good manager is managing that dependence. Managers who say that they cannot delegate because they have poor staff may genuinely be unfortunate in the calibre of the staff that they have inherited or been given. More often this view is a criticism of themselves: a criticism either of their unwillingness to delegate when they could and should do so, or a criticism of their selection, training and development of their staff.*[56]

The process of empowerment entails the removal of constraints and the granting of autonomy for independent actions. As part of her discussion on the democratic enterprise, *Gratton* refers to the importance of trust and power.

> The re-appropriation of choice from senior members of the organization to individuals themselves implies trust on both parts, but particularly on the part of senior members. It is they who have to cede power to individual employees and to trust them to behave in an autonomous manner and make decisions and take action that serve their personal good and the good of the organization. Democracy implies the giving of authority to individuals to make choices within the context of obligations and accountabilities. Authority, obligations and accountability are deeply bound up with trust. Trust without accountability and obligation is likely to become one-sided, that is, to slide into dependence. Accountability without trust is impossible because it would mean the continual scrutiny of the motives and actions of individuals.[57]

According to *Watson*, there has been a growing trend of questioning the extent to which social science study of work behaviour and managerial practice has been sufficiently critical.

> The crux of the problem that all writers and researchers interested in managerial issues have to face up to is the fact that managerial activities are always and inevitably implicated in issues of power and relative advantage and disadvantage between human groups and human individuals . . . Helping make work organisations more efficient or more effective is not a politically neutral matter.[58]

THE ART OF DELEGATION

Empowering other people is a matter of judgement and involves the question of discretion. Delegation is not an easy task. It involves behavioural as well as organisational and economic considerations, and it is subject to a number of possible abuses. Effective delegation is a social skill. It requires a clear understanding of people-perception, reliance on other people, confidence and trust, and courage. It is important that the manager knows what to delegate, when and to whom. Matters of policy and disciplinary power, for example, usually rest with the manager and cannot legitimately be delegated.

Training and learning experience

Delegation involves subordinates making decisions. For example, as *Guirdham* points out: 'A strict separation of manager and subordinate roles sends the message to workers that they are only responsible for what they are specifically told to do. Managers who neglect to, or cannot, delegate are failing to develop the human resources for which they have responsibility.'[59]

Mistakes will inevitably occur and the subordinate will need to be supported by the manager, and protected against unwarranted criticism. The acceptance of ultimate responsibility highlights the educational aspect of the manager's job. The manager should view mistakes as part of the subordinate's training and learning experience, and an opportunity for further development. 'Even if mistakes occur, good managers are judged as much by their ability to manage them as by their successes.'[60]

Individual characteristics

Notwithstanding any other consideration, the extent and nature of delegation will ultimately be affected by the nature of individual characteristics. The ages, ability, training, attitude, motivation and character of the subordinates concerned will, in practice, be major determinants of delegation. An example is where a strong and forceful personality overcomes the lack of formal delegation; or where an inadequate manager is supported by a more competent subordinate who effectively acts as the manager. Failure to delegate successfully to a more knowledgeable subordinate may mean that the subordinate emerges as an informal leader and this could have possible adverse consequences for the manager, and for the organisation. Another example, and potential difficulty, is when a manager is persuaded

to delegate increased responsibility to persons in a staff relationship who may have little authority in their own right but are anxious to enhance their power within the organisation.

The need for control

Authority, responsibility and accountability must be kept in parity throughout the organisation. This is essential in order to maintain effective co-ordination and control, and to maintain the chain of command. The manager must remain in control. The manager must be on the lookout for subordinates who are more concerned with personal empire building than with meeting stated organisational objectives and prevent a strong personality exceeding the limits of formal delegation. We have said that delegation creates a special manager–subordinate relationship and this involves both the giving of trust and the retention of control. Control is, therefore, an integral part of the system of delegation. However, control should not be so close as to inhibit the effective operation or benefits of delegation. It is a question of balance.

A SYSTEMATIC APPROACH TO EMPOWERMENT AND DELEGATION

In order to realise the full benefits of empowerment and delegation without loss of control, it is necessary to adopt a planned and systematic approach. Setting up a successful system of delegation involves the manager examining four basic questions.

- What tasks could be performed better by other staff?
- What opportunities are there for staff to learn and develop by undertaking delegated tasks and responsibilities?
- How should the increased responsibilities be implemented and to whom should they be given?
- What forms of monitoring control system would be most appropriate?

In order to set up an effective system of delegation, subordinates should know exactly what is expected of them, what has to be achieved, the boundaries within which they have freedom of action, and how far they can exercise independent decision-making. It is possible to identify six main stages in a planned and systematic approach to delegation (*see* Figure 17.6).

- **Clarification of objectives and suitable patterns of organisation.** Policies and procedures must be established and defined in order to provide a framework for the exercise of authority and the acceptance of responsibility.
- **Agreement on terms of reference and acceptance of authority and responsibility.** The manager can then negotiate and agree the subordinate's role prescription and terms of reference. Those areas of work in which the subordinate is responsible for achieving results should be identified clearly. Emphasis should generally be placed on end-results rather than a set of detailed instructions.
- **Guidance, support and training, and patterns of communication.** When subordinates have agreed and accepted the delegation, they should be properly briefed, given guidance and support and any necessary training. They should be advised where, and to whom, they could go for further advice or help.
- **Effective monitoring and review procedures.** The manager should agree time limits for delegation (such as a target date for completion of a specific task or a specified time period). It is necessary to agree the level and nature of supervision, and to establish a system to monitor progress and provide feedback. **Delegation is not an irrevocable act; it can always be withdrawn.** It is also important to make clear expected levels of achievement and agree on performance standards (wherever practically possible in quantitative terms), and how performance in each area is to be measured and evaluated.

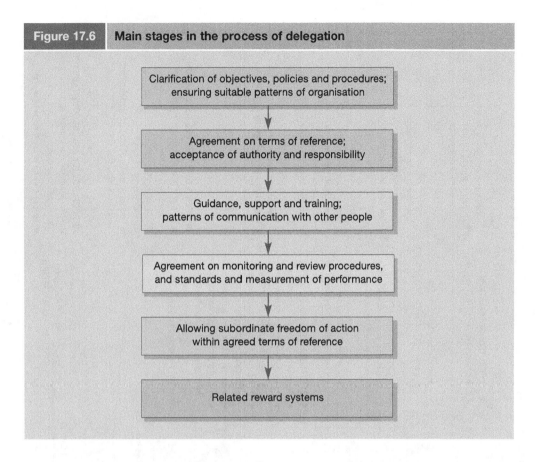

Figure 17.6 Main stages in the process of delegation

- **Freedom of action within agreed terms of reference.** The subordinate should then be left alone to get on with the job. One of the most frustrating aspects of delegation is the manager who passes on authority but stays close behind the subordinates' shoulders keeping a constant watch over their actions. This is contrary to the nature of delegation. The true nature of successful delegation means that the subordinate is given freedom of action within the boundaries established and agreed in the previous stages.
- **Related reward system.** Wherever possible, the process of delegation should be related to some form of associated 'reward' system. Examples could include bonus payments, improved job satisfaction, reduction of work stress and enhanced opportunities for promotion or personal development, including further delegation.

A planned and systematic approach means that effective delegation can be achieved within the formal structure of the organisation and without loss of control. It is important, however, to make sure that subordinates accept the extent of, and any restrictions on, the authority and responsibility delegated to them. Subordinates should feel a sense of commitment to their new tasks or assignments and should feel free to discuss any doubts or concerns. Delegation involves the acceptance theory of authority. *Davis and Newstrom* explain this as follows:

> *Although authority gives people power to act officially within the scope of their delegation, this power becomes somewhat meaningless unless those affected accept it and respond to it. In most cases when delegation is made, a subordinate is left free to choose a response within a certain range of behaviour. But even when an employee is told to perform one certain act, the employee still has the choice of doing it or not doing it and taking the consequences. It is, therefore, the subordinate who controls the response to authority. Managers cannot afford to overlook this human fact when they use authority.*[61]

A summary of delegation, authority, power and responsibility is given in the concept map set out in Figure 17.7.

Figure 17.7 Concept map of delegation, authority, power and responsibility

DELEGATION, AUTHORITY, POWER AND RESPONSIBILITY

- DELEGATION
- AUTHORITY
- POWER
- RESPONSIBILITY

DELEGATION
'Delegation is part of the managerial function involving some element of risk'
- EFFECTIVE DELEGATION
- REASONS FOR INEFFECTIVE DELEGATION

EFFECTIVE DELEGATION
- Understanding the task
- Identifying the correct person(s) to perform the task
- Communicating the task
- Setting and discussing the objectives for the task
- Monitoring progress
- Evaluation and feedback

Both the delegator and the person(s) to whom the work is delegated

Based on
- *Previous performance*
- *Special skills*
- *Special circumstances*

Using appropriate communication methods
- *Verbal/Written/Diagrammatic*

Objectives require
- *time scales*
- *quality of the results to be quantified*

AUTHORITY
The RIGHT to authority
- Given to the subordinate to do the manager's job (otherwise formal organisations cannot exist)
- Extent of delegated authority
- Anything the manager has the right to do (except where the manager is specifically prohibited from doing)
- Cannot totally delegate authority of performing the managerial functions viz:
 planning
 organising
 motivating
 communicating
 controlling

INEFFECTIVE DELEGATION of – manager – subordinates
- Heavy work loads
- Lack appropriate staff
- Unfamiliarity with the task — staff not trained — staff not in post
- Personal characteristics
- Fear of subordinate doing undesirable things of – manager – subordinate
- Liking by the manager for the actual job

DELEGATION OF AUTHORITY AND POWER
Authority and Power relationships
A manager must possess both otherwise conflict occurs. Subordinates must be provided with equal authority and power at all levels of an organisation
= legitimate power of workable authority
- Managers have the right to require accounting for the authority delegated and tasks assigned to a subordinate
- Subordinates must answer to the manager concerning the stewardship of the authority granted to him or her by the manager

RESPONSIBILITY
- The obligation to do something
- The duty to perform the job or function in the organisation
- An individual's obligation to her or himself to perform the task
- Responsibility cannot be delegated
- Delegating authority can increase the manager's responsibility since there is additional responsibility for the subordinate's task

BENEFITS OF EFFECTIVE DELEGATION
- Efficient use of manager's and subordinates' time
- Motivation of staff
- Development of staff
- Reducing levels of stress in managers and subordinates

RESPONSIBILITY AND ACCOUNTABILITY
- Accountability – a person is accountable to higher authorities
- Responsibility is created **within** a person when accepting a task and the appropriate delegation of authority

POWER
The ABILITY to influence another measured in terms of:
- giving rewards
- promising rewards
- threat to withdraw current rewards
- withdrawing current rewards
- threat of punishment
- punishing

influenced by
- Subjective factors – ethical/moral. For example, how much power should a manager have?
- Extent of power significantly determined by the person being controlled
- May be more important what a person thinks the manager's power is than what it actually is

POWER

ALL RETAINED BY MANAGEMENT

Management controls every detail

NONE RETAINED BY MANAGEMENT

Management loses control

Zone of INSTRUCTION	Zone of DELEGATION	Zone of EMPOWERMENT	Zone of ANARCHY

DOES EMPOWERMENT DELIVER?

Effectively managed, empowerment can offer a number of potential benefits throughout all levels of the organisation. But does empowerment promote greater motivation and increase job satisfaction and work performance? Does empowerment deliver? From a study of 171 employees in a major Canadian life insurance company, *Thorlakson and Murray* found no clear evidence for the predicted effects of empowerment. However, they suggest that the potential effectiveness of empowerment should not be ruled out. The larger the organisation, the more difficult to institute participatory management. In this study, the participants were members of a large organisation and corporate size, together with the top-down implementation of empowerment, could have played a major role.[62]

Although there is a continuing debate about the real benefits of empowerment there appears to be a general assumption that 'empowerment programmes will result in motivated staff, quality customer service and improved profits'.[63] From a discussion of the benefits and problems of empowerment and a review of its operation in a number of companies, *Pickard* concludes that empowerment does appear to be having a radical effect on the way people work. As an example, Pickard describes improved job satisfaction and the changing attitude of staff arising from the introduction of empowerment at Harvester restaurants. Within a framework handed down from head office, staff work in teams which are responsible for making decisions on the running of individual restaurants.[64]

Peiperi poses the question 'Does empowerment deliver the goods?' and concludes:

> *Empowerment says that employees at all levels of an organization are responsible for their own actions and should be given authority to make decisions about their work. Its popularity has been driven by the need to respond quickly to customer needs, to develop cross-functional links to take advantage of opportunities that are too local or too fleeting to be determined centrally. Better morale and compensation for limited career paths are other advantages. Potential difficulties include the scope for chaos and conflict, a lack of clarity about where responsibility lies, the breakdown of hierarchical control, and demoralization on the part of those who do not want additional authority. Successful empowerment will typically require feedback on performance from a variety of sources, rewards with some group component, an environment which is tolerant of mistakes, widely distributed information, and generalist managers and employees. The paradox is that the greater the need for empowerment in an organization, the less likelihood of success. It has to be allowed to develop over time through the beliefs/attitudes of participants.[65]*

According to *Erstad*, among the many fashionable management terms, empowerment refers to a change strategy with the objective of improving both the individual's and the organisation's ability to act. In the service sector, for example, empowerment is often seen as a way to gain competitive advantage but the true potential is broader. From the context of articles specialising in this area, Erstad concludes that empowerment is a complex process. In order to be successful it requires a clear vision, a learning environment both for management and employees, and participation and implementation tools and techniques.[66]

Potential benefits of empowerment

Empowerment makes greater use of the knowledge, skills and abilities of the workforce; it encourages teamworking; and if there is meaningful participation, it can aid the successful implementation of change programmes.[67] *Wall and Wood* suggest that although few manufacturing companies empower their staff, research shows that empowerment can be one of the most effective tools in raising both productivity and profit. Empowerment improves performance because of the opportunities empowerment provides for them to do their work more effectively. It develops an individual's knowledge so they take a broader and more

proactive orientation towards their job and are more willing to suggest new ways of doing things and to engage in meaningful teamworking.[68] Findings from a Whitehall II study of over 10,000 civil servants on work-related stress suggests that giving people more control over their jobs can greatly benefit their health.[69]

The police custody officer and empowerment

The Police Service has statutory responsibility for the treatment of persons detained by them (and other agencies such as HMRC which brings people into a police station). These people must be treated in accordance with the Police & Criminal Evidence Act 1984 (PACE) that was enacted in January 1986 and any code of practice issued under the Act.

Section 39 of PACE specifies that these duties should be the duty of the custody officer at a police station. The same section goes on to declare where

*an officer of **higher** rank than the custody officer gives directions . . . which are at variance with any **decision** or **action** taken by the custody officer in the performance of a duty imposed on him under this Act the matter **shall** be referred at once to an officer of the rank of Superintendent or above who is responsible for that police station.*

There is statutory backing for the decisions and actions taken by custody officers in the performance of their duties.

PACE sets out the provisions regarding the appointment of custody officers (Section 36). Custody officers are appointed to designated police stations, which are effectively police stations equipped to receive and house detained persons in the conditions that PACE requires. Subject to limited exceptions all detained persons must go to a designated police station. Custody officers are appointed by the Chief Officer of Police for that area or by an officer directed by that Chief Officer of Police to do so. Importantly no police officer may be appointed a custody officer unless at least the rank of sergeant, and significantly none of the functions of a custody officer shall be performed by an officer who is involved in the investigation of an offence for which the person is in detention (and there is case law that identifies what being involved in an investigation entails).

Most forces have adopted the sergeant rank as the best suited to the custody officer role (custody officers no longer have to be a police officer). On appointment training is given in the role of sergeant and specifically custody officer duties. Custody officers, though they work for the same organisation, have an element of impartiality through the statement that they must not be involved in the investigation of an offence for which that person is detained. This allows for their decision-making to be non-partisan. There is an argument perhaps that for the decision-making to be completely impartial custody provisions should be independent of the police service but in practice it is argued that custody officers value their impartiality and their decision-making is reflected in this.

The Act clearly defines the process for any challenge to custody officers' decision-making and that is by appeal to the station commander, a Superintendent. As well as providing support for custody officers in their decision-making it also affords protection for them from **rank pulling** in a hierarchically structured organisation such as the police.

Custody officers deal with people's liberty and determine whether they enter the legal process by charging them to appear at court. This is serious business and in practical terms it is taken very seriously. Their decision-making in this process is subject to periodic review. In the first 24 hours of a person's detention that review is undertaken at the 6-, 15- and 24-hour stages. Any detention beyond 24 hours requires the authority of a Superintendent and any detention beyond 36 hours requires a warrant from a court. The custody officer's decision-making is subject to close scrutiny through the training process, accreditation process and local inspection processes. Most importantly, it is a legal requirement now that all designated custody centres are videotaped, which is perhaps the ultimate scrutiny. The arrival of video recording tapes in custody centres was welcomed by custody officers as it saw a corresponding fall in the number of complaints against them in the charge room process.

In practical terms it is rare that decisions of a custody officer are challenged by a more senior officer (a Detective Chief Inspector). The fact that these occasions are so rarely reported is evidence of the seriousness and professionalism adopted by Custody Sergeants in their decision-making process. **A process that would only work with empowerment.**

(I am grateful to Sergeant Robert Collier of The Hampshire Constabulary for providing this information.)

Control versus autonomy

Whatever the extent of employee empowerment, there is still a requirement for some form of management control and this gives rise to a number of important behavioural considerations. From their study of top-performing companies in the 1990s, *Goldsmith and Clutterbuck* refer to the sharing of power, and to the balance between control and autonomy. They question how companies manage to balance giving people maximum freedom against exerting controls to ensure the benefits of size and a common sense of direction. The more managers share power, the more authority and resources they gain:

> *The way to exert the most effective control is to limit it to the few simple, readily understandable processes that have the greatest impact on group performance, and to maximise the freedom that managers at all levels have to achieve clear goals in their own way. And the more rigidly those core controls are enforced, the greater are the freedoms people need in order to compensate and to release their creativity, initiative and proactivity. Control and autonomy are therefore two sides of the same coin . . . What do we mean by control and autonomy? Formal control seems to be exercised in three main ways: through setting or agreeing targets for performance (mainly but not exclusively financial); through measurement and reporting systems; and through certain decisions to be made centrally or corporately. Autonomy is, in essence, an absence of formal control: once clear goals are set, the individual manager has greater or lesser freedom to determine how they will be met. There are still controls in place, but they are much less obvious or intrusive.*[70]

Critical reflection

'Some form of hierachical power and order is an essential feature of effective work performance, but the nature of modern organisations has noticeably diminished demands for management control over the actions and behaviour of people at work.'

What is your considered opinion? Do you favour more or less control over your work activities?

SYNOPSIS

■ Control is an integral part of the process of management. There are, however, varying connotations of the meaning and exercise of control. It is often interpreted in a negative manner to suggest direction or command, the restriction of behaviour or even exploitation of employees. However, control is not only a function of the formal organisation, it is also a function of interpersonal influence. Control is a general concept that is applied both to individual behaviour and organisational performance.

■ Control can serve many important functions and be manifested in a variety of forms. There are a number of important characteristics of an effective control system. The system should be understood, conform with the structure of the organisation, report deviations quickly, draw attention to critical activities of the organisation, be flexible, consistent with the activity to which

it relates and subject to continual review. If control systems are to be successful in leading to improved performance, then attention must also be given to the factors which influence human behaviour.

■ Work organisations are not only systems of hierarchical structure, they are also systems of social relationships, status and power. Power is an inherent feature of work organisations and an underlying reality behind the decision-making process. Organisations can be classified in terms of the relationship between power, involvement and the compliance of their members. The pluralistic approach, however, recognises power as a social process. Power is a major organisational variable that derives from a multiplicity of sources and situations. A dilemma that underlies the nature of control is finding the right balance between order and flexibility.

■ Management control systems are frequently thought of in terms of accounting or financial systems. The reasons are easy to understand but accounting control systems tend to operate in a negative way, and to give little specific recognition from management and only a limited sense of achievement. What need to be considered are behavioural factors and the manner in which control systems motivate people to improve their performance. To do this, they must take account of individual, social and organisational factors that determine people's patterns of behaviour.

■ Discussion on the balance between control and autonomy draws attention to the importance of empowerment and allowing employees greater freedom. Attempting to distinguish between empowerment and delegation is not easy but empowerment can be viewed as the more embracing process that gives rise to delegation. At the individual level, delegation is the process of entrusting authority and responsibility to others but ultimate accountability cannot be delegated. A planned and systematic approach to delegation means that it can be achieved without the loss of management control.

■ In order to realise the full benefits of empowerment and delegation without loss of control it is necessary for the manager to examine four basic questions and to adopt a planned and systematic approach with six main stages. Despite the continuing debate about whether empowerment actually delivers, effectively managed it does offer potential benefits throughout all levels of the organisation. However, whatever the extent of employee empowerment there is still a requirement for some form of management control and there are a number of behavioural considerations.

REVIEW AND DISCUSSION QUESTIONS

1 Give your own views on the controversial nature of management control. What do you see as the purposes of management control in work organisations?

2 Detail with supporting examples the essential elements of a management control system.

3 Discuss the main factors that are likely to affect resistance to, and the successful implementation of, management control systems.

4 Explain fully the importance of the concept of power to management and organisational behaviour.

5 Discuss critically the nature of pluralistic approaches to power and give your own practical examples.

6 How would you explain the organisational and personal relationships between a manager and subordinate staff that are created by the process of empowerment?

7 As a departmental manager explain fully how you would attempt to realise the full advantages of delegation without loss of control over subordinate staff.

8 Discuss critically what you see as the likely consequences of a manager exercising close personal supervision as a means of maintaining control and power over the work of subordinate staff.

MANAGEMENT IN THE NEWS

The undercover boss

FT

Stefan Stern

Employee attitude surveys, brown bag lunches, focus groups, informal chats: managers try quite hard to find out what their staff are thinking. But the results are mixed at best. What are your staff thinking? Admit it – you don't really know. Is there any way of finding out? Electronic surveillance would be a bad idea. Cloaks of invisibility work for Harry Potter, but are not available to the rest of us. One chief executive has done the next best thing. He went undercover in his own business for two weeks, disguised as an office worker, completing shifts on ten different sites. He has heard for himself what his people really think. It has been

Management in the news – continued

Source: INSADCO Photography/Alamy

A CEO dons a disguise and learns that an effective, open dialogue is the solution to communicating key messages to staff.

a revelatory experience. Stephen Martin is the 43-year-old CEO of the Clugston Group, a medium-sized civil engineering and logistics company based in the north of England. But for two weeks earlier this year, as far as his colleagues were concerned he was 'Martin Walker', an ordinary co-worker trying to earn a living like everybody else.

How did Mr Martin avoid being found out? He is still a relatively new CEO, having started in December 2006. He grew a beard and turned up to work in protective clothing rather than a suit. His down-to-earth, approachable style does not mark him out immediately as 'boss class'. 'This was a once-in-a-lifetime opportunity to hear unfiltered what my employees were really thinking,' Mr Martin told me last week. 'They said things to me that they would never have told their managers.' What lessons has he learned? 'Our key messages were just not getting through to people,' Mr Martin says. 'People working a shift on a large site do not have time to read newsletters or log on to websites. You have to communicate with people on their terms, and it is different for every location. One size does not fit all.'

For example, Mr Martin found that an apparently sensible idea – encouraging his workers to take a tea-break where they were working rather than coming back to a canteen – was taken to mean that the break had been cut. What is more, having worked these physically demanding shifts, which involved pouring concrete, laying kerbs and clearing drains, the boss now has a better informed view of the job. His conclusion: 'We were asking the impossible of some of them.' This experiment has highlighted a classic management problem. Leaders may know exactly what they want to see happening. They send out messages down the management line. Employees ought to understand. But between the top table and the shopfloor something goes wrong. And right now there is a bigger, more urgent point. In a recession it is even harder to have an effective, open dialogue with an anxious workforce.

Mr Martin feels he needs to 'over-communicate' to reassure staff who have seen big redundancies in recent months. 'If you don't pass on enough information, even if it is bad news, they will fill the gap with something else, probably worse than the truth.' Key messages to staff should never go undercover, even if one boss had to don a disguise to find this out.

Source: Stern, S. 'The Undercover Boss', *Financial Times*, 8 June 2009. Copyright © 2009 The Financial Times Limited, reproduced with permission.

Discussion questions

1 What does Stephen Martin's experience tell us about the problems associated with both direct (notice boards, websites) and indirect (delegated via managers) systems of organisational communication and control? How can they be overcome?

2 Use either Table 17.1 or Figure 17.3 to suggest which sort of control system you believe is best suited to organisations like the Clugston Group, and why.

ASSIGNMENT

The Empowerment Questionnaire

The following questionnaire consists of managerial behaviours that promote empowerment. Think of any work experience you have had – even a short-term, vacation or part-time job. How frequently did your manager do each of the following? Please mark the response that best describes the manager's behaviour.

My Manager	Very infrequently	Infrequently	Sometimes	Frequently	Very frequently
1 Lets me do my job without interfering	☐	☐	☐	☐	☐
2 Makes an effort to locate and remove barriers that reduce efficiency	☐	☐	☐	☐	☐
3 Encourages all of us to work as a team	☐	☐	☐	☐	☐
4 Clearly defines what is expected of me	☐	☐	☐	☐	☐
5 Provides me with honest feedback on my performance	☐	☐	☐	☐	☐
6 Openly recognises work well done	☐	☐	☐	☐	☐
7 Keeps me focused on customer needs	☐	☐	☐	☐	☐
8 Encourages me to monitor my own efforts	☐	☐	☐	☐	☐
9 Makes sure I have the training I need to do my job	☐	☐	☐	☐	☐
10 Allows me to make decisions about my own work	☐	☐	☐	☐	☐
11 Listens to me before making decisions affecting my area	☐	☐	☐	☐	☐
12 Provides me with an environment conducive to teamwork	☐	☐	☐	☐	☐
13 Rewards me for meeting company goals	☐	☐	☐	☐	☐
14 Informs me regularly about the state of business	☐	☐	☐	☐	☐
15 Encourages me to make suggestions	☐	☐	☐	☐	☐
16 Makes sure I have all the information I need to do my work	☐	☐	☐	☐	☐
17 Behaves in ways that demonstrate respect for others	☐	☐	☐	☐	☐
18 Explains how my job fits into the company objectives	☐	☐	☐	☐	☐

Source: Osland, Joyce S., Kolb, David A. and Rubin, Irwin M. *Organizational Behaviour: An Experimental Approach*, seventh edition, Prentice Hall (2001). Copyright © 2001. Reproduced with permission from Pearson Education, Inc.

a If this was *not* a permanent, full-time position, to what extent do you think this influenced your manager's behaviour towards you?

b How did your experience compare with the manager's behaviour to other members of staff in the same department/section?

c How would you describe the manager's general belief in, and approach to, empowerment? And what was your perception of the manager's overall effectiveness?

PERSONAL AWARENESS AND SKILLS EXERCISE

Objectives

Completing this exercise should help you to enhance the following skills:

■ Assess the extent to which you are in danger of becoming a control freak.

■ Review honestly and reflect upon features of your own personality.

Exercise

Working in small self-selected groups, individually answer the following questions honestly. If necessary think how you would be likely to behave in the given situation. Then compare and discuss responses with your colleagues. (Your tutor will provide one suggested set of guidelines.)

I trust others to get the work done on time and to a good standard

(a) rarely

(b) generally

(c) always

I find other people have better ideas than me

(a) rarely

(b) sometimes

(c) often

I normally find I am right

(a) mostly

(b) sometimes

(c) it depends on your perspective

During the course of a meeting, do you:

(a) Take notes, because someone has to?

(b) Take down the important points?

(c) Assume someone else is paying attention?

At the end of the day are you more likely to:

(a) Stay until you have returned every email before going home?

(b) Make a list of relevant things to tackle tomorrow?

(c) Start calling around your colleagues to see who wants to go out for a drink?

When faced with a menu in a restaurant, do you:

(a) Think it is sensible to order for everyone to save time?

(b) Ask everyone else what they would like first and then order?

(c) Wait until it's your turn to order?

Do you feel that if you were to take a holiday your business would:

(a) Fall apart because no one knows how to do anything properly?

(b) Suffer a bit, but not as much as it would were you not to have a holiday?

(c) Allow others a chance to take charge and show what they can do?

When planning a trip, do you:

(a) Allow extra time for traffic and unexpected delays and bring a briefcase full of work to occupy your time in case you arrive early?

(b) Follow the airline's instructions?

(c) Wait until the last minute, at which point you rush like mad?

When setting off on holiday, do you:

(a) Go through everyone's suitcase to make sure it is packed properly before heading off?

(b) Pack your suitcase and figure everyone else can do their own?

(c) Pack when the taxi arrives?

Source: For exercise questions, Kirwan-Taylor, H. 'People Who Can't Let Go', *Management Today*, March 2007, p. 47. Reproduced from *Management Today* magazine with the permission of the copyright owner, Haymarket Business Publications Limited.

Discussion

■ Do you think you have controlling issues or can you exercise flexibility?

■ How would you draw the line between being easygoing and being irresponsible?

■ To what extent do you see yourself as a team player and how does this fit with your answers?

CASE STUDY

What You Say Is What You Get . . . ?

The onset of the financial crisis which hit the banking and finance sector in 2007 has had dramatic repercussions in most areas of working life. The inquest has thrown up many questions about the decision-making process and the degree of responsibility exercised by top finance teams. Some of the fallout is suggesting that a big part of the problem was the lack of women at the top. Women are showing themselves to be a significant presence in the financial sector; it is argued that they do not exercise power as recklessly as men, take fewer risks and are a potential source of organisational stability. So why don't they make it to the top? For a number of researchers and campaigners in the field, it's all about what you say. The way in which people in organisations communicate, and how those communications are perceived and acted upon can have a major impact on individual success, team performance and personal career paths. Whilst questions of perception and communication may not tell the whole story about the position of women in organisational life, they do tell part of it. Many women may not be able, or even wish, to challenge the dominant masculine model of society in general and work organisations in particular (this dominance of a male paradigm is often termed patriarchy). Nevertheless, information about gender-related differences in matters of perception and communication can help individuals, both men and women, to become more effective in their working lives.

Learning two languages

In August 2006 Alison Maitland, writing for the *Financial Times*, reported on a training event held for

Coming to a boardroom near you; women learn the language of business leadership.

Source: © Jon Feingersh/Blend Images/Corbis

a group of 20 high-ranking female executives at a venue just outside Paris.[71] The course was run by a Paris-based training consultancy called Diafora,[72] which has links to the European Professional Women's Network[73] via one of its founding partners, Avivah Wittenberg-Cox. Wittenberg-Cox is co-author of the book *Why Women Mean Business*, and CEO of 20-first, a consulting organisation which aims to work

> with organisations that seek to move from 20th century mindsets, management styles and marketing approaches into more progressive 21st century forms – and to stay first at the game.[74]

At the session described the women were practising saying 'no' in a language which would get the message across clearly to a bullying male boss who was trying to offload his unfinished work. They were learning to

speak 'masculine'. The session was addressing a problem which stems from the tendency for women and men to learn different ways of speaking which reflect differing assumptions about the purpose of communication. Women, it has been discovered, tend to communicate in order to make people feel at ease, to include people and to create a sense of harmony. Men tend to communicate as a means of getting a point across, or making an argument. This is part of the socialisation process and is based on common conventions about the role of women and men in society. It results in differences both in the language used and the linguistic structures and habits employed. Deborah Tannen,[75] an American professor of linguistics, who has researched and written extensively on the nature of communication patterns between men and women, notes that women tend to use more 'tag' questions at the end of sentences as a way of attempting to draw the other party into further discussion. Men tend to make statements or express opinions without these mechanisms for encouraging further discussion. For instance, where a woman might say:

> I thought the report John gave into the problems at the Zurich office was very clear, didn't you? Should we act on his recommendations?

a man might simply state:

> John's Zurich report was very clear. We'll do what he suggested.

Both might actually wish to convey the same message; that the report was clear and the recommendations sound. However, the 'female' version, which aims to elicit an opinion or confirm agreement, contains what to the 'male' listener sounds like uncertainty or hesitancy. By contrast, to the female listener, the 'male' version might seem abrupt or arrogant and convey an impression that her views on the subject were irrelevant. Either way, the unconscious message behind the speech pattern can be damaging to the image of the speaker in the eyes of their colleague.

Tannen also noted that women were much more likely to use 'weak' words and phrases in their conversation.

> A woman manager might say to her secretary, 'Could you do me a favor and type this letter right away?' knowing that her secretary is going to type the letter. But her male boss, on hearing this, might conclude she doesn't feel she deserves the authority she has.[76]

Another illustration is the phrase 'I'm sorry', which women often use to smooth conversation or to express regret that something has happened and to minimise it, not as an admission of error. For men, 'I'm sorry' is often used to mean something much tougher; it equates to admitting a mistake and apologising for it. Women

who are 'always apologising' thus give an impression of incompetence.

How to make an impression

Training women to say no to an unreasonable demand is only part of the agenda addressed by the Diafora programmes. Beefing up their language to avoid weak phrases such as 'as soon as possible' or 'I don't know but . . .' or 'I guess I could . . .' might help women limit some of the day-to-day perceptual damage, but there are other more fundamental problems to consider. One of them is the issue of women's self-promotion and their approach to achieving career success. Wittenberg-Cox finds that many young men have already learned what is known as the 80/20 rule of power politics by the time they embark on their careers: that you should spend 80 per cent of your time at work actually working, and 20 per cent communicating your achievements and gaining visibility.

> This appears to be news to the women on the [Diafora] course, but may be more familiar to their male colleagues back at the office. Guys have told me this rule as if they were fed it with their mother's milk.[77]

These anecdotal findings are supported by those of senior academic researcher Dr Val Singh, working at Cranfield's International Centre for Women Leaders. Writing about the question of impression management (IM)[78] she reports that the young men in one of her research samples had learned to use IM at a younger age than their female counterparts, and might therefore be getting a head start on the career ladder. For instance, 60 per cent of the junior males in her sample actively sought out key people for the purpose of networking whereas very few junior females did so.

> Some men and women trust the formal HRM systems to provide career opportunities, underestimating the importance of informal networks . . .

Women tended to adopt IM strategies later in their careers, usually having noticed their equally capable male colleagues achieving more and more rapid promotions. The Cranfield studies identify three types of IM: self-focused (which is to do with packaging and 'branding' oneself), manager-focused (which is about building and maintaining relationships in a fairly instrumental way) and job-focused (which is about delivering extra levels of job performance).[79] Men appear to be readier to engage in manager-focused IM, even if they don't like it much, than women. Also, according to research done internally for Hewlett-Packard, men apply earlier for promotion.

> women apply for open job positions if they think they respond to 100% of the criteria listed, while men respond as soon as they feel that they cover 60% of the requirements. Worse though, she noted, is that hiring

managers do the same. They recruit women if they respond to 100% of the criteria, but they are ready to recruit men as long as they respond to 60% (and women recruiters are tougher on women candidates than men are).[80]

Women managers and cultural difference

Both Diafora and 20-first suggest that the cultural difference between men and women is as tangible as that between different nationalities, and should be treated as such. The group hopes to encourage and train not only women, but also men, to become 'gender bilingual' in the search for managerial talent and business success. And indeed national cultural difference itself should not be forgotten as something which might affect perceptions and behaviours, not necessarily to the detriment of women. Some research into both managerial effectiveness and the perception of what makes a good manager is beginning to reveal different levels of sex stereotyping in different cultures. For instance, a study by Chow[81] seems to indicate that in Hong Kong financial and telecommunications businesses, the perceptions of both men and women about the characteristics of an effective business leader are substantially gender neutral;

A less assertive and more individualist, more gender egalitarian culture may offer a favourable and women-friendly culture toward female leaders in management positions in Hong Kong organisations in the future, especially if women aspiring to become leaders demonstrate the attributes that subordinates seek.

On a lighter note, Wittenberg-Cox recently perceived a difference between French female managers and those from the US or the UK in relation to the way in which they assert femininity. In an article celebrating the apparent return of high heels to businesswomen's wardrobes at a conference involving the CEOs of some very substantial companies, she observed that they no longer signified the 'dumb-blond plaything of yesteryear' but power. But only, so far, for French women:

American women have been forced to adapt too much to the male model in their rise to power . . . Frenchwomen, in particular, were never asked, like their unfortunate Anglo-Saxon sisters, to choose between family and career, and between femininity and power. Despite the supposed macho nature of Latin men, France has created one of the world's only societies where women work full-time (80% of women between 25 and 50), have lots of children (the highest birth rate in Europe after Ireland) and still look and sound like – and are loved for being – women.[82]

Your tasks

1 Analyse the issues raised in this case using the concepts of legitimate (organisational) power and personal (informal) power. What can we learn about the relationship between perception, communication, status and power in organisations?

2 How should senior managers, in particular those who are responsible for the assessment and promotion of staff, act in the light of the concept of the '80/20' rule?

3 Discuss the reasons for and against the use of women-focused training such as that offered by Diafora and the Cranfield International Centre for Women Leaders. How else might organisations ensure that opportunities for career enhancement are fair? How important is this for organisational effectiveness?

Notes and references

1 See, for example, Salaman, G. *Class and the Corporation*, Fontana (1981).

2 For a discussion on management control and an understanding of behaviour at work, see, for example, Johnson, P. and Gill, J. *Management Control and Organizational Behaviour*, Paul Chapman (1993).

3 Tannenbaum, A. S. *Control in Organizations*, McGraw-Hill (1968), p. 3.

4 Drummond, H. *Introduction to Organizational Behaviour*, Oxford University Press (2000), p. 25.

5 Child, J. *Organization: Contemporary Principles and Practice*, Blackwell Publishing (2005), p. 112.

6 Lawler, E. E. 'Control Systems in Organizations', in Dunnette, M. D. (ed.) *Handbook of Industrial and Organizational Psychology*, Rand McNally (1976).

7 For example, see Mullins, L. J. and Banks, G. 'How Well Am I Doing?', *Euhofa Journal*, Association Internationale des Directeurs d'Écoles Hoteliers, Lausanne, Switzerland, no. 18, June 1986.

8 Tulgan, B. 'Winning the Talent Wars', in Crainer, S. and Dearlove, D. (eds), *Financial Times Handbook of Management*, second edition, Financial Times Prentice Hall (2001), p. 351.

9 Wilson, F. *Organizational Behaviour and Work: A Critical Introduction*, second edition, Oxford University Press (2004), p. 183.

10 Lorange, P. 'Ultra-Rapid Management Processes', in Chowdhury, S. (ed.) *Management 21C*, Financial Times Prentice Hall (2000), p. 157.

11 Zimmermann, J. 'The Different Centres of Control', *Mastering Management*, Financial Times/Pitman Publishing (1997), p. 21.

12 For examples, see Tibballs, G. *Business Blunders*, Robinson Publishing (1999).

13 'Untapped Potential: The Barriers to Optimum Corporate Performance', Proudfoot Consulting, October 2002.

14 Obeng, E. 'New World Organization', in Crainer, S. and Dearlove, D. (eds), *Financial Times Handbook of Management*, second edition, Financial Times Prentice Hall (2001), p. 85.

15 Lucas, E. 'Tooling Up for Leadership', *Professional Manager*, September 2000, p. 10.

16 Cloke, K. and Goldsmith, J. *The End of Management and the Rise of Organizational Democracy*, Jossey-Bass (2002), p. 5.

17 McKenna, R. *New Management*, Irwin/McGraw-Hill (1999), pp. 430–1.

18 Shovelton, Dame H. 'Accountable to Some?', *Chartered Secretary*, September 2001, pp. 24–6.

19 See, for example, Report of 'The Victoria Climbié Inquiry', Chairman Lord Laming, Department of Health, January 2003. For a summary, see: Dobson, N. 'Gross Failure', *Chartered Secretary*, July 2003, pp. 24–6.

20 Reeves, T. K. and Woodward, J. 'The Study of Managerial Control', in Woodward, J. (ed.) *Industrial Organization: Behaviour and Control*, Oxford University Press (1970)

21 Wilson, F. *Organizational Behaviour and Work: A Critical Introduction*, second edition, Oxford University Press (2004), p. 170.

22 Nordström, K. and Ridderstråle, J. 'Funky Inc.,' in Crainer, S. and Dearlove, D. (eds), *Financial Times Handbook of Management*, second edition, Financial Times Prentice Hall (2001), p. 72.

23 See, for example, Sparrow, A. 'Watching Brief', *Professional Manager*, November 2002, pp. 20–1.

24 Child, J. *Organization: Contemporary Principles and Practice*, Blackwell Publishing (2005).

25 Luthans, F. *Organizational Behavior*, fifth edition, McGraw-Hill (1989), p. 547.

26 Hicks, H. G. and Gullett, C. R. *The Management of Organizations*, third edition, McGraw-Hill (1976), p. 502.

27 Knights, D. and Willmott, H. *Management Lives: Power and Identity in Work Organizations*, Sage Publications (1999), p. 31.

28 Robbins, S. P. and Judge, T. A. *Organizational Behaviour*, thirteenth edition, Pearson Prentice-Hall (2009), p. 485.

29 Etzioni, A. *A Comparative Analysis of Complex Organizations: On Power, Involvement and Their Correlates*, revised edition, Free Press (1975).

30 'Sex and Power 2008', Equality and Human Rights Commission, September 2008.

31 Fincham, R. 'Perspectives on Power: Processual, Institutional and Internal Forms of Organizational Power', *Journal of Management Studies*, vol. 29, no. 6, 1992.

32 Pfeffer, J. *Power in Organizations*, Pitman (1981).

33 French, J. P. and Raven, B. 'The Bases of Social Power', in Cartwright, D. and Zander, A. F. (eds) *Group Dynamics: Research and Theory*, third edition, Harper and Row (1968).

34 For an account of the use of power, see, for example, Guirdham, M. *Interactive Behaviour at Work*, third edition, Financial Times Prentice Hall (2002), Chapter 9.

35 Parker, L. D. 'Shock of the New a Century On', *Professional Manager*, November 2005, pp. 34–5; and 'Mary Parker Follett: Prophet of Management', Thinkers Checklist No. 24, Chartered Management Institute (1998).

36 Handy, C. B. *Understanding Organizations*, fourth edition, Penguin (1993), p. 131.

37 Green, J. 'Who Wields the Power in Your Organisation?' *Administrator*, February 1996, pp. 21–2.

38 Mann, S. 'Oh I Heard It On the Grapevine', *Professional Manager*, July 1997, p. 33.

39 Kirwan-Taylor, H. 'People Who Can't Let Go', *Management Today*, March 2007, pp. 45–7.

40 Stewart, R. *Managing Today and Tomorrow*, Macmillan (1991).

41 Reeser, C. and Loper, M. *Management: The Key to Organizational Effectiveness*, Scott, Foresman (1978), p. 437.

42 Allen, D. 'There's More to Accountancy Than Accounting', *Administrator*, March 1992, p. 6.

43 Goldsmith, W. and Clutterbuck, D. *The Winning Streak Mark II*, Orion Business Books (1998).

44 Berry, A. J., Broadbent, J. and Otley, D. (eds), *Management Control: Theories, Issues and Practices*, Macmillan (1995), p. 77.

45 Hannagan, T. *Management: Concepts and Practices*, fifth edition, Financial Times Prentice Hall (2008), p. 560.

46 Ezzamel, K., Lilley, S. and Wilmott, H. 'Be Wary of New Waves', *Management Today*, October 1993, pp. 99–102.

47 Gretton, I. 'Taking the Lead in Leadership', *Professional Manager*, January 1995, p. 22.

48 Wilkinson, A. 'Empowerment: Theory and Practice', *Personnel Review*, vol. 27, no. 1, 1998, pp. 40–56.

49 Mills, D. Q. and Friesen, G. B. 'Empowerment', in Crainer, S. and Dearlove, D. (eds) *Financial Times Handbook of Management*, second edition, Financial Times Prentice Hall (2001), p. 323.

50 Tulgan, B. 'Winning the Talent Wars', in Crainer, S. and Dearlove, D. *Financial Times Handbook of Management*, second edition, Financial Times Prentice Hall (2001), p. 348.

51 Crainer, S. *Key Management Ideas: Thinkers That Changed the Management World*, third edition, Financial Times Prentice Hall (1998), p. 126.

52 Mooney, J. D. *The Principles of Organization*, revised edition, Harper & Row (1947), p. 17.

53 Urwick, J. F. *Notes on the Theory of Organization*, American Management Association (1952).

54 See, for example, Waterman, R. H. *The Frontiers of Excellence*, Nicholas Brearley (1994); and Yukl, G. and Fu, P. 'Determinants of Delegation and Consultation by Managers', *Journal of Organizational Behavior*, vol. 20 (1999), pp. 219–32.

55 McGregor, D. *The Human Side of Enterprise*, Penguin (1987).

56 Stewart, R. *The Reality of Management*, third edition, Butterworth Heinemann (1999), p. 180.

57 Gratton, L. *The Democratic Enterprise*, Financial Times Prentice Hall (2004), pp. 188–9.

58 Watson, T. J. *Organising and Managing Work*, second edition, Financial Times Prentice Hall (2006), p. 12.

59 Guirdham, M. *Interactive Behaviour at Work*, third edition, Financial Times Prentice Hall (2002), p. 569.

60 Gracie, S. 'Delegate Don't Abdicate', *Management Today*, March 1999, p. 94.

61 Davis, K. and Newstrom, J. W. *Human Behaviour at Work*, eighth edition, McGraw-Hill (1989), pp. 336–7.

62 Thorlakson, A. J. H. and Murray, R. P. 'An Empirical Study of Empowerment in the Workplace', *Group & Organization Management*, vol. 21, no. 1, March 1996, pp. 67–83.

63 Jamison, C. 'Top 10 Myths of Customer Service', *The British Journal of Administrative Management*, July/August 1999, p. 20.

64 Pickard, J. 'The Real Meaning of Empowerment', *Personnel Management*, vol. 25, no. 11, November 1993, pp. 28–33.

65 Peiperi, M. 'Does Empowerment Deliver the Goods?', *Mastering Management*, FT/Pitman Publishing (1997), p. 287.

66 Erstad, M. 'Empowerment and Organizational Change', *International Journal of Contemporary Hospitality Management*, vol. 9, no. 7, 1997, pp. 325–33.

67 See, for example, Sell, R. 'Empowerment', *QWL News and Abstracts*, ACAS, no. 133, Winter 1998, pp. 7–11.

68 Wall, T. and Wood, S. 'Delegation's a Powerful Tool', *Professional Manager*, November 2002, p. 37.

69 Wheatley, R. 'Stress and Delegation', *Professional Manager*, vol. 12, no. 3, May 2003, p. 22 (The Whitehall II Study, HSE Contract Research, Report 422/2002).

70 Goldsmith, W. and Clutterbuck, D. *The Winning Streak Mark II*, Orion Business Books (1998), pp. 12–13.

71 Maitland, A. 'Learn the Masculine Imperative', *FT.com*, 1 August 2006.

72 See www.diafora-leadership.com.

73 See www.europeanpwn.net.

74 20-first website, http://www.20-first.com (accessed 3 August 2009).

75 Tannen, D. *Talking from 9 to 5: Women and Men at Work*, HarperCollins (2001).

76 Tannen, D. 'The Talk of the Sandbox: How Johnny and Suzy's Playground Chatter Prepares Them for Life at the Office', *Washington Post*, 11 December 1994.

77 Maitland, A. 'Learn the Masculine Imperative', *FT.com*, 1 August 2006.

78 Singh, V. 'Impression Management', Cranfield International Centre for Women Leaders, 2000.

79 Singh, V., Kumra, S. and Vinnicombe, S. 'Gender and Impression Management: Playing the Promotion Game', *Journal of Business Ethics*, vol. 37, no. 1, 2002, pp. 77–89.

80 Wittenberg-Cox, A. and Maitland, A. *Why Women Mean Business*, Jossey-Bass (2008), p. 114.

81 Chow, I. 'Gender Differences in Perceived Leadership Effectiveness in Hong Kong', *Women in Management Review*, vol. 20, no. 4, 2005, pp. 216–33.

82 Wittenberg-Cox, A. 'High Heels Scale New Heights', European Professional Women's Network, 2005, http://www.europeanpwn.net/index.php?article_id=144 (accessed 3 August 2009).

19

ORGANISATION CULTURE AND CHANGE

A central feature of the successful organisation is the diagnosis of its culture, health and performance, and the ability of the organisation to adapt to change. It involves the applications of organisational behaviour and recognition of the social processes of the organisation. The manager needs to understand the nature and importance of organisational culture and climate, employee commitment, and the successful implementation and management of organisational change.

Learning outcomes

After completing this chapter you should be able to:

- outline the meaning and nature of organisation development;

- examine the nature, types and main features of organisational culture;

- evaluate influences on the development of culture and the importance of culture;

- detail the characteristics of organisational climate and employee commitment;

- explore the nature of organisational change and reasons for resistance to change;

- examine the management of organisational change, and human and social factors of change;

- review the importance of organisational culture and the ability of the organisation to adapt to change.

Critical reflection

'An organisation cannot develop, or change. It is the people comprising the organisation who determine the culture of the organisation, develop and change. The study of organisation culture and change should therefore concentrate on the actions, behaviour and effectiveness of individuals.'

What is your view? What does organisation development mean to you?

ORGANISATION DEVELOPMENT, CULTURE AND CHANGE

Organisation development (OD) is a generic term embracing a wide range of loosely defined intervention strategies into the social processes of an organisation. These intervention strategies are aimed at the development of individuals, groups and the organisation as a total system. In a very general sense, OD is concerned with attempts to improve the overall performance and effectiveness of an organisation. Essentially, it is an applied behavioural science approach to planned change and development of an organisation. A goal of OD can be seen as the transformation of an organisation into a learning organisation, discussed in Chapter 20.

The broad nature of OD means that many interrelated topics could be included under this heading or 'label'. Given the importance of people, topics that are normally included under the heading of organisational behaviour can also be seen as relevant to the study of OD. However, the emphasis of OD is more on the development of the organisation than the actual processes of organisation and management. **Organisational culture and organisation change are two major topics that are central and critical features of OD.**

Organisation culture

An example of a comprehensive definition of OD in the behavioural science sense of the term is given by *French and Bell*:

> *Organization development is a long-term effort, led and supported by top management, to improve an organization's visioning, empowerment, learning, and problem-solving processes, through an ongoing, collaborative management of organization culture – with special emphasis on the culture of intact work teams and other team configurations – utilizing the consultant-facilitator role and the theory and technology of applied behavioral science, including action research.*[1]

French and Bell include culture prominently in their definition as they believe that culture is the bedrock of behaviour in organisations. They summarise the primary distinguishing characteristics of organisation development in terms of the following:

- a focus on culture and processes with specific encouragement of collaboration between leaders and members;
- a focus on the human and social side of the organisation, the importance of teams of all kinds, and participation and involvement in problem-solving and decision-making;
- a focus on total system change with organisations viewed as complex social systems;
- OD practitioners as facilitators, collaborators and co-learners with the overarching goal to make the client able to solve problems on their own;
- a reliance on an action research model and the adoption of a developmental view that seeks betterment of both individuals and the organisation.[2]

Organisation change

The relationship between OD and change is emphasised by *Hamlin, Keep and Ash*, who maintain that 'For organisations that do manage change effectively, change itself becomes the driving force that perpetuates future success and growth. In these organisations, every change becomes welcomed as an opportunity for increasing efficiency and building new organisational success.'[3]

According to Church, OD ought to be about large-scale organisational change that is based on people's perceptions and behaviours – human data.

> *I would draw the line at that kind of work. I would say that downsizing is not OD. I would say that a lot of training and development is not OD. Process consultation is, in my way of thinking, not OD. It's a skill that OD practitioners have, but it's not doing OD. I really think of OD as being systematic organisational change.*[4]

The implementation of OD

In order to bring about effective change, OD makes use of a number of approaches – often referred to as **intervention strategies** – including survey research and feedback, T-groups, team building and grid training.

■ **Survey research and feedback** involves the use of questionnaire surveys to help determine the attitudes of members to the functioning of the organisation. Results of the surveys are fed back to top management and then to work groups for interpretation and analysis. Group members participate in discussions on the implications of the information, the diagnosis of problems and the development of action plans to help overcome the problems identified.

■ **T-groups (or sensitivity training)** involve small, unstructured, face-to-face groupings who meet without a planned agenda or set activities. Training is intended to concentrate on process rather than content: that is, on the feeling level of communication rather than the informational value of communication. With the guidance of the trainers, participants' patterns of behaviour become the focus of attention for the group. The objectives are usually to increase participants' sensitivity to the emotional reactions in themselves and others, their diagnostic ability, and their behavioural flexibility and effectiveness. (T-groups are discussed in Chapter 9.)

■ **Team building** is the process of diagnosing task procedures and patterns of human inter-action within a work group. The basic objective is to improve the overall performance of the organisation through improvements in the effectiveness of teams. Attention is focused on work procedures and interpersonal relationships, and especially the role of the leader in relation to other members of the group.

■ **Grid training** is a development from the *Blake and Mouton* Managerial Grid® approach (discussed in Chapter 12). An implied goal of grid training is that changes are aimed at attaining a 9,9 orientation (maximum concern for both production and people) on the Grid.[5]

There are, however, a number of other possible intervention strategies. *Naylor* refers also to the following 'OD techniques':

■ **role analysis** – the systematic clarification of roles and allocation of them among group members;

■ **life and career planning** – people are encouraged to develop and express personal goals with strategies for integrating these goals with those of the organisation;

■ **quality of work life** – links between quality of work life and career planning, and a philosophy of improving the climate in which work occurs; and

■ **counselling** – to help individuals better understand what it is like to work with them and, through this, assist them to attain their goals.[6]

A pluralistic approach

No two organisations are the same. Each organisation has its own types of problems and most appropriate remedies. OD is action-oriented and tailored to suit specific needs. It takes a number of forms with varying levels of intervention. OD concerns itself with the examin-ation of organisational health and the implementation of planned change. This may include training in interpersonal skills, sensitivity training, and methods and techniques relating to motivational processes, patterns of communication, styles of leadership and managerial behaviour.

Although an OD programme is legitimised by the formal system, it focuses on both the formal and the informal system. The initial intervention strategy is usually through the informal system, which includes feelings, informal actions and interactions, group norms and values, and forms part of the culture of an organisation. In Chapter 1, it was suggested that the term 'organisational behaviour' is a misnomer. The same caveat also applies to the

term 'organisation development'. An organisation is made up of people. When we talk about organisation development it is important to emphasise a pluralistic approach and remember that, in practice, we are referring to the development and performance of those individuals and groups of people who comprise the organisations.

The ethical nature of OD

Although the OD approach should care about people as the instrument of improved productivity, the wide range of activities and attention to organisation change, values and attitudes inevitably give rise to questions about the ethical nature of OD. In addition to organisational issues, the interventions target interpersonal behaviour and the development of individuals and teams. Critics may view OD as serving the best interests of management and little more than an exercise in the manipulation of employees. For example, *Woodall* notes that most culture change initiatives assume that strong cultures are associated with successful organisations and that the values held by employees should match with the management vision.[7]

ORGANISATIONAL CULTURE

Although most of us will understand in our own minds what is meant by **organisational culture**, it is a general concept with many different meanings and difficult to define or explain precisely. The concept of culture has developed from anthropology. Although people may not be aware consciously of culture, it still has a pervasive influence over their behaviour and actions. There is, however, no consensus on its meaning or its applications to the analysis of work organisations.[8] Furthermore, there is sometimes confusion over the difference between the interpretation of organisational culture and organisational climate (discussed later in this chapter). A popular and simple way of defining culture is 'how things are done around here'. For example, *Atkinson* explains organisational culture as reflecting the underlying assumptions about the way work is performed; what is 'acceptable and not acceptable'; and what behaviour and actions are encouraged and discouraged.[9]

A more detailed definition is:

The collection of traditions, values, policies, beliefs, and attitudes that constitute a pervasive context for everything we do and think in an organisation.[10]

The culture of an organisation is also often likened to the personality of an individual[11] (*see* Assignment 1 at the end of this chapter).

Charters questions the extent to which the concept of 'folklore' offers the potential to explore the existence of company myths and legends. Dictionary definitions, and discussions of the term in research papers, point to its close connection with culture.

Elements of folklore include myths and legends, and hence the concept of folklore appears to validate the exploration of organisational stories as part of cultural research . . . If folklore really is an expression of culture, then it could be argued that it should be possible to discern aspects of the culture of an organisation through the legends and myths of that organisation, the stories told which may or may not have a foundation in history.[12]

System of management authority

Cartwright sees culture as a system of management authority. When accepted by employees, cultural values increase the power and authority of management in three ways. Employees

- identify themselves with their organisation and accept its rules when 'it is the right thing to do';
- internalise the organisation's values when they believe they are right; and
- are motivated to achieve the organisation's objectives.[13]

Levels of culture

Schein suggests a view of organisational culture based on distinguishing three levels of culture, from the shallowest to the deepest: artefacts and creations; values; and basic assumptions.[14]

- **Level 1: Artefacts.** The most visible level of the culture is artefacts and creations – the constructed physical and social environment. This includes physical space and layout, the technological output, written and spoken language and the overt behaviour of group members.
- **Level 2: Espoused values.** Cultural learning reflects someone's original values. Solutions about how to deal with a new task, issue or problem are based on convictions of reality. If the solution works, the value can transform into a belief. Values and beliefs become part of the conceptual process by which group members justify actions and behaviour.
- **Level 3: Basic underlying assumptions.** When a solution to a problem works repeatedly it comes to be taken for granted. Basic assumptions are unconsciously held learned responses. They are implicit assumptions that actually guide behaviour and determine how group members perceive, think and feel about things.

Schein suggests that the basic assumptions are treated as the essence – what culture really is – and values and behaviours are treated as observed manifestations of the culture essence.

TYPES OF ORGANISATIONAL CULTURE

There are a number of ways to classify different types of organisational culture. Developing the ideas of *Harrison*,[15] *Handy* describes four main types of organisational cultures: power culture; role culture; task culture; and person culture.[16]

- **Power culture** depends on a central power source with rays of influence from the central figure throughout the organisation. A power culture is frequently found in small entrepreneurial organisations and relies on trust, empathy and personal communications for its effectiveness. Control is exercised from the centre by the selection of key individuals. There are few rules and procedures, and little bureaucracy. It is a political organisation with decisions taken largely on the balance of influence.
- **Role culture** is often stereotyped as a bureaucracy and works by logic and rationality. Role culture rests on the strength of strong organisational 'pillars' – the functions of specialists in, for example, finance, purchasing and production. The work of, and interaction between, the pillars is controlled by procedures and rules, and co-ordinated by the pediment of a small band of senior managers. Role or job description is often more important than the individual, and position is the main source of power.
- **Task culture** is job-oriented or project-oriented. In terms of structure the task culture can be likened to a net, some strands of which are stronger than others, and with much of the power and influence at the interstices. An example is the matrix organisation. Task culture seeks to bring together the right resources and people, and utilises the unifying power of the group. Influence is widely spread and based more on expert power than on position or personal power.
- **Person culture** is where the individual is the central focus and any structure exists to serve the individuals within it. When a group of people decide that it is in their own interests to band together to do their own thing and share office space, equipment or clerical assistance, then the resulting organisation would have a person culture. Examples are groups of barristers, architects, doctors or consultants. Although it is found in only a few organisations, many individuals have a preference for person culture, for example university professors and specialists. Management hierarchies and control mechanisms are possible only by mutual consent. Individuals have almost complete autonomy and any influence over them is likely to be on the basis of personal power.

Every organisation will have its own unique culture and most large businesses are likely to be something of a mix of cultures with examples for each of the four types in varying areas of the organisation. Different people enjoy working in different types of organisation culture and they are more likely to be happy and satisfied at work if their attributes and personalities are consistent with the culture of that part of the organisation in which they are employed.

Four generic types of culture

From an examination of hundreds of business organisations and their environments, *Deal and Kennedy* categorise corporate cultures according to two determining factors in the marketplace:

- the degree of risk associated with the organisation's activities; and
- the speed at which organisations and their employees receive feedback on the success of decisions or strategies.

These factors give rise to four generic types of culture: the tough-guy, macho culture; the work-hard/play-hard culture; the bet-your-company culture; and the process culture.[17]

- **Tough-guy, macho culture** – an organisation of individualists who frequently take high risks and receive quick feedback on the right or wrong of their actions. Examples cited include police departments, surgeons, construction, cosmetics, management consulting and the entertainment industry. Financial stakes are high and there is a focus on speed. The intense pressure and frenetic pace often results in early 'burn-out'. Internal competition and conflict are normal, stars are temperamental but tolerated. A high staff turnover can create difficulties in building a strong cohesive culture.
- **Work-hard/play-hard culture** – characterised by fun and action where employees take few risks, all with quick feedback. There is a high level of relatively low-risk activity. Examples include sales organisations such as estate agents and computer companies, mass consumer companies such as McDonald's, office equipment manufacturers and retail stores. Organisations tend to be highly dynamic and the primary value centres on customers and their needs. It is the team who produce the volume, and the culture encourages games, meetings, promotions and conventions to help maintain motivation. However, although a lot gets done, volume can be at the expense of quality.
- **Bet-your-company culture** – where there are large-stake decisions with a high risk but slow feedback so that it may be years before employees know if decisions were successful. Examples include oil companies, investment banks, architectural firms and the military. The focus is on the future and the importance of investing in it. There is a sense of deliberateness throughout the organisation typified by the ritual of the business meeting. There is a hierarchical system of authority with decision-making from the top down. The culture leads to high-quality inventions and scientific breakthroughs, but moves only very slowly and is vulnerable to short-term fluctuations.
- **Process culture** – a low-risk, slow-feedback culture where employees find difficulty in measuring what they do. Typical examples include banks, insurance companies, financial services and the civil service. The individual financial stakes are low and employees get very little feedback on their effectiveness. Their memos and reports seem to disappear into a void. Lack of feedback forces employees to focus on how they do something, not what they do. People tend to develop a 'cover your back' mentality. Bureaucracy results with attention to trivial events, minor detail, formality and technical perfection. Process cultures can be effective when there is a need for order and predictability.

Note, however that in a subsequent publication, *Deal and Kennedy* suggest revisions to the original typology. For example, under process cultures, banks might not yet fit into the work-hard/play-hard culture but have evolved more into sales-type organisations.[18]

INFLUENCES ON THE DEVELOPMENT OF CULTURE

The culture and structure of an organisation develop over time and in response to a complex set of factors. We can, however, identify a number of key influences that are likely to play an important role in the development of any corporate culture. These include history, primary function and technology, strategy, size, location, management and leadership, and the environment.[19]

- **History**. The reason, and manner in which, the organisation was originally formed, its age, and the philosophy and values of its owners and first senior managers will affect culture. A key event in the organisation's history such as a merger or major reorganisation, or a new generation of top management, may bring about a change in culture. Corporate history can be an effective induction tool to assist a growth programme, and to help integrate acquisitions and new employees by infusion with the organisation's culture and identity.[20] Failure in mergers and acquisitions can arise from cultural clashes and failure to integrate different cultures.[21]

- **Primary function and technology**. The nature of the organisation's 'business' and its primary function have an important influence on its culture. This includes the range and quality of products and services provided, the importance of reputation and the type of customers. The primary function of the organisation will determine the nature of the technological processes and methods of undertaking work, which in turn also affect structure and culture.

- **Strategy**. Although a business organisation may pursue profitability, this is not by itself very clear or a sufficient criterion for its effective management. For example, to what extent is emphasis placed on long-term survival or growth and development? How much attention is given to avoiding risks and uncertainties? Or how much concern is shown for broader social responsibilities? The organisation must give attention to objectives in all key areas of its operations. The combination of objectives and resultant strategies will influence culture, and may itself be influenced by changes in culture. (See also Chapter 14 and Chapter 18.)

- **Size**. Usually larger organisations have more formalised structures and cultures. Increased size is likely to result in separate departments and possibly split-site operations. This may cause difficulties in communication and inter-departmental rivalries with the need for effective co-ordination. A rapid expansion, or decline, in size and rate of growth, and resultant changes in staffing will influence structure and culture.

- **Location**. Geographical location and the physical characteristics can have a major influence on culture – for example, whether an organisation is located in a quiet rural location or a busy city centre can influence the types of customers and the staff employed. An example could be a hotel or restaurant. Location can also affect the nature of services provided, the sense of 'boundary' and distinctive identity, and opportunities for development.

- **Management and leadership**. Top executives can have considerable influence on the nature of corporate culture. Examples are the key roles played by Sir Richard Branson, Anita Roddick, founder of The Body Shop,[22] and Marjorie Scardino and her change of style when she took over as the new chief executive of Pearson.

Her candour works . . . As an example of straight talking winning over a sceptical City and press, it is brilliant. As an example of just how much a company's culture can change under a new chief executive, it is breathtaking.[23]

Another example is *Louis Gerstner*, who defined a strategy for the computing giant IBM and remade the ossified culture bred by the company's success, rebuilt the leadership team and gave the workforce a renewed sense of purpose.[24]

However, all members of staff help to shape the dominant culture of an organisation, irrespective of what senior management feel it should be. Culture is also determined by the nature of staff employed and the extent to which they accept management philosophy and policies or pay only 'lip service'. Another important influence is the match between corporate culture and employees' perception of the psychological contract (discussed in Chapter 1).

■ **The environment**. In order to be effective, the organisation must be responsive to external environmental influences. For example, if the organisation operates within a dynamic environment it requires a structure and culture that are sensitive and readily adaptable to change. An organic structure is more likely to respond effectively to new opportunities and challenges, and risks and limitations presented by the external environment.

THE CULTURAL WEB

In order to help describe and understand the culture of an organisation, *Johnson, Scholes and Whittington* present a cultural web, which brings together different aspects for the analysis of organisational culture (*see* Figure 19.1).

Figure 19.1	The cultural web of an organisation

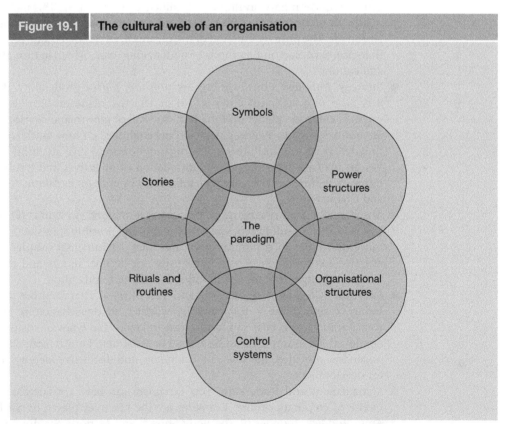

Source: Johnson, G., Scholes, K. and Whittington, R. *Exploring Corporate* Strategy, seventh edition, Financial Times Prentice Hall (2005), p. 202. Reproduced with permission from Pearson Education Ltd.

- **Routine behaviours** – the ways in which members of the organisation behave towards each other and towards those outside the organisation and which make up how things are done or how things should happen.
- **Rituals** – the particular activities or special events through which the organisation emphasises what is particularly important; can include formal organisational processes and informal processes.
- **Stories** told by members of the organisation that embed the present and flag up important events and personalities, and typically have to do with successes, failures, heroes, villains and mavericks.
- **Symbols** – such as logos, offices, cars, titles, type of language or terminology commonly used – which become a shorthand representation of the nature of the organisation.
- **Power structures** – the power of the most powerful individuals or groups in the organisation may be based on management position and seniority, but in some organisations power can be lodged with other levels or functions.
- **Control systems** – the measurement and reward systems that emphasise what it is important to monitor, and to focus attention and activity upon – for example, stewardship of funds or quality of service.
- **Organisation structure** – which reflects power structures and delineates important relationships and activities within the organisation, and involves both formal structure and control and less formal systems.
- **The paradigm** of the organisation, which encapsulates and reinforces the behaviours observed in other elements of the cultural web.[25]

Other interpretations of culture

There are, however, many other ways in which people attempt to describe and understand what constitutes organisational culture, and different areas of attention for analysing the elements of culture. *Wilson* suggests that culture is a characteristic of the organisation, not of individuals.

> *One way of examining the culture of an organization is to look at its corporate image to see what and who is valued in the organization. A corporate image is the mental picture the clients, customers, employees, and others have of an organization. The impression is the combination of unconscious, unintended, conscious, and intended factors that arise.*[26]

ACAS distinguishes two different organisation cultures and different ways of doing things:

- **Control culture** with the emphasis on rules and procedures, control and compliance with precedent providing guidelines; and
- **Quality of working life culture** with the emphasis on core values, with mission statements providing guidance and commitment via shared goals, values and traditions.[27]

Naylor suggests that seeing quite what forms organisational culture is difficult, and to make a start we need to recognise both the visible and invisible layers. On the surface is the visible layer made up of elements such as artefacts, symbols, languages, stories and activities which can be collected, compared and assembled into a description of the organisation. Underpinning this 'visible culture' is the invisible layer of beliefs, values, norms, basic assumptions and understanding.[28]

THE IMPORTANCE OF CULTURE

Applications of organisational behaviour and the effective management of human resources are dependent not only upon the nature of the industry or business, but also upon the characteristic features of the individual organisation – and its culture. The pervasive nature of culture in terms of 'how things are done around here' and common values, beliefs and

attitudes will therefore have a significant effect on organisational processes such as decision-making, design of structure, group behaviour, work organisation, motivation and job satisfaction, and management control. For example, many managers claim that their organisation's culture contributes considerably to their stress.[29]

Harrison and Stokes maintain that organisational culture influences the behaviour of all individuals and groups within the organisation.

> *Culture impacts most aspects of organizational life, such as how decisions are made, who makes them, how rewards are distributed, who is promoted, how people are treated, how the organization responds to its environment, and so on.*[30]

A similar point is made by *Reigle*, who refers to culture as an important factor in successful technology implementation, innovation, mergers, acquisitions, job satisfaction, organisational success and team effectiveness, and to the importance of determining whether organisations exhibit organic or mechanistic cultures.[31]

Culture and organisation control

Egan refers to culture as the largest organisational control system that dictates how crazy or idiosyncratic people can be. Companies and institutions have both an overt and covert culture that influences both business and organisational behaviour.

> *The covert set can be quite dysfunctional and costly. Culture – the assumptions, beliefs, values and norms that drive 'the way we do things here' – is the largest and most controlling of the systems because it affects not only overt organisational behaviour but also the shadow-side behaviour . . . Culture lays down norms for the social system. In one institution you had to be an engineer to rise to the top. There was no published rule, of course, it was just the way things were. In one bank you could never be made an officer of the company if you wore polyester clothes. Culture tells us what kind of politics are allowed and just how members of an organisation are allowed to play the political game.*[32]

Egan also distinguishes between the 'preferred culture' which serves the business and the 'culture-in-use'. This culture-behind-the-culture carries the real beliefs, values and norms that drive patterns of behaviour within the company. These remain unnamed, undiscussed and unmentionable and these covert cultures lie outside ordinary managerial control. The first step in changing such limiting behaviour features is to identify the preferred culture and to ensure that the company's way of operating effectively serves the business right now.[33]

Culture and work ethic

Culture can influence people's attitudes and behaviour at work. For example a report from the Chartered Management Institute found that one in three managers felt that in their organisation there was a culture of not taking time off for sickness and nearly half felt they would not be treated sympathetically if they took sick leave.[34] *Bunting* draws attention to the link between work ethic (discussed in Chapter 1) and culture, and the extent to which people have a choice over how hard they work. Although some people have no choice, for the vast majority of people there is a degree of choice but the choices are not made in isolation:

> *they are the product of the particular organisational culture of our workplaces, which promote concepts of success, of team spirit so that we don't let colleagues down, and a powerful work ethic. We are also influenced by a culture that reinforces that work ethic and its cycle of continual achievement and consumption as measures of self-worth.*

Bunting maintains that it is through work that we seek to satisfy our craving for a sense of control, mastery and security and that clever organisations exploit this cultural context by designing corporate cultures that meet the emotional needs of their employees.[35]

Culture in short-life organisations

The importance of culture raises interesting questions relating to its nature and influence in 'short-life' organisations – that is, organisations created to run for only a short period of time such as arts festivals or national garden festivals. For example, how does culture develop when the organisation has little or no prior history, has short-term goals and objectives and has only limited time for top management to exercise influence? How do managers in such organisations attempt to inculcate culture? From a study of Garden Festival Wales, *Meudell and Gadd* found that success in creating a culture occurred as a direct result of their recruitment and training initiatives. However, it is not only culture but climate that is important for organisational effectiveness.

> *Rigorous training in customer care/corporate culture might produce an automatic 'Have a nice day' but only the engendering of a suitable climate will encourage people to say it and mean it.*[36]

Culture and organisational performance

Culture is clearly an important ingredient of effective organisational performance. In commenting, in a study of Europe's top companies, on Heineken's superiority in world markets, *Heller* makes the point that it rests in part on its remarkable corporate culture:

> *There is nothing accidental about cultural strengths . . . There is a relationship between an organisation's culture and its performance.*[37]

In their original study of highly successful companies, *Goldsmith and Clutterbuck* identified eight characteristics built into the day-to-day culture of the organisation. From their subsequent study of the world's top companies, it appears that a key characteristic of high-performing companies is a challenge culture. All the companies are very demanding of the people who work for them but this is balanced by a nurturing culture that shows that they also care for their employees in numerous ways.[38]

And according to *Cummings and Worley*:

> *An organization's culture is the pattern of assumptions, values and norms that are more or less shared by an organization's members. A growing body of research has shown that culture can affect strategy formulation and implementation as well as a firm's ability to achieve high levels of excellence.*[39]

Use of managerial tools

Chatman and Cha suggest that every company has a culture – good or bad. However, there is more to a good culture than happy staff. In order to aid long-term performance, there are three main criteria needed to develop a suitable culture:

- it must be strategically relevant;
- it needs to be strong in order that people care about what is important; and
- the culture must have an intrinsic ability to adapt to changing circumstances.

In order that leaders can develop, manage and change their culture for better performance, Chatman and Cha refer to the use of three managerial tools:

- **Recruitment and selection** – hire people who fit the company's culture even if this may involve overlooking some technical skills for a better cultural fit. Look carefully at the characteristics of your recruiters and consider your selection decision in the light of culture.
- **Social tools and training** – develop practices that enable new people to understand the values, abilities, expected behaviour and social knowledge in order to participate fully as an employee, and to create strong bonds among members.
- **Reward system** – culture is an organisation's informal reward system but it needs to be intricately connected to formal rewards. Examples include staff meetings where the seating arrangement is in accordance with level of sales, name badges that include inventory losses, and payments of large commissions in front of customers and other staff.[40]

Culture change

The pervasive nature of organisational culture means that if change is to be brought about successfully, this is likely to involve changes to culture. For example, *Stewart* makes the following comment on the relationship between culture and change:

> In recent years attention has shifted from the effects of the organization of work on people's behavior to how behavior is influenced by the organizational culture. What is much more common today is the widespread recognition that organizational change is not just, or even necessarily mainly, about changing the structure but often requires changing the culture too.[41]

A similar view is held by *Naylor*, who points out that 'In the holistic system, any change will affect the culture and the culture will affect or constrain the change . . . Cultural change is intimately bound up with the process of organisational change.'[42]

However, although attention is often given to shifting the prevailing activities and atmosphere of an organisation to a brighter future, changing the ethos and culture of an organisation is not easy. In practice, organisations usually appear to alter their underlying ethos only on a gradual basis and the complexity of environmental pressures may itself hinder rapid change. Culture is often deep-rooted and commitment to the objectives and policies of the organisation, people's cognitive limitations and their uncertainties and fears, may mean a reluctance to accept a change in behaviour. Culture is reinforced through the system of rites and rituals, patterns of communication, the informal organisation, expected patterns of behaviour and perceptions of the psychological contract.

> *Clearly most organisations are not the stable, predictable structures of the past. Keeping followers motivated and committed in an era of unrelenting change, means that leaders must be able to create organisational cultures that foster not only performance, but also a sense of pride and fun. Because cultures evolve over many years and are usually deep-rooted, they can be difficult to change. Some commentators have observed that it is easier to change behaviour by changing processes and systems in an organisation than it is to change people's attitudes. While goals change in the course of a person's life, values tend to remain constant and help determine an employee's attitudes to their employer.*
>
> DTI (2004)[43]

The nature of organisational change is discussed later in this chapter.

National and international culture

Culture helps to account for variations among organisations and managers, both nationally and internationally. It helps to explain why different groups of people perceive things in their own way and perform things differently from other groups.[44] With greater international competition, an understanding of national culture has become of increasing importance for managers. According to *Siddall*, for example, 'International business, the issue of culture and the need for better understanding have become major parts of organisational behaviour.'[45] Cultural practices vary widely among different countries and because of our own values may be difficult to understand.

Schneider and Barsoux suggest that cultural beliefs and values influence the meaning of management and also show up differences in conceptions of organisations. National differences and cultural reasons raise concerns about the transferability of organisational structures, systems and processes and question the logic of universal 'best practice'.[46] *Cheng, Sculli and Chan* also question the universality of theories of management and organisational behaviour on the grounds that they have not adequately addressed the factor of culture.[47] Those fortunate enough to have shared the experience of the author in visiting both Walt Disney World Resort in Florida and Disneyland Resort Paris would probably have witnessed

the cultural differences in the attitudes to, and acceptance of, the Disney approach and procedures between American and French employees.

According to *Francesco and Gold*, culture has recently been accepted as an explanation of organisational behaviour. One reason is the increase in competitiveness of nations and a second reason is that managers encounter different cultures in their contacts with people from other nations. However, there are limits to the use of culture to explain organisational behaviour, and the relationship between national cultural values and actual behaviour in organisations is complex.[48]

Recall also the discussion on the international context of management and organisational behaviour in Chapter 1.

Critical reflection

'The proliferation of definitions and explanations of culture, its anthropological origins and lack of clarity undermines its value to our understanding of organisational behaviour. It is too ambigious a concept for the effective day-to-day management of the organisation.'

Do you agree? What role do you think culture plays in the management of modern work organisations?

ORGANISATIONAL CLIMATE

In addition to arrangements for the carrying out of organisational processes, management has a responsibility for creating a climate in which people are motivated to work willingly and effectively. **Organisational climate** is another general concept and difficult to define precisely. It is more something that is felt. It can be likened to our description of the weather and the way in which the climate of a geographical region results from the combination of environmental forces. Some of these forces are better understood than others. In a similar way that culture was defined simply as 'how things are done around here', climate can be defined as 'how it feels to work around here'.

Applied to organisations, **climate** can be said to relate to the prevailing atmosphere surrounding the organisation, to the level of morale, and to the strength of feelings of belonging, care and goodwill among members. Climate will influence the attitudes that members of the organisation bring to bear on their work performance and personal relationships. The extent to which employees accept the culture of the organisation will have a significant effect on climate. Whereas organisational culture describes what the organisation is about, organisational climate is an indication of the employees' feelings and beliefs of what the organisation is about. Climate is based on the perceptions of members towards the organisation.

> Organisational climate is a relatively enduring quality of the internal environment of an organisation that (a) is experienced by its members, (b) influences their behavior, and (c) can be described in terms of the values of a particular set of characteristics (or attributes) of the organisation.[49]

From a detailed study of approaches to organisational climate, *Moran and Volkwein* conclude that:

> since climate operates at a more accessible level than culture, it is more malleable and, hence, the more appropriate level at which to target short-term interventions aimed at producing positive organisational change . . . [however,] interventions to change climate must consider the deeper patterns embedded in an organisation's climate.[50]

Climate also relates to the recognition of the organisation as a social system and the extent to which membership is perceived as a psychologically rewarding experience. It can

be seen as the state of mutual trust and understanding among members of the organisation. For example, *Rentsch* suggests that 'One assumption of climate theory is that organizational members perceive and make sense of organizational policies, practices, and procedures in psychologically meaningful terms'.[51]

Characteristics of a healthy organisational climate

Organisational climate is characterised, therefore, by the nature of the people–organisation relationship and the superior–subordinate relationship. These relationships are determined by interactions among goals and objectives, formal structure, the process of management, styles of leadership and the behaviour of people. Although similar types of organisations will share certain common features and norms, each organisation will have its own different and distinctive features. In general terms, however, a healthy organisational climate might be expected to exhibit such characteristic features as:

- the integration of organisational goals and personal goals;
- the most appropriate organisation structure based on the demands of the socio-technical system;
- democratic functioning of the organisation with full opportunities for participation;
- justice in treatment with equitable HRM and employment relations policies and practices;
- mutual trust, consideration and support among different levels of the organisation;
- the open discussion of conflict with an attempt to avoid confrontation;
- managerial behaviour and styles of leadership appropriate to the particular work situations;
- acceptance of the psychological contract between the individual and the organisation;
- recognition of people's needs and expectations at work, and individual differences and attributes;
- concern for flexibility and the work/life balance;
- opportunities for personal development and career progression;
- a sense of identity with, and loyalty to, the organisation and a feeling of being a valued and important member.

Climate and organisational performance

If organisational climate is to be improved, then attention should be given to the above features. A healthy climate will not by itself guarantee improved organisational effectiveness. However, an organisation is most unlikely to attain optimum operational performance unless the climate evokes a spirit of support and co-operation throughout the organisation, and is conducive to motivating members to work willingly and effectively. *Gray* maintains from his research to have found a clear correlation between successful workplace outcomes and a range of climate characteristics and that a climate conducive to successful outcomes also tends to be conducive to individual happiness. The climate of an organisation has a significant impact on the quality and quantity of work that gets done and on the well-being of employees.[52]

EMPLOYEE COMMITMENT

Among the factors that contribute to a healthy organisational climate is the extent to which members of staff have a sense of commitment to the organisation. The extent of their commitment will have a major influence on the level of work performance. The concept of **employee commitment** itself, and the manner in which it is actually created, is not easy to describe. There does, however, appear to be a growing acceptance of the notion of **engagement** or attachment and loyalty. *O'Reilly* refers to the term 'organizational commitment' as 'typically conceived of as an individual's psychological bond to the organization, including a sense of job involvement, loyalty, and a belief in the values of the organization'.[53]

People clearly differ in what motivates them and what they are seeking from work. But unless people feel fully engaged with the organisation they will not be intellectually and emotionally committed or motivated to give willingly of their best. *Walton* suggests that a significant change in approaches to the organisation and management of work is from organisational control to commitment in the workplace. The evidence is well grounded that underlying all the policies of commitment strategy is a management philosophy at the centre of which 'is a belief that eliciting employee commitment will lead to enhanced performance'.[54]

Securing the commitment of staff

Genuine commitment requires not just a recognition or understanding of what the organisation expects but an emotional and behavioural response from staff. After the downsizing, de-layering, streamlining and outsourcing of recent years, *Altman, Cooper and Garner* question whether companies can continue to count on commitment from employees when they are no longer seen to be committed to them. The more companies downsize, the more they are seen to be breaking the psychological contract. A new psychological contract needs to consider the organisation of the future.

> *The old 'command and control' interpretation of loyalty in the workplace needs to be replaced with an attitude of commitment by both sides which leads to a more pragmatic relationship within the limited horizons against which businesses are being managed today worldwide. Employers will still commit themselves to their employees but employment can no longer be guaranteed.*[55]

Galunic and Weeks suggest that with the demise of job security, companies need other strategies to encourage commitment. Examples include paying more attention to compensation, flexible working, spending to support telecommuting and lifestyle-friendly perks. However, while such initiatives may encourage employees to work hard, they are no substitute for job security. In order to help restore commitment without again offering job security, Galunic and Weeks propose that in addition to company-specific training, there is a programme of investment in generic training that focuses on general skills and education to raise the professional level of employees. By developing 'employability' and the ability to earn a living through professional or occupational – not job – security, employees are in turn likely to respond with greater commitment to the company.[56]

According to *Gratton*, the obligations of the firm to individual members are expressed continuously and the first obligation is true commitment to people.

> On the face of it 'true commitment to people' is an overused phrase, appearing as it does on every CEO's annual business report. The obligation or 'true commitment' is tested, not when times are good, but when times are hard.[57]

Circle of employee engagement

De Vita suggests that after the cost-cutting and downsizing of the 1990s, how we feel about work is becoming the prime concern of a growing number of companies. Employee engagement should not be written off as just another HR fad but neither should it be viewed as a quick fix. Engagement relates to the core of a business – its values, culture and way of managing, and changing that is a tall order. But a truly engaged company is likely to be a 'great' one. As an example De Vita quotes the success of the John Lewis Partnership as a result of its co-ownership by employees combined with a collective management approach and the full engagement of employees.[58] The positive behaviour of a deeply engaged employee will rub off on clients, customers and colleagues. A highly engaged company is known to perform better; enjoy high staff retention; sustain long-term success; display energy, productivity and innovativeness; and win regard as an attractive place to work. *See* Figure 19.2.

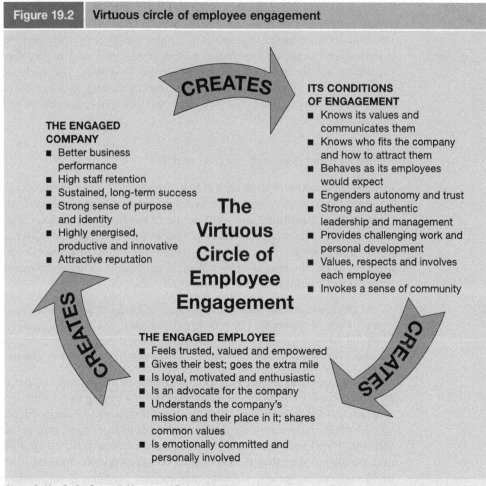

Figure 19.2 Virtuous circle of employee engagement

Source: De Vita, E. 'Get Engaged', *Management Today*, April, 2007, p. 40. Reproduced from *Management Today* magazine with the permission of the copyright owner, Haymarket Business Publications Limited.

Underlying influences

In addition to the above, there are a number of underlying influences on the extent of employees' commitment to the organisation.

■ People differ in their **work ethic** and the manner of their involvement with, and concern for, work and the extent to which they have an instrumental, bureaucratic or solidaristic orientation. Some people may well have a set attitude to work, whatever the nature of the work environment.

■ People's behaviour and the level of their commitment is also influenced by the nature of the **psychological contract** and the degree to which it is perceived as fair by both the individual and the organisation.

■ In terms of their relationship with the work organisation, employees may reasonably have the approach of 'what's in it for me?'. An important influence on the strength of commitment is the **nature of the reward system** and the satisfaction of needs and expectations at work in terms of economic rewards, intrinsic satisfaction or social relationships (*see* Chapter 7).

THE NATURE OF ORGANISATIONAL CHANGE

Change is an inevitable and constant feature. It is an inescapable part of both social and organisational life and we are all subject to continual change of one form or another.

Like it or not, change happens. Change is also a pervasive influence and much of the following discussion provides links with other topics in other chapters. The effects of change can be studied over different time scales, from weeks to hundreds of years, and studied at different levels. Change can be studied in terms of its effects at the individual, group, organisation, society, national or international level. However, because of its pervasive nature, change at any one level is interrelated with changes at other levels, and it is difficult to study one area of change in isolation. At the individual level there could for example, be a **personal transformational change** where circumstances have not changed but because of some emotional or spiritual happening the individual was transformed or changed. This transformation may have some effect on their behaviour and actions at work and relationships with colleagues. But our main focus of attention is on the management of organisational change. Organisational change can be initiated deliberately by managers, it can evolve slowly within a department, it can be imposed by specific changes in policy or procedures or it can arise through external pressures. Change can affect all aspects of the operation and functioning of the organisation.[59]

The forces of change

An organisation can perform effectively only through interactions with the broader external environment of which it is part. The structure and functioning of the organisation must reflect, therefore, the nature of the environment in which it is operating. There are factors which create an increasingly volatile environment, such as:

- uncertain economic conditions;
- globalisation and fierce world competition;
- the level of government intervention;
- European Union social legislation;
- political interests;
- scarcity of natural resources;
- rapid developments in new technologies and the information age.

In order to help ensure its survival and future success the organisation must be readily adaptable to the external demands placed upon it. The organisation must be responsive to change. Other major forces of change include:

- increased demands for quality and high levels of customer service and satisfaction;
- greater flexibility in the structure of work organisations and patterns of management;
- the changing nature and composition of the workforce; and
- conflict from within the organisation.

According to a survey from the Management Consultancies Association, four interrelated forces are driving change, each of which brings organisations and individuals into conflict:

1 outsourcing and the continual redefinition of what constitutes an organisation's core business;
2 the distribution of work across different people, organisations and locations, and the extent to which this makes work fragmented;
3 changing demographics and expectations that create an employees', rather than employers', market;
4 the double-edged sword of technology, which enables people to do more but tempts organisations to do too much.[60]

Change within the organisation

Change also originates within the organisation itself. Much of this change is part of a natural process of ageing – for example, as material resources such as buildings, equipment or machinery deteriorate or lose efficiency; or as human resources get older, or as skills and abilities become outdated. Some of this change can be managed through careful planning

– for example, regular repairs and maintenance, choice of introducing new technology or methods of work, effective human resource planning to prevent a large number of staff retiring at the same time, and management succession planning – training and staff development. However, the main pressure of change is from external forces. The organisation must be properly prepared to face the demands of a changing environment. It must give attention to its future development and success; this includes public sector organisations and the armed forces.[61]

> Public sector executives face unique obstacles in leading organisational change, in part because of entrenched civil service bureaucracies, procedural constraints such as managing performance and firing employees, and dealing with many different stakeholders with competing priorities.[62]

A concept map of needs and drivers of organisational change is presented in Figure 19.3.

Critical reflection

'Change is nothing new and a simple fact of life. Some people actively thrive on new challenges and constant change, while others prefer the comfort of the status quo and strongly resist any change. It is all down to the personality of the individual and there is little management can do about resistance to change.'

To what extent do you accept this contention? What is your attitude to change?

PLANNED ORGANISATIONAL CHANGE

Most planned organisational change is triggered by the need to respond to new challenges or opportunities presented by the external environment, or in anticipation of the need to cope with potential future problems, for example, uncertain economic conditions, intended government legislation, new product development by a major competitor or further technological advances. Planned change represents an intentional attempt to improve, in some important way, the operational effectiveness of the organisation.

The basic underlying objectives can be seen in general terms as:

■ modifying the behavioural patterns of members of the organisation; and
■ improving the ability of the organisation to cope with changes in its environment.

ACAS refers to initiating and maintaining a Quality of Working Life (QWL) change programme. Such initiatives could stem from a variety of issues that might provide 'a window for change' to management and/or worker representatives. Examples include:

■ a general sense that the organisation could perform better;
■ the need to improve organisation flexibility, quality or to develop new customer concern;
■ a sense that skills and abilities of people are under-utilised or concerns about a lack of commitment from employees;
■ the need to introduce changes in technology or working practices;
■ workers feeling over-controlled by supervision or by the process or jobs seen as being boring;
■ concerns about ineffective communications or poor performance indicators;
■ fractious relationships between managers and the managed.[63]

Behaviour modification

A programme of planned change and improved performance developed by *Lewin* involves the management of a three-phase process of behaviour modification:

Figure 19.3 Concept map of organisational change – needs and drivers

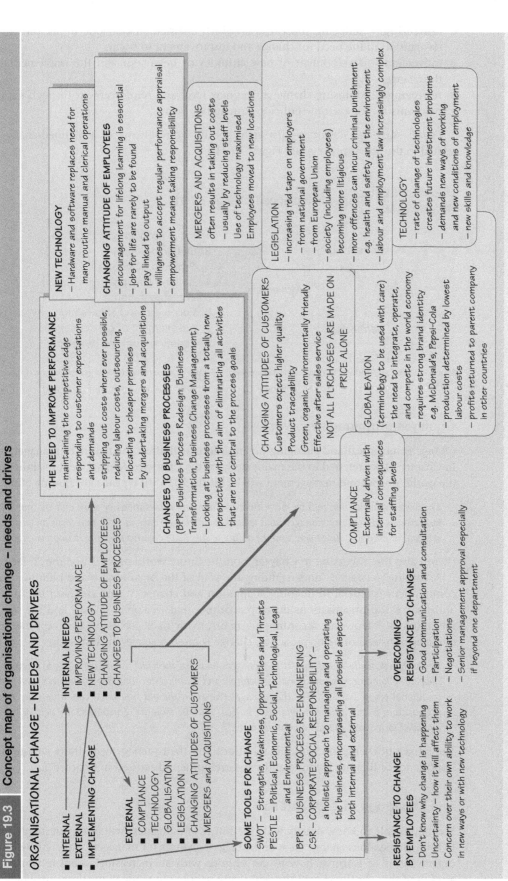

ORGANISATIONAL CHANGE – NEEDS AND DRIVERS

■ INTERNAL
■ EXTERNAL
■ IMPLEMENTING CHANGE

INTERNAL NEEDS
■ IMPROVING PERFORMANCE
■ NEW TECHNOLOGY
■ CHANGING ATTITUDE OF EMPLOYEES
■ CHANGES TO BUSINESS PROCESSES

EXTERNAL
■ COMPLIANCE
■ TECHNOLOGY
■ GLOBALISATION
■ LEGISLATION
■ CHANGING ATTITUDES OF CUSTOMERS
■ MERGERS and ACQUISITIONS

SOME TOOLS FOR CHANGE
SWOT – Strengths, Weakness, Opportunities and Threats
PESTLE – Political, Economic, Social, Technological, Legal and Environmental
BPR – BUSINESS PROCESS RE-ENGINEERING
CSR – CORPORATE SOCIAL RESPONSIBILITY – a holistic approach to managing and operating the business, encompassing all possible aspects both internal and external

RESISTANCE TO CHANGE BY EMPLOYEES
– Don't know why change is happening
– Uncertainty – how it will affect them
– Concern over their own ability to work in new ways or with new technology

OVERCOMING RESISTANCE TO CHANGE
– Good communication and consultation
– Participation
– Negotiations
– Senior management approval especially if beyond one department

NEW TECHNOLOGY
– Hardware and software replaces need for many routine manual and clerical operations

CHANGING ATTITUDE OF EMPLOYEES
– encouragement for lifelong learning is essential
– jobs for life are rarely to be found
– pay linked to output
– willingness to accept regular performance appraisal
– empowerment means taking responsibility

MERGERS AND ACQUISITIONS
– often results in taking out costs
– usually by reducing staff levels
– Use of technology maximised
Employees moved to new locations

LEGISLATION
– increasing red tape on employers
 – from national government
 – from European Union
 – society (including employees) becoming more litigious
– more offences can incur criminal punishment e.g. health and safety and the environment
– labour and employment law increasingly complex

TECHNOLOGY
– rate of change of technologies creates future investment problems
– demands new ways of working and new conditions of employment
– new skills and knowledge

THE NEED TO IMPROVE PERFORMANCE
– maintaining the competitive edge
– responding to customer expectations and demands
– stripping out costs where ever possible, reducing labour costs, outsourcing, relocating to cheaper premises
– by undertaking mergers and acquisitions

CHANGES TO BUSINESS PROCESSES
(BPR, Business Process Redesign: Business Transformation, Business Change Management)
– Looking at business processes from a totally new perspective with the aim of eliminating all activities that are not central to the process goals

CHANGING ATTITUDES OF CUSTOMERS
Customers expect higher quality
Product traceability
Green, organic, environmentally friendly
Effective after sales service
NOT ALL PURCHASES ARE MADE ON PRICE ALONE

GLOBALISATION
(terminology to be used with care)
– the need to integrate, operate, and compete in the world economy
– requires strong brand identity e.g. McDonald's, Pepsi-Cola
– production determined by lowest labour costs
– profits returned to parent company in other countries

COMPLIANCE
– Externally driven with internal consequences for staffing levels

(Note that the examples are illustrative and not exhaustive.)
Source: Copyright © 2008 The Virtual Learning Materials Workshop. Reproduced with permission.

- **unfreezing** – reducing those forces which maintain behaviour in its present form, recognition of the need for change and improvement to occur;
- **movement** – development of new attitudes or behaviour and the implementation of the change;
- **refreezing** – stabilising change at the new level and reinforcement through supporting mechanisms, for example policies, structure or norms.[64]

French, Kast and Rosenzweig list eight specific components of a planned-change effort related to the above process (*see* Figure 19.4).[65]

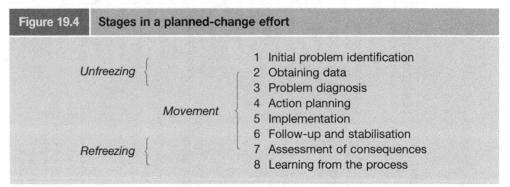

Figure 19.4	Stages in a planned-change effort

Unfreezing {

Movement {

Refreezing {

1 Initial problem identification
2 Obtaining data
3 Problem diagnosis
4 Action planning
5 Implementation
6 Follow-up and stabilisation
7 Assessment of consequences
8 Learning from the process

Source: Adapted from French, W. L., Kast, F. E. and Rosenzweig, J. E. *Understanding Human Behavior in Organizations*, Harper and Row (1985), p. 9.

Changes in managerial work

Change is reciprocal and changing organisations will affect the nature of managerial work. In Chapter 11 we referred to the major study by the Chartered Management Institute on what the world of work and management will be like in 2018. To repeat a key finding of the study:

> *The working population will be more diverse. Changing expectations of work and the impact of new technologies will require managers and leaders to develop a range of skills that focus on emotional and spiritual intelligence, judgement and the ability to stimulate creative thinking to improve productivity.*[66]

(Recall also the discussion in Chapter 3 on the future world of work and the 'Y' factor.)

According to *Gratton*, 'understanding the soul of the organisation and building trust and commitment is crucial to ongoing adaptation and change'.[67] And *Lockhead* maintains that 'most successful organisations develop a culture that welcomes change and the opportunities it brings'.[68] However, according to *Crainer*, many managers refuse to accept the necessity of change. Instead of being proactive, change is often reactive, the last resort.

> *Research repeatedly shows that it is managers who are the chief stumbling block to making change happen. Changing organizational structures and managerial thinking challenges and undercuts traditional power bases . . . For the manager reared on the old functional certainties, the new world organization is very difficult to manage. Indeed, the vast majority of managers are neither trained nor equipped to manage in such an environment.*[69]

The impact of change on work organisations and their management draws attention to the importance of lifelong learning and self-development discussed in Chapter 5.

The challenge of e-business

It is impossible to know exactly what the future of e-business will bring but it will continue to bring tremendous change. One of the biggest changes for managers, especially within large organisations, is learning how to get to grips with an increasingly flexible workforce. As a result of the e-business environment many people can work at any time, anywhere and at

any place. Many employees work at home but although the virtual office may help organisations to cut costs, it also poses many management challenges including the challenge to put structures in place to ensure regular meetings take place. Flexible working calls for flexible managers. This means that the traditional line managers need to become leaders, coaches and facilitators. Given the accelerating rate of change, particularly with the internet, it is essential that organisations invest in and develop their managers to succeed with this change.

RESISTANCE TO CHANGE

Despite the potential positive outcomes, change is often resisted at both the individual and the organisational level. Resistance to change – or the thought of the implications of the change – appears to be a common phenomenon. As long ago as 1970, *Toffler* wrote about the psychological dimension of 'future shock', and that people are naturally wary of change. 'Among many there is an uneasy mood – a suspicion that change is out of control.'[70]

Resistance to change can take many forms and it is often difficult to pinpoint the exact reasons. The forces against change in work organisations include: ignoring the needs and expectations of members; when members have insufficient information about the nature of the change; or if they do not perceive the need for change. Fears may be expressed over such matters as employment levels and job security, de-skilling of work, loss of job satisfaction, wage rate differentials, changes to social structures and working conditions, loss of individual control over work, and greater management control.

Individual resistance

Some common reasons for individual resistance to change within organisations include the following:

■ **Selective perception.** People's interpretation of stimuli presents a unique picture or image of the 'real' world and can result in selective perception. This can lead to a biased view of a particular situation, which fits most comfortably into a person's own perception of reality, and can cause resistance to change. For example, trade unionists may have a stereotyped view of management as untrustworthy and therefore oppose any management change, however well founded might have been the intention. Managers exposed to different theories or ideas may tend to categorise these as either those they already practise and have no need to worry about or those that are of no practical value and which can be discarded as of no concern to them.

■ **Habit.** People tend to respond to situations in an established and accustomed manner. Habits may serve as a means of comfort and security, and as a guide for easy decision-making. Proposed changes to habits, especially if the habits are well established and require little effort, may well be resisted. However, if there is a clearly perceived advantage, for example a reduction in working hours without loss of pay, there is likely to be less, if any, resistance to the change, although some people may, because of habit, still find it difficult to adjust to the new times.

■ **Inconvenience or loss of freedom.** If the change is seen as likely to prove inconvenient, make life more difficult, reduce freedom of action or result in increased control, there will be resistance.

■ **Economic implications.** People are likely to resist change that is perceived as reducing either directly or indirectly their pay or other rewards, requiring an increase in work for the same level of pay or acting as a threat to their job security. People tend to have established patterns of working and a vested interest in maintaining the status quo.

■ **Security in the past.** There is a tendency for some people to find a sense of security in the past. In times of frustration or difficulty, or when faced with new or unfamiliar ideas or methods, people may reflect on the past. There is a wish to retain old and comfortable ways. For example, in bureaucratic organisations, officials often tend to place faith in well-established ('tried and trusted') procedures and cling to these as giving a feeling of security.

- **Fear of the unknown**. Changes which confront people with the unknown tend to cause anxiety or fear. Many major changes in a work organisation present a degree of uncertainty, for example the introduction of new technology or methods of working. A person may resist promotion because of uncertainty over changes in responsibilities or the increased social demands of the higher position.

Organisational resistance

Although organisations have to adapt to their environment, they tend to feel comfortable operating within the structure, policies and procedures which have been formulated to deal with a range of present situations. To ensure operational effectiveness, organisations often set up defences against change and prefer to concentrate on the routine things they perform well. Some of the main reasons for organisational resistance against change are as follows.

- **Organisation culture**. Recall that the culture of an organisation develops over time and may not be easy to change. The pervasive nature of culture in terms of 'how things are done around here' also has a significant effect on organisational processes and the behaviour of staff. An ineffective culture may result in a lack of flexibility for, or acceptance of, change.
- **Maintaining stability**. Organisations, especially large-scale ones, pay much attention to maintaining stability and predictability. The need for formal organisation structure and the division of work, narrow definitions of assigned duties and responsibilities, established rules, procedures and methods of work, can result in resistance to change. The more mechanistic or bureaucratic the structure, the less likely it is that the organisation will be responsive to change.
- **Investment in resources**. Change often requires large resources that may already be committed to investments in other areas or strategies. Assets such as buildings, technology, equipment and people cannot easily be altered. For example, a car manufacturer may not find it easy to change to a socio-technical approach and the use of autonomous work groups because it cannot afford the cost of a new purpose-built plant and specialised equipment.
- **Past contracts or agreements**. Organisations enter into contracts or agreements with other parties, such as the government, other organisations, trade unions, suppliers and customers. These contracts and agreements can limit changes in behaviour – for example, organisations operating under a special licence or permit, or a fixed-price contract to supply goods/services to a government agency. Another example might be an agreement with unions that limits the opportunity to introduce compulsory redundancies, or the introduction of certain new technology or working practices.
- **Threats to power or influence**. Change may be seen as a threat to the power or influence of certain groups within the organisation, such as their control over decisions, resources or information. For example, managers may resist the introduction of quality circles or worker-directors because they see this as increasing the role and influence of non-managerial staff, and a threat to the power in their own positions. Where a group of people have, over a period of time, established what they perceive as their 'territorial rights', they are likely to resist change.

Perceptions and change

Although change is often resisted, *Cunningham* maintains that one of the greatest myths in management is the generalisation that people resist change. In fact people love change. The commonest reason for resistance is where people perceive a potential loss. For example, because of negative rumour-mongering, people may perceive that they will be worse off from a proposed change even if the opposite is in fact true. In a different context, changes that result, for example, in the loss of one's job, can create real, fact-based resistance. While people welcome change that they want, they have to be careful about the pace of change. In a more general context people may be enthusiastic for change, for example in large organisations where some people want to see changes and improvements in communication.

What seems to get in the way is the continual chanting of the untrue generalisation that 'people resist change'. People resist some change – if they perceive that they are going to lose out. People welcome change that makes things better.[71]

Neuroscientific approach to resistance to change

Riches questions why some organisations struggle to change and applies an interesting approach to resistance to change based on a neuroscientific understanding. Whether consolidating a merger, re-engineering business processes, restructuring, changing value propositions, introducing new IT systems, relocating premises, or changing the culture – all too often the process is derailed by the resistance of employees. Resistance to change is one of the most powerful drivers of human behaviour, and the key to dealing with it effectively is to understand both its physical and emotional components. Most organisations make two fatal errors when dealing with resistance. First, they underestimate the strength of current patterns that employees are comfortable and familiar with. Second, they underestimate what will be required to change those patterns and deal with the automatic, though sometimes subtle, fight or flight responses that occur when employees interpret changes as threats.

The amygdala and The Almond Effect®

According to Riches, our brains are hard-wired to do three things: match patterns, resist or fight any threats to survival, and respond first with emotion over logic. Our neural pathways and amygdalae are the key players in these reactions. The amygdala is an almond-shaped piece of the brain that triggers the 'fight or flight' reaction. Your brain has two amygdalae, and they play a fundamental role in ensuring your survival. Sometimes, though, the amygdalae set off a false alarm. This is what Riches calls The Almond Effect®. Put simply, you act without thinking and get it wrong. You can probably think of many times when this has happened, times when you said or did something in the heat of the moment, and almost immediately afterwards regretted it.

The Almond Effect® is critical if survival really is at stake, but at work it often gets in the way. It is the reason why all too often, human beings automatically react to change with resistance, even before they fully understand the nature of the change. The amygdala has activated the fear response based on previous memories of change (old neural pathways) associated with, for example, job losses, more work, new skills required, change of roster, cost cutting and so on. Stress hormones are released as part of the inbuilt flight/fight mechanism and show up at work as anger, anxiety, lethargy, poor performance and reluctance to change.

The only way to overcome this resistance is to convince employees that the changes or new initiatives enhance their ability to 'survive'. If you don't convince them, they may comply with changes for a while but will soon fall back into the old way of doing things. Their older, established neural-pathway patterns are simply more hard-wired than the new ones. Neuroscientists show us that although rational decision-making is inextricably intertwined with emotions, human beings are primarily emotional and secondarily rational, so emotions call the shots in business and in life. Unless an organisation accepts and addresses this reality, managing change with an emphasis on logic rather than emotion will not diminish resistance to organisational change.[72]

Critical reflection

'The biggest difficulty with change is the associated fear and uncertainty. If management maintains effective and continuous communications at all levels of the organisation before and during the introduction of change this would minimise any problems.'

What is your view? What has been your experience of organisational change?

THE MANAGEMENT OF ORGANISATIONAL CHANGE

The successful management of change is clearly essential for continued economic performance and competitiveness and is the life-blood of business success. New ideas and innovations should not be perceived as threats by members of the organisation. The efforts made by management to maintain the balance of the socio-technical system will influence people's attitudes, the behaviour of individuals and groups, and thereby the level of organisational performance and effectiveness.

Stewart is among those writers who point out how changes in technology and in domestic government policies have had a radical impact on managers in many companies and in public service organisations.

> *One of the most difficult problems for managers is rapid change. How British managers react to change will have an important influence on Britain's economic future. This is true for managers in the public service as well as for those in industry and commerce. The tempo of change has speeded up; hence the demands made on managers to plan for, and adjust to, change are greater. All change requires both abilities.*[73]

Organisational responses to change

Christensen and Overdorf suggest a framework to help managers understand what types of change the organisation is capable and incapable of handling. They identify three factors that affect organisational responses to different types of change and what an organisation can and cannot do:

- **resources** – access to abundant, high-quality resources increases an organisation's chances of coping with change;
- **processes** – the patterns of interaction, co-ordination, communication and decision-making employees use to transform resources into products and services. Processes may be formal and explicitly defined and documented, or informal and routines or ways of working that evolve over time;
- **values** – the standards by which employees set priorities that enable them to judge whether an order is attractive, whether a customer is more or less important, whether an idea for a new product is attractive or marginal.

The factors that define an organisation's capabilities and disabilities evolve over time – they start in resources, then move to visible, articulated processes and values, and finally migrate to culture. Christensen and Overdorf maintain that when an organisation faces the same sort of problem that its processes and values were designed to address, managing can be straightforward. However, when the problem facing the organisation is fundamentally different these same factors constitute disabilities, especially when the organisation's capabilities have come to reside in processes and values. There are three possible ways in which managers can develop new capabilities to cope with change:

- create organisational structures within corporate boundaries in which new processes can be developed;
- spin out an independent organisation from the existing organisation and develop new processes and values;
- acquire a different organisation whose processes and values match closely the new requirements.[74]

Actions to secure effective change

Many books and articles refer to the steps or actions to be taken to secure successful and sustainable change.[75] For example, *Kotter and Cohen* list the following eight steps for successful large-scale change:

1 **Create a sense of urgency** among relevant people, whatever the nature or size of the organisation.
2 **Build a guiding team** with the credibility, skills, connections, reputations and formal authority to provide change leadership.
3 **Create visions** which are sensible, clear and uplifting, and sets of strategies.
4 **Communicate** the vision and strategy in order to induce understanding and commitment.
5 **Empower action** and remove obstacles that stop people acting on the vision.
6 **Produce short-term wins** that help to provide credibility, resources and momentum to the overall effort.
7 **Don't let up** but maintain the momentum, consolidate early changes and create wave after wave of change.
8 **Make change stick** by nurturing a new culture, and developing group norms of behaviour and shared values.[76]

Change and the environment

Newton points out that change takes many forms and, typically, organisations are undertaking many changes in parallel all the time. Newton provides a variety of optional guidance to help review the nature of change being made and the environment in which one is working.

> *The central point is: there is not one type of change, and there is not a single way to approach change. Change management methodologies are only helpful if they are applicable both to the change you want to make and the environment in which you work. The approach you take to change must be tailored depending on the nature of the change you are making and the character of your organisation.*[77]

Minimising the problems of change

Activities managed on the basis of technical efficiency alone are unlikely to lead to optimum improvement in organisational performance. A major source of resistance to change arises from the need of organisations to adapt to new technological developments. The following discussion on how to minimise the problem of change centres on the example of the impact of information technology. The general principles, however, apply equally to the management of change arising from other factors.

■ **An important priority is to create an environment of trust and shared commitment, and to involve staff in decisions and actions that affect them.** It is important that members of staff understand fully the reasons for change. Organisations should try to avoid change for the sake of change as this can both be disruptive and lead to mistrust. However, considerations of the need to change arising from advances in information technology simply cannot be ignored.

■ **There should be full and genuine participation of all staff concerned as early as possible, preferably well before the actual introduction of new equipment or systems.** Information about proposed change, its implications and potential benefits should be communicated clearly to all interested parties. Staff should be actively encouraged to contribute their own ideas, suggestions and experiences, and to voice openly their worries or concerns.

■ **Team management, a co-operative spirit among staff and unions and a genuine feeling of shared involvement will help create a greater willingness to accept change.** A participative style of managerial behaviour that encourages supportive relationships between managers and subordinates, and group methods of organisation, decision-making and supervision, are more likely to lead to a sustained improvement in work performance. There is an assumption that most people will direct and control themselves more willingly if they share in the setting of their objectives.

- As part of the pre-planning for new technology there should be a carefully designed 'human resource management action programme'. The action programme should be directed to a review of recruitment and selection, natural wastage of staff, potential for training, retraining and the development of new skills, and other strategies to reduce the possible level of redundancies or other harmful effects on staff. Where appropriate, arrangements for greater flexibility or a shorter working week, and redeployment of staff, should be developed in full consultation with those concerned.

- The introduction of incentive payment schemes may help in motivating staff by an equitable allocation of savings which result from new technology and more efficient methods of work. Incentive schemes may be on an individual basis, with bonuses payable to each member of staff according to effort and performance; or on a group basis, where bonuses are paid to staff in relation to the performance of the group as a whole. By accepting changes in work methods and practices, staff share in the economic benefits gained from the improved efficiency of information technology and automated systems.

- Changes to the work organisation must maintain the balance of the socio-technical system. Increased technology and automation may result in jobs becoming more repetitive and boring, and providing only a limited challenge and satisfaction to staff. It is important, therefore, to attempt to improve the quality of work, to remove frustration and stress from jobs, and to make them more responsible and interesting. Actual working arrangements rely heavily on the informal organisation and effective teamwork and can have a significant influence on the successful implementation of change.

- Careful attention should be given to job design, methods of work organisation, the development of cohesive groups, and relationships between the nature and content of jobs and their task functions. The introduction of new technology has also highlighted the need to give attention to the wider organisational context including the design of technology itself, broader approaches to improved job design, employee involvement and empowerment, the development of skills and problem-solving capacity, and the effective management of change. (The subject of technology and organisations is discussed more fully in Chapter 16.)

Style of managerial behaviour

One of the most important factors in the successful implementation of organisational change is the style of managerial behaviour. Some members may actually prefer, and respond better, to a directed and controlled style of management. (Recall, for example, the discussion on Theory X and Theory Y styles of managerial behaviour in Chapter 12.) In most cases, however, the introduction of change is more likely to be effective with a participative style of managerial behaviour. If staff are kept fully informed of proposals, are encouraged to adopt a positive attitude and have personal involvement in the implementation of the change, there is a greater likelihood of their acceptance of the change. However, *Reis and Pena* maintain that too often, management ignores human resistance issues and the need to address them in the implementation plan.

> *The success of any change depends on the willingness of employees to accept it with enthusiasm and implement it with care. Yet, business changes at times are undertaken without understanding how the human element influences the success or failure of a project. Frequently, companies develop impressive technical plans and simply assume the change – technical or organizational – will occur. The difficult and often neglected part of such initiatives is leading and managing behavioural change with those persons who interface with the new technology or the new initiatives.*[78]

OVERCOMING RESISTANCE TO CHANGE

The effective management of change must be based on a clear understanding of human behaviour at work. Most people are not detached from their work but experience a range of

emotional involvements through their membership of the organisation, and they feel threatened and disoriented by the challenge of change. Emotions such as uncertainty, frustration or fear are common reactions. It is understandable therefore that people often adopt a defensive and negative attitude, and demonstrate resistance to change. It is important to remember that change is a complex and powerful psychological experience, and that individuals react internally to change.

According to *Atkinson*, a major problem in driving change in organisations is dealing with and managing the resistance that will be encountered – but that resistance should be welcomed as a healthy response. Resistance is natural and should not be viewed only as a negative response to change. In the absence of really positive benefits from the proposed change, the 'default' response of resistance is acceptable.

> It is unusual for any change not to attract some resistance. Even with foresight, pre-planning and all the apparent logic behind the need to change, you should expect some resistance as the norm. Recognise and welcome it as a healthy response and an opportunity to openly debate possibilities and treat resistance as a powerful ally in facilitating the learning process.[79]

People are the key factor

The successful implementation of new work methods and practices is dependent upon the willing and effective co-operation of staff, managerial colleagues and unions. People are the key factor in the successful management of change. If change is to work, it must change the perceptions, attitudes and behaviour of people.

However, *Lucas* reminds us that a high proportion of change initiatives fail, derailed by the people factor.

> Given that change has become such a fact of business life, it is worrying that so many change management programmes fail to fulfil their potential. The consensus among the experts is that it is often the people factor that derails the effort. Put simply, organisations know where they want to go – but they are not taking their people with them.[80]

Taylor points out that one of the most stressful aspects of change is often the sense of loss of control that accompanies it. The individual can feel powerless and helpless. Many organisations spend a great deal of attention and energy focusing on the operational outcomes of proposed changes but often pay scant attention to enabling employees to adapt psychologically to the new situation.[81] *Reeves and Knell* suggest that 'knowledge leaders understand that change provokes an emotional response, that successful change involves allowing people to feel angry, resentful and afraid as well as excited, hopeful and energised'.[82]

> Behaviour change is a personal issue. Groups don't change, teams don't change, companies don't change: individuals change. Teams change the way they operate when every member of the team changes the way he or she operates. Companies change the way they operate when the people in them change the way they behave.[83]

Responsibilities of top management

The successful management of change is a key factor of organisational performance and effectiveness and should emanate from the top of the organisation. Top management has a responsibility for the underlying philosophy and attitudes of the organisation, for creating and sustaining a healthy climate, and for establishing appropriate and supportive organisational processes. The successful implementation of change demands positive action from top management and a style of transformational leadership in order to gain a commitment to change.

> ### Managing change in the workplace is dependant on good people management
>
> Effective development of people in line with business ambitions is central to managing change and ensuring competitive edge during times of economic uncertainty. Organisations face tough decisions in times of change. These can involve business refocusing, rationalisation and restructuring, innovating, seizing new market opportunities, and re-engineering the skills base to boost competitiveness. However all will include engaging the workforce. Organisations need to be responsive to changing conditions but also to acknowledge what this means to their people.
>
> The Investors in People approach recognises that, in order to get the best out of your people, it is vital that all employees are clear about the goals of the organisation as well as their individual workplace objectives. Cascading the vision and direction of the organisation is one of the strongest levers you can pull to generate improved business performance. During times of change it is key that these objectives are regularly reviewed to ensure they remain up to date and relevant. It is also critical that people are kept informed of organisation-wide goals so they are clear about how their role contributes to these.
>
> Changing goals can also create a need for investment in training and development to ensure the workforce has the ability to meet new objectives. The importance of developing new skills to respond to change and of supporting the workforce to work in new ways should not be underestimated. However, this investment will not provide a sustained impact on performance unless underpinned by strong leadership and communication. Managers need to be able to support their teams effectively. What this means in practice is being able to explain to employees both the reason for change and the effect it will have on them; creating a culture where feedback is given on a regular basis and acted upon; one where people are encouraged to give their ideas for working smarter and take responsibility for their objectives. The role of inspirational leadership and effective communication is vital.
>
> By getting the people management practices right, you open the way to a responsive and flexible workforce which is able to respond effectively to a changing business environment. Once this culture has been created, organisations cannot afford to stand still. Effective people management needs to be seen as an ongoing project rather than one with an end date to ensure that organisations stay ahead of the competition and continue to perform whatever the market conditions.
>
> *Source*: Investors in People. © Investors in People, July 2009.

Leading IT change

A report published jointly by the Chartered Management Institute, the British Computer Society and the Change Leadership Network refers to challenges facing senior executives to ensure they are better prepared to lead technological change. Change always involves risk and on the basis of examination of ten detailed organisational case studies the report identifies five key challenges in obtaining best value from IT-enabled change:

- Creating transformational value rather than just implementing IT projects.
- Building capability for ongoing change. Being able to predict future business needs and how IT can help shape new business models and deliver the desired benefits.
- Creating a climate of open communication.
- Managing confidence and trust – understanding the impact of external changes.
- Building personal capability, learning and confidence.[84]

Change leaders

An interesting proposition is put forward by *Drucker*, who contends that 'one cannot manage change. One can only be ahead of it. We do not hear much anymore about "overcoming resistance to change".' Everyone now accepts that change is unavoidable.

*But in a period of upheavals, such as the one we are living in, change is the norm. To be sure, it is painful and risky, and above all it requires a great deal of very hard work. But unless it is seen as the task of the organization to **lead change**, the organization – whether business, university, hospital and so on – will not survive. In a period of rapid structural change, the only ones who survive are the **Change Leaders**. It is therefore a central 21st-century challenge for management that its organization become a change leader. A change leader sees change as opportunity. A change leader looks for change, knows how to find the right changes and knows how to make them effective both outside the organization and inside it. This requires:*

1 Policies to make the future.
2 Systematic methods to look for and to anticipate change.
3 The right way to introduce change, both within and outside the organization.
4 Policies to balance change and continuity.[85]

Critical reflection

'The socialisation of new members into an organisation's culture and climate is no more than a management control system and manipulation of the individual. It is therefore unethical and should be condemned.'

How would you challenge the validity of this statement? What has been your personal experience?

SYNOPSIS

■ Organisation development (OD) is a generic term embracing a wide range of intervention strategies into the social processes of an organisation. In a very general sense, OD is concerned with attempts to improve the overall performance and effectiveness of an organisation. The broad nature of OD means, however, that many interrelated topic areas could be included under this heading. OD makes use of a number of intervention strategies, and is action-oriented and tailored to suit specific organisational needs. Two central and critical features of OD are organisational culture and organisational change.

■ Organisational culture helps to explain how things are performed in different organisations. Culture is, however, a general concept, and difficult to explain precisely. There are a number of ways to classify different types of organisation culture. It develops over time and in response to a complex set of factors. There are a number of different ways in which to understand what constitutes organisational culture.

■ Applications of organisational behaviour and the effective management of human resources are dependent upon the characteristic features of the individual organisation – and its culture. The pervasive nature of culture has an important effect on the behaviour and actions of individuals, on the process of management and on organisational performance. It describes what the organisation is all about. Culture helps to account for variations among organisations and managers, both nationally and internationally.

■ Organisational climate is based on the perception of members towards the organisation, and can be seen as the state of mutual trust and understanding among members of the organisation. Climate influences the attitudes that staff bring to bear on their work performance and personal relationships. Among the factors which contribute to a healthy climate is the extent to which employees have a sense of commitment to, and psychological bond with, the organisation.

■ Organisations operate within an increasingly volatile environment and are in a state of constant change. Change is a pervasive influence and an inescapable part of social and organisational life. There is a wide range of forces acting upon organisations which make the need for change inevitable. Change can affect all aspects of the operation and functioning of the organisation. Planned organisation change involves a process of behaviour modification. Change is reciprocal and changing organisations may affect the nature of managerial work.

■ Despite the potential positive outcomes, change is often resisted at both the individual and the organisational level. Resistance to change can take many forms

and it is not always easy to pinpoint the exact reasons. It is important that management adopt a clearly defined strategy for the successful initiation of change, including attention to the style of managerial behaviour, and the human and social factors of change. The effective management of change is a key factor of organisational performance and competitiveness, and should emanate from the top of the organisation.

REVIEW AND DISCUSSION QUESTIONS

1 Explain fully what you understand by the meaning and nature of organisation development (OD).

2 Suggest how you would attempt to explain the concept of organisational culture. What factors might influence the development of culture?

3 Discuss critically the importance of culture for effective organisational performance. Give practical examples from your own organisation.

4 What do you understand by organisational climate and what do you think are its main characteristic features? From your own organisation, give examples of features that have contributed to and/or detracted from a healthy climate.

5 Explain the concept of employee commitment and suggest how it might actually be created. Give examples of factors that have contributed to your own strength of commitment in any work situation.

6 Give specific examples of major changes confronting management today and their probable implications for an organisation of your choice.

7 Why do individuals and organisations tend to resist change? To what extent do you believe such resistance can be effectively overcome?

8 Explain fully what *you* believe are the most important features in the successful implementation of organisational change.

MANAGEMENT IN THE NEWS

The time is ripe for fresh ideas

Lynda Gratton

Forget business workshops and case studies – recessions provide real-time opportunities for executive learning as old myths are brought into question and management innovations emerge. Historically a downturn has been a time when business models, organisational structures, labour markets and employee contracts come under immense strain. Accepted wisdoms are challenged and this break in thinking can result in the adoption of new practices and the adoption of new habits and skills. There are two points of tension emerging in this recession that may allow for innovation in management practices.

Recessionary times can act as the catalyst to spur changes in organisational cultures.

Wider distribution of leadership

This recession has brought into stark perspective the role of the leader. Up to this point, the dominant norm has been the 'command and control' leadership style. In this model, the organisation is viewed as a hierarchy in which decisions are escalated to the top, where a CEO makes the decisions. But many people are now questioning the wisdom of placing so much power in

the hands of so few. At the same time, insights from research in decision sciences and technological advances have shown that often the best decisions are made by an 'intelligent crowd', rather than one all-powerful individual.

Management in the news – continued

Senior leadership cadres have traditionally been essentially homogeneous – middle-aged men with similar backgrounds. Research on innovative teams has shown that such groups are likely to be less competent in decision-making than diverse teams. With the dominant model under question, this is a good time to bring diversity back on to the agenda.

Creating flexible virtual teams

Past recessions have often served to accelerate the adoption of management practices and processes that already had some popularity pre-recession. The same is true of virtual working. Assembling teams to work on projects and task forces has become more viable in the past decade, often hastened by the pressures of globalisation. Yet while virtual working is emerging as a trend, there is still an assumption that face-to-face working trumps virtual working. As a result, every Sunday night thousands of executives board aircraft and trains to get to Monday morning meetings. With many companies freezing travel budgets, this is likely to change and many executives will have to do more work virtually.

At the same time, the entry and exit roads of the world's big cities are clogged from early dawn with commuters hurrying to and from work. This movement of people has been based on two assumptions: that people need to meet every day to get their work done; and that when at home, they are likely to slack and need the discipline of an office to ensure they perform.

Both assumptions are wrong. First, people do not need to meet every day to get their work done. Our research has shown that virtual teams – where members rarely meet – can be highly productive. What is important in these teams is that they are all inspired by a meaningful task, fascinating question or compelling vision. The second assumption – that people need the discipline of an office to ensure they perform – is also a myth. Much research has shown that when people have the opportunity to work on engaging, well-planned tasks at home they are significantly more productive and committed than those who toil through the commuter traffic every day.

Source: Gratton, L. 'The Time Is Ripe for Fresh Ideas', *Financial Times*, 5 February 2009. Copyright © 2009 The Financial Times Limited, reproduced with permission from Lynda Gratton.

Discussion questions

1 With reference to Lewin's model of change management, as shown in Figure 19.4, suggest the steps that would need to be taken by an organisation to introduce the two innovatory management practices advocated by Gratton.

2 Crainer suggests that managers are themselves often the source of resistance to change. Using the information in the chapter about resistance to change as the basis for your analysis, explain why managers might resist such changes.

3 What steps would you take to overcome these types of resistance?

ASSIGNMENT 1

Understanding your organisation's personality

An important part of any manager's, sales person's or frontline staff's role is to be an ambassador for the organisation. This means representing its values, its image and its style in a variety of situations.

In each case, you represent the personality not only of yourself, but of your organisation – and one of the most effective ways to explore the personality of your organisation is by describing it as if it were a person.

Ask yourself the following questions about your organisation.

- What gender would it be?
- How old would it be?
- Where would it live?
- Where would it prefer to holiday?
- What car would it drive?
- What interests or hobbies would it have?
- If it were to win the lottery, what would it do?

Source: Reproduced with permission from David Hill, Director, Echelon Learning Ltd.

(Some feedback may be given by your tutor.)

ASSIGNMENT 2

Rate your readiness to change – a quiz

The left-hand column lists 17 key elements of change readiness. Rate your organisation on each item. Give three points for high ranking ('We're good at this; I'm confident of our skills here'), two for medium score ('We're spotty here; we could use improvement or more experience') and one point for a low score ('We've had problems with this; this is new to our organisation'). Be honest. Don't trust only your own perspective; ask others in the organisation, at all levels, to rate the company too. The consultants at Symmetrix believe – no surprise – it helps to have an outsider do the assessment with you.

Readiness scoring

How to score: High = 3, Medium = 2, Low = 1.

Category		Score
Sponsorship	The sponsor of change is not necessarily its day-to-day leader; he or she is the visionary, chief cheerleader, and bill payer – the person with the power to help the team change when it meets resistance. Give three points – change will be easier – if sponsorship comes at a senior level; for example, CEO, COO, or the head of an autonomous business unit. Weakest sponsors: mid-level executives or staff officers.	☐
Leadership	This means the day-to-day leadership – the people who call the meeting, set the goals, work till midnight. Successful change is more likely if leadership is high-level, has 'ownership' (that is, direct responsibility for what's to be changed) and has clear business results in mind. Low-level leadership, or leadership that is not well connected throughout the organisation (across departments) or that comes from the staff, is less likely to succeed and should be scored low.	☐
Motivation	High points for a strong sense of urgency from senior management, which is shared by the rest of the company, and for a corporate culture that already emphasises continuous improvement. Negative: tradition-bound managers and workers, many of whom have been in their jobs for more than 15 years; a conservative culture that discourages risk-taking.	☐
Direction	Does senior management strongly believe that the future should look different from the present? How clear is management's picture of the future? Can management mobilise all relevant parties – employees, the board, customers, etc. – for action? High points for positive answers to those questions. If senior management thinks only minor change is needed, the likely outcome is no change at all; score yourself low.	☐
Measurements	Or in consultant-speak, 'metrics'. Three points if you already use performance measures of the sort encouraged by total quality management (defect rates, time to market, etc.) and if these express the economics of the business. Two points if some measures exist but compensation and reward systems do not explicitly reinforce them. If you don't have measures in place or don't know what we're talking about, one point.	☐
Organisational context	How does the change effort connect to other major goings-on in context of the organisation? (For example: Does it dovetail with a continuing total quality management process? Does it fit with strategic actions such as acquisitions or new product lines?) Trouble lies ahead for a change effort that is isolated or if there are multiple change efforts whose relationships are not linked strategically.	☐

Assignment 2 – continued

Category		Score
Processes/ functions	Major changes almost invariably require redesigning business processes that cut across functions such as purchasing, accounts payable, or marketing. If functional executives are rigidly turf-conscious, change will be difficult. Give yourself more points the more willing they – and the organisation as a whole – are to change critical processes and sacrifice perks or power for the good of the group.	☐
Competitor benchmarking	Whether you are a leader in your industry or a laggard, give yourself points for a continuing programme that objectively compares your company's performance with that of competitors and systematically examines changes in your market. Give yourself one point if knowledge of competitors' abilities is primarily anecdotal – what salesmen say at the bar.	☐
Customer focus	The more everyone in the company is imbued with knowledge of customers, the more likely that the organisation can agree to change to serve them better. Three points if everyone in the workforce knows who his or her customers are, knows their needs, and has had direct contact with them. Take away points if that knowledge is confined to pockets of the organisation (sales and marketing, senior executives).	☐
Rewards	Change is easier if managers and employees are rewarded for taking risks, being innovative, and looking for new solutions. Team-based rewards are better than rewards based solely on individual achievement. Reduce points if your company, like most, rewards continuity over change. If managers become heroes for making budgets, they won't take risks even if you say you want them to. Also: If employees believe failure will be punished, reduce points.	☐
Organisational structure	The best situation is a flexible organisation with little churn – that is, reorganisations are rare and well received. Score yourself lower if you have a rigid structure that has been unchanged for more than five years or has undergone frequent reorganisation with little success; that may signal a cynical company culture that fights change by waiting it out.	☐
Communication	A company will adapt to change most readily if it has many means of two-way communication that reach all levels of the organisation and that all employees use and understand. If communications media are few, often trashed unread, and almost exclusively one-way and top-down, change will be more difficult.	☐
Organisational hierarchy	The fewer levels of hierarchy and the fewer employee grade hierarchy levels, the more likely an effort to change will succeed. A thick impasto of middle management and staff not only slows decision-making but also creates large numbers of people with the power to block change.	☐
Prior experience with change	Score three if the organisation has successfully implemented major changes in the recent past. Score one if there is no prior experience with major change or if change efforts failed or left a legacy of anger or resentment. Most companies will score two, acknowledging equivocal success in previous attempts to change.	☐
Morale	Change is easier if employees enjoy working in the organisation and the level of individual responsibility is high. Signs of unreadiness to change: low team spirit, little voluntary extra effort, and mistrust. Look for two types of mistrust: between management and employees, and between or among departments.	☐

Category		Score
Innovation	Best situation: the company is always experimenting; new ideas are implemented with seemingly little effort; employees work across internal boundaries without much trouble. Bad signs: lots of red tape, multiple signoffs required before new ideas are tried; employees must go through channels and are discouraged from working with colleagues from other departments or divisions.	☐
Decision-making	Rate yourself high if decisions are made quickly, taking into account a wide variety of suggestions; it is clear where decisions are made. Give yourself a low grade if decisions come slowly and are made by a mysterious 'them'; there is a lot of conflict during the process, and confusion and finger pointing after decisions are announced.	☐
	Total score	☐

If your score is:

41–51: Implementing change is most likely to succeed. Focus resources on lagging factors (your ones and twos) to accelerate the process.

28–40: Change is possible but may be difficult, especially if you have low scores in the first seven readiness dimensions. Bring those up to speed before attempting to implement large-scale change.

17–27: Implementing change will be virtually impossible without a precipitating catastrophe. Focus instead on (1) building change readiness in the dimensions above and (2) effecting change through skunkworks or pilot programmes separate from the organisation at large.

After completing your total score, compare and discuss your response with those of your collegues.

Source: Stewart, T. A. 'Rate Your Readiness to Change', *Fortune*, 7 February 1994, pp. 63–4. Copyright © 1999 Time Inc. All rights reserved. Reproduced with permission.

PERSONAL AWARENESS AND SKILLS EXERCISE

Objectives

Completing this exercise should help you to enhance the following skills:

■ Relate classifications of culture to different types of organisations.

■ Assess influences on the development of culture.

■ Evaluate the appropriateness of culture for specific organisations.

Exercise

Using the classifications of organisational culture proposed by Handy, and by Deal and Kennedy, you are required to:

1 Compare and contrast influences on the development of culture in any two different types of organisations. Your two organisations could be, *for example*:

 private and public sector; for-profit and not-for-profit; service sector and manufacturing sector; production and academic; private enterprise and one other different type.

2 Suggest, with supporting reasons, which of **either** the Handy or the Deal and Kennedy typologies you would try to foster if you were appointed as a senior manager in any *three* of the following organisations:

 – wheel-clamping contractor;

 – research laboratory;

 – naval submarine;

Personal awareness and skills exercise – continued

- private hospital;
- second-hand car business;
- high-fashion clothing store;
- fast-food chain;
- advertising agency.

Discussion

■ How important is organisational culture? How would you attempt to foster a change in the prevailing culture of an organisation?

■ To what extent do textbook classifications aid our practical understanding and analysis of organisational culture?

■ Should there be/is there a most 'suitable' culture for specific organisations?

CASE STUDY

Moving with the times

The NHS Workforce Review Team (WRT) is a group of dedicated health-care workforce planners who provide objective modelling, analysis and evidence-based recommendations in order to enable patient-centred and clinically driven strategic decision-making across the health-care workforce. WRT was established in 1999 by Dr Judy Curson, a medical doctor turned specialist in workforce planning and staff development. Today, WRT comprises an experienced team of analysts, data modellers and professional health-care advisers.

In early 2007 it was clear that WRT would need to relocate its main office within the following 12 to 24 months. Consequently, two conflicting needs emerged: to improve the standard of the facilities available to staff, and to maintain costs at an appropriate and affordable level.

An important first step in planning and delivering an office environment that allowed the team to perform well but remain cost-effective was recognising some of the key features of the organisation and its staff. The culture of the organisation was characterised by a strong belief in the values of public service combined with a drive to be successful. It also had a reputation for delivering projects effectively. It was crucial to maintain flexibility both in organisational terms to allow responsiveness to business needs, and on an individual level within the team. It was also important to maintain its reputation for efficiency.

Source: Courtesy of NHS Workforce Review Team (WRT)

One team of professionals shows the way to make hot-desking really work.

WRT in Winchester comprised 40–45 staff, with four individuals located in a satellite office in Leeds who were not directly affected by this relocation. A significant proportion of the WRT team worked part-time and/or were frequently out of the office for business reasons. The total number of staff fluctuated according to the demands of the business through the use of a small pool of temporary workers. An early list of essential needs in the new accommodation included:

- approximately 45 desk units
- three meeting rooms
- accessibility via public transport
- availability of staff parking.

However, it became clear that it would be costly to lease an office that would provide all these features. A more innovative approach was needed, so WRT gave all staff the opportunity to put forward ideas and suggestions. The relocation project group proposed a solution which extended the use of open-plan office space together with a hot-desking system for the majority of staff. This would reduce both the number of desks and the total floor space required, therefore reducing the cost to an affordable level. Once it was agreed that this would form the basis of the office system, suitable premises were located and the final selection was made by the senior management team using a points system.

Implications of adopting a hot-desking system

The decision to move the whole team to hot-desking could not be made in isolation. It was anticipated that it would have a wide-ranging impact on most other office systems. The WRT team as a whole recognised the potential effect the physical work environment could have on its effectiveness and cohesion. The diagram below shows other working practices that had to be developed either to support hot-desking directly or to improve the team's efficiency. The design of the new working area provided 26 standard desk units for the 40–45 staff, situated in an open-plan office. To support this area and necessary new working practices, WRT planned the following additional facilities:

- five small to medium-sized meeting rooms, including one with soft seats intended for one-to-one discussions, and two rooms with a moving divide between them to extend the room when needed;
- a central area where printers, fax, scanner and small photocopier machines were located in an 'S'-shaped curve to serve all staff;
- a bistro-style kitchen area with essential facilities and seating for use during breaks;
- a tea bar area of six to seven seats equipped with power and telephone sockets as an overflow area for busy days, intended for use by staff who are only in the office for a short time or who were mainly in scheduled meetings;
- an enclosed bank of built-in, full-height storage cupboards on one wall to provide a range of storage options.

Follow me!

A key part of the success of hot-desking lay in ensuring that the IT and telephone system could 'follow' an individual as they moved from one desk to another and as they worked in the office or at home. This was achieved relatively inexpensively as all staff were given laptops. However it was essential that staff working remotely could still access the main shared drive because data and information cannot be carried out of the office, for example on memory sticks, for reasons of confidentiality and security.

The telephone system was adapted to allow allocation of an extension number (rather than a specific handset) to each individual. The software allows staff to remain on the same extension number when

working from home. On arrival at a desk the individual logs into the telephone system and calls are routed to that handset until they log out. All hot desks are equipped identically with power and network points, an adjustable mounted screen, keyboard and mouse. The whole office area is covered by wireless access allowing those temporarily working from the tea bar or elsewhere full access to WRT systems and the internet.

Where am I sitting today?

A total of six members of staff were allocated permanent desks spaced throughout the open office area. These were all administrative members of the operations/business support team who are office-based. Other team members, including senior management and the WRT directors, are allocated a hot desk. After considering other options such as a first come first served system, it was decided that desks would be allocated each day by a simple rota system scheduled a week at a time by each member of the operations team in turn. This system was felt to be fairer as it would avoid small groups/teams colonising preferred areas. It also ensured that staff who chose to start and finish later under the existing flexitime system were not disadvantaged.

Guidelines were drawn up requiring staff to move around the office each day and not sit in the same place throughout a working week. On the occasions when the tea bar was needed as overflow space, staff members with the most meetings in their diaries were allocated the space. In practice this tends to mean that members of the senior management team are most often allocated this area, providing further high-level, visible management support for the policy. The next day's seating allocation is displayed every afternoon.

Where's my stuff?

One of the logistical challenges WRT faced in introducing the hot-desking system was how to provide storage for items such as working documents and laptops (although staff members are encouraged to take their laptops home). The solution was to provide a plastic storage box with handles for each person – these are stored in a section of the storage wall and have become known as the 'blue boxes'. They have the capacity to store a laptop, a good number of files and paperwork, and personal effects. To achieve this change in working practices WRT undertook a comprehensive review of all the material it held prior to moving and dramatically reduced the volume of material held in hard copy. Material that needed to be retained for any

reason and was not available electronically was archived and kept in remote storage. A central resource centre of key reference material was developed, and is maintained in a designated part of the storage wall to provide an up-to-date resource for the whole team. It includes a single printed copy of many official publications, articles and 'grey' literature not widely available otherwise.

But will I like it?

One of the challenges WRT faced in developing this working practice was the doubt felt by some team members prior to the changes; the loss of their 'own' desk and therefore their own personal space was one such concern. These concerns had to be recognised and addressed as far as possible as they had important implications not only for individuals but for the cohesiveness of the whole team.

In order to allay the concerns and provide an overview of how the new office would function, a draft office systems document was developed and circulated to all staff giving them an opportunity to comment, raise questions or make suggestions. Following this consultation a final working draft was agreed that formed the basis of the office systems in the period immediately after the move. A comprehensive review after three months in the new premises, involving all team members, was also planned. The Leeds office staff were involved in this process, as it was recognised that the changes in the main office, and to IT systems, could affect those working more remotely. It was felt to be important that the Leeds staff should not be alienated by the Winchester group's preoccupation with their approaching move and new working practices.

How do I get to work?

The new office is located in central Winchester and has only two parking spaces. It is, however, situated close to a railway and bus station, and is within 30 minutes of an airport. There are 'park and ride' sites around the city and several car parks in close proximity. To encourage other methods of travel, one of the two car parking spaces was turned into a bicycle rack. The one remaining car park space is allocated on a rota basis to individuals travelling long distances. This rota is done at the same time as the seating plan. The team's acceptance of this plan was influenced by the range of travel options available and a perceived fairness and flexibility in the allocation of parking spaces.

Source: The case study was provided by Donna and Chris of WRT.

Your tasks

1 Review the case study organisation in the light of the 'cultural web' (Figure 19.1) and try to pick out examples of each aspect.

2 Write a brief description of WRT's culture based on your findings and show how the aspects fit together.

3 Summarise the evidence you can find in the case about the use of the managerial tools (recruitment and selection, social tools and training, reward system) considered by Chatman and Cha.

4 Choose a model of change or change management from the chapter and use it to analyse the content of the case. Write a short report explaining how the model can help managers to manage major workplace changes such as this one.

Notes and references

1 French, W. L. and Bell, C. H. *Organization Development: Behavioral Science Interventions for Organization Improvement*, sixth edition, Prentice Hall (1999), pp. 25–6.

2 Ibid., p. 29.

3 Hamlin, B., Keep, J. and Ash, K. *Organisational Change and Development*, Financial Times Prentice Hall (2001), p. 13.

4 Maier, D., Leban, B. and Orr-Alfeo, D. 'A Values Statement on OD: An Interview with Practitioner-Scholar Dr Allan Church RODC', *Organization Development Journal*, vol. 19, no. 3, Fall 2001, pp. 69–74.

5 Blake, R. R. and Mouton, J. S. *The Managerial Grid III*, Gulf Publishing Company (1985).

6 Naylor, J. *Management*, second edition, Financial Times Prentice Hall (2004), pp. 645–6.

7 Woodall, J. 'Managing Culture Change: Can It Ever Be Ethical?', *Personnel Review*, vol. 25, no. 6, 1996, pp. 28–40.

8 See, for example, Smircich, L. 'Concepts of Culture and Organizational Analysis', *Administrative Science Quarterly*, vol. 28, 1983, pp. 339–58.

9 Atkinson, P. E. 'Creating Cultural Change', *Management Services*, vol. 34, no. 7, 1990, pp. 6–10.

10 McLean, A. and Marshall, J. *Intervening in Cultures*, working paper, University of Bath, 1993.

11 See, for example, Oswick, C., Lowe, S. and Jones, P. 'Organisational Culture as Personality: Lessons from Psychology?', in Oswick, C. and Grant, D. (eds) *Organisation Development: Metaphorical Explorations*, Pitman Publishing (1996), pp. 106–20.

12 Charters, J. 'Are You a "Woodentop?"', *The British Journal of Administrative Science*, May/June 2000, p. 20.

13 Cartwright, J. *Cultural Transformation*, Financial Times Prentice Hall (1999), p. 34.

14 Schein, E. H. *Organizational Culture and Leadership: A Dynamic View*, third edition, Jossey-Bass (2004).

15 Harrison, R. 'Understanding Your Organization's Character', *Harvard Business Review*, vol. 50, May/June 1972, pp. 119–28.

16 Handy, C. B. *Understanding Organizations*, fourth edition, Penguin (1993).

17 Deal, T. E. and Kennedy, A. A. *Corporate Cultures: The Rites and Rituals of Corporate Life*, Penguin (1982).

18 Deal, T. E. and Kennedy, A. A. *The New Corporate Cultures*, Perseus Books (2000).

19 See, for example, Handy, C. B. *Understanding Organizations*, fourth edition, Penguin (1993); and McLean, A. and Marshall, J. *Cultures at Work*, Local Government Training Board (1988).

20 Kransdorff, A. 'History – A Powerful Management Tool', *Administrator*, October 1991, p. 23.

21 See, for example, Beckett-Hughes, M. 'How to Integrate Two Cultures', *People Management*, vol. 11, no. 5, 10 March 2005, pp. 50–1.

22 Roddick, A. *Body and Soul*, Ebury Press (1991); Roddick, A. *Business As Unusual*, Thorsons (2000).

23 Blackhurst, C. 'Up Front at Pearson', *Management Today*, May 1997, pp. 50–7.

24 Gerstner, L. V. Jr. *Who Says Elephants Can't Dance?: Inside IBM's Historic Turnabout*, HarperBusiness (2002).

25 Johnson, G., Scholes, K. and Whittington, R. *Exploring Corporate Strategy*, seventh edition, Financial Times Prentice Hall (2005).

26 Wilson, F. *Organizational Behaviour and Work: A Critical Introduction*, second edition, Oxford University Press (2004), p. 185.

27 'Effective Organisations: The People Factor', Advisory Booklet, ACAS, November 2001.

28 Naylor, J. *Management*, second edition, Financial Times Prentice Hall (2004).

29 Oliver, J. 'Losing Control', *Management Today*, June 1998, pp. 32–8.

30 Harrison, R. and Stokes, H. *Diagnosing Organizational Culture*, Pfeiffer & Company (1992), p. 1.

31 Reigle, R. F. 'Measuring Organic and Mechanistic Cultures', *Engineering Management Journal*, vol. 13, no. 4, December 2001, pp. 3–8.

32 Egan, G. 'The Shadow Side', *Management Today*, September 1993, p. 37.

33 Egan, G. 'Cultivate Your Culture', *Management Today*, April 1994, pp. 38–42.

34 Worrall, L. and Cooper, C. *The Quality of Working Life 2007*, Chartered Management Institute (2007).

35 Bunting, M. *Willing Slaves*, HarperCollins (2004), p. xxiii.

36 Meudell, K. and Gadd, K. 'Culture and Climate in Short-Life Organizations: Sunny Spells or Thunderstorms?', *International Journal of Contemporary Hospitality Management*, vol. 6, no. 5, 1994, pp. 27–32.

37 Heller, R. *In Search of European Excellence*, HarperCollins Business (1997), p. 229.

38 Goldsmith, W. and Clutterbuck, D. *The Winning Streak Mark II*, Orion Business Books (1998).

39 Cummings, T. G. and Worley, C. G. *Organization Development and Change*, eighth edition, Thompson South-Western (2005), p. 509.

40 Chatman, J. A. and Cha, S. E. 'Culture of Growth', Mastering Leadership, *Financial Times*, 22 November, 2002, pp. 2–3.

41 Stewart, R. *The Reality of Management*, third edition, Butterworth Heinemann (1999), p. 123.

42 Naylor, J. *Management*, second edition, Financial Times Prentice Hall (2004), p. 79.

43 'Inspired Leadership: Insights Into People Who Inspire Exceptional Performance', DTI, August 2004.

44 Potter, C. C. 'What Is Culture: And Can It Be Useful For Organisational Change Agents?', *Leadership and Organization Development Journal*, vol. 10, no. 3, 1989, pp. 17–24.

45 Siddall, P. 'Working With Cultural Differences', *Chartered Secretary*, February 1998, p. 30.

46 Schneider, S. C. and Barsoux, J. *Managing Across Cultures*, second edition, Financial Times Prentice Hall (2003).

47 Cheng, T., Sculli, D. and Chan, F. 'Relationship Dominance – Rethinking Management Theories from the Perspective of Methodological Relationalism', *Journal of Managerial Psychology*, vol. 16, no. 2, 2001, pp. 97–105.

48 Francesco, A. M. and Gold, B. A. *International Organizational Behavior*, second edition, Pearson Prentice Hall (2005).

49 Tagiuri, R. and Litwin, G. H. (eds) *Organizational Climate*, Graduate School of Business Administration, Harvard University (1968), p. 27.

50 Moran, E. T. and Volkwein, J. F. 'The Cultural Approach to the Formation of Organizational Climate', *Human Relations*, vol. 45, no. 1, 1992, p. 43.

51 Rentoch, J. R. 'Climate and Culture: Interaction and Qualitative Differences in Organizational Meanings', *Journal of Applied Psychology*, vol. 75, no. 6, 1990, p. 668.

52 Gray, R. *A Climate of Success*, Butterworth-Heinemann (2007).

53 O'Reilly, C. 'Corporations, Culture and Commitment: Motivation and Social Control in Organizations', in Steers, R. M., Porter, L. W. and Bigley, G. A. (eds) *Motivation and Leadership at Work*, sixth edition, McGraw-Hill (1996), p. 374.

54 Walton, R. E. 'From Control to Commitment in the Workplace', in Steers, R. M. and Porter, L. W. (eds) *Motivation and Work Behavior*, McGraw-Hill (1991), p. 448.

55 Altman, W., Cooper, C. and Garner, A. 'New Deal Needed to Secure Commitment', *Professional Manager*, September 1999, p. 40.

56 Galunic, C. and Weeks, J. 'Survey – Mastering People Management', *Financial Times*, 12 November 2001.

57 Gratton, L. *The Democratic Enterprise*, Financial Times Prentice Hall (2004), p. 184.

58 De Vita, E., 'Get Engaged', *Management Today*, April 2007, pp. 38–43.

59 For a discussion of change in relation to the complexities of organisational life, see Senior, B. and Fleming, J. *Organizational Change*, third edition, Financial Times Prentice Hall (2006).

60 Czerniawska, F. *From Bottlenecks to BlackBerries: How the Relationship between Organisations and Individuals Is Changing*, Management Consultancies Association (September 2005).

61 See, for example, Henderson, H. (Squadron Leader) 'Flying High', *Manager: The British Journal of Administrative Management*, January/February 1998, pp. 10–13.

62 Fenlon, M. 'The Public Spirit', Mastering Leadership, *Financial Times*, 22 November 2002, p. 4.

63 'Effective Organisations: The People Factor', Advisory Booklet, ACAS, November 2001.

64 Lewin, K. *Field Theory in Social Science*, Harper and Row (1951).

65 French, W. L., Kast, F. E. and Rosenzweig, J. E. *Understanding Human Behavior in Organizations*, Harper and Row (1985).

66 'Management Futures: The World in 2018', Chartered Management Institute, March 2008.

67 Gratton, L. *Living Strategy: Putting People at the Heart of Corporate Purpose*, Financial Times Prentice Hall (2000), p. 191.

68 Lockhead, Sir M. 'In My Opinion', *Management Today*, September 2008, p. 12.

69 Crainer, S. *Key Management Ideas: Thinkers That Changed the Management World*, third edition, Financial Times Prentice Hall (1998), pp. 144–5.

70 Toffler, A. *Future Shock*, Pan Books (1970), p. 27.

71 Cunningham, I. 'Influencing People's Attitudes to Change', *Professional Manager*, vol. 14, no. 3, May 2005, p. 37.

72 Material in this section reproduced with kind permission of Anne Riches, creator of The Almond Effect®. For further information see www.AnneRiches.com.

73 Stewart, R. *The Reality of Management*, third edition, Butterworth Heinemann (1999), p. 161.

74 Christensen, C. M. and Overdorf, M. 'Meeting the Challenge of Disruptive Change', *Harvard Business Review*, vol. 78, no. 2, March–April 2000, pp. 67–76.

75 See, for example, Covington, J. and Chase, M. L. 'Eight Steps to Sustainable Change', *Industrial Management*, vol. 14, no. 6, November/December 2002, pp. 8–11 and 'Implementing an Effective Change Programme', *Management Checklist 040*, Chartered Management Institute, July 2008.

76 Kotter, J. P. and Cohen, D. S. *The Heart of Change*, Harvard Business School Press (2002).

77 Newton, R. *Managing Change: Step by Step*, Pearson Prentice Hall (2007), p. 215.

78 Reis, D. and Pena, L. 'Reengineering the Motivation to Work', *Management Decision*, vol. 39, no. 8, 2001, pp. 666–75.

79 Atkinson, P. 'Managing Resistance to Change', *Management Services*, Spring 2005, p. 15.

80 Lucas, E. 'Riding the Change Roller-Coaster', *Professional Manager*, September 2002, pp. 27–9.

81 Taylor, G. 'Managing the Situational and Psychological Pressures Brought About by Change', *Professional Manager*, vol. 16, no. 4, July 2007, p. 14.

82 Reeves, R. and Knell, J. 'Your Mini MBA', *Management Today*, March 2009, pp. 60–4.

83 Stuart-Kotze, R. *Performance: The Secrets of Successful Behaviour*, Financial Times Prentice Hall (2006), pp. 17–28.

84 Tranfield, D. and Braganza, A. *Business Leadership of Technological Change: Five Key Challenges Facing CEOs*, Chartered Management Institute (2007).

85 Drucker, P. F. *Management Challenges for the 21st Century*, Butterworth Heinemann (1999), p. 73.

Index